routard

Paris

Series director: Philippe Gloaguen
Series creators: Philippe Gloaguen and Michel Duval
Chief editor: Pierre Josse
Assistant chief editor: Benoît Lucchini
Coordination director: Florence Charmetant
Editorial team: Yves Couprie, Olivier Page, Véronique de Chardon, Amanda Keravel, Isabelle Al Subaihi, Anne-Caroline Dimas, Carole Foucault, Bénédicte Solle, André Poncelet, Jérôme de Gubernatis, Marie Lung and Thierry Brouard.

English translation: Nick Halliwell
Managing editor: Liz Coghill
Editorial: Sarah Hudson, Suzanne Juby, Chris Bagshaw, Sofi Mogensen and Jane Franklin
Additional research and assistance: Christine Bell, Penny Langton, Tamsin Black and Zack Taylor
Proofreader: Simon Tuite
Index: Dorothy Frame

We have done our best to ensure the accuracy of the information contained in this guide. However, addresses, phone numbers, opening times etc. do invariably change from time to time, so if you find a discrepancy please do let us know and help us update the guides. You can contact us at: hachetteuk@orionbooks.co.uk or write to us at Hachette UK, address below. Hachette UK guides provide independent advice. The authors and compilers do not accept any remuneration for the inclusion of addresses in this guide. Please note that we cannot accept any responsibility for any loss, injury or inconvenience sustained by anyone as a result of any information or advice contained in this guide.

Hotels, restaurants, B&Bs – price guide
Because of rapid inflation in many countries, it is impossible to give an accurate indication of prices in hotels and restaurants. Prices can change enormously from one year to the next. As a result we have adopted a system of categories for the prices in the guides: 'Budget', 'Cheap', 'Moderate', 'Chic' and 'Très Chic' (in the guides to French-speaking countries), otherwise 'Expensive' and 'Splash out' in the others. These categories do vary from guide to guide, however. If the 'Budget' or 'Cheap' hotels start at £2/$3 per night, then those costing £5/$7.50 per night will belong to the 'moderate' category and those costing £10/$15 and upwards will belong to the 'chic' or 'expensive' category. It therefore follows that in a guide where the 'Budget' option costs £10/$15 per night, the price ranges in the other categories will increase accordingly.

As prices may change so may other circumstances – a restaurant may change hands, the standard of service at a hotel may deteriorate since our researchers made their visit. Again, we do our best to ensure information is accurate, but if you notice any discrepancy, do let us know at the address already given above. The only thing we can't predict is when a hotel or a restaurant changes its standing (gets better or worse) and moves into a different category. If this happens, then we look forward to hearing from you, either by e-mail (see above) or by post (see below for address).

First published in the United Kingdom in 2000 by Hachette UK.

Distributed in the United States of America by Sterling Publishing Co., Inc.
387 Park Avenue South, New York, NY 10016-8810.

A CIP catalogue for this book is available from the British Library.

ISBN 1 84202 027 7

Typeset by WestKey Ltd, Falmouth, Cornwall.
Printed and bound in France by Aubin Imprimeur, Poitiers.

Hachette UK, Cassell & Co, Wellington House, 125 Strand, London WC2R 0BB.

Cover design by Emmanuel Le Vallois (Hachette Livre) and Paul Cooper.
Cover photo © Tony Stone.
Back cover photo of La Grande Arche de la Défense at night © Derek Croucher.

routard

Paris

The guides for travellers

CONTENTS

JUST EXACTLY WHO OR WHAT IS A ROUTARD?

You are. Yes, you! The fact that you are reading this book means that you are a Routard. You are probably still none the wiser, so to explain we will take you back to the origin of the guides. Routard was the brainchild of a Frenchman named Philippe Gloaguen, who compiled the first guide some 25 years ago with his friend Michel Duval. They simply could not find the kind of guide book they wanted and so the solution was clear – they would just have to write it themselves. When it came to naming the guide, Philippe came up with the term Routard, which at the time did not exist as a bona fide word – at least, not in conventional dictionary terms. Today, if you look the word up in a French-English dictionary you will find that it means 'traveller' or 'globetrotter' ... so there you have it, that's what *you* are!

From this humble beginning has grown a vast collection of some 100 titles to destinations all over the world. Routard is now the bestselling guide book series in France. The guides have been translated into five different languages, so keep an eye out for fellow Routard readers on your travels.

What exactly do the guides do?
The short answer is that they provide all the information you need to enable you to have a successful holiday or trip. Routards' great strength however, lies in their listings. The guides provide comprehensive listings for accommodation, eating and drinking – ranging from campsites and youth hostels through to four star hotels – and from bars, clubs and greasy spoons to tearooms, cafés and restaurants. Each entry is accompanied by a detailed and frank appraisal of the address, rather like a friend coming back from holiday who is recommending all the good places to go (or even the places to avoid!). The guides aim to help you find the best addresses and the best value for money within your price range, whilst giving you invaluable insider advice at the same time.

Anything else?
Routard also provides oceans of practical advice on how to get along in the country or city you are visiting plus an insight into the character and customs of the people. How do you negotiate your way around the transport system? Will you offend if you bare your knees in the temple? And so on. In addition, you will find plenty of sightseeing information, backed up by historical and cultural detail, interesting facts and figures, addresses and opening times. The humanitarian aspect is also of great importance, with the guides commenting freely and often pithily, and most titles contain a section on human rights.

Routard are truly useful guides that are convivial, irreverent, down-to-earth and honest. We very much hope you enjoy them and that they will serve you well during your stay.

Happy travelling.

The Hachette UK team

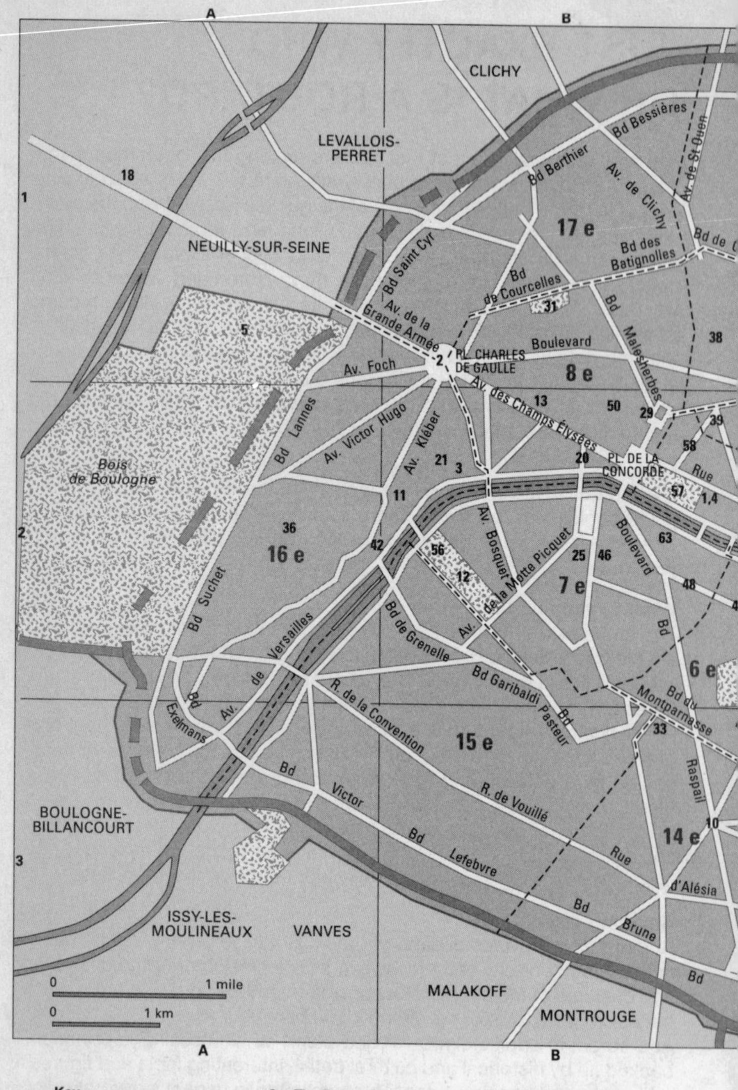

Key

1 Musée de la Publicité
2 Arc de Triomphe
3 Musée d'Art moderne de la Ville de Paris
4 Musée des Arts décoratifs
5 Musée national des Arts et Traditions populaires
6 The Georges-Pompidou Centre (Beaubourg)
7 La Bourse (Stock Exchange)
8 The Buttes-Chaumont quarter
9 Musée Carnavalet
10 The Catacombs
11 Palais de Chaillot
12 Champ-de-Mars
13 Champs-Élysées
14 Le Châtelet
15 Île de la Cité
16 Musée national du Moyen Âge et des thermes de Cluny
17 Musée Cognacq-Jay
18 La Défense
19 The Grands Boulevards
20 Grand Palais, Petit Palais
21 Musée Guimet
22 Les Halles
23 Hôtel de Ville (town hall)
24 Institut de France
25 Les Invalides
26 Jardin des Plantes
27 The Louvre
28 Luxembourg

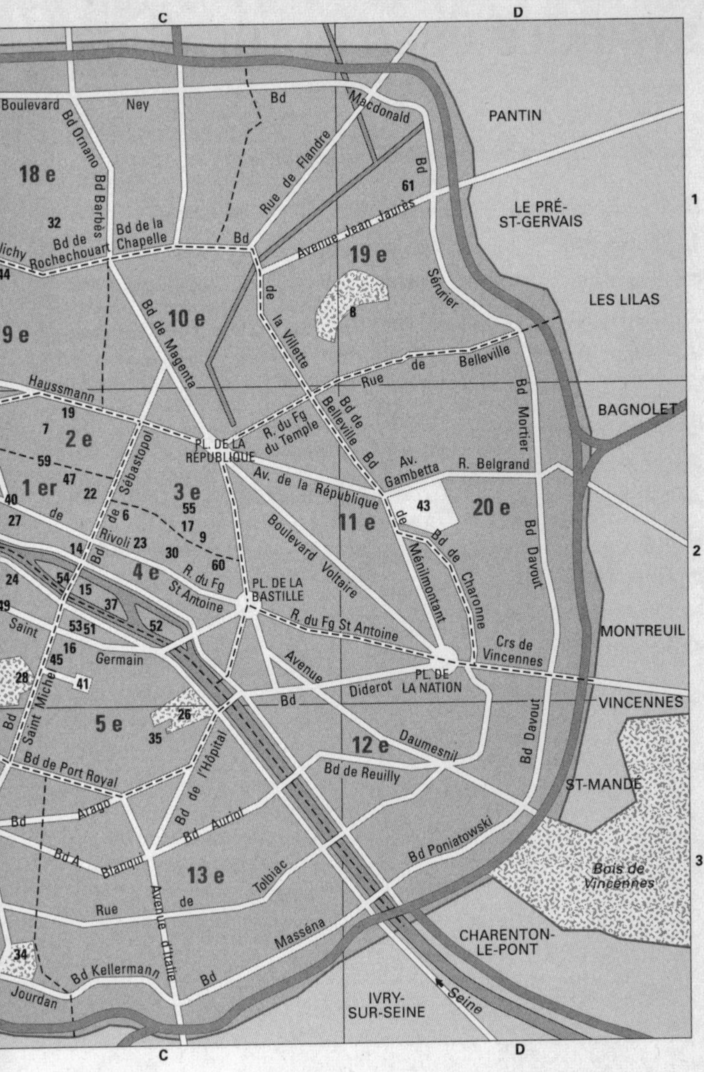

29 Madeleine
30 Le Marais
31 Parc Monceau
32 Montmartre
33 Montparnasse
34 Parc Montsouris
35 Mosquée de Paris
36 La Muette
37 Notre-Dame
38 'Nouvelle-Athènes'
39 Opéra
40 Palais-Royal
41 Panthéon
42 Passy
43 Père-Lachaise cemetery
44 Pigalle
45 Latin Quarter
46 Musée Rodin
47 Église St-Eustache
48 The Faubourg St-Germain
49 St-Germain-des-Prés
50 Faubourg St-Honoré
51 Église St-Julien-le-Pauvre
52 Île St-Louis
53 Église St-Séverin
54 Ste-Chapelle
55 Musée national des Arts et Métiers
56 The Eiffel Tower
57 Tuileries
58 Place Vendôme
59 Place des Victoires
60 Place des Vosges
61 Cité de la Musique (Parc de la Villette)

SYMBOLS USED IN THE GUIDE

Please note that not all the symbols below appear in every guide.

- ■ Useful addresses
- Tourist office
- Post office
- Telephone
- Railway station
- Bus station
- Metro station
- R.E.R station
- Shared taxi
- Tram
- River transport
- Sea transport
- Airport
- Airfield
- Where to stay
- Where to eat
- Where to go for a drink
- Where to listen to music
- Where to go for an ice-cream
- ★ To see
- Shopping
- ● 'Other'
- Parking
- Castle
- Ruins
- Diving site
- Shelter
- Camp site
- ▲ Peak
- ● Site
- ○ Town
- Hill
- Abbey, chapel
- Lookout
- Beach
- Lighthouse

GETTING THERE

GETTING TO PARIS FROM THE UK

BY AIR

Flying to Paris from the UK can take less time than a rush-hour tube journey. From London it is a 45-minute flight, from Manchester 1 hour 25 minutes. Depending on where you live in relation to the airport, however, the overall journey may take the same time by train.

The airline industry is fiercely competitive, which is clearly good news for the consumer, who benefits from the wide range of discounts and from airlines constantly undercutting each another. For those looking for the lowest fare to Paris, it's a good idea to pick up a copy of the London *Evening Standard* or have a look in the travel sections of the Sunday papers.

Alternatively, various on-line travel agents offer excellent value fares when tickets are booked on-line (see below under *Travel Agents*). Make sure that the company is approved by ABTA/ATOL. The major airlines can also be contacted for bookings direct by phone or through their websites. If booking in advance, expect to pay between £80 and £120 for a return flight from London to Paris and about £10 to £30 more from Birmingham, Manchester, Leeds or Glasgow. Some of the best fares to Paris are from Glasgow International Airport.

The smaller regional airports around the UK, such as Cardiff or Bristol, also have regular air services to Paris, but these are considerably more expensive when booked through the major airlines. They do, however, offer frequent, reliable and cost-efficient charter flights that can be booked through local high-street travel agents, such as Thomas Cook or Going Places.

London is the hub for flights between the UK and Paris, with scores of flights every day. British Airways, British Midland and Air France dominate the UK–France airline market, serving London Heathrow, Gatwick and London City airports. The vast majority of UK flights arrive at Paris' Roissy-Charles-de-Gaulle Airport, with only a handful going to the smaller Orly Airport.

Of course, the arrival of the *Eurostar* train has provided strong competition in the south and southeast, and the airlines are looking increasingly to the north of England for business.

Airlines

- **Air France** (Birmingham, Dublin, Edinburgh, Glasgow, Humberside, London [City, Gatwick, Heathrow], Manchester, Newcastle, Southampton). Reservations and information: ☎ (0845) 0845 111; ☎ (01) 605 0383 (Ireland). Website: www.airfrance.co.uk
- **British Airways** (Aberdeen, Belfast, Birmingham, Bristol, Edinburgh, Glasgow, London [Gatwick and Heathrow] Manchester, Newcastle, Plymouth, Southampton). Reservations and information: ☎ (0345) 222 111. Website: www.british-airways.com

● **British Midland** (Belfast, Dublin, East Midlands, Edinburgh, Glasgow, Leeds/Bradford, London Heathrow, Manchester, Teeside). Reservations and information: ☎ (0870) 607 0555. Website: www.iflybritishmidland.com

BY TRAIN

Eurostar is a practical, comfortable and stylish way to travel to Paris and its popularity is continually on the increase.

For those travelling from the UK, Eurostar is particularly convenient as connections are available throughout the country via regional train operators. There is also a service from Ashford in Kent serving the south-east. The 186mph/300kph Eurostar service whisks you from London's Waterloo station (connections via Northern, Waterloo and City, Jubilee and Bakerloo underground lines) to Paris' Gare du Nord (2, 4, 5 Metro and B, D RER lines connect you to the rest of Paris) in just under 3 hours (including the one hour time difference). This figure will be cut by a further 35 minutes once the British side of the track is finally upgraded to meet French standards. There are 20 trains per day Monday to Friday (15 on Sunday), roughly one an hour beginning at about 5am and ending around 8pm. On a cautionary note, be sure to arrive at the station at least 25 minutes prior to departure as you may not be allowed to board after this time; the Eurostar staff are quite strict about this.

At the time of writing prices range between £70 and £270 for a standard, second-class return from London. However, reduced fares are available for the under–26s, seniors, groups and advance booking. Fares remain constant throughout the year; however, demand increases during the peak travel seasons.

There are often some very good promotional offers available. For example: at the time of writing an outward journey on a Saturday night followed by an early morning return cost £29, and the standard youth fare (no railcard necessary) was £75 return. For further details contact Eurostar direct. Alternatively, high-street travel agents such as Thomas Cook can make reservations on your behalf, but will charge you a booking fee of around £10.

🚆 **Eurostar** (London Waterloo-Paris), Waterloo International Terminal, London, SE1 (Waterloo tube). Reservations: ☎ (0990) 186 186 (01233) 617 575 (7am–10pm). Website: www.eurostar.co.uk

BY COACH

Eurolines, a subsidiary of National Express, offers a long-distance coach service between London Victoria Coach Station (a short walk from Victoria Railway Station and accessible via the Victoria, Circle and District underground lines) and Paris. In addition, the company connects other principal cities in the UK with its London terminus through the National Express network. Coach travel is certainly the cheapest way to get to Paris; however, it is not the fastest. The journey, leaving London at 9am, takes between 7 and 9 hours, depending on the traffic. This is three times as long as the Eurostar journey.

Coach travel is, however, still affordable! At the time of writing the return fare from London to Paris was £33 – definitely the most economical way to get there. To maximize value it is advisable to avoid the peak seasons of July,

August and December, and to purchase tickets in advance in order to get the cheapest fare. There is a minor reduction for the under 26s and the over 50s.

Eurolines (London Victoria-Paris), Victoria Coach Station, 52 Grosvenor Gardens, London, SW1 (Victoria tube). Reservations: ☎ (0990) 143219. Website: www.eurolines.com

BY CAR

British driving licences are valid in France, although it is always a good idea when travelling abroad to purchase an International Driving Permit (IDP) from the Automobile Association (AA) before leaving home (call ☎ 0990 500 600 for details).

France's motorways (*autoroutes*) are well maintained and largely traffic-free; however, tolls are expensive and should be included in the cost of taking a car to Paris. Parking costs also need to be accounted for in your budget. Almost everywhere within the city (even residential neighbourhoods) charges for the privilege of parking. Permits are available from grey ticket machines situated on most streets. The speed limit on France's motorways is 130kph (80mph) and therefore driving is a considerably slower endeavour than the 300kph (180mph) train. Driving in Paris can be a challenge and is not for the faint-hearted as Parisians famously drive according to their own idiosyncratic standards (just take a look at the other cars around you and you'll see how many bumps take place!). As in the UK, French law requires that all drivers have at least third-party insurance in order to drive on French roads.

If you do decide to take a car to Paris, there are three ways you can travel: by ferry, by hovercraft/catamaran or by train.

Ferry: whichever operator you choose to cross the Channel depends on where you are in the UK; the Dover–Calais route remains the most popular as it is the shortest at 90 minutes. Ferries remain a sensible alternative to the Channel Tunnel, especially for people starting their journey in the west of the country. Furthermore, the frequent promotions offered by the ferry companies, often through national newspapers, mean ferry travel remains, by and large, more economical than the Eurotunnel car-train service.

Portsmouth and Southampton are the chief points of departure for ferries to Caen and Le Havre, both convenient points for driving to Paris; however, crossings last between 5 and 7 hours and therefore make the day a long one.

Prices vary enormously and discriminate against those who travel at convenient times, such as weekends, holidays and even mornings. Most operators also divide the year between low, medium and high seasons, but the proportional difference in price is far less than is the case with airlines – usually around £10. The fare structure is geared towards single journeys, although there are good 5-day deals. Expect to pay between £40 and £100 for a car and two passengers between Dover and Calais and between £70 and £200 for longer crossings. As a general rule, extra passengers cost only £1. For detailed information on fares, contact the ferry companies direct; most of them have well-organized websites that offer on-line booking. Alternatively, most high-street travel agents are able to provide comprehensive information on particular crossings.

☛ **Brittany Ferries** (Portsmouth–Caen), Wharf Road, Portsmouth PO2 8RU. Reservations: ☎ (0990) 360 360. Website: www.brittanyferries.com
☛ **P&O Stena Line** (Dover–Calais), Channel House, Channel View Road, Dover, Kent CT17 9TJ. Reservations: ☎ (0870) 600 0600. Website: www.posl.com
☛ **P&O Portsmouth** (Portsmouth-Le Havre), Peninsula House, Wharf Road, Portsmouth, PO2 8TA. Reservations: ☎ (0990) 980 555. Website: www.poef.com
☛ **Sea France** (Dover–Calais), Eastern Docks, Dover, Kent CT16 1JA. Reservations: ☎ (08705) 711 711. Website: www.seafrance.co.uk
Hovercraft and Seacat (catamaran): Faster than the traditional drive-on/drive-off ferry, both the hovercraft and the catamaran are especially practical for those who live don't live near to the Eurotunnel and, compared to ferries, they represent a considerable reduction in the time spent at sea. On a good day the hovercraft can do the Dover–Calais crossing in as little as 22 minutes. However, more frequently it takes about 35 minutes, while the Seacat covers the same route in around 50 minutes. While on board, passengers sit in airline-style seats from where they are served refreshments. For those who have never 'flown' in a hovercraft it remains a novel and exciting experience (but if the weather is rough, flights will be cancelled). The Newhaven–Dieppe route is a longer crossing of 4 hours, but Dieppe is closer to Paris than the more northern ports. Again, fares are geared towards single-journey travel with good deals on 1- and 5-day returns. Expect to pay between £90 and £180 for a standard single fare, and a little less for a 5-day return.
☛ **Hoverspeed** (Dover–Calais, hovercraft; Folkestone–Boulogne, Seacat; Newhaven–Dieppe, Seacat), International Hoverport, Dover, Kent CT17 9TG. Reservations: ☎ (0870) 240 8070. Website: www.hoverspeed.co.uk

Taking the car on the train: Eurotunnel's auto-train service from Folkestone to Calais/Coquelles carries cars and their passengers under the Channel in about 35 minutes, and runs 24 hours a day. Departures are twice hourly during the day and once hourly at night. The service connects the UK's M20 with northern France's network of motorways. Eurotunnel's fare structure does not discriminate against those wishing to purchase a return ticket (for stays of more than 5 days). As a guideline expect to pay between £200 and £250 for a return ticket including a car and passengers, depending on the time of year and the time of day. Again, there are good deals for 5-day (mini-break) returns and Eurotunnel occasionally offers promotional fares.

Be sure to arrive at least 25 minutes prior to departure, as boarding may be denied after this time.

🚆 **Eurotunnel** (Folkestone–Calais), Customer Service Centre, Junction 12 of the M20, PO Box 300, Folkestone, Kent CT19 4DQ. Reservations: ☎ (08705) 353535. Website: www.eurotunnel.co.uk

TRAVEL AGENTS IN THE UK

There are masses of travel agents in the UK which, because of their size and global reach, can pass on savings to the traveller. Alternatively, there are a number of very good internet-only sites that are able to provide economic rates because of their low overheads. The following are a selection of the best and most reputable travel agents in the UK, all approved by ABTA/ATOL in Britain.

- **Council Travel** (discount flights), 28a Poland Street, London W1V 3DB. ☎ (020) 7287 9410 (offices also in Birmingham, Edinburgh, Glasgow, Manchester, Newcastle and Oxford)
- **STA Travel** (discounts for Youth and non-Youth tickets/packages) (nationwide) 86 Old Brompton Road, London SW7 3LQ. ☎ (020) 7581 4132 (37 branches). Website: www.statravel.co.uk
- **Thomas Cook** (flights/holiday packages/last minute bookings), branches nationwide. Information and bookings: ☎ (0990) 666 222. Website: www.thomascook.co.uk
- **Trailfinders** (discounts and tailor-made travel), 42–50 Earl's Court Road, London W8 6FT. ☎ (020) 7938 3366 (offices also in Birmingham, Bristol, Dublin, Glasgow, Manchester, Newcastle). Website: www.trailfinder.com

Internet-only companies: www.armchair.com; www.a2btravel.com; www.cheapflights.co.uk; www.deckchair.com; www.lastminute.com

GETTING TO PARIS FROM THE REPUBLIC OF IRELAND

BY AIR

The short (90 minutes) and inexpensive flight from one of Ireland's three major airports to Paris makes air travel the most sensible option for individual passengers travelling to Paris. The 10- to 20-hour land and sea option can be quite exhausting, especially for those on a short trip, and is essentially designed for those taking a car.

Dublin is the busiest international airport in Ireland, with five airlines connecting to Paris several times a day. Shannon and Cork airports also have daily direct flights, however, the frequency of flights and choice of airlines is fewer than from Dublin.

There is plenty of competition, which means that bargains are relatively easy to find. The Irish-based discount airline Ryan Air flies direct from Dublin to Paris' small Beauvais-Tille Airport four-times a day and provides the most economical option. At the time of writing it was possible to purchase a return ticket for IR£50. Other airlines with direct flights to Paris are Air France, British Midland and Aer Lingus (from Shannon). British Airways and Jersey European also fly from Ireland but you have to connect in the UK, adding to the length of the journey.

Airlines

- **Air France** (Dublin). Reservations and information: ☎ (01) 844 5633. Website: www.airfrance.com
- **British Airways** (Cork, Dublin, Shannon). Reservations and information: ☎ (1800) 626747. Website: www.british-airways.com
- **British Midland** (Dublin). Reservations and information: ☎ (01) 283 8833. Website: www.iflybritishmidland.com
- **Jersey European Airlines** (Cork, Dublin, Shannon). Reservations and information: ☎ (1890) 925 532. Website: www.jea.co.uk
- **Ryan Air** (Cork, Dublin, Kerry, Knock). Reservations and information: ☎ (01) 609 7800. Website: www.ryanair.ie

BY TRAIN

It is possible to travel from Dublin to Paris (via London) by train in around 11 hours. The entire trip can be arranged in Ireland through the Continental Rail Desk of Iarnrod Éireann in Dublin (details below). Alternatively, the companies responsible for the individual parts of the journey may be contacted independently in Britain or from Ireland. For those outside Dublin, Ireland's efficient national railway system (Iarnrod Éireann) provides frequent, reliable, although fairly expensive services though its Intercity network. Once in Dublin you have to go to the Port (for Irish Ferries services) or Dun Laoghaire (for Stena Sealink services) for the 3 and a half hour ferry ride from Dublin to Holyhead in Anglesey. From Dublin train station, the Port is an easy 15-minute bus ride and Dun Laoghaire is accessible via the 20-minute DART train. On reaching the UK, it takes 4 hours from Holyhead to London Euston on Virgin trains. To connect to Eurostar at London Waterloo, for the final 3-hour leg of the journey, passengers must take the Northern Line tube south (about a 15-minute journey), which connects Euston and Waterloo stations. Be sure to check-in for the Eurostar at least 25 minutes before departure as you may be denied boarding after this time.

🚆 **Eurostar** (trains from London Waterloo to Paris Gare du Nord), Waterloo International Terminal, London SE1 (Waterloo underground station). Reservations: c/o Alan Lynch: ☎ (01) 670 8877. Website: www.eurostar.co.uk
🚆 **Iarnrod Éireann** (Continental Rail Desk), 35 Lower Abbey Street, Dublin 1. Reservations and information: ☎ (01) 677 1871. Website: www.irishrail.ie
🚆 **Virgin Trains** (Holyhead–London Euston). Reservations and information: ☎ (0345) 222 333 (in UK). Website: www.virgintrains.co.uk

BY COACH

🚌 **Bus Éireann/Eurolines** (coach services throughout Ireland via Dublin to Paris Bagnolet), Central Bus Station (Busaras), Store Street, Dublin 1. Reservations and information: ☎ (01) 830 2222. Website: www.buseireann.ie. Bus Éireann is affiliated to Eurolines, Europe's largest long-distance coach company, and operates a Paris service (via London) from Dublin twice daily. As Ireland's largest national coach operator, Éireann also serve every large city in Ireland via Dublin. Departures for Paris leave early morning or evening and the journey takes a rather exhausting 22 hours. The journey is a through service with only an hour's break at London's Victoria Coach Station.

Adult return fares range from IR£90–110 (July and August only) and IR£50–70 for a youth ticket, making it the most economical route to Paris from Ireland.

BY CAR

Taking a car to Paris is not cheap; drivers have to pay for either the long Ireland to France crossing or the shorter Ireland to UK crossing and then the cross-Channel ferry, or Eurotunnel, to France.

The most frequently-travelled route for taking a car from Ireland to Paris is via the UK; however, it is possible to avoid the UK altogether by sailing direct from Rosslare to either Cherbourg or Le Havre in Brittany and driving to Paris from there. The real advantage of this is that the expense of the cross-Channel ferry or Eurotunnel connecting the UK and France is avoided altogether. However, this sailing is not for everyone as it is long and infrequent (between 16 and 22 hours, departing between three times a week and once fortnightly). It is a route that is especially practical for those living in the south and south west of the Republic. Expect to pay from IR£200–300 for a standard single, and about the same for a 5-day return.

From southeast Ireland, the Rosslare–Fishguard route is very good for driving to Paris. The journey takes 3 and a half hours on the ferry and 1 hour 40 minutes on the catamaran. Once in the UK, Fishguard is well situated for access to the M4 to London, from where Dover is about a 2 hour drive. Expect to pay from IR£80–240 for a single ticket for a car and its passengers, slightly more for the catamaran and a 5-day return.

From the Dublin area, the Holyhead route remains the most time-efficient as it is only a 3 and a half hours crossing on the ferry. Irish Ferries and Stena Lines serve the route. Stena Lines have recently introduced a 'Superferry' which sails from Dublin Port and makes the trip in 1 hour 40 minutes. Expect to pay from IR£100–250 for a standard single of a car and up to four passengers and about the same for a 5-day return. The fare depends greatly on when you travel, but both operators frequently run special offers and promotions. Once in the UK, drivers must either take one of the cross-Channel ferries or the Eurotunnel to France. The auto-train service from Folkestone to Calais takes 35 minutes and costs from IR£200–250 for a return ticket including a car and passengers.

There are a number of ferry routes to choose from between the UK and France. The two most sensible routes are either Dover–Calais or Dover–Boulogne, which take around 90 minutes. The ferry operators often have promotional offers (frequently through the national press), so it is wise to check before travelling.

Irish Ferries (Dublin–Holyhead, Rosslare–Cherbourg/Le Havre). Reservations and information: (Dublin) ☎ (01) 638 3333; (Rosslare) ☎ (053) 33158. Website: www.irishferries.ie

Stena Lines (Dun Loaghaire/Dublin Port–Holyhead, Rosslare–Fishguard). Reservations and information: (Dun Loaghaire) ☎ 01 204 7700; (Rosslare) ☎ (053) 33115. Website: www.stenaline.co.uk

TRAVEL AGENTS IN THE REPUBLIC OF IRELAND

- **American Express Travel**, 116 Grafton Street, Dublin 2. Reservations and information: ☎ (01) 677 2874
- **Budget Travel**, 134 Lower Baggot Street, Dublin 2. Reservations and information: ☎ (01) 661 3122
- **Budget Travel Shops**, 63 Main Street, Finglas 11, Dublin (seven offices in Dublin and throughout Ireland). Reservations and information: ☎ (01) 834 0637
- **Hello France**, The Mill Crosses Green, Cork, County Cork. Reservations and information: ☎ (021) 378 404

GETTING TO PARIS FROM NORTH AMERICA

BY AIR

Flying is the only practical way to travel from North America to Europe. For those with more time and money on their hands, taking a boat across the Atlantic is still a feasible and exciting option, but for the majority, air travel is the only option. More Americans visit France than any other country in the world; because of this, the route from the US to western Europe, in particular the eastern seaboard, is one of the world's most competitive air routes, providing the consumer with a wealth of carriers and agents from which to choose. All the airlines given below offer daily flights between the cities listed and Paris. Most cities have at least two or three flights per day and New York and Boston have around 10. Most of the lowest fares are offered from the east coast gateways of Atlanta, Boston, Miami, New York, Philadelphia and Washington. However, direct (and often affordable) services are also offered from Chicago, Cincinnati, Dallas, Houston, Los Angeles and San Francisco. It is even often more cost-effective to fly to another European city (London, Frankfurt or Brussels, for instance) and then connect with the same carrier to Paris (British Airways, Lufthansa and Sabena are good bets).

Smaller US cities also have good connecting services to major US cities but try to stay with the same airline as changing lines will result in higher fares. Moreover, the smaller the regional airport, the more it will cost for a connecting flight, so in some cases it may be worthwhile finding other means of transportation to the major airports.

When booking flights, it is often a good idea to check the Internet first for the cheapest available flight, and then call the airline as often they will match or better their original quote. Alternatively, many airlines offer what they call 'Dot-Com' specials, which are 5–10 per cent discount incentives for booking online.

Another option is flying to London first. From the east coast, London is the cheapest place to fly to in Europe, and many airlines (particularly Virgin) regularly offer promotional fares. It may be worthwhile, therefore, flying to London, then hopping on a plane, train or bus to Paris.

If you are planning to combine a trip to Paris with hotel accommodation and/or car rental it is certainly a good idea to look into package deals offered by the airlines, and increasingly by travel agents. They work out to be very good value for money as these companies bulk-buy and can pass on some of the savings to the consumer. When arranging a package deal, make sure the agent is a member of the United States Tour Operator Association (USTOA) or approved by the American Society of Travel Agents (ASTA).

Airlines

- **Air France** (Atlanta, Boston, Chicago, Houston, Los Angeles, Miami, New York, San Francisco, Washington DC). Reservations and information: ☎ (1800) 237 2747. Website: www.airfrance.com

• **American Airlines** (Boston, Chicago, Dallas, Miami, New York). Reservations and information: ☎ (1800) 443 7300. Website: www.americanair.com
• **Continental Airlines** (Boston, Houston, Miami, New York, Washington DC). Reservations and information: ☎ (1800) 525 0280. Website: www.continental.com
• **Delta Airlines** (Atlanta, Boston, Chicago, Cincinnati, Los Angeles, New York, San Francisco, Washington DC). Reservations and information: ☎ (1800) 221 1212. Website: www.delta-air.com
• **TWA** (Boston, New York). Reservations and information: ☎ (1800) 892 4141. Website: www.twa.com
• **US Airways** (Philadelphia). Reservations and information: ☎ (1800) 428 4322. Website: www.usairways.com
• **United Airlines** (Chicago, Los Angeles, San Francisco, Washington DC). Reservations and information: ☎ (1800) 241 6522. Website: www.ual.com

TRAVEL AGENTS IN NORTH AMERICA

• **Council Travel** (students and those under 26)
65 offices nationally, in most large cities. National Reservations ☎ (800) 226 8624. Website: www.counciltravel.com
• **STA Travel** (students and those under 26). Reservations and information: ☎ (1800) 781 4040. Website: www.statravel.com
• **Travel Avenue** (Discounters), 10 South Riverside, Suite 1404, Chicago, IL 60606. Reservations and information: ☎ (1800) 333 3335
• **UniTravel** (Consolidators), 1177 North Warson Road, St. Louis, MO 63132. Reservations and information: ☎ (1800) 325 2222
• **Internet-only companies:**
www.lowestfare.com; www.priceline.com (name your own price/last-minute deals); www.previewtravel.com (very competitive)

GETTING TO PARIS FROM CANADA

BY AIR

Montreal and Toronto are Canada's two major cities for direct flights to Paris. The main European airlines fly at least once daily to Paris, while the smaller ones offer between two and four flights per week. The main airlines to and from Paris are the state airline Air Canada, as well as Air France, British Airways and KLM Royal Dutch Airlines.

The national airlines (Air Canada and Canadian Airlines) offer extensive domestic services from regional cities to the major international cities. Even airlines flying from other main Canadian cities such as Vancouver or Calgary are forced to fly through one of the two international cities.

There is less international competition on flights from Canada than from the US. This means that ticket prices are less likely to be discounted and rigid fare structures are usually only relaxed during off-peak times. One way around this is to travel from one of the northern US cities; a feasible prospect for 90 per cent of the Canadian population who live within 100 miles of the US border. There are also no immigration problems for Canadians wanting to cross what is the largest undefended international border in the world. It is quite practical for someone living in Hamilton, Ontario, for example, to travel to Detroit in Michigan and connect with a US airline for the 9-hour flight to Paris.

The major US cities that are practical for Canadian residents to fly from are Buffalo, Cleveland, Detroit, Minneapolis, Seattle, and possibly even Boston. At the time of writing it was possible to fly from Buffalo, New York to Paris on Continental Airlines (via Newark) for around US$400; a considerable saving in comparison to the corresponding fare from Toronto. Unfortunately, public transportation between Canada and the US is not particularly good; there are typically once-daily bus or train services across the border to the major cities. Passengers wishing to fly from US cities, therefore, often have to organize their own transportation to US airports.

If you do fly from either Montreal or Toronto expect to pay around CAN$700 in the winter (except at Christmas) and CAN$800 during the peak months of summer. Flight time from Montreal is 6 and a half hours, 7 and a half from Toronto, and 12 and a half from Vancouver.

Airlines

- **Air Canada** (nationwide; Montreal and Toronto for direct international flights). Reservations and information: ☎ (1888) 247 2262 (Canada and US). Website: www.aircanada.ca
- **Air France** (Calgary, Montreal, Toronto). Reservations and information: ☎ (1800) 667 2747. Websites: www.airfrance.com (in English); www.airfrance.fr (in French)
- **American Airlines** (nationwide). Reservations and information: ☎ (1800) 443 7300. Website: www.americanair.com
- **British Airways** (Montreal, Toronto, Vancouver). Reservations and information: ☎ (1800) 247 9297. Website: www.british-airways.com
- **KLM** (Montreal, Toronto, Vancouver). Reservations and information: ☎ (1800) 374 7747. Website: www.klm.com

TRAVEL AGENTS IN CANADA

- **Collacutt Travel** (general travel services), The Bayview Village Centre, 2901 Bayview Avenue, Toronto, Ontario, M2K 1E6. Reservations and information: ☎ (1888) 225 9811. Website: www.collacutt-travel.com
- **Sears Travel** 81 offices throughout Canada. Reservations and information: ☎ (1888) 884 2359. Website: www.sears.ca
- **Travel House** (tours, packages and consolidators), 1491 Yonge Street, Suite 401, Toronto, Ontario, M4T 1ZR. Reservations and information: ☎ (416) 925 6322. Website: www.travel-house.com

Additionally, many of the travel agents listed in the North America section may be used for travelling from Canada.

GETTING TO PARIS FROM AUSTRALIA AND NEW ZEALAND

BY AIR

The major cities in Australia and New Zealand are well served by European, and particularly Asian airlines, making it possible to fly from Auckland, Brisbane, Melbourne, Perth and Sydney to Paris any day of the week, and always including an Asian stop-over. Since the flight is so long and gruelling (between 19 and 25 hours), the stop-over is actually pretty welcome and many arrange to spend a night or two in one of the many Asian cities served by the airlines, such as Bangkok, Hong Kong, Kuala Lumpur and Singapore. There is usually little or no extra cost for arranging this.

Asian airlines such as Air Lanka, Malaysia Airlines and Singapore Airlines usually offer the best fares. British Airways and Qantas tend to be more expensive, although they offer more frequent flights: British Airways have one flight per day, whereas some of the smaller Asian airlines have two or three per week. Expect to pay between Aus$1,400 and Aus$2,000 for a return flight to Paris in low season, and about Aus$400 more in high season; a little less for student, youth and senior fares. Charter flights operate regularly from Australia (less so in New Zealand) and are certainly worth considering. Sydney, with the greatest concentration of airlines, is the cheapest city to fly from, but really the difference tends to be marginal.

Airlines

- **Air Lanka** (Sydney). Reservations and information: ☎ (02) 9244 2111. Website: www.airlanka.com
- **British Airways** (Brisbane, Perth, Sydney). Reservations and information: ☎ (02) 8904 8800. Website: www.british-airways.com
- **Cathay Pacific** (Australia – Adelaide, Brisbane, Cairns, Melbourne, Perth, Sydney; New Zealand – Auckland, Christchurch). Reservations and information: Australia ☎ (131) 747; New Zealand ☎(0800) 800 454. Website: www.cathaypacific.com
- **Malaysia Airlines** (Australia – Adelaide, Cairns, Darwin, Melbourne, Sydney; New Zealand – Auckland, Christchurch; Tasmania – Hobart). Reservations and information: Australia ☎ (132) 627; New Zealand ☎ (09) 373 2741. Website: www.malaysiaairlines.com
- **Qantas**. Reservations and information: Australia ☎ (131) 211; New Zealand ☎ (0800) 808 767. Website: www.qantas.com
- **Singapore Airlines** (Australia – Adelaide, Brisbane, Cairns, Melbourne, Perth, Sydney; New Zealand – Auckland, Christchurch). Reservations and information: Australia (Sydney) ☎ (02) 9350 0100; New Zealand ☎ (0800) 808 909. Website: www.singaporeair.com.au

TRAVEL AGENTS IN AUSTRALIA AND NEW ZEALAND

- **STA Travel** (discounts for Youth and non-Youth tickets/packages), 855 George Street, Sydney 2000. ☎ (02) 9212 1255 (72 branches); 90 Cashel Street, Christchurch, New Zealand. ☎ (03) 379 9098 (13 branches). Website: www.statravel.com.au
- **Thomas Cook**, 175 Pitt Street, Sydney. ☎ (1300) 728 747 (nationwide); 96 Anzac Avenue, Auckland, New Zealand. ☎ (0800) 500 600 (nationwide). Websites: www.thomascook.com.au; www.thomascook.com.nz
- **Trailfinders** (discounts and tailor-made travel), 91 Elizabeth Street, Brisbane, Queensland, 4000. ☎ (07) 3229 0887 (also in Sydney and Cairns). Website: www.trailfinder.com/australia/travelc.htm

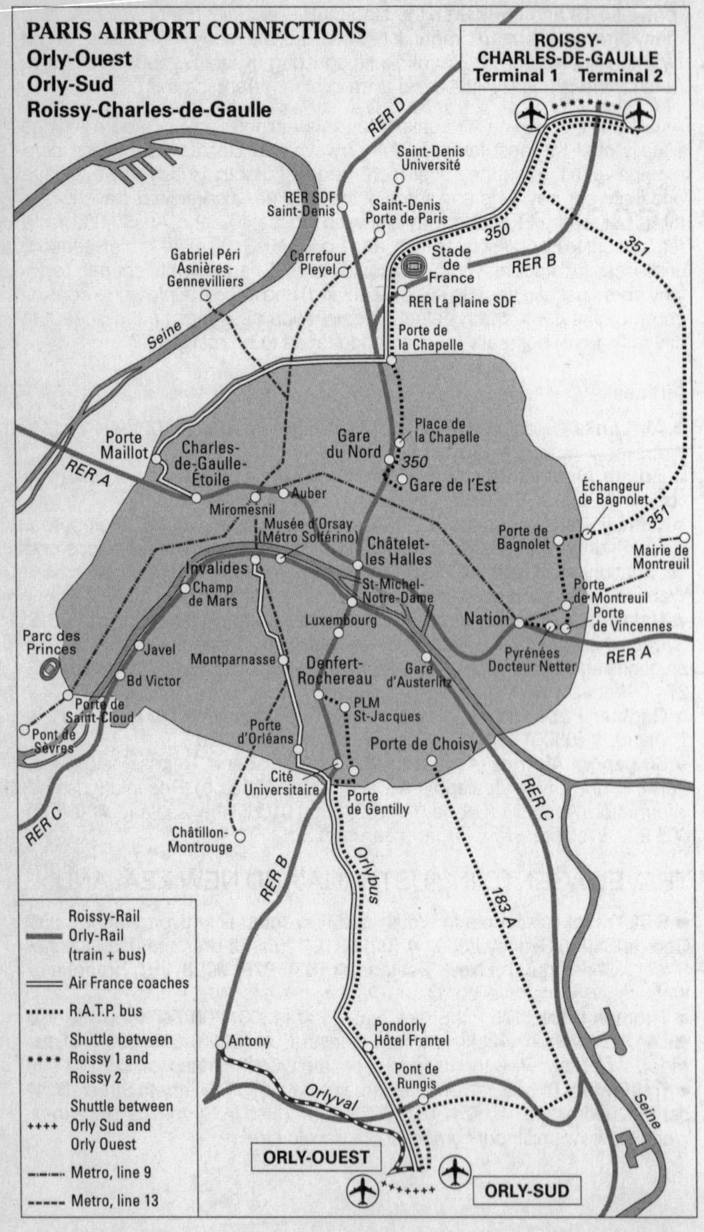
PARIS AIRPORT CONNECTIONS
Orly-Ouest
Orly-Sud
Roissy-Charles-de-Gaulle
ROISSY-CHARLES-DE-GAULLE
Terminal 1
Terminal 2
RER D
Saint-Denis Université
RER SDF Saint-Denis
Saint-Denis Porte de Paris
350
351
Stade de France
RER B
RER La Plaine SDF
Gabriel Péri Asnières-Gennevilliers
Carrefour Pleyel
Seine
Porte de la Chapelle
Place de la Chapelle
Gare du Nord
350
Gare de l'Est
Porte Maillot
Charles-de-Gaulle-Étoile
RER A
Miromesnil
Auber
Musée d'Orsay (Métro Solférino)
Châtelet-les Halles
Échangeur de Bagnolet
351
Porte de Bagnolet
Mairie de Montreuil
Invalides
Champ de Mars
St-Michel-Notre-Dame
Porte de Montreuil
Porte de Vincennes
Nation
Luxembourg
Pyrénées Docteur Netter
RER A
Parc des Princes
Javel
Montparnasse
Denfert-Rochereau
Gare d'Austerlitz
Bd Victor
Porte de Saint-Cloud
PLM St-Jacques
Pont de Sèvres
Porte d'Orléans
Porte de Choisy
Cité Universitaire
Porte de Gentilly
RER C
RER C
Châtillon-Montrouge
RER B
Orlybus
183 A
Antony
Pondorly Hôtel Frantel
Pont de Rungis
Orlyval
Seine
ORLY-OUEST
ORLY-SUD
Roissy-Rail
Orly-Rail
(train + bus)
Air France coaches
R.A.T.P. bus
Shuttle between Roissy 1 and Roissy 2
Shuttle between Orly Sud and Orly Ouest
Metro, line 9
Metro, line 13

GENERAL INFORMATION

ACCOMMODATION

Please note: during important events (trade fairs, sporting events, and so on), many Paris hotels tend to be booked up a long way ahead. Make sure you check accommodation well in advance if you want to find somewhere to stay at these times.

Paris offers a huge variety of accommodation for those on a budget, from youth hostels and hotels for young people to classic 1- or 2-star hotels. Those included here (*see* the separate sections on the arrondissements) have been chosen according to the following criteria: value for money, central position, charm and attractiveness. Some have all of these qualities, or most of them.

A word of advice: do book ahead! When you're sure of your dates, phone first to make the booking and then send a letter to confirm your reservation details, along with the required guarantee, such as a credit card number. Ring before you arrive to double-check everything is confirmed and to ensure that the establishment where you'll be staying will accept your chosen method of payment.

The following are useful organizations for booking budget accommodation:

• **La Fédération Unie des Auberges de Jeunesse** (FUAJ) (youth hostel association): 27 rue Pajol 75018. ☎ 01-44-89-87-27. Fax: 01-44-89-87-10/49. Metro: La Chapelle, Marx-Dormoy, or Gare-du-Nord (RER B). Website: www.fuaj.org. The FUAJ's central booking office allows you to make reservations at all the youth hostels in the Paris area (*see* '11th, 17th and 20th arrondissements').

• **Paris Loc'Appart:** 125 avenue Mozart 75016. ☎ 01-45-27-56-41. Telephone service Monday to Friday 2–7pm. Fax: 01-42-88-38-89. For further information, e-mail italielocappart@infonie.fr. Visits by appointment only. This small Parisian agency offers flats for rent, for a range of periods, from a minimum of three nights up to a few months. The flats are centrally located, particularly in the 5th and 6th arrondissements, or in touristy areas such as Montmartre. Prices are competitive, from 400F for a studio flat to 750F for three rooms for one night. It's a good deal if you take into account the money you'll save on restaurants and the convenience of having a flat instead of a hotel room.

ARRIVING

See map on p.24 for airport connections.

ARRIVING BY AIR

● **Roissy-Charles-de-Gaulle** (terminals 1 and 2): information ☎ 01-48-62-12-12. Flight information ☎ 01-48-62-22-80.
● **Orly-Sud** and **Orly-Ouest:** information ☎ 01-49-75-52-52. Flight information ☎ 01-49-75-15-15.

Roissy-Charles-de-Gaulle 1 and 2 to the city centre

The **Air France coach** leaves Charles-de-Gaulle Airport, goes to place de la Porte-Maillot in the city centre, stopping in place du Général-Koenig, close to the Méridien Hotel, and then on to the terminus at place de l'Étoile, on the corner of avenue Carnot and rue de Tilsitt (this is also the pick-up point for the return journey). Departures every 12 minutes from Terminals 2A (gate A5) and 2C (gate C5) or 2B (gate B6) and 2D (gate D6) and from Terminal 1 (gate 34, Arrivals level). Journey time: around 35 minutes.
Roissy Bus: leaves from Terminal 1, gate 30, Arrivals level ; T9, gate A, and from Terminals 2A, gate 10 and 2D, gate 12 (6am to 11pm). Departures every 15 minutes to place de l'Opéra (corner of rue Scribe and rue Auber). Journey time: 45 minutes. Return journeys between 5.45am and 11pm from place de l'Opéra (opposite American Express).
RATP buses: No. 350 goes to Gare du Nord (75 minutes) and No. 351 goes to place de la Nation (90 minutes). The cheapest option but also the slowest.
RER line B 'Roissy-Rail': the quickest way to get to the centre. Departures every 15 minutes, journey time around 30 minutes, including the shuttle bus service between the terminals and the station. Arrives at Gare du Nord to connect with city-centre Metro and RER trains.
● **By taxi:** allow for around 180F to the centre of Paris.

Orly-Sud and Orly-Ouest to the city centre

The **Air France coach** leaves from Orly-Sud, gate F, or Orly-Ouest, gate E, Arrivals level, every 20 minutes from 6am to 11pm. Arrival in the city centre is at the Aérogare des Invalides, with stops at rue du Commandant-Mouchotte, Montparnasse, on the station side. Journey time: 30 to 40 minutes. Same for the return journey.
The **Orly-Rail train** leaves every 20 minutes or so from the Pont de Rungis and stops at stations on the RER line C (Boulevard-Victor, Javel, Champ-de-Mars, Pont-de-l'Alma, Invalides, Quai-d'Orsay, Pont-St-Michel, Austerlitz). There is a connecting shuttle service between the airport and the station. The journey to Gare d'Austerlitz takes around 35 minutes in total. Highly recommended for those days when the whole of France is heading south on the motorway.
The **Orly Bus** leaves Orly-Sud, gate H, platform 4, or Orly-Ouest, gate J, Arrivals level between 6am–11.30pm. The cheapest option. Departures are every 15 minutes to place Denfert-Rochereau, where there are good links to the rest of Paris via the RER, two Metro lines and two bus lines. Allow 25–30 minutes for the journey from the airport to place Denfert-Rochereau. For the return journey, buses run from place Denfert-Rochereau between 5.35am and 11pm.
The **Jet Bus** runs every 12 minutes from Orly-Ouest, gate C, Arrivals

level, and Orly-Sud, gate H to the Villejuif-Louis-Aragon (line 7) metro station. The service runs from 6am to 10.15pm Monday to Friday, Saturday until 10.10pm and Sunday from 6.10am to 10.15pm. Allow between 15 and 20 minutes for the journey. ☎ 01-69-01-00-09.

Orlyval allows you to get from Orly to the centre of Paris and vice versa in less than 30 minutes. Departures are from Orly-Sud, gate K, near the baggage reclaim, or at Orly-Ouest, gate W, Departures level, every 4 to 7 minutes from 6am to 10.30pm daily (Sunday 7am to 11pm). The shuttle service operates between Orly and Antony station, from where you can pick up the RER line B without having to wait. The ticket gives access, for no extra charge, to first class travel over the whole of the RER and SNCF network in Paris and the suburbs. With the same ticket you can get from Orly to anywhere in the Île-de-France, including Roissy-Charles-de-Gaulle Airport. For the return journey the automatic metro is easily accessible from anywhere in the capital or the Paris region via Antony (RER, Metro stations, SNCF stations). ☎ 08-36-68-77-14.

RER line C trains depart every 15 minutes between 5.20am and 12.20am. A shuttle bus service runs from the airport to Pont-de-Rungis from where you can pick up the RER to Paris-Austerlitz. Allow 15 minutes for the bus and 25 minutes for the train journey.

● **By taxi:** allow for around 130F to the centre of Paris.

Between Roissy-Charles-de-Gaulle 1 and 2 and Orly

The **Air France** coach to Orly leaves from Roissy-Charles-de-Gaulle, Terminal 1 (gate 36, Arrivals level), 2A and 2C (gate C2) and 2B and 2D (gate B1). Departures to Roissy-Charles-de-Gaulle go from Orly-Sud (gate F) and Orly-Ouest (gate D, Arrivals level). The service runs from 6am to 11pm every 20 minutes (in both directions). Journey time: 50 minutes. Connecting passengers can get a transit ticket from the connection services (follow the signs at the airport).

Roissy-Rail + Orlyval: this is a shuttle service from Roissy-Charles-de-Gaulle airport to Denfert-Rochereau followed by the RER, line B to Antony and then the Orlyval between Antony and Orly. Runs daily from 6.30am to 10.30pm (Sunday 7am to 10.55pm).

● **By taxi:** budget for around 300F.

For those on a budget

● The Carte Orange (*see* 'Getting around') is valid for Roissy-Rail and Orly-Rail, as long as you have a *coupon* covering zone 4 for Roissy and zone 3 for Orly.

● The Orly-Rail ticket gives access to the Metro and RER networks, at no extra cost.

● Regular visitors to France might consider the *Carte Multipass*, valid for a year on Air France coaches. This can be bought on board the coaches or at Air France agencies and works using a system of units which are deducted from the card after each Air France coach trip. The card costs 200F for 50 credits and 398F for 100 credits. The journey from Montparnasse to Roissy-Charles-de-Gaulle uses 13 credits, which is 52F instead of 70F.

ARRIVING BY TRAIN

The *Eurostar* train links London's Waterloo station with the Gare du Nord in Paris in just 3 hours, with about 20 trains a day. The Gare du Nord has rapid connections with the centre of Paris, on the RER D line, among others. For schedules and fares ☎ (UK) (0990) 186 186. Website: www.eurostar.com

Rail Europe in the UK has information on train travel to Paris from the rest of France. ☎ (020) 7730 3402. Website: www.raileurope.com. Before boarding your train in France, don't forget to punch (*composter*) your ticket in one of the orange machines at the station. If you don't, your ticket is not valid. All Paris train stations have excellent bus and Metro connections with the rest of the city.

BUDGET

Paris is not necessarily any more expensive than other European capital cities. However, the twin temptations of its wonderful restaurants and more than 30,000 shops, many of them graciously accepting credit cards, mean that, in spending terms, the sky's the limit. There is plenty of accommodation for those on a shoestring, but for a little more comfort, you should find a double room in an appealing 3-star central hotel for 600F–900F. If the tariff doesn't include breakfast, you might prefer to venture out to a nearby café for your coffee and croissant; hotel breakfasts charged separately tend to be rather pricey.

If you do need to keep an eye on the *centimes*, be wary of resting your sightseeing legs too frequently in those alluring cafés. Remember that bar and café prices are lowest when you stay standing, and highest when you're sitting outside. A cup of coffee in the legendary Café de Flore or Café de la Paix is shockingly overpriced, but how can you resist the sense of history?

CLOTHING

Christian Lacroix, Christian Dior, Jean-Paul Gaultier, Yves Saint-Laurent, Agnès B, Comme des Garçons, Hermès, Givenchy, Pierre Cardin, Louis Vuitton . . . the list of Paris-based designers is seemingly endless. Although casual style is now accepted almost everywhere in the city, Paris is still the *haute couture* capital of the world. Twice a year, the fashion circus comes to town, to attend the ritual shows held at the Carrousel du Louvre. In tow is the press pack, there to capture on film every shimmy, pout and (God forbid!) stumble of the top models.

You'll have to go to some lengths of preening and grooming before you feel overdressed here. French women are renowned for displaying a certain *je ne sais quoi* in their style, mixing classic clothes with the chicest of accessories. They'll add a chiffon scarf here, a tiny handbag there, and generally achieve a neat, fashionable look. Personal appearance is very important to Parisian men, too, and, along with the Italians, they are probably the best-dressed chaps in Europe. Perhaps surprisingly, there's something of a trend for *le style anglais*. Traditional brogues, English-style shirt collars and waxed country coats are all popular, and worn with a French swagger.

Wealthy Parisians insist on nothing but the best for their darling offspring. You will often see children looking like miniature fashion models, in adorable outfits, with hair perfectly cut and styled. Paris has many boutiques and designer ranges to tempt indulgent parents and grandparents – at a price!

As for what to take with you (rather than what to take away in those lovely shopping bags!), compact Paris is an ideal city for walking, so you'll really appreciate a pair of comfortable shoes at the end of a day's sightseeing. A light overcoat might help you to keep your belongings well hidden from pickpockets. In the evenings, enjoy making a bit of an effort; you won't feel out of place. Men should wear a jacket and tie to a smart restaurant, but people rarely dress up to the nines for the opera or theatre nowadays, except on opening nights. Even so, scruffiness is never welcomed. Trainers are not always viewed with admiration, even in a casual setting, so consider your footwear carefully if you want to make an impression.

COMMUNICATIONS

INTERNET

E-mail your holiday snaps of one of Europe's most photogenic cities straight to your family and friends while you're still in Paris. The French are mad about technology – indeed, they have had access to online information for more than 15 years, with France Telecom's Minitel service – and Paris has a number of cybercafés. They're friendly places, serving coffee and other drinks, and sometimes sandwiches and snacks. They also provide computer terminals by the hour, so that you can pick up and send e-mails, and surf the Net at your leisure. You'll also find terminals for public use in many of the larger post offices.

- **Web Bar:** 32 rue de Picardie 75003. Metro: République. ☎ 01-42-72-66-55. Website: www.webbar.fr
- **Café Orbital:** 13 rue de Médicis 75006. Metro: Odéon. ☎ 01-43-25-76-77. Website: www.cafeorbital.com. The first cybercafé in Paris, set up in 1995, 200m from the Sorbonne University. Serves hot drinks, fruit juices, beers and 'cyberwiches'.
- **Travel Café:** 2 ruede l'Alleray 75015. Metro: Vaugirard. Website: www.abcvoyage.com/travelcafe.html

POST

Stamps are available at post offices (closed Sunday and Saturday after 12pm) and at tobacco shops (*tabacs*). Letterboxes on the streets are yellow. Last pick-up is around 6 or 7pm at post offices and from 8 to 10pm at the main post office. Outgoing post can also be left at the reception desk of your hotel. The main post office is at 52 rue du Louvre 75001 ☎ 01-40-28-20-00. It is open 24 hours a day in case you need to make a phone call or buy a stamp when the other offices are closed.

When you go to collect any *poste restante* (which can be received at any post office, as long as you know the address and postcode of the office), ask them to check under the initial for your first name as well as your surname. The French often write their name with their family name first, so you may find your letters filed under 'J' for 'John' rather than 'S' for 'Smith', for example.

- **Telegrams:** for telegrams overseas: ☎ 0800-33-44-11.

TELEPHONE

Phone calls in France cost roughly the same as in the US and UK. Few phone boxes take coins, with phone cards (*télécartes*) being far more widely used. These cards, which represent good value for money, are available from *tabacs* all over Paris, or from post offices. Phoning from a hotel is expensive, as in all countries.

For all calls within France – both local and long-distance – dial all 10 digits of the phone number. Phone numbers are broken up into five sets of two, and each set is spoken as a whole number. The number 02-25-30-55-68, for example, would be said 'zero-two, twenty-five, thirty, fifty-five, sixty-eight'. If you do say it as individual numbers, however, you will be understood!

Dialling codes from France:

United Kingdom: 00 44
Republic of Ireland: 00 353
United States: 00 1
Canada: 00 1
Australia: 00 61
New Zealand: 00 64
South Africa: 00 27

Dialling codes to France:

From United Kingdom: 00 33
From Republic of Ireland: 00 33
From United States: 011 33
From Canada: 011 33
From Australia: 0011 33
From New Zealand: 00 33
From South Africa: 09 33

Most people in Paris (like everywhere else!) seem to live by (and through) their mobile phones. Many British-registered mobile phones will be usable in Paris, but most mobile phones from the US don't work in Europe, so check with your supplier before you leave.

ELECTRICITY

Voltage is 220V and sockets accept plugs with two round pins. Adaptors can be bought at the airport before you leave, or try the BHV department store (52/64 rue de Rivoli 75004. Metro: Hôtel-de-Ville) if you forget. It opens late on Wednesdays.

EMBASSIES AND CONSULATES

IN PARIS

United Kingdom: 35 rue du Faubourg-St-Honore 75383. ☎ +33-1-44-51-31-00. Fax: +33-1-42-66-91-42. Consulate: ☎ +33-1-44-51-31-02. Website: www.amb-grandebretagne.fr (Consulates-General in Bordeaux, Lille, Lyon, Marseille and Paris).

Republic of Ireland: 12 avenue Foch 75116. ☎ +33-1-44-17-67-00. Fax: +33-1-44-17-67-60
United States: 2 avenue Gabriel 75008. ☎ (and Consulate) +33-1-43-12-22-22. Fax: +33-1-42-55-97-83. Website: www.amb-usa.fr (Consulates in Marseille, Paris and Strasbourg).
Canada: 35 avenue Montaigne 75008. ☎ +33-1-44-43-29-94. Fax: +33-1-44-43-29-99. Website: www.amba-canada.fr
Australia: 4 rue Jean Rey, Cedex 15, 75015. ☎ +33-1-40-59-33-00. Fax: +33-1-40-59-33-10. Website: www.austgov.fr
New Zealand: 7 ter, rue Léonard de Vinci 75116. ☎ + 33-1-45-00-24-11. Fax: +33-1-45-01-26-39.
South Africa: 59 quai d'Orsay 75007. ☎ +33-1-45-55-92-37. Fax: +33-1-47-05-51-28 (Consulates in Le Havre, Lille and Marseille).

FRENCH EMBASSIES AND CONSULATES ABROAD

United Kingdom: French Embassy, 58 Knightsbridge, London SW1. ☎ (020) 7201 1000. Website: www.ambafrance.org.uk
Republic of Ireland: French Embassy, 36 Ailesbury Road, Dublin 4. ☎ (01) 260 1666
United States: French Embassy, 4101 Reservoir Road NW, Washington DC 20007. ☎ (01) 202 944 6000/6212. Website: www.info-france-usa.org (Consulates in Atlanta, Boston, Chicago, Houston, Los Angeles, Miami, New Orleans, New York, San Francisco and Washington DC)
Canada: French Embassy, 42 Promenade Sussex, Ottawa K1M 2C9. ☎ (613) 789 1795. Fax: (613) 562 3704. Website: www.amba-ottawa.fr (Consulate-General in Moncton, Montreal, Quebec, Toronto and Vancouver)
Australia: French Embassy, 6 Perth Avenue, Yarralumla, Canberra, ACT 2600. ☎ (43) 2216 0100. Fax: (43) 2216 0156. Website: www.france.net.au (Consulates-General in Sydney and Melbourne)
New Zealand: French Embassy, 34–42 Manners Street, PO Box 11–343, Wellington. ☎ (04) 384 2555/2577. Website: www.ambafrance.net.nz (Consulate in Auckland)
South Africa: French Embassy, 807 George Avenue, Arcadia, Pretoria, 0083, Gauteng. ☎ (12) 429 7000/7029. Website: www.france.co.za (Consulates in Johannesburg and Cape Town)

EMERGENCIES

- For the police, call 17
- Emergency help in English **SOS Help** ☎ 01-47-23-80-80
- **SAMU** (ambulance): ☎ 15
- **Emergencies:** ☎ 18 or 01-48-28-40-04
- **SOS Médecins** (emergency doctors): ☎ 01-43-37-77-77/01-47-07-77-77
- **SOS Dentistes** (emergency dentists): ☎ 01-47-07-44-44. Daily 8am to 10pm
- **24-hour pharmacies** (open daily): 6 place Félix-Éboué 75012. ☎ 01-43-43-19-03. Metro: Daumesnil-Félix-Éboué; 84 avenue des Champs-Élysées 75008 (in the Les Champs shopping arcade). F 01-45-62-02-41. Metro: George-V.

ENTRY FORMALITIES

CUSTOMS AND DUTY FREE

No matter where you are travelling from, the importing of narcotics, copyright infringements, fakes and counterfeit goods is strictly prohibited for anyone travelling to France. Firearms and ammunition are also forbidden unless accompanied by specific authorization from the appropriate Ministry in Paris.

When returning to the UK, obscene material and offensive weapons are prohibited in addition to those items listed by French customs.

UK (EU) citizens: Any goods that are for personal use are free from both French and UK customs duty. To meet the criteria of 'personal use' there is a set of guidelines that is used by all EU customs officers. These guidelines include up to 800 cigarettes or 1kg of loose tobacco, 10 litres of spirits, 90 litres of wine and 110 litres of beer. Despite the liberalized restrictions on importing and exporting tobacco and alcohol, the removal of duty-free allowances for EU visitors means that prices in France now include duty, which cannot be reclaimed.

At any port of entry, those with nothing to declare should use the 'Green Channel' and those with goods in excess of their allowance should use the Red Channel, both marked clearly after passport control. There is a separate 'Blue Channel' for members of the EU (*see* 'Passports and visas').

For further information and clarification, in the UK contact the Excise and Inland Customs Advice Centre ☎ 020 7202 4227, or visit their website at www.hmce.gov.uk. In France, call the customs information centre in Paris ☎ 01-40-01-02-06.

All other citizens: The limitations on import and export outside the EU are far more stringent than within it, but visitors from outside the EU may bring back goods free of duty or tax. To qualify, you must spend more than 1,200F at a single store; the retailer will supply a Retail Export Form, called a *bordereau de détaxe*, which must be endorsed by customs and will be returned by them to the retailer, who will in turn refund the tax portion (20.6 per cent) of your purchase. Visitors over 15 may take up to 1,200F worth of articles back home with them free of duty or tax. In addition they may leave France with 200 cigarettes or 250g of smoking tobacco, 2 litres of wine, 1 litre of spirits and 50g of perfume. Those under 17 may not export tobacco or alcohol from France.

PASSPORTS AND VISAS

In 1985, France signed the Schengen Agreement, which means that a visa issued by a French Embassy includes entry not only to France, but also to Austria, Belgium, Germany, Italy, Luxembourg, The Netherlands, Portugal and Spain. There is no longer any formal border between many of these countries and flights between them now take off and land from domestic terminals.

The UK did not sign the Schengen Agreement and has maintained inter-EU immigration control. However, many UK ports of entry have a separate passenger exit, marked by a blue sign with yellow stars, where EU members can simply wave their passports at an immigration officer.

Citizens of the UK and any other EU country may remain in France for as long as they wish without a visa and may also be employed while abroad.

Citizens of Australia, New Zealand and the US do not require a visa for short stays (up to three months), but they must apply to their nearest consulate or embassy for long-stay visas or a *Carte de Commerçant*, which permits employment in France.

Canadian citizens do not need a visa to visit France; they are at liberty to remain in the country for a period of up to three months providing they are in possession of a passport valid up to six months after the end of the intended visit. For longer (and working) stays a visa will be required and may be obtained at the French embassy or consulate.

Citizens of South Africa need a visa to enter France and must apply at least three weeks before leaving South Africa. Applicants must have a valid passport that does not expire within three months of the expiry date of the French visa. A visa can be issued for either three or six months, unless the applicant is a student, diplomat or has business interests in France. If this is the case, contact your local French embassy before you depart.

FESTIVALS AND EVENTS

6 January: Epiphany, or Fête des Rois
This religious date is celebrated by the eating of the *Galette des Rois*, a traditional cake with a crown and a hidden charm. The child who finds the charm wears the crown and becomes king or queen for a day.

First week in March: Salon de l'Agriculture (Paris Agricultural Fair), Porte de Versailles 75015
Fine beasts and a vast food and drink hall celebrating the French agricultural industry.

End of March to end of May: Foire du Trône, Bois de Vincennes 75012
The largest traditional funfair in France, with everything from carousels to candy floss.

Second half of April: Paris Marathon
In the style of the New York, London, Boston . . . .

1 May: Labour Day
Processions and marches organized by trade unions, and gifts of bouquets of lily-of-the-valley.

May to end of July: Paris Jazz Festival
Programme of jazz performances, including many free concerts, based around the Parc Floral de Paris 75012.

Last Saturday in May: Grand Steeplechase de Paris, Auteuil Racecourse 75016
Steeplechase-style racing (over fences) was introduced to Auteuil in the late 19th century, making a change from the trotting style that is more usual in France.

Last week in May–first week in June: French Open, Roland Garros

France's own Grand Slam men's and women's tennis tournament, on the red clay courts of the Stade Roland-Garros.

Mid-June to end of August: Traditional funfair, Jardin des Tuileries 75001

Midsummer (around 21 June): Fête de la Musique, all over Paris
On the evening of the longest day, musicians take to the streets and stages of Paris, to take part in this government-inspired annual festival. This social phenomenon dates back to 1981.

21 June: International rose competition, Jardin de Bagatelle, Bois de Boulogne
Prizes for the best blooms, then the rose garden stays open until October.

Late June: Course des Garçons de Café, start and finish at Hôtel de Ville.
Hundreds of waiters and waitresses in uniform test their balancing skills, and fitness, in races through the streets of Paris.

14 July: Bastille Day
The most important day in French revolutionary history is celebrated on the evening of the 13th with wild festivities, including a gay and lesbian bash for 20,000 people on the Quai de la Tournelle, and traditional parties (*bals populaires*) in Parisian fire stations. The day after is reserved for a military parade on the Champs-Élysées, led by the President, followed by a huge firework display over the Trocadéro.

Mid-July: Final of the French National Rugby Cup, Stade de France, St-Denis-la-Plaine 93216

Mid-July to mid-August: 'Paris Quartier d'Été'
Month-long programme of unusual events to liven up the summer, when traditionally Parisians evacuate the city for their holiday on the coast.

Mid-July to beginning of September: Festival of Open-Air Cinema, Parc de la Villette
Special outdoor summer screenings of selected films.

Around 23 July: Tour de France
The legendary cycling race culminates with the survivors tearing up and down the Champs-Élysées in front of thousands of passionate spectators.

End of September: Paris Gardens Festival
A weekend with hundreds of free events in parks and gardens all over the city, and the chance to see secret gardens that are rarely open to the public.

End of September to end of December: Autumn Arts Festival
One of Paris' most high-profile cultural events, with a vast range of performances, from singing and dancing to theatre and film.

1 October: Prix de l'Arc de Triomphe, Hippodrome de Longchamp, Bois de Boulogne
France's most important horse race, marking the start of the racing season, and a significant event on the French social calendar.

First Saturday of October: Montmartre Village Festival
Celebrations in this village-like quarter of the city, for the harvesting of its own tiny vineyard, which produces 500 bottles of suspect wine every year.

Third weekend in October: FIAC Paris (Contemporary Art Fair), Pavillon du Parc de Paris, Place de la Porte de Versailles

Amost 100 dealers from all over the France, and further afield, meet to buy and sell modern art.

Third week in December: Christmas crib
Giant nativity scene set up under a tent in front of the Hôtel de Ville; proceeds go to charity and queues are long.

24 December: Christmas Eve
Many Parisians have a big blow-out meal on the evening before Christmas Day, rather than on the day itself. For some, the Christmas Midnight Mass at Notre-Dame is more of a priority.

End December: International Circus Festival, Big Top, Pelouse de Reuilly, Porte Dorée 75012
Competitions and shows put on by the best circus performers of today and the future.

GETTING AROUND

PUBLIC TRANSPORT

The city of Paris has an extremely efficient public transport network, with **Metro** and **RER** trains, and day and night **buses**. The Metro trains run from 5.30am to around 12.30am; to use the system, simply identify your line number and the correct terminating station for the direction you want to take, and follow the signs indicating *direction*. Hail a bus from a bus stop, and make sure you punch individual tickets in the machine by the door.

There are a number of different **tickets** and **travel passes** available for use on the RATP network of buses, Metro and RER trains. Single tickets can be bought for each journey, but it's much cheaper to buy them in a *carnet* (or book) of 10, from Metro stations, *tabacs* or tourist offices. Alternatively, if you're staying a few days, or planning to use the transport system to the full on any particular day, consider one of the travel cards or passes, which are excellent value.

- **Carte Orange:** the weekly, monthly or annual travel pass that's an essential item in every carless Parisian's wallet. The daily version, which tourists might find useful, is known as the *Formule 1*. The Carte Orange entitles the holder to travel on the buses, Metro and RER trains.

- **Carte Paris-Visite:** perfect for visiting Paris and the surrounding area, this non-transferable pass is used in conjunction with a *coupon* covering a choice of zones 1 to 3, 1 to 5 (including use of the line to Orly airport) or 1 to 8. The *coupon* is valid for 1 to 5 consecutive days and allows an unlimited number of journeys within the chosen zones, over the whole of the RATP network. Prices: 55F for one day, 90F for two days, 120F for three days and 175F for five days. Reductions for children. The Paris-Visite card also entitles the holder to a discount on 14 tourist activities, including the Cité des Sciences, the Musée Grévin and the Pont-Neuf boat trips.

- **Mobilis:** cheap and practical, the *Mobilis* pass comprises a non-transferable card (without photo) and a *coupon* covering a choice from zones 1 to 2 up to 1 to 8, which may be purchased in advance. The two-zone *coupon*, for example, costs 30F for one day. It allows an unlimited number of journeys within the chosen zones, on the RATP and SNCF Île-de-France networks, except for the Roissy-Charles-de-Gaulle and Orly airport lines. Unlike the *Paris-Visite* card, it does not give any discounts on tourist sites.

● **SNCF information and ticket sales:** ☎ 08-36-35-35-35

● **RATP Information:** 53 quai des Grands-Augustins 75006. ☎ 01-43-46-14-14 or 08-36-68-77-14. Metro: St-Michel. Information on timetables, ticket prices and routes on the Metro, RER or buses, available 6am to 9pm daily. Metro and bus maps are distributed free of charge from here, and can also be found at Metro and bus stations.

TAXIS

Taxis can be hailed on the street (when the light on the top is on) or at one of the city's taxi ranks, which are marked with a sign. The meter starts running with an initial fare of about 13F. The rates go up after 7pm and outside the city limits. Drivers generally expect to be paid in cash, and it is usual to add a 10 per cent tip.

FOR ARMCHAIR TRAVELLERS

● **Paris Story:** 11 *bis,* rue Scribe 75009. ☎ 01-42-66-62-06. Metro: Auber or Opéra. Open daily 9am to 8pm from 1 April to 31 October, 9am to 6pm the rest of the year. A 45-minute film tracing 2,000 years of Parisian history. One showing every hour. Entrance fee: 50F for adults; 30F for those between 6 and 18; free for under–6s.

Take a trip around Paris in just 45 minutes, comfortably seated in a cinema. Awarded a prestigious prize for innovation when it first opened, this wide-screen montage has lost a little of its freshness, but remains popular with tourists. It shows the different faces of Paris – artistic, historic, poetic, mysterious and roguish – and is accompanied by superb music by Rameau, Debussy, Ravel, Verdi, Gounod and Édith Piaf, telling the story of a village which became a great capital.

At the end of the show, there is an free (rather scholarly) exhibition called *Paristyles*, for keen historians, which offers photos, graphics and comments on the evolution of Parisian urban planning over 2,000 years.

ON FOOT

● *Paris à pied* ('Paris on foot') **topoguide**, from the **Fédération Française de Randonnée Pédestre** (the French ramblers' federation): 14 rue Riquet 75019. Information: ☎ 01-44-89-93-93. Open Monday to Friday 10am to 6pm. Metro: Riquet.

Paris is the perfect city for visitors who love walking, with its neat and compact centre. There are two main FFRP routes, both clearly signposted with yellow and red markers, each around 20km (12 miles) long. The first goes from the Parc Montsouris to La Villette (you can then come back by boat if you time it right); the other takes you to the Bois de Vincennes from Porte Dauphine.

The *Topoguide*, on sale for 99F from all large bookshops and at the Fédération (*see above*), provides accurate maps, and gives detailed historical comments on the quarters through which the routes pass.

• **Promenades parisiennes** (Parisian walks, from the organization of the Musées de la Ville de Paris): 37 rue des Francs-Bourgeois 75004. ☎ 01-42-76-47-42. Brochures available from 31 rue des Francs-Bourgeois, town hall and tourist offices.

Each route covers a particular quarter where walkers can discover the historical and architectural heritage of Paris. Unfortunately, most of the brochures (which were free) are now out of print individually and have been published instead in a complete illustrated edition priced at 159F. For the moment, only the following walks are still available free of charge: *La République to La Villette; Les Tuileries to Le Louvre; The banks of the Seine.*

• **Service des Visites des Parcs et Jardins de la Ville de Paris** (parks and gardens department): 1 avenue Gordon-Bennett 75016. ☎ 01-40-71-75-60 or 01-40-71-75-23. Metro: Porte-d'Auteuil. Publishes a free series of brochures (although a few have now gone out of print) for lovers of contemporary parks and gardens, with detailed information on some of the city's most recent projects, including the Parc André-Citroën, the Promenade Plantée (Floral Walkway), and the Parc de Bercy.

Nature-trail leaflets are available from the *Maison Paris-Nature* (pavillon 1, Parc Floral de Paris 75012), the *Maison de l'Air* (27 rue Piat 75020. ☎ 01-43-28-47-63) and the *Parc de Bercy*, 41 rue Paul-Belmondo. Cost is 5F per leaflet, 120F for all 24. The town halls in each of the arrondissements distribute the leaflets which deal with their areas free of charge (the leaflet on the Bois de Vincennes, for example, is distributed by the town hall of the 12th arrondissement).

The leaflets were designed to help walkers to find traces of nature in the urban environment. There are 24 itineraries, one for each arrondissement, plus one each for the Bois de Boulogne, the Bois de Vincennes, the Forêt de Beauregard and the arboretum de l'École du Breuil. Regularly updated, they include a map and an aid to identifying plants, and spotting insects and birds, and fossils.

• **Walks and guided visits in the parks and gardens:** programme information ☎ 01-40-71-75-60. 38F per walk, 26F for under–25s, no advance booking. The parks of Paris hide a thousand and one curiosities and nearly all of them have a tale to tell. From March to the end of autumn, a variety of walks, lasting around 2 hours, give visitors a chance to discover their secrets in the company of knowledgeable botanists or historians.

BY BIKE AND SCOOTER

• **Escapade Nature:** reservations ☎ 01-53-17-03-18, or fax: 01-43-45-57-19. This very professional association organizes guided rides around Paris, lasting between 90 minutes and 3 hours according to the programme you choose. Tariffs include the hire of the bike: *relaxing ride* lasting 90 minutes 105F; *discovery ride* lasting 3 hours 165F. A bit cheaper if you bring your own bike. Reduced rates for under 12s.

• **Paris à vélo c'est sympa!:** (Paris is fun on a bike!) 37 boulevard Bourdon 75004. ☎ 01-48-87-60-01. Fax: 01-48-87-61-01. Metro: Bastille. Take a 3-hour bike ride around Paris with a guide and discover an unknown and unusual side of the capital. During the week, every morning at 10am; 'Paris by night' (reservations only) at 8.30pm on Tuesday, Thursday, Saturday and Sunday; Saturday departures at

10am, 3pm and 8.30pm (summer only); Sunday departures at 6am (summer only), 10am and 3pm. A range of themed rides includes *Paris insolites* ('Unique Paris') in the 13th arrondissement; *Paris contrastes* ('The Paris of contrasts') in the 19th and 20th arrondissements; *Paris-village: Montmartre* ('Paris as a village: Montmartre') in the 18th arrondissement; *Paris Art-nouveau* in the 16th arrondissement; and *Paris s'éveille* ('Paris awakes') from 6 to 9am. Budget for between 150F to 170F (plus an annual subscription of 20F) inclusive of bike, guide and insurance; 130F for groups. There are also rides in the Île-de-France (trips around the Marne and Versailles). Bicycle hire also possible (60F per half-day, 80F per day).

● **Paris-vélo:** 2 rue du Fer-à-Moulin 75005. ☎ 01-43-37-59-22. Fax: 01-47-07-67-45. Metro: Censier-Daubenton. This bike-hire shop has been in business for more than 20 years, and now also offers bike trips around the capital. There are a number of accompanied rides for groups (minimum seven people), including *Paris insolite* ('Unique Paris') or *Circuit grands monuments ('The great monuments'), leaving at 10am. 'Paris by night', leaves at 8.30pm.* À la carte trips are also available. The price (120F to 180F; student discounts available) includes guide, bike and insurance. Reservation necessary. Bike hire also available: 90F per day from 10am to 7pm, 75F per half-day, 420F per week (2,000F deposit required).

● **RATP-Roue libre** ('freewheeling'): ☎ 08-36-68-77-14. From March to October you can hire bikes from the Eiffel Tower, Châtelet, St-Germain-en-Laye, the Bois de Boulogne and the Bois de Vincennes, for around 45F per half-day. A free guide to cycle routes is available from RATP ticket offices.

● **Vélo-Taxi** (bike-taxi): ☎ 01-47-42-00-01.

● **Scooter hire:** L'Atelier de la Compagnie des Scooters Parisiens, 13 rue Legrand 92240 Malakoff. ☎ 01-46-55-72-32. Metro: Porte-de-Vanves; 57 boulevard de Grenelle 75015. ☎ 01-45-79-77-24. Metro: Dupleix. When the weather is fine, scooters become less readily available.

BUS AND COACH TOURS

Balabus de la RATP (RATP's 'Wanderbus'): under the Grande Arche de La Défense. Metro: Grande-Arche; and at the Gare de Lyon 75012. Information: ☎ 08-36-68-77-14. Metro: Gare-de-Lyon. All Sundays and Bank Holidays, from the first Sunday in April to the last Sunday in September. Departures leave approximately every 20 minutes from 12.30pm from La Défense and from 1.30pm from the Gare de Lyon, until 8pm at the Défense and 8.30pm at the Gare de Lyon. The hour-long trip costs three single RATP tickets (one-way), and is free for those in possession of a *Carte Orange* (zones 1–3 minimum), and *Paris-Visite* or *Mobilis* cardholders. No reduction for children.

The Balabus travels right across Paris, passing the most interesting sites and monuments. You can hop on and hop off but, unless you've got one of the travel passes, you have to pay with one to three RATP tickets, depending on the length of the journey, each time you do so. If you don't have a travel pass, it's perhaps better to take the whole superb ride in one go.

● **Noctambuses** (night buses): from 1am to 6am, leaving from

Châtelet, for night owls or early birds.

● Some **regular bus lines** allow you to visit the length and breadth of Paris on a single Metro ticket. For example, see the Champs-Élysées on the No. 73, travel along the Seine via place de la Concorde and the Louvre on the No. 72), or visit Paris from north to south by way of the Opéra, the Île de la Cité and boulevard St-Michel on the No. 21. You can also take a tour of Paris with the **Metro Aerien** (overhead Metro), going from Nation to Charles-de-Gaulle-Étoile by way of Denfert-Rochereau on line 6, or from Charles-de-Gaulle-Étoile to Nation, via Barbès-Rochechouart, on line 2.

Cityrama: 4 place des Pyramides 75001. ☎ 01-44-55-61-00. Metro: Pyramides, Palais-Royal or Tuileries. Open daily 7am to 8.30pm 1 November to 31 March; 7am to 10pm 1 April to 31 October. Open-top coaches.

Paris-Vision: 214 rue de Rivoli 75001. ☎ 01-42-60-31-25. Metro: Tuileries. Open-top coaches departing every hour, daily, between 9.30am and 5pm, April to October and four times a day from November to March. The 2-hour tour costs 100F (free for under–11s).

BY BOAT

The 13km (8 miles) of the River Seine have been gradually conquered and tamed over a period of roughly 2,000 years, and today this wide waterway is one of the city's most beautiful avenues. When Queen Elizabeth II came to Paris in 1953, one of the priorities of her hosts was to take her on a *bâteau-mouche* trip of the Seine. You can do the same, choosing from a number of boat companies (*see below*).

Bateaux Parisiens: port de la Bourdonnais, near the Eiffel Tower, on the Left Bank. ☎ 01-44-11-33-44. Metro: Bir-Hakeim-Grenelle. Prices: 50F for adults and 25F for under 12s for a traditional boat trip. An excellent service with 3 hours' free parking, and 1-hour trips departing every 30 minutes in peak season, from 10am to 10pm (no departure at 7.30pm). Between November and March departures are every hour between 10am and 9pm. This company is very close to the Eiffel Tower. Park your car, go on the boat trip and then, from the third level of the tower, take a look at the route you've just followed.

Bateaux-mouches: port Conférence 75008. ☎ 01-42-25-96-10/40-76-99-99-99.

La Guêpe Buissonnière and Le Canotier: ☎ 01-42-40-96-97. Fax: 01-42-40-77-30. Trips on the Parc de la Villette ornamental lake and the Canal St-Martin (*see* '10th arrondissement, Canal St-Martin' *and* '19th arrondissement, Parc de la Villette').

Batobus: the boat shuttles run between six stops – the Eiffel Tower, Musée d'Orsay (quai de Solférino), St-Germain-des-Prés (quai Malaquais), Notre-Dame (quai de Montebello), Hôtel de Ville (quai de l'Hôtel-de-Ville) and the Louvre (quai du Louvre). ☎ 01-44-11-33-99. Fax: 01-45-56-07-88. Cost: 20F for the first stop and then 10F for each extra stop; fixed daily price for the whole round trip at 65F, and 35F for under–12s. Daily trips, 1 April to 30 September, 10am to 7pm (9pm in July and August), one about every 25 minutes.

BY HELICOPTER

Paris Hélicoptère: Zone aviation d'affaires, aéroport du Bourget, 93350 Le Bourget. ☎ 01-48-35-90-44. Website: www.paris-helicoptere.com. Metro: Le Bourget. Bus No. 350 goes to the terminal. All flights leave from the airport at Paris-Le Bourget and have to be booked in advance. A 25-minute flight encompassing an 80-km loop of the capital costs 800F per person. This exhilarating excursion provides an exceptional panoramic view of Paris that you would otherwise see only in a photo.

HEALTH AND INSURANCE

France has a very good public health service, and standards are comparable with those found in other western European countries and the US. For minor ailments, go in the first instance to a pharmacy (look out for the green cross), where highly qualified pharmacists should be able to give you valuable advice. Many medicines are available over the counter in France.

In an emergency, doctors' and dentists' services are available at the end of the phone (*see* , 'Emergencies').

Hospitalized visitors will be expected to make immediate payment for any treatment, but hospital staff will help with arrangements with insurance companies.

Statistically speaking, you are far more likely to encounter accidents or fall victim to some form of crime when abroad than at home. Travel and health insurance is therefore highly recommended. It is available through airlines, credit card companies, travel agents and student and senior-affiliated organizations (such as STA and SAGA). Insurance may be included in the price of your ticket or package, or you may be covered by your credit card company (particularly American Express) if your ticket was purchased with that card.

For South Africans coming to Paris, the French Embassy will insist on proof of insurance before issuing a visa.

UK and Ireland visitors: Form E111 entitles the holder to free or reduced-cost emergency medical treatment when in France. If a visitor becomes hospitalized, he or she can expect approximately the same level of care and treatment as in the UK. Available at any main post office, E111s must be filled out and stamped by the post office before you leave the UK; they are issued free of charge and are valid indefinitely, or until used to claim treatment.

North American visitors: whereas Canada's public health service will pay a proportion of its citizens' medical costs while abroad, the US Medicare/Medicaid programme does not cover health expenses outside the US, and US medical insurance is not always valid in France. It is advisable to check the nature and extent of foreign coverage with individual insurance companies; often, the visitor will have to pay first and claim reimbursement later.

Australia, New Zealand and South Africa visitors: citizens of these countries are on their own if they need treatment and do not have health insurance. French hospitals demand on-the-spot payment for medical care, so insurance is vital.

LANGUAGE

France has an enviable education system, which puts a good emphasis on the learning of English. As a result, especially in the capital city, you should be able to communicate successfully with most people under a certain age (and many who are older!). Hotel reception staff are almost always multilingual. Waiters and waitresses will usually know enough to take your order in English, but it's fun to attempt to get to grips with the menu in French. You may meet with a fairly dismissive response, but it's worth a try!

HANDY WORDS AND PHRASES

Over the next few pages you'll find a selection of very basic French vocabulary, and many apologies if the word you are looking for is missing. For those struggling with French menus, there is more help at the back of the book in the detailed menu decoder.

Let us begin, however, with a very basic guide to some French grammar: All French nouns are either masculine or feminine and gender is denoted as follows: 'the' singular is translated by le (m), la (f) or l' (in front of a word beginning with a vowel or mute 'h'; 'the' plural = les (whatever gender and in front of a vowel or mute 'h'). 'A' = un (m), une(f) (no exceptions for vowels or mute 'h').

There are two forms of the word 'you' – tu is 'you' in the singular, very informal and used with people you know, vous is 'you' in the singular but is used in formal situations and when you don't know the person vous is also the plural form. Young people often address each other as 'tu' automatically, but when in doubt and to avoid offence, always use 'vous'.

Adjectives agree with the gender of the accompanying noun. For a singular masculine noun there is no change to the adjective, but to indicate the masculine plural, an 's' is added to the end of the adjective; an 'e' is usually added for a feminine noun and 'es' for the plural. If you are not very familiar with French don't worry too much about gender agreement when talking (unless you wish to perfect your pronunciation, as 'e' or 'es' usually makes the final consonant hard). We have used feminine versions where applicable simply to help with the understanding of written French. These are either written out in full or shown as '(e)'. Finally, if you do not know the right French word try using the English one with a French accent – it is surprising how often this works.

THE VERB 'TO BE':

I am	je suis
you are (informal/sing.)	tu es
he/she/it is	il(m)/elle(f)/il est*
we are	nous sommes
you are (formal/plural)	vous êtes
they are	ils(m)/elles(f) sont*

When you are in a hurry gender can complicate things – just say le or la, whichever comes into your head first and you will sometimes be right and usually be understood.

* The most common forms use the masculine: 'it is' = il est, 'they are'= ils sont. C'est = 'that is' or 'this is', and is not gender specific.

ESSENTIAL VOCABULARY

Yes/No	Oui/Non
OK	D'accord
That's fine	C'est bon
Please	S'il vous plaît
Thank you	Merci
Good morning/Hello (during the day)	Bonjour
Good evening/night/Hello (during the evening)	Bonsoir
Hello/Goodbye (very informal)	Salut
Goodbye	Au revoir
See you soon	À bientôt
Excuse me	Excusez-moi
I am sorry	Je suis désolé(m)/désolée(f)
Pardon?	Comment?

Handy phrases

Do you speak English?	Parlez-vous anglais?
I don't speak French	Je ne parle pas français
I don't understand	Je ne comprends pas
Could you speak more slowly please?	Pouvez-vous parler moins vite s'il vous plaît?
Could you repeat that, please?	Pouvez-vous répéter, s'il vous plaît?
again	encore
I am English/Scottish/ Welsh/Irish/American/ Canadian/Australian/ a New Zealander	Je suis anglais(e)/écossais(e)/ gallois(e)/irlandais(e)/américain(e)/ canadien(ne)/australien(ne)/ néo-zélandais(e)
My name is . . .	Je m'appelle . . .
What is your name?	Comment vous appelez-vous?
How are you?	Comment allez-vous?
Very well, thank you	Très bien, merci
Pleased to meet you	Enchanté(e)
Mr/Mrs	Monsieur/Madame
Miss/Ms	Mademoiselle/Madame
How?	Comment?
What?	Quel (m)/Quelle (f)?
When?	Quand?
Where (is/are)?	Où (est/sont)?
Which?	Quel (m)/Quelle (f)?
Who?	Qui?
Why?	Pourquoi?

Essential words

good	bon/bonne
bad	mauvais/mauvaise
big	grand/grande

small	petit/petite
hot	chaud/chaude
cold	froid/froide
open	ouvert/ouverte
closed	fermé/fermée
toilets	les toilettes/les w.c.
women	dames
men	hommes
free (unoccupied)	libre
occupied	occupé/occupée
free (no charge)	gratuit/gratuite
entrance	l'entrée
exit	la sortie
prohibited	interdit/interdite
no smoking	défense de fumer

TIME AND SPACE

Periods of time

a minute	une minute
half an hour	une demie-heure
an hour	une heure
week	une semaine
fortnight	une quinzaine
month	un mois
year	un an/une année
today	aujourd'hui
yesterday/tomorrow	hier/demain
morning	le matin
afternoon	l'après-midi
evening/night	le soir/la nuit
during (the night)	pendant (la nuit)
early/late	tôt/tard

Telling the time

What time is it?	Quelle heure est-il?
At what time?	À quelle heure?
(at) 1 o'clock/2 o'clock etc.	(à) une heure/deux heures etc.
half past one	une heure et demie
quarter past two	deux heures et quart
quarter to three	trois heures moins le quart
(at) midday	à midi
(at) midnight	à minuit

GETTING AROUND

by bicycle	à bicyclette/en vélo
by bus	en bus
by car	en voiture
by coach	en car
on foot	à pied
by plane	en avion
by taxi	en taxi
by train	en train

In town

map of the city	un plan de la ville
I am going to . . .	Je vais à . . .
I want to go to	Je voudrais aller à . . .
I want to get off at . . .	Je voudrais descendre à
platform	le quai
return ticket	un aller-retour
single ticket	un aller simple
ticket	le billet
timetable	l'horaire
airport	l'aéroport
bus/coach station	la gare routière
bus stop	l'arrêt de bus
district	le quartier/l'arrondissement
street	la rue
taxi rank	la station de taxi
tourist information office	l'office du tourisme
train station	la gare
underground	le métro
underground station	la station de métro
bag/handbag	le sac/le sac-à-main
case	la valise
left luggage	la consigne
luggage	les bagages

Directions

Is it far?	Est-ce que c'est loin?
How far is it to . . .?	Combien de kilomètres d'ici à . . .?
Is it near?	Est-ce que c'est près d'ici?
here/there	ici/là
near/far	près/loin
left/right	gauche/droite
on the left/right	à gauche/à droite
straight on	tout droit
at the end of	au bout de
up	en haut
down	en bas
above (the shop)	au-dessus (du magasin)
below (the bed)	au-dessous (le lit)
opposite (the bank)	en face (de la banque)
next to (the window)	à côté (de la fenêtre)

Driving

Please fill the tank (car)	le plein, s'il vous plaît
car hire	la location de voitures
driver's licence	le permis de conduire
petrol	l'essence
rent a car	louer une voiture
unleaded	sans plomb

IN THE HOTEL

I have a reservation for 2 nights	J'ai une réservation pour 2 nuits

I leave	Je part . . . . .
I'd like a room	Je voudrais une chambre
Is breakfast included?	le petit-déjeuner est inclus?
single room	une chambre à un lit
room with double bed	une chambre à lit double
twin room	une chambre à deux lits
room with bathroom and toilet	une chambre avec salle de bains et toilette/W.C.
a quiet room	une chambre calme
bath	le bain
shower	la douche
with air conditioning	avec climatisation
1st/2nd floor etc	premier/deuxième étage
dining room	la salle à manger
ground floor	le rez-de-chaussée (RC)
key	la clef
lift/elevator	l'ascenseur

Paying

How much?	C'est combien, s'il vous plaît?/Quel est le prix?
Do you accept credit cards?	Est-ce que vous acceptez les cartes de crédit?
Do you have any change?	Avez-vous de la monnaie?
(in) cash	(en) espèces
coin	la pièce de monnaie
money	l'argent
notes	les billets
price	le prix
travellers' cheques	les chèques de voyage

EATING OUT

General

Do you have a table?	Avez-vous une table libre?
I would like to reserve a table	Je voudrais réserver une table
I would like to eat	Je voudrais manger
I would like something to drink	Je voudrais boire quelque chose
I would like to order, please	Je voudrais commander, s'il vous plait
The bill, please	L'addition, s'il vous plait
I am a vegetarian	Je suis végétarien(ne)

Meals and mealtimes

breakfast	le petit-déjeuner
cover charge	le couvert
dessert	le dessert
dinner	le dîner
dish of the day	le plat du jour
fixed price menu	la formule/le menu à prix fixe
fork	la fourchette
knife	le couteau

lunch	le déjeuner
main course	le plat principal
menu	le menu/la carte
(Is the) service included?	Est-ce que le service est compris?
soup	la soupe/le potage
spoon	la cuillère
starter	l'entrée/le hors-d'oeuvre
waiter	Monsieur
waitress	Madame, Mademoiselle
wine list	la carte des vins

Cooking styles

baked	cuit/cuite au four
boiled	bouilli/bouillie
fried	à la poêle
grilled	grillé/grillée
medium	à point
poached	poché/pochée
rare	saignant
steamed	à la vapeur
very rare	bleu
well done	bien cuit

Meat, poultry, game and offal

bacon	le bacon
beef	le boeuf
chicken	le poulet
duck	le canard
frogs' legs	les cuisses de grenouilles
game	le gibier
ham	le jambon
kidneys	les rognons
lamb	l'agneau
meat	la viande
pork	le porc
rabbit	le lapin
salami style sausage (dry)	le saucisson-sec
sausage	la saucisse
snails	les escargots
steak	l'entrecôte/le steak/le bifteck
veal	le veau

Fish and seafood

cod	le cabillaud/la morue
Dublin bay prawn/scampi	la langoustine
fish	le poisson
herring	le hareng
lobster	le homard
mullet	le rouget
mussels	les moules
oysters	les huîtres
pike	le brochet
prawns	les crevettes
salmon (smoked)	le saumon (fumé)

sea bass	le bar
seafood	les fruits de mer
shellfish	les crustacés
skate	le raie
squid	le calmar
trout	la truite
tuna	le thon

Vegetables, pasta and rice

cabbage	le chou
cauliflower	le chou-fleur
chips/french fries	les frites
garlic	l'ail
green beans	les haricots verts
leeks	les poireaux
onions	les oignons
pasta	les pâtes
peas	les petits pois
potatoes	les pommes-de-terre
rice	le riz
sauerkraut	la choucroute
spinach	les épinards
vegetables	les légumes

Salad items

beetroot	la betterave
cucumber	le concombre
curly endive	la salade frisée
egg	un oeuf
green pepper/red pepper	le poivron/poivron rouge
green salad	la salade verte
lettuce	la laitue
tomato	la tomate

Fruit

apple	la pomme
banana	la banane
blackberries	les mûres
blackcurrants	les cassis
cherries	les cerises
fresh fruit	le fruit frais
grapefruit	le pamplemousse
grapes	les raisins
lemon/lime	le citron/le citron vert
orange	l'orange
peach	la pêche
pear	la poire
plums	les prunes/les mirabelles (type of plum)
raspberries	les framboises
red/white currants	les groseilles
strawberries	les fraises

Desserts and cheese

apple tart	la tarte aux pommes
cake	le gâteau
cheese	le fromage
cream	la crème fraîche
goat's cheese	le fromage de chèvre
ice cream	la glace

Sundries

ashtray	un cendrier
bread	le pain
bread roll	le petit pain
butter	le beurre
crisps	les chips
mustard	la moutarde
napkin	la serviette
oil	l'huile
peanuts	les cacahuètes
salt/pepper	le sel/le poivre
toast	le toast
vinegar	le vinaigre

DRINKS

beer	la bière
a bottle of	une bouteille de
black coffee	un café noir
coffee	un café
with cream	un café-crème
with milk	un café au lait
a cup of	une tasse de
decaffeinated coffee	un café décaféiné/un déca
espresso coffee	un express
freshly-squeezed lemon/ orange juice	un citron pressé/une orange pressée
a glass of	un verre de
herbal tea	une tisane/infusion
with lime/verbena	au tilleul/à la verveine
with mint	à la menthe
with milk/lemon	au lait/au citron
milk	le lait
(some) mineral water	de l'eau minérale
orange juice	un jus d'orange
(some) tap water	de l'eau du robinet
(some) sugar	du sucre
tea	un thé
wine (red/white)	le vin (rouge/blanc)

SHOPPING (*SEE ALSO* 'PAYING')

Useful shopping vocabulary

I'd like to buy . . .	Je voudrais acheter . . .
Do you have . . .?	Avez-vous . . .?
How much, please?	C'est combien, s'il vous plaît?

I'm just looking, thank you Je regarde, merci
It's for a gift C'est pour un cadeau

Shops

antique shop	le magasin d'antiquités
baker	la boulangerie
bank	la banque
book shop	la librairie
cake shop	la pâtisserie
cheese shop	la fromagerie
chemist/drugstore	la pharmacie
clothes shop	le magasin de vêtements
delicatessen	la charcuterie
department store	le grand magasin
gift shop	le magasin de cadeaux
the market	le marché
newsagent	le magasin de journaux
post office	la poste/le PTT
shoe shop	le magasin de chaussures
the shops	les boutiques/magasins
tobacconist	le tabac
travel agent	l'agence de voyages
expensive	cher
too expensive	trop cher
cheap	pas cher, bon marché
sales	les soldes
size (in clothes)	la taille
size (in shoes)	la pointure

TELEPHONING

telephone/phone booth	le téléphone/la cabine téléphonique
phone card	la carte téléphonique
post card	la carte postale
stamps	les timbres

Days of the week

Monday	lundi
Tuesday	mardi
Wednesday	mercredi
Thursday	jeudi
Friday	vendredi
Saturday	samedi
Sunday	dimanche

Colours

black	noir/noire
blue	bleu/bleue
brown	brun/brune
green	vert/verte
orange	orange
pink	rose

red	rouge
white	blanc/blanche
yellow	jaune

Numbers

enough	assez
zero	zéro
one; first	un/une; premier/première
two/second	deux/deuxième
three/third	trois/troisième
four/fourth	quatre/quatrième
five/fifth	cinq/cinquième
six/sixth	six/sixième
seven/seventh	sept/septième
eight/eighth	huit/huitième
nine/ninth	neuf/neuvième
ten/tenth etc.	dix/dixième etc.
eleven	onze
twelve	douze
thirteen	treize
fourteen	quatorze
fifteen	quinze
sixteen	seize
seventeen	dix-sept
eighteen	dix-huit
nineteen	dix-neuf
twenty	vingt
twenty-one	vingt-et-un
twenty-two/three etc.	vingt-deux/trois etc.
thirty	trente
forty	quarante
fifty	cinquante
sixty	soixante
seventy	soixante-dix
eighty	quatre-vingts
ninety	quatre-vingt-dix
hundred	cent
thousand	mille

MEDIA

BOOKS

Paris maintains its lifelong literary connections in some wonderful bookshops and, on weekends, a huge covered second-hand book market in George Brassens park (Metro: Porte de Vanves). And then, of course, there are the famous *bouquinistes*, who sell second-hand books, posters and postcards from green wooden boxes along the left and right banks of the Seine.

● **Galignani:** 224 rue de Rivoli 75001. Metro: Tuileries. ☎ 01-42-60-76-07. First, in 1802, a publishing company, then a reading room, and now one of the great bookshops of Paris, with 1930s woodwork.

- **Brentano's:** 37 avenue de l'Opéra 75001. Metro: Opéra. ☎ 01-42-61-52-50. American bookshop with a good travel section.
- **Fnac:** 136 rue de Rennes 75006. Metro: St-Sulpice. ☎ 01-49-54-30-00. The main branch of this nationwide chain of stores, which offers good value and good advice.
- **La Hune:** 170 boulevard St-Germain 75006. Metro: St-Germain-des-Près. ☎ 01-45-48-35-85.

PRESS

Daily newspapers in France have a relatively small circulation in comparison with those in other European countries, but the French do like their weekly news magazines, such as *Le Nouvel Obs*, *L'Express* and the gossipy *Paris-Match*. You will see traditional *kiosques* (newsstands) on many Paris street corners, stocked to overflowing with the dailies – *Le Monde*, *Le Figaro* (both quite conservative) and the more left-wing *Libération*, or *Libé*, as it is known – magazines covering every subject, from weekly listings of cultural events (*Pariscope* or *L'Officiel des Spectacles*, every Wednesday) to sex and health, via nature, travel and cycling, as well as foreign-language newspapers, children's books and comics, and the ubiquitous postcards. For night owls, the **Drugstore Publicis** branches at 133 avenue des Champs-Élysées and 1 avenue Matignon are open every day 9am–2am, for all sorts, from coffee and snacks to novels and videos.

TELEVISION

France has four television channels in the public sector – *France 2*, *France 3*, *Arte* and *La 5ème* – and three private channels in *TF1*, *M6* and *Canal Plus*. Viewing reaches its peak at 8pm every day when the French gather round their sets to watch the news either on *TF1* or *France 2*. As well as these channels, there are some 250 available on cable or via satellite.

Frankly, the output on French television is horribly 'dumbed down', and your evenings would be much better spent venturing out to one of Paris' many cinemas.

MONEY

The currency in France is the French *franc*, usually shown in prices as 'F' 'FF'. It is divided into 100 *centimes*. Foreign currency or travellers' cheques can be exchanged at banks displaying a *Change* sign (closed Saturday and Sunday), or at Bureaux de change all over the city. You will need a passport for bank transactions. *Bureaux* in popular tourist areas are likely to stay open even on Sundays, but their rates will not be as favourable as the banks'.

- **Thomas Cook:** 8 place de l'Opéra 75009. ☎ 01-47-42-46-52.
- **American Express:** agency for the purchase and exchange of travellers' cheques at 11 rue Scribe 75009. ☎ 01-47-77-77-07. Metro: Opéra. Open Monday to Friday 9am to 6.30pm, Saturday 9am to 5.30pm, Sunday (exchange only) 10am to 5pm. Branch at 38 avenue de Wagram 75008. ☎ 01-42-27-58-80. Freefone (24 hours a day): ☎ 0800-90-86-00. Service to clients (24 hours a day): ☎ 01-47-77-70-00. Metro: Charles-de-Gaulle-Étoile.

MUSEUMS

Parisian museums are sometimes rather expensive, although the city's policy is actually to reduce entrance fees. If cultural visits are a priority for you, it might be worth investing in the *Carte Musées et Monuments* (museums and monuments card), a pass valid for a single day (80F), three (160F) or five consecutive days (240F). The card gives free access to the permanent collections of 70 museums, and to some of the most important monuments in and around Paris. It is also a way of queue jumping, which you'll certainly appreciate when you see the crowds waiting outside the Musée d'Orsay or the Louvre.

The card can be bought from nearly all the museums and monuments in Paris, at Fnac shops, in around 100 Metro stations and at the Paris Tourist Office.

Individual museum entrance fees range from around 12F to 40F, according to their importance and whether they are private or public and subsidized or not. Most of them offer reductions to students and some of them are free to under–18s. Some are also free on Sundays.

• **Caisse Nationale des Monuments Historiques et des Sites** (CNMHS) (National Organization for Historic Monuments and Sites): Centre d'Information, Hôtel de Sully, 62 rue St-Antoine 75004. ☎ 01-44-61-20-00/01-44-61-21-50. Fax: 01-44-61-20-36. Metro: St-Paul. The CNMHS offers a pass (280F), which is valid for a year for entry to 100 national monuments throughout the whole of France (including eight in Paris). The advantages are no queuing and free entry to exhibitions at the monuments listed. You can buy the pass at the cultural sites involved or by post from the CNMHS.

• **Association Inter-Musées** (museums association): 4 rue Brantôme 75003. ☎ 01-44-61-96-60. Fax: 01-44-61-96-69. Metro: Rambuteau. Website: www.intermusees.com

MUSIC AND OPERA

This city has it all for music lovers, with classical concerts, innovative and traditional opera performances, lively or moody jazz clubs, and world-renowned cabaret.

Paris' *Opéra Bastille* (120 rue de Lyon 75012. Metro: Bastille) is housed in an extraordinary and controversial curved glass building, a legacy of Mitterrand and his great projects. It is now the largest opera house in the world, with an auditorium that seats 2,700 people. It stands in stark contrast to the opulent *Opéra Garnier* (place de l'Opéra 75009. Metro: Opéra), which holds an audience of 'only' 2,200, and boasts chandeliers, gilded mirrors, gold-leaf decoration and red-velvet seats. This was the first place where Rudolf Nureyev danced in the West.

If you don't fancy either of these, what about opera on a renovated barge? *Péniche Opéra*, near the Hotel du Nord (Quai de Jemmapes 75010. Metro: Jaurès), puts on daily performances at 9pm.

Paris is a great place for jazz fans, with many different kinds of venue, from smoky basement bars to newer places playing world music and North African rock as well as modern jazz.

- **Le Duc des Lombards:** 42 rue des Lombards 75001. ☎ 01-42-33-22-88. Metro: Châtelet. Improvizations, Latin American and French jazz in a lively club. Concerts at 10pm.
- **Le New Morning:** 7/9 rue des Petites-Ecuries 75010. ☎ 01-42-23-51-41. Many big names in jazz, including Dizzy Gillespie, have played at this very popular club, where the décor is reminiscent of a converted garage. Concerts at 9pm.
- **Le Baiser Salé:** 56 rue des Lombards 75001. ☎ 01-42-33-37-71. Metro: Châtelet. A wide range of jazz from Africa, South America, USA and Europe, and contemporary French songs at 8pm Thursday, Friday and Saturday. Jazz concerts start at 10pm.

TICKETS

- For last-minute half-price theatre tickets try the Kiosque de la Madeleine, every day noon to 8pm, Sunday to 4pm, the Kiosque du Chatelet (12.30pm to 4pm, except Sunday and bank holidays), or the Kiosque de Montparnasse (12.30 to 8pm, Sunday to 4pm)
- **Shows at rock-bottom prices:** Minitel: 36–15, SPECTATEL; or 36–15 SORTEZ. A 35 to 40 per cent reduction on theatre seats, concerts, the circus, café-theatre, ballet and festivals. Seats are made available 48 hours in advance and up until 6pm on the day of the performance. Despite the discounts, tickets can still end up costing an arm and a leg, as they are often for the best seats.
- **Globaltickets:** Maison de la Grande-Bretagne, 19 rue des Mathurins 75009. ☎ 01-42-65-39-21. Fax: 01-42-65-39-10. Metro: Havre-Caumartin. This international agency offers telephone booking for seats for the theatre, musicals, the opera, classical concerts, rock concerts and variety shows, sporting events and tickets to museums (for any large exhibitions currently on show).

OUTDOOR ACTIVITIES

- **Allô Sports:** ☎ 01-42-76-54-54. Open Monday to Thursday 10.30am to 5pm and Friday to 4.30pm. Everything you ever needed to know about sport (indoor and outdoor) in Paris.

PARKS AND GARDENS

Paris is at the heart of a horticultural region, and the names of some of its southern suburbs – l'Hay-les-Roses and Fontenay-aux-Roses are just two – remind us that this is still the rose-growing centre of France. The horticulturists and gardeners of the city council lovingly look after 400 public gardens, covering some 7,600 acres. Every year, they plant over 3,000 new trees, 215,000 perennials and climbing plants, and 3 million green or flowering plants. Wherever they can save a green space or add a touch of nature to the urban environment, landscape designers do all they can. The most recent project is the *coulée verte* ('green trail') along the Daumesnil viaduct, which runs from the Bastille to the forest of Vincennes.

All Parisian parks have their own character. In the English-style Parc

Monceau, impeccably dressed children are promenaded by their private-school teachers around Ledoux's rotunda. In contrast, the huge Bois de Boulogne, on the outskirts of the city, boasts more than 140,000 trees – some more than 200 years old – and offers Parisians endless outdoor entertainment, from boating to clay-pigeon shooting. The floral park at Vincennes is a must when it is ablaze with stocks, tulips, pansies and a unique collection of irises. Right in the centre of the city, the formal Jardin des Tuileries, where roof tiles or *tuiles* were made from the clay in the ground, is like an outdoor museum, with alleyways lined with around 100 sculptures and statues. In the 1980s, the *jardin* was transformed into a night-time catwalk for gay men. The most recent of all the parks, the Parc André-Citroën, a sort of modern Versailles, has vast green lawns and a multitude of water features.

Perhaps the most beautiful and romantic of Parisian parks, the Jardin du Luxembourg (*Le Luco* to old hands) has always been popular with creative types – Baudelaire, Verlaine, George Sand, Delacroix and Watteau, Gide, Sartre and Simone de Beauvoir all wandered here, or sat and painted, or met and talked. Come here to watch the comings and goings, to dream under a chestnut tree, to play tennis, or bring the children to see a Punch and Judy show (school holidays; for programme information ☎ 01-43-26-46-47), ride a pony or eat candy floss.

ROLLERBLADING

This mode of transport is popular in Paris, and it's definitely worth a try – but only with the right protection (kneepads, elbow pads and wrist protection), even though it may not be the height of fashion.

For experienced rollerbladers, every Friday since February 1998, come rain or shine, people have met at 40 avenue d'Italie (on the square of the same name, on the esplanade in front of the cinema) at 10pm. The lively procession, escorted by the police, goes up and down the streets of Paris following an itinerary which varies every week. It's a real pleasure to enjoy Paris without cars, who are obliged to wait for the end of the procession! The rollerbladers often take over the boulevards St-Michel, St-Germain, or even the rue de Rivoli before going right past the Louvre across the Cour Napoléon.

You do need a certain amount of stamina, and plenty of water, if you want to complete the whole route (25km/15 miles or so in 3 hours), but there's nothing to prevent you from dropping out along the way. If you do get left behind, don't worry, as the leaders do wait for slower bladers. The atmosphere is fun and relaxed, with rollerblading pros mixing with grandads trying to get back in shape.

For the less experienced, or for those who want to skate somewhere a bit quieter, the *Rollers et Coquillages* association offers a different 3 and a half-hour route every Sunday, at around 2pm. Meet in front of *Nomades*, the rollerblade hire shop (*see below*). There's a good atmosphere here too, with enthusiasts, young couples and families. The pros are easily recognizable by their yellow T-shirts, and show admirable patience in waiting for and helping the less experienced. For a while now this route has been open to all, made safe by the presence of the police.

• **Ilios Roller Shop:** 4 allée Vivaldi 75012. ☎ 01-44-74-75-76. Half-day hire (10am to 3pm): 30F per day, 60F for 2 days, 100F per week, 250F for 7 days

• **Nomades:** 37 boulevard Bourdon 75004. ☎ 01-44-54-07-40. Monday to Friday 50F per day or 30F per half-day. Saturday and Sunday: 60F per day (half-days on Saturday 40F). Members of the *Rollers et Coquillages* association (membership about 100F), which shares its premises with the shop, get a 10 per cent reduction on the hire of blades.

• **Vertical line roller:** 60 avenue Raymond-Poincaré 75016. ☎ 01-47-27-21-21. 30F per half-day, 60F per day and 100F per weekend, including protection. Also offers routes for all levels.

PARTYING

Once upon a time, nightclub clients would be loyal to one place for at least three years. Nowadays, the absolute maximum is six months. This is a result of the phenomenon whereby special parties are organized for one night only at unusual venues, cabarets or dance halls, capitalizing on a certain dissatisfaction with some of the more squalid clubs and with the entry restrictions at some of the bigger clubs (such as *Les Bains*).

The Paris nightclub scene has become even more transient since the arrival of raves, which are set up on park corners or on derelict sites and attract enormous crowds of people who spend the night drinking and dancing to house or techno music.

The success of a new venue is down to the trendsetters, who create the atmosphere and pass on the information, and there are now around 200 in Paris. Among these venues are 50 traditional dance halls, which have stood the test of time in an amazing way, increasing in number from 130 in 1879 to over 200 in 1900. The trick of the networking trendsetter is to get everything for free, establish what's fashionable and what's not, and then move on and let the masses in.

Each club has its own system of selecting its clientele. There are two types of bouncers – the heavies and the physionomists, who judge people on their appearance. They are responsible for making sure that the club gets the right mix of punters. If they refuse you entry, either you've turned up at the wrong moment or else your style is not in keeping with the club. Going to a club with a tough door policy requires a certain amount of preparation. Make sure you check out the dress code for the night you want to go, find out which times are least busy and when you are more likely to get in. Then, be confident, but never aggressive. One way around the problem of gaining entry is to book a table at the club's restaurant – then they *have* to let you in!

To find out more about where to go and what to do in Paris at night, check out the daily listings in the newspapers and scour the *What's On*-type magazines, such as *Pariscope.*

POLICE

The main *Préfécture de Police* is at 7 bd du Palais 75004. ☎ 01-42-60-33-22. ☎ 17 for emergencies.

Public disorder in Paris is strongly discouraged by the presence of the *CRS* (Compagnie Républicaine de Sécurité), who are known for their tough approach. Do your best not to annoy them, as they carry big sticks and aren't afraid to use them. The regular police have the right to stop anyone and ask to see ID (the French have identity cards, which they are obliged to carry with them at all times).

If you're unlucky enough to have to report a crime at a police station, you will need to be patient. It's also helpful to speak some French. Try not to be offended by their apparent lack of interest.

POLITESSE (OR LACK OF IT)

French hospitality is often much maligned abroad, probably because when tourists think of France they think of Paris. In fact, in the provinces, visitors generally encounter a warm welcome, and people who have mastered the art of the smile, and of saying 'hello', 'goodbye' and 'thank you'.

In Paris it can be a different story. Inevitably, prices are higher – rent is, after all, more expensive – but this is sometimes allied with a noticeable lack of welcome, arrogant service, and miscalculated bills (which are corrected only with a pout and a shrug). Often it seems that the Parisian attitude is that if you don't like it, you can go somewhere else.

Don't be downhearted. Maintain your own standards – always say 'hello' and 'goodbye' in shops, call waiters *Monsieur* or *Madame* (clicking your fingers and shouting '*Garçon*' is *not* recommended!), and use the *vous* form of address, not *tu*, until encouraged to do otherwise – and you should get a reasonable response.

PUBLIC HOLIDAYS

Banks, shops and museums will be closed on the following public holidays, but most restaurants will stay open.

1 January (New Year's Day); Easter Monday (March or April); 1 May (Labour Day); 8 May (VE Day); last Thursday in May (Ascension); Pentecost (*Pentecôte*) and Whit Monday (May or early June); 14 July, National Day (Bastille Day); 15 August (Assumption); 1 November (All Saints) (*Toussaint*); 11 November (Armistice Day); 25 December (Christmas Day).

Where a national holiday falls on a Sunday, the next day is taken as a holiday instead. If a national holiday falls on a Thursday, the French often take the Thursday and the Friday off, making a four-day weekend. This is known as *faire le pont*, 'to make the bridge' over the Friday.

RESTAURANTS

Paris is one of the great eating capitals of the world, catering for every price range and all kinds of tastes. Here, you can eat typically French or exotic cuisine, gourmet dishes or regional specialities. You'll find small *bistrots* (the original deliverers of fast food, whose name derives from the Russian for 'quickly, quickly'), lively *brasseries* and sophisticated restaurants (originally established for the purpose of 'restoring' – *restaurer* – customers). If your chosen place is well known, you should book as far ahead as possible; it's not only the tourists who treat themselves in the capital city of a whole country of gourmets and food experts.

Unfortunately, the tourist areas, particularly in Montmartre, and around Montparnasse and Les Halles, are not always the best places to eat. There are exceptions, of course, but you will need to choose carefully.

A *prix fixe* menu offers a rather limited choice of dishes at a set price, which may or may not include drinks. The average price of a good meal in Paris is higher than elsewhere in France, but it's still possible to have lunch for 70F in a basic restaurant. The cost of dinner can be anything from 100F–120F to over 1,000F per person.

Some of the classic (and most expensive) eating addresses in Paris include *Maxim's*, *Le Procope* (the oldest restaurant in the city), *Lipp*, *La Tour d'Argent*, *Polidor* and *Le Train Bleu*. *La Coupole* is a traditional brasserie, while *Chartier* is a 105-year-old cafeteria that still serves more than 1,500 meals a day. Some of these are listed in our selections. Please note that all the French dishes mentioned in the restaurant listings are listed in the menu decoder at the back of the book.

SAFETY

You need take no more precautions in Paris than in any other European city, and it's unlikely that anything untoward will happen to you. However, do keep a vigilant eye out for pickpockets (sometimes quite young children), particularly on the rail links from the airports, where gangs have been known to operate; on the Metro line number 1, which runs by many tourist attractions; in the major department stores, where tourists often leave wallets, passports, and credit cards on counters during transactions; and in all touristy areas, of course. It is safe for women to move about on their own in the city. They may be subject to unwelcome attention, but this can be dealt with firmly.

If you do suffer some kind of loss, make a report to the local police station (*commissariat*), and keep a copy for any insurance claim.

SHOPPING

This city is a Mecca for the shopping junkie, who will never run out of things to buy or treasure troves to browse. Paris has over 30,000 shops, large and small, as well as numerous markets – this is the place, after all, that gave the world the expression 'flea market', or *marché aux puces* – modern malls and ancient arcaded *galeries*, food stores and antiques auctions.

Opening hours are usually 10am to 6.30 or 7pm (department stores stay open late once a week and on Sundays for a few weeks before Christmas). Chain stores such as Monoprix and Prisunic stay open till 9 or even 10pm. Smaller shops may close for an hour or so at lunchtime, and some close altogether for the whole of August. Food stores usually close from 1–3pm or 4pm, as well as Sunday afternoons and Mondays.

If you don't have cash, you can usually pay by credit card (*carte de crédit*). Few shops accept Eurocheques or travellers' cheques, although the larger department stores probably will. Paying for goods in Paris can involve two operations – first you choose your item, which is then wrapped by one assistant while you pay a cashier at the *caisse*. Then you return to the first assistant to claim the goods with your stamped receipt.

If you are resident outside the European Union you can claim a tax refund on goods that you are taking back with you. *See* 'Entry formalities' above.

WHAT AND WHERE TO BUY

The most interesting items to track down in Paris are fashion, food and 'style', whether that means contemporary interior design, gorgeous tableware or antique furniture. If your cash supplies are running low, or your credit card is screaming in pain, you can always have a wonderful time simply window-shopping. But beware! Window-dressing is a real art here, and shopfronts are hard to resist.

Fashion

For *haute couture* (*see also* 'Clothing', above), saunter down the rue du Faubourg St-Honoré 75008, passing a succession of exquisite palaces showcasing the work of world-famous designers. Don't be afraid to push open the door of *Dior* and *Hermès*, for example, and step right into their refined worlds. Their well-trained, uniformed staff may seem intimidating, but they are discreet, and there's no obligation to buy. If the Faubourg St- Honoré gives you an insatiable appetite for luxury, you could also seek out the avenue Montaigne, rue François–1er, rue Royale and the place Vendôme.

Many high-quality designers have recently opened shops across the river in the St-Germain area, but generally the Left Bank is the place to find more affordable French chic. The streets of the Marais, too, are full of boutiques providing ample inspiration for achieving that certain look. Just a few suggestions: *Big Ben Club* (72 rue Bonaparte 75006. Metro: St-Sulpice) was the first shop in Paris to specialize in white blouses, and is now an institution, offering more than 80 styles; *Comme des Femmes* (31 rue St-Placide 75006. Metro: St-Placide) sells big-name lingerie at 30–50 per cent less than elsewhere; *Être Ronde en Couleurs* (1 rue de Rivoli 75004. Metro: St-Paul) is the place for fuller-figured women to buy lovely underwear and evening clothes; *Mosquitos* (25 rue du Four 75006. Metro: Mabillon) sells multi-coloured shoes that are as original as the shop's name.

Men are well catered for at *Brummell*, the menswear department of the enormous *Printemps* store (61 rue Caumartin 75009. Metro: Havre-Caumartin). Find a shirt in a fine fabric at *Le Fou du Roi* (55–57 rue de Vaugirard. Metro: Rennes), and something to go with it at *Cravatterie Nazionali* (249 rue St-Honoré. Metro: Concorde or Madeleine), which has an impressive selection of 5,000 ties in 600 styles, displayed in wooden cabinets and drawers.

Paris has clothes to suit every child, and every budget, from casual T-shirts and jeans to cute smocked dresses for special occasions. Many designers of adult clothes now have children's ranges too, though not at insignificant prices. At the top of the range is *Poême* (71 ave P. Doumer 75016. Metro: La

Muette), the place to go if nothing but the best will do. Their ranges go up to age 12, with pinafore dresses, dungarees and formal concoctions in silk and velvet. At the other end of the scale, *Lara et les Garçons* (60 rue St-Placide 75006. Metro: St-Placide) has a constant stock of discounted designer seconds, both clothes and shoes, for children aged 0–16.

Food

France is a country of natural riches, where chefs have invented the best ways to use its superb produce, and master pastry-makers have created the delicious cakes still enjoyed today. It's no surprise that Paris is a paradise for gourmets. The two main temples at which those gourmets worship are *Fauchon* (*see* '8th arrondissement'), and nearby *Hédiard*, whose founder in the mid–1800s was the first to introduce tropical fruits to France. Fauchon sells honey made by bees from the Garnier Opéra that have gathered pollen from the flowers in the Tuileries gardens. Both establishments have a restaurant, and Fauchon also boasts a particularly hedonistic patisserie.

French bread is renowned the world over; the sweet *brioche* was invented in Paris in 1690, but the *baguette* is a newer addition to the range, first appearing in the city in the 1960s. *Poilâne* (8 rue du Cherche-Midi 75006) is Paris' favourite bakery, dating from 1936. Its famous round sourdough loaves are baked in wood-fired ovens, and the bread is often mentioned by name on restaurant menus.

Anne of Austria first brought chocolate to Paris via Spain and the conquistadors. The first manufacturer of chocolate liqueur and pastilles opened its doors in 1659, and became the ultimate in chic. Nowadays, at *Jadis et gourmande* (88 bld du Port-Royal 75005. Metro: Port-Royal), chocolate in all shapes and sizes is displayed on wooden shelves. The specialities include twists of plain or milk chocolate with dried fruit, orange-flavoured chocolate in the shape of a crown, and a chocolate birthday postcard complete with envelope. Cheese lovers and connoisseurs will be in heaven at *Androüet* (6 rue Arsène Houssaye 75008. Metro: Liège). This highly acclaimed shop boasts 150 varieties of cheese, from classic Camembert to the unusual Lou Picadou, and sells delightful wooden selection boxes that are perfect as gifts.

Parisian food markets date back to the Middle Ages, but many of them are still the lifeblood of the capital. You'll enjoy both the atmosphere and the wonderful produce. Try the *Mouffetard* market ('La Mouff') (rue Mouffetard 75005) for fruit, vegetables and charcuterie, the *Raspail* organic market (bd Raspail, between rue du Cherche-Midi and rue de Rennes, 75006) for unusual, organically grown vegetables such as squash and Chinese cabbage, the *Belleville* market (central section of bd de Belleville 75020) for plantains, yams and exotic fruits, and the incredible Asian supermarket of *Tang Frères* (48 avenue d'Ivry 75013), which is open on Sundays for everything Asian from kumquats and dim sum to bonsai. The oldest and most crowded of the Parisian flea markets is the *Marché aux Puces de St-Ouen* (rue des Rosiers, St-Ouen 75018. Metro: Porte de Clignancourt), which consists of several separate specialist markets, and is a favourite Sunday outing for local people all year round.

Department stores

Parisian style is epitomized in a seemingly endless choice of shops, from vast department stores to the tiniest boutiques. In fact, you could describe Paris as one large department store. In the Middle Ages, various trade associations grouped together in guilds set up their stalls in districts according to their products. This tradition continues today to a large extent, with specialist shops giving a particular character to different areas of the capital. Jewellers have gathered in the rue de la Paix and the place Vendôme; fabric shops are found around the Marché St-Pierre, near the Sacré-Coeur; musical instruments and sheet music are on sale in the rue de Rome, while the Faubourg St-Antoine is the place for furniture; rue de Paradis is the street to find fine crystal and porcelain, and the shop windows of the avenue de la Grande-Armée are full of gleaming cars and bicycles.

Most of the department stores in Paris are now over one hundred years old. Visiting them is rather like visiting a historic monument, but without the entrance fee (unless you give in to temptation!). The first of its kind, and still the most chic, *Au Bon Marché* (22 rue de Sèvres 75007. Metro: Sèvres-Babylone) was founded in 1852 by Aristide Boucicaut. It was designed by Gustave Eiffel, and recently renovated by Andrée Putman, who designed the unusual central escalator. *Au Printemps* (64 bld Haussmann 75009. Metro: Havre-Caumartin) was founded by an ex-employee, Jules Jaluzot, in 1865. *La Samaritaine* (19 rue de la Monnaie 75001. Metro: Pont-Neuf) was started in 1870 by Ernest Cognacq, a street vendor who sold ties on the Pont-Neuf. It is now the biggest department store in Paris, with a great view of the Seine from its restaurant. Its No. 2 store (1904) has the most beautiful Art Deco-style façade in the city. The 'newest' store is *Galeries Lafayette* (40 bld Haussmann 75009. Metro: Chaussée d'Antin), founded in 1899, and worth visiting for its giant double glass dome alone. Each of the stores has its specialist subject: *Samaritaine* is famous for its hardware and gardening departments and its work wear; *Printemps* is popular for wedding lists; *Bon Marché* is very upmarket, with an excellent food hall; and *Galeries Lafayette* is better known for its fashion. The fifth store, the *Bazar de l'Hôtel de Ville* (always called the 'BHV') is a favourite with DIY enthusiasts; its basement is a treasure trove of nails, screws, nuts and bolts, and all sorts of gadgets.

Specialist shops

Luxury is the watchword in Paris' specialist shops. *Guerlain* (68 ave des Champs-Élysées 75008. Metro: Franklin D. Roosevelt) is the most beautiful perfume shop in the city, with original 1912 décor of marble and mirrors. *À la Mère de Famille* (35 rue du Faubourg, Montmartre 75009. Metro: Le Peletier) has a turn-of-the-century interior with blue and white tiles. It sells traditional confectionery from the provinces, strictly only for those with a sweet tooth!

Many shops specialize in beautiful tableware, producing new collections twice a year. *Gien* (18 rue de l'Arcade 75008. Metro: Madeleine) sells attractive patterned pieces from its earthenware factory, and personalized and collectors' plates. At *La Maison Ivre* (38 rue Jacob 75006. Metro: St-Germain-des-Près) you'll find handcrafted china in the vivid blue, yellow and green colours of Provence, as well as printed tablecloths.

Some of the most appealing shops in Paris are the smaller ones, owned and run by individual enthusiasts selling an eclectic range of goods.

Galeries

About 200 years ago, the Right Bank of Paris was covered by an extensive network of arcades, known as *galeries* or *passages*. Arcades were a Parisian invention, and threaded their way between houses or formed secret passageways from one street to another. They became fashionable during the Restoration, and were popular places to meet, to see and be seen. Forerunners of modern malls, they housed fashionable shops selling everything from millinery to wine, restaurants and cafés, and reading rooms. In the evening, they often provided a venue for elegant balls.

The Vivienne, Colbert and Vero-Dodat arcades opened in 1826. Today, some of the boutiques lining the glass-roofed, mosaic-floored Galerie Vivienne (4 rue des Petits-Champs 75001) have remained unchanged since that time. Enjoy a brownie and a cup of tea English-style at the *galerie*'s tea-room, eavesdropping on journalists and fashion *aficionados* at neighbouring tables.

SMOKING

Cigarettes are still relatively inexpensive in France, and the French remain inveterate smokers. Smoking is quite common in business meetings, for example, and you will often come across that familiar image of the archetypal Frenchman, Gauloise stuck to his bottom lip, eyes screwed up against the blue smoke. Some restaurants offer non-smoking (*non fumeur*) areas, but the rules are not always observed. If you need an ashtray, ask for a *cendrier*; if you need a light, simply say '*Vous avez du feu?*'

TIME

France is one hour ahead of GMT (Greenwich Mean Time), and changes its clock in spring and autumn.

TIPPING

There are no strict rules for tipping in France, as there are in the USA, for example. In bars, it's quite common to leave the smallest bits of change for the waiter, but not necessarily expected. Waiting at tables in France is a respected profession, with special colleges and exams, and waiting staff are paid properly, and do not have to rely on tips (not always the case in some countries). Unscrupulous waiters may, however, return your change to you on a saucer with the coins hidden on the bottom, then the bill, then the notes. Remember to check underneath, or you could be leaving a very generous tip indeed.

In restaurants, a 15 per cent service charge is already included in the price, but it is customary to tip the waiter or waitress, especially if the food or service was exceptional (up to 10F in a *bistrot*, more in a nice restaurant). It's a similar situation in hotels, where standard service is included, according to law, and a tip is proffered only for special service. Taxi drivers do expect a tip of 10 per cent.

Until recently, there was a long-held tradition in France of tipping cinema ushers or usherettes 1 or 2F after they had shown you to your seat, but this is no longer the case.

TOILETS

The infamous French *toilettes à la Turque* – two footprints, a hole in the ground and a ferocious flushing system that always splashes your shoes – is less common these days in most of France, although you'll still find them in the dark basements of some Parisian bars and cafés. They're almost always accompanied by a bright-yellow oval soap on a stick above the basin. However, these days you're likely to find a more conventional and familiar arrangement. Bear in mind that it's considered impolite to use these toilets without ordering something. Museum and department store facilities might be a better bet, or one of the coin-operated public booths that you'll see on many corners (although these are not suitable for unaccompanied children).

TOURIST OFFICES

Office du tourisme et des congrès de Paris: Central Office, 127 avenue des Champs-Élysées 75008. ☎ 08-36-68-31-12, or 01-49-52-53-54. Metro: George-V or Charles-de-Gaulle-Étoile. Website: www.paris-touristoffice.com. Open daily 9am to 8pm in peak season, 9am to 8pm Monday to Saturday and 11am to 7pm on Sundays and bank holidays out of season. Closed 1 May. Staffed by a multilingual team.

- **24-hour tourist information** ☎ 01-49-52-53-56.
- **Gare de Lyon office:** open 8am to 8pm, closed Sunday, except May to September. ☎ 01-45-51-22-15. Metro: Gare-de-Lyon. Friendly and competent staff, and a range of leaflets, most for a small charge. The *Paris Mode d'Emploi* ('User's Guide') is free and has around 100 pages listing all the things to do and see in the capital, as well as many useful addresses. There's also an interesting *Plan Vert de Paris* showing the city's green spaces (5F).
- Other offices at **Gard du Nord** 75010 ☎ 01-45-26-94-82, **Gare de l'Est** 75010 ☎ 01-46-07-17-73, **Gare d'Austerlitz** 75013 ☎ 01-45-84-91-70, **Gare Montparnasse** 75014 ☎ 01-43-22-19-19, and **Tour Eiffel** (May to September) 75007 ☎ 01-45-51-22-15.

Espace du tourisme d'Île-de-France: Carrousel du Louvre, 99 rue de Rivoli 75001. Metro: Palais-Royal-Musée-du-Louvre. ☎ 0803-818-000/01-44-50-19-98. Website: www.paris-ile-de-france.com. Open daily 10am to 7pm except Tuesday. A wide choice of literature covering events, shows, visits and activities in the Île-de-France. The staff speak English, German, Spanish and Italian

- **Mairie de Paris:** Salon d'Accueil ('welcome centre'), 29 rue de Rivoli 75004. ☎ 01-42-76-43-43. Fax: 01-42-76-58-15. Metro: Hôtel-de-Ville. Open Monday to Saturday 9am to 6pm. Website: www.paris-france.org.

Information also available from the **Direction des Affaires Culturelles de la Ville de Paris:** 31 rue des Francs-Bourgeois 75004. ☎ 01-42-76-67-00. Metro: Hôtel-de-Ville. Open Monday to Friday 9am to 5.30pm

TOURS

There are lots of associations offering guided tours around the monuments of Paris. Private guides and conference organizers also run tours around the less well-known areas of Paris (for example, the Père-Lachaise Cemetery, and the place des Victoires quarter). Dates, timetables, meeting places and prices can be found in the entertainment guides *L'Officiel des Spectacles, Pariscope, Arts Programme,* the 'Paris' supplement of *Télérama* and *Le Figaroscope.* It's worth a little perseverance to discover the few secrets that Paris still has tucked away. A guided tour is the perfect way to do this.

• **Caisse Nationale des Monuments Historiques et des Sites** (CNMHS) (National Organization for Historic Monuments and Sites): Hôtel de Sully, 62 rue St-Antoine 75004. ☎ 01-44-61-21-50. Fax: 01-44-61-20-36. For tours: ☎ 01-44-61-21-69/70. Fax: 01-44-61-21-62. Metro: St-Paul. Don't be put off by the long-winded name. This organization publishes a free brochure every two months which gives a day-to-day listing of their various tours. It is available from museums and libraries in Paris, at town halls and at tourist information offices. These tours can also be found in *L'Officiel des Spectacles* and in *Arts Programme* (exhibitions brochure published six times a year). Tours cost 50F (40F for under-25s), not including the entrance fee to the place you visit.

From April to October, CNMHS also organizes one-day and half-day coach excursions in the Île-de-France and Paris' surrounding areas. Do book in advance.

• **Service des Relations avec le Public des Musées de la Ville de Paris** (public relations service of Parisian museums): 37 rue des Francs-Bourgeois 75004. ☎ 01-42-76-47-42. Metro: St-Paul. Offers cultural walks allowing visitors to get to know the city's various quarters (*see* 'Getting around'), and organizes events at the municipal museums for adults, children and visitors with disabilities. Write to the above address for a brochure listing the available programmes.

As part of the 'Music and Heritage' series, free classical music concerts are held one Sunday every month at 4pm in a Parisian church. They are worth catching. ☎ 01-42-76-56-18. Also worth attending are the *Le Point de Vue du Conservateur,* free presentations of the religious and secular works of art from the municipal heritage.

WHEN TO GO

Paris is a year-round tourist destination, with no climatic extremes, and there's not much chance of getting away from other overseas visitors, who number 20 million annually. Everyone loves 'Paris in the springtime', and this – usually mid-May and June – is one of the best times to go. In the summer (July and especially August), Parisians leave the city in droves, heading in all directions to the coast. The streets are less congested, and it's easier to find accommodation, but some restaurants and bars may be closed for their annual month-long holiday. The city fills up again in September. Autumn is trade fair time, and accommodation is in short supply. Wait until November and December, and hope for some cold, crisp days, when Paris can be at its most beautiful.

BACKGROUND

VITAL STATISTICS

Population: 2.1 million within the city itself; 10.6 million in the Île de France
Size: 100 square kilometres (39 square miles)
Status: capital of France and of the Île de France region.
Density: 21,000 inhabitants per sq km
Religion: Catholic; 10 per cent of Parisians regularly attend Mass
Tourism: 20 million visitors annually
Sanitation: in 1954, 80 per cent of Parisian homes had no bathroom; today, there are 600km (400 miles) of underground sewers

GEOGRAPHY

ORIENTATION

Orientation in this relatively small and compact city is easy. Its main thoroughfare, and point of reference, is the river Seine, which flows roughly westwards here. The Seine divides Paris into two halves, north and south. It is both the heart and mirror of Paris, and the quarters around it are those that have played the most significant role in the city's history. Wandering around the river's two islands is like stepping back in time – Notre Dame and its surrounding streets belong to the Middle Ages, while the Île St-Louis is steeped in 17th-century history, and the place de la Concorde is a prime example of 18th-century sophistication in architecture. Marie-Antoinette and Robespierre were held in the riverside Conciergerie prison before their execution; the grand and spectacular palace of Marie-Antoinette's royal predecessors – now the Louvre Museum – stands a couple of hundred metres downriver on the opposite bank. The Tuileries gardens, where the royal courtiers strolled in splendour, run alongside the river right to the place de la Concorde. Today, more modern structures overlook the water – the Institut du Monde Arabe (inaugurated in 1980) towards the eastern end of the city, and Eiffel's tower (built for the Exposition Universelle of 1889) and the Palais de Chaillot (constructed for the 1937 exhibition) towards the west.

DIVISIONS

The two halves of the city, on either side of the river, are known as the *Rive Droite* (Right Bank) and the *Rive Gauche* (Left Bank). They are entertainingly different in character. The Right Bank is associated more with the establishment, and here you'll find some of the city's most significant monuments, its grandest buildings and its wealthiest quarters. *Rive droite* has come to be used to describe anything with a certain level of sophistication, and this area north of the river is also the location for smart squares, and expensive shops, cafés and restaurants. The Right Bank's exception to the rule is probably the *Marais*, which has become achingly hip over the last decade or so, and popular with the gay community, and is the venue for the outrageous annual Bastille Ball. For most people, however, locals included, it is the Left Bank that has always been the place for unconventional behaviour. It's been home to scholars and intellectuals since the 12th century, and more recently to dissidents, beatniks, writers, philosophers and artists. Its *Latin Quarter* is so called because it has been the centre of university teaching, originally all carried out in Latin, for over 700 years.

Outside these two broad areas, village-like Montmartre, rising up to the north of the centre, and topped by the white, domed Sacré-Coeur, has an almost rural atmosphere. The working-class quarters of eastern Paris offer a rich ethnic mix, and are becoming cool places for more adventurous Parisians to hang out in the evening.

LAYOUT

Paris is divided up into twenty arrondissements or districts. The 1st is in the centre of the city, and the others are numbered from it in a clockwise, snail-like manner. They are a basic unit of orientation in the city, and are constantly referred to in guides and literature, almost always using simply their associated number (1er, for Premier, or 2ème, for Deuxième, and so on). The last two digits of a Paris address give the arrondissement; 8 rue du Cherche Midi 75006 is in the 6th, for example.

The arrondissement system dates from the time of Baron Haussmann, who was responsible for the hugely significant urban planning project of 1852–70. Paris owes much of its current street layout to Haussmann, who tore down old, squalid sections of the city on the orders of Napoleon III, and replaced many of the ancient narrow streets with the boulevards you see today. This had the effect of subduing revolutionary activity – these main arteries were too wide for the putting up of barricades. Haussmann also created gardens and open spaces, a proper sewage system and reservoirs for the provision of clean water to the city. It was only after this shake-up that Paris was able to take on its role as the 'City of Light'.

HISTORY

EARLY TIMES

The original Parisians were a Celtic tribe known as the *Parisii*, who lived on the island in the River Seine that is now called the Île de la Cité. Julius Caesar arrived with his soldiers in 53 BC, liked the site, on the lucrative trade route between the south of France and Britain, creating a settlement. The Romans called the place *Lutetia Parisiorium*, gradually took over the Celtic tribe, and stayed for another 300 years. They built up the town, mainly on the Left Bank, with markets, temples, sturdy bridges over the Seine, and straight streets. Today you can still see vestiges of the Roman era at the Arènes de Lutèce, the arena dating from the 2nd century AD, and in the rue St Jacques, which, in true Roman style, runs straight as a die.

Under an imperial decree of 212, Lutetia was renamed Paris. The city was to remain subject to Roman law until it finally succumbed to persistent barbarian invasions. During the governorship of Julian, nephew of Constantine the Great, Paris had resisted the advances from the north and northeast. But in 508 it finally became the capital of Clovis, the Frankish king, and his dynasty, the Merovingians. These unsophisticated and bloodthirsty 'long-haired kings' imposed Salic Law, and ruled Paris until the succession of the second Frankish dynasty, the Carolingians. Emperor Charlemagne was a Carolingian descendant. He ruled from 800–814, but spent little time in Paris. It was the Carolingians, however, who created the office of Count of Paris, which was to prove significant in the city's history.

Towards the end of the 9th century, the Vikings turned their attention on Paris. They held the city under siege for ten months in 885. Inspired by the strength of their new Count of Paris, Odo, the Parisians resisted and finally saw the Vikings and their 700 ships retreat and move on to attack Burgundy.

Left largely to its own devices by the Carolingians, over time Paris gradually developed into a provincial city, governed by its counts. The Francians (from the western part of the Franks' kingdom) began to prefer the leadership of the counts of Paris to that of Charlemagne's successors. In 888, they decided to elect Count Odo as their king. A century later, in 987, Hugues Capet, descendent of one of the counts of Paris, assumed the crown of West Francia, and made Paris the capital of his (limited) kingdom. He was to prove to be France's first significant king, and his dynasty was to remain in power for the next 800 years.

MEDIEVAL PARIS

From the end of the first millennium to the late 15th century Paris grew considerably in power and influence. The energetic king Philippe-Auguste (1180–1223) instigated the first street-paving programme, built the market at Les Halles (where it would remain for nearly 800 years), approved the charter for the University of Paris and commissioned a new palace on the Right Bank – the Louvre. He also decided to re-do the city's defences, building new 2.5-m (8-ft) thick ramparts that enclosed an area of almost a square mile, including the Left Bank, and took nearly 20 years to build. It wasn't only the city of Paris that expanded during Philippe-Auguste's reign; his kingdom also began to grow, to include much of southern France.

The medieval city of Paris was divided into three parts: the Île de la Cité, with the first royal palace and Notre Dame, the Right Bank, and the Left Bank, where the university was established. Paris soon became the centre of learning in Europe. Students began to arrive from all over Europe to join with the intellectual revolutionaries who were breaking away from the dogma of the church. The university offered four main areas of study: medicine, the arts, theology and church law. One of the first colleges, or student residences, was founded in 1253 by Robert le Sorbon; now known as the Sorbonne, it still exists today as a world-famous college of the University of Paris.

The next important king, Louis IX (1226–70), led an excessively pious life, earning himself a sainthood after his death. His rigid regime consisted of constant genuflections, reciting of prayers, the wearing of a hair shirt and washing of the feet of abbots. It was Louis who had the spectacular Sainte-Chapelle constructed close to the royal palace.

Throughout the medieval period, Paris developed and evolved. There was much activity all over the city. The university was booming. There were tradesmen everywhere buying and selling foodstuffs (recalled in street names to this day, such as rue la Grande Boucherie, or Butcher's Road), money, and services, from scribing to prostitution. Crafts – tapestry-making, gold-smithing, illumination, candle-making – were taught and learned by masters and apprentices, and guilds were established to oversee quality and methods, and examinations. Amid all this activity, the population of Paris continued to grow – from 1200 to 1300, it increased from around 200,000 to 300,000 – and a kind of class system began to emerge.

Philippe IV's reign (1285–1314) was marked by economic difficulties, with bad weather and harvests, and too much involvement in expensive wars. It was to be the beginning of a difficult period for France and the French.

DECLINE

In 1338, Edward III of England, grandson of Philippe IV, came to France to claim 'his' throne. France and Paris were to suffer greatly. Many were lost at the battles of Crécy, Poitiers and Agincourt, and then the 1348 Black Death devastated the people further.

Charles V ascended the throne in 1364. He was a skilful ruler, who managed to regain some of France's lost territory, and built new ramparts in the capital, but his was a short reign, ending with his death in 1380. He was succeeded by Charles VI, the boy-king, who was ill equipped to cope with the fighting between rival factions from Burgundy and Armagnac. The unrest spread to Paris and control of the city changed hands several times around the turn of the 14th century. It was a time of mayhem, murder and atrocities; buildings were destroyed, and the people began to run out of resources. When the English, who had made an alliance with the Burgundians, marched on Paris again, in 1420, they found the city in a state of disrepair. Henry VI of England was crowned king in Notre-Dame, then installed the Duke of Bedford as Regent and made the Parisians swear an oath of allegiance to the Plantagenets. Charles VII, the legitimate French king, remained in Bourges during this time under the English – a period of terrible deprivation – and finally liberated Paris again in 1436.

THE RENAISSANCE

Charles VII was succeeded on the throne by his son Louis XI (1461–83), and by the late 15th century Paris was beginning to see something of an improvement. In the early 1470s Louis XI introduced printing to the city from Germany and the first presses were set up in the rue St-Jacques. The Left Bank, with its thousands of students, became a centre for the book trade. Trade prospered and the city grew.

As the 16th century progressed, the gap between the classes grew, too. Wealthy Parisians built themselves fine mansions, and conspicuously consumed imported goods, particularly from Italy. Under the reign of François I, who ascended the throne in 1515, Paris became a true Renaissance city. The key word of the court of François I (and of his son and successor Henri II) was ostentation. François liked to be seen as a great patron of the arts and education. He established a humanist university in Paris, and encouraged an intellectual freedom that allowed the rise to fame of such writers as Rabelais and Montaigne. Although he preferred to live in the Marais, where many of Paris' *haute bourgeoisie* had their residences, he went to work on the Louvre palace, pulling the old one down and having a new one built in Italian Renaissance style. He also commissioned extensive work on the beautiful chateau at Fontainebleau.

After the death of Henri II and François II, Charles IX became the new monarch. Because he was only a child of ten, Henri II's widow, Florentine Catherine de' Medici, was made Regent, and the fashion for Italian style continued.

THE REFORMATION

The arrival of the Reformation in the 1520s became the cause of a terrible conflict throughout France – the Wars of Religion between French Catholics and Protestants (or Huguenots). There was terror and suspicion in Paris, where the Protestants were as fanatical as the Catholics of the orthodox church, the university and the monarchy. Protestants were persecuted, and many were murdered, and Huguenot armies threatened Paris with invasion or siege more than once in the 1560s. In 1572, it all came to a head with the St Bartholomew's Day Massacre, on 23 August. More than 3,000 Huguenots were slaughtered in Paris, by Catholic citizens on the rampage. They had been led to believe that the life of their king, and their city, was in danger. (The dead almost included Henri de Navarre, brother-in-law of Charles IX, and future king of France, who only escaped by promising to renounce his Protestantism.)

The massacre led to years of war in France, and severe deprivation in Paris. In 1588, the Parisians rose in revolt against Henri III, forcing him to withdraw from the city. In 1589, with Henri III assassinated, Henri de Bourbon, King of Navarre, claimed the throne. The religious war continued to rage until 1593, when Henri (originally a Huguenot) was received into the Catholic church. In 1598, his Edict of Nantes decreed that there must be religious tolerance.

RENOVATION

Henri IV's main priority was the renovation of his ravaged capital city. His second wife; Marie de' Medici, was not happy with the Louvre, so Henri became the latest in a long line of kings to leave their mark on the royal palace. He also constructed the Place Vendôme, commissioned the harmonious arcaded Place des Vosges, which remains astonishingly unchanged today, and began the development of the Île St-Louis – originally the Île aux Vaches, or 'Cow Island' – as a high-class residential area. Under his reign, the aristocracy returned to Paris (many had been living away from the troubles in their Loire Valley chateaux), building elegant mansions all over the city, particularly in the Marais.

Henri's Huguenot past finally caught up with him in 1610, when he was assassinated by a Catholic fanatic. Henri's son, Louis XIII, was just eleven years old, so his widow Marie was appointed Regent. She commissioned the Palais du Luxembourg, in the style of her childhood home in Florence. Marie and Louis ruled France with the invaluable assistance of Armand Jean du Plessis, Duc de Richelieu, as chief minister. Richelieu was an able and loyal administrator, and he and his successor Mazarin restored the country to a powerful and successful state.

The 'Sun King'

Louis XIV succeeded his father in 1643 at the age of five. History seemed to be repeating itself as his mother, Anne of Austria, became Regent and Italian-born Giulio Raimondo Mazzarino, (aka Mazarin), was appointed as chief minister. Cardinal Mazarin was corrupt but clever, and served his country well. He repelled a Spanish invasion, negotiated peace in Europe, and guided the royal court through the threat of the *Fronde* of 1648. During this time, the privileged classes, opposed to royal policies that might affect their own wealth, stirred up civil unrest. Louis felt it necessary to flee Paris for a time, but was eventually able to return in safety.

After Mazarin's death, Louis came of age and chose the energetic and ambitious Jean-Baptiste Colbert to be his new chief minister. Colbert reformed the economy and contributed to France's prosperity by founding state-run companies, such as the Gobelins tapestry factory. He was also responsible for new projects in Paris; the old city walls were replaced by vast tree-lined *grands boulevards* such as the Champs-Élysées, the Hôtel des Invalides (barracks for old soldiers) and the place des Victoires were built, and the Louvre was furnished with an elegant colonnade.

Louis XIV's reign was extraordinarily lavish and splendid. He saw himself as the 'Sun King', bringing light and life to his country and his people, and believed royal power to be absolute. He encouraged artistic endeavour, and the early years of his reign were a time when writers, painters and sculptors flourished. However, he increasingly lost touch with reality; he spent more of his time at his palace at Versailles, where he drained the state coffers renovating the buildings and creating gardens for his court of some 10,000 members to enjoy. There, they lived surrounded by frivolity in a milieu where extravagant dress and appearance counted for everything, for both men and women. State funds were also directed towards 35 years of warring.

As Louis XIV continued to spend the country's *livres*, and Colbert's well-meaning policies began to cripple the economy, Paris degenerated into a stinking mess of gambling, poverty and unemployment, muggings and traffic jams, despite the efforts of the new Lieutenant General of Police Nicholas de la Reynie. There was human excrement in the streets, and life in the city was uninspired and stultified. Meanwhile, Louis carried on creating his myth of a golden age and a great monarch.

The *Ancien Régime*

In 1715, Louis XIV was succeeded by another five-year-old, his great-grandson Louis XV. The royal court, under the Regent, Philippe d'Orléans, moved back from Versailles to Paris, where it presided over a new age of enlightenment. The significant change in attitude stimulated the flourishing of literary salons, attended by philosophers such as Jean-Jacques Rousseau, Diderot, Voltaire and Montesquieu, and there was an important move towards reason, science and an understanding of the natural world. Paris was a city of contrasts. The gap between the rich and poor continued to widen. The rich, becoming ever richer, built new mansions in the Faubourg St-Germain and the Faubourg St-Honoré. The poor lived in squalid conditions, were barely able to afford a loaf of bread, and were regularly struck down by infectious diseases.

When he was old enough to rule in his own right, Louis XV – despite being nicknamed 'Le Bien-Aimé' ('the well-beloved') at first – proved himself to be lazy and weak, allowing his favourites to gain the upper hand in governmental decisions. His mistresses Mme de Pompadour and, later, Mme du Barry were both notable figures at court, and particularly well able to influence him. When the place Louis XV, now the place de la Concorde, was laid out, in 1748, its huge statue of the king was immediately vandalized by the people. Louis made an unwise marriage to an unpopular wife, lost French colonies in America and India, and did nothing for the poor; he died in 1774 detested and unlamented, and had to be buried under cover of darkness.

One of the most significant structures of the Ancien Régime was the new 25-km (16-mile) city wall of the Fermiers-Généraux (tax collectors), built in 1784. It was not for defence, but acted instead as a tollbooth for the payment of duty on goods entering the city from the provinces. It followed the line of many of today's boulevards, passing via Nation, Stalingrad, Anvers, Pigalle, place Blanche, and so on. Finished in 1789, it was to play an important role in the birth of the Revolution, symbolizing the oppressive tax rules under which the poor were suffering.

The Ancien Régime continued with the accession to the throne of Louis XVI and his silly wife, 'that Austrian woman', Marie-Antoinette. Their incompetent and frivolous behaviour only served to exacerbate the class war between the rich and the poor. The starving Parisians knew only that their uncaring queen spent her time at Versailles dressed as a milkmaid and playing at rural life, and believed the rumours that she was sleeping with guards and other women at the court. Meanwhile, they hated her hopeless husband for not standing up to the Paris *Parlement*, which would only approve the levying of taxes on the poor.

The last straw came when, in 1789, after several successive bad harvests, the price of bread rose again. Paris was desperate, and ripe for change.

REVOLUTION

Louis was ill equipped to deal with the problems faced by his country. His response was to call a meeting at Versailles of the Etats-Généraux (Estates General), representatives of the clergy, nobility and ordinary citizens (the Third Estate, or 96 per cent of the population). Following a dispute between the Estates over electoral reform, the Third Estate swore the Tennis Court Oath, promising to create a proper constitution for France. Louis eventually agreed to the transformation of the Estates General into a National Assembly.

The theory dealt with, practical considerations now came to the fore. On 14 July 1789, the desperate *sans-culotte* Parisians ('without knickers', because they wore long trousers, unlike the aristocracy, who wore knee breeches) took up arms and attacked Les Invalides, and, most famously, stormed the Bastille prison, releasing its inmates (actually only seven in number). They made their way to Versailles, forced the king to accept the tricolour, which they had created as their flag, and brought Louis and Marie-Antoinette back in procession to Paris.

A year later, the king and queen attended a celebration mass in Paris on 14 July, and Louis pledged to support the new constitution. In fact, neither of the royals had accepted their reduced role, and plans were afoot for their escape from France. The revolutionaries caught up with them at Varennes, and they were returned in utter shame to Paris, mocked and despised along the way. From then on, they were prisoners of the revolution.

Republican feeling was growing. In June 1791, members of the National Assembly called for an end to absolute monarchy. The government managed to control unrest for the time being, but the seeds had been sown. On 22 September 1792, the elected National Convention (which had replaced the Assembly) formally abolished the monarchy, declared the first day of Year One of the French Republic, and established a new calendar. By January 1793, Louis had been found guilty of 'crimes against the French people', and had been put to death by the guillotine in the place de la Concorde. Eight months later, the Musée du Louvre was opened to the public for the first time. During the two-month Great Terror, in 1794, when extremists took over the Convention, Marie-Antoinette and thousands of others, including some of the original revolutionaries, followed Louis to the scaffold. Ironically, main Terror committee member Robespierre himself was also destined to suffer the same fate.

With the demise of the Terror, Paris was ruled by a number of different systems. Some *nouveaux riche* young citizens adopted an outrageous and extravagant way of life. Buildings were renamed to reflect the original values of the Revolution – the Palais Royal became the Palace of Equality – and it was the norm to address fellow citizens as *citoyen* or *citoyenne*, rather than *Monsieur* or *Madame*. In 1795, the Constitution of Year Three of the Republic was passed. Conditions were still worsening, however, and the *sans-culottes* again attacked the Convention. One of the soldiers who was detailed to protect the Convention was a young Corsican commander called Napoleon Bonaparte. A new player had entered stage left.

NAPOLEON BONAPARTE

Napoleon, trained at the École Militaire in Paris, was, it seemed, the only man who could unite the citizens of France's capital city, and of the whole country. Following a *coup d'état* on 9 November 1799, he became first Consul and then, on 18 May 1804, was declared Emperor of the French. His contribution to French history is immense. He centralized power, founded the Bank of France, extended the empire, brought internal peace, and promoted commerce so that the economy was soon back in the healthy state that it had enjoyed in the mid–17th century. He also drew up a civil code (the *Code Napoléon*), which has since been used as a model for legal systems in many countries. His contribution to Paris was equally significant. Once he and his empress Josephine had been crowned in a spectacular ceremony in Notre-Dame, he was able to set about turning Paris into his vision of an imperial capital. He commissioned the Arc de Triomphe and the Arc du Carrousel (memorials to his many military victories), the column in the place Vendôme (made from melted-down gunmetal taken from the Battle of Austerlitz), the temple-like Madeleine church, the Bourse (the stock exchange), the arcaded rue de Rivoli, and a number of new bridges over the Seine.

Napoleon's imperial interlude ended with his disastrous 1812 invasion of Russia. He lost more than half a million soldiers and Paris was to suffer retaliation on the part of the allies from Russia, Prussia, Austria and Britain. In March 1814, the city was occupied by the Prussians, Napoleon was forced to abdicate, and banished to the island of Elba, and the Bourbon royal house was restored to the throne. Louis XVIII (brother of XVI) reluctantly became constitutional monarch.

In 1815, Napoleon had a final fling – his 'Hundred Days'. He escaped from Elba and returned to Paris, where, with the support of Bonapartists, he reclaimed his throne. In June, however, he met his Waterloo against the

British and the Prussians, and was finally and firmly sent off further afield, this time to St Helena in the South Atlantic. He would only return to Paris after his death in December 1840, to be buried with great ceremony in a red granite sarcophagus in Les Invalides.

RESTORATION, ROMANTICISM AND REVOLT

Louis XVIII, restored by the European allies, lasted only 10 years, and did not make much of a mark on the capital. He commissioned little in the way of public building, but private developers were active, gas-lighting was introduced in the city, and a public bus route started up, taking passengers from place de la Bastille to the Madeleine. There were new pavements, the markets were busy, and the theatres and opera houses were full. Restoration Paris was comfortable for many of its 700,000 citizens, although the gap between the rich and the poor still existed.

Louis' successor, the reactionary Charles X, was narrow-minded, selfish and thoroughly unpopular. His first minister Polignac inevitably caused a stir when he removed the freedom of the press in July 1830; printers and journalists rose up in revolt against this policy. Charles was persuaded to abdicate and went into exile. Louis-Philippe, Duc d'Orléans, was brought in at the suggestion of the ageing revolutionary Lafayette. He was rather middle class in his attitudes; a financially aware man, and a great supporter of industrialization. Under his reign, France's first railways were built, and primary education was made mandatory, but the working classes still did not have the vote – they were not even allowed to discuss politics among themselves – and trade unions were illegal. Paris developed slowly, and there was a gradual increase in the number of its businesses. In a great wave, country people came to the city in search of jobs, so that the population of the capital reached one million in 1844. Unemployment grew, and living conditions in Paris deteriorated once again.

Paradoxically, even though the king was a dull man, Romanticism was at the heart of Paris culture and intellectual life during the July Monarchy. Delacroix, feminist writer George Sand, her lovers Chopin and de Musset, Victor Hugo and Dumas all displayed a social conscience, a hatred of the dishonourable, and an empathy with the poor.

The press was to play a significant role in inspiring the second revolution of the 19th century. Opposition newspapers had made sure that their readership knew about the corruption of politicians and the weakness of the regime, and had reported on the growth in unemployment. The turning point came in February 1848, when royalist troops fired on demonstrators and citizens in the boulevard des Capucines, killing around 50 people. Louis-Philippe immediately sacked his unpopular first minister Guizot, but it was too late; the monarchy was destined to fall, and the king had to leave Paris in disguise. The Second Republic was proclaimed.

A provisional government was unsuccessful, and there was persistent conflict between the National Guard and demonstrators, between the *bourgeoisie* and the National Guard, and between government officials and conservatives and moderates. Severe rioting was the result of the closure in June 1848 of the National Workshops, which had provided employment for many Parisian poor. Barricades went up in the Faubourg St-Antoine, but the insurgents were crushed after six days of fighting by the National Guard, reinforced by troops brought in from outside the city. Over

4,000 were killed, and many more were arrested and subsequently deported to Algeria.

THE SECOND EMPIRE

In this climate of crisis, Louis-Napoleon Bonaparte, nephew of the first Napoleon, won the first presidential elections of the Second Republic by a margin of four to one. At the end of his first term, in December 1851, he announced his intention to carry out a *coup d'état*, and to allow a plebiscite for its approval. There was little resistance – partly because of his associations with the Napoleonic myth, and partly because he had tens of thousands of troops supporting him – and the plebiscite did not take place until a year later. By then he had already proclaimed himself Emperor Napoleon III, and Paris became an imperial city once again.

Fortunate to come to power at a time of growing economic prosperity – displayed in two great exhibitions, in 1855 and 1867 – Napoleon III was responsible for the most incredible modernizing transformation of Paris and its street layout. The architect and engineer of his plan was Georges Haussmann (later Baron Haussmann). Narrow medieval streets and tottering buildings were swept aside, to be replaced by boulevards that were wide enough to take the increasing traffic. He laid out the Bois de Boulogne and Bois de Vincennes, built railway stations, and opened up new spaces, such as the place de l'Opéra. (Although a new opera house was Haussmann's idea, Garnier's astonishingly opulent building was not finished until after the Baron's death.) He added seven new avenues radiating out from the Arc de Triomphe. New structures, such as the reading room at the Bibliothèque Nationale, were built using iron and glass. Schools, churches, synagogues and hospitals were constructed, and the city was divided into twenty arrondissements, or administrative quarters. Haussmann also developed new water and sewage systems – much needed. On the down side, 200,000 poor Parisians found themselves banished to miserable slums on the outskirts of the city.

This was a glittering era for the privileged classes. Napoleon's Spanish empress, Eugenie, presided over a court of vulgar *nouveaux riches*. Suddenly, shopping and consumerism became easy, with the opening of the first department store, *Au Bon Marché*, in 1852, and the setting up of the first fashion houses. The 'City of Light' was the glamour capital of Europe.

THE THIRD REPUBLIC

The 1870 Franco-Prussian war brought about the end of an empire that had already lost its shine. By 19 September, Prussian troops had secured the surrender of the emperor himself, and had surrounded Paris. They were unable to capture the well-defended city – even though its citizens were reduced to eating sewer rats – but it had to capitulate when Thiers established a government at Versailles, having signed a treaty with the German emperor. The Parisians of the radical left were angry, rose up to demand a free municipal government, and declared the Paris Commune in March 1871. The Communards were extremists, and prepared to fight against Versailles. It was a ghastly and ruthless period, with more than 20,000 Parisians killed, and thousands more fleeing the city for ever. Paris was eventually retaken by Versailles, and the Third Republic was established in an atmosphere of suspicion and hatred.

The government would remain at Versailles until 1879, but it continued work in Paris following Haussmann's plans, and restored the damage done during the fighting of 1871. Despite terrible debts, the aim was to enable Paris to present an impressive face to the world for a great exhibition in 1878. They completed the avenue de l'Opéra and the boulevard Henri IV, improved access to Les Halles, and constructed many buildings divided into units for lease as small shops or apartments. The Sacré-Coeur basilica was designed for the Montmartre hill in expiation for the events of 1871. The underground rail system was begun, and scores of schools and hospitals were built. By the 1880s, Parisians were able to choose from a range of department stores, some of which still exist today.

At the same time as it was carrying through Haussmann's plans, the French government was also hurtling towards the new century, with the industrialization of Paris' suburbs, and the inevitable formation of trade unions. Further exhibitions followed in 1889 and 1900. The star of the former was the world-famous icon of Paris, Gustave Eiffel's metal tower. The Grand Palais and the Petit Palais were constructed for the latter, using the very latest in metal structures and glass skylights.

THE *BELLE ÉPOQUE*

The exuberant period from the 1880s to the outbreak of the First World War in 1914 was known in Paris as the *Belle Époque* (the 'Fine Time'). Around the turn of the century, the population of Paris passed the figure of two million. Despite industrial action and random assassinations, the middle classes had no trouble enjoying themselves in Paris, where new dance halls, cabarets and cafés were being built all the time. An outrageous new dance called the can-can was invented, and was on show nightly at the Moulin Rouge and the Folies-Bergères.

Paris became the European capital of the arts. A new decorative style called *Art Nouveau* was born – based on nature, its motifs soon flourished on the new Metro stations and in the construction of department stores, such as *Galeries Lafayette* – as was Symbolist poetry, and, later, Modernism. The Lumière brothers showed their new invention – a cinema in a café – in 1895. Picasso (still relatively poor) reigned over his artist's studio in Montmartre, laying the foundations of 20th-century art, and counting in his circle of friends Henri Rousseau, Apollinaire, Gertrude Stein and Max Jacob. Here, in the *Bateau Lavoir*, Picasso and Braque explored the fundamentals of Cubism. At the same time, Stravinsky, Diaghilev, Eric Satie and Marcel Proust changed the face of music, ballet and iterature. Imagination was all, and fun was the name of the game.

TWO WORLD WARS AND IN BETWEEN

In September 1914, Paris was forced to defend itself against an invasion that was part of a war that no European nation wanted. The German troops were turned back at the Marne by French reinforcements brought to the site in a fleet of Paris taxis. Although the Louvre's treasures had been packed away, just in case, the city remained largely untouched – physically – by the conflict. The Parisians suffered a tough three-year period, and there was terrible loss of French life, but Clemenceau, elected as head of government, was able to restore the country's confidence. In 1920, the 'Unknown Soldier' was interred under the Arc de Triomphe.

Following the 1919 peace treaty at Versailles, the city of Paris entered into a crazy period. Ideas associated with surrealism began to spread. The city became a magnet for dissident Americans – mostly ex-pat writers who based their life around Sylvia Beach's Left Bank bookshop *Shakespeare and Company*. Sylvia was devoted to them; Hemingway describes how she would let them use her shop as a reading room, or just to get warm, and she was extremely generous with credit. The American soldiers of the Great War had brought jazz music to the French capital, and clubs were springing up everywhere. Black American Josephine Baker, from St Louis, Missouri, danced naked, and became the leading figure of a fascination with jazz and black culture. The cafés and lodgings of Montparnasse thronged with modern young things, setting new trends and having a wild time.

It couldn't last, could it? Sure enough, the thrill of the Paris scene was destroyed in the 1930s, as a consequence of the Great Depression. Unemployment rose, there were strikes and demonstrations (a million people took to the streets on one day in 1934), and Parisians turned to the Communist Party. The Party came together with Socialists and Radicals, forming the Popular Front that came to power under Léon Blum in 1936. Many workers went in completely the opposite direction, joining newly formed Fascist organizations. Extremism grew on either side, and violent political unrest in Paris was the norm during Blum's year-long government. The modernization of Paris continued, with the completion of the Metro system, and more housing for working people, but a 'Great Exhibition' of 1937 was noticeably not that great. Within three years, Paris had been surrendered by its country's government to the Germans.

After more or less six months of phoney war (called the *drôle de guerre*, or 'funny war', by the French), in spring 1940, the Germans began to advance towards France. By mid-May, they were just 110km (70 miles) from Paris. Children were evacuated, concrete barriers were set up in the suburbs of the city, and the great escape began. By the summer, the population of Paris had decreased from almost 5 million in 1936 to around 1 million.

It was inevitable. On 14 June, the swastika flag was raised over the Hôtel de Ville, and the German occupation of Paris began; it was to last for four years. It was a strange, painful period. German soldiers installed themselves in the city's fine hotels, while the Luftwaffe settled in to the Palais du Luxembourg. Their officers ate in the best restaurants, while the German rank and file revelled in the luxury items to be found in the shops. Although a curfew and rationing had been imposed, and there were prohibitive signs in German everywhere, a bizarre kind of truce was established between the occupiers and many of the Parisians who had fled the city, who now returned to live side by side with the enemy. The university reopened, and Paris' writers and philosophers appeared again in their favourite cafés on the Left Bank. They were the intellectual supporters of a growing underground movement. In July 1942, the rounding-up and deportation of 13,000 Jews had been a major inspiration for the Resistance. Coordinated initially by Jean Moulin, and motivated by de Gaulle's Algiers-based government-in-exile, its exploits against the occupying force became legendary. Full-scale insurrection became increasingly likely.

De Gaulle was also working hard elsewhere, persuading the Allies that they *had* to liberate Paris if France was to survive. Between 19 and 24 August, with the Allies heading their way, the Parisians took to the streets, setting up barricades, and defending themselves against German attack. On the

24th, French and Allied soldiers swept into the city; the Germans capitulated and, on 25 August, de Gaulle drove to his old office in rue St-Dominique. On 26 August, there was an emotional parade down the Champs-Élysées, from the Arc de Triomphe, where de Gaulle laid a wreath to the Unknown Soldier, to Notre-Dame, where a service was held. Ernest Hemingway, at the head of a band of Free French irregulars, went straight to the Ritz to celebrate Paris' Liberation. General de Gaulle is said to have preferred the Café de la Paix.

POST-WAR PARIS

The capital recovered slowly from the ravages of war. There was much rebuilding to be done, both physically and psychologically. The economy was understandably in complete disarray, but the Marshall Plan pumped millions of dollars into the country. Women were given the vote for the first time in 1945, in recognition of their contribution to the war effort. The Fourth Republic was founded in 1946; de Gaulle resigned, protesting that they had merely resurrected the constitution of the Third Republic, and formed a new party, the RPF (Rassemblement du Peuple Français). Over the next 13 years, governments (mostly coalitions) came and went with alarming regularity. Many lasted only a matter of months. The people were dismayed by problems in the old colonies, particularly Algeria, strikes in Paris, and an expensive foreign policy in Indo-China. In 1958, de Gaulle presented a new constitution to the people. He received 80 per cent approval, and was accordingly elected head of government of the Fifth Republic in 1959. Now Paris could return to a state of peace, and its economy was able to recover.

De Gaulle – unlike many of his predecessors, and one notable successor – had no great ambition to leave monuments behind him. New construction work was carried out almost exclusively in concrete, and this period produced some of the most significant architectural landmarks of Paris today – the Montparnasse tower is a typically ugly example. The belief was that useful was beautiful. Paradoxically, during his time in power, a number of conservation laws were passed, ensuring the survival of historic areas such as the Marais.

Post-war intellectual life in Paris revolved around the philosophers of the Left Bank. Sartre and his existentialist clique continued the work they had begun between the wars, while Sartre's lover Simone de Beauvoir produced the feminist treatise *Le Deuxième Sexe* (The Second Sex). As the economy took its upward turn, however, out went existentialism, and in came the *Nouvelle Vague* ('New Wave') of the arts of the early 1960s. The cafés filled with earnest young beatniks – and the smoke from their Gauloises – and schools began to creak at the seams as the post-war baby boom took hold. The atmosphere was brooding, and getting warmer.

In May 1968, the cauldron bubbled over, first in Nanterre and then on the Left Bank. Students rioted in protest at the conditions in their universities, and at the war in Vietnam; they burned cars, fought with the police in the streets, and demanded the end of de Gaulle's increasingly authoritarian government. They were joined after a week or so by trade unions all over the city, and Paris came to a standstill as workers in all industries came out on strike. The May 68 events ground to a halt in the face of public opposition, but de Gaulle's number was up. By spring 1969, he had been the subject of a vote of no confidence, and was forced to resign.

The demonstrators of 1968 had hoped for a more liberal society after the devastating war, but they had been disappointed. Their actions in May marked the end of Left Bank idealism. Intellectual radicalism was replaced in the 1970s and '80s by a new materialism, largely inspired by imports from across the Atlantic. Fast food outlets – a travesty, surely, in this city of gourmet eating – became a common sight in Paris.

De Gaulle's successor, Georges Pompidou, was a right-wing conservative, yet he was responsible for commissioning one of the most innovative and extraordinary buildings in Paris, indeed, in Europe – the Centre Georges Pompidou, more commonly referred to these days as 'Beaubourg', after the area where it's located. Designed by Richard Rogers and Renzo Piano, this immensely controversial structure was the first to display its services on the outside in a labyrinth of pipes and tubing. Pompidou died suddenly in 1974, leaving the way open to Valéry Giscard d'Estaing. Giscard's major contribution to the Parisian plan was the acclaimed transformation of the Gare d'Orsay railway station into one of the world's finest art museums.

Giscard was of the old school, and would prove to be France's last Gaullist president. In 1981, the Socialists, with Francois Mitterrand at their head, were swept into power. Paris was overjoyed, but during his two terms in office *Tonton* (or 'Uncle', as he was known) proved that this socialist certainly did not ignore his own interests. He spent lavishly on what he called *Grands Projets*, embellishing the city with the controversial new Bastille Opera House (2,500 million francs), the transformation of the Louvre complex, including the extraordinary glass pyramid (loathed by some, loved by others), and, most spectacular and triumphant of all, the vast 25-storey Grande Arche at la Défense. His last project before his death was a brand-new (and, again, controversial) Bibliothèque Nationale (National Library) on the banks of the Seine. Certainly, his work injected new life into the capital, but Mitterrand's time in power was also marked by excessive corruption, and constant strife between him and his conservative rival, mayor of Paris, prime minister and subsequently President, Jacques Chirac.

PARIS TODAY

Many would argue that the Paris of Chirac lacks real soul. As mayor, he made the trains and buses run like clockwork, and spruced up the streets and boulevards so that the city could present an irreproachable face to world. During his time, the population of central Paris has become almost exclusively middle-class, comfortable in its conservatism, and protected from the grim outer reaches of the city by the *boulevard périphérique*. Although it still has its students, the Left Bank is less of a hotbed of radical thought and new ideas. The intellectuals coming out of the school of political science are more likely to be carrying a Hermès Kelly bag under their arm than a copy of *Das Kapital*. These days, it's in the city's neglected multicultural suburbs that the real innovations – cultural and political – are taking place.

The age-old divide between rich and poor – Paris' splendid city centre, adorned with Mitterrand's expensive monuments, and its suburbs, where families live squeezed into *grand ensemble* tower blocks – may have threatened to erupt in some kind of political uproar. But some would say that one spectacularly symbolic event has taken the pressure right off President Chirac. In July 1998, hundreds of thousands of Parisians thronged the Champs-Élysées to see a spectacular light show on the Arc de Triomphe.

They were celebrating the World Cup victory of a multi-racial French soccer team, whose star player, Zinadine Zidane, had risen to fame from the humblest of backgrounds in Marseille. Zidane's team-mates included Karembeu from New Caledonia, Lama from French Guyana, the Basque Lizarazu, and Thuram from Guadaloupe. Two years later, *Les Bleus* won football's Euro 2000 competition. Chirac must have thought that all his birthdays had come at once as he presided over an exuberant civic reception in Paris for his victorious boys. They were proof positive (according to him) that modern France is a country where even the most deprived can achieve their dream. That inspirational slogan, *La Victoire est en Nous* ('Victory is within us'), should run and run – at least for the time being.

CAFÉ SOCIETY

Paris would not be Paris without its cafés. From Trocadéro to St-Germain, from Montparnasse to the Bastille, they have been the silent witnesses to the city's most interesting, and sometimes most creative and inspirational, conversations and debates. In the 18th century, Voltaire and Rousseau met at the Procope café in the rue des Fosses-St-Germain. The tradition continues today, and great ideas are still conceived over a glass of French wine in a smoky atmosphere.

Venice and Marseille were enjoying café life quite some time before Paris, which had to wait until 1684 for its first. It was opened by a Sicilian, Francesco Procopio, and was an instant and huge success. Punters and professionals from the nearby Comédie Française would stop at the Procope between shows to enjoy the newly imported drink from the East. Racine is reputed to have written his plays with a cup of coffee always to hand.

The café soon became an ideal place for debating and fashionable ideas. Diderot and d'Alembert are said to have launched their great philosophical work, the *Encyclopédie*, at the Procope, and revolutionaries frequented the cafés of the Palais-Royal, led by Camille Desmoulins. In the 19th century, the Tortoni café was a popular meeting place for great minds, and later Trotsky chose the Closerie des Lilas as a base for spreading his politics. The Café de Flore became famous through customers Jean-Paul Sartre and Simone de Beauvoir, who developed their existentialist philosophy there over many a glass of wine.

The cafés in Montparnasse and St-Germain became regular watering holes for writers and painters. Modigliani settled his bills at La Rotonde with a total of 14 paintings, which were all burned when he died. Truman Capote and Ernest Hemingway had regular tables at the Closerie des Lilas, and also went to the Café de Flore, as did André Breton, Albert Camus and others.

When it isn't raining, tables and chairs spill out of the cafés on to Paris' pavements, leaving just enough room for pedestrians (who are entitled to 1.4–1.6 metres (4.6–5.3 feet) according to a decree from the city council). These popular Parisian *terrasses* are places to see and be seen, particularly if you have the latest in mobile phones, which must be used at every available opportunity for the ultimate in chic. Alternatively, you can use that other traditional Parisian accessory, the small dog, to sit on a chair next to you and eat titbits from your plate.

BOOKS AND LITERATURE

BOOKS SET IN PARIS

La Force de l'Age (The Prime of Life), Simone de Beauvoir; intellectual life on the Left Bank in the 1960s, when Simone and Jean-Paul Sartre would meet regularly in the Café de Flore to discuss

Nadja, André Breton; surrealist account of the encounter between the narrator and a young unknown woman wandering the streets of Paris.

A Tale of Two Cities, Charles Dickens; the gap between the rich and poor in Paris and London.

A Moveable Feast, Ernest Hemingway; account of bohemian life in Paris between the wars, when Hemingway spent time in St-Germain with Gertrude Stein and F. Scott Fitzgerald. They would spend hours at the bookshop-cum-library of *Shakespeare and Company*, owned by American Sylvia Beach.

Les Misérables, Victor Hugo; *Notre-Dame de Paris*, Victor Hugo; monumental and romantic evocations of the Paris of the mid–1800s, with a strong sense of social injustice, poverty and revolution.

Parisian Sketches, Henry James; another American in Paris.

Down and Out in Paris and London; George Orwell's account of a struggle for survival in the two cities during the late 1920s.

A La Recherche du Temps Perdu (Remembrance of Things Past), Marcel Proust; astonishing autobiographical narrative written in Paris and about Paris by the most important 20th-century French writer. Evoking the old-fashioned atmosphere of the *bourgeois* 16th arrondissement, private mansions, and promenades on the Champs-Élysées.

Maigret stories of Georges Simenon; the seamier side of Paris is the background for Simenon's stories about his famous detective.

A Sentimental Journey, Laurence Sterne; the British author's description of a trip to Paris in 1768.

Nana, Emile Zola; detailed descriptions of the Paris of Napoleon III, following the story of Nana the courtesan.

BOOKS ABOUT PARIS, FRANCE AND THE FRENCH

France Today, John Ardagh; *The New French Revolution*, John Ardagh; the politics, people and peculiarities that make up modern France.

Architect's Guide to Paris, Renzo Salvadori.

The French, Theodore Zeldin; erudite, witty and deeply researched biography of a country and its people. Recently updated.

Reflections on the Revolution in France, Edmund Burke; written in 1790, Burke's book predicted the Terror which followed the Revolution. This British political thinker analysed events in Paris, and related them to the contemporary situation in London.

Paris in Time, Marshall Dill, Jr; the history of Paris, from its origins on the Ile de la Cité, with perceptive comments along the way.

Sylvia Beach and the Lost Generation, Noel Riley Fitch; literary Paris of the 1920s and, 30s, when Sylvia owned the bookshop Shakespeare and Co. and looked after impoverished American writers like Hemingway and Ezra Pound.

Americans in Paris, Brian N. Morton; Paris through the eyes of dozens of Americans, from Louis Armstrong to Isadora Duncan.

WRITERS AND PARIS

The reputation of Paris as a city of philosophical trends, literary and artistic creativity, and protest movements, has always reached far beyond its own frontiers. For the past 150 years, the City of Light has been a beacon for writers and artists, who have reached out for it as a symbol of intellectual freedom.

During the first half of the 19th century, the new social order created by the Industrial Revolution was consolidated in Paris, as it was all over Europe. Society was more mobile than ever before, and a rich source of inspiration for writers such as Victor Hugo, who took the misery of Paris' poor as his subject, and Balzac and Flaubert, who wrote about the pretensions of the newly ascendant bourgeoisie. In the 1880s, Guy de Maupassant exposed the cynicism and corruption of the so-called *Belle Époque*, marking the golden age of the realist novel. Their message was spread in the literature that was widely circulated at the time, either via the dozens of *bouquinistes* already in existence by the mid–1800s, or through reading rooms and literary *salons* or the lending libraries of the city's publishing houses.

In the last two decades of the century, the symbolist poets clustered like devoted courtiers at the feet of their 'master', Stéphane Mallarmé. Some, particularly Arthur Rimbaud and Charles Baudelaire – whose masterpiece was called *Les Fleurs du Mal* (The Flowers of Evil) – were as famous for their dissolute lifestyle as for their poetry. English writer Oscar Wilde also claimed to be a disciple of Mallarmé. He wrote his play *Salomé* in Paris, chose to live in the city after his release from prison, and died in 1901 at the Hôtel d'Alsace, on the rue des Beaux Arts.

An ever-increasing sense of impending doom marked the work of some of these writers. Marcel Proust's seven-volume masterpiece *À La Recherche du Temps Perdu* (Remembrance of Things Past) (1913–27) was the first great work in French of the new century, but, as its title suggests, it is an extended elegy. The world it mourns was shattered forever in 1914 by the seismic shock of the First World War. The impact of war was reflected during the following decade, firstly by the movement known as Dada, a rebellious anti-art group, from which grew Surrealism. The publication of the Surrealist Manifesto in 1924 by André Breton signified the birth of this art and literary movement, which dominated Parisian literary life throughout the 1920s. Many of the most distinguished French writers of the early part of the century were at one time connected with the movement.

During this post-war period, many foreign writers began to be attracted to the French capital. It was a stimulating and liberating place to write, and rates of exchange made it relatively cheap. American writer Gertrude Stein established a kind of *salon*, and a call on her was a rite of passage for all English-speaking writers in the 1920s. Ernest Hemingway and F. Scott Fitzgerald were among those who came with letters of introduction to her legendary studio on the rue de Fleurus. (Curiously, Hemingway was later to attack her in his memoir of life in Paris, *A Moveable Feast.*) Ms Stein also wrote one of the classic books about ex-pat life in Paris, *The Autobiography of Alice B. Toklas* (1933).

The irascible Hemingway was kinder in retrospect about Ezra Pound, who was then living in Paris and making something of a vocation of helping young writers. Another kindly mentor was the Irish writer James Joyce. His unconventional *Ulysses* was first published in 1921 by the American Sylvia Beach, founder of the *Shakespeare and Co* bookshop formerly in rue de l'Odéon in the Latin Quarter, and now in rue de la Bûcherie. Other Irish writers, including Samuel Beckett, came to Paris because Joyce was there. The city's other major attraction was the distinct possibility of getting published. The Paris media included avant-garde magazines such as *Transition*, and countless other short-lived but influential periodicals through which the modernist movement was able to define itself.

These immigrant writers preferred the bargain-basement rents and prices, and the classlessness, of Paris' Left Bank. They congregated in the many cafés and bistros on the narrow streets around Montparnasse, particularly the Closerie des Lilas, La Coupole, the Dôme, the Sélect and the Rotonde. Here, they were far from the *haut-bourgeois* areas on the Right Bank, and the constraints of respectability. Paris was famous then, as it is now, for its atmosphere of sexual freedom and, as writers like Henry Miller were to discover, that freedom could be a stimulus to art as well as a source of personal pleasure.

The character of the Montparnasse quarter was completely destroyed in the 1970s, with the rebuilding of the station and the tower, but Baudelaire, Sartre and de Beauvoir have not left – they are all buried in the cemetery on boulevard Edgar Quinet.

English writer George Orwell was less enchanted with the Paris of the 1930s. He worked as a *plongeur* (washer-upper) in the kitchen of a hotel on the rue de Rivoli. The scathing account he gave of his experiences in *Down and Out in Paris and London* is characteristic of the more socially committed writing of the period.

The Second World War and the occupation of Paris by the Germans gave rise to a style of writing that brooded on the essential nature of existence. The axis of intellectual and literary life shifted from Montparnasse, northwards to St-Germain des Prés, and two cafés – the Flore (172 boulevard St-Germain 75006) and the Deux Magots (6 place St-Germain-des-Prés 75006) – witnessed the birth of 'existentialism'. Jean-Paul Sartre and Albert Camus became the key figures in this new philosophical and literary movement. Both had been active in the Resistance during the war, and Camus' *The Plague* was a metaphor for that terrible trauma. Sartre's lover Simone de Beauvoir was an equally important member of the group, subsequently producing the seminal feminist work *Le Deuxième Sexe* (The Second Sex), and, later, *La Force de l'Age* (The Prime of Life), her evocative account of intellectual life on the Left Bank. The Brasserie Lipp (151 boulevard St-Germain 75006) was sometimes the lunchtime venue for the philosophical clique. de Beauvoir and Sartre's disciples wore black polo-necks and black eye make-up, and had long, languid discussions on the meaning of life – or its utter lack of meaning – before strolling off to catch the latest Godard film of the *nouvelle vague*.

In existentialist accounts, Man's condition was said to be 'absurd'. Accordingly, in the late 1940s and throughout the 1950s, Paris became the nexus of what became known as 'absurdist' theatre. Beckett's *Waiting for Godot*, along with works by Eugène Ionesco and Jean Genet, caught the post-war mood of uncertainty, and took it further, to mock the very idea of meaning.

The French existentialists were joined in Paris in the 1950s by a new generation of American poets and novelists. Jack Kerouac, Allen Ginsberg, Neal Cassady and William Burroughs were the self-styled Beat Generation, who wrote about an unrestricted life *On the Road*. Unsurprisingly, they were too restless to make Paris their home for very long.

In the decade that followed, the single most important cultural and political event was the major student uprising of 1968. It may have failed in its immediate goals, but its impact can be traced in the 'democratization' which has been a feature of the arts ever since. Barthes, Derrida and Foucault challenge the distinctions between 'creative' and 'critical' texts, and between 'fiction' and 'fact'. Simultaneously, the *nouveau roman* ('new novel') pioneered by Alain Robbe-Grillet and Nathalie Sarraute undermines the authority of the author, giving the reader a more active role.

These recent writings may seem to mark a complete break with tradition. In another sense, they are absolutely in keeping with the tradition of freedom. They could only have come from Paris.

ART AND ARTISTS

Many consider Paris to be the birthplace of modern art. By the mid-19th century, the French capital was Europe's centre of intellectual activity, a city where artists gathered to participate in the creative revolution that was gathering pace. The *salon* system had reigned supreme for centuries, but painters – first Manet and then the Impressionists – began to step forward to challenge every rule in the book. The work of these artistic revolutionaries was ground-breaking, both in terms of its subject matter and in its representation, and the Establishment was profoundly shocked.

These were intense years of artistic experimentation, following a route via Impressionism, Post-Impressionism, Fauvism and Cubism, to the first examples of abstract art, which appeared in the second decade of the 20th century. Picasso, Braque and Miró developed their own brands of abstraction between the wars, and the anti-art movement of Dadaism arrived briefly, only to be supplanted by Surrealism. After the Second World War, a circle of artists gathered around the Left Bank's Existentialist writers, but, as the years went by, many artists left Paris. New York took over the lead in artistic innovation, and Paris never regained its supremacy as world capital of art.

Today, Paris is still the most obvious, and best place to follow the long, rich and complicated history of French art, which has been so influential throughout the world. The Musée du Louvre, which started life as a royal collection, when French king François I bought Leonardo da Vinci's *Mona Lisa* for himself, has grown to accommodate the most comprehensive art collection in the world. The Musée d'Orsay is the city's temple to the art and design of the 19th century, with a superb collection of Impressionist paintings. Its scope is very precise: from 1850, the beginning of Courbet's realism and 19th-century art, to 1905, the birth of Cubism and the beginning of 20th-century art. To see more 20th-century work, and Matisse's famous *The Dance*, make for the Musée d'Art Moderne (Palais de Tokyo east wing, 11 ave du Président-Wilson 75016).

PAINTING

Nicolas Poussin (1594–1665) was one of the first French painters not to be under the thumb of a patron. He spent little time in Paris, preferring the artistic freedom of Rome, where he expounded on the heroic themes of Roman moral victory, while his contemporary Claude Lorraine (1600–82) painted delicate, idyllic Roman landscapes. In 1648, the Académie Royale de Peinture et de Sculpture was set up, with the purpose of establishing and maintaining quality in art. Almost a century later, the Academy provided its first showcase for painters, in *salons*, or public rooms.

Ardent Bonapartist, and influential artist Jacques-Louis David (1748–1825) closed down the *salon* in 1792, and opened the Académie des Beaux-Arts, which had the same format and aims. David's severe Neoclassical style was much in vogue at the time, and particularly popular with the new Emperor. The painter's representation of Napoleon's coronation was monumental. David was to teach many of the next generation's finest painters, including Jean-Auguste-Dominique Ingres (1780–1867), who carried on where his teacher left off, and continued to demonstrate a rigid Classicism. His exquisite portraits remained in complete opposition to Romanticism, which was beginning to develop at around the same time.

The first great canvas of the Romantic movement was exhibited in the *salon* in 1819. Paris society was shocked by the powerful immediacy of Théodore Géricault's *The Raft of the Medusa*, which illustrated a political and scandalous event. The painting still hangs in the Louvre. Eugène Delacroix (1798–1863) became the major figure of the Romantic movement in Europe. His passionate evocation of historical, bibilical, mythological and literary subjects, and his use of colour, were to exert a huge influence on Cézanne and Van Gogh, two of the founders of modern painting. His *Liberty Guiding the People*, showing revolutionary Parisians at the barricades, was considered dangerous, and hidden away by the authorities for 20 years. Delacroix worked from 1844 to 1857 in a studio at 58 rue Notre-Dame, which may be visited today. He spent the last six years of his life at 6 place Furstenberg, in St-Germain, where a small museum now displays his personal effects and his studio.

Delacroix also shared a studio in Paris with Camille Corot (1796–1875), at 13 quai Voltaire. Corot's poetic landscapes, painted in soft grey-greens, became immensely popular towards the middle of the century. The Romantic painters, and one group in particular – the landscapists who went to Barbizon in the Fontainebleau forest – began to be seen as eccentric bohemians. The leading member of the Barbizon group was Jean-François Millet (1814–75), the son of a rural worker who sought to portray honest, unprettified scenes of peasant life and labours. Versions of his *The Sower* (1850) are on display in the Louvre. Millet was much influenced by the work of caricaturist Honoré Daumier (1808–79), who satirized Parisian life – the theatre, the art world, politics and the law courts – in the spirit of Balzac and his Comédie Humaine. He eventually made over 4,000 lithographs, which reached a vast audience via various journals, and led to his spending six months in prison. His picture of Parisian life in the mid–19th century can still be seen in the Petit Palais in the Louvre.

The main legacy of the Barbizon group was their habit of painting in the open air; this was later adopted as one of the key principles of Impressionism.

With Millet and Gustave Courbet (1819–77), Romanticism gave way to Realism. Courbet's images of abject poverty include *Stonebreakers* (1850) and *Burial at Ornans* (1850), which features more than 50 life-sized figures at a peasant funeral, and hangs in the Louvre. Courbet was perceived as a dangerous socialist, and the Academy would not present his work at the *salon*. The painter was forced to set an example for his successors by putting on shows at his own expense.

Edouard Manet (1832–83) was the next painter to scandalize Paris, when his work was viewed in the *Salon des Refusés* ('Rejects' Salon'), set up by Napoleon III. Manet began in the academic tradition, but soon developed his own methods, including painting directly from the model, using a restricted palette, particularly black, and handling paint quite loosely. He exhibited with (and inspired) the Impressionists, although he was never really one of them, and created outrage with his *Déjeuner sur l'Herbe* ('Picnic on the Grass') (1863) and *Olympia* (1865), which presented naked women in an extraordinarily direct manner. *Olympia* was considered so shocking that it was not hung in the Louvre until 1907. It's now exposed to the eyes of the world in the Musée d'Orsay, along with Manet's *Déjeuner sur l'Herbe*.

The *salon* continued to refuse work that it saw as unacceptable, so in 1874 the *Société Anonyme des Artistes* held its own 'rebel' exhibition, in a photographers' studio at 35 boulevard des Capucines. Claude Monet (1840–1926) was the leader of the new group of artists, and his painting *Impression: Sunrise* (1872) gave its name to the movement; they were described by one critic as 'lunatics'. The Impressionists – Monet, Renoir, Sisley, Pissarro, Morisot and Degas – painted everyday scenes directly from nature, banishing earth colours from their palette, and sometimes employing small dabs of loose paint (pointillism) to capture the play of light on the surface of objects. Monet's *Impression: Sunrise* can be seen in the Musée Marmottan (2 rue Louis-Boilly 75016), along with his world-famous water-lilies series of paintings, dating from his last years at Giverny. The shimmering pools of colour are near-abstract and represent naturalism taken to its logical conclusion.

Some sort of art-world backlash against Impressionism was inevitable. 'Post-Impressionism' is the broad term given to the work of various important figures, who were reacting against what they saw as the superficiality of their predecessors. Gauguin, Van Gogh, Georges Seurat, Toulouse-Lautrec, Cézanne and Degas (one of the original exhibitors on the boulevard des Capucines) were among those seeking a more formal conception of art or a new emphasis on the subject. Vincent Van Gogh arrived in Paris in 1886, and soon began using vivid colour and pointillism in his views of the city. He later moved to the south of France, where he suffered mental illness and died an early death. Painter and sculptor Edgar Degas (1834–1917) had been a pupil and admirer of Ingres, but developed his own style to create unusual compositions influenced by Japanese prints and photography. His favoured subjects were ballet dancers, working girls and racehorses; his *L'Absinthe* hangs in the Musée d'Orsay, alongside some of his beautiful sculptures.

Henri de Toulouse-Lautrec (1864–1901) recorded the *demi-monde* of Paris' Belle Epoque with masterly sinuous lines and bold, flat colour. His dynamic images, many of which were used on posters advertising cabarets and dance halls, have come to personify this period. His subjects were the seedy characters he encountered in bars, circuses and brothels all over the city.

Paul Cézanne (1839–1906) was the most radical of the Post-Impressionists, devoting his life to working out how to represent the underlying structure of objects by use of colour alone. He was not a Parisian artist, but had his first big show in the capital in 1895. He described how he saw Nature in terms of cones, spheres and cylinders – a fascinating concept to the creators of Cubism in the early 20th century.

The commercial success of some of the Impressionists and Post-Impressionists, and the Parisian lifestyle of even the poorest artists, attracted creative types from all over the world. Even the least successful painters could afford to live in the artistic quarters of the French capital – the Latin Quarter and Montmartre – and enjoy the decadence of the period leading up to the turn of the century.

SCULPTURE

The work of French sculptors has largely followed the style of painting through the centuries. The major work in Paris of François Rude (1784–1855), the principal sculptor of the early 19th century, is *his Volunteers of 1792 (The Marseillaise)* on the Arc de Triomphe. Rude combined the romanticism of Delacroix with the classicism and Napoleonic enthusiasm of David. One of his pupils, Jean-Baptiste Carpeaux (1827–75), was also heavily influenced by Delacroix. He created *The Dance* (1865) for the Paris Opera House; it was considered highly immoral. Carpeaux was a precursor of the most celebrated sculptor of the 19th century – Auguste Rodin (1840–1917). By returning to a close study of nature, Rodin liberated sculpture from the sentimental idealism of the academicians. His figures were so lifelike and so full of movement and emotion that some critics refused to believe that he hadn't cast them directly from models.

Rodin's genius is celebrated in one of Paris' most delightful museums, the Musée Rodin, at the 18th-century Hôtel Biron (77 rue de Varenne 75007). The sculptor actually lived and worked in the mansion, and some of his best-known pieces are on display here, inside the house and around the garden, including *The Thinker, The Kiss*, *The Gates of Hell* and *The Burghers of Calais*. His controversial portrait of writer Balzac is the closest anyone came in 19th-century sculpture to pure abstract symbol.

THE BIRTH OF MODERN ART

In 1905, another new painters' movement caused a furore in Paris. This group, led by Henri Matisse (1869–1954), exhibited paintings characterized by their violent use of colour, flat pattern and unconventional distortions at the *Salon d'Automne*. They were called the *Fauves* (or 'wild beasts') by the critics, who were struck by their lack of inhibition. The Fauvists were all painters who had been struggling to make a living in turn-of-the-century Paris – Matisse, Derain, Vlaminck, and Dufy, among others – and who had been greatly influenced by Van Gogh and Gauguin. Fauvism lasted just a few years, but it was quickly followed by a new 'ism' that would last longer, and have a most profound influence on the course of 20th-century art.

Pablo Picasso (1881–1973) is surely the most significant figure in the development of modern art. He spent much of his life in Paris and, together with Georges Braque (1882–1963), developed Cubism, the parent of abstract art, while living and working in the city. Their aim was to capture several viewpoints of a subject simultaneously, to break down an object into facets, and thus represent it not as it appears, but to show the way that it exists in space. Cézanne had influenced the first phase of the movement. Picasso and Braque developed Analytical Cubism (1909–12), which excluded colour, and then Synthetic Cubism (1912–14) which reintroduced colour and added new elements such as newspaper cuttings and cane.

From 1904 to 1912, Picasso had a tiny studio in the Bateau-Lavoir lodging house in Montmartre's place Emilie-Goudeau. The house quickly became a gathering place for many of the major figures of avant-garde and experimental art and literature. Here, Picasso painted his hugely significant *Demoiselles d'Avignon*, a key painting in the journey towards Cubism and abstract art. Today, although new artists' studios have been built on the site of the fire-damaged Bateau-Lavoir, the spirit of the Montmartre of Picasso, Modigliani, Utrillo, Dufy and Van Gogh lives on in the neighbourhood Musée du Vieux Montmartre, at 12 rue Cortot.

By the 1920s, the Paris art scene had de-camped across the river to Montparnasse, where the Montmartre artists were joined in the cafés and brasseries by refugees from eastern and central Europe. Picasso and Braque rented *ateliers* (studios) in La Ruche, a beehive-shaped pavilion salvaged from the 1900 Exhibition, and made available to poor artists by the sculptor Alfred Boucher. Among the Cubists' neighbours were Romanian sculptor Constantin Brancusi (1876–1957), Russian Marc Chagall (1887–1985) and Lithuanian Chaim Soutine (1893–1943). The 'Beehive' stands in an overgrown garden off the narrow passage de Dantzig, south of Montparnasse, and still provides space for painters and sculptors.

These post-war years also saw the rise of 'anti-art' movements intended specifically to shock the Establishment. Parisian Marcel Duchamp (1887–1968) used lavatory seats as art to challenge traditional ideas about taste; Dadaist 'art events' arrived in the city in the persons of Picabia and Tristan Tzara; in 1925, Surrealism took over from Dadaism, with a scandalous show in Paris exhibiting the work of American photographer Man Ray, Picasso, Catalan Joan Miró (1893–1983) and Max Ernst (1891–1976). Salvador Dali (1904–89) arrived from Spain in 1929; a genius of self-publicity, he was to become the embodiment of the Surrealist movement. Dali was just one of the struggling artists who lived and worked at the ateliers of the Villa Seurat near the Parc Montsouris.

Picasso remained in Paris throughout the Second World War occupation of the city, becoming something of a symbol of the Resistance. He is honoured today in a lovely one-man museum, housed in the beautiful 17th-century Hôtel Salé mansion (5 rue de Thorigny). The large collection, mostly handed over to France by the estate of Picasso in lieu of death duties, covers the artist's entire career, as well as displaying work by his circle of friends. It's a must, if only to see Picasso's *Self-Portrait* from his blue period, his *Still Life with Cane Chair* from his Cubist years and *Pan's Flute* from his classical period, as well as Matisse's exquisite *Still Life with Oranges*.

After the occupation, the Paris art scene fell into the doldrums. Many of the most innovative artists, including Matisse, Picasso and Chagall, had left the city, and abstract art was recognized as New York's baby. Paris – the city of David, Delacroix and Manet, the birthplace of Impressionism, Post-Impressionism, Fauvism and Cubism, the place where Picasso the consummate artist felt most at home – had lost its slot as art capital of the world.

CINEMA

THE BIRTH OF CINEMA

At 14 boulevard des Capucines there's a plaque that reads 'Here, on 28 December 1895, the first public showings of moving pictures took place with the aid of the cinematograph, a device invented by the Lumière brothers.' Cinema was born in the basement of a Parisian café, and since then Paris has played a leading role in the world of film. For the first few years of cinema's development, 90 per cent of all the films shown throughout the world were made in France. During the 1920s, Hollywood got in on the act and by the end of the decade, 85 per cent of the world's films came from the USA.

Atmospheric Paris continued to inspire countless French-born and foreign film-makers, however, as it rode a rollercoaster of changing moods, from the First World War to the student riots of the late 1960s. Throughout the century, French film-makers have been closely linked with both political and artistic movements. The Avant-Garde, influenced by 1920s Surrealism, gave way to poetic realism, in the 1930s and 1940s, when film-makers such as René Clair (*Sous les toits de Paris*), Jean Renoir and Marcel Carné tried to give cinema-goers a social conscience. Films such as Carné's *Les Enfants du Paradis* made Parisian cinema-goers aware of the poverty that existed practically next door to them, while Renoir's *La Règle du Jeu* and *Le Crime de Monsieur Lange* satirized the bourgeoisie and encouraged social revolution.

After the darkness and pessimism of post-war French cinema, artistic revolution arrived in the 1950s in the form of *the nouvelle vague* ('new wave'). Claude Chabrol, Jean-Luc Godard, Louis Malle, Jacques Rivette and François Truffaut made their base with other directors at the Cinémathèque, and in the *ciné-clubs* of Paris' Left Bank. Their films, often autobiographical, were full of references to other cinematic work. The landmark film of the movement was Godard's *À Bout de Souffle*. Premiering in Paris in March 1960, it was a critical and commercial success, a pastiche of American cinema, with jump-cut editing and a romantic approach. Godard's black-and-white images of Paris are enduring: Jean Seberg selling the *New York Herald Tribune* on the Champs-Élysées and night-time shots of café terraces and rooftops.

Many of the *nouvelle vague* directors continued to work into the 1970s and 1980s, being joined by auteur directors such as Eric Rohmer, who created intimate, perceptive studies of relationships, in a naturalistic style. In the

1980s, newer directors turned a sympathetic eye again on marginalized Paris – in *Loulou* (1980), Maurice Pialat gave a portrait of blue-collar France, and the darkness of life in the Parisian suburbs; Jean-Jacques Beneix made a stylish debut with his ingenious Paris-set fantasy-thriller *Diva* (1981); and Luc Besson triumphed with his 'punk-chic' film *Subway* (1985), with spiky-haired Christopher Lambert living in a strange underworld society in the Parisian Metro.

Some of France's biggest film stars – Montand, Depardieu, Deneuve, Belmondo, Delon, Adjani – enjoy near-icon status in their own country. Yet today only a small percentage of French-made films are successful at the box office. French film-making, it seems, survives by specializing. Helped by state subsidies, the industry produces a range of films for a variety of limited audiences. It follows, then, that even successful French films are rarely seen outside France. French directors' films are often perceived as too individualistic, sometimes shocking, and at times difficult to understand – no wonder then that they don't always travel very well!

PARIS AS A FILM SET

Historic and picturesque Paris has provided the perfect backdrop for film-makers for a century. American producers sealed their love affair with the city with *An American in Paris* (1951), which set Gene Kelly and Leslie Caron against the sights and sounds of Paris, using Impressionist and Post-impressionist images. In *Funny Face* (1956), the charm of the city was matched with that of its star, Audrey Hepburn, and Hepburn appeared in the French capital again the following year in Billy Wilder's *Love in the Afternoon*.

Despite the obvious surface beauty of Paris, more recent directors haven't shied away from showing all its complex layers. A number of films of the 1990s have shown that, although Paris is a place of romance, it has its fair share of social problems – *La Haine* (1995), *J'embrasse pas* (1991) and *Les Amants du Pont-Neuf* (1991) all depict another side of Paris, portraying the harsher realities of life, set against its streets, skies and waterways of the urban environment.

ON VA AU CINOCHE?

Paris is *the* city for the film-lover, with 300-plus screens. Every day cinema-goers can choose from one of the most exciting and wide-ranging programmes in the world – from big Hollywood blockbusters and home-grown releases, to films from all countries and all eras, showing at small, independent venues. There may not be an international film festival in Paris on the scale of Cannes, but that's because the festival of cinema in the capital is permanent.

The city's mainstream cinemas (or *cinoches*, to the slang-loving French) are located around the Champs-Élysées, the Grands Boulevards, the place de la Bastille, Montparnasse and the Odéon crossroad. Gaumont and UGC are the best-known names. In the last few years, a couple of vast multiplexes have landed (seemingly from outer space) outside the city's traditional 'cinema' locations, and a new complex has been built at the foot of the Grande Bibliothèque.

Fans of arthouse, classic and experimental films turn their back on these multi-screen monsters, and head instead for the boulevard St-Michel. In the side-streets all along the length of the boulevard, from the Seine right up to the Jardin du Luxembourg, filmhouses (often called *studios*) show oldies and classics, as well as newer films that aren't on general release. These cinemas might lack the comfort and projection quality of the big multi-screens, and offer less choice at the snack counter, but they more than make up for it in ambiance.

Film buffs visiting Paris will love the Cinémathèque Française (7 ave Albert de Mun 75016; ☎: 01 56 26 01 01; Metro: Trocadéro), at one end of the Palais de Chaillot. Around 40,000 films, many of them classics or rare pieces of work, are housed in its library. They are restored and shown to the public in screenings from Wednesday to Sunday, at 7pm and 9pm. The Vidéothèque de Paris (Forum des Halles, 2 Grande Galerie 75001; Metro: Les Halles) has a collection of over 3,500 videos of footage (television, film, or newsreel) featuring Paris. For a small fee, visitors may view any video on the spot, from Tuesday to Sunday, 12.30 to 8.30pm.

The week's programme of cinema screenings throughout Paris can be found in the two main listings magazines – *L'Officiel des Spectacles* and *Pariscope* – which are both available from news-stands (*kiosques*) all over the city. Non-French films are usually presented subtitled in their original version (marked 'VO' in the listings), rather than being dubbed, so film fans can easily catch up on films missed at home on a wet afternoon. 'VF' indicates a soundtrack in French (either dubbed or original).

1ST ARRONDISSEMENT

THE LOUVRE ● THE PALAIS-ROYAL ● LES HALLES ● ÎLE DE LA CITÉ

The Palais-Royal is surrounded by a bustling area: lively during the day with employees from insurance companies, travel agencies and banks milling about together with the Japanese who work in the area and in particular frequent the rues Ste-Anne and Faubourg-St-Honoré. At night it turns into something of a ghost town. It does, however, have some nice walks through charming streets and nostalgic passageways.

WHERE TO STAY

☆ BUDGET

Hôtel de Lille (map C2, **1**): 8 rue du Pélican 75001. ☎ 01-42-33-33-42. Metro: Palais-Royal, Louvre or Pyramides. Double room with washbasin 250F, with shower 300F. Shower available on the landing for 30F. Situated in a quiet and historic street, this small hotel has 14 rooms, with a romantic and old-fashioned feel to it, well cared for by a very nice family. Rooms 1, 4, 7 and 10 are a bit gloomy but incredibly quiet. No breakfast, but there is a hot-and-cold drinks machine. Ideal if you're on a budget.

BVJ Centre International (map C2, **2**): 20 rue Jean-Jacques-Rousseau 75001. ☎ 01-53-00-90-90. Fax: 01-53-00-90-91. Metro: Louvre or Palais-Royal. Single room 120F, including bed and breakfast. Meals from 40F to 60F. No meals on Sunday. Left luggage 10F. Half board 160F or 180F; full board 220F or 240F. Youth-hostel style rooms have 200 beds in all, in rooms with from one to eight beds. Open to anyone aged between 18 and 35. No card required, but there is a 10 per cent reduction with the *Carte Jeune* and FYITHO (GO and Euro 26). It's best to reserve two to three days in advance. Turn up or ring between 9 and 9.30am to find out about vacancies. Open 24 hours. If it's full the same organization also has a similar hotel in the Latin Quarter. Check-out at 9am.

Hôtel de la Vallée (map D2, **3**): 84–86 rue St-Denis 75001. ☎ 01-42-36-46-99. Fax: 01-42-36-16-66. Metro: Châtelet, Étienne-Marcel, Les Halles. Double room 220F to 300F, according to level of comfort. Shower on each floor 15F. Right in the heart of Les Halles, you won't find a better location! Very good for the price, even if the 'sex shop' environment won't be to everyone's taste. If you want peace and quiet, although the rooms do have double-glazing, choose one of the rooms overlooking the courtyard (unfortunately there aren't very many of these). Otherwise, ask for one on the higher floors. All rooms have television. Frankly, it's not easy to find anything cheaper in this area. Note that they don't take cheques, but they do take credit cards. Rooms have to be paid for in advance.

Hôtel du Palais (map D3, **4**): 2 quai de la Mégisserie 75001. ☎ 01-

42-36-98-25. Fax: 01-42-21-41-67. Metro: Châtelet. Double room 256F to 406F, depending on toilet facilities. TV included. A modest hotel boasting rooms (with double-glazing), which have fantastic views over the Seine, the Eiffel Tower, the Conciergerie and Notre-Dame. People mainly come for the view and the perfect location. The highest rooms are the quietest, but also the most modest, and therefore less expensive. On the fifth floor there's no TV. And all you can see is the sky . . . but if you get up onto a chair you can see a bit of Châtelet, which is some compensation! Antiquated but on the whole, it's pretty clean. Watch out, there have been mistakes with bookings.

☆ ☆ MODERATE

Hôtel Lescot (map D2, **7**): 26 rue Pierre-Lescot 75001. ☎ 01-42-33-68-76. Fax: 01-42-33-97-10. Metro: Étienne-Marcel. Single room 425F; double room 460F with bath and toilet. For three people, budget for 580F. Small, modern, comfortable hotel, 50m (164ft) from the Forum des Halles. Pleasant decor, TV in all rooms and double-glazing. The rooms are rather small and have no particular charm of their own. Definitely haggle on price if the hotel isn't full. The establishment is linked to a restaurant which provides room service.

☆ ☆ ☆ CHIC

Hôtel Londres St-Honoré (map B1, **8**): 13 rue St-Roch 75001. ☎ 01-42-60-15-62. Fax: 01-42-60-16-00. Metro: Tuileries. Double room 490F to 590F, all with shower or bath and toilet. Charming hotel, very friendly, with a family atmosphere, in a quarter which doesn't usually

Where to stay
- **1** Hôtel de Lille
- **2** BVJ Centre International
- **3** Hôtel de la Vallée
- **4** Hôtel du Palais
- **7** Hôtel Lescot
- **8** Hôtel Londres St-Honoré
- **10** Hôtel du Cygne
- **11** Hôtel Agora

Where to eat
- **21** Café Véry
- **22** Higuma
- **23** Universal Restaurant
- **24** Foujita 1
- **25** Foujita 2
- **26** Le Palet
- **27** Osaka
- **28** Foyer Concorde
- **29** Chicago Meatpackers
- **30** Davé
- **31** La Mousson
- **32** L'Ardoise
- **33** Le Béarn
- **34** Ca d'Oro
- **35** Lescure
- **36** Macéo
- **37** La Fresque
- **38** Nodaïwa
- **39** Juvéniles
- **40** Au Petit Bar
- **42** Le Café Marly
- **43** Willi's Wine Bar
- **44** Toupary
- **45** Le Comptoir Paris-Marrakech
- **46** L'Ostréa
- **49** La Robe et le Palais
- **50** Le Rubis
- **53** À la Cloche des Halles
- **54** Le Relais Chablisien
- **55** Taverne Henri IV
- **56** Au Pied de Cochon
- **57** À la Tour de Montlhéry, Chez Denise
- **58** La Poule au Pot

Where to go for a drink/ Going out
- **70** Flann O'Brien
- **72** Le Café du Pont 9
- **73** Colette
- **74** Bar de l'Hôtel Costes
- **75** Banana Café
- **76** Carr's
- **77** Tropic Café
- **79** Le Sunset
- **80** Le Duc des Lombards
- **81** Le Petit Opportun
- **82** Le Slow-Club
- **83** La Scala
- **84** Le Fumoir

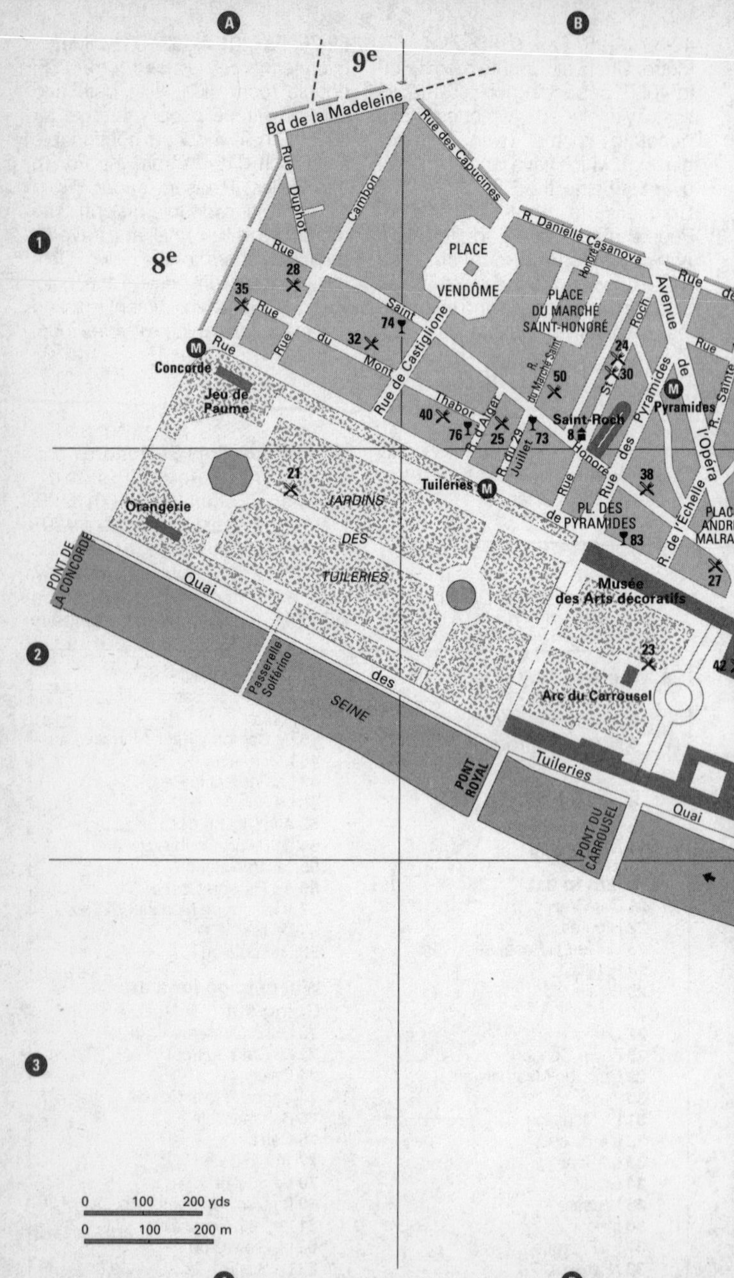
A
B
9e
8e
1
2
3
Bd de la Madeleine
Rue Duphot
Cambon
Rue des Capucines
R. Danielle Casanova
PLACE
VENDÔME
PLACE DU MARCHÉ SAINT-HONORÉ
Rue Saint Roch
Avenue de l'Opéra
Rue des Pyramides
Rue Sainte Anne
Rue du Mont Thabor
Rue de Castiglione
R. d'Alger
R. du 29 Juillet
Rue Saint Honoré
Concorde
Jeu de Paume
Orangerie
Saint-Roch
Pyramides
Tuileries
JARDINS DES TUILERIES
PL. DES PYRAMIDES
PLACE ANDRÉ-MALRAUX
R. de l'Échelle
Musée des Arts décoratifs
Arc du Carrousel
PONT DE LA CONCORDE
Quai des Tuileries
Passerelle Solférino
SEINE
PONT ROYAL
PONT DU CARROUSEL
Quai
0 100 200 yds
0 100 200 m

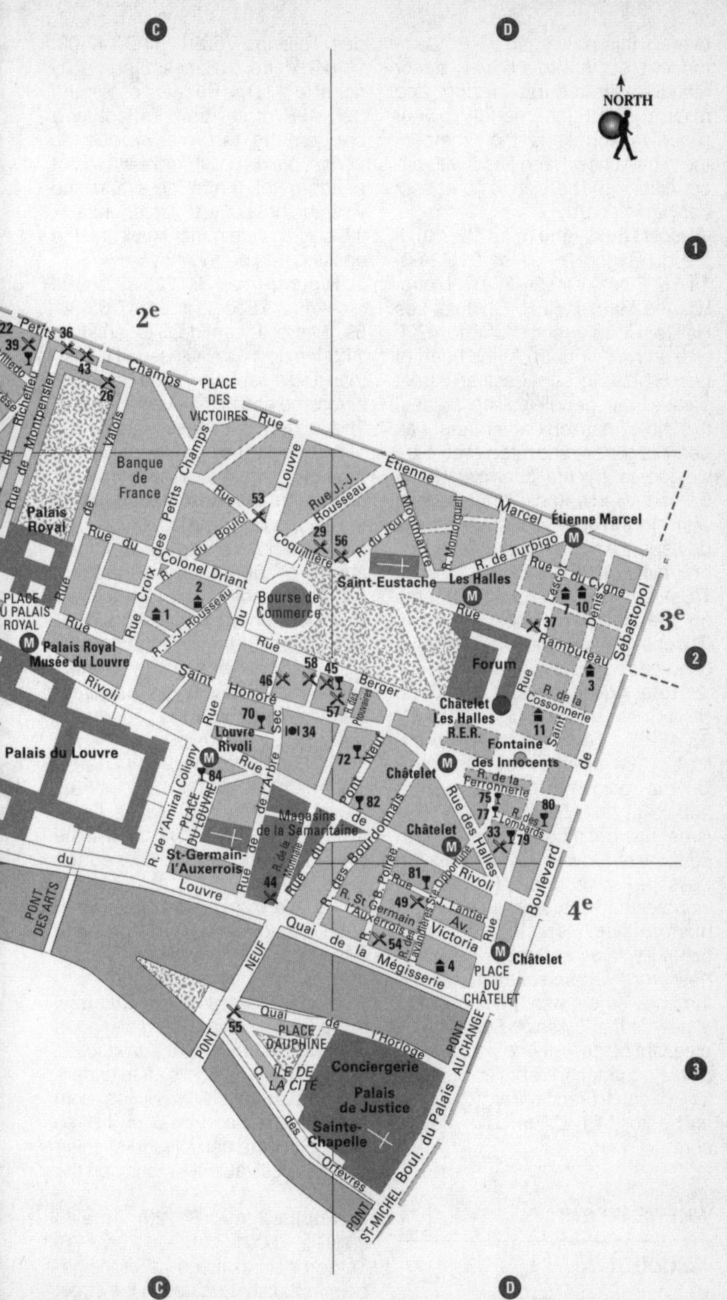

C
D
NORTH
1
2
3
2e
3e
4e
PLACE DES VICTOIRES
Banque de France
Palais Royal
PLACE DU PALAIS ROYAL
Palais Royal Musée du Louvre
Palais du Louvre
Bourse de Commerce
Saint-Eustache
Les Halles
Étienne Marcel
Forum
Châtelet Les Halles R.E.R.
Fontaine des Innocents
Châtelet
Louvre Rivoli
Magasins de la Samaritaine
St-Germain-l'Auxerrois
PLACE DU LOUVRE
PONT DES ARTS
PONT NEUF
PLACE DAUPHINE
ÎLE DE LA CITÉ
Conciergerie
Palais de Justice
Sainte-Chapelle
PLACE DU CHÂTELET
PONT AU CHANGE
PONT ST-MICHEL
Rue de Rivoli
Rue St-Honoré
Rue Étienne Marcel
Rue du Louvre
Quai du Louvre
Quai de la Mégisserie
Quai de l'Horloge
Quai des Orfèvres
Boul. du Palais
Boulevard de Sébastopol
Rue Rambuteau
Rue Berger
R. de Turbigo
R. Montmartre
R. Montorgueil
Rue Coquillière
Rue J.-J. Rousseau
R. du Jour
Rue du Bouloi
Rue Croix des Petits Champs
Rue des Petits Champs
Rue de Valois
Rue de Montpensier
Rue de Richelieu
Rue du Colonel Driant
Rue de l'Arbre Sec
R. de l'Amiral Coligny
Rue du Pont Neuf
Rue des Bourdonnais
Rue des Halles
R. de la Ferronnerie
R. des Lombards
R. de la Cossonnerie
Rue St-Denis
Rue Lescot
Rue du Cygne
R. des Prouvaires
R. de la Monnaie
Rue J. Lantier
Av. Victoria
R. St Germain l'Auxerrois
Rue Ste Opportune
R. des Lavandières
Rue B. Poirée
Q. de l'Horloge

overdo things warmth-wise. Comfortable rooms with a flowery decor (satellite TV, double-glazing and minibar) and the friendly owner proudly informs us that some of them have now been fitted with air-conditioning. There are a number of car-parks nearby.

☗ **Hôtel du Cygne** (map D2, **10**): 3 rue du Cygne 75001. ☎ 01-42-60-14-16. Fax: 01-42-21-37-02. Metro: Étienne-Marcel. RER: Châtelet-Les Halles. Double room 420F to 490F with shower or bath. At the heart of Les Halles, in a pedestrian street packed with people selling clothes, this hotel has character and has been recently renovated. You'll be welcomed by the charming Mme Remont. Comfortable lounge areas with old furniture to rest on after a day spent wandering around Paris, and nicely laid out rooms: satellite TV, safe, hairdryer and open beams on the ceiling in most of them. Choose No. 16 with its attractive sandy coloured decor.

☗ **Hôtel Agora** (map D2, **11**): 7 rue de la Cossonnerie 75001. ☎ 01-42-33-46-02. Fax: 01-42-33-80-99. Metro: Les Halles or Châtelet. Double room with shower or bath and toilet from 530F to 690F. This street has been here since the 12th century and owes its name to the *cossons*, or second-hand dealers, who settled here. A well-renovated modern hotel. There is a small, tastefully laid out lobby. Pleasant, basic rooms, some of them with old furniture, others with a balcony and a view of the Église St-Eustache. A pleasant place, rather quiet for such a lively quarter. Celebrities such as film director Francis Ford Coppola and actor Matt Dillon have stayed here.

1ST

WHERE TO EAT

☆ BUDGET

✕ **Café Véry** (map A2, **21**): jardin des Tuileries 75001. ☎ 01-47-03-94-84. Metro: Tuileries. Open daily noon to 11pm. Budget for around 80F; 49F for children. Perfect for a bite on the terrace (*croque au comté*, chicken with morels and hot peach gateau) after an exhausting visit to the Louvre. Unfortunately, the portions are rather small and the cooking can be rushed.

✕ **Higuma** (map B1, **22**): 32 *bis* rue Ste-Anne 75001. ☎ 01-47-03-38-59. Metro: Pyramides. Open daily 11.30am to 10pm. Closed at Christmas and 1 January. Menu served at lunchtime and in the evening at 63F. This is a little Japanese place, a sort of spruced up canteen, where employees from Japanese companies in the area descend *en masse* to refuel quickly but copiously. The menu includes bowls of varied soups or generous helpings of sautéed noodles (48F) and a few gourmet dishes such as fried ravioli (32F). If you can, sit at the counter and watch the Japanese chefs knead the noodles or make the vegetables waltz around enormous pans.

✕ **Foujita 1** (map B1, **24**): 41 rue St-Roch 75001. ☎ 01-42-61-42-93. Metro: Pyramides or Tuileries. Open at lunchtime until 2.15pm and in the evening until 10pm. Closed on Sunday. Menu at 70F at lunchtime. In the evening budget for 110F to 120F. One of the best sushi bars in Paris, with very reasonable prices. Very substantial menus at lunchtime: *sushi*, *sashimis* or *natto* (raw fish on a bed of rice). A really good deal and an excellent introduction to this cuisine, which is often expensive. Unfortunately, the dining room is pretty small and it's often full, so try to get there early. In the evening you get less value for money on the menus.

✕ **Foujita 2** (map B1, **25**): 7 rue du 29 juillet 75001. ☎ 01-49-26-07-70. Same opening times as its neighbour, but daily. Located in the street running parallel, this restaurant is a lot bigger but not as pleasant as Foujita 1. Same menus.

✕ **Le Palet** (map C1, **26**): 8 rue de Beaujolais 75001. ☎ 01-42-60-99-59. Metro: Palais-Royal. Closed Saturday afternoon and Sunday, at lunchtime on public holidays, and also at Christmas and New Year. At lunchtime, there's a menu at 70F; in the evening there are menus at 80F or 100F. In this quarter, which is great for just strolling around, the restaurants are all fairly expensive. In fact, the choice is really between the sandwich bars and the Japanese restaurants specializing in bowls of noodles. This small, modest, country-style establishment, with its dining rooms in 18th-century cellars, will appeal to many.

✕ **Osaka** (map B2, **27**): 163 rue St-Honoré 75001. ☎ 01-42-60-64-29. Metro: Palais-Royal. Open from noon to 9pm. Closes at 4pm on Tuesday. Menus at 58F at lunchtime and 62F in the evening. This is a Japanese institution in Paris. A good snack bar specializing in noodle soups, livened up with vegetables, meats, bamboo shoots and many other tempting things. The dish with noodles and pork is great (42F), and the Japanese ravioli is sublime (40F). Popular with coach-loads of Japanese, who add atmosphere when they come pouring in. *The sushi bar* next door with the same name restricts itself to *tempura* and Japanese fondues. Prices are competitive: menu at 80F at lunchtime.

✕ **Chicago Meatpackers** (map C2, **29**): 8 rue Coquillière 75001. ☎ 01-40-28-02-33. Metro: Les Halles or Louvre. Open daily 11.30am to 1am. Closed 24 December in the evening. No reservations at the weekend. At lunchtime, there are menus at 59F and 74F; in the evening there's a set menu at 125F. One of the sunniest terraces (in the summer anyway!) in front of Les Halles, with all the refinements of the 'American way of life': cold beers, western decor and plastic bibs for the children. In fact, this is a great place for taking the kids because they can wander freely around the dining room. Everyone loves the spare-ribs, every type of burger imaginable, nachos and the enormous onion pie. American cuisine, which means it's simple fare but well done – and service comes with a smile. Wednesday, Saturday and Sunday at 1pm and 2pm is kids' hour. For 59F they have their own special menu and a show.

✕ **Le Béarn** (map D2, **33**): 2 place Ste-Opportune 75001. ☎ 01-42-36-93-35. Metro: Châtelet. Open lunchtime and evening, last orders at 8pm in winter and 9pm in summer. Closed Sunday and from 10 to 17 August. À la carte from 85F, drinks not included. A tiny, local bistro which regulars rush to at lunchtime for a hot meal on the hoof. Good cuisine and service with a smile around the bar, which is made of real zinc. Dishes include *salé aux lentilles* (streaky salted pork with lentils), cod fillet with sorrel and stuffed tomatoes. Produce is always fresh. At lunchtime try the dish of the day from 50F to 55F. A bit more expensive in the evening.

✕ **Foyer Concorde** (map A1, **28**): 263 *bis* rue St-Honoré 75001 (entrance in the place Maurice-Barrès, to the left of the church). ☎ 01-42-60-43-33. Metro: Concorde or Tuileries. Open Tuesday to Saturday noon to 3pm and in the evening 7 to 10pm. Open all day Sunday. Closed Monday. Menus at 55F, 76F and 85F. Budget for 220F à la carte, including drinks. This Polish association restaurant is housed in a 13th-century former crypt, which is part of the church of Notre-Dame-de-l'Assomption (this is the Poles' church in Paris). Don't expect any culinary miracles, but a good opportunity to discover traditional Polish cuisine without breaking the bank. On the menu are Polish herring, red beetroot soup and goulash. If you're really broke, there's a great value menu of the day, served lunchtime and evening at 28F (and no, that's not a printing error!). It's very simple fare, accompanied by a glass of wine. Polish beers and French wines, but no vodka. Waiter service is provided by the members of the association, who are volunteers and give a warm welcome.

✕ **La Mousson** (map C1, **31**): 9 rue Thérèse 75001. ☎ 01-42-60-59-46. Metro: Pyramides or Palais-Royal. Open until 10pm. Closed Sunday and for two weeks in August. Menu 67F at lunchtime, 92F in the evening. À la carte, budget for 100F to 120F. Lucile, whose smile and charming chatter used to enchant many stars when she worked at the Grand Chinois, set up this restaurant a while ago. Of Chinese-Cambodian origin, her specialities include *luk-lak* (beef sautéed in garlic), *amok* (steamed fish with Cambodian sauce), *sach tcha kapit* (minced pork with lemongrass), grilled pork spare-ribs and *bò bún* (pieces of beef with chinese pasta). There is a dish of the day from 43F to 49F (chicken or beef curry, *calamari* with basil or beef satay), with dessert, available from Monday to Saturday.

✕ **Universal Resto** (map B2, **23**): galerie du Carrousel du Louvre 75001 (entrance through the pyramid or at 99 rue de Rivoli). ☎ 01-47-03-96-58. Metro: Palais-Royal or Louvre. Open daily 8am to 11.30pm. Closed between Christmas and 1 January. Menus from 45F to 80F. Budget for a maximum of 100F. An immense space entirely given over to an eclectic menu. You'll find Lebanese, Mexican, Chinese and Italian cuisine, but also roast chicken and plates of cheese. Inexpensive and really practical (especially if you've got children with you).

✕ **Au Petit Bar** (map B1, **40**): 7 rue du Mont-Thabor 75001. ☎ 01-42-60-62-09. Metro: Tuileries. Closed Sunday, public holidays and in August. Open lunchtime and evening until 10.30pm. Dishes around 45F; salads around 20F. Hidden behind the luxurious Hôtel Meurice, this is a tiny local bistro of the type you don't find any more. The setting is simple, but great. A family affair, with dad at the till, mum in the kitchen and the son is the waiter. People come here for the unpretentious authentic French cuisine, with no frills and no hefty prices. Dish of the day is usually something like an escalope in breadcrumbs with dandelion salad from the garden (in season). Desserts are traditional, but home-made (excellent apple tart). Come early because the dining room soon fills up.

☆☆ MODERATE

✕ **Ca d'Oro** (map C2, **34**): 54 rue de l'Arbre-Sec 75001. ☎ 01-40-20-97-79. Metro: Louvre. Open until 11pm. Closed on Sunday and from 7 to 22 August. Menu at 85F at lunchtime, otherwise budget for 160F à la carte. A discreet and welcoming place. You go through a tiny room and a narrow corridor and out into a dining room with Venetian decor (the chef hails from Venice). Treat yourself to a *bruschetta* (grilled bread rubbed with garlic, covered in olive oil, basil and tomato) or maybe a few peppers grilled with basil, before going for pasta or maybe risotto for two (mushroom or seafood). The full lunch menu (wine extra) is really good.

✕ **Lescure** (map A1, **35**): 7 rue de Mondovi 75001. ☎ 01-42-60-18-91. Metro: Concorde. Open lunchtime and evening. Closed Saturday and Sunday, as well as for three weeks in August and two weeks at

Christmas. Menu at 100F lunchtime and evening. À la carte, budget for around 140F. A warm welcome for regulars, a little less for others, but this is a good location, considering the quarter. In fact, it's unusual to find a *poule au pot farcie Henri IV* at less than 50F in the financial district. The set menu at 100F offers some good starters (delicious mackerel), generous main courses (haddock *à l'anglaise*), cheese or dessert, and wine (37cl). At lunchtime, even the suits and ties come here, which is saying something! The dining room is rather mock provincial, but that doesn't really matter. In the evening the large *table d'hôte* at the back fills up, which makes things a bit more relaxed, and in summer people fight over who gets the terrace!

✕ **La Fresque** (map D2, **37**): 100 rue Rambuteau 75001. ☎ 01-42-33-17-56. Metro: Étienne-Marcel or Les Halles. Open lunchtime and evening (service until midnight). Closed Sunday lunchtime and for one week in August. Set menu at 68F at lunchtime; à la carte around 120F. A nice little restaurant with a small terrace, in the premises of a former snail vendor (yes, really, a former *escargot* shop). Lovely decor: white earthenware antique tiles, colourful frescoes and long wooden tables. Relaxed ambiance, of the elbow-in-your-neighbour's-dish type, but at the same time hip, fun and cosmopolitan. The attentive service always comes with a smile. Each lunchtime there's a quick but consistent set menu: starter, main course, a carafe of wine and a cup of coffee. In the evening there's no set menu. There are great starters every day, three or four traditional dishes spiced up by a touch of originality, and, unusually, there is always a vegetarian dish.

☆ ☆ ☆ CHIC

✕ **Toupary** (map C3, **44**): on the fifth floor of the shop 2 de La Samaritaine, 2 quai du Louvre 75001. ☎ 01-40-41-29-29. Metro: Pont-Neuf. Open 11.45am to 3pm and 7.30pm to 11.30pm. Tea-room open from 3.30 to 6pm. Closed Sunday. At lunchtime there's a set meal at 75F and menus at 99F and 149F. In the evening there's an à la carte menu at 199F. Children's menu 45F, lunchtime only. The terrace is open to those who love a view of the Parisian rooftops (in summer only, 9.30am to 7pm), but the true star here is the panoramic restaurant, which appeals to those who like watching the Seine and its boats. The decor is anti-minimalist and neo-modern, with sophisticated lighting and an explosion of colour, designed by Hilton McConnico, the darling of American design made famous by the film *Diva* (1981) by Jean-Jacques Beneix. Nothing outstanding on the menu, except for the prices, but the view really is amazing. If you're broke come for a cup of tea or make do with the first set meal at noon, which is actually the best.

✕ **Le Comptoir Paris-Marrakech** (map C2, **45**): 37 rue Berger 75001. ☎ 01-40-26-26-66. Metro: Les Halles. Open 11am to 2am (3am at weekends). Set lunchtime menu at 89F. On Sundays and public holidays, brunch at 110F. In the evenings budget for between 150F and 200F, drinks excluded. Tapas from 30F. With its eclectic Franco-Morrocan cuisine, musical ambiance, candlelight and *joie de vivre* both at night and during the day, this famous Les Halles tapas bistro is worth a visit. The menu gives you a chance to sample dishes such as *tajine de lotte*, tandoori chicken and Mediterranean prawns infused with Sechuan pepper, not forgetting the dried fruit tart or yogurt with rose syrup.

Clientele of young trendsetters after a sexy cocktail or something a bit different from the norm.

✕ **L'Ardoise** (map A1, **32**): 28 rue du Mont-Thabor 75001. ☎ 01-42-96-28-18. Metro: Tuileries. Open daily lunchtime and evening until 11pm. Closed Monday, one week in May and in January, and three weeks in August. Menu is à la carte at 170F. Pierre Jay, the young chef, has concocted a single menu (served each lunchtime and evening) nicely put together and bursting with ideas. Dishes include marinated fresh anchovies served in a terrine, a crispy spiced pear-sausage compote, *mitonnée de joue de porc,* pâté and mashed sweet potatoes, Challans duckling with figs (for two). There are two starters, three main courses and a dessert on the blackboard. Nice presentation, produce cooked intelligently with a hint of inventiveness and interesting wines, with prices kept on a tight rein. The clientele is rather strait-laced, and it has a kind of hushed atmosphere.

✕ **Davé** (map B1, **30**): 39 rue St-Roch 75001. ☎ 01-42-61-49-48. Metro: Pyramides. Closed Saturday lunchtime and on Sunday. No set menu; à la carte at around 220F. You don't really need to know the honourable Davé, the lucky owner of this humble Chinese restaurant, to recognize him in all the framed photographs hanging all over the dining room. Pictured with Catherine Deneuve, again with David Bowie, and then with Serge Gainsbourg . . . he'll come up and ask 'What would you like?' after seeing you settled in his monochrome world of red velvet walls, red carpet and red hangings. People from the fashion and showbiz worlds come here to eat prawns in breadcrumbs, steamed rolls, prawn crackers and coconut balls. The bill tends to be a little high for such a modest meal, but at least you can say that you've dined in the same place as all those stars!

✕ **Macéo** (map C1, **36**): 15 rue des Petits-Champs 75001. ☎ 01-42-97-53-85. Metro: Pyramides. Open lunchtime and evening until 11pm. Closed on Sunday. Lunch menu at 195F, dinner at 220F. Vegetarian menu 180F at lunchtime, 220F in the evening. This superb restaurant, which dates back to 1880, for a long time enjoyed the favours of a smart clientele keen on the setting. Taken over by Mark Williamson, the owner of the nearby Willi's, and re-christened Macéo (after Macéo Parker, a member of James Brown's first group, the Famous Flames), the place has been touched up with a peculiarly British style. Remodeled gradually, the decor has recovered its former grace, enhancing a tempting menu which plays its flavours off against one another, e.g. lamb's sweetbread salad with marinated fennel, roast back of brill with lemon-flavoured spices, and *pain perdu crème au jasmin sauce anglaise*. The wine list is in the image of the owner: impeccable. There's an amazing vegetarian menu which has been a big hit. When you come in, there's a bar area which means you can calmly wait for your table while enjoying a drink.

✕ **L'Ostréa** (map C2, **46**): 4 rue Sauval 75001. ☎ 01-40-26-08-07. Metro: Louvre or Châtelet. Open lunchtime and evening until 11.30pm. Closed Saturday lunchtime and Sunday, and also during the first three weeks of August. No set menu; budget for 200F excluding drinks. Steadily run by its manager, Jean-Pierre Devaux, the actual bar of this rather ordinary looking sailor's bar has not changed since it opened, which was quite a few years ago now. The fish is always fresh and the prices are quite high, especially the special oysters No. 2, the *fines de claires*

No.3 and the Belon oysters. For a reasonable bill, go for the herrings (35F), followed by lots of *moules marinières* (65F), washed down by two glasses of Pouilly Fuissé at around 25F each and, to finish, an excellent coffee. The fish soup, the haddock *à l'anglaise*, the sole *meunière* and the plate of seafood for two (350F) have also been tried and tested.

At No. 14 in the same street, the lady of the house runs **Le Paquebot** (☎ 01-42-21-19-00, closed Saturday lunchtime and Sunday), which has a menu at 170F.

✗ **Le Café Marly** (map B2, **42**): 93 rue de Rivoli 75001. ☎ 01-49-26-06-60. Metro: Palais-Royal or Louvre. Open daily 8 to 2am. Located in the same square as the Louvre pyramid. Budget for around 250F. Fairly expensive, but with sumptuous decor (gilding and contemporary furniture) and a typically Parisian crowd (journalists, artists, curators from the Louvre and trendy young things). Good dishes: steak tartare, *pavé de cabillaud purée* and Caesar salad. Very crowded.

✗ **La Robe and le Palais** (map D3, **49**): 13 rue des Lavandières-St-Opportune 75001. ☎ 01-45-08-07-41. Metro: Châtelet. Closed on Sunday. Menus at lunchtime at 79F and 99F. In the evening budget for at least 200F. A restaurant whose name is not without a touch of humour for the lovers of fine wine who settle down here for a drink, just a few steps away from the Palais de Justice (Law Courts). After having earned their stripes at the Carré des Feuillants and at L'Ébauchoir, the two hosts, Patrick Gras in the kitchen and Olivier Schvitz at front of house, have created this little bistro where homage is paid to the vine, a passion they share. They've put everything they learned in their former employment into practice here. The set lunch menu (dish and glass of wine) is excellent value. Every day there is a star dish. À la carte, the prices start to get a bit steep.

✗ **Nodaïwa** (map B2, **38**): 272 rue St-Honoré 75001. ☎ 01-42-86-03-42. Metro: Tuileries or Palais-Royal. Open lunchtime and evening until 10pm. Closed Sunday and in August. Menus from 85F to 350F. À la carte, budget from 130F to 150F excluding drinks. This tiny restaurant has only one thing on its mind: eels. It is the Parisian branch of a famous Tokyo restaurant which, since the 18th century, has been serving nothing else. Very oily, yet delicate and tasty, appreciated by the Romans and also widely eaten in both Charente and in the Basque Country, eels are treated like royalty by the Japanese chefs here – they are served grilled with a sauce on a bed of rice with soup and salad, or as *sushi* or *sashimi*.

RESTAURANTS OPEN THROUGHOUT THE NIGHT

✗ **Au Pied de Cochon** (map D2, **56**): 6 rue Coquillière 75001. ☎ 01-40-13-77-00. Website: www.blanc.com. Metro: Louvre or Les Halles. Open 24 hours, all year round. Menu at 146F until 7pm; à la carte at around 250F. This world-famous, venerable institution is still one of the cornerstones of Les Halles. People come from far and wide to taste the famous pigs' trotters, the *andouillette tirée à la ficelle*, the *fort des Halles* (sirloin steak served with a shallot sauce) or perhaps a 'Temptation of St Anthony', which brings together grilled pork snout, ears, trotters and tail (not for the fainthearted!). The simple seafood dish at 198F or the 'Royal' at 488F (for two) are also popular. There's a terrace available when the weather is good. It's best to make a reservation.

✕ **À la Tour de Montlhéry, Chez Denise** (map D2, **57**): 5 rue des Prouvaires 75001. ☎ 01-42-36-21-82. Metro: Louvre, Châtelet or Les Halles. Open 24 hours. Closed on Saturday, Sunday and from mid-July to mid-August. Budget for at least 250F, including wine. One of the oldest night-time restaurants in Paris, packed out round the clock, this is a former Les Halles bistro which has managed to hold on to something of the atmosphere of the old days. The waiters tend to bully the regulars a bit and the welcome can sometimes be a little oafish, but that's part of the character of the place. On the walls there are paintings, drawings by Moretti and posters, while the rest of the decor includes imitation leather seats, hams hung from the ceiling and ceiling fans. Very lively. Generous and truly French cuisine: *andouillette*, tripe, *gigot-flageolets*, *bœuf gros sel* and brain, all washed down with a bottle of Brouilly. No set menus. Most of the dishes cost between 90 and 130F, so it's a bit of a bargain find. Main courses around 50F.

✕ **La Poule au Pot** (map C2, **58**): 9 rue Vauvilliers 75001. ☎ 01-42-36-32-96. Metro: Louvre or Les Halles. Open from 7pm to 6am. Closed Monday. Menu at 160F; à la carte budget for around 220F. If you're feeling peckish after 2am, this is the perfect place in the Les Halles area. There's a long dining room decorated with posters, copperware and back lighting, which manages to give a certain intimacy with a pleasant brasserie atmosphere. The service is good, which doesn't always go without saying in this quarter, and the menu brings together tried and trusted dishes such as *pot-au-feu* and marrow-bone *entrecôte*, not forgetting the famous *poule au pot* which gives its name to the restaurant.

WINE BARS

✕ 🍷 **Juvéniles** (map C1, **39**): 47 rue de Richelieu 75001. ☎ 01-42-97-46-49. Metro: Palais-Royal. Open until 11.30pm. Closed Sunday. Menu at 128F; à la carte at around 150F. A very Parisian wine bar, run by a joyously Rabelaisian Scot, with a very British sense of humour. The clientele is made up of people in the know who come for a good bottle or a few glasses while munching on some excellent *tapas* – grilled squid, chicken wings grilled with spices and Pierre Oteiza salami. Main courses include lamb's sweetbread curry, tuna steak grilled in a vinaigrette of fresh herbs and, to finish, an admirable Stilton straight from England. Good selection of wines and sherry by the glass, as well as spirits with, of course, Scottish malts chosen with love. Reservations are a must because space is at a premium.

✕ 🍷 **Willi's Wine Bar** (map C1, **43**): 13 rue des Petits-Champs 75001. ☎ 01-42-61-05-09. Metro: Bourse or Palais-Royal. Open 11am to 11.30pm for the kitchen, until midnight for the bar. Closed Sunday. Menus at 148F at lunchtime and 185F in the evening. The quintessential smart wine bar. Exquisite surroundings, with warm wood tones. Large round tables for chatting to friends, perfect lighting and nice posters on the walls. Willi's appeals to all the British businessmen in the capital who love good wine, as well as yuppies from the Stock Exchange. A number of sophisticated dishes and original salads accompany the fantastic Côtes-du-Rhône, of which the owner is one of the finest connoisseurs, but there are also Spanish, Californian or Italian wines. A large choice of wines by the glass. Excellent choice of cheeses.

✂ 🍷 **Le Rubis** (map B1, **50**): 10 rue du Marché-St-Honoré 75001. ☎ 01-42-61-03-34. Metro: Pyramides. Open until 10pm (4pm on Saturday). Closed Sunday and public holidays, as well as for two weeks in August and two weeks at Christmas. Dish of the day at around 50F to 60F. This is real Parisian life, complete with Gallic outbursts, sandwiches at the bar and *vin rouge* 'straight from the vineyard'. An old-established and excellent wine bar, run by really welcoming people. Dining room upstairs. In summer, it's so packed that you may want to sit and have a drink outside.

✂ 🍷 **À la Cloche des Halles** (map C2, **53**): 28 rue Coquillière 75001. ☎ 01-42-36-93-89. Metro: Louvre or Les Halles. Only serves until around 9pm. Closed Saturday evening and Sunday, as well as for two weeks in August. Budget for around 60F for one course and a glass of wine. It would be easy to pass by this wine bar without ever noticing it! The bell (*cloche*) of the restaurant name, which once announced the beginning and end of the market day, hangs over the entrance. The tradition was that as it tolled, you could go and help yourself to any leftovers (this is where the French word *clochard*, meaning 'tramp', comes from). The bar is run by Annie and Serge Lesage and has received an award for agricultural merit for the quality of its produce. The landlord himself bottles all the non-vintage wines and the food which accompanies them is always amazingly fresh – solid dishes of *charcuterie*, ham on the bone and farmhouse cheese, served in generous portions. At lunchtime, the local suits are three deep at the bar. Not particularly eye-catching, but a great place to meet for something to eat without breaking the bank.

✂ 🍷 **Le Relais Chablisien** (map D3, **54**): 4 rue Bertin-Poirée 75001. ☎ 01-45-08-53-73. Metro: Châtelet or Pont-Neuf. Open lunchtime and evening until 9.30pm. Closed Saturday and Sunday, as well as for three weeks in August. 175F menu including wine; à la carte at around 220F, excluding drinks. A friendly *bon-viveur*, Christian Faure celebrates Chablis – his native part of France – in his restaurant wine bar. The menu varies with the seasons and the wine list includes Irancy, Chablis premier cru, Sauvignon, Chardonnay and Pinot Noir from St-Bris. Regulars at the Théâtre de la Ville come here for a sandwich and a glass of wine before going to see one of their favourite plays. The decor is that of a rustic inn (people sit down rather than prop up the bar) with a gentrified welcome. *Charcuterie* costs 55F, the dish of the day is around 90F and wine by the glass is between 16 and 22F.

✂ 🍷 **Taverne Henri IV** (map C3, **55**): 13 place du Pont-Neuf 75001. ☎ 01-43-54-27-90. Metro: Pont-Neuf. Open noon to 9pm (4pm on Saturday). Closed Sunday and during August. Average price for a meal à la carte is 125F. In this wine bar, set in a magnificent Louis XIII house, you won't really find much privacy, but there's a real 'Old-France style' landlord, and the kind of people you probably won't mix with every day on your travels (lawyers and policemen from the quai des Orfèvres). The wines served at the bar (Loire, Bordeaux, Alsace and Burgundy) are excellent. The landlord recommends that you give him a ring before you come, so that he can have the bottle you want waiting for you and ready to drink. Good *charcuterie*. Half a dozen snails *en croquille* (in pastry), *tripoux de l'Aveyron*, excellent *tartines* and wine by the glass from 20F to 24F.

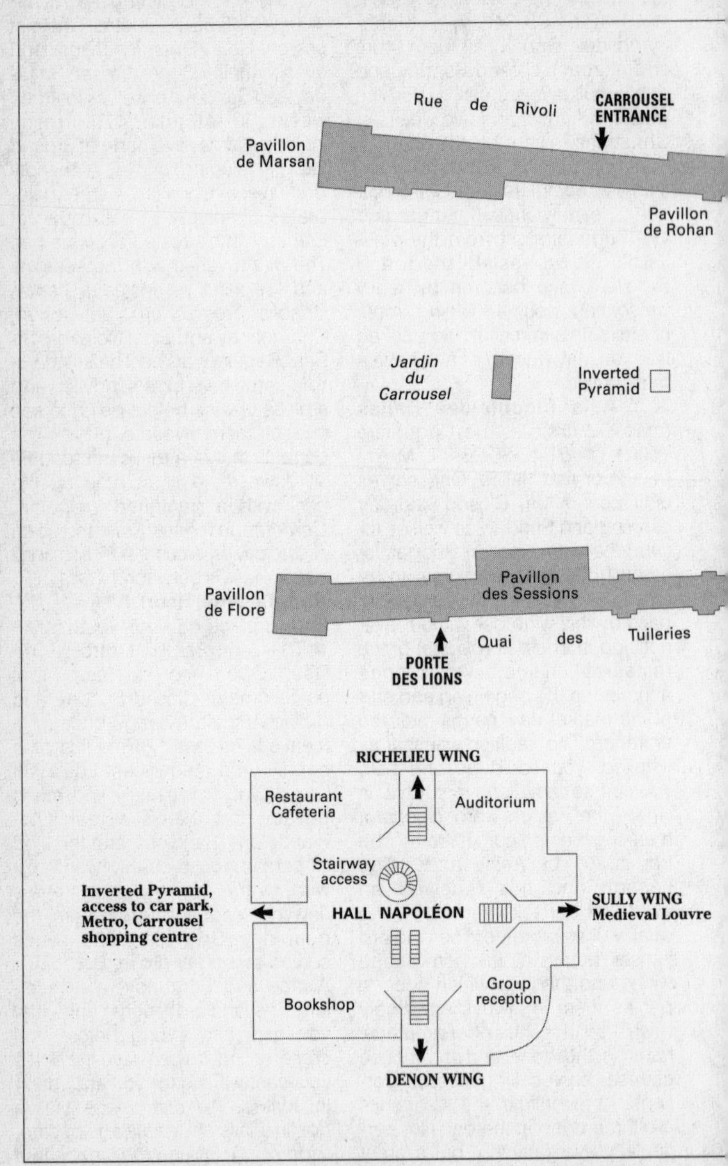

Rue de Rivoli
CARROUSEL ENTRANCE
Pavillon de Marsan
Pavillon de Rohan
Jardin du Carrousel
Inverted Pyramid
Pavillon de Flore
Pavillon des Sessions
Quai des Tuileries
PORTE DES LIONS
RICHELIEU WING
Restaurant Cafeteria
Auditorium
Stairway access
Inverted Pyramid, access to car park, Metro, Carrousel shopping centre
HALL NAPOLÉON
SULLY WING Medieval Louvre
Group reception
Bookshop
DENON WING

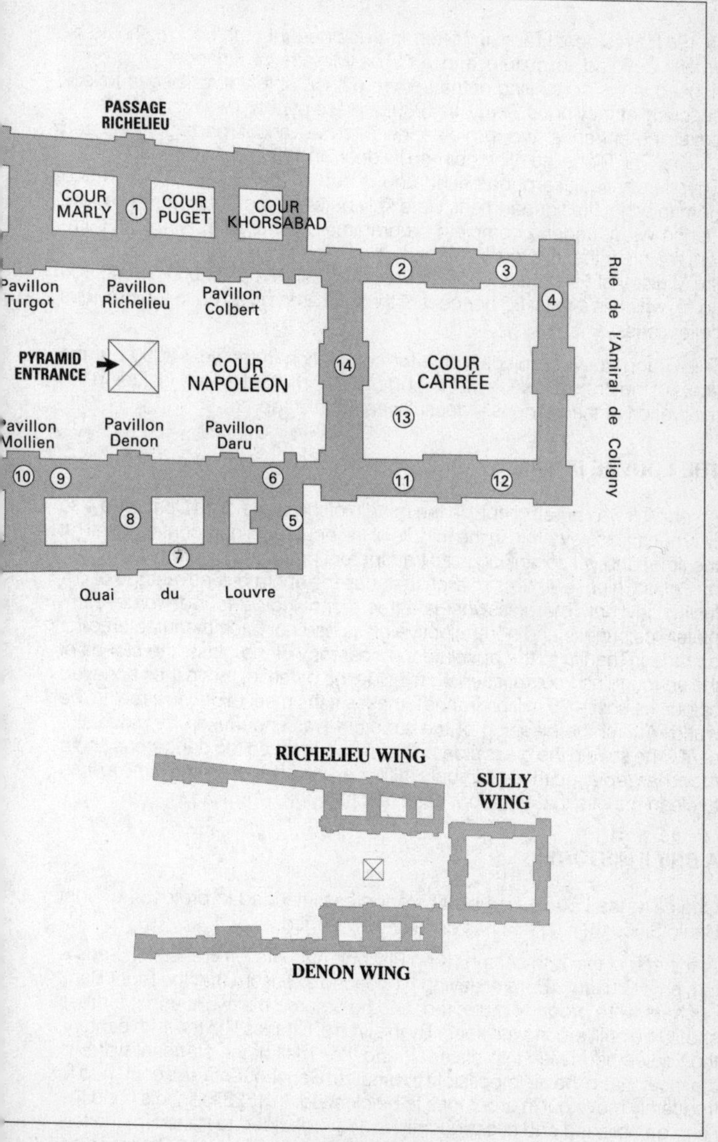

THE LOUVRE MUSEUM

THE LOUVRE MUSEUM

In 1981, President François Mitterrand decided that the Louvre should be wholly devoted to culture and art. The Ministry of Finance, which was housed in the north wing of the Louvre palace at that time, began to look seriously at moving to Bercy. In 1989, a glass pyramid was constructed to cover the entrance and to give access to the various parts of the Grand Louvre. The Richelieu Wing opened its doors in 1993, whilst the whole of the Egyptian antiquities department, and a part of the Greek, Etruscan and Roman antiquities department, were split between the Cour Carrée and the Denon Wing, under a complete programme of renovation. Museum curators maintain that the rooms formerly occupied by the top civil servants of the Ministry of Finance have freed up a surface area of 22,000m^2 (240,000 sq ft), which is almost 82 per cent of the total area given up to the previous collections.

The Grand Louvre project is due for completion in the year 2000 but the scale of the project is such that the bill of 7,000 million francs – including the renovation of the gardens – doesn't seem too steep.

THE LOUVRE PYRAMID

An obelisk was erected right in the middle of the place de la Concorde – so why not a glass pyramid in the middle of the Louvre? Highly controversial (at the time) and yet so striking in its transparent purity, the pyramid, designed by Pei, a Chinese-American architect, has the enormous advantage of diffusing daylight. The glasswork is a true technological *tour de force:* completely colourless and non-reflective glass had not been manufactured for decades. Thanks to the absolute transparency of the glass, the stones of the surrounding Louvre, seen from inside the pyramid, retain their honeyed colour. Its cost – 75 million francs – makes it the most expensive roof in the world. At first the cleaning of the structure was undertaken by mountaineers, who scaled the glass sides. This method proved too dangerous and a robot has replaced these climbers, although they do return from time to time to clean the bits that the robot can't reach!

1ST

A BRIEF HISTORY

Originally, the Louvre was built as a fortress intended to protect the Right Bank. Since then its role has constantly changed.

At the end of the 12th century, King Philippe Auguste left France for Jerusalem on a Crusade. Before leaving he needed to ensure that the Right Bank quarters were properly protected, and he ordered that walls and a fortress should be built around the keep. By the time of Charles V in the 14th century, the Louvre had fallen into disrepair and the smell of the stagnant water in the moat made the air impossible to breathe. Consequently the court had to frequently move out in order for it to be cleaned. In 1528 François I had the keep demolished and subsequently, in 1546, decided to transform the fortress into a luxury residence. The work took years to complete. Catherine de Médicis instigated the construction of a huge palace in the Tuileries, which later Henri IV decided to join with the Louvre to make a gigantic royal palace. This was known as the 'Grand Design'. Subsequent kings embellished and enlarged the Louvre, but its golden age came to an end when Louis XIV moved his court to Versailles.

The Louvre was never intended to be a museum and the collections of antiques and paintings were only available to a privileged few. The idea that the palace could open to the public, who could view the royal collections, was first conceived in 1747, but it was under the Revolution that the plans were finally realised. Louis XVI was assigned the Tuileries as his place of residence in 1793, on the initiative of the constituent Assembly wishing to ensure his safety, and this led to the creation of a commission to organize the 'Central Museum of Arts', which opened the same year. The museum was considerably enriched by the spoils of the Napoleonic wars and was renamed the 'Musée Napoléon', but in 1815 the museum was forced to return many of these works. The museum continued to be altered and collections were augmented and improved. Napoleon III commissioned the architect Visconti to complete the palace and the section which separated the two palaces was torn down, the façades were redecorated, the North wing was closed off and a new courtyard was constructed. The new Louvre, inaugurated in 1857, finally completed the 'Grand Design'. In 1869 more improvements were made to the Southwest wing, but these transformations did not last for long as the Tuileries palace was destroyed by fire in 1871.

The fire put paid to the use of the Louvre as a palace, and henceforth it became solely a museum. The collections continued to grow and by the 1970s it was no longer able to cope with the number of exhibits and the number of visitors. Most of the post 1848 pieces were moved to the Musée d'Orsay, which was created on the opposite bank of the Seine, and restoration work began on the Louvre itself.

PRACTICAL INFORMATION

Access

Metro: Palais-Royal-Musée-du-Louvre. From the metro, there is direct access to the Carrousel-du-Louvre shopping arcade. Main entrance: the pyramid (cour Napoléon). Bus Nos. 21, 24, 27, 39, 48, 68, 69, 72, 81 and 95. Underground car-park: Carrousel-Louvre, access by the avenue du Général-Lemonnier, open from 7am to 11pm. Pedestrian access: two stairways, located either side of the Arc du Carrousel.

TIP For groups and those holding free access booking, enter through the shopping arcade (99 rue de Rivoli; Metro: Palais-Royal), which is a lot less crowded. A new entrance, located at the Porte des Lions (Denon Wing), has been open since May 1999.

Information

- *Recorded information:* ☎ 01-40-20-51-51
- *Switchboard:* ☎ 01-40-20-53-17
- *Individual:* visits/conferences for individuals: ☎ 01-40-20-52-09
- *Groups:* all groups must book in advance. Information: ☎ 01-40-25-57-60 for independent groups or ☎ 01-40-20-51-77 for guided tours.
- *Auditorium information:* ☎ 01-40-20-52-99
- *Website:* www.louvre.fr
- *E-mail:* info@louvre.fr

Opening hours

Open 9am to 6pm Thursday to Sunday, 9am to 9.45pm on Monday (short tour) and Wednesday (the whole thing). Ticket offices shut 45 minutes before closing time (the rooms begin to be cleared 30 minutes before closing). Closed on Tuesday and some public holidays (phone the information line for more details). Temporary exhibitions located in the Napoleon Hall, along with the bookshop and the restaurants under the pyramid and the Medieval Louvre and History of the Louvre are open from 9am to 9.45pm.

TIP For those of you who don't like crowds, the Louvre is much quieter (and cheaper) on Monday and Wednesday between 5pm and 9.45pm – useful to know when you've seen the crush some mornings! The 'First Visit to the Louvre' tour offers just the absolute must-see exhibits, such as the *Mona Lisa,* Vermeer's *La Dentellière* and *Le Scribe.* On Monday evening there's a short tour, when only the main halls are open, allowing you to visit the major works in an atmosphere which is ideal for quiet contemplation. Ask for the free mini-guide 'Monday Evening Itinerary'. You can bring a friend for free on Monday evening if you have the *Louvre Jeunes* card (see below).

Prices

Free for under 18s, people with disabilities and art students, otherwise it's a fixed price for everyone: 45F until 3pm, 26F after 3pm and all day Sunday. **Note that the Louvre is free to all on the first Sunday of every month.** Young Louvre 'addicts' can purchase the *Louvre Jeunes* card which is valid for a year, for people under 26. For 100F, you can visit the *Mona Lisa* every day if you wish, and the temporary exhibitions as often as you like. If you're planning a lot of visits, the *Louvre Jeunes* card soon pays for itself. The *Carte de la Société des Amis du Louvre* (300F) allows you to visit whenever you want, without queuing, to see both the permanent and temporary exhibitions.

Temporary exhibitions in the Napoleon Hall cost 30F. A double ticket covering both permanent collections and temporary exhibitions costs 60F before 3pm, 40F after 3pm and Sunday. The ticket remains valid for the whole day, even if you leave the museum and come back later.

TIP To avoid queues at the Louvre, you can purchase tickets in advance on ☎ 0803-808-803, via the Louvre website www.louvre.fr, or at Fnac shops and certain department stores. Tickets are valid any day up until 31 January in the year following the date of purchase

The CyberLouvre

The Louvre's multimedia area, located in the passage which connects the Napoleon Hall to the Galerie du Carrousel, is accessible free of charge during the museum's opening hours. It allows visitors to surf the Louvre's websites: one site presents the museum's collections and news in four languages (www.louvre.fr), whilst the other is an educational site which provides an introduction to art for children (www.louvre.edu).

CD-ROMs covering the Louvre's collections, and databases listing all the works of art, are accessible from 10 computers at the CyberLouvre.

Where to eat/Where to go for a drink

✕ Ɪ If you're feeling peckish, you can always drop into the café Mollien (Denon Wing, first floor), the café Richelieu (Richelieu Wing, first floor), the café Denon (Denon Wing, ground floor), the café Marly or the **Universal Restaurant** in the Carrousel shopping arcade (*see* Where to eat).

HOW TO GET AROUND

The museum is spread across three wings: Denon, Sully and Richelieu, all clearly signposted from the pyramid entrance.

There is a system of seven different colours over several floors, each of which correspond to one of the seven departments: *Oriental Antiquities* (including the *Arts of Islam*), *Egyptian Antiquities, Greek, Etruscan and Roman Antiquities, Sculptures, Objets d'Art, Paintings* and *Graphic Arts.* The *Medieval Louvre* and the rooms dedicated to the *History of the Louvre* are set apart in two different halls. The works of art are not just hung randomly: the ground floor is set aside for heavier works and those which need less lighting, and the second floor is devoted to paintings which require natural light (zenithal lighting).

Ask for the small information map (available in seven languages) which tells you how to use the colour-coded and numbered signposting system. A guide for visitors with disabilities is available in English and French and there are also two tours specially designed for those with disabilities, including an audio-guide (10,000 works of art with a French commentary and 300 with a commentary in other languages).

Aside from its interior treasures, the Louvre is fortunate enough to be one of the few museums in the world which has hundreds of windows overlooking three exceptional landmarks: the Seine, the pyramid and the rue de Rivoli.

PUBLIC INFORMATION

A database available on 14 screens and updated daily, is accessible in the Napoleon Hall, and shows, almost in 'real time', all the things visitors can do in the museum at any given time. It provides information on which collections are accessible, the current exhibitions on display and their location, the programmes on show in the Louvre auditorium until the evening, and the workshops running that day.

The following tour is just a suggestion and it is worth noting that sometimes particular works of art are removed from display, or certain halls may be closed from time to time.

A 'QUICK' TOUR

The following itinerary (1–15) will take around 4 hours, and will allow you to visit the essential parts of the museum's seven departments mentioned above (drawings are on show in the permanent halls on the Paintings route). The numbering on the map will help you to find your way around.

A serious visit to the Louvre requires at least a couple of days. There are fuller details on the halls in the next section, but note that some works may have been transferred.

(1) From the Napoleon Hall, head for the Richelieu Wing, admiring the Cours Marly, Khorsabad and Puget. At the Cour Marly, take the Ministry staircase and go up to the first floor (Napoleon III's apartments), then backtrack and take the escalator to the second floor. Go into the *Médicis Gallery* to see the immense compositions which Rubens painted to the glory of Marie de Médicis to decorate his palace at Luxembourg. Before leaving, Hall 38 – Dutch paintings – containing *La Dentellière* by Vermeer, is worth a short detour.

(2) Return via the escalator and take the French paintings tour which continues in the Sully Wing (works from the 14th to 16th centuries). In Hall 16, before the rotonda, you can see Poussin's *Les Quatre Saisons*, and in Sully 4 you can admire *St Thomas* by Georges de La Tour, bought by the Louvre for 32 million francs, thanks to public donation. The apostle has become worth more than a rock star, and has to be seen to be believed, as Doubting Thomas himself would have said.

(3) Walk through Sully 4 and 5 until you reach the enormous *Batailles* by Le Brun, representing the story of Alexander the Great and inspired by Raphaël's fresco in the Vatican. These paintings belonged to Louis XIV who loved to be compared to the ancient hero, although he never really conquered anything other than Alsace!

(4) The French paintings tour continues in the 36 halls devoted to the 18th and 19th centuries. Here you'll find Watteau's *Le Pèlerinage à l'Île de Cythère* as well as *Gilles* (also known as the *Pierrot*), and *Le Bain Turc* by Ingres, among other masterpieces.

(5) The French paintings route (in the Cour Carrée up to Hall 73) ends here. To continue, turn round and go up the Henri II or Henri IV staircase.

(6) Enter the medieval part of the Louvre on the mezzanine floor, where you can admire the extraordinary *fossés de Philippe Auguste*, the *donjon* and *Hall St-Louis* (open daily until 9.45pm). Excavations here have brought to light remains of the old fortress. You can walk alongside the ramparts erected by Philippe Auguste in 1200 to reinforce the city's protection. Later, Charles V transformed the fortress into a royal residence. On the walls of the fortress, you can still see the various signs carved by the masons, such as a heart and a star. Later on, the imposing keep was used as a prison and then for protecting the royal treasury, which was the financial heart of the kingdom. From the keep, continue to St-Louis Hall. It is still not known what this room was used for or the exact date of its construction, but its architectural style dates it to the reign of St Louis (1226–1270).

Here, you'll find the helmet of Charles VI (1380–1422), who was mad (maybe the helmet had something to do with it!), and various objects (ceramics, glassware, pennants) found during the excavations in the Carrée.

(7) Return to the mezzanine of the Denon Wing, passing through the Napoleon Hall. Opposite the escalator, in Hall A, admire the funeral art of Roman Egypt. On the way out, on the right, there are four superb halls of Greek antiquities with curious cycladic idols; on the right is the Coptic art gallery and the re-creation of the church of Baouit. Retrace your steps to the Denon entrance.

(8) On the ground floor, walk through the collections of Etruscan and Roman Antiquities and stop on the landing in front of the *Victoire de Samothrace.* Dedicated to a naval victory in the second century BC, this is a good example of a ship's figurehead. Make a U-turn to come back to the Greek Antiquities Hall. At the end you'll see the *Venus de Milo* carved from fine Paros marble.

(9) Behind the *Venus*, go down the staircase, pass in front of the sphinx and enter the department of Egyptian Arts. In Hall 4, the mastaba of Akhéthétep has been restored. Don't forget to visit the Trail of the Sphinxes.

(10) The Egyptian tour continues, documenting daily life in Ancient Egypt. You can see the funeral trappings and the *Book of the Dead,* as well as macabre mummies of animals. At the back, take the northern staircase.

(11) On the first floor, follow the chronological tour of the Egyptian Pharaohs, including funeral furniture, bas-reliefs, *objets d'art,* jewels dating from 4000 to 30 BC, and earthenware from the second century BC in Hall 23.

(12) Leaving Hall 30, go straight ahead until you reach the landing opposite the one which houses the *Victoire*. You should now be at the entrance to the Red Halls. The first one, the Daru Hall, houses the *Sacre de Napoléon* by David and then, in the Mollien Hall, look out for *Le Radeau de la Méduse* by Géricault, a macabre illustration of a tragic event. In the same room Delacroix's monumental work *Mort de Sardanapale* is on display, depicting violence and voluptuous pleasure.

(13) Retracing your steps, in the Denon Hall, there's a door to the left which takes you to the Hall of States, where the unmissable *Les Noces de Cana* by Veronese is on display. An immense, breathtaking canvas, which has been lovingly restored. Behind the reinforced display case you'll find (at last!) da Vinci's **Mona Lisa** (Department of Paintings), a portrait of the wife of a Florentine nobleman, considered to be a masterpiece, even by the artist himself. Leonardo refused to give it to the husband who had commissioned it, and took it to Amboise with him when François I invited him to France. When Leonardo died, the King purchased the painting.

(14) On leaving this hall, enter the Grande Galerie where you can see the Italian sketches. From there, go down the Mollien staircase to see *Les Esclaves* by Michelangelo (Department of Sculptures). An artist of great genius, he was one of the great Italian-born masters of the High Renaissance

(15) Reach the exit by going down to the mezzanine floor and coming out under the pyramid.

AN IN-DEPTH VISIT

The short tour is designed to ensure that you see all of the Louvre's most interesting works. Although far more of the treasures in the museum are covered in the following section, we have not drawn up an exhaustive catalogue of all the works of art, as this would fill a book in itself!

The tour runs as follows: Greek, Etruscan and Roman Antiquities; Egyptian Antiquities; French Paintings; Paintings from the Northern Schools; Italian and International Paintings; Italian and Nordic Sculpture; French Sculpture; Objets d'Art; and Oriental Antiquities and Islamic Arts.

GREEK, ETRUSCAN AND ROMAN ANTIQUITIES

Mezzanine floor (Denon Wing *Halls 1 to 4*)

To go round in chronological order, which is probably the best way to visit the collections, enter via the Denon Wing on the mezzanine floor, Lower Daru Gallery. To gain access to the halls dealing with pre-classical Greece (3000 to 480 BC), enter the pyramid and use the Denon escalator. Halls 1a to 2 are situated in Napoleon III's former stables. Note the tiled floor, which is quite unique.

– **Cycladic idols (Hall 1a):** These marble sculptures from the Cyclades are presented in a very modern setting. Lots of nudes, with an amazingly stylized elegance, such as the *Head of a large female statuette* from Kéros, or the large kandela, a curious vase in the shape of a sea urchin.

– **Minoan and Mycenaean civilizations (Hall 1b):** ceramics and bronzes dating from the second century BC. Admire *L'Adorant de Psychro* and the collection of vases from Rhodes.

– **Geometric Age (Hall 1c):** small, minimalist sculptures and bronze and clay animals.

– **Oriental Age (Hall 1d):** decorative trends began in the seventh century BC, and the *Dame d'Auxerre*, found in Crete, is a good example. The white limestone figurine is surrounded by more imposing works, some of which show the progress of casting techniques.

– **Archaic Age (Hall 1e):** examples of the development of funerary and votive art in the fifth century BC. Admire the sculpture from Samos from all angles.

– **Epigraph Gallery (Hall 2):** on the left, the Greek Inscriptions Hall is parallel to the Pre-Classical Greece Hall. Twenty-four inscriptions in Greek are dissected and explained.

– **The Age of the Severe Style (Hall 3):** well named as here is the famous *Torse de Milet*, which illustrates the transition from the archaic period to the more realistic period of classicism. Follow the staircase at the end of the gallery.

Ground floor (Denon and Sully)

– **Olympia Hall (Hall 4):** here you will find three of the twelve sculptures representing the labours of Hercules from the temple of Zeus on Mount Olympus. They depict the fight with the Cretan Bull, the combat against Geryon and the massacre of the birds at Lake Stymphale. There is also an explanatory model.

– **The Rotunda of Mars (Hall 5):** note the superb ceiling (from the former apartments of Anne of Austria).

– **Hall of Diana (Hall 6):** this restored hall has become the site for temporary exhibitions situated around one of the department's famous works. From here, visit the former Greek Antiquities Halls.

– **Parthenon Hall (Hall 7):** here you can admire the *Panathénées*, part of the famous monument's frieze (440 BC), where young girls from noble families went to make offerings to Athena. The art of sculpture reaches its highest level here. The following halls **(Nos. 14, 15 and 16)** contain further original works (from the fourth and third centuries BC).

– **Hall 12:** the *Venus de Milo.* This famous figure needs no introduction. Found in 1820 on the island of Milos, it is a symbol of sculptural perfection.

– **Halls 9, 10 and 11:** opposite the Cour Carrée, these halls bring together copies of original works of art (especially from the Roman period).

– **Cariatides Hall (Hall 17):** this hall, richly decorated by Jean Goujon, was used for royal weddings and other regal celebrations. Several notable events have taken place here. Henri III had 120 pages assembled here and whipped for making fun of him in public. During a ball held in the same year, he caused a scandal by insulting his sister, Marguerite de Valois, in front of the whole Court, about her immoral behaviour. Following the king's death in 1610, people came here to pay their respects as his coffin lay in state, while 100 masses a day were said. In 1658, Molière made his debut in the Cariatides Hall in front of Louis XIV.

Here, too, there are copies of Roman works which have long since disappeared. These copies were originally meant to be decorative, which sometimes led the artists to neglect the back of them. Among the most significant works are the *Gaulois blessé, Artémis* (also known as 'Diane de Versailles'), *Les trois Grâces, Silène portant Dionysos enfant, Hermès attachant sa sandale* and *Hermaphrodite endormi.*

Return to Anne of Austria's apartments, after the Rotonda of Mars. **Halls 22 to 29** cover the Roman period, with sculpted sarcophagi. **Halls 18 to 20** are devoted to the Etruscan period: Volterra alabaster urns and clay sarcophagi, engraved bronze mirrors, remarkable little bronzes, and gold and silver work. In the middle lies the famous sarcophagus known as *Sarcophage des époux* ('The husband and wife').

– **Hall 21:** in the display cases there are fine clay vases, glasswork, gold jewellery, ewers and silver vases (including one in the shape of a horse).

– **Hall 30:** contains Roman mosaics, as well as frescoes from Pompeii, a lovely mosaic of Daphne (close to Antioch) and the superb *Triomphe de Neptune et Amphitrite.*

– **Cour du Sphinx (Hall 31):** the high point, with the mosaic of the *Saisons* (from a Roman villa in Antioch). Note the beautiful interior façade by Le Vau.

First floor (Sully Wing *Halls 32 to 44*)

The Greek Antiquities end here with the *Trésor de Boscoreale.* At the top of the great stairway stands the famous *Victoire de Samothrace,* a statue from the second century BC, discovered on the island of Samothrace. It is meant to symbolize a naval victory (showing the prow of a ship, note the body taut against the wind, the clothing soaked by the spray).

– **Hall des Bronzes (Hall 32):** contains decorated and engraved mirrors. Don't miss the delightful little group with Bacchus and Apollon de *Lillebonne*, a fine, bronze statue discovered in Seine-Maritime.

– **Hall Henri II-Orfèvrerie Romaine (Hall 33):** the *Trésor de Boscoreale*, a very important set of silverware and Roman furniture, occupies a large part of this hall. A prodigious discovery from a villa destroyed by the eruption of Vesuvius (in 79 AD). There are dozens of superb silver objects, richly decorated, forming a unique collection which rather curiously seems to have more to do with the Renaissance than with the Hellenic tradition. *Les Oiseaux*, a vast composition by Georges Braque, adorns the ceiling.

– **Hall of Antique Glassware:** kept in the former Grand Cabinet of the king, this collection of Greek and Roman glassware includes hand-blown glass, covering the whole of the Roman period. Glass blowing allowed the manufacture of objects in all kinds of shapes, including glasses with engraved decorations.

– **Former Charles X Museum (Halls 35 to 38):** a collection of figurines made from baked earthenware, stucco and wood, stretching over four halls. The majority of the collection comes from the former Charles X Museum. The figurines were generally found in tombs, but their religious importance evolved over time towards a more aesthetic function.

– **Galerie Campana (Halls 39 to 47):** Greek ceramics stretching over nine halls, including a themed hall and three study halls. This collection of Greek vases is one of the richest in the world, both in terms of quantity and quality. These vases are both works of art and historical documents, allowing us to get a better idea of daily life in classical Greece. The most commonly used themes for illustration are sport, social activities, the gods and myths.

EGYPTIAN ANTIQUITIES

Ground floor and first floor, Sully Wing

The department of Egyptian Antiquities 4,200 metres square (45,200 square feet) forms one of the largest Egyptian collections in the world, along with those in Cairo and Berlin. There are 30 halls in all. On the ground floor is a thematic tour and on the first floor a chronological tour. Starting with the Nile, this tour, covering 4,000 years, attempts to retrace the everyday life of ancient Egypt. There are numerous texts on display which explain the history behind the works and visual aids which help the overall understanding of the objects on display.

The main entrance is through the Hall Napoleon. Underneath the pyramid, take the escalators, in the direction of Sully Wing.

– Past the Medieval Louvre is the great Sphinx of Tanis **(Hall 1)**.
– Then take the staircase on the left. At the entrance to the department, *Nakhthorheb* awaits you**(Hall 2)**.

– **Hall 3:** the Nile, the life-blood of Egypt is the subject of this collection, including scale models of boats from the Middle Empire, and figurines.

– **Hall 4:** work in the fields; the mastaba of Akhéthétep. Beautiful coloured bas-reliefs. The rest of the hall is devoted to agriculture.

– **Hall 5:** farming, hunting and fishing. An insight into Egyptian food, including the unusual 'ideal mummies' menu', made up of the most delectable dishes of the day.

– **Hall 6:** writing and the scribes. Everything you always wanted to know about the essential workings of the Egyptian government, which had a considerable ability for organization, inventories and accounts. A display case is devoted to weights and measures and, most amazing of all, the scribes' palettes.

– **Hall 7:** materials and techniques, artists and artisans. Here you'll find a fine, bronze statue of the god Horus reaching out to you.

– **Hall 8:** house and home. Domestic objects found in tombs give an insight into the Egyptians' home life.

– **Hall 9:** jewels, clothing, body care. Here you'll discover some very rare pieces: the fish necklace, the necklace of Pinedjem and the ring of Horemheb and an exceptional collection of toiletry items. At the far end there is a display case containing rare costumes.

– **Hall 10:** leisure, music and games. Proof that the Egyptians had no lack of distractions. Display cases holding games and musical instruments.

– **Hall 11:** with the forecourt of the temple and the path of the Sphinxes, you can almost imagine that you are in Karnak. There are six limestone sphinxes from the Serapeum excavations, as well four large, pink baboons from Luxor! The large staircase leads to the first floor, directly into Hall 27 (the beginning of the chronological presentation). Don't take this route if you want to see the whole of the museum.

– **Hall 12:** the temple. The largest sculptures are set up to give you an idea of what an Egyptian temple looked like. Porticoes, columns and statues of divinities such as those of *Sekhmet*, colossuses of *Sethi II* and *Ramses II*, and a fine head of *Aménophis III*. Sandstone relief sculptures conjure up the god Montu. Situated in Hall 12 *bis* are the chapels, the chamber of the ancestors and the zodiac of Dendera on the ceiling, all richly engraved and decorated.

– Return to the back of the Henri IV Gallery to descend into the crypt of Osiris **(Hall 13)**, whose tragic fate led to his becoming the ruler of the after-life. There's a magnificent pink granite sarcophagus of Ramses III. The mythology and rites involved in a royal burial are illustrated in display cases.

– **Hall 14:** the sarcophagi, which were supposed to protect the person who had died in his or her voyage to the other world.

– **Hall 15:** the mummy. Embalming before burial was carried out in order to prevent the body from physically decaying and to ensure the survival of the soul.

– **Hall 16:** the tombs.

– **Hall 17:** the *Book of the Dead* and funeral trappings. The length of the hall makes it possible to display the entire of the *Book of the Dead* by Hornedjitef (over 20m/65ft).

– **Hall 18:** the gods and magic. A truly wonderful 'healing statue', plus objects and texts reflecting the importance of magic in everyday life. Statuettes representing the various divinities and their attributes.

– **Hall 19:** animals and gods, sacred animals, Serapeum from Memphis. Don't miss the fascinating exhibit of animal mummies. From the Montou bull to the Sobek crocodile, they represent all the Egyptian gods. Superb statue of the Apis bull. Now retrace your steps, take the Northern staircase and rejoin the chronological route.

The chronological route

A small chronological frieze gives an idea of just how long the Egyptian civilization lasted. Almost 3,000 years separate Cheops from Cleopatra, the last pharaoh. There are two ways to follow the tour: either via the short presentation of a selection of works, or by going through the more in-depth galleries.

– **Hall 20:** the end of prehistory. The age of Nagada (around 4000–3100 BC) saw the appearance of the first hieroglyphics. One of the masterpieces of this period is the *Poignard du Gebel el Arak.* Beautifully painted hard-stone vases.

– **Hall 21:** the Thinite age (around 3100–2700 BC). The first two dynasties. Interesting *Stèle du Roi-Serpent*, a symbol of the unification of Egypt and the birth of writing. Stunning ivory furniture, as well as colourful vases.

– **Hall 22:** the Old Empire (around 2700–2200 BC). This is the period of the splendour of powerful kings, during which the first pyramids were built. There's a really fine head of the pharaoh Didoufri and the famous *Crouching scribe,* depicted in a suggestive pose, with his expressive eyes and amazing face. The Raherka and Merséankh couple is striking in its finesse.

– **Hall 23:** around 2033–1710 BC, the Middle Empire. Two large wooden statues: the chancellor Nakhti and the governor of Hapydjefaï province. The display cases contain lovely earthenware, such as the blue hippopotamus. Further on there are portraits of kings, and steles.

– **Hall 24:** the New Empire (from the reconquest to Amenophis III, 1550–1353 BC). This hall lets you see how the style developed from the rigid archaism of the *Statue of Prince Lahmès* to the sensual *Portraits of King Amenophis III.* Superb golden goblet of the great Djehouty and fine statuettes of the scribe Nebmeroutef.

– **Hall 25:** the New Empire, the Akhenaton period and Nefertiti (1353–1337 BC), also known as Amenophis IV. There is a fine colossus against the back wall. Amongst the Louvre's must-sees, you'll find the body sculpted in red quartzite (probably of Queen Nefertiti), the head of the princess and the statuette of the royal couple holding hands.

– **Hall 26:** the New Empire, around the reign of Tutankhamen (1337–1295 BC). Tutankhamen initiated a return to traditional politics and religion, after the upheavals caused by Akhenaton. On display you can see a delicate glass head in two different shades of blue and the majestic statue of the god Amon. Next come the original Egyptology halls, created by Champollion in 1827.

– **Hall 27:** the New Empire at the time of Ramses (1295–1069 BC). The pharaohs. The pinnacle of the 19th and 20th dynasties is marked by an unequalled architectural richness. Splendid fragment of painted relief representing Sethi I and the goddess Hathor.

– **Hall 28:** the New Empire at the time of Ramses. Princes and courtiers. Very fine stone statuette of Amon and his wife Mout. Jewels from the Serapeum of Memphis. Breastplates in gold encrusted with earthenware.

– **Hall 29:** 1069–404 BC. This is the period of the first Persian domination. On the right, *Statue of Karomama*, the finest Egyptian bronze, encrusted in gold and silver. Stunning golden jewel showing the triad of Osiris-Isis-Horus. Also admire the ivory *Statuette of naked woman.*

– **Hall 30:** the last pharaohs of Egypt up to Cleopatra (404–30 BC). Fine torso of Nectanébo I. The influence of Greek art is evident on the body of the goddess Isis (wet drape).

The funeral gallery of Roman Egypt

Located around the Cour Visconti, in the Denon area, entrance to this gallery is from the pyramid – head for the Denon Wing. After the second escalator and an antichamber, enter the hall devoted to funeral rites in Egypt during the Roman period (first to fourth centuries AD). This is part of the late antiquity tour which covers the oriental Mediterranean between the first and ninth centuries AD.

This small corner is full of architecture ideal for displaying objects connected with the cult of the dead. Its huge, low arches conjure up a sort of crypt. Here you'll find a painted shroud, the coffin of Chenptah, and a funeral papyrus illustrating the Ptolemaic period, as well as portraits painted on wax or in tempera, masks and breastplates in wood, plaster and tissue, stuccoed and painted. The portraits known as 'du Fayoum' are proof of the high level of painting achieved by the Greeks and Romans.

Coptic halls

The prodigious art of the Copts is housed in the wing next to the Cour Visconti, on the ground floor to the east. Entrance is from the pyramid, towards the Denon Wing and through the Pre-Classical Greece Halls (which you go through before turning right). Coptic art represents the art of the first centuries AD, especially that of the earliest Christians, followed by that of the monks.

– **Coptic Art Gallery:** famous Coptic fabrics with their fine colours, one of the specialities of Coptic art. Superb bronze censer, topped off by an eagle holding a snake. Remarkable tapestries from the fifth to the eighth centuries. Printed flax panel, depicting the legend of Dionysius. Also tells of the 'shawl' of Sabina, evoking themes from pagan mythology on Nilotic decor.

Baouit Hall

Access is through the back of the Coptic Art Gallery. Re-creation of one of the churches of the monastery of Baouit, founded in the fourth century and abandoned in the twelfth century. Sculpted wooden and limestone interiors. Beautiful paintings from Kellia, another monastic site. A large display case shows a rich collection of Coptic draperies and clothes.

FRENCH PAINTINGS

The tour begins in the Richelieu Wing, Hall 3, on the second floor and continues (still on the second floor) in the Sully Wing, Halls 4, 5, 6 and 7, ending on the first floor in the Denon Wing, Halls 8 and 9, where you'll find works of the 19th century.

The Richelieu Wing

Spread across 18 halls, there are 200 works from the primitives to Poussin.

– **Hall 1:** the *Portrait of Jean le Bon,* painted around 1350. The earliest French portrait retained from the 14th century.

– **Hall 4:** the famous *Pietà de Villeneuve-lès-Avignon*, the summit of heart-rending pathos in Christian art.

– **Hall 6:** French painting experiences a revival towards the mid-15th century through important regional schools. Earliest influences of the Renaissance can be seen in *Charles VII* by Jean Fouquet.

– **Halls 7 and 8:** portrait painters of the 16th century represented by artists like Clouet. Portrait of *François I* (life-size painting).

– **Halls 9 and 10:** the arrival of Italian artists (Leonardo da Vinci, Rosso, Il Primatice) in France changed the course of French painting, which went from medieval art to Mannerism. *Diane Chasseresse* and *Gabrielle d'Estrées et une de ses Sœurs* are representative of this school of Fontainebleau.

– **Hall 11:** as a reaction against the excesses of Mannerism, the generation of artists such as Vouet, Valentin and Poussin turned towards the naturalist movement, emerging from the art of Caravaggio.

– **Halls 13, 14, 16 and 18:** a quarter of the work of Nicolas Poussin is on show at the Louvre, which allows us to follow the evolution of this 'philosophical' 14th-century artist: from his first 'Roman' years (*Les Bacchanales*) to the paintings of his maturity *(Self-portrait)* and to the works from the end of his career *(Les Saisons* and *Apollon et Daphné).* A splendid octagonal hall (Hall 16) has been specially designed for Poussin's *Les Quatre Saisons.*

– **Hall 15:** another artist who was a genius with light: Claude Gellée, known as 'le Lorrain', with his *Port de Mer au Soleil Couchant.*

– **Rest Hall (Hall 17):** this contains information about the 'painting of the month'.

The Sully Wing

– **Hall 28:** admire the marvellous light of Georges de La Tour in *La Madeleine à la Veilleuse*, *L'Adoration des Bergers, St Thomas* and above all *Le Tricheur.*

– **Hall 29:** the Le Nain brothers, 'painters of reality' in the 17th century, recognized for their sincerity and sense of observation in *La Tabagie, La Forge* and *Famille de Paysans dans un Intérieur.*

– **Halls 31 and 32:** portraits and religious painting in the 17th century. Giant canvases by Le Sueur and Le Brun (*Histoire d'Alexandre,* Hall 32). Philippe de Champaigne with *Ex-voto* from 1662 and *Christ Mort.*

– **Halls 34 and 35:** displays the famous *Louis XIV* by Rigaud, *Charles le Brun* by Nicolas de Largillierre, *Athalie Chassée du Temple* by Antoine Coypel (full of theatricality), as well as his *Démocrite* with its vibrant colours close to the style of Rubens. *Louis XV,* a fine pastel by Quentin de La Tour, can be seen, along with pastels and miniatures from the 18th century.

– **Watteau Hall (Hall 36):** contains the famous *Pierrot* known as 'le Gilles', *Pèlerinage à l'Île de Cythère* and *Nymphe et Satyre.* Also Nicolas Lancret, Nicolas de Largillierre and his unusual *Étude de Mains.* There are also good examples of De Troy and the painters of the reign of Louis XV such as Van Loo, Boucher and Lemoyne.

– **Hall 39:** in the *Déjeuner de Chasse* by De Troy, note the carefree attitude of the aristocracy. Painted in 1737 (the first rumbles of the Revolution could be heard).

– **Hall 40:** *Le Buffet, La Raie* and *L'Enfant au Toton* by Chardin.

– **Boucher Hall (Hall 46):** *L'Enlèvement d'Europe* and *Les Forges de Vulcain* (charming and fresh in its approach).

– **Hall 47:** you can already see something of Renoir in the sad face of *L'Oiseau Mort.* Also on dislpay are *L'Accordée du Village* painted by Greuze and the famous *Diderot* by Van Loo.

– **Fragonard Hall (Hall 48):** you'll be amazed by this collection: Fragonard's *Grand Prêtre Corésus,* full of heavy theatricality with an unreal light, the *Leçon de Musique,* his *Baigneuses* rich with sensuality, the famous *Verrou* and *L'Adoration des Bergers* (with a light and a mystery reminiscent of Rembrandt). There are also works by Élisabeth Vigée-Lebrun, who painted a superb portrait of *Hubert Robert* and several works by Hubert Robert himself, renowned for his paintings of ruins.

– **Greuze Hall (Hall 51):** paintings by Greuze with a moral message: *La Malédiction Paternelle* and its logical sequel *Le Fils Puni.*

– **Vien Hall (Hall 53):** works by François-André Vincent and Regnault, among others. Very academic, as with Pajou and Lagrenée, they foreshadow the cold manner of David. Others who are less well-known include Pierre-Paul Prud'hon, the painter of *Monsieur Vallet* (wonderfully natural, ruffled hair, nonchalant pose), Vivant Denon and Boilly, a painter of country life scenes.

– **Ingres Hall (Hall 60):** *E. Bochet, La Baigneuse*, the famous *Louis-François Bertin,* a symbol of the bourgeoisie, established and triumphant, are all on display here. Note the great care that has been taken over the details in these paintings, for example the reflection of the window on the back of the chair. In *Le Bain Turc,* almost 50 years later, the famous bathing woman's back makes a return appearance.

– **Géricault Hall (Hall 61):** Géricault's *Scène de Déluge* and *Officier de Chasseur à Cheval* are full of lyrical spirit and flamboyance. There are many horses in Géricault's work, so it's no surprise to learn that he died falling off of one! *La Mort de Géricault*, painted by Ary Scheffer, can also be seen here.

– **Delacroix Hall (Hall 62):** as with Géricault, Delacroix's great works (such as *Femmes d'Alger* and *La Liberté*) have stayed on the first floor of the Denon Wing. Here you'll find, however, *L'Assassinat de l'Évêque de Liège, Léon Riesener,* the famous self-portrait (a mysterious air, intense stare and an expression which is even vaguely disturbing), *Frédéric Chopin* and *Noces Juives au Maroc.*

– Then to the **Barbizon School:** *Folles Filles* by Narcisse Diaz de la Peña and *Botteleurs de Foins* by Millet. It is incredible to think that in 1850 this pleasant painting had people quaking in their boots! The middle classes accused Millet of being a socialist painter – some of them even took his work to be a call to revolt!

– Ending this section are almost 100 works by **Corot**. *Velléda* (from 1868), painted in the artist's twilight years, depicts a melancholic face, against a background of drizzling rain and winter landscape. Other masterpieces include: *Zingara au Tambour Basque, Jeune Fille Grecque à la Fontaine, Souvenir de Castelgandolfo, Femme à la Perle, La Dame en Bleu* and *Souvenir de Mortefontaine.*

– These last halls are somewhat unusual as they show the **works of donors** (notably Thomy Thiéry and Moreau-Nélaton). One of the conditions imposed by these donors was that the works should remain together, which explains the somewhat mixed nature of these presentations. These collections also offer plenty of works by Corot.

– The **Beistegui Collection** is located in Sully Wing, Hall 4. Twenty-one paintings by portrait painters of the 18th and 19th centuries. In particular *La Marquise de Solana,* a masterpiece by Goya, and *Bonaparte* by David, which was never finished.

As a sequel to the period covering the 14th to the 17th centuries, 39 halls are devoted to French painting of the 18th to the 19th centuries. The Italian architect Italo Rota provided the layout and the terracotta tones go remarkably well with the Corots and the Barbizon School.

– For those of you who would like to connect this panorama of 19th-century painting with the great works from the same period, continue to the Red halls: **Daru Hall (Hall 75), Denon Hall (Hall 76)** and **Mollien Hall (Hall 77)** in the Denon Wing (Halls 8 and 9) on the first floor. These halls present, among other things, the immense French paintings of the latter half of the 18th and the first half of the 19th century. They need to be displayed in a large area to ensure you can stand back as far as possible.

– *Murat, Roi de Naples* and *Les Pestiférés de Jaffa* by Antoine-Jean, Baron Gros. Géricault spent 16 months painting the famous *Radeau de la Méduse* (1819). Depicting the horrific drama when 149 shipwrecked sailors were abandoned for 12 days on a raft, the public was shocked by the realism of the corpses and the dark tones. Only 15 sailors survived, and extraordinary dramatic tension is rendered by the exhausted bodies rising to hail the rescue boat.

– On to the more famous **Delacroix:** *Dante et Virgile, Le Massacre de Scio, Femmes d'Alger, La Liberté Guidant le Peuple, La Prise de Constantinople* and *La Mort de Sardanapale.* The demise of this Assyrian king, who had the throats of all his wives and horses cut, before committing suicide himself, is depicted with a violence tinged with romanticism, provided by the red, gold, brown and black tones and the aesthetic curves and rounded shapes which flow through the painting.

– *Jeanne d'Arc* by Ingres. It's hard to believe that this work is by Ingres as it seems surprisingly academic. A bit further on, you'll find the *Grande Odalisque*, a painting in which Ingres was seeking perfection. On closer inspection, an expert revealed the presence of three extra vertebrae in the seated figure which add to the lasciviousness of the pose. Also here are *Œdipe* and the portrait of *Mademoiselle Rivière.*

David's works include *Madame Récamier,* the conformist *Serment des Horaces* (it looks like something by Vernet) and the very famous *Sacre de Napoléon.*

PAINTINGS FROM THE SCHOOLS OF THE NORTH

It's now possible to view these collections together since they've been moved to the second floor of the Richelieu Wing. **Halls 1 to 3** are common to the French Painting and Flemish Painting tours. Further on, the Schools of the North tour continues on the left.

– **Halls 4 to 6:** at the end of a joint section with the French school, devoted to international Gothic art, you'll find first of all the Dutch primitives, in particular the triptych of the *Famille Braque* by Van der Weyden and the admirable *Vierge au Chancelier Rolin* by Jan Van Eyck. Note the luminous and exquisite landscape in the background. The artist was one of the first to use oils. Further on are the Memling series with *Portrait d'une Dame Âgée* and the very famous *Nef des Fous* by Bosch.

– **Halls 7 to 16:** the Flemish painters of the 16th century and the beginning of the 17th century, and a small selection of sketches. Masterpieces here include *Les Mendiants* by Brueghel the Elder and *La Tireuse de Cartes* by Lucas Van Leyden. There are also works from the German school by Dürer, Cranach, and the incomparable group by Holbein, including the portrait of the humanist Erasmus.

Next we come to the great transverse spaces.

– **Halls 17 and 19** (including the **Médicis Gallery**): houses the large Flemish works of the 17th century. Don't miss the Médicis Gallery with 24 canvases by Rubens telling the life story of Marie de Médicis. The best-known episode, *Le Débarquement de Marie de Médicis au Port de Marseille,* inspired many French artists.

– **Halls 21 and 22** (after the sumptuous Le Fuel staircase): other masterpieces by Rubens. *La Kermesse,* the portrait of his second wife, *Hélène Fourment*, and many other sketches. After Rubens is his pupil Van Dyck, portrait artist of the English royal court *(Charles I* and *La Vierge aux Donateurs*) and David Teniers, a specialist in the rustic genre (*Intérieur de Cabaret*).

– **Halls 31 and 32:** dedicated to Rembrandt and his followers. *Autoportrait à la Tête Nue, Philosophe en Méditation, Ste Famille, Pèlerins d'Emmaüs,* the unforgettable *Bethsabée au Bain* and, in another style, *Bœuf Écorché.*

– **Hall 38:** Vermeer, the painter of intimate enclosed spaces, for example, *La dentellière et l'Astronome.*

In the Salon Carré, the Hall des Sept Mètres and the first third of the Grande Gallerie (eastern part) in the Denon Wing on the first floor, are Italian paintings of the 13th, 14th and 15th centuries.

The Salon Carré now houses the Florentines Cimabue, Giotto, Fra Angelico, Uccello and Botticelli. On the northern wall of the Grande Gallerie is Pérugin, Leonardo da Vinci and the young Raphael. On the opposite wall, Antonello da Messina, Mantegna and Bellini. In the Hall des Sept Mètres are the small-format works: Pisanello, Piero della Francesca and Sassetta.

The next part of the tour completes the chronological presentation of the Italian paintings. The Hall of States is mainly devoted to the large-format works of the Venetian school, including *Les Noces de Cana* by Veronese. With the exception of the world-famous *Mona Lisa*, most of Leonardo da Vinci's works are in the Hall of States. The collection of Raphaels occupies half of the tour then, around the *Portrait de Baldassate Castiglione*, we find the master's pupils: Pontormo, Bronzino, Correggio, Arcimboldo, and Baroche, whose painting *La Circoncision* ends the section.

Canvases by Anibal Carrache and Caravaggio illustrate the Italian pictorial revolution in the 17th century. There are also works by their followers: Manfredi, Reni and Guerchin. Smaller-format works include Gentileschi, inspired by Caravaggio, Lanfranco, Dominiquin and Borgianni. Finally there are a majestic group of Bolognese large-format works by Reni, Guerchin and Cortone.

The other regional schools are represented in the Small Exhibition Halls and the former Van Dyck Hall. This forms a more coherent collection with the former Rubens Hall, where Italian and Spanish paintings of the 18th century are exhibited.

ITALIAN DRAWINGS

Adjacent to the Grande Gallerie, the Mollien Halls house sketches drawn in the 16th and 17th centuries. There are a number of drawings showing the story of Scipio, a few gouaches and paintings from the workshops of Raphaël (*La Modération* and *La Tempérance*, around 1520), as well as the *Allégorie des Vices* and its counterpart, *L'Allégorie des Vertus*, by Correggio (painted around 1530 in Mantua).

ITALIAN AND NORDIC SCULPTURE

Situated in the Denon Wing, on the ground floor mezzanine, Nordic sculpture from the 12th to the 16th centuries is displayed along with Italian sculpture from the 11th to the 15th centuries. Sculpture up to the 19th century continues on the ground floor. The famous *Slaves* by Michelangelo has pride of place in the Mollien Gallery. Two works you shouldn't miss are *Psyché Ranimée par le Baiser de l'Amour* by Canova and the lovely *Nymphe au Scorpion* by Bartolini.

FRENCH SCULPTURE

French sculpture is housed on the ground floor of the Richelieu Wing, in and around the two large covered courtyards. From Hall 20, known as the Girardon Crypt, go through to the Cour Puget and the Cour Marly at the lowest level, which allows you an overall view of the monumental sculptures.

– On the right, the **Cour Puget** houses many open-air sculptures from the 17th to the 19th centuries. On the middle level is the *Milon de Crotone* by Puget, where Milon, an arrogant athlete, is held prisoner by the tree trunk he wished to chop down.

– On the left is the **Cour Marly**, with the *Chevaux de Marly* by Coustou.

– Go to the upper terrace of the Cour Marly, then turn left. The chronological tour starts in the lobby. For the medieval part **(Halls 1 to 10)**, each hall is organized around a work or a theme (the *Vierge à l'Enfant*, the altarpieces and the recumbent effigies).

– The halls devoted to modern times are organized around a sculptor and his work, including Jean Goujon and Germain Pilon. From **Hall 21**, the tour circuit continues around the Cour Puget and you have to return through the

Girardon Crypt where you can see Pigalle (*Mercure Attachant ses Talonnières*), Houdon and Chaudet (*La Paix* and *L'Amour*).

– The small gallery of the Royal Academy of Painting and Sculpture **(Hall 25)** groups together the pieces submitted by sculptors during the 18th century. Sometimes the work submitted actually represented the sculptor's lifetime's work.

OBJETS D'ART

The Objets d'Art department's collections are spread between the Richelieu Wing (first floor), the Sully Wing (first floor) and the Denon Wing (first floor).

From the Middle Ages to the Renaissance

(Richelieu 3, Halls 1 to 33, on the Cour Puget side)

Merovingian, Carolingian, Byzantine, Roman and Gothic art are on show in the first halls which lead into one another. Note the *Patène de Charles le Chauve*, which comes from the treasure of St-Denis, the *Vases de Suger* and the *Vierge de Jeanne d'Évreux* in gilded silver. Even the sword of Charlemagne – nicknamed 'Joyous' – which was used in the coronation of many kings of France (Louis XIV, among others) is displayed here.

– **Hall 9:** the tapestries known as *Mille Fleurs* (the rarest have a pink background) constitute one of the most attractive furnishings created in the late Middle Ages.

– **Hall 11:** an admirable selection of Limoges enamels from the 16th century. *La Résurrection* by Léonard Limousin is in Hall 22.

– **Halls 19 and 20:** two very famous wall-hangings are beautifully displayed: *Les Chasses de Maximilien* (12 works illustrating a hunting scene for each month of the year) and *L'Histoire de Scipion* (eight tapestries woven at Les Gobelins from 1688 to 1690).

– **Halls 27 and 28:** treasure, wall-hangings and cloaks of the order of the Holy Ghost.

– **Hall Mazarin** (at the junction with the Sully Wing)**:** an evocation of the royal collections under Louis XIII and Anne of Austria. The golden coffer and Anne of Austria's golden goblet are particularly memorable.

1ST

The 17th and 18th centuries (*Sully, Halls 34 to 61*)

This section presents one of the finest collections of furniture and *objets d'art* from the period of Louis XV. Works from the 19th century, which were housed in Halls 62 to 65, have been transferred to the Rohan section in the Richlieu Wing.

The 19th century and the Apartments of Napoleon III

(Return to the Richelieu Wing, on the Cour Marly side)

– **Halls 67 to 73** are devoted to the 19th century, including the *Chambre de Mme Récamier.* In **Hall 73**, the impressive jewel cabinet of the Empress Josephine is on show and there is a fine collection of porcelain in **Hall 71**.

– The **Apartments of Napoleon III** (the end of the visit) were fitted out to accommodate Minister Fould, although he never actually lived in these sumptuous apartments, which he had designed with Lefuel. Gold and illusion are dominant features of this Louis XIV-style palace, characteristic of the Second Empire.

The introductory gallery **(Hall 80)** leads to the family lounge and the theatre. The family lounge serves as a transition between the large and the small apartments **(Halls 83 to 88)**. The largest of the rooms, and the most sumptuous, is the *Grand Salon* or *Salon d'Angle,* which could be transformed into a theatre and hold up to 265 spectators. Note the splendid Baccarat crystal chandelier, the painting on the ceiling by Maréchal and the padded pieces of furniture which were evocatively known as 'confidants' or 'indiscreets'. In the small dining room **(Hall 76)** a charming *trompe-l'œil* painting can be seen. The large dining room **(Hall 75)** displays a more severe style.

– To finish the tour of the Objets d'Art department, when visiting the Italian Paintings go into the **Gallery of Apollo** (Denon 8, first floor, **Hall 66)**. Here you will find Louis XIV's collection of precious and semi-precious stones and jewels, as well as the Crown jewels of the kings of France, and magnificent cut stones and rock crystals. You'll also find the *Regent*, a 140-carat diamond discovered in India in the 18th century.

ORIENTAL ANTIQUITIES AND ISLAMIC ARTS

The Islamic section, on the mezzanine floor of the Richelieu Wing, is accessible by the two escalators leading to the upper floors. It brings widely varying works together: carpets (including the carpet from Iran known as *de Mantes*, **Hall 11**), textiles, weapons, miniatures, ceramics, glasswork and *objets d'art* (e.g. the copper alloy bowl, encrusted with gold and silver, known as the *Baptistère de St Louis*, **Hall 8**).

1ST

– On the ground floor, around the Cour Khorsabad **(Halls 1 to 6)** are the Mesopotamian works and, further on, those from Iran **(Halls 7 to 10)**.

– The **Sackler Wing** (Sully, ground floor) and the 11 new halls following the Iran tour (which begins in the Richelieu Wing), house the collection of Oriental Antiquities. Here you will find over 2,000 works from fallen empires such as the Babylonian empire. Don't miss the most important exhibit here: the statue discovered at Aïn Ghazal (Jordan), dating from the seventh century BC. Loaned to the Louvre for 30 years by the Hashemite kingdom, it is 1.05m (3ft) high and characteristic of pre-ceramic Neolithic culture. Oddly enough it shows a modern-looking relaxed pose, with a slight hint of irony in the expression.

The first hall is dedicated to Iron-Age Iran: baked earthenware and horses' bits with engraved motifs. Artefacts from the Palace of Suse follow, with magnificent friezes showing hunters and animals and the famous cornice of the Apanada (7m/23ft high). From Achememide Iran, we move on to the Parthian period and its alabaster statuettes. Further on are Phoenician sarcophagi and a display showing the importance of funeral rites. Finally, in the halls devoted to the countries of the Levant and to Carthage are steles which were used for religious rites. The tour ends with Arabia (a fine evocation of the desert and the nomads) before Islam and Cyprus.

The high point of the visit is in the **Cour Khorsabad** where the entrance to the palace of the Assyrian king Sargon II has been re-created. The two original winged bulls, which line the covered passage, act as palace guards. If you look closely, you'll see that they've each got five feet – seen from the front they are motionless, but from the side they appear to walk. The other three (one original, one 19th-century copy, and one a cast from 1992) are laid out in a frieze and give an idea of the bas-reliefs which decorated the 2km (1 mile) of indoor and outdoor walls of the palace.

– Around the Cour Khorsabad are artefacts which date from the second century BC: *La Stèle des Vautours,* countless statuettes from Goudea, the statue of Ebih-Il with its eyes encrusted with lapis-lazuli and a stele in basalt on which the first laws ever known to man are engraved (the *Code of Hammourabi*).

THE PALAIS-ROYAL QUARTER

A single ticket allows access to the three museums of the Central Union of Decorative Arts (Musée des Arts décoratifs, Musée de la Mode et du Textile and Musée de la Publicité). Full price 35F, concessions 25F. Free access to the permanent collections for under 18s.

★ **Musée des Arts décoratifs:** Union Centrale des Arts décoratifs, palais du Louvre, 107 rue de Rivoli 75001. ☎ 01-44-55-57-50. Fax: 01-44-55-57-84. Website: www.ucad.fr. Metro: Palais-Royal or Tuileries. Access for visitors with disabilities through Hall 105. Open 11am to 6pm (9pm on Wednesday); Saturday and Sunday 10am to 6pm. Closed Monday.

The Musée des Arts décoratifs is continuing with important renovation work as part of the Grand Louvre programme and the opening of its new halls has been put back to the end of 2002. This means that the chronological tour of the permanent collections has been reworked in order to free up new spaces for the thematic presentation of the collections, in particular the 20th-century ones, and to modernize the public reception area with new signs, a restaurant and lifts.

1ST

It must be said that this museum deserves to be better known. It has been in existence in the Marsan Wing of the Louvre since 1905, and has over 220,000 works tracing the art of living from the 13th century up to the present day. The permanent collections are partly closed (the halls devoted to the 17th, 18th, 19th and 20th centuries will not re-open until the end of 2002). However, those concerning the Middle Ages and the Renaissance re-opened in January 1998. This is the oldest section in the museum, with collections of religious and secular art covering a period of 400 years (13th to 16th centuries), displayed in nine superb new rooms, stunningly designed and laid out. The sculptures and paintings originating from religious establishments are presented against a medieval backdrop, whilst everyday objects are on display, representing the daily life of that time.

THE MIDDLE AGES AND THE RENAISSANCE

– Opposite the main staircase, on the first floor, **Hall 1** hosts a collection of tapestries, earthenware and furniture. These depict fantasy animals, monkeys, owls, men with the bodies of animals, and so on. This style, known to man since the Classical Age, was rediscovered during the Renaissance following excavations at Nero's Golden House around 1480. One of the most remarkable works in this hall is a tapestry from the 16th century showing an allegory of the *Vanité des Voluptés*.

– Now go straight on to **Hall 3**, turning left, then left again. There's a re-creation of the bedroom of a member of the 15th-century Court with Gothic-style furniture. There are five tapestries illustrating the famous *Roman de la Rose*, and also the varnished Italian majolicas.

– Retrace your steps to the Hall of the Master of the Madeleine **(Hall 2)**, offering painting and sculpture from the 13th to the 15th centuries. While Europe was undergoing a troubled period, art was experiencing a golden age. Here you'll find superb Italian altarpieces and refined Italian panels including the fine stone *Angel*, a Parisian sculpture from the 13th century made of polychrome oak, and a polychrome *Vierge Allaitant* from the 15th century.

– Situated at the end is the Hall Jules Maciet **(Hall 4)**, re-creating the reign of Louis XII with the beginning of the dominance of Italian art and the introduction of agricultural themes. A tapestry allegedly shows Charles of Orleans and his wife, Marie of Cleves.

– Next, go into the altarpiece gallery **(Hall 5)**, which re-creates the central nave of a church. You'll find religious art from the 14th, 15th and 16th centuries. Admire the altarpieces shown in their entirety – which is a rare occurrence – *Diptyque de la Vierge à l'Enfant* by Antonio by Carro (1398) and *Retable de Saint Jean Baptiste* by Luis Borrassa, which measures more than 3m (10ft).

– **Hall 6**, at the end on the right, shows the art of firing from the 13th to the 16th centuries: glassware, enamels and earthenware. There is also a superb cross with a double crosspiece in enamelled copper, dating from 1250. Very fine bronzes from the Renaissance period.

– On the left, enter **Hall 7**, known as Émile Peyre, the donor of all the Italian paintings in the collection. The pupils of the greatest painters of the 16th century are represented here. From the school of Donatello, there is a splendid *Vierge à l'Enfant* in painted baked earth from the 15th century.

– Go back to the previous hall and, on the left, look at the study **(Hall 8)**. This room was originally located close to the bedroom and reserved for honoured guests. Fairly rare intarsia (an elaborate form of 15th-century marquetry) panels. A chest shows four of the Labours of Hercules, a fine work of the French Renaissance (1546).

– The last hall on the floor **(Hall 9)** is a reconstruction of a room from the time of Henri II. You'll find six seats *(sgabello)* made of polychrome wood, from the 16th century, which come from the Doges' Palace in Venice. There are also rare stained-glass windows in yellow silver from the workshop of Dirck Crabeth, made in Leyden, in the Netherlands, in 1543. French furniture of the same period is also on display, including dressers, chests, extending tables and a superb Île-de-France wardrobe, not forgetting two paintings by Cranach, one of which, *Adam and Eve*, is attributed to his workshop.

TEMPORARY EXHIBITIONS AND ACTIVITIES

In spite of a number of halls being closed, the **temporary exhibitions** remain open 11am to 6pm Tuesday to Friday, and 10am to 6pm on Saturday and Sunday, as do the **documentation centres** (glass, toys, drawings, wallpaper, 20th century objects). Late night opening on Wednesday until 9pm. **Artdécojeunes** offers activities for children aged from 4 to 18. Information and reservations: ☎ 01-44-55-59-25.

★ **Musée de la Mode et du Textile:** Union Centrale des Arts décoratifs, palais du Louvre, 107 rue de Rivoli 75001 (access for visitors with disabilities at No. 105). ☎ 01-44-55-57-50. Website: www.ucad.fr. Metro: Palais-Royal, Pyramides or Tuileries. Same opening hours, prices and premises as the Musée des Arts Décoratif (see above), but situated on the first floor.

A result of pooling the funds of the Union Centrale des Arts Decoratifs and the Union Française des Arts du Costume, the collections at this museum of fashion and textiles allow you to trace the evolution of fashion. The building has been completely renovated and redesigned. Originally the museum exhibited mainly women's fashion from the 17th century to the present day, with costumes and accessories, focusing on middle-class fashion and *haute couture*. Textiles and the techniques involved in its manufacture were only briefly covered by a few looms (e.g. the pleating loom) and a display of silhouettes noting the key dates: 1760, the manufacture of painted tissue by Oberkampf in Jouy; 1801, Jacquard weaving techniques; 1817, first tulle looms secretly transported from Britain to France, dye colouring using aniline (the era of chemical dyes); 1860, mass production of the sewing machine; end of the 19th century, appearance of the great couturiers (such as Charles Worth and Paul Poiret); 1937, birth of nylon. Since the renovation, exhibitions are presented over two levels (providing around one per cent of the collection), and are renewed every year according to different themes: *Geometry* in 1997, *Touches of Exoticism* in 1998 and *Wardrobe* in 1999. The museum is made up of around 40 collections given by various donors.

★ **Centre de Documentation sur la Mode et le Textile:** open to enthusiasts, researchers and professionals, ensuring the conservation, improvement, use and communication of reference material on fashion and textiles. Open on Thursdays from 2pm to 5pm, by appointment only: ☎ 01-44-55-58-57.

★ **Musée de la Publicité:** same address, telephone number and opening times as the Musée des Arts décoratifs: ☎ 01-44-55-57-50. Website: www.museedelapub.org. This space on the 3rd floor of the Musée des Arts décoratifs is entirely given over to an art which is, by its very nature, ephemeral – advertising. It is currently the only museum in the world solely dedicated to this subject. There are two very separate parts: first, a cafeteria, designed as an open agora in a multimedia space where the light filters in through red blinds. In this incandescent atmosphere, there are two rows of computer screens by which you can pay a virtual visit to the amazing database of a collection of 15,000 indexed and numbered advertising posters and 10,000 publicity films. In a few years' time a hundred thousand additional ads will be included, the result of two major legacies. It is a shame you need to queue for so long to access these gems. From posters advertising cough sweets to TV ads for cars costing millions, from the Laughing Cow cheese to Dim stockings and tights, all the fantasies and desires of an industrial society are just a mouse-click away.

The second part is the exhibition space – a number of rooms opening off a main corridor, whose walls are covered in aluminium plates between which visitors can glimpse, as if in some dilapidated squat, remnants of the building's old décor: torn wallpaper, decorative woodwork, old gilded moulding and the marble of battered fireplaces . . . the day-to-day backdrop for the civil servants of the old Ministry of Finance! Metal pipework and colonnades covered in leopard-skin add a further wild touch to this impressive set designed by Jean Nouvel. These rooms will house themed exhibitions – definitely worth keeping a close eye on the listings.

★ **Bibliothèque des Arts décoratifs:** 107 rue de Rivoli 75001. Metro: Palais-Royal or Tuileries. Premises are currently under renovation and collections are being computerized. Due to re-open in 2001.

★ **Les Ateliers du Carrousel:** 111 rue de Rivoli 75001. ☎ 01-44-55-59-02. Metro: Palais-Royal or Tuileries. Children, teenagers and adults can perfect their drawing, painting, sculpture, modelling, watercolours, cartoon strips and other artistic disciplines, while discovering the history of art. Preparation for studies in plastic arts for schoolchildren and students. Holiday workshops.

There is also a second site at the *École Camondo* (*see* 14th arrondissement).

★ **Jardins des Tuileries:** These gardens were orginally known as the Tuileries – a word meaning tile-making factories – because the clay-based earth here was used to manufacture tiles. This former public tip was bought by Catherine de Médicis to be made into a park. Embellished by André Le Nôtre a century later, the garden soon became very popular. The arrangement of the flowerbeds is a prime example of formal French garden design.

As you enter the garden, you will pass the imposing and pretentious Arc de Triomphe, built in 1808 in honour of the no-less-pretentious Napoleon. The horses, sculpted by Bosio, are copies of the originals brought from Italy by Napoleon. The Venetians had taken them from Constantinople and the Roman Empire, in turn, had stolen them from Delphi. But their journey did not stop there, because Louis XVIII finally returned them to the Venetians. It was in the little streets which criss-cross this quarter that Marie-Antoinette got lost in June 1791, when she was fleeing Paris. As a result, she was late for her rendezvous and missed her escort, the Duc de Fersen, which led to her arrest at Varennes.

Until recently, the statue of Captain Dreyfus, with his broken sword symbolizing his infamy, stood in the gardens. In 1985, however, Jack Lang, then Minister of Culture, asked for the statue to be transferred to the courtyard of the *École Militaire*, but Charles Hernu, the Minister of Defence, objected, judging this to be a rather contentious decision. In 1994, there was a new twist to the story, this time because the statue's sculptor, 75-year-old Tim, still did not meet the criteria of exhibiting his work in the Tuileries – only the work of deceased artists is displayed in the garden. 'As far as I'm concerned this would be too much of a sacrifice!', said Tim. The bronze has therefore been moved to place Pierre-Lafue, in the 6th arrondissement.

On 24 December 1800, the attempted assassination of Napoleon took place in this neighbourhood, on rue St-Nicaire. The royalists St-Régant and Carbon almost succeeded in killing Napoleon, then First Consul. Barrels of gunpowder and scrap iron hidden on a cart exploded, but not quite at the right moment, as Bonaparte's carriage, coming out of the Tuileries, turned left to head towards the Opéra located in place Louvois. Several people were killed and 44 houses were damaged. When Napoleon became Emperor he had the buidlings razed to the ground in 1806.

From the terrace of the Bord-de-l'Eau, there is a fine view over the octagonal ornamental lake, with superb statues by Coysevox and Coustou, amongst others. At certain times of year, a mini-funfair takes possession of the northern end of the garden for a few weeks. Don't miss the big wheel, just like the one in the film *The Third Man*, which, from the top, allows you to enjoy a view over the whole of Paris and the green terraces of the quarter's more affluent residents.

Over the years, the Tuileries have fostered desire, passion and love, perhaps because of the trees, the wildlife or maybe the statues. On the eve of the Revolution, well-to-do families would come to take the air here on Sundays. They would greet one another formally, while beneath these polite rituals young men and women would exchange furtive, flirtatious looks. The Tuileries of French author and doctor Céline, who lived nearby in the passage Choiseul, are more surreal in character. During the 1980s, the gardens became a gay cruising park at night, but since then the nature of the place has changed. However, for those in the know, the terraces along the Seine remain an amazing spectacle, and the banks of the Seine have been christened 'Tata Beach' like the surfer's beach (with a fashion show of male models presenting the latest mini-briefs!).

On each side of the western exit (on the Place de la Concorde side) are the Jeu de Paume and the Orangerie, two museums dedicated to the arts. The Musée du Jeu de Paume's collections were moved to the Musée d'Orsay (*see* '7th arrondissement') in 1987, since when it has been used as an exhibition hall for contemporary art.

★ **A walk around the Tuileries:** 1.5km (1 mile); 30 minutes from the Concorde metro station to the Palais-Royal metro station by way of the pyramid in the Louvre. Open 7am to 8.30pm (9pm for the main gate) from 31 March to the last weekend in September, and 7.30am to 7pm (7.30pm for the Grille d'Honneur) the rest of the year. Free guided tours: ☎ 01-40-20-90-43.

Enter through the Grille d'Honneur de la Concorde. Opposite, the famous Paris axis continues, starting from La Défense, and heading straight towards the Louvre pyramid. Pay homage on your left to the bust of André Le Nôtre, creator, in 1664, of the gardens which stretch out before you (23ha/57 acres). Heading past the octagonal ornamental lake, where ducks from the Seine like to come and rest, and the Élysée Palace, you'll enter the 'Grand Couvert' planted with banana trees and horse chestnuts. '3,000 trees for the Year 2000' was the slogan of the Public Establishment of the Grand Louvre. These trees line the way to the Solférino path, which is linked to the Musée d'Orsay via a pedestrian passage opened in December 1999. Known as the Passerelle Solférino, this avoids the need for detours.

Note the discreet style of the cafés which have sprung up in this area. The round ornamental lake comes alive from 3pm onwards with brightly coloured little sailing boats which can be hired for children. Summer meetings of the Club des Parisiens Bronzés (the Sunbathing Club of Paris) are also held here. The almost white gravelly ground is a marvellous reflector for the sun, useful to know if you want people to think you've spent your holiday in the Seychelles, instead of Paris!

The numerous statues (around 100) from the 18th and 19th centuries are all copies, their precious originals now safe in the Louvre. In the garden of the Carrousel are 12 rows of trimmed yews which make a fantastic 6-ha (14-acre) maze. To get there, go past the little moats, dug in the 19th century to keep the crowds away from the former castle of the Tuileries, walk up the 12 steps of the terrace of the Tuileries and head towards the pyramid of the Louvre. The famous castle of the Tuileries used to stand between the two pavilions by Marsan and Flore, but it was burned down under the Commune in 1871. As you can see, the moats provided little defence. Turn around to admire the view of the Tuileries and the English-style gardens, created by Napoleon III. There are a few blue tits' nests hidden in the tree trunks. Over 23 species of birds have been seen in the Tuileries, including a kestrel in the nearby Tour St-Jacques, who comes looking for food early in the morning. The northern terraces of the Feuillants and south of the Bord de l'Eau have been replanted with lime trees and mulberry trees, in memory of Henri IV. The flowerbeds, planted with perennials and biennials, are changed twice a year: there are 16 gardeners tending almost 60,000 plants!

★ **Musée de l'Orangerie:** on the corner of the quai des Tuileries and the place de la Concorde, in the Jardin des Tuileries. ☎ 01-42-97-48-16. Metro: Concorde. This little museum is a well kept secret. It contains a highly coherent group of canvases from the Impressionists up to 1930. The museum is closed for renovation work until 2001. This is a shame for lovers of the *Nymphéas* by Monet or Cézanne's *Baigneurs*, as you'll have to wait until then before being able to view them again.

★ **Galerie Nationale du Jeu de Paume:** 1 place de la Concorde 75008. ☎ 01-47-03-12-50. Metro: Concorde. Open Tuesday noon to 9.30pm, Wednesday to Friday noon to 7pm, and Saturday and Sunday 10am to 7pm. Closed Monday. Entry fee 38F; concessions 28F. Group tours by reservation only.

Since the departure of its Impressionist canvases to the Musée d'Orsay, this gallery has devoted itself to contemporary art, playing host exclusively to temporary exhibitions such as Dubuffet in 1991, Nan Goldin in 1992, Takis in 1993, Tàpies in 1994, a century of British sculpture in 1996, César in 1997, and Alechinsky and Arman in 1998 and the Icelandic painter Erro in 1999. There is a hall in the basement showing work by independent film-makers. The thematic programmes, (for example *Un Été Portugais* and *Les Essais* by Jean-Luc Godard in 1997, and independent Japanese cinema in 1999), are separate from the temporary exhibitions.

The royal game of real tennis (*jeu de paume*), which was born in France – although it is hardly played any more outside Britain – is a forerunner to today's modern game of tennis. The construction of the Jeu de Paume courts were authorized by Napoleon III in 1851, on the proviso that they respected the main decorative guidelines of the Orangerie. As the popularity of the game began to wane, the buildings were converted into a gallery, and the Jeu de Paume hosted its first exhibition at the beginning of the century. It was closed in 1986, and was completely renovated. The modern style and spirit of the gallery can be seen in the superb façade, the entrance which is in perfect perspective, and the large glass wall overlooking the Jardins des Tuileries. There's also a pleasant tea-room, an art bookshop and an audiovisual room.

★ **Palais-Royal:** Metro: Palais-Royal-Musée-du-Louvre. The Palais Royal, which has been occupied since Roman times, was probably Paris's first spa. A villa and enormous bathing pools have been found during excavations. The current building was the former palace of Cardinal Richelieu, during which time it was known as the Palais-Cardinal. Louis XIV lived there for the first few years of his life; he played kings and queens in the grounds of the palace with the daughter of a servant whom he called 'Queen Marie'. Henriette de France also lived here, and during the Regency years it played host to many libertine dinners. Louis-Philippe-Joseph, the future Philippe Égalité, short on cash, reduced the size of the garden and built shops and apartments all around it, which he then rented out. Charlotte Corday bought the knife which she used to killed Marat in one of the Palais' shops. In 1786, the old Comédie-Française theatre was built.

TIP If you haven't got a seat for a show at the Comédie-Française, 112 tickets go on sale 45 minutes before the curtain rises, at rock-bottom prices, in rue de Montpensier, at the corner of rue de Richelieu.

Before the French Revolution, the Palais-Royal was very much alive and sported a *very* bad reputation as a place where people went to drink, gamble and flirt. Underneath the galleries, the cafés and gambling dens attracted the crowds. The most famous, the Café de Foy, even offered rum. The area was renowned for its debauchery: licentious plays were staged and an MP was even thrown into the ornamental lake where Louis XIV, as a child, had almost drowned. In this den of vice and iniquity, ideas started to take shape. It was here that Camille Desmoulins, on 12 July 1789, called on the people of Paris to take up arms after the sacking of the liberal minister Necker, sparking events that were to lead to the Revolution. It is said that in 1815, the Russians and the Prussians, who had defeated Napoleon, gambled away all the war damages they were paid by France here. It is also said that Marshal Blücher lost several million in the gambling dens. The gambling craze spread to the well-heeled youth and, in the 1830s, so many ruined gamblers committed suicide that Louis-Philippe had to kick out the prostitutes and close the drinking and gambling establishments, 'whose orgies,' wrote Balzac, that had 'started with wine, decided to end in the Seine'. Eventually, as fashions changed, the Grands Boulevards became the more popular haunt for those seeking illicit pleasures, and the Palais-Royal lost its reputation as well as its customers.

Restif de La Bretonne, an explorer of the streets of Paris, was full of praise for the prostitutes who, during the Revolution, occupied the galleries of this royal palace. Many guides were published, giving detailed descriptions of the 'lovelies' and their prices: 'Marie, a big blond girl, pale complexion, broken teeth . . . 3 *livres*. If you haggle you can get her down to 1 *livre* 4 *sols*'.

Certainly, from the Restoration onwards, the boulevards took over in reputation from the Palais-Royal. However, in 1852 the Palais-Royal quarter was still the one with the most brothels and prostitutes. From 1910 to 1912, Céline gives us the clearest description of the arcades of the Palais-Royal, at around 11pm: 'It was full of tarts . . . every few yards . . . or even less . . . one every three or four pillars with one or two punters'. It's interesting to get an insight into what the young Céline got up to!

Today the Palais-Royal is a quieter place. The green enclosure now only plays host to nannies, children and office workers. Writers Jean Cocteau and Colette lived here for many years, which gives you an idea of how fashionable the area is, and it is still only the privileged who live here – the former heir to Maxim's restaurant, the current heir to the Véfour restaurant, M.

Taittinger of the great champagne house, the singer Mireille, and the interior designer and friend of royalty, Inès de La Fressange, to name but a few.

So what is left of the Palais-Royal? Today it is home to the Councils of State (visits by appointment) and the Constitutional Council. In other words, it is much more straight laced these days.

– **Opposite the Théâtre-Français:** at 157 rue St-Honoré cigar-smokers will find their idea of heaven in *La Civette*, one of the oldest shops in Paris. It was opened in 1756 by the Duchess of Chartres, and rapidly took advantage of the fashion for tobacco.

– **Also worth seeing:** *Le Grand Véfour*, a famous restaurant in the 18th century, where Voltaire would treat himself; the café *Cuorazza*; and the amazing Didier Ludot, who sells designer clothing, including unusual Hermès scarves and Dior court shoes designed by Roger Vivier.

★ **Place Vendôme:** a fine architectural structure from the end of the reign of Louis XIV (the work started in 1686), this octagonal square, surrounded by Corinthian-style façades, has had lots of names, including place de Conquête and place Louis-le-Grand. It was part of the first property promotion where private houses could be built behind the façades, according to the purchasers' plans.

The history of the square charts the idiosyncratic consequences of political change. At the end of the 17th century it was decorated with a statue of Louis XIV, wearing an enormous wig. From 1793 to 1799, during the Revolution, the statue was demolished and the square renamed place des Piques. Napoleon created the Vendôme column, 43.5m (143ft) high, made from melted down Russian and Austrian cannons. He commissioned Chaudet to sculpt his statue, posing as Caesar, for the top. The Fall of Napoleon's Empire resulted in the fall of the column, but as its foundations were buried 9m (30ft) under the ground, nothing could destroy it completely, so only the bronze Napoleon was removed. During the Restoration, a white flag was planted on the column and was later transformed into a gigantic *fleur de lys*. A wave of nostalgia eventually restored Napoleon to the top, wearing a cocked hat, but as the two horns of the hat all too easily gave rise to sexual allusions to Josephine, the hat was removed and Napoleon adopted the bourgeois headgear of a hosier. Finally, a standard Napoleon was hoisted to the top – and it's still there today!

On 16 May 1871, the painter Courbet organized one of the most spectacular events of the Commune at the place Vendôme. In front of more than 100,000 Parisians, the statue of the Emperor was toppled onto a bed of manure which had been specially prepared for the purpose. However, the people made him pay dearly for toppling this 'symbol of despotism' and, having seized all the canvases from his workshop, threw him into prison, then forced him into exile in Switzerland, where he died a broken man a few years later. As for Napoleon, he was already back on his pedestal!

Wandering around the square, you will see the elegant young jet-set coming out to play. This is still the place for luxury mansions and exclusive jewellers (Boucheron, Cartier, Mauboussin, Van Cleef and Arpels, and Bulgari and Chaumet, installed in Chopin's former apartment), plus the banks and the mythical Ritz hotel. At the Ritz you can have a drink in the tiny but superb Bar Hemingway, where the famous American writer, F. Scott

Fitzgerald, often whiled away the time and wrote *A Diamond As Big As The Ritz*. As for the local restaurants, – most of them are incredibly expensive (*see* 'Where to eat'), as are the shops.

Every year (usually in December), there's an open-air exhibition of sculptures by contemporary artists, organized by the Vendôme Committee.

★ Adjoining the place Vendôme, **rue de la Paix** used to house the Capuchin monastery. Louvois, Louis XIV's minister, and the Marquise de Pompadour are buried at the site of Nos. 2 to 6 in this road.

★ Diametrically opposite, on the other side of the place Vendôme on the corner with rue St-Honoré, is the **private residence of the Sultan of Brunei**, the richest man in the world. It was sumptuously restored, over four years, by an architect from the Bâtiments de France. His home isn't open to the public, but its façade in dressed stone is worth taking a look at.

★ **La Fontaine Molière:** on the corner of the rues de Richelieu and Molière. Built in the monumental style by Visconti and situated very close to the site of the house where the great actor and playwright died (Molière, not Visconti!). The statue is oddly lit from the back by rather gaudy spotlights.

★ **Church of St-Roch:** on the corner of the rues St-Roch and St-Honoré. One of the prettiest Parisian churches, Louis XIV laid the first stone. Due to a lack of funds, a lottery was organized in order to continue with the construction work. The church was finished in 1722, after numerous chapels had been added. Famous for its acoustics, concerts are regularly held here. In the chancel, a rather demonstrative pulpit rests on the shoulders of the Virtues and, above it, the Angel of Truth brandishes his trumpet! From the steps of the church, priests and parishioners could watch the disquieting passage of the carts carrying condemned prisoners on their way to the guillotine at the Place de la Révolution.

It was at the foot of the church of St-Roch that Napoleon Bonaparte, on 5 October 1795, had royalist insurgents who were trying to enter the Hall of the Convention at the Tuileries shot.

★ The quarter also has its share of **passages**, glass-topped 19th-century arcades (N.B. many are closed in the evening). Start with the ones that zigzag between rue Montpensier and rue de Richelieu: the Passage de Richelieu, the Passage Hulot, the Passage Potier and the Passage de Beaujolais.

Along the way, there are some fine sights: in rue de Montpensier stands the superb **Palais-Royal theatre** (especially stunning in the evening, when it's all lit up). On the outside, there is a strange, baroque façade, with a very modern fire escape (almost a work of art), while the inside has a rich decor in deep red and rose tones.

Nearby, in rue de Beaujolais, is the restaurant of **Le Grand Véfour**, established in 1760. On the first floor are *salons* where Marat and Desmoulins, amongst others were once received. The decoration is sumptuous: lace curtains and brass curtain rails, glass ceilings painted with arabesques, ceramics and gilded mouldings. Slip behind the restaurant to rejoin the Passage du Perron, on the left; a festival of light and colour will greet you from the shops selling music boxes, toys and antiques.

Coming out of rue de Beaujolais through an elegant little stairway, turn right; 30m (100ft) further, on the left, is the Passage des Pavillons, very short and rather crooked, which soon leads you into the traffic of rue des Petits-Champs.

★ **Place des Victoires:** built in 1686 by Marshal de La Feuillade, in honour of the victories of Louis XIV. One of the first statues of Louis XIV stood here until 1792, when it was melted down by the revolutionaries. The current statue dates from 1822. The square boasts a harmonious layout and is now one of the headquarters of the fashion world, a famous creative centre with, in particular, Kenzo and Thierry Mugler's boutiques. Unfortunately, the fashion houses have chased out a number of restaurant owners and antiques' dealers whose trade brought the quarter alive in the evening and at weekends, thus dealing a fatal blow to the soul of the square.

★ **Galerie Vero-Dodat:** 2 rue du Bouloi. Dating from 1826 and undeniably beautiful, even in its noble decline. Admire the fine mahogany panelling, the little columns decorated with friezes separating the shops and the gilded, rusting signs, with damaged and missing letters. There are some interesting little shops – especially the puppet repair shop, bursting with life and colour. Porcelain cherubs beckon you from the windows, while further on there's a stringed-instrument maker.

THE LES HALLES QUARTER

Since the demise of Les Halles market in 1969, the new Les Halles quarter has gradually taken over from the Latin quarter as the supreme fashion area in Paris – at least until a few years ago, as the Bastille quarter and the rue Oberkampf are now putting up quite a fight for this position, not to mention the 9th and 10th arrondissements and Belleville.

In almost a quarter of a century, Les Halles has been turned upside down. Many people who arrive in rue Rambuteau are seduced by its friendly village look, but those who knew it in the old days and older local residents know that the original village is no more than a distant memory. In the 1950s, fruit and vegetable merchants stood side by side. Now they've all gone and buildings which formerly housed slums have been renovated, sometimes quite sumptuously, and the working-class community have been exiled to distant suburbs. 'By knocking down Les Halles, they have spat in Paris's coffin', wrote the French author René Fallet. Yet if the quarter *has* lost its soul, it does seem to be gaining a different one with a new way of life being created.

A BRIEF HISTORY

The birth of Les Halles

The 'heart of Paris', dear to Émile Zola, whose novel, *Le Ventre de Paris*, was set in the quarter, goes back 800 years to when Philippe Auguste had the first Halles built. From one century to another, they became more and more important. Splendid private residences were built, artisans and traders moved in, and the poor were also integrated into the community with the famous Court of Miracles, immortalized in Victor Hugo's *Notre Dame de Paris* (The Hunchback of Notre Dame).

There were public stocks for dishonest traders, blasphemers and pimps, but the edict from the king stated that 'only mud and other filth might be thrown at their eyes, not stones or things which might do them injury'. The stocks remained in place until the Revolution. In one bizarre episode, a cheese-seller who had tampered with his butter was exposed to the jeers of the crowd, until the slab of butter placed on his head had melted!

The Innocents

It is curious to note that for a long time Les Halles cohabited with the famous Cemetery of the Innocents (which was situated more-or-less on the site of the present-day Fountain of the Innocents). Fenced in by high walls and rather cramped, the creation of mass graves was soon required. Holes were dug 10m (32ft) deep, left open and bodies were piled one on top of the other, covered with just a thin layer of earth. For five centuries, the inhabitants of the quarter and the traders from Les Halles lived surrounded by the appalling smell of death. The cemetery received bodies from 22 parishes, and the area became a hub of activity with street vendors, letter-writers, onlookers, thieves and prostitutes.

It's easy to imagine the charming view offered to tenants at the time. At least they had the advantage of being able to chuck their slop buckets out of the window without anyone complaining! By 1780, the situation had become unbearable for the residents of the quarter and the traders at Les Halles. Millions of bodies buried over a period of seven centuries had raised the cemetery 2m (6ft) above ground level and the stench of rotting bodies was polluting the environment. The collapse of a mass grave into the cellars of a nearby house brought about the graveyard's final closure, as the inhabitants almost died of asphyxia!

An edict issued by Louis XVI gave the cemetery land to the herb and vegetable market, which was just nearby. Bones from the graveyard were removed, loaded onto carts and tipped into the quarries at the Tombe-Issoire (the current catacombs, located at Place Denfert-Rochereau). Over three years, a total of 12,000 journeys by cart were made during the day and 3,500 by night to transport all the remains. During the great construction work of 1860, another 800 cartfulls of remains were sent to the catacombs.

The heart of Paris

In the 19th century Les Halles began to expand, taking over a considerable area. The wine market was moved to Jussieu as a result. In 1851, Napoleon III appointed the architect Victor Baltard to design permanent buildings capable of housing the market. He created airy pavilions, offering maximum light, with a practical design.

The quarter has always been filled with colourful and truculent personalities, characteristic of the extraordinary hustle and bustle of the place: local merchants with their own rituals, customs, and languages, small businesses connected to the activities of Les Halles, café owners, seedy hotels, prostitutes, tramps, and thieves, all indispensable to the social life and folklore of the area.

Despite the lively nature of this exceptional quarter, there was a time when Les Halles seemed to have reached the point of no return. The authorities no longer appeared capable of supporting a city which was constantly expanding to the point of suffocation and where the turnover and storage of goods was always on the increase. The heavy traffic flooding into the centre of Paris exacerbated the problem to such a degree that in 1969 the market at Les Halles was moved out of the city centre and transferred to Rungis, 15km south of Paris. Controversially, the ten pavilions, commissioned by Napoleon III in 1851 from the architect Baltard, were destroyed, despite a huge public outcry.

LES HALLES TODAY

Despite having never found a proper identity of its own, Les Halles is still in existence today. If you find the Forum rather depressing, there are plenty of other things to entertain you here – including the Pompidou Centre, which is an undeniable cultural success in its own right.

TIP It is best to avoid the shopping centre of Les Halles and the area immediately around it and go north or east. In spite of the demolition and reconstruction work, there are still many old houses, private residences, narrow streets, fountains and architectural features worth seeing.

The restaurants offer an amazing range of culinary possibilities, and in spite of the loss of the original Les Halles, there are still plenty of old bistros which have retained the atmosphere of the 'good old days'. Take a walk along rue Montmartre or rue Montorgueil at 6am and there are plenty of cafés which are already open and buzzing. Even today, Les Halles is still a place to be seen in.

A SHORT WALK AROUND THE QUARTER

This short tour passes a few landmarks and historical points of interest and as you look around you'll see fine wrought-iron balconies, friezes and caryatids (columns in the form of draped female figures).

★ **Rue St-Honoré:** from the Palais-Royal to the rue des Halles, there are lots of old houses and picturesque shops. This was one of Paris's busiest streets. For traders, the idea was to be as close to the hustle and bustle of Les Halles as possible. Every day, during the Reign of Terror, prisoners condemned to the guillotine were transported to their execution along this street.

Lavoisier, who was responsible for the discovery of oxygen, lived at No. 47 until he was condemned to death during the Reign of Terror. At No. 93 there is an old shop sign *Au Bourdon d'Or*, which dates back to 1637 while a succession of wrought-iron work can be seen at Nos. 97 to 105. In 613, Queen Brunehaut was executed on the site of No. 111, at the crossroads with rue de l'Arbre-Sec (a name which indicates the presence of a gallows at one time). At 70 years old, poor Brunehaut was tied by her hair to the tail of a wild horse. It was also at this crossroads that the Battle of the Fronde started in 1648, when a riot broke out following an increase in taxes. As for Cyrano de Bergerac, he was born in rue des Prouvaires, and Molière was born in rue Sauval (not at 31 rue du Pont-Neuf, as one 19th-century fraudster tried to con people into thinking, in order to make his house rise in value!). At No. 43 in rue Sauval there is also a shop, La Galcante, which is like a little museum dedicated to the press, housing copies of every daily newspaper and magazine since the beginning of the century. The *Fontaine du Trahoir* on the corner was rebuilt in the 18th century by Soufflot and No. 115 has been a chemist's since 1715.

★ **Rue de la Ferronnerie:** in the 17th century, this road was a narrow extension of rue St-Honoré. It was here, at No. 11, on 14 May 1610, that Henri IV was assassinated by Ravaillac in front of an inn bearing the prophetic name *'Au Cœur Couronné Percé d'une Fleche'* ('The Crowned Heart Pierced by an Arrow'). Poor old Henri was rather unlucky: 50 years earlier a previous king had ordered the road to be widened, but the work was never carried out. As a result, Henri's carriage was caught in traffic allowing Ravaillac the time to fulfil his task. Ravaillac had arrived on foot from Angoulême in order to assassinate the king, having been ordered to do so in a dream. When he got to Paris, however, he had another dream telling him not to kill the king and he set off back home. At Étampes, a further dream convinced him that the crime was necessary, so he went ahead with his plan! As punishment for the assassination he was cut into five pieces.

Today this is a pedestrian street with trendy boutiques, and few people notice the marble plaque which bears the arms of France and Navarre, in memory of the departed Henri.

★ **Fontaine des Innocents:** this is the only surviving fountain from the Renaissance era in Paris. The work of Jean Goujon, from a design by Pierre Lescot, initially it had only three sides because it was joined to a church next to the Cemetery of the Innocents. At the end of the 18th century, when the cemetery was removed, the church was demolished and the land was handed over to Les Halles, the fountain was moved and a fourth side was sculpted in the same style as the other three. When the fruit and vegetable markets were moved into one of the Baltard pavilions, however, the fountain was moved again, this time to its current site. Tourists, punks and small-time dealers now occupy the area during long summer evenings.

★ **Rue St-Denis** *(up to Étienne-Marcel):* this is one of the oldest streets in Paris. The tumbrels (horsedrawn carts), taking condemned men and women to the gibbet at Montfaucon, passed along this route. It was also the 'royal way' along which sovereigns made their triumphal entrance into Paris after being crowned – and also the one they took to be buried at the Basilica of St-Denis. These processions were the cause of great rejoicing, and wine and milk would flow from the fountains. Even the windows were rented out at very high prices so that people could watch the parades go by. There was a saying that: 'anyone who comes down this way in happiness will go back up in sadness'.

The rue St-Denis has always been a lively street, with plenty of trading and an enormous, noisy crowd milling about all year round. At one time beartamers and *trouvères* (poets) dazzled passers-by with their talents, whilst the streets all around bore witness to a myriad of professions and businesses.

Many streets still have their original names, representing the trade that was carried out there: the rue des Lombards (pawnbrokers, originally from Lombardy), the rue de la Cossonnerie (*cossons* handled stolen goods) and the rue de la Grande-Truanderie (which means the 'street of the great swindle'!). The development of Les Halles and the great building project carried out by Haussmann resulted in the disappearance of local trades and craftspeople. Shops were transformed into fruit and vegetable depots or into storage refrigerators for butter.

When the market of Les Halles moved to Rungis in 1969, however, the small businesses returned, taking over the former banana warehouses and other depots. Nowadays, boutiques selling the latest clothes, retro or hip, furniture shops, gadget boutiques and avant-garde hair-stylists, are once more bringing in the crowds. The area has almost regained the liveliness which it knew in the Middle Ages, except that it has been rather strangely stripped of its residents, as is reflected at St-Leu, the only church in rue St-Denis, which has lost its status as a parish.

Although the building work in the avenue Victoria, the rue de Rivoli, rue Rambuteau, rue Étienne-Marcel, rue Turbigo and rue Réaumur has destroyed many of the old houses, there are still several which are worthy of attention. Take a look at those between rue des Prêcheurs and rue du Cygne where there is a harmonious merging of different styles: gables from the Middle Ages, stone skylights from the 17th century and eaves from the 18th century.

★ **Rue du Jour:** this is the former 'ring road' within Philippe Auguste's city walls. Charles V had a home built here, known as the *Séjour du Roi* (the King's Retreat), and the 'Jour' was retained for the street name. At No. 4 stands the Hôtel de Royaumont. The present building is a reconstruction of the one dating from 1612, although the porch and the cellars are original.

★ **Church of St-Eustache:** one of the finest churches in Paris, its construction deserves a mention. In the 13th century, Jean Allais (head of the craft guild for the mystery plays) loaned Philippe Auguste – who was short of cash – a sum which the king repaid by authorizing him to take one *denier* (French currency of the time) for each basket of fish sold at Les Halles. He took so much that he suffered from remorse and built a little chapel dedicated to St Agnes. The little chapel was enlarged when, in the hope that their wealth would bring them closer to heaven, the merchants of Les Halles adopted the church.

St-Eustache owes something to the plan and proportions of Notre-Dame. Due to lack of money it was to take more than a century to complete, with the façade incomplete until the mid–18th century, and is built in the classical style, whilst the structure and interior are Gothic and the decor is Renaissance. There have been a few famous parishioners including Richelieu (who was baptized here in 1586) and Louis XIV, who took his First Communion here in 1649.

The church of St-Eustache also has remarkable acoustics. It's well worth going along to the organ concerts which take place here or the choirs of the High Mass on Sunday (11am High Mass with the great organ and the choir of St-Eustache; from 5.30pm to 6pm the great organ, followed by a mass). Musicians have always appreciated this church; in 1855 Berlioz heard his *Te Deum* here for the first time, whilst Liszt had his *Messe de Gran* perfomed here in 1886.

A swift mass was held at the St-Eustace on 21 February 1673 for a certain Jean-Baptiste Poquelin (better known as the playwright Molière). His profession was officially recorded as upholsterer, because as an actor he had no right to a religious service.

Inside are remarkable stained-glass windows and many high-quality works. Starting from the left (from the entrance in rue du Jour) are the *Martyre de Saint Eustache* by Simon Vouet and a fine *Adoration des Mages* by Rubens (or by someone from his school). In the choir chapel, successively displayed are the *Extase de Madeleine* by Manetti and *Les Disciples d'Emmaüs* (school of Rubens). The stained-glass windows of the choir date from the 17th century from designs reputedly drawn by Philippe de Champaigne. There is a curious stained-glass window close to the door leading out of the choir stalls, donated by the butchers' corporation. The great organs comprise no fewer than 7,000 pipes. There is an amazing ribbed vault which is 33.5m (110ft) high, and the whole building has a unity of style which is exceedingly rare. The pillars have been richly sculpted, and heavy, majestic keystones hang from the choir and the ambulatory. In a chapel on the left-hand aisle, don't miss the touching modern, naïve sculpture, *Le Départ des Fruits et Légumes du Cœur de Paris* (1969), by Raymond Mason – a poignant testimony to the exodus of the market traders to Rungis.

★ **La Bourse du Commerce:** along with the surrounding streets, La Bourse (the Stock Exchange) offers some interesting archictectural features. The Hôtel de la Reine, built for Catherine de Médicis, originally stood here. Razed to the ground, it was replaced in the 18th century by a corn exchange which was succeeded by the present rotunda in 1889, designed in the neo-Classical style. The semi-circular rue de Viarmes is lined with buildings decorated with Doric columns. The fluted column at the side of the Stock Exchange is the last vestige of the Hôtel de la Reine. It had been built to slake Catherine de Médicis's passion for astrology, as it housed the observatory of Ruggieri, her astronomer. After the St Bartholomew's Day Massacre, the queen, thrown into a panic by the eccentric Ruggieri's sorcery and his predictions such as 'You will die near St-Germain', moved into St-Eustache.

Further on, the rue du Louvre marks the beginning of the Palais-Royal quarter.

In front of St-Eustache lies the **Jardin des Halles**, a vast, formal garden that plays an important social and cultural role in the community. François-Xavier Lalanne was entrusted with the design of what he defined as an 'urban garden', where plants grow from trellises and arbours. In the centre of this green space lies a circular area, with a gentle slope, punctuated by strips of lawn. With a wonderful view of St-Eustache, this is a popular meeting place.

An enormous sculpted monolith (designed by Henri de Miller) in the shape of a monumental head accompanied by a hand stands here, fitting in perfectly with the grand materials chosen for this site. On the left (as you look at the church), a sundial reflects onto a curved concrete slab, situated in an area which children have transformed into a skateboard park. Behind there are glass pyramids housing a tropical greenhouse, the largest greenhouse built in Europe since the 19th century. You can go inside or just admire the palms, papaya and banana trees from the outside. There are also plenty of green spaces accessible to the public, with trees and pretty modern fountains. It is a delightful place to stroll around, away from the mad frenzy of the adjacent Forum des Halles. (The various points of interest situated underneath the Garden of Les Halles are dealt with below; *see* 'Forum des Halles'.)

★ **Pavillon des Arts:** 101 rue Rambuteau, terrasse Lautréamont 75001. ☎ 01-42-33-82-50. Close to the Church of St-Eustache. Metro and RER: Les Halles or Châtelet. Bus: Nos. 29 and 38. Open daily except Monday and public holidays, from 11.30am to 6.30pm. The Pavilion of the Arts museum regularly organizes temporary exhibitions dedicated to the heritage of Paris. It houses all forms of art – painting, graphic arts, sculpture, applied arts and photography – and covers all cultures, from Antiquity to the 20th century.

★ **Jardin des Enfants aux Halles:** 105 rue Rambuteau 75001. ☎ 01-45-08-07-18. Metro and RER: Les Halles or Châtelet. Bus: Nos. 42, 72, 73, 80 and 83. This garden is for 7 to 11 year-olds. Try to go in the afternoon as schools use it in the mornings. The opening hours are a little complicated: 10am to 4pm on Wednesday and Saturday all year round; Tuesday, Thursday and Friday, 9am to noon and 2pm to 4pm (November to March), until 6pm (April to June) and until 7pm (July and August). Closed Mondays and on Friday mornings in the summer. Access every hour during peak times (maximum stay 1 hour). Entry fee 2.50F. At weekends, you need to get there early and queue (you'll be given a token). An event organizer is on hand on Wednesday, Saturday and Sunday. There's a fun walk organized around the mazes and lots of games on offer as well as a swimming pool, the 'volcanic world' or the 'wild world', and the seven musical steps, among other marvels created by Claude Lalanne, wife of the sculptor and designer of the Garden of Les Halles. A victim of its own success, the garden can only hold 60 children at any one time and there's often quite a queue.

★ Around St-Eustache, things hot up a bit at night as the large food factories work 24-hour shifts. Get up at 6am to experience the goings on in **rue Montmartre** and **rue Montorgueil**, the last vestiges of the original activities of Les Halles, with wholesale butchers' shops. Some cafés open at 4.30am.

1ST

FORUM DES HALLES

Out of the famous *trou des Halles* (the local nickname for the large space left behind after the markets were moved to Rungis) rose the Forum des Halles. Large glass galleries surrounding a patio allow natural light to enter the first two levels of the shopping centre. The Forum is full of shops selling clothing, jewellery, perfume and gadgets, plus a number of restaurants and Fnac (a huge chainstore selling books, CDs and computer software).

After initial problems, the commercial profit per square metre is now twice the national average. Its concrete architecture and maze of internal streets on four levels attracts plenty of young people, although some find it a rather Kafkaesque experience! Those who love it are drawn to its liveliness – the kind of atmosphere which inspired the film *Subway* by Luc Besson.

A short tour round the Forum

On the ground floor, situated on the Pierre-Lescot side, are screens providing information about the museums, monuments, exhibitions and workshops available.

★ **The patio:** when the weather is fine people gather around the marble *Pygmalion* by Julio Silva. Sometimes you'll find an orchestra playing here.

★ On Level 3, rue des Piliers, there's a long, coloured **fresco** by Moretti tracing the progress of Man since prehistory. Look for the faces of Victor Hugo and Louis Armstrong.

The New Forum

The areas around the Place Carrée, underneath the Jardin des Halles between the Forum and the Stock Exchange, are constructed from stone, glass and grass and provide a welcome relief from all the concrete. One can sense how the architects have tried to respond to the practical demands as well as the aesthetic requirements of such a busy and important space. The resolutely modern, large-scale design is quite daring and the concept of turning it into a space for cultural and sports events, rather than an arrivals hall for the large Châtelet-les-Halles station situated underneath it, can only be applauded. There is a video library, a disco, a swimming pool and a photo space, all of which provide a welcome relief from the 'everything to buy' philosophy of the neighbouring Forum.

★ **Forum des Images:** 2 Grande Galerie du Forum des Halles (between the swimming pool and the place Carrée) 75001. ☎ 01-44-76-62-00 or 01-40-26-34-40 (recorded information). Website: www.forumdesimages.com.

Open 1pm to 9pm (10pm on Thursday). Closed Monday. Entry fee 30F, reduced rate 25F for under 30s, students, the unemployed and over 60s. It is also possible to take out a subscription. When it was created ten years ago, this place was one of the first cultural establishments in France to specialize in the field of audiovisual technology.

In this somewhat futuristic environment, around 40 individual video screens allow you to select your programme directly. You can view almost anything: TV programmes, old Gaumont news, video documentaries or films. There is a very up-to-date search-by-subject facility, and all the documents are connected with the city of Paris (around 6,000). Viewing is limited to 2 hours for non-subscribers and although you don't need to make an appointment, you may have to queue; subscribers don't have to wait. There are several sorts of subscription allowing free access to the whole of the Forum des Images.

Opened in October 1999, the Cyberport is a sort of cyber café dedicated to the Internet and multimedia. You'll find around 10 workstations and, more importantly, highly competent training staff. The entry fee includes half an hour at a terminal, and whilst you are there you can open an e-mail account.

There is also a videothèque showing unreleased films and films on current affairs, with a different theme each month. Access is included in the entry fee. Sessions run from 2.30pm until 9pm (beginning of the last session). The Forum also organizes and produces a series of festivals, including the *Rencontres Internationales de Cinéma à Paris* designed to promote previously unreleased films, the annual multimedia festival and *Les Rendez-vous sur le Cinéma* on Wednesday, Thursday and Friday at 7pm.

★ **Médiathèque Musicale de Paris:** Forum des Halles, 8 porte St-Eustache 75001. ☎ 01-55-80-75-30/32. Open Tuesday to Saturday noon to 7pm. Yearly subscriptions (valid for the whole of the Paris library network) of 200F allow you to borrow CDs while videos cost 400F. Audio tapes are free. A collection of 30,000 CDs, 5,000 cassettes, 1,800 videos, 8,000 books on music and 10,000 music scores are available on loan. You can borrow five of each type, plus five books, for three weeks or two videos for a week only. They have a very wide selection of works covering all styles of music.

★ **The swimming pool:** 10 place de la Rotonde, porte du Jour, Level 3. ☎ 01-42-36-98-44. Open Tuesday, Thursday and Friday 11.30am to 10pm,

Monday 11.30am to 8pm, Wednesday 10am to 7pm and at weekends 9am to 5pm. A 50m (165ft) pool. Part of it is equipped with lanes for serious swimmers. It's a semi-private pool, so it's quite expensive.

TOWARDS LE CHÂTELET

★ **St-Germain-l'Auxerrois:** place du Louvre. Metro: Louvre. At first sight you might think you have two churches here side by side, but the one on the left is actually the town hall for the 1st arrondissement. No doubt more than one couple about to get married have gone to the wrong one by mistake!

The real church dates from the 12th century and used to be the parish church of the kings of France in the 14th century. A Gothic masterpiece, the nave displays a great sculptural richness, and the detail on the gate touches on the humorous – note the imp trying to blow out the candle which St Genevieve is holding in her hand. Interesting architectural diversities include a Renaissance gate, a Roman bell-tower and a flamboyant 15th-century Gothic porch.

The Revolution transformed the place into a fodder store, before Baltard and Lassus gave it its current appearance. The bells in the tower had the sad privilege of sounding the alarm for the St Bartholomew Massacre. Molière got married here and many artists and architects have been buried within the church. On the buttresses, which end in miniuature steeples, is one of the richest bestiaries ever seen, depicting wolves, bears, dogs, monstrous birds and griffins. The gargoyles also feature in mysterious scenes involving animals.

Inside the church there are a number of works worthy of interest. On the left, as you come in, there is a Flemish altarpiece from the 16th century. The chapel on the right, known as the parish chapel, has an altar and Gothic altarpieces, frescoes and interesting statues from the 13th to 15th centuries. Also note the superbly sculpted royal workbench and throne, and the fine 17th-century organ case.

★ **La Samaritaine:** 19 rue de la Monnaie 75001. Metro: Pont-Neuf. Open daily except Sunday, from 9.30am to 7pm. Late night opening on Thursday until 10pm. Located in 3 buildings.

The name of this famous department store comes from the enormous water pump that Henri IV had built at the end of the Pont-Neuf depicting the women of Samaria offering Jesus a drink of water. It was designed to supply water to the fountain of the Croix du Tahoir, as well as the Louvre and the Jardin des Tuileries. In 1869, a certain Ernest Cognacq sub-let a café on the corner of the rue de la Monnaie and rue du Pont-Neuf and began trading. After barely two years, he had established a nice little nest egg and married Louise Jay, the head saleswoman of the clothing department of the *Bon Marché* (another department store). In 1903 he built the current *Samaritaine*, in art-nouveau style. Although many of the elements of the original decoration have faded or disappeared, it is possible to imagine what Ernest Cognacq meant when he said: 'The department store of our age must not be afraid to be showy. Quite the contrary, it needs to attract attention and bring in customers!'

From the fifth floor of the shop, you can admire the superb glass roof and its iron Art Nouveau frame. You can also stop and eat at the Toupary restaurant (*see* 'Where to eat').

Le Sand's cafeteria is also on this floor as well and is open during shop hours. For around 50F you can eat well, but if the weather's fine, don't miss the terrace restaurant on the 10th floor, with its superb views over Paris. Open Easter to October, except when it's raining.

It is also worth visiting the eighth floor of Shop 2, where you'll find the story of 'The Exemplary Life of Ernest Cognacq and Louise Jay', the founders of the store, told through figurines.

★ **Quai de la Mégisserie:** Metro: Châtelet or Pont-Neuf. A paradise of flowers, plants, budgerigars, canaries and other singing birds. There used to be many other animals here – dogs, cats, rabbits, squirrels, monkeys, white mice, fish and tortoises – but recently the police closed down this animal market, for hygiene reasons.

Nearby, at No. 31 rue du Pont-Neuf, a plaque commemorates the birth of Molière in 1620. Rather strangely, at No. 96 rue St-Honoré there is another plaque commemorating the same event but in 1622 (the second date is the correct one!).

★ **Place du Châtelet:** on the whole this area of Paris is the one which has undergone the most change. Today there is nothing left as a reminder of the sinister Châtelet prison, with its towers and dungeons, which was demolished at the beginning of the 19th century. There are also no traces of the butchers' blocks and stalls of the Grande Boucherie, the oldest market on the Right Bank. In 1860, during the great Haussmann renovation projects, the square's two great theatres were built.

For decades the Théâtre du Châtelet was the most beautiful 'dreaming machine in France', transporting audiences away from reality into the all-singing, all-dancing world of operettas.

On the site of the Théâtre de la Ville (formerly the Sarah Bernhardt) ran the little street where the poet Gérard de Nerval hanged himself in the early hours of one cold morning. The priest accepted that his death was an accident so that he could be buried at Père-Lachaise Cemetery (*see* '20th arrondissement').

ÎLE DE LA CITÉ (1ST ARRONDISSEMENT)

It's well worth taking the time to stroll around the Île de la Cité. In spite of the daily influx of thousands of tourists rushing to visit the imperial monuments, you can't help thinking about that little tribe, the *Parisii*, who lived peacefully on this small island over 2,000 years ago. The Île stretches over two arrondissements – Notre-Dame is covered in the section on the 4th arrondissement.

★ **Ste-Chapelle:** 4 boulevard du Palais 75001. ☎ 01-53-73-78-50. The high chapel can be visited by appointment only ☎ 01-53-73-78-51. Metro: Cité, Saint-Michel of Châtelet. Bus: nos. 21, 27, 38, 85, 96. Enter through the Palais de Justice (on the left in the courtyard), then go around the chapel. Open daily 9.30am to 6.30pm April to September and 10am to 5pm

October to March for individual visitors; last entry 30 minutes before closing. Closed on certain public holidays. Entry fee 35F; reduced (18 to 25 years) 23F; free for under 12s. You can buy a ticket for both the Ste-Chapelle and the Conciergerie (50F). There are guided tours (several daily of which two are at a fixed time: 11am and 3pm) as well as conference visits organized by Les Monuments Historiques (information ☎ 01-44-61-20-69).

A jewel of Gothic architecture, completed in 1248, the Ste-Chapelle has a gigantic reliquary, a perfect example of craftsmanship from the Middle Ages. It was built by St Louis to provide a home for the Crown of Thorns and a fragment of the True Cross. These relics are now in Notre-Dame.

The Ste-Chapelle was used as a grain store and an archive storage site during the French Revolution. Restored in 1837, it became a victim of its own success: humidity damaged the paintings and the stained-glass windows deteriorated. A ventilation system was installed to counteract the humidity and gradually the frescoes were repaired.

The chapel is a unique testimony to medieval art. The most striking thing is the flight of fancy in the stained-glass windows. The building comprises two superimposed chapels of which the upper level communicated directly with the Palais de Justice.

– *The lower chapel:* low-ceilinged, this chapel was used by servants, soldiers and the working classes. The floor is constructed from tombstones.

– *The upper chapel:* the royal family's place of worship. Superbly restored, this chapel boasts an extraordinary panorama of 15-m (50-ft) high stained-glass windows, punctuated by small, fine columns. These frail stone structures are only capable of supporting the building because the stone is cut in the direction of the quarry vein. The superb stained-glass work depicts over 1,000 scenes from the Old and New Testaments, and the colours and delicate images make it one of the world's oldest and finest examples of stained-glass work. Standing against the pillars are the statues of the Apostles – the recess was reserved for the king. In 1871 the Sainte-Chapelle narrowly escaped being burnt down when Communists doused it in petrol.

★ **Palais de Justice:** boulevard du Palais 75001. ☎ 01-44-32-50-00. Guided tours available. To watch a trial, go between 1.30 and 6pm, except on Sunday. Avoid Tuesday, as this is the day for schoolchildren. Entry is free.

The Law Courts don't attract the same crowds of visitors that go to the Ste-Chapelle and the Conciergerie), but there is definitely something fascinating about seeing justice at work, if your French is good enough.

For something more calming outside of the lunchtime period, you can visit the two immense naves of the salle des Pas-Perdus and the Chambre Dorée (Gilded Chamber), which was undoubtedly St Louis's bedroom. In the salle des Pas-Perdus, on the statue of the lawyer Berryer to the right of the figure representing Law, there is a small tortoise, symbolic of the speed of justice! Don't forget to look at the Palais de Justice clock which has been telling Parisians the time for over 600 years. Its face, which is the original, is the oldest in Paris.

The Palais was once the dwelling place of the medieval Capetian Kings until it underwent significant modifications. During the Revolution, the revolutionary tribunal sat in the Chambre Dorée (the highest chamber of the civil court) and it was here that Fouquier-Tinville sent Marie-Antoinette and many others to the scaffold. Although defence counsel were allowed to speak at the beginning of the tribunal's proceedings, the whole process was very soon reduced to a sort of ticket system for the guillotine. Once inside the Conciergerie, there was little chance of ever coming out in one piece.

★ **Conciergerie:** 1 quai de l'Horloge 75001 ☎ 01-53-73-78-50. On the corner with boulevard du Palais. Open April to September 9.30am to 6.30pm and October to March 10am to 5pm. Last entry 30 minutes before closing. Same entry fees as the Ste-Chapelle. Guided tours and conference visits are available (same details apply as with the Ste-Chapelle).

To mark the bicentenary of the Revolution, the cells in this prison were renovated and several dungeons were re-opened. Almost all the heroes or victims of the Revolution (the latter having previously been the former!) passed through here before losing their heads. The most famous inmate was Marie-Antoinette, but Ravaillac and Montgomery (who accidentally killed Henri II) also spent some time here.

The Conciergerie takes its name from its *concierge*, a powerful lord who collected the rents from the ground floor shops of the Palais de Justice. Later on, when the building became a prison, he also collected the rent for the dungeons and the furniture inside them.

– *The outside:* on the quays, there are four fine towers. Their simplicity lends a certain majesty to the banks along this part of the Seine. The foot of the towers originally used to be submerged in the water and one of the two twin towers held Fouquier-Tinville during the Terror. The one on the right was known as 'Bonbec' (which means something like 'good mouth'), because this was where the prisoners were made to talk!

On the corner of the quay stands the Tour de l'Horloge, erected in the 14th century. This was the first clock tower in Paris and has an elegantly sculpted dial which still works.

– *The interior* (entrance through the quai de l'Horloge): this leads to the salle des Gardes, which then extends into the rue de Paris. On the left is the vast salle des Gens-d'Armes. These three Gothic spaces possess some very fine arches. On two pillars of the salle des Gens-d'Armes, you can see the level that the Seine reached in 1910. The pillars were added in the 19th century to help the building withstand the test of time. This hall was used as a refectory, and at the back were the kitchens with their vast chimneys. The rue de Paris was originally used as a dormitory by poor prisoners – those with money had an individual cell and were known as *pistoliers* (the *pistole* was a unit of currency).

The condemned men and women would have to cross the prisoners' gallery to have their hair cut evenly before they were loaded into carts for the final leg of their journey. Whilst here you can visit the dungeon where Marie-Antoinette spent two-and-a-half months before her execution in 1793. Whether it was just amazing coincidence or part of a malicious plot, less than a year later, Robespierre, one of her most fervent accusers, was to occupy the dungeon next door. The Chapelle des Girondins was once the setting for a night of partying for 22 prisoners who were going to die at dawn. Wax figures are used to bring the dungeons to life and there is a permanent exhibition on the Revolution (with audio visuals).

★ **Square du Vert-Galant:** at the end of the Île de la Cité, the Square du Vert-Galant is like a ship's figurehead, a meeting point popular with fishermen, lovers and tramps. Behind the square, a staircase leads onto Paris's oldest bridge which, paradoxically, is known as the Pont-Neuf (meaning 'New Bridge'). Two elegant Louis XIII houses give way to the charming **Place Dauphine**. Only the houses at Nos. 14 and 26 still retain the primitive appearance of the houses from that period.

– **Bateaux-Vedettes du Pont-Neuf:** boarding at Square du Vert-Galant. ☎ 01-46-33-98-38. Boats depart every 30 minutes. In summer, trips are from 10am to noon, 1.30pm to 6.30pm and 9pm to 10.30pm. In winter the timetable varies a bit because the departures are every 45 minutes; it's advisable to ring first.

The word *bateau-mouche* comes from the engines of the boats which were manufactured at la Mouche, a suburb of Lyon – nothing to do with flies!

★ **Pont-Neuf:** as its name fails to indicate, this is the oldest bridge in Paris. When the first stone was laid, on 31 May 1578, Henri III, dressed in black, held a set of ivory rosary beads shaped as skulls and simply burst into tears. He had just been to the burial of one of his favourite beaux, who had died in a duel. Originally the bridge was known as the Pont des Pleurs (Bridge of Tears), but its construction was not completed until 1607.

Originally built to improve communications between the Louvre and the Abbey of St-Germain, the Pont-Neuf was the first bridge without any houses and the first to have pavements. Frequently used, the bridge became a very fashionable and lively place where merchants, fire-eaters, bear-tamers and cabaret artists would come and congregate. At any hour of the day you'd be sure to find 'a monk, a white horse and a whore'. Prisoners were executed here by hanging or decapitation, and it was the height of fashion to fight a duel on the bridge.

The tradition of Parisian cabaret singers, known for their criticism of political life, was born here. 'Le Savoyard' was the first artist to note that the public applauded far more when he poked fun at lords of the Court than when he recited old songs from the Middle Ages. Others imitated him and soon the Pont-Neuf became the only place in Paris where people made fun of everything – for example, the king, his ministers, the clergy and the police. The young Molière was brought here by his grandfather and no doubt he found plenty to feed his imagination. Under Louis XIV, the least malicious names applied to Mme de Maintenon were 'the old cow' or 'the king's dirty tart'. Those who had disgraced themselves would often come along to encourage the cabaret singers. Even the Revolution couldn't discourage this popular attraction; it was Napoleon's police who eventually cleared the Pont-Neuf of all these anti-establishment activities. In 1818, the statue of Napoleon in the place Vendôme was removed and the bronze was melted down to recast the statue of Henri IV which had been swept away by the Revolution. The sculptor, Mesnel, a fierce supporter of Bonaparte, placed a little statue of the emperor in Henri's arms!

Today it's the longest bridge in Paris. In 1985, it had the honour of being wrapped in cloth for a couple of weeks by the modern American artist

Christo. Pissarro, Derain and Victor Hugo have all also rendered homage to this amazing monument through their art. in 1999, it underwent an 'end of the century' makeover which brought a gleam to the stone. Once again it is a new Pont-Neuf!

★ **The booksellers:** the *bouquinistes* (antiquarian booksellers) have been here since the Pont-Neuf was first constructed. At the time, books were very expensive and so the second-hand market flourished from about 1539 onwards. To control the book pedlars, who sometimes broke the law, it was decided, in the 17th century, to keep them in the area around the Pont-Neuf. Following changes to the law, little boxes started appearing in which the booksellers would display their wares and by the turn of the century it was obvious that they were here to stay.

Today, there are no booksellers actually on the bridge. Instead, the boxes (which only measure 4 x 2m/13 x 6ft), painted in bottle green, stretch out for over 3km (2 miles) along both the Left and the Right Bank. There are around 242 of them, representing around 300,000 books – the largest open-air bookshop in the world.

WHERE TO GO FOR A DRINK

🍸 **Flann O'Brien** (map C2, **70**): 6 rue Bailleul 75001. ☎ 01-42-60-13-58. Metro: Châtelet or Louvre-Rivoli. Open daily 4pm to 2am. Closed at Christmas. 22F for half a pint of beer, 38F for a pint. One of the first Irish pubs in Paris. Has a beautiful stone cellar. People come here for the craíc, to drink a pint of Guinness and listen to traditional Irish music. Every evening, except Monday and Thursday, there's a jam session.

🍴 🍸 **Le Café du Pont 9** (map D2, **72**): 27–29 rue du Pont-Neuf 75001. ☎ 01-40-26-30-74. Metro: Pont-Neuf. Closes at 2am. Closed for 2 days at Christmas. Set menus at 70 and 80F served at lunchtime and in the evening. À la carte, budget for around 150F. This is an old Les Halles bistro converted into a restaurant with singing and dancing every Wednesday evening, a writing workshop on Sunday at 4pm and Tuesday at 7pm, music some weekends, a florist annex for those last-minute flower purchases, and above all, some very good things on the menu – service stops at midnight. Like the bric-à-brac decor, the clientele is a mixture – Les Halles stalwarts, lawyers, doctors and students.

🍸 **Bar de l'Hôtel Costes** (map A-B1, **74**): 239 rue St-Honoré 75001. ☎ 01-42-44-50-25. Metro: Tuileries. Cocktails around 70F. Located in the fashion and business quarter, this bar draws suits and those working in the fashion world. The restaurant is full every evening, and the patio opens as soon as the weather allows. Evening dress is not insisted on as long as you're hip, known or with someone who is! Many people just come for a drink as the prices are steep.

🍸 **Colette** (map B1, **73**): 213 rue St-Honoré 75001. ☎ 01-55-35-33-90 or 93 for the bar. Metro: Tuileries or Pyramides. Open 10.30am to 7.30pm. Closed Sunday and public holidays. Bottled water starts at 8F. In the basement you'll find what people say is the most 'in' boutique of the moment, selling books, hi-tech gadgets, cosmetics and fashion items. This is the leading 'water bar' in Paris (60 types of mineral water from all over the world), but it also offers delicious pastries by Jean-Paul Hévin, vegetable flans, pasta dishes and compotes. You'll either love it or hate it.

🍸 **Banana Café** (map D2, **75**): 13–15 rue de la Ferronnerie 75001. ☎ 01-42-33-35-31. Metro: Châtelet.

Open daily 4.30pm to dawn. Drinks around 30F to 40F. This is a showbiz bar with a gay tendency (in every sense of the word). Mainly regulars, but it doesn't take long to become one. Tropical decor and a great atmosphere on every floor: on the ground floor there's techno music, while in the basement a pianist plays well-known songs. Famous for its theme nights – each wilder than the last. Non-stop happy hour from 6.30pm to 9.30pm: two drinks for the price of one.

🍸 **Tropic Café** (map D2, **77**): 66 rue de Lombards 75001. Metro: Châtelet. ☎ 01-40-13-92-62. Open every evening 5pm until very late. Beers from 22F, other drinks at 48F. The Tropic is a kind of anti-Banana Café (see above), a showbiz bar which has become impossible to get into because everyone has already got in. No go-go dancers here, no stars, but the staff are friendly and the clientele is fairly varied. The terrace is just as pleasant in winter as in summer. Bingo every Wednesday, DJs on Friday and Saturday for the latest house and garage sounds.

✕ 🍸 **Carr's** (map B1, **76**): 1 rue du Mont-Thabor 75001. 01-42-60-60-26. Metro: Tuileries. Open daily all year round, noon to 2am. Lunch menu at 100F. Set menu at 135F, 155F menu also available. À la carte, budget for around 220F. The Irish pubs are not all full of hordes of thirsty football supporters, getting off the coach with scarves and banners. At Carr's the setting is cosy, with a lovely chimney and a large library. It is slightly reminiscent of the inside of a student bar at a traditional British university. Lovers of whisky will be in seventh heaven with the wide range on offer – around 40F per glass. If you're hungry there are sandwiches to soak it all up (from 30F to 48F), as well as Irish specialities such as Irish stew.

🍸 **Le Fumoir** (map C2, **84**): 6 rue de l'Amiral-de-Coligny 75001. ☎ 01-42-92-00-24. Metro: Louvre-Rivoli or Châtelet. Open to 2am. Set menus at 105F at lunchtime, 170F in the evening. À la carte, budget for around 200F. Cocktails from 65F, this drops to 35F during Happy Hour between 6pm and 8pm. A stylish ambiance is guaranteed in this splendid café strategically located on the place du Louvre. The library corner, with international newspapers, and the view over the place, make it worth a detour. Unfortunately, the cooking is not up to much so it's best to go for brunch or in the afternoon.

GOING OUT

🍸 **Le Comptoir Paris-Marrakech** (map C2, **45**): 37 rue Berger 75001. ☎ 01-40-26-26-66. Metro: Les Halles. Open 11am to 2am (3am at weekends). For brunch or a 'sexy' drink such as a tequila with ginger ale, allow between 55F and 84F. Cocktails during the Happy Hour (6 to 8pm) cost 35F. Nice terrace, French-oriental atmosphere. See entry in 'Where to eat? – chic' for more details.

WHERE TO HEAR JAZZ

– **Le Sunset** (map D2, **79**): 60 rue des Lombards 75001. ☎ 01-40-26-46-60. Metro: Châtelet. Open daily 9.30am until dawn. Entry from 50F to 100F, according to who's playing. Drinks from 25F. This little underground jazz club has forged a solid clientele of *aficionados*. From doctors to models, a whole world of jazz fans meet in the basement to enjoy the music. Fusion, classical jazz, free jazz or jazz rock, there's something for everyone (three 1-hour sets from 10pm to 9pm on Sunday). Although people listen in an almost religious silence, the atmosphere is fairly relaxed and big names quite often come to jam as surprise guests. You can also dine in the restaurant (89F and 130F menus).

– **Le Duc des Lombards** (map D2, **80):** 42 rue des Lombards 75001. ☎ 01-42-33-22-88. Metro: Châtelet. Open daily 7.30pm to 3am (4am at the weekend). Occasionally closed Sunday. Entry 80F to 100F, according to what's on. Drinks, which are not obligatory, from 28F. The first set starts at 10pm. Since its beginnings in 1985, this jazz pub has never looked back, staging good shows with prestigious jazz musicians. If you're planning to stick around, ask for the loyalty card, which means every fifth concert is free.

– **Le Petit Opportun** (map D3, **81**): 15 rue des Lavandières-Ste-Opportune 75001. ☎ 01-42-36-01-36. Metro: Châtelet. Open 9pm until dawn. Closed Sunday and Monday, as well as in August. Entry 50F or 80F; drinks from 25F. Groups of friends and large families squeeze into this wonderful 13th-century cellar to listen to their favourite jazz. The place is designed to hold 35 people, but some evenings there are three times as many there. The first set starts at 10.45pm.

NIGHTCLUBS

– **Le Slow-Club** (map D2, **82):** 130 rue de Rivoli 75001. ☎ 01-42-33-84-30. E-mail: slowclub@aol.com. Metro: Châtelet or Pont-Neuf. Open 10pm until 3am (4am at the weekend). Closed Sunday, Monday and Wednesday, except the night before public holidays. Drinks are optional and cost from 19F. During the week, the entry fee is 60F; on Friday, Saturday and the night before public holidays it's 75F. There is a reduction for students under 25 (55F), except at the weekend. Jazz, blues, dixieland or rock groups every night. As the oldest jazz club in Paris, this is more than just a club, it's an institution.

– **La Scala** (map B2, **83):** 188 *bis* rue de Rivoli 75001. ☎ 01-42-61-64-00. Metro: Palais-Royal. Open daily 10.30pm to 6am. Entry 80F during the week, 100F on Saturday; free for women except Friday, Saturday and the night before public holidays. Popular with youngsters and foreigners, this is one of the most amazing discos in the capital, with six bars on three levels organized around a giant screen outlined in gold and black where Jules the DJ will display personalized messages on request. He will also play any music you want.

2ND ARRONDISSEMENT

THE BIBLIOTHÈQUE NATIONALE ● LES PASSAGES ● THE QUARTIER DE LA PRESSE

Between rue Étienne-Marcel and the Grands Boulevards there stretches a mainly working-class and highly commercial district that provides the chance to take a few picturesque walks through narrow and lively streets.

WHERE TO STAY

☆ CHEAP

Tiquetonne Hôtel (map D3, **1**): 6 rue Tiquetonne 75002. ☎ 01-42-36-94-58. Fax: 01-42-36-02-94. Metro: Étienne-Marcel or Réaumur-Sébastopol. Double rooms with washbasin 146F, or with shower and toilet 246F; almost all with double-glazing. Closed in August and between Christmas and 1 January. Close to Les Halles and the Pompidou Centre. Before booking in at this one-star hotel, take time to enjoy the calm and beauty of this area's pedestrian streets. The rooms have retained a retro style, although the bathrooms are a little more bland. Charming and very peaceful, with a warm welcome.

Hôtel Ste-Marie (map D1–2, **2**): 6 rue de la Ville-Neuve 75002. ☎ 01-42-33-21-61. Fax: 01-42-33-29-24. Metro: Bonne-Nouvelle. Double room without shower 260F, with shower and toilet 320F. Triple room with shower and toilet 450F. In a quiet street just off the Grands Boulevards, the hotel has around 20 well-equipped rooms with satellite TV and direct telephone although not all of the rooms are in the same condition. No. 8, with its open beams has a certain charm, but mind your head in the two rooms on the top floor, which are right up in the attic. These, however are quite light and airy, unlike those overlooking the courtyard. Breakfast available for children.

Hôtel des Boulevards (map D1, **3**): 10 rue de la Ville-Neuve 75002. ☎ 01-42-36-02-29. Fax: 01-42-36-15-39. Metro: Bonne-Nouvelle. Double room with separate toilet from 200F to 220F, with shower and toilet 285F, with bathroom from 310F. Twin room 320F. Direct telephone, TV and fax service. A small, unpretentious and recently renovated hotel with 18 rooms. Quiet and rather functional, close to the Opéra and Les Halles. The decor is rather anonymous, but the rooms are clean. Breakfast is included. There's a car-park 200m (220yds) from the hotel. Friendly and relaxed welcome, but rather a lot of readers have mentioned bookings which have been forgotten. Book a week to 10 days in advance. Credit cards accepted.

☆☆ MODERATE

Hôtel Bonne Nouvelle (map D1, **4**): 17 rue Beauregard 75002. ☎ 01-45-08-42-42. Fax: 01-40-26-05-81. Metro: Bonne-Nouvelle, Sentier or Strasbourg-St-Denis. Double room with washbasin 280F, with shower or bathroom from 350F to 600F. Admire the pretty screen with a *trompe-l'œil* of a building in the moonlight. Each room is individual with a mix of traditional and modern (bath, toilet, cable TV, modem sockets, direct telephone, hairdryer). Unfortunately, some are quite small and may feel little damp. One suite is ideal for four people and offers a splendid view over the Pompidou Centre, the Montparnasse Tower and the old Parisian rooftops. Very warm welcome. The breakfast, which is very good, is available in the dining area or in your bedroom.

☆☆☆ CHIC

Hôtel Vivienne (map C1, **5**): 40 rue Vivienne 75002. ☎ 01-42-33-13-26. Fax: 01-40-41-98-19. E-mail: paris@hotel-vivienne.com. Metro: Grands-Boulevards, Richelieu-Drouot or Bourse. Double room with shower 370F, with shower and toilet 450F, with bath and toilet from 470F to 515F. This hotel is very near the Hard Rock Café, the Musée Grévin, the Théâtre des Variétés and a myriad of passages and galleries. The welcome is young and friendly. The 44 rooms, which are clean and well lit, offer peace and comfort (direct telephone, satellite TV and double-glazing). No. 14 is the most popular because of its specially well-thought-out decor and because it communicates with No. 15, which means you can make it into a suite. On the fifth and sixth floors there's a fine view over Paris. Some rooms have a balcony. You can have breakfast in your room at no extra charge.

☆☆☆☆ TRÈS CHIC

Hôtel France d'Antin (map A2, **6**): 22 rue d'Antin 75002. ☎ 01-47-42-19-12. Fax: 01-47-42-11-55. Metro: 4-Septembre or Opéra; or RER: Opéra or Auber. Around 880F for a double room with bath. About 100m (330ft) from the Opéra Garnier and close to the Louvre, this is a very pleasant three-star hotel with tapestries, a pianola, and marble and armchairs in the lobby. The 30 pretty rooms are air-conditioned and have the usual creature comforts: mini-bar, TV (satellite, Canal+) and a safe.

Hôtel Victoires Opéra (ex Grand Hôtel de Besançon) (map C2, **7**): 56 rue Montorgueil 75002.

Where to stay

1 Tiquetonne Hôtel
2 Hôtel Ste-Marie
3 Hôtel des Boulevards
4 Hôtel Bonne Nouvelle
5 Hôtel Vivienne
6 Hôtel France d'Antin
7 Hôtel Victoires Opéra (*ex* Grand Hôtel de Besançon)

Where to eat

20 Au Pays de Cocagne
21 Le Petit Vendôme
22 Dilan
23 Chez Danie
24 Le Tambour
25 La Bocca
26 Bar-restaurant Les Variétés
27 Le Gavroche
28 L'Arbre à Cannelle
29 Chez Clément
30 Voyageurs du Monde, Le Restaurant
32 Le Grand Colbert
33 A Priori Thé
34 L'Ange Vin
35 La Grille Montorgueil
36 Le Moï
37 Le Canard d'Avril

Where to go for a drink/ Going out

51 Kitty O'Shea's
52 Le Café
53 The Frog and Rosbif
56 Le Rex-Club
57 Pouchla
58 Le Café Noir
59 Le Port d'Amsterdam

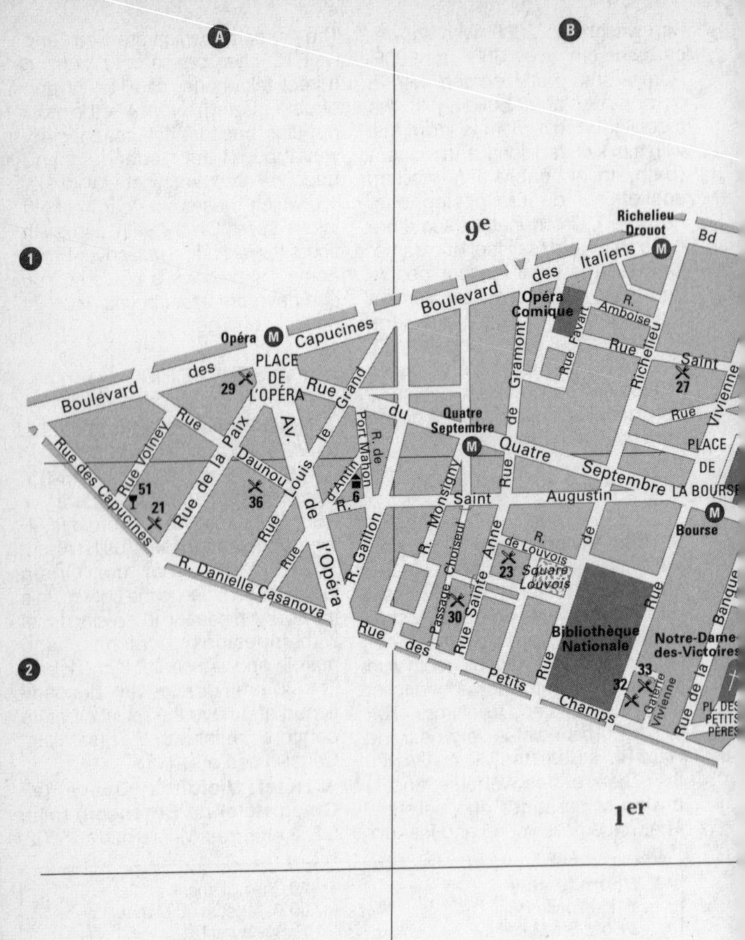
A
B
1
2
3
9e
1er
Richelieu Drouot
Bd
Italiens
des
Boulevard
Opéra Comique
R. Amboise
Rue Favart
Rue de Gramont
Rue Richelieu
Rue Saint
27
Vivienne
Opéra
Capucines
Boulevard des
PLACE DE L'OPÉRA
29
Rue du Quatre Septembre
Rue Grand
Quatre Septembre
PLACE DE LA BOURSE
Bourse
Rue Volney
51
21
Rue des Capucines
Rue de la Paix
Rue Daunou
36
Av. Louis le Grand
R. de Port Mahon
R. d'Antin
6
Rue Saint Augustin
R. Monsigny
Rue de l'Opéra
R. Gaillon
R. de Louvois
23
Square Louvois
Rue Sainte Anne
Passage Choiseul
30
Rue des Petits Champs
R. Danielle Casanova
Bibliothèque Nationale
Notre-Dame des-Victoires
Rue de la Banque
33
32
Galerie Vivienne
PL. DES PETITS PÈRES
0 100 200 yds
0 100 200 m

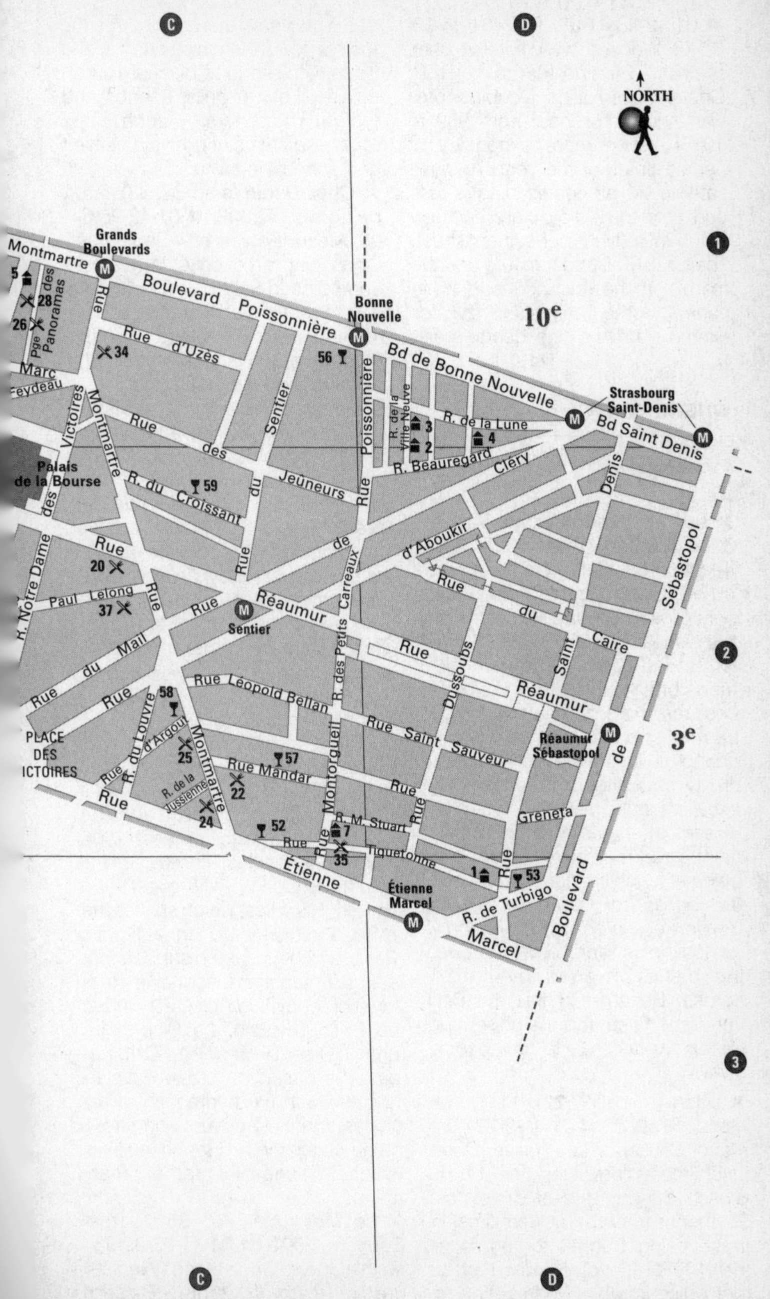
C
D
NORTH
1
2
3
C
D
10e
3e
Grands Boulevards
Bonne Nouvelle
Strasbourg Saint-Denis
Sentier
Réaumur Sébastopol
Étienne Marcel
Palais de la Bourse
PLACE DES VICTOIRES
Boulevard Poissonnière
Bd de Bonne Nouvelle
Bd Saint Denis
Boulevard de Sébastopol
Rue Réaumur
Rue d'Uzès
Rue des Jeûneurs
R. du Croissant
Rue du Sentier
Rue Poissonnière
R. de la Lune
R. Beauregard
R. de la Ville Neuve
Cléry
Rue d'Aboukir
Rue du Caire
Rue Saint Denis
Rue Dussoubs
Rue Léopold Bellan
Rue Saint Sauveur
Rue Mandar
R. M. Stuart
Rue Tiquetonne
Rue Greneta
R. de Turbigo
Rue Étienne Marcel
Rue Montorgueil
R. des Petits Carreaux
Rue Montmartre
Rue du Mail
Paul Lelong
R. Notre Dame des Victoires
R. du Louvre
d'Argout
R. de la Jussienne
Feydeau
Pge des Panoramas
56
59
58
57
52
53
34
28
26
20
37
25
22
24
35
1
2
3
4
5
7

☎ 01-42-36-41-08. Fax: 01-45-08-08-79. Website: www.hotel.vo.com. Metro: Étienne-Marcel. RER: Châtelet-Les Halles. Double rooms with shower or bath from 980 to 1080F, even more expensive at certain times of the year. All have satellite TV, air conditioning, a safe and a minibar. A tidy, clean and new hotel, in a lively pedestrian street. The Louis-Philippe furniture and the marble in the entrance add to its charm. Some rooms (No. 22, for example) have a nice lounge area.

WHERE TO EAT

☆ BUDGET

✕ **Le Petit Vendôme** (map A2, **21**): 8 rue des Capucines 75002. ☎ 01-42-61-05-88. Metro: Opéra or Madeleine. Open 7am to 8pm. Lunch only. Closed Sunday. No set menus, but dishes from 65F to 75F. Budget for around 110F. Come here for a tasty bite – they offer different cheeses and cold meats which can be made up into thick sandwiches during the lunchtime rush (they use crusty baguettes from Julien's, an excellent bakery in the 1st arrondissement – *see* '1st arrondissement'). You may have to fight for a place at lunchtime for *civet de porc au bergerac* (pork stew with Bergerac), *pied de porc grillé* (grilled pig's trotters) and tripe. Even the bar is invaded by hungry hordes. Because of this, Le Petit Vendôme, like the neighbouring Olympia, often has to turn people away.

2ND

✕ **Dilan** (map C2, **22**): 11–13 rue Mandar 75002. ☎ 01-40-26-81-04. Metro: Sentier or Les Halles. Open lunchtime and evening until 11pm. Closed Sunday and at Christmas. Set menus from 62F at lunchtime; in the evening budget for no more than 130F. A friendly Kurdish restaurant which is really worth checking out. You get a warm welcome, the food is good, there's plenty of it, and it's fairly close to traditional Turkish cuisine. Lots of grills, kebabs and typical starters such as *taramasalata*, stuffed vine leaves and aubergine caviar.

✕ **Chez Danie** (map B2, **23**): 5 rue de Louvois 75002. ☎ 01-42-96-64-05. Metro: Bourse or 4-September. Open lunchtime only, 11.30am to 3pm. Closed Saturday, Sunday and public holidays. Set menu 50F, menu at 54F. Close to the Bibliothèque Nationale, this tiny place is a godsend. Danie offers a set meal consisting of a starter, choice of two dishes and dessert (all desserts are home-made). *Foies de volaille persillade, agneau aux trois parfums, lapin en gibelotte, bœuf carottes à l'estragon* are just some of the things on offer – but it's different every day. In this area, where there are so many mediocre and expensive sandwich bars, Chez Danie's value for money speaks for itself.

✕ **Le Tambous** (map C2, **24**): 41 rue Montmartre 75002. ☎ 01-42-33-06-90. Metro: Châtelet, Les Halles or Sentier. Open daily 24 hours. Closed for two days after Christmas. Set lunch menu at 55F. À la carte, budget for at least 150F. André Camboulas, known as the 'urban bucolic', will greet you warmly. His voice, which shakes the rafters, conjures up an authentic Paris which is fast disappearing. This self-taught philosopher is a true 'creator' of bistros (his CV includes Le P'tit Gavroche, Le Pick-Clops and L'Oiseau Bariolé). Original decor is based on urban Parisian furniture with fire hydrants, paving stones, manhole covers and street name-plates. Very French cuisine which is cheerful rather than refined.

✕ **Le Moï** (map A2, **36**): 5 rue Daunou 75002. ☎ 01-47-03-92-05. Metro: Opéra. Open Monday to Saturday 12 to 10.30pm. Closed

Sunday. Set menus from 65F to 98F, served at lunchtime and in the evening. This two-floor Vietnamese restaurant looks like a colonial villa, with its walls covered in rice leaves, dark flooring, tropical maps and pretty crafts. All dishes are attractively presented. As a starter try the Van Than soup or the Bi-Bun salad with five flavours. Follow this with the delicious chicken kebabs with coconut milk, steamed dishes or other mouth-watering specialities, such as the Vietnamese fondue (120F). The set menus (starter, main course and dessert) are excellent value for money.

☆☆ MODERATE

✕ **La Grille Montorgueil** (map C2, **35**): 50 rue Montorgueil 75002. ☎ 01-42-33-21-21. Metro: Les Halles or Étienne-Marcel. Open daily at lunchtime and in the evening until midnight. On Saturday and Sunday, the lunchtime shift happily carries on until 5pm. No set menus – choose from the blackboard each day. Budget for around 120F to 140F. This 100-year-old local café offers a traditional Parisian bistro's menu. Starters include herrings, fried potatoes, *meurette* of snails or celery *rémoulade* (between 35F and 45F), followed by small dishes (from 50F to 75F) like leg of lamb, veal, *gigotine de canard*, and grilled meats and fish. Good, plain cooking. There are always a few cheap things on offer. When the weather's good, there's a nice sunny terrace.

✕ 🍸 **Bar-restaurant Les Variétés** (map C1, **26**): 12 passage des Panoramas 75002. ☎ 01-42-36-98-09. Metro: Bourse or Grands-Boulevards. Open lunchtime and evening until 10 or 11pm. Closed on Saturday and Sunday, as well as in August. Budget for 100F. Near the fast-food smells of the Grands Boulevards, well hidden under one of the most charming passages in the quarter, this is an old-style Parisian bar with bevelled mirrors and a real Formica bar, where the local workforce take refuge. A great place to stop off before or after the theatre. Starters and desserts from 25F; dish of the day at 55F.

✕ **Le Gavroche** (map B1, **27**): 19 rue St-Marc 75002. ☎ 01-42-96-89-70. Metro: Richelieu-Drouot or Bourse. Open 7am to 2am. Closed Sunday and in August. Set menu 75F, served lunchtime and evening. À la carte, budget for around 130F. This bistro sings the praises of Beaujolais. At lunchtime, auctioneers from Drouot, Stock Exchange brokers and insurance brokers enjoy a typical French meal: *coq au vin* and rib of beef for two. The welcome is sometimes also very Parisian, that is to say, surly! In the evening, before and after the shows at the nearby theatres, young trendies meet around the tables covered with the classic red-and-white Vichy fabric. It's also occasionally frequented by journalists. There is an intimate and cosy back room. Eleven vintages of Beaujolais. At the bar, an 8cl glass of wine costs less than 10F.

✕ **L'Arbre à Cannelle** (map C1, **28**): 57 passage des Panoramas 75002. ☎ 01-45-08-55-87. Metro: Grands-Boulevards. Open until 6pm; meals served 11.30am to around 3.30pm (a bit later on Saturday). Closed Sundays and public holidays. Budget for around 130F. More like a tea-room than a restaurant. The superb façade with sculpted woodwork fits in perfectly with the old-style charm of this arcade. There's a terrace outside so that you can enjoy watching the world go by, but you can also sit inside (there are superb coffered ceilings). Sweet or savoury tarts: *Maraîchère*, salmon or Provençal, chocolate gâteau and a fine red-fruit crumble. A number of gourmet salads from 59F to 112F are a light lunch in themselves.

✕ **La Bocca** (map C2, **25**): 59 rue Montmartre 75002. Metro: Sentier. ☎ 01-42-36-71-88. Open at lunchtime and in the evening, but it's best to call and book. Budget for around 180F. A good Italian restaurant with an elegant decor full of ceramics, which gives it a Spanish look. A slightly hip atmosphere – a bit noisy and a bit smoky – but the service is relaxed. You suddenly find yourself in Calabria and Umbria, Sicily and Tuscany. The pasta is perfectly cooked with a different daily sauce. There are tasty mozzarella tomatoes, antipasti or *scalopine al limone* (escalopes with lemon). No set menu, but there are special offers on starters and dishes of the day on the blackboard. A few wines from Italy by the glass. The only downside is the price – a small plate of pasta costs 75F. A shame, because it's really good.

✕ **Chez Clément** (map A1, **29**): 17 boulevard des Capucines 75002. ☎ 01-53-43-82-00. Metro: Opéra. Open daily 7.30am to 1am (*see Chez Clément* in '17th arrondissement').

✕ **Voyageurs du Monde, Le Restaurant** (map B2, **30**): 51 *bis* rue Ste-Anne 75002. ☎ 01-42-86-17-17. Metro: Pyramides. Open Monday to Friday for lunch only, from noon to 2.30pm. Closed at the weekend, in August and between Christmas and 1 January. You are strongly advised to book because it soon fills up here. Set menu at 100F with starter, main course and dessert at lunchtime; à la carte the price is about the same. Ideal for a spot of culinary travelling. The travel agency, shop and restaurant show just how entrepreneurial the owner is. The cosy, colonial decor adds a pleasant note. There's a different culinary destination every day, and it's always an exotic one. One day it's Brazil and its *feijoada* (beans with tongue and sausage), sometimes it's the West Indies and a few *accras* (fried fish), or it might be Indonesia via the satay kebabs, not forgetting India, Cuba and Africa. The menu is set on a weekly basis so you can find out where they're off to in advance.

✕ **Au Pays de Cocagne** (Espace Tarn; map C2, **20**): 111 rue Réaumur 75002. ☎ 01-40-13-81-81. Metro: Bourse, Grands-Boulevards or Sentier. Closed on Saturday lunchtime, Sunday, August and the last week of December. Set menus at 98F and 160F, served lunchtime and evening. Entrusted with the economic and cultural promotion of this region of France, the Espace Tarn is close to the Stock Exchange. They may regret that they've gone for modern furnishings (a way of saying 'we're not a load of yokels!'), giving the restaurant a look which gives a fairly distant reflection of the warmth of the inhabitants of the Tarn. But the cuisine has genuine regional accents (*cassoulet*, *confit*), and there are Gaillac wines and pleasant service.

✕ **Le Canard d'Avril** (map C2, **37**): 5 rue Paul-Lelong 75002. ☎ and fax: 01-42-36-26-08. Metro: Sentier or Bourse. Closed at weekends, Monday evening and public holidays. Menus of the day at 89F and 129F. Patrick in the kitchen and Bruno front of house, from Pau and Aveyron respectively, have refurbished this former bistro. They opened on 1 April and duck, in all shapes and varieties, is their main dish (hence the restaurant's name). The blackboard menus change daily according to what's available, but there's always room for the cuisine of the south west, including *magret de canard 'au foin'* (duck braised in a casserole), *cassolette de pétoncles* and the delicious *crème brulée à la fleur de lavande*. Booking at lunchtime is recommended.

☆☆☆ CHIC

✕ **Le Grand Colbert** (map B2, **32**): 2 rue Vivienne 75002. ☎ 01-42-86-87-88. Metro: Bourse. Open daily noon to 1am. Set menu at 155F, including coffee, served at lunchtime and evening. This brasserie is part of the Colbert Gallery, and you'll find your way in through the gallery. It has recaptured its golden youth (friezes repainted, immense bronze counter and Café de Paris lamps) and, in a superb 1830s setting, offers all the classic brasserie standards (including lentil salad and lamb curry); unfortunately a little rushed.

WINE BAR

✕ 🍷 **L'Ange Vin** (map C1, **34**): 168 rue Montmartre 75002. ☎ 01-42-36-20-20. Metro: Grands-Boulevards or Sentier. Open 11am to 2am (kitchen open until 11.30pm). Closed Sunday and Monday. Set menu at 150F served lunchtime and evening. Dish of the day 70F. Budget for 230F à la carte, including drinks. This is a large, high-ceilinged place, intelligently restored but still with a few items of decor from the 1930s, such as the balustrade on the mezzanine. The rest of the setting, post art-deco and modern, merges in easily. Excellent wines to wash down sophisticated dishes (not always cheap) or *charcuterie*, cheese or pâté. You can buy wine to take out if you want to extend your enjoyment.

TEA-ROOM

– **À Priori Thé** (map B2, **33**): 35–37 galerie Vivienne 75002. ☎ 01-42-97-48-75. Metro: Palais-Royal or Bourse. Open Monday to Friday 9am to 6pm, Saturday 9am to 6.30pm, and Sunday 12.30pm to 6.30pm. Closed on 25 December, 1 January, 1 May and 14 July. Brunch 135F on Saturday and 146F on Sunday. With its terrace tables in the heart of the Galerie Vivienne and under the glass roof of the covered arcade dating from the early 19th century, this tea-room has an eccentric charm. The salads are as delicious as they are generous. The same goes for the brunch, which will really fill you up. There's also an excellent children's menu at 50F.

BIBLIOTHÈQUE NATIONALE DE FRANCE

58 rue de Richelieu 75002. ☎ 01-47-03-81-26. Metro: Bourse or Palais-Royal. Reading rooms open 9am to 6pm Monday to Friday, 9am to 5pm on Saturday. The National Library has moved. Since October 1998, all that's been left on this site are the specialized departments which are only open to accredited researchers and students. The crowds which used to meet here have gone to the Bibliothèque Nationale de France François-Mitterrand in Tolbiac. There are also guided tours. Phone the Caisse Nationale des Monuments Historiques for information: ☎ 01-44-61-20-00.

Before moving the printed material to Tolbiac, the Richelieu site housed several million books and newspapers which it had accumulated over a number of centuries. Initially, they were stored in a fine private residence at 8 rue des Petits-Champs but as the premises expanded the library ended up by occupying the whole of the block, plus two annexes. It has also housed almost every kind of printed matter (books, newspapers etc.) since the time of Francis I, thanks to the formal system of depositing a copy of every book, film, record etc., plus a priceless collection of original editions of the works of the greatest authors (e.g. a Gutenberg Bible, and writings by Rabelais and François Villon). In the old days, works which were judged to be too erotic by the censors disappeared into 'Hell', a room to which hardly anyone had access. The manuscripts department includes papyrus scrolls, parchments with illuminated letters, the correspondence of great writers and original manuscripts by Victor Hugo and Proust, amongst others. There is the world's richest exhibition hall of engravings, not to mention the music, theatrical arts and maps departments, as well as the Medals Exhibition Hall (see below). The beautiful Galerie Mazarine and the Galerie Mansart show temporary exhibitions. Open daily 10am to 8pm.

The collections at Richelieu comprise 530,000 manuscripts, 11 million engravings and photographs, 580,000 coins and medals, 880,000 maps and over 2 million musical pieces, collections and scores. (Don't worry, the highly efficient staff will be able to help you find exactly what you are looking for!) This site will also eventually hold theatrical arts documents from the Bibliothèque de l'Arsenal. Eventually it is planned that it will be home to the future National Institute of the History of Art, which will bring together the resources of various libraries, including those at the Louvre and Jacques-Doucet.

Don't forget to have a look through the window of the Labrouste lecture theatre (on the right in the main courtyard). This amazing glass superstructure, supported by thin iron columns and sporting frescoes and and golden tinting, has more security guards than you'd find at an embassy.

– **Musée des Médailles** (Medals Exhibition Hall): open daily 1pm to 5pm (12pm to 6pm on Sunday and public holidays). ☎ 01-47-03-83-34 (for group bookings). Entry fee 22F, concessions 15F. Exhibitions of medals, cameos and jewels. In all, the department has 40,000 works dealing with coin collecting. There's a short film lasting 20 minutes.

★ **Square Louvois:** this has one of the most attractive fountains in Paris, representing the four 'feminine' French rivers: the Loire, the Seine, the Garonne and the Saône – hence the exclusion of the Rhône, which is masculine in French. When you come out of the square opposite the Bibliothèque Nationale, take rue Colbert on the left to see, at No. 4, the vestiges of a fountain. The water came from the Seine via the Notre-Dame pump. The tank was on the first floor and an icebox (a forerunner of our refrigerators) was in the basement. This made it possible to keep some of the ice amassed during the winter through into the summer.

LES PASSAGES

Follow the **passages** through the 2nd arrondissement for a walk with a difference, tinged with mystery.

Along this route you'll relive the supposedly 'good old days' when Paris had neither pavements nor electricity. These *passages* were built on plots of land requisitioned by the Revolution, in order to protect people passing through them from the mud and the rain. These narrow arcades were one of the first pedestrian areas, with elegant vaulted roofs made from wrought-iron and glass. Their popularity soon grew and the Restoration and the July Monarchy were to see the creation of around 20 of these miniature villages. This area had the first restaurants worthy of the name, cafés where people played draughts or dominoes and saw the beginnings of theatres, balls and inns where people drank *absinthe*. The middle-classes, poets and thespians, factory workers and the working-classes all rubbed shoulders together.

The *passages* had their golden age in the 19th century. At the time, building an arcade and then leasing the shops and their accommodation was the most profitable investment you could make, so it should come as no surprise that by 1840 there were more than 130 of them. Eventually shoppers began to desert the arcades for the new-fangled department stores. As the city grew, trains pushed travellers out towards the countryside, and cars passed by these arcades without even noticing them. These days however, traffic jams have brought pedestrians back onto the pavement, and the *passages* have been rejuvenated. They're not all business premises, however, some of them are simply a means of communication between two streets. One of the benefits of taking this route is that if it rains you'll be under cover!

★ **Galerie Vivienne** at 4 rue des Petits-Champs has had a long convalescence, but it has now been restored to its former old-world charm. It is worth visiting for its mosaic floor with large geometric shapes, rotundas, glass roofs, fine forged-iron staircases, and its refined tranquillity. At the end of the gallery is a beautiful clock.

A favourite *passage* with Parisians up until the Second Empire, Galerie Vivienne awoke from a long sleep in the 1980s with the arrival of designer shops such as Casa Lopez, Jean-Paul Gaultier, Emilio Robba and Christian Astuguevieille. Upmarket businesses have replaced the humbler professions that used to be here.

Opposite, **Passage des Petits-Pères** leads to the church of Notre-Dame-des-Victoires, which is unique because it is decorated with around 36,000 thanksgiving plaques. Its neighbour, **Galerie Colbert**, has had a facelift as well. Nicely restored, it houses the **Musée des Arts du Spectacle** (Theatre Museum), with a fine rotunda. The way out is in rue de la Banque, where you rejoin **Place des Petits-Pères**. At No. 7, take a look at the Ionic cornices of the Hotel Colbert; at the middle of the highest part the stone scrolls are formed by grass snakes.

★ **Passage Choiseul:** begins with an elegant façade at 23 rue St-Augustin and ends at 40 rue des Petits-Champs, protected by an iron structure. The opposite of its predecessor, it's flashy, busy and crowded. Local employees with no time to do their shopping on the avenue find almost all the shops they need here.

★ **Passage des Panoramas:** 11 boulevard Montmartre 75002. Metro: Grands-Boulevards. The circular panoramas gave their name to a *passage* which combined the atmosphere of the wooden galleries of the Palais-Royal with that of the boulevards. New alleys have expanded the original arcade. It is a scale model of a *grand boulevard* – animated, colourful and sparkling, with some amazing shops.

The unique engraver's shop owned by Stern is a must-see. The shop hasn't changed since 1840. Its windows are like little museums, from old engraved maps to 'livery buttons'. Inside there's magnificent sculpted woodwork.

There are also a number of philatelists, from the popular discount trader to the Cartier of stamps, displaying his certificates of authenticity. Exit at 10 rue St-Marc.

★ **Passage des Princes:** between 97 rue de Richelieu and 5 boulevard des Italiens 75002. Metro: Richelieu-Drouot. After six years of work and around 300 million francs invested in its restoration, the latest of the *passages* (1860) has finally rediscovered its 19th-century style. If the decrepit shop windows have now disappeared, giving way to trendy shops, the architects have made it a point of honour to save most of the original items (such as the marble bases and Napoleon III staircase) and to preserve the original atmosphere as much as possible.

★ Continuing to the east of the 2nd arrondissement, there's the **Tour de Jean-sans-Peur**, at 20 rue Étienne-Marcel. People used to live in this tower, which along with the Hôtel de Clisson (*see* North of the Marais in '3rd arrondissement'), is the only real vestige of feudal Paris. Built in 1408, it lost the private residence to which it belonged, and since then has been adopted by a primary school. No tours. Coming through rue Française, rejoin rue Tiquetonne, with fine 18th-century houses on each side (at No. 10 there's an unusual shop sign: 'The cork tree').

★ Heading along rue Greneta, there's a fountain at the corner of the street, which dates back to the 16th century. Opposite the Grand-Cerf is **Passage du Bourg-l'Abbé**. A round arched glass roof, an old barometer and a forlorn broken clock look at one another wearily. The *passage* is becoming rather decrepit.

★ **Passage du Grand-Cerf:** entrance through 145 rue St-Denis. It was built in 1825 on the site of the hostelry of the same name, which was used as a mail staging-post until the Revolution. The *passage* was reopened in 1992, after being given an end-of-the-century makeover which has perhaps turned out a bit too clean and academic. Certainly the glass roof is superb, but the rather dreary uniformity of the shops have made it lose some of its charm.

★ Through rue de Palestro, as far up as No. 21, is **Passage de la Trinité**. This is the only vestige of the former Trinité hospital, as well as the church which was built there in 1817. Even though the public urinals have been removed, it is still used for this purpose by people walking down the rue St-Denis (fortunately it still has a central gutter!). At night it's pretty gloomy. Exit at 164 rue St-Denis. The light from the sex shops is oddly reassuring.

★ **Passage Basfour**, as far up as 178 rue St-Denis, is a 12th-century lane which originally bordered the former Trinité hospital. There are some superb 14th-century gabled houses. Return by rue de Palestro (at No. 27), which you can also find from the other side of rue de Réaumur. There's a superb ceramic clock on the corner of rue Réaumur and rue St-Denis.

Take a look at the 1900 architecture of the *Monoprix* shop on the corner with boulevard Sébastopol, before being swallowed up by rue de Ponceau, a street where there is always something happening. One morning the body of a famous archbishop was found here, but there's no plaque on the wall to commemorate him!

★ **Rue du Caire:** the whole quarter was given Egyptian names after the Bonaparte expedition in 1798. This is where the famous **Cour des Miracles** (Court of Miracles) was held in the 17th century. It probably owed its name to the fact that once night had fallen 'the blind could see clearly . . . cripples regained the use of their limbs'. Victor Hugo placed it in the Middle Ages in his novel *Notre-Dame de Paris* (*The Hunchback of Notre Dame*). At the time there were thousands of beggars, thieves and pickpockets here, as well as con artists who pretended to be blind or disabled, as well as army deserters and prostitutes. The beggars elected a king and a queen, nicknamed 'Rolin-Trapu' and 'Catin Bon-Bec'.

In 1668 the first Lieutenant of Police, La Reynie, cleaned up the Court of Miracles in 24 hours, promising that the last six beggars he found there would be hanged on the spot.

DID YOU KNOW?

The word *argot* (meaning 'slang') originates from 16th-century beggars. Under Francis I, a group of beggars who had their own language and laws nicknamed their leader the Rajot (hence *argot*). Every evening he was given a percentage of the takings and the rest was spent on food and drink.

★ **Place du Caire:** the most beautiful entrance to **Passage du Caire**, this square is bordered by an Egyptian-inspired building, complete with a sphinx, a lotus, imitation-hieroglyphics and three enormous heads of scribes. The square and the quarter, lively during the day (but hell for cars), enjoy an almost provincial calm in the evening and are totally deserted at night. In the *passage* (which closes at 7pm), there are a number of streets covered with glass roofs with shops selling clothing.

This is where the **Sentier** area starts, the realm of off-the-peg clothing. There are plenty of ways out in rue du Caire, but leave the *passage* via 239 rue St-Denis.

★ A few yards along is **Passage du Ponceau**, at No. 212. Exit onto the boulevard Sébastopol and it's a short walk up to No.135.

A large iron gate opens onto **Passage Lemoine**. Exit at 230 rue St-Denis.

Almost opposite is **Passage Ste-Foy**, at No. 261. This is a strange, narrow, mysterious, dirty and slightly scary *passage* which springs out at 14 rue Ste-Foy. No. 13 leads to rue d'Aboukir.

★ From rue d'Aboukir, go to 57 rue de Cléry. This is the entrance to **Passage de Cléry**. At night this is the most sinister *passage* in the quarter: dark, narrow, twisting and dotted with steep, dimly lit stairways. At the end there's a prison grill and the starred arch of rue Beauregard. At No. 32 there's a small statue of Joan of Arc in the façade.

Go towards Porte St-Denis; at No. 50, on the right, towards rue de Cléry, is the smallest street in Paris (5m/16ft). Rue des Degrès consists of a stairway with 14 steps but no road surface, pavement, or street numbers.

THE HEADQUARTERS OF THE 'MADAMES'

★ **Rue St-Denis**, between rue de Turbigo and Porte St-Denis, is where 80 per cent of Parisian prostitution is concentrated. On payday business is brisk: at night you'll find the prostitutes crowding the pavement, spaced about a yard apart. As early as the 14th century, the Provost of Paris, Aubriot, noting that the prostitutes dressed in a flamboyant way, decreed an order 'prohibiting gilded belts, upturned collars and jay feathers on dresses'.

The rue St-Denis has always had a vocation for the business of 'personal services', the Cemetery of the Innocents being one of the favourite places for soliciting. The prostitutes have always been a headache for the authorities. Charlemagne tried in vain to kick them out and St Louis, infuriated by these 'women so free with their bodies', drove them outside Philippe Auguste's city walls.

The word *bordel*, meaning 'brothel', comes from this time. The prostitutes built houses from *bords* (an old French word meaning planks) outside the city walls and punters soon started calling these houses *bordes*.

Highly organized, they held their annual celebrations under the aegis of their patron saint, St Madeleine, complete with a procession. They have never felt the need to keep themselves hidden. It's curious to note how history repeats itself: chased out of the city centre some time in the Middle Ages, the prostitutes returned when Les Halles became an area of importance. They were once again expelled when Les Halles was moved, and in particular when the quarter was renovated, and have now returned, buying up all the bedsits in rue St-Denis and the neighbouring streets.

DID YOU KNOW?

Shirley Maclaine, a highly conscientious actress, who was given the role of Irma la Douce in Billy Wilder's eponymous film, came for a bit of 'work experience' to rue St-Denis to study the language, behaviour and customs of Parisian prostitutes.

★ **Rue des Petits-Carreaux and rue Montorgueil:** very lively street markets with lots of traditional trades and old shops. There are a few original façades, such as the Rocher de Cancale, on the corner of rue Montorgueil and rue Greneta. This was also the road used by wholesalers providing fish and lobster from the coasts of the English Channel and the North Sea.

★ **Rue Damiette:** a little street running parallel to the rue des Petits-Carreaux. In the 18th century the chevalier du Barry placed Jeanne Bécu, then Mlle Lange, as a 'hostess' here. Her speciality was supplying pretty girls to the rich and the nobility. But she had a slight problem: she needed a title. She solved this by marrying Guillaume du Barry, brother of Jean, and sent the count off to his estates near Toulouse. The new Countess was thus able to set up in Versailles.

THE QUARTIER DE LA PRESSE

During the French Revolution, a site in the Passage du Caire was made into a printing works. Later, under the Second Empire, the *passage* itself was home to many lithographers and printers. At 100 rue Réaumur, *L'Intransigeant* set up shop in a new building in 1924. *France-Soir* followed suit, before leaving in 1988. *Le Figaro* is still located in this area in rue du Louvre, as is *l'AFP*, in place de la Bourse.

★ **Rue du Croissant:** going back to the 18th century, the road owes its name to a shop sign. At No. 8 is a fine house with a convex façade. At No. 16, the Imprimerie de la Presse, which prints many daily newspapers, occupies a large private residence that used to be home to the newspaper *Le Siècle*, then more recently *Combat*.

All night long, delivery men load up the newspapers, making this little street a huge contrast to the rest of the Sentier area, which is completely dead at night.

On the corner of rue du Croissant and rue Montmartre is La Chope du Croissant, a café where, on 31 July 1914, Jean Jaurès, the founder of *L'Humanité*, was murdered. A large marble plaque commemorates the event.

★ **Rue Réaumur:** some of the finest examples of the art of ironwork in Paris are to be found here. It owes its existence to an architectural competition. Whether Art Nouveau, as at No. 118, or modern simplicity, as at No. 124, these superb houses are all glass, metal and light. It makes you wish they'd never invented concrete.

The **Bourse** (Stock Exchange), the temple of business, is built in heavy pseudo-Greek style. You can tour the visitors' gallery from Monday to Friday, except on public holidays, from 1.15pm to 4pm; by appointment for groups. There is a charge for entry. The tour is every 15 minutes. During the week you can get information in the visitors' gallery between 9.30am and 5pm: ☎ 01-40-41-62-20.

★ **Les Étoiles du Rex:** 1 boulevard Poissonnière 75002. ☎ 08-36-68-05-96. Website: www.legrandrex.com. Metro: Grands-Boulevards or Bonne-Nouvelle. Tours every 5 minutes (20 people maximum) from 10am to 7.30pm from Wednesday to Sunday, public holidays and school holidays. From 6 years and upwards. Entry fee 45F; 40F for under 12s; 75F with a cinema ticket. The Rex was a sensation on the day it opened in 1932: it offers a huge auditorium, an immense screen and, overhead, a ceiling covered with stars. There is also a nursery and a kennel on the ground floor, so you don't have to worry about your kids, or the dog. Guided by a voice off-stage, the tour begins with a trip behind the screen and into the wings of the great cinema. It covers the cutting room, the projectionist's workshop, and you can even sit in the director's seat. There is a simulation of special effects and sound effects.

WHERE TO GO FOR A DRINK

🍸 **Kitty O'Shea's** (map A2, **51**): 10 rue des Capucines 75002. ☎ 01-40-15-00-30. Metro: Madeleine or Opéra. Open daily noon to 2am. Closed for a week at Christmas. 22F for half a pint of beer. This little bit of Ireland in the Opéra quarter offers a chance for a complete change of scene. It's a genuine, lived in place. The star at the bar is Guinness. On the first floor, a second bar welcomes people who want a bit of peace and quiet. At weekends, it'll take you around 15 minutes to get to the bar, and there's traditional Irish music every Sunday from 9pm to 11pm.

🍸 **Le Café** (map C2, **52**): 62 rue Tiquetonne 75002. ☎ 01-40-39-08-00. Metro: Étienne-Marcel. Open daily 9.30am to 2am. Full meal 50F. Perhaps the hippest café in Paris, with the ubiquitous minimalist name! With its sunny terrace, open 9am to 6pm, charming waiters, vegetarian *croques* and half pints of beer at

16F, this charming bistro attracts crowds every day, and not just anyone – stars who have been spotted here include supermodel Naomi Campbell, fashion designer John Galliano and actress Emma Thompson.

🍸 **The Frog and Rosbif** (map D3, **53**): 116 rue St-Denis 75002. ☎ 01-42-36-34-73. Metro: Étienne-Marcel or Les Halles. Open daily noon to 2am. At lunchtime, there's a set menu at 69F: starter and main course, or main course and dessert. *Rosbif* is the French slang for the British. The Frog produces beers the way others produce their food: home-made! White, red, amber or brown, 100 per cent unpasteurized pure malt, the beers are unreservedly popular (35F per pint). A guarantee of quality is the high proportion of Brits amongst the clientele! British crisps, British cooking, British service. Brunch on Sunday from noon to 4pm.

✕ **Le Café Noir** (map C2, **58**): 65 rue Montmartre 75002. ☎ 01-40-39-07-36. Metro: Sentier. Open until 2am. Closed Sunday. 11F per half pint. This is one of the nicest bars in the quarter and yet not a slave to fashion. A cross-section of people make up the clientele, all mixing happily together around the old bar.

🍸 **Pouchla** (map C2, **57**): 10 rue Mandar 75002. ☎ 01-40-26-40-75. Metro: Les Halles or Étienne-Marcel. Open daily 5pm to 1am. Pints cost 30F. Close to rue Montorgueil, an atypical bar where all they serve is excellent draught German beers (the owner is Bavarian). In the middle of the room is a *Stammtisch*, a typically Germanic locals' table. There are around 30 games available to customers, including dominoes, draughts and backgammon. Games and beer, what more could you want?

🍸 **Le Port d'Amsterdam** (map C2, **59**): 20 rue du Croissant 75002. ☎ 01-40-39-02-63. Metro: Sentier. Open daily 5pm to 2am. Set menu at 65F, served lunchtime and evening. 15F for half a pint of beer (11F on Monday evening). Happy hour between 5pm and 8pm with pints at 22F and cocktails at 30F. Dutch number plates, ads for Grolsch and a portrait of the Queen of the Netherlands on the wall, make it easy to guess the owners' nationality. Richard and Roderick, two young Dutchmen, who are experts in draught beers and *bitterballen*, also serve meat croquettes. On Monday evening, at 10pm on the dot, the tables and chairs give way to young students who have come to strut their stuff.

NIGHTCLUB

– **Le Rex-Club** (map C1, **56**): 5 boulevard Poissonnière 75002. ☎ 01-42-36-10-96 or ☎ 01-40-28-95-62 (programme information) or ansaphone on ☎ 01-42-36-83-98 (the week's programmes). Fax: 01-42-36-55-72. Metro: Bonne-Nouvelle. Open 11pm to 6am Wednesday to Saturday. For the rest of the week you'll need to phone as it depends on the programme. Closed in August. Entry from 50F to 80F. Located beside the Grand Rex, this club was opened in 1932 by Louis Lumière and Jacques Haïk, the owners of the finest cinema of the day. A large, but slightly cold, dance hall, which can hold up to 500 people. The Rex is now devoted exclusively to DJs; no more live rock concerts, except for one-off events. Techno was first heard here soon after its birth in Detroit in 1985. The age range of the clientele is from 18 to 35. A lively atmosphere where music comes first.

3RD ARRONDISSEMENT

THE MARAIS ● NORTH OF THE MARAIS ● THE TEMPLE DISTRICT

THE MARAIS

The Marais is one of the oldest and most attractive quarters in Paris. It is almost equally divided between the 3rd and 4th arrondissements and, broadly speaking, is bordered by the rue Beaubourg to the west, the boulevard Beaumarchais to the east, the Seine to the south and the rue de Réaumur and the rue de Bretagne to the north. There is a great deal of architectural consistency and the area has become one of most sought-after in Paris. There are some superb walks through streets dotted with fine private residences, and along narrow passages and fine medieval lanes. Push open the heavy doors to discover paved courtyards and indoor gardens. At night it changes into something else altogether.

FROM MARSHES TO MANSIONS

As its name, which means 'marsh', indicates, the quarter was originally a swampy area between the Seine and one of its tributaries, which up to the 12th century often flooded when the waters were high. Religious institutions were the first to move in, then came the Jewish community. The nobles had their country houses here (the Temple district took its name from the Knights Templar). When the monarchy left the Louvre for the Hôtel St-Pol, the Court followed and when Henri IV decided upon the construction of the Place Royale (now the Place des Vosges), the nobility had sumptuous houses built all around it.

At the end of the 12th century, with the growing importance of Versailles, the Marais was abandoned. The Faubourg St-Germain and the Faubourg St-Honoré streets developed around this time ('faubourg' meaning suburb). The nobles sold their houses to the rich middle-classes and merchants, and the district lost its shine. The French Revolution further hastened its decline.

By the 19th century, the Marais had become full of craftsmen, warehouses and small-scale industries, and the quarter's architectural heritage gradually deteriorated. This is where almost all of the rather tacky 'souvenirs of Paris' were manufactured. Gradually, the working-class took over the quarter, while property developers and unscrupulous speculators continued to do whatever they liked. In 1962, the Malraux Law finally put an end to the demolition and renovation work by declaring the Marais to be a wholly listed area. In fact, the Marais is lucky in that it contained so many fine houses in the first place that, even after many buildings were demolished, there are still a good number of them left.

THE MARAIS TODAY

The houses here have regained their lustre and their fine, paved courtyards. Some of them are home to museums, while others, split into flats, have been sold as second homes or apartments for young singles. Still, you can admire the porches and ironwork from the outside. In the evening rue de Turenne turns into something of a ghost town and sadly the lively St-Paul quarter has seen almost the whole of its permanent population leave.

However, lower down, in the 4th arrondissement, the Jewish community is hanging on, in rue des Rosiers and rue des Écouffes. The atmosphere here is as lively as a square in Provence, and the market of les Enfants-Rouges continues to offer delicious smells, a riot of colour and a friendly local population. The gay community have colonized some of the streets of the Marais and brought many cafés and meeting places back to life. The area also has all sorts of restaurants, from charming to cheap.

WHERE TO STAY

☆ BUDGET

Hôtel du Marais (map C2, **1**): 16 rue de Beauce 75003. ☎ 01-42-72-30-26. Metro: Temple, Arts-and-Métiers, Rambuteau or Filles-du-Calvaire. Rooms with washbasin only, from 13F for a single room to 180F for a double. Don't miss the tiny entrance which, rather oddly, is half hidden behind a wall. The hotel is above the bistro of the same name, where you can have your breakfast in the morning. Basic, with small rooms.

☆☆ MODERATE

Paris-Bruxelles Hôtel (map C1, **3**): 4 rue Meslay 75003. ☎ 01-42-72-71-32. Fax: 01-42-77-62-33. Metro: République. Single rooms with washbasin (but without TV) 170F to 190F; with shower, toilet, telephone and TV 280F. Double rooms 300F to 400F with shower, toilet, telephone and TV; with bathroom 350F to 400F. A classic but likeable hotel in a street specializing in shoes. The rooms on the road side (sound-proofed) are nicer because they're larger and lighter than those on the courtyard side. Those on the top floor have good views. Family rooms (for three or four people) are more spacious, from 500F. Good value for money, but note that they don't take cheques.

Hôtel Picard (map C2, **4**): 26 rue de Picardie 75003. ☎ 01-48-87-53-82. Fax: 01-48-87-02-56. Metro: Temple, République or Filles-du-Calvaire. Double room with toilet but no shower 250F; with shower, toilet and TV 330F. The largest rooms, with bathroom, toilet and TV, are 400F. Located just opposite the famous Carreau du Temple, in an area unfrequented by tourists, this simple hotel has well-kept rooms.

☆☆☆ CHIC

Hôtel du Vieux Saule (map C2, **5**): 6 rue de Picardie 75003. ☎ 01-42-72-01-14. Fax: 01-40-27-88-21. Metro: Temple, République or Filles-du-Calvaire. Double rooms which are modern and very comfortable, with shower and toilet 490F, or with bathroom and toilet 590F. Fine, quiet and elegant hotel with a façade covered in flowers in the summer. There's a nice, quiet flower garden. All rooms are air-conditioned and equipped with hairdryer, trouser-press, telephone, safe and cable TV. Avoid the ones on the ground floor because they have bars on the windows. Free sauna. Breakfast costs 50F, served in an arched, 16th-century cellar. The car-park costs 65F.

WHERE TO EAT

☆ BUDGET

✕ **Chez Léon and Francine** (map C2, **20**): 24 rue de Poitou 75003. ☎ 01-42-71-88-65. Metro: St-Sébastien-Froissart. Open 10am to 6.30pm. Closed Saturday and Sunday, and in August. Budget for around 50F to 60F. A delicatessen with a family feel, here you can try Yiddish specialities in a tiny dining room, at very reasonable prices. Francine, a member of the Leikowitz family of excellent butchers from the rue des Rosiers, naturally offers products from her brother's establishment, but also serves stuffed turkey fillet (38F), *krepler* broth (beef and chicken soup with ravioli, 38F), stuffed carp (45F), as well as a fine house strudel or poppy cake (12F). Dish of the day costs 38F.

✕ **Hôtel du Mont-Blanc** (map C2, **21**): 17 rue Debelleyme 75003. ☎ 01-42-72-23-68. Metro: Filles-du-Calvaire. Open at noon only for lunch, but opens as a bar until around 9pm. Closed on Sunday and in August. Main courses around 50F. It looks like an old-style café, with oilcloths on the tables and the Formica bar, behind which stands Mme Morvan, queen of all she surveys (she's been here since 1959). Artists, artisans, workers – they all come for lunch – crudités or egg mayonnaise (15F), followed by bavette pommes *sautées*, *pot-au-feu* or *morue provençale*. Home-made desserts include stewed apple or chocolate mousse (15F). The cuisine and the prices are as old-style Paris as the decor. After a stroll around the Picasso Museum nearby, come and have an Italian coffee (6.50F) and a rest.

✕ **Pachamanca** (map B2, **26**): 2 impasse Berthaud 75003. ☎ 01-48-87-88-22. Metro: Rambuteau. Open noon to 11pm. Closed Monday, and also in August. Set menu 55F at lunchtime; à la carte around 120F; main courses for about 49F. Tucked away close to Beaubourg, this hospitable, tiny Peruvian *cantina* is just the ticket if you're feeling a little peckish after doing the rounds of the area. For a modest sum, you can take a culinary trip through the Cordillière, which is every bit as good as the one offered by the Auvergnat bars all around, which have interchangeable and frequently mediocre dishes of the day.

☆☆ MODERATE

✕ **La Fontaine Gourmande** (map C2, **23**): 11 rue Charlot 75003. ☎ 01-42-78-72-40. Metro: Rambuteau or Arts-and-Métiers. Open until 10.30pm. Closed Saturday and Sunday, and in August. If you're feeling hungry as you come out of

Where to stay
- **1** Hôtel du Marais
- **3** Paris-Bruxelles Hôtel
- **4** Hôtel Picard
- **5** Hôtel Vieux Saule

✕ **Where to eat**
- **20** Chez Léon and Francine
- **21** Hôtel du Mont-Blanc
- **23** La Fontaine Gourmande
- **24** Chez Nénesse
- **26** Pachamanca
- **27** Chez Omar
- **28** Au Bascou
- **29** Le Baromètre
- **30** L'Ambassade d'Auvergne
- **31** Anahi
- **32** Les Caves St-Gilles
- **33** Chez Janou
- **35** À la Mexicaine
- **36** Gli Angeli

Where to go for a drink/ Going out
- **40** The Quiet Man
- **41** Le Web Bar
- **42** Les Bains
- **44** L'Apparemment Café

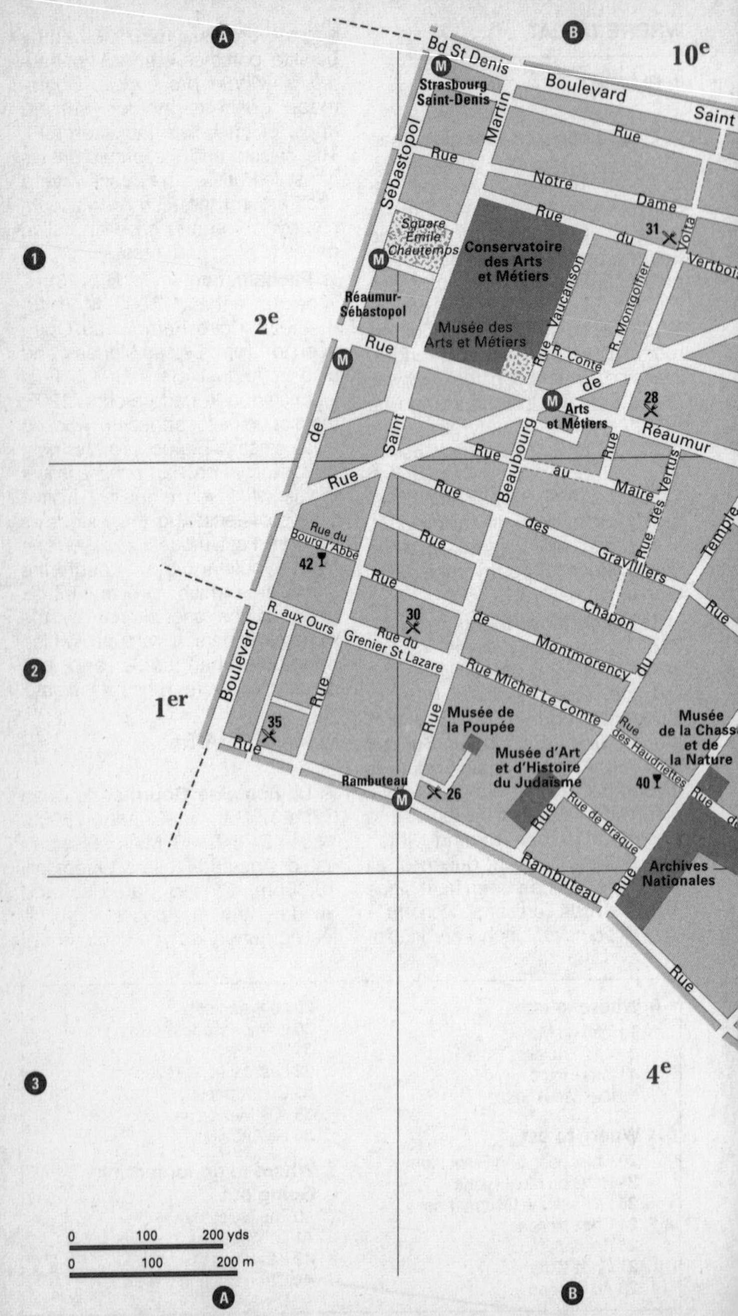
A
B
1
2
3
10e
2e
1er
4e
Bd St Denis
Boulevard Saint
Strasbourg Saint-Denis
Martin
Sébastopol
Rue Notre Dame
Rue du Vertbois
Volta
31
Square Emile Chautemps
Conservatoire des Arts et Métiers
Musée des Arts et Métiers
Réaumur-Sébastopol
Vaucanson
R. Montgolfier
R. Conte
Arts et Métiers
28
Rue de Réaumur
Rue Saint
Beaubourg
Rue au Maire
Rue des Vertus
Rue des Gravilliers
Rue Chapon
Rue de Montmorency
Temple
Rue du Bourg l'Abbé
42
R. aux Ours
30
Rue du Grenier St Lazare
Rue Michel Le Comte
Boulevard
35
Rambuteau
26
Musée de la Poupée
Musée d'Art et d'Histoire du Judaïsme
Rue des Haudriettes
Musée de la Chasse et de la Nature
40
Rue de Braque
Archives Nationales
Rue Rambuteau
0 100 200 yds
0 100 200 m

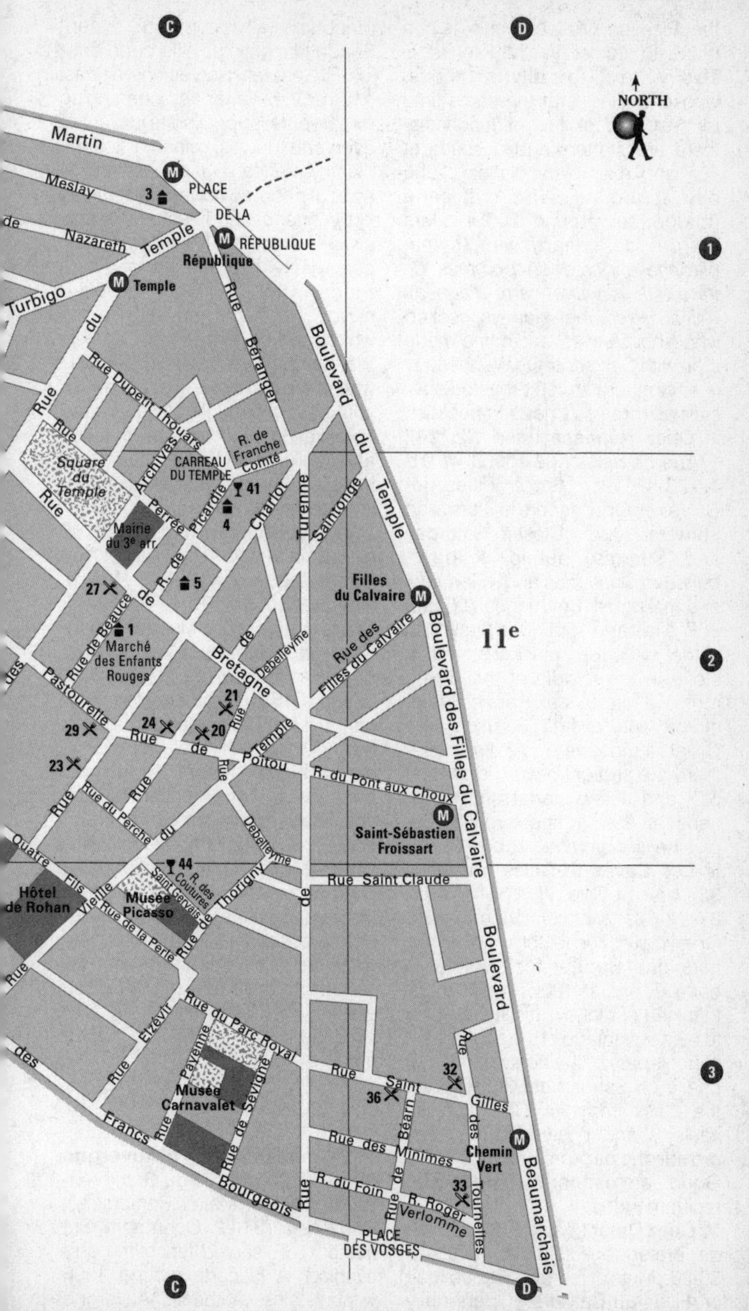

C
D
NORTH
1
2
3
Martin
Meslay
Nazareth
Temple
Turbigo
PLACE DE LA RÉPUBLIQUE
République
Temple
Rue du Temple
Rue Béranger
Boulevard du Temple
Rue Dupetit Thouars
Square du Temple
CARREAU DU TEMPLE
R. de Franche Comté
Rue Perrée
Rue de Picardie
Rue Charlot
Rue de Turenne
Rue de Saintonge
Mairie du 3e arr.
Filles du Calvaire
Boulevard des Filles du Calvaire
11e
Rue des Filles du Calvaire
Rue de Bretagne
R. de Beauce
Marché des Enfants Rouges
Rue Pastourelle
Rue Debelleyme
Rue de Poitou
R. du Pont aux Choux
Saint-Sébastien Froissart
Rue du Perche
Rue Saint Claude
Rue Vieille du Temple
Rue des Quatre Fils
R. des Coutures Saint Gervais
Rue de Thorigny
Hôtel de Rohan
Musée Picasso
Rue de la Perle
Rue Elzévir
Rue du Parc Royal
Rue Payenne
Rue de Sévigné
Musée Carnavalet
Rue des Francs Bourgeois
Rue Saint Gilles
Rue de Béarn
Rue des Minimes
R. du Foin
R. Roger Verlomme
Rue des Tournelles
Chemin Vert
Boulevard Beaumarchais
PLACE DES VOSGES

the Picasso Museum, this is the place to come. In the kitchen is Thierry Odiot, formerly of Lenôtre, whose cuisine is at the same time modest and skilful. At lunchtime, there are starters and desserts at 18F and exemplary dishes of the day at around 55F. À la carte (budget for around 200F) offers *magret de canard* with thyme, *citronnelle purée de pommes de terre à la verveine, carré d'agneau rôti au miel*, veal kidneys cooked whole house-style, and home-made tripe with Calvados. On Wednesday evening there are spit-roasted specialities (but you'll need to book).

✕ **Chez Nénesse** (map C2, **24**): 17 rue de Saintonge 75003. ☎ 01-42-78-46-49. Metro: Filles-du-Calvaire. Open noon to 2pm and 8pm to 10pm. Closed Saturday and Sunday, public holidays, between Christmas and 1 January, and in August. Set menus 70F and 80F; à la carte 180F. This place has a feel typical of old Paris, with a stove in the middle of the dining room, a tiled floor, fabric tablecloths and a fine Formica bar. Great atmosphere. At lunchtime there are straightforward dishes at 52F and a few starters and desserts at 20F. In the evening the cuisine is a bit more elaborate.

✕ **Les Caves St-Gilles** (map D3, **32**): 4 rue St-Gilles 75003. ☎ 01-48-87-22-62. Metro: Chemin-Vert. Open daily noon to 3pm and 8pm to midnight. Budget for 150F à la carte. Tapas at 100F. If you've got that kind of money, this is the place to take advantage of the assortment of hot tapas, or the richly garnished paella on Sunday at 98F. Rioja by the glass from 18F. The Spanish azulejos and posters for *corridas* provide the backdrop for local VIPs. Good atmosphere. Booking is recommended.

✕ **Chez Omar** (map C2, **27**): 47 rue de Bretagne 75003. ☎ 01-42-72-36-26. Metro: Temple, République or Filles-du-Calvaire. Open daily lunchtime and evening, except Sunday lunchtime. À la carte only, 150F. Generally serves until at least 11pm. Chez Omar has been going for 20 years, appealing to just about everyone: locals, cinema technicians, Americans, Japanese and all sorts of people who've come across it by chance and just can't stay away. An old-style Paris bar, it has a conviviality straight out of North Africa. High ceilings, bevelled mirrors, and packed with tables which people tend to talk across, thanks to the smiling, friendly waiters who are ready to admonish you if you haven't finished your (excellent) couscous (between 60F and 105F). It can be a rushed experience, so if you want to take your time come early or late.

✕ **À la Mexicaine** (map A2, **35**): 68 rue Quincampoix (corner of rue Rambuteau) 75003. Metro: Rambuteau. ☎ 01-48-87-99-34. Open daily except Monday lunchtime and Sunday evening. Set menus at 45F and 59F at lunchtime, 95F and 155F in the evening. How can this be a truly Mexican restaurant with no chilli con carne, you may ask. The owners will tell you: because it's an American dish! If you're fed up with margaritas, you'll soon find something else at this typical Mexican place. Let yourself be blown away by the chalupitas (stuffed tortillas), or the rather baroque *sopas* with black beans, with corn or pig's ears. The menu is an encyclopedia of Mexican cuisine, and everything is well explained. The tortillas are home-made.

☆☆☆ CHIC

✕ **L'Ambassade d'Auvergne** (map B2, **30**): 22 rue du Grenier-St-Lazare 75003. Metro: Rambuteau. ☎ 01-42-72-31-22. Open daily. Set menu 170F, served lunchtime and evening. À la carte around 190F without wine. Authentic Auvergne cooking – heavily involving pork in all its forms – ham, braised pork, Auvergne sausage, you name it! There are also some excellent white wines and delicious green lentils from the Puy region. Who said that tradition equals a lack of refinement? Almost all the local wines are served by the glass (22F) and the plum brandy is strong enough to make you forget that the bill is a bit steep!

✗ **Anahi** (map B1, **31**): 49 rue Volta 75003. ☎ 01-48-87-88-24. Metro: Arts-and-Métiers. Open daily 8pm to half past midnight. Closed between Christmas and 1 January, and for a few days around 15 August. Budget for 200F without drinks. This restaurant has always attracted the super-hip crowd – director Quentin Tarantino and fashion designer Thierry Mugler have been spotted here. A bit expensive but with a charming welcome. Essential to book.

✗ **Au Bascou** (map B1, **28**): 38 rue Réaumur 75003. ☎ 01-42-72-69-25. Metro: Arts-and-Métiers. Open until 10.30pm. Closed Saturday lunchtime and Sunday, for four weeks in August and a week at the end of the year. Budget for around 250F including wine. À la carte only, both at lunchtime and in the evening: starters 55F, main courses 85F and dessert 40F. Rather expensive for lunch. Jean-Guy Loustau, originally from the Basque Country, defends his region with a passion. Here are some of the best Basque *charcuteries*, excellent *chipirons sautéed à la luzienne* as well as fish dishes worthy of the ones found in the Basque Country itself. This former wine steward has not lost his passion for good wines, and his cellar is a clear reflection of this. Wines from the south west are also well represented, with Madiran, Jurançon and Irouléguy.

✗ **Chez Janou** (map D3, **33**): 2 rue Roger-Verlomme 75003. ☎ 01-42-72-28-41. Metro: Chemin-Vert. Open daily noon to 2am. Lunch from noon to 3pm and dinner from 8pm to midnight. Budget for 160F. The atmosphere is fantastic in this old bistro which has been boosted by the new landlord and backed by a team of hip young people. In summer the terrace is packed; in winter everyone squeezes into the little lounge, a glass of *génépi* liqueur in one hand and a *pastis* in the other. Try the Provençal tuna steak or the flaked cod.

✗ **Gli Angeli** (map D3, **36**): 5 rue St-Gilles 75003. ☎ 01-42-71-05-80. Metro: Chemin-Vert. Open daily to 11.30pm. Closed for a fortnight in August. Budget for at least 200F per person. Pasta dishes are around 70F. Close to the Place des Vosges, this little restaurant, decorated with the warm colours of Italy, is very popular with the locals. There's a wide choice of genuine pasta dishes. For lovers of Italian wines, try their Lacrima de Christi (Christ's Tears); the vineyards are on Vesuvius.

WINE BAR

✗ 🍷 **Le Baromètre** (map C2, **29**): 17 rue Charlot 75003. ☎ 01-48-87-04-54. Metro: Temple. Open until 9 to 9.30pm. Closed Saturday and Sunday, and in August. Budget for around 120F; à la carte only. Very lively at lunchtime. This is a fairly anonymous bar, but popular with locals. Dishes of the day such as skate with *beurre blanc* tagliatelli, Auvergne tripe and *gratin d'andouillette* for around 60F, are all cooked with an angelic simplicity. In the afternoon and evening it's just a wine bar, with bread and *charcuteries* or cheeses to accompany the reasonably priced wines selected by the landlord (including Irancy, Beaujolais and Alsace).

NORTH OF THE MARAIS

★ **Musée Carnavalet, Histoire de Paris:** 23 rue de Sévigné. ☎ 01-42-72-21-13. Metro: St-Paul or Chemin-Vert. Bus Nos. 29, 69, 76 and 96. Open Tuesday to Sunday 10am to 5.40pm. Entry fee 30F; concessions 20F; free for 7 to 26-year-olds. Closed Monday and some public holidays. Guided tour around the permanent collections on Saturday at 2.45pm, and around the temporary exhibitions on Wednesday and Saturday at 3pm. Themed tours on Tuesday and Thursday at 2.45pm.

Some of the rooms have been recently renovated, maps of its various sections are available and there is an audioguide in the archaeological rooms. (Note the alternating opening times of the rooms dedicated to the 17th and 18th centuries: they're only open in the afternoons, from 1.10pm to 5.40pm.) There are several workshops for children on Wednesday, Saturday and during the school holidays, which last 1 hour 30 minutes (30F for a fun show for kids or a story, 55F for a workshop).

This is one of the finest museums in Paris, not only because of its setting and architectural proportions, but also because of the value of its collection, which covers Paris from its conception to the present day. The story of the capital is told through paintings, sculpture, furniture and everyday and decorative objects. The Carnavalet often only gets a look in if the 'big boys' (such as the Louvre or the Musée d'Orsay) leave people with enough time, but it's a mistake so see the Carnavalet as a minor museum. It is fascinating to discover the history of Paris from its early beginnings, through the Middle Ages, the Revolution, the Terror and the Romantic era. Allow your imagination to wander from one age to another as you walk through each room.

The museum's name doesn't let on, but it is made up of two private residences: Carnavalet and Le Peletier de St-Fargeau. The former is home to the exhibits on the origins of Paris up to the reign of Louis XVI. The second houses the collections from the Revolution to the present day. The entrance to the museum is through the Carnavalet residence, which adjoins Le Peletier de St-Fargeau via a passage through the Lycée Victor-Hugo. A superb example of Renaissance architecture, it was altered and embellished by Mansart and the home of Mme de Sévigné for around 20 years. The historic courtyard of the residence is on the corner of rue de Sévigné and rue des Francs-Bourgeois. There are a number of sculptures by Jean Goujon (including the Renaissance entrance gate and the four characters symbolizing the seasons on the central façade). The bronze statue of Louis XIV, in the paved courtyard, is the work of Coysevox and was the only one to escape being melted down during the Revolution. It was situated in the town hall, which doubled as the headquarters of the Commune of Paris, but no one ever thought to check there, so the statue was saved.

There follows a quick tour through the main sections of the museum, beginning with the very first archaeological discoveries made in the 19th century, as well as those made much more recently in the rue de Lutèce. There are explanatory notes in Braille and visually impaired visitors can touch some of the original sculptures.

– **Hall 1:** models, objects from the Bronze Age and superb jewels owned by the city's first inhabitants, the *Parisii.*

– **Hall 2:** amazing gold coins dating from the beginning of Paris but showing a Jean Cocteau-style human profile. Two other rooms house items from the Middle Ages (Merovingian and Carolingian periods) to the 15th century.

– **Hall 3:** a well-preserved eighth-century belt, as well as the impression of the face of a six-month-old baby found in a sarcophagus, said to be the first known Parisian.

– Also noteworthy are the rooms displaying Renaissance painting (magnificent works from the workshops of François Clouet and his school), the rooms of the former Municipality and those of the trades and professions of Paris.

On the **first floor** are dozens of rooms which allow visitors to follow decorative techniques and fashion in detail from the Renaissance to the end of the 18th century. Access is through the 16th-century halls on the ground floor or the escalier Luynes.

– **Cabinet des Arts Graphiques et Numismatiques:** traces the evolution of Paris through paintings and engravings. 'Photographs' from the period include *View of Paris Taken from the Quai de la Rapée,* by Pierre-Denis Martin. Open by appointment from 2 to 5pm Tuesday to Friday. Information: ☎ 01-42-72-21-13.

– **Cabinet Colbert de Villarcef (Hall 17)**: comes from a private residence in the rue de Turenne. The decor is characteristic of the Louis XIII style (flowers, ribbons, grotesques, masks and lovers). On the mantelpiece is a portrait of Mazarin, the Italian-born Cardinal who virtually ruled France during the minority of Louis XIV.

– **Cabinet Doré de l'Hôtel La Rivière:** decor from a residence in the Place des Vosges (1653). Architecture by Le Vau, paintings by Le Brun. Superb ceiling.

– Halls with interior design carried out under Louis XVI: among others is the **Salon du Graveur Demarteau** with doors painted by Boucher. The fourth is said to be by Fragonard, and the animals by J.-B. Huet.

– **Escalier de Luynes:** sole survivor of all the staircase decors from the 18th century. Murals from the Hôtel de Luynes (1747). Note the figures which seem to be watching the people climbing the staircase.

– **Salle des Philosophes:** items such as Jean-Jacques Rousseau's inkwell and collection of dried plants, and Voltaire's snuffbox. A fine room with chiselled Louis XV panelling.

– The superb **Salon Jaune** originates from the Hôtel Lally-Tollendal and the **Salon Bleu** dates from Louis XV. In **Hall 40**, there's an unusual 'regulator' in a violin-type case, a device which is in fact a clock. **Salon Lilas** contains some superb furniture.

– **Hall 41:** contain scenes from earthy Parisian life, such as *Dispute at the Fountain.*

– **Salon Chinoise (Hall 42)**: this is the only hall with original panelling plus a fine set of 'exotic' furnishings.

– **Hall 22:** devoted to Madame de Sévigné. With the notable inclusion of the 'sloping' desk with her arms, the portrait of her daughter by Pierre Mignard and the portrait of Mme de Sévigné and Claude Lefèvre.

★ Taking the passage, you return once more to the **Hôtel Le Peletier de St-Fargeau** where you can find many emotive symbols and souvenirs from the Revolution and the end of Louis XVI's reign. A host of objects recalls this period: a scale Bastille cut from one of the stones of the famous prison; a fine collection of patriotic earthenware; the tables of the Constitution and the Rights of Man which used to be placed behind the President of the Convention; an original red cap worn by one of the famous *'sans-culottes'*, a fine wardrobe decorated with revolutionary maxims inlaid in marquetry; portraits of Danton, Robespierre, Mme Récamier and others. Whole rooms have been reconstructed, such as the rooms of Marcel Proust.

The jeweller Fouquet's Art Nouveau shop, originally designed by Mucha in 1900, has been recreated, as well as the ballroom of the Hôtel de Wendel. There are also some exhibits from the last century, evoking the Saint-Germain-des-Près of Juliette Greco, Cocteau and Poiret.

Finally, don't miss the temporary exhibitions and displays of photographs of old Paris.

★ **Hôtels de la rue du Parc-Royal:** a unique succession of magnificent houses from the 17th and 18th centuries; and, at night, one of the most romantic walks you can imagine. At No. 4 is the Hôtel Canillac, one of the rare houses whose gate is usually left open. On the left, don't miss the unique Louis XIII staircase, with wooden banisters carved with tracery and flower-shaped ornamentation. At No. 8 is the former Hôtel Duret de Chevry, now renovated; at No. 10 and 12 are two more fine façades.

★ **Rue Payenne:** this street runs right along on the left-hand side of the Parc Royal. At No. 13 is the elegant Hôtel de Châtillon, covered with ivy and Virginia creeper, which boasts a fine courtyard and, on the right, a staircase with a superb banister. At No. 11, the Hôtel de Marle is well restored and now houses the Swedish Cultural Centre. The architect Mansart died at No. 5, a curious 17th-century residence. It houses the only chapel of the 'religion of humanity', based on the positivist thought of Auguste Comte. Note the profession of exalted faith on the façade.

★ **Rue de Turenne:** one of the main north-south axes of the Marais is bordered by many former fine residences. At No. 67 are the remains of a vast butcher's shop which occupied the whole lower part of the building. Of the original *six têtes de bœufs-consoles* (cows' heads) which held up the balcony, only two remain, as well as a piece of the bar used to hang the meat.

On the corner of rue de Turenne and rue Villehardouin there is a fine recess holding a 17th-century Virgin.

★ **Musée Cognacq-Jay:** 8 rue Elzévir 75003. ☎ 01-40-27-07-21. Metro: St-Paul or Chemin-Vert. Reinstalled in the superb Hôtel Donon. Open Tuesday to Sunday 10am to 5.40pm. Closed Monday and public holidays. Entry fee 22F; concessions 15F; free to under 26s and those over 60.

A splendid 16th-century residence, built for Médéric de Donon, an adviser to Henri III. This admirable museum is devoted to the private collection of Ernest Cognacq. Along with Louise Jay, his wife, he founded the department store *La Samaritaine* overlooking the Seine by the Pont Neuf. An orphan, he was forced to leave school at the age of 11 and tried to make his fortune by selling clothes, opening the '*Samar*' in 1869. He began acquiring 18th-century works of art, and eventually donated them to the City of Paris.

The 20 halls of the museum essentially house works from the 18th century, the period about which Cognacq was most passionate. There are exquisite *salons* and former bedrooms, all decorated with quality works of art, and even a few masterpieces. Each is based around a theme, such as bourgeois life, 18th-century childhood, a sculpture gallery, an English gallery, to name but a few. The paintings, porcelain, everyday and decorative objects make up whole displays.

Amongst the painters represented are Rembrandt (Hall 4, *L'Ânesse du Prophète Balaam*), Fragonard (Hall 6, *L'Heureuse Famille* and Hall 8, *Perrette and le Pot au Lait),* Chardin (Hall 4, *Le Chaudron de Cuivre*), as well as Boucher, Watteau, Greuze and Canaletto.

There is also porcelain from Saxony and a series of small, rococo objects: boxes, small bottles, cases and small pots. Climb right up to the top (Hall 20) to discover the superb wooden roof.

There are changing temporary exhibitions as well as stories and pastel workshops for children.

★ On the corner of rue des Francs-Bourgeois and rue Vieille-du-Temple, is the **Maison de Jean Hérouet**, the home of Louis XII's treasurer. It is a typical early 16th-century house, with a magnificent turret and Gothic sculptures.

★ **Musée d'Art et d'Histoire de Judaïsme** (map **B2**): Hôtel de St-Aignan, 71 rue du Temple 75003. ☎ 01-53-01-86-60. Metro: Rambuteau or Hôtel-de-Ville. Bus Nos. 29, 38, 47 and 75. Open Monday to Friday 11am to 6pm and on Sunday 10am to 6pm. Disabled access. Entry fee 40F; reductions for 18 to 26-year-olds; free for under 18s, the unemployed and visitors with disabilities.

This magnificent, 17th-century private residence (which has been undergoing restoration since 1978!) is home to the Museum of the Art and History of Judaism. It's been worth the wait. Inside are the remains of the original architecture, such as the great staircase, which has been entirely reconstructed, and the antique frescoes which were discovered during restoration work.

The museum brings together the Isaac Strauss-Rothschild collections from the Musée de Cluny and the former Museum of Jewish Art as well as donations, loans and around 30 classic MNR works. (MNR stands for *musées nationaux recuperation* meaning 'national museum recovery'. These works were confiscated from Jews by the Nazis and are being held until their owners are found.) The history of the Jewish people from the Middle Ages to today is traced throughout the four levels of the museum. The most important events in Judaism (persecution, the Dreyfus affair, the Holocaust) are recorded chronologically and geographically. There are archaeological items, religious furniture and medieval funeral steles discovered around rue de la Harpe, as well as the cultural items and canvases by Modigliani, Marc Chagall and Lipchitz, bearing witness to the Jewish contributions to 20th-century art. The most spectacular pieces on display are the 3,000 or so items left to the museum by the grandchildren of Captain Dreyfus (papers from Devil's Island, where he was imprisoned, letters of support and personal souvenirs). One of the walls of the inner courtyard is covered with small plaques bearing the names of Jewish immigrants living there just before the World War II.

The museum has an auditorium, a media library (books, videos and photographs) and a documentation centre. There is also a bookshop, a café and temporary exhibitions. A huge garden next to the museum is opening soon. A flowerbed in the Le Nôtre style will be a reminder of how the original garden must have looked in the 17th century.

★ **Rue des Francs-Bourgeois:** straddling the 3rd and 4th arrondissements, there are prestigious private residences on both sides of this street. We've dealt with both sides in the section on the 4th arrondissement.

★ **Hôtel Libéral-Bruant:** 1 rue de la Perle. ☎ 01-42-77-79-62. Metro: Chemin-Vert or St-Paul. Built in the 17th century by the architect of the Invalides, today, after restoration (an elegant façade with a sculpted pediment), it is home to the **Musée de la Serrurerie** (museum of Locksmiths). Open 10am to noon and 2pm to 5pm. Closed Monday mornings, Saturday, Sunday and public holidays. Entry fee 30F and 15F. Five small rooms are packed with locks, latches, bolts and door hammers in all shapes and sizes and from all eras. Note the curious lock in the shape of a huge lion's mouth and whose jaws brutally close on the hand of anyone who might try to break in.

★ **Musée Picasso:** Hôtel Salé, 5 rue de Thorigny. ☎ 01-42-71-25-21. Metro: St-Sébastien-Froissart. Open 9.30am to 6pm (5.30pm from 1 October to 31 March) and until 8pm on Thursdays. Closed Tuesday. Entry fee 30F; 20F for those aged 18-25. Prices increased by 8F for temporary exhibitions. Free for under 18s. This superb residence was built in the 17th century for a nouveau-riche gentleman who had made his fortune by levying the unpopular salt tax, and the house became known as the *Salé* or 'Salty' residence. The doors of the house open onto a magnificent inner staircase, and the exhibition rooms, which are very well lit, have an excellent selection of old and new. Designed by Roland Simounet, the architect entrusted with the renovation of the museum, the rooms provide a perfect setting for Picasso's works of art.

Information panels, photographs, letters and other documents help the visitor to understand the various turning points in the life and work of the famous artist: the young Picasso arriving penniless from Barcelona, mad about art, painting his drinking companions; the revelation of cubism and the *Bateau-Lavoir* era; the succession of love affairs and political adventures, all translating into new shapes and accents, from neoclassicism to surrealism, to the violent baroque of the *Grands Nus*; the extraordinary fecundity of the man who once said: 'I don't look for things, I find them'. This is a unique collection, housed in a beautiful buiding, which covers Picasso's entire output from 1905 to 1973.

★ **Palais de Soubise:** 60 rue des Francs-Bourgeois. ☎ 01-40-27-60-96. Metro: Rambuteau or Hôtel-de-Ville. Open noon to 5.45pm, at weekends from 1.45pm to 5.45pm. Closed Tuesday and public holidays. Entry fee 20F; concessions 15F. A superb residence, through the half-moon gate you can see the magnificent horseshoe-shaped courtyard, flanked by a gallery of columns. The façade of the building is a masterpiece of symmetry and elegance. The manor house of Olivier de Clisson occupied this site before the current house was built, and a door and two turrets (see below) still remain. It was here that the St Bartholomew's Day Massacre of the Hugenots was plotted in 1672. At the beginning of the 18th century the building, which had been bought by the Rohan-Soubise family, was knocked down and rebuilt by the architect Delamair and redecorated by Boffrand. Many members of the Rohan family subsequently lived here. There is a sumptuous Louis XV-style interior.

The Hôtel de Soubise and its adjacent buildings have housed the **Musée de l'Histoire de France** since 1808. It forms of the **Archives Nationales** (containing millions of ministerial documents and private archives). Some of the most original (and sometimes moving or amusing) documents from the National Archives can be seen here. The museum offers a programme of temporary exhibitions with themes of a historical nature: the problem of municipal water in Paris, lighting and so on. There is a superb map of Paris dating from 1676. The last hall, decorated with gilded panelling, was the drawing room of the Princess de Soubise. There is a fine balustrade to be seen in her bedroom.

★ **Hôtel de Clisson:** 58 rue des Archives. One of the oldest examples of Parisian civil architecture. Built in 1380, all that remains today of the home of the supreme commander of the French armies, Olivier de Clisson, a companion of Du Guesclin, is the ogival gate topped by two corbelled pepperpot towers.

★ **Hôtel de Guénégaud:** 60 rue des Archives; on the corner with rue des Quatre-Fils. ☎ 01-53-01-92-40. Open 11am to 6pm. Closed Monday and public holidays. Entry fee 30F; reduced rate for children and school groups. A magnificent 17th-century house, the work of François Mansart. Saved *in extremis* by the Malraux Law, it now houses the **Musée de la Chasse et de la Nature** (Museum of Hunting and Nature), with an elegant courtyard and splendid interior staircase. Whatever you may think about hunting, there is some magnificent weaponry here from all ages, as well as interesting paintings by Oudry, Chardin, Vernet and Brueghel de Velours. And naturally, there are all sorts of trophies on display. Admire the perfect reconstruction of the French-style gardens, the tracery of the ironwork balcony and the ornate designs of the flowerbeds. As you leave, note the pretty *fontaine des Haudriettes* from the 18th century.

★ Behind the Archives, in rue des Quatre-Fils, it's worth making a detour to the **Centre d'Accueil et de Recherche des Archives Nationales** because of its highly modern architectural style, which contrasts with the rigorously classical Archives building to great effect.

★ **Hôtel de Rohan:** 87 rue Vieille-du-Temple. Currently closed for work – end date not confirmed at time of writing. Once it opens, you'll be able to admire the high-relief of the *Chevaux d'Apollon* by Le Lorrain, which seems to burst out of the stone. The apartments with the splendid *cabinet des Singes* can only be seen during temporary exhibitions. There are tapestries by de Beauvais and some fine panelling.

★ **Musée de la Poupée, Au Petit Monde Ancien:** impasse Berthaud (go as far as 22 rue Beaubourg) 75003. ☎ 01-42-72-73-11. Metro: Rambuteau. Open 10am to 6pm including public holidays. Closed Monday and 25 December and 1 January. Entry fee 35F; concessions 25F; children aged 3–18 years 20F. Established in 1994 by two passionate collectors, this museum traces the history of puppets from 1860 to 1960. There are temporary exhibitions and a shop, as well as courses and workshops. You can also bring any puppets which need repairing to the 'clinic'.

★ **The Horloge area:** bordered by rue St-Martin, rue Rambuteau, rue

Beaubourg and rue du Grenier-St-Lazare. See the *horloge à automates* (automata clock) which is 4m (13ft) high, entitled 'The Defender of Time'. The automata are set in motion at noon, 6pm and 10pm, when the defender of time is attacked by three creatures: a crab, a dragon and a bird. Unfortunately the Horloge area doesn't have much else to offer, with concrete façades fast deteriorating. It lacks soul and for this reason is usually deserted at night.

★ **Passage Molière:** begins at 82 rue Quincampoix, and rejoins rue St-Martin. During the Revolution this was known as the passage des Sans-Culottes. These days it has a quiet old charm and an almost provincial air, with washing drying in the wind and shrubs growing on the balconies.

A bit further up, if you take rue Quincampoix again, you'll find the **rue aux Ours;** nothing to do with bears, as you may think if your French vocabulary stretches that far, but a corruption of the word *oues* which meant *oies*, or geese. They were a very popular grilled dish in this area during the Middle Ages.

★ Walk along the **rue Michel-le-Comte** and admire some of the houses. No. 16 is the 15th-century Auberge de l'Ours et du Lion. At No. 19, there's a lovely inner courtyard. At No. 25 a sign and a long passage dotted with houses leads to a courtyard with little workshops, which is typical of the old Marais. Don't miss No. 27, which has been superbly renovated. At No. 28 is the Hôtel d'Hallwyll with a fine porch framed by columns and a sculpted pediment.

★ The **rue du Temple** also has its share of fine private houses. No. 71 is the Hôtel St-Aignan, the headquarters of the Municipality from 1795 to 1800, then town hall of the old 7th arrondissement. Opposite is the passage St-Avoye. No. 79 is the Hôtel de Montmor (1623) and is where Molière wrote *Tartuffe*. There's a monumental porch and two elegant wings on the Louis XV-style courtyard. From the bottom of rue de Braque there is a lovely view of the Hôtel de Clisson. At No. 7 there's an attractive courtyard, whilst Nos. 4 and 6 boast two superb doors topped with wrought-iron balconies.

★ **Maison de Nicolas Flamel:** 51 rue de Montmorency. Built in 1407, which makes it one of the oldest houses in Paris. Much restoration work was carried out in the 18th century, and the pseudo-Gothic elements of the façade are obviously later than the construction date. Nicolas Flamel, a great 15th-century academic, was believed to have invented the philosopher's stone.

A WALK AROUND THE 'FRENCH PROVINCES'

This walk is a little off the beaten track. There are no spectacular private residences but fine courtyards with hanging gables, ornate staircases and picturesque old lanes. Most of the streets bear provincial names.

★ Take the **rue Charlot** which, contrary to appearances, is not a well-deserved homage to the great comedian, Charlie Chaplin (known to the French as 'Charlot'), but the name of an obscure 17th-century financier. At No. 5 is the beginning of the ruelle Sourdis, unfortunately now closed off by an iron gate.

Almost opposite, the **Church of St-Jean** used to be a Capuchin monastery, then a chapel, which Mme de Sévigné often attended. There's an iron gate and an old fountain in a quiet little courtyard. The porch was reworked by Baltard. Inside are some fine paintings, remarkable panelling in the chancel and *St Francis of Assisi* by Germain Pilon. Your only chance to see them is at High Mass on Sunday, from 10.30am to noon.

★ On the way, cross the **rue du Perche**. Mme de Maintenon lived at No. 9. On the left is the **rue Pastourelle** (Pastoral), which has born this name, evoking meadows and country lanes in the heart of the city, since 1330. Opposite is rue de Beauce, which you come into from the **ruelle de Sourdis** (closed off by an iron gate in the evening). It looks just as it did 300 years ago, with its corbelled houses and central gutter. Unfortunately, a wall at the end of the street prevents you from rejoining rue Charlot.

★ On the corner of the **rue de Beauce** and **rue Pastourelle** the former names of the streets are engraved in the stone: Beausse and rue d'Anjou. The rue de Beauce is narrow but, unlike the ruelle de Sourdis, it has not kept its medieval look. Before you reach rue de Bretagne, take the tiny rue des Oiseaux to reach the Marché des Enfants-Rouges, one of the oldest and little known markets in Paris. During the 17th century it was known as the 'little market of the Marais' before being renamed after a neighbouring children's hospital where the patients wore red clothing. The market has been rather distastefully modernized, but it's lively at weekends with a café and an antiques shop.

Emerging back onto the **rue de Bretagne**, you'll find many shops. Opposite the market, on the corner with rue Charlot, there's a bakery with an attractive interior: ceramics decorated with flowers, stuccoes and a marble counter. But the best bakery in the quarter is on the corner of rue de Saintonge.

It would be impossible to list all the houses of interest in the other 'provincial streets', as there are too many of them, but to get an idea of what a typical house in the Marais was like before renovation, take a look at 8 **rue de Saintonge**. In the courtyard on the left is a huge staircase with a wrought-iron banister, as well as fading inscriptions indicating the presence at one time of the concierge and a certain patina of time on the walls. At No. 13, you can imagine the 17th century mathematician Blaise Pascal in his little room, young and full of ideas, inventing the first adding machine.

On the corner with the **rue du Poitou**, there's a bakery with an interior of ceramics and painted mirrors. Robespierre lived at No. 64 from 1789 to 1791.

THE TEMPLE DISTRICT

Although a street, a boulevard, a faubourg and a square have been named after them, there is nothing else to remind you that the Knights Templar once inhabited this area or that this was the location of the keep from where Louis XVI set off for the scaffold. However, it was the Templar monks who originally made the area habitable, the Temple quarter existing as a city within the city, a sort of free zone for artisans and debtors, until the time of the Revolution. It was made up of a keep, a church and a prison, as well as the Palais du Grand Prieur, where the royal family would spend time. The doomed Louis XVI, Marie Antoinette and their immediate family were imprisoned in the keep and spent the whole period of their detention here before the final march to the scaffold. The 10-year-old heir to the Revolutionary throne, Louis XVII, died here after being walled up and allowed no communication with the outside world. Napoleon had the palace and keep destroyed in 1808, probably due to superstition. There are a number of interesting things to see around the fine place du Temple.

There is still an established population, giving the area around rue Volta, rue des Vertus and rue des Gravilliers a lived-in feel. The **rue des Vertus** itself is reminiscent of the trading which used to go on here and today numerous bistros and Arab, Chinese and Vietnamese restaurants make up the oldest Asian community living in Paris. To replace the workers who left for the Front in 1914, the government brought over 100,000 Chinese from Sun Yat Sen's Republic (including two young men called Den Xiao Ping and Zhou Enlai!). Many of them remained after the war and set up home in the 3rd arrondissement. Today, their descendents run many of the cafés in the district.

The area has also been discovered by young trendies and the success of Tango, the best African nightclub in town, no doubt has something to do with it (see below).

★ Very lively during the day, the **rue des Gravilliers** specializes in jewellery, trinkets and leather articles. It has many fine 17th- and 18th-century façades. There's a beautiful house at No. 14, on the corner of rue des Gravilliers and rue des Vertus. The name of the latter street is an ironic reference to the profession which used to be practised there – you don't need to understand French to work that one out! No. 29 has fine wrought-iron work and at No. 19 there is a dark paved passageway, with a drain in the middle, which leads on to the rue Chapon. Members of the trade union movement may feel moved at No. 44, the Association Internationale des Travailleurs (International Association of Workers); the first Internationale (supported by Karl Marx) had its headquarters here.

From here, descend the rue Beaubourg and turn right into rue du Grenier-St-Lazare, which takes you back to the rue aux Ours.

★ The **rue Au-Maire**, one of the liveliest in the quarter, has popular bistros, cheap restaurants and many old houses. At No. 15 there is an old passageway through to 34 rue des Gravilliers, but the iron gate at the bottom is often closed.

★ The **rue Volta** has what is thought to be the oldest house in Paris, although some people insist that honour should go to the house of Nicolas Flamel, at 51 rue de Montmorency (dating from 1406). Whether it is the oldest in Paris or not, it certainly has characteristics typical of the Middle Ages, such as the two former shops which have a stone rim on either side of the door, which was closed with horizontal shutters. The lower one was used as a counter. The ceilings were barely 2m (6ft 6in) high. The half-timbering has recently been renovated. After the 14th century, the use of wood for walls was banned, because of the fear of fire. They were probably right, given the devastation caused by the Great Fire of London in 1666!

★ **Le Musée des Arts et Métiers** (Museum of Arts and Professions): 60 rue Réaumur, 75003. ☎ 01-53-01-82-00 (recorded information). Website: www.cnam.fr/museum. Metro: Arts-et-Métiers. Bus 20, 38, 39, 47. Open Tuesday to Sunday 10am to 6pm, and late-night opening on Thursday until 9.30pm. Closed Monday and public holidays. Entry fee 35F, concessions 25F, family tickets (two adults and two children) 100F. Free for the under fives.

Founded in 1794 by Abbot Gregoire (the first priest to agree to swear an oath of allegiance to the new social order issuing from the Revolution), the aim of the Conservatoire National des Arts et Métiers was to bring together 'all the newly invented and perfected tools and machines' and to promote demonstration and instruction aimed at training skilled craftsmen and providing them with 'good models' to copy. In 1798 the abbey of Saint-Martin-des-Champs was chosen to house this Conservatoire. The church then became a temple to a new religion – progress. Throughout the 19th century, the collections continued to expand and the teaching practices became ever more popular. Rail tracks were even installed around the buildings (and can still be seen today), allowing demonstrators to transport cumbersome objects to the lecture halls with ease. In 1988 the decision was taken to completely revamp the museum. Renovation works are now complete; the restored buildings have retained their integrity while their contents have been expanded and enhanced with the inclusion of contemporary items.

Visits are based around seven different areas. Each of them (structured chronologically) consists of an exhibition hall where you can handle the models and carry out experiments (very popular with the kids) and also an interactive information kiosk. Another novelty is that 150 'key objects' have been equipped with individual explanatory devices, illustrating their activity in context.

– **2nd floor:** on the left coming out of the lift is the astonishing *Cabinet des curiosités (chamber of curiosities)* which contains, among other things, a machine for forecasting tides.

The first area is *Scientific Instruments*: a full range of devices for measuring, counting, forecasting and evaluating dating back to the 17th century, from measuring jugs to microscopes through to Pascal's astonishing calculating machine (1642), Bürgï's celestial globes and vacuum machines. Also an attractive reconstruction of Lavoisier's laboratory.

Next is *Materials:* this area covers textiles, with Vaucanson's superb loom (1746); paper (a very attractive mock-up of a paper factory); glassworks (a magnificent collection of items by Gallé). There are also blast furnaces and more modern composite materials: aluminium and early examples of Bakelite, when chemistry came to the aid of physics.

– **1st floor:** You begin with *Construction.* Wooden frames that look like concrete and cement. A superb mock-up of the construction of a building in rue de Rivoli, with the use of a steam-powered device to move the winches. Bridges and bridge-building techniques are tackled on a mezzanine floor. Finally, the display of modern construction techniques includes a superb model of a tunneller.

The next area, *Communication* (a very large section, 10 per cent of the whole collection), stretches the full length of the building. It is divided into a number of different themes: on the left, the written word, graphic arts and printing (particularly noteworthy is the first printing press, designed by Marinoni, and Comté's etching machine). On the left is a history of the audio-visual arts: their debut with the magic lantern, then photography (Daguerre's chamber), Marey's 'gun' (forebear of the cinema), the first tentative steps in cinema itself with one of the Lumière brothers' prototypes. The section on sound features phonographs, while long-distance communication includes Wheatstone and Cooke's magnetised needle telegraph,

Ferrié's wireless, and Barthélémy's first television (1935). Finally all the modern technical advances, including a mock-up of the Telstar telecommunications satellite.

This is followed by the *Energy* section, from animal or natural power through to nuclear. There are lots of models in this section, starting with Marly's machine (which provided all the ornamental lakes in the gardens of Versailles with water), then paddle wheels and Papin's steam lifting machine. The evolution of electricity from Volta's battery to Gramme's dynamo and objects of grandeur such as Diesel's engine and a model of a nuclear power station.

The last area on this floor is *Mechanics*, which includes the body of trades covering precision craftsmanship and the start of mechanisation. From gears, levers and ball bearings: everything involved in mechanised movement. Also displayed are the workings of small mechanisms: wrought locks (with the chequering machine manufactured by Mercklein for Louis XVI), watch mechanisms, spheres of boxwood, ebony or ivory, masterpieces of fine craftsmanship by François Barreau. There are also some magnificent machine tools, almost works of art in themselves, such as Senot's screw-making tower.

Half-way through this section is the marvellous *Théâtre des Automates (theatre of automata)*, where a nine minute film gives you an introduction to the items on display in the hall before you take a look at the amazing objects themselves. Music boxes, animated pictures (some of which belonged to Marie-Antoinette) and all manner of magical and marvellous items.

– **Ground Floor:** the final section, *Transport*, a field initially dominated by ships and horses, then by the arrival of the railway and finally the all-conquering car. Some exceptional items illustrate this evolution: Cugnot's artillery carriage (1796), the first genuine automobile land vehicle (steam-driven), an astonishing collection of velocipedes (with and without pedals), and a Model-T Ford. From more recent times there is a model of a cross-section of the Météor metro line.

Finally, the museum tour is rounded off beautifully with a visit to the fully restored **chapel**, whose 12th century chevet (given over to a display of the remains of the Merovingian burial ground discovered in the course of restoration work) makes a happy marriage with flamboyant 19th century colour work: Foucault's pendulum has been reinstated in its original location in the centre of the choir. Some larger items are displayed in the nave where a walk-way allows visitors to see them close-up from an impressive angle. Further exhibits include old vehicles, planes (such as Blériot's, in which he made the first flight across the Channel) and a preparatory scale model for Bartholdi's Statue of Liberty. There are also many more exhibits from modern times including, for example, the Vulcain d'Ariane 5 rocket engine.

There is also a cafeteria (just before *Transport*, on the ground floor), a documentation centre open to all and sundry (and another more specialised one to which visits are by appointment only) and a small shop/bookshop at the entrance.

★ **Carreau du Temple:** rue Dupetit-Thouars and rue Perrée. Under this beautiful metallic structure, with its glass roof and arabesque wrought-iron work, there is an old clothes market, carrying on the tradition of the fair which was held here in the Middle Ages.. Open 9am to 12.30pm (1pm on Sunday). Closed Monday.

Throughout the 19th century, hard-up Parisians have shopped for clothes here. The current building replaced a 1900 Baltard-type structure, built under Napoleon III in 1900. The market has its own 19th-century based argot; a shirt is a *'limace'*, a female trader is *'une râleuse'* and a male client is *'un gonce'*. Today, most of the clothes are new and traders and second-hand dealers are gradually leaving the area, but the atmosphere is as lively as ever. The old custom of haggling lives on and pitches are still allocated according to an old tradition. Every morning at 8am each trader places an aluminium medallion into a basket and then they are picked out one by one. The first chooses the best pitch, and so on. Along the rue Dupetit-Thouars there are shops selling the cheapest leather jackets in Paris. The local motto is: 'Anyone who hesitates will spend an hour here, anyone who stops is lost!'

★ The area still has a fair number of craftspeople and cottage industries, which hark back to the days of the Temple enclosure, which, until the Revolution, enjoyed special tax privileges. You can take a walk (during the week) in the **cité Dupetit-Thouars,** flanked by paved courtyards and old workshops, some of which are being renovated. Note the old billiard factory, Hénin Aîné, which still retains a former charm, with its neatly laid out ancient tools.

The **rue de la Corderie** is an odd shape. It starts with a bottleneck and then opens out into a lovely square with old bars.

WHERE TO GO FOR A DRINK

🍸 **The Quiet Man** (map B2, **40**): 5 rue des Haudriettes 75003. ☎ 01-48-04-02-77. Metro: Rambuteau or Hôtel-de-Ville. Open daily 4pm to 2am (5pm to 2am on Thursday and Friday). Closed 24 and 25 December. 19F for half a pint of beer, 35F for a pint. If you have a sudden desperate urge to forsake Parisian cafés for a touch of the Emerald Isle, this is the place to come. The welcome is as charming as the locals. Games of darts are closely fought. Last orders at 1.30am. Traditional Irish, Quebec or French music in the evening.

🍸 **Le Web Bar** (map C2, **41**): 32 rue de Picardie 75003. ☎ 01-42-72-66-55. Metro: Temple or République. Open daily 8.30am to 2am. Set menus: 51F lunchtime; 59F in the evening. The hippest cyber café, but luckily also the cheapest! Situated in a former goldsmith's workshop converted into an art gallery, you can surf the net for only 40F per hour or 250F for 10 hours. There are permanent exhibitions on various floors, short films are shown on the third Friday of every month, and readings every Sunday afternoon. Good food (sandwiches and *bruschetta*), including Sunday brunch. Set menu served at lunchtime and in the evening. If possible, sit at one of the tables under the large glass roof which dates from the last century.

🍸 **L'Apparemment Café** (map C2-3, **44**): 18 rue des Coutures-St-Gervais 75003. ☎ 01-48-87-12-22. Metro: St-Sébastien-Froissart. Closed Saturday lunchtime. Brunch 90F and 120F; à la carte 90F. Right in the heart of the historic Marais, just down the road from the Picasso Museum – and yet it's not a new gay or intellectual bar. View works by local young artists from the comfort of velvet armchairs and 1930s American sofas. There is also a lounge area with a well-stocked library and a choice of games (free with a drink). Generous portions of good food (cheese, *charcuterie*, fish, crudités). A large choice of cocktails at around 50F.

NIGHTCLUB

– **Les Bains** (map A2, **42**): 7 rue du Bourg-l'Abbé 75003. ☎ 01-48-87-01-80. Metro: Étienne-Marcel. Open daily midnight to dawn. Restaurant open from 8.30pm, last orders at midnight; budget for 250F per person. Entrance including a drink 120F on Saturday and Sunday, 100F the rest of the week. 50F per drink during the week, 70F at the weekend. The capital's VIP club – musicians Prince and Lenny Kravitz, plus fashion designer Jean-Paul Gaultier, are often seen here. It's quite difficult to get in. If you do manage it, you can sample the French-Thai cuisine which is not of the highest standard – but remember, it's not the food that matters, it's the people!

4TH ARRONDISSEMENT

THE POMPIDOU CENTRE ● BEAUBOURG ● THE ST-GERVAIS – ST-PAUL DISTRICT ● ÎLE DE LA CITE ● ÎLE ST LOUIS ● PLACE DES VOSGES

This is the heart of the Marais, with narrow streets, fine private residences and picturesque passages between rue des Francs-Bourgeois and the Seine and the sublime place des Vosges. To the south of rue de Rivoli, the St-Paul quarter used to be one of the most popular Parisian districts, whilst the Beaubourg is full of cafés, shops and galleries and home to the famous *Centre Georges-Pompidou.* The two islands in the Seine are connected by a bridge. The Île de la Cité was home to the first Parisians and boasts the Notre-Dame as its considerable and renowned centrepiece, while the Île St-Louis is a sheer delight, with ancient houses, charming shops and hotels.

WHERE TO STAY

☆ BUDGET

The **MIJEs** *(Maison Internationale de Jeunesse et des Étudiants)* offer three excellent places to stay in 16th- and 17th-century private residences, superbly renovated, in the heart of historic Paris. You won't find anywhere better. Arrive as soon as you can after 7am to get a bed, as you can't reserve a place in advance. Most of the rooms are occupied by groups – French or other nationalities. Group reservations: ☎ 01-42-74-23-45; fax: 01-42-74-52-05. For individuals, fax: 01-40-27-81-64. E-mail: MIJE@wanadoo.fr. In summer they are very busy, but with the rapid turnover you have a fairly good chance of finding accommodation. Single bed 138F in rooms for four or more (including breakfast). Double room with shower 180F. Maximum stay is seven nights. Half board 190F, obligatory for groups of over 10 people. Curfew is at 1am. Check-out is between noon and 3pm. Free left luggage service. Meals at the Fourcy (see below) with MIJE *table d'hôte* (the host's table) for guests of the other two MIJEs (and for anyone else). Set menus 50F and 65F.

Hôtel MIJE Maubuisson (map B2, **1**): 12 rue des Barres 75004. For contact details, see above. Metro: St-Paul or Pont-Marie. A magnificent house with corbels, half-timbering and sawtooth gables. Interior decorated in Gothic style with old furniture in solid wood. A quiet street, with a view over the rooftops and the stained-glass windows of the church of St-Gervais.

Le Fauconnier MIJE (map C2, **2**): 11 rue du Fauconnier 75004. For contact details, see above. Metro: St-Paul. A former 17th-century townhouse which has been superbly renovated. There's an imposing sculpted wooden gate and inside are huge old wardrobes, chests, long rustic tables and a magnificent staircase with a wrought-iron banister. In summer, you can have your breakfast in the paved courtyard. Rooms have from one to eight beds. Washbasin and shower en suite. Toilets in the corridor.

Hôtel MIJE de Fourcy (map C2,

3): 6 rue de Fourcy 75004. For contact details, see above. Metro: St-Paul or Pont-Marie. A former 17th-century private residence. Magnificently renovated, it now houses young people astonished to find themselves staying in such a palace. Good location between the Place des Vosges and the Île St-Louis. There's a little garden on the corner of rue Charlemagne. Rooms have from four to eight beds with mezzanine, washbasin and shower. Toilets on each floor. Medieval-looking wooden footbridges link the two buildings. You eat in a fine arched dining room with exposed stones, which is common to all three MIJEs.

HOTELS

☆ MODERATE

Grand Hôtel Jeanne d'Arc (map C2, **4**): 3 rue de Jarente 75004. ☎ 01-48-87-62-11. Fax: 01-48-87-37-31. Metro: St-Paul, Chemin-Vert, Marais or Bastille. Bus Nos. 96, 69, 76 or 29. Double room 305F to 500F. For three people 540F; for four 600F. Extra bed 75F. This well-kept and charming hotel is situated in a quiet location just off the lovely Place Ste-Catherine. The decor was created by a local artist; murals in the lounges and dining rooms, door numbers, banisters and decorative furniture, even the enormous mirror in reception. Children's beds can be provided on request. Pets are accepted. Booking is essential. All the rooms have been refitted with a shower or bathroom. Cable TV. First breakfast is free.

Grand Hôtel du Loiret (map B1, **5**): 8 rue des Mauvais-Garçons 75004. ☎ 01-48-87-77-00. Fax: 01-48-04-96-56. Metro: Hôtel-de-Ville. Double room with washbasin 230F, with shower 320F and with bathroom 420F. This hotel has been entirely renovated and tastefully redecorated. There's a fine wooden staircase and marble-style walls. The rooms on the first to the fourth floors have been repainted in warm, rather masculine colours, but the cheaper rooms on the upper floors (the shower is in the corridor) are no less attractive. For example, the room for four on the seventh floor (no lift) offers a wonderful view over the rooftops of Paris from the Panthéon to Sacré-Cœur, via Beaubourg and Notre-Dame.

Hôtel Andréa (map A1, **6**): 3 rue St-Bon 75004. ☎ 01-42-78-43-93. Fax: 01-44-61-28-36. Metro: Châtelet or Hôtel-de-Ville. Double room with shower or bathroom and toilet from 330F to 360F. For three people 435F; for four 500F. This hotel is housed in a 19th-century building in a quiet street, just off the bustling rue de Rivoli. Fairly cheap for the area and reasonably comfortable. Rooms 203, 603 and 604 have a fine view over Paris.

Hôtel Sansonnet (map B1, **7**): 48 rue de la Verrerie 75004. ☎ 01-48-87-96-14. Fax: 01-48-87-30-46. Metro: Hôtel-de-Ville or Châtelet. Double room with toilet, shower or bathroom from 400F to 440F. A well-kept little hotel with tasteful decor and a charming welcome from the landlord.

☆☆☆ CHIC

Hôtel de Nice (map B2, **9**): 42 *bis* rue de Rivoli 75004. ☎ 01-42-78-55-29. Fax: 01-42-78-36-07. Metro: Hôtel-de-Ville. Double room with shower or bathroom, hairdryer and TV 500F. Elegance, refinement, discretion (in fact so much that you might find it difficult to locate the entrance!) and a smiling welcome. The owners used to be antiques' dealers and they've put their taste for beautiful things to good use. In the TV lounge, where breakfast is served, soft fabrics, 18th-century engravings and a portrait of a dandy with his dog and cat, are reminiscent of the time when conversation was still an art. The rooms are soundproofed, with well-designed bathrooms. In summer go for the rooms looking out over the pretty Place du Bourg-Tibourg. Excellent value for money.

Hôtel St-Louis Marais (map D2, **10**): 1 rue Charles-V 75004. ☎ 01-48-87-87-04. Fax: 01-48-87-33-26. E-mail: slmarais@cyber.com. Metro: Bastille or Sully-Morland. Closed in August. Single room from 400F to 550F. Double room (all small) 650F with shower and toilet, 750F with toilet and bathroom. The hotel has an old-world charm and only a few rooms, which adds to the discreet family atmosphere. The attic rooms are really charming. Breakfast is served in a lovely arched cellar.

Hôtel de la Place des Vosges (map D2, **11**): 12 rue de Birague 75004. ☎ 01-42-72-60-46. Fax: 01-42-72-02-64. Metro: St-Paul or Bastille. From 545F to 610F for a double room with bathroom, including breakfast. In the prestigious street which leads to the Hôtel du Roi in the Place des Vosges. Sixteen rooms, which are not terribly spacious but comfortable and quiet, with satellite TV. The decor is fresh and blends in well with the exposed beams.

Where to stay

1 Hôtel MIJE Maubuisson
2 Le Fauconnier MIJE
3 Hôtel MIJE de Fourcy
4 Grand Hôtel Jeanne d'Arc
5 Grand Hôtel du Loiret
6 Hôtel Andréa
7 Hôtel Sansonnet
9 Hôtel de Nice
10 Hôtel St-Louis Marais
11 Hôtel de la Place des Vosges
12 Hôtel du 7e Art
13 Hôtel St-Merry
14 Hospitel
15 Hôtel Spéria
17 Hôtel St-Louis
18 Hôtel des Deux Îles
19 Hôtel de Lutèce

Where to eat

20 Le Ravaillac
21 Le Soleil en Coin
22 Au Jambon de Bayonne
23 À L'Escale
24 Le Petit Picard
25 Le Temps des Cerises
26 Le Café de la Poste
27 Le Grand Appétit
28 Aux Vins des Pyrénées
30 Au Canard Laqué
31 Bistro Tokyo
32 L'Ostéria
34 Les Fous de l'Île
35 Brasserie de l'Isle St-Louis
36 La Taverne du Nil
37 Isami
39 The Studio
40 Chez Marianne
42 Thanksgiving
43 Chez Clément
45 Le Grizzly
46 Brasserie Bofinger
48 L'Enoteca
49 Baracane
50 Amadéo
51 Le Loir dans la Théière
52 La Charlotte de l'Isle
53 Le Coude Fou
55 L'Alivi

Where to go for an ice-cream/ Where to go for a drink/ Going out

60 Berthillon
63 Les 7 Lézards
64 Le Petit Gavroche
65 Le Lizard Lounge
66 Le Petit Fer à Cheval
67 Café Klein Holland
68 La Tartine
69 The Auld Alliance
70 Les Étages
71 Ma Bourgogne
72 Le Pick-Clops
73 L'Illustre
74 Les Marronniers
75 Chez Richard
76 La Belle Hortense
77 Le Café du Trésor
78 Café Martini
82 Café des Phares

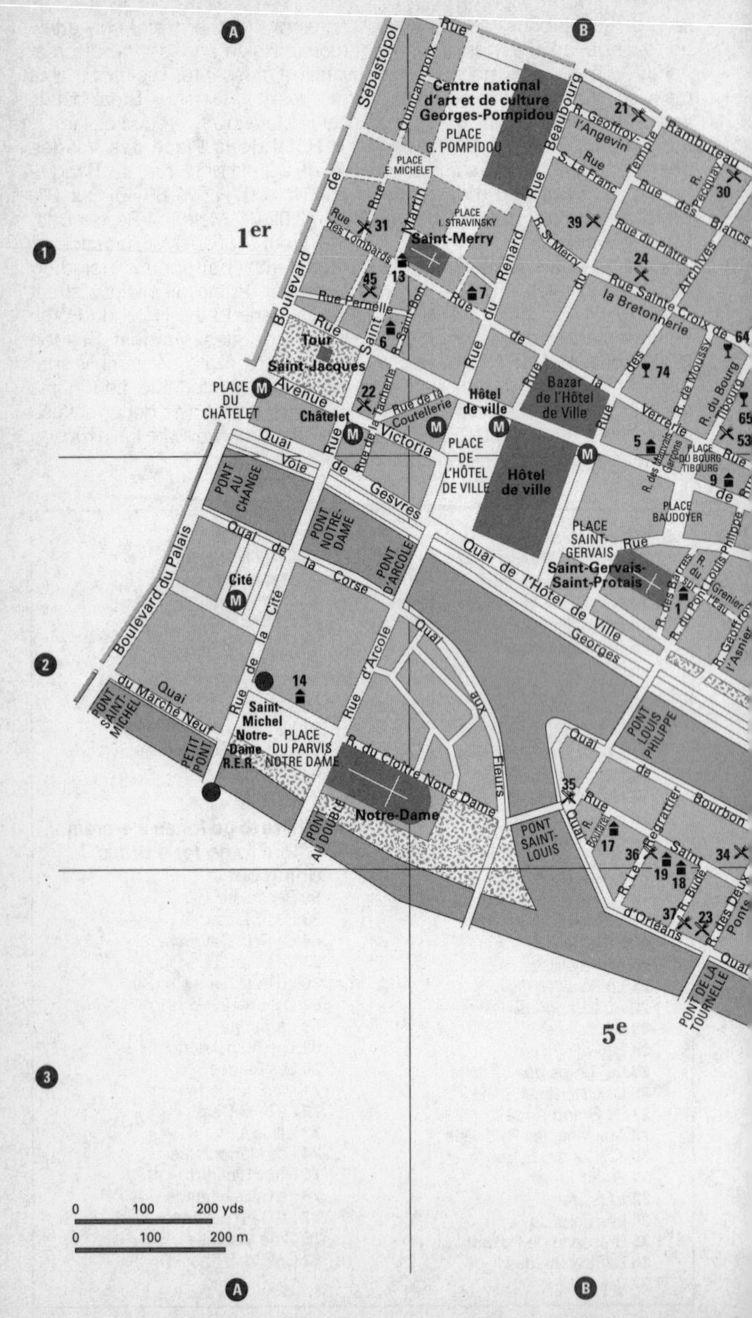
Centre national d'art et de culture Georges-Pompidou
PLACE G. POMPIDOU
PLACE E. MICHELET
PLACE I. STRAVINSKY
Saint-Merry
1er
Tour Saint-Jacques
PLACE DU CHÂTELET
Châtelet
Hôtel de ville
Bazar de l'Hôtel de Ville
PLACE DE L'HÔTEL DE VILLE
PLACE BAUDOYER
PLACE SAINT-GERVAIS
Saint-Gervais-Saint-Protais
PLACE DU BOURG TIBOURG
Cité
Saint-Michel Notre-Dame R.E.R.
PLACE DU PARVIS NOTRE DAME
Notre-Dame
PONT AU CHANGE
PONT NOTRE-DAME
PONT D'ARCOLE
PONT SAINT-MICHEL
PETIT PONT
PONT AU DOUBLE
PONT SAINT-LOUIS
PONT LOUIS PHILIPPE
PONT DE LA TOURNELLE
Boulevard de Sebastopol
Boulevard du Palais
Quai du Marché Neuf
Quai de la Corse
Quai de Gesvres
Quai de l'Hôtel de Ville
Quai aux Fleurs
Quai de Bourbon
Quai d'Orléans
Avenue Victoria
Rue Rambuteau
Rue Beaubourg
Rue du Renard
Rue Saint-Martin
Rue Quincampoix
Rue des Lombards
Rue Pernelle
Rue de la Verrerie
Rue Sainte Croix de la Bretonnerie
Rue du Temple
Rue des Archives
Rue des Blancs
Rue du Plâtre
Rue de la Cité
Rue d'Arcole
R. du Cloître Notre Dame
Rue Saint-Louis
5e
0 100 200 yds
0 100 200 m

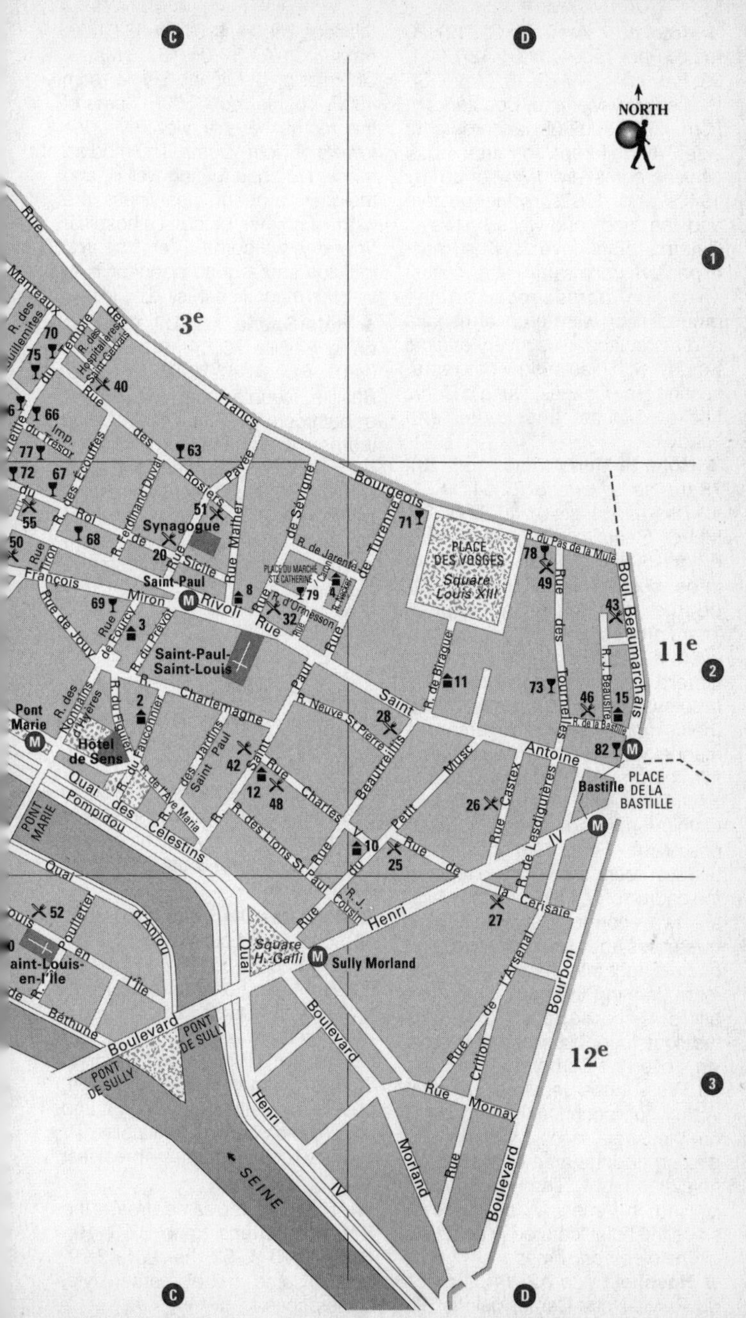

NORTH
3e
11e
12e
PLACE DES VOSGES
Square Louis XIII
Synagogue
Saint-Paul
Saint-Paul-Saint-Louis
Hôtel de Sens
Pont Marie
PLACE DE LA BASTILLE
Bastille
Sully Morland
Square H.-Galli
PONT MARIE
PONT DE SULLY
SEINE
Saint-Louis-en-l'Île
Rue Francs Bourgeois
Rue de Rivoli
Rue Saint Antoine
Boul. Beaumarchais
Boulevard Henri IV
Boulevard Morland
Boulevard Bourbon
Quai des Célestins
Quai d'Anjou
Quai Pompidou
Rue des Rosiers
Rue du Roi de Sicile
Rue François Miron
Rue Charlemagne
Rue Saint Paul
Rue Charles V
Rue du Petit Musc
Rue Beautreillis
Rue de Turenne
Rue de Sévigné
Rue des Tournelles
Rue Castex
Rue de la Cerisaie
Rue de l'Arsenal
Rue Crillon
Rue Mornay
Rue des Lions St Paul
Rue de Jouy
Rue Pavée
Rue Mahler
Rue des Écouffes
Rue de Birague
R. Neuve St Pierre
R. du Pas de la Mule
R. de Jarente
R. d'Ormesson
R. de Lesdiguières
R. J. Beausire
R. de la Bastille
R. Ferdinand Duval
R. du Prévôt
R. du Figuier
R. du Fauconnier
R. des Nonnains d'Hyères
R. de l'Ave Maria
R. des Jardins Saint Paul
R. J. Cousin
Rue de Fourcy
Rue Saint Louis en l'Île
Rue Poulletier
Rue de Béthune
Rue des Blancs Manteaux
Rue Vieille du Temple
R. des Hospitalières Saint Gervais
Imp. du Trésor
PLACE DU MARCHÉ STE CATHERINE
C
D
1
2
3

☗ **Hôtel du 7ᵉ Art** (map C2, **12**): 20 rue St-Paul 75004. ☎ 01-42-77-04-03. Fax: 01-42-77-69-10. Metro: St-Paul or Sully-Morland. Double room from 430F to 690F, according to size. A well-kept, original hotel whose rooms are livened up by 1940s and 1960s movie posters and the black-and-white hallways. Cinema buffs love it. The most expensive rooms are attic suites. There's a bar/tea-room on the ground floor with large armchairs and a fireplace, plus a very original window with plaster figurines representing Ray Charles, Donald Duck, Mickey Mouse, and Laurel and Hardy.

☗ **Hôtel St-Merry** (map A-B1, **13**): 78 rue de la Verrerie 75004. ☎ 01-42-78-14-15. Fax: 01-40-29-06-82. Metro: Châtelet or Hôtel-de-Ville. From 450F to 1,800F (for two or three people) according to size, degree of comfort and aspect. There are rooms to suit all pockets, even if some of them are most suited to rich honeymooning medievalists, who'd better keep their more acrobatic amorous manoeuvres to a minimum since this is a former 17th-century presbytery! There are 12 rooms, all with Gothic furnishings and all at different prices. For 1,100F go for the unusual room above the chapel of the church of St-Merri, across which are two enormous sculpted flying buttresses (they start at the wall and plunge right into the middle of the room, framing the bed). If you can afford it, choose room 12, with its fabulous four-poster bed and great view over the Sorbonne. There are no TVs – these people have taste! Watch out, because the bedrooms on the street don't have double-glazing and the area can get quite noisy at night. The hotel is not lacking in American clients ever since the hotel featured in an article in *The New York Times*.

☗ **Hospitel** (map A2, **14**): 1 place du Parvis-Notre-Dame, galerie B2, 6th floor, 75004. ☎ 01-44-32-01-00. Fax: 01-44-32-01-16. Metro: Châtelet or St-Michel. Single room 480F, double room 550F. Some of the rooms have a view over the towers of Notre-Dame. The modern rooms are cheerful and well lit, and the standards of cleanliness are high, of course, being in a hospital! Friendly welcome. Very central location and a good opportunity to visit this magnificent listed building.

☗ **Hôtel Spéria** (map D2, **15**): 1 rue de la Bastille 75004. ☎ 01-42-72-04-01. Fax: 01-42-72-56-38. Metro: Bastille. Double room with shower or bathroom 600F and 680F. Large leather armchairs and modern decor feature at this clean and functional hotel. Telephone, TV and mini-bar in every room. Some of them have particularly spacious bathrooms, others have open beams. In a good location.

☆☆☆☆ TRÈS CHIC

☗ **Hôtel St-Louis** (map B2, **17**): 75 rue St-Louis-en-l'Île 75004. ☎ 01-46-34-04-80. Fax: 01-46-34-02-13. Metro: Pont-Marie. Rooms with bathroom and toilet from 775F to 875F. An elegant hotel which fits in with the quarter. The rooms are not very spacious, but they are comfortable.

☗ **Hôtel des Deux Îles** (map B2-3, **18**): 59 rue St-Louis-en-l'Île 75004. ☎ 01-43-26-13-35. Fax: 01-43-29-60-25. Metro: Pont-Marie. RER: St-Michel-Notre-Dame. Double room with bathroom and toilet 870F. Very popular with visitors from the United States. Elegant and comfortable, but quite small rooms. Beams and undeniable charm, with satellite TV in every room. Grandiose breakfast room.

☗ At No. 65 in the same street is the **Hôtel de Lutèce** (map B2-3, **19**): ☎ 01-43-26-23-52. Fax: 01-43-29-60-25. Same owner, same style, same prices.

WHERE TO EAT

☆ BUDGET

✗ **Au Jambon de Bayonne** (map A1, **22**): 6 rue de La Tacherie 75004. ☎ 01-42-78-45-45. Metro: Hôtel-de-Ville. Open until 10pm. Closed Saturday and Sunday and in August. The Bayonne isn't worth crossing Paris for, but if you find yourself at the town hall, the Marché aux Fleurs (flower market), or at Beaubourg or Marks & Spencer, it's worth a visit for the menu at 57F, served at lunchtimes and evenings until 8.30pm. They also have a menu at 72F and 115F, served at lunchtime and in the evening. À la carte 130F. Dish of the day 65F. Daily there's a star dish, a classic among classics, such as dried sausage, tongue salad, *blanquette de veau* or *rognons à la berrichonne*, with crème caramel to follow. Usually very busy.

✗ **À l'Escale** (map B3, **23**): 1 rue des Deux-Ponts or 2 quai d'Orléans 75004. ☎ 01-43-54-94-23. Metro: Pont-Marie. Open lunchtime only, daily except Wednesday. Closed in August. No set menu, budget for around 150F without drinks. At this friendly café (with the sunny side looking out over the Seine), provincials passing through Paris who've just 'done' Notre-Dame and the Île St-Louis will find all the reassurance they need with a dish of the day (70F to 75F) cooked with love by Mme Tardieu, 'mother' to her clients. *Pot-au-feu*, lamb curry, Lyons sausage, *andouillette* and grills are a pleasure to eat and can be accompanied by a glass of Irancy, Touraine or many other kinds of wine, chosen by M. Tardieu, who is something of a connoisseur. They don't do ice-creams or sorbets from Berthillon's, unlike all the other bars and restaurants on the Île St-Louis, but there are iced delicacies from Pascal's.

✗ **Le Petit Picard** (map B1, **24**): 42 rue Ste-Croix-de-la-Bretonnerie 75004. ☎ 01-42-78-54-03. Metro: Rambuteau or Hôtel-de-Ville. Open to 11pm. Closed Saturday lunchtime, Sunday lunchtime, all day Monday and in July. Set menus at 64F at lunchtime and 89F and 129F in the evening. Three-course à la carte 150F to 200F. At lunchtime, the house is packed out thanks to its menus: starter, main course, dessert and a carafe of red wine. This is one of the best restaurants in the quarter, even if the food hasn't quite scaled the heights of some other establishments; it is really quantity rather than quality. There are around ten starters, five main courses and five desserts. Portions are very generous. In the evening, the set meal includes vegetable soup, salmon escalope with sorrel and lamb curry. If the lunchtime clientele is mixed, in the evening it's mainly single men.

✗ **Le Temps des Cerises** (map D2, **25**): 31 rue de la Cerisaie 75004. ☎ 01-42-72-08-63. Metro: Bastille or Sully-Morland. Open lunchtime only. Closed Saturday, Sunday and public holidays, as well as in August. Menu 68F. Located in a pretty, low-ceilinged, late 18th-century house, they don't serve food in the evening, but the bar is open until 8pm. It has been a bistro since 1910. Photos of old Paris and the good humour of the proprietors recall the old tradition of Parisian conviviality, as does the zinc bar, and traditional café-style tables. There's a good set menu at an unbeatable price: egg mayonnaise, *andouillette grillée purée*, *pot-au-feu* or lasagne. There's a small menu with three courses at around 63F and an eclectic selection of wines at all sorts of prices (including Clos Vougeot, Gaillac, Chablis, Bourgueil and St-Joseph). If you want a seat you'll have to get here at noon on the dot.

✕ **Le Café de la Poste** (map D2, **26**): 13 rue Castex 75004. ☎ 01-42-72-95-35. Metro: Bastille. Open until 11pm. Closed Saturday and Sunday. Budget for around 120F. Opposite a post office whose 1930s-style brick façade owes its survival to the preservation efforts of the locals, this café looks more neo-Bastille than the postmen's café that its name suggests, whatever one of those might look like. Tastefully converted, there are some interesting mosaics and a fine wooden bar. On the blackboard there is usually a pasta dish (44F at lunchtime and 48F in the evening) such as tagliatelle with mushrooms, or macaroni with aubergines, and a few meat dishes at around 70F, including *émincé de bœuf Strogonoff* and *massalé d'agneau*, as well as salads (Niçoise, Italian, etc.) which go down well in summer. Starters and desserts at around 30F. The menu changes on a daily basis.

✕ **Le Grand Appétit** (map D3, **27**): 9 rue de la Cerisaie 75004. ☎ 01-40-27-04-95. Metro: Sully-Morland or Bastille. Open Monday to Thursday noon to 3pm and Friday noon to 2pm. Closed at weekends. Budget for around 70F per person. A Parisian macrobiotic classic with a different dish daily, such as thick vegetable tart (48F). Also sells groceries (next door). Very Zen. A restful and very healthy spot after a walk around the Marais.

✕ **Au Canard Laqué** (map B1, **30**): 5 rue Rambuteau 75004. ☎ 01-42-78-22-42. Metro: Rambuteau. Open until 11pm. Closed Sunday lunchtime. Express menu at 38F served lunchtime and evening; other menus from 47F to 75F. A rather anonymous Chinese restaurant which offers Thai, Vietnamese and Chinese specialities. Very good value though. Varied à la carte as well as five set menus. Attentive service. Free liqueur if you spend over 100F.

✕ **Bistro Tokyo** (map A1, **31**): 20 rue des Lombards 75004. ☎ 01-42-72-11-11. Metro: Châtelet or Hôtel-de-Ville. Service from 11am to 3pm and 6pm to midnight. Open daily. Set menus at 44F, 79F and 132F, lunchtime and evening. At lunchtime there is also the Tokyo Express menu at 49F. A small Japanese restaurant offering a culinary journey without the price of the airline ticket. Original food is served in a simple decor. For 44F: four chicken kebabs, meatballs, a bowl of rice, a soup and the chef's salad. But there is also a wide choice of *sushi* (with salmon, bream, mackerel or seaweed) and *sashimi*. Wash it all down with some *sake* or a bottle of Japanese beer.

☆☆ MODERATE

✕ **Le Ravaillac** (map C2, **20**): 10 rue du Roi-de-Sicile 75004. ☎ 01-42-72-85-85. Metro: St-Paul. Open lunchtime and evening until 11pm (last orders). Closed Sunday evening and the first two weeks in August. À la carte only, budget for around 120F. This Polish restaurant doesn't appeal much from the outside. However, there are many different Polish specialities (between 59F and 78F) such as cabbage soup, *pierogi* (stuffed dumplings), *pozarsky* (veal with buckwheat and sautéed potatoes), special sauerkraut (grilled pork rib, pork breast, Polish sausage) and *golabki* (cabbage stuffed with meat and rice). Polish beers are a good idea instead of vodka if you want to be able to find your way back to your hotel but don't want to see the bill hit the stratosphere!

✕ **Le Soleil en Coin** (map B1, **21**): 21 rue Rambuteau 75004. ☎ 01-42-72-26-25. Metro: Rambuteau. Open until 10.30pm (11pm on Friday and Saturday). Closed Saturday lunchtime and Sunday. Set menu 126F lunchtime and evening. À la carte, budget for around 140F excluding drinks. Dish of the day 70F at lunchtime and 74F in the evening – if there's any left. Provençal warmth and mainly Mediterranean cuisine greets you here. Try a country salad, a *terrine du soleil* or a terrine of courgettes with tomato sauce as a starter, and follow with leg of lamb with herbs or *blanquette de veau à l'ancienne*. Good home-made desserts. There's a big noticeboard where you can pick up information on concerts, things for sale or swaps. Pretty full at lunchtime, quieter in the evening, except on Saturday.

✕ **Aux Vins des Pyrénées** (map D2, **28**): 25 rue Beautreillis 75004. Metro: Bastille or Sully-Morland. ☎ 01-42-72-64-94. Open daily to 11.30pm except Sunday evening and from 10 to 20 August. At lunchtime there's a set menu at 75F. À la carte, budget for around 130F without drinks. An old wine shop which has metamorphosed into a neo-bistro while retaining the same name. There's a very friendly atmosphere (the owner greets half the clients with a kiss – as is the tradition in France of course). A clever mix of the Parisian with the provincial and little dishes that you can order from the board. The menu is simple and effective: quality meats, mainly grilled, with accompaniments which come in generous portions, as well as vegetarian and low-fat choices. Brunch on Sunday. Interesting selection of wines.

✕ **Baracane** (map D2, **49**): 38 rue des Tournelles 75004. ☎ 01-42-71-43-33. Metro: Bastille. Open noon to 2.15pm and 7pm to midnight. Closed Saturday lunchtime and Sunday. Booking is advisable. At lunchtime there are set menus at 52F and 82F. In the evening there's a set menu at 135F and *menu-carte* at 215F. This tiny bistro owes its cuisine to Gascony. There's leg of lamb from Lozère or house *cassoulet* with tasty *confits*. The two set menus at lunchtime include either a dish made with fresh ingredients from the local market, plus a glass of wine and coffee, or a main course, starter or dessert and a glass of wine. In the evening there's a set menu with starter, main course and a choice of desserts, which changes regularly. If you're feeling flush, try the *menu-carte* which includes three courses as well as an aperitif, a half bottle of wine (which you can choose – pretty unusual) and coffee. Very good value, especially considering the quality of the cooking.

✕ **Les Fous de l'Île** (map B2, **34**): 33 rue des Deux-Ponts 75004. ☎ 01-43-25-76-67. Metro: Pont-Marie. Open noon to 11pm. Closed Saturday lunchtime, Sunday evening and all day Monday. Set menu 78F at lunchtime; in the evening à la carte is around 150F to 180F. Mainly a restaurant, this becomes a tea-room in the afternoon. At lunchtime there's a good set menu. Dishes of the day cost between 60F and 85F. Simple but good cooking, occasionally taking its inspiration from outside France (e.g. fricassée of *langoustines à l'indienne*). Brunch on Sunday: three set meals at 100F, 125F and 150F. They also have live music including jazz and blues every other day from 10pm. The programme is varied and the atmosphere is relaxed and upbeat, aided by enthusiastic support from friends of the musicians and a music-loving clientele. On music night, there's a set menu at 100F.

✕ **The Studio** (map B1, **39**): 41 rue du Temple 75004. ☎ 01-42-74-10-38. Metro: Hôtel-de-Ville. Open every evening until midnight and at lunchtime for brunch on Friday, Saturday and Sunday. Closed at Christmas. Budget for at least 150F à la carte. Located in the superb paved courtyard of the Café de la Gare, the atmosphere is quite nostalgic. Music joyously escapes from the rooms where dance classes are held on the first floor, while on the ground floor people rush to see the Café de la Gare show. The restaurant is always busy, with waiters rushing around while diners sip margaritas and wait for their tables. You dine in a large room with a high ceiling, surrounded by the sound of conversation and music reverberating around the walls. Decor is Tex-Mex and when the weather is fine eat on the superb terrace. The menu covers tacos and tortillas, chilli con carne and spare-ribs, costing between 69F and 89F, while the excellent meat dishes, such as T-bone steak, are from 145F. Straightforward, unrefined cooking. Three very Mexican brunches are served at the end of the week, from 75F to 115F.

✕ **Chez Clément** (map D2, **43**): 21 boulevard Beaumarchais 75004. Metro: Bastille. ☎ 01-40-29-17-00. Open daily until 1am (*see* Chez Clément in the '17th arrondissement').

☆☆☆ CHIC

✕ **Isami** (map B3, **37**): 4 quai d'Orléans 75004. ☎ 01-40-46-06-97. Metro: Pont-Marie. Open noon to 2.30pm and 7pm to 10.30pm. Closed Sunday lunchtime and Monday, as well as in August. Set menus at 160F and 180F; à la carte budget 200F. Right in the heart of the Île St-Louis, this authentic Japanese restaurant is a haven for lovers of raw fish. If this is your first experience of Japanese food, or if you're not sure about the appeal of raw fish, the *sushi* and *sashimi* menus are a good introduction. But the best idea is to take a little of whatever you fancy from the *sushi* (10F to 35F): perhaps eel or omelette, octopus or *coquille St-Jacques*, not forgetting oysters and salmon.

✕ **L'Alivi** (map C2, **55**): 27 rue du Roi-de-Sicile 75004. ☎ 01-48-87-90-20. Metro: St-Paul or Hôtel-de-Ville. Open daily lunchtime and evening. Two set menus at 122F and 175F. À la carte, budget for at least 250F including wine. A Corsican restaurant with a small, cosy dining room. Good traditional Corsican food, including roast kid with Corsican herbs and *poivrons à la bonifacienne*.

✕ **Chez Marianne** (map C1, **40**): 2 rue des Hospitalières-St-Gervais 75004. ☎ 01-42-72-18-86. Metro: St-Paul or Hôtel-de-Ville. Open daily 11am to midnight. Dishes from 55F to 75F. Booking is highly recommended. Central European specialities are on offer in these two restaurants next door to one another. At Chez Marianne, you get a choice of three dishes: aubergine caviar, delicious taramasalata, excellent tzatziki, pastrami or *falafel*. Or try the salmon, which melts in the mouth. In the summer there's a terrace which is very pleasant in the evening. If you don't have time to eat in, you can try a take-away *falafel* (22F).

✕ **Thanksgiving** (map C2, **42**): 20 rue St-Paul 75004. ☎ 01-42-77-68-28. Metro: St-Paul. Open daily except Sunday evening and Monday. Closed from 1 to 20 August and 1 to 7 January. At lunchtime set menu at 79F, in the evening premier set menu at 155F. À la carte, budget for 170F. Brunch at weekends from 11am to 4pm. This excellent American food shop (located at 14 rue Charles-V 75004) has opened a restaurant where you can indulge in the joys of an American brunch while you're antiques hunting (90F to 110F – the food, not the antiques, which will set you back a touch more). There's a choice of a number of set menus or individual courses with tea or coffee. During the week, the menu is based around Cajun (Louisiana) and Deep South dishes.

✂ **La Taverne du Nil** (map B2, **36**): 16 rue Le Regrattier 75004. ☎ 01-40-46-09-02. Metro: Pont-Marie. Open until 11pm. Closed Monday lunchtime. At lunchtime there's a set menu at 90F, in the evening there are set menus at 140F and 187F. À la carte, budget for 160F. An authentic Lebanese restaurant, despite the name. Excellent kebabs and a good deal for two in the evening: a set menu at 140F with an assortment of *hors-d'œuvres* and kebabs, and different grilled meats from the menu. The two set menus offer *mezze*, kebabs, wine and dessert. Avoid the table under the loudspeaker!

✂ **Brasserie de l'Isle St-Louis** (map B2, **35**): 55 quai de Bourbon 75004. ☎ 01-43-54-02-59. Metro: Pont-Marie. Open noon (6pm on Thursday) to around 1am. Closed Wednesday, Thursday lunchtime and in August. Budget for 150F to 160F, including drinks. The waiters have purportedly been here for an average of around 25 years, but they still haven't lost their enthusiasm and good humour. There's a stuffed stork above the bar, and a clock from the Vosges keeps time. The menu is based around the excellent sauerkraut, but you'll also find haddock and, as a starter, Welsh rarebit. Wash it all down with a good Alsace wine. You can also make do with a good omelette *aux fines herbes* while contemplating the back of Notre-Dame and the banks of the Seine. Packed on evenings when France is playing rugby in Paris.

✂ **Le Grizzly** (map A1, **45**): 7 rue St-Martin 75004. ☎ 01-48-87-77-56. Metro: Hôtel-de-Ville or Châtelet. Open until 11pm. Closed Sunday. Set menus 120F at lunchtime, 160F in the evening. À la carte, budget for around 170F without drinks. This Basque-Béarnais spot is as popular for its welcoming terrace near the church of St-Merri as for its cuisine, which is inspired by its native region. Ratatouille with poached egg, *cassoulet* with Tarbes beans, *fricot* of veal with *ceps* or squid in their own ink – these are just a few of the good things on the menu.

✂ **Brasserie Bofinger** (map D2, **46**): 5–7 rue de la Bastille 75004. ☎ 01-42-72-87-82. Metro: Bastille. Open Monday to Friday noon to 3pm and 6.30pm to 1am, and on Saturday and Sunday noon to 1am. Set meal 119F at lunchtime, or set menu at 178F. This famous brasserie, opened originally in 1864 and transformed in 1919, has a lovely glass roof and a first-floor lounge decorated by Hansi. The undisputed stars here are sauerkraut and seafood. Try the 'Country' sauerkraut at 98F, the 'Special' at 118F and the seafood: 'Mareyeur' at 235F and 'Royal' at 295F.

✂ **Amadéo** (map C2, **50**): 19 rue François-Miron 75004. ☎ 01-48-87-01-02. Metro: St-Paul or Pont-Marie. Closed Monday lunchtime and Sunday, as well as a fortnight in August. Set menus 75F and 95F at lunchtime; in the evening there's a gastronomic menu at 185F. With a name like this it's hardly surprising to find an operatic atmosphere, which is accompanied by quality service, even if the dining room is hardly bigger than a diva's dressing room! The menu is pretty adventurous, mixing original flavours according to the inspiration of the moment and the season. Try the fish *rillette*, shellfish or orange crème caramel. Twice a month there's an original menu, a wonderful lyrical experience at 285F, soprano and piano included.

✂ **L'Ostéria** (map C2, **32**): 10 rue de Sévigné 75004. ☎ 01-42-71-37-08. Metro: St-Paul. Open lunchtime and evening until 10.30pm (last orders). Closed at weekends and in August. À la carte, budget for around 200F without drinks. This restaurant is renowned for serving the best gnocchi in Paris, although to find the place you'll need to keep your eyes peeled as it's hidden behind anonymous lace curtains and there's no sign! Starters from 65F, main courses from 80F and the desserts are all at 50F (even the compôte of seasonal fruits). Simple decor but, nevertheless, the dining room is always packed with contented diners (booking is essential). There's a delicious salad of warm octopus with lemon and olives, *al dente* spaghetti with clams, the inevitable gnocchi *au naturel* (with sage butter) and of course the famous tiramisu *della casa*.

WINE BARS

✕ 🍷 **L'Enoteca** (map C2, **48**): 25 rue Charles-V 75004. ☎ 01-42-78-91-44. Metro: St-Paul. Open daily lunchtime and evening (service until 11.30pm). Set lunch, including drinks, during the week at 75F; in the evening you can eat à la carte for between around 160F and 200F. Almost unmissable, this Italian wine bar is packed out every evening with a very Parisian clientele. It is not uncommon to see a few faces from French TV. Surrounded by a warm decor, very definitely the Marais, with its old stonework, visible beams and patinated walls, people come to discover the richness of the Italian wines. Each week the wines by the glass are different, allowing you to travel from north to south in bibulous terms, from the white wines of Trentino to those from Sicily, or reds from Piedmont and those from Basilicate. The menu includes antipasti (60F), mozzarella with tomato (65F) or fresh pasta, which the chef creates according to his fancy that day (60F). Lovers of Italian wine can choose from over 450 bottles on the wine list.

✕ 🍷 **Le Coude Fou** (map B1, **53**): 12 rue du Bourg-Tibourg 75004. ☎ 01-42-77-15-16. Metro: Hôtel-de-Ville. Open daily lunchtime and evening all year round. Set menus 90F at lunchtime, 115F and 140F in the evening; à la carte at around 160F without drinks. A successful wine bar, whose fame attracts many real connoisseurs as well as the curious. An original list covers wines which are off the beaten vineyard track. There are pretty, naïve frescoes running along the two dining rooms. Traditional dishes include lamb with sautéed potatoes or kebab of monkfish with Nantes butter. A definite Marais atmosphere. At lunchtime, the set meal is a main course and starter or dessert, with a glass of wine.

TEA-ROOMS

– **Le Loir dans la Théière** (map C2, **51**): 3 rue des Rosiers 75004. ☎ 01-42-72-90-61. Metro: St-Paul. Open Monday to Friday 11am to 7pm and at weekends 10am to 7pm. Dish of the day 60F to 70F. A charming tea-room which serves hot dishes at lunchtime, in particular savoury tarts at 48F. The atmosphere is cosy and relaxed, although service isn't always with a smile. Soft old armchairs into which you can sink deliciously or more conventional seating; it's up to you. The spinach pie *(pascualina)* and the tarts, such as potato and bacon or curried chicken and mushroom, are enough on their own to make you want to come back. But the real stars are the delicious cakes, including apple, nut and cinnamon, chocolate fondant and bitter chocolate *noisetin*. There's a good selection of teas at 20F and brunch for around 100F at weekends.

– **La Charlotte de l'Isle** (map C3, **52**): 24 rue St-Louis-en-l'Île 75004.

☎ 01-43-54-25-83. Metro: Pont-Marie or Sully-Morland. Open noon to 8pm. Closed Monday, Tuesday and Wednesday and in July and August. Budget for 50F for tea and a cake. The daughter of a *pâtissier*, Sylvie Langlet has followed in her parent's footsteps. For 25 years she has lovingly created delicious cakes which transport her customers to seventh heaven. Florentines, chocolate or lemon tarts, cakes – everything is irresistible. Look out for the window display, which is quite something – most people spend quite a while staring at it. The tiny interior is charming. On Wednesday (you have to book), you can have a birthday tea with a puppet show. On Friday from 6pm to 8pm there's a tea dance which is open to all.

THE GEORGES-POMPIDOU CENTRE (BEAUBOURG)

A BRIEF HISTORY

In 1969, President Georges Pompidou dreamed of giving France an art centre capable of taking up the torch of artistic and cultural creation from other capitals. The result was the Centre Georges-Pompidou. Over 600 architects from all over the world pitched for the work but it was an Italian-British union that got the job: Renzo Piano and Richard Rogers.

The work was carried out quickly and one morning in 1977 Parisians woke up and couldn't believe their eyes. Some of them threw their hands up in horror, calling it a monstrosity, while others thought the architecture was challenging. The more pragmatic among them, at the time of an oil crisis, thought that the presence of a refinery right in the middle of Paris was a good idea.

An immense blue structure of metal, glass, piping, rails, nozzles and enormous hatches, brightens up the old quarter. All the technical elements (lifts, ventilation, heating) are on the outside, leaving the maximum amount of space for exhibitions inside. 'A building with its guts quite literally ripped out', said one wag.

SUCCESS

Today, twice as many people visit the Pompidou Centre as the Eiffel Tower and almost as many as Disneyland Paris – 8 million on average every year. All the elements of modern culture have been brought together in a single place and in an extraordinarily accessible way. The centre has won the public over by the way it deals with a traditionally serious subject, and one of the miracles of the centre is that it has earned a dominant, indispensable place in French culture, despite its controversial beginnings.

Not only is the centre a lively and fun place, but it also benefits from the streetlife in the square in front of it. Street singers, poets, escapologists and fire-eaters all perform to the crowd, while African speakers hold forth passionately about subjects dear to their hearts, to the amazement of passers-by.

PRACTICAL INFORMATION

Beaubourg is a cultural centre, with more to offer than just a museum.

– **Opening times:** open daily, except Tuesday, from 11am to 10pm. The Musée d'Art Moderne shuts at 9pm. The only day of the year it is expected to be closed is 1 May.

– **Information:** ☎ 01-44-78-12-33. Metro: Rambuteau or Hôtel-de-Ville. RER: Châtelet-Les Halles. Bus Nos. 21, 29, 38, 47, 58, 69, 70, 72, 74, 75, 76, 81, 85, 96.

- www.centrepompidou.fr (for events at the centre, the museum's collection and documentation), but also:
- www.ircam.fr (for Ircam activities and concerts)
- www.bpi.fr (for BPI activities and its catalogue)
- www.cnac-gp.fr (for the Musée d'Art Contemporain).

– **Reception:** on Level 0, via a wider entrance with an awning. There's an excellent new guide to the centre on a pleasant yellow background.

In the enlarged forum on three levels (-1, 0 and 1), a centuries' old olive tree stands resplendent in a gigantic pot of earth.

At the back is the information desk, ticket stand, cloak rooms and an area of general services with a stamp and cash machine. On Level 0 are the *Espace éducatif* and the *Galerie des enfants*. To the right is the Flammarion bookshop.

On Level 1, to the left, is Cinema 1, a designer shop on a mezzanine floor and the main entrance to the BPI, Bibliothèque publique d'information (the public library). To the right are the *Nouveau Café* and a gallery of temporary exhibitions.

If you are planning to return within the year, buying an annual pass has several advantages: free entry to all exhibitions without having to queue, and the centre's programme sent to you in advance; priority bookings and reductions on dance and theatre shows, concerts and cinema, and reduced prices for young people. Information: ☎ 01-44-78-14-63.

– You can also join the *Societé des Amis du Musée National d'Art Moderne* and the *Association des Amis du Centre Georges-Pompidou*. There are several options ranging from 120F to 140F per year, offering benefits not to be sneezed at if you're likely to be paying a lot of visits to the Pompidou or if you're an art student, teacher or are simply under 26. For information: ☎ 01-44-78-12-76; fax: 01-44-78-12-22 or visit their website or drop in at Level 0 every day from 1–7pm, except Tuesday and Sunday.

2000: A FRESH DEPARTURE WITH A VISION OF THE FUTURE

★ **Musée National d'Art Moderne (MNAM) – Centre de Création Industrielle (CCI)**: Open 11am–9pm every day except Tuesday. Longer opening hours for temporary exhibitions. Entry fee 30F; concessions 20F. For exhibitions, prices range between 40F and 50F. A ticket to an exhibition also gets you into the Musée, the Atelier Brancusi and the Galerie des enfants. Free for the unemployed or under 13s. Access via the outside caterpillar walkways.

– **Level 4**, dedicated to contemporary collections from 1960 to the present day. The idea is to mix genres: painting, sculpture, architecture, design, photography, film and video, to show the impact of new techniques on artistic creation and the diversity of the latter. The exhibits change frequently.

The visit begins with a homage to the Swiss engineer-cum-sculptor, Jean Tingueély (several of his works are dotted around the capital such as the Stravinsky fountain, a joint project with Niki de St-Phalle, near the Pompidou Centre, see below). Then you go on to the 'classics' of the centre's collections: pop art, new realists, kinetic art, *arte povera* and conceptual art, ending with the latest trends in figurative and abstract painting.

If you stick to the numerical order of the rooms, you then arrive, somewhat arbitrarily, granted, at *Compression* by César in the room devoted to Pop Art, *Déjeuner sur l'herbe* by Alain Jacquet, and a not very appetizing *Repas hongrois* (Hungarian Meal) by Daniel Spoerri. Things get even more disquieting with Andy Warhol's awesome *Electric Chair*, and your mind boggles still more before somewhat disturbing interior reconstructions (Room 8) by Dorothea Tannings and Edward Kienholz. It doesn't get any better with Diane Arbus' photos, reflecting an American society that's gone off the rails.

Geometric abstraction and the optical and kinetic arts follow on from this – you may need to keep asking yourself what on earth got into Georges Pompidou when he commissioned Yaacov Agam to design the antechamber to his flat in the Élysée in 1974? A nerve-crunching exercise, if ever there was one!

Room 10 provides an exciting overview of the development of architecture and design in the '60s and '70s. Looking at the models on display, the more cautious may experience relief that some projects never progressed beyond the conceptual stage.

In room 13, the piano wrapped in felt with a red cross on it by the prolific Joseph Beuys is explained by a biographical note about the artist. A Luftwaffe pilot during the Second World War, he crashed in 1943 in the Crimea, but was saved from the intense cold by the Tartars who covered him in fat and felt. An odd beginning to an artistic career, so what do you know, in Room 15, there's the piano and the felt, but this time, Beuys has added a thermometer and blackboard. A display cabinet of swaddled birds, *Les Messagers* (by Anette Messager, no less) lends a touching and feminine note to Room 20.

With the Italians and *Arte Povera* in Room 21, it's back to basics: wood, glass, stone, animals and vegetables. In Italy, the so-called 'years of lead' constituted a political statement against mass-consumer art.

Pure abstraction makes a come-back in room 24 with the works of Richter.

Then you're faced with the spine-chilling works of Baselitz and Kieffer, and their worrying incursions into the human psyche. The masks and portraits of Marlène Dumas and Amulf Rainer emphasise this obsession with the macabre.

Room 33 brings you up to the latest trends in architecture and design, dominated by weightlessness and immateriality. Philippe Starck reveals his wide-ranging artistic talent.

– **Level 5** is divided into two sections. In the first is a demonstration and illustration of the links between art and technique, while the second is devoted to the various movements of the 1950s. This level also covers the spectacular heritage of the MNAM/CCI, with amazing cubist sculptures (presented alongside several original pieces from the collections of the artists themselves) and a complete set of the works of each of the great masters of the 20th century – Matisse, Picasso, Braque, Duchamp, Kandinsky, Léger, Miró, Giacometti and Dubuffet – as well representing the groups and movements which have truly marked the century (e.g. dadaism, abstraction, informal art). The chronological tour includes a number of 'breaks': such as certain movements like the Union of Modern Artists, reconstructions such as André Breton's workshop, and quiet areas.

The paintings on display change every 18 months. Here's a quick canter through the current ones. The first you come across is the impressive *Femme debout* by Miró, which gazes down over the terrace surrounded by water. Ordered chronologically, you then arrive at *La Guerre* by Rousseau Le Douanier, one of the founding paintings of modern art, before crossing to Room 2 opposite, for the Fauvists, where Marquet and Derain's paintings erupt in a riot of colour.

The birth of Cubism follows, probably the greatest artistic revolution since the Renaissance, and the impact of other civilizations is shown, such as the influence of African masks on the vision of Braque and Picasso, all of which changed the face of artistic creation forever. With Rouault, there's a return to Christianity and the painting of a martyr flayed alive.

In Room 5, Juan Gris and Fernand Léger rush headlong into the trap set by Picasso, and Cubism descends into optical puns and geometric patterns. Braque and Picasso rival one another in their exploration for new techniques of collage. In Room 7, values are overturned in the Roaring Twenties. Many an artist found his imagination unlocked by the traumas of the First World War. Dada set out to provoke and lobby right-minded folk. Arp, Duchamp, Picabia and Man Ray followed suit and clearly had an absolute field day.

Chagall and the Russians explored popular themes, and Matisse flirted with figurative art. In Rooms 10 and 11, you can trace the first steps of the three great 'K's, Klee, Kandinksky and Kupka, towards abstraction, while in Room 12, the radicalism of the Soviet Revolution starts to make itself felt with the work of Malevitch, and a black stick on a white background becomes a work of art.

The Dutch have their say in Room 13, and the De Stijl school contributes to the abstract movement with its strict geometrical patterns. Then Mondrian and Van Doesburg whittle painting down to the three primary colours plus black and white and a few intersecting straight lines. It's quite a surprise to find that the stark lines of Marcel Breuer and Mies Van der Roe's chairs were produced as early as 1927 and 1932. Austere, functional designs become the trend in the architecture of the inter-war years. In Room 16, the Delaunay husband-and-wife team create striking concentric patterns, and in Room 17, Fernand Léger lends a harmonious dimension to his perception of modernity.

In Room 19, an absolute must is Max Ernst's *Capricorne*, where the figures stand like a couple of awesome guardians to the realm of the bizarre and peculiar. In the wake of Freud's probings into the human psyche, the Surrealists went behind reality to tackle the ins and outs of the waking dream. De

Chirico, Magritte, Ernst, Tanguy, Dalí, Miró and even Giacometti all figure among the stars of the 20th century. André Breton, who theorised the movement, occupies a central place with the weird decor of his studio. Max Ernst pushed the absurd to extremes with his explorations on the theme of collage: his *Roman-collage* consists of 150 pieces.

Rooms 27, 28 and 29 cover the 1920s and '30s and show figurative art making a comeback in Europe. Montparnos, Soutine, Foujita, Modigliani, Balthus, Bellmer and the sculptor Brancusi made Paris the worldwide centre for Art.

Rooms 30 to 32 cover the 1930s and '40s, including works by Matisse and Bonnard, with their exploding colours. Even Picasso and Braque finally returned to figurative art and it's a delight to find the work of Nicolas de Staël (Rooms 32–34) in the middle of non-figurative, abstract painters whilst Dubuffet tackled popular culture. After the Second World War, Belgian, Dutch and Danish members of CoBrA skillfully straddled abstract and figurative art, but after these lyrical developments, it's back to the theme of the human body with Giacometti and Francis Bacon in Room 36. While Giacometti pared it down to the nth degree, Francis Bacon gave it a ghostly and disturbing quality.

In Room 38, artistic movements seem to disperse. Fontana and Klein offer new perspectives in the plastic arts, changing the spectator's conception of art. In Room 39 and 40–45, we find altered political and economic contexts. New York has become the centre of world art and the new melting pot for ideological and aesthetic debate. Jackson Pollock has developed a theory of spontaneous painting, splattering his canvases with paint, then covering them with sand and broken glass in total disorder. The three marvellous *Bleus* by Miró mark a significant point in Spanish painting.

In Room 41 are Matisse's *Nu bleu* and Brancusi's *Muse endormie*, two masterpieces that complement one another admirably for the clarity of their forms and make a superb end to the visit. A real treat.

★ **The Bibliothèque publique d'information** is bigger and better than ever. Open 12 noon–10pm (11am Saturday and Sunday). Entry is free. The library occupies Levels 1, 2 and 3 and has its own entrance on Level 1. It also has its own lift between the three levels. Famed for the wealth of its resources, the library offers everyone free access (it can seat 2000) to its collections of encyclopedias and multimedia in printed, audial, visual, computer or digital format. You can consult its catalogue on Minitel or the Internet.

★ The **new restaurants:** On Level 1 is a theatre-bar in the foyer of the *Espace-spectacle*, but if you are looking for real refinement, you should go to the *Restaurant Georges* on Level 6 where the splendid terrace commands a panoramic view over the rooftops of Paris. The restaurant was placed in the hands of the Costes family, and has seating for 200 diners inside, 150 outside; it also has its own entrance in the evening via the *porte Rambuteau*. The setting, designed by Jacob-McFarlane, is superb, consisting of vast aluminium shells that either look like cocoons, or for the more sceptical, gigantic molars. On the subject of which, if you're hoping for something to eat around here, you should look under 'Where to eat' in the addresses given in the '4th arrondissement'.

– **Level 6** covers an area of 3,400 square metres (4066 square yards) and is used for temporary exhibitions. Notice the mirror of water and the mobile by Calder.

★ **The new entertainment complex** brings together the four halls that were previously scattered around the Pompidou Centre in an area covering 3000 square metres (3588 square yards). These comprise the *Grande Salle* for theatre, dance and concerts, with seating for 440; the *Salle Parole* or conference and seminar room with seating for 160; the *Salle de Cinéma 2*, which seats 150, and the *Studio* intended for research and development. A large entrance hall and a gallery round off this part of the complex.

– **Shows:** Visitors to the Centre can also attend various shows in the teepee outside on the piazza, including dance, seminars and spoken reviews.

The Centre's events sometimes take place in the Espace Électra, the Musée du Jeu de Paume, the Musée d'Art moderne de la Ville de Paris and the Grand Palais.

OTHER THINGS TO SEE

★ Beaubourg is also home to **Ircam** *(l'Institut de Recherche et de Coordination Acoustique-musique)* in Place Igor-Stravinski. Open 9.30am to 7pm. Its activities are centred around three objectives: research, creation and sharing. The music of the future is made here using 20th-century technology. Ircam has set up a course for composers, a summer school and two doctorate training courses. For the general public, it organizes courses and conferences. Their concerts attract many music lovers.

★ **Atelier Brancusi:** entry on the piazza. Same opening hours as the Pompidou Centre. Born in Romania in 1876, Constantin Brancusi lived in Paris from 1904 until his death. He was one of the century's most important sculptors, and most of his work was carried out in his workshop in the 15th arrondissement. In his will, he left the workshop to the State, but it was only in 1997 that it was rebuilt on the piazza. You'll find over 140 sculptures, as well as drawings and photographic works here.

★ Alongside the Pompidou Centre, in a large **pool** which pays homage to **Igor Stravinsky,** Niki de St-Phalle and Jean Tinguely, the exponents of new realism, have dreamed up prehistoric animals with mechanisms which make them appear to be drinking the water. They spit and belch out jets of brightly coloured water and each sculpture, created from scrap materials and iron, is related to a work by the Russian composer, such as *The Firebird* and *The Rite of Spring*. Best seen at night, when projectors flash over the explosive colours.

THE BEAUBOURG DISTRICT

An extension of the Les Halles quarter, bordering the Marais, this area has a series of narrow lanes which allow you to make a quick escape from the 'refinery' – if you feel the need. To the south are rue de la Reynie, rue Quincampoix, rue des Lombards, rue de la Verrerie (with numerous restaurants) and the Hôtel de Ville (town hall).

★ **Rue Quincampoix:** for a long time this was one of the most picturesque streets in Paris. To the north it crosses the boundary with the 3rd arrondissement. There are many fine houses and private residences. The street is still linked with the Scottish banker, Law, who was involved in a forerunner of Wall Street's Black Thursday, albeit some 200 years earlier. He set up a bank at No. 65 and created the India Company, a joint stock company, which controlled all external trade. A huge share speculation multiplied their value 10-fold in a matter of days, causing chaos when Law was unable to pay out the promised dividends, lost his investors' confidence, and the system crashed overnight, ruining a great deal of lives. It is even said that the scandal may have hastened the Revolution. In any case, the French owe Law their lasting mistrust of securities, deeds and shares.

Above No. 27, on the corner with rue Aubry-le-Boucher, there's a pretty *trompe-l'œil* façade.

By the 1970s, the fine houses in the street had fallen on hard times and a number of them were home to some legendary houses of ill-repute. However, recent renovations have revealed the richness of the façades once more: corbels, gables, wrought-iron balconies and monumental studded doors. There are also a number of art galleries along the street.

★ **Église St-Merri:** entrance in rue St-Martin and rue de la Verrerie. Dating from the mid-16th century, the northern side of the church is in flamboyant Gothic style, although during that period it was the Italian Renaissance style that was in fashion. As often was the case at the time, the southeastern side is abutted by houses. The nearby rue St-Martin (the oldest street in Paris, along with rue St-Jacques), rue de la Verrerie, rue du Cloître-St-Merri and rue des Juges-Consuls are lined with old houses and fine mansions. Inside the church there's a lovely series of pillars which taper due to the absence of capitals. The decorative style is quite sober, the nave and choir are very deep and there is some fine panelling and stained-glass windows to be seen in the first few chapels.

Two streets further up, rue Geoffroy-Langevin has retained its picturesque medieval layout. At 41 rue du Temple, enter the fine courtyard of the former inn, the L'Aigle d'Or, which belonged to one of the great stagecoach companies serving the provinces. It has some fine façades. The building at the end is occupied by Romain Bouteille's Café de la Gare. The others house various *Fame*-style dance schools. The courtyard here is always lively. On the corner of rue Ste-Croix-de-la-Bretonnerie, there's a curious corner turret dating from 1610.

★ The **rue St-Merri**, at the end of the cul-de-sac du Bœuf, has hardly changed since the Middle Ages: large paving stones and a central gutter remain.

DID YOU KNOW?

Voltaire protested against the term *cul-de-sac* and wrote to the Prefect of Police: 'I don't believe that a road resembles a bottom (*cul*, as in backside) or a bag (*sac*). I beg you to use the word *impasse* (blind alley), which is noble, sonorous and intelligent.'

★ **Tour St-Jacques:** an important stage on the pilgrimage to Santiago de Compostela that also had an unlikely hand in the course of scientific progress as Pascal, the French Mathematician, carried out experiments on the pull of gravity from the tower. The church to which it was originally attached was demolished during the Revolution, but the tower, left all alone, was rented by an armourer who manufactured his hunting shot by letting drops of lead fall down the drop. Rather ingenious. During the 19th century, it was restored and is now used as a meteorological observatory. A technician goes up the tower every morning to take readings and he or she is obviously fit as there's no lift.

★ **Hôtel de Ville (town hall)**: Headquarters of the Paris City Council. Metro: Hôtel-de-Ville, obviously! Access to the halls only on organized tours, which are free. Groups must make appointments from Monday to Friday, one or two months in advance: ☎ 01-42-76-50-49 or 01-42-76-54-04. There are visits for private individuals on the first Monday of each month, by appointment at least a week in advance: ☎ 01-42-76-50-49 or 01-42-76-54-04 for the exact timetables. The tour takes 1 hour. Advance bookings at 5 rue Lobau. The halls are accessible to visitors with wheelchairs.

Burned down during the Paris Commune, the town hall was rebuilt in a neo-Renaissance style which was even more grandiose than the previous one. On the inside, it's a perfect masterpiece of the 'pompous' style. Frescoes, gilding, precious woods and crystal chandeliers are crammed into a true decorative obsession.

Temporary exhibitions about Paris are held regularly at 29 rue de Rivoli. Open 9am to 6pm daily except Sunday and public holidays. ☎ 01-42-76-43-43 to find out the subject of the next exhibition.

★ Until the mid-ninth century the **Place de l'Hôtel-de-Ville** was known as the Place de Grève (because it ran gently down towards the Seine – *grève* means bank or seashore). It is why the word 'grève' also means strike, since, as a focus point of activity along the river, those who were searching for work tended to congregate here. The Paris Commune installed its headquarters here from 1789 to 1795. It was here on 17 July 1789 that the Commune gave Louis XVI their insignia, the tricolour cockade, the receipt of which would prove his acceptance of the Revolution. The Hôtel de Ville was a hive of activity throughout the Revolution. Robespierre took refuge here before it was his turn to be arrested and many of the major executions took place here. Some very famous people lost their heads, were broken on the wheel, hanged or quartered: Ravaillac, Brinvilliers (the female poisoner), the bandit Cartouche, Damiens (who tried to kill Louis XV) and Fouquier-Tinville to name only a few. On a happier note, it was here that on 25 August 1944 General de Gaulle celebrated the Liberation of Paris in front of 200,000 people.

★ **Cloître des Billettes:** 22–26 rue des Archives 75004. This was the last medieval cloister to be built in Paris (in 1427), with beautiful and flamboyant arched arcades. It can be visited during temporary exhibitions. The Billettes church, which now houses the cloister, dates from the 18th century. Concerts are regularly held in the church.

★ **Maison de Jacques Cœur:** 40 rue des Archives 75004. Today this old residence houses a state primary school. Much to everyone's amazement, during recent clearance work traces of moulding and mullioned windows were found which made it possible to date the house to the 15th century and to discover that it had belonged to either Jacques Cœur – a financier and minister to Charles VII – or his son. This makes it one of the oldest houses in Paris.

The rings that are topped by huge bollards at the entrance to some of the streets in this area were not intended for tethering horses, but to hang chains across the streets. In the Middle Ages, many people lived in fear of Parisian rioting, so, in case of trouble, they tried to restrict the freedom of movement of those on foot or horseback. On another tack, the central gutter caused problems for refined ladies if it had been raining as it was quite difficult to cross wearing long skirts and high heels, so they were obliged to pay strong men to carry them across to the other side. How romantic!

THE ST-GERVAIS – ST-PAUL DISTRICT

To the south of the Marais, and separated from the north Marais by rue St-Antoine and rue de Rivoli, this quarter has undergone a great sociological change in the last 20 years, as it has almost entirely lost its popular atmosphere and a lot of its old houses. However, there is a superb architectural walk and plenty of bookshops to be discovered.

★ **Church of St-Gervais-St-Protais:** located behind the Hôtel de Ville, this church, set on its mound, is pretty imposing. The approach is via a great staircase and the façade is classical, superimposing the three Greek orders: Doric, Ionic and Corinthian. Inside there is a superb 16th-century slender arch, a flamboyant Gothic-style nave, and an 18th-century organ case, one of the last remaining organs from this era in Paris. (The oldest dates from the 16th century and can be found in the Chapelle de la Salette, 55 boulevard de Belleville.) At the entry to the chancel, there are some fine 16th-century stalls whilst behind it there is a superb chapel of the Virgin, as well as magnificent stained-glass windows, a Christ on the Cross from the 19th century and a finely wrought grill from the 17th century. All the chapels contain interesting paintings, sculptures or stained-glass windows. In 1918, a shell from the German gun known as 'Big Bertha' brought down part of the arch, killing 51 people.

★ The architectural walk around the quarter begins with the superb 18th-century building that stretches from No. 2 to No. 14 **rue François-Miron**. It is quite unbelievable that there were serious plans to demolish it in the 1940s. There is some fine ironwork on the façade and the old inscription 'place Baudoyer'. Not far from here, in 1993, a Carolingian dwelling was discovered during the construction of an underground car-park. A few metres underneath the pavement, a rare Merovingian burial ground (fourth to seventh centuries) was also found. But, to the great displeasure of the residents, most of the remains were once again buried under tons of concrete, because the incompetent authorities failed to react quickly enough.

To the right **rue des Barres** leads to rue de l'Hôtel-de-Ville and down to the Seine. It is a curious street, bordered as it is by new and rather graceless constructions, but with some fine medieval buildings such as the one which houses the Accueil des Jeunes en France (Welcome for Young People to France) on the corner of rue du Grenier-sur-l'Eau.

★ The **rue de l'Hôtel-de-Ville** has been restored for the most part. Originally known as rue de la Mortellerie from 1212 until the 19th century, there is an inscription engraved in the stone at No. 95 (the *mortelliers* were masonry workers and mortar plasterers and *mortel* means mortal). After the cholera epidemic of 1832 which decimated Paris, the surviving inhabitants, finding the name of their street a bit too morbid, changed it to its present name. The headquarters of the Compagnons du Devoir du Tour de France, the oldest corporation and guardian of traditions in the country, is at No. 84 (sculpted pillars). At No. 62, on the corner with rue des Barres, a restaurant occupies the former shop of a wine merchant (with a splendid finely wrought external grill) and that of a baker (with a fine ceramic ceiling).

★ Having followed rue du Grenier-sur-l'Eau and crossed rue du Pont-Louis-Philippe, you reach **rue Geoffroy-l'Asnier**. Several superb buildings have survived, such as the Hôtel de Châlons-Luxembourg at No. 26. There is a splendid gate dating from the time of Louis XIII with a sculpted tympanum (not Louis XIII's) decorated with a lion's head. Gabriele D'Annunzio lived here in 1914. At No. 22, there's a staircase with a wooden balustrade in the entrance and an elegant dwelling at the end with a sculpted garland above the door. The houses nearby have been charmingly renovated. In the small courtyard, there is a 17th-century building with a standing lantern.

★ **Mémorial du Martyr Juif Inconnu et le Centre de Documentation Juive Contemporaine:** corner of rue du Grenier-sur-l'Eau and rue Geoffroy-l'Asnier 75004. ☎ 01-42-77-44-72. Website: www.memorial-cdjc.org. Metro: Pont-Marie or St-Paul. The memorial is open Sunday to Friday 10am to 1pm and 2pm to 6pm (5pm on Friday). Closed Saturday. The Documentation Centre is open Monday to Thursday 2pm to 6pm. Entry fee 30F; annual subscription 80F.

The Contemporary Jewish Documentation Centre is the largest centre in Europe for research on the Shoah, with over a million unpublished archives and a library of 50,000 works on the Holocaust and anti-Semitism. The file drawn up by the French Government between 1941 and 1944 for the arrest and internment of French Jews is part of the memorial. There is a crypt with the Tomb of the Unknown Jewish Martyr.

Each of the floors has themed temporary exhibitions, telling the tale of the suffering and struggles of the Jewish people during World War II through poignant images, photographs and text. Sadly, there are plenty of them.

★ Return to **rue François-Miron**, an old Roman road leading to Melun, a suburb of Paris. Lined with medieval houses, it still retains remnants of the quarter as it used to be. At Nos. 11 and 13, on the corner of rue Cloche-Perce, are two lovely gabled houses from the 13th century whose half-timbering has recently been rediscovered. At No. 30, in the little courtyard located at the other end of the corridor, there is part of a 15th-century house in the Renaissance style, with two façades with sculpted wood sections (they are listed façades). Marie Touchet lived here, the mistress of Charles IX and mother of his illegitimate son, Charles de Valois.

After the death of the king, Marie Touchet had two daughters. The first, Henriette, the Marquise de Verneuil, was enshrined in history when she dared to comment on the personal hygiene of Henri IV. It was she who said to the king: 'Sire, you stink like a rotting carcass.' 'Rotting carcass perhaps,' replied the king, 'but a royal rotting carcass', thereby making it fairly clear who wore the trousers in the kingdom. Continuing on the theme of smells – but infinitely more pleasant ones – today, at the same address, lovers of spices and products from all over the world stop at Izrael, a 'world grocer's', with a bazaar-like atmosphere. There are hundreds of amazing foods: Brazil nuts, pine kernels from China, pistachios from Iran, rice from Pakistan, herrings from Norway and French olives. At Nos. 44 and 46 are two 16th-century houses with skylights with triangular pediments and an odd modern weathervane above the roof. They are home to *Sauvegarde et Mise en Valeur du Paris Historique,* an organisation dedicated to safeguarding and protecting historical Paris, a fascinating information centre (☎ 01-48-87-74-31; open 2pm to 6pm). Apart from the free visit to the cellar and the little courtyard, there are many documents on old Paris and they organize informative tours across the capital.

★ **Hôtel de Beauvais:** at 68 rue François-Miron, this is the finest building in the district. Mozart stayed here during one of his visits to Paris. It dates from the 17th century and was the property of Pierre Beauvais and his wife Catherine. Not exactly an oil painting, she was nicknamed Cateau la Borgnesse (One-Eyed Kate), but nonetheless took the virginity of Louis XIV when he was 16. People say that his mother, Anne of Austria, was mad with joy at such early proof of her son's virility, as she had had to live for so many years with his father, Louis XIII, who was impotent. In 1660, on the triumphal entry into Paris of Louis XIV with his young wife, Marie-Thérèse, there was a good line-up on the balconies of the house: Anne of Austria, the Queen of England, Cardinal Mazarin and, of course, Cateau la Borgnesse (who must surely have given the king a lewd wink!). Apparently, she later began collecting archbishops.

The house has some interesting features. As land was limited, the architect (Lepautre) was unable to put the traditional plan (outbuildings in front, main residence, then garden) into practice. The main building therefore gives onto the street. Inside is an immense porch leading to an elegant hall in the shape of a rotunda, surrounded by Doric columns. On the left, there is a superb stone staircase with Corinthian cornices and a sculpted ceiling. The oval courtyard is surrounded by newels and Ionic columns with a balcony in the middle, topped by an odd skylight.

– From Nos. 72 to 78 are fine 18th-century façades. All the buildings have been superbly renovated.

★ **Hôtel d'Aumont:** just down the road, at 7 rue de Jouy, this building is lit up at night from the quai de l'Hôtel-de-Ville. Very chic, though rather cold and conservative, it is the work of Le Vau, one of the architects of Versailles. Today it houses the administrative court. Opposite, on the corner of rue de Jouy and rue de Fourcy, there's a fine stone sign, representing a grinder, set in a new building.

★ **Maison Européenne de la Photographie:** 5–7 rue de Fourcy 75004. ☎ 01-44-78-75-00. Website: www.mep-fr.org. Metro: St-Paul. Open 11am to 7.45pm. Closed Monday, Tuesday and public holidays. Entry fee 30F; reduced rate 15F; free for children under eight. In a restored private residence, the Hôtel Hénault de Cantobre, this is a large collection of original contemporary photographs, plus themed exhibitions, a gallery for new talent, a library, a video library, a bookshop and an auditorium – in fact everything you could possibly hope for if you are interested in photography. There is a small café open from 11am to 7pm Thursday to Sunday and on Wednesday until 5pm.

★ At 22 bis **rue du Pont-Louis-Philippe** you can admire, if the door is open, a magnificent Renaissance house with sculpted half-timbering which is almost unique in Paris. The first courtyard is also of interest with its cornices built into the stone.

★ **Hôtel de Sens:** 1 rue du Figuier 75004. ☎ 01-42-78-14-60. Open 1.30pm (10am on Saturday) to 8.30pm. Closed Sunday and Monday. One of the last testaments to medieval civil architecture, transformed into a library specializing in the fine and decorative arts. Guided tours (broadly speaking) on the third Friday of every month at 3pm. Register at the Caisse des Monuments Historiques. The Hôtel de Sens was actually built on the order of the Archbishop of Sens, but he died before he got the chance to move in. It looks simultaneously like a house and a fortress, in many ways being strongly reminiscent of the latter with corner turrets, bartizans, and a tower with a balcony with ornamental openings and corbelling. The building has superb windows, skylights and above all a remarkable Gothic porch. Queen Margot lived here upon her return from captivity after Henri IV divorced her, and she collected hair from her lovers with which she is reputed to have made wigs.

★ **Bibliothèque Forney:** housed in the Hôtel de Sens since 1961, it was founded at the end of the 19th century and is essentially devoted to fine arts (architecture, painting, engraving and drawing), decorative and graphic arts and the craft industry. The collection has some 200,000 books, 2,200 newspaper titles, 400 annual subscriptions and 40,000 catalogues from exhibitions in France and abroad. There are also 5,000 posters from the 1880s to 1945, 10,000 more recent posters and over a million postcards, slides, engravings and labels. There are also temporary exhibitions. This museum is not very well known, but is worth a visit as it is quite fascinating.

★ The rue du Figuier leads to **rue Charlemagne**. No. 20 is an old house at the beginning of rue du Prévôt. On the corner note the old names engraved in the stone: rue Percée and rue aux Prestres. The rue du Prévôt has kept its authentically medieval character (at No. 5, there is a vast porch which was used to let the carriages out). At 16 rue Charlemagne, there's a Franco-Polish café, Karine, which is a hangover from the large Polish community that once lived in this area, serving generous sandwiches and Polish and French dishes at lunchtime. Destruction of the houses on the whole of one side of rue des Jardins-St-Paul has at least allowed a large portion of Philippe Auguste's city wall to be brought to light. The resulting space is great for local kids, who now have a playground. Finally, at No. 12 there is a pretty fountain.

★ **Cimetière St-Éloi** used to be on the corner of rue Neuve-St-Pierre and rue Hôtel-St-Paul. Closed in 1791 to allow building work to take place, this cemetery was never moved, so beneath your feet lie occupants as famous as the Man in the Iron Mask, Jean Nicot (who died in 1600, and who gave us the word 'nicotine'), François Rabelais (died in 1553) and Madeleine Béjart (both mistress and mother-in-law of Molière).

★ **Village St-Paul:** between quai des Célestins, rue St-Paul and rue Charlemagne. Open daily except Tuesday and Wednesday 11am to 7pm. The 16th-century condemned buildings and fountains have been given a makeover and the lovely little inner courtyards, invaded by antiques' dealers, have become a meeting place for the start of guided walks, which are highly prized in the quarter. There are around 60 antiques' dealers and bric-à-brac stalls, which are well established. The market is worth a visit, if only for its provincial charm, provided by the traders, and for its fantastic twice-yearly jumble sale when temporary stalls are set up by locals and by provincial traders who come to Paris specially.

★ A splendid renovated house on the corner of rue Charlemagne and rue Eginhard is even more striking at night, when the light shows up the warm tones of the stone. In the twisting, narrow **rue Eginhard** there are huge paving stones, an axial gutter and the vestiges of an old fountain in a cul-de-sac.

★ **Église St-Paul-St-Louis:** in rue St-Antoine, this is a Jesuit church, built in 1627 in the so-called 'Jesuit' style, on the orders of Louis XIII. It has a fine façade on three floors topped by Corinthian columns and an unusual dome. Richelieu laid the first stone, paid for the magnificent sculpted doors and said the first mass. Bossuet gave famous sermons here and the nobles sent their valets several hours in advance to get the best seats! The hearts of Louis XIII and Louis XIV were laid to rest here but were later stolen during the Revolution by a 'patriot' to make dye. A somewhat extraordinary story.

The interior is influenced by Italian baroque, with sculpted ceilings and a 55m (180ft) high cupola, which at the time was considered to be a great technical feat. The drum of the cupola is painted as a beautiful trompe-*l'œil*. The two great fonts at the entry were donated by Victor Hugo, whose local parish this was. Above the arcade leading to the sacristy is *Le Christ au Jardin des Oliviers* by Delacroix. Opposite is *St Louis Recevant la Couronne d'Épines du Christ*.

On leaving the church, try taking the side door (on the left as you look towards the altar). You will rejoin rue St-Paul through the picturesque **passage St-Paul**, which has barely changed since the 18th century. Leave the passage at 45 rue St-Paul.

★ **Rue St-Paul:** this, the main road in the quarter, was already in existence bearing this name in 1350, and the surrounding streets have been relatively untouched over the centuries. On the corner of rue des Lions-St-Paul, there is a 16th-century quadrangular turret. A famous doctor who was a strong supporter of the practice of bleeding lived in this house. One of his clients was Louis XIII himself, whom he bled 47 times in a single year.

★ **Musée de la Curiosité et de la Magie:** 11 rue St-Paul 75004. ☎ 01-42-72-13-26 and 01-42-77-45-62. Metro: St-Paul. Open Wednesday, Saturday, Sunday, some public holidays and during some school holidays, 2pm to 7pm. Tour and show 45F; reduction for children aged 3 to 12.

Hidden in 16th-century arched cellars, this museum holds many surprises. Dive into the bizarre world of illusions and the history of magic. This unique collection was assembled in 1993 by Georges Proust, a relative of the famous writer Marcel. There are over 3,000 objects and documents dating from 1800 to 1950, presented in a fairground atmosphere. Try and get the better of the optical illusions, scientific devices and magic tricks. There is a conjuring show (both on stage and up close) at the end of the tour, which puts visitors' powers of observation to the test, as well as animated historical tableaux and a hall of mirrors. There is also a history of magic – the earliest traces of magic go back to Egyptian priests who fooled the crowds with bottomless vases.

– Conjuring courses are available on Saturday between 11am and 1pm (card tricks), or at 2pm and 3.15pm (general magic), according to your level. Price 100F.

– Children's workshops are held during the school holidays, with an afternoon party and show for 200F. Phone in advance.

★ **Rue des Lions-St-Paul:** there are a number of houses which are worthy of interest along this street. No. 11 is the house where Mme de Sévigné lived as a young bride and where – as she had nothing better to do – she spent her time writing. Her daughter, Mme de Grignan, the recipient of a good number of her famous letters, was born here. Behind the great studded door is a charming paved inner courtyard and a fine staircase with wrought-iron banisters at the end on the right.

★ **Rue Charles-V:** No. 12 is the house of the Marquise de Brinvilliers, the famous poisoner, who practised on the patients at the hospital and on her servants before removing her first victim, her father, in order to get the family fortune. She was decapitated in the place de Grève, now known as the place de l'Hôtel-de-Ville, for her sins. In the courtyard on the left, there is also a vast staircase with a superb wrought-iron banister. There is a garden inside, but the door is almost always closed.

★ On the corner of rue St-Paul and rue Neuve-St-Pierre you can see a section of the wall of the former Église St-Paul, destroyed after the Revolution. All that remains is a vestige of the clock-tower. In the corner, you can still glimpse the first steps of the staircase to the tower.

★ **Rue Beautreillis:** the charm of the provinces in Paris. This is where Jim Morrison of *The Doors* was officially found dead in his bath from a heart attack in early July 1971. According to other, less official, sources, Jim died not in his bath, but in the toilets of a club then known as the Rock'n'Roll Circus, probably as a result of an overdose. He is buried in the Père Lachaise cemetery (*see* '20th arrondissement').

★ **Rue du Petit-Musc** there is a rich profusion of sculptures, garlands and fruits on the façade of the Hôtel Fieubet (17th century), on the corner of the quai des Célestins, and a lovely house dating from the end of the 18th century on the corner of rue de la Cerisaie (today it's a restaurant-bistro, one of Paris's oldest and best).

★ **Pavillon de l'Arsenal:** 21 boulevard Morland 75004. ☎ 01-42-76-33-97. Website: www.pavillon-arsenal.com. Metro: Sully-Morland or Bastille. Open Tuesday to Saturday 10.30am to 6.30pm and Sunday 11am to 7pm. Closed Monday. Entry is free.

Exhibits devoted to Paris, the planning of the city and its architecture. On the ground floor there are photographs, maps and models which bring the history of the capital from the 12th to the 21st centuries back to life, through a tour entitled 'Paris, the city and its projects'. It traces the evolution of the capital through its successive city walls, explains the current state of affairs and presents large-scale architectural and urban projects. A 40m (130ft) model of Paris, with a touch screen, gives you access to over 3,000 images of the city projected onto nine screens.

On the first floor there are large temporary exhibitions offering a more thematic tour through Parisian architecture and town planning.

The second floor is on two mezzanines, with exhibits of current projects showing the results of tenders for building work and construction.

The documentation centre and photograph library are open Tuesday to Friday 2pm to 6pm.

★ On the corner of rue St-Antoine is the **Hôtel de Mayenne**, dating from 1612 and now housing a school, École des Francs-Bourgeois. A little further along, on the corner of rue Castex, is the **l'Eglise Réformée de Ste-Marie** whilst opposite is Beaumarchais on his pedestal, and nearby is a structure you certainly can't miss, the column of the Bastille (*see* '11th arrondissement').

★ **Rue St-Antoine** still has many interesting houses. This old Gaulish-Roman street was the east axis of the city – to the west is rue St-Honoré, to the north rue St-Martin, and to the south rue St-Jacques. The precise location of the ramparts of the Bastille has been traced to the beginning of the street. In the courtyard of No. 111, on the right, there is a high-ceilinged staircase with a wrought-iron banister and antique columns supporting a round terrace, whilst at No. 119 there is an old passageway leading to rue Charlemagne, which is currently being renovated. At No. 133 there is a splendid wrought-iron balcony supported by fantastic creatures.

ÎLE DE LA CITÉ (4TH ARRONDISSEMENT)

The eastern half of the island was almost wiped out by Haussmann in order to install his bland buildings to house the Prefecture de Police and law courts. Fortunately, the truly marvellous cathedral of Notre-Dame is there to save the island's reputation

★ **Notre-Dame:** place du parvis de Notre-Dame 75004. Metro: Cité or St-Michel. Open Monday to Saturday 8am to 6.45pm, closed Sunday except between 1pm and 3.30pm. Free guided tour of the cathedral daily at noon Monday to Friday, at 2.30pm Saturday and Sunday. Meet at the bottom of the nave. The tour takes 1 hour 30 minutes. School groups daily 10am to noon and 2pm to 4pm except on Monday, Saturday and Sunday and during the school holidays. Information and reservations: 6 place du Parvis 75004; ☎ 01-42-34-56-10.

People usually approach Notre-Dame from the Place du Parvis, at the centre of which is a point from where all distances in France are measured – look out for the plaque on the ground. This square is another creation of the rapacious Haussmann who cleared away the maze of medieval lanes and houses that previously occupied it.

The cathedral took almost 200 years to build, beginning in the mid-12th century when the Bishop of Paris, Maurice de Sully, decided to build a prestigious cathedral. Initially an architect whose name has been lost to us, then Jean de Chelles and Pierre de Montreuil (the architect of Ste-Chapelle), were entrusted with directing the work, but it was not until towards 1340 that it was finished.

Many events have taken place over its long career. Among the most striking are the depositing of the Crown of Thorns by St Louis in 1239, the rehabilitation of Joan of Arc and the marriage of Marguerite de Valois and Henri de Navarre in 1572. The cathedral was looted during the Revolution, the bells were melted down and the heads of the kings of Judah and Israel were torn off the hinges of the Portal of St Anne. The 19th-century architect Viollet-le-Duc reinstated their heads. Not long ago, the real heads were found in the basement of a bank, and they are now on show at the Musée de Cluny (*see*

'5th arrondissement'). Napoleon had himself crowned Emperor of France in 1804 and in August 1944, during the Liberation Mass, General de Gaulle escaped his first assassination attempt. Some years later, in 1970, the state funeral of De Gaulle was conducted in the cathedral.

– **The archaeological crypt:** located under the square, this is one of the largest crypts in Europe. ☎ 01-43-29-83-51. Open daily from 10am to 4.30pm in winter and until 6pm in summer. Closed on public holidays. It contains relics from as far back as the third century and Gaulish-Roman remains from the cellars of the old rue Neuve-Notre-Dame.

– **The exterior:** Notre Dame is a Gothic masterpiece that ranks as one of the the world's most magnificent religious buildings. The main façade is made up of three huge doors: the Portal of the Virgin (on the left), the Portal of the Last Judgement and the Portal of St Anne. The grey statues you see today didn't always look that way. At one time they were highly coloured, set against a gold background.

The Portal of the Virgin contains a remarkable tympanum with statues restored and replaced by Viollet-le-Duc in the 19th century. The Portal of the Last Judgement portrays the Demons of Hell (on the left) and Paradise (on the right), whilst on the Portal of St Anne there are even more angels, saints and kings. Above the portals stretches the Gallery of the Kings, from where 28 regal statues stare down at the tourists, then there's the famous rose window, a blaze of coloured glass depicting the Virgin Mary. It has an astonishing diameter of 10m (33ft) proving the ambition, and even the audacity, of the architects of the time.

– **The towers:** access by the corner of rue du Cloître-Notre-Dame. Normally open daily from 10.30am to 4.15pm in winter, and 9.30am to 5.30pm in summer, but overall the opening times are pretty random. Information: ☎ 01-44-32-16-70. Entry fee 32F. Overhanging the magnificent west front, the south tower houses the famous tenor Emmanuel Bell, which weighs 13 tons and whose clapper alone weighs 500 kilos (over 1,100lbs). The second tower houses a staircase with 387 steps from which you can access a platform to enjoy the fantastic view over the Île de la Cité and the whole of Paris. From the vantage point of the south tower you will be able to take a closer look at the splendid gargoyles with their monstrous heads that give the building a touch of humour, also by Viollet-le-Duc. The spire, which is 45m (147ft) high, and 90m (295ft) above ground, was destroyed during the Revolution and rebuilt at the end of the 19th century. It is made entirely of oak covered with lead and weighs almost 750 tons.

– **The interior:** once inside the first thing you notice is how wide the nave is, bolstered by enormous pillars bearing the load, with spectacular flying buttresses on the outside. The chancel screen is 14th century with some 17th century restoration. It tells the story of the life of Christ. In the panel of the *Last Supper*, Judas, breaking the rules of polite etiquette, serves himself before anyone else. Notice the very maternal face of the Virgin. The choir stalls are exquisite; carved in wood, they were commissioned by Louis XIV, whilst behind the altar is a 'Pietà' by Nicholas Couston. There is a series of paintings on a religious theme by Charles Le Brun hanging in the chapels at the side and two further statues of note, the Virgin and Child dating from the 14th century close to the transept, and that of Louis XIII located beside the altar.

– **The treasury:** after the south transept on the right-hand side as you come in. Open from 9.30am to 11.30am and 1pm to 5.30pm. Closed Sunday and on Christian festivals. Entry fee from 5F to 15F. As you might guess, this houses religious treasures, reliquaries and ancient manuscripts.

★ **Square de l'Île-de-France:** behind Notre-Dame, once you've crossed the Pont de l'Archevêché. This was originally a separate island known at the end of the 13th century as the *Motte aux Papelards* (the Hypocrites' Lawn), and used as the dumping-ground for the debris from the Notre-Dame construction site. It now houses the Memorial to the Martyrs of Deportation. Some 200,000 points of light symbolize the 200,000 people who died as a result of deportation during the Second World War. A single chamber with adjacent cells, with a single opening at the end, it looks out over the river, barred by an iron grille. A symbolic and evocative place, it makes you think of all the people who suffered. Emerging once more into the daylight, it seems incongruous to see people sunbathing on the banks of the Seine close by.

★ The **rues des Ursins, Chanoinesse** and **de la Colombe**, which escaped Hausmann's building clearance, still give you some idea of the atmosphere of the Île de la Cité in former days. The playwright Racine lived at 16 rue Chanoinesse, and also at 7 rue des Ursins.

ÎLE ST-LOUIS

The Île St-Louis has an interesting history. Originally known as the Île-Notre-Dame, it was divided in two by a canal around 1360 (along what is now rue Poulleiter). The island remained largely unused, frequented only by washerwomen and lovers until the early 17th century, when Christophe Marie commissioned some elegant town houses. The canal was filled in and private homes sprang up all over the island, and from 1725 it became known as the island of St-Louis.

The only public monument on the island is the church of the same name, visible from afar thanks to its large clock-tower at the entrance. The interior is Baroque and consequently richly decorated. The island's inhabitants, the Ludoviciens, whose apartments now change hands for millions of francs, might be supposed to still enjoy a village-like atmosphere, given the island's delightful little shops and absence of monuments. However, the art shops and other local products now attract fair numbers of tourists, but, nevertheless, it is a charming place for a stroll and a spot of window shopping.

The island's quays tend to be quieter. Their façades, nearly all dating from the 17th century, present an elegant, uniform aspect when viewed from the river banks.

★ **Hôtel Lambert**, at 1 quai d'Anjou, is named after its first owner, an adviser to Louis XIII. It is undoubtedly the most beautiful house in Paris. Its oval gallery (with a terrace and a sculpted frieze) overlooking the quai d'Anjou and the Seine, is not open to the public because the house now belongs to Guy de Rothschild. There is another entrance at 2 rue St-Louis-en-l'Île.

At 3 quai d'Anjou is the **Hôtel de Louis Le Vau**, named after the talented and clever architect who was to carry out many other projects on the island and give it its style. The balcony is the longest on the island. Built in 1657, the interior is magnificent, with decorative panelling and painted ceilings.

Baudelaire wrote *Les Fleurs du Mal* while living here. At 5 quai d'Anjou is the little Hôtel de Marigny (with a fine wrought-iron grille) and at No. 7 the Siège du Syndicat des Maîtres Boulangers de Paris (Headquarters of the Trade Union of Master Bakers of Paris). In the entrance hall, on the right, there are some interesting historical commentaries and a collection of old baking troughs. The 19th century painter and caricaturist Honoré Daumier once lived at No. 9.

★ **11 quai de Bourbon** is the Hôtel de Philippe de Champaigne. De Champaigne was a great painter and valet to Marie de Médicis. In the courtyard, there is a staircase with a balustrade. At No. 15 is the Hôtel le Charron, dating from 1637, with an interesting courtyard. On each side lie elegant staircases with wrought-iron banisters. At No. 19, there is the attractive façade of the Hôtel de Jassaud with three pediments and a fine door. Here too you can see a courtyard with a little garden and statue. Camille Claudel, the sculptor and mistress of Auguste Rodin, worked here from 1899 to 1913.

★ **Rue St-Louis-en-l'Île:** the Hôtel de Chemizot, at No. 51, is a fine building, remarkable for its façade: a vast door topped by a sculpted tympanum, a wrought-iron balcony supported by mythical beasts and, above, an ornamented triangular pediment. In the courtyard, you'll find the same proliferation of plants as on the façade.

★ **Église St-Louis-en-l'Île:** built in 1644 to plans by Le Vau, this church has an interesting interior design. Beside the entrance is a chapel with baptismal fonts showing eight scenes from the Life of Christ on wood (Flemish school, 16th century). The *Baptême du Christ* is by Stella. Following the left-hand side (towards the chancel) is *St Jean et St Pierre Guérissant un Paralytique* by Van Loo. On the right-hand side, in the Chapelle Ste-Thérèse, there are some attractive 17th-century Italian earthenware works (in the middle is the *Adoration des Bergers*). In the Chapelle St-Vincent-de-Paul there is a Holy Virgin attributed to Canova, whilst in the Chapelle de la Communion, above the altar, is *Les Pèlerins d'Emmaüs* by Coypel. Finally, in the third chapel, there is a splendid bas-relief in gilded and coloured wood, *La Mort de la Vierge* (16th century, Flemish school).

★ **Quai d'Orléans:** at No. 18 is the very fine Hôtel Rolland. At No. 6 is the Musée Adam-Mickiewicz, dedicated to the great Polish poet who lived in Paris in the 19th century.

The **quai de Béthune** also has its share of elegant private houses. President Georges Pompidou lived and died at No. 24. At Nos. 20 and 22 there are identical houses and at Nos. 16 and 18 is the Hôtel de Comans or Hôtel de Richelieu – the powerful Cardinal Richelieu owned it at one time.

★ **Théâtre de l'Île-St-Louis:** 39 quai d'Anjou 75004. Metro: Pont-Marie. ☎ 01-46-33-48-65. Installed in the former carriage house of a private home, this is a charming little theatre (the only one on the island), which is a showcase for young writers and musicians from all over the world. It has a very interesting programme if you would like to try out your French comprehension in intimate surroundings, and there are concerts at the weekend.

THE OLD JEWISH QUARTER AND THE PLACE DES VOSGES

Bordered to the west by the rue des Archives, to the north by the rue des Francs-Bourgeois, and to the south by the rue de Rivoli and the rue St-Antoine, this is the heart of the Marais, still surprisingly working-class in places, and also the heart of the old Jewish quarter. One of the most colourful areas in Paris, there are some lovely restaurants and interesting shops dotted about the quarter.

★ **Rue Ste-Croix-de-la-Bretonnerie:** deep in the heart of the Marais, this area has been colonized by the gay community. Some of the established residents have had trouble accepting this social change, so there is occasional friction, but this change has made it one of the liveliest parts of the Marais. Lots of little restaurants, bars, café-theatres and pretty shops (although they are often rather expensive).

★ **Église des Blancs-Manteaux:** at 12 rue des Blancs-Manteaux and 53 rue des Francs-Bourgeois 75004. Metro: St-Paul. Although the architecture is not terribly original, the façade originates from a church on the Île de la Cité and there are some lovely details inside. The baroque pulpit is stunning and inlaid with ivory, and there is a 17th-century communion balustrade and some interesting paintings from the same period, *Multiplication des Pains* (Christ multiplying the loaves) and, above the door, *Adoration des Bergers*.

Opposite the church is the **rue Aubriot**, one of the streets of the Marais that has kept most of its character.

★ **Mont-de-Piété:** 55 rue des Francs-Bourgeois 75004. ☎ 01-44-61-64-00. Metro: St-Paul. Open 9am to 4.30pm (3.30pm on Friday). Closed Saturday and Sunday. This is a municipal pawnbrokers, more familiarly known as *Ma Tante* (meaning 'My Aunt' as all students familiar with the phrase *'la plume de ma tante'* will know – it's interesting to note that in English the pawnbroker was referred to as 'Uncle'!). It was created in 1777 to compete with and try to regulate the morals involved in the activities of pawnbrokers. When times were hard, this is where people came to pawn jewels, paintings, cameras and furs. If whatever you brought was good quality, you could expect to be loaned up to 50 per cent of its sale value at public auction. Only objects which are not redeemed by their owners are finally sold; sometimes you can find a real bargain.

★ **Rue Vieille-du-Temple:** lined with 13th-century houses and private residences, the main one to note is No. 47, the 17th-century Hôtel Amelot de Bisseuil, known as the 'Dutch Ambassadors'. Another sculpted tympanum and one of the finest doors in the Marais, with medallions and Medusa heads. Beaumarchais lived here while he was writing *The Marriage of Figaro* and organizing arms trafficking for the American insurgents during the War of Independence. He almost ruined himself in the process as the insurgents, after their victory, never actually paid him!

Walk past the Hôtel de Rohan (*see* '3rd arrondissement'), and slip into the rue de la Perle. This was known as rue Crucifix-Maquereau in the 16th century because of the cross in the centre, which prostitutes used to gather around (*maquereau*, literally 'mackerel', also means pimp).

★ **Rue du Roi-de-Sicile:** a higgledy-piggledy street that weaves its way with nothing but contempt for the term 'alignment'. Today, the street still has many attractive shops and traditional traders, such as the cake shop at No. 30 (a gabled house) and the former horsemeat butcher's on the corner of rue Vieille-du-Temple (decorated with mosaics).

★ **The old Jewish quarter: the rue des Rosiers** is the epicentre of the Jewish quarter. One of the most attractive and liveliest streets in the Marais, the rue des Rosiers was the former ring road of Philippe Auguste's city wall, taking its name from the gardens planted with rose bushes. This was one of the main areas of the Jewish community in the 12th century. In the Middle Ages they were forbidden from practising most 'noble' professions (such as teaching and law), so they switched to commercial trading and pawnbroking instead. The Jewish community was expelled from the area at the end of the 14th century, but by time of the Revolution it had managed to reinstate itself to some extent and comprised a few hundred people and, until the end of the 19th century, the place St-Paul was nicknamed 'place aux Juifs' (the Jews' square). In 1900 the name was changed from rue aux Juifs to rue Ferdinand-Duval, as France was gripped by anti-Semitism following the Dreyfus Affair.

During the 20th century, the district saw its population increase, first with the arrival of Jews from the USSR (Ashkenazis) and Poland fleeing the pogroms, then with those driven out of Germany by the Nazi regime. One of the darkest moments in the history of France was the Vél'd'hiv' raid. On the night of 16 July 1942, Jews in the area around rue des Rosiers and rue de St-Paul were arrested by the French police. The German authorities had told the police that any children under the age of 14 were not to be brought in. However, the police were particularly zealous that night and arrested everyone, regardless.

Today the Sephardic Jews, repatriated from North Africa, reinforce the old Ashkenazi community. Shops selling *falafel* (chickpea balls in pitta bread) now jostle with the older Ashkenazi shops with their traditional inscriptions in Hebrew.

The community spirit has protected the area from the depopulation which the rest of the Marais has suffered and allowed it to retain its popular, villagey feel. Everyone knows one another here and the spirit of solidarity shows. The rue des Écouffes, in summer, takes on the look of a Mediterranean square. However, recently, elegant boutiques have been trying to buy out the little shops, bringing more middle-class businesses into the area.

The streets are lined with lots of picturesque old houses. Strolling along rue des Hospitalières-St-Gervais, you may wonder about the origin of the two Egyptian-inspired bulls' heads decorating the school between Nos. 6 and 10 (from where all the children were deported during the Second World War). They indicated the former butchers' section of the Marché des Blancs-Manteaux. You can still make out, at Nos. 6 and 10, the inscriptions 'École primaire de jeunes israélites' or 'Primary school for young Israelites'.

If you're in the mood for a cake, cross the road to Chez Finkelsztajn at 27 rue des Rosiers. They have also opened a branch at 24 rue des Écouffes. There is a fine mosaic façade.

★ **Rue Pavée:** it has borne this name since 1450 because it was the first paved street in Paris. At No. 22, on the corner with the Hôtel Lamoignon, you can see the remains of a section of wall and a plaque. This is where the La Force prisons stood where many victims of the Revolution were held. The Petite-Force prison housed 'women of ill-repute', and the Grande-Force prison was for male debtors. When the massacres of 2 September 1792 took place, 60 people were murdered here, including the Princess de Lamballe. Her head was presented to Marie-Antoinette on a spike. At No. 12 there's a pretty courtyard framed by a private house from the mid-17th century, where Tronchet, Louis XVI's lawyer, lived. On the right, there is a small 18th-century staircase held up by a supporting beam and a corbelled façade. On the left, there is another impressive staircase. At No. 10, there is a synagogue created by Guimard at the turn of the century. The architect designed a curved façade to give an impression of width in this narrow space.

★ **Hôtel de Lamoignon:** 24 rue Pavée 75004. ☎ 01-44-59-29-40. Metro: St-Paul. One of the oldest private houses in Paris (1585). Today it is home to the **Bibliothèque Historique de la Ville de Paris,** the Historical Library of Paris. Open from 9.30am to 6pm except Sunday. There are interesting temporary exhibitions which can be seen from 10am to 6pm except on Monday, but the interior of the building cannot be visited. The house was built between 1585 and 1590 for Diane of France, the Duchess of Angoulême, an illegitimate daughter of Henri II; on her death it passed to her nephew, Charles de Valois. Prestigious past inhabitants of the house have included Guillaume de Lamoignon, the first President of the Parliament of Paris, Malesherbes and Alphonse Daudet, the writer. The square turret on the corner of rue Pavée and rue des Francs-Bourgeois made it possible to observe the two streets in all four directions. In the courtyard, there is a façade with Corinthian pilasters, decorated with lions' heads, bows, arrows.

★ **Rue des Francs-Bourgeois:** is split between the 3rd and 4th arrondissements. Take rue Pavée and then rejoin rue Vieille-du-Temple. Fortunately the new fashion boutiques that have moved into the area have not decimated the old shop interiors, so at No. 7 you can still see hooks left from its days as a butcher's and, on the corner of rue de Sévigné and rue des Francs-Bourgeois, there's a former baker's shop with an old-fashioned external decor, and at No. 29 a baker's with a fine flour mill in enamel.

From here on there is a succession of private residences with highly original façades. At No. 31, the Hôtel d'Albret (headquarters of the City's Board of Cultural Affairs) has a sculpted gate, lions with tympanum and a wrought-iron balcony. It dates from 1550 (the façade on the street is from 1700). In the 19th century, it contained a light-fittings factory. At No. 26 is the Hôtel de Sandreville (with Louis XVI façade) and at No. 30 stands the Hôtel d'Almeyras, which boasts a large door and a stone and red brick courtyard.

A little further on, at No. 34, there is an old pharmacy with sculpted wooden counters and ancient chemists' jars. In the 14th century, there was a medieval almshouse at Nos. 34–36 which sheltered the poor who were exempt from taxes. They were immortalized in the name of the street: *'franc'* means free.

At No. 38 is the picturesque passage des Arbalétriers which links up with the rue Vieille-du-Temple. The houses on the right-hand side of the street have been restored while those on the left date from 1600.

★ **Place du Marché-Ste-Catherine:** between rue de Sévigné and rue de Turenne. Built on the site of the former priory and the former church of St

Catherine, demolished in 1783, this attractive square has recently been transformed into a pedestrian area. It also joins the rue de Jarente, which is itself bordered by courtyards and an old fountain.

★ **Hôtel de Sully:** 62 rue St-Antoine 75004. ☎ 01-44-61-21-75. Metro: St-Paul. Now houses the Caisse Nationale des Monuments Historiques et des Sites. Bookshop open from 10am to 6pm. Closed Monday. The information centre (same address) is open from Monday to Friday 9am to 6pm. Information: ☎ 01-44-61-21-50. The most prestigious house in the area, built at the beginning of the 17th century in the purest Renaissance style, and acquired by Sully, Henri IV's minister in 1634. Restoration work has been particularly well carried out here.

Skylights and sculptures in the main courtyard represent the four seasons. To gain access to the second courtyard, cross the central building to a French-style garden, at the end is of which is the orangery, which was intended to protect the exotic trees. On the façade of the building there is a little sundial (take off 1 hour in winter and 2 hours in summer to discover the correct time).

★ **Place des Vosges:** arguably the most beautiful square in Paris, its symmetrical appearance was the result of new town planning regulations as, up until then, you could build exactly how and where you liked, which is why the old medieval streets looked so disorderly.

On 30 June 1559 Henri II organized a tournament to celebrate the double marriage of his children. It was held in front of the Hôtel des Tournelles, on the edge of the site of the present day square. Henri competed well but then challenged Montgomery, the captain of his guard. Montgomery accidentally hit him in the eye and Henri died in agony 10 days later. Catherine de Medicis, Henri's widow, had the Hôtel des Tournelles demolished and the resulting space became a horse market, until Henri IV selected it as the perfect site for his new square. Work began on the place Royale, as it was originally called, in 1605.

It was inaugurated in 1612, two years after Henri's death, on the occasion of the marriage of Louis XIII and Anne of Austria. Gloriously symmetrical and neatly laid out (108m/355ft each side), the square is surrounded by some 36 mansions, nine on each side, built over arcades. The roofs are made from blue sloping Angers slate and the window frames are white stone and red brick, though some of the buildings were just faced with imitation brick. The pavilions of the king and queen, to the north and south, stand a little higher than those east and west.

Festivals and tournaments were regularly held in the central space that is today occupied by a formal garden. Victor Hugo lived on the square from 1832 to 1848 (see below), the writer Alphonse Daudet lived at No. 8 and Madame de Sévigné was born here in 1626. The statue of Louis XIII on a horse that you see in the centre of the square is a mediocre 19th-century copy of the original bronze statue which was melted down during the Revolution.

Above the monumental arch in rue de Béarn, is the Pavillon de la Reine (Queen's Pavilion – currently a hotel), with rounded and triangular pediments. During the reign of Louis XIII, the whole of the Court vied to live here, but when they left for Versailles, the upper middle-classes, financiers and rich merchants moved in. There is a pretty verdant courtyard at No. 21, the former Hôtel de Richelieu, where the Cardinal lived whilst waiting for his Cardinal's Palace to be finished (the present Palais-Royal – *see* '1st arrondissement').

During the Revolution the square was renamed the Place de l'Indivisibilité, and eventually took the name of Place des Vosges in honour of the first French *département* to pay taxes in 1800. Nobody had paid any since the Terror, so the Republic was extremely grateful. There are some fine shops, antiques' dealers and tea-rooms under the arcades. Today the place des Vosges is still an extremely prestigious Parisian address and a very pleasant place to stroll and relax away from the bustle of the livelier parts of the Marais.

★ **Maison de Victor Hugo:** 6 place des Vosges 75004. ☎ 01-42-72-10-16. Metro: Bastille or St-Paul. Bus Nos. 20, 29, 65, 69, 76 and 96. Open from 10am to 5.40pm. Closed Monday and public holidays. Entry fee 22F; 15F reduced rate; free for under 27s.

Victor Hugo's home is located inside the Hôtel de Rohan-Guéménée, which was transformed into a museum in 1902, the year of the centenary of the birth of the writer. Victor Hugo lived on the second floor of this house from 1832 to 1848. He wrote all of his great plays here – *Marie Tudor, Ruy Blas* and *Les Burgraves* – as well as collections of poetry – *Les Chants du Crépuscule, Les Voix Intérieures* and *Les Rayons* and *les Ombres* – and a large part of *Les Misérables.*

The first floor contains a fascinating mix of documents, drawings and photographs of the writer, as well as temporary exhibitions. On the second floor there is an organized tour following the three broad stages into which Victor Hugo's life can be divided, including the unusual Chinese lounge which he designed during his exile. The library is open by appointment.

WHERE TO GO FOR AN ICE-CREAM

🍦 **Berthillon** (map C3, **60**): 31 rue St-Louis-en-l'Île 75004. ☎ 01-43-54-31-61. Metro: Pont-Marie. For ice-creams to take away and to eat in, open from 10am to 8pm Wednesday to Sunday. Closed Monday, Tuesday and during part of the school holidays, except for the Christmas holidays (which is a bit crazy for an ice-cream maker!). 9F, 16F and 20F per cone for one, two or three scoops. Berthillon affords itself the luxury of not opening slavishly during the holiday season; mad or arrogant – you decide. This establishment doesn't really care because it's an institution. Many restaurants boast 'ice-cream from Berthillon's' on their menus. Loads of flavours (wild strawberry, banana, peach) and a sublime *pear granita* – and there are always new concoctions. Consistent quality explains the long patient queues.

WHERE TO GO FOR A DRINK

🍸 **Le Lizard Lounge** (map B1, **65**): 18 rue du Bourg-Tibourg 75004. ☎ 01-42-72-81-34. Metro: St-Paul. Open daily noon to 2am. Set menu 45F at lunchtime, brunch on Sunday from 50F. Half a pint of beer from 16F. Something of a fish out of water this – a straight bar located between the bisexual and gay bars, it has become the enfant terrible of the quarter. Owned by a young Englishman, Irishman and American, the clientele is young and hip, and there's a techno lab in the basement from Wednesday to Saturday. Happy hour from 5pm to 7pm upstairs and 8pm to 10pm in the cellar.

🍸 **Le Petit Fer à Cheval** (map C1, **76**): 30 rue Vieille-du-Temple 75004. ☎ 01-42-72-47-47. Metro: St-Paul or Hôtel-de-Ville. Open daily 9am to 2am. Glass of wine from 16F. Nothing much has changed in this venerable establishment, opened in 1903. A local bistro and 100 per cent Parisian, the old wooden benches come from disused metro trains and the original bar is in the shape of a horseshoe (*fer à cheval* means horseshoe). The music is jazzy but not loud enough to drown out your conversation. Dishes of the day at around 60F. An old-fashioned bar that reminds you of the good old days that you never knew, but can imagine.

🍸 **La Belle Hortense** (map C1, **76**): 31 rue Vieille-du-Temple 75004. ☎ 01-48-04-71-60. Metro: St-Paul or Hôtel-de-Ville. Open until 2am. Glass of wine from 14F to 35F. Spirits from 40F. Just opposite the Petit Fer à Cheval (same owner, see above), this is a literary bar popular with writers. Ask to see the landlord's cellar, apparently it's worth it (Côtes du Rhône Guigal at 36F).

🍸 **Les 7 Lézards** (map C1, **63**): 10 rue des Rosiers 75004. ☎ 01-48-87-08-97. Metro: St-Paul. Open daily 11am to 2am (from 6pm on Monday and Tuesday). The name is usually a talking-point and that's exactly why people come here to chat and generally mull over the state of the world in general. 'World' snacks from 25F, except at weekends when there's jazz instead. The stage is open to anyone on Thursday and professionals at weekends (entry 70F). No draught beer, but ginger juice and tea provide the stimulants.

🍸 **Le Petit Gavroche** (map B1, **64**): 15 rue Ste-Croix-de-la-Bretonnerie 75004. ☎ 01-48-87-74-26. Metro: Hôtel-de-Ville. Closed Saturday lunchtime and Sunday; in August open evenings only. Set menu 48F at lunchtime, 50F in the evening. À la carte, the bill doesn't go above 100F. There's a homely atmosphere here, a refuge for the locals that gets busy, as you'll discover when you're pressed against the bar – it's been going for 20 years now. On the wall are two amusing educational pictures dealing with the dangers of alcoholism! Over the counter there's a drawing signed by Poulbot, but it isn't the genuine article.

🍸 **Café Klein Holland** (map C2, **67**): 36 rue du Roi-de-Sicile 75004. ☎ 01-42-71-43-13. Metro: St-Paul. Open daily 5pm to 2am. 14F for half a pint of beer at any time of the day, or 140F for a yard of ale. More cheerful than a Belgian bar, less noisy than an Australian watering hole, but as friendly as an Irish pub, this Dutch bar is always full. The welcome is friendly, the decor a touch on the sober side, but nevertheless pleasant, and the clientele native to the Low Countries. The beers are obviously Dutch, as is the gin (15F) and the bar snacks (*bitter ballen* at 25F).

🍸 **L'Illustre** (map D2, **73**): 11 rue des Tournelles 75004. ☎ 01-40-27-04-40. Metro: Bastille. Open daily 6pm to 2am. Spirits 45F, half a pint of beer 22F. Neither a hip bar, nor a select bar, just a place for friends to meet, with the added benefit of Canal+, the French pay-per-view channel.

🍸 **La Tartine** (map C2, **68**): 24 rue de Rivoli 75004. ☎ 01-42-72-76-85. Metro: Hôtel-de-Ville or St-Paul. Open until 10pm. Closed Tuesday, Wednesday mornings and for a fortnight in August. Various sandwiches at 14F. An old café which has been here for centuries, this is one of the original Parisian wine bars. The walls are stained by the nicotine of regulars, and smoke from the pipes of intellectuals, artists and journalists. Large mirrors and old gas lighting, art-deco tables and a service which is as crabby as you could wish, for that real Parisian experience. They specialize in wines from the Rhône Valley and Bordeaux accompanied by *charcuterie.*

🍸 **Les Marronniers** (map B1, **74**): 18 rue des Archives 75004. ☎ 01-40-27-87-72. Metro: Hôtel-de-Ville. Open daily 8am to 2am. 19F for half a pint of beer, food from 35F to 75F. In the heart of the Marais, this famous terrace is filled, both in winter and summer, with a clientele which seems to be half gay and half straight. People come here to have a drink and nibble an omelette or *Croque Monsieur* whilst eyeing up the sex of their choice. On Wednesday evening, the action is on the first floor from 8pm to 1am for the *Revue Perpendiculaire.*

🍸 **The Auld Alliance** (map C2, **69**): 80 rue François-Miron 75004. ☎ 01-48-04-30-40. Metro: St-Paul. Open daily 11am to 2am. Half a pint of beer from 18F, dishes from 25F to 60F. To the numerous English and Irish pubs in Paris can be added this Scottish one, which has wisely chosen the Marais in which to set up. There is a large selection of Scottish single malts (sold in shots of 3cl) and traditional Scottish dishes such as the famous haggis (stuffed sheep's stomach – and you thought the French ate anything that moved!). On the walls hang clan tartans as well as pictures showing scenes from the Battle of Culloden, full of blood and thunder. There's quite an atmosphere, especially if there's a football match on.

🍸 **Les Étages** (map C1, **70**): 35 rue Vieille-du-Temple 75004. ☎ 01-42-78-72-00. Metro: St-Paul or Hôtel-de-Ville. Open daily 5pm to 2am (noon to 2am at weekends). 35F for bottled beers. Tapas from 10F. Brunch at weekends for 95F. An original concept in an old 18th-century private house that has been transformed into a bar. A waiter will give you the menu on arrival at the ground floor, from where a staircase leads to the two upper floors and rooms furnished in post-war style. You place your orders via an old bakelite wall telephone. As the tables are quite close to one another, it's easy to start up a conversation with your neighbours.

🍸 **Ma Bourgogne** (map D2, **71**): 19 place des Vosges 75004. ☎ 01-42-78-44-64. Metro: Bastille or St-Paul. Open daily until 1am. Closed in February. Set menu at 195F; 250F for à la carte with wine. You can come here to admire the splendid arcades on the Place des Vosges in one of the most beautiful parts of Paris, while drinking wine from a list which has a number of interesting bottles as well as a good choice of Beaujolais served by the glass. The wine is accompanied by the excellent house steak *tartare* or *tripoux du Rouergue.*

🍸 **Le Pick-Clops** (map C2, **72**): on the corner of rue Vieille-du-Temple and rue du Roi-de-Sicile 75004. ☎ 01-40-29-02-18. Metro: St-Paul. Open 8am to 2am (on Sunday, from 2.30pm in winter, and 10am in summer). Half a pint of beer 11F at the bar, 15F after 10pm. This is a meeting place for regulars or trendies in-the-know, with neon signs, mirrors and Formica. Sometimes it's a bit hot and can get a bit out of control.

🍸 **Le Café du Trésor** (map C1, **77**): 5–7 rue du Trésor 75004. ☎ 01-44-78-06-60. Metro: St-Paul. Open daily until 2am, but opening times vary according to the seasons. Set menu 100F at lunchtime and evening; brunch 90F and 100F on Sunday. À la carte, budget for 150F. Without doubt, one of the most sought-after spots in Paris with one of the nicest terraces in summer and a good sprinkling of 'the beautiful people'. Brunch at weekends, snack café, dinner (not that great), post-show and organized fiestas punctuate the life of this bistro which already has a cult following.

If the Café du Trésor is full – the terrace often is when the weather is good – try **La Chaise au Plafond** opposite, a trendy terrace café.

🍸 **Café Martini** (map D2, **78**): 11 rue du Pas-de-la-Mule 75004. ☎ 01-42-77-05-04. Metro: Bastille or Chemin-Vert. Open daily 8.30am to 2am. Half a pint of beer from 13F. Paris? Milan? New York? This compact bar is a perfect hotchpotch, with a rather international atmosphere. Try a draught Pelforth beer, a glass of wine or an Italian espresso coupled with *panini* from 20F. If you need to stretch your legs afterwards in classical French surroundings, the place des Vosges is the proverbial stone's throw away.

🍸 **Café des Phares** (map D2, **82**): 7 place de la Bastille 75004. ☎ 01-42-72-04-70. Metro: Bastille. Non-stop service. There's a philosophical debate every Sunday at 11am. Dish of the day and a cup of coffee 48F. 19F for half a pint of beer; cocktails 40F. A vast room with Mediterranean colours (bright yellows and blues) and very lively at lunchtime with students, tourists and regulars. And as it's the first philosophical café in Paris, there is a veranda and a terrace in summer so that you can give yourself up to deep thought! In case you need food for the body as well as the mind, there is a selection of salads and snacks to choose from. Discussions are always lively, but it's best to arrive early if you want a seat.

GOING OUT

🍸 **Double Fond** (map C2, **79**): 1 place du Marché-Ste-Catherine 75004. ☎ 01-42-71-40-20. Metro: St-Paul. Open daily 7pm to dawn except Sunday and Monday in winter; in summer the terrace opens at 3pm (last orders 1.30am). Closed 1 January. Drinks from 30F to 60F. Three shows per evening at 8.30pm, 10pm and midnight (at 10pm only on Wednesday; at 9pm and 11pm on Friday) in this den of magic run by a team of 10 professionals. Their shows work in two ways: *klip-poupes* is a house speciality show-casing close-up magic with conjuring tricks for groups seated at the tables, and the show itself is in the cellar, where you sit around a heart-shaped table. At the bar, on the ground floor, you can take advantage of all kinds of practical jokes and tricks. On the terrace, eccentric, smiling performers show off their art. There's something of the spirit of the music hall and the café-theatre about this place. Show 100F; reduced rate for students. At the bar, depending on what time it is, soft drinks cost 29F, cocktails around 55F.

🍸 **Chez Richard** (map C1, **75**): 37 rue Vieille-du-Temple 75004. ☎ 01-42-74-31-65. Metro: Hôtel-de-Ville. Open daily from 5pm to 2am; midnight for food. Closed for a week at the beginning of August. Full meal 110F without drinks. A good example of the successful renovation of a place which had become very run-down. Over three levels (basement, ground floor, first floor), the walls are exposed stone, lit by soft golden lighting which makes the place at the same time both intimate and convivial. The basement is particularly good, dominated by a superb wrought-iron chandelier sculpture and enlivened by brightly coloured mosaics made by friends of the landlord. The very mixed clientele, aged from 25 to 50, come here for, apart from the obvious classics, a *mojito* (50F), which is the landlord's pride and joy. Cocktails and spirits 25F. You can eat a few dishes such as quiche and *bavette*, a cut of red meat where the grain goes lengthways.

GAY PAREE!

Always on the move, a gay night out in Paris tends to change as often as the bars in the Marais, opening, closing, changing the name or landlord. Therefore it's impossible to supply an accurate lasting list of gay bars, though there are many of them. The growing success of Radio FG 98.2 – originally 'Fréquence Gay' – following the progress of all sorts of electronic music (from house to techno by way of trance, ambient or drum 'n' bass), and also the annual Gay Pride march, have given the gay community such publicity that bars have sprung up all over the place in an almost *fin-de-siècle* frenzy.

At the time of writing the following were popular spots for men: the **Cox** (15 rue des Archives); the **Amnésia** (42 rue Vieille-du-Temple); the **Okawa** (40 rue Vieille-du-Temple); the **Coffee Shop** (5 rue du Bourg-Tibourg); the **QG** (12 rue Simon-Lefranc); and **Skeud** (35 rue Ste-Croix-de-la-Bretonnerie).

For girls, there's **Scandaleuses** (8 rue des Écouffes), which is the hippest bar.

5TH ARRONDISSEMENT

THE CONTRESCARPE ● THE MOUFF' ● THE LATIN QUARTER

A lot of water has flowed under the bridges of Paris since the early 12th century, when Abélard led 3,000 pro-Fronde students onto the Montagne Ste-Geneviève to deliver a sermon in Latin. The area gained a reputation for learning towards the mid–13th century through its prestigious university. Today the university is popularly known by the name of just one of its faculties, the Sorbonne, named in its turn after the college for poor students created by the theologian Robert de Sorbon, located not far from the Maubert quarter. Despite the commercialisation of the 'Boul'mich' (the Parisians' name for the boulevard St-Michel), now largely taken over by fast-food outlets and High Street fashion shops, and the general gentrification of the arrondissement, the Sorbonne remains one of the most significant testimonies to the *Grande Époque* and continues to attract lecturers and students from all over the world. As a result much of the area is always guaranteed to be lively. However, for those of you who can't stand too much hustle and bustle or the fast-food school of cooking, the 5th arrondissement also has some more traditional restaurants and a number of quiet walks. The areas around the Panthéon and nearby place de la Contrescarpe are full of ancient buildings and interesting nooks and crannies, and the Jardin des Plantes and Arenes de Lutèce are welcome open spaces in which to relax in the heart of the city.

WHERE TO STAY

☆ BUDGET

Young and Happy Hostel (map B3, **1**): 80 rue Mouffetard 75005. ☎ 01-45-35-09-53. Fax: 01-47-07-22-24. Website: www.youngandhappy.fr. Metro: Monge. Budget for 107F for a bed in a dormitory, 127F for a bed in a double room. You can make reservations in writing, paying up front for the first night, or come along in the morning between 11am and 4pm. Closed from 2am to 8am. Payphone in the entrance, cold drinks machine, TV. If you want to tune straight into what's going on in the district, this is the perfect hotel. However, the street is pretty noisy, so be warned. There are 70 beds in basic rooms with showers and toilet facilities. The atmosphere is relaxed and international and you can eat at the nearby university restaurant.

☆☆ MODERATE

Hôtel Le Central (map B2, **2**): 6 rue Descartes 75005. ☎ 01-46-33-57-93. Metro: Maubert-Mutualité or Cardinal-Lemoine. Single rooms from 150F to 198F and double room with shower from 220F to 246F. A family hotel in a good location, just opposite the École polytechnique. Good value for those on a shoestring, but a bit noisy.

Hôtel Marignan (map B1, **3**): 13 rue du Sommerard 75005. ☎ 01-43-54-63-81 or 01-43-25-31-03. Metro: Maubert-Mutualité. For a double room, budget for 300F to 330F with washbasin and toilet, and from 390F to 460F with shower and toilet. For three, from 400F. For four or five people there are family rooms with a shower on each floor at 490F and with a private bathroom and toilet at 650F. Breakfast is included. Backpackers from all over the world have been meeting here for over 30 years. There's a dining room where you eat your own food, a microwave and fridge. There's also a washing machine, clothes dryer and ironing board. Friendly welcome and lots of info about Paris.

Hôtel de l'Espérance (map B3, **4**): 15 rue Pascal 75005. ☎ 01-47-07-10-99. Fax: 01-43-37-56-19. Metro: Censier-Daubenton or Gobelins. Bus Nos. 21, 27, 83 or 91. Double room with shower and toilet 450F, with bath and toilet 500F. In a little one-way street (so it's pretty quiet) this two-star hotel is wedged between the boulevard de Port-Royal and the square St-Médard (at the bottom of the very lively rue Mouffetard). There are 38 elegant rooms with marble bathrooms, assorted fabrics, four-poster beds (for the most part), hairdryer, cable TV and direct telephone. On the ground floor is a charming garden for breakfast in the spring, lounge and TV.

Where to stay

1 Young and Happy Hostel
2 Hôtel Le Central
3 Hôtel Marignan
4 Hôtel de l'Espérance
7 Hôtel St-Jacques
8 Hôtel du Esmeralda
9 Familia Hotel
10 Hôtel de la Sorbonne
11 Hôtel des Grandes Écoles
12 Hôtel du Levant

Where to eat

20 Foyer du Vietnam
21 Mexi and Co
22 Au Bistro de la Sorbonne
23 Le Reflet
24 Le Volcan
25 L'Époque
26 Pema Thang
27 Au Bon Coin
28 El Picaflor
29 Au Jardin des Pâtes
30 Han Lim
31 Restaurant Perraudin
32 Le Mauzac
33 ChantAirelle
34 Joël D, le Bistro de l'Huître
35 Le Port du Salut
36 Savannah Café
37 Tashi Delek
38 Machu-Picchu
39 Au Coin des Gourmets
40 Le Buisson Ardent
41 Le Languedoc
42 Chez Laurette
43 Le Petit Prince
44 L'Atlas
45 Mavrommatis-Le Restaurant
46 Coco de Mer
47 Les Bouchons de François Clerc
48 Le Vigneron
49 Le Balzar
50 La Rôtisserie du Beaujolais
51 Le Fogon St-Julien
53 Chez Flavien and Songmala
54 Anahuacalli
55 Le Petit Navire
56 La Papillote

Where to go for an ice-cream

80 Gelati d'Alberto

Where to go for a drink/ Going out

60 Finnegan's Wake
62 Taverne Daubenton
63 Café Égyptien
64 Le Verre à Pied
65 Le Bistro de la Huchette
66 Connolly's Corner
67 Le Requin Chagrin
68 Le Rallye
69 L'Envol Québécois
70 Café de la Nouvelle Mairie
71 Le Café Maure de la mosquée de Paris
73 Le Piano Vache
74 Le Café Oz
75 Polly Maggoo
77 Le Petit Journal
78 Caveau de la Huchette
79 The Rocky Horror Picture Show

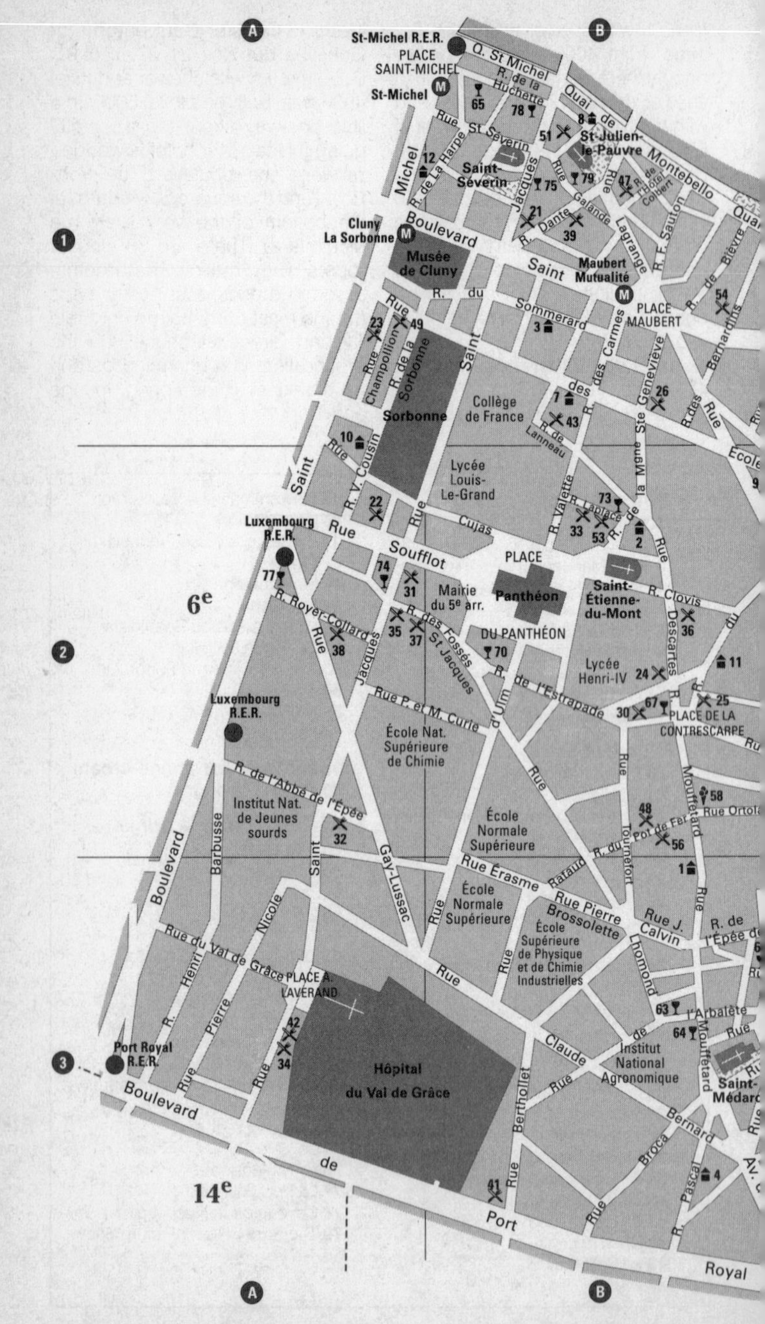
St-Michel R.E.R.
PLACE SAINT-MICHEL
St-Michel
Q. St Michel
R. de la Huchette
Quai de Montebello
St-Julien-le-Pauvre
Saint-Séverin
Rue St Séverin
Cluny La Sorbonne
Musée de Cluny
Boulevard Saint Michel
Maubert Mutualité
PLACE MAUBERT
R. du Sommerard
Sorbonne
Collège de France
Lycée Louis-Le-Grand
Luxembourg R.E.R.
Rue Soufflot
PLACE DU PANTHÉON
Panthéon
Mairie du 5e arr.
Saint-Étienne-du-Mont
Lycée Henri-IV
PLACE DE LA CONTRESCARPE
6e
École Nat. Supérieure de Chimie
Institut Nat. de Jeunes sourds
École Normale Supérieure
École Supérieure de Physique et de Chimie Industrielles
PLACE A. LAVERAND
Hôpital du Val de Grâce
Institut National Agronomique
Saint-Médard
Port Royal R.E.R.
Boulevard de Port Royal
14e
Rue Mouffetard
Rue Gay-Lussac
Rue Claude Bernard
Rue Pierre Brossolette
Rue Érasme
Rue d'Ulm
R. de l'Estrapade
Rue P. et M. Curie
R. Royer-Collard
R. de l'Abbé de l'Épée
Rue du Val de Grâce
Boulevard Barbusse

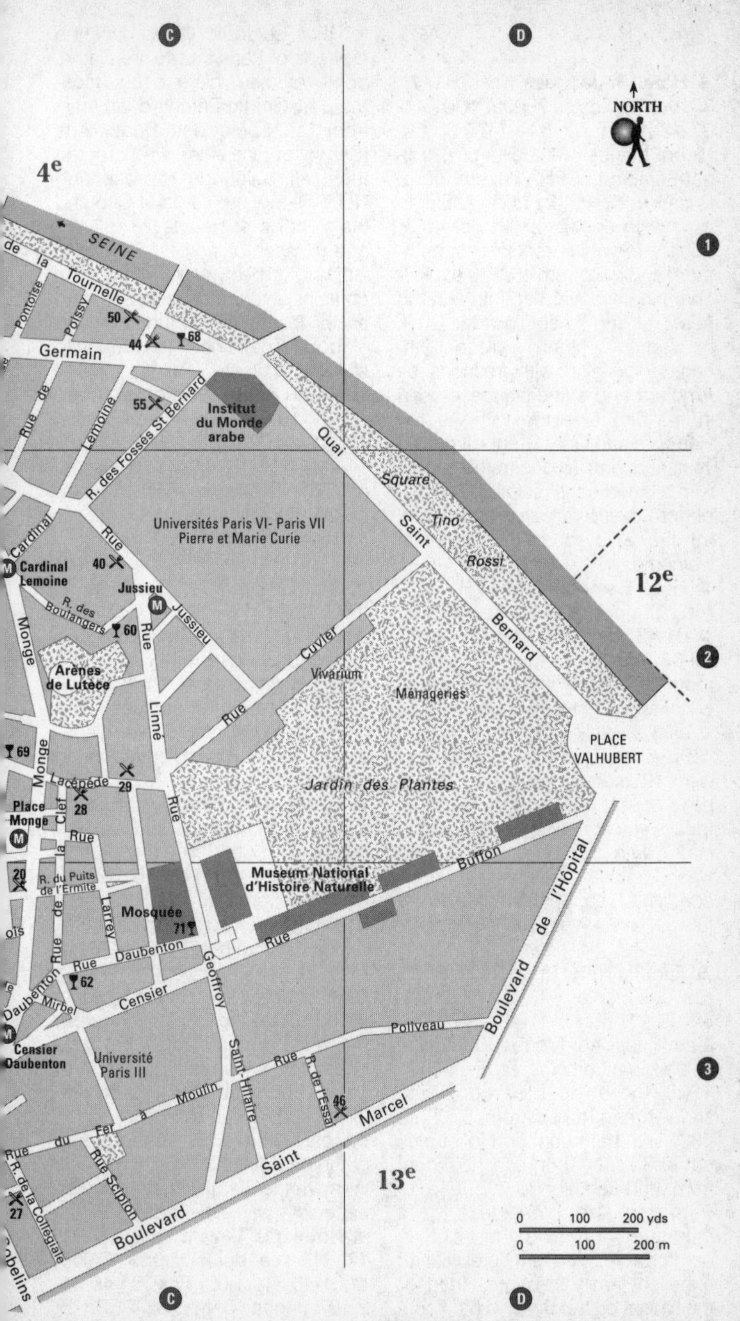

C
D
NORTH
4e
12e
13e
SEINE
1
2
3
de la Tournelle
Pontoise
Poissy
Germain
Rue de
Lemoine
R. des Fossés St Bernard
Institut du Monde arabe
Quai
Square
Saint
Tino
Rossi
Bernard
Universités Paris VI- Paris VII Pierre et Marie Curie
Cardinal
Cardinal Lemoine
Rue
Jussieu
R. des Boulangers
Rue
Jussieu
Monge
Arènes de Lutèce
Cuvier
Vivarium
Ménageries
Rue
Linné
PLACE VALHUBERT
Monge
Lacépède
Place Monge
Clef
Rue
de la
Rue
Jardin des Plantes
R. du Puits de l'Ermite
Larrey
Mosquée
Museum National d'Histoire Naturelle
Buffon
Rue
Boulevard de l'Hôpital
Rue Daubenton
Rue
Daubenton
Mirbel
Censier
Geoffroy
Censier Daubenton
Université Paris III
Poliveau
Saint-Hilaire
Rue
R. de l'Essai
Moulin
à
Fer
du
Rue
Rue Scipion
R. de la Collégiale
Marcel
Saint
Boulevard
Gobelins
50
44
68
55
40
60
69
29
28
20
71
62
46
27
0 100 200 yds
0 100 200 m

☆☆☆ CHIC

Hôtel St-Jacques (map B1, **7**): 35 rue des Écoles 75005. ☎ 01-44-07-45-45. Fax: 01-43-25-65-50. Metro: Maubert-Mutualité or Cardinal-Lemoine; RER: Luxembourg. Bus Nos. 63, 38, 21 and 27. Single room with shower and toilet 400F, double room with shower or bathroom and toilet from 450F to 610F. A charming two-star hotel right in the heart of the Latin Quarter. It is housed in a highly stylized 19th-century building with frescoes by Amblard and a fine staircase used in the film *Charade* with Audrey Hepburn and Gary Grant – it has 35 vast and prettily decorated rooms with all mod cons: satellite TV, telephone, hairdryer and toilet. Ask for the attic rooms. Exceptional welcome.

Hôtel Esmeralda (map B1, **8**): 4 rue St-Julien-le-Pauvre 75005. ☎ 01-43-54-19-20. Fax: 01-40-51-00-68. Metro: St-Michel. Double room (bathroom and toilet), some with views over Notre-Dame and the square Viviani, between 420F and 490F. A neat little 17th-century hotel with 19 rooms, decorated like a doll's house, with a listed staircase. Ideal if you are not too critical of furniture with the lived-in look and wash basins and baths in a similar condition. The location ensures it's full up every year, so booking is essential.

Familia Hotel (map B-C2, **9**): 11 rue des Écoles 75005. ☎ 01-43-54-55-27. Fax: 01-43-29-61-77. Metro: Jussieu, Maubert-Mutualité or Cardinal-Lemoine. From 390F to 450F for a double room with shower and toilet, from 500F to 580F with bathroom and toilet plus cable TV. Ten per cent discount from mid-January to the end of February and in August for a minimum of two nights. A comfortable, pleasant hotel with an excellent family welcome. Head for the rooms on the 5th and 6th floors for their splendid views over the rooftops of Paris and Notre-Dame. Some of them have been decorated by Gerald Pritchard, an artist from the Ecole des Beaux-Arts (School of Fine Arts), who created the wall paintings representing Notre-Dame, the Île de la Cité and the Pont-Neuf. Rooms 23, 52, 53 and 61 have balconies. The stone stairway is lovely and the entrance contains an ancient bookcase, and as for the Louis XV furniture and elaborate paintings, they're quite something else!

Hôtel de la Sorbonne (map A1–2, **10**): 6 rue Victor-Cousin 75005. ☎ 01-43-54-58-08. Fax: 01-40-51-05-18. Metro: St-Michel or Cluny-Sorbonne; RER: Luxembourg. Double room with shower and toilet from 420F, with bathroom 460F. In the heart of the student quarter, where it all happens. A clean hotel in a nice building. The prices are pretty reasonable and the place is quiet, well run, with a pleasant welcome. Each room has TV, telephone, hairdryer. The highest prices are for very spacious rooms with a bathroom in marble.

Hôtel des Grandes Écoles (map B2, **11**): 75 rue du Cardinal-Lemoine 75005. ☎ 01-43-26-79-23. Fax: 01-43-25-28-15. Metro: Cardinal-Lemoine or Monge. Rooms situated on each side of a cul-de-sac, with shower or bathroom and toilet between 530F and 690F. Located in a private lane just off the place de la Contrescarpe, this hotel is charming, with great character, a verdant garden and paved courtyard. The countryside in Paris! You can take your tea in the garden, even if you're not one of the hotel's customers. Book well in advance as it's very popular, especially with Americans.

Hôtel du Levant (map A–B1, **12**): 18 rue de la Harpe 75005. ☎ 01-46-34-11-00. Fax: 01-46-34-25-87. Metro: St-Michel; RER: St-

Michel and Cluny-Sorbonne. E-mail: hlevant@club-internet.fr. Single room with shower and toilet 385F, double room from 560F. Breakfast included. A charming hotel, not really for the most budget-conscious backpackers, but definitely worth seeking out in the rue de la Harpe. The rooms have been renovated in modern colours, and there is satellite TV with Canal + for insomniacs. An excellent buffet for breakfast.

WHERE TO EAT

☆ BUDGET

✕ **Foyer du Vietnam** (map C3, **20**): 80 rue Monge 75005. ☎ 01-45-35-32-54. Metro: Monge. Last orders at 10pm. Closed Sunday, Bank Holidays and from the end of July to the end of August. Set menus 57F and 68F served lunchtime and evening. À la carte around 70F. There is a TV to entertain the regulars and the waiters that may be a little off-putting, and this place really doesn't look anything special from the outside, but it does provide an opportunity to eat good traditional Vietnamese cooking. There's an excellent and filling pork and noodle soup, and the steamed ravioli is delicious. Or why not try fish simmered in spicy sauce, pork kebabs, Hanoi soup, rice soup with tripe, duck soup or grilled prawns with vermicelli.

✕ **Mexi and Co** (map B1, **21**): 10 rue Dante 75005. ☎ 01-46-34-14-12. Metro: Maubert-Mutualité. Open from 10.30am to midnight all the year round except 25 and 31 December. Set menus from 50F to 90F, children's menu 40F. Budget for around 80F à la carte. Mexican cuisine has been very popular in Paris for several years, but here it takes an original turn. This spot is like a sort of sunny grocer-cum-café, where you are welcomed by tropical music with lots of '*ay ay ay*' and traditional good food: chicken or beef *tacos*, *guacamole*, *burritos* and beef or chicken *tamales* and *empanadas*. Wash it all down with Mexican or Peruvian beer from the bottle, just like a real *hombre*. Tables on the pavement so you can sit out in the sun.

✕ **Au Bistro de la Sorbonne** (map A2, **22**): 4 rue Toullier 75005. ☎ 01-43-54-41-49. Metro: Cluny-La Sorbonne; RER: Luxembourg. Open lunchtime and evening until 11pm. Closed Sunday. Set menus 95F and 140F, à la carte in the evening – budget for 150 to 180F. The students at the nearby Sorbonne University know this place very well, as it offers good value for money. Pleasant decor in the two connecting dining rooms – the walls of one of them depicting the Sorbonne back in the 14th century.

✕ **Le Reflet** (map A1, **23**): 6 rue Champollion 75005. ☎ 01-43-29-97-27. Metro: Cluny-La Sorbonne. Open from 9am to 2am. Budget for around 80F for a full meal. This is a good spot for combining a visit to one of the many cinemas near by. The decor is cinema inspired and the food is varied, ranging from sandwiches at 15F, starters such as potatoes stuffed with cheese, savoury tart, salad, to main courses (including a glass of wine): lasagne, chilli con carne and the like. In conjunction with the cinema opposite, the Reflet Médicis, they organize theme nights: see three films in one night, with intervals and breakfast (free) at *Le Reflet*.

✕ **Chez Flavien and Songmala** (map B2, **53**): 9 rue Laplace 75005. ☎ 01-43-29-47-86. Metro: Maubert-Mutualité or Cardinal-Lemoine. Open Monday to Friday, closed weekends from 25 December to 2 January and for the whole of

August. Set menu 78F at lunchtime, à la carte budget for a maximum of 100F. A small road located towards the top of rue de la Montagne Ste-Geneviève, (the *Montagne* part of this road's name is distinctly misleading, though it does run up a small hill), the eponymous owners have turned what used to be their home into a French/Cambodian restaurant. At lunchtime there is *quenelles de brochet*, fresh green bean salad with hot sausage, veal escalopes with ravioli, and *clafoutis* and *crème brûlée à l'ancienne*. In the evenings the restaurant is transformed with Buddhas and batiks and offers traditional home Cambodian cooking.

☆☆ MODERATE

✕ **Restaurant Perraudin** (map A2, **31**): 157 rue St-Jacques 75005. ☎ 01-46-33-15-75. RER: Luxembourg. Last orders 10.15pm. Closed Saturday and Monday lunchtime, all day Sunday, and for the second fortnight in August. No reservations. At lunchtime, there's a set menu at 63F with starter, main course and dessert. There's a gourmet menu at 150F. À la carte, budget for around 110F. Near the Panthéon and the Jardin du Luxembourg, this is an unpretentious, modest bistro with traditional old-style French cooking. Publishers and students from the Sorbonne meet to chat over *tarte à l'oignon*, *œufs cocotte aux lardons*, *gigot au gratin dauphinois*, *confit de canard* and *bœuf bourguignon*. There's a little indoor garden. If this place is full, try the Port du Salut (see below).

✕ **Le Volcan** (map B2, **24**): 10 rue Thouin 75005. ☎ 01-46-33-38-33. Metro: Monge or Cardinal-Lemoine. Last orders 11.30pm. Closed Monday. Menus served lunchtime and evening at 59F, 95F and 145F. An old-established place which has lost none of its natural character. Good Greek and French dishes, including an excellent moussaka. Main courses for around 80F. Three set menus each with a starter, main course and dessert (drinks are included with lunch).

✕ **Chez Laurette** (map A3, **42**): 283 rue St-Jacques 75005. ☎ 01-43-29-63-48. Metro: Port-Royal. Open daily lunchtime and evening at least until midnight. Closed Sunday and in August. Set meal 39F for main course and drink. Budget for an average of 80F à la carte. *Cordon bleu* cooking from Algeria includes *chorba* (soup) and couscous with delicate, hand-rolled semolina. Couscous royal (kebabs, *merguez* sausages, chicken) or with two types of meat at 65F. Delicious *tajines* too, but you need to order them. The Franco-Algerian dishes of the day are also excellent.

✕ **L'Époque** (map B2, **25**): 81 rue du Cardinal-Lemoine 75005. ☎ 01-46-34-15-84. Metro: Cardinal-Lemoine. Service from noon to 3pm and from 7pm to 11pm. Closed Sunday and for a fortnight in August. Set menu 68F at lunchtime, in the evening the set menu begins at 78F. Surrounded by Greek restaurants whose reasonably-priced cuisine has drawn quite a few people away, here is a bistro worthy of its name. Set menus served until 10pm offer *blanquette de veau*, *gigot d'agneau rôti au four* or *soupière de poisson à l'étouffée*. There are also set menus at 118F and 165F. The atmosphere is friendly and unpretentious with attentive service and a few good wines at reasonable prices.

✕ **Pema Thang** (map B1, **26**): 13 rue de la Montagne-Ste-Geneviève 75005. ☎ 01-43-54-34-34. Metro: Maubert-Mutualité. Service from noon to 2.30pm and from 7pm to 11pm. Closed Sunday and Monday lunchtime. Set menu 67F at lunchtime, in the evening 79F and 110F (one for meat-eaters, the other for vegetarians). One of the set menus at 105F allows you to try the various Tibetan specialities. Testament to the fact that the Latin Quarter is at the crossroads of Paris' different cultures, this restaurant is straight from the high plateaux of Tibet. Tibetan cuisine turns out to be subtle and every bit as good as its Asian cousins. Steamed dishes are the speciality and, while original, are a sort of cross between Chinese, Japanese and Indian food. At lunchtime, people from the Sorbonne come to discover new horizons with *sha momok* (steamed beef ravioli), *then thouk* (noodle soup) and *pemathang* (sweet and sour meatballs with sautéed vegetables).

✕ **Au Bon Coin** (map C3, **27**): 21 rue de la Collégiale 75005. ☎ 01-43-31-55-57. Metro: Gobelins or Censier-Daubenton. Open noon to 2.30pm and 7pm to 11pm. Closed Sunday and for the first three weeks in August. Set menus 65F at lunchtime, 75F and 100F in the evening. With the evocative name of a roadside café or a provincial restaurant on the edge of a quiet river, this *Bon Coin* (literally a 'good corner') isn't actually full of fishermen moaning about the one that got away, but rather a more business-like clientele, attracted by the carefully chosen and reasonably priced menus. Try *terrine de lièvre, confit de canard, raie aux câpres, cuisses de grenouilles provençale.* Don't expect miracles, but simply good pub style cooking that has its good and bad days. Friendly service and slightly rustic decor. A pleasant place for a night out with friends without breaking the bank.

✕ **El Picaflor** (map C2, **28**): 9 rue Lacépède 75005. Metro: Monge. ☎ 01-43-31-06-01. Open lunchtime and evening until 11pm. Closed Sunday evening and Monday. At lunchtime there's a set menu at 59F including starter, main course and drink. In the evening and Sunday lunchtime there is a set menu at 79F. À la carte, budget for 150–200F. The best Peruvian restaurant in Paris and probably the whole of France (mind you, there aren't that many!). A warm welcome and setting. À la carte, try *aji de gallina, ceviche* (marinated fish with green lemon), *chupe de camarones* (soup with shrimps, prawns, fish, vegetables and a poached egg), *chicharron de mariscos* (fried seafood, octopus, squid, small scallops and so on). There are plenty of specialities from Peru and other South American countries available on request, such as *adobo a l'arequiperia* (ragoût of pork with onions and lemon), *picante de conejo* (rabbit marinated in spices and peanut sauce) and the mysterious *quinua atamalada*, a pre-Hispanic dish of Inca corn in a cheese sauce, ratatouille and potatoes. Wash it down with a light Peruvian red and the whole evening should remind you of your trip to Machu Picchu. Music on Friday and Saturday evening. Booking is advised.

Incidentally, there is a boutique full of excellent South American products at 5 rue Tiquetonne 75002. ☎ 01-42-33-10-08.

✕ **Au Jardin des Pâtes** (map C2, **29**): 4 rue Lacépède 75005. Metro: Monge or Jussieu. ☎ 01-43-31-50-71. Open daily from noon to 2.30pm and 7pm to 11pm. No à la carte, budget for around 100F per person. A few yards from the Jardin des Plantes (could there be a smidgeon of a pun in the air here?) this house is given over, body and soul, to *pâtes* (pasta – this time home-made from organic flour). It also serves organic beer and wine. Try buckwheat pasta with chicken livers, sesame butter and prunes, rice pasta with sautéed vegetables, ginger and tofu. It is advisable to book.

✕ **Han Lim** (map B2, **30**): 6 rue Blainville 75005. ☎ 01-43-54-62-74. Metro: Monge. Closed Monday and during August. No credit cards. Set menu 73F at lunchtime. À la carte budget for around 120F. This is one of the oldest Korean restaurants in Paris. There's an interesting menu at lunchtime, with *potage au pot-au-feu*, sautéed seafood (whelks and cuttlefish), rice and an assortment of Korean vegetables, dessert and a carafe of red wine or a half bottle of Évian water, and a Korean barbecue at 82F. A good opportunity to dive into an unknown cuisine. After the restaurant, why not go for a pint of beer a few streets away, at Connolly's Corner, one of the best Irish pubs in Paris? (*see* 'Where to go for a drink?')

✕ **Le Mauzac** (map A2, **32**): 7 rue de l'Abbé-de-l'Épée 75005. ☎ 01-46-33-75-22. RER: Luxembourg. Open daily from 6.30am to 10pm, Thursday and Friday to 11pm. Closed Saturday evening, Sunday and during August. Budget for 100F at lunchtime and 160F in the evening. This is an authentic bistro with rare 1950s furniture (tables and bar). It has delighted its faithful band of regulars, who attend assiduously (especially in the evening), for some time. The wines are rich and fruity (35 wines from 12F to 19F per glass), and the dishes on Thursdays and Fridays interesting, dependent on what the patron has selected from the market at Rungis that morning. On other evenings Le Mauzac usually simply offers plates of *charcuterie* and cheeses up until 10pm. Prompt and friendly service.

✕ **ChantAirelle** (map B2, **33**): 17 rue Laplace 75005. ☎ 01-46-33-18-59. Metro: Cardinal-Lemoine or Maubert-Mutualité. Open until 10.30pm. Closed Saturday lunchtime and Sunday. Set menu 80F at lunchtime, in the evening there are two set menus at 105F and 150F. À la carte, budget for around 140F to 180F. Everything here comes direct from the Auvergne (apart from the meat and ice-creams and sorbets). The owner is a fanatical advocate of his homeland's products, which you can also buy to take away (honey, jam, meats and cheeses). Rustic specialities will warm your heart: cabbage stuffed in the old 'Yssingeaux' style (the filling is based on beef, mushrooms, sausage meat and cabbage), and *potée* from the Haute-Loire (knuckle of ham, sausage, streaky salt pork, cabbages, turnips, white beans, carrots and marrow), which is generous and fortifying. For vegetarians we recommend the *gratin forézien* (cheese, lentils and potatoes). You can share a plate of *charcuterie* as a starter, as you can the excellent cheeses – Ambert blue cheese, *salers*, St-Nectaire farmhouse, Auvergne blue. There is a lovely restful garden terrace where it's a good idea to book a table in advance. Good wine list and four types of mineral water. There's a 5 per cent reduction on the menu prices if you book over the internet: website: www.asterion.fr/chantairelle.

✕ **Le Port du Salut** (map A2, **35**): 163 *bis* rue St-Jacques 75005. ☎ 01-46-33-63-21. RER: Luxembourg. Service from noon to 2.30pm and 7pm to 10.30pm. Closed Sunday evening and Monday, as well as for a fortnight in August. Set menus 67F and 94F served lunchtime and evening. Budget for 120F à la carte. This is a great alternative if the Perraudin is too full (see above). A charming setting with huge beams, a tiny staircase, a piano and paintings showing country scenes. All the great French singers have played here (Jacques Brel to name but one). There's a large cellar for groups (set menus at 120F or 150F). A lovely venue with an intimate feel.

✕ **Tashi Delek** (map A2, **37**): 4 rue des Fossés-St-Jacques 75005. ☎ 01-43-26-55-55. RER: Luxembourg. Open until 10.30pm. Closed Sunday and during August. Set menu 56F at lunchtime and evening. Other set menus from 58F to 65F at lunchtime and 105F in the evening. The first Tibetan restaurant in Paris, run by real Tibetans who have been here ever since the Chinese invaded their own country. The decor is unsurprisingly Tibetan and the cuisine is made up of regional dishes from U-Tsang, Kham and Amdo. Try a few dishes so that you can familiarize yourself: *momok* (beef ravioli), *chabale* (stuffed omelettes), *baktsa markou* (pasta balls with melted butter and goat's cheese). For the brave there's the salted butter tea.

✕ **La Papillote** (map B2, **56**): 13 rue du Pot-de-Fer 75005. ☎ 01-43-36-66-46. Metro: Place-Monge. Open daily except Sunday evening and Monday from November to the end of March. Closed for two weeks in February. Set menus 65F at lunchtime, 70F, 98F and 145F in the evening. À la carte, budget for 160F to 180F for a full meal, without drinks. La Papillote is proof of the culinary renewal of the Mouf' (as the locals call the area) in the last two years. In surroundings slightly reminiscent of a cave-dweller's house (at least in the room at the back), it has a generous and varied menu consisting of a market-inspired cuisine: duck breast with honey, *marbré de poireaux* and *foie gras*, trout in a foil parcel and *fondante tulipe de mousse glacée au chocolat*. Discreet but attentive service and a few tables on the terrace when it's fine.

✕ **Machu-Picchu** (map A2, **38**): 9 rue Royer-Collard 75005. ☎ 01-43-26-13-13. RER: Luxembourg. Closed Saturday lunchtime, Sunday and during August. Set menu 48F at lunchtime, à la carte only in the evening, budget for around 150F. Mannequins in ponchos welcome you on the mezzanine and the South American theme is continued with multicoloured tablecloths, a warm, Latin welcome, appropriate background music and Latin American singers (on Friday and Saturday evening). As a starter, try the *ceviche de pescado*. Then, there's a tough choice between the generous dishes of *lomo soltado* (fillet of minced beef with onions) and *arroz con pato* (duck with rice). The dishes are copious and the beer hails from Peru and the wine from Chile and Argentina. Friendly service.

✕ **Au Coin des Gourmets** (map B1, **39**): 5 rue Dante 75005. ☎ 01-43-26-12-92. Metro: Maubert-Mutualité or St-Michel. Open daily except at lunchtime on New Year's Day. Set menus 69F at lunchtime, from 105F to 145F in the evening. À la carte around 150F. 'Indo-Chinese specialities' is written on the menu and this really is a melting-pot of delicious specialities from the peninsula. The dining room is always full and the welcome is jovial and friendly. It's impossible to list the whole menu, but the grated green papaya, the *tea khtoeun* (stuffed braised duck with mushrooms), the Cambodian crêpe *(bank xeo)*, the minced pork rice flakes *(natin)* and the Cambodian *amok* give diners a good idea of Indochina.

✕ **Anahuacalli** (map B1, **54**): 30 rue des Bernardins 75005. ☎ 01-43-26-10-20. Metro: Maubert-Mutualité. Closed lunchtime Monday. At lunchtime there's a set meal at 75F. Budget for 150F à la carte without drinks. A truly Mexican restaurant – not one of those fake Tex-Mex places. Obviously there are *tacos* and *burritos*, but there's also the *mole poblano* (turkey with chocolate) and specialities from Veracruz and Merida which you don't often find on the menu at Tex-Mex restaurants. There's also a good choice of tequilas and *cervezas* (beers).

Le Languedoc (map B3, **41):** 64 boulevard de Port-Royal 75005. ☎ 01-47-07-24-47. Metro: Gobelins; RER: Port-Royal. Last orders at 10pm. Closed Tuesday and Wednesday, and also in August and for a fortnight at Christmas. Set menu 105F served lunchtime and evening. À la carte, budget for between 110F and 150F. A satisfying south-western cuisine in a setting reminiscent of an old provençal house. The *confit de canard-pommes sarladaises* and the *cassoulet au confit d'oie* are the stars of the menu, but the meat dishes can hold their own too. Wash it all down with a good Rouergue wine or the white Gaillac. A comprehensive menu with starter, main course, cheese or dessert and half a bottle of wine; excellent value for money.

5TH

☆☆☆ CHIC

Joël D, le Bistro de l'Huître (map A3, **34**): 285 rue St-Jacques 75005. ☎ 01-43-54-71-70. RER: Port-Royal. Open until midnight. Closed Sunday, Saturday lunchtime and in August. Budget for around 180–200F per person. This tiny bistro, just a few yards from the Val-de-Grâce, is often packed out. There are two good reasons for this: the warm loquacity of Daniel, the owner, and the oysters (the restaurant's only dish) which are fresh and delicious. They come either from Quiberon, Marennes-Oléron or Normandy. The clientele is very 'Left Bank' (mainly TV and media people, artists and the like) , watching their collective figure, so oysters are the perfect choice.

Savannah Café (map B2, **36**): 27 rue Descartes 75005. ☎ 01-43-29-45-77. Metro: Cardinal-Lemoine. Open until 11pm. Closed Sunday, Monday lunchtime and between Christmas and New Year's Day. Set menu at 85F served until 8pm, then at 137F. À la carte, budget for at least 150F without drinks. If you absolutely have to dine in the Contrescarpe-Mouffetard district (which can be a bit 'touristy'), we recommend this place. Cosmopolitan cuisine covers *tabouleh*, *houmous*, *kebbé*, *ceviche*, *carpaccio*, lamb curry with fresh coriander, *chilli con carne*, fruit and vegetable curry (with cardamom, coconut and chutney), and dishes of the day such as chicken liver fried *à la libanaise* (with garlic and lemon), and roasted stuffed aubergines.

L'Atlas (map C1, **44):** 10–12 boulevard St-Germain 75005. ☎ 01-46-33-86-98. Metro: Maubert-Mutualité. Open daily, lunchtime and evening except Monday. Set menu 98F at lunchtime; in the evening, à la carte only, budget for at least 200F. After a visit to the Institut du Monde arabe (Institute of the Arab World), try this restaurant, whose sign conjures up *wadis* and palm groves. Morroccan cuisine, but without the traditional sugar and fat, results in dishes like a light couscous served with excellent meats and vegetables, and wonderful *tajines* (a choice of 16). Apart from these classics, you can treat yourself to prawns grilled with paprika, lamb *à la mauve*, seafood or partridge with chestnuts (in season). Warm welcome and attentive service, which, after all, is never a given.

Mavrommatis-Le Restaurant (map B–C3, **45**): 42 rue Daubenton 75005. ☎ 01-43-31-17-17. Metro: Censier-Daubenton. Open until 11pm. Closed Monday. Set menu 150F at lunchtime, à la carte budget for 200F without drinks. Greek gastronomy in the setting of an Athenian house dating from the early 20th century. Delicious Greek and Cypriot specialities, that you can eat on the terrace when the weather's fine. Try the moussaka, obviously, *coulis* of shellfish with feta cheese, quails roasted in honey and thyme, or the excellent corn balls crushed and stuffed with meat. If there are at least four of you, try the *mezze* (160F per person: 16 hot and cold dishes).

✕ **Coco de Mer** (map C3, **46**): 34 boulevard St-Marcel 75005. ☎ 01-47-07-06-64. Metro: St-Marcel. Open lunchtime and evening until midnight. Closed all day Sunday and Monday lunchtime. Set menus at 135F and 170F. Budget for around 200F à la carte. An essential stop-off for locals, so it's a good idea to book. Specialities from the Seychelles (unique in Paris): excellent grouper grilled *au rougail* (with tomato and garlic sauce), *cari zourite-coco* (based on octopus), delicious bream. Several dishes of marinated raw fish for starters, exquisite cream *gratiné* with banana as a dessert. There's a video showing the magic of the Seychelles – lounge on real white sand and sip rum or a cool fruit juice.

✕ **Les Bouchons de François Clerc** (map B1, **47**): 12 rue de l'Hôtel-Colbert 75005. ☎ 01-43-54-15-34. Metro: Maubert-Mutualité. Service until 10pm. Closed Saturday lunchtime and Sunday. Set menu 227F lunchtime and evening; less elaborate set meal 137F weekday lunchtime. À la carte, budget for around 300F. The setting of this fine 16th-century house is perfect for an evening around a good bottle of well-priced wine. There are Graves, St-Estèphe, Margaux, Pauillac and other St-Juliens on the wine list. The menu is almost incidental! For starters there's cannelloni of warm lamb or *marinière* of small scallop with tamarind; as main meals try the pigeon casserole with mushrooms and wine, or *aïoli* of cod flavoured with saffron and coconut. For dessert there is pineapple roasted in *piña colada* sauce or banana ice-cream with cinnamon. The wine is the thing here, so obviously the degree of painfulness of the bill will be affected by the bottle, or two, that you choose.

✕ **Le Fogon St-Julien** (map B1, **51**): 10 rue St-Julien-le-Pauvre 75005. Metro: St-Michel or Maubert-Mutualité. ☎ 01-43-54-31-33. Open until half past midnight. Closed Sunday as well as from the end of August to the beginning of September. Set menus 120F at lunchtime and 180F in the evening. À la carte, budget for 150F. At last, a traditional Spanish restaurant that doesn't play on the stereotypes, but gives you a good impression of Spain as it is today, close to the square and the pretty church of St-Julien-le-Pauvre. Well-chosen products such as marvellous *charcuterie* and quality *tapas*. There's a choice of *paella* (all at 110F): *valenciana* (saffron, snails, rabbit, vegetables), mixed (saffron, poultry, seafood), *arroz negra* (squid in its ink cooked in the oven); or else try some excellent *tapas* from 45F to 120F: small stuffed peppers, a plate of *charcuterie*, cold tuna with *confit* of onions or *tortilla*. Pineapple with liqueur is one of the very welcome desserts. Add to that a short but interesting wine list and good service and you have several good reasons to visit this restaurant nestling in the shade of the square.

✕ **Le Vigneron** (map B2, **48**): 18–20 rue du Pot-de-Fer 75005. ☎ 01-47-07-29-99. Metro: Place-Monge. Open daily. Set menus at 118F and 148F, à la carte budget for 230F. The La Mouff' quarter can be rather disappointing, so this is a real find. The menu offers good things in general, such as *terrine de campagne* with compôte of caramelized onions, ox cheek *à l'ancienne*, house *cassoulet*, *tarte fine aux pommes maison* served warm. Everything is tasty and well presented. The wine list is slightly disappointing. On the stone walls there are photos of the great chefs of France.

✕ **Le Balzar** (map A1, **49**): 49 rue des Écoles 75005. ☎ 01-43-54-13-67. Metro: Odéon or Cluny-La Sorbonne. Open daily until midnight. No set menu, budget for around 180F per person, excluding drinks. Taken over by the Café Flo group, this famous brasserie is still a pleasant place to dine after the cinema or theatre. The décor and ambiance are reminiscent of the Lipp, but the bill is likely to be on the slightly cheaper side. At lunchtime all the publishers from the nearby publishing houses and professors from the Sorbonne come here. There's traditional plush brasserie decor with imitation leather wall seats, large mirrors and waiters in white aprons. There's a very pleasant indoor area with large windows where you can sit in the warm in winter and watch the world go by. Specialities include skate with melted butter and *sauerkraut*. Nourishing, classic French cuisine, but what counts is to be there.

✕ **La Rôtisserie du Beaujolais** (map C1, **50**): 19 quai de la Tournelle 75005. ☎ 01-43-54-17-47. Metro: Cardinal-Lemoine or Pont-Marie. Closed Monday. À la carte only, budget for around 250F. An annexe of the famous and highly expensive Tour d'Argent restaurant. From the covered terrace here there's a view over the elegant facades of the Île St-Louis, lit up by the lights of the passing bâteaux-mouches that ply the Seine until about 10.30pm. The spit-roast specialities (chicken, duckling, pigeon) and the prepared dishes (*andouillette*, *steak tartare*, *coq au vin*, *tête de veau sauce gribiche*) are good value. The wine list has a plethora of beaujolais wines, but is otherwise a little lacking in character. Good ambiance and rapid service with a smile.

✕ **Le Petit Prince** (map B1, **43**): 12 rue de Lanneau 75005. ☎ 01-43-54-77-26. Metro: Maubert-Mutualité. Open in the evening only until midnight (half past midnight Saturday and Sunday). Set menus 82F and 118F lunchtime and evening. À la carte, budget for 150F. Close to the Panthéon, the Petit Prince has a relaxed feel to it. The posters for the *Orient-Express*, the old and rather dented spice boxes and the subdued fabrics all give a family feel to this local bistro with a cosy setting and efficient service. Generous, but light dishes which move between fashionable dishes and traditional food. Booking is advisable.

✕ **Le Buisson Ardent** (map C2, **40**): 25 rue Jussieu 75005. ☎ 01-43-54-93-02. Metro: Jussieu. Open lunchtime and evening until 10pm. Closed Saturday lunchtime and Sunday, and also in August. Set menus 90F at lunchtime, 160F lunchtime and evening. Good quality home cooking in a pleasant setting. An excellent set menu comprising a starter, a delicious *confit de canard* with garlic potatoes, cheese (or salad) and dessert (charlotte, chocolate gâteau). There's a large choice à la carte, with *ris de veau à la crème* and *magret de canard au poivre* notable highlights.

✕ **Le Petit Navire** (map C1, **55**): 14 rue des Fossés-St-Bernard 75005. ☎ 01-43-54-22-52. Metro: Jussieu. Closed Sunday and Monday, and for three weeks in August. Set menu 150F at lunchtime and evening, à la carte budget for 250F. Jean-Claude Cousty and his wife have had their hands on the tiller of their Petit Navire ('little ship') for over 30 years. As soon as you come in, the lovely smells and the rather traditional provincial-style decor create a feeling of really good French cooking that is not let down by the quality and the freshness of the dishes, which are essentially seafood orientated. The *tapenade* (49F), *bourride sètoise* (110F), and full menu are all delicious. Good value for a fish restaurant.

TEA-ROOM

– **Le Café Maure de la mosquée de Paris** (map C3, **71**): 39 rue Geoffroy-St Hilaire 75005. ☎ 01-43-31-38-20. Metro: Jussieu or Place-Monge. Open daily 9am to 11.30pm. Tea and pastries 10F. A real haven of peace, this place instantly whisks you away to the gardens of the Alhambra or to the court of a rich caliph. With its columns, arcades, fine ceramics and patio, the Café Maure is perfect for relaxing and dreaming. The mint tea is probably the best in Paris. The coffee's also pretty good and very reasonably priced. The restaurant serves *tajines* (different sorts of spicy ragout) and couscous though the patisseries are probably better.

WHERE TO GO FOR AN ICE-CREAM

Gelati d'Alberto (map B2, **58**): 45 rue Mouffetard 75005. ☎ 01-43-37-88-07. Metro: Place-Monge. Open daily in the summer, closed Monday in winter and during January and February. 9F for small ices and 15F for big ones. If the name of this ice-cream maker makes you think of Italy, his products are reminiscent of the Venice Carnival. Here the range of flavours is like a multicoloured bouquet. Every morning Alberto makes around 15 flavours: the classics (lemon, raspberry), gourmet (caramelized cream, Nutella) and originals (allow yourself to be tempted by the yoghurt one). There are a few tables and the helpings are very generous. Excellent value for money. They also sell by the litre if you just can't get enough and have the use of a freezer in your accommodation.

THE CONTRESCARPE, THE MOUFF'

If you take the rue de la Montagne Ste-Geneviève heading upwards, you will find the bustle of the busy boulevards being temporarily left behind. Temporarily because, athough there are some charming little streets to explore off the main drag, the rue Mouffetard, or La Mouff', and the place de la Contrescarpe, are often just as lively as the winding lanes of the Latin Quarter. Some of the streets and little squares have lost their village character with the departure of the traditional working class residents who couldn't afford the new rents, but there are still a few areas left where you can wander uninterrupted in the real Paris and among real Parisians.

★ Heading along the rue des Écoles towards the East, you'll see the place Marcellin-Berthelot. As you pass by you'll notice the imposing mass of the **Collège de France**, founded by François I. The greatest French intellectuals have taught here: Ampère, Champollion, Bergson, Paul Valéry, Roland Barthes, Michel Foucault, François Jacob, Pierre Boulez and Emmanuel Le Roy Ladurie, to name a few. One exception, and a big one, was Einstein, who turned down the post he was offered there. To spite him, there isn't a single street, square or even so much as a gymnasium named after him in the whole of Paris! Was revenge sweet? Turn right onto the rue Jean de Beauvais and then left onto the rue de Lanneau, one of the oldest streets in the city, that turns into the rue de l'École-Polytechnique after the crossroads.

★ **Le couvent des Bernardins:** 24 rue de Poissy 75005. Did you know that one of the most resplendent buildings of the Middle Ages is off limits to the public? Until 1993, it was a fire station!

In the 13th century, the Abbé de Clairvaux built a college inside Philippe Auguste's city walls. The church, which fell into disuse during the Revolution, was destroyed. However, the refectory is still there, as is the magnificent Gothic crypt, one of the longest in Paris, and a splendid 18th-century staircase. The City of Paris, which owns it, still has no intention of opening it up to the public and there are even plans to turn it into an accommodation centre for the police. The whole thing seems a great pity.

★ The **place de la Contrescarpe:** one of the prettiest squares in Paris. All the houses have been restored, with varying degrees of success. Have a drink at La Chope, on the terrace. Rabelais and his friends came to chew the fat and to talk about the finer points of the French language at No. 1.

★ The **rue Mouffetard:** originally a Roman route and therefore one of the city's oldest, the Mouff' is a long, narrow and sloping street. Despite the determined efforts at renovation, it's still one of the most picturesque, if only because of all the remnants from the Middle Ages: old shop signs, the names of the streets, little passages and courtyards. Unfortunately fast-food outlets are starting to take over.

On the corner with the rue du Pot-de-Fer, there's a small fountain commissioned by Marie de Médicis (17th century). Old houses line the street – but sometimes the restoration work seems a to have been a bit too polished. There are some little courtyards such as the one at No. 52.

Opposite No. 66, there is a little crêperie, an absolute institution here as it has been selling crêpes and various sandwiches until 2am for many years, in winter as well as summer, and at very reasonable prices. At No. 69, there's a bas-relief representing a magnificent oak tree. The restaurant above called Au Vieux Chêne (The Old Oak Tree), has been trading for 100 years or more. A ball was held here from 1844 to 1880 that was as famous as it was notorious.

Before the street became pedestrian only, there were two old **passages** on each side: the **passage des Patriarches** and the **passage des Postes** (at Nos. 101 and 104 respectively). At No. 100, the cinema L'Épée de Bois (The Wooden Sword) showed the sort of films you'd imagine from the name. One of the most colourful markets in Paris is held in the last section of the rue Mouffetard. To take full advantage arrive early in the morning and preferably on a Saturday, and if you happen to be in the city in the last few days before Christmas, watch out for the odd chunk of wild boar (complete with hair and trotters) and other edible animal parts proudly on display. The old houses leaning over the proceedings give the whole thing a distinctly medieval feel. The market packs up at around 1.30pm. On the corner with the rue Daubenton, look out for the rather chubby house that looks fit to burst. At No. 122, the sign of the Bonne Source dates from the time of Henri IV. At No. 134, admire the fine arabesque façade of the Facchetti charcuterie, decorated using the *sgraffito* process (cement sculpted and enhanced by baroque-inspired decor) by Adhigeri in the 17th century, which led to the building being listed in 1990.

Right at the bottom of La Mouff' is the charming **église St-Médard** (entrance through 41 rue Daubenton, through a door with columns). In the 18th century its cemetery was the scene of mass hysteria around the tomb of a

Jansenist (a member of the religious movement, Jansenism) whom people believed could help to cure illness. The authorities had the cemetery closed and, shortly after, graffiti appeared on a nearby wall: 'By order of the King, God is forbidden to perform miracles in this place.'

★ **A walk around the montagne Ste-Geneviève area:** (2km (1 1/4 miles, 45 minutes without stops, from the Cardinal-Lemoine Metro station to the Censier-Daubenton Metro station). This pleasant and easy walk can be enlivened in the mornings by taking in the market in the rue Mouffetard.

On leaving the Cardinal-Lemoine Metro station, walk up the street of the same name (Hemingway lived at No. 74 from 1921 to 1923) towards the rue Clovis and Philippe Auguste's ancient city walls, the Hôtel des Grandes Écoles and its frontispiece. You can begin to feel the atmosphere of ancient Paris even before you enter the Mouff' imagining the poets of the *Pléiade* and Rabelais sitting at bistrot tables in the place de la Contrescarpe. At No. 39 rue Descartes stands the building in which the poet Verlaine rented a room to work and where he later died in 1896. Continue along the rue Mouffetard until you reach rue Blainville, then take the rue de l'Estrapade, the rue Laromiguière and the rue Amyot. In the rue Tournefort look for the old name of the street engraved in stone. There's a bird's eye view over the dome of the Panthéon from here. On the other side of the street is the restaurant Le Zénith, which has a little terrace on the place Lucien-Herr. Many years ago this was the route taken by the wine growers of the Faubourg St-Médard. On the corner there is a fountain, built by Marie de Médicis, which supplied water to the palais de Luxembourg.

If you've had enough by now you can get back onto the Metro at Monge; if not, follow the old Roman road towards Lyon (*via Lugdunum*) from the bottom of rue Mouffetard. They discovered an amazing 3,000 pieces of gold at No. 53 when demolition work was carried out in 1938 . . . so keep your eyes peeled for any they missed. Continue along rue Jean-Calvin and place Lucien-Herr, planted with lovely trees whose blue flowers enliven the terraces. Finally, the rue Lhomond and the passage des Postes allow you to rejoin the rue Mouffetard towards the bottom. Follow the narrow rue Daubenton to the Censier-Daubenton Metro station, past the église St-Médard.

★ **Les arènes de Lutetia:** on rue Monge and rue de Navarre (entrance through the rue de Navarre). Located in the centre of a public garden, and dating from the 1st century AD, the Roman amphitheatre was discovered when the street was being cleared in 1869. Its existence had been suspected for a long time, although nobody had ever been sure of the exact location. The relatively modest size of the arena proves that Lutetia, at the time, was a far less important city to the Roman occupiers than, say, Arles. Nevertheless, apparently the terraces were able to hold up to 17,000 people who would have witnessed both theatrical performances and gladiator contests there. The amphitheatre was almost demolished in 1980 to make way for a housing estate, but the plan became the subject of passionate controversy between developers and defenders of history and heritage and, evidently, the latter won. Today the arena is used as a playground by the local children and is a little haven of peace in the middle of the busy city, very popular for walks or games of *boules*.

★ If you walk through the little **rue des Boulangers** you reach **place Jussieu** and the faculté des Sciences. There's some most unusual graffiti on both façades above the square – old Maoist incendiary slogans from the 1970s. The Jussieu site of the university is the largest 'academic factory' in Paris with over 10,000 researchers, professors, students and administrative employees working there.

★ The **quai St-Bernard:** in the 17th and 18th centuries people used to bathe here. The rich undressed in their carriages, the poor undressed wherever they could; but they all bathed naked.

AROUND THE INSTITUT DU MONDE ARABE

★ The **Institut du Monde Arabe (IMA):** 1 rue des Fossés-St-Bernard 75005. ☎ 01-40-51-38-38. Information (answering machine): ☎ 01-40-51-38-11. Metro: Jussieu, Cardinal-Lemoine or Sully-Morland. Website: www.imarabe.org. Bus Nos. 24, 63, 67, 86, 87, 89. Open 10am to 6pm. Closed Monday. Entry is free. Entry charge for the museum and some exhibitions; free for under 12s. The Institute comprises a museum (Occupying the 4th to 7th floors), a library, a Sound and Image area, a number of exhibition halls, an area for young people, a restaurant and a cafeteria (9th floor). On the ground floor there is a bookshop/general shop as well as a literary café, where you can drink mint tea.

A competition was launched in 1981 for the construction of this amazing building which was won by Jean Nouvel and his Architecture Studio team. They did well to come up with a modern building which could curve around the quai St-Bernard and also manage to conjure up the Arab world at the same time. This amazing building of glass, aluminium and concrete is the result, three resolutely modern materials that are used to superb effect. The south façade is a particular success and the north building, which looks as sharp as the blade of a knife, describes a delicate curve. Between the two buildings is a deep and narrow chasm with a walkway joining them above.

The institute aims to explore the many facets of Arab culture. Created with the initiative of France and 19 Arab States (it now brings together the 22 member States of the League of Arab States), over the last 12 years the IMA has put on some very successful exhibitions promoting the Arab world, some of them receiving over 400,000 visitors.

● **The museum:** start the tour on the 7th floor, where you can see examples of Arab-Islamic art from the 9th to 19th centuries. The objects are well displayed with clever lighting. Architecture and mosaics are showcased on the 7th floor. On the 6th floor the salle Khalifa Abdul Aziz al-Moubarak has superb illuminations, ornate plates from the *Koran*, geometric panelling, religious books from the 12th and 14th centuries, carpets, ceramics, coins, etc. There are interesting displays on mathematics, weights and measures, and astrolabes (including one from the 10th century). On the 4th floor are some inlaid wooden chests. In the hall on the left there is a splendid collection of *objets d'art*: jewels, miniatures, ancient carpets, pilgrimage ewers (Turkey, 18th century), a Dervish's axe, etc. In the largest room is a 12th-century engraved water jar, and chiselled basins inlaid with gold and silver.

● **The Library:** access through the 3rd floor. Open from 1pm to 8pm.

Closed Sunday and Monday. An amazing library in the shape of a tower where a gigantic spiral staircase is covered with thousands of books: from the book of *pied-noir* (the term for Algerians of European origin) cuisine to a cartoon book on Mohammed. You can view them on the spot, but some can be sent out on loan. There's also a quiet reading room available. The IMA publishes a number of magazines on and around the Arab world: *Qantara, Mars, Al-Moukhtarat.*

- **The Sound and Image area:** in the 1st basement you can view, without an appointment, hundreds of films, photographs and sound documents connected with the Arab world.

- **The Cinema Section:** this has turned out to be one of the IMA's greatest successes. With few resources, it nevertheless manages to offer superb programmes. Information: ☎ 01-40-51-39-68. Ticket office on Level 0.

- **Thursdays at the IMA:** set up in 1990 to develop discussion about Arab society, history and culture. It holds debates and meetings with Arab, French and European writers and personalities. Information: ☎ 01-40-51-34-68 or 01-40-51-38-04.

- **Shows:** a meeting point for all the different kinds music of the Arab world, popular or avant-garde, urban or rural, plus those from neighbouring countries: Turkey, Iran, Africa. Themed musical events and concerts at 8.30pm in the auditorium. Reservations: ☎ 01-40-51-38-14 Tuesday to Sunday from 2pm to 5pm.

✕ Ɪ Don't miss the opportunity to sip some mint tea in the **tea-room** (in the afternoon) on the 9th floor. There's also a restaurant and an exceptional view.

★ The **Jardin des Plantes** (*Natural History Museum*): Entrance on the corner with the rue Cuvier and the rue Geoffroy-St-Hilaire (Metro: Jussieu) or in the place Valhubert (Metro: Gare-d'Austerlitz). ☎ 01-40-79-30-00. Open 7.30am to 5.45pm (7.45pm in summer).

A lovely place to walk in the heart of the city, the idea for this garden (in 1635) came from Guy de La Brosse, who was physician to Louis XIII. He obtained permission to create a herb garden, and a school of botany and natural history for the medical and chemistry students of the time, so the Jardin des Plantes is akin to being the oldest natural history museum in the world. Buffon was a naturalist who devoted himself to the study of science. He was made director of the King's garden in 1739 during the reign of Louis XV and continued in the role for some 50 years into the reign of Louis XVI. The area doubled in size during his directorship. Daubenton took over after him.

Almost all great French naturalists and botanists have worked here: Jussieu, Geoffroy St-Hilaire, Lamarck, Lacépède, Cuvier . . . . It has been a truly experimental garden, to which explorers and missionaries have brought plants and seeds from all over the world. Nicot planted tobacco here and a cocoa tree was brought back from the West Indies. There are plants from the Himalayas, the Alps and Morocco and a wonderful display of wild plants.

If you approach the gardens through the Cuvier gate, to the left you'll see the great amphitheatre and Cuvier's house and, to the right, a shady, cool and peaceful mound with very old trees, including a cedar planted in 1734.

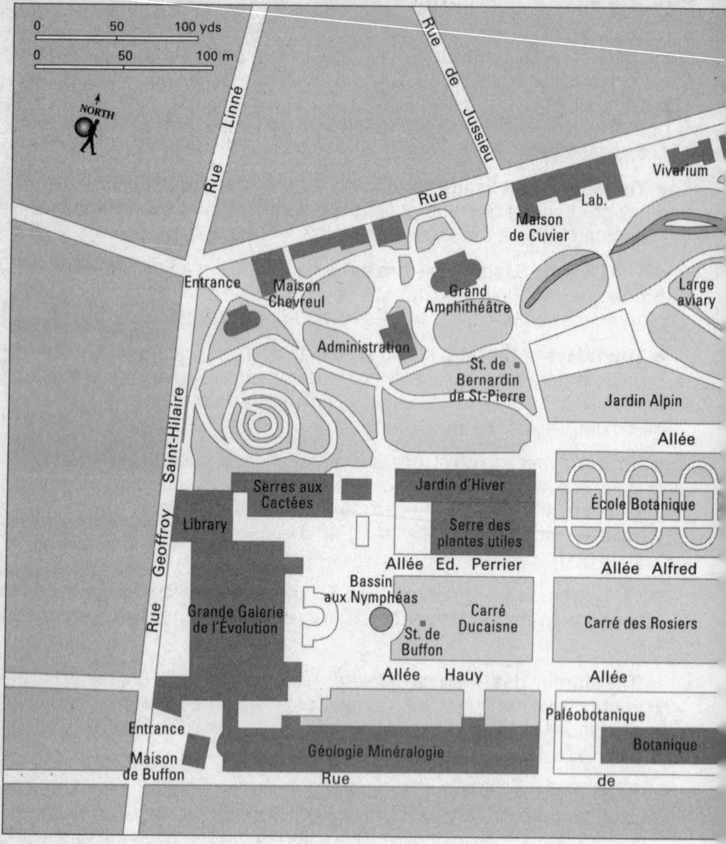

It is interesting to note that the gardens were laid out on the site of a refuse dump, so, by the 18th-century, they were already beginning to be concerned about ecology and improving the look of the city. However, surprisingly, this concern is not always prevalent today, as you will see if you enter one of the pavilions housing some of the priceless collections, some of which are in a terrible state of neglect. The paintings disappeared a long time ago, rust is eating away at the metallic structures, and the plaster is peeling.

● **La Menagerie:** access on the corner of quai St-Bernard and also in rue Cuvier. ☎ 01-40-79-37-94. Open 9am to 5pm (6pm in summer). Entry fee 30F; reductions 20F. There's a free map indicating the location of all the animals.

The Menagerie is the oldest public zoo in the world, founded in 1794 with the aim of giving 'philosophers, artists and men of science food for thought

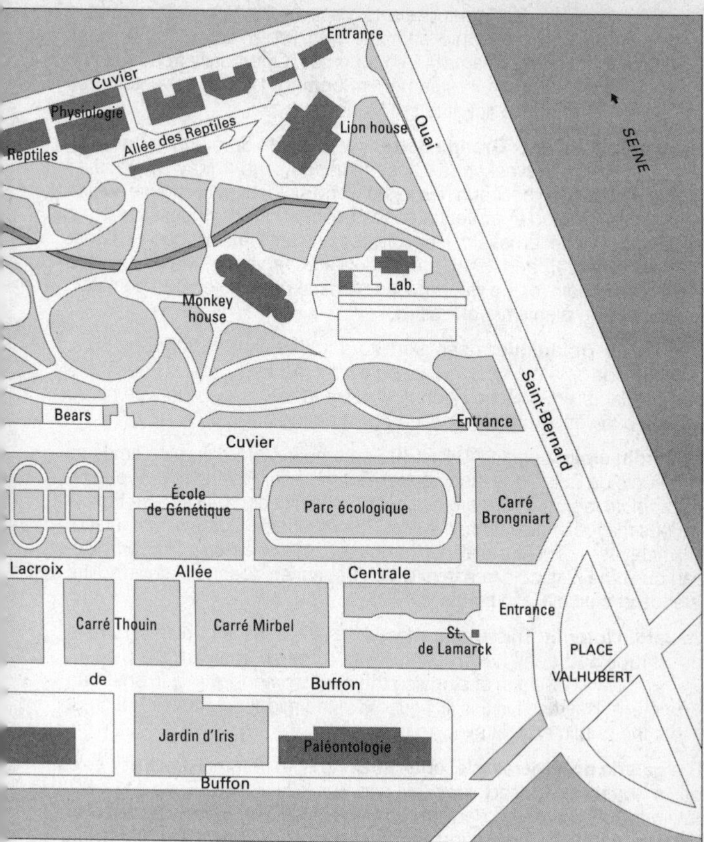

THE JARDIN DES PLANTES

and creation' and to house survivors from the Royal Menagerie at Versailles and other exotic animals that were dotted around France at the time, from circuses and fairgrounds. Among the most famous and surprising animal pairings were the lion and his dog. The story goes that they were presented to the king, but the dog eventually died, leaving his grieving playmate. To console the lion, he was given another little dog, whom he appears to have liked excessively because he promptly ate it. During the siege of Paris by the Prussians in 1870, since the people even ate their pets and rats, it is hardly suprising that almost all the animals in the Menagerie were also eaten and even took pride of place on the menus of the great restaurants. While we're on the subject, there's a refreshment area and a crêperie available, so you won't have to resort to eyeing up the bison!

Today you can see llamas, camels, monkeys, lions, bears, porcupines, bears, reptiles, and so on. Also, don't miss the *vivarium* that contains snakes, tarantulas, chameleons and stick insects.

• The **Microzoo:** this is a great place to discover the fascinating world of the creepy-crawly microscopic animals, who live in forests and, more uncomfortably for the squeamish, in our homes. Open daily from 10am to noon and 2pm to 5.15pm in summer, 1.30pm to 4.45pm in winter. Free access with the entrance ticket to the Menagerie.

• The **Jardin d'Hiver** or **Grande Serre:** open 1pm to 5pm during the week and 10am to 5pm at weekends. Closed Tuesday and 1 May. There is an entry fee. Plants from hot countries in the world's oldest glass house (which was originally created to protect a coffee bush) and today houses banana trees, bamboo, tree ferns, etc. Humidity is constantly maintained at 90 per cent. Between 1945 and 1946, the cold killed everything. Make sure you climb the rock, both for the view and to reach the pavilion located behind it, where other rare plants are exhibited.

• **L'école de Botanique:** open 9am to 11.30am and 1.30pm to 5pm. Closed Tuesday, Saturday, Sunday and Bank Holidays. Entry is free. Thousands of plants arranged by genus and by family, under the weathered branches of a venerable old Corsican pine dating from 1774.

• **Le Jardin alpin:** open 1 April to 30 September. Same opening times as for the École de Botanique (see above). Entry is free. Plants are grouped by geographical region. There are over 2,000 species cohabiting here thanks to various microclimates, from the Alps, the Pyrenees, Corsica, Greenland, the Himalayas . . . There are also a number of trees of historical importance, in particular the pistachio tree from which Sébastien Vaillant discovered the existence of sexual life in plants in 1720.

• **Le Jardin interdit:** This is an enclosure reserved just for botanists where ferns, shrubs and trees have been allowed to grow freely for the past 45 years, simply with the aim of studying the development of flora in an urban environment. The result is this little jungle in the middle of Paris; it's a great pity that the public are not allowed to enter.

• The **galerie de Minéralogie:** open 10am to 5pm (11am to 6pm at weekends in summer). Closed Tuesday and Bank Holidays. Entry fee 30F; reductions 20F. The only collection of its kind in the world, this museum was created in order to understand the importance of minerals through the ages, from prehistory to the discovery of the diffraction of x-rays by crystals. As you enter via the hall, you notice immediately the enormous crystals on show, including the largest natural crystal in the world that has remained uncut. Apart from its size, its value comes from its transparency. On the other side of the hall there is a fine geode of amethyst (a geode is a former gas bubble in which crystals form). In the basement are the 'Museum's Treasures'. On the left of the entrance, 300 years of mineralogy are brought together with a collection of amazing stones, whilst right at the back on the left is the 'paleo-botanical' section.

• The **galerie d'Entomologie:** ☎ 01-40-79-30-00. As we go to press it is closed, and is not due to reopen in the near future.

• The **galerie de Paléontologie et d'Anatomie comparée:** open 10am to 5pm (11am to 6pm at weekends in summer). Closed Tuesday and 1 May. Georges Cuvier was assistant professor of comparative anatomy at the Jardin des Plantes. He originated the natural system of animal classification and established the science of palaeontology. You can find thousands of fossils in this gallery, including the famous coelacanth skeleton (a fish which was thought to have become extinct but which was found to be still alive even today), a mammoth skeleton from Siberia, and casts of prehistoric animals. The exhibits here cover over 600 million years of history.

• **La Grande Galerie de l'Évolution:** 36 rue Geoffroy-St-Hilaire 75005. Metro: Jussieu or Censier-Daubenton. Open 10am to 6pm (late opening Thursday to 10pm). Closed Tuesday. This superb zoology gallery, closed since 1965, reopened its doors in June 1994 after an investment of 400 million francs. Its history has been a long one. In 1635, the Royal Garden of Medicinal Plants, inaugurated during the reign of Louis XIII, housed the first natural history collections. It grew quickly, augmented by donations from travelling naturalists who brought back previously unknown animals from their expeditions. In 1793, a decree by the Convention prohibited animals from being exhibited at fairs and even from being kept on royal estates. One such creature was the rhinoceros that was presented to Louis XV in 1770. The poor thing had been kept at Versailles, but died in 1793. The museum's naturalists lost no time, setting to work to stuff it with the only resources they had available, namely four wooden table legs to support the animal's legs and two barrels for the body. The skin was stretched over this improvised frame and painted to better resemble the animal's healthy glow in real life and hey presto, the result was the world's first stuffed rhinoceros. It has since been reworked from time to time, but remains on display on the last floor of gallery.

After a gap of a century, the rhinoceros could have had an equally impressive royal neighbour, a giraffe presented in 1826 to Charles X by the Pasha of Egypt with the aim of improving relations between the two countries. Atir, an Egyptian groom entrusted with the care off the precious animal, spent his time feeding and brushing it, and the giraffe lived for 18 years. Upon its death it was duly stuffed under the supervision of Buffon's team and is now at the Musée de La Rochelle.

At the end of the 19th century, Buffon's Cabinet d'histoire naturelle (Natural History Exhibition Room), as it was now named, enriched by various expeditions, including the one Napoleon made to Egypt, listed more than a million specimens from all over the world, albeit rather tightly packed in. The Zoology Gallery was built and inaugurated by President Fallières in 1889. After bombing had damaged the façade in 1940, the gallery, poorly repaired because of lack of funds, began to deteriorate alarmingly. The animals became covered in dust and their fur faded and damaged by rain. In 1965 came closure, and the gallery was plunged into darkness, to the great regret of the public who were upset to see one of the most prestigious zoological collections disappear.

The relatively recent renovations have enabled the museum to improve the organisation and display of its exhibits. Rather than simply displaying by genus, today they are based around one theme, evolution. The message is clear: it is to make visitors aware of the enormous diversity of the natural world and Man's responsibility towards preserving it. It is impossible to display all the museum's exhibits, so many of them are still in the *zoothèque*, a sort of museum antechamber reserved for scientists, located underneath the gallery. There are interactive terminals, a media library, laboratories for students, and a *son-et-lumière* show at 11am and 4pm (and 8pm Thursday). The exhibits range over four levels, divided into three main areas, in addition to the temporary exhibitions: 'The diversity of life', 'The evolution of life' and 'Man's role in evolution'.

– **The basement:** temporary exhibition. Access past the skeletons of a whale and a sperm whale.

– **The ground floor:** 'The diversity of the living world in a marine environment' presents an impressive whale's skeleton at the entrance, the reconstruction of a heap of sand enlarged 800 times, that may put you off lying on the beach for a while, and a narwhal (at the back, on the left), a marine mammal hunted for its twisted horn and brought back from Spitzbergen by the Duke of Orleans himself. You return to the 1st level by passing the ice 'desert'.

– **1st level:** 'The diversity of the living world on land'. Over 3,000 specimens from the Arctic and Antarctic, the African savannah, the Saharan desert and the tropical forests of South America. The flora and fauna of France can be viewed on an interactive terminal.

Look out for the Duke of Orleans' elephant seat on the right. Perched up high and off to hunt for a tigress, the Duke probably wasn't expecting a memorable face-to-face meeting, but, in a single bound, a tigress jumped onto the ducal seat. A gun went off and, scared witless, the elephant charged off into the jungle, His Grace hanging on for dear life. The next day, a bit shaken, he finally managed to shoot the tigress. The scene is now immortalised in the Gallery.

Also on the 1st level is the *mediathèque* (media gallery). Take note of the fact that when you enter the gallery you can't go back into the museum, so it's better to take a look around after the tour. There's another entrance (free) via 36 rue Geoffroy-St-Hilaire.

– **3rd level:** 'The evolution of life'. This is the heart of the museum, showing how animals have evolved since the dawn of time and how they have constantly adapted to their environment. A whole host of animals are on display, showing evolutionary progress since the primeval swamp. The coelacanth, which first appeared 380 million years ago, was thought to have been extinct for 65 million years. Imagine the amazement when, in 1938, a specimen was found in the Indian Ocean. During this time the species has only evolved slightly however, (something of a let down bearing in mind the millions of years that have elapsed) and it now has the beginnings of lungs and the movement of its fins is identical to that of the legs of a lizard. However, what is striking is that the coelacanth shows all the characteristics necessary for leaving the water and beginning a life on land, except . . . that it remains underwater. Another interesting exhibit is the gavial from the Ganges (*Gavialis gangeticus*). A sort of enormous crocodile, it is the only specimen of its kind in a museum.

There are also exhibits dedicated to genetics and how, by the mutation of their DNA, animals have adapted to their environment.

– **2nd level:** 'The gallery of Man' presents human evolution and our effect on the environment. The hall, displaying extinct animals, or endangered species, is hidden in a corner of the gallery. You can find it thanks to the dodo placed symbolically at the entrance. The plump dodo, whose short wings prevented it from flying, lived on the island of Mauritius. It became extinct in the late 17th century after the arrival of explorers and sailors, who found it very tasty. The cast here was made in 1901. The next hall is large, with subdued lighting, where you can see more unique creatures such as the black emu, of which only the skeleton remains (hunted for its flesh on

Kangaroo Island, near Australia, the species had become extinct by 1840), or the Tasmanian wolf, compared to a vampire because it drank the blood of its prey. The last of the species was killed in 1961. There is also an example of the Seychelles turtle (there are only three of these on display in the museums of the world) which became extinct in the early 19th century; the Cape lion, which disappeared shortly afterwards, and the Schomburgk stag, the last of which died at the Jardin des Plantes. In all there are 120 specimens to remind us of the richness of nature and Man's destructive presence in the world.

● **The flowerbeds:** from place Valhubert there's a magnificent view over the flowerbeds bordered by aisles of banana trees. From May to October this is the prettiest display of flowers in Paris.

★ The **mosqueé de Paris:** place du Puits-de-l'Ermite 75005. ☎ 01-45-35-97-33. Metro: Monge or Jussieu. Open 9am to noon and 2pm to 6pm. Closed Friday and in the morning on Islamic holidays. Access to the first garden is free. Entry to the mosque and guided tour: 15F; reduced rates for children, students and groups. Maximum wait of 15 minutes between each group.

The mosque was built in 1922 by three French architects and several hundred North African artisans in a pretty Andalusian style, in recognition of the aid given to France by the countries of North Africa during the First World War. It also houses a library, a Turkish bath, a restaurant and a tea-room, Café Maure (*see* 'Tea-room'). It is sumptuously decorated with huge gates of sculpted and chiselled wood, ancient carpets and richly ornate cupolas. There are also superb inner patios with luxuriant plant life and cedar wood ceilings, and in front of the mosque is a fine inner courtyard with sculpted arcades, ceramics and marble slabs. At the end is the *mihrab* pointing the way to Mecca and a rostrum *(minbar),* from where the Friday sermon is traditionally given. You can also visit the conference hall.

● **Hammam de la mosquée de Paris:** 39 rue Geoffroy-St-Hilaire 75005. ☎ 01-43-31-18-14. Metro: Jussieu or Monge. Women's days: Monday, Wednesday, Thursday, Friday and Saturday from 10am to 9pm. Men's days: Tuesday and Sunday 10am to 9pm. A very pleasant resting room with a little fountain in the middle. Have tea served while you recline on a mattress.

★ The **musée de Sculpture en plein air:** quai St-Bernard. Metro: Gare-d'Austerlitz or Jussieu. Bus Nos. 24, 63 and 89. A walk along the banks of the Seine with modern sculptures dotted here and there. Very pleasant on a fine day.

THE LATIN QUARTER

It is sometimes difficult to tell just exactly where the Latin Quarter begins and ends; is it bordered by St Michel and the Luxembourg gardens, or does it stretch further out towards the rue Mouffetard? Wherever its borders do lie, and they are probably something of a moveable feast, what is certain is that the presence of the university, where teaching was carried out in Latin in the Middle Ages, led to the area being dubbed the Latin Quarter and the name has stuck ever since. To some extent the area is still living on the memory of the university and its – at times – unruly students, even though the Sorbonne has not played such a central role for many years now. Despite the fact that many of its streets are now packed with designer shops, fast-food outlets and cafés better known for the steep rise in their prices than for the warmth of their welcome, there's still an indefinable *je ne sais quoi* that fascinates. The streets seem to be permanently thronged with people, even in winter and at 2 or 3 in the morning. Narrow roads twist and turn, lined with old houses, faded stonework, cobbled courtyards and leaning wooden doors. In many places the buildings have been spruced up, from the outside at least, but the area has lost none of its charm nonetheless.

A LITTLE HISTORY

Abélard, a 12th-century theologian and philosopher, was the first to colonise the area, bringing with him his students from the Île de la Cité, where the university had been based until then, following a philosophical dispute. He is more remembered, however, for his doomed love affair with his pupil, Héloïse. Her family ordered Abélard to be castrated, an extreme form of chastisement indeed, and Héloïse spent the rest of her life in a convent. All very sad. Robert de Sorbon created a college for poor theology students and the university grew rapidly, becoming renowned throughout Europe. However, the Sorbonne, as it became popularly known, eventually sank into conventionality and began to oppose new trends in philosophical thought, rather than welcoming them – first the Jansenists (who believed there could be no good act without the will of God), and then the 18th-century philosophers.

By the latter half of the 20th century there was a great deal of unrest at the university based on criticism of traditional teaching methods and disenchantment with the establishment in general, in keeping with the times. The real crisis broke out in March 1968 at the faculty of Nanterre, and moved to the Sorbonne the next day. For the first time ever, the police dared to violate the traditional immunity of the campus by arresting students inside its walls. What followed was reported world-wide – demonstrations, repression and barricades in the streets on the nights of the 10th and 11th May. In the resulting mayhem, 400 people were injured and hundreds were arrested in what later came to be termed the *événements* of May '68.

WHAT TO SEE

★ This is a very pleasant place to stroll around, looking out for the fine doors and sculpted façades of old houses and private residences. There are hardly any traditional small traders and craftsmen left, but, nevertheless, this is one of the few areas of Paris, along with the Marais, which haven't been too badly hit by architectural atrocities committed since Baron Haussmann began cutting great swathes through the medieval streets. Starting from the fountain in the place St-Michel, you'll be drawn to the narrow streets of the Îlot St-Séverin: **rue de la Huchette**, **rue de la Harpe**, **rue St-Séverin**, and **rue Xavier-Privas**. There are at least 10 restaurants per square metre here, with restaurateurs standing at their doorways to entice you in as you amble by. Crowded on summer evenings with a healthy mix of tourists and young people, if you like it to be lively then you're going to like it here, but select your restaurant with care – the quality is not always of the highest standard. The rue de la Huchette has borne the same name for

800 years and has had one of the most illustrious of residents – Napoleon Bonaparte lived at No. 10. One of the smallest streets in Paris, and certainly the most charmingly named, is the **rue du Chat-qui-Pêche** (the cat who fishes). It measures just 20m (65ft) long and 1.50m (5ft) wide and leads from the rue de la Huchette and to the quai St-Michel. It is probably best observed from one end though, rather than descended, as it sometimes looks a bit dank.

★ The **église St-Séverin:** dates from the 13th century, but is mainly in the Flamboyant Gothic style. The church holds regular concerts and is considered to have a far more progressive clergy than nearby St-Nicolas-du-Chardonnet. There's a fine façade with a wide Flamboyant bay, and a 13th-century tower and gate from a church that was demolished on the Île de la Cité. To the right, on the side of the church, you can see a number of gargoyles. Part of the last charnel house in Paris, dating from the 15th century, is to be found in the garden. Inside is a magnificent reception hall, also in the Flamboyant style, and a superb organ case dating from Louis XV (unfortunately it hides the finest stained-glass window in the church). The first columns of the bays have cornices, the others don't. This clearly shows the difference between the construction processes of the 13th and 15th centuries. There is also a fine *triforium* with slender bays and a lovely Flamboyant arch. The ribs in the central hall radiate with great suppleness and in a superbly flowing style. As for the stained-glass windows, there is an interesting series of apostles in the first three rows (14th century), whilst those on the apse date from the 15th century.

★ The **rue du Petit-Pont** and **rue St-Jacques**, into which it runs, follow the old Roman road. These were the first streets in Paris. The boulevard St-Germain, which cuts across them, and the boulevard St-Michel, were built centuries later during Napoleon III's rule.

★ The **Musée national du Moyen Âge et des thermes de Cluny (National Museum of the Middle Ages and the Cluny Baths)**: 6 place Paul-Painlevé 75005. ☎ 01-53-73-78-00. Metro: St-Michel. Open 9.15am to 5.45pm. Closed Tuesday. Entry fee 30F; 20F for everyone on Sunday; free for under 18s and the unemployed as well as on the first Sunday of the month. Guided tours Wednesday, Saturday and Sunday at 3.45pm for the medieval collections and the private residence, 2pm for the Lutetian baths and their underground galleries (full price: 36F on top of entry to the museum). Themed tours on Saturday and Sunday 10.30am (full price: 24F on top of entry to the museum).

At the junction of boulevard St-Michel and boulevard St-Germain, the museum is one of the finest in the district and set in a wonderful late 15th – century building. To be absolutely precise, it is in fact made up of several different buildings. The oldest is the Gallo-Roman thermal bath, dating from the 1st and 2nd centuries, though from the ruins you can see today you don't really get much of an idea of what the scale and grandeur of the buildings must have been like when they were whole. Thirteen centuries later, the abbé de Cluny bought the site in 1330 to build a private residence accommodating priests passing through Paris. At the beginning of the 16th century, the building housed Louis XII's widow, who spent her mourning period here.

The collection housed here is one of the finest of medieval art in the world and also offers a complete survey of the history of monumental sculpture.

The **Hôtel de Cluny** is one of three Parisian medieval residences which are still standing. Once you have passed through the pretty gate with its plant fresco, you will discover a rich façade with finely chiselled arches, corner turrets with crested doors, a Flamboyant balustrade, decorated skylights, gargoyles and mullioned windows. On the right in the courtyard there is also a fine 15th-century well.

– On the *ground floor*, there are three halls presenting 15th- and 16th-century furniture and tapestries including chests, tables and an altarpiece of the Passion which displays an incredible sculptural richness. In Hall 2 admire the tapestry at the back, which tells a story very much in the manner of today's cartoons. In Hall 4 there are several 15th-century tapestries known as *mille fleurs* (a thousand flowers) from Flanders. Entitled 'The Noble Life', they depict scenes of aristocratic life in which upper-class ladies in voluptuous dresses and silken drapes pass their lives in the pursuit of pleasure – times were obviously rather good. The next hall has 12th- to 15th-century stained-glass windows, most of them from the Sainte-Chapelle. From here you descend to the Cluny baths.

– *Hall of tapestries:* Coptic Egyptian fabrics (the only ones to have retained their colours).

– *Hall of stained-glass windows* dating from the 12th and 13th centuries.

– *Hall 8:* a series of *heads of the Kings of Judah.* These were originally attached to statues in the Gallery of the Kings at Notre-Dame, but were brought here after being decapitated during the Revolution.

– The cold room of the baths, the *frigidarium (Hall 10)*, contains the largest Gallo-Roman arch in France and a fine example of the period. In order to be able to bathe in good, fresh water, the Romans built an aqueduct to transport water from Rungis 12km (7.5 miles) away. A few steps further down is the warm room or *tepidarium.* Wood ovens used to heat the water are visible as openings underneath the walls. All the basement parts of the baths are open to the public.

– On the 1st floor in *Hall 11* is the star attraction of the museum: the tapestry *La Dame à la Licorne* (The Lady with the Unicorn), from the 15th century. The tapestry depicts six romantic paintings displayed in a rotunda to illustrate the theme of the five senses. The arms shown are those of a rich family from Lyon. The *mille fleurs* style highlights a natural gaiety and a closeness to nature. The Lady is always surrounded by a lion and a unicorn. From the left, in the first scene, the Lady brushes against the unicorn's horn (Touch), in the second, a monkey smells a flower that he has stolen from a basket (Smell) while the Lady plaits a garland of carnations; in the centre, the third, the unicorn is looking at itself in the mirror held out to him by the Lady (Sight); the fourth depicts Hearing with the music of an organ; the fifth evokes Taste through a budgerigar, a monkey and a dog receiving treats. Finally, the last scene counteracts the previous ones. The Lady places her jewels in a chest as a sign of the renunciation of the subjection of the senses, according to her 'only desire', for spirituality.

– The other halls also display a multitude of objects such as sculptures, ivories, altarpieces, steles, tapestries and stained-glass windows.

– The *jardin médiévale,* which opened in September 2000, unites the public garden (which stretches between the boulevard St-Michel and the rue de la Cluny along boulevard St-Germain) with a new space, previously forbidden to the public. Covering 5,000 square metres (5,450 square yards), this is a delightful place for a stroll.

★ The **Sorbonne:** on the corner of rue des Écoles and rue St-Jacques. Entrance in the rue des Écoles or access through the main courtyard, in rue de la Sorbonne. In the Middle Ages, classes were given in the open air, and centred around theology, but by the end of the 19th century, the fine 17th-century buildings had become too small. They were replaced by this unforgettable 'masterpiece' which looks rather like an army barracks. All that remains of the 17th-century building is the great chapel built in 1635 in the Jesuit style. Inside are paintings of Philippe de Champaigne and the superb tomb of Richelieu in white marble. The chapel is only open on certain occasions (and houses temporary exhibitions), but you can wander freely through the courtyard and the galleries. *Le Bois sacré*, a fresco by Puvis de Chavannes, can be seen in the great lecture theatre. In the courtyard, there are statues of Victor Hugo and Pasteur.

★ The Sorbonne is only a stone's throw from the Panthéon. On the way you'll walk past the grey mass of the **lycée Louis-le-Grand**. Molière, Robespierre, Victor Hugo, Baudelaire (who was expelled), Pompidou and Senghor, the Senegalese statesman, were all pupils here, and Jean-Paul Sartre was one of the lecturers. Today it is still a breeding ground for first prizes at the 'Concours général' (a prestigious competitive examination for pupils in top streams at French secondary schools).

★ **Le Panthéon:** entrance in rue Soufflot 75005. ☎ 01-44-32-18-00. Open 9.30am to 6.30pm 1 April to 30 September; the rest of the year 10am to 6.15pm; the ticket office closes 45 minutes before closing time. Closed on national holidays. Full-price tour: 35F, free for under 12s, reduction for people between the ages of 12 and 25. Guided tours by reservation.

A solid edifice, built in the form of a Greek cross, the Panthéon has had a curious history. Louis XV had vowed to build a church following his recovery from an illness, and entrusted the work to Soufflot, the leading French exponent of Neoclassicsm of the time. However, finances were severely lacking, so a lottery was organized to raise the capital. The building was thus finished in 1789, but very shortly afterwards, during the Revolution, it was secularised and transformed into a mausoleum intended for the great men of the time: Mirabeau (who was the first of these illustrious occupants), Voltaire, Jean-Jacques Rousseau and Marat. However, at the beginning of the 19th century, the building was de-secularised and became a church again, then a secular building once more from 1831 to 1852, then a church again. In 1885, on the occasion of the funeral of Victor Hugo, they plumped for a church again and so it has remained ever since. Later figures from public life to be interred were Gambetta (statesman), Jean Jaurès (politician and newspaper editor), Émile Zola (writer), Braille (inventor of the reading system for the blind), the Abbé Grégoire, Victor Schœlcher (who abolished slavery in the French colonies) and Jean Moulin, hero of the Resistance. The most recent interments have been Pierre and Marie Curie and André Malraux (statesman and novelist), on 23 November 1996.

The church is currently being restored. Some of the stones have cracked and fallen 40m (130ft) or more, so it's not surprising that the public is no longer allowed into part of the nave and the transepts, but you can still see the whole of the church if you stay in the aisles, which are protected by netting. This is also now the way into the crypt. Visitors can learn more from the interactive terminals and multimedia displays, which are freely accessible.

The **Crypt:** there are over 70 of the great and the good buried here. Although the tombs of Voltaire, Rousseau, Jaurès and Hugo are easy to find, the last resting place of Jean Moulin is less obvious.

A former chapel contains a model of the Panthéon made by the architect Rondelet, Soufflot's successor. (Soufflot died 10 years before the building was completed.) From there you have a partial view over the building. On the right-hand side is the famous fresco of *Sainte Geneviève ravitaillant Paris* (this translates literally as 'the revictualling of Paris by St Geneviève') by Puvis de Chavannes. The inner architecture is fairly heavy and pretentious. A series of columns with friezes supports the rounded arches, and the 83m (272ft) high central cupola is impressive, particularly from the outside. The walls were painted by various 19th-century artists. A staircase leads to the gallery from where you have a fine view of the church. A second, spiral staircase leads to the terrace for a view over the surrounding rooftops, but if you want to climb even higher you can reach the gallery of the recently renovated cupola, which has a wonderful panoramic view of Paris.

★ The **place de l'Estrapade:** just down the road from the Panthéon, the place de l'Estrapade runs alongside rue St-Jacques. The *estrapade*, (strappado) was a brutal punishment for soldiers who had deserted or robbed, which involved the dislocation of limbs by pulling with a rope. Louis XI – always up-to-date in such matters – abolished this form of torture, which was Italian in origin, and replaced it with the chain gang, forcing condemned prisoners to work for the state.

★ The **église St-Étienne-du-Mont:** behind the Panthéon. Work began during the reign of Charles VIII in 1492, but was not finished until 1626, by which time Louis XIII had become King. It was built on the site of a former abbey where Sainte Geneviève, who had come to the aid of Paris against Attila and his barbarian army and a later Frankish invasion, had been venerated. Her prayers were thought to have saved the city. The church was rebuilt in the 15th century and the new building took the name of St-Étienne-du-Mont.

The charming façade is a mix of Renaissance, Baroque and Gothic styles. On the tympanum is the *Martyre de St Étienne*. The bell-tower is 16th century. The Gothic interior has a lovely Flamboyant arch (and note the curious passageway between the pillars), but the star attraction of the church is the fine Renaissance *jubé* (rood screen) separating the chancel from the nave – the only one left in Paris. There's also a fine organ case surmounted by 17th century cherubs and 17th-century pulpit made of sculpted wood. Around the chancel can be seen some interesting 16th-century stained-glass windows. Pascal, the mathematician and Racine, the playwright, are interred in the chapel of the Virgin, behind the chancel. There are also frescoes by Caminade (on the right are the Three Kings).

The remains of Sainte Geneviève are enshrined in a small chapel, but don't miss the *chapelle des Catéchismes* (Chapel of Catechisms) where there are some superb 17th-century stained-glass windows. The work is so fine that the effect is to make them almost look like paintings, in particular *L'Arche de Noé* and *Le Vaisseau de l'Église*. Next to it is *La Multiplication des pains*, another fine composition. In the Salle des Catéchismes, on the right, there are frescoes by Giacometti (*La Pentecôte*, etc.).

– As you leave the church, emerging onto rue Clovis, make sure you look at No. 3 where there is a small piece of Philippe Auguste's city walls.

★ To reach **place Maubert**, walk down **rue de la Montagne-Ste-Geneviève**, one of the oldest streets in Paris. During the Wars of Religion this was the scene of the hanging of two young men. Incredibly, one of them survived the rope and used his miraculous survival as a divine sign that he should be saved and protested his innocence. An enquiry duly showed that the young man was indeed innocent and he was spared. A lucky escape, but justice was cruel in the Middle Ages: the gallows, the wheel and the stake were common forms of punishment for the least of crimes.

In the 19th century, this road was also a meeting place for tramps who would collect cigarette ends from the streets, extract the tobacco and then sell it on. Times must have been hard indeed. The notorious lover of the Marquise de Brinvilliers, Godin de Sainte-Croix, had his laboratory at No. 4 impasse Maubert. He died there suddenly, and the police finally discovered the horrific secret of the crimes committed by this pair of poisoners. The Marquise's father and brothers had all been murdered.

The so-called Maub', the area around the place Maubert, is another old part of Paris, though one that has changed a lot. The **rue de Bièvre** where students used to eat couscous for next to nothing, is still affordable, even though former president François Mitterrand lived there for many years. The restaurant near his former residence naturally has 'President's couscous' on the menu. A hundred years ago, it was still just a narrow passage, bordered by a river, the Bièvre, which flowed down from the heights of the Butte-aux-Cailles. (For more on this area *see* 'Les Gobelins' in '13th arrondissement'.)

★ The twisting **rue Maître-Albert** has been in existence since the 13th century. No. 7 is the finest residence in the street (17th century). The former 15th-century faculty of Medicine is located in *rue de la Bûcherie,* and in the *rue de l'Hôtel-Colbert,* there are a number of superb private residences (this street used to be called the rue des Rats, which shows that the Maub' was not always a fashionable area).

★ Return via **rue Galande**, where there are still some interesting old houses. Note that in keeping with the general rather 'gothic' ambiance of the area the Studio Galande cinema often shows the *Rocky Horror Picture Show* (*see* 'Something different').

The rue St-Julien-le-Pauvre also has a series of elegant and well-restored houses.

★ The **église St-Julien-le-Pauvre:** one of the most charming little churches in Paris, with a small, tranquil garden in the shade of Notre-Dame and also one of the oldest. Building commenced in 1170 with the stones left over from the construction of Notre-Dame and finished in 1220, though the current façade is 17th century. The St Julien referred to in the name of the church is probably Julien the Hospitaler, mentioned in *The Golden Legend* by Jacques de Voragine. As a stag had predicted that he (Julien) would kill his mother and father, Julien left the family home and led an exemplary life. One day, without Julien himself being aware of it, Julien's wife invited his parents into their home. The young man, surprised by these strangers, fulfilled the terrible prophecy. In great despair, he renounced all material wealth and from then on lived as a hermit.

The church has suffered many slings and arrows of its own during its very long existence, as you can see from the stump of wall in front of the entrance. There are also the remains of a well, today located on the outside. On the right, you can see a slab of the old Roman road that led from Paris to Orléans. Once inside, the church has an intimate feel. It has belonged to Greek Catholics since 1889, as some features of the interior indicate. The iconostasis (screen containing icons, common in Eastern churches) separating the chancel is the work of a Syrian artist. This Eastern aspect may well be what gives the church some of the feeling of warmth that is missing from many Western places of worship. There is a fine 15th-century tombstone on the right-hand side and remarkable 12th-century cornices in the chancel with monstrous figures (harpies) and acanthus leaves. On the left-hand wall, there is a very fine 17th-century forged iron lectern.

In the adjacent **square** lives a 400-year-old tree. It is the oldest in Paris, so it is quite understandable that it needs a concrete support to prop it up.

★ The **musée de l'Assistance Publique – Hôpitaux de Paris:** 47 quai de la Tournelle 75005. ☎ 01-40-27-50-05. Metro: Maubert-Mutualité or St-Michel. Open 10am to 5pm. Closed Sunday and Monday. Allow 90 minutes for a visit.

This is an odd little museum that deserves to be better known, situated in the 17th-century Hôtel de Miramion. It follows the entire history of Parisian hospitals over the centuries, with documents, first-hand accounts and paintings.

The exhibits depict the role of the Church in the founding of the first hospitals with rare pieces such as: the *Livre de Vie active* from 1482, whose rich illuminations show scenes from hospital life; 14th-century accounts; statutes of the Hôtel-Dieu (the principal Parisian Hospital) from 1535; a superbly illustrated *Antiphonaire de la Charité*, the letter of expulsion from Clemenceau to the nuns at the beginning of the anti-clerical 20th century; and *lettres de cachet* signed by Louis XIV and Colbert, the great 17th-century statesman. Among unusual objects on display are surgical instruments, an antique electrocardiagraph and an amazing collection of babies' bottles made of earthenware, tin and iron, the oldest dating from the Gallo-roman era. There is fine painting by Vuillard, *Le Docteur Vaquez opérant à la Pitié* and on the way out, note the touching *Sortie de maternité*.

The museum also features a programme of temporary exhibitions on subjects chosen for their particular relevance to, or resonance with, the world of contemporary medicine.

★ The **musée de la Préfecture de police:** 1 *bis* rue des Carmes 75005. ☎ 01-44-41-52-50. Fax: 01-44-41-52-58. Metro: Maubert-Mutualité. Open Monday to Friday 9am to 5pm and Saturday 10am to 5pm (please note that on Saturday, entrance is through 5 rue de la Montagne-Ste-Geneviève). Entry free. Access is through the police station serving the 5th arrondissement. You will need to show some form of identification to enter the hall on the 2nd floor, where the history of the Paris police from the 16th century to present day is exhibited, so make sure you have been good recently. This museum was created by the Chief Commissioner Lépine, to whom Paris is also indebted for *hirondelles* (policemen on bicycles) and the white baton.

There's a short talk about the various functions and wide remit of the Paris police force (uniformed police, civil defence, the fire brigade, hygiene, the police internal investigation body, transport, etc.) and portraits of the 78 *Préfets*, who have been appointed by the Minister of the Interior since 1800. This is followed by exhibits of miscellaneous objects and documents, including an executioner's sword, a display about the Marquise de Brinvilliers, the woman who poisoned her brothers and her father (see also 'Place Maubert') and two decrees issued by the Convention summoning Louis XVI to be brought to the witness box during the Revolution.

In the more contemporary section are documents on Vidocq, a famous convict who became the head of the Sûreté (1832), and a rather odd menu offering 'kebabs of dog's liver *à la maître-d'hôtel*', 'cat stew' and 'salami of rat *à la Robert*'. This was the 'nouvelle cuisine' of the Commune era. The menu was stained with the blood of President Paul Doumer when he was assassinated in 1871.

There are some instructive showcases on technical anthropometry, the scientific measurement of the human body, developed by Bertillon, which laid the foundations for the French system of establishing legal identity. There are also showcases with weapons of all types and a parade of famous murderers. All in all, an unexpected and interesting little museum, even if the presentation is rather austere.

★ Towards boulevard St-Michel, you won't want to miss the extraordinary **Shakespeare & Co** in rue de la Bûcherie. An American-run bookshop selling English language books, it is one of the haunts of ex-pats in Paris, who come to pick up a second-hand or new novel, or catch up on some news from home. The original shop, launched by the American Sylvia Beach (publisher of Joyce's *Ulysees*) was in the rue de l'Odéon, patronised by Hemingway, Scott Fitzgerald, Gertrude Stein, T.S.Eliot and others doing their 'stint' in Paris.

★ From the Jardins du Luxembourg, you can complete your visit to the Latin Quarter by heading down to the **Val-de-Grâce** via rue St-Jacques. A former 17th-century abbey, the Val-de-Grâce has been a military hospital since 1793. Its dome is reminiscent of the dome of St Peter's in Rome. The interior of the dome contains an enormous fresco, with over 200 huge figures. At the age of seven, Louis XIV, the son of Anne of Austria, laid the first stone himself, the Queen having commissioned the abbey, designed by François Mansart, to give thanks for Louis's birth.

As can be seen from the names of the streets, rue des Ursulines and rue des Feuillantines, the area contained many convents at one time.

★ The **musée du Service de santé des armées:** 1 place Alphonse-Laveran 75005. ☎ 01-40-51-51-92. Metro: Gobelins; RER: Port-Royal. Bus Nos. 91 and 83. Open Tuesday and Wednesday noon to 6pm, Saturday 1pm to 6pm and Sunday 1.30pm to 6pm (the ticket office closes at 5pm). Entry fee: 30F, half price for under 12s, free for children under 6 and members of the armed forces.

This surprising museum is situated in the cloister of the abbey Val-de-Grâce. It has a rich collection of objects, drawings and uniforms illustrating the various roles of medicine in the army, from helping the wounded on the battlefield to life in hospital. You can learn about the 'abdominal protection' used during the First World War, the research carried out with anatomical figures made of wax, and see an amazing 16th-century German surgical kit in gold plate engraved with the busts of various queens.

More modern research into the physical effects of being underwater or high in the sky explain the presence of a single-seater decompression chamber and the head of the rocket *Véronique* launched on 22 February 1961 at Hammaguir in the Sahara. There is also a splendid and unique collection of pharmaceutical jars and pestle and mortars belonging to a Dr. Debat.

WHERE TO GO FOR A DRINK

🍸 **Finnegan's Wake** (map C2, **60**): 9 rue des Boulangers 75005. ☎ 01-46-34-23-65. Metro: Jussieu or Cardinal-Lemoine. Open daily 11am to 1.30am, at weekends from 6pm. Half a pint of beer 18F, a pint 25F and a pint of Guinness 38F. Cheaper during the day. Happy hour 6pm to 8pm. This Irish pub plays the celtic cultural card to the full. Language courses are offered in Breton on Monday, in Gaelic on Wednesday, in Welsh on Thursday and there are concerts on Friday. Basically, it's like being in 19th-century Dublin. Two stone-clad rooms with visible beams create the atmosphere.

🍸 **Taverne Daubenton** (map C3, **62**): 25 rue Daubenton 75005. ☎ 01-43-31-44-00. Metro: Censier-Daubenton. Open daily 10am (3pm on Sunday) to 2am. Budget for 130F à la carte. If a car happens to be parked in front of this tiny place, you might miss it, so keep your eyes peeled. Built on a street corner, this former pub has been taken over by arts students (the faculty is nearby), 'bar-room philosophers' and Brazilian-Cape-Verdo-Portuguese. The Brazilian souvenir posters add colour, as does the cuisine, and the musicians who play some evenings. There's a small but well proportioned terrace in the summer.

🍸 **Le Bistro de la Huchette** (map B1, **65**): 27 rue de la Huchette 75005. ☎ 01-53-10-83-26. Metro: St-Michel. Open daily to 2am. Half a pint of beer from 15F. Dishes at around 40F. The owner has a taste for good wines, a sense of conviviality and a warm and smiling welcome. There are some good beers as well: Bruges *blanche* and draught Grimbergen, Kilkenny, Krieg and others. It's a nice place to have breakfast too. In the afternoons it's pretty quiet, but things start to pick up around apéritif time and at night. There are exhibitions of paintings and excellent music on the sound system, blues or Latin, depending on who's behind the bar. Small-scale catering: good *charcuterie* and cheeses, *tartines de pain Poilâne* and generous mixed salads. A trendy 'Latin Quarter' and international clientele, which gives the place a true Parisian touch.

🍸 **Le Verre à Pied** (map B3, **64**): 118 *bis* rue Mouffetard 75005. ☎ 01-43-31-15-72. Metro: Censier-Daubenton. Closed Sunday afternoons, Monday, 1 May, New Year, Easter Monday, and from 16 to 18 August. Set meal with main course and dessert 55F at lunchtime only. An old bistro with a bar that is so narrow that you can hardly fit a glass on it. Tiled floor, an old stove, and classic café tables where regulars and students rub shoulders – so it hasn't changed much since the First World War. At lunchtime only, try the *croûte montagnarde* (grated cheese and ham on rustic bread and butter) served with a salad, or a set dish of the day plus cheese or dessert, and *au p'tit Léon* at 14F (cane sugar, white rum and green lemon).

🍸 **Connolly's Corner** (map B3, **66**): 12 rue de Mirbel 75005. ☎ 01-43-31-94-22. Metro: Censier-Daubenton. Open daily 4pm to 2am. Happy hour 4pm to 8pm. You can drink a pint of Guinness (38F) and have a game of darts in the purest Irish tradition. A collection of cut-off ties to admire at the bar. Pop or traditional music concerts on Tuesday, Thursday and Sunday, plus certain Wednesdays.

🍷 **Le Requin Chagrin** (map B2, **67**): 10 rue Mouffetard 75005. ☎ 01-44-07-23-24. Metro: Monge. Open daily 4pm to 2am (5am at the weekend). Half a pint of beer 16F before 9pm, 22F afterwards. The action takes place around the magnificent wooden bar where students and connoisseurs of draught beers (nine different types) meet to celebrate one of the liveliest happy hours in the Contrescarpe area, from 4pm to 9pm. Small groups of chess players are dotted around. There's a carefully planned music programme.

🍷 **Café Égyptien** (map B3, **63**): entrance in the rue de l'Arbalète 75005. Metro: Censier-Daubenton. Open daily except Monday, 11.30am to 1.30am. Egyptian menu at 45F, drinks from 15F. A little room that doesn't look anything special and another which is hardly any bigger in the basement, where you can smoke *chicha* (hookah) with honey, apple or strawberry (20F), while drinking a cup of tea (18F per pot), or sipping a drink with hibiscus *(karkadet),* anis or cinammon. Otherwise there are fruit juices to go with an eastern-style pastry (10F). There are also a few dishes priced at between 18F and 20F (salads, *falafel*, etc.). On the walls a few photos and drawings add to the decor.

🍷 **Le Rallye** (map C1, **68**): 11 quai de la Tournelle 75005. ☎ 01-43-54-29-65. Metro: Maubert-Mutualité. Open daily 7.30am (9.30am at weekends) to 2am. Half a pint of beer 15F, dishes of the day 45F. A crazy bar entirely dedicated to the adventures of *Tintin*, the Belgian boy detective (there's an amazing collection of gadgets and posters of the cartoon hero) and the music of Mano Negra and Les Négresses Vertes. The slightly rowdy clientele runs on beer and there's a terrace that is very popular when the weather is fine. One of the best Parisian grunge-style places.

🍷 **L'Envol Québécois** (map C2, **69**): 30 rue Lacépède 75005. ☎ 01-45-35-53-93. Metro: Monge. Open daily 4pm to 2am. Closed in August. Set menu 69F served lunchtime and evening, with a Quebec menu at 99F. Antoine Larose is a native of Montreal. Exhibitions of the work of Quebecois artists and poetry and discussions over glasses of beer, draught Belgian or bottled beer from Quebec. Try the Quebec *kir*, a glass of Sauvignon with maple syrup, or one of the many cocktails, and a few dishes such as the *hambourgeois* (around 70F), generous Quebec-style hamburgers served with salad and oven chips, or broad beans with bacon and maple syrup. The background music is mainly American rock and songs from Canada.

🍷 **Café de la Nouvelle Mairie** (map B2, **70**): 19 rue des Fossés-St-Jacques 75005. RER: Luxembourg. ☎ 01-44-07-04-41. Open 9am to 8pm, later on Tuesday and Thursday evenings, and some evenings in the summer (it is advisable to check). Closed at weekends. A glass of wine costs from 15F to 30F. This wine bar, located behind the Panthéon, pays tribute to the kings of groove and swing. There's a simple reason for this: the Polygram building (Barclay, Polydor, Phonogram), which is home to an army of young people mad about music, is just the other side of the street. In between listening to new talent or thinking about how to promote their latest artists, music industry folk come to sip a glass of Anjou or Faugères wine. When a British or American rock group is in town, you can often see them sharing a bottle around a table. The welcoming terrace is great in the evening, when the place de l'Estrapade, just opposite, is at its most charming.

GOING OUT

Le Piano Vache (map B2, **73**): 8 rue Laplace 75005. ☎ 01-46-33-75-03. Metro: Maubert-Mutualité. Open daily noon (9pm at weekends) to 2am. Half a pint of beer from 20F. Over the past 20 years, this place has seen more students and hordes of rockers than most other bars in Paris. There's a very curious animal, known as the Tibetan gnu, above the bar, and some nostalgic photos of rock groups underneath it. Evenings with different DJs several times a week: Latin on Tuesday, Goth on Wednesday, reggae on Thursday, and techno-rock on Friday.

To vary things a little, take a trip to the **Violon Dingue**, rue de la Montagne-Ste-Geneviève. It's just down the road. Open 6pm to 2am. Happy hours 6pm to 10pm. Along with Le Piano Vache, this is the place to go for a wild night out on the town.

Le Café Oz (map A2, **74**): 184 rue St-Jacques 75005. ☎ 01-43-54-30-48. RER: Luxembourg. Open daily 4pm to 2am. 15F for half a pint of beer. This establishment seems to be reserved for Paris' Australian community, and there are lots of them! From the draught beer to wine – don't miss the champagne (36F) – everything is 100 per cent Australian. You can almost feel the wide open spaces of the bush. The welcome from the staff is very convivial and lovers of Australian rock won't find much to complain about. Midnight Oil and INXS are on tap. The best time to come is between 8pm and 10pm; later on it gets very crowded. Boosted by their success, the owners have opened a similar bar at 18 rue St-Denis.

The rue du Petit-Pont, just before the beginning of the rue St-Jacques, has a few nightspots which are always lively. Night owls, insomniacs, nocturnal philosophers and noisy groups meet at the **Cloître**, open to 2am, or the **Polly Maggoo (map B1, 75),** open to 4am. Old Stones, Led Zeppelin or even Jacques Brel on the dance floor.

WHERE TO GO FOR LIVE MUSIC

Le Petit Journal (map A2, **77**): 71 boulevard St-Michel 75005. ☎ 01-43-26-28-59. Metro: St-Michel or Odéon; RER: Luxembourg. Bus Nos. 27, 21, 38, 82, 84, 85. Open every evening except Sunday. Closed in August. Set menu 69F at lunchtime. New Orleans jazz is played here from 9.30pm to 2am. Entrance fee plus drink: 100F. You can also eat pretty well for 200F or 270F, drink and show included. Student rate: entrance fee plus drink 70F. Second drink from 40F.

NIGHTCLUB

– **Caveau de la Huchette** (map B1, **78**): 5 rue de la Huchette 75005. ☎ 01-43-26-65-05. E-mail: huchette@aol.com. Metro: St-Michel. Open daily 9.30pm to 2, 3 or 4am. Drinks from 26F. Entry fee: 60F Sunday to Thursday (55F for students, on presentation of their ID card), 75F Friday, Saturday and the nights before public holidays. You can dance to the most prestigious American and European jazzmen, as well as the indestructible Maxim Saury. Covering two floors, it is usually peopled by a compact throng of tourists and smart students.

SOMETHING DIFFERENT

– **The Rocky Horror Picture Show at the Studio Galande** (map B1, **79**): 42 rue Galande 75005. ☎ 01-43-26-94-08. Metro: Maubert-Mutualité or St-Michel. Shows at 10.30pm on Friday and midnight on Saturday. 44F; reduced rate for students, the unemployed and members of the military, 34F. Cult cinema *par excellence*. From *Crash* to *Priscilla, Queen of the Desert*, via *Métropolis*, *Easy Rider*, *Pulp Fiction*, *A Clockwork Orange* or *Brazil*, this old cinema in the rue Galande clearly doesn't bother with weepies in the *Officer and a Gentleman* style.

Resolutely trashy, every weekend it shows *The Rocky Horror Picture Show*, the musical comedy of, by now, world renown, that needs no introduction. People dress up in the costume of the character of their choice and jump around, dance, sing and generally enjoy themselves. So, don't forget to pack the fishnet stockings. A great excuse to make a racket, and an opportunity for chance meetings . . . . The best session is at 10.30pm. You'll need an umbrella and a change of clothing for when the proceedings get a little wild, with water and rice sometimes being involved. So, consider yourself warned.

– **The banks of the Seine (map C1):** quai St-Bernard, at the foot of the Université de Jussieu 75005. Metro: Jussieu. Every evening from 15 July to 15 August and some weekends. If the weather is good, there are 'improvised' soirées of salsa and tango where the dancers will mesmerise you with their sensuous swaying. You can even bring a picnic, and why not try a few steps yourself, if you're not feeling too inhibited, that is. Entrance is free and all this takes place in the open air on the banks of the Seine, opposite one of the finest sights in Paris – Notre-Dame and the Île St-Louis. What a fantastic setting for a warm summer's evening!

6TH ARRONDISSEMENT

THE ODÉON QUARTER • ST-GERMAIN-DES-PRÉS

The 6th arrondissement, like its great rival, the 5th, is a real mix of the private and the public. The area around the Odéon Theatre is full of life, with people coming and going at all times of day and night, whilst St-Germain-des-Prés is smaller and slightly more arty. The rue du Cherche-Midi marks the beginning of several streets lined with private residences, as well as the odd convent, close to the 7th arrondissement.

WHERE TO STAY

☆ BUDGET TO MODERATE

Association des étudiants protestants de Paris (map C2, **1**): 46 rue de Vaugirard 75006. ☎ 01-43-54-31-49. Fax: 01-46-34-27-09. RER: Luxembourg; Metro: Mabillon, Odéon or St-Sulpice. Literally an 'association for protestant Parisian students', but in reality open to all denominations, the dormitories in this hostel are open all year round: 82F per person. Double room from 95F to 105F per person, and single room from 110F to 120F available in July, August and September only. It is advisable to call before turning up (the opening times are given on the answering machine – in French). Located in a charming, large old building opposite the Jardin du Luxembourg, it takes students aged from 18 to 26. The rooms are well situated, especially the ones higher up, with views over St-Sulpice and the Jardin du Luxembourg. There are communal facilities in the form of TV rooms, games rooms and common rooms for those whose feet begin to tire of trudging around the streets. It costs 10F to register with the association, plus a deposit of 150F. Breakfast included.

Delhy's Hotel (map D1, **2**): 22 rue de l'Hirondelle 75006. ☎ 01-43-26-58-25. Fax: 01-43-26-51-06. Metro: St-Michel. Single room 250F, double rooms with washbasin 310F, double rooms with shower 390F. Close to place St-Michel, this hotel is in one of the lesser-known streets of Paris. Crammed with old buildings and walls, the area is full of the ambiance and flavour of a Paris centuries old. Back in the 16th century, the hotel was a private residence (along with No. 20) which François I gave to his favourite, the Duchess of Étampes, Anne de Pisseleu. Some original stones and beams can still be seen in the rooms, which are simply furnished, with a bathroom or shower. TV in all rooms.

Hôtel des Académies (map B3, **3**): 15 rue de la Grande-Chaumière 75006. ☎ 01-43-26-66-44. Fax: 01-43-26-03-72. Metro: Vavin. Bus Nos. 58, 68 and 91. Double room 300F with shower, from 345F to 360F with shower and toilet. A small family-style hotel in a quiet street with an atmosphere redolent of the 1950s. There are a few single rooms with washbasins at a reduced rate, though you do need to book well in advance for these.

Hôtel de Nesle (map C1, **5**): 7 rue de Nesle 75006. ☎ 01-43-54-62-41. Fax: 01-43-54-31-88. Metro: Odéon or Pont-Neuf. You cannot book in advance here, so it's best to turn up before 10am. Double room with sink 350F overlooking the street, 450F with shower and 550F with shower and toilet, overlooking the little garden. Situated in a small, quiet, historical street off the rue Dauphine and close to the river, this charming little hotel offers a series of rooms which have been decorated around a theme: Africa, the Orient, Egypt and Molière, whose plays were performed at the Comédie Française at No. 14 in the nearby rue de l'ancienne Comédie. The Sahara room even has its own private Turkish bath. There's a little indoor garden with an overhanging terrace, where you can relax in peace. Credit cards are not accepted.

Hôtel des Canettes (inset map, **6**): 17 rue des Canettes 75006. ☎ 01-46-33-12-67. Fax: 01-44-07-07-37. Metro: St-Germain-des-Prés or Mabillon. Double room 460F. A

Where to stay

1 Association des étudiants protestants de Paris
2 Delhy's Hotel
3 Hôtel des Académies
5 Hôtel de Nesle
6 Hôtel des Canettes
7 Hôtel du Globe
8 Hôtel du Lys
9 Hôtel La Louisiane
10 Hôtel Louis II
11 Grand Hôtel des Balcons
12 Hôtel Le Clos Médicis
13 Hôtel des Marronniers

Where to eat

21 Le Golfe de Naples
22 Le Petit Vatel
23 Orestias
24 L'Assignat
27 La Tourelle
28 Indonesia
29 La Crêperie des Canettes
30 Le Vavin
31 Yamani
32 Bistro de la Grille
33 Bistro Mazarin
34 Le Machon d'Henri
35 Le Nemrod
36 La Lozère
37 Aux Trois Canettes
38 Noura
40 L'Arbuci
41 Positano
42 Le Petit Mabillon
43 Aux Charpentiers
44 Nouvelle Couronne Thaïe
45 Marmite et Cassolette
46 Le Montagnard
47 L'Épi Dupin
48 La Rôtisserie d'En Face
49 Les Bookinistes
50 La Cafetière
51 Bouillon Racine
52 L'Alcazar
53 Le Coffee Room M's
54 Wadja
56 La Table d'Aude
57 Le Procope
58 Le Petit Lutétia
61 Le Petit Zinc
62 La Bauta
63 Brasserie Lipp
64 La Méditerranée
65 Chez Albert
66 Le Rond de Serviette
67 La Muraille de Jade
70 Tch'a
71 Restauration Viennoise
72 La Tour de Pierre

Where to go for a drink/ Going out

80 The Frog Princess
81 La Bibliothèque
82 Le Lucernaire
83 Chez Georges
84 La Palette
85 La Rhumerie
86 Les Étages St-Germain
87 Le Flore
88 Les Deux Magots
89 Bob Cool
90 Le Bar du Marché
91 Le Sélect
92 La Closerie des Lilas
93 Le Bilboquet
94 Cubana Café
95 Le Shannon Pub
97 Caveau de la Bolée
98 Le Pousse au Crime
99 Coolin
101 Le Petit Suisse
102 La Taverne de Nesle

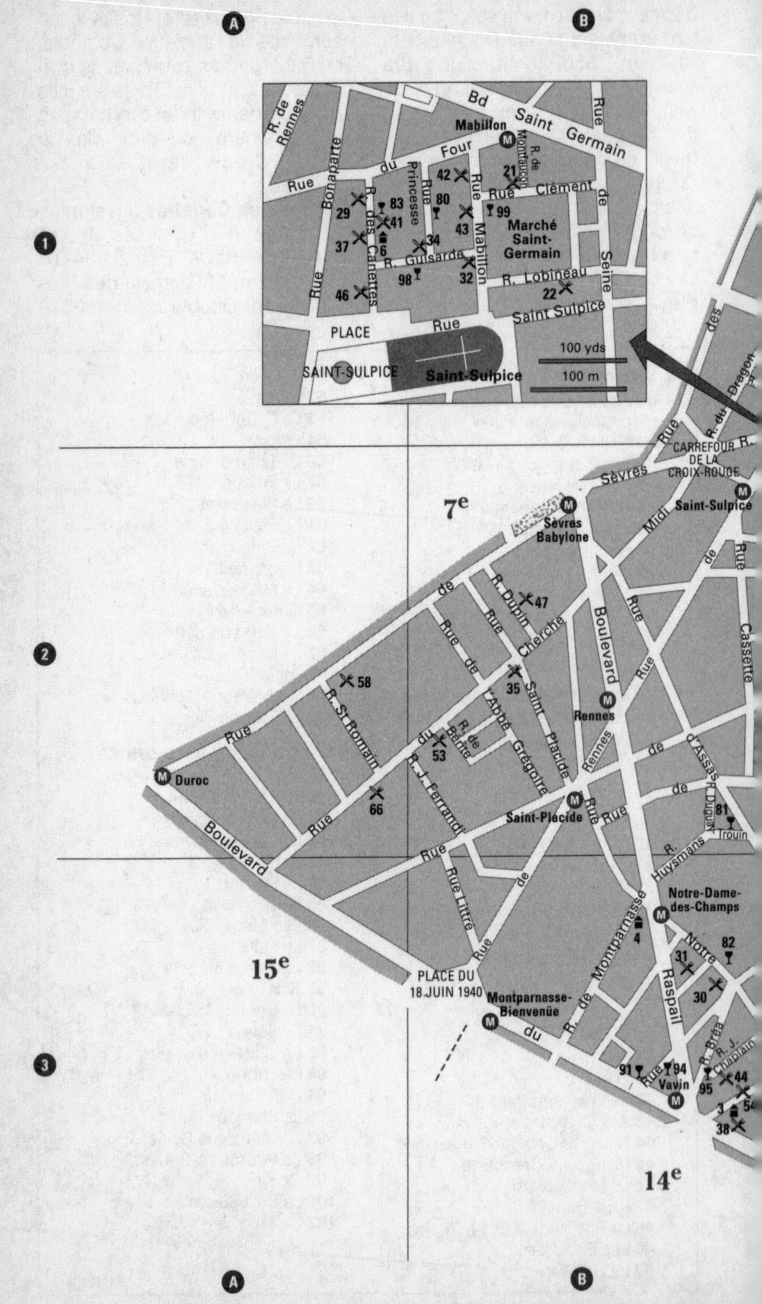
A
B
1
2
3
Bd Saint Germain
Mabillon
R. de Montfaucon
Rue du Four
R. de Rennes
Rue Bonaparte
R. des Canettes
Rue Princesse
Rue Mabillon
Rue Clément
Rue de Seine
Marché Saint-Germain
R. Guisarde
R. Lobineau
Rue Saint Sulpice
PLACE SAINT-SULPICE
Saint-Sulpice
100 yds
100 m
7e
15e
14e
Sèvres Babylone
CARREFOUR DE LA CROIX-ROUGE
Saint-Sulpice
Rue de Sèvres
R. du Dragon
Rue du Cherche Midi
R. Dupin
Rue de l'Abbé Grégoire
Rue Saint Placide
R. de Bérite
R. St Romain
R. J. Ferrandi
Boulevard Raspail
Rue de Rennes
Rue Cassette
Rennes
Rue d'Assas
R. Duguay Trouin
R. Huysmans
Saint-Placide
Duroc
Rue de Vaugirard
Rue Littré
Boulevard du Montparnasse
Notre-Dame-des-Champs
Rue Notre
Rue de Rennes
R. de Montparnasse
PLACE DU 18 JUIN 1940
Montparnasse-Bienvenüe
Vavin
R. Bréa
R. J. Chaplain
Rue Vavin

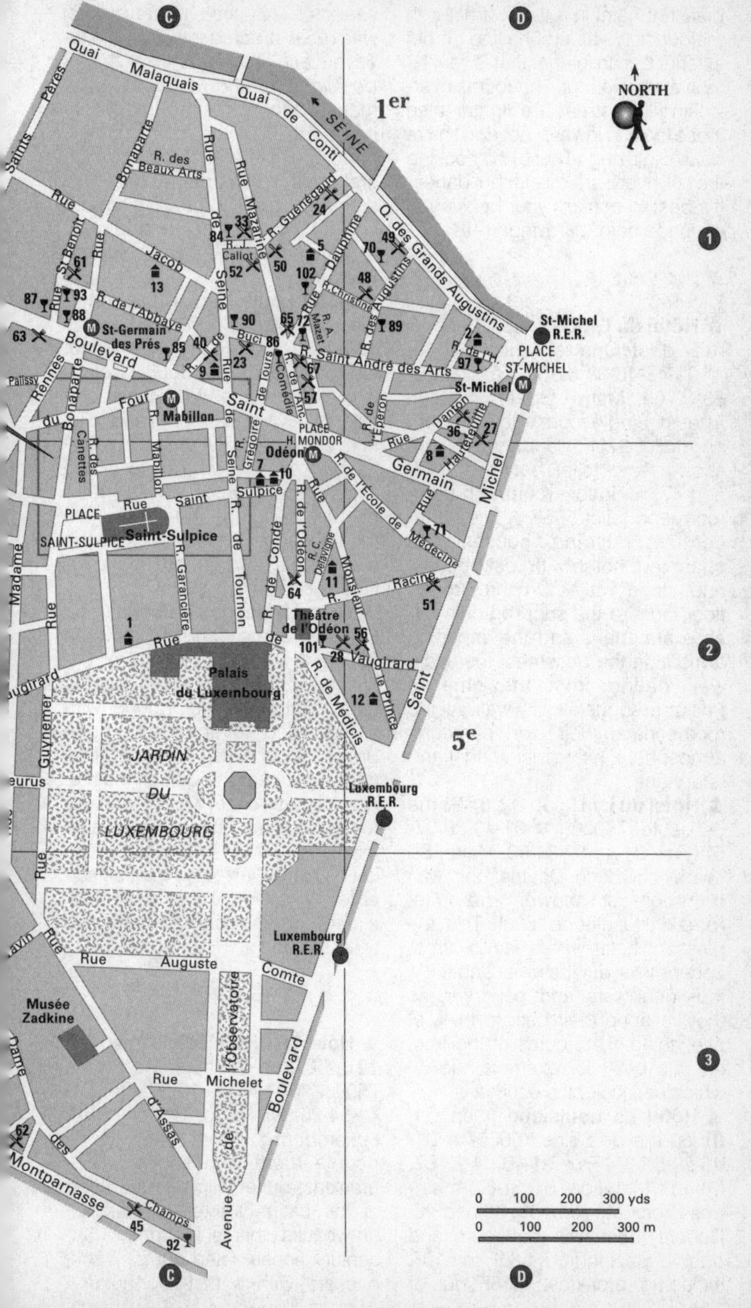

NORTH
1er
5e
SEINE
Quai Malaquais
Quai de Conti
Q. des Grands Augustins
St-Michel R.E.R.
PLACE ST-MICHEL
St-Michel
St-Germain des Prés
Mabillon
Odéon
PLACE H. MONDOR
PLACE SAINT-SULPICE
Saint-Sulpice
Théâtre de l'Odéon
Palais du Luxembourg
JARDIN DU LUXEMBOURG
Luxembourg R.E.R.
Musée Zadkine
Boulevard Saint Germain
Boulevard Saint Michel
Boulevard Montparnasse
Rue de Vaugirard
Rue Bonaparte
Rue de Seine
Rue Mazarine
Rue Dauphine
R. Guénégaud
R. Christine
R. des Grands Augustins
R. Saint André des Arts
Rue Jacob
R. de l'Abbaye
Rue St Benoit
R. des Beaux Arts
Rue de Buci
Rue du Four
Rue de Rennes
R. des Canettes
Rue Mabillon
Rue Saint Sulpice
R. Garancière
Rue de Tournon
Rue de Condé
R. de l'Odéon
Rue Monsieur le Prince
R. de l'École de Médecine
Rue Racine
Rue Danton
Rue Hautefeuille
R. de l'Éperon
R. de Médicis
Rue Madame
Rue Guynemer
Rue Auguste Comte
Rue Michelet
Rue d'Assas
Avenue de l'Observatoire
Rue Notre Dame des Champs
0 100 200 300 yds
0 100 200 300 m

pleasant hotel in a lively street with the curiosity value of having an old exterior but an interior that is very hi-tech and colourful. The rooms overlooking the street are lighter than those looking inward, but don't have double-glazing. Those overlooking the courtyard are quieter but darker. It's best to confirm your booking in advance before arriving.

☆☆☆ CHIC

Hôtel du Globe (map C2, **7**): 15 rue des Quatre-Vents 75006. ☎ 01-43-46-33-62-69. Fax: 01-46-33-62-69. Metro: Odéon. Shut in August. Single room with bathroom and toilet 275F; double room with shower and toilet between 390F and 475F; double room with bathroom and toilet 565F. A fine, 16th-century building houses this charming hotel with oak beams and stone walls. On the ground floor, admire the superb Louis XV-style armchairs and the imposing armour. In the basement there is a well dating from the time of Philippe Auguste's city wall. All the rooms have their own particular atmosphere, not to mention TV and telephone.

Hôtel du Lys (map D2, **8**): 23 rue Serpente 75006. ☎ 01-43-26-97-57. Fax: 01-44-07-34-90. Metro: St-Michel or Odéon. Double room with bathroom or shower and toilet (breakfast included) 520F. This is a pleasant hotel with a family atmosphere in a quiet street. Cable TV, individual safe and hairdryer, so they've done their best to think of everything. The rooms at the front are the best; for example, No. 9, which overlooks the courtyard.

Hôtel La Louisiane (map C1, **9**): 60 rue de Seine 75006. ☎ 01-43-29-59-30. Fax: 01-46-34-23-87. Metro: Mabillon or St-Germain-des-Prés. Bus Nos. 63, 87 and 96. Double room with bathroom and double-glazing from 585F to 610F, including breakfast; 535F out of season. This well-located hotel was reconstructed in the studio for Tavernier's film about jazz, *Autour de minuit* (*Round Midnight*). Minimalist decor, to the extent of having no TV in the rooms (shock, horror!). There are 70 rooms which are small, comfortable and well sound-proofed. Expensive unless you're looking for peace and quiet at any price. They don't accept cheques.

Hôtel Louis II (map C2, **10**): 2 rue St-Sulpice 75006. ☎ 01-46-33-13-80. Fax: 01-46-33-17-29. Metro: Odéon. E-mail: louis2@club-internet.fr. Rooms with shower and toilet 580F, with bathroom and toilet from 645F to 820F. A charming hotel for backpackers who have a little extra to spend. Situated in an 18th-century building, the rooms are modern and comfortable, though retaining a certain nostalgia for times gone by.

Grand Hôtel des Balcons (map C2, **11**): 3 rue Casimir-Delavigne 75006. ☎ 01-46-34-78-50. Fax: 01-46-34-06-27. Metro: Odéon. Double room from 600F to 1,060F with shower and toilet or bathroom. Breakfast-buffet free if it's your birthday! Right near the Odéon theatre, in a quiet little street which leads into rue Monsieur-le-Prince. Good value for money, which is unusual in the Latin Quarter. Art-deco interior, satellite TV. Credit cards accepted, except for American Express and Diner's Club.

☆☆☆☆ TRÈS CHIC

Hôtel Le Clos Médicis (map D2, **12**): 56 rue Monsieur-le-Prince 75006. ☎ 01-43-29-10-80. Fax: 01-43-54-26-90. Metro: Odéon; RER: Luxembourg. From 790F for a double room with shower. Free breakfast-buffet. Right in the heart of the Latin Quarter, without the drawbacks, this is a superb 18th-century house, fitted out for backpackers with a taste for luxury!

There is a fireplace in the huge lobby with comfortable sofas. In summer, there's a terrace where you can have breakfast or a drink. The 38 rooms are delightfully decorated, inspired by Provence. Double-glazing, air-conditioning, satellite TV, direct telephone, hairdryer, mini-bar and lovely tiled bathrooms.

Hôtel des Marronniers (map C1, **13**): 21 rue Jacob 75006. ☎ 01-43-25-30-60. Fax: 01-40-46-83-56. Metro: St-Germain-des-Prés. Double room with shower and toilet from 855F to 955F, with bathroom and toilet from 905F to 1,005F. Lurking at the end of a small courtyard, this place has a certain rustic charm. Behind it, there's a little garden with a veranda where you can have breakfast. You need to book a long time in advance. Ask for a room overlooking the St-Germain bell tower. The rooms are air-conditioned and there's satellite TV. Ask for room 12, all in red, with a four-poster bed and overlooking the garden.

WHERE TO EAT

☆ BUDGET

Orestias (map C1, **23**): 4 rue Grégoire-de-Tours 75006. ☎ 01-43-54-62-01. Metro: Odéon. Open lunchtime and evening until 11.30pm (last orders). Closed Sunday. Set menu 41F served lunchtime and evening (except Friday and Saturday evening). Plus a menu at 48F served every evening. À la carte, budget for a maximum of 100F. One of the last cheapish places still to be found in the Latin Quarter. On the 1st floor there is a room which can accommodate groups. Greek food but also some classic French dishes, try the *taramasalata, pikilia* (an assortment of Greek hors-d'œuvres), and *moussaka* and in season you'll find *marcassin* (young wild boar). À la carte there's sautéed veal, *keftedes*, roast shoulder of lamb. Very generous portions at low prices, which explains why it is always full, both with the local workforce and young tourists.

L'Assignat (map C1, **24**): 7 rue Guénégaud 75006. ☎ 01-43-54-87-68. Metro: Odéon. Open 7.30am to 8.30pm for the bar and noon to 3 or 3.30pm for the restaurant. Closed Sunday and in July. Set menu 60F at lunchtime, otherwise budget for a maximum of 75F. À la carte main course around 40–45F. A discreet local restaurant and a refuge for art dealers who've had enough of blowing 200F on lunch, as well as employees from the Monnaie de Paris and students from the Beaux-Arts who can still practise a pre-war form of payment, namely credit. Students on grants eat and then write what they've had in a notebook and then settle up at the end of the month. Weekly rehearsals of brass bands, such as the one from the Beaux-Arts, in the bistro cellar. Simple dishes in a crowded, fun atmosphere. Watch out for the owner's mother, who likes to look after the locals.

Le Golfe de Naples (inset map, **21**): 5 rue Montfaucon 75006. ☎ 01-43-26-98-11. Metro: Mabillon. Open daily until 11pm. Closed 24 December in the evening and all day on 25 December. À la carte only, budget for between 50F and 120F. Pizza lovers will be in seventh heaven in this simple *trattoria*. The pizzas are cooked on a wood fire and are amazingly good. Slightly brusque service though.

Le Petit Vatel (inset map, **22**): 5 rue Lobineau 75006. ☎ 01-43-54-28-49. Metro: Mabillon. Closed Sunday and Monday, as well as for a month around mid-January. Set meal 70F at lunchtime. À la carte, budget for 100F. This St-Germain-

Des-Prés institution is worth a visit. Pocket sized (and a small pocket at that!), it has recently been renovated, but has kept its low prices. Try the house *terrine*, the *tartines de tapenade*, *rognons aux vin blanc* (kidneys in white wine), *bœuf mironton*, sautéed lamb. Excellent value for money. Some good wines, choose between Gaillac, Cahors, etc. or a glass of Minervois or white Bergerac for 12F.

✕ **La Tourelle** (map D1-2, **27**): 5 rue Hautefeuille 75006. ☎ 01-46-33-12-47. Metro: Odéon or St-Michel. Open lunchtime and evening until 10.30pm. Closed Sunday, Bank Holidays and from the end of July to mid-August. Set menus 68F at lunchtime, 85F and 119F in the evening. À la carte around 120F. An old-style Paris restaurant situated in a 500-year-old house, with a magnificent corbelled turret and a little square dining room with a low ceiling. The clientele is made up of workers and regulars. Quick service and a good place to go for a filling lunch.

✕ **Indonesia** (map C-D2, **28**): 12 rue de Vaugirard 75006. ☎ 01-43-25-70-22. Metro: Odéon; RER: Luxembourg. Last orders 10.30pm (11pm Friday and Saturday). You're advised to book in the evening. Set menus 89F, 99F and 129F, à la carte around 150F. This is the only Indonesian restaurant in Paris that is organized as a workers' co-operative. The food is good and you are welcomed with a smile. There are a number of set menus in the form of *rijstafel* (literally rice-meal or rice-table). This comprises a whole series of little dishes typical of the islands of Java, Sumatra, Bali and the Celebration Islands: fish with coconut milk, *rendang* (beef with spices and coconut milk), *nasi goreng* (Indonesian sautéed rice), *balado ikan* (fish with peppered tomato sauce). The more expensive menus offer a greater diversity of dishes. An explanation about how to eat rice properly is provided! Delicious curries and kebabs with satay (peanut) sauce. Every Friday evening they have Balinese dance soirées.

✕ **La Crêperie des Canettes** (inset map, **29**): 10 rue des Canettes 75006. ☎ 01-43-26-27-65. Metro: Mabillon or St-Germain-des-Prés. Open until 11pm. Closed Sunday and Monday evening. Set menu 52F, à la carte budget for 100F including drinks. A little restaurant which also doubles as a tea-room and an ice-cream parlour. The *galette* (around 40F) and the *crêpe* reign supreme here (between 15F and 45F). There's nut salad and filled buckwheat *galettes* on the menu. The landlord's son took over recently, so there may be changes ahead!

✕ **Le Coffee Room M's** (map B2, **53**): 71 rue du Cherche-Midi 75006. ☎ 01-45-44-20-57. Metro: St-Placide or Sèvres-Babylone. Open daily except in August. Set menu 78F at lunchtime, budget for a maximum of 100F à la carte. Run by a former pastry chef for the Duke of Marlborough, this is a very cosy place, with Chesterfields and odd armchairs, offering excellent Anglo-French cuisine. Set meals during the week at lunchtime: dish of the day, dessert, coffee or tea, a glass of bordeaux wine at 20F. In the evening there are grills: chicken with barbecue sauce, coleslaw, roast potatoes, spare-ribs. On Sunday, there's a solid brunch at 120F.

☆☆ MODERATE

✕ **Le Vavin** (map B3, **30**): 18 rue Vavin 75006. ☎ 01-43-26-67-47. Metro: Vavin. Closed Sunday, Saturday evenings and in August. Set menu at lunchtime 100F; in the evening à la carte only, budget for 150F. A well-run brasserie full of students from the nearby colleges.

With the first rays of sun, the vast, south-facing terrace generally fills up straightaway with sun-worshippers. À la carte, the French brasserie classics include *andouillette de Troyes*, *entrecôte* with marrowbone, *coq au vin* with fresh pasta. For less ravenous appetites there are *croques au pain Poilâne* and a variety of salads.

✕ **Yamani** (map B3, **31**): 8 rue Ste-Beuve 75006. ☎ 01-45-48-49-80. Metro: Vavin. Open lunchtime and evening until 11pm. Closed Sunday and Bank Holidays, and for two weeks in August. There are a number of set menus from 60F to 200F. Kebab menus at 75F or 90F; 85F and 100F in the evening, which includes house soup with *tofu* and seaweed and a generous bowl of salad, followed by a series of kebabs. Amazing value for money and well known to everyone who goes to the cinema in Montparnasse in the evening. At lunchtime, there's an even cheaper menu to attract students and teachers from the nearby Assas college.

✕ **Bistro de la Grille** (inset map, **32**): 14 rue Mabillon 75006. ☎ and fax: 01-43-54-16-87. Metro: Mabillon. Open daily lunchtime and evening. Offers excellent cuisine from Lyons. Set menu 105F at lunchtime and 155F in the evening. For an à la carte meal, budget for 150F, wine extra. Interesting decor with walls covered in black-and-white photos of French cinema actors, as well as former French presidents. Try the ragout of duck with olives or the grilled *andouillette* with mustard sauce. In the evening there's à la carte or a set menu, as well as fine oysters and game in season. A tried and tested restaurant which has always been full during the 20 years that it's been here.

✕ **Marmite et Cassolette** (map C3, **45**): 157 boulevard du Montparnasse 75006. ☎ 01-43-26-26-53. Metro: Vavin or Raspail; or RER: Port-Royal. Closed Saturday and Sunday. Set menu 80F including a starter and a main course or a main course and a dessert, 100F with starter, main course and dessert. A kind of bistro annex to the gourmet O à la Bouche (*see the* '14th arrondissement'), this restaurant has inherited the efficient touch of its big brother while adding a little tradition. There are herrings and potatoes with oil, caramelized pork cheeks with cumin carrots, and apple with white cheese sorbet. Dishes of the day on the blackboard and a few wines by the glass. It is advisable to book in advance.

✕ **Bistro Mazarin** (map C1, **33**): 42 rue Mazarine 75006. ☎ 01-43-29-99-01. Metro: Odéon or Mabillon. Open until 11pm. Budget for around 100F without drinks. A little bistro on the corner of the rue Jacques-Callot, where the menu includes *andouillette*, steak tartare with chips, macaroni with gorgonzola. Neo-bistro decor, prompt service and a terrace where it's pleasant to sit in hot weather.

✕ **Le Machon d'Henri** (inset map, **34**): 8 rue Guisarde 75006. ☎ 01-43-29-08-70. Metro: St-Germain-des-Prés. Open lunchtime and evening until 11.30pm. Budget for around 150F for a full meal. A charming bistro with old stone and beams offering classic and generous dishes: lamb, *gratin dauphinois*, terrine of courgettes with tomato *coulis*, crispy fruit tart of the day. You are strongly advised to book.

✕ **Le Nemrod** (map B2, **35**): 51 rue du Cherche-Midi 75006. ☎ 01-45-48-17-05. Metro: St-Placide. Open 7am 10.30pm (8.30pm on Saturday). A corner café/brasserie that offers a full restaurant menu on Saturday lunchtimes only. Closed Sunday and some Bank Holidays, as well as for three weeks in August. Set menu 155F in the evening;

budget for 150F à la carte. Situated between rue St-Placide and rue du Cherche-Midi and proud owner of a lovely terrace, the Nemrod is a favourite place to eat in the area at lunchtime. A series of dishes of the day (eight every day) may include: steamed sautéed beef with paprika, Auvergne savoury with lentils, *confit de canard pommes à l'ail*, Auvergne sausage with white wine, mushroom omelette, or stuffed cabbage. Cheeses from the Auvergne and *charcuterie* from Mas-Rouget, in the Cantal. The wine list also looks good: an excellent Pouilly Fumé from Blondelet, Meursault and Burgundy whites from Roussilat, Morgon from Thévenet.

✕ **La Lozère** (map D1, **36**): 4 rue Hautefeuille 75006. ☎ 01-43-54-26-64. Metro: St-Michel or Odéon. Open lunchtime and evening until 10pm. Closed Sunday and Monday, in August, for a week at Easter and between Christmas and New Year's Day. Set menus 95F at lunchtime only, 130F and 160F in the evening. This is the restaurant of the Maison de la Lozère, and acts as a culinary ambassador for the *département* of the same name which is reminiscent, to a certain extent, of Ireland. An opportunity to taste delicious regional specialities in a rustic setting. À la carte, soup, *tripoux vinaigrette*, lamb from Lozère, *entrecôte fleur d'Aubrac* and white wine from the Aubrac every Thursday. Opposite is a co-operative shop where you can find all the regional products used in the cuisine you have just sampled, and next door is the tourist office and the booking service for rural *gîtes* – so the Lozère tourist authority is obviously on its toes!

✕ **Aux Trois Canettes** (inset map, **37**): 18 rue des Canettes 75006. ☎ 01-43-26-29-62. Metro: St-Germain-des-Prés or Mabillon. Service until 10.30pm. Closed Saturday lunchtime and Sunday, and also in August. Set menu 85F, à la carte budget for around 160F. Antonio, who is a genuine Neapolitan, has reigned here since the 1960s. The place has barely changed since then, and probably not much since the 1920s, when this 19th-century former wine depot first became a restaurant. On the ground floor, the decor has a nautical and volcanic theme, appropriate to the Naples region. Antonio remains faithful to the culinary traditions of his own country, so try black chick pea salad, sardines marinated in coarse salt, aubergines with olive oil, or *saltimbocca* of veal au San Daniele. In June, when the marché de la Poésie (literally Poetry Market) is held in place St-Sulpice, the Trois Canettes gives an international literary prize.

✕ **Noura** (map B3, **38**): 121 boulevard du Montparnasse 75006. ☎ 01-43-20-19-19. Metro: Vavin. Open daily noon to midnight. Set menus 97F at lunchtime and 149F in the evening. À la carte around 120F to 130F without drinks. Less refined than its namesake on the Right Bank, this restaurant does have one bonus, a little courtyard-garden where you can have lunch or dinner in summer. The Lebanese specialities are plentiful. Well-designed set dishes (with photos to back them up) allow beginners to make their choice quickly: *hors-d'œuvres* (small or large at 66F and 67F), mixed *chawarma* (thinly-sliced sirloin steak) (98F) or *chawarma houmous* (88F). Try *jellab*, a syrup of dates and pine-nuts, or Lebanese beer.

✕ **L'Arbuci** (map C1, **40**): 25 rue de Buci 75006. ☎ 01-44-32-16-00. Metro: Mabillon. Open daily noon to 1am. Set menu 77F at lunchtime, à la carte, budget for 150F. The set meal consisting of 'as many oysters and kebabs as you can eat' (146F) has become very popular here, along with the kebabs cooked on a spit for 87F. For anyone who is hungry but indecisive, the set meal of oysters and kebabs combines both for 137F. For those with a big appetite, the slab of beef is good and thick and the 'crispy' spareribs are very tasty. The basement houses a jazz group.

✕ **Le Petit Mabillon** (inset map, **42**): 6 rue Mabillon 75006. ☎ 01-43-54-08-41. Metro: Mabillon. Open lunchtime and evening. Closed Sunday and Monday lunchtime, as well as for two weeks at Christmas. Set menu 77F lunchtime and evening, à la carte around 130F. This cosy Sicilian restaurant makes the most of what little space it has – two dining rooms containing a dozen tables. The room in the basement has the advantage of being less noisy, and its windows have a view over the courtyard. There's excellent *bocconcini* and home-made fresh pasta. Come early if you have forgotten to book.

✕ **Aux Charpentiers** (inset map, **43**): 10 rue Mabillon 75006. ☎ 01-43-26-30-05. Metro: Mabillon, Odéon or St-Germain-des-Prés. Open lunchtime and evening until 11pm. Closed on the evening of 24 December, all day on 25 December and 1 May. Set menus 120F at lunchtime and 158F in the evening. Dishes of the day 76F and 89F, à la carte at least 89F. Full à la carte around 200F to 220F. A good restaurant in the former premises of a company of carpenters, with a fine bar, models, souvenirs, and photos connected with the profession. Traditional bourgeois cuisine with a dish for every day: on Monday, it's veal *marengo*; on Tuesday, *bœuf à la mode* with carrots; Wednesday, a savoury dish of lentils; Thursday, *pot-au-feu* and vegetables, etc. During the week, there's a set meal at lunchtime with specialities from Limousin.

✕ **Nouvelle Couronne Thaïe** (inset map B3, **44**): 17 rue Jules-Chaplain 75006. ☎ 01-43-54-29-88. Metro: Vavin. Open lunchtime and evening until 11pm. Closed Monday and Sunday lunchtime. At lunchtime, set menus 45F and 52F. In the evening there are set menus at 69F and 98F. À la carte around 120F. This is an excellent Thai restaurant with soft colours, subdued tones and tables well separated, situated in a quiet street. Good specialities at reasonable prices include fish soup with coconut milk, seafood or prawns with satay, chicken glazed with citronella, peppered sautéed duck with bamboo shoots. Lots of Chinese dishes too and a few steamed specialities. Wines at very reasonable prices: a quarter litre of red wine at 12F, Côtes-du-Rhône at 48F. Chinese and Thai beers.

✕ **Le Montagnard** (inset map, **46**): 24 rue des Canettes 75006. ☎ 01-43-26-47-15. Metro: St-Sulpice. Open daily until 11.30pm. Set menus 95F and 120F. Right in the heart of St-Germain-des-Prés, a true Savoy chalet with nourishing cuisine, useful after long walks in the forest, though the nearest you'll get to woodland in Paris is the Bois de Boulogne! Set menu with onion soup, *fondue savoyarde* or *escalope savoyarde*. À la carte, *fondue bourguignonne* at 98F (based on two people sharing) and *assiette du montagnard* (cold meats) at 92F.

✕ **La Muraille de Jade** (map C1, **67**): 5 rue de l'Ancienne-Comédie 75006. ☎ 01-46-33-63-18. Metro: Odéon. Open daily. Budget for around 120F. The regulars create a relaxed atmosphere here, where you can eat excellent Vietnamese, Thai or Chinese food. Attentive service, and the prices are reasonable.

✕ **La Table d'Aude** (map D2, **56**): 8 rue de Vaugirard 75006. ☎ 01-43-26-36-36. Metro: Odéon. Closed Sunday and the first three weeks in

August. Set menus from 65F during the week, at lunchtime 175F, with as much wine as you can drink. A rather unusual but good place to eat with simple, gourmet traditions hailing from Cathar country: *cassoulet de Castelnaudary, charcuterie* from the Black Mountain *à la poule grand-mère de l'Alaric*. The owner is fiercely proud of his region's heritage but expert at putting everyone at ease. One speciality which is not to be missed are the *haricots du père Falcou*, cooked with garlic and olive oil, served cold, as a starter.

☆☆☆ CHIC

✕ **Positano** (inset map, **41**): 15 rue des Canettes 75006. ☎ 01-43-26-01-62. Metro: St-Germain-des-Prés. Open lunchtime and evening (last orders midnight). Closed Sunday. Budget for a total of 150F. Without a doubt, one of the best pizza houses in Paris (from 55F to 75F). Try the *margherita* (tomato, mozzarella), *marinara* (tomato, garlic, oregano, basil), four seasons (tomato, ham, artichokes, mozzarella, mushrooms), *calzone romano* (pizza-turnover). The decor is pared down to the essential: a wood oven, butcher's hooks, check tablecloths and, of course, a smattering of Italians. It's best to arrive either very early or very late to get a seat.

✕ **L'Épi Dupin** (map B2, **47**): 11 rue Dupin 75006. ☎ 01-42-22-64-56. Metro: Sèvres-Babylone. Open until 10.30pm. Closed Saturday and Sunday, and also for three weeks in August. Set meal 110F at lunchtime, menu-carte 165F in the evening. This restaurant is full lunchtime and evening – you'll need to book at least a week in advance for the first service of the evening. The menu features daily finds from the market at Rungis market and offers a choice of six starters, eight main courses and six desserts every day. Try *tatin* of endives and caramelized goat's cheese, *croustillant de St-Jacques* with lemon and green peppers, *feuillantine* of warm potatoes and *mascarpone* sorbet. Great value for money and friendly and efficient service.

✕ **La Rôtisserie d'en Face** (map D1, **48**): 2 rue Christine 75006. ☎ 01-43-26-40-98. Metro: St-Michel or Odéon. Service noon to 2.30pm and 7.30pm to 11pm (11.30pm Friday and Saturday). Closed Saturday lunchtime and Sunday. Set menus 100F to 210F. Budget for around 250F à la carte. This restaurant has been a big hit, and has become a Left Bank institution in just a few years. The menu offers such delights as barbary duck with *gratin de blettes* and parmesan, *pastilla* (a sort of pie) of guinea fowl with aubergines and onions, pork cheek with carrots and fondant potatoes, and rotisseries. The only drawback is that it can be a bit noisy.

✕ **Les Bookinistes** (map D1, **49**): 53 quai des Grands-Augustins 75006. ☎ 01-43-25-45-94. Metro: Pont-Neuf or Odéon. Open until midnight. Closed Saturday and Sunday lunchtime. Set menus 160F at lunchtime, 180F Sunday evening. À la carte, budget for 300F. Consistently good, even if the bill can be a bit steep. A cheerful atmosphere makes it full every evening. The main courses are well thought out and the desserts are sublimely light.

✕ **La Cafetière** (map C1, **50**): 21 rue Mazarine 75006. ☎ 01-46-33-76-90. Metro: Odéon. Open until 11pm. Closed Sunday, Monday, two weeks between Christmas and New Year's Day, and for three weeks in August. Budget for between 190F and 230F for a full meal. Adored both for its caviar and its salmon, but there's nothing too snobbish about the atmosphere. The landlord welcomes everyone with the same courtesy. The tables, which are pretty close together, give the place a sort of roguish bistro chic. The menu is inspired by Italy: tagliatelle *à la sicilienne*, *penne arrabbiata*, mushroom risotto . . . but the blackboard regularly changes, offering various meat and fish dishes prepared in traditional French style. As you might imagine from the name, there is a collection of old coffee pots adorning the walls.

✕ **Bouillon Racine** (map D2, **51**): 3 rue Racine 75006. ☎ 01-44-32-15-60. Metro: Cluny-Sorbonne or Odéon. Open daily from 11am to 1am. Set menus 79F at lunchtime, from 107F to 218F in the evening. À la carte around 170F. A really good restaurant in the Latin Quarter is something of a rarity. Dating from the beginning of the 20th century and having endured several years as a humble works canteen, it was bought by Belgian investors, and has now been restored to its former Art Nouveau glory. The Belgian-inspired menu includes *goujonnettes* of Zeebrugge sole, *fumet* with grapefruit and beer, venison stew, crêpe with cinnamon ice-cream, apples caramelized *à la Rodenbach*. Beers include Rochefort, Chimay, Orval. There are tarts served at tea-time (4–6pm), and the famous Liège coffee is available by the jug all day.

✕ **Chez Albert** (map C1, **65**): 43 rue Mazarine 75006. ☎ 01-46-33-22-57. Metro: Odéon. Open until 11pm. Closed Sunday and Monday lunchtime, and also in August. Set menu 90F served until 8pm; 135F in the evening. À la carte, budget for somewhere between 160F and 200F. Always packed out, this Portuguese restaurant specializes in fresh fish: cod croquettes, grilled sardines or clams with coriander, followed by cod grilled over a wood fire, pork with clams, grilled squid sautéed with garlic and parsley and strips of potato, or grilled sea bass. You can also order a dish to be shared by two people: rice with seafood (*gambas*, crab, prawns, clam shells; 260F) or *catamapa* (monkfish with clams; 260F). Wash them down with a little Vinho Verde or Dao, an excellent red.

✕ **Wadja** (map B3, **54**): 10 rue de la Grande-Chaumière 75006. ☎ 01-46-33-02-02. Metro: Vavin. Open until 11pm. Closed Sunday and Monday lunchtime, and also in August. Set menu 89F with starter, main course and dessert at lunchtime, and starter and main course in the evening. À la carte meals at around 180F excluding drinks. This venerable institution, where a good number of poor artists used to come to eat for a few francs is, like La Coupole, one of the historic landmarks of Montparnasse (*see* '14th arrondissement'). The menu is good value for money, with good food a remarkable wine list. Chicken terrine with mushroom truffle jelly, crunchy sweet pepper with beef and *foie gras*, roast wild duck, leg of lamb with *carré rosé*. The service is fast and cordial.

✕ **Le Procope** (map C1, **57**): 13 rue de l'Ancienne-Comédie 75006. ☎ 01-40-46-79-00. Fax: 01-40-46-79-09. Metro: Odéon. Open daily from 11am to 1am. Set menus 130F and 178F. À la carte, budget for around 260F. The oldest café in Paris, and it's even air-conditioned. In 1686, one Francesco Procopio dei Coltelli came from Italy and opened a bar in Paris, introducing a new drink which was an enormous hit: coffee. The proximity of the Comédie Française made this a very literary and artistic place. In the 18th century, philosophers met here and it is believed that the idea behind the *L'Encyclopédie* originated from a conversation between Diderot and d'Alembert in this establishment. The French dramatist Beaumarchais sipped his coffee while waiting here to find out what the verdict was on his plays, staged at the nearby Odéon, and Danton, Marat and Camille Desmoulins came to discuss the Revolution here. Later, Musset, Sand, Balzac, Huysmans, Verlaine and many others liked to meet here. Today, it has kept its role as a place for intellectual meetings and even has a 'Presidential table'. The prices are still reasonable – the first menu comes with a starter, main course and dessert, served until 8pm every day. There's nothing particularly special about the cooking – the main thing is to be here!

✕ **Le Petit Lutétia** (map A2, **58**): 107 rue de Sèvres 75006. ☎ 01-45-48-33-53. Metro: Vaneau. Open daily lunchtime and evening. Last orders 11pm. Closed 1 May and at Christmas. Set menu 150F served lunchtime and evening. À la carte, budget for around 180F excluding wine. The dining room is retro, reminiscent of the good old inns of the provinces: engraved mirrors, green plants, proper tablecloths (and napkins!). Among the specialities, is duck *confit* with sautéed potatoes, calves' liver with grapes and potato gratin, beef steak, stuffed mussels and crème brûlée. There's a good selection of red meats. The dishes of the day on the blackboard are reasonably priced.

✕ **Le Petit Zinc** (map C1, **61**): 11 rue St-Benoît 75006. ☎ 01-42-61-20-60. Metro: St-Germain-des-Prés. Open daily noon to 2am. Set menu 168F served lunchtime and evening. À la carte around 260F. A classic restaurant with superb 1900s decor. Tables on a mezzanine or in corners. Quiet and intimate with soft lighting. A fine menu: fisherman's soup (with *rouille* – a garlic mayonnaise made with red chillies), fried side of beef, roast leg of lamb from the Baronet du Limousin, fisherman's pot. In the summer there are a few tables on the pavement.

✕ **La Bauta** (map C3, **62**): 129 boulevard du Montparnasse 75006. ☎ 01-43-22-52-35. Metro: Vavin. Open noon to 2pm and 7.30pm to 10.45pm. Closed Saturday lunchtime and Sunday, and from 8 to 22 August. At lunchtime, there's a set menu at 149F, in the evening à la carte at around 250F. If the decor is inspired by Venice (there is a fine collection of Venetian masks on the walls), the menu changes daily and takes its inspiration from Italian cuisine. Remarkably fresh produce is cooked with finesse and the list of pastas will please all spaghetti lovers. They are perfectly *al dente* but it's a shame that the portions are so small.

✕ **La Méditerranée** (map C2, **64**): 2 place de l'Odéon 75006. ☎ 01-43-26-02-30. Metro: Odéon; RER: Luxembourg. Open daily lunchtime and evening. Set meal starter plus main course or main course plus dessert at 150F, set menu at 180F. À la carte, budget for 230F per person. Years ago this restaurant would be filled with stars: Orson Welles, the French poet Louis Aragon, Picasso, Chagall, Man Ray and the actor Jean-Louis Barrault. Now back on its feet after a discreet makeover, whilst retaining the original charming decor created by Vertès, Bérard and Cocteau, this is a place for die-hard fans of Parisian life and style. À la carte, there's a handful of seductive starters, main courses and desserts: kipper *rémoulade* with apples, cod *brandade*, pan of squid with vegetables, fillet of roast seabass with dried tomatoes, *croustillant* of rhubarb and banana. There's valet parking for anyone determined to come by car.

✕ **Brasserie Lipp** (map C1, **63**): 151 boulevard St-Germain 75006. ☎ 01-45-48-53-91. Metro: St-Germain-des-Prés. Open daily until half past midnight. Set menu 196F, à la carte budget for around 250F. The most famous Parisian brasserie

– in fact almost a legend – the Lipp serves 500 meals a day and employs almost 80 people. François Mitterrand was an assiduous client and, since the 1920s, many famous people have been regulars here, from the writer François Mauriac to Georges Pompidou. No reservations, so the best idea is to come early or be willing to wait – it's worth it. The decor – large mirrors, fine ceramic panels, frescoes which are becoming blurred – is straight out of the 1900s, and is listed as a historic monument. Today, writers and stars of stage and screen are part of the clientele, but they still don't detract from the traditional-style menu, which offers few surprises and is not for the extremely figure-conscious. You won't find any artichokes (they create too much waste) nor mussels (because they need to be scraped)! A few years ago a revolution broke out with the arrival of four new dishes: roast pork, *navarin* of lamb, monkfish and calves' liver. Nothing like it had been seen for 20 years. Things are decidedly on the move, since they're now even changing the menu four times a year according to the seasons. Expensive wines, but there are half bottles of claret or Coteaux d'Aix.

✕ **Le Rond de Serviette** (map A2, **66**): 97 rue du Cherche-Midi 75006 ☎ 01-45-44-01-02. Metro: Vaneau. Open lunchtime and evening. Closed Saturday lunchtime, Sunday and three weeks in August. Set menus from 98F to 280F. Regulars can have their own *rond de serviette* (napkin ring) here. However, even if you're a new client, the welcome is excellent (though the napkin ring won't be granted until much later). A cosy setting, with harmonious pastel tones and a menu with wine included at 280F: red mullet tart with basil, roast sea-bream with fennel and poppy seeds, fillet of beef fried with wild mushrooms.

✕ **L'Alcazar** (map C1, **52**): 62 rue Mazarine 75006. ☎ 01-53-10-19-99. Metro: Odéon. Open daily lunchtime and evening (last orders 1am). Set menu 120F at lunchtime, 150F in the evening. Brunch 160F on Sunday (80F for children). Budget for at least 350F. The first French step for British restaurateur and style guru Sir Terence Conran, who dared to open this establishment in the heart of one of the most popular areas of Paris. An immense, immaculate white space which offers, on the first floor, a bar where you can have a drink and a few nibbles for around 150F and, on the ground floor, under a huge glass roof, a restaurant with French culinary classics (kidneys, *pot-au-feu*, grilled entrecôtes, etc.). Very fashionable and expensive, but at least the apéritif is free.

WINE BAR

✕ 🍷 **La Tour de Pierre** (map C1, **72**): 53 rue Dauphine 75006. ☎ 01-43-26-08-93. Metro: Odéon or Pont-Neuf. Open lunchtime and evening until 9pm. Closed Sunday, for a week between Christmas and New Year's Day, and for two weeks in August. Budget for 150F per person excluding drinks. Dish of the day 60F. Don't look for the *tour de pierre* (stone tower), you won't find it, though the cellar is original. There are newspaper articles and wine diplomas adorning the walls as well as the cup for Meilleur Pot (Best Bar) 1992 and the Gault et Millau Georges Dubœuf 1995 cup for the best bistro. Good atmosphere and generous food with excellent terrines, Lyons sausage, *andouillette*, duck *confit*.

TEA-ROOMS

– **Tch'a** (map D1, **70**): 6 rue du Pont-de-Lodi 75006. ☎ 01-43-29-

61-31. Metro: Odéon or Pont-Neuf. Open from 11am to 7.30pm. Closed Monday and the whole of August. Set menu 75F, à la carte around 130F. Gallery, tea-room, restaurant and shop, this minimalist space attracts a mainly female clientele, who appreciate its serenity. Run by a high priestess of tea hailing from Hong Kong, it is worth a visit not only for its amazing range of teas – green, white, yellow, blue-green, red, compressed and perfumed black – with unusual names: 'eyebrows of longevity', 'silver needles from Mount Jun', 'jade dragon', etc., but also for its lean cuisine: poached ravioli, turnip pâté, 'five flavours' sautéed in basil (leek, carrot, dry tofu, flavoured mushrooms, bamboo shoots), duck with salted prunes. A good place for thinkers and aesthetes. Included in the set menu is a main course, rice, a dessert and a cup of tea.

– **Restauration Viennoise** (map D2, **71**): 8 rue de l'École-de-Médecine 75006. ☎ 01-43-26-60-48. Metro: Odéon. Set menu 50F until 7pm. Budget for 50F on average for a meal. Open 9am to 7.15pm. Closed Saturday and Sunday, and in August. A real institution, opened in 1928 by two Hungarians. Two small dining rooms and an expensive menu. A hang-out for students from the Sorbonne or the British Institute, who are lured by the cakes – *strudel, flanni, kifli* – covered with raspberries and macaroons and accompanied by a small selection of teas or a thick Viennese hot chocolate.

THE ODÉON QUARTER

The Odéon district nestles between the Luxembourg gardens and the Seine. It keeps an academic toe in the water with the British Institute, the rue des Écoles and the Descartes Faculty of Medicine, but also has more commercial matters at heart, with a string of bars, pavement fast-food outlets, cinemas and shops. It fairly buzzes at all times of the day and night and is a great place to watch busy Parisians relaxing after work, though there are always a great many tourists around too, winter and summer, doing exactly what you are doing of course, so it would be hardly fair to grumble about them, would it?

★ Beyond the St-Michel fountain, there's another picturesque little jumble of streets, the **îlot St-André-des-Arts.** As you walk you'll notice vestiges of the past everywhere – a medieval turret, wrought-iron balconies and ancient, leaning walls. There are also some fine façades in rue St-André-des-Arts where Picasso had one of his studios, and little cafés and shops abound.

At No. 1 rue Danton stands the first house to be made of reinforced concrete, dating back to 1898. Surprisingly early for a material generally considered to be modern, it is the work of the architect François Hennebique, the inventor of concrete.

★ **La cour de Rohan:** entrance through rue du Jardinet or through the courtyard of Commerce-St-André. A good many visitors pass by this charming succession of little courtyards bordered by elegant middle-class 16th-century dwellings without really noticing them. The former locksmith's workshop, in the courtyard of the cour de Commerce-St-André, gives access to the first little courtyard, and has a tower which was once part of Philippe Auguste's city ramparts.

★ **La cour du Commerce-St-André:** built in 1776, it provides a very evocative image of old Paris, with its old houses, leaning walls and irregular partially cobbled street. Marat's former printworks, from where he published *L'Ami du peuple,* is at No. 8, whilst the first guillotine was built in the workshop of the joiner Tobias Schmidt at No. 9. It is said that Dr Guillotin carried out experiments on some unfortunate sheep here with his 'philanthropic decapitation machine'. In truth, the unfortunate doctor protested right up until his death in 1814 about the place history had accorded him in adopting his name for this ruthlessly efficient killing machine. All he did was to propose it to the Assembly; it was a certain Dr Louis who was entrusted with getting the machine ready, hence its first name of *louisette* or *louison*.

FROM ODÉON TO THE JARDIN DU LUXEMBOURG

★ The **carrefour de l'Odéon** is one of the liveliest areas in Paris. When the weather is fine, there are still crowds at two o'clock in the morning and even occasionally traffic jams. Danton lived in a house on the exact site of his statue and many of his fellow revolutionaries also lived around here, including Marat, who was famously murdered in his bath by Charlotte Corday.

★ The **rue Monsieur-le-Prince**, which used to be called rue des Fossés – meaning the Street of Ditches (because it followed Philippe Auguste's city wall) – has a number of fine dwellings. At No. 4, there is the superb gate of the Hôtel de Bacq (1750). Blaise Pascal, the French philosopher and mathematician, lived at No. 54, but practically every house has a plaque. In this same street, at No. 20, Malik Oussekine died under the blows of the military forces which rained down on rioting students in December 1986. And in the courtyard of No. 14, during excavation work carried out in December 1997, a Gallo-Roman dwelling was found. It appears to have been on the western edge of the former *Lutetia*, the first Paris, a large part of which lies under the modern city. Once the excavations have finished, the site is due to become a car-park – *quelle horreur!*

★ The **rue de l'École-de-Médecine** used to be called rue des Cordeliers, then later rue Marat. It was in the former Couvent des Cordeliers, from No. 15 to No. 21, that Danton founded his revolutionary club in 1790. There are interesting temporary exhibitions of contemporary art. ☎ 01-40-46-05-47. Open daily 11am to 7pm.

★ The **musée d'Histoire de la médecine:** 12 rue de l'École-de-Médecine 75006. ☎ 01-40-46-16-93. Open 2pm to 5.30pm. Closed Saturday in summer, Thursday in winter and Sunday all year round. Entry fee 20F. To reach the museum, go along the corridor, take the staircase passing *La Nature se dévoilant devant la Science*, then follow the arrows. In this unique hall, dating from the beginning of the 19th century, there is a series of cases in which all the major medical instruments are displayed, including the scalpel used to carry out the autopsy on Napoleon, the kit used by Littré (who wrote the acclaimed *Dictionnaire de la langue française*) and Laennec's stethoscope (Laennec was the inventor of this instrument). There is also a fine selection of absolutely terrifying forceps and scalpels and other 'instruments' used to open up bodies for embalming, etc.

To end with, there's a really choice item: the instrument which carried out a successful operation on Louis XIV for an anal swelling! This operation was important, because it led to the establishment of surgery as a medical practice, rather than allowing it to continue being carried out by barbers, as was the practice at that time. Also important is a wooden anatomical dummy made up of 3,000 separate parts, commissioned by Napoleon.

★ The **musée de la Minéralogie de l'école des Mines de Paris:** 60 boulevard St-Michel 75006. ☎ 01-40-51-91-39. RER: Luxembourg. Open Tuesday to Friday 1.30 to 6pm, Saturday 10am to 12.30pm and 2pm to 5pm. Guided tours by appointment. Entry fee 30F; reduced rate for students and carte Vermeil.

Founded in 1794, this museum has a collection of minerals which places it amongst the top five collections in the world. There are rocks, ores, gemstones and meteorites on display in the gallery (5,000 pieces). The museum has a total of 100,000 samples including 80,000 minerals and 15,000 rocks.

★ The **théâtre de l'Odéon** was built in 1808 in the rather heavy style typical of the period. It was memorably occupied in May 1968 by the rebelling students during the *événements* when left-wing idealism swept the country. The Roman helmets then used for theatrical performances protected many a student's head on the barricades. On the inside there's a fine ceiling by André Masson.

Listed houses line the square. At No. 2 lived one of the most charismatic heroes of the Revolution: Camille Desmoulins. At No. 1 stood the former Café Voltaire, a literary centre for 150 years, where the Americans of the Lost Generation used to meet (Scott Fitzgerald, Hemingway, Sinclair Lewis, etc.). You'll find superb 17th- and 18th-century private residences (in particular in rue de Condé and rue de Tournon, etc.) absolutely everywhere in this quarter. A clairvoyant reputed to have a certain Bonaparte as a client lived at 5 rue de Tournon and No. 17 is where Gérard Philipe, a French actor, died at home.

★ The **jardin** and the **palais du Luxembourg:** one of the most beautiful gardens in Paris and as romantic as you could wish for. The large, formal French-style flowerbeds have been loved by Baudelaire, Verlaine, George Sand and many others. Set right in the middle of the Latin Quarter, the Luxembourg (known as the 'Luco' to the older generation) has always been the chosen place of both writers and lovers. If it could talk, it would have wonderful tales to tell of the historical and literary life of France. Rousseau and Diderot walked through these gardens which Watteau painted in his youth, as did David and, to a lesser extent, Delacroix. They fell somewhat into disuse during the Revolution, but by the 19th century had become a great favourite with the chattering classes once more. The characters in Victor Hugo's *Les Misérables* also visited the gardens during the course of their struggles, as did Balzac in real life who, they say, used to walk along past the railings in his dressing-gown, a chandelier in his hand. The writer André Gide is another of the great literary figures who were 'Luco' regulars. During the Second World War the gardens concealed the clandestine meetings of Resistance fighters who might have run into yet more artistic figures in the shape of Kessel, Modigliani or Zadkine. Hemingway came to practise his painting and Lenin to see the chair attendant with whom he had fallen in love.

● On the left of the entrance through the place Edmond-Rostand is the superb fontaine de Médicis, a popular meeting-place surrounded by plane trees. It dates from 1624, but the sculptures are 19th century.

• On a lawn on the rue Guynemer side you'll find the original *statue de la Liberté,* (albeit a much smaller version than the famous one in New York harbour) by its creator, sculptor Bartholdi. Above the balustrade which runs around the central ornamental lake are statues of the queens of France. Carps splash about in the lake and there's an open-air kiosk and refreshment area.

• There are a number of unexpected things in this garden, including a school of horticulture, and beehives which produce several hundred kilos of honey every year. The garden's orchard has 200 varieties of apples and pears, some of which are very rare.

• For children there is the famous *guignol* (puppet show), which seems to have been going on forever, and shows no sign of packing up. There are shows on whenever kids have a day off school (Wednesday, Saturday, Sunday and in the holidays) from 11am. Entrance fee: 24F, 18F for groups. ☎ 01-43-26-46-47 (to find out what the programme and show times are). For groups, book on: ☎ 01-43-29-50-97. Nearby there's a children's garden (you have to pay to get in). They can also go pony riding or play on the seesaw while eating candyfloss. The roundabout, designed by Charles Garnier (the architect of the Opéra), is more than a century old and still working.

• If you fancy a game of tennis, there are courts available to book – usually on the day you want to play at the tennis chalet beside the courts. They are very much in demand so you can only play for 30 minutes, but what a chic venue. You will also be surprised to learn that the garden is home to a 'real tennis' court. Of course, there's no longer anyone who plays it with the 'palm of the hand' – its name in French, *jeu de longue paume*, means game of the long palm. Information: ☎ 01-45-34-27-84.

You will also sometimes see people practising Tai Chi Chuan near the tennis courts.

• The **palais du Luxembourg**, which houses the **Sénat**, was commissioned by Marie de Médicis, Henri IV's second wife, who was getting bored at the Louvre after his death. The architect was inspired by the Pitti Palace in Florence, which was the Queen's home town. Rubens decorated it with paintings tracing the life of Marie de Médicis (they are now in the Louvre). The palace was later used as a prison during the Revolution. One of its famous occupants, Jaques-Louis David, was recognized by his jailer as having been the latter's son's teacher. The jailer therefore gave him some brushes, enabling David to occupy himself during his incarceration. This resulted in his finest self-portrait and a unique landscape, today also displayed in the Louvre. It was also at the Palais du Luxembourg that Talleyrand and Napoleon plotted the Coup d'État. After the upheavals of the revolutionary era, the palace was restored to more peaceful political matters and the garden to the people. There are organized tours. For information ring: ☎ 01-42-34-20-60.

• Next to the Senate, at 19 rue de Vaugirard, is the **musée du Luxembourg** (temporary exhibitions). Open 11am to 6pm (8pm on Thursday). Closed Monday. ☎ 01-42-34-25-94.

• As you come out, don't forget to measure yourself against one of the metres of marble placed at head height at 36 rue de Vaugirard (on the right of the coach entrance). These were installed during the revolutionary period in order to get the people accustomed to the new measurements, first introduced at that time.

★ The **musée Zadkine:** 100 *bis* rue d'Assas 75006. ☎ 01-43-26-91-90. Metro: Vavin or Notre-Dame-des-Champs; RER: Port-Royal. Bus Nos. 38, 82, 83 and 91. Open 10am to 5.40pm. Closed Monday and Bank Holidays. Entry fee 22F; concessions 15F. Groups must book.

Lovers of sculpture will adore this delightful museum at the end of a narrow alley. Set in a marvellous garden, you are welcomed by numerous works by Ossip Zadkine, positioned around a charming country house which is a real surprise in this part of Paris. Of Russian origin, Zadkine arrived in Paris in 1909. In 1928, along with his wife Valentine Prax, who was also a painter, he moved into his 'Assas folly', where he lived until his death in 1967. Zadkine was a famous figure in Montparnasse in the 1920s. A friend of Guillaume Apollinaire, Blaise Cendrars and Max Jacob, he also rubbed shoulders with the likes of Braque, Chagall, Kessel, Modigliani and Soutine.

Open to the public since 1982, the museum shows almost 100 works laid out in chronological order over five halls. All of Zadkine's creative periods are represented: primitivism, cubism, the period inspired by mythological antiquity and abstract art. There are also some of his works in wood on show, such as *Prométhée* (1955), *les torses de Pomone* (1960), *d'Éphèse* (1920), *d'Hermaphrodite* (1925); and in bronze, *Formes et Lumières* (1923), *Femme à l'éventail* (1923), *La Naissance de Vénus* (1950), *Les Ménades* (1929). Works in stone include *Tête héroïque* (1908) and *La Sainte Famille* (1912). Finally, Zadkine's plans for monuments, such as *La Ville détruite* (1947) or *Van Gogh marchant à travers champs* are also displayed.

The museum has renovated and opened 'the workshop' and three or four times a year plays host to French and overseas contemporary artists.

ST-GERMAIN-DES-PRÉS

St-Germain has a personality all of its own. It's quite hard to actually mark out the boundaries (Philippe Auguste's city wall, which was on a level with the rue de l'Ancienne-Comédie, set the boundaries between the Latin Quarter and the Faubourg St-Germain in 1200), but this quarter has a history and a culture which are in many respects very different from those of the adjacent Latin Quarter. Sadly, little by little, the spirit of St-Germain-Des-Prés, as personified by Sartre, Simone de Beauvoir and playwright Boris Vian – among others – is fading away. Luxury shops are taking over from cultural institutions and the literary world is finding itself increasingly sidelined. However, it's still an interesting area to explore, full of antique shops, art galleries, shops selling soft furnishings and chic decorations for the home and, still, some bookshops.

A BRIEF HISTORY

Initially the whole history of St-Germain-des-Prés was centred around its abbey. From 555 AD (the date on which St Germain, bishop of Paris, built the first basilica) to the Revolution, the abbey's intellectual influence never faded. In the Middle Ages the St-Germain Fair was a great success, with gambling, acrobats, animal trainers (a rhinoceros was put on show for the first time) and fire-eaters all attracting huge crowds. Henri IV came here to gamble – and lost. He was forced to ask his chief minister, Sully, to lend him 3,000 *écus* because, as he put it, 'the merchants have got me by the short and curlies'.

During the 18th and 19th centuries the middle-classes and the publishers of the Faubourg St-Germain reigned supreme, before giving way to the intellectuals of the 20th century. 'It's never been a real quarter, you could never find whores, or peanut sellers', said the poet Jacques Prévert before moving out to Montmartre, whilst Boris Vian defined it as an island, the last haven of creativity and non-conformism.

At the end of the 1930s, Le Flore (see below) picked up the rowdier elements who had been kicked out of the Deux Magots (see below). This Prévert contingent was joined in 1939 by Jean-Paul Sartre and Simone de Beauvoir, who provided the quarter's intellectual input. Paradoxically, the Occupation during the Second World War was a rich moment in the life of St-Germain. The Germans, surprisingly, were thin on the ground here, leaving the poets and writers to meet and work in the cafés as usual, though over almost empty plates. Simone de Beauvoir always arrived first at Le Flore in winter, to be sure of a place near the stove. 'Fiestas' brought everyone together to listen quietly to jazz, to read poems and put on little plays.

With the Liberation began St-Germain's golden age, being colonized by young people who, after the dark days of the war, wanted to party. Vian noted ironically: 'Everyone's coming here because this is where the works that the whole world is talking about are created and because they want to see the painters and intellectuals, but they've already gone!' This was also the age of the clubs. Be-bop was all the rage. The press invented orgies and produced exaggerated reports about the excesses of the 'nightclub rats': frenetic dancing, eccentric clothes and morals, graffiti and existentialist poetry were the order of the day. This was also the period that gave us the mime artist Marcel Marceau and Juliette Gréco, the nightclub muse, dressed all in black.

Like many other quarters of Paris, clothes shops, fast-food outlets and banks have invaded St-Germain. The first victims of the resulting spiralling rents were the bookshops, and then came the sociological changes as the original population was forced to move out and flashy signs and commercialism descended.

However, if St-Germain is no longer quite what it was in its heyday, there are still some traces left. The famous cafés of the Left Bank – Les Deux Magots, Le Flore and the Brasserie Lipp – are still going strong, frequented by publishers, writers, artists and politicians.

WHAT TO SEE

★ The **église St-Germain-des-Prés:** the oldest church in Paris. Between the 8th and the 13th centuries the abbey had great influence and became an important seat of learning. Unfortunately there's not much left of the great abbey, though it prospered until the Revolution and almost managed to survive those very turbulent times. However, in 1802 the chapel of the Virgin, the cloister and the chapter were demolished. The great tower and the chancel still remain from the 12th century, whilst the presbytery on the right dates from the 18th century.

Inside there are a few 'salon' frescoes from the 19th century, but their somewhat cold and pretentious style contrasts greatly with the naïve and spontaneous simplicity of the Roman sculptures. The nave is Gothic, replacing the previous one, which was Roman. The chancel and the ambulatory are 12th century. In the latter is the tomb of the poet Nicolas Boileau and the tomb of the great 17th-century philosopher, René Descartes, is also here. On the left of the church there is a little square with a sculpture by Picasso, a homage to Apollinaire and the ruins of the chapel of the Virgin. The *palais abbatial*, a fine stone and brick house, home to the abbots from 1586 until the Revolution, stands at the corner of the rue de l'Abbaye and the passage de la Petite-Boucherie.

There is a fine original fountain presented to Paris by the Canadian province of Quebec on the corner of rue Bonaparte and place du Québec. It is the very image of the ice which covers the rivers in Canada for parts of the year.

★ The **place de Furstenberg:** this is one of the loveliest squares in Paris, and often a summertime venue for groups of musicians who 'jam' in the centre. The ornate street lamps give the whole area a lovely romantic atmosphere but the benches have been removed by the police, who thought that the local tramps were spending too much time on them.

There are a number of picturesque streets around the square, lined with 17th- and 18th-century houses, such as the twisting rue Cardinale, rue de l'Échaudé and rue de Bourbon-le-Château. In the rue de Seine there are some fine private residences, and the occasional little courtyard with façades covered in moss. The rue Jacob has numerous elegant interior design shops and the whole area is full of little art galleries. Important business is conducted at La Palette, over a glass of Cabernet Sauvignon, naturally. This is a lovely spot to sit on a sunny afternoon, but if it's raining there is an atmospheric backroom in which to sup your *express* and draw on your Gauloise with suitable Gallic aplomb.

★ The **musée Delacroix:** 6 rue de Furstenberg 75006. ☎ 01-44-41-86-50. Metro: Mabillon or St-Germain-des-Prés. Open 9.30am to 5pm (last entry 4.30pm). Closed Tuesday, as well as 1 January, 1 May and Christmas Day. Groups must book in advance: ☎ 01-40-13-46-46. The museum occupies three rooms of the apartment that the painter had converted in 1857 in order to be closer to the church of St-Sulpice, one of whose chapels he had been entrusted with decorating (the Chapel of Holy Angels). Unfortunately by this time he was already ill and it proved to be his last work.

As well as the numerous paintings, engravings, sketches, watercolours and pastels on display, there are also letters and documents that show his ties with Baudelaire, George Sand and Théophile Gautier, and offer a slightly more intimate view of the man. You can also see items of furniture, including his painting table, and a few objects from his trip to Morocco. The workshop, located in the private garden, was built according to Delacroix's own plans.

The museum is a relatively young one, having been opened in 1971, and is quite small, but nevertheless it is worth a look round before you let yourself be lured away by his major works on show at the Louvre.

★ The **marché de Buci:** although the stalls are mainly set up in the rue de Seine, it is still known as the 'Buci market' after the rue de Buci. It's quite small, but picturesque for the visitor – normally offering a choice of fresh fruit, cheese, wine and flowers, with prices about on a par with any other Parisian market, despite its central tourist location. There are also a couple of small supermarkets and several other shops in the nearby roads. The terraces of the restaurants Le Dauphin and the Bistro du Marché in the rue de Buci, are particularly popular when the weather is fine. An ideal place to watch the street theatre and the world going by in general. There are also two excellent pâtisseries, luxury charcuteries, and superb bakeries. The market is usually shut for a couple of hours early afternoon, but opens again at around 4pm, and on Sunday, when the larger Parisian markets are cleaning up and pulling down the shutters, late risers can still find plenty to buy here.

★ The **rue des Saints-Pères:** on the corner of rue Jacob is a Mussolini masterpiece mixed with a touch of Stalinism: the Faculty of Medicine. You may feel utterly staggered that this monstrosity was allowed to be built, but it does have one saving grace: the fine bronze door by the sculptor Paul Landowski, who sculpted the *Christ* of Corcovado, in Rio de Janeiro.

Opposite the Faculty of Medicine, at 30 rue des Saints-Pères, is 'Debauve et Gallais, selling fine and hygienic coffees, vanillas, teas and chocolates'.

★ **Towards the quais:** leaving the rue Dauphine, turn left. You'll find the Impasse de Nevers, built in the 13th century and still lined with old houses. It's adjacent to a vestige of Philippe Auguste's city wall.

6TH

★ The **musée de la Monnaie:** 11 quai Conti 75006. ☎ 01-40-46-55-35. Open Tuesday to Friday 11am to 5.30pm, Saturday and Sunday noon to 5.30pm. Closed Monday. Free on Sunday. Guided tour around the workshops, in which commemorative medals are still manufactured, at 2.15pm, Wednesday and Friday plus a film lasting 30 minutes.

This museum houses a complete collection of coins, medals, machines, tools, documents, and paintings. All coins used to be minted here, but today only collectors' medals and coins are made. Among the exhibits there is the '*franc à cheval*', minted in 1360 to celebrate the liberation of Jean II le Bon (the Good). The collections of medals are excellent, and La Monnaie is the world's leading publisher of art medals. There are also activities and workshops for children.

Until 2002 you will be able to see an exhibition on the theme of 'The Euro and the coins of Paris'. Guided tours on Sunday at 3pm: 18F. Information: ☎ 01-40-46-55-35.

★ Slightly further along the quai past La Monnaie is the **Institut de France**, a splendid Baroque building crowned with a famous cupola (1663). This is the site of the former Tour de Nesle, where the three daughters-in-law of Philippe le Bel met their lovers.

Today, it houses the **bibliothèque Mazarine** and the 40 'Immortals' of the **Académie française** – although many French people have only actually heard of maybe half of them. Created by Richelieu in 1635, this noble institution, whose main task is to defend the French language, particularly from the pervasive invasion of Anglo-American terms such as 'le walkman', 'le parking' etc., finally accepted a woman – Marguerite Yourcenar – into its ranks, after thinking about it for three centuries. Two more followed: Jacqueline de Romilly and Hélène Carrère d'Encausse, though it still couldn't be claimed that the floodgates have exactly opened. Every Thursday, the academicians meet to work on a new dictionary. The last anyone heard they were said to be up to 'E' and they reckon they'll be finished in about 50 years.

In front of the Institute is the pedestrian bridge called the Pont-des-Arts, the last bastion for romantics, painters and lovers, that leads to the Louvre. It was erected a number of years ago to replace the former walkway, which had succumbed to repeated blows from barges.

A little further on is the École des Beaux-Arts with one entrance in rue Bonaparte and another on the quai Malaquais. This is the principal school for fine arts in France.

★ The **rue Visconti:** between rue de Seine and rue Bonaparte, this is a narrow little street almost entirely lined with 16th-century residences. Racine died at No. 24. Balzac set up a print works at No. 17.

★ The **rue du Dragon:** contains numerous old and elegant houses. Two picturesque streets nearby have retained the silhouette they had in the Middle Ages: **the rue du Sabot** and the **rue Bernard-Palissy**. The **rue du Four**, which runs from the carrefour de la Croix-Rouge, takes its name from the French word for oven (*four*), as it was at one time the property of the abbey of St-Germain-des-Prés, where the local inhabitants had to go to bake their bread.

★ **The area around St-Sulpice:** there's a guided tour of the church of St-Sulpice and the crypts on the 2nd Sunday of each month at 3pm. This massive building is of little interest apart from its five bells. Baudelaire and de Sade were baptized here and Camille Desmoulins and Victor Hugo were married here. On the inside there is a very fine fresco by Delacroix, *La Lutte de Saül avec l'Ange* (first chapel on the right as you go in). On a level with the chancel, inlaid in the floor, there is a brass line representing the Paris zero meridian.

Kestrels have built their nests inside the church towers. It's a perfect site for birds which are said by the French to be 'making the sign of the Holy Ghost' when they hover over a single spot for several seconds.

On a much more secular and earthy note, there was a famous brothel called Chez Miss Beety at No. 36 rue St-Sulpice beside the church. Priests formed a not insubstantial part of its clientele, as well as at a similiar establishment called Chez Alys, at No. 15.

The little **rue des Canettes** runs from place St-Sulpice to the rue du Four. It is very old indeed (13th century), and has a number of fine houses. Its name is thought to come from the superb bas-relief on the façade of No. 18 which represents three ducklings (*canettes*) playing in the water.

The rue Guisarde and the **rue Princesse** also contain some charming old houses. The 18th-century painter Chardin, who assisted in restoring the paintings at the Château of Fontainebleau, lived at 13 rue Princesse.

★ The **rue du Cherche-Midi:** starting at the carrefour Croix-Rouge, this old Roman road was known as the Chemin de Vaugirard in the 14th century. It is lined with elegant private residences, many of which have interesting connections with the past. At No. 18 there is a lovely 18th-century decorated façade, whilst at No. 19 there's a sign from the same period.

On the corner of boulevard Raspail there is a memorial to the writer François

Mauriac and at No. 40 there is a fine residence dated 1710 which belonged to Rochambeau, who won the Battle of Yorktown (in the American War of Independence). Garat, the Minister of Justice who read Louis XVI's death sentence out, lived in the 18th-century residence at No. 44, and in 1831 the abbé Grégoire, another figure from the Revolution and founder of the Conservatoire des Arts and Métiers, died there. Laennec (the inventor of the stethoscope) lived on the corner of rue de l'Abbé-Grégoire. At No. 72, at the end of the courtyard, there is a lovely private garden whilst at No. 86, right at the end, there is a picturesque fountain showing Jupiter.

★ The **hôtel du Petit-Montmorency:** 85 rue du Cherche-Midi 75006. Built in 1743, the building now houses the musée Hébert. Nearby, at No. 89, there is a house from the same period which was home to Madame Sans-Gêne, the wife of Marshal Lefebvre. In the hall, on the right, there is an elegant stairway with wrought-iron banisters and a statue of Napoleon at its foot. Today it is the Embassy of Mali.

★ The **musée Hébert:** 85 rue du Cherche-Midi 75006. ☎ 01-42-22-23-82. Metro: Duroc, Vaneau or St-Placide. Open 12.30 to 6pm; Saturday, Sunday and certain Bank Holidays, 2pm to 6pm. Last entrance at 5.30pm. Closed Tuesday. Full price entry fee 16F. This is another of those odd little museums showing interesting collections of work, this time by the 19th-century painter Hébert (1817–1908). Like his cousin, the novelist Stendhal, Hébert fell in love with Italy and worked there for many years. He managed to capture its light and colours, and created a body of work which is highly original (although not very well known). In some ways this is a museum of the Italian people and landscape. There is a fine series on peasant women and children as well as moving portraits such as *Le Petit Brigand* and *Le Petit Violoneux endormi.* The sensuality of Italy is apparent in the languid pose of *Rosa Nera à la fontaine.* Other remarkable canvases include the disturbing and tragic *Ophelia, Les Joueuses de harpe,* and *Vierge entre deux anges.* The apartments are filled with fine furniture, period oak panelling and there is a gorgeous portrait of the *Comtesse Pastré* and a remarkable nude, *La Fille aux joncs.*

6TH

★ The **hôtel Lutétia:** 45 boulevard Raspail 75006. ☎ 01-49-54-46-46. Fax: 01-49-54-46-00. Metro: Sèvres-Babylone. Some of the sculptures on the façade are by the sculptor Paul Belmondo (father of the actor Jean-Paul). General De Gaulle and his wife spent their wedding night here.

During the Second World War, the hotel was requisitioned by the German Army. In order not to let the occupying forces get their hands on the best wines, the owner had the cellar walled up. The scheme appeared to have worked until one day a German officer happened to see an old menu offering some excellent vintages. The hotel staff were all interrogated to discover what had happened to these treasures . . . but without success, and the wine was preserved for French rather than German palates. In 1945 the Lutétia accommodated some of the French who had managed to survive the concentration camps and its rooms were transformed into an infirmary. The lists of these temporary inhabitants were displayed on the street, enabling families to search for news of their loved ones.

Today, the Lutétia is once again a superb four-star hotel, and has been entirely renovated. The rooms are cheaper at weekends, but everything is relative and you'll still need to budget for around 1,250F for a double room.

CULTURE

– **Le Lucernaire** (map B3, **82**): 53 rue Notre-Dame-des-Champs 75006. ☎ 01-42-22-26-50 and 01-45-44-57-34. Metro: Notre-Dame-des-Champs or Vavin. Open until 1am. Closed Sunday for theatre performances. The National Centre of Art and one of the liveliest places in Paris. All year round, there are more than 30 plays, a selection of the best art and a gallery with paintings. After the show you can eat at the restaurant of the same name (except Saturday lunchtime and Sunday) (☎ 01-45-48-91-10). Set menu 98F, and à la carte around 180F.

WHERE TO GO FOR A DRINK

There are lots of bars in this area, though the quality isn't always too high. So, if **Pousse au Crime** is a bit full, and if there's no room at **Chez Georges**, try the **Frog Princess** for some home-brewed French beer or the **Shannon** to experience the French version of an Irish pub.

🍸 **Le Flore** (map C1, **87**): 172 boulevard St-Germain 75006. ☎ 01-45-48-55-26. Metro: St-Germain-des-Prés. Open daily 7am to 1.30am. A large café absolutely loaded with history. Opened in 1890, it was first frequented by the founders of Action française, and had a clientele inclined towards the left-wing, including Sartre, Camus, Jacques Prévert and his brother Pierre. It was sold a few years ago for a staggering sum, reputed to be some 14 million francs. Why would anyone pay such a fortune? Well, obviously coffee, cakes and champagne sell well. There is a very pleasant outside area with tables giving on to the street, open in summer but protected by glass in the winter. The café itself has a classic art-deco interior, little changed since the War.

🍸 **Les Deux Magots** (map C1, **58**): 6 place St-Germain-des-Prés 75006. ☎ 01-45-48-55-25. Metro: St-Germain-des-Prés. Open daily 6.30am to 1.30am. Coffee 22F, salads from 40F to 90F, a glass of wine from 35F to 60F. An institution in Paris, Les Deux Magots is the best observation post over the St-Germain *passeggiata*; watching passers-by is a national sport here. Delicious and timeless in the afternoons, the dining room on the 1st floor is less well known.

Les Deux Magots derives its name from the 19th-century shop originally on the site which sold Chinese silk and fabrics. When, in 1875, a café also selling spirits took over, it kept the name. The current decor dates from 1914. By 1885 it had become established as a meeting place for the literary glitterati and the poets Verlaine, Rimbaud and Mallarmé liked to meet here. In 1925 it was the turn of the Surrealists: Breton, Desnos, Bataille, Artaud, as well as Picasso, St-Exupéry, Giacometti and Hemingway. The writer and diplomat Jean Giraudoux, who was for a time head of the French Ministry of Information during the Second World War, used to take his breakfast here at 10am on the dot every morning. In 1933 the Prix des Deux-Magots, a prize for literary excellence, was created and proved to be adept at selecting the best of contemporary French writing. In the 1950s Sartre and Simone de Beauvoir would spend two hours writing non-stop every day, whilst inevitably filling three ashtrays with cigarette butts.

Les Deux Magots has always prided itself on the quality of its service, to such an extent that for a long time the famous chocolate, made on the premises, was served in silver pots and, as elsewhere in

Paris, the waiters are resplendent in their black suits and starched white aprons, taking great pride in their art. It is said that they cover an average of 12km (over 7 miles) during the course of a day. In summer the terrace is taken by storm but it is large and you should not have to wait too long for a seat. Come early in the morning; you'll be able to have a memorable breakfast for 80F. However, do be aware that everything is pretty expensive here.

🍸 **Le Sélect** (map B3, **91**): 99 boulevard du Montparnasse 75006. ☎ 01-45-48-38-24. Metro: Vavin. Open daily 8am to 2.30am (3.30am at weekends). Set menu 90F served lunchtime and evening. À la carte, the bill comes to around 120F excluding drinks. A rendezvous for artists (or those who pose as artists), between 1918 and 1930 Le Sélect was one of the leading bars in French artistic life. Invaded by students in the early evening, the place fills up with regulars later on. You can engage a great painter-to-be in conversation over a cocktail (60F).

🍸 Younger and funkier is the **Café de l'Atelier**, nearby, open 24 hours a day, seven days a week.

🍸 **La Closerie des Lilas** (map C3, **92**): 171 boulevard du Montparnasse 75006. ☎ 01-43-54-21-68. Metro: Port-Royal. Open daily 11am to 1.30am. A classic and former *guinguette* (small restaurant with music and dancing) and staging post. Members of the 19th-century Parnassian poetry movement, with Leconte de Lisle at their head, were regulars, as were Verlaine, Baudelaire, Mallarmé, etc. Later the Surrealists took over, but there are many others of an artistic persuasion whose names are engraved on the tables: Max Jacob, Modigliani, Strindberg, etc. Everyone except Hemingway, who had a brass plate fixed on the counter of the famous American bar instead. He wrote *The Sun Also Rises* here. Behind the red imitation leather seats is a traditional brass hat stand and on the floor are mosaics. The walls are lined with old mirrors and wooden panelling.

There are some good stories attached to the bar. One evening Fernand Léger, already famous as one of the founders of the Cubist movement, was having a drink on the terrace here. He saw a ravishing bride pedalling along on a brand new bike. Out of breath, she dropped into the chair next to him and told him her amazing adventure: she had got married that very morning, several hundred miles away in Normandy. Among the wedding presents she found a bicycle. Unable to stand any more, she leapt onto the bike and, drunk with the summer (and the wine), she returned to Paris . . . . The ravishing bride never went back to Normandy and . . . well, she married Fernand Léger.

Another fairly expensive place – cocktails are around 70F to 80F. There's a tea-room open until 7pm. If you want to eat the restaurant is very pricey, so it's best to eat in the brasserie, which is better value, more relaxed and, of course, more crowded! Egg mayonnaise at 40F, steak tartare, one of the best in Paris, at 90F.

🍸 **La Taverne de Nesle** (map C1, **102**): 32 rue Dauphine 75006. ☎ 01-43-26-38-36. Metro: Odéon. Open daily 9.30pm to 4am (6am at weekends). 25F for half a pint of beer. Sample beers from all over the world for around 50F. You can also find a complete collection of the beers brewed in France, such as the superb Bavaisienne from the Theillier brewery in Bavay, Hommelpap by Ferme Beck (made from hops harvested on the farm) and St-Martial by the Limoges micro-brewery. The choice of Belgian and German beers is also very good.

The Frog Princess (inset map, **80**): 9 rue Princesse 75006. ☎ 01-40-51-77-38. Metro: Mabillon. Open daily 6pm (noon at weekends) to 2am. Budget for between 100F and 130F for a full meal, excluding drinks. At weekends, brunch from 42F to 105F. Like its big brother at Les Halles, the Frog Princess brews its own beer on the premises – Frog natural blonde, Dark de Triomphe, Raspberet in Seine. There are around 15 bottled beers to choose from and various spirits. For sports fans, there are four screens permanently showing the best football, rugby, etc. matches. The atmosphere is young and relaxed.

Bob Cool (map D1, **89**): 15 rue des Grands-Augustins 75006. ☎ 01-46-33-33-77. Metro: Odéon or Pont-Neuf. Open daily 5pm to 2am. Cocktails 40F, beers from 15F to 25F and a good choice of tequilas. Far from those fashionable bars where the barmen think they're Tom Cruise, here is a real bar, with a real barman who really knows his job. Ask him for a mint julep or a *mojito*, a Margherita or a Daquiri, and you won't be disappointed. Happy hour is from 5pm to 9pm. The background music is blues and rock.

Cubana Café (map B3, **94**): 47 rue Vavin 75006. ☎ 01-40-46-80-81. Metro: Vavin or Montparnasse-Bienvenüe. Open daily 11am to 2am (at least!). At lunchtime, there's a set menu at 89F, otherwise budget for 150F à la carte excluding drinks. Brunch at 110F. A restaurant-bar which is both elegant and not too expensive, where you nibble Latino classics *tête-à-tête* with the *caballero* of your choice or, better still, with the Che Guevara of the *casa*. The decor is a mish-mash of cigar rings, photos, posters and revolutionary slogans scratched onto the ochre walls. A *mojito* costs 39F. Sets of Cuban dominos are available and happy hour is 5.30pm to 7.30pm. Cuban coffee costs 10F. There is a cigar cellar where you will find the great classics and a neo-Cuban menu with a guaranteed '*coco loco*' service.

Le Shannon Pub (map B3, **95**): 23 rue Bréa 75006. ☎ 01-43-26-34-70. Metro: Vavin. Open daily 5pm to 4am (5am at weekends). A pint of beer costs 27F, cocktails 45F. The prices reduce to 22F and 30F respectively during happy hour from 5pm to 8pm. Boosted by their success at the Bréguet (*see the* '15th arrondissement'), the owners have installed lots of rock music (Pixies, Smashing Pumpkins, etc.). But Le Shannon is a lot smarter than its big brother, as befits the quarter, and has quickly become Paris' leading 'urban' pub for Anglophiles.

La Bibliothèque (map B2, **81**): 52 rue d'Assas 75006. ☎ 01-42-22-89-52. Metro: Notre-Dame-des-Champs. Open 2pm to 8pm. Closed weekends, Wednesday and July and August. Coffee 8.50F, beers from 18F. Opened in 1994 by M. Zrehen, a lecturer in communication at the University of Valenciennes, La Bibliothèque has the subtitle 'beau bar et librairie improbable', or 'fine bar and improbable bookshop'. The shelves pay homage to the crime novel and are lined with 'Série noire', 'Spécial Police', 'Fleuve noir' detective novels. Fans of French detective stories need look no further!

Le Petit Suisse (map C2, **101**): 16 rue de Vaugirard 75006. ☎ 01-43-26-03-81. Metro: Odéon; RER: Luxembourg. Open Monday to Friday 7am to 8pm. Coffee 12F, 18F for half a pint of beer. Sandwiches at around 20F. Very pleasant when the weather is nice, because the terrace is opposite the Jardin du Luxembourg. A student bar which is fairly typical but of a dying breed, even in this Sorbonne-dominated part of the quarter. A former meeting point for Marie de Médicis' Swiss Guards, nowadays it's full of budding philosophers, writers and rather elegant young people. Light snacks (sandwiches, charcuterie) at modest prices.

🍸 **Chez Georges** (inset map, **83**): 11 rue des Canettes 75006. ☎ 01-43-26-79-15. Metro: St-Germain-des-Prés. Open noon to 2am. Closed Sunday and Monday, and in August. Bottled beers 17F to 25F. The eponymous owner died in 1999, but the place's spirit remains intact. Generations of nicotine addicts and smoky intellectuals have given the walls and ceiling something of a sheen. The fine bar dates from 1928, though the Germans cannibalized the old zinc counter during the Second World War to make new aeroplanes. There is a charming old arched cellar. Popular with almost everyone, including the occasional chess fan. There are some cheap but good wines to take away and big '*Canettes* sandwiches' if you're feeling peckish.

🍸 **La Palette** (map C1, **84**): 43 rue de Seine 75006. ☎ 01-43-26-68-15. Metro: Odéon. Open 8am to 2am. Closed Sunday, 25 December, 1 January, Easter Monday and Whitsun. Dishes of the day 60F, house tarts 35F. Drinks around 20F. Tucked away on the corner of a side street with a wonderful terrace and a back room that is full of charm. However, the welcome can be a little brusque, though typically Parisian, and some might say it's quite expensive. Try a glass of Sancerre or Brouilly accompanied by a 'guillotine' (ham on Poilâne bread). The atmosphere is lively and very French.

🍸 **La Rhumerie** (map C1, **85**): 166 boulevard St-Germain 75006. ☎ 01-43-54-28-94. Metro: Mabillon. Open daily 9am to 3am. There's a West Indian dish at lunchtime at 73F including drinks, a Creole dish at 68F in the evening, otherwise it's salads (50F) and à la carte dishes. An institution, La Rhumerie was created in 1932 and still belongs to the same family. Redecorated a few years ago in neo-colonial style (green and yellow wicker), there is a vast terrace under a glass roof and two dining rooms. You can stay here for hours just sipping excellent cocktails (40F) or trying the 20 types of rum on offer if your head is up to it. The clientele is mixed, all ages and styles.

🍸 **Coolin** (inset map, **99**): 15 rue Clément 75006. ☎ 01-44-07-00-92. Metro: Mabillon. Open daily 10am (1pm on Sunday) to 1.30am. Spirits from 38F. A haven of conviviality in the rather soulless marché St-Germain, which now seems entirely devoted to designer boutiques and clothes. The feeling of warmth is reinforced by the ochre walls, pale wooden tables and benches and a vast, dark bar. You can try their whiskey (38F to 55F) on its own or with hot snacks (15F to 35F), such as the Coolin stuffed potato. From 5pm to 8pm Monday to Saturday it's happy hour (pints, vodkas and whiskeys 25F); concerts from 6pm to 8pm on Sundays and traditional Irish music on Mondays until 9pm.

🍸 **Le Bar du Marché** (map C1, **90**): 75 rue de Seine 75006. ☎ 01-43-26-55-15. Metro: Mabillon. Open daily until 2am. Coffee 12F, half a pint of beer from 20F. The waiters zigzag between the tables at speed, looking cool. It's very lively, a bit like the huge poster of the Frères Jacques (a very popular French group) taped onto the mirror.

🍸 **Les Étages St-Germain** (map C1, **86**): 5 rue de Buci 75006. ☎ 01-46-34-26-26. Metro: Mabillon. Open daily 11am to 2am. Tapas at 15F, set menu 49F at lunchtime, cocktails 25F until 9pm. A bustling place bursting with colour and good humour, on two floors. There's no sign (the neighbours wouldn't like it) as the place has already lowered the tone of the area! Good beers, house cocktails with quite a kick, original tapas (kebabs, *tians* (gratin of fish or vegetables), aubergine fritters) and, free of charge, as many peanuts as you can eat.

WHERE TO GO FOR LIVE MUSIC

🍸 **Le Bilboquet** (map C1, **93**): 13 rue St-Benoît 75006. ☎ 01-45-48-81-84. Metro: St-Germain-des-Prés. Open 8pm to 3am; for food until 1am. Set menu 157F, à la carte budget for 250F per person. One of the oldest jazz clubs in the area (1947), this place jealously guards a fine mezzanine under which you can have a drink or eat, and a small stage devoted exclusively to the most classical jazz (from the '20s to the '50s). On top of this you can add shoulder of lamb with vegetables for two, or the famous steak tartare or just a drink (120F). The band plays from 10.30pm onwards, in three one-hour sessions. You'll meet a cosmopolitan clientele, both adopted and native Parisians.

GOING OUT

🍸 **Caveau de la Bolée** (map D1, **97**): 25 rue de l'Hirondelle 75006. ☎ 01-43-54-62-20. Metro: St-Michel. Open 6.30pm to 4am. Closed Sunday. Dinner and show 260F, 300F at weekends. Popular with students. A very Parisian welcome, on the ground floor you can dine for 100F among chess players who are 'blitzing' one another. In the basement there's a rather amateurish but heartfelt cabaret, held in what was a prison in the 14th-century cellar.

NIGHTCLUB

– **Le Pousse au Crime** (inset map, **98**): 15 rue Guisarde 75006. ☎ 01-46-33-36-63. Metro: Mabillon or St-Sulpice. Open every night 11pm until dawn (2am Tuesday and Wednesday). Closed Sunday and Monday. No entry fee during the week, 80F with a drink at weekends. Fancy the life of a convict for an evening? That's what Le Pousse offers. The stone arched walls, especially in the basement, and the sculpted wooden panels will transport you to medieval times. You can almost believe that you're in the dungeons of a castle. Sometimes frequented by the B.C.B.G. (bon chic, bon genre – the French equivalent of Sloane Rangers or yuppies) during the week, at weekends it's usually packed out.

7TH ARRONDISSEMENT

THE EIFFEL TOWER ● LES INVALIDES ● THE FAUBOURG ST-GERMAIN ● THE MUSÉE D'ORSAY

Much of the 7th arrondissement is hidden behind high walls and heavy doors housing ministries and international institutions. However, as with many parts of central Paris if you peer past the imposing and sometimes forbidding doors you'll find fine courtyards and indoor gardens which are particularly splendid in the spring. The 7th arrondissement locals tend to be conservative people who have elected the same member of parliament for several decades. For the tourist, the main attractions of the arrondissement are the Eiffel Tower and Les Invalides.

WHERE TO STAY

☆☆ MODERATE

Hôtel Eiffel Rive Gauche (map B2, **1**): 6 rue du Gros-Caillou 75007. ☎ 01-45-51-24-56. Fax: 01-45-51-11-77. E-mail: eiffel@easynet.fr. Metro: École-Militaire. Budget for 325F to 490F for a double room. Off season there is a 10 per cent reduction. A small hotel in a quiet street where cars are not allowed to park. Four floors connected by walkways surround a patio which overlooks an inner courtyard, topped by a glass ceiling. Ochre and rose pink are the predominant colours and, with a little imagination, you could be in Andalucía – it's just a shame that the plants and flowers are plastic! Having said that, from the top floor you can indeed see the top of the Eiffel Tower. Thirteen rooms overlook the patio. Booking is recommended.

Hôtel du Palais-Bourbon (map C2, **2**): 49 rue de Bourgogne 75007. ☎ 01-44-11-30-70. Fax: 01-45-55-20-21. E-mail: htlbourbon@aol.com. Website: www.hotel-palais-bourbon.com. Metro: Varenne. Double room with shower and toilet 405F, with bathroom and toilet 610F. Rooms for three people 710F and for four 780F. Breakfast included. There's a lovely little room near the reception with high ceilings and open beams. Some rooms are truly immense – one of the advantages of old buildings – but this doesn't prevent it from being comfortable: the windows have double-glazing and all rooms have air-conditioning. There's a mini-bar, TV (with CNN) and newly renovated bathrooms.

Grand Hôtel Lévêque (map B2, **3**): 29 rue Cler 75007. ☎ 01-47-05-49-15. Fax: 01-45-50-49-36. Website: www.hotel-leveque.com. Metro: École-Militaire or Latour-Maubourg. Double room with shower and toilet 420F to 470F. Breakfast included. The Eiffel Tower is nearby, but the market in the rue Cleris is equally picturesque. People fight over the rooms on the street side! There's a feel of real local life here. A one-star hotel with 50 rooms, entirely renovated and with reasonable prices, the rooms are clean and comfortable, with satellite TV. Book ahead as it's popular.

Hôtel Malar (map B1, **4**): 29 rue Malar 75007. ☎ 01-45-51-38-46. Fax: 01-45-55-20-19. Metro: Latour-

Maubourg. Double room 360F with shower, 420F with shower and toilet, 520F with bathroom. Close to the Eiffel Tower. Convivial and cosmopolitan atmosphere (they speak English, Italian, Spanish and Brazilian Portuguese) with a family charm and atmosphere. Direct telephone, double-glazing, satellite TV and hairdryer in all the rooms. Go for the rooms on the courtyard side, which are a lot quieter, pleasanter and are more spacious.

Hôtel Le Pavillon (map B1, **5**): 54 rue St-Dominique 75007. ☎ 01-45-51-42-87. Fax: 01-45-51-32-79. Metro: Invalides. Room with shower, TV and toilet 460F. Three double rooms with bathrooms, toilet and TV at 575F. There's a 10 per cent reduction January to March. A small, quiet two-star hotel, set back from the street, with an inner patio. This is a former convent and has retained an almost provincial charm. There are only 18 rooms, all clean and comfortable. The room in which the Mother Superior lived is the most in demand! Nos. 10 and 14 have two double beds and a large bathroom. You will need to make it quite clear that you want to keep the same room if you're staying for a number of days.

☆☆☆ CHIC

Hôtel St-Dominique (map B1, **6**): 62 rue St-Dominique 75007. ☎ 01-47-05-51-44. Fax: 01-47-05-81-28. Metro and RER: Invalides. Budget for 460F for a single room, 540F to 580F for a double. Near the Eiffel Tower, a charming establishment installed in a former 13th-century convent, which has retained its superb exposed beams. There's a little flower-filled patio where you can have breakfast or a quiet drink in summer. Comfortable rooms with rustic furniture. The bathrooms have been tastefully refitted and there is cable TV, mini-bar and direct telephone in all rooms. Breakfast is served in a 17th-century arched dining room.

Hôtel Lindbergh (map D2, **7**): 5 rue Chomel 75007. ☎ 01-45-48-35-53. Fax: 01-45-49-31-48. E-mail: infos@hotellindbergh.com. Website: www.hotellindbergh.com. Metro: Sèvres-Babylone. Double room with bath or shower 520F to 570F. Near the Bon Marché. A charming little hotel on a quiet street run by three very pleasant young women who have decided to renovate from top to bottom, bringing it up to date. The attic rooms on the top floor are fun. You get a free half-bottle of champagne per person if you stay for more than three nights.

Hôtel Bersoly's St-Germain (map D1–2, **8**): 28 rue de Lille 75007. ☎ 01-42-60-73-79. Fax: 01-49-27-05-55. E-mail: bersolys@easynet.fr. Metro: Rue-du-Bac. Double room 600F to 650F with shower and toilet, between 700F and 750F with bath. Closed in August. A former 18th-century private residence, completely renovated, in the heart of historic Paris and near the quarter's antique dealers. The rooms may be small, but they're spotless, each named after a famous painter, with a corresponding reproduction of that artist's work. The 'Gauguin' and the 'Turner' are particularly good rooms. The atmosphere is hushed, with exposed beams and stylish furniture. There is cable TV in all rooms and a small bar near reception.

Hôtel du Quai Voltaire (map D1, **9**): 19 quai Voltaire 75007. ☎ 01-42-61-50-91. Fax: 01-42-61-62-26. E-mail: info@hotelduquaivoltaire.com. Metro: Rue-du-Bac. Double room with sink 400F, with shower or bath and toilet from 720F to 770F. A two-star hotel which is magnificently located on the banks of the Seine, opposite the *bouquinistes* (antiquarian booksellers) and the Louvre, and close to the Musée d'Orsay. Built in the 19th century, many famous people have stayed here, including Wagner, Baudelaire, Oscar Wilde and Pissarro. Rooms 14 and 24 are spacious. Still a little noisy despite the double-glazing.

Hôtel St-Thomas-d'Aquin (map D2, **10**): 3 rue du Pré-aux-Clercs 75007. ☎ 01-42-61-01-22. Fax: 01-42-61-41-43. Metro: Rue-du-Bac or St-Germain-des-Prés. Double room with bath or shower, toilet and satellite TV between 500F and 600F. A two-star hotel in a quiet and well-located street in the heart of Paris. Twenty modern, well-lit rooms, with large windows and impeccable bathrooms. Some rooms have balconies. Lovely attic rooms on the fifth floor.

Hôtel Muguet (map B2, **11**): 11 rue Chevert 75007. ☎ 01-47-05-05-93. Fax: 01-45-50-25-37. Website: www.hotelmuguet.com. Metro: École-Militaire or Latour-Maubourg. Double rooms with shower or bath 580F, all with satellite TV and Canal+. In a very quiet street, away from the traffic, with a small garden where you can sunbathe when the weather is fine. There are three rooms on the sixth floor with a view of the Eiffel Tower, others overlook Les Invalides. Cheerful welcome.

☆☆☆☆ TRÈS CHIC

Hôtel d'Orsay (map C1, **12**): 93 rue de Lille 75007. ☎ 01-47-05-85-54. Fax: 01-45-55-51-16. Metro: Solférino or Assemblée-Nationale. Single room 485F to 700F, double room with shower 485F to 800F. Very close to the Seine and the Musée d'Orsay, a comfortable and quiet hotel, born out of the marriage between the former Hôtel Solférino and the Résidence d'Orsay. Has been entirely renovated. Not cheap, but for the area, what do you expect? Booking recommended.

Hôtel St-Germain (map D2, **13**): 88 rue du Bac 75007. ☎ 01-49-54-70-00 or 01-45-48-62-92. Fax: 01-45-48-26-89. Website: www.hotel-saint-germain.fr. Metro: Rue-du-Bac. Budget for 600F for a double room with shower and 850F for a double room with shower and toilet. With a bath and a view over

7TH

Where to stay

1 Hôtel Eiffel Rive Gauche
2 Hôtel du Palais-Bourbon
3 Grand Hôtel Lévêque
4 Hôtel Malar
5 Hôtel Le Pavillon
6 Hôtel St-Dominique
7 Hôtel Lindbergh
8 Hôtel Bersoly's St-Germain
9 Hôtel du Quai Voltaire
10 Hôtel St-Thomas-d'Aquin
11 Hôtel Muguet
12 Hôtel d'Orsay
13 Hôtel St-Germain
14 Hôtel Lenox

Where to eat

20 Chez Germaine
21 Au Pied de Fouet
22 Au Babylone
23 Le Roupeyrac
25 Le Poch'tron
26 Au Bon Accueil
27 Le Café des Lettres
28 Casa Pasta
29 L'Affriolé
30 7eSud
31 Thoumieux
32 Au Petit Tonneau
35 La Maison des Polytechniciens
36 La Maison de l'Amérique Latine
37 Le Rouge Vif
38 L'Œillade
39 Apollon
40 Le Basilic
41 Il Girasole
43 La Maison de Cosima
44 Le P'tit Troquet

Where to go for a drink/ Going out

51 Master's Bar
54 Club des Poètes
55 O'Brien's
56 Le Café du Marché

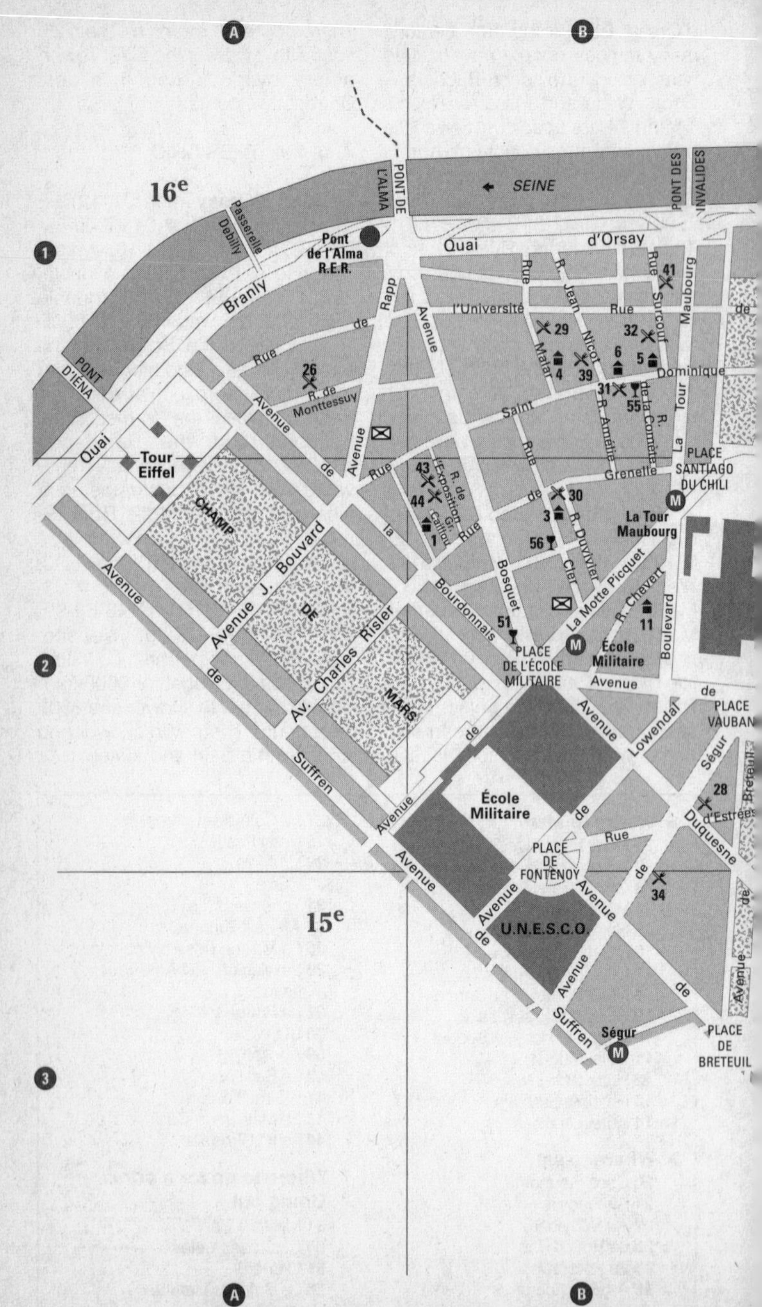
16e
15e
SEINE
PONT DE L'ALMA
PONT DES INVALIDES
PONT D'IÉNA
Passerelle Debilly
Pont de l'Alma R.E.R.
Quai Branly
Quai d'Orsay
Tour Eiffel
CHAMP DE MARS
Avenue J. Bouvard
Av. Charles Risler
Avenue de Suffren
Avenue de la Bourdonnais
Avenue Rapp
Avenue Bosquet
Rue de l'Université
Rue Saint Dominique
Rue de Grenelle
R. de Monttessuy
R. de l'Exposition
R. Jean Nicot
Rue Malar
Rue Surcouf
R. Amélie
R. de la Comète
R. Duvivier
Rue Cler
Gr. Caillou
La Motte Picquet
R. Chevert
Boulevard La Tour Maubourg
PLACE SANTIAGO DU CHILI
La Tour Maubourg
PLACE DE L'ÉCOLE MILITAIRE
École Militaire
Avenue Lowendal
PLACE VAUBAN
Avenue de Ségur
Rue d'Estrées
Duquesne
Breteuil
PLACE DE FONTENOY
U.N.E.S.C.O.
Ségur
PLACE DE BRETEUIL
A
B
1
2
3
41
29
32
6
5
4
39
31
55
26
43
44
1
3
30
56
11
51
28
34

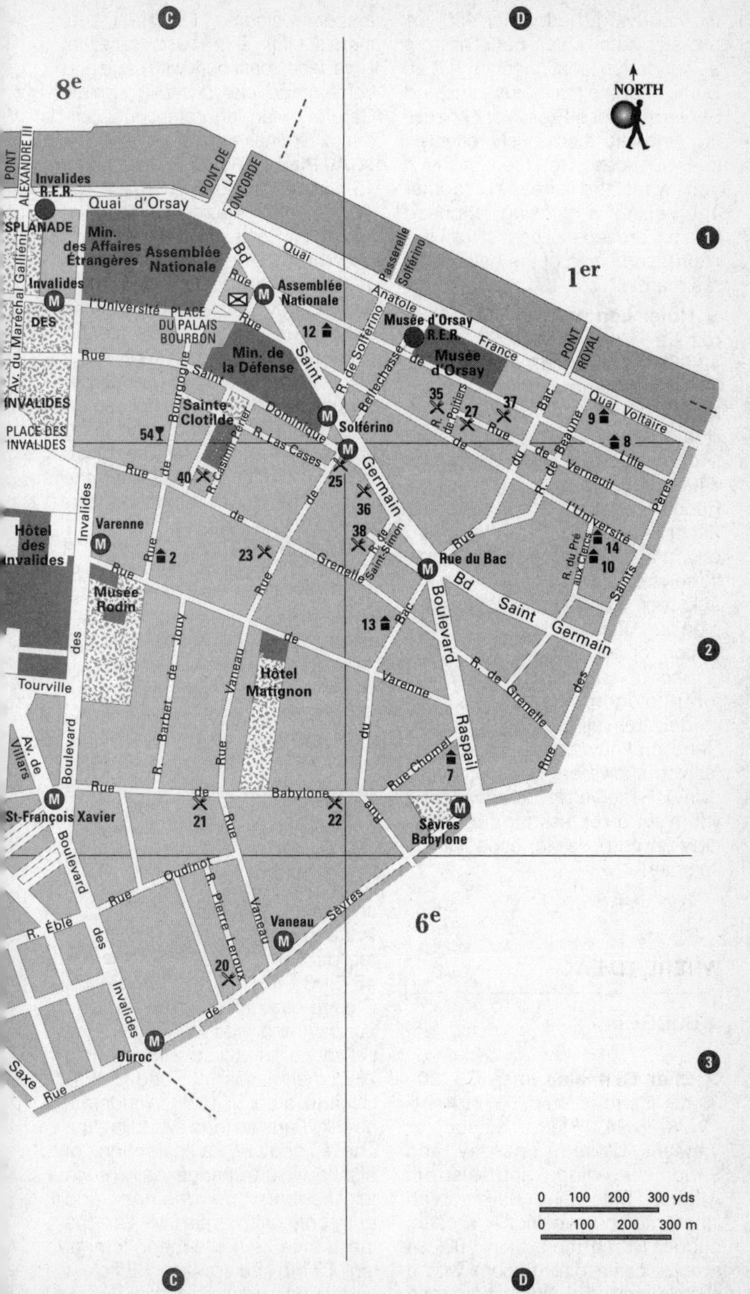

8e
1er
6e
NORTH
Invalides R.E.R.
Quai d'Orsay
Min. des Affaires Étrangères
Assemblée Nationale
Assemblée Nationale
Musée d'Orsay R.E.R.
Musée d'Orsay
Min. de la Défense
Sainte-Clotilde
Solférino
Varenne
Hôtel des Invalides
Musée Rodin
Hôtel Matignon
Rue du Bac
St-François Xavier
Sèvres Babylone
Vaneau
Duroc
PLACE DU PALAIS BOURBON
PLACE DES INVALIDES
Quai Voltaire
Bd Saint Germain
Boulevard Raspail
Rue de Grenelle
Rue de Varenne
Rue de Babylone
Rue de Sèvres
0 100 200 300 yds
0 100 200 300 m

the courtyard, budget for 950F. A two-star hotel which benefits from a wonderful location on the Left Bank, near the main museums and St-Germain-des-Prés. Very charming, and this is obviously reflected in the prices. Get there early if you want the cheaper rooms! The setting is stunning: exposed beams, arched ceilings, stylish furniture, and some of the bathrooms are marble.

Hôtel Lenox (map D2, **14**): 9 rue de l'Université 75007. ☎ 01-42-96-10-95. Fax: 01-42-61-52-83. E-mail: lenox@gofornet.com. Metro: St-Germain-des-Prés or Rue-du-Bac. Double room with shower and toilet 680F. Budget for 740F to 890F with a bathroom. Recently renovated, sophisticated decor and a distinguished retro charm are the main features at this three-star establishment. There are attic rooms on the fifth floor and a pleasant, intimate bar, with 1930s decor, open 5pm to 2am. This is one of the favourite locations for photographers, stylists and models from all over the world (the Carré du Louvre, where numerous fashion shows are held, is not far away). Reserve well in advance. If you want quiet, ask for a room as high up as possible, especially in summer!

WHERE TO EAT

☆ BUDGET

Chez Germaine (map C3, **20**): 30 rue Pierre-Leroux 75007. ☎ 01-42-73-28-34. Metro: Duroc or Vaneau. Closed Saturday and Sunday evening, and also in August. Set menu 65F served lunchtime and evening. À la carte, budget for no more than 100F. A simple, clean dining room with a slightly provincial atmosphere, and friendly welcome. On the menu, there's *bitok à la russe*, excellent *brandade*, roast pork with sage and home-made *clafoutis* with apples. Carafe of an unpretentious Bordeaux Ordinaire at 18F.

Au Pied de Fouet (map C2, **21**): 45 rue de Babylone 75007. ☎ 01-47-05-12-27. Metro: St-François-Xavier or Sèvres-Babylone. Open noon to 2.30pm and 7pm to 10.30pm. Closed Saturday evening and Sunday, as well as in August. Set menu 73F; à la carte the bill should be no more than 100F. A tiny place with a real zinc bar, proper tablecloths, imitation leather seats – and unbeatable prices; the living image of the old Parisian bistro which is so popular all over the world. The cuisine blends in perfectly with the decor.

Au Babylone (map C2, **22**): 13 rue de Babylone 75007. ☎ 01-45-48-72-13. Metro: Sèvres-Babylone. Open lunchtime only. Closed Sunday and public holidays, as well as in August. Set menu 100F; not much more à la carte. The dining room is larger than the one at the Pied de Fouet, with a quaint, old-world charm. The paintings have become yellow with age and there is an imitation leather wall-seat. Good home-cooking. Dishes between 55F and 60F. The set menu includes starter, main course, cheese and drinks.

Le Roupeyrac (map C2, **23**): 62 rue de Bellechasse 75007. ☎ 01-45-51-33-42. Metro: Solférino. Closed Saturday evening and Sunday, and also in August. First set menu lunchtime and evening 78F, other menus 110F and 150F. À la carte around 140F. Wonderful, no-frills Parisian food including 'the chef's choice', a selection of dishes which change daily, such as *haricots de mouton* and *entrecôte* with marrow. On the menu there is home-made terrine, leg of lamb and apple tart. Efficient and friendly service

✕ **Le Café des Lettres** (map D1, **27):** 53 rue de Verneuil 75007. ☎ 01-42-22-52-17. Metro: Rue-du-Bac. Open daily noon to 11pm. Closed Sunday evening from 4pm and between Christmas and 1 January. Set menus 150F to 200F; brunch 160F on Sunday. Budget for around 120F à la carte. Enter the Café des Lettres via the porch of the Avejan private residence, which has now become the Centre National des Lettres. For the last 10 years the café has been full of writers and regulars in the street where the notorious French singer Serge Gainsbourg used to live (at No. 7). The conviviality of the bar and the Swedish ambiance and menu will take you far away from St-Germain. Dish of the day 78F. Offerings include chicken *à l'indienne*, herrings and gravlax. Finish with a *vaffla* (waffle) served with Chantilly cream. In summer there's a lovely terrace. Every month there's a different exhibition of paintings.

☆☆ MODERATE

✕ **Le Poch'tron** (map C2, **25**): 25 rue de Bellechasse 75007. ☎ 01-45-51-27-11. Metro: Solférino. Closed Saturday and Sunday. Budget for around 150F. There's nothing terribly refined about the name of this bistro, but the welcome is friendly. Traditional cooking includes warm *tartine corrézienne*, terrines and farmhouse rib of veal. Some pleasant wines from Alsace.

✕ **7ᵉSud** (map B2, **30):** 159 rue de Grenelle 75007. ☎ 01-44-18-30-30. Metro: École-Militaire. Open lunchtime and evening all week, and for brunch from noon to 5pm on Sunday. Closed 15 days in August. À la carte only, budget for around 150F without wine. A bistro with lamps in the shape of gypsum flowers, ochre walls, and scenes from North African life. Mediterranean-style menu: Greek salad, *tajine* and penne *all'arrabbiata*. From Greece to North Africa, via Italy, the South of France and Spain – this bistro offers a range of dishes from hot places. Carefree but smiling staff.

✕ **Casa Pasta** (map B2, **28):** 35 avenue Duquesne 75007. ☎ 01-45-55-43-43. Metro: St-François-Xavier. Last orders 10.45pm. Closed Saturday lunchtime, as well as for one week in the middle of August and a week over Christmas and New Year. Set menu 95F at lunchtime, main courses from 72F. This pocket-sized *trattoria* specializes in pizzas. Its big sister, which is nearby and is more elegant, offers a superb old *prosciutto* machine – where you'll find more fine pasta and delicious gnocchi with basil and pepper. Several outside tables are available in hot weather.

✕ **Il Girasole** (map B1, **41**): 9 rue Surcouf and 8 rue Desgenettes 75007. ☎ 01-45-50-20-69. Metro: Latour-Maubourg. Open until 11pm. Closed Saturday and Sunday. Budget for around 200F per person. Run by two Sardinian brothers and offering pasta and antipasti. The atmosphere has the warmth of Italy, but there's no menu, so when you ask about the dishes make sure you also enquire about the prices! Spaghetti *alla vongole* (with clams), tagliatelli with mushrooms, *orecchiette primavera* (pasta with seasonal vegetables) and rigatoni *all'arrabbiata*, preceded by rocket and parmesan salad, all accompanied by a glass of Montepulciano, make for a good meal.

✕ **Le P'tit Troquet** (map B2, **44**): 28 rue de l'Exposition 75007. ☎ 01-47-05-80-39. Metro: École-Militaire. Open to 11pm. Closed Sunday and Monday lunchtime, the first three weeks of August and for a week at Christmas. Set menu 159F at lunchtime and evening. A typical small Parisian bistro with a single menu. Dishes include *quenelle* of salmon and goat's cheese, duck breast with honey and chocolate fondant.

✕ **Au Bon Accueil** (map A1, **26**): 14 rue de Monttessuy 75007. ☎ 01-47-05-46-11. RER (Line C): Pont-de-l'Alma. Open until 11pm. Closed Saturday lunchtime and Sunday. Set menus 135F at lunchtime, 155F in the evening. À la carte, budget for around 250F. A name which smacks of the type of restaurant you get along the 'Nationale 20' (a major road), this is a tongue-in-cheek country stop-off in the heart of the very aristocratic 7th arrondissement. The Rungis market is scoured for the best products. Excellent *menu-carte,* and from the terrace there is a superb view over the Eiffel Tower, which is only a few hundred yards away. Sadly the welcome (*acceuil*) does not quite live up to its name!

✕ **La Maison de Cosima** (map B2, **43**): 20 rue de l'Exposition 75007. ☎ 01-45-51-37-71. Metro: École-Militaire. Open in the evening only until 10.30pm. Closed Sunday, between Christmas and New Year, as well as for 10 days in February and August. Open lunchtime by reservation only. Three-course menu lunchtime and evening 159F. In a tiny street with a certain gastronomic reputation, this place, named after the owners' daughter, has only subtle dishes on the menu. Try *pâté en croûte* with duck and *foie gras* or a *terrine de foie gras* and pork cheeks, *noisettes de rognons* fried with citrus fruits, followed by liquorice tart. The dining room is pretty small, so you need to book.

7TH

☆☆☆ CHIC

✕ **La Maison des Polytechniciens, restaurant le Club** (map D1, **35**): 12 rue de Poitiers 75007. ☎ 01-49-54-74-74. Metro: Rue-du-Bac. Open lunchtime and evening until 10pm. Closed weekends. Budget for 200F to 250F. In the former Hôtel de Poulpry, this is a fine 18th-century building where Watteau practised his talents (there is still a ceiling painted with arabesques). It was here that a meeting of Monarchist chiefs chose to make Louis-Napoleon Head of State on the basis that 'He's an idiot and we'll be able to do what we want with him'! In 1920 it was bought by La Maison des Polytechniciens and it has just been renovated. Light, generous, fresh and inspired cuisine. You just have to try the pumpkin and langoustine soup with pine-nuts and coriander, the shellfish *marinière*, the artichoke and spinach mousse, and *mitonnée* of veal kidneys flavoured with truffles. And as if that's not enough, there are remarkable desserts, a finely tuned wine list and impeccable service.

✕ **Les Olivades** (map B3, **34**): 41 avenue de Ségur 75007. ☎ 01-47-83-70-09. Metro: École-Militaire. Open until 11pm. Closed Saturday and Monday lunchtime, Sunday and also the second fortnight in August. Set menu 179F at lunchtime and evening, set lunch 130F. À la carte, budget for 200F without drinks. The menu here is inspired by the south – *croustillant* of mullet and sardines with balsamic vinegar, crab *rémoulade*, quail *confite* with olive oil and apples, and *coquilles St-Jacques* fried in their shells. For dessert try the *compôte de vieux garçon* in a *millefeuille d'oreillette fleur d'oranger.* The wine list is off the beaten track – follow the owner's advice. Eat out on the terrace when the weather is fine.

✕ **La Maison de l'Amérique Latine** (map D2, **36**): 217 boulevard St-Germain 75007. ☎ 01-45-49-33-23. Metro: Solférino or Rue-du-Bac. Open lunchtime only, 1 October to 1 May; lunchtime and evening the rest of the year. Closed Saturday, Sunday and public holidays, as well as in August. Set menu 230F at lunchtime. In the evening there's à la carte only between 300F and 350F. At lunchtime on a sunny day you could be forgiven for thinking you were in a park in the Île-de-France. Inventive French cuisine by a Japanese chef. Visit the bar as well, open 8.30am to 7pm, which offers South American specialities and a few brasserie dishes. Book at least three days in advance.

✕ **Le Rouge Vif** (map D1, **37**): 48 rue de Verneuil 75007. ☎ 01-42-86-81-87. Metro: Rue-du-Bac. Last orders midnight. Closed Saturday lunchtime, Sunday and between Christmas and the New Year. Set menu 90F in the evening; budget for 180F à la carte. A lively place run by a couple of chaps who know the nightlife around here pretty well. A few 'Lyons specialities', dishes straight from the roasting spit, and a host of inventive ideas from the market.

✕ **L'Œillade** (map D2, **38**): 10 rue St-Simon 75007. ☎ 01-42-22-01-60. Metro: Rue-du-Bac. Closed Saturday lunchtime, all day Sunday, the second fortnight in August and for Christmas and New Year. Set menu 168F served lunchtime and evening. À la carte around 200F to 220F. There are always plenty of people in the two dining rooms here. Not surprising, given the robust dishes such as stuffed cabbage, braised calves' sweetbreads with morel mushrooms, *foie gras*, lobster and sea bream roasted with olive oil and basil.

✕ **Thoumieux** (map B1, **31**): 79 rue St-Dominique 75007. ☎ 01-47-05-49-75. Metro: Latour-Maubourg. Open Monday to Saturday noon to 3.30pm and 6.45pm to midnight, Sunday noon to midnight. Set menus 82F and 160F at lunchtime and evening. À la carte, budget for around 180F without drinks. A charming, large brasserie founded in 1923 with a lively atmosphere and very popular with tourists. The mushroom omelette and fillet of duck with olives are greatly appreciated. The place is also a hotel, with double rooms all with bath, toilet and telephone for 600F. Breakfast at 35F.

In an adjoining street there is an annex which is something between a cosy bar and an elegant bistro, the **Café Thoumieux** (4 rue de la Comète 75007; ☎ 01-45-51-40-40). Every Monday, there's a drinks and jazz event from 7.30pm.

✕ **Au Petit Tonneau** (map B1, **32**): 20 rue Surcouf 75007. ☎ 01-47-05-09-01. Metro: Invalides or Latour-Maubourg. Open daily noon to 3pm and 7pm to 11.30pm. Closed for a week in August. Set menu 110F at lunchtime and in the evening. À la carte between 200F and 250F. This restaurant is worth a visit both for the personality of the owner and for the quality of her cuisine. The dishes are cooked in a traditional way, and the fish and the shellfish are remarkably fresh. The set meal changes every day: Bresse salad with poultry livers, sautéed lamb with gratin and crème caramel. The wine list has an emphasis on the Loire.

✕ **Apollon** (map B1, **39**): 24 rue Jean-Nicot 75007. ☎ 01-45-55-68-47. Metro: Latour-Maubourg. Open until 11pm. Closed Sunday and 20 December to 10 January. Set menus 69F at lunchtime and 128F in the evening. Budget for 200F à la carte. Located near the famous bakery, Poujauran, this Greek restaurant offers generous portions on a generous menu. The set menu includes starter, main course and drinks at lunchtime, and there's a more developed menu in the evening (until 10.30pm). À la carte, it's a lot more expensive: the best idea is to share a *pikilia* (an assortment of hors-d'œuvres) or a generous Greek salad (tomato, cucumber, onion, sweet pepper, feta cheese and olives), and then follow it with a *kleftiko* (lamb with feta cheese, garlic, herbs and tomato) served with saffron rice. There's an excellent house *au torchon* (yoghurt with honey, pine-nuts and pistachios). Credit cards are not accepted.

✕ **Le Basilic** (map C2, **40**): 2 rue Casimir-Périer 75007. ☎ 01-44-18-94-64. Metro: Solférino. Open daily noon to 2.30pm and 7.30pm to 10.30pm. Budget for around 220F. The elite of the 7th arrondissement like to meet in this comfortable brasserie, whose welcoming terrace is opposite the Church of St-Clotilde. The menu changes with the seasons, but for the faithful there are a few essentials: leg of lamb roasted with *sel de Guérande*, aubergine terrine, sole *meunière* and ice-creams. Only for those with some money to spare!

✕ **L'Affriolé** (map B1, **29**): 17 rue Malar 75007. ☎ 01-44-18-31-33. Metro and RER: Invalides. Open until 11pm. Closed Saturday lunchtime and Sunday. Set menus 120F at lunchtime, 190F in the evening. The decor here is 1940s and the innovative menu is definately worth a try. The beetroot *millefeuille* and *foie gras* with hazelnuts or duck, whole roast plaice and caramelized Jerusalem artichokes, baked apple or raisin and vanilla ice-cream are all recommended. Kind welcome.

THE EIFFEL TOWER

☎ 01-44-11-23-13; group information: ☎ 01-44-11-23-11. Website: www.tour-eiffel.fr. Metro: Bir-Hakeim-Grenelle, Trocadéro, or École-Militaire. RER: Champ-de-Mars-Tour-Eiffel (LineC). Bus Nos. 42, 69, 72, 82 and 87.

7TH

First and second floors: tours daily 9.30am to 11pm for the first, second and third floors (until midnight from mid-June to the end of August). Access by lift: for the first, second and third floors respectively: 22F, 44F and 62F, concessions: 13F, 23F and 32F. Using the stairs, one price only 18F. Free for the under 3s.

– On the **first floor**, at 57m (186ft): restaurants, bar, tea-room.

– On the **second floor**, at 115m (377ft): the famous Jules Verne gourmet restaurant, a buffet and a glazed lower gallery.

– On the **third floor**, at 214m (700ft): an open upper gallery with telescopes. Enjoy a panorama of up to 90km (55 miles) over Paris when the weather is clear; the best time to come is an hour before sundown.

The lighting system was completely changed in 1986. The Champ-de-Mars floodlights were replaced with sodium lamps in the superstructure of the tower and the resulting effect was a complete success. The illuminated screen installed in 1997, marking the countdown in days to midnight of 31 December 1999, was unfortunately hit by a bug a few hours before the crucial moment. The Eiffel tower played an important role in events marking the year 2000 in Paris, and boasts some new features in the form of both temporary and permanent changes to its illumination. Permanent installations include a giant new beacon (made up of four projectors), replacing the one which it which sported until 1970, whilst throughout the year 2000, the tower flashed with golden lights for 10 minutes every hour, from nightfall until 1am, the time when the illuminations on the Tower go out for the night.

For the record, 20 abseilers worked every night for three months to attach these bulbs to the 18km of electrics running off 30km of power cables.

FACTS ABOUT THE TOWER

The extraordinary birth of the Eiffel Tower was the crowning glory of the epic 19th-century Industrial Revolution. All good guidebooks pay homage to Gustave Eiffel, its engineer, but in fact the Eiffel Tower could well have been named something completely different. It was two engineers from Eiffel's workshops, Kœchlin and Nouguier, who thought up the idea of a very high iron tower, and won the competition for the Universal Exhibition. Then Gustave Eiffel leapt onto the bandwagon. He decided he would finance the project and in exchange his name would be associated with those of his two engineers every time their work was mentioned – very clever! Before the official inauguration at the Universal Exhibition, Eiffel organized a more intimate party for the site workers on 31 March 1889 and climbed the 1,710 steps of the Tower to plant the French flag on the top of 'his' invention. The first visitors were welcomed on 15 May 1889.

Always ahead of its time, in 1907 the Tower was given a clock, showing the time in giant luminous figures 6m (19ft) high. In 1909 the Tower was threatened with demolition but was saved by the invention of wireless telegraph, as it proved the perfect location for transmitting signals. From 1910 it became part of the International Time Service and it then played its part in National Defence as a radio transmitting station during the First World War. French radio since 1918 and French TV since 1957 have made use of the Tower and today it broadcasts six French TV channels.

When first built it was criticized and called a 'hollow chandelier', or 'an ugly skeleton', according to the writer Guy de Maupassant. The writer Huysmans had even sharper words: 'You can't believe that this shapeless grill is finished and that this vulgar suppository riddled with holes will last long.' And yet the Eiffel Tower also won over many artists including Seurat, Rousseau and Utrillo.

In line with the four points of the compass, four blocks of masonry serve as supports for the Tower's four 318m (1,040ft) legs. Its total weight is 10,100 tons, including 60 tons of paint. It is repainted every seven years – or actually slightly less than that, as the work tends to last for 15 to 16 months – in three graduated colours from the lightest (at the top) to the darkest (at the bottom). This accentuates the perspective and the impression of vertigo which you get from the ground.

DID YOU KNOW?

In hot weather the top of the Eiffel Tower expands by up to 18cm (7in), while the wind moves it by 6 to 7cm (2 to 3in). The Tower receives over 6 million visitors per year.

The Tower has also been involved in some amazing stories. In 1912, Reisfeldt, the 'birdman', unfortunately failed to fly as he leapt from the Tower with his artificial wings; he made a hole 35cm (13in) deep in the frozen ground. Marc Gayet, a hunchback trying to jump off the Tower with a parachute, fared no better when his parachute failed to open due to a technical fault. There have been some more amusing events too: there was the journalist who cycled down the steps from the first floor and reached the bottom triumphant, only to be arrested by the prefecture of police for 'causing a crowd to gather'.

Among the more tragic events, there have been only two survivors out of the 370 who have attempted suicide. Gustave Eiffel, who lived to the ripe old age of 91, was right when he said: 'I ought to be jealous of the Tower, it's more famous than I am.'

★ The **Champ-de-Mars:** surrounded by vines in the 15th century, it was occupied by market gardeners growing vegetables for the Parisians. In the 18th century it was used as a parade ground for the pupils at the École Militaire.

In 1785 the Champ-de-Mars was given an unusual assignment: the cultivation of the potato. Apparently the plantations were enclosed to encourage the Parisians to take an interest. It worked. The Parisians naturally began to covet what was forbidden to them, leading to demand for and even theft of the new vegetable. Publicity guaranteed!

In 1790, in the middle of the Revolution, the Festival of the Federation was held here. A year later, Bailly, the first Mayor of Paris, had demonstrators shot who were demanding the forfeiture of Louis XVI's rights. In 1793 the king was condemned to the guillotine, which was then set up on the Champ-de-Mars, but the people asked for it to be placed in the moat around the edge to avoid the Champ being soiled with the blood of a criminal.

★ **École Militaire:** built in 1752 to a design by Jacques-Ange Gabriel, the school was Mme de Pompadour's idea, to initiate 500 poor gentlemen into the military. 'I've approved the project, my little beloved, seeing as you're so keen on it', Louis XV wrote to her. Napoleon was one of the pupils here in 1784 and left a year later, aged 16, with the rank of sublieutenant and the comment: 'Will go far if circumstances allow it.'

LES INVALIDES

☎ 01-44-42-37-72. Metro: Invalides, Varenne, Latour-Maubourg. RER: Invalides. Bus Nos. 28, 49, 63, 69, 82, 83, 87, 92 and 93. Open daily 10am to 5pm between October and March and 10am to 6pm April to September. Closed 25 December, 1 January, 1 May and 1 November.

The entrance gate of this imposing building opens on to flowerbeds, which used to be tended by disabled soldiers. Imagine the little vegetable plots and Parisians walking around on Sunday and stopping to chat with the old soldiers. Begun in 1671, it was Louis XIV's idea to build a magnificent home for his wounded and homeless veterans as he felt that those who had served their country should be rewarded in some way. At the end of the imposing esplanade (500m/1,640ft long and 250m/820ft wide) stands the *hôtel* with its dome and the Église Saint-Louis. In the main courtyard look for the bull's eye surrounded by two wolves' paws. These are a pun on the name of the creator of the Invalides. He was called Louvois – *loup* in French means wolf and *voit* means see, hence the 'wolf sees all'. It was Jules Hardouin-Mansart, however. who finished the work of the Invalides. Construction work started on the *hôtel* in 1671, designed by Libéral Bruant.

★ **The *hôtel*:** tours daily 7.30am to 7pm. Disabled old soldiers and the poor were cared for and up to 5,000 pensioners were accommodated in this military hospital. Since the start of the last century, the military administration have gradually taken over the buildings and there are barely a hundred occupants left. The 195m (640ft) façade has a very pure line and the gate is magnificent. There is an imposing main courtyard where military parades and prestigious marriages take place surrounded by the buildings housing the Musées de l'Armée et des Plans-Reliefs (*see below*).

★ The **Église St-Louis** stands at one end of the main courtyard: there are tours 10am to 4.30pm (5.30pm in summer), except when there is an important ceremony taking place. Entry is free. This is the soldiers' church, with a military coldness; the only decoration in the long nave consists of flags captured from the enemy. The church was begun in 1677 under the direction of Jules Hardouin-Mansart. It is a fine example of Classical architecture with 107m (350ft) high lantern towers. The exterior and interior of the dome were re-gilded in 1989, and required 12kg (27lb) of gold and weeks of work. Don't miss the remarkable organ case dating from 1679 and look out for the white marble pulpit.

It was only in 1840 that the decision to transfer the body of Napoleon I to the Invalides was taken. The tomb, ringed by a crown of laurels and engraved with the names of the victories of the Empire, was finished in 1861. It is accessible until 7pm from 15 June to 15 September. The church has become a military burial place and houses many vaults containing the tombs of famous marshals: Turenne, Vauban, Foch and Lyautey.

★ **Musée de l'Armée:** ☎ 01-44-42-37-72. Website: www.invalides.org. Tours 10am to 5.45pm from 1 April to 30 September; 10am to 4.45pm the rest of the year. Closed 1 January, 1 May, 1 November and 25 December. The ticket (38F; concessions 28F, free for under 12s) gives you access to the Musée de l'Armée, the Musée des Plans-Reliefs (scale models), the Dome (Napoleon's tomb) and to the Musée de l'Ordre de la Libération. There are conferences and a musical season from October to June in the main hall and the Église St-Louis. ☎ 01-44-42-48-14. There are tours and stories for children aged from 7 to 12 (30F for children; 38F for adults). ☎ 01-44-42-51-73.

– **Western wing of the ground floor:** there are many weapons and suits of armour, mainly from the 16th century, as well as some historical pieces such as the armour and sword used by François I, the armour worn by Charles IX, Louis XIII and Louis XIV (pieces from the former royal collections). There's an interesting little section of antiquities with flints, ancient bronze weapons, a Corinthian helmet, a Greek crown and other fine articles from the Roman age. The oriental collections are magnificent, in particular the Turkish quiver and bows (17th century), superb Balinese ceremonial kriss, Chinese imperial swords, 16th century Samurai armour, and guns inlaid with mother-of-pearl and precious stones.

– **On the second floor:** halls devoted to the two world wars. From the First World War there are documents, photographs, paintings, drawings, weapons, uniforms and miscellaneous souvenirs, including a poster calling people to join up (dated 2 August 1914). The Second World War collection can either be viewed as a continuation from the Frist World War section, or it can be visited separately as part of the new wing on the third floor (*see below*).

– **On the third floor:** after a closure lasting 30 years, in a light and well-ventilated setting, the Salle Gribeauval offers a complete retrospective on the artillery of the French Land Army from 1550 to 1914.

– **New wing:** opened in June 2000, this wing houses collections covering the period from 1939 to 1945: the Second World War, the rise of the free French forces and the France Combattante. Key moments in French history are well-documented – for example, DeGaulle's rallying call to the French nation, the Battle of Britain and the Liberation of Paris. The museum has chosen a hi-tec approach, with videos and multimedia interactive equipment.

– **Eastern wing:** the tour continues on the other side of the main courtyard with the Salle Turenne dedicated to the emblems of the French Army from the 17th century to the present day. There is a remarkable set of weapons from the 17th and 19th centuries, a series of unique French uniforms (1767–1870) and portraits of famous military men. Finally, there are the Napoleonic souvenirs: hat, waistcoat and his military room (not forgetting his tomb in the Dome).

★ **Musée des Plans-Reliefs:** Hôtel National des Invalides, 6 boulevard des Invalides 75007. ☎ 01-45-51-95-05. Open daily 10am to 5pm from 1 October to 31 March and 10am to 6pm from 1 April to 30 September. Closed 1 January, 1 May, 1 November and 25 December. The entry ticket is combined with the Musée de l'Armée. Entry fee 37F; reduced rate for children under 12, and the over 60s. Educational activities available with advance booking, ☎ 01-45-51-92-45.

Situated on the top floor of the Invalides, this museum was opened in its present position in 1977 and houses models of fortified cities. The scale models were created on Louvois' initiative in the 17th century in order to compensate for the inaccurate maps of the period. Military commanders realised the need to be precisely aware of the location of a particular place (in minute detail: hills, plains, and so on) in order to be able to both defend and attack strategic points. They soon became a symbol of royal power and were proudly shown off to visiting VIPs. Apart from the military aspect, this museum is also a very interesting repository of urban history, with human and physical geography and sociology. There are plenty of maps and prints and detailed records on the façades of streets. The museum's collection, which comprises more than 100 scale models as well as models and other maps, was classified as a historic monument in 1927.

★ **The Dôme Church:** tours around the tomb daily 10am to 5.45pm from 1 April to 30 September; 10am to 6.45pm from 15 June to 15 September; 10am to 4.45pm the rest of the year. Closed 25 December, 1 January, 1 May and 1 November. Last entry half an hour before closing time.

Forming a central part of the existing buildings of Les Invalides (1679–1706) by Hardouin-Mansart, this is one of the finest monuments erected since the Renaissance. The building is perfectly adapted for its intended use, which was rare in the buildings of Louis XIV – Versailles, for instance was impossible to heat, a typical example of one of his monumental errors. It is not certain what Louis intended this second church for; perhaps it was to replace the St-Denis basilica, but it was used exclusively by the king himself and became a tomb for the Bourbon family.

The interior is very ornate, and certainly more interesting than the famous **tomb of Napoleon**, which has a more symbolic than an aesthetic value. Note that Napoleon's mortal remains actually rest in six concentric coffins, with his feet pointing towards the altar. The innermost is made of tin, the next of mahogany, the next from lead, the next from ebony, and the last from oak. He was in fact buried with his boots unstitched – when he was exhumed on St Helena in 1840 it was revealed that his toenails had grown after his death, making holes in his socks.

AROUND LES INVALIDES

★ **Musée Rodin:** 77 rue de Varenne 75007. ☎ 01-44-18-61-10. Fax: 01-45-51-17-52. Website: www.musee-rodin.fr. Metro: Varenne. Open 9.30am to 5.45pm (4.45pm 1 October to 31 March). Last entry 30 minutes before closing time. Closed Monday and public holidays. Entry fee 28F; concessions 18F; reduced rate on Sunday. Free for under 18s and on the first Sunday of every month. Entry to the park 5F.

Rodin, who rented part of the Hôtel Biron in order to set up his workshop, donated all his works to the State in 1916 with a view to creating this museum. It was opened to the public three years later and he could hardly have dreamed of a better setting. Ten days before he died he married his lifelong companion, Rose Beuret. You will find his most famous works here: *Le Baiser* (The Kiss), *Les Bourgeois de Calais* (The Burghers of Calais) and *Le Penseur* (The Thinker) are among those on display both inside and outside in the rose garden. All in all there are some 500 works to be seen.

There are also works throughout the building from Rodin's personal collection. It's impossible to list everything, so below is a selection of what the museum holds.

– **Ground floor:** Here you'll find *La Jeune Femme au Chapeau Fleuri*, *L'Âge d'Airain*, *Madame Roll*, and a few of Rodin's canvases: *St Jean-Baptiste Prêchant* and *Le Baiser*. Also *Rodin*, a portrait by John Sargent. In the Camille Claudel hall is the admirable *Âge Mûr*. On the staircase, *Les Trois Ombres*.

– **First floor:** On the right is *L'Illusion, Sœur d'Icare*, some variations on Balzac and three superb works by Van Gogh: *Le Père Tanguy*, *Vue du Viaduc d'Arles* and *Les Moissonneurs*. Also *Femme Nue* by Renoir and *Belle-Île* by Monet. *Le Théâtre de Belleville* is by Eugène Carrière, and there are paintings by Charles Cottet. On the left are the *Enfant Prodigue* and *La Toilette de Vénus* by Rodin and the plaster casts for *La Porte de l'Enfer*. There is the prodigious *Penseur* by Edvard Munch and *Tête d'Homme Blessé* attributed to Géricault.

– **The park:** The central garden has been completely restructured. On the western side (or on the right with your back to the museum) a winding path has been created on the theme of water springs. On the other side there's a special setting for *Orpheus*, where plant-life reinforces the dramatic character of the work. Right at the bottom there are three arches in a lattice fence, echoing the three bays of the garden façade. There is a remarkable view over the garden and the house and more sculptures: *La Porte de l'Enfer*, the famous *Bourgeois de Calais* and *Le Penseur*.

✕ Why not admire the works of the Master while dining in the shady **café** in the museum's park? Open 10am to 6pm. Often deserted, this is a wonderful spot when the weather's fine. There is a shop selling books and souvenirs.

★ **Le Bon Marché:** rue de Sèvres, on the corner with the rue du Bac 75007. Metro: Sèvres-Babylone. Paris's first department store. The metallic roof is by Gustave Eiffel. M. Boucicaut was the first to offer free entry with no obligation to purchase, to display prices and to offer exchange and refund, all revolutionary. As with so much of this quarter, the atmosphere is somewhat hushed. It inspired Émile Zola's novel *Au Bonheur des Dames* (The Ladies' Paradise), and when writing the book he often came in to talk to the staff.

The walk through the public garden just opposite the *Bon Marché* is more interesting. There is an enormous statue showing Mme Boucicaut (symbol of goodness and charity) 'giving food to the poor'.

★ **Jardin de Babylone:** 33 rue de Babylone 75007. Metro: Sèvres-Babylone. Formerly a cloister garden, this is now practically an orchard. At the entrance there is a row of cherry trees; apple trees line the avenues; on the pergola on the right there are vines and there is also a double hedgerow of hazel trees and redcurrant bushes.

★ **Rue du Bac:** this street was used to take stones from the quarries of Montrouge for the construction of the Tuileries. It quickly became the link between the Left and Right Banks.

★ **Chapelle de la Médaille Miraculeuse:** 140 rue du Bac 75007. ☎ 01-49-54-78-88. Fax: 01-49-54-78-89. Metro: Rue du Bac. Open 7.45am to 1pm and 2.30pm to 7pm; Tuesday all day; Friday closed 1pm to 4pm. There are Masses at 8am, 10.30am and 12.30pm; Tuesday, also at 4pm and 6.30pm; Saturday, there is also a Mass at 5.15pm; Sunday at 7.30am, 10am and 11.15am. It was here that the Virgin appeared to a nun, Catherine Labouré, on 27 November 1830. Ever since then the chapel has been full. Over 2 million people come here every year and at the 12.30pm Mass you'll see a cross-section of the local population together with pilgrims. The chapel is of considerable interest, with the bodies of St Catherine and St Louise, the founder of the Daughters of Charity, kept in reliquaries.

THE FAUBOURG ST-GERMAIN

Between the esplanade of Invalides and the boulevard St-Germain is the area of government ministries and the embassies – over 150 of them in 200 hectares (500 acres). They occupy most of the large private residences built here in the early 18th century, when the Marais was in decline. During the week you can see courtyards and gardens, but at weekends everything is closed and the area is like a ghost town. Only the rue du Bac, with its own particular charm, retains some interest. There's a superb 18th-century fountain at 59 rue de Grenelle. At 57 rue de Varenne stands the **Hôtel Matignon**, where the Prime Minister lives.

A SOCIAL STUDY

A study of the privileged people who are hidden away behind the façades of the Faubourg is quite fascinating, because you'll find, side by side, members of all the classes who have successively dominated French political life over the last 300 years. If the top civil servants make do with a five-room apartment in the avenue Rapp or avenue Bosquet, a few millionaires can afford their own private residence, such as the Greek ship-owner Niarchos, whose residence in the rue de Chanaleilles houses one of the finest private collections of 17th-century French furniture and 10 or so Van Goghs! Their neighbours, the Republican ministers, hang out between the boulevard St-Germain and Les Invalides – an incessant parade of cars with official badges on them. All these people know one another – the garden parties must be spectacular! The latest inhabitants are the heirs of the great French families; dozens of them still live here, even after several revolutions and despite quite a lot of problems with the houses their ancestors had built over 300 years ago.

★ **Musée Maillol and the Fondation Dina Vierny:** 59–61 rue de Grenelle 75007. ☎ 01-42-22-59-58. Fax: 01-42-84-14-44. Metro: Rue-du-Bac. Bus Nos. 63, 68, 69, 83, 84, 94. Open 11am to 6pm. Closed Tuesday and public holidays. Entry fee 40F; concessions 30F; free for under 16s.

This museum is the result of Dina Vierny's extraordinary passion for art, and for Aristide Maillol in particular. The great sculptor's favourite model (she also sat for Matisse, Dufy and Bonnard), Dina fought to set up this little-known museum over a period of 30 years. The collection is housed in a superb private residence adorned by the *Fontaine des Quatre Saisons* by Bouchardon. Maillol features large, with his *Monumentales* on the ground floor, but there is also room for Marcel Duchamp (the admirable *Boîte en Valise* and *La Mariée*), Oscar Rabin (*Le Passeport*) and Vladimir Yankilevski (*La Porte, Derrière la Porte, la Plage*, executed during the Brezhnev period).

– **The first floor:** here there are charcoal nudes by Maillol, red chalk drawings, superb charcoals and chalk on packaging paper, and pastels. Admire the strange *Dos Couché*, several bronzes, the voluptuous *Grand Nu Jaune* in oil, ceramics, *Grand Nu Sombre* by Pierre Bonnard and works by Gauguin, Renoir, Odilon Redon and Maurice Denis (*Nono au Bain*).

– **The second floor:** more oils (an exquisite portrait of Mme Maillol), tapestries by the Master, large bronzes (*L'Été, Le Printemps*, *Flore* and *Pomone*) and terracottas. In an elegant panelled hall, there is a rich exhibition of works by Picasso, Ingres, Degas, Foujita, Cézanne, Pascin and Suzanne Valadon. And, in other halls, Pougny, Poliakoff and Kandinsky (*Aigles Rouges*).

✕ In the basement, if you fancy a snack, there is a charming **café** offering dishes of the day, salads, sandwiches, quiches, cakes and ice-cream. You can eat in the café without paying the museum entry fee (tell them at reception).

THE MUSÉE D'ORSAY

The Musée d'Orsay has quite simply created a fantastic niche for itself as one of the finest museums in the world. Covering the whole of the second half of the 19th century, it spans under one roof the entire range of the visual arts produced from 1848–1914, namely sculpture, painting, architecture, the decorative and graphic arts and photography. It is also a genuine interdisciplinary museum, with cross-references to literature, music and daily life under the Second Empire (1852–1870) and the early years of the Third Republic (1870–1940). The museum successfully represents the challenge to official and academic art by encouraging the innovative trends that completely altered the history of art. Its collections were built up from the state collections in the Louvre (for artists born after 1820), and from the Impressionist collections of the Musée du Jeu de Paume and the Musée d'Art Moderne (for those born before 1870), and augmented by recent acquisitions. Visitors can trace in detail the path taken by those artists and sculptors who caused the greatest artistic revolution since the Renaissance at the start of the 20th century. The museum regularly features themed exhibitions, which place these radical changes in their historical, economic and social contexts.

Established during three terms of French presidency, it is the result of an unusual political co-operation.

If France preens its feathers, it's not without justification: every art specialist the world over recognises that France, along with the United States, the UK and Spain, is one of the few countries to have a long tradition of establishing outstanding museums; the most recent include the Pompidou Centre, the Musée Picasso and the Musée d'Orsay. Since December 1986, Orsay has seen nearly 2 million visitors a year pass through its doors.

PRACTICAL INFORMATION

62 rue de Lille 75007. Main entrance: 1 rue de la Légion-d'Honneur 75007. ☎ 01-40-49-48-14: general information: ☎ 01-45-49-11-11. Website: www.musée-orsay.fr. Metro: Solférino. RER: Musée-d'Orsay (line C). Bus Nos 24, 63, 68, 69, 73, 83, 84 and 94. Open Tuesday, Wednesday, Friday and Saturday, 10am to 6pm; Thursday until 9.45pm; Sunday, 9am to 6pm. Between 20 June and 20 September, open from 9am. Closed Monday. N.B.: the ticket office closes half an hour before closing time. Themed guided tour from Tuesday to Saturday (for information: ☎ 01-45-49-45-46 for school parties and ☎ 01-45-49-16-15 for all other groups). There's a special introduction to a particular work every day except Saturday at 12.30pm. Admission: 40F and 30F on Sundays and for concessions. Free for under-18s and the first Sunday in the month. A bookshop and boutique selling cards and gifts gives you the chance to bring a souvenir away from your visit.

✕ When you get hungry there is a **restaurant** at 1 rue de la Légion-d'Honneur 75007. Access through the museum entrance. Closed Monday. Open Tuesday to Sunday 11.30am to 2.30pm; there's a tea-room in the afternoons (except Thursday) 3.30pm to 5.30pm; dinner only Thursday 7pm to 9.30pm. In a luxurious setting (decorated ceiling, painted panels and gildings) you can enjoy good food at reasonable prices. Set menu of the day 89F (main course and dessert) or you can choose just the main course for 71F, or the themed buffet with around 15 dishes at 96F (buffet and dessert).

✕ On the upper level is the **Café des Hauteurs** (near Degas' pastels just behind the great clock). Open 11am to 5pm (9pm Thursday), and less expensive than the restaurant.

The food's very good: salads and snacks such as country-style or seafood open sandwiches, quiches or pizzas in the price range 32F to 66F (only served at lunchtime or dinner time). For tea, there are muffins with tea or coffee for 28F.

– There are numerous **activities and events**: themed films and documentaries are shown in the auditorium (the documentaries are free with the entry ticket), as well as conferences, concerts and courses in cultural history.

A BRIEF HISTORY

The Orsay was originally a station, built in record time between 1898 and 1900 on the charred remains of the Palais d'Orsay, burnt down during the Paris Commune. The construction was daring for the time, with an enormous metallic structure even heavier than the Eiffel Tower. The nave is even bigger than the one in Notre-Dame! The building, although constructed at the end of the 19th century, is definitely in the '1900 eclectic-rococo-Napoleon-III' style, which is closer to a palace than a railway station. The architect who won the tender did so thanks to his idea of a stone façade, intended to make the station blend in with its environment. Later on, a luxury hotel was added (this was where General de Gaulle announced his return to power in 1958, declaring: 'Do you really think that at the age of 67 I'm going to start out on a career as a dictator?'). However, the station was little used by 1939 as trains became too long for the platforms. The main rail connection to the south west fell naturally to the Gare d'Austerlitz, and Orsay was used as a reception centre for concentration camp prisoners when Paris was liberated, and was also temporarily occupied by the Théâtre Renaud-Barrault. In 1962, Orson Welles filmed *The Trial* and Bertolucci shot a few scenes of *The Conformist* here.

Lots of plans for converting the station were put forward and finally it was decided to construct a large hotel and in 1970 planning permission for the demolition of the station was granted. But public opinion began to turn against the disappearance of such a shining example of the metallic architecture of the 19th century, and in 1973, under President Georges Pompidou, the Minister of Culture, Jacques Duhamel, listed the station in the Inventory of Historic Monuments. But no one knew quite what to do with it. The idea of creating a museum gained momentum in 1977, and the Museums Board of France launched a study to look into it. Two years later, President Valéry Giscard d'Estaing organized a consultation, following which an architectural firm was chosen for the job. The design was entrusted to Renaud Bardon, Pierre Colboc and Jean-Paul Philippon, and the interior conversion to the Italian architect Gae Aulenti. The problems were not easy to solve. They had to fill a structure which had not been designed to house a museum, think about preventing any rises in the water level of the Seine, compensate for the vibrations of the RER, and adapt the air-conditioning and lighting to such an enormous structure. In addition, there were huge financial problems. When François Mitterrand came to power he put a stop to the uncertainties and demanded that the project was to be completed – he tripled the budget.

Priority was given to the architectural continuity of the station. The great nave was kept in its entirety and highlighted by the creation of a longitudinal axis. As for the interior, Gae Aulenti dreamed up a museum on five levels. In the nave, there is a central aisle, on ascending platforms, leading on each side to suites of halls, followed by a series of terraces, interspersed with more halls. Obviously there was no lack of critics; they denounced Gae Aulenti's 'pharaoism' (sharper tongues called it a 'Mussolini style'). But today it is widely accepted as an architectural masterpiece, with the works presented over 17,000m (55,700ft) of floor space and in natural light.

WHAT TO SEE

The museum has an excellent free leaflet with maps of each level and descriptions of the halls. Below is a selection of what there is to see.

● *Presentation of collections*

The great artistic movements are laid out in chronological order, although the need to leave some major collections grouped together means that the pattern is disrupted from time to time.

● *Sculpture*

The sculptures are splendidly displayed down the central aisle, where you can see *La Danse* by Carpeaux, from the façade of the Garnier Opéra, and the *Ugolin*, which once adorned the Opéra's balcony, as well as David d'Angers' *Goethe*, Pradier's *Sapho* and Mercier's *David*. There's an unusual plaster haut-relief of the *Gates of Hell* (*Porte d'Enfer*) by Rodin as well as his amazing statue of Balzac, followed by dozens of bronzes by Degas and busts by Dalou. The stylised forms of Maillol, Pompon and Bourdelle round off the sculptures.

● *Painting*

Painting is classified by themes and schools. Unusually, the *pompiers* – the official and academic painters of the 19th century – are on display here. The decision to show them was not unanimous and caused a great deal of controversy. Many of the painters who triumphed at the end of the 19th century and were then forgotten were actually pretty poor painters, but others did have something to say before slipping away into dull academicism. Other artists represented a sort of compromise, bridging the gap between contemporary and past artists, but producing works that were nonetheless worthy of interest. There were debates about whether these artists should be hung in the large halls on the Seine side (with the stable light from the north, so dear to painters), thus relegating the Impressionists to the fifth floor, in halls at least as cramped as the Jeu de Paume (with severe problems with the lighting and the setting). However, it doesn't seem to have made a difference to attendance figures!

● *Architecture*

Right at the back of the main aisle is an area permanently devoted to architecture where, beneath a glass paving slab, you can see a model of the

Opéra district and a cross-section of the Opéra building as it was when it was opened in 1875. Along with the plans, drafts and model, there's also a panoramic aerial view of Paris seen from the south which shows the extent of the city before the time of Haussmann's alterations.

Ornamentation runs riot in the ballroom upstairs, which positively drips with gilt moulding. It's a fitting backdrop for a few gems of 'Third Republic' academic art.

● *Decorative Arts*

For once, these are not the poor relations. After a spell in purgatory due to a previous generation's dim view of the lifestyle of the upper middle classes, they have now found their place naturally enough in the middle of a vast stylistic wheel that rotates through the neo-Renaissance and Classicism to the heights of Art Nouveau via the excesses of Orientalism and Chinoiserie. Soon to appear in the museum are the works of the Wiener Werkstätte school that will complement well those of William Morris and Frank Lloyd Wright.

● *Photography*

Dating from 1839, photography is also represented in the Musée d'Orsay, which holds nearly 30,000 photos. As well as providing invaluable insight into ages past, the photos reflect both the speed of technological advancement and the aesthetic concerns of talented portrait and landscape artists like Nadar, Regnault, Nègre, Stieglitz and, not least, Man Ray, with his 1922 photograph of Marcel Proust on his deathbed. Photography has its own room, number 49 on the fourth floor.

Apart from all that, as you wander round, armed with the museum's excellent plan, you're more than likely to come across a group being lectured by an official guide. Their commentaries are usually very interesting, and it's amazing what you can learn from them.

● **Ground Floor:**

The museum's central aisle leads you in stately style past the marble, bronze and onyx statues that line the edges; you get a sense of the solemnity that must have reigned in the official salons of the 19th century. On either side passageways lead off between great blocks of marble resembling the entrance to an Egyptian temple, to smaller rooms that cover an admirable range of works.

– Begin to the right of the main aisle (rooms 1–3) with the **great Classical and Romantic painters**, both of which schools were a major influence on the Impressionists. In the first part of this section are some major 'official' painters, like Ingres, represented by *La Source*, and Chassériau's *Le Tepidarium*, jaunty pieces that delighted the authorities of the day as they strolled about in their top hats and tails twiddling their moustaches. Baudelaire waxed lyrical about the intense colours of Delacroix' *Chasse aux lions*, while Cabanel's *Naissance de Vénus* (acquired by Napoleon III, and looking like an advert for Lancôme) had a whole generation of students from the academy of Fine Arts positively drooling. Then there's Paul Baudry's portrait of his friend *Charles Gamier*, who designed the Paris Opéra, and you start to see early hints of Symbolism in *Jeunes filles au bord de la mer* by Puvis de Chavannes (vulgarly dubbed '*Pubis de Cheval*' by Dalí) and Gustave Moreau's *Orphée*. Notice the pre-1870 paintings by

Degas, clearly already obsessed with race horses. Behind this section, the decorative arts of the Second Empire are in full swing with an eclectic riot of outrageous cabinets, wallpaper and porcelain.

Return to the bottom of the steps of the central aisle.

– On the left is the **Salle Daumier** (4),dedicated to the extraordinary talent of this painter and caricaturist. You can see his *Parlementaires*, an amazing series of terracotta statuettes, painted in oils and used as models for cartoons in the *Charivan*, as well as his baroque but expressive paintings, *Scènes de comédie, Les Voleurs de l'âne, Don Quichotte et la mule morte, Crispin et Scapin*, and so on. Daumier died in penury, misunderstood by his contemporaries.

Next, you come to the **Cauchard collection** (5), put together by this enlightened collector who founded the great workshops of the Louvre and championed the work of Millet, Rousseau, Corot and the Barbizon school. Millet is represented by *Angélus du soir*, a vision of peasants hankering after the countryside they had abandoned for the city, and *by Le Printemps*, where the unearthly effects of the light after a storm are not dissimilar to the techniques used by Constable or Reynolds. Then there's *Le Palais des Doges* by Ziem and *Campagnie de France*, 1814, by Meissonier, a strikingly realistic work that captures the characters' disenchantment with war.

– In the aisle on the Seine side of the museum the paintings glorify agriculture and animal husbandry, the mainstays of French rural life in the 19th century. Of note are Daubigny's *Les Vendanges en Bourgogne*, Troyon's *Boeufs allant au labour* (you can really sense the animals straining with the effort), Rosa Bonheur's *Labourage nivernais*, and so on.

– The rotunda (7) is devoted to masterpieces by the father of Realism, Courbet. *Un enterrement à Omans* was the movement's manifesto, but it was savaged by the critics in 1850 who wanted to know how 'anyone could paint such hideous people'. *La Falaise d'Etretat* is an overt hymn to nature devoid of the presence of man. *L'Atelier du peintre* is an unintentionally visionary work in spite of the realism of the portrait and still life; Baudelaire can be seen reading on the right. Finally, there's a stark realism about *L'Origine du monde* though no lack of feeling; one of its former owners, the psychoanalyst Jacques Lacan, is reputed to have allowed only specially chosen friends to see it.

– Still on the left, alongside the central aisle (rooms 14–18), are the wonderful, all-encompassing rooms of the **Impressionists before 1870**. In the Manet room, you can see his *Olympia*, which caused such a scandal. Strangely enough, it wasn't the model with the simple choker round her neck symbolising the immorality of prostitution (Goya had set the precedent here) that got the painting refused by the 1865 Official Salon, but the fact that the painting was 'unfinished' in the eyes of the jury. Take a look at the bunch of flowers; it consists of splashes of colour and is why *Olympia* is considered the painting with which Impressionism really began. Zola came to the defence of *Olympia*, and, in return, Manet painted his portrait, including, in the middle of some Japanese engravings, a reproduction of the prostitute who had caused such a rumpus. Other no less famous Manets include *Le Balcon*, where the mathematical structure reveals a modernity that was truly revolutionary for 1869; here the painter Berthe Morisot is depicted leaning on the railings surrounded by oddly static characters. *Le Fifre* (refused by the Official Salon in 1866) is similarly avant-garde, with its uniform background and challenge to the established rules of perspective.

Like the early works of Bazille and Renoir, *Déjeuner sur l'herbe* shows Monet clearly following in Manet's footsteps, and the influence is still more apparent in the wonderful winter landscape of *La Pie*, where the subtle play on the monochrome white provides the only contrast with the vibrant colours of the other works. Nonetheless it, too, was refused by the jury of the 1869 Salon.

– Come back to the Seine side where, in addition to the little rooms of pastels (17–21), mostly by Redon, Millet and Degas, is a room devoted to the work of Fantin-Latour (number 15), a great friend of the Impressionists. *Un coin de table* depicts the ill-starred duo, Verlaine and Rimbaud. The Belgian Alfred Stevens, darling of Parisian women, was the regular portrait artist of Second Empire high society ladies.

– In room 16, Boudin and Jongkind explore the infinite nuances of the Normandy coast at the time when Deauville and Trouville were becoming fashionable seaside resorts.

Next comes room 19 and the collection of the Basque Personnaz, a friend of Degas. You can trace the works of Guillaumin and Pissarro between 1870–1902 in 14 paintings, which show how Pissarro's work evolved from Impressionism to Pointillism. Beside these is *Jeune fille au jardin* by an American friend of Degas, Mary Cassat.

– Room 20 brings together the works assembled by the Argentine collector Edouardo Mollard, who favoured landscape paintings by the Barbizon school and Alfred Sisley, an Englishman who fell in love with the Île de France.

– In the last part on this level, beside the forbidding works of the **Realists**, are the fascinating paintings of the **Orientalists**. In the wake of Napoleon's visit to Egypt, the distant vision of the Middle East had became a popular subject. Paintings of note include *Pèlerins allant à la Mecque* by Léon Belly, *Le Pays de la soif* by Eugène Fromentin, and *Sahara ou Le Désert* by Guillaumin, an amazing painting where you get a real sense of the desolate emptiness of the desert.

– As you go up the escalator to the upper level, don't miss the opportunity to look down into the vast nave of the museum, rustling with the muffled whispers and footsteps of visitors coming in.

● **The Upper Level:**

Most of the **Impressionist** and **Post-impressionist** paintings, which used to be on display in the Musée du Jeu de Paume, are now hung in rooms on the upper level. N.B.: the sheer numbers of so many masterpieces makes it totally impossible to list them all.

One historical point to note is that Monet's *Impression, soleil levant*, formerly displayed in the Musée Marmortan, a gallery much maligned by contemporary critics, involuntarily gave its name to the movement.

– Begin in Room 29 with the Moreau-Nélaton Collection. Two years before the *Olympia* scandal Manet had already made enemies by displaying his *Déjeuner sur l'herbe*. Originally called *Partie carrée*, it was declared 'indecent' by Napoleon III. The subject, a naked woman flanked by two men in a wood, provoked violent controversy, but the innovative sweeping brush strokes and the absence of perspective so adored by the Classical painters brought it to the attention of the critics. The irony was that it was rejected by the Salon of 1863 although it was inspired by a work by Raphaël, a painter the Academicians positively worshipped. Also in this room are two major Monets: *Coquelicots* and *Le Pont de chemin de fer à Argenteuil*, as well as the touching *Blonde aux seins nus* by Manet, bathed in a pearly light.

– Following on is Room 30, where you can see Monet's friend Whistler's *La Mère de l'artiste* and Caillebotte's *Les Raboteurs de parquet*, important not only because it was influenced by photography and revolutionised the concept of framing, but because it took as its subject the world of work. The blinding light portrayed in it was also innovative.

– In the following room are paintings by Degas, including *L'Absinthe*, with its haggard, listless characters, a work inspired by Baudelaire's search for an artificial paradise. Or there's *Les Repasseuses* depicting the dull, monotonous chores of the world of women's work, and evoking the novels of Zola, who used the theme repeatedly.

One display case is devoted to dance: numerous terracottas, later recast in bronze, illustrate Degas' mission to capture the movement of the body as it strained with the effort of exercise. The thespian world is also represented, with *Orchestre de l'Opéra*, a striking piece that looks like a photograph, where everything is crammed into a confined space.

There's a very obvious Japanese influence about *Sur la plage* by Manet, while sketches of *Stéphane Mallarmé* and *Georges Clémenceau* reveal the painter's commitment to portrait painting.

– Room 32. The 1870 war with Germany dispersed the Impressionists, but in the decade that followed they were reunited thanks to several exhibitions financed by philanthropists and critics who were scandalised to see their works systematically refused by the Official Salons.

The panoply of impressive works here is almost overwhelming. In no particular order are: the portrait of *Alphonsine Fournaise* by Renoir, who had also joined the movement; the masterly *Bal du Moulin de la Galette*, where you feel drawn into the dance by the bustle and gaiety of the scene; *La Balançoire*, and *Torse au soleil*, with its experimental bluish shadows cast by the light falling through the leaves.

The electrifying colours of the red, white and blue flags *in Rue Montorgueil pavoisée* create a striking impact, while, in *Dindons*, Monet gives free rein to his quest to capture the light. Not to be missed are *Les Toits rouges* by Pissarro, a real landlubber who devoted himself to the agricultural world, and next to it, Sisley's *Régates à Molesey* and *Le Givre*, typically English works that evoke the inconstancy and inclemency of the weather.

Another Monet, *La Gare Saint-Lazare*, illustrates that poetry really can be found in an industrial setting; the train appears as a vague apparition, a hazy outline against clouds of steam. Zola raved about it. With the series of *Cathédrales de Rouen* and variations on *Meules de foin* (Haystacks), painted at different times of day, Monet pushed his search for coloration to its limits. Subjectivity reigned supreme.

Next are paintings by Renoir, and you can see the influence of his travels in Algeria and his discovery of the rich Mediterranean colours in *Fêtes arabes à Alger*, and in *Les Baigneuses*, a work that's positively drenched in colour. Further on are *Jeunes Filles au piano* and *Danse à la campagne* coupled with *Danse à la ville*, where you'll be amused to note how the same man holds a different partner according to the social setting: in one, a white goose and in the other, a courtesan.

– Colour reaches its apotheosis in the **Van Gogh room**. Fifteen paintings trace his short career, first in the Belgian Borinage, where he applied thick layers of paint and browns predominated, as in *La paysanne hollandaise*, and then in his Parisian period, where he came under the influence of the Impressionists (*Restaurant de la Sirène*, for example). Later he met Gauguin, and their brief life together in Provence is represented *by La chambre à Arles*, *Salle de danse* and *Les Roulottes*, where the brilliant colours shimmer in the white heat of midday, enhanced with flat tints and picked out in black like a stained-glass window. The magnificent *Nuit étoilée* recalls the work of Munch. Other paintings are a reminder of the times when he was shut away during outbursts of madness, such as *Portrait de l'artiste peint à Saint-Rémy*, where the artist seems to cast a questioning glance at his own image; there's a terrible look of lucidity and torment in his eyes, emphasised by the background pattern of intense, swirling blues. His physician, Dr Gachet, who treated him in Auvers, was also a friend. His portrait of the doctor is a work that's full of compassion, but the crazed, dramatic vision of *L'Église d'Auvers-sur-Oise* gives more of a sense of the artist's approaching end and suicide.

– **Cézanne room** (36). Cézanne also stayed in Auvers-sur-Oise in company with Pissarro. He developed his own concept of perspective, which you can see in the famous *Joueurs de cartes*, *L'Estaque* and *La Maison du pendu*. His still lifes border on geometric painting and influenced the Cubists.

Cast your eye over the panels painted by Toulouse-Lautrec for the Foire du Trône, where he's depicted characters such as La Goulue and the acrobat Valentin together with Jane Avril and Oscar Wilde.

– On the same level as the **Café des Hauteurs** are the darkened rooms containing pastels by Degas (37 and 38). They lead straight into room 39, devoted to the **last years of Monet and Renoir**, including, among other things, *Londres*, *Le Parlement* and, from his time at Giverny, *Les Nymphéas bleus* by Monet. Here you can also see *Les Grandes Baigneuses* by Renoir, painted when he was crippled with rheumatism. All the faces look the same, suggesting that, presumably, he only had one model to work from.

– Turn a corner and you'll find more pastels in Room 40, with Odilon Redon's delicate *Coquille* and the mysterious *Parc de Bruxelles* by William de Gouve de Nuncques, a precursor of Magritte.

– Behind the great glass panelling is a series of rooms starting with Room 42 and the naïve, primitive paintings of Le Douanier Rousseau, including *La Guerre* and *La Charmeuse de serpents*. The French poet, Apollinaire, considered him the most genuinely modern painter of his time.

– The **School of Pont-Aven**. Pont-Aven was the idyllic Breton harbour chosen by painters as a refuge from the Academy and its critics, where they could get on with their work in peace. At the time, Brittany was thought of as an unusual and exotic place that exuded the very essence of primitivism.

– Room 43. This room includes paintings by Gauguin, among others, such as *Portrait de l'artiste* and a masterpiece, *La Belle Angèle*, showing Miss Pont-Aven in her Sunday best, that is somewhere between a Russian Icon and the *Mona Lisa*. To her left, notice the Peruvian idol, a souvenir of

Gauguin's childhood. *Aréaréa* and *Vaïrumati* date from his time in Tahiti, and the geometrical bodies are reminiscent of Amerindian art. The lizard captured by a white bird is a theme that crops up in Polynesian fairy stories and represents the struggle of the light against the shadows. Opposite are paintings by Emile Bernard, the first artist to develop a 'cloisonné' style of painting, using flat tints in random colours and thick black lines like a stained-glass window. *Lutte bretonne* looks like an illustration for a Tintin album.

– Continue on to the Neo-Impressionists where the Pointillists totally deconstructed light. Of note are *Femmes au puit* and *Bouée rouge* by Paul Signac, and Seurat's marvellous but unfinished *Cirque*, an attempt to reconcile scientific theories about the division of light with the psychology of vision. Don't miss the sunset in *La Plage à Heist* by Georges Lemmen.

– Before reaching the small paintings of the **nabis** – Maurice Denis, Félix Vallotton, Bonnard, Vuillard and Sérusier (*Le Talisman*) – a whole hall is dedicated to **Toulouse Lautrec pastels**, including *Jane Avril, La Clownesse Cha-U-Kao, La Toilette* and *Le Lit*.

– Going back down to the mid-level, **the Max and Rosy Kaganovitch Collection** includes works by Bonnard, Derain, Vlaminck and Cézanne, *L'Hôpital St-Paul à St-Rémy* by Van Gogh and *Paysannes Bretonnes* by Gaugin.

● **Mid-level Gallery**

– On the Seine side you'll find all the gilt, pomp and splendour of the Third Republic in the Salle des Fêtes (551), oozing allegorical subjects in the finest pretentious style, like the idealised nude of *Naissance de Vénus* by William Bouguereau. Move on to rooms 55–60, devoted to **naturalism,** which have some remarkable works (even if they are too academic or outrageously lyrical for some tastes). See *La Paye des Moissonneurs* by Léon L'hermitte (1882), *The Docks of Cardiff*, a fantastic fresco of popular life by Lionel Walden, *Le Rêve* by Édouard Detaille, *L'Excommunication de Robert le Pieux* by Albert Laurens and *Caïn* by Fernand Cormon. The world of work is glorified, on the other hand, in the sculptures by Constantin Meunier and the monumental triptych *Âges des ouvriers* by Léon Frédéric. Of interest are a sculpture of Madame Ettore Bugatti, wife of the famous car manufacturer, by Rembrandt Bugatti, a marble bust of Sarah Bernhardt and a portrait of Marcel Proust by Emile Blanche.

– Rooms 59 and 60 are devoted to French **Symbolists**, among them Eugène Carrière, with his *Paul Verlaine*; Delville's languid adonises evoking Platonic love; Ménard; the decorative panels for the Château de Domecy by Redon, and non-French artists, like Gustave Klimt *(Rose bushes beneath the Trees*), the Alpine landscapes of the Swiss Ferdinand Hodler, *Marie Monnom* by the Belgian Ferrand Khnopff, the English Pre-Raphaelites and *Summer Night in Aasgaarstrand* by the Norwegian, Edvard Munch.

Rooms 61–66 cover the decorative arts.

– Halls devoted to the **Symbolists and decorative arts** include Carrière, Verlaine, Delville, Ménard, Klimt (*Rosiers Sous les Arbres*), Munch (*Nuit d'Été à Aasgaarstrand*) and Redon.

The foreign schools also offer a number of interesting works.

Rich collections of **Art Nouveau** include panelling from Charpentier's dining-room and superb marquetry furniture by Émile Gallé as well as decorative glass by Decorchemont, and stained-glass windows by Jacques Gruber and the political leader, Guimard, from the Nancy School of art. Belgian Art Nouveau is represented by the furniture of Serrurier-Bovy, the workshop of Paul Hankar, wood panelling from the Hôtel Aubecq by Victor Horta and the office of Van de Velde. The Art Nouveau of Vienna, Glasgow and Chicago is in the Pavillon Amont.

– On the balcony-cum-gallery on the Seine side of the museum are Rodin's major works, including *Ugolin*, *Âge d'airain*, his imposing statue of Balzac and the monumental plaster sculpture of the *Porte d'Enfer* (Gates of Hell). Don't miss *Gérôme Exécutant les Gladiateurs*, a fine bronze by J.-L. Gérôme, and the admirable *Âge Mûr* by Camille Claudel.

– On the other side of the middle level, on the Lille terrace, are sculptures by Maillol, Bourdelle and Bartholomé, Pompon's delightful *Ours blanc* and at the back, if you've still got the energy, rooms 67–72 are the last rooms devoted to painting, with post–1900 artists: Bonnard's *La Partie de Croquet*, Denis's *Les Muses*, Vallotton's *Le Ballon* and Vuillard's *Les Jardins Publics*.

AROUND THE MUSÉE D'ORSAY

★ **Musée de la Légion d'Honneur:** 2 rue de Bellechasse 75007. Opposite the Palais d'Orsay. ☎ 01-40-62-84-25. Metro: Solférino. RER: Musée-d'Orsay (Line C). Open 11am to 5pm. Closed Monday. Entry fee 25F; concessions 15F. Free entry for under 18s and on the first Sunday of every month. Occupies the fine Hôtel de Salm, burned down under the Commune and then rebuilt. It has a superb façade (at 64 rue de Lille) with a courtyard and colonnades. Because of the variety and quality of the documents on show, it is both a museum of history and a museum of society.

Fans of Napoleon will find a large number of objects which belonged to the Emperor (pistols, sword, breast-plate, his portrait by Gros). There are also souvenirs from the training academies of the Légion d'Honneur; French orders and decorations from the 16th to the 20th centuries; and a large exhibition of foreign orders: *objets d'art*, manuscripts, paintings, tapestry and popular art. There is also the President of the Republic's huge chain of the Order of the Légion d'Honneur.

★ **L'Assemblée Nationale:** 33 *bis* quai d'Orsay 75007. Metro: Assemblée-Nationale or Invalides. Attend a parliamentary session. For all information: ☎ 01-40-63-64-08 or 01-40-63-99-99 (recorded message). You can attend a session of government if you wish in the semi-circular room of the **Palais Bourbon**; be sure to bring your passport or identity card with you (sessions are on Tuesdays, Wednesdays and Thursdays at 3pm between 1 October and 30 June). If you just want to look around the building there are three guided tours on Saturdays at 10am, 2pm and 3pm (maximum 30 people per group). Entry is of course free!

★ The 7th arrondissement has some superb examples of **Art Nouveau** architecture. Art Nouveau, created in reaction to the academic forms of the end of the 19th century, was largely inspired by Japanese art. At 29 avenue Rapp there is an exquisite example of an art-nouveau door – a lovely nymphet tempting passers-by. This most frequently photographed monument in the 7th arrondissement (after the Eiffel Tower, of course) is the work of architect Jules Lavirotte. If you are a fan, there are further examples at 3 square Rapp and 12 rue Sédillot.

★ **The sewers (égouts) of Paris:** opposite 93 quai d'Orsay 75007. ☎ 01-53-68-27-81. RER: Pont-de-l'Alma (Line C). Open 11am to 4pm (5pm from May to the end of September). Closed Thursday, Friday and for two weeks in January. Entry fee 25F; free for under fives, reductions for children and students. A tour of Paris underneath the city, explaining the whole history of the Parisian sewer system, 5m (16ft) underground. The tour lasts 1 hour 15 minutes and is supplemented by a film on Paris and its water system with explanatory visual aids and sometimes smells . . . which need no explanation!

WHERE TO GO FOR A DRINK

🍸 **Master's Bar** (map B2, **51**): 64 avenue Bosquet 75007. ☎ 01-45 51-08-99. Metro: École-Militaire. Open 5pm to 2am. Beers from 22F, cocktails 48F. Prices increase at the weekend. An American-style piano bar. The owner used to work at Harry's Bar (the bar at the Ritz Hotel in Paris), so expect excellent cocktails. There's also a huge choice of whiskies (around 100) and an arched cellar with piano music at the weekend. A chic bar in an otherwise low-key area for nightlife. Snacks from 30F.

🍸 **O'Brien's** (map B1, **55**): 77 rue St-Dominique 75007. ☎ 01-45-51-75-87. Metro: Invalides or La Tour-Maubourg. Open daily 6pm (4pm Friday, Saturday and Sunday) to 2am. Beer is 29F per pint during happy hour. This Irish pub, run by a Welshman and his Irish wife, is a big hit. It's always packed, but that's not surprising given that the 7th arrondissement has a singular lack of anywhere else young and lively. Happy hour until 8pm. Guinness, Killkenny and cider on draught; Corona, Carlsberg, Becks and Labatt Ice bottled.

🍸 **Le Café du Marché** (map B2, **56**): 38 rue Clerc 75007. ☎ 01-47-05-51-27. Metro: École-Militaire. Open daily 7am to midnight (4pm Sunday). Main courses 50F at lunchtime, 60F in the evening. The terrace and colourful street are very lively. A great spot to stop for a drink before getting your photo taken at the nearby Eiffel Tower.

GOING OUT

– **Club des Poètes** (map C1–2, **54**): 30 rue de Bourgogne 75007. ☎ 01-47-05-06-03. Metro: Assemblée-Nationale, Invalides or Varenne. Closed Sunday and in August. Set menu 96F at lunchtime, 120F in the evening. Children's menu 80F. Drinks from 60F to 90F; 45F for students. Dinner at 8pm, including a show at 10.15pm. This place is for poetry lovers; the aim is to spread the poetic word to as many as possible. Surrounded by the decor of a country inn, everyone reads their own work and that of the great poets of the past: Victor Hugo, Rimbaud, Aragon, Vian and Villon. On certain Wednesdays there is a poetic tea-party for children from 4.30pm to 6pm. The programme includes spiritual nourishment, a piece of cake and fruit juice – all for just 35F. Monday is talent night, with unknown (for the moment!) contemporary poets holding forth.

8TH ARRONDISSEMENT

ARC DE TRIOMPHE ● THE CHAMPS-ÉLYSÉES ● PARC MONCEAU ● PLACE DE LA CONCORDE ● THE MADELEINE

In the *beaux quartiers* of the 8th arrondissement you'll find smart shops, *haute couture* fashion houses and important art galleries, and, in the cafés and bars of the Champs-Élysées, the most expensive freshly squeezed orange juice in the world! All around are towering buildings full of the capital's workers who then rush off at the end of the day to get their train home from the Gare St-Lazare. Apart from the *Champs* and its neighbouring streets, the quarter is quite deserted at night.

WHERE TO STAY

☆ BUDGET

Hôtel Wilson (map D1, **1**): 10 rue de Stockholm 75008. ☎ 01-45-22-10-85. Metro: St-Lazare. Double room 245F, with shower and toilet 260F. Room for three people 360F and for four (two double beds in two rooms) 395F. The *Wilson* has nothing special to offer, other than its location, close to the Gare St-Lazare. Having said that, it's very clean and is an affordable one-star hotel if you want to stay fairly near the city centre without breaking the bank. It offers a friendly welcome and breakfast included in the tariff, which is rare. There's no lift, and it's quite a climb up to the rooms on the fifth floor, which are well lit and offer interesting views.

Hôtel Bellevue (map D2, **2**): 46 rue Pasquier 75008. ☎ 01-43-87-50-68. Fax: 01-44-70-01-47. Metro: St-Lazare (exit on the rue de Rome side). Double room 225F to 360F, according to level of comfort (washbasin, shower or bath), with direct telephone, satellite TV and Canal+. On the Place de la Gare St-Lazare, an excellent base for visiting the Opéra and Madeleine quarters and also the Grands Boulevards. There are 46 rooms over seven floors (there's a lift). Those overlooking the courtyard are darker but also quieter. Double-glazing throughout and air-conditioning in the rooms with shower and bath.

☆☆☆ CHIC

Hôtel des Champs-Élysées (map B2, **3**): 2 rue d'Artois 75008. ☎ 01-43-59-11-42. Fax: 01-45-61-00-61. Metro: St-Philippe-du-Roule or Franklin-D.-Roosevelt. RER: Charles-de-Gaulle-Étoile. Double rooms with air-conditioning and shower 495F or bath 580F. All fully equipped with TV and Canal+. A comfortable two-star place, clean and welcoming, away from the noise of the nearby Champs-Élysées. The 36 rooms are soundproofed and are all different and spacious. There is a nice arched breakfast room. Book well in advance because this hotel is popular.

WHERE TO EAT

☆ BUDGET

✕ **La Fontaine Vignon** (map D2, **20**): 21 rue Vignon 75008. ☎ 01-42-65-26-95. Metro: Madeleine or Havre-Caumartin. Open noon to 3pm. Closed in the evening, Sunday and in August. A warm welcome, and a number of good-value set menus from 78F to 98F, with generous servings. Choose salads from 44F to 55F, dish of the day at 52F (*coq au vin* with fresh pasta or fillet of smoked hake and spinach) or a set meal including main course and dessert. This is a former bakery and the dining room in the basement used to house the bakehouse.

✕ **Chez Léon** (map D2, **21**): 5 rue de l'Isly 75008. ☎ 01-43-87-42-77. Metro: St-Lazare or Havre-Caumartin. Last orders around 10pm. Closed Sunday and in August. Budget for less than 100F à la carte. Although this place is very close to the Gare St-Lazare, and is not on a motorway, it has an intriguing real *Relais Routier* (transport café) sign. And it's just like a transport café – the menu, the plastic covers protecting the tablecloths, the hole-in-the-ground toilets, the 1950s black-and-yellow refrigerators – all it needs is a big bloke propping up the bar with a glass of red wine and a Gitanes cigarette in his mouth! This unique place was an annexe of the Fédération des Transports Routiers (Road Transport Federation), which used to have its headquarters opposite. Try the *hors-d'œuvres* at 20F and the dish of the day for around 65F: *hachis Parmentier* (shepherd's pie), *pot-au-feu garni* and *blanquette de veau*. Obviously, considering the prices, you can't expect too much.

✕ **Radis Olive** (map B3, **29**): 27 rue de Marignan 75008. ☎ 01-42-56-55-55. Metro: Franklin-Roosevelt. Open daily noon to midnight. Set menus 70F at lunchtime, 76F or 88F in the evening. If you've just come out of one of the many cinemas around here, or have been sightseeing and are starving, this Lebanese place can be very useful. There are a number of set menus with two starters, and a choice of a meat or a vegetarian menu (unusual in France) which has been quite a hit. *Mezze-découverte* (a selection of *mezze*, or Lebanese snacks) for a minimum of two people.

✕ **The Chicago Pizza Pie Factory** (map B2, **31**): 5 rue de Berri 75008. ☎ 01-45-62-50-23. Metro: George-V. Open daily until 1am. Closed evening on 24 December and lunchtime on 25 December, as well as the morning of 1 January. Set meals 51F to 71F at lunchtime. Budget for around 110F in the evening. Children's menu 56F. Introduced by an ad man from Chicago, the American pan-pizza bears little relation to its authentic Italian rival. In this huge, typically American basement dining room, the waiters (mostly students) frequently stop in the middle of their shifts and dance to very loud music. When it's someone's birthday (23F per slice of cake), they switch out the lights and process across the dining room to the sound of *Happy Birthday* by Stevie Wonder, until they reach the birthday boy or girl. Half-price pizzas between 4pm and 7pm and happy hour at the bar from 6pm to 9pm (4pm to 8pm in the dining room). Children are especially welcomed on Saturdays and Sundays at 1pm and 2pm, with lots of special events.

☆☆ MODERATE

✕ **Le Boucoléon** (map C1, **30**): 10 rue de Constantinople 75008. ☎ 01-42-93-73-33. Metro: Europe. Last orders 11pm. Closed weekends and in August. Budget for around 140F, excluding drinks. A real local bistro where you can come in your shirt-sleeves and eat some first-rate food. The curious name comes from one of the gates of the city of former Constantinople (Istanbul). Simple decor with green-and-white checked tablecloths and a few tables on the terrace in summer. Starters include *tartare de saumon* (35F) or duck *foie gras* (65F); main courses include calf's liver fried with juniper berries (78F) or duck *pot-au-feu* with celery (75F). For dessert, go for the hot chocolate *financier* (a cake made with ground almonds and egg white).

✕ **Chez Clément** (map B3, **23**): 19 rue Marbeuf 75008. ☎ 01-53-23-90-00. Metro: Franklin-Roosevelt. Open daily noon to 1am (*see* also Chez Clément *in the* '17th arrondissement').

✕ **Plaza Berri** (map B2, **24**): 4 rue de Berri 75008. ☎ 01-43-59-46-20. Metro: George-V or Franklin-Roosevelt. Open daily at lunchtime and in the evening until 11pm. À la carte only; budget for around 200F for a starter, main course, dessert and drinks. Eating around the Champs-Élysées quarter is never cheap, but this is a good find. Armand, an affable Turk, loves Italian cuisine, having spent many years working in Italian restaurants, and now offers good pizzas (52F to 80F), beef carpaccio (68F) and pasta (68F and 88F). And the waiters don't mind if a pizza is all you want.

✕ **Bar à Huîtres Garnier** (map D2, **26**): 111 rue St-Lazare 75008. ☎ 01-43-87-50-40. Metro: St-Lazare. Open daily 11.30am to midnight. Closed in August. Single set menu (195F) served lunchtimes and evenings. Budget for 210F à la carte, excluding drinks. Perfectly located (opposite the Gare St-Lazare and not far from the big department stores), this mini oyster bar (there are around 10 seats) has an almost exclusively female clientele who treat themselves to superb plates of Belon oysters or specials from Marennes-Oléron. There are also crabs, prawns, clams or sea urchins, and seafood served on the fisherman's platter (130F), the mini platter (280F) or the giant platter (450F for two).

✕ **La Maison de l'Aubrac** (ex-Petit Berry; map B3, **27**): 37 rue Marbeuf 75008. ☎ 01-43-59-05-14. Metro:

Where to stay

1 Hôtel Wilson
2 Hôtel Bellevue
4 Hôtel des Champs-Élysées

Where to eat

20 La Fontaine Vignon
21 Chez Léon
23 Chez Clément
24 Plaza Berri
26 Bar à Huîtres Garnier
27 La Maison de l'Aubrac
28 Virgin Café
29 Radis Olive
30 Le Boucoléon
31 The Chicago Pizza Pie Factory
32 Chez Clément
33 Planet Hollywood
34 La Fermette Marbeuf
35 Le Berry's
36 La Maison d'Alsace
37 Chez Tante Louise
39 Brasserie Lorraine
41 Asian
42 Spoon
44 L'Appart

Where to go for a drink/ Going out

45 The Cricketer Pub
47 Le Buddha Bar
48 Le Cabaret (Le Milliardaire)
49 Le Man Ray
50 Montecristo Café
51 Chesterfield Café
52 Le Mathis
53 Le Queen
55 Le Forum
56 Villa Barclay
57 Café Indigo

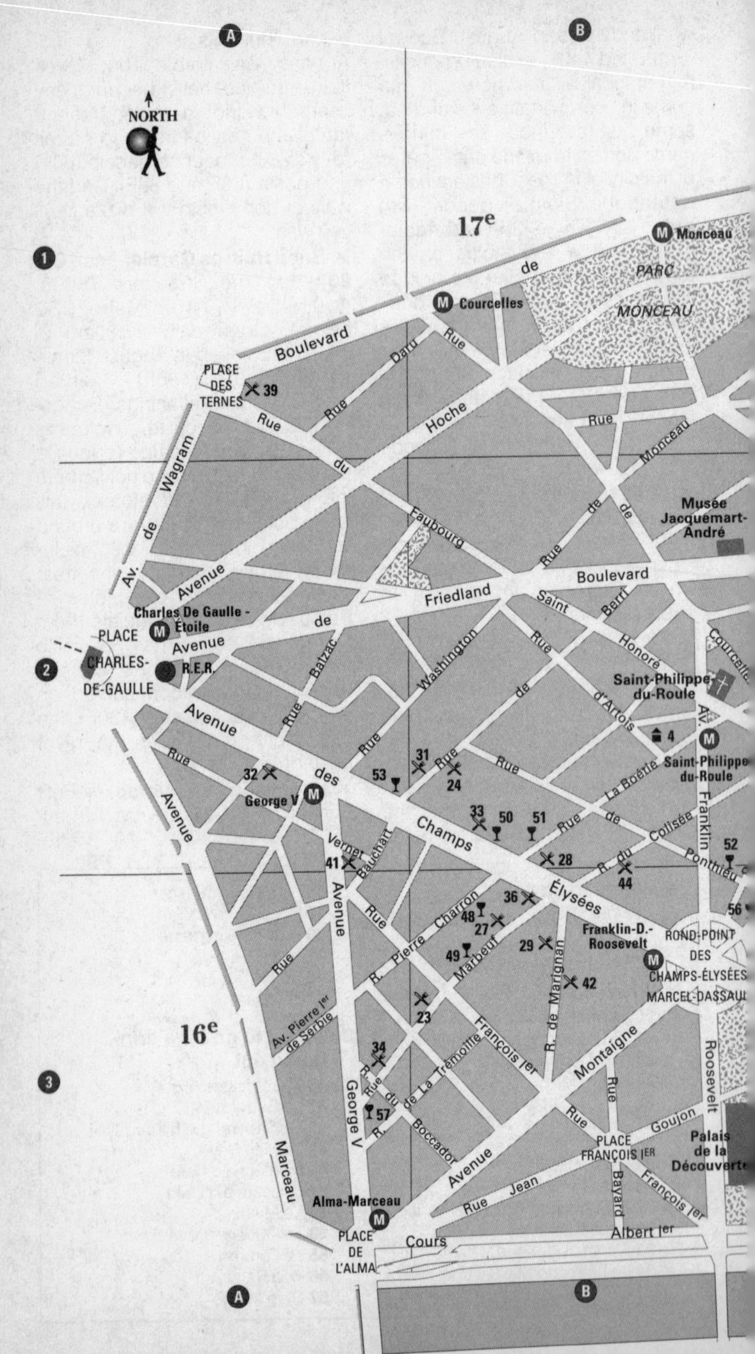

A
B
NORTH
1
2
3
17e
16e
Monceau
PARC
MONCEAU
Courcelles
Boulevard de
PLACE DES TERNES
39
Rue Daru
Rue de Courcelles
Rue du Faubourg
Hoche
Rue de Monceau
Musée Jacquemart-André
Av. de Wagram
Avenue
Boulevard
Friedland
Rue de Berri
Saint Honoré
Charles De Gaulle - Étoile
PLACE CHARLES-DE-GAULLE
Avenue de
R.E.R.
Rue Balzac
Rue Washington
Rue de
Saint-Philippe-du-Roule
Av. Courcelles
d'Artois
4
Saint-Philippe du-Roule
Avenue des Champs Élysées
Rue
32
George V
53
31
24
Rue La Boétie
Rue de Colisée
33
50
51
52
Franklin
Ponthieu
Vernet
41
Bauchart
28
R. du
44
Avenue
36
Avenue
56
Rue Pierre Charron
48
27
Franklin-D.-Roosevelt
ROND-POINT DES CHAMPS-ÉLYSÉES MARCEL-DASSAULT
49
Marbeuf
29
R. de Marignan
42
Rue
23
Av. Pierre Ier de Serbie
François Ier
Rue de La Trémoille
34
R. du Boccador
George V
57
Montaigne
Rue
Roosevelt
Rue Goujon
PLACE FRANÇOIS IER
Palais de la Découverte
Marceau
Avenue
Rue Jean
Bayard
François Ier
Alma-Marceau
PLACE DE L'ALMA
Cours
Albert Ier
A
B

Boulevard des Batignolles
PLACE PROSPER-GOUBAUX
Courcelles
Rue de Constantinople
Rue de Saint Pétersbourg
Rue de Moscou
Liège
Europe
R. de Liège
Rue d'Amsterdam
Rue Monceau
Rue de Naples
Rue du Général Foy
Musée Cernuschi
Musée Nissim-de-Camondo
Rue de Madrid
R. de Londres
Lisbonne
Rue du Rocher
Rue de Vienne
Rome
9e
Rue de Stockholm
Gare Saint-Lazare
Rue Treilhard
Bienfaisance
Rue de la Boétie
Saint-Augustin
Malesherbes
Saint-Lazare
Av. de Messine
Téhéran
Laborde
COUR DE ROME
Haussmann
Boulevard
PLACE SAINT-AUGUSTIN
R. de la Pépinière
26
R. de l'Isly
21
Saint-Augustin
Haussmann
Av. Percier
Miromesnil
La Boétie
Rue Pasquier
Rue de l'Arcade
Rue de Rome
Rue
Avenue Delcassé
Rue Cambacérès
R. Roquépine
Boulevard Malesherbes
Rue des Mathurins
Penthièvre
45
Rue d'Anjou
R. de Castellane
Rue Tronchet
20
Vignon
Rue Mermoz
Matignon
Rue du Faubourg Saint Honoré
PLACE BEAUVAU
R. de Duras
Rue de Surène
Sainte-Marie-Madeleine
PLACE DE LA MADELEINE
55
37
Avenue
Av. Gabriel
Av. de Marigny
Palais de l'Élysée
Rue de l'Élysée
Rue d'Anglas
Madeleine
Rue Boissy
Rue Royale
Avenue Gabriel
Avenue des Champs Élysées
Champs Élysées Clemenceau
1er
47
Grand Palais
Univ. Paris IV
Av. Winston Churchill
Petit Palais
Concorde
PLACE DE LA CONCORDE
Cours La Reine
0 100 200 300 yds
0 100 200 300 m

Franklin-Roosevelt. Open daily 24 hours. Set menu 160F, served lunchtime and evening. À la carte, budget for around 180F. The main selling point of this brasserie, located just off the Champs-Élysées, is the fact that it's open round the clock. The Auvergne-inspired menu includes beef (entrecôte and sirloin), *morue aveyronaise*, *poêlon de cochon* and steak *tartare*. At around 3am the place gradually fills up with shift workers and starving night owls, who come to enjoy a glass or two from a selection of 65 wines.

✕ **Virgin Café** (map B2, **28**): 52–60 avenue des Champs-Élysées 75008. ☎ 01-42-89-46-81. Metro: Franklin-Roosevelt. Open daily 10am (midday Sunday and public holidays) to midnight. Closed 1 May, Christmas and 1 January. Budget for around 120F for a full meal. One of the best eating places around the Champs-Élysées, located on the second floor of the Virgin Megastore, this is a relaxed place. The age of the customers averages 25 to 35, and you're quite likely to see some famous faces among them. Try the *tempura* of vegetables (deep-fried) or beef carpaccio, or you can have just a cocktail (47F to 49F). The selection of wines by the glass is remarkable. Happy hour Monday to Friday 5pm to 7pm. Brunch on Sunday, noon to 5pm (86F and 125F). Children's menu at 65F.

✕ **Planet Hollywood** (map B2, **33**): 78 avenue des Champs-Élysées 75008. ☎ 01-53-83-78-27. Metro: George-V. Open 11.30am to 1am except the evening of 24 December. Budget for 150F, excluding drinks. The Planet Hollywood chain is dedicated to the cinema, to the point that French movie star Gerard Depardieu is a supplier, selling his own Château de Tigné wine here. The Hollywood bar is in the basement. Go down a floor to the restaurant for American cuisine and ersatz French cuisine (*boeuf bourguignon* and *pot-au-feu*). Contrary to popular belief, it wasn't Schwarzenegger, Stallone and Willis who created this restaurant chain, but a smart catering entrepreneur, who offered the movie stars a few shares in exchange for their presence at the launch. Annoyingly, the staff do tend to bully you into ordering drinks.

✕ **La Fermette Marbeuf** (map A3, **34**): 5 rue Marbeuf 75008. ☎ 01-53-23-08-00. Metro: Alma-Marceau. Open daily until 11.30pm and 12.30am Thursday, Friday and Saturday. Set menu for 148F at lunchtime, including drinks, and 178F in the evening. À la carte, budget for around 280F. The dining room here is a masterpiece of art nouveau style, rediscovered by chance in 1978 during building work, and now listed in the Inventory of Historic Monuments. A must-see 'museum-restaurant' that is inextricably linked with the heritage of Paris. Essential dishes such as *magret de canard* (duck) with figs, *filet de canette fermière rôti 'façon gibier'* (roast duckling), whole grilled turbot with *sauce béarnaise*, *tournedos* of salmon with broad beans or a simple steak *tartare* enter a new dimension in this magical place. The wine list is expensive and offers a limited choice.

✕ **Le Berry's** (map C1, **35**): 46 rue de Naples 75008. ☎ 01-40-75-01-56. Metro: St-Augustin. Last orders at midnight. Closed Saturday lunchtime and Sunday, and also Christmas and New Year. Set meal 100F; à la carte, budget for 150F. A contemporary-style bistro where the cooking is inspired by the cuisine of the chef's home region of Berry. The owner is a great fan of rugby, and there are international team shirts on the walls. On the menu are veal with red wine and fricassée of poultry with Sancerre.

Daily specials might include *paleron de bœuf topinambours*, *entrecôte de Salers pommes à l'ail* and *travers de porc riz*. For dessert there's *poirat berrichon* or *chanciau*. There's a good set meal (starter plus main course, or main course plus dessert), which is changed daily. Good, reasonably priced wines.

✕ **La Maison d'Alsace** (map B3, **36**): 39 avenue des Champs-Élysées 75008. ☎ 01-53-93-97-00. Metro: Franklin-Roosevelt. Open daily 24 hours. Set menu 178F; à la carte, budget for at least 250F. The 'Alsace', as it's known to its regulars, offers a reasonable meal of sauerkraut accompanied by a glass or carafe of white wine. Its fine decor, based on bevelled mirrors, *trompe-l'œil* and marquetry, contributes to the warm atmosphere. A rich culinary heritage is represented on the menu by steamed sauerkraut accompanied in traditional style by smoked bacon, and *montbéliard* cheese, as well as plenty of other meat, fish and seafood dishes, and some wonderful desserts.

☆ ☆ ☆ CHIC

✕ **Chez Tante Louise** (map D3, **37**): 41 rue Boissy-d'Anglas 75008. ☎ 01-42-65-06-85. Metro: Madeleine. Closed in August. Set menu for 190F lunchtimes and evenings. À la carte, budget for 250F excluding wine. Just down the road from Place de la Madeleine, this well-known art deco-style restaurant has a relatively new chef, who remains faithful to the repertoire of the original restaurant. He's added a few Burgundian specialities, such as *œufs en meurette*, veal kidney cooked in its own fat, braised cheek of beef with carrots or *navarin* of lamb. Excellent wines and quality.

✕ **Asian** (map A2, **41**): 30 avenue George-V 75008. ☎ 01-56-89-11-00. Metro: George-V. Open daily noon to 2am, last orders 1am. 'Four-seasons' dishes from 80F to 155F or a choice of two set menus: '*Asie du Monde*' 178F and 'Dynasty' 350F. For à la carte main courses (meat or fish) 88F to 144F. The latest of the hip restaurants where it's good to be seen plays on the idea of travel in Asia. Its decor is ultra-trendy, with a mezzanine bar and restaurant in the basement reached via a magnificent red-lacquered wood staircase, and bouquets of bamboo in fine, imposing vases. However, the service is not great and the tables are rickety (perhaps meant to be part of the charm, but not really in keeping with the prices). Starters, main courses and desserts hover between Japanese, Chinese, Thai and Vietnamese cuisine. Try the *chariot vapeur*, a variety of steamed dishes. The pasta is made on the premises.

✕ **Spoon** (map B3, **42**): 14 rue de Marignan 75008. ☎ 01-40-76-34-44. Metro: Franklin-Roosevelt. Open lunchtime and evening until 11.30pm. Closed Saturday and Sunday. À la carte 300F to 400F. The Zen-like atmosphere here is created by an elegant, minimalist decor, carried through in the furniture, the shape of the cutlery and the lighting. *Spoon* is run by one of the leading lights of *nouvelle cuisine*, who has invented the new concept of 'world food', or the art of bringing flavours, spices, smells and techniques from all over the world and subtly mixing them together. It's proved a hit, and many customers – except perhaps celebrities – have to wait at least a fortnight for a table. If you do manage to get in, you can indulge yourself in the 'vegetable garden', with its maelstrom of flavours, or the roast rack of lamb. It seems a shame that some of the dishes are presented as if for a gastronomic competition, and you can end up still feeling a bit peckish. A real gimmick is the mineral water list, which some of the waiters will talk about as though they were wine connoisseurs discussing the merits of a particular vintage! You might as well be in California, where many of the wines come from too.

✗ **Brasserie Lorraine** (map A1, **39**): 2 place des Ternes 75008. ☎ 01-42-27-80-04. Metro: Ternes. Open daily to 1am. Set menu 228F. À la carte, budget for 300F with drinks. A classic Parisian brasserie and a pillar of the Place des Ternes. The Lorraine has been here for over 70 years and offers good-quality cooking, served by attentive staff, in a vast retro dining room with red seats and white tablecloths. On the menu are sauerkraut (120F) and various seafood dishes. There's a pleasant terrace in summer.

✗ **L'Appart** (map B2–3, **44**): 9 and 11 rue du Colisée 75008. ☎ 01-53-75-16-34. Metro: Franklin-Roosevelt. Open 11am to 2.30pm and 7.30pm to 11.45pm. Closed Sunday and Monday afternoons. Budget for 350F for two people, juggling the set menu and à la carte, and you won't be disappointed. There are four rooms offering modern cuisine: the dining room, the kitchen cellar, a little lounge on the first floor or the library in the basement. The lounge is the most intimate and romantic, and the library has a trendy neon bar. Booking is essential to secure your first choice. There's a choice of a set menu (180F) with limited dishes, or a lovely à la carte with, among other things, an excellent fillet of bream (115F) or shoulder of lamb and vegetables with thyme (125F). On the cheese front, lovers of Stilton (40F) will be able to treat themselves. The service could be a bit friendlier.

THE CHAMPS-ÉLYSÉES AND THE SURROUNDING AREA

★ The vast **place de l'Étoile**, officially re-christened **place Charles-de-Gaulle** (Metro and RER: Charles-de-Gaulle-Étoile) is the crossroads of the 8th, 16th and 17th arrondissements, measuring 240m (790ft) in diameter. Twelve avenues radiate away from it, and it gives an extraordinary feeling of open space in a busy city.

The most famous attribute of the *place* is the **Arc de Triomphe**, built to commemorate the Napoleonic armies. 'A piece of stone on a pile of glory', as Victor Hugo called it, it is a reflection of the great megalomaniac Imperial era. Napoleon decreed on 18 April 1806 that it should be built, but he never saw the finished monument. The definitive draft by the architect was only accepted in 1809, and when Empress Marie-Louise arrived in 1810 only the foundations were finished, and a fake arch of wood covered in canvas had to be erected. The Emperor's abdication stopped the work and it was Louis-Philippe who finally inaugurated it in 1836.

Four years later, Napoleon's ashes were exhibited here before being transferred to the Invalides (*see* '7th arrondissement'). Since then, the Arc de Triomphe has witnessed all the great events in Paris. France's most important writer of the 19th century, Victor Hugo, who had criticized it because the name of his father did not appear among those of the 660 generals engraved in the stone, was given a state funeral there. In 1919 the First World War victory parade was held here and on 11 November 1920 the remains of the Unknown Soldier were laid under the arch. An eternal flame, rekindled every evening, has watched over him ever since. The tomb has become one of the most important French national symbols. On 26 August 1944, the day after the Liberation of Paris, General de Gaulle came to kneel at it before making his triumphant walk down the Champs-Élysées to Notre-Dame. Another well-known visitor had followed the same route four years previously, but Adolf Hitler took his walk earlier in the morning and in a deserted city.

The Arc de Triomphe has also seen some entertaining happenings. One odd fellow decided to fry eggs over the sacred flame. In 1919 aviator Charles Godeffroy, protesting against the lack of space dedicated to aviation at the Bastille Day parades, flew, in front of a number of photographers, under the arch in his aeroplane. It was a tight fit, with a margin of just 3m (10ft) on each side!

You can visit the platform (which offers splendid views) and the museum daily except on public holidays. Open 10am to 10.30pm (6pm Sunday and Monday) 1 October to 31 March, and 9.30am to 11pm (6.30pm Sunday and Monday) 1 April to 30 September. Ticket office shuts half an hour before closing. Entry fee 35F; concessions 23F; free for under-12s. You can also visit the museum room, which offers documents and photographs tracing the history of the Arc de Triomphe, and a film in French and English.

DID YOU KNOW?

- The Arc de Triomphe measures 49.5m (162ft) in height, 44m (147ft) in width, and the height of the arch measures 29m (95ft) from the ground. From the terrace there's a panoramic view along the Louvre–Champs-Élysées–La Défense axis.
- One of the finest examples of monumental sculpture on the Arc de Triomphe is *La Marseillaise* by Rude.
- One original project of the 18th century was to erect a colossal elephant here; the body would contain lounges, a ballroom and a vast dining room, and the ears would be used as acoustic horns in order to broadcast orchestral music. Once the work was suspended, another architect came forward with the more prosaic proposition of putting up a gigantic water tower on the foundations, from which an artificial river would flow right along the Champs-Élysées!

★ The **Champs-Élysées:** in 1670 Le Nôtre designed the Jardin des Tuileries and extended the central aisle with an opening into the forest. This was the Grand Cours, so called to distinguish it from the Cours-la-Reine, which ran along the banks of the Seine. The kings of France would ride down here on their way to hunt at Versailles. This route was also called the Champs-Élysées ('Elysian Fields'), a Greek term referring to the heavenly place inhabited by heroes and virtuous men after death. In 1770, in spite of the levelling of the promontory by the Marquis de Marigny, brother of Mme de Pompadour, the avenue was still 'a torrid or glacial area, a field of mud or dust, exhausting both horses and pedestrians'. The Cossacks and British troops set up camp here during the occupation of Paris in 1815, and fed their campfires with trees from the gardens – it took two years to repair the damage. In the same year, the Champs-Élysées roundabout was built and cafés and shops began to flourish on the avenue.

Due to its exemplary layout – with its width of 71m (232ft) – this triumphal Parisian route remains prestigious. During the day it's a business quarter, but the work is forgotten in the evening at the *Drugstore Publicis*, the first late-night 'drugstore/café/newsagent' in France, *Le Lido*, the rather sanitized cabaret with its prim nudes, large cafés such as *Le Fouquet's*, numerous multi-screen cinemas, and restaurants, which are gradually being replaced by fast-food establishments.

On significant national occasions – such as Bastille Day on 14 July and Armistice Day on 11 November – it is on the Champs-Élysées that emotional parades take place. On the roundabout on the left as you head up the avenue is the former private residence of the Le Hon family, subsequently occupied by *Jours de France* (a national newspaper), which added a wing to it. Countess Le Hon, the wife of an ambassador, was particularly famous because of her love affair with her neighbour, the Duc de Morny. At No. 25 lived the Marquise de Païva, a famous adventuress. Her residence, in the style of the Second Empire, now houses the headquarters of the very male and exclusive Traveller's Club. At No. 68 is the Guerlain building, dating from 1913, a beautiful example of the architecture of the period.

The roundabout, with its beautifully lit fountains, the work of Max Ingrand in 1958, is an important crossroads on the Right Bank. It's hard to imagine today that the avenue Montaigne used to be lined with highly suspect dance halls and down-at-heel bars. It was once known as the *Allée des Veuves* ('Widows' Alley'), because widows who couldn't show themselves in town during their period of mourning used to come here for consolation, to look for a lover. The famous *Mabille* ballroom, which opened around 1840, was at or near the current No. 51. It was *the* place to go at the time, where all the dandies and their ladies used to meet to dance the polka. Baudelaire, who knew a thing or two about pleasure, loved this place, but it was destroyed during the First World War.

Under Napoleon III the Champs-Élysées reached its peak of importance, developing into a focus of luxury and elegance. Many personalities chose to live here, and bankers and financiers had splendid mansions built. Members of high society would regularly saunter down the avenue and the descriptions given by Marcel Proust of his outings give an idea of its former splendour.

By the turn of the century changes were under way and commercial buildings began to take over from the luxury townhouses. Bit by bit tradespeople and restaurants moved in and people were already saying in the 1930s that the Champs-Élysées 'was no more'. The first shops were followed by cinemas and the avenue became a paradise for those connected with the world of movies. Le Fouquet's restaurant was a favourite with famous French actors of the time such as Raimu, Abel Gance, Guitry and even Charlie Chaplin.

The second half of the 20th century was less glorious for the lovely avenue, due to increased traffic and some savage urban planning. In 1994 ideas were put forward for redevelopment – doubling the row of plane trees, the building of new urban housing, and better organization of parking. *Les Champs* has been treated to a well-deserved facelift, using a combination of tradition and modernity. New shops and companies have set up – Arthur Andersen Consulting renovated a fine art deco building on the corner of avenue George-V, luxury leather-goods manufacturer Louis Vuitton moved in just down the road, at No. 101, and the luxury Marriott hotel opened its doors, a worthy successor to the Carlton, the Astoria and Claridges (which have all disappeared one by one). A new store of the Fnac chain (an institution in France, selling music, books, stationery, computer software) was installed in the Claridges arcade, quickly followed by the famous Ladurée tea-rooms, a temple to *gourmandise* behind superb green and gold windows.

Even if the Champs-Élysées has lost some of its former splendour, with the installation of the inevitable Virgin Megastore and McDonald's, it remains the busiest place in France, with 300–500,000 people passing through every day. One of the most famous avenues in the world, and since its inception always the scene of royal and victory parades, the Champs-Élysées has never been out of the limelight and is still changing and developing every day.

★ **Théâtre des Champs-Élysées:** avenue Montaigne 75008. Metro: Alma-Marceau. Built by the Perret brothers, just before the First World War, in a revolutionary style using concrete. The architects called upon Bourdelle for the façade and Maurice Denis and Vuillard for the interior frescoes. The whole thing comprises three performance spaces; the Grand Théâtre seats 2,000, the Comédie, 655, and the Studio, 257. On 11 December 1957 it became the first building constructed in the 20th century to be listed as an Historic Monument.

★ **Grand Palais:** avenue Winston-Churchill, 75008. Metro: Franklin-D.-Roosevelt or Champs-Élysées-Clemenceau. Opening times vary according to which exhibitions are on. This colossal palace – a marriage of iron, glass and stone – was built for the 1900 Universal Exhibition, at the same time as the magnificent **Pont Alexandre-III**. Once the exhibition was over, nobody had the courage to take it down, and it remains as a testimony to the extravagance of Paris' *Belle Époque*. Don't miss the superb art nouveau two-flight staircase. The palace's pillars are weakening and it is gradually falling down, so some parts are closed to the public, but, along with the Palais de la Découverte, it still houses some prestigious temporary exhibitions.

★ **Palais de la Découverte:** in the western part of the Grand Palais. ☎ 01-56-43-20-21. For group bookings and information ring: ☎ 01-56-43-20-25. Website: www.palais.decouverte.fr. Metro: Franklin-D.-Roosevelt or Champs-Élysées-Clemenceau. RER: Invalides. Bus Nos. 28, 42, 49, 52, 63, 72, 73, 80, 83, 93. Open daily (except Monday) 9.30am to 6pm; Sunday and some public holidays 10am to 7pm. The entrance ticket also gives access to the hands-on halls (supplement of 15F for the planetarium).

The aim of this scientific cultural centre is to promote public interest in science, and hopefully to encourage young people to consider science as a field of study or career. Exhibits on static electricity and natural history (rats, ants, fish, frogs) are among the most popular. 'Planet Earth' is devoted to earth sciences, and, by 2001, will occupy over 1000 square metres (3,200 square feet) of space. It offers a permanent exhibition on meteorology, the climate and problems relating to the environment. In one hall, a 70-m (230-ft) long geological scale traces the world's evolution and the species that live in it.

– **Ground floor:** include exhibits on animal life, electricity, electrostatics, sound, and the Eureka hall for the discovery of physics and perception. The *Espace Cybermétropole* is the largest space in France devoted to the Internet and multimedia and open to the general public. Dynamic staff look after all interested visitors, of all ages, offering them an initiation into new technologies. Twenty-four computer terminals are available, so that visitors can surf the Internet or try out the latest scientific, educational and leisure CD-ROMs, all free of charge.

– **First floor:** in the planetarium visitors can enjoy an unmissable 45-minute journey, learning about the planets, the sun, human biology and heredity, the atom and chemistry. The planetarium allows you to travel the universe and to understand astronomical phenomena as a whole.

★ **Petit Palais, Musée des Beaux-Arts de la Ville de Paris:** opposite the Grand Palais; entrance in avenue Winston-Churchill 75008. ☎ 01-42-65-12-73. Metro: Champs-Élysées-Clemenceau. Bus Nos. 42, 72, 73, 80 and 83. Paris' Fine Arts Museum, closed for renovation until 2003.

★ Not far away, at the end of the avenue Montaigne, is the **Pont de l'Alma**. Built between 1854 and 1856, it takes its name from the victory of Britain and France over the Russians at Alma in the Crimean War. Nothing remains of the original structure, except the 6m (19ft) *Zouave*, a statue by Georges Diébolt representing the men who fought in the battle.

More recently, the bridge has been associated with another tragic event. On 31 August 1997 Diana, Princess of Wales, and Dodi Al-Fayed, met their death in a car accident in the tunnel of the same name. Since then, dozens of visitors come every day to leave flowers at the Flame of the Statue of Liberty, at the avenue de New-York end of the bridge in remembrance. Many seem to believe that this monument was erected in memory of Princess Diana, but in fact it was built and given to Paris 10 years before the accident by American associations, to commemorate the friendship between France and the United States.

AROUND PARC MONCEAU

★ **Musée Jacquemart-André:** 158 boulevard Haussmann 75008. ☎ 01-42-89-04-91. Metro: Miromesnil or St-Philippe-du-Roule. Bus Nos. 22, 43, 52, 80, 84, 83, 93 and 54. Open daily 10am to 6pm. Entry fee (audio-guide included) 48F; 36F for children and the unemployed; free for children under seven. For group visits and information ring: ☎ 01-45-62-39-94. A delightful museum, the former residence of M. and Mme André, who were great collectors and scoured Europe to buy all the works of art which you can see here. When it was opened, in 1913, it was immediately considered to be one of the centres of art in Paris, and a recent facelift has given it back its former charm.

Take time to stroll in the garden and have a cup of tea in the dining room with its Tiepolo ceiling, or on the terrace. The rooms on the ground floor are devoted, in succession, to 18th-century French art, with paintings by Fragonard, Boucher and Chardin, and sculpture by Pigalle; to Flemish and Dutch schools of the 17th century, with Van Dyck, Ruysdaël and Rembrandt represented; and a British collection includes works by Reynolds and Gainsborough. The tour is a perfect opportunity to see the living space of a large 19th-century residence, with its sumptuous lounges, private apartments and a winter garden. The monumental staircase gives access to the rooms on the first floor, which contain a magnificent collection of Italian Renaissance works, with beautiful paintings by Botticelli, Carpaccio and

Bellini, with sculpture by Verrocchio and Donatello, to name but a few.

There is a very well-stocked shop at the exit with gifts as well as maps, posters and books.

✕ **Café Jacquemart-André:** 158 boulevard Haussmann 75008. ☎ 01-45-62-04-44. Open daily 11.30am to 5.30pm (11am at the weekend for brunch). The café is in the sumptuous dining room of the former Jacquemart-André residence, and is worth making a detour for in itself. It has a beautiful painted ceiling, tapestries, gilded bronze, and a view over the very pleasant courtyard. Locals often meet here for brunch (140F) or a light meal. Dish of the day costs between 65F and 100F, salads from 65F. The *tartes* are to die for, with the great classics mingling with adventurous newcomers.

★ **Musée Nissim-de-Camondo (map C1): 63 rue de Monceau 75008.** ☎ 01-53-89-06-50. Website: www.ucad.fr. Metro: Villiers or Monceau. Open 10am to 5pm. Closed Monday, Tuesday and public holidays. Audio-guide available. Groups by appointment: ☎ 01-44-55-59-26. In building this residence, now a museum that is part of the Union Centrale des Arts Décoratifs (Central Association of Decorative Arts), the Pereire brothers were inspired by a desire to make the Plaine Monceau the finest quarter in Paris.

Brothers Abraham and Nissim de Camondo, from a rich family of Levantine origin, nicknamed 'the Rothschilds of the East', moved in here during the Second Empire. Their son, Count Moïse de Camondo, who had both good taste and ample resources, was responsible for the current building, and for the superb collection seen today. His private residence was built in 1912, modelled on the Petit Trianon at Versailles. He was passionate about art – especially French art of the late 18th century – and assembled the finest furniture, paintings, sculpture, ornaments and silverwork available on the art market. The result is a monumental collection of 800 pieces bringing together the biggest names and the best artists of the time, from Vigée-Lebrun and Oudry to Pigalle and Huet. Among the best exhibits are a roll-top desk by Oeben, an embroidery frame commissioned by Marie-Antoinette and a Sèvres dinner service.

The count left the whole collection to the French State in 1935, in memory of his son Nissim, killed in action in during the First World War, under the condition that it should remain as it was. Since 1986 the museum has been entirely restored thanks to sponsorship, and it looks today just as it always did.

★ **Musée Cernuschi** (map C1): 7 avenue Velásquez 75008. ☎ 01-45-63-50-75. Metro: Monceau or Villiers. Bus Nos. 30 and 94. Open 10am to 5.40pm. Entry fee 22F; free for under-26s for the permanent collections; reductions for 7- to 25-year-olds for the temporary exhibitions. Closed Monday and public holidays. Located on the edge of the Parc Monceau, in the magnificent residence of Henri Cernuschi, humanist financier of Milanese origin.

Traumatized by the repression of the Commune of Paris, in 1871 Cernuschi left France for two years to travel across Asia. He brought back a unique collection of *objets d'art*, which he left to the City of Paris, including prehistoric painted pottery, little items made of Chang jade, ancient vases dating from the 12th century BC, bronze mirrors, painted or varnished clay figurines and animals, and silk paintings. The museum holds a remarkable collection of Ancient Chinese art and, in the central hall, there is an immense

Japanese bronze Buddha. It's impossible to mention everything, but take a look at the 17th-century, 12-leaf screen in engraved lacquered wood (not always on view) and the pair of 12th-century *bodhisattvas* in wood from northern China. This museum is an essential complement to the Musée Guimet, which is also dedicated to Asiatic art (*see* '16th arrondissement').

The Cernuschi puts on regular exhibitions of arts from the Far East, as well as conferences and workshops, tours for those with hearing difficulties and events for children, and also has a documentation centre.

★ **Parc Monceau:** open 7am to 8pm (10pm April to the end of October). Gates shut 15 minutes before closing time. The former park of the Château de Mousseaux, which stood here before 1300, is a fine representation of the Second Empire's taste for gardens in the English style – informal in design, unlike the geometric French design. In around 1780 it was the private park of the Duc d'Orléans, who added an Egyptian pyramid, a Greek temple, grottoes and artificial waterfalls. Some of these exotic buildings are still here, but the park itself has been reduced in size. A few dozen hectares were sold off, allowing the banker Pereire and a few others to make a lot of money in property speculation. The houses in the surrounding streets – which bear the names of painters Murillo, Van Dyck, Ruysdael and Velásquez – were the homes of the *cocottes* (mistresses) of Emperors, bankers and the first great industrialists.

To give you an idea of the extravagance of the time, go and see the little *palais* that overlooks the park on the corner of avenue Van Dyck, the house of the chocolate-maker Menier. The kitchen in the house was so far from the dining room that a little railway was used to bring the dishes to the table. M. Menier's second home was the Château de Chenonceaux.

In the park the little walkway that leads to the central path is enhanced by the Renaissance arcade of the original town hall, burned down during Commune. Chopin and Guy de Maupassant are celebrated in monuments in the shade of large trees. As a child Marcel Proust used to play here before going to school at the Lycée Condorcet; later, he would withdraw to 102 boulevard Haussmann to write. Among the park's other bits and pieces are the elegant Rotunda of Chartres, surrounded by 16 columns and opening out on to the boulevard de Courcelles; a pond adorned with a Corinthian colonnade, said to come from the remains of a chapel built by Catherine de Medicis; tombs housing the remains of unknown people (although it isn't clear why they were brought here); a curious pyramid, covered with the patina of age; and a Japanese funeral lamp, a present from Tokyo to Paris. The Parc Monceau is the perfect place to people-watch at almost any time of day – you'll see everything from well-behaved children from private schools and lovers on benches, to elegant joggers and worthy old gentlemen reading *Les Échos* or *La Tribune de Genève*.

★ **Cathédrale Alexandre-Nevsky:** 12 rue Daru 75008. Metro: Ternes or Courcelles. Open to visitors Tuesdays to Fridays, 3pm to 5pm. Between the Parc Monceau and the Étoile, behind the Salle Pleyel, this cathedral was built in the Byzantine-Muscovite style in 1861 with five amazing gilded domes. In the 1950s, following water seepage, the crypt was completely renovated. The wall paintings, reminiscent of the era when Christianity was first taken to Russia, were produced by Albert Alexandrovitch, and led to the cathedral's listing as an Historic Monument in 1981. Every Sunday, from 10am to 12.30pm, the faithful of Russian origin attend services under the cupolas, where candles light up the religious icons. The most famous service is celebrated at Easter, with plenty of emotion and nostalgia.

DID YOU KNOW?

There are more Russian orthodox churches active in Paris than in Moscow. In total, there are said to be over 150 in France.

PLACE DE LA CONCORDE

This symmetrical square was designed by the architect Gabriel between 1753 and 1763 in honour of Louis XV, after whom it was originally named. It was to be the location for an important statue of the king on his horse. The fountains, copies of those that adorn St Peter's Square in Rome, were added later, between 1836 and 1846.

Unrestricted in terms of space, and working on marshland, Gabriel wanted to create some kind of equivalent of the huge park of Versailles, but without the grass. He had two buildings with columns, inspired by the Louvre, built opposite the Seine; today, one houses the headquarters of the Navy and the other is the Hôtel Crillon. (In 1792 there was a series of thefts from the then Ministry of the Navy, which kept the Crown Jewels; the Regent, a 150-carat diamond, was found later under a pile of rubble in the avenue Montaigne, and is now displayed in the Louvre.)

During the Revolution the guillotine was set up in the square, which was then re-christened place de la Révolution, then place Louis XVI. The place de la Concorde has consequently witnessed its share of historic moments, particularly executions – of Louis XVI on 21 January 1793, then of Robespierre in 1794, and, between the two, the death by guillotine of over 1,100 people. It was the setting for right-wing rioting on 6 February 1934, fighting during the Liberation of Paris and some of the passionate student demonstrations of 30 May 1968.

★ In the middle stands a column known as the **Obélisque de Louxor**, which gives motorists trapped in traffic jams an opportunity to learn a few rudiments of Egyptian hieroglyphics; it dates from around 1250 BC, and the carvings on it tell stories of the reign of Ramses II and Ramses III. The obelisk, 4m (13ft) and 230 tons of pink granite, was a gift in the 1830s from the Viceroy of Egypt. A special ship had to be constructed to transport it to France; it took two years and 25 days for the ship to reach Toulon, but then it was another three years before it was finally moved into place, completing its journey from the Temple of Thebes to Paris. The lifting work was entrusted to a M. Lebas, an engineer who prepared a very complicated set of machinery, requiring the aid of 240 artillerymen. The various phases of the transportation and the erection process are actually engraved on the base. Incidentally, the granite base for the obelisk originally came from the Île Melon in northern Finistère, Brittany.

★ For the **Galerie Nationale du Jeu de Paume**, which overlooks place de la Concorde, *see under* '1st arrondissement, Jardin des Tuileries'.

★ All around the *place* are large **statues** representing eight important French cities. It is said that Juliette Drouet posed for 'Strasbourg', while the wife of the Prefect of Police of Lille served as the model for the statue representing that city. The statues stand on bases known as *guérites* ('sentry boxes' or 'booths'), which were actually once inhabited. When the *place* underwent development work, it proved rather difficult to evict the occupants, who were growing vegetables and fruit trees in nearby ditches. The *guérite* of the city of Bordeaux was, unsurprisingly, occupied by a wine merchant. In March 1871 the statues were draped in black veils as the Kaiser travelled across Paris following France's surrender to the Prussians in the Galerie des Glaces at Versailles.

The place de la Concorde was lit by electricity for the first time in 1866.

★ The **Chevaux de Marly**, at the entrance of the Champs-Élysées, have been replaced after being eaten away by pollution. In the 1950s these equestrian groups by Coustou were the subject of a fraud carried out by a conman, who sold them for a very high price to a rich but naïve American collector. When the purchaser wanted to take delivery of his horses, he couldn't understand why the French government was against it and had to leave the country with a fake receipt as his only souvenir!

★ The **Pont de la Concorde** was built with stones from the Bastille prison. The revolutionary leaders wanted the people to be able to walk over this former symbol of royal power.

THE MADELEINE AND THE SURROUNDING QUARTER

★ **Église de la Madeleine:** Metro: Madeleine. Open 7.30am to 7pm during the week, 8am to 1pm and 4pm to 7pm on Sunday. The Madeleine is the great grey Greek-style temple that you can see from place de la Concorde. It took no less than 80 years to build, undergoing a number of changes of architect and of use along the way. It was begun in 1764, modified 10 years later and abandoned during the Revolution. Later, Napoleon wanted to make it a temple to the glory of the soldiers of his Grande Armée. However, his fall meant that the building was returned to its original intended use, and was finally finished as a church in 1842. In the meantime there had been proposals for it to be used as a Stock Exchange, as a library and as a community centre – and trees had grown up in the middle of the site.

It is worth climbing the steps to admire the impressive sculpted bronze doors. Inside, you'll find no better example of the 'pompous' style, yet the cupola, with its diameter of 18m (60ft), was greatly admired by the congregation when it was unveiled at the consecration ceremony. The painter had represented, in an immense fresco, all the figures of Christianity mingling with characters from French history – Mary Magdalene, Charlemagne, St Catherine, Richelieu, St Louis, Clovis, the Emperor Constantine and, of course, Napoleon crowned by Pope Pius VII. The magnificent organ, dating from 1846, is by Cavaillé-Coll, and lends the appropriate note of pomp to the splendid ceremonies held here.

On one side there is a well-established flower market (open daily except Monday), on the other a ticket kiosk offering 50 per cent off theatre seats for plays on the same day (open Tuesday to Saturday 12.30pm to 8pm, Sunday 12.30pm to 4.30pm; the queues are especially long on Saturdays). (There is another ticket office on the square in front of the Gare Montparnasse, in the 15th arrondissement).

Under the Madeleine itself, among the flowers, there is a little door leading to the foyer in the vaulted cellars where you can eat at lunchtimes, Monday to Friday, for less than 50F. ☎ 01-42-65-52-17.

● Opposite the Madeleine, at 9 boulevard Malesherbes, stands the house where Marcel Proust spent his childhood. And at 11 rue de l'Arcade stood the brothel owned by Albert Le Cuziat, which Marcel Proust furnished with money from his mother's legacy.

Not far away, in the rue d'Anjou, is the Square Louis-XVI, located on the site of the former cemetery where Louis XVI and Marie-Antoinette were buried. The floral decoration of the square is almost entirely white, the colour of royalty.

★ The area around the **Madeleine** has more to offer than just its church. There are also the most amazing luxury shops. If you love the finer things in life, or want to window-shop in the footsteps of wealthy Parisians, try the following:

– **Fauchon:** 26–30 place de la Madeleine 75008. ☎ 01-47-42-60-11. Metro: Madeleine. Open 9.40am to 7pm. Closed Sunday. The temple to sophisticated food, where you can buy cherries, apricots, peaches and exotic fruits such as lychees from Madagascar, passion fruit from Kenya and papayas all year round. The grocery opposite sells flavoured teas (such as blueberry, mango, caramel and a Caribbean blend) by weight, and many flavours of jam, from carrot, nectarine and black fig, to Provençal almond and hazelnut. Don't miss out on a visit to Fauchon's nearby *pâtisserie*, where all the products are delicious.

– **Hédiard** is the other foodie paradise on place de la Madeleine, known for its ready-made meals, cakes, confectionery (particularly marzipan), and its wide-ranging grocery section, with unusual jams, such as wild rose, pink sweet potato, wild strawberry and kiwi, as well as the more usual cherry flavour. In the 1850s Ferdinand Hédiard was a true pioneer, the first person to introduce tropical fruits into France, and famous for having offered the first fresh pineapple to Alexandre Dumas. The shop today has a restaurant on the first floor where you can have an elegant nibble while breathing in the smell of leaf tea or freshly ground coffee, and watch the regulars do their shopping below.

– The **Maison de la Truffe** sells the best truffles in Paris as well as many other things, particularly the famous Rodel preserves.

The only problem is that at the end of your tour of the above you may not be hungry enough to manage supper at Maxim's, in rue Royale. That'll save your wallet, at least.

★ The **Madeleine public toilets:** place de la Madeleine 75008. Metro: Madeleine. Open 9.30am to 11.30am and 12.30pm to 7pm. It might be unusual to include public toilets on a tourist itinerary, but these are the finest in Paris and compete with many other places in terms of decor. These conveniences were built in 1905 in a very elegant art nouveau style. The cubicle doors, made of dark wood decorated with beautiful glass windows, are original, as is the tiled ceiling and the frieze. There's also a kind of throne where you can have your shoes shined.

★ **Passage de la Madeleine:** place de la Madeleine 75008. Metro: Madeleine. Built in 1845, this passageway links place de la Madeleine and rue Boissy-d'Anglas. In this elegant and peaceful alleyway you'll find a lovely but very expensive shop, *Territoire*. The world-famous Hermès shop (of elegant handbags and scarves fame) stands on the corner of rue Boissy-d'Anglas and the faubourg St-Honoré.

★ **Marché de la Madeleine:** entrance in rue Tronchet and rue de Castellane 75008. Metro: Madeleine. Well known to lovers of the quarter, who come for a little escapism between 11am and 3pm. The old shops have given way to Vietnamese, Chinese, Japanese, Greek and Italian restaurants where you can eat informally, elbow-to-elbow, on benches or at the bar. Chez Van is the oldest seller of Chinese soups in the area.

WHAT TO DO

– **Bateaux-Mouches** (boat trips on the Seine): boarding at Pont de l'Alma, on the Right Bank. ☎ 01-42-25-96-10. Metro: Alma-Marceau. Departures every 30 minutes (every 15 minutes in the evening) from 10am to noon and 1.30pm to 11pm in summer; in winter 11am, 2.30, 4, 6 and 9pm. The trip takes 1 hour 10 minutes. Price 40F; children and over-65s 20F. Buy your ticket 15 minutes before departure.

WHERE TO GO FOR A DRINK

Remember that most of the establishments listed below have a strict door policy. Unless you have the right look for a particular time and place, or you're on the arm of a supermodel, you may be left on the doorstep, especially at the Buddha Bar, Villa Barclay and Barfly.

🍸 **The Cricketer Pub** (map D2, **45**): 41 rue des Mathurins 75008. ☎ 01-40-07-19-97. Metro: Madeleine. Open daily 11am to 2am. Budget for around 100F for lunch. Unlike some British pubs, this one isn't dark and secretive. On the contrary, its wide bay windows open on to the outside to allow passers-by to see exactly what sort of people come here. The clientele is mainly English in the evening (traders, bankers and executives of British companies), but more diverse at lunchtime. This difference can be explained by the food (75F per course) for lunch (in the evening, only crisps are available to accompany the beer). Once a week there's a quiz night, when the prize is a bottle of champagne. This place and its twin, The Bowler Pub (13 rue d'Artois 75008; ☎ 01-45-61-16-60), are the only venues in Paris offering English real ale (35F).

🍸 **Villa Barclay** (map B3, **56**): 3 avenue Matignon 75008. ☎ 01-53-89-18-91. Metro: Franklin-D.-Roosevelt. Open daily 11.30pm to late. Club Thursday to Saturday. Entrance fee including drink 100F. Cocktails from 80F. The place to be for the city's gilded youth. Rich young things, future execs and their bosses spend loads of money in opulent red-velvet surroundings. The rest – the restaurant, the bar, the piano bar, the disco – are just incidental.

🍸 **Le Buddha Bar** (map D3, **47**): 8 rue Boissy-d'Anglas 75008. ☎ 01-

53-05-90-00. Metro: Concorde. Open lunchtime (noon to 3pm) and in the evening (6pm to 2am). Closed Saturday and Sunday lunchtime. Set menu 190F at lunchtime. À la carte, budget for at least 350F without drinks. There's no lack of style here, with a monumental staircase, 250-seater dining room, 150-seater mezzanine bar, a gigantic Buddha and clouds of smoke from sticks of incense, but the bill for your sweet and sour Chinese-American dinner will be a hefty one. Some might think it's worth it for the chance to see some of Paris celebs (Isabelle Adjani), but you'll need to look pretty hip to get in. Drinks are around 80F.

🍸 **Le Forum** (map D2–3, **55**): 4 boulevard Malesherbes 75008. ☎ 01-42-65-37-86. Metro: Madeleine. Open daily 11.30am to 2am (Saturday 5.30pm to 2am). Closed Sunday. Cocktails from 70F to 80F. Defining itself as the most British of American bars, Le Forum is a luxury pub dedicated to lovers of whisky. Its list is well supplied with Scottish, Canadian and even Japanese versions of the amber liquid, as well as almost 200 cocktails. With its original decor, dating from 1930, mahogany panelling and leather armchairs, it is elegant and refined, and a perfect spot at the end of a busy day.

🍸 **Café Indigo** (map A3, **57**): 12 avenue George-V 75008. ☎ 01-47-20-89-56. Metro: Alma-Marceau. Open daily noon to 2am. Set menu 150F. À la carte, budget for around 200F excluding drinks. The last really hip restaurant bar around the Champs-Élysées, with trendy music, interior design by a promising architect, attractive staff and some good wines (try a glass of Chilean Terra Noble) and food such as carpaccio of salmon and *coquilles St-Jacques* (scallops). All of this is (naturally) offered in a soothing indigo setting.

🍸 **Le Man Ray** (map B3, **49**): 34 rue Marbeuf 75008. ☎ 01-56-88-36-36. Fax: 01-42-25-36-36. Metro: George-V or Franklin-D.-Roosevelt. Restaurant open daily noon to 2pm and 7pm to 12.30am. À la carte 95F to 160F. The bar is open 6pm to 2am. 65F per cocktail. This restaurant is owned by the well-known names of Johnny Depp, Sean Penn, John Malkovich and Mick Hucknall, so it has no trouble attracting a classy clientele, and already has its regulars. If you manage to get in, you'll probably have to make do with having a drink at the bar. Few come here for the food, anyway, preferring to be seen at aperitif time in the company of a model or a star of the small screen. The service is surprisingly friendly. Friday is disco night, from 1.30am onwards.

GOING OUT

🍸 **Montecristo Café** (map B2, **50**): 68 avenue des Champs-Élysées 75008. ☎ 01-45-62-30-86. Metro: Franklin-Roosevelt. Open daily 24 hours. Set menu 85F at lunchtime, 95F and 150F in the evening. À la carte, budget for 130F. Crammed in between the fast-food outlets and the encroaching Tex-Mex establishments, this little *nuevo musico oportunisto cubano* has opened its doors to lovers of Cuba. There's a complete change of scenery as soon as you enter. Avoid the restaurant on the ground floor, with its sunny terraces, and head for the basement, where salsa and reggae, cocktails and cigars are on offer under the gaze of Che Guevara, Fidel Castro and other bearded men. Hemingway has a little lounge in the shape of a library, where you can skim a few pages of his novels while eating tapas and enjoying *mojitos.*

🍸 **Chesterfield Café** (map B2, **51**): 124 rue La Boétie 75008. ☎ 01-42-25-18-06. Metro: St-Philippe-du-Roule or Franklin-Roosevelt. Open daily 9am to 5pm. Budget for around 130F. Brunch 75F and 109F. One of the many Tex-Mexes near the Champs-Élysées, but quite a nice one, with red-brick walls and round wooden tables, bistro chairs and nostalgic cowboy posters. Every evening at around 11.30pm (except Sunday and Monday) there are American-style rock and blues concerts on a tiny stage. The programme is mostly made up of groups that are largely unknown in Europe, but there are mementoes on the walls of rare appearances by stars (the Spin Doctors, Keanu Reeves). Gospel brunch on Sunday and happy hour during the week from 4pm to 8pm (with 50 per cent reduction on drinks).

🍸 **Le Mathis (map B-C2–3, 52)**: 3 rue de Ponthieu 75008. ☎ 01-53-76-01-62. Metro: Franklin-D.-Roosevelt. Open every evening (except Sunday) until dawn. Cocktails for around 70F, alcohol-free drinks 50F. There's a certain boudoir ambiance in this hotel bar, which is fitted out in kitschy disco red. You might even bump into someone famous.

NIGHTCLUBS

– **Le Cabaret** or **Le Milliardaire** (map B3, **48**): 68 rue Pierre-Leroux 75008. ☎ 01-42-89-44-14. Metro: George-V. Open daily 11pm to dawn. Cocktails from 80F. When the boss of the Queen nightclub (*see below*) decided to launch a new VIP den in partnership with a former employee of the Elite model agency and an artistic director who gave Paris the Folies, the gossip columns went berserk. If you can believe the photos, everyone – Catherine Deneuve, Charlotte Rampling, John Galliano, Mickey Rourke – has been here. Le Cabaret is kitsch, with red-velvet walls, brass friezes, old leather armchairs and deliberately tacky acts (such as knife throwers, pom-pom girls). Obviously you'll need to be dressed up to the nines if you want to stand any chance of getting in, preferably accompanied by somebody famous or a Parisian aristocrat.

– **Le Queen** (map A2, **53**): 102 avenue des Champs-Élysées 75008. ☎ 01-53-89-08-90. Metro: George-V. Open every evening from midnight to dawn. Entrance free Tuesday to Thursday, 50F on Monday, and 100F at the weekend, including one drink. Drinks cost 50F. Not for the faint-hearted, this place has techno to tear you apart. There's a disco evening every Monday and 'secret' evenings on Wednesdays (drum 'n' bass, ambient). Most other evenings are designated gay nights.

9TH ARRONDISSEMENT

THE GRANDS BOULEVARDS ● 'NOUVELLE-ATHÈNES'

The 9th arrondissement has more architectural harmony than the 10th, but it isn't much frequented by tourists. People come here for shopping in the big department stores, or to wander along the boulevards, or around the Opéra quarter and Pigalle, but there's nothing really worth exploring in any great depth. However, you may come across some pleasant surprises, especially in the northern part of the quarter.

WHERE TO STAY

☆ BUDGET

■ **Woodstock Hostel** (map C2, **1**): 48 rue Rodier 75009. ☎ 01-48-78-87-76. Fax: 01-48-78-01-63. Website: www.woodstock.fr. Metro: Anvers. It's 87F per night, from November to March, and 97F from April to October. Budget for 10F more for a double room. Closed noon to 4pm (but the telephones are always manned for bookings) and at night from 2am. A student hotel (more of a youth hostel, actually) for those on a budget, with rooms with bunk beds. The small inner patio is lovely in summer, but closes at 9.45pm (the neighbours have complained about the noise). Plenty of showers on each floor, and breakfast included.

■ **Perfect Hotel** (map C1, **2**): 39 rue Rodier 75009. ☎ 01-42-81-18-86. Fax: 01-42-85-01-38. Metro: Anvers or Cadet. Double room with shower or bath 280F. A single room (which can be occupied by two people) costs 180F. Just opposite the Woodstock (*see above*), this nice hotel has a Montmartre ambiance that you can feel as soon as you enter the reception, with an immense mural of the Moulin Rouge. There's a pleasant lounge on the ground floor with an old piano, and another cosy lounge in the basement with soft sofas and paintings of Montmartre. No TV or mini-bar in the rooms, but the hotel bar is open all night.

☆☆ MODERATE

■ **Hôtel des Croisés** (map B2, **4**): 63 rue Saint-Lazare 75009. ☎ 01-48-74-78-24. Fax: 01-49-95-04-43. Metro: Trinité. Double rooms from 460F to 490F with full bathroom facilities and direct telephone. In a wonderful location, this hotel is almost worth a visit in its own right as it is quite beautiful. It has a superb reception, with old panelling and soft carpeting, and a fabulously retro lift, all wood and wrought-iron grills. The rooms (double beds only) are as spacious as you could wish, with an eccentric idiosyncratic charm – period furniture, art deco panelling (in some) and marble fireplaces. The rooms on the fifth and sixth floors have an alcove that serves as a sitting area. The bathrooms are typically 1950s in style and some of them are enormous. There is satellite TV in all the rooms. Breakfast can be served in your room. This excellent two-star hotel gives amazing value for money, but it only has 26 rooms, so you'll need to book.

☗ **Hôtel des Arts** (map C3, **5**): 7 cité Bergère 75009. ☎ 01-42-46-73-30. Fax: 01-48-00-94-42. Metro: Grands-Boulevards or Cadet. Double room with shower, toilet, TV and Canal+ 400F, with bath 420F. A two-star hotel in a charming passage with a convivial welcome. The rooms are clean and quiet, away from the hustle and bustle of the Faubourg. The staircase is lined with old posters of stage shows, and the grey parrot in reception talks and sings *La Marseillaise*.

☗ **Hôtel Victor Massé** (map B1, **6**): 32 *bis* rue Victor-Massé 75009. ☎ 01-48-74-37-53. Fax: 01-44-53-96-22. E-mail: vicmasse@club-internet.fr. Metro: Pigalle or Saint-Georges. Double room 420F, all mod cons with TV and direct telephone. Triple room 490F. A comfortable hotel located near Place Pigalle, which is perfect for those who love the nightlife. Double-glazing is an essential factor.

☗ **Hôtel de Hollande** (map C3, **7**): 4 rue Cadet 75009. ☎ 01-47-70-50-79. Fax: 01-42-46-56-77. Metro: Cadet or Grands-Boulevards. Double room with washbasin 250F, with shower and toilet 350F and 360F, with bath and toilet 440F. This pleasant two-star hotel is at the heart of the streets near the capital's biggest shops, and has TV in all rooms. In an area where there are many awful hotels, it's worth making a note of. Best to book.

☆☆☆ CHIC

☗ **Hôtel Chopin** (map C3, **9**): 46 passage Jouffroy 75009 (on a level with 10 boulevard Montmartre). ☎ 01-47-70-58-10. Fax: 01-42-47-00-70. Metro: Grands-Boulevards or Bourse. Double room with shower or bath 450F or 490F, all with excellent bathroom facilities. This jewel of a 19th-century hotel is located at the end of a pretty passage, which means that it's a veritable oasis of peace and quiet, just off the Grands Boulevards, near the Musée Grévin. Step back in time at this hotel, where the façade dates from 1850. Inside there is old panelling and a large bay window through which you can see the receptionist, who almost disappears behind the vast counter. The view over the rooftops is reminiscent of impressionist paintings, particularly at sunset. The attic rooms on the fourth floor are charming and well lit, as they overlook the glass roof of the arcade and the rooftops of the Musée Grévin. Avoid those overlooking the courtyard, which have a magnificent view of an enormous wall.

☗ **Hôtel du Léman** (map D3, **10**): 20 rue de Trévise 75009. ☎ 01-42-46-50-66. Fax: 01-48-24-27-59. E-mail: lemanhot@aol.com. Metro: Cadet or Grands-Boulevards. Double room from 490F to 540F depending on the season (prices can climb alarmingly in high season), with all mod cons. Five minutes from the Grands Boulevards, this is a comfortable, quality hotel. Satellite TV and mini-bar, and buffet breakfast. Booking is essential.

☗ **Hôtel de la Tour d'Auvergne** (map C2, **11**): 10 rue de la Tour-d'Auvergne 75009. ☎ 01-48-78-61-60. Fax: 01-49-95-99-00. Metro: Cadet. Double room from 550F to 750F. A three-star hotel overlooking a quiet street near the Sacré-Cœur. The rooms (all with four-poster beds) have all mod cons (bath, TV and hairdryer) and are spacious and beautifully decorated. Bar open and room service available 24-hours a day. Breakfast is particularly nice. The fifth floor is reserved for non-smokers.

☗ **Hôtel du Square d'Anvers** (map D1, **12**): 6 place d'Anvers 75009. ☎ 01-42-81-20-74. Fax: 01-48-78-

47-45. Metro: Anvers. Double room from 460F to 550F, with full bathroom facilities and direct telephone. This hotel benefits from being on the delightful Place d'Anvers. The very comfortable rooms on the sixth floor are splendid, with a 180-degree view over the Sacré-Cœur, the Tour Montparnasse and the Eiffel Tower.

Hôtel Corona (map C2, **13**): 4 rue Rodier 75009. ☎ 01-42-80-53-00. Fax: 01-42-85-42-29. Metro: Notre-Dame-de-Lorette. Double room from 520F to 590 F. A three-star hotel, well located between Sacré-Cœur and the Opéra. There's a large marble reception area and the rooms are functional, modern and nicely refurbished with satellite TV and hairdryer. Paying car park opposite the hotel.

Hôtel Winston (map B1, **14**): 4 rue Frochot 75009. ☎ 01-48-78-05-28. Fax: 01-48-78-06-07. Metro: Pigalle and Saint-Georges. Double room 320F, with full bathroom facilities, telephone, satellite TV and radio. A three-star hotel in a good location, with the Moulin Rouge, the Sacré-Cœur, the Opéra, and the Pigalle metro station near by. If you look closely, you might discover its rather outdated charm!

WHERE TO EAT

☆ BUDGET

Au P'tit Creux du Faubourg (map C2, **20**): 66 rue du Faubourg-Montmartre 75009. ☎ 01-48-78-20-57. Metro: Notre-Dame-de-Lorette or Cadet. Open at lunchtime only. Closed Sunday and from mid-July to mid-August. Set meals 50F and 65F. Full of regulars daily, this unpretentious place offers a very reasonable set menu, with a starter (celery *rémoulade*, tomato vinaigrette or fillet of herring), followed by a meat or fish dish (sautéed veal macaroni, *pot-au-feu* or fillet of scorpion fish with basil), and finishing with a traditional dessert such as crème caramel.

Chartier (map C3, **21**): 7 rue du Faubourg-Montmartre 75009. ☎ 01-47-70-86-29. Metro: Grands-Boulevards. Open daily from 11.30am to 3pm and 6pm to 10pm. No bookings. Set menus at 85F and 110F served lunchtime and evening. Push open the big revolving door to discover this immense 19th-century 'stockpot' (mentioned in the 1863 *Blue Guide* to Paris, and now listed on the Inventory of

Where to stay

- **1** Woodstock Hostel
- **2** Perfect Hotel
- **4** Hôtel des Croisés
- **5** Hôtel des Arts
- **6** Hôtel Victor Massé
- **7** Hôtel de Hollande
- **9** Hôtel Chopin
- **10** Hôtel du Léman
- **11** Hôtel de la Tour d'Auvergne
- **12** Hôtel du Square d'Anvers
- **13** Hôtel Corona
- **14** Hôtel Winston

Where to eat

- **20** Au P'tit Creux du Faubourg
- **21** Chartier
- **22** La Fermette d'Olivier
- **23** Le Choron, Chez Saïd
- **26** Le Bistro du Curé
- **27** Lou Cantou
- **28** Lycée 43
- **29** Le Grand Café Capucines
- **30** Bistro Valparaiso
- **32** Le Sinago
- **33** Le Café Sushi
- **35** Mi Ranchito
- **36** Le Relais Beaujolais
- **38** Le Roi du Pot-au-Feu
- **40** Chez Catherine
- **41** I Golosi
- **42** Au Petit Riche
- **43** Bistro des Deux Théâtres
- **45** La Clairière
- **47** La Table de la Fontaine

Where to go for a drink/ Going out

- **51** Au Général La Fayette
- **52** Le Bar des Roses
- **53** Le Dépanneur
- **55** Le Moloko

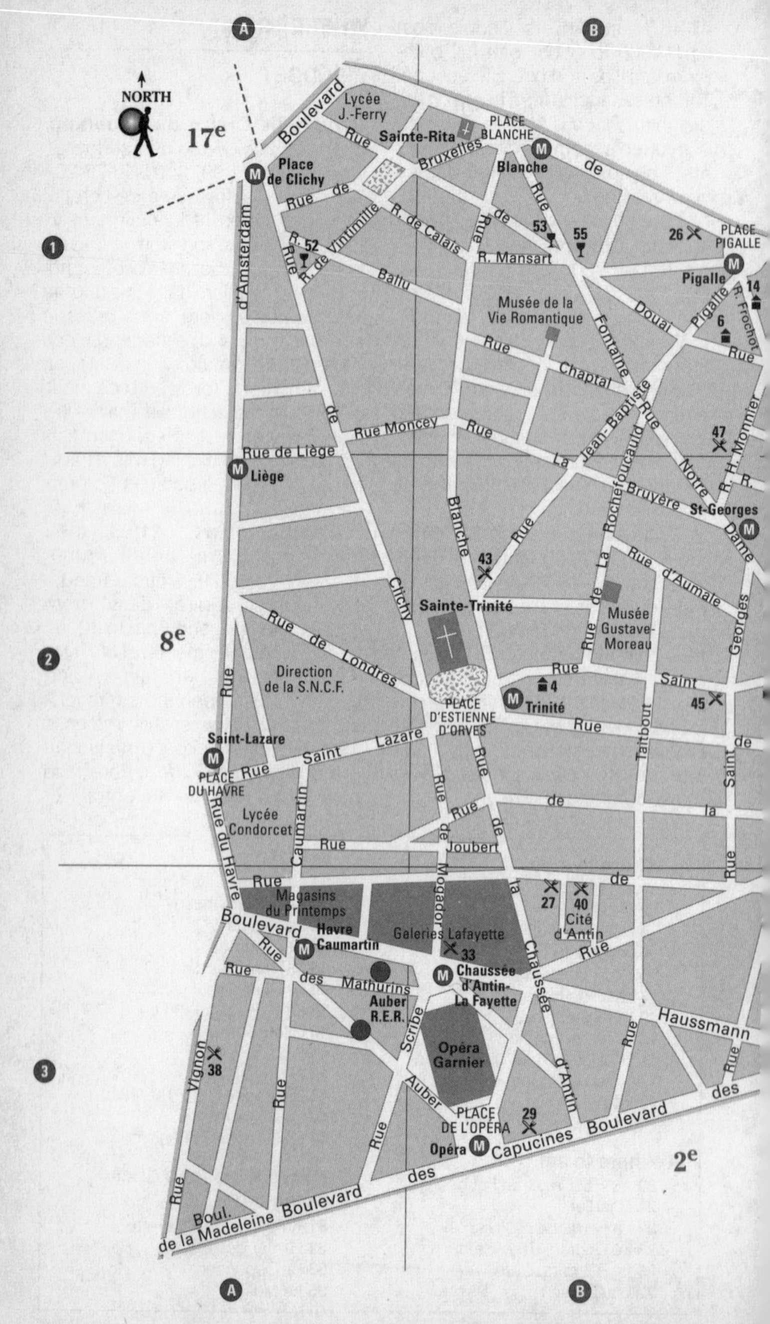

NORTH
17e
8e
2e
A
B
1
2
3
Boulevard
Lycée J.-Ferry
Sainte-Rita
PLACE BLANCHE
Blanche
Place de Clichy
Rue de Bruxelles
Rue de Vintimille
R. de Calais
R. Mansart
Rue Ballu
R. de Vintimille
d'Amsterdam
52
53
55
26
PLACE PIGALLE
Pigalle
14
6
R. Frochot
Rue Pigalle
Douai
Fontaine
Musée de la Vie Romantique
Rue Chaptal
Rue Moncey
Rue de Liège
Liège
Rue La Bruyère
Jean-Baptiste
Rochefoucauld
Rue Notre Dame
47
R. H. Monnier
St-Georges
Blanche
43
Rue d'Aumale
Sainte-Trinité
Musée Gustave-Moreau
Georges
Clichy
Rue de Londres
Direction de la S.N.C.F.
PLACE D'ESTIENNE D'ORVES
Trinité
4
Rue Saint
45
Taitbout
Rue Saint Lazare
Saint-Lazare
PLACE DU HAVRE
Rue du Havre
Lycée Condorcet
Caumartin
Rue Joubert
Rue de Mogador
Rue de la Chaussée d'Antin
27
40
Cité d'Antin
Magasins du Printemps
Boulevard Haussmann
Havre Caumartin
Galeries Lafayette
33
Chaussée d'Antin-La Fayette
Rue des Mathurins
Auber R.E.R.
Scribe
Opéra Garnier
Vignon
38
Rue Auber
PLACE DE L'OPÉRA
29
Opéra
Boulevard des Capucines
Boul. de la Madeleine
Boulevard des

C
D
18e
10e
Boulevard de Rochechouart
Clichy
Anvers
Barbès Rochechouart
Square d'Anvers
PL. D'ANVERS
12
Lycée J.-Decour
Rue Bochart de Saron
Martyrs
Avenue Trudaine
Rue de Dunkerque
Rochechouart
Poissonnière
Victor Massé
28
Rue Rodier
Rue Turgot
R. de Navarin
Rue de La Tour d'Auvergne
2
1
Condorcet
Clauzel
des
Milton
11
Rue de Maubeuge
R. Manuel
Faubourg
Rue de Bellefond
Rue Choron
13
23
32
Lorette
36
Poissonnière
Square de Montholon
Fayette
Lazare
Notre-Dame-de-Lorette
Rue Lamartine
Rue de Montholon
35
PLACE KOSSUTH
Châteaudun
Cadet
Rue Bleue
Rue Trévise
20
Rue Saulnier
Victoire
Le Peletier
51
Laffitte
Pelletier
22
7
Chauchat
Provence
Rue Richer
Faubourg
du
Hôtel des ventes Drouot-Richelieu
Passage Verdeau
Rue Geoffroy-Marie
10
Rue de la Grange Batelière
41
R. de Montyon
Rue Sainte Cécile
42
Rossini
30
Mairie du 9e arr.
9
Musée Grévin
Jouffroy
Passage
Montmartre
Rue Bergère
5
Cité Bergère
21
Italiens
Richelieu Drouot
Boul. Montmartre
Grands Boulevards
Boulevard Poissonnière
Bonne Nouvelle
0 100 200 yds
0 100 200 m
1
2
3

Historic Monuments). Its original decor is intact, it has 350 seats, 16 waiters, and serves 1,500 meals a day. Full of regulars, ageing locals, starving students and artists, and tourists, who are all guaranteed decent food (although not always piping hot) for less than 90F. What really matters is being able to say that you've visited this institution at least once.

✕ **La Fermette d'Olivier** (map C2–3, **22**): 40 rue du Faubourg-Montmartre 75009. Metro: Grands-Boulevards or Le Peletier. ☎ 01-47-70-06-88. Open noon to 3pm and 7pm to 10pm. Closed Saturday, Sunday and public holidays, for 10 days in March and a fortnight in October. In an old quarter, which is mainly given over to kosher food, this organic *fermette* (farmhouse-style cottage), tucked away at the back of a courtyard, is a rarity, with a macrobiotic menu at 80F served lunchtime and evenings, and a more traditional menu at 98F. Vegetarians can treat themselves to generous servings for around 50F – Japanese (omelette, courgette fritters, cereals, vegetable *accras*), or Zen (rice, bulghur wheat, semolina, buckwheat, vegetables) – or a Zen menu with main course, dessert and drinks. The more traditional menu consists of onion soup *au gratin*, goose cutlet with thyme or veal kidneys with mustard, followed by dessert. Fairly quiet in the evening.

✕ **Le Choron, Chez Saïd** (map C2, **23**): 9 rue Choron 75009. ☎ 01-48-78-58-97. Metro: Notre-Dame-de-Lorette. Open lunchtime and evening until 9.30pm. Closed Sunday and in August. Single menu at 42F. Basic food, but it must be doing something right as all the workers in the area come at lunchtime. As many crudités as you can eat, house couscous on Thursday, fish and paella on Friday.

✕ **Le Bistro du Curé** (map B1, **26**): 21 boulevard de Clichy 75009. ☎ 01-48-74-65-84. Metro: Pigalle. Open until 11pm. Closed Sunday and public holidays, and also in August. Set menus 64F and 95F served lunchtime and evening. Dish of the day 43F; express menu 51F. In this former bar (now a House of God, called 'The Priest's Bistro') you can eat at angelic prices. A large stone statue of the Virgin Mary stands in front of the counter, the priest goes from table to table to say hello (inwardly blessing your meal) and the service is supplied by benevolent Christians – and all this so close to the sex shops! There are two set menus. One carries a choice such as *potage* (soup of the day) or egg mayonnaise, roast beef *à la poivrade purée* (dressing with crushed peppercorns) or *blanquette* of turkey with saffron rice, and dessert. On the other is shrimps with mayonnaise, assorted crudités, *pavé* (fillet) of beef with green pepper, braised saddle of lamb, veal escalope and dessert. If you have anything to confess, the priest will see you on the first floor.

✕ **Lou Cantou** (map B3, **27**): 35 cité d'Antin 75009. ☎ 01-48-74-75-15. Metro: Chaussée-d'Antin. Open lunchtime only 11am to 3pm. Closed Sunday and public holidays, as well as for the first three weeks of August. Lunchtime menu at 64F. À la carte from 90F. Since the 1920s this fine restaurant with its rural decor (ox yoke, horse's harness, pots and pans) has been providing sustenance at low prices. There's a single set menu including drinks, on which you can find all the staples of the *bouillon* (rustic) genre: beetroot or red cabbage salad, grated carrot, garlic sausage with potato salad, followed by *boeuf bourguignon* with noodles, Basque chicken and rice, and crème brûlée to finish. Credit cards not accepted.

✕ **Lycée 43** (map C1, **28**): 43 avenue Trudaine 75009. ☎ 01-48-78-43-25. Metro: Anvers or Pigalle. Closed Saturday and Sunday evening, and also in August. Set menus at 70F and 100F served lunchtime and evening. À la carte, between 120F and 150F. This former coach drivers' meeting place is said to have been feeding the coachmen at the turn of the century, before attracting wrestlers performing at the Élysée-Montmartre in the 1950s. Tourists passing through on their way to Montmartre (or on their way back) are received with the same amiability as the regulars. Generous menus and wines at very reasonable prices in a warm, family atmosphere.

✕ **Mi Ranchito** (map C2, **35**): 35 rue de Montholon 75009. ☎ 01-48-78-45-94. Metro: Cadet. Open daily except Saturday lunchtime and from mid-August to mid-September. On Sunday, non-stop service from 1pm. Set menus 65F at lunchtime, 90F in the evening. À la carte, budget for around 130F. Children's menu at 50F. Pay no attention to the pseudo-Colombian decor, what counts here is the Colombian cuisine and the ambiance. The *ceviche* (seafood) or *empanadas* are nicely prepared, while novelty seekers will go for the *comelones* (for big eaters) and the dish of chicken with hot sauce or *churrasco* (chicken grilled with cassava). On Friday and Saturday evening there's a Colombian *pot-au-feu* (stew).

☆ ☆ MODERATE

✕ **Le Sinago** (map C2, **32**): 17 rue Rodier 75009. ☎ 01-48-78-11-14. Metro: Cadet or Notre-Dame-de-Lorette. Last orders 10pm. Closed Sunday and in August. Set menu 65F at lunchtime. À la carte, budget for around 130F. Behind the banal look of this restaurant is a hidden treasure dishing up authentic Cambodian cuisine. There's a wonderful soup with ravioli, fresh spring rolls, Cambodian pancakes with meat and vegetables, and lemongrass chicken. Many dishes, such as the *amok* (spiced catfish wrapped in banana leaves), pepper salad or the Khmer fondue, are only available if ordered in advance. Come for the peaceful atmosphere.

✕ **Le Café Sushi** (map B3, **33**): *Galeries Lafayette* (fifth floor), 40 boulevard Haussmann 75009. ☎ 01-42-82-34-56. Metro: Chaussée-d'Antin. Open at lunchtime only 11.30am to 6pm (8pm on Thursday). Set menus from 98F to 120F. After a shopping spree at the wonderful *Galeries Lafayette* why not eat here too? A short trip on the escalator to the fifth floor, a slalom through the rugs and sofas, and you come out into a Japanese-style area where, from some of the tables, you can admire the rooftops of Paris. You may have to queue for a bit, because the café is very popular. There are a number of set menus: 'Sushi' or 'Sashimi', both with a bowl of soup and salad, 'Fuji' *(yakitoris)* or 'Kyoto' with a choice of *sushi* and *sashimi*, five kebabs, rice and salad. To drink, there's Japanese beer at 35F, *sake* at 40F and green tea at 15F.

✕ **Le Relais Beaujolais** (map C2, **36**): 3 rue Milton 75009. ☎ 01-48-78-77-91. Metro: Notre-Dame-de-Lorette or Le Peletier. Open lunchtime and evening until 10pm. Closed Saturday and Sunday, and also in August. Budget for between 160F and 200F. A serious restaurant in a quiet street with a provincial atmosphere. The landlord is a lover of Beaujolais wines and will always find you the right bottle of Chenard or Fleurie. The cuisine is inventive and the service diligent and friendly. You get a free aperitif, so why not try a little *Beaujolais-fraise*?

✕ **Le Roi du Pot-au-Feu** (map A3, **38**): 34 rue Vignon 75009. ☎ 01-47-42-37-10. Metro: Havre-Caumartin. Open until 10.30pm. Closed Sunday and public holidays, and from 15 July to 15 August. Budget for 150F for a three-course meal. A very small place with an old-style bistro feel, a zinc bar and Vichy tablecloths. The jewel in the crown is the excellent *pot-au-feu* which comes in three versions: *pauvre* (literally, 'poor') at 85F, which is a single course; *classe moyenne* ('middle-class') at 120F with dessert; and *riche* (obvious, really) at 145F, for soup, *pot-au-feu* and dessert.

✕ **La Clairière** (map B2, **45**): 43 rue Saint-Lazare 75009. ☎ 01-48-74-32-94. Metro: Trinité. Open at lunchtime only. Closed Saturday and Sunday. Set menu 130F served lunchtime and evening. À la carte, budget for 200F without drinks. A good place to eat at lunchtime although you may have to use your elbows, because the place soon fills up, both in the dining room and at the bar. The menu includes excellent home-cooking such as knuckle of ham with potatoes, Lyonnais sausage, shoulder of lamb and steak *tartare*. The blackboard, which is always heaving with choices, is cleverly reproduced all over the dining room, which means that everyone can see what's on it. The wine list (wines are available by the glass) is another reason to be cheerful: Marcel Lapierre's Beaujolais-Villages, 'Clos Seguier' '95 Cahors, 'Château d'Aydie' Madiran, 'Château Sepian' '95, 'Mehaye', or Claude Courtois's wonderful 'Clos du Paradis' white (Quartz) and red (Racines).

✕ **Bistro Valparaiso** (map D3, **30**): 15 rue Sainte-Cécile 75009. ☎ 01-48-01-02-75. Metro: Grands-Boulevards. Closed Saturday lunchtime and Sunday, and also in August. Set meals from 55F to 75F; à la carte at around 110F. This old bistro in an out-of-the-way street has been taken over by a Latin American. If the place itself – a large dining room with evenly spaced tables – is lacking a little in warmth, the food and the welcome make up for it. The wine list is somewhat minimalist, but the list of beers and Latin cocktails will soon make you forget that. Generous portions of delicious Chilean, Argentinean or Mexican dishes – *empanadas*, *pastel de choclo*, *ceviche* – are served at very reasonable prices. At the weekend, there's usually someone playing the guitar or the piano.

✕ **La Table de la Fontaine** (map B1, **47**): 5 rue Henri-Monnier 75009. ☎ 01-45-26-26-30. Metro: Saint-Georges. Closed Saturday lunchtime and Sunday. There are two set menus, one at 108F at lunchtime only and the other at 148F. À la carte, budget for around 150F without wine. Close to the Saint-Georges and Labruyère theatres, this restaurant is very popular with actors. The *trompe-l'oeil* hangings, discreet lighting and muffled conversations all contribute to the theatrical illusion. The cuisine fits in perfectly, being classical but refined. The menu might include ravioli *à la crème d'herbes*, haddock carpaccio, grilled salmon, or rabbit casserole with sage and polenta *au gratin*.

☆☆☆ CHIC

✕ **Chez Catherine** (map B3, **40**): 65 rue de Provence 75009. ☎ 01-45-26-72-88. Metro: Chaussée-d'Antin. Service until 11pm. Closed Saturday and Sunday, public holidays, in August and the first week in January. Budget for around 250F including drinks. This well-established, attractive Parisian bistro has undergone a revolution. Whereas the cuisine used not to be up to much and the wine list was mediocre, today the cooking is spot on, and the cellar is full of amazing wines. The *terrine aux tourteaux* and *foie gras* (80F) is wonderful, along with the *saucisson vigneron pommes à l'huile, filet de loup aux épices* and *magret de canard du Gers grillé.* As well as a few wines served by the glass or the jug (such as Cairanne from the Richaud estate or Coteaux de l'Ardèche from the Colombier estate), you can find Robert Michel's Cornas, the Côteaux-d'Aix, the Clos Milan Baux-de-Provence, or the superb Clos Rougeard Saumur-Champigny at very reasonable prices.

✕ **I Golosi** (map C3, **41**): 6 rue de La Grange-Batelière 75009. ☎ 01-48-24-18-63. Metro: Richelieu-Drouot or Grands-Boulevards. Open until 11pm. Closed Saturday evening and Sunday, and also in August. No set menu. Budget for somewhere between 180F and 220F. This restaurant pays homage to Italy with seductive dishes. Risotto, fresh pasta with tomato sauce and artichoke hearts, or gnocchi of potatoes with duck ragout (the menu changes every week). The wine list offers the best Italian wines. I Golosi is also a wine merchant's, with some excellent products. The decor is pure Venetian. On Saturday lunchtime, it is busy with regulars from the nearby auction houses, and families with their children.

✕ **Le Grand Café Capucines** (map B3, **29**): 4 boulevard des Capucines 75009. ☎ 01-43-12-19-00. Metro: Opéra. Open 24 hours a day, all year round. There's a set menu at 178F served lunchtime and evening. À la carte, budget for 260F without drinks. The decor sparkles like a Christmas tree, with Mucha-style frescoes and furniture in the floral style of the Belle Époque. The waiters are busy but remarkably attentive and considerate. Seafood is top of the bill here, but if that doesn't take your fancy, there is a *Privilège* menu with all the brasserie classics. At the end of the meal, when you order your coffee, you're given two cups: a very strong Italian espresso in the first one, and a high-quality coffee, generally not as strong, in the second. The clientele tends to be mainly night owls.

✕ **Au Petit Riche** (map C3, **42**): 25 rue Le Peletier 75009. ☎ 01-47-70-68-68. Metro: Richelieu-Drouot. Last orders 12.15am. Closed Sunday. Set menus from 140F to 180F; children's menu at 70F. À la carte comes to around 200F without drinks. Founded in 1880, the Petit Riche, with its string of Belle-Époque lounges, harks back to the days of society dinners and elegant women in the fashions of the day. There's a 'traditional' set menu at 180F with a number of starters, main courses and a choice of desserts, including veal, fillet of perch and *tarte fine aux pommes* (apple tart). The restaurant is close to several theatres, and, in association with many of them, offers a special all-in price for theatre and dinner.

✕ **Bistrot des Deux Théâtres** (map B2, **43**): 18 rue Blanche 75009. ☎ 01-45-26-41-43. Metro: Trinité. Open daily until 12.30am. Set menu 169F served lunchtime and evening, including aperitif, wine and coffee. An essential stopping-off point for night owls and thespians, on the slopes of Pigalle. In this quarter it sticks out like a sore thumb because of its rather English elegance. The service has its good and bad days. Mainly of interest because you can eat here after midnight.

THE GRANDS BOULEVARDS

FROM THE BOULEVARD DU CRIME TO THE BOULEVARD DU KITSCH

From the Bastille to the Madeleine, the Grands Boulevards follow the route of Charles V's former city ramparts, which were extended by Louis XIII. When the fortifications became unnecessary, Louis XIV had them converted into promenades lined with trees, and large houses with enormous gardens were built along the edges. In the 19th century the Boulevards were swallowed up in the urban sprawl and filled with dance halls and theatres, where the most amazing melodramas were staged (the famous 'boulevard du Crime', towards the place de la République, which disappeared in Haussmann's reconstruction, was brought back to life with panache by Marcel Carné and Jacques Prévert for the film *Les Enfants du Paradis*). Today, there is a still a succession of so-called 'boulevard' cafés, large brasseries, restaurants, cinemas and theatres. The latter specialize in light, slightly racy comedy, mainly aiming to provide undemanding escapist entertainment without any intellectual pretensions. The heyday of the Boulevards was in the second half of the 19th century, when they became a symbol of elegance and fashion.

Towards the 1950s, the Boulevards gradually became more working-class, with the big department stores preferring, at around the same time, to move to the Faubourg Saint-Honoré and the Champs-Élysées. One of France's best-known actors and singers, Yves Montand, sang about this period, when working men would go out walking with their families on a Sunday, sometimes taking potshots at fairground stalls, or listening to the patter of street traders. Nowadays, few bother to stroll around here like they used to – young people tend to be attracted to the livelier quarters like Les Halles, Saint-Michel or Saint-Germain – but this doesn't mean that the Boulevards are finished. It's still worth taking a tour around the *passages*, delightful 19th-century glass-roofed shopping arcades.

★ **Passage Jouffroy:** this arcade, built in 1847, is a bit like a provincial street market, and yet it has retained something of a shady past. At the end of the last century it had a reputation for harbouring prostitutes, as well as for restaurants and the Musée Grévin. It is more welcoming if you enter from the boulevard Montmartre side, but either way it could do with a bit of a facelift. At No. 34 there's an interesting shop selling walking sticks and, at the end, an elegant retro hotel. When you get to the rue de la Grange-Batelière, dive down the Passage Verdeau opposite for shops full of priceless treasures – musical instruments, old cameras and books. *La France Ancienne* offers a vast array of postcards, posters and old newspapers, all at very reasonable prices.

★ **Musée Grévin:** 10 boulevard Montmartre 75009. ☎ 01-47-70-87-99 and 01-47-70-85-05. Metro: Grands-Boulevards. Open daily 1pm to 7pm between April and August, 1pm to 6.30pm from September to March. Opens at 10am during the school holidays. Ticket sales end an hour before closing. Entry fee 58F; reduction for children aged between six and fourteen (the price may be a bit steep, because it is a private museum, but it does include a 90-minute guided tour). In 1882, when photography was taking its first tentative steps, Arthur Meyer created a waxworks museum to introduce Parisians to the celebrities of the day. It was an immediate hit. Today it still attracts young and old alike, and is careful to stay up to date. The first hall has recently welcomed – with some considerable ceremony – Zidane from France's 1998 World Cup-winning football team. You'll also see Madonna, Michael Jackson, Leonardo Di Caprio and 50 stars of the silver screen such as Charlie Chaplin, Boris Karloff, Alfred Hitchcock and Marilyn Monroe, along with famous French celebrities such as Josiane Balasko and Thierry L'Hermitte. In the basement there are scenes from the French Revolution.

During the tour don't miss the two smaller, permanent exhibits, 'The Palace of Mirages', a sound-and-light show that dates from the 1900 Universal Exhibition but is still not showing its age and, in the Museum of the Theatre, a mime show, popular with children.

★ **Department stores:** the growth of the department store in France dates from 1852, when Aristide Boucicaut opened *Au Bon Marché*. Imitators soon followed: in 1864, Jules Jaluzot opened *Le Printemps*; in 1870, Ernest Cognacq and Louise Jay opened *La Samaritaine*, opposite the Pont-Neuf; and in 1894 *Les Galeries Lafayette* was launched, aimed at a working-class public.

This was the golden age of trade, when ornate façades, gilding and statues were considered *de rigueur*. Refurbishment has removed the splendid central staircase at *Le Printemps*, as well as the one at *Les Galeries Lafayette*, just a few months before it was listed as an historic monument. However, the flamboyant decoration of *Le Printemps*, with its central cupola's glass roof, can still be seen from boulevard Haussmann. The best way to appreciate it is in the café under the dome.

Right next door to these temples of consumerism, and around the same time, the world of finance was erecting huge buildings with guilded balconies to house the captains of industry and the upwardly mobile *nouveau-riche* businessmen. The stars among these are the Compagnie des Wagons-lits (one of the original railway companies), opposite the square Louis XVI; the headquarters of the Crédit Lyonnais bank (17 boulevard des Italiens); the headquarters of the Banque Nationale de Paris; the Maison Dorée (20 boulevard des Italiens), and the Société Générale bank (29 boulevard Haussmann) whose magnificent 1900 decor of marble and glass hasn't changed a bit.

★ At 14 boulevard des Capucines is a **plaque** that reads: 'Here, on 28 December 1895, the first public showings of moving pictures took place with the aid of the cinematograph, a device invented by the Lumière brothers.'

★ **L'Opéra Garnier:** ☎ 01-40-01-17-89 or 08-36-69-78-68 (reservations). Metro: Opéra. Unguided tours daily from 10am to 5pm (doors close at 4.30pm), except on days when there is a matinée or a one-off performance. There are a number of ways of getting tickets for performances. The most common one is to queue when the box office opens, a fortnight before the first night. Tickets are scarce, so get there at 9am (even though the box office opens at 10am) and expect to spend some time waiting. Tickets can be expensive, too (60–670F for operas, and 50–420F for ballets). If you can't actually get there in person you can try telephoning, but as there is only a limited quota of tickets they are likely to have been snapped up already. The third solution is to write six months in advance, giving various alternative dates and the prices you're prepared to pay, or to try to get tickets from Fnac and Virgin shops and ticket agencies – again, these are fairly scarce. If you don't manage to get tickets (some people wait two years for them, so don't be surprised), there is a guided tour daily (except Monday) at 1pm (entry fee 60F; concessions 45F), which is definitely worthwhile. Come between 1pm and 2pm if you aren't taking the guided tour, so that you can get into the theatre itself and admire Chagall's painted ceiling, which is the highlight of the tour. Rehearsals in progress often prevent visitors from seeing the theatre, but at lunchtime the stage empties. If you arrive after 2pm, find out before buying your ticket whether you'll be able to see the ceiling.

A masterpiece of the decorative and flamboyant architectural style of the Second Empire, the Paris Opera House still has its admirers. Designed by Charles Garnier, work began in 1860 and it was opened in 1875 as the supreme achievement of Haussmann's town-planning project. The main façade of the building sets the tone of the place, not to mention that of the avenue and the whole of the Opéra quarter. The rather overblown style of the main staircase, the great foyer and the auditorium is typical of the time. On the day of the inauguration, Garnier paid for his own ticket, a second-class box at 120F. Despite its size, and the extent of its site – it covers an area of 11,000 square metres (36,000 square feet) – the Opéra has a seating capacity of just 2,200 spectators, whereas the stage can hold 450 performers.

Badly damaged by pollution, the Opéra has been undergoing renovation work since spring 1999.

The Opéra has its serious side, but there are also some entertaining anecdotes connected with it. Its legendary underground lake (which is, in fact, a reservoir) does exist. It was used to drain water off underneath the building, and would of course be of great use if there were ever a fire. One technician had the bright idea of farming trout in the water. They flourished rather too well, with the result that his colleagues used to come and fish for them at lunchtime. The story goes that the cunning technician then replaced the tasty trout with barbel, a much less popular fish. If you were able to cross the rooftops of the Opéra, you might come across M. Paucton, a beekeeper in his spare time who, for the last 16 years, has been tending two hives that he built here. Apparently, his bees love it, and the proof of the pudding is in the eating. He collects almost 200kg (440lb) of honey every year, and it's on sale at *Fauchon*, in place de la Madeleine in the 8th arrondissement, or in the Opéra's own shop.

★ **Musée et la Bibliothèque de l'Opéra:** you can visit the restored Museum and Library of the Opéra along with the Opéra itself, but the reading room of the library is open to the public only on special Heritage Days. Unlike the rest of the theatre, the buildings, which were never totally converted by Garnier, are far less ornate.

The museum has a temporary exhibition space and a permanent gallery (upper floors), where the pastels and paintings on the theme of dance and Russian ballet include the famous *Portrait de Wagner* (1893) by Renoir and the *Danseuse s'Exerçant au Foyer* by Degas. You can also see the scale model of Lenepveu's original ceiling, which is hidden beneath the one by Chagall. The museum has thousands of reproductions of miniature stage sets from the last century in the Galerie des Guignols; models were always made before the full-sized versions were built. They are put on display in rotation. The library has high wooden shelves, which contain general works on the theatre and dance, plus several music scores.

'NOUVELLE-ATHÈNES'

THE SUBTLE CHARM OF THE NEO-CLASSICAL

This quarter, around rue Notre-Dame-de-Lorette and rue des Martyrs, is full of provincial charm and tranquillity. There are many 18th- and 19th-century private residences. Its soubriquet 'Nouvelle-Athènes' ('New Athens') derives from the neo-Classical style of the buildings, erected during the Restoration, and broadly inspired by ancient Greece. A veritable 'Republic of Arts and Writing' was established here during the period of triumphant Romanticism, with, among others, George Sand, Alexandre Dumas, Berlioz, Delacroix and Chopin in residence. A number of the significant sites connected with this period are worth seeing.

★ **Place Saint-Georges:** Metro: Saint-Georges. There is a fine house in Romantic-Gothic style at No. 28, while Thiers' house is now a museum. On one street corner there is a lovely antiques shop under a veranda. The rue Saint-Georges has housed a number of prestigious, if not infamous, residents – No. 50 was first a theatre, then a brothel called *Chez Marguerite*, and Goering had a room there during the Second World War.

★ The **rues Rodier, Milton, de l'Agent-Bailly** and the **cité Charles-Godon** have retained their village feel, giving a foretaste of Montmartre, further up the hill. At 3 rue de l'Agent-Bailly, a large porch opens into one of the loveliest courtyard-gardens in the 9th arrondissement. A former 17th-century monastery, then Napoleon's stables, then a mail staging-post, it now houses workshops and offices. Note the fine façade at the end with a weathervane, little steeple and clock. No. 18 rue Rodier has a façade sculpted with medallions and at No. 20 a series of courtyards lead into one another. At 3 **rue de la Tour-des-Dames**, there is a curious private residence with a concave façade. Opposite, at Nos. 2 and 4, there are several typically 19th-century follies.

★ **Musée de la Vie Romantique** (museum of romantic life): 16 rue Chaptal 75009. ☎ 01-48-74-95-38. Fax: 01-48-74-28-42. Metro: Saint-Georges, Blanche, Liège or Pigalle. Open 10am to 5.40pm. Closed Monday and public holidays. Entry fee 22F, 15F concessions; 15F for temporary exhibitions.

Painter Ary Scheffer lived in this lovely house, at the end of a romantic alley, and it hasn't changed since 1830. Every Friday, the most important creative figures of the day – Ingres, Delacroix, Liszt and Chopin – used to come to Scheffer's *salon*. Writer George Sand was another frequent visitor, and it is to her that the museum is largely devoted. The rooms, decorated in the style of the day, are full of objects, portraits and furniture that were part of her life. There are a few paintings and drawings, such as the *Parc de Nohant* and *L'Education de la Vierge* by Delacroix, *Maurice Sand* by Thomas Couture (who was Manet's teacher), several watercolours and *Dendrites* by George Sand. On the other side of the main house is Scheffer's workshop, which is also full of memorabilia.

Temporary exhibitions bring the broad aspects of Romanticism and its echoes in the 20th century back to life. There is a tea-room in summer.

★ **Hôtel des Ventes Drouot** (Drouot auction rooms): 9 rue Drouot 75009. Metro: Richelieu-Drouot or Le Peletier. ☎ 01-48-00-20-20. Website: www.gazette-drouot.com. Open daily from 11am to 6pm and one Sunday a month. Closed in August. The auctions take place in the afternoon, from 2pm onwards. There are a number of ways of getting hold of the catalogue: the *Gazette Drouot* is available in bookshops or on the company's website, and the schedule is given away free at the auction house. The auctions are open to everyone.

There's something of a theatrical touch to this auction house. It's a good opportunity to see the professionalism of the auctioneer, who skilfully leads the bidding, as well as to see some of the unusual items that come up. The lots are put on show the day before they are sold, when potential buyers are allowed to handle some of them.

★ **Musée Gustave-Moreau:** 14 rue de La Rochefoucauld 75009. ☎ 01-48-74-38-50. Metro: Trinité. Open from 10am to 12.45pm and 2pm to 5.15pm; Monday and Wednesday from 11am to 5.15pm. Closed Tuesday. Entry is free to under-18s; there's a reduced rate for those under 25, and for everyone on Sunday. This museum has an amazing history. It was designed and created by Gustave Moreau during his own lifetime so that 'future generations will be able to see where the artist's work came from and the efforts he made during his lifetime'. Much misunderstood, Moreau's work was judged to be strange by most of his contemporaries and, when he left the museum to the State, the legacy was only accepted after five years of consideration. However, he did become a leader for a generation of symbolists and provided the inspiration for several painters who soon got themselves noticed, notably Matisse and Rouault (who was the museum's first curator). Gustave Moreau was born in 1826 and died in 1898. He chose to live in the Nouvelle-Athènes quarter, where he spent his last few years classifying his works and conceiving other, even larger ones, more in keeping with the museum's dimensions.

– **On the first floor** there is a tour of what remains of the rooms where Moreau lived with his parents, which he converted into a 'personal museum' in 1897. For a long time closed to the public, these apartments are now open, exhibiting small, intimate works, paintings, drawings and engravings by Poussin, Rembrandt, David d'Angers, and a few finished works by Gustave Moreau himself.

– **On the second floor** is the great workshop, with its magnificent spiral staircase. *Le Retour des Argonautes* is a vast painting representing a boat 'loaded with all the chimera of youth', according to a comment made by the painter himself. The artist's wax sculptures are in a large showcase: Moreau wanted to cast them in bronze, which he felt would be better than paint to give 'the measure of the qualities and science in the rhythm and the arabesque of the lines' (!). The main characters are Prometheus, Jacob and the Angel, Moses, and Salome and the head of John the Baptist. Revolving panels display studies, sketches and drawings, listed, dated and annotated by the painter.

– **On the third floor** are sliding panels designed by Moreau displaying small paintings, as well as revolving frames and a revolving case showing watercolours. The main exhibit here is Moreau's masterpiece *Jupiter et Sémélé*, a riot of colours and exuberant detail. The characters' voluptuous pose, the remarkable balance of the bodies and the drape of their clothing all contribute to an admirable composition. The polyptych *Vie de l'Humanité* represents humanity, from the Golden Age to the Iron Age, the Fall of Man, and, right at the top, Redemption. Finally, there is the fascinating *Triomphe d'Alexandre* with an amazing perspective.

WHERE TO GO FOR A DRINK/ GOING OUT

🍸 **Au Général La Fayette** (map C2, **51**): 52 rue La Fayette 75009. ☎ 01-47-70-59-08. Metro: Cadet or Le Peletier. Open daily noon to 4pm. Set menus at 100F and 120F. This brasserie, opened in 1896, is an institution at the business heart of Haussmann's Paris. The fact that one of the first barrels of Guinness in the capital was opened here after the war should tell you all you need to know. Gilded stucco work and mouldings have been left intact. Here, solitary writers rub shoulders with actors from the theatres on the Boulevards and antique dealers from the Drouot, all in a laid-back jazzy atmosphere. At any time of the day you can try 100 varieties of beer (from 23F to 114F) and Auvergne-style snacks, with some good wines. Dish of the day 69F.

🍸 **Le Bar des Roses** (map A1, **52**): 66 boulevard de Clichy 75009. ☎ 01-48-74-91-71. Metro: Place-Clichy. Open daily 7am to 10pm, 11pm or midnight. Half a pint of beer 14F, coffee in the dining room 8.50F. The owner's heroes of stage or screen – Clint Eastwood, Ornella Mutti, Isabelle Adjani – adorn the walls here, giving the place a rather out-of-date atmosphere which seems to be popular with both visiting VIPs and locals. There's a superb south-facing terrace in summer and also a well-stocked jukebox (10F for five selections).

🍸 **Le Dépanneur** (map B1, **53**): 27 rue Fontaine 75009. ☎ 01-40-16-40-20. Metro: Pigalle. Open daily all day. Set menus at 70F and 99F. A local classic, people often meet at the Dépanneur because all the other bars are closed. Groups coming out of the nearby nightclubs make up most of the clientele from 3am onwards. There's a DJ at weekends, and frequent theme nights.

🍸 **Le Moloko** (map B1, **55):** 26 rue Fontaine 75009. ☎ 01-48-74-50-26. Metro: Pigalle or Blanche. Open daily 9.30pm to 7am. 30F for a beer, 55F for cocktails. People chatter upstairs while the jukebox plays downstairs (select from 1,200 songs, free of charge) in this former meeting place for Russian exiles at the turn of the century. There are some rather odd African masks together with some strange Asian statues. Gets very crowded at weekends, with theme nights from Thursday to Sunday.

10TH ARRONDISSEMENT

RÉPUBLIQUE ● CANAL SAINT-MARTIN ● THE 'BAS DE BELLEVILLE'

The 10th arrondissement is like the railway waiting room of Paris, with its two major stations, the Gare de l'Est and the Gare du Nord. It's not really a tourist area, but you might find yourself having a look around if you're staying in a hotel near here. It's rather squeezed in between more interesting quarters (Les Halles, Montmartre, the Marais), while the Grands Boulevards to the east and Belleville to the west tend to encroach upon some of its territory. There's a limited cultural life, but you can follow the locals and find a few good spots and colourful walks if you look hard enough. This sort of 'tourism' will appeal to those who like to get well off the beaten track.

WHERE TO STAY

☆ BUDGET

☗ **Hôtel Vicq d'Azir** (map D2, **1**): 21 rue Vicq-d'Azir 75010. ☎ 01-42-08-06-70. Fax: 01-42-08-06-80. Metro: Colonel-Fabien. Open 8am to 10pm. Double room 125F to 195F, depending on degree of comfort. There's a shower which you have to pay for and toilet on each landing for those rooms with fewer facilities. A modest hotel in the northeast of Paris with 70 rooms, including some that overlook the charming small inner courtyard. You pay when you arrive. No breakfast, but a friendly welcome.

☆ CHEAP

☗ **Hôtel de Milan** (map B2, **2**): 17–19 rue Saint-Quentin 75010. ☎ 01-40-37-88-50. Fax: 01-46-07-89-48. Metro: Gare-de-l'Est or Gare-du-Nord. Double room 186F to 316F, with either washbasin, washbasin and toilet, or bathroom. Rooms at 429F for three or four people. A warm welcome. Double-glazing, lift, satellite TV in most of the rooms. All credit cards are accepted, except American Express.

☗ **Hôtel Palace** (map B3, **3**): 9 rue Bouchardon 75010. ☎ 01-40-40-09-45/46. Fax: 01-42-06-16-90. Metro: Strasbourg-Saint-Denis or Jacques-Bonsergent. Double room 133F to 236F with toilet, shower or all mod cons. There is also a shower, which you have to pay to use, on the landing. The flowered wallpaper may not be to everyone's taste, but this family hotel in a quiet street is still one of the cheapest in Paris. The small inner courtyard is attractive and well maintained. This place is already a landmark for many backpackers, as it's in a lively quarter where there are lots of theatres, five minutes from the Gare de l'Est and the République.

☗ **Hôtel Moderne du Temple** (map D3, **4**): 3 rue d'Aix 75010. ☎ 01-42-08-09-04. Fax: 01-42-41-72-17. Metro: République or Goncourt. Double room 160F to 240F with washbasin, shower or full bathroom facilities. A really pleasant surprise, situated between the Canal Saint-Martin lock and the sloping part of the Faubourg-du-

Temple, this hotel is in a narrow, working-class street with ageing façades. It has 43 rooms, with facilities roughly equivalent to what you'll find at the nearby youth hostel. There's a small bar. Direct telephone in every room.

☆☆ MODERATE

Hôtel-Gilden Magenta (map C3, **5**): 35 rue Yves-Toudic 75010. ☎ 01-42-40-17-72. Fax: 01-42-02-59-66. E-mail: hotelgildenmagenta@compuserve.com. Metro: République or Jacques-Bonsergent. Double room 390F to 410F, with shower and toilet. Room for three people 465F, or for four 550F. A real find, this small two-star hotel is in a quiet street between the Place de la République and the Canal Saint-Martin. If you take the rue de Marseille opposite the hotel, you'll enter a new world on the footbridges of the Canal Saint-Martin. When the weather is fine you can have your breakfast on the lovely little patio, which is on a level with Rooms 3 and 5. All the rooms have cable TV and direct-dial telephone, and the owners are friendly, smiling and helpful. It's best to book at least eight days in advance.

New Hotel (map B1, **6**): 40 rue Saint-Quentin 75010. ☎ 01-48-78-04-83. Fax: 01-40-82-91-22. E-mail: info@newhotelparis.com. Metro: Gare-du-Nord. Double room 390F to 490F, with shower or bath. The areas around railway stations are never the best a city has to offer, but this establishment is surprisingly quiet. Some of the functional rooms have a balcony, and you'll find everything you'd expect from a two-star hotel, from satellite TV to a hairdryer, in most rooms. The cellar has been converted into three small vaulted rooms, with medieval-style decor and a small fountain in a recess, where generous breakfasts are served (*croissants*, *brioches*, cornflakes, orange juice). At the end of the short street on the right of the hotel there is terrace overlooking the trains at the Gare de l'Est, and offering a magnificent view over Paris.

Hôtel Mazagran (map A3, **7**): 4 rue de Mazagran 75010. ☎ 01-48-24-25-26. Fax: 01-42-47-17-96. Metro: Strasbourg-Saint-Denis, boulevard Bonne-Nouvelle exit. Double room 295F to 400F, from the most basic (without private facilities) to the best equipped. All have TV and double-glazing. The Mazagran has been completely renovated, but the decor is still as bland as ever! It's mainly of interest because of the nearby theatres and boulevards – which are good for a stroll – the Grand Rex, the largest cinema in Europe, and the Sentier quarter for shopping. The rue Mazagran is very quiet, especially in the evening, and you'll be greeted at the hotel with a smile; it's a good idea to make a reservation.

Hôtel Royal Magenta (map B2, **8**): 7 rue des Petits-Hôtels 75010. ☎ 01-42-46-33-00. Fax: 01-42-46-38-76. Metro: Gare-du-Nord or Gare-de-l'Est. Double room 260F to 500F, either with washbasin, or with shower or bath and toilet. A maze-like, two-star hotel, with medium-sized, functional rooms, all with TV. It has the advantage of being close to the stations, to the Marché Saint-Quentin, and away from the noise, and, for those travelling by car, there is a private garage adjacent to the hotel.

Hôtel Excelsior République (map B3, **9**): 4 rue de Lancry 75010. ☎ 01-42-06-23-30. Fax: 01-42-06-09-80. Metro: République or Jacques-Bonsergent. Budget for 350F to 400F for two, with shower, toilet, TV and direct telephone. This two-star hotel close to the Grands Boulevards, theatres and the Place de la République has been completely renovated. It has 35 modern, functional and very clean rooms, all with double-glazing. There is a garage and car park near by.

☗ **Hôtel Parisiana** (map A2, **10**): 21 rue de Chabrol 75010. ☎ 01-47-70-68-33. Fax: 01-48-00-00-67. Metro: Gare-de-l'Est. Double room 466F with bath and toilet or shower and toilet, including breakfast. This two-star hotel is actually two buildings separated by a charming small garden where generous breakfasts (*croissants*, orange juice, *fromage frais*, Gruyère) are served. The dining room is decorated with a pretty mural. The rooms facing the road have recently been double-glazed. All rooms have TV and a hairdryer and the bathrooms are spacious.

☗ **Nord-Est Hôtel** (map B2, **11**): 12 rue des Petits-Hôtels 75010. ☎ 01-47-70-07-18. Fax: 01-42-46-73-50. Metro: Gare-du-Nord or Gare-de-l'Est. Double room 380F to 410F, with shower and toilet or bath and toilet. There is satellite TV in all the rooms. This small, two-star is well situated between the Gare du Nord and the Gare de l'Est, in a quiet street close to the Marché Saint-Quentin. It has a provincial charm, squeezed in behind a small garden where you can relax in fine weather. Friendly welcome. Clean, functional rooms. Reserve well in advance.

☗ **Hôtel Nord et Champagne** (map B2, **12**): 11 rue de Chabrol 75010. ☎ 01-47-70-06-77. Fax: 01-48-00-95-41. Metro: Gare-de-l'Est and Gare-du-Nord. Double room 330F to 400F, with shower or bath, toilet, direct telephone, TV and Canal+. Centrally located, sitting snugly between a winebar-restaurant and a take-away, this two-star hotel has contemporary-style rooms, most of which open on to a blooming indoor garden. Rooms overlooking the busy street have double-glazing. There's a car park 50m away.

WHERE TO EAT

☆ BUDGET

✕ **Dishny** (map B1, **20**): 25 rue Cail 75010. ☎ 01-42-05-44-04. Metro: La Chapelle. Open daily from 7am to midnight. Set menus 40F at lunchtime, 55F and 99F in the evening. The average price for an à la carte meal is 55F excluding drinks. You can hardly miss this restaurant, in the heart of the Indian-Sri Lankan business quarter. Its frontage is flashy pink, although the decor inside is quite basic. From morning to night there's a constant toing and froing, particularly of the Tamil community. Early in the morning, workers come for a Tamil-style breakfast; at lunchtime, and again in the evening, the French join in, attracted by impeccable menus at unbeatable prices. À la carte is only marginally more expensive than a set menu; choose from meat or vegetable samosa (15F and 12F), chappati (12F), cheese-nan (20F), or curries (20F to 40F) with a choice of chicken, beef, squid. Drinks are also reasonably priced, with Indian beer at 18F, and cardamom tea at 10F. The take-away option is very popular with Tamil families at the weekend.

✕ **Yasmin** (map B3, **21**): 71–73 passage Brady 75010. ☎ 01-45-23-04-25. Metro: Château-d'Eau. Open lunchtime and evening until 11.30pm. Set menus 45F at lunchtime, from 59F in the evening. At Yasmin you can eat your fill for under 90F. It may not have the refinement of the great Indian restaurants, but the menu is varied (a choice of five or six dishes, accompanied by Basmati rice or a nan) and people love it. Walking through the colourful and fragrant Passage Brady, with its Indian spice stalls and barbers' shops, you can easily imagine yourself in another country.

✕ **Pooja** (map A-B3, **40**): 91 passage Brady 75010. ☎ 01-48-24-00-83. Metro: Château-d'Eau. Closed Monday. Set menus 45F and 65F at lunchtime; in the evening there are set menus from 89F. A tiny restaurant whose owner is from Uttar Pradesh. The reviewers are unanimous – press cuttings singing his praises are displayed on the front window. The tried-and-tested evening set menu, with samosas and raita, lamb curry and chicken curry, gives a good taste of India, and the polite service is more reminiscent of that country than of Paris.

✕ **Ajmeer** (map C2, **22**): 159 quai de Valmy 75010. ☎ 01-42-05-67-05. Metro: Louis-Blanc or Château-Landon. Open until 11.30pm. Closed Monday lunchtime. Set menu 49F at lunchtime and 80F in the evening. But for the boats sometimes glimpsed on the Canal Saint-Martin, or the Parisians walking their dogs along the banks of the Seine, you might think you were in India. This is a sort of cabin with walls covered in Indian fabrics and sculpted wooden panels where, for less than 100F, you can eat good food in generous portions. There's a good vegetarian biryani.

✕ **Restaurant de Bourgogne** (map C3, **23**): 26 rue des Vinaigriers 75010. ☎ 01-46-07-07-91. Metro: Jacques-Bonsergent or Gare-de-l'Est. Open until 10pm. Closed Saturday evening, Sunday and public holidays, and also from the last week of July to the third week of August. Set menus 55F and 60F at lunchtime, 60F and 65F in the evening. Close to the Hôtel du Nord and the romantic Canal Saint-Martin, this tiny local restaurant has not changed a jot over the last few years. There's still an old provincial feel, and a working-class clientele. The owner's waistline is the best recommendation for the cooking here! House

Where to stay

1 Hôtel Vicq d'Azir
2 Hôtel de Milan
3 Hôtel Palace
4 Hôtel Moderne du Temple
5 Hôtel-Gilden Magenta
6 New Hotel
7 Hôtel Mazagran
8 Hôtel Royal Magenta
9 Hôtel Excelsior République
10 Hôtel Parisiana
11 Nord-Est Hôtel
12 Hôtel Nord and Champagne

✕ **Where to eat**

20 Dishny
21 Yasmin
22 Ajmeer
23 Restaurant de Bourgogne
24 Tokioyaki
25 Kibélé
26 Au Vieux Bistro
27 Café Panique
29 Le Cambodge
30 Chez Kolia
31 Le Réveil du Xe
32 Arthur
33 La Vigne Saint-Laurent
34 Le Parmentier
35 Boua Thaï
36 La Chandelle Verte
37 Le Petit Café
38 Le Coin de Verre
39 China Town Belleville
40 Pooja
41 L'An II
42 Chez Michel
43 Le Baalbek
44 Flo
45 Terminus Nord
46 Julien
47 Le Palet Lafayette
48 La Marine
49 Purple Café

Where to go for a drink/ Going out

55 Chez Adel
56 La Patache
57 L'Atmosphère
58 La Java
59 Les Étoiles
61 L'Apostrophe
62 Chez Prune
64 Le Galopin

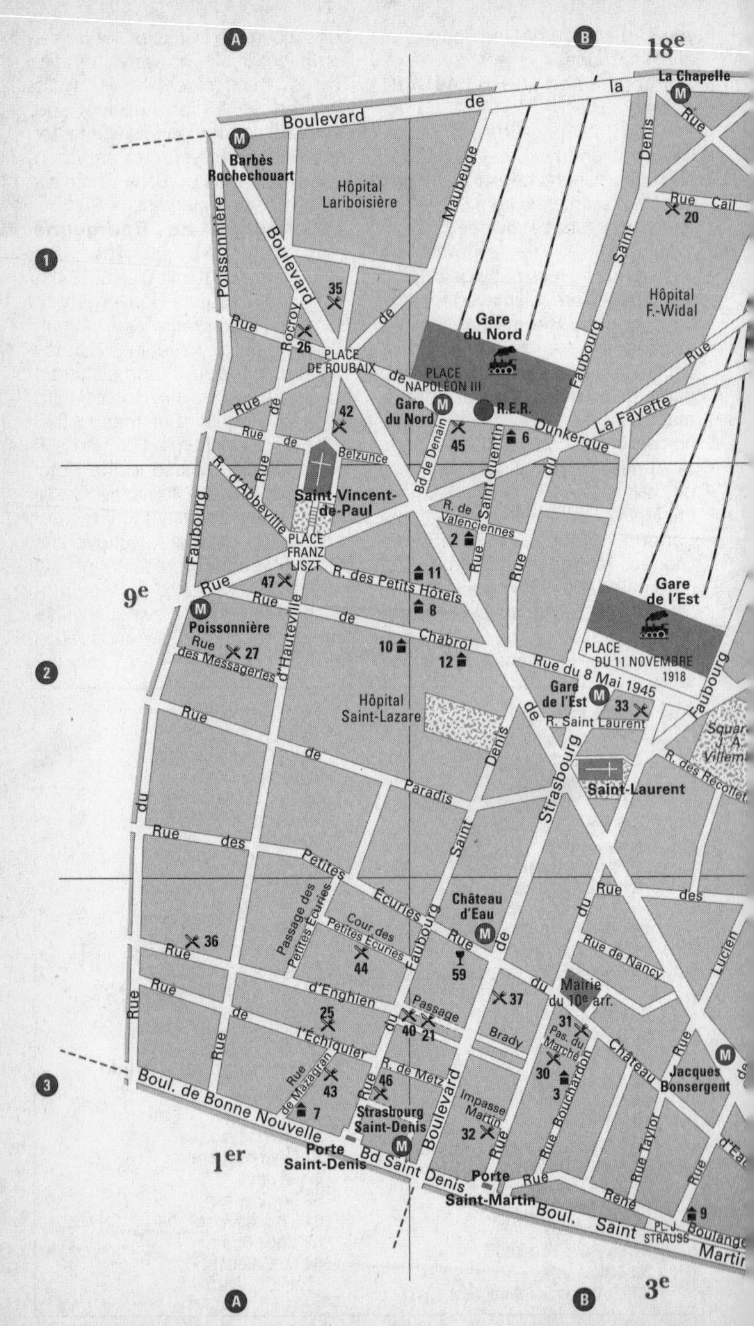
A
B
18e
La Chapelle
Boulevard de la
Barbès Rochechouart
Hôpital Lariboisière
Poissonnière
Boulevard
Maubeuge
Denis
Rue
Rue Cail
20
Saint
1
35
Hôpital F.-Widal
de
Gare du Nord
Rue
Rocroy
26
PLACE DE ROUBAIX
de
PLACE NAPOLÉON III
Faubourg
Rue
Gare du Nord
R.E.R.
Rue de
42
45
6
Dunkerque
La Fayette
Rue de Belzunce
Bd de Denain
Saint Quentin
du
R. d'Abbeville
Rue
Saint-Vincent-de-Paul
R. de Valenciennes
Faubourg
PLACE FRANZ LISZT
2
Rue
Rue
11
47
R. des Petits Hôtels
Gare de l'Est
9e
Rue
8
Poissonnière
Rue de Chabrol
10
12
PLACE DU 11 NOVEMBRE 1918
Rue des Messageries
27
d'Hauteville
Rue du 8 Mai 1945
2
Gare de l'Est
33
Faubourg
Hôpital Saint-Lazare
R. Saint Laurent
Square J. A. Villem
Rue
de
Denis
de
R. des Récollet
Paradis
Strasbourg
Saint-Laurent
du
Rue des
Saint
Petites
Rue des
Passage des Petites Écuries
Écuries
Château d'Eau
du
Cour des Petites Écuries
Faubourg
Rue
Rue de Nancy
Lucien
36
Rue
44
59
de
Rue
Rue
d'Enghien
du
Mairie du 10e arr.
37
25
Passage
Brady
31
Pas. du Marché
Château
Rue
de
l'Échiquier
40
21
du
Rue
3
R. de Metz
30
Jacques Bonsergent
Rue de Mazagran
43
46
Impasse Martin
3
Rue Bouchardon
Boul. de Bonne Nouvelle
7
Strasbourg Saint-Denis
Boulevard
32
Rue Taylor
d'Eau
Porte Saint-Denis
Rue
1er
Bd Saint Denis
Porte
Rue René
Rue
Saint-Martin
Boul. Saint
9
PL. J. STRAUSS
Boulange
Martin
3e
A
B

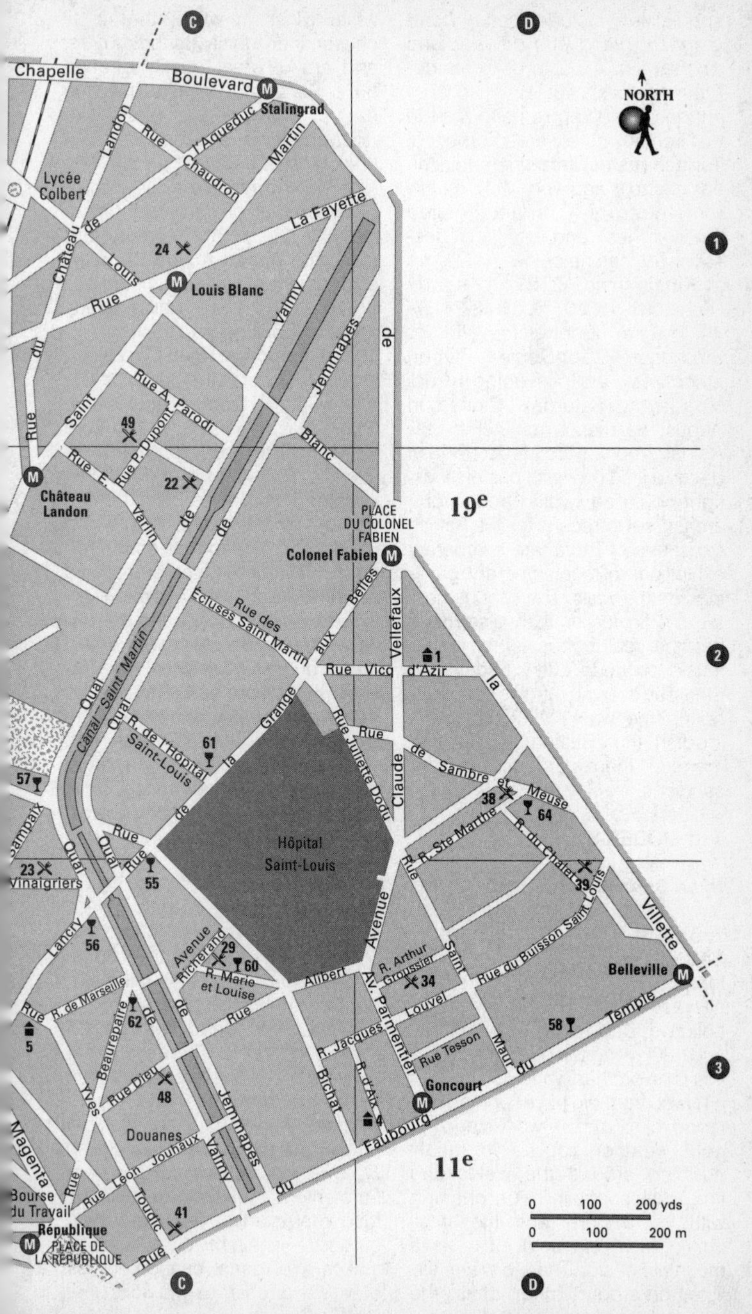
C
D
NORTH
1
2
3
Chapelle
Boulevard
Stalingrad
Rue Landon
Rue de l'Aqueduc
Chaudron
Martin
Lycée Colbert
Rue du Château Landon
La Fayette
24
Louis Blanc
Rue Louis Blanc
Valmy
Jemmapes
de
Rue A. Parodi
Rue P. Dupont
Saint
49
Rue E. Varlin
22
Château Landon
19e
PLACE DU COLONEL FABIEN
Colonel Fabien
Belles
Rue des Écluses Saint Martin
aux
Vellefaux
1
Rue Vicq d'Azir
la
Quai de Valmy
Canal Saint Martin
Quai de Jemmapes
Rue Grange aux Belles
R. de l'Hôpital Saint-Louis
61
Rue Juliette Dodu
Rue de Sambre et Meuse
Claude
38
64
57
Sampaix
R. du Chalet
R. Ste Marthe
Hôpital Saint-Louis
23
Vinaigriers
55
39
Villette
Lancry
56
Avenue Richerand
29
60
R. Marie et Louise
Alibert
Avenue
R. Arthur Groussier
34
Saint Maur
Rue du Buisson Saint Louis
Belleville
Temple
R. de Marseille
62
5
Beaurepaire
R. Jacques Louvel
Av. Parmentier
Rue Tesson
58
Rue Dieu
48
Yves
Bichat
R. d'Aix
Goncourt
4
Faubourg
Douanes
Magenta
Rue Léon Jouhaux
11e
Bourse du Travail
Toudic
41
République
PLACE DE LA RÉPUBLIQUE
0
100
200 yds
200 m

specialities include *boeuf bourguignon*, *blanquette de veau* and *coq au vin*. A bottle of Côtes-de-Provence costs 48F.

– In the rue d'Enghien and the rue de l'Échiquier there are a number of **Turkish restaurants** where you can eat cheaply and very well: *mezze* (hors-d'œuvres), *adana* (grilled meat dishes) and delicious desserts. Try the one below:

✕ **Kibélé** (map A3, **25**): 12 rue de l'Échiquier 75010. ☎ 01-48-24-57-74. Metro: Bonne-Nouvelle or Strasbourg-Saint-Denis. Open lunchtime and evening from Monday to Saturday. Closed in August. Set menus from 49F to 89F. A long room with Mediterranean decor, a tiled floor with pastel tones, light-coloured walls and stone arches, set the scene for this Turkish experience. There are temporary exhibitions of contemporary paintings on the walls. The kebabs here are a little tastier than elsewhere, but the real bonus is the world music concerts every Friday and Saturday evening (and occasionally during the week) at 9.30pm – a Yiddish trio, Balkan jazz or flamenco, there's something for everyone.

☆☆ MODERATE

✕ **Le Coin de Verre** (map D2, **38**): 38 rue de Sambre-and-Meuse 75010. ☎ 01-42-45-31-82. Metro: Belleville or Colonel-Fabien. Open Monday to Saturday 8pm to 1am, all year round. Closed on public holidays. Budget for between 90F and 130F. Ring the bell to be let in – this is no ordinary wine bar. It offers a refuge from the never-ending city round of commute-work-sleep. In cold weather you'll find locals huddled around the welcoming fire, philosophizing, or chatting with the owners, and the small dining room starts to look like a mountain chalet. The red wines are listed on a board in red chalk, the white wines in white; they're all chosen individually by the owners, and are of great quality (around 80F). So as not to keel over too early, have a plate of *cochonnailles* or cheese (60F) (including a fabulously rich and smelly *tome de Savoie*), all accompanied by excellent bread. Occasionally, there are some more elaborate dishes (made to order) such as *andouillettes* or *potée aux choux*. You'll have gathered by now that booking is essential.

✕ **Le Cambodge** (map C3, **29**): 10 avenue Richerand 75010. ☎ 01-42-41-90-78. Metro: République. Open daily noon to 3pm and 8pm to 11pm. The average price for a meal is 65F without drinks. Main courses from 30F to 48F. The first version of this restaurant, which used to be in a former pottery on the boulevard du Montparnasse, is remembered with affection by those who used to go there regularly. The dining room was a real mess, but the soup was amazing! Here the Vietnamese/Cambodian dishes are as tasty as ever, and the old spirit is still there. Choose from 'Phnom Penh' soup, *natin* (cream of pork with satay and coconut milk accompanied by crunchy prawn crackers), *bò bún* or fish with ginger.

✕ **La Marine** (map C3, **48**): 55 *bis* quai de Valmy 75010. ☎ 01-42-39-69-81. Metro: Jacques-Bonsergent or République. Open daily 8.30am to 2am. Last orders at midnight. Set meal 68F at lunchtime only. In the evening, budget for 170F excluding drinks. There's a great atmosphere in this restaurant, run by three brothers, and every evening the place is packed. A huge mural shows the *Joven Dolores*, the boat which goes from Formentera to Ibiza, the owners' favourite island. The retro-style cuisine – snail ravioli to tuna – makes a pleasant change. Glass of whisky or champagne 35F.

✕ **Tokioyaki** (map C1, **24**): 231 rue du Faubourg-Saint-Martin 75010. ☎ 01-46-07-67-91. Metro: Louis-Blanc. Open daily. Set menu for two 158F, set meals 45F to 78F. With its handful of well-planned kebab set meals and its *sushi* and *sashimi*, this Japanese restaurant has no problem filling its tables. It's packed at lunchtime with a cross-section of clientele – old and young, men and women, executives and workers. The *yakitori* set menus offer a wide variety of Japanese cuisine, or you can go for the mixed meals of *sushi* or *sashimi* kebabs, served (as are all the set menus) with a bowl of soup, rice and a salad. The set menu for two offers an assortment of raw fish *(sushi-sashimi-maki)* and eight kebabs.

✕ **Au Vieux Bistro** (map A1, **26**): 30 rue de Dunkerque 75010. ☎ 01-48-78-48-01. Metro: Barbès-Rochechouart or Gare-du-Nord. Closed Saturday evening and Sunday. Set menus 59F and 68F served lunchtime and evening. It's unusual to find a typically French restaurant in this area of Barbès, but that's what this is. Really good home-cooking including *andouillettes* and *confit de canard* served with potatoes and mushrooms. The price is very reasonable for this sort of food. There's a set meal at 59F with starter and main course, including the house *confit de poule* served with *pommes sarladaises*.

✕ **Chez Kolia** (map B3, **30**): 5–7 passage du Marché 75010. ☎ 01-42-01-03-57. Metro: Château-d'Eau. Open lunchtime and evening. Closed Sunday. Budget for 130F, including wine. Tucked away at the end of a forgotten passage, this timeless Balkan tavern is hard to find. There are two small dining rooms. The bric-à-brac decor is a bit surprising, but the welcome is friendly and the cuisine quite unusual. *Tchevaptchitchi*, grilled pork and beef sausages, Slavonic *cassoulet* (in comparison, the Toulouse version looks like a dish for anorexics), and stuffed cabbage and vine leaves, will transport you to the former Yugoslavia. A gargantuan experience which, obviously, you have to finish off with a plum *eau-de-vie* like they do in the Balkans.

✕ **Le Réveil du Xe** (map B3, **31**): 35 rue du Château-d'Eau 75010. ☎ 01-42-41-77-59. Metro: Château-d'Eau or République. Open Monday to Saturday at lunchtime only, and Tuesday evening until 9.30pm. Closed Sunday and public holidays, and for a fortnight around 15 August. Dish of the day at lunchtime from 56F. In the evening, a meal costs from 100F to 130F including drinks. A nice bistro run by real fans of good wine, this is a lovely place – simple, authentic and typically French. The menu offers dishes such as *confit de canard*, *joue de bœuf à l'auvergnate* with steamed potatoes, *aligot-saucisse* (on the first Tuesday of every month), succulent *charcuterie* and creamy cheeses from the Auvergne. Excellent selection of wines at very reasonable prices. To add to the start or finish of your meal there's a free house aperitif or coffee.

✕ **Le Petit Café** (map B3, **37**): 14 boulevard de Strasbourg 75010. ☎ 01-42-01-81-61. Metro: Strasbourg-Saint-Denis. Open until midnight. Closed Saturday lunchtime, Sunday and Monday, and also in August. Set menu 58F at lunchtime. In the evening à la carte only; budget for 120F. This bistro next to the Théâtre Antoine, of which it is part, is named after a play written by Tristan Bernard. On the walls are posters of plays once staged at the theatre as well as photographs of the players (Paul Meurisse, Louis Jouvet with Jean-Paul Sartre, and so on). The food is Bayonne-based. As a starter there are *chipirons amatxis*, *pied du contrebandier* (pork trotters) and marinated salmon with lentils *à la navarraise* (lentils cooked with chorizo). Main courses include *marmitako* (tuna ragout) and *axoa* d'Espelette (minced veal casserole). For dessert, don't miss out on the classic *ardi gasna* with cherry jam. There are a few nice wines by the carafe (50F per 50cl).

✕ **Le Palet Lafayette** (map A2, **47**): 89 rue d'Hauteville 75010. ☎ 01-48-24-20-22. Metro: Poissonnière or Gare-de-l'Est. Closed Saturday lunchtime and Sunday. This restaurant, which looks like an English pub, is the little brother of the *Palet* (*see* '1st arrondissement'). Same price, same service.

✕ **Arthur** (map B3, **32**): 25 rue du Faubourg-Saint-Martin 75010. ☎ 01-42-08-34-33. Metro: Strasbourg-Saint-Denis. Restaurant open every lunchtime except Saturday, and in the evening until 11.30pm from Tuesday to Saturday. Closed Sunday and in August. Set meal 115F (starter and main course or main course and dessert); set menu 144F (starter, main course and dessert). Close to the theatres on the boulevards (there are five in the immediate vicinity), this is the archetypal classic French restaurant. The setting is gently provincial – coffee-coloured walls, posters and portraits from the theatres, small lamps on the tables and a bulging bar. Classic cuisine is mixed with a splash of creativity, resulting in dishes like warm red mullet salad with balsamic vinegar, roasted cod with *sauce vierge*, and crème caramel with fresh vanilla pods. Even the wine by the carafe is agreeable and there are also some really good vintages, plus a few quality aperitifs and liqueurs. As a bonus, around 11pm the theatre performers come in and provide some off-stage entertainment, as you can see from the photographs displayed in the window. Albert Camus, author of *The Outsider*, used to eat here.

✕ **Café Panique** (map A2, **27**): 12 rue des Messageries 75010. ☎ 01-47-70-06-84. Metro: Poissonnière. Open noon to 2.30pm and 7.30pm to 9.30pm. Closed Saturday, Sunday and public holidays. A cosy setting, with regularly changing displays of contemporary works, and the restful atmosphere of a place far removed from the hustle and bustle of the boulevards. In the evening there's a single three-course set meal at 130F. At lunchtime, it's a lighter version (starter and main course or main course and dessert) for 98F. You can't go wrong here; everything is delicious, whether you go for *émincé* of haddock with ginger and lime or leg of lamb with cumin and almonds. Some nice surprises on the wine list.

✕ **La Vigne Saint-Laurent** (map B2, **33**): 2 rue Saint-Laurent 75010. ☎ 01-42-05-98-20. Metro: Gare-de-l'Est. Open noon to 2.30pm and 7pm to 10.30pm. Closed Saturday and Sunday, for three weeks in August and between Christmas and 1 January. One-course meal at 69F served lunchtime and evening; à la carte, budget for around 140F. If you have a train to catch, instead of diving into the first brasserie you come across around the Gare de l'Est, take a couple more minutes and seek out this small wine bistro. The mainstays of the menu are *charcuterie* and cheese. The *grelots de Savoie* fight it out for top of the bill with *demi-saint-marcellin affinés à la lyonnaise* and *demi-arôme-de-Lyon aux gènes de marc*, which are very tasty, and, of course, extremely smelly Reblochon and Camembert. In addition there is a dish of the day, such as boned and stuffed pig's trotters with purée of peas. Wash it down with a Cairanne '92 (Côtes du Rhône) or a Bourgueil '95. Most of the wines cost less than 100F per bottle. The one-course meal comprises two types of cold meats, green salad, two cheeses and a glass of wine.

✕ **Le Parmentier** (map D3, **34**): 12 rue Arthur-Groussier 75010. ☎ 01-42-40-75-75. Metro: Goncourt. Open lunchtime and evening until 10.30pm. Closed Saturday lunchtime and Sunday, and also in August. Set menu 128F served lunchtime and evening, set lunch 80F (also an à la carte menu). A discreet little spot, in a street that does not attract much attention, near the Sainte-Marthe quarter, which has recently become quite fashionable. The azure blue façade and multicoloured mosaics, the small dining room with its yellowing walls and the fresh gourmet cuisine make this new restaurant a pleasant place to stop off. On the blackboard there's a *menu-carte* (starter, main course and dessert) or another set menu at 150F, plus 25cl of wine and a cup of coffee. It might include the following, depending on what's fresh at the market: a salad of Puy lentils, cream of pumpkin soup, salmon poached in Maussane olive oil (perfectly cooked, still slightly pink inside), different types of ravioli or crème brûlée with ginger.

✕ **Boua Thaï** (map A1, **35**): 15 rue Saint-Vincent-de-Paul 75010. ☎ 01-48-78-41-88. Metro: Gare-du-Nord. Open until 11pm. Closed Sunday lunchtime and the last two weeks of August. Set menus at lunchtime 59F and 85F; in the evening it's à la carte only. Budget for around 110F, excluding drinks. Close to the Hôpital Lariboisière and five minutes on foot from the Gare du Nord, the setting here is warm, hushed and peaceful, and the tables are well spaced out. The grilled beef salad with spicy sauce (which you can also eat raw, Lao-style, as well as other dishes; just ask the chef), the special house salad with seafood, and the beef satay are the most popular starters. As main courses, cod fillet with garlic and pepper, house seafood and the beef sautéed with Thai pepper sauce are all musts. The sautéed Thai vegetables are perfect, as is the sticky rice.

✕ **La Chandelle Verte** (map A3, **36**): 40 rue d'Enghien 75010. ☎ 01-47-70-25-44. Metro: Bonne-Nouvelle. Open Monday to Friday noon to 2.30pm, and on other days or in the evening by reservation (for 10 or more people). Closed Saturday and Sunday, and for three weeks in August. Set menu 82F at lunchtime, with starter, main course and dessert. In the evening, there's a set menu at 122F. The cuisine in this colourful place varies according to the seasons, what's available and the inspiration of the day. There's a large selection of salads (with a mixture of spices and always full of flavour) and regional dishes. The set menu at 82F can be reduced to a version at 72F with starter and main course or main course and dessert. There's a large, well-lit dining room, with walls decorated with posters.

✕ **China Town Belleville** (map D3, **39**): 27–29 rue du Buisson-Saint-Louis 75010. ☎ 01-42-39-34-18 Metro: Belleville. Open daily from noon to 3pm and 7pm to 2am. Set lunch menu at 52F, 55F and 58F and 'Karaoke' set menus from 100F. Although it looks like a Chinese temple, this is actually a karaoke restaurant with an amazing musical menu. There are almost 9,000 titles in French, English, Spanish, Italian, Chinese and Japanese. In the room at the back noisy groups of friends, or brave (or drunk!) souls, push on to the stage to sing good old classics between mouthfuls of food. If you're shy, or allergic to karaoke, you can have the sound without the visuals in the main dining room, which is for food only. People come here more for the singing than the cooking, although the latter is perfectly acceptable.

✕ L'An II (map C3, **41**): 9 rue du Faubourg-du-Temple 75010. ☎ 01-40-40-70-76. Metro: République. Open 6am to 9.30pm. Closed Sunday. Dish of the day 50F. À la carte, budget for around 95F. On the corner of the rue Yves-Toudic, this unpretentious café-brasserie has been nicely renovated in the old style, with a fine brass counter and wooden flooring, and appeals to unpretentious customers. The cuisine has a definite southwest bias, with a remarkable *confit de canard*, succulent terrines, *gamelle auvergnate* (cold meats), *gamelle du berger* (cheeses) and dishes with mushrooms and poultry. With a glass of wine (of which there is a fine selection), a meal rarely costs more than 100F. If you just want to slake your thirst, try a half of Bombardier at the bar, an English beer that is sold in only two places in Paris.

☆☆☆ CHIC

✕ Chez Michel (map A1, **42**): 10 rue de Belzunce 75010. ☎ 01-44-53-06-20. Metro: Gare-du-Nord. Open until 11pm. Closed Sunday and Monday, and also at Christmas and in August. Single set menu 180F; children's menu 50F. This restaurant looks like a small farmhouse and seems out of place among the other restaurants in the area. The menu comes from Brittany and includes *terrine d'andouille aux baies de poivre*, *galette de beurre demi-sel* and marinated fillet of herring. You'll enjoy these to such a point that you'll have to loosen your belt by a notch to make room for the traditional Breton dish *kig ha farz* (a kind of savoury pudding), Breton lobster *au gratin* with parmesan or Saint-Jacques lobster roasted in herb butter. For dessert, traditional *Paris-Brest* or *kouign-aman* served warm are worth their weight in sugar.

✕ Le Baalbek (map A3, **43**): 16 rue de Mazagran 75010. ☎ 01-47-70-70-02. Metro: Bonne-Nouvelle. Open until 1am. Closed Sunday. Set menu 59F at lunchtime. In the evening à la carte only; budget for 130F. This Lebanese restaurant is one of the best in Paris. To avoid getting lost in the maze of the menu, adopt the *mezze* formula. For 325F for two or 595F for four, you will get to taste a dozen hors-d'œuvres followed by five or six types of barbecued meat (it doesn't sound like a lot, but don't worry, you won't go hungry). Follow this Middle-Eastern feast with a mint tea and a few *pâtisseries* (extra). The belly dancing (evenings only) begins around 10pm. Budget for 200F per person with wine or *arak*, not forgetting a tip to the dancers (100F notes are accepted, but not obligatory). Booking is essential.

✕ Flo (map A3, **44**): 7 cour des Petites-Écuries 75010. ☎ 01-47-70-13-59. Metro: Château-d'Eau. Open daily until 1.30am. Closed on Christmas night. Set menus 132F at lunchtime and 179F in the evening. À la carte between 160F and 200F. This classic night-time *choucroute* (sauerkraut) venue dates from 1886, when it was owned by a German restaurateur. In the past, the *Flo* would send meals to the actors' dressing rooms in the theatres on the nearby boulevards; Sarah Bernhardt was a regular customer when she was playing at the Renaissance theatre. The restaurant has superb 1900 decor, with glass walls separating the rooms, richly decorated ceilings, leather *banquettes*, and a brass hat stand. A seafood platter costs 259F, and there's also excellent country sauerkraut for two, mussels with Riesling and pig's trotters in breadcrumbs. Considering the setting, the set menus are pretty reasonable, offering starter and main course or main course and dessert, including drinks.

✕ **Terminus Nord** (map B1, **45**): 23 rue de Dunkerque 75010. ☎ 01-42-85-05-15. Metro: Gare-du-Nord. Open daily until 1am. Set menus 138F at lunchtime and 189F in the evening. Budget for around 250F à la carte. Another superb brasserie, in 1920s style, with fine flowered tiling. Lively atmosphere and excellent food with specialities such as seafood, sauerkraut, hot *foie gras* with potatoes, grills and steak *grillé maître d'hôtel*.

✕ **Julien** (map A3, **46**): 16 rue du Faubourg-Saint-Denis 75010. ☎ 01-47-70-12-06. Metro: Strasbourg-Saint-Denis. Open daily until 1.30am. Set menu 132F at lunchtime and 189F in the evening. À la carte, budget for 170F to 260F. Another conversion of one of the oldest establishments in Paris. The successful ingredients of dazzling Art Nouveau decor with baroque stucco work and panelling, and service that is as quick as it is efficient, have been preserved, as well as good-value dishes.

TEA-ROOM

– **Purple Café** (map C1, **49**): 9 rue Pierre-Dupont 75010. ☎ 01-40-34-14-64. Metro: Château-Landon. Open 2pm to 7pm Tuesday to Saturday. Closed in August. Drinks from 18F. A small space furnished with two or three wooden tables and benches, and shelves stocked with CDs, magazines (including the art review *Purple*, after which the café is named) and beautiful 'alternative' books. Apart from tea there is 'Iced flames' or, better still, 'Floral fluid' to drink, two visually arresting, alcohol-free cocktails designed by the artist Martine Aballéa.

WINE BAR

✕ 🍷 **Le Coin de Verre** (map D2, **38**): 38 rue de Sambre-and-Meuse 75010. ☎ 01-42-45-31-82. Metro: Belleville or Colonel-Fabien. Open Monday to Saturday 8pm to 1am all year round. *See* 'Where to eat'.

WHAT TO SEE

★ **Place de la République:** urban planner *extraordinaire* Baron Haussmann was responsible for the place de la République, and also added the barracks. A number of thoroughfares (Magenta, République, Voltaire, Turbigo) fan out from here in a star shape, designed (according to Haussmann's intentions) to limit the possibilities of popular insurrection. In the middle stands the *Republic* statue, decorated by a bronze frieze that traces a century of Republican history in France.

★ **Rue du Château-d'Eau:** linking the boulevard Magenta to the rue du Faubourg-Saint-Denis. At No. 39 is the smallest house in Paris, with a width of just over 1m (3.5ft), and one floor which is 5m (16.5ft) high.

★ The **boulevard Saint-Martin**, with its unusual raised pavements, is one of the oldest thoroughfares in the city. It still has two theatres where tragedies and melodramas were staged in the 19th century. The Théâtre de la Renaissance, with its rich ornament (intertwined caryatids, corniches with cherubs) by Lalande, dates from 1872. The famous melodramatic actress Sarah Bernhardt ran the theatre, and often appeared here too. Edmond Rostand's *Cyrano de Bergerac* was staged here for the first time in 1897; the theatre director had so little faith in the play that he had another one on standby in case. He needn't have worried. Other celebrated playwrights, such as Feydeau, Labiche and Offenbach, had works performed at this mythical theatre in their day. Boulevard Saint-Martin's other theatrical establishment is the Théâtre de la Porte-Saint-Martin, born from the rubble of the Commune in 1873. Sarah Bernhardt, Marie Dorval (Alfred de Vigny's muse) and Coquelin all appeared here.

★ Porte Saint-Martin and Porte Saint-Denis were built to celebrate the victories of Louis XIV. **Porte Saint-Denis**, the larger of the two, commemorates the taking of 40 cities during the Battle of the Rhine, and displays some quite remarkable reliefs.

★ **Atelier-Hoguet-Musée de l'Éventail (Hoguet workshop and fan Museum)** (map B3): 2 boulevard de Strasbourg 75010. ☎ 01-42-08-90-20. Metro: Strasbourg-Saint-Denis. Closed in August. Open Monday, Tuesday and Wednesday 2pm to 6pm. Entry fee 30F, concessions 15F. Groups by appointment. Fan-making workshop for children on Wednesday afternoons (phone in advance).

This fascinating little museum, consisting of three rooms, was created by fan-maker Mme Hoguet. First, it displays mountings and the traditional materials (horn, wood, mother-of-pearl, bone, ivory) used in their production, then tools, fabrics and pleating devices. Finally, visitors may see the showroom created by fan-makers Lepault and Deberghe in 1893, which is preserved in its original state. Big walnut and glass chests of drawers display at least 50 of the 1000 items in the Hoguet collection, dating from the 17th century to the present day. Silk and mother-of-pearl fans dating from the 18th century are shown alongside contemporary models made of Plexiglas. The items on display are changed twice a year. There are humorous paper advertising fans from the 1920s and 1930s, a 4cm (1.5in) doll's fan, and formal dance fans that doubled as dance cards, for signing up potential partners. For real 'fan fans' there are two points of interest: a shop selling souvenirs, books and, of course, fans, and Mme Hoguet's lively workshop, where she not only makes new creations but also restores old fans.

★ **Gare de l'Est:** place du 11 novembre 1918. The most recent of the great Parisian stations, completed in 1850, the Gare de l'Est was extended several times between 1895 and 1931. It is now Paris' largest station in terms of surface area; Saint-Lazare is the most important in terms of volume of traffic and number of travellers. Situated right at the top of boulevard de Strasbourg, its two wings and glass and ironwork façade are visible from some distance. All that remains of the original building is the left-hand wing, with one statue representing Strasbourg (one of the station's destinations) and another Verun. In times gone by it was the point of arrival in the capital for people from the Alsace-Lorraine region, and as a result there are many traditional brasseries in the area.

★ **Marché Saint-Quentin:** just beside the Gare de l'Est, this covered market extends over some 2,500m (8,200ft). It's the largest in Paris, built in 1865 and renovated in 1982. Behind the huge sliding glass doors you'll find a bit of countryside in the heart of the city. Wandering among the stalls selling fresh produce is a great pleasure, especially on Sunday mornings (until 1pm).

★ **Marché du Faubourg-Saint-Denis:** discover sights and smells from all over the world at this lively and cosmopolitan market.

★ The **passage Brady** has become a sort of 'Little India', bringing colour to a dusty old street. There are shops selling Indian and Pakistani foods, as well as some good restaurants. Always lively, it really wakes up in the evening.

★ The **rue de Paradis** is renowned for trade in luxury porcelain, so take some time to stroll down it. At No. 18, the former Museum of Advertising, there is a magnificent art deco façade, which is worth a look for its exuberant style and for the superb tiling in the porch, a fine example of the work of the Choisy-le-Roi ceramics factory. A modern art gallery, Le Monde de l'Art, has been set up here (open daily except Sunday; Tuesday to Saturday 1pm to 7.30pm, Monday 2 to 7pm; entrance free). The building that houses it is also decorated with some remarkable tiling.

★ There are some interestingly named streets in the area. Check out the enticing sounding **passage du Désir** ('Passageway of Desire'), between the boulevard de Strasbourg and Faubourg Saint-Martin, the nearby **rue de la Fidélité** ('Faith Street'), and further up the more prosaic **rue des Petits-Hôtels** ('Street of the Small Hotels').

★ **Hôtel de Bourrienne:** 58 rue d'Hauteville 75010. ☎ 01-47-70-51-14. Metro: Poissonnière or Château-d'Eau. Mansion open all year round by appointment (without an appointment from 1 to 15 July and the whole of September) from 1pm to 7pm. Entry fee 30F; 25F for under-18s. As you step across the threshold of this beautiful mansion, the noise of the city suddenly fades away, as if you've entered into another world. The *hôtel* is the former residence of Napoleon's private secretary, with old-style parquet flooring, period furniture and a small garden. The owner herself often gives the guided tour of this house, which is full of history; if only the walls could speak, surely they'd tell all sorts of tales about Empress Joséphine, statesman and diplomat Talleyrand and the other historical figures who used to come here.

CANAL SAINT-MARTIN

Work on the Canal Saint-Martin, originally conceived by Louis XIV, began during Napoleon's reign and finished in 1825. It remains one of the most picturesque and, paradoxically, one of the least-known urban landscapes in Paris. It has always inspired poets, writers (such as Georges Simenon) and artists, and its banks have long been the setting for intense activity. Once, dozens of barges transported sand and coal daily along the canal, which is partly underground, and the nine locks were worked by hand. Today the goods are carried on the roads, and the canal is no longer used commercially. Now only a couple of barges a day pass under its walkways and use its swing bridges.

The canal almost met its end when, at the beginning of the 1970s, the Council of Paris adopted a proposed four-lane motorway project which would have passed right over it. The president of the time was much in favour of the move. However, an energetic campaign by riverside residents, which highlighted the obvious idiocy of the project, meant that it was never carried out. Suddenly Parisians rediscovered the canal, and began once again to enjoy its nine locks, tree-lined banks, and small squares, Venetian-style metal bridges and its swing bridges. The whole ensemble makes up one of the most romantic and unexpected landscapes in the capital. It stretches from the Seine to the Bassin de la Villette in the north, where it joins the Canal de l'Ourcq.

WHAT TO DO

– You can take a delightful **3-hour trip** up the Canal Saint-Martin, through the locks. *La Guêpe Buissonnière* and *Le Canotier* leave from the quai Anatole-France (near the Pont de la Concorde). ☎ 01-42-40-96-97. Metro: Solférino. RER: Musée-d'Orsay (Line C). Boats depart from the Musée d'Orsay at 9.30am daily from the end of March to mid-November. You can also choose to go down the canal. Boats depart at 2.30pm daily from the Parc de La Villette in front of La Folie des Visites Guidées ('Mad about guided tours') centre. Metro: Porte-de-Pantin. The boat arrives 3 hours later at the quai Anatole-France. Price 100F; children aged 4 to 11 55F; those from 12 to 25, 75F. Book by telephone.

Heading northwards, after going through the locks in the Bassin de l'Arsenal, you travel under the Bastille Column (*see* '11th arrondissement'), then through a 2-km (1.5-mile) underground archway. A substantial part of the trip is actually underground, below the street. There are light-holes every 50m (165ft) allowing shafts of sunlight to pierce the darkness and the murky water, making the trip even more magical and mysterious; take a warm sweater or jacket.

THE 'BAS DE BELLEVILLE'

This is an old working-class quarter to the south of the boulevard de Belleville and broadly framed by rue Sainte-Marthe and rue Saint-Maur. Another part extends over the 11th arrondissement, on the other side of the Faubourg du Temple, and was part of Belleville until the construction of the tax collectors' wall, which split the area in two. This division became official in 1860, when all the outlying villages were annexed to Paris and the arrondissements were created.

This area has seen the immigration of many different peoples over the years. First, Jewish people came from Russia and Poland, then Tunisian Jews arrived in the early 1950s, along with North Africans and Yugoslavs, who came to work in the motor industry. Subsequently Turks came here to settle in the clothing industry, and more recently Pakistanis, Sri Lankans and Asians have moved into the quarter. The old French proletariat work in small factories around here, or in the many local workshops, and the area has remained deeply working-class. The redevelopment of the quarter has not gone as far as the brutal renovation that has swept through the other side of the boulevard de Belleville.

Of course, this quarter is rarely visited by 'tourists' in the normal sense of the word. Its main attractions are an atmosphere and a way of life that, along with the cultural diversity of its population, make it a very lively part of town. On your trip between the Marais and the Hill of Belleville, take the opportunity to stop off at one of the area's many excellent restaurants. Along the way you can take in some fine courtyard gardens, quaint old shops and cafés from a bygone era (with a patina of grime and nicotine).

A SHORT WALK AROUND THE 'BAS DE BELLEVILLE'

★ Come out of the Belleville Metro station and head down the **rue du**

Faubourg-du-Temple into a fine old working-class area. Here, in the space of a just few hundred metres, you can get a fairly good idea of what Belleville used to be like. On the left a sign indicating 'Aux Cent Culottes' links the area's commercial and revolutionary traditions; it's a play on words, recalling the French revolutionaries, who were known as *sans-culottes* (*see* 'History'). At No. 129, the poetically named Cour de la Grâce de Dieu ('Courtyard of the Grace of God') has been nicely renovated. The Galerie du Commerce, at No. 105, still has its retro architecture. At the end is La Java, one of the 200 pre-war *bals musettes* (dance halls, where customers would be entertained by accordion music). Right at the bottom, at No. 48, is a gateway leading to a small villa, around which stand a few small houses with tiny gardens. One of the proprietors, from Normandy, had his residence built in the style of his own region. The back of the building has a lovely sundial.

★ **Hôpital Saint-Louis:** entrance at 2 rue Bichat. It was at the Saint-Louis that gas lighting was tried out for the first time, in 1818. The hospital complex is an architectural masterpiece, built during the reign of Henri IV. It has a central courtyard with gardens and benches, surrounded by the hospital buildings. The walls have been cleaned up, revealing an attractive red brick beneath the grime, and the elegance and harmony of the façades. The architects of the new hospital skilfully built on to an old building and reintroduced elements of its architecture, which is why there are more skylights than usual.

★ Go back up the *rue de la Grange-aux-Belles* as far as the intersection with the **rue des Écluses-Saint-Martin**. This was the spot where the infamous Montfaucon gibbet stood; up to 50 brigands, rebels and knaves could be hanged on it at any one time. François Villon, the poet, is known to have escaped it twice.

Further up, in the place du Colonel-Fabien, fans of Brazilian architect Oscar Niemeyer will enjoy the undulating architecture of the Communist Party headquarters.

WHERE TO GO FOR A DRINK

🍸 **La Patache** (map C3, **56**): 60 rue de Lancry 75010. No telephone. Metro: Jacques-Bonsergent. Open (almost) daily 6pm to 2am. A turn-of-the-century café, yellowed with age and nicotine, rescued seven years ago. The old stove still runs on coal and the drinks prices haven't changed for ages (everything is 10F!). This is a kind of theatre bar, where the spontaneous improvization (particularly on Tuesdays) by a few actors often surprises those who aren't in the know. Warning: the owner could do with a stint at charm school, but don't let that put you off. This place is worth a detour.

🍸 **L'Atmosphère** (map C2, **57**): 49 rue Lucien-Sampaix 75010. ☎ 01-40-38-09-21. Metro: Gare-de-l'Est. Open from 11pm to 2am (10pm on Sunday). Closed Monday and for a fortnight in August. Beer is 12F per half-pint at the bar. Budget for 40F tops for a few nibbles. Originally a quiet, unassuming spot serving a few market specialities, this place was revolutionized in 1994 and set alight to the rhythm of well-organized concerts featuring world, jazz, alternative and typically French music (drinks increase by 3F on concert evenings).

🍸 **Chez Adel** (map C2–3, **55**): 10 rue de la Grange-aux-Belles 75010. ☎ 01-42-08-24-61. Metro: Jacques-Bonsergent or Colonel-Fabien.

Open 10am to 3pm Monday, 10am to 2am Tuesday to Friday, 5pm to 2am Saturday and 7pm to 10pm Sunday. Drinks cost around 12F. Set menu 50F and dish of the day 40F. You can eat well and cheaply here in an up-to-date version of the local Parisian restaurant. In the evening people come for a drink and to listen to live music (Tuesday to Saturday from 8pm), or to see a play on Sundays at 8pm. Syrian food specialities at the weekend.

🍸 **L'Apostrophe** (map C2, **61**): 23 rue de la Grange-aux-Belles 75010. ☎ 01-42-08-26-07. Metro: Colonel-Fabien. Open daily 7am (4pm on Sunday) to 2am. Couscous from 40F to 70F; half a pint of beer 14F. Jazz, rock, *guinguette* (dance hall music) and funk – this is a lively spot, part of the alternative scene of the Canal Saint-Martin (like its neighbour, Chez Adel, above). Free live music every evening at 10pm, Thursday to Saturday, and French billiards (10F per game). It gets a bit out of hand some evenings. Jeans and trainers are *de rigueur.*

🍸 **Chez Prune** (map C3, **62**): 36 rue Beaurepaire 75010. ☎ 01-42-41-30-47. Metro: Jacques-Bonsergent. Open daily until 2am. Dishes from 35F to 45F; spirits from 14F to 30F served at your table. The last hip Parisian café on the Canal Saint-Martin. A former bar-tobacconist, this café was opened, after a speedy renovation, to take advantage of the 1998 football World Cup. Whether you choose a glass of Ardèche or one of the special concoctions of the house, you'll get your money's worth. Tuck into plates of *charcuterie* or a vegetable basket with house dip. The service is young and good-looking!

WHERE TO SPEND AN EVENING

✕ **Le Galopin** (map D2, **64**): 34 rue Sainte-Marthe 75010. ☎ 01-53-19-19-55. Metro: Belleville, Goncourt or Colonel-Fabien. Closed Monday. Set menus 75F including starter or dessert and 95F for the full menu. Music on Friday and Saturday nights from 9pm. Friendly, bohemian atmosphere – very cool, but the food is not great.

NIGHTCLUBS

– **La Java** (map D3, **58**): 105 rue du Faubourg-du-Temple 75010. ☎ 01-42-02-20-52. Metro: Belleville or Goncourt. Entry fee (plus 20F for one-off concerts) 80F on Thursday, 100F on Friday and Saturday. Cocktails 35F. Inaugurated in the 1920s in the heart of Belleville, this is now the oldest disco in the capital. By turns cabaret (Édith Piaf started her career here), retro *bal-musette* (accordion music) and psychedelic, it's now hip in spite of itself and offers Cuban fiestas to a mixed clientele, including some of the latest chic French actors. Thursday and Friday evening is the time for Cuban jam sessions, or there's salsa, with live performances until 3am with the best Latino bands, and clubbing until dawn with the best DJs. A must for anyone who can't keep still.

– **Les Étoiles** (map B3, **59**): 61 rue du Château-d'Eau 75010. ☎ 01-47-70-60-56. Metro: Château-d'Eau. Entry fee 60F, or 120F with dinner. Drinks from 40F. South American evenings on Thursday, Friday and Saturday from 9pm (for those having dinner) or 11pm (for those who just come to dance) until dawn. Ride the Latino wave that's breaking over Paris. This former local cinema has been transformed into a combined bar, restaurant and salsa club, to transport customers straight to the hot and sultry atmosphere of Cuba or Puerto Rico. You can either book a table, where you'll be served exotic cuisine, or just come for a drink and a dance.

11TH ARRONDISSEMENT

THE BASTILLE ● THE FAUBOURG ST-ANTOINE

THE BASTILLE AND THE BASTOCHE

Constructed between 1356 and 1383, overlooking the Faubourg St-Antoine in the east of Paris, the Bastille was conceived as a medieval fortress and built as part of the defensive outer walls of the city to protect Paris from attack.

The surrounding area was known as the Bastoche, a lively part of Paris, renowned for its drinking and partying, and its brothels and pimps, especially around rue Lesdiguières, rue Jean-Beaucine and rue des Tournelles.

During the 16th century, under Louis XII, the Bastille was turned into a state prison, and the character of the surrounding area soon began to change. The rue de la Roquette became a rather sinister street along which prisoners were marched to their execution and the dead were taken to Père Lachaise cemetery. For a long time after the demise of the prison rue de la Roquette still bore the stigma of its rather macabre role.

The population of the Bastoche has always been very mixed. During the 19th century the area was inundated with migrants from the Auvergne region. Once settled, they soon developed the tradition of music and dance in this quarter in the form of the *'bal-musette'* (literally the bagpipes ball). The area around the rue de Lappe was the scene of much dancing to traditional music played on a type of bagpipe known as the *cabrette*. With the introduction of the accordion into France by the Italians, however, the principal instrument of the *'bal-musette'* was soon replaced.

The rue de Lappe was described by Alphonse Daudet, in 1870, as 'a sort of Auvergnat ghetto'. In 1886, in the Faubourg St-Antoine, out of over 46,000 woodworkers more than 8,000 were foreigners: Belgians, Germans, Italians and Russians. Around the rue Sedaine and the rue de la Popinque lies the Jewish-Spanish community. Jews also emigrated from Turkey between 1914 and 1940; their ancestors, originally from Spain, had fled from the Inquisition in the 16th century. Today the houses once occupied by the poor, who gave both the quarter and Paris itself such a unique flavour, are now disappearing. In the rue de Charonne, rue Daval, rue de Lappe and rue Keller a new artistic quarter is being born. But, ever-faithful to its cosmopolitan past, the Bastille and the rue de la Roquette continue to shelter immigrants from all over the world, from the North Africans (who arrived in the 1920s), to Turks, West Indians, Vietnamese, Indians and Thais.

Nevertheless, the whole area is undergoing rapid change. Property speculation is booming; over the past 10 years, the price per square metre has multiplied 10-fold.

A BRIEF HISTORY

As a prison, the Bastille was used initially for incarcerating upper class criminals who had committed crimes against the state and so came to represent a symbol of absolute power as wielded at will by the monarchy. It housed many famous prisoners, such as Nicolas Fouquet, the Superintendent of Finances and guilty of being richer than Louis XIV, and the mysterious 'Man in the Iron Mask'. The satirical writer Voltaire also stayed here twice (once for a year and once for a month). Only later did the prison admit criminals from the lower classes.

It is ironic that by the time of the storming of the Bastille on 14 July 1789 it was hardly in use. Louis XVI was even thinking of demolishing the building, as it was preventing the development of the city. So the attack in July 1789 was more of a symbolic protest. Only seven prisoners were found inside, and most of them had to be hurriedly imprisoned again, having gone mad during their incarceration. The storming of the Bastille doesn't appear to have made much of an impression on Louis XVI though – his diary entry for 14 July 1789 was: 'Today, nothing.'

It took 700 revolutionaries over two months to ensure there was no trace of the hated prison remaining and the place de la Bastille was created in its place. Today, all that remains of the Bastille are a few blocks on the Pantin-Italie metro line, a few vestiges in the Square Galli, at Sully-Morland, a souvenir cut from one of the prison's stones (at the Musée Carnavalet), and the former bell of the Bastille, displayed at the Hippopotamus restaurant. Several plans were made for the place de la Bastille, but due to changes in power and the 1830 July Revolution, none of these came to fruition. Eventually it was Louis-Phillipe, wanting to pay homage to the Revolution that brought him to power in 1830, who decided that a monument should be erected in the place de la Bastille to commemorate the events of the July Revolution and those who died in the battle. The 'Colonne de Juillet' was built between 1831 and 1840. The bodies of the victims, originally buried at the Louvre, were moved to this site and reinterred in a crypt underneath the column. It is also believed that two decomposing Egyptian mummies, which were being held at the Louvre at the same time, were simultaneously transferred to this site for burial. This meant that during the solemn burial ceremony the two pharaohs also received full military honours as heroes of the French Revolution!

During the Second Republic the government organized for the victims of the 1848 Revolution to be buried under the column in a second vault alongside those from 1830. It wásn't until 1880, during the Third Republic, that the storming of the Bastille was turned into a national day of celebration – Bastille Day, celebrated each year on 14 July.

The place de la Bastille went on to become a symbol for activists, and, along with the Place de la République, became the favourite starting point for political marches and demonstrations Over time, however, people got bored with this tradition and the processions became smaller and smaller. Change came again on 11 May 1981 with François Mitterrand's socialist victory at the polls; this time the place de la Bastille was the scene of an enormous party. For many people this was the rebirth of a certain utopia following 23 years of conservative government. People from the world of showbusiness, the arts and academia met at Bofinger to celebrate the event. Since then there have been other rallies, marches and huge parties – the *Beurs* (second-generation North Africans living in France), students in 1986 and SOS Racisme (an anti-racist organization). In January 1996 people gathered at the place de la Bastille to pay their respects to François Mitterrand on his death.

The opening of the ultra-modern Opéra de Paris Bastille in 1989 was to definitively mark the renewal of the area, as well as to guarantee its sociological repositioning. Inevitably, the image of the working-class and revolutionary Faubourg St-Antoine has disappeared with the gradual gentrification of the area.

WHERE TO STAY

☆ BUDGET TO CHEAP

🏠 **Auberge de Jeunesse** (map A1, **1**): 8 boulevard Jules-Ferry 75011. ☎ 01-43-57-55-60. Fax: 01-43-14-82-09. Metro: République. Double room 236F, otherwise 120F per person for multiple rooms, including breakfast and linen. It's an official youth hostel, so you must have a membership card (you can buy one when you arrive). The door is locked between noon and 2pm. There's free access to the rooms during the day, but you have to be out before 10am. There are around 100 beds in rooms for two, four or six people. The atmosphere is warm and relaxed and they've made a real effort with the decor, with walls rough-cast in cream and terracotta tones. The rooms overlooking the square are very well lit. Left luggage (10F), launderette (20F for the washing machine, 10F for the dryer) and a bike shed. Lots of opportunities to meet new people. When the youth hostel is full, they'll try to find you somewhere else to stay for the same price.

🏠 **Maison Internationale des Jeunes pour la Culture et la Paix** (map C3, **2**): 4 rue Titon 75011. ☎ 01-43-71-99-21. Fax: 01-43-71-78-58. Metro: Faidherbe-Chaligny or Boulets-Montreuil. Price 110F per person, breakfast included. Operates like a youth hostel, all year round. There's a little inner courtyard with a bit of green. Accepts people from 18 to 30 years of age. No card required. Friendly ambiance. An opportunity to meet young people from all over the world. Closes at 2am. Rooms with two, three, five or eight beds, some of them with a mezzanine. Basic comfort and hygiene; toilet facilities on the landing.

🏠 **Auberge Internationale des Jeunes Ste-Marguerite** (map B3, **3**): 10 rue Trousseau 75011. ☎ 01-47-00-62-00. Fax: 01-47-00-33-16. E-mail: aij@aijparis.com. Website: www.aijparis.com. Metro: Bastille or Ledru-Rollin. Price 91F per night (81F from November to February). Breakfast included. The cheapest of all the youth hostels, and nice with it, in a wonderful lively quarter, near the Aligre market. Rooms with two to six beds, including a few laid out on two floors. The ones with five and six beds have their own showers and toilets. For the rooms with two, three and four beds, the toilet facilities are in the corridor. A new Internet terminal allows you to surf the web and to check your mailbox. Another advantage is that this youth hostel is open round the clock, so there's no curfew. Bank cards are accepted.

🏠 **Hôtel du Monde** (map B2, **4**): 15 rue Pasteur 75011. ☎ 01-49-29-50-00. Fax: 01-47-00-71-09. Metro: St-Ambroise, Parmentier or Richard-Lenoir. Bus Nos. 46, 56, or 69. From 200F to 350F for two people, according to degree of comfort; 450F for three and 550F for four or five. This residence, which is rather reminiscent of a youth hostel (but more cheerful), is clean and comfortable, even if the flooring and the paint have faded a bit. A real find for young backpackers who want to maintain their independence and keep the costs down. Studios for two, three or four people, all fitted with kitchenettes (with fridge, hotplates and all you need to cook yourself a meal). Direct telephone. Washing and drying machines (30F) and free ironing board. Linen supplied free of charge. Young and cosmopolitan. Fixed prices for long stays.

☗ **Hôtel Printania** (map A1, **5**): 16 boulevard du Temple 75011. ☎ 01-47-00-33-46. Fax: 01-49-23-05-19. Metro: République or Filles-du-Calvaire. Double rooms from 201F (bathroom and toilet), 281F with shower and toilet. Larger rooms at 329F for three people and 422F for four. There are 54 rooms in this 'little' hotel. Simple, slightly dated decor, with lots of paintings by – justly – unknown artists. The prices are extremely reasonable for the area and the welcome is charming. Right next to République and at the gates to the Marais.

☗ **Hôtel des Arts** (map C3, **6**): 2 rue Godefroy-Cavaignac 75011. ☎ 01-43-79-72-57. Metro: Charonne. Double rooms with bathroom 176F (some of them with a toilet), and around 250F with shower and toilet. An unpretentious but clean and welcoming one-star hotel. The corner rooms are nicer, but they're also noisier.

☗ **Pax Hôtel** (map B3, **7**): 12 rue de Charonne 75011. ☎ 01-47-00-40-98. Fax: 01-43-38-57-81. Metro: Ledru-Rollin or Bastille. Double room with washbasin 250F; double room with shower, toilet, TV and hairdryer between 280F and 300F. This well-run little family hotel is right near the Opéra-Bastille, in a busy and lively street. Some people may regret the lack of peace and quiet, but, having said that, some rooms have double-glazing and the area is really lively and friendly.

☆☆ MODERATE

☗ **Hôtel Mondia** (map A1, **8**): 22 rue du Grand-Prieuré 75011. ☎ 01-47-00-93-44. Fax: 01-43-38-66-14. Metro: République. Double rooms 340F to 380F, depending on size and aspect. In a quiet little street, a lovely little hotel with an outdated and retro ambiance right down to the smallest detail. Also nicely located since Belleville, Ménilmontant and the Bastille aren't far off and Marais-Les Halles is also nearby. Charming welcome, charming decor: stencilled paintings and pretty stained-glass effects, especially in the breakfast room. The rooms are in the same style, comfortable with full bathroom (shower or bath), hairdryer, direct telephone, personal safe deposit, TV with Canal+ and full-length mirror; marble fireplace in some rooms. Three attic rooms on the sixth floor. Prices are negotiable according to the length of your stay. Highly recommended.

☗ **Hôtel Notre-Dame** (map A1, **9**): 51 rue de Malte 75011. ☎ 01-47-00-78-76. Fax: 01-43-55-32-31. Metro: République or Oberkampf. Double room with washbasin or shower 210F to 320F. Doubles with shower and toilets or bathroom and toilet 380F. A well-run two-star, in a good location. The rooms, tastefully decorated, are fitted with all mod cons: direct telephone, automatic alarm and TV. Go for the street side as it's brighter. Note: cheques are not accepted. It's best to book.

☗ **Hôtel Beauséjour** (map B1, **10**): 71 avenue Parmentier 75011. ☎ 01-47-00-38-16. Fax: 01-43-55-47-89. Metro: Parmentier or Oberkampf. 380F for two people, 480F for three and 550F for four. A hotel with 31 rooms over six floors (don't worry, there *is* a lift!), all with bath or shower, double-glazing, TV and direct telephone. There's a little bar at reception which is open 24 hours a day and you can ask to be served in your room. The welcome is charming.

Hôtel Daval (map B3, **11**): 21 rue Daval 75011. ☎ 01-47-00-51-23. Fax: 01-40-21-80-26. Metro: Bastille. The double rooms with shower are 415F and there's a special breakfast for 50F. At the heart of the liveliest part of the Bastille area, alongside the bars in the rue de Lappe and the rue de la Roquette, a nice two-star place, with modern decor and all mod cons: TV (with satellite and Canal+), double-glazing and mini-safe. Don't worry about the Alsatian dog, he doesn't bite!

Where to stay

1 Auberge de Jeunesse (youth hostel)
2 Maison Internationale des Jeunes pour la Culture and la Paix
3 Auberge Internationale des Jeunes Ste-Marguerite
4 Hôtel du Monde
5 Hôtel Printania
6 Hôtel des Arts
7 Pax Hôtel
8 Hôtel Mondia
9 Hôtel Notre-Dame
10 Hôtel Beauséjour
11 Hôtel Daval
12 Hôtel Beaumarchais
13 Hôtel Verlain

Where to eat

20 Paris-Hanoï
21 À la Flanquette
22 Sizin
23 À l'Ami Pierre
24 Le Petit Keller
25 L'Engizek
26 Le Sot-L'y-Laisse
27 Les Cinq Points Cardinaux
28 Zagros
29 Le Scarbo
30 Dong Huong
31 Montpoupon
32 Au Trou Normand
33 Le Waly Fay
34 Au Vieux Chêne
35 Les Uns et les Autres
36 Un Saumon à Paris
37 Loulou de Bastille
38 Yakitang
39 La Plancha
40 Le Vieux Byzantin
41 L'Homme Bleu
42 La Folie Milon
43 Pause Café
44 Paris Main d'Or
45 New Nioullaville
46 Chez Raymonde
48 Suds
49 Anjou-Normandie
50 Le Repaire de Cartouche
51 Traiteur d'Italie Ristorante
52 L'Occitanie
53 Le Camelot
54 Le Villaret
55 Les Amognes
56 Blue Elephant
57 Dame Jeanne
58 Cefalù
59 Restaurant Cartet
60 Astier
61 La Barcarola
62 Mansouria
64 Le Passage
65 Restaurant de la Réunion
70 Jacques Mélac
71 Le Clown Bar

Where to go for a drink/ Going out/Nightclubs

70 Jacques Mélac
80 Le Réservoir
81 Satellit Café
82 Le Bar Sans Nom
83 Le Kitch
84 Le Cannibale Café
85 Le Robinet Mélangeur
86 Le Café Charbon
87 Le Cithéa
88 Le Blue Billard
89 Le Balajo
90 La Chapelle des Lombards
91 La Casbah
92 L'Électron Libre
93 Le Sherkhan
94 Le Mécano-Bar
95 Le Tamla
96 La Fabrique
97 L'Armagnac
98 Café de l'Industrie
99 Le Troisième Bureau
100 Le Lèche-Vin
101 Havanita Café
102 Sanzsans

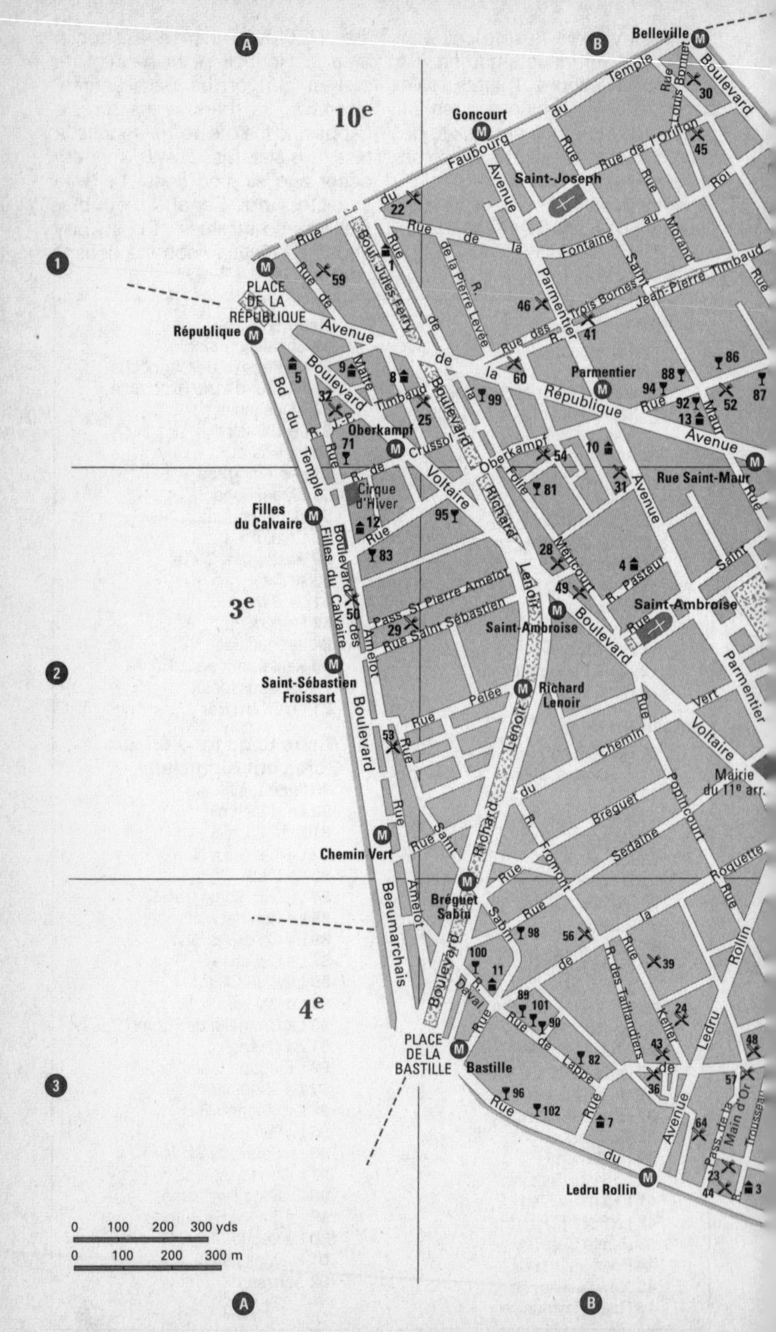

10e
3e
4e
Goncourt
Belleville
Saint-Joseph
PLACE DE LA RÉPUBLIQUE
République
Parmentier
Oberkampf
Cirque d'Hiver
Filles du Calvaire
Rue Saint-Maur
Saint-Ambroise
Saint-Sébastien Froissart
Richard Lenoir
Mairie du 11e arr.
Chemin Vert
Bréguet Sabin
PLACE DE LA BASTILLE
Bastille
Ledru Rollin
Boulevard Richard Lenoir
Boulevard Voltaire
Avenue de la République
Avenue Parmentier
Boulevard Beaumarchais
Boulevard des Filles du Calvaire
Bd du Temple
Rue du Faubourg du Temple
Rue Oberkampf
Rue Jean-Pierre Timbaud
Rue de la Roquette
Avenue Ledru Rollin
Rue de Lappe
0 100 200 300 yds
0 100 200 300 m

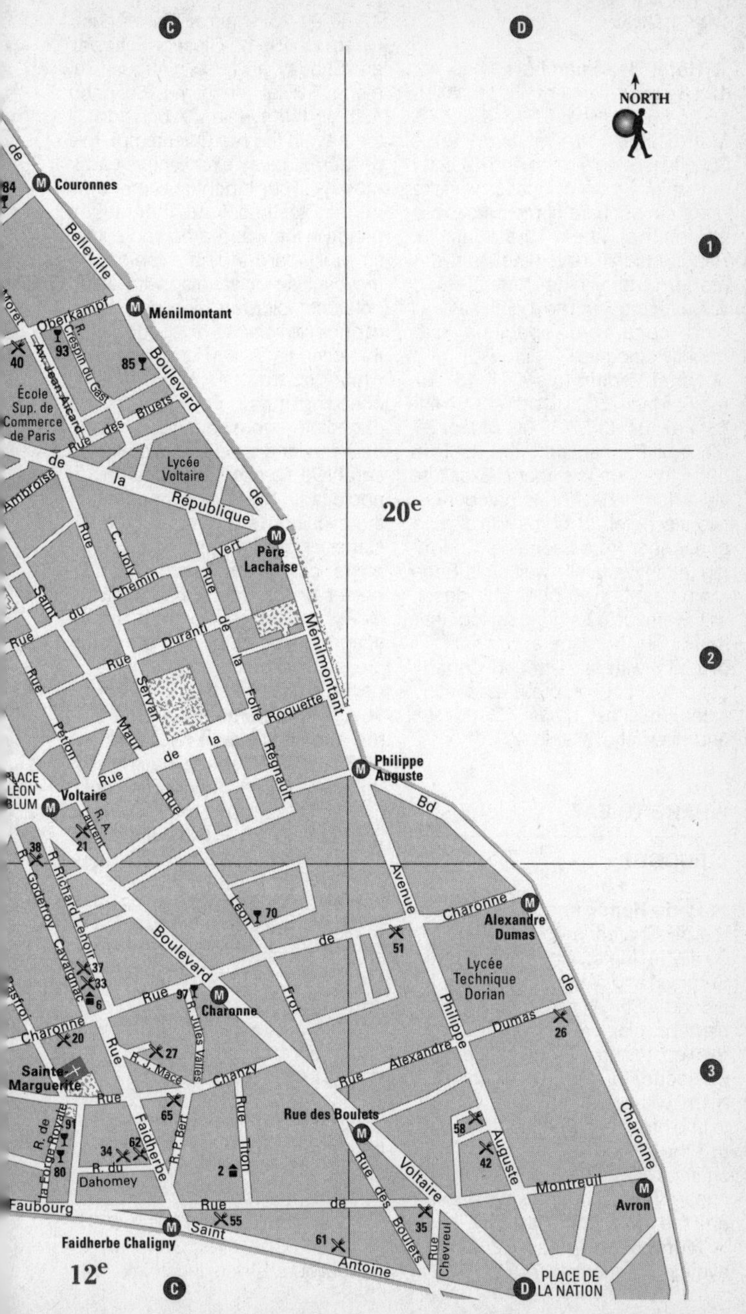
NORTH
Couronnes
Belleville
Ménilmontant
Oberkampf
Boulevard
École Sup. de Commerce de Paris
Rue des Bluets
Lycée Voltaire
de la République
20e
Père Lachaise
Chemin Vert
Rue du
Rue Saint Maur
Rue Duranti
Rue Servan
Rue de la Folie Regnault
Roquette
Ménilmontant
Philippe Auguste
Voltaire
PLACE LÉON BLUM
Boulevard Voltaire
Rue Léon Frot
Avenue Philippe Auguste
Bd de Charonne
Alexandre Dumas
Lycée Technique Dorian
Rue Alexandre Dumas
Charonne
Rue de Charonne
Sainte-Marguerite
Rue Faidherbe
Rue Chanzy
Rue Titon
Rue des Boulets
Rue de Montreuil
Avron
Rue du Faubourg Saint Antoine
Faidherbe Chaligny
Rue Chevreul
PLACE DE LA NATION
12e
R. Godefroy Cavaignac
R. Richard Lenoir
R. J. Macé
R. Jules Vallès
R. P. Bert
R. de la Forge Royale
R. du Dahomey
C
D
1
2
3

☆☆☆ CHIC

Hôtel Beaumarchais (map A2, **12**): 3 rue Oberkampf 75011. ☎ 01-53-36-86-86. Fax: 01-43-38-32-86. Metro: Filles-du-Calvaire. Price 350F for a single room and 490F for a double. A perfect location with the great atmosphere of the bars in rue Oberkampf, near the Bastille, République and even the Marais. A modern, charming hotel. Good value for money. The rooms have all mod cons, are spacious and brightly coloured.

Hôtel Verlain (map B1, **13**): 97 rue St-Maur 75011. ☎ 01-43-57-44-88. Fax: 01-43-57-32-06. Metro: St-Maur or Parmentier. From 450F to 520F for a double room. Excellent value for money for its category. A two-star hotel, 38 rooms with all mod cons, near Père-Lachaise. Charming, attentive family welcome. Each room has its own particular decor, with warm colours bringing together mahogany, cream and midnight blue: TV with satellite and Canal+, hairdryer, trouser press and mini-safe. Breakfast buffet 45F. Minitel and Internet available.

WHERE TO EAT

☆ BUDGET

Paris-Hanoï (map C3, **20**): 74 rue de Charonne 75011. ☎ 01-47-00-47-59. Metro: Charonne. Closed Sunday and August. Budget for around 80F. A pocket-sized Vietnamese place which is cool and relaxed, taking you straight from the Bastoche to the quarter of Hoa Kiem, without jet lag. Treat yourself to one of the excellent house soups, or the noodles sautéed with shrimps. It's good, simple and really cheap. This place is always packed and the atmosphere is lively.

Montpoupon (map B2, **31**): 73 avenue Parmentier 75011. ☎ 01-47-00-94-25. Metro: Parmentier. Open to 10pm. Closed Saturday and Sunday, and also in August. Set menu 54F at lunchtime, 80F and 100F in the evening. Alongside all the bars in the rue Oberkampf, this restaurant gives excellent value for money. The lunchtime menu is perfect testimony to the fact: it brings in the whole area and sometimes it's hard to find a table. Egg mayonnaise or saveloy with warm potatoes, followed by a pork stew, or duck with chips – it depends what the chef finds at Rungis market, which guarantees a constantly changing menu. To follow there's chocolate mousse and fromage frais and for a supplement of 8F you can have an excellent home-made apple tart – the pastry is perfect. In the evening it's quieter, but the set starter or dessert and main course offers *cuisse de canard confite*, *onglet* or *bavette*. Fine paintings nicely framed on the walls. Landscapes inspired by Monet, which are the work of a talented chef, who paints in his time off.

À la Flanquette (map C2, **21**): 9 rue Auguste-Laurent 75011. ☎ 01-43-79-16-66. Metro: Charonne or Voltaire. Open lunchtime only. Closed Saturday and Sunday. Single menu at 80F. Old France in all its splendour – with its loyal regulars. There's a single menu for all with cheese and dessert, and a whole host of dishes straight out of an old housewife's cookery book. Milanese *osso bucco* (veal knuckle with vegetables), house rib of veal and chips, wing of skate with capers, pheasant roasted with cabbage, streaky salted pork with lentils – all traditionally cooked. Establishments like this one are becoming rare nowadays. Don't miss it.

Sizin (map A1, **22**): 36 rue du Faubourg-du-Temple 75011. ☎ 01-48-06-54-03. Metro: Goncourt or République. Open lunchtime and evening to midnight. Closed Sunday lunchtime. Set menu 51F at lunchtime. À la carte, budget for 80F without drinks. Located practically on the corner of the quai de Jemmapes and opposite the Palais des Glaces. À la carte, you get the whole range of Turkish cuisine: wood-stove cooked pizzas, *böreky*, stuffed vine leaves, *kanarya* (aubergine and pepper with yoghurt) and other *mezze*, dishes based on minced meat and lamb, not forgetting the creamy house yoghurts and the *baklava* with honey and nuts. Coffee is free to all.

✕ **Le Scarbo** (map A2, **29**): 1 *bis* passage St-Sébastien 75011. ☎ 01-47-00-58-59. Metro: St-Sébastien-Froissart or St-Ambroise. Restaurant open during the week and at lunchtime only. Set menu 60F and dish of the day 35F. Bar open to 2am (at weekends, they open at 6pm). Hidden away in a passage, near Emmaüs, Le Scarbo cleverly hangs on to its clientele of regulars who come here for the excellent menu with a starter, a main course and dessert or 25cl of wine. Great value for money. The cuisine is of the classic sort, *boeuf bourguignon*, salmon with dill, chocolate mousse or home-made tart. There's a very reasonably priced dish of the day, which is worth checking out. Music or theatre on Monday evening (and some others).

✕ **À L'Ami Pierre** (map B3, **23**): 5 rue de la Main-d'Or 75011. ☎ 01-47-00-17-35. Metro: Ledru-Rollin. Open to 2am. Closed Sunday and Monday, and also from 17 July to 17 August. No set menu; a meal costs around 90F to 100F plus drinks. A bistro with a warm atmosphere. The dish of the day costs around 60F – wonderful *magrets* and *confits* of duck, lamb ribs and various *andouillettes*.

✕ **Le Petit Keller** (map B3, **24**): 13 rue Keller 75011. ☎ 01-47-00-12-97. Metro: Bastille. Open to 11pm. Closed Sunday. Set menu 50F at lunchtime and 75F in the evening, including drinks. In an area where there are an increasing number of pseudo-modern establishments, here is a great place which has invented an odd sort of hip transport-bar formula, perfect if you're broke but still want to try out the Bastille without having to pay the normal prices. The set menu at 75F has a lot to do with it. Fresh spinach with Auvergne blue cheese, *terrine de campagne*, sautéed pork with olives, and, to finish, crumble or chocolate *fondant* with custard. To slake your thirst go for beer or a bottle of red at 60F. The ambiance is relaxed.

✕ **L'Engizek** (map A–B1, **25**): 24 rue Jean-Pierre-Timbaud 75011. ☎ 01-48-06-65-65. Metro: Oberkampf. Open to 11.30pm. Closed Sunday. Set menus 54F at lunchtime, 79F and 96F in the evening. Budget for around 120F à la carte. Children's menu 39F. The reputation of this Turkish restaurant, which has been open for around 15 years, is still excellent. In the two brightly coloured dining rooms, lulled by Turkish music, all you have to do is make a choice from the two set evening menus or the varied à la carte menu. The many wood-stove specialities (such as the kebabs) are the tried and trusted favourites.

✕ **Le Sot-L'y-Laisse** (map D3, **26**): 70 rue Alexandre-Dumas 75011. ☎ 01-40-09-79-20. Metro: Alexandre-Dumas. Last orders 10pm. Closed Saturday lunchtime and Sunday, between Christmas and 1 January, and in August. Set menu 85F lunchtime and evening. The *sot-l'y-laisse* is the particularly tasty bit of flesh hidden above the 'parson's nose' on a chicken. The blackboard has daily specials, starters, main courses, and desserts, in this bistro with an unpretentious setting. Budget for 100F, including cheese. Otherwise, the dish of the day costs 45F at lunchtime – try cream of mussels, roast pork with onions or lamb casserole and, to finish, mandarin mousse or fresh grapefruit salad.

✕ **Les Cinq Points Cardinaux** (map C3, **27**): 14 rue Jean-Macé 75011. ☎ 01-43-71-47-22. Metro: Faidherbe-Chaligny or Charonne. Open to 10pm. Closed Saturday and Sunday, and also in August. Set menus 60F at lunchtime, 65F and 99F in the evening. A nice bistro that welcomes everyone. On the ceiling are the old tools used by local artisans. Fillet of herring, sausage and lentils for the first set menu of the evening, avocado *au gratin* with Roquefort, *confit de canard* or Auvergne tripe for the next one. Really simple traditional cuisine and a friendly atmosphere.

✕ **Zagros** (map B2, **28**): 21 rue de la Folie-Méricourt 75011. ☎ 01-48-07-09-56. Metro: St-Ambroise or Richard-Lenoir. Open noon to 2.30pm and 7.30pm to 11.30pm. Closed Sunday. Set menus 60F at lunchtime and 95F in the evening. Budget for around 120F à la carte. Greek-Kurdish cuisine in a simple, but warm decor. The owner is friendly and so are the locals. Boosted by his success, he has opened a new dining room on the first floor. Starters include taramasalata, stuffed aubergine and mint fromage frais. There's a large choice of grilled meat or traditional meatballs (52F to 70F), served with baked potatoes and bulghur (crushed wheat). Filling and tasty.

✕ **Au Trou Normand** (map A1, **32**): 9 rue Jean-Pierre-Timbaud 75011. ☎ 01-48-05-80-23. Metro: République or Oberkampf. Open lunchtime and evening to 11.30pm. Closed Saturday lunchtime and Sunday, and also in August. Set meal with main course and dessert 45F, served lunchtime and evening. À la carte, budget for 60F. A small, basic restaurant (with pre-war prices!). There are 22 starters from 10F to 15F and 10 main courses from 30F to 39F. During the week, at lunchtime, it's full. Hardly surprising.

✕ **Au Vieux Chêne** (map C3, **34**): 7 rue du Dahomey 75011. ☎ 01-43-71-67-69. Metro: Faidherbe-Chaligny. Open lunchtime and evening to 10.30pm (11pm weekends). Closed Saturday lunchtime and Sunday, and also 25 December and 1 January. Set menus, including drinks, 65F at lunchtime and 120F in the evening. Dish of the day is around 40F. Don't miss the discreet little street which leads to this charming bistro, a survivor from the age of woodworkers. Furniture is from the 1950s. The clientele is made up of regulars.

✕ **Les Uns et les Autres** (map D3, **35**): 15 rue Chevreul 75011. ☎ 01-43-70-22-40. Metro: Boulets-Montreuil or Nation. Closed Sunday, Monday evening, Tuesday evening and in August. Complete set menus 87F at lunchtime and 105F in the evening. If there's a show on, a set meal is 119F. A nice little bistro which is transformed every evening into a literary or musical cabaret. There are readings from short stories and other literary works on Thursday evening from October to April, singers or musicians on Thursday the rest of the year, and on Wednesday, Friday and Saturday evening from 10pm. Classic menus on the blackboard but, frankly, that isn't the attraction of the place. Couscous on Friday. More than 30 wines served by the glass.

✕ **Yakitang** (map C2–3, **38**): 52 rue Godefroy-Cavaignac 75011. ☎ 01-43-67-08-39. Metro: Voltaire. Open noon to 2pm and 7pm to 10.30pm. Closed Monday lunchtime and Sunday, at Christmas, 1 January and for three weeks in August. Set menus 43F to 88F. A Japanese place with very reasonable prices. The set menu at 68F (nine kebabs, rice, soup and salad) will easily fill you up.

✕ **Dong Huong** (map B1, **30**): 14 rue Louis-Bonnet 75011. ☎ 01-43-57-42-81. Metro: Belleville Open daily except Tuesday. À la carte only; count on spending 100F. This restaurant is a real success story. Twenty years ago it was just another family shop. Now there are four large dining rooms and almost 25 people working here. And the reason for this success? The food. All the tried and trusted favourites of Vietnamese gastronomy are here, with excellent *banh xéo* (filled and grilled crêpes, at 45F) as a bonus. In fact, the Vietnamese community in Belleville come here at lunchtime, and that's always a good sign.

☆☆ MODERATE

✕ **La Plancha** (map B3, **39**): 34 rue Keller 75011. ☎ 01-48-05-20-30. Metro: Bastille. Open 6pm to 2am. Last orders 1.30am. Closed Sunday and Monday, and also for a week in August. Budget for between 150F and 200F, including drinks. A real Basque place run by a real Basque (and a very friendly one, at that). Small, warm, intimate, and often packed out. When you try the first tapas, you realize why! It's all simply exquisite: tortilla, mussels, *chipirons*, sardines or *gambas a la plancha* and fresh tuna when in season. Don't miss the lamb's cheese *(antigasma)*, and the succulent Basque cake. All washed down with a good sangria, of course!

✕ **Loulou de Bastille** (map C3, **37**): 11 rue Richard-Lenoir 75011. ☎ 01-40-09-03-31. Metro: Voltaire. Open daily and all year round to midnight. Set meal 68F at lunchtime. À la carte, budget for around 130F. Run by an American from Manhattan, who took over the business from Loulou, the original owner. Happy service and atmosphere. Straightforward cuisine which appeals to the loyal regulars. Home-made bread, among other things.

✕ **La Folie Milon** (plan D3, **42**): 33 avenue Philippe-Auguste 75011. ☎ 01-43-70-01-76. Metro: Nation. Open lunchtime and evening (last orders 11pm) except Sundays and Mondays. Set menu 85F at lunchtime. À la carte, budget for 130F without drinks. A restaurant warmly set out between yellow and orange walls. Eclectic menu which is full of surprises. There's a superb marinade of squid in its own ink, which looks odd (at first sight!), entrecôte with *civet d'andouille* and thick fondant with warm chocolate and Jamaican spices. Add to this a charming terrace and permanent exhibitions of paintings and you'll understand the popularity of this place. Wines from 80F.

✕ **Le Waly Fay** (map C3, **33**): 6 rue Godefroy-Cavaignac 75011. ☎ 01-40-24-17-79. Metro: Charonne. Open every evening 8pm to 2am. À la carte, budget for 150F. Three friends run this 'Afro-soul-West Indian' restaurant which plunges you into its ethnic-urban environment. The all-black cuisine – Creole black pudding, *cod accras*, Senegalese soya, vegetable *maffé*, *yassa* chicken and kid *colombo* – is great. There's jazz and hip soul. Booking is advisable.

✕ **Le Vieux Byzantin** (map C1, **40**): 128 rue Oberkampf 75011. ☎ 01-43-57-35-84. Metro: Ménilmontant or Parmentier. Open noon to 3pm and 6.30pm to 2am (later on busy evenings). Closed Sunday lunchtime. Set menus 53F at lunchtime, 83F and 97F in the evening. Don't be put off by the rather old-looking front. This is a very welcoming Turkish restaurant, with a pleasant setting: photographs on the walls, rugs, and *kilims* on the tables. Good, simple and generous dishes: taramasalata, aubergine caviar, kebabs and grills. À la carte, it rarely costs more than 100F, unless you go over the top with the raki or the ouzo.

✕ **Pause Café** (map B3, **43**): 41 rue de Charonne 75011. ☎ 01-48-06-80-33. Metro: Bastille. Open to 2am. Closed Sunday evening and 25 December. Budget for no more than 120F. One of the hip young meeting places in the Bastille, and featured as such in Cedric Klapisch's offbeat hit film *Chacun cherche son chat*, which is set in the area. Several dishes of the day (55F to 65F), including a *tartare*, a hot *tartine* or a mixed platter. There are also good home-made desserts, such as chocolate tart.

✕ **Un Saumon à Paris** (map B3, **36**): 32 rue de Charonne 75011. ☎ 01-49-29-07-15. Metro: Bastille. Last orders 11pm. Closed Sunday lunchtime and lunchtime daily in August. Set menus 69F at lunchtime and 79F in the evening. À la carte, budget for 130F. The same name and the same deal as the excellent shop specializing in products from Eastern Europe and Scandinavia in the rue Monge, in the 5th arrondissement. Halfway between a bistro and a delicatessen. Dishes include the plate of three taramasalatas (46F), plate of three herrings flavoured with paprika, dill, curry or marinated (48F), *maatje* herrings and hot potatoes (49F), *borscht* (beetroot soup) (44F), baked egg with caviar (70F) and salmon marinated Scandinavian style (68F). And of course, vodka and aquavit (3cl, 20F) to warm the cockles of your heart. The set menu in the evening is more generous, but it is only served during the week.

✕ **Paris Main d'Or** (map B3, **44**): 133 rue du Faubourg-St-Antoine 75011. ☎ 01-44-68-04-68. Metro: Ledru-Rollin. Open noon to 3pm and 8pm to midnight. Closed Sunday and in August. At lunchtime there's a set menu at 65F; in the evening budget for 150F. A pleasant Corsican restaurant, designed by an Argentine! Ask for the menu and take your pick: *brocciu omelette, brocciu cannelloni, Bonifacio-style aubergine, kid fressure* fried with *chanterelles* or cod with Swiss chard. The *charcuterie*, cheese and wines all come straight from Corsica. At lunchtime it's absolutely packed out with people trying out the continental menu. In the evening it becomes Corsican again.

✕ **New Nioullaville** (map B1, **45**): 32 rue de l'Orillon 75011. ☎ 01-40-21-96-18 and 01-40-21-98-38. Metro: Belleville Open daily to 1am. Set menus from 48F to 78F, served lunchtime only. This immense restaurant (around 500 seats) has been renovated. The kitchen has been entirely redone, the ceiling and the lighting of the dining rooms redesigned, and air-conditioning installed. Specialities from Canton and Sichuan, with dishes based on tofu, noodles and soup. Also dishes from Cambodia, Vietnam and Thailand. Peking duck for four people costs 268F. High chairs available (a service which is extremely rare in French restaurants).

✕ **Chez Raymonde** (map B1, **46**): 119 avenue Parmentier 75011. ☎ 01-43-55-26-27. Metro: Parmentier or Goncourt. Open to 11pm. Closed Monday and Tuesday. Menus for around 130F during the week; around 185F at the weekend, drinks not included. An original place which recalls the Paris of old. Tables surround the dance floor and at around 10pm every night, Yannick, the chef, puts his arms around Benoît, his front of house partner, to start off the dancing, and everyone is invited to join in. An accordionist regularly plays waltzes and tangos. People leave their grilled *andouillette* with mustard sauce to dance. The best thing is to come in a large group and create your own ambiance.

✕ **Suds** (map B3, **48**): 55 rue de Charonne 75011. ☎ 01-43-14-06-36. Metro: Ledru-Rollin. Open every evening 7.30pm to 1am. Bar open to 1.30am. Closed Monday. À la carte, budget for 150F; no set menu. Delicacies and drinks whisk you away to the south of France, through Spain and Portugal, towards Latin America. Those of you with a touch of wanderlust on your palate will feel at home here. Try salad of *gambas* with bacon and poached egg (42F) and *magret de canard* with honey (88F). Every Sunday evening there's excellent Latino music from the best current DJs. The *mojito* is almost as good as in Cuba.

✕ **L'Homme Bleu** (map B1, **41**): 55 *bis* rue Jean-Pierre-Timbaud 75011. ☎ 01-48-07-05-63. Metro: Couronnes. Open 7.30pm to 1am. Closed Sunday. Budget for around 160F per person; à la carte only. A change from the usual couscous restaurants of the Bastille, the menu here includes well-seasoned *kefta*, perfectly cooked *tajines* and tasty little stuffed dishes *(boreks* and *briks)*.

✕ **Anjou-Normandie** (map B2, **49**): 13 rue de la Folie-Méricourt 75011. ☎ 01-47-00-30-59. Metro: St-Ambroise. Closed in the evening and at weekends, and also in August. Set menus 76F and 110F. Children's menu 60F. À la carte, budget for 150F. Advisable to book. A distinguished fake rustic setting, but the beams are original. An old place which has kept its reputation for the warmth of its welcome and specializing in grilled *andouillette*.

✕ **Restaurant de la Réunion** (map C3, **65**): 23 rue Paul-Bert 75011. ☎ 01-43-70-94-11. Metro: Faidherbe-Chaligny. Closed Sunday and Monday evening, and also from mid-August to early September. Budget for around 150F à la carte for a meal with a starter, main course and dessert, excluding drinks. The setting is rather elegant, and yet, with a little imagination, you could believe you were at the heart of Réunion Island. The ceilings are painted to look like skylights opening on to the sky of Réunion, with palm branches and toucans flying overhead. There are two aquariums in the background and the cuisine is tasty and scented. As a starter, there's *vindaye* of fresh fish and gratin of *chouchou* with shrimps, unless you go for the Réunion or local platter, which is more expensive, but undoubtedly a good introduction to the gastronomic pleasures of the island. Then there's marlin or swordfish with *combava* curry, both delicious and original. Efficient service.

✕ **Traiteur d'Italie Ristorante** (map D3, **51**): 152 rue de Charonne 75011. ☎ 01-43-71-32-50. Metro: Alexandre-Dumas. Closed Sunday and Monday evening, and also in August. Budget for 150F; à la carte only. Huge pizzas and lots of seafood specialities (at weekends) for a perfectly reasonable price. Family ambiance and a bustling atmosphere.

✕ **L'Occitanie** (map B1, **52**): 96 rue Oberkampf 75011. ☎ 01-48-06-46-98. Metro: Parmentier. Open lunchtime and evening (last orders 10.30pm). Closed Saturday lunchtime, at Christmas, 1 January and also in August. Set menus 65F at lunchtime, 93F and 139F in the evening. Enjoy the sun of Toulouse, the Languedoc and garlicky cooking in a quaint and rustic setting, around little tables with flowered tablecloths. Nobody here knows the meaning of the word 'cholesterol', or if they do they're ready to fight it with garlic and Cahors! Hearty cuisine, with generous set menus at 52F or 54F at lunchtime. The welcome is as warm as the cuisine.

☆☆☆ CHIC

✕ Le Camelot (map A2, **53**): 50 rue Amelot 75011. ☎ 01-43-55-54-04. Metro: Chemin-Vert or St-Sébastien-Froissart. Open to 11pm. Closed Sunday and Monday, and also in August. Set menus 140F at lunchtime and 160F in the evening. The menu changes daily – *coquilles* St-Jacques roasted with vermicelli of celery, followed by pigeon *confit* with chips and, to finish, *clafoutis* (fruit baked in batter) with chocolate and rice pudding with caramelized clementines.

✕ Le Villaret (map B1, **54**): 13 rue Ternaux 75011. ☎ 01-43-57-75-56 or 01-43-57-89-76. Metro: Parmentier. Open lunchtime and evening; last orders 1am. Closed Saturday lunchtime and Sunday, for two weeks in May, the whole of August and 10 days over Christmas and New Year. Set menus 150F and 120F (main course and starter or dessert) at lunchtime. À la carte, budget for around 220F. A wonderful bistro. The dishes vary depending on what's available at the market and the 'house medicines' (the wine list, plus a list of 'exceptional medicines', which is full of great vintages at attractive prices) keep everyone happy. Depending on when you go, and on what the chef's found at Rungis market, you may be treated to a foil parcel of clams with thyme, a fricassée of mushrooms with garlic and parsley, big green asparagus, medallions of monkfish with cream of crab, calves' liver with endives or sirloin with shallots, accompanied by a gratin of Jerusalem artichokes. One of the best places in Paris at night, with a warm welcome.

✕ Les Amognes (map C3, **55**): 243 rue du Faubourg-St-Antoine 75011. ☎ 01-43-72-73-05. Metro: Faidherbe-Chaligny. Open lunchtime and evening to 10.30pm. Closed Sunday, Saturday, and for three weeks in August. À la carte, budget for around 200F. Children's menu 150F. Superb menu and great value for money. Fillet of roast lamb, skate and red cabbage will tempt you, with crêpes for dessert. There is a very fine selection of wines. A warm welcome.

✕ Dame Jeanne (map B3, **57**): 60 rue de Charonne 75011. On the corner of the passage de la Main-d'Or. ☎ 01-47-00-37-40. Metro: Charonne or Ledru-Rollin. Closed Saturday lunchtime and Sunday. Booking is recommended at weekends. 'Fruit and vegetable' menu 111F. *Menu-carte* at 138F (two main courses) or 168F (three main courses). Mexican hacienda decor with ochre walls decorated with dark-red stencils and a wrought-iron screen. The 'fruit and vegetable' menu offers, for a very reasonable price, a good chance to sample the fare of this young creative chef who plays with scents and spices with daring mixes of unexpected flavours. Dishes on the now traditional *menu-carte*, plus new ideas daily (and there are plenty of them), include: *croustillant* of pig's trotters and roast goat, braised *coquilles* St-Jacques, fried ginger and mashed potato with olive oil, French toast with caramelized apples, and grapefruit and bitter cocoa *brandade*. Original presentation.

✕ Le Passage (map B3, 64): 18 passage de la Bonne-Graine 75011. ☎ 01-47-00-73-30. Metro: Ledru-Rollin. Closed Saturday and Sunday. No set menu; budget for at least 150F without wine. Dish of the day around 75F; *andouillettes* between 80F and 100F. There are almost 300 wines in the cellars of this wine bistro. The decor is typically bistro, with old beams and bottles containing all sorts of things on show here and there. If you look hard enough, there is even a salmanazar by Laurent-Perrier (a Champagne bottle 12 times bigger than the normal size!). The sort of place where ordering a cheap wine is almost frowned upon! The trend here is towards Côtes-du-Rhône, with a particularly interesting selection of Côtes-Rôtie. To go with the wine (and not vice versa), there are eight sorts of *andouillette* prepared by top *charcutiers* from all over France, and the blackboard offers well-cooked traditional dishes, such as farmhouse chicken *en barbouille* (with black pudding), rabbit sautéed with spice bread and prunes, and fillet of roasted red mullet with purée of Jerusalem artichokes.

✕ **Cefalù** (map D3, **58**): 43 avenue Philippe-Auguste 75011. ☎ 01-43-71-29-34. Metro: Nation. Open noon to 2.30pm and 7.30pm to 10.30pm. Closed Saturday lunchtime and Sunday, as well as the second fortnight in August. Set menu 89F, and a *menu dégustation* at 180F. Budget for at least 150F à la carte. Ten minutes from Père-Lachaise and five minutes from the Place de la Nation. A Sicilian place with antipasti, sole with caviar of aubergines, Sicilian-style spaghetti and 'four flavours' of tagliatelle. For dessert, *cannoli*, a delicious Sunday treat in Sicily, is highly recommended – a crunchy roll filled with fresh ricotta and dried fruit, usually accompanied by a glass of Marsala. Set menu (except on Friday evening and Saturday) offers: antipasto, *osso buco* and cheese (pecorino). The gourmet menu (without wine) is a bit expensive. Book in the evening (even during the week).

✕ **Restaurant Cartet** (map A1, **59**): 62 rue de Malte 75011. ☎ 01-48-05-17-65. Metro: République. Last orders 10.30pm. Closed Saturday and Sunday, and in August. Budget for 300F. A long dining room, with just 16 covers. The Lyons-style tripe and sheep's trotters are two dishes which you really should not miss. Otherwise there are generous pâtés and terrines. Desserts include excellent floating islands, lemon tart and chocolate mousse. Round off with *bugnes*, sweet fritters from Lyons, which will be authoritatively placed on your table at the end of the meal.

✕ **Astier** (map B1, **60**): 44 rue Jean-Pierre-Timbaud 75011. ☎ 01-43-57-16-35 or 01-43-38-25-56. Metro: Parmentier. Open lunchtime and evening to 11pm. Closed Saturday, Sunday and public holidays, as well as during the spring school holidays, in August and for two weeks between Christmas and 1 January. Set menus 115F at lunchtime, 140F in the evening. A typical Parisian bistro with classic prices, proper tablecloths and serviettes. It's full every night. The *menu-carte* offers classic dishes (starter, main course, amazing cheese – all you can eat – and a choice of desserts) and changes daily.

✕ **La Barcarola** (map C3, **61**): 275 rue du Faubourg-St-Antoine 75011. ☎ 01-43-72-24-76. Metro: Faidherbe-Chaligny. Open to 1am, or later. Closed Sunday and Monday evening, and in August. Set menu 130F lunchtime and evening. Budget for 180F to 200F à la carte. Far from the hustle and bustle of the Bastoche, this restaurant has a laid-back atmosphere, helped by the loyal regulars, including lots of Italians. It looks like a fine country inn (visible beams, old stones) with flowers everywhere. It is famous for its remarkable minestrone, pasta, and seafood lasagne. None of the regulars would miss the polenta *alla bergamasca* on Wednesday, served at 9pm (plain with a fricassée of mushrooms). They also do excellent tiramisu.

✕ **Le Repaire de Cartouche** (map A2, **50**): 99 rue Amelot 75011. ☎ 01-47-00-25-86. Metro: Filles-du-Calvaire. Closed Sunday, Monday and from mid-July to mid-August. Budget for around 180F à la carte. Dishes full of flavour and beautifully presented. Seasonal cuisine (during the shooting season, the grouse is excellent) always based on the best produce. The wine list is well thought out, and goes perfectly with the cooking. Unfortunately, the service is not always as good as the cuisine.

☆☆☆☆ TRÈS CHIC

✕ **Blue Elephant** (map B3, **56**): 43 rue de la Roquette 75011. ☎ 01-47-00-42-00. Metro: Bastille. Open lunchtime and evening, last orders midnight. Closed Saturday lunchtime, 1 May, and 24 and 25 December. Set menu 150F at lunchtime. Budget for 230F à la carte (including a Thai beer). In the evening there are set menus at 275F and 300F. This place conjures up a relaxed image of Thailand: tropical plants, a waterfall, plus well-spaced tables and Asian-style service with a smile. The cuisine features spices discreetly adapted for all palates (on the menu, the very hot dishes are shown by three elephants). If you like pepper, start your meal with *tom yam khung* (spicy soup of giant shrimps with lemongrass) and follow with *chiang rai* (pork with green pepper and basil), or Thai curried chicken (with coconut), or 'Blue Elephant' rice (rice sautéed with crab meat). As for the wines, they've selected some reds and whites which go perfectly with the dishes. Booking is essential at weekends. Women customers are offered an orchid!

✕ **Mansouria** (map C3, **62**): 11 rue Faidherbe 75011. ☎ 01-43-71-00-16. Metro: Faidherbe-Chaligny. Open to 11pm. Closed Sunday and Monday lunchtime. Set menu lunchtime and evening 182F. À la carte budget for 300F. The trendiest Moroccan restaurant in Paris. You'll need to book. Excellent *tajines* and couscous in a variety of styles: Fez style, Casablanca style, Oujda style or *voilé*. *Menu-dégustation* 210F, for at least two people.

WINE BARS

✕ 🍷 **Jacques Mélac** (map C3, **70**): 42 rue Léon-Frot 75011. ☎ 01-43-70-59-27. Metro: Charonne. Open 9am to 10.30pm. Closed Sunday and Monday evening, as well as August and between Christmas and 1 January. No set menu; budget for 100F to 120F. There's a climbing vine which runs right along the house, revealing Jacques Mélac's passion. He is one of the few Parisian bistro owners who harvest and produce their own wine. Bottles are sold in the shop, in aid of charity. Grape harvesting takes place in the second fortnight of September, so don't miss it! Mélac has set up an association, 'The Winegrowers of Paris', in order to bring together people involved in wine in Paris and those who want to get started (all you need is a large tray to grow a vine stock). The headquarters of the association and the shop are at: 42 rue Léon-Frot 75011. For information: ☎ 01-40-09-93-37. As an aside, there are some typical bistro dishes.

🍷 **Le Clown Bar** (map A1, **71**): 114 rue Amelot 75011. ☎ 01-43-55-87-35. Metro: Filles-du-Calvaire. Open noon to 3pm and 7pm to 1am. Closed all day Sunday in summer (generally open in the evening in the winter, depending on whether the owners feel like it or not) as well as the week of 15 August. You can get a complete meal for around 180F to 200F. A wine bistro frequented by actors from the neighbourhood, between rehearsals. Not surprisingly, you may detect a slight clown theme in the decor. They're all over the place – on the superb ceramic frieze, on the ceiling, on the old posters stuck all over the wall and in the windows. There's a fine selection of wines by the glass (20F to 25F) or bottled (from 100F for the wine of the day). The cuisine is not particularly exciting, but there's *charcuterie* (56F) or house terrine served in an unlimited supply (35F).

AROUND THE PLACE DE LA BASTILLE

★ **Place de la Bastille:** following the demolition of the prison, work began in 1803 on the construction of the place de la Bastille. It wasn't until 60 years later, however, that it took on its definitive shape with the building of boulevard Henri-IV and the construction of the Caserne des Célestins (the barracks of the Republican Guard) and the Gare de la Bastille. Although the latter has been demolished, there has never been any question of doing the same with the Caserne, which is built on part of the old Célestins convent. The Colonne de Juillet embodies the collective spirit of the 1789 Revolution. It is instantly recognizable with its elegant parapet (50m/164ft high), the fine lions' heads decorating the cornice and the Spirit of Liberty (symbolizing the struggle against oppression) crowning the top of the monument, clutching the broken chain of despotism in his left hand and the torch of civilization in his right. In 1989 the monument and the names inscribed on it were beautifully re-gilded for the Republic's bicentennial celebrations.

★ The **Opéra-Bastille** *see the* 12th arrondissement.

★ **Rue de Lappe:** One of the prettiest streets in Paris. It had a bad reputation at the end of the 19th century when the 'apaches' (the ruffians of the day) ruled the roost, a time when the road was also lined with popular dance halls. It is the 'capital', along with the rue de la Roquette, of businesses supplying cafés and restaurants. Full of lively, noisy bars, the old Parisian courtyards in the street are not without a certain charm, bringing a much needed respite from the hellish traffic of the Bastille. At No. 18 there are artists' workshops. At No. 24 the concierges have added some colour by planting lots of flowers and hazel, lilac, ash, willow and birch trees which they've brought from the countryside. At No. 34 stands the prettiest courtyard in the street, and at No. 41 there is a narrow alleyway leading to the passage Thiéré.

★ **Rue de la Roquette:** a very long street which goes as far as Père-Lachaise. There are old houses, restaurants, shops and alleyways all along the street. The Théâtre de la Bastille is nearby. Chances are that you'll enjoy it if you like innovative theatre and experimental dance.

When you come out, you can always go for a drink at No. 74, La Taverne. Mainly frequented by young people, rockers and leather-clad bikers. A bit noisy, but lively.

Take a tour around the street's courtyards and alleyways to get to know this old area better. At No. 43 there's a fine sculpted gable. At No. 41 there are large workshops which have been converted into lofts, and a curious clock without hands. On the corner of rue du Commandant-Lamy, one of the ugliest churches in Paris has been replaced by a very modern one. The locals miss the old church – they used to like the Breton lighthouse which seemed to be watching over them when they'd been up all night! On the way to Père-Lachaise, via Place Voltaire, there's a large public garden situated on the site of the former Prison de la Roquette, the porch of which is still intact. Opposite, on the corner of rue de la Croix-Faubin, there are five unusual, wide, flat stones which provided the foundations for the guillotine. There were public executions in the rue de la Roquette until the early 20th century.

★ **Rue de Charonne:** this is the former road leading to the village of Charonne. Here too, there are old passageways, houses and shops. On the corner with rue du Faubourg-St-Antoine stands the Fontaine Trogneux, built in the 18th century (marking the 1910 flood level). At No. 37 there is a pleasant courtyard with a splendid loft on the right hand side with original carvings on the façade. Other tenants, however, have chosen to decorate their homes in a more rustic country-style. Finally, at the crossing with the avenue Ledru-Rollin, stands Le Bistro du Peintre, a bar which still has its fine 1900 decor, its wrought-iron veranda and the old sign in gold lettering: 'Coffee: 10 centimes per cup'.

THE FAUBOURG ST-ANTOINE

★ **The passageways of the Faubourg-St-Antoine:** one of the most charming streets in Paris, the Faubourg-St-Antoine is very long and will take you as far as Place de la Nation. It forms the backbone of this large area of artisans and cottage industries. Thanks to Louis XI, who licensed the establishment of craftsmen in the 15th century, the wood and furnishing trades developed. Skilled artisans, released from former constraints, were able to give free rein to their creativity, and this is where the first decorations in bronze and the first inlay work were created, and where the finest Louis XIV, Louis XV and Louis XVI furniture was made and sent to decorate Versailles or other palaces.

Today it is hard to imagine the strictness of the rules which were imposed on artisans. Most of them had to work with 'an open shop' so that passers-by could see the quality of the materials used, and working at night was severely punished, because it could have led to defects! Supporting an enormous working-class population, the Faubourg supplied the largest battalions of all for the popular revolts: the storming of the Bastille, the anti-Louis-Philippe riots in 1832, the revolution in 1848, and resistance to the Coup d'État by the future Napoleon III in 1851. In fact, this is why the Canal St-Martin is covered over 2km (1 mile) from the Bastille – to allow troops to cross it more quickly if rioting broke out!

Throughout the area there are many narrow little streets where you can still see a few cabinetmakers, upholsterers and gilders working, often in superb courtyards lined with fine houses and private residences.

Here is a short route through what remains of this artisans' heritage, which is rapidly disappearing. Just like everywhere else, trade is taking over from craftsmanship.

• Starting at the Bastille, take the **passage du Cheval-Blanc** on the corner of the Faubourg Ste Antoine and rue de la Roquette. There's a network of little courtyards all bearing the names of the months of the year. You come out again at No. 21 in the Faubourg.

• At No. 33 stands the splendid building, a former factory, that housed the trendy magazine *Actuel*, that has since folded. In the courtyard there is a fine renovated building, an old well, a corbelled house and a staircase with a 17th-century wooden balustrade. At the end on the right there is a collection of garden gnome-style dwarves, surrounding their very own Snow White.

• At No. 56, do not miss the superb **cour du Bel-Air**, one of the most attractive in the Faubourg. Nicely renovated and planted with trees, its façades are covered in Virginia creeper.

• At No. 66, **passage du Chantier** still looks as it did in the 19th century. Large paving stones, narrow pavements lined with polishing and varnishing workshops, storehouses, old furniture stores, and a maze of flower-filled little courtyards. Don't miss the one at No. 2, behind its heavy wrought-iron grill. The passage comes out at 55 rue de Charenton.

• **Cour de l'Étoile-d'Or,** from the 18th century, is at No. 75. On the façade of an old house at the end of the first courtyard there is a sundial dating from 1751.

• **Passage de la Main-d'Or:** starts at No. 133 and goes as far as rue de Charonne. The name is taken from an old shop. There are some traditional bars here from the last century, in the street of the same name (Aux Petits Joueurs and À l'Ami Pierre).

• There are other similar courtyards and buildings. The area is full of passages, unusual terraced houses and secret courtyards.

★ **Église Ste-Marguerite:** 36 rue St-Bernard 75011. Metro: Faidherbe-Chaligny. Open from Monday to Saturday 8.30am to noon and 2pm to 7pm. Open on Sundays from 9am to noon. In the middle of the polishers' and varnishers' workshops there is a church which, although not famous, is one of the most attractive in Paris. Although from the outside it looks like a large village church, on the inside it has a certain architectural refinement. Built in the 17th and 18th centuries, it was the church's first vicar who himself sculpted the fine bas-reliefs on the exterior of the transept. In the afternoon, when the sun is in the west, the inside is flooded with light through the fine stained-glass windows. The Chapelle des Âmes, a masterpiece of *trompe-l'œil*, is amazing. There is a fine sculpted wooden pulpit.

On the left of the church is the cemetery, known as the 'cimetière Louis XVII'. It is here that the young son of Louis XVI, aged 10, is said to have been buried. Mystery surrounds this story as the remains, which were exhumed later, were those of a much older boy. This gave rise to the theory that the prince's body had been substituted for another and led to a long list of false Louis XVII claimants in the 19th century. The tomb is just behind the Chapelle des Âmes (to see it, ask the curate).

WHERE TO GO FOR A DRINK

Le Réservoir (map C3, **80**): 16 rue de la Forge-Royale 75011. ☎ 01-43-56-39-60. Metro: Ledru-Rollin. Open 8pm to 2am (4am at weekends). Closed 10 to 20 August. Average price for a meal without drinks 250F. A fashionable caf'-conc' (café with live music). Cheap cocktails (50F a glass; plus 20F on evenings when there's a concert) in a fantastic setting: an immense semi-grotto, with a crumbling old water tank (hence the name – *reservoir*) over the bar and wooden tables, wrought-iron chandeliers and stone walls which give the whole thing a very medieval feel. On the musical programme there are some surprises – there have been some legendary jam sessions here!

Café de l'Industrie (map B3, **98**): 16 rue St-Sabin 75011. ☎ 01-47-00-13-53. Metro: Bréguet-Sabin or Bastille. Open noon to 2am. Closed Saturday and 1 January. Budget for 120F to eat. Beers cost around 15F. Packed out every night (you almost have your nose in your neighbour's drink), this bistro is part of Paris's neo-working-class circuit. Take note of the latest styles in leather jackets. The welcome is friendly and the service is quick. At the bar, order a *caïpiroska* (40F) or a *ti punch* (28F). There's also a restaurant, but it's incidental.

Le Troisième Bureau (map B1, **99**): 74 rue de la Folie-Méricourt 75011. ☎ 01-43-55-87-65. Metro: Parmentier or Oberkampf. Open daily 11.30am to 2am. Set menu 115F lunchtime and evening. À la carte, budget for no more than 120F. Young and relaxed, this place is divided into two sections. At the front part you drink (13F for half a pint of beer), out back you eat, or sometimes both at the same time. Less flashy and cooler than all the bars in the rue Oberkampf, which is nearby.

Le Lèche-Vin (map B3, **100**): 13 rue Daval 75011. ☎ 01-43-55-98-91. Metro: Bastille. Open daily 8pm to 2am except Sunday. Drinks cost around 20F. The walls are covered with hundreds of pious images in which Jesus Christ, the Virgin Mary and all the saints appear in front of Buddha and Vishnu. A magnificent statue of St Theresa (life-size!) has pride of place in the dining room. If the owner has transformed his establishment into a theological shambles, it's more because of his taste for provocative kitsch, rather than sacrilege. If you don't believe us, visit the toilets! Over 18s only.

Havanita Café (map B3, **101**): 11 rue de Lappe 75011. ☎ 01-43-55-96-42. Metro: Bastille. Open daily 5pm to 2am. Closed 24 December. Cuba for under 50F! Comfortably installed in a leather armchair, in just a couple of minutes you'll find yourself transported to Havana, surrounded by fans and palm trees. Excellent daiquiris and *mojitos* (45F). On the musical front, a talented DJ plays salsa, mambo, cumbia and other funky sounds. A place devoted to fashionable exoticism. Every week there are deliveries of Cuban cigars. The establishment is also a restaurant (just!).

Sanzsans (map B3, **102**): 49 rue du Faubourg-St-Antoine 75011. ☎ 01-44-75-78-78. Metro.: Bastille. Open 9am to 2am. Closed Christmas. 22F for half a pint of beer. Budget for around 120F for a meal. One of the grooviest places in Paris. Just down the road from Radio Nova, this cool bar attracts a wide cross-section of the community. The decor is cheap (mainly from the flea markets), the level of comfort is basic (wobbly chairs, elbow to elbow), the menu is international and the music is rap, acid, jazz and hip hop.

Le Mécano-Bar (map B1, **94**): 99 rue Oberkampf 75011. ☎ 01-40-

21-35-28. Metro: Parmentier. Open daily 9am to 2am. Salad or main course from 50F, drinks around 20F. A former toolstore 'aux arts mécaniques', founded in 1832, the new owners have hung onto the retro façade and moved the decor about. There are a few broken old machine tools to set the tone, with a 10m (30ft) bar taken by storm every evening by an ethnic hip crowd from all over Paris who come to mix with the locals. DJs in the evening, cocktails, musical brunch on Sunday from noon (80F), philosophers' café, salsa lessons, book signings and rotating exhibitions the rest of the time (time permitting).

Le Tamla (map B2, **95**): 44 boulevard Voltaire 75011. ☎ 01-43-38-61-05. Metro: Oberkampf. Open daily to 2am (midnight on Sunday). Set menu 55F at lunchtime, 60, 70 and 75F in the evening. À la carte, budget for 100F without drinks. A little bistro where you can have a quick snack and a toast to anything you can think of (15F for a planter's punch). Board games, permanent exhibitions and the music is half Tamla Motown, half Nova. Appreciated by all sorts of people (including trendies and locals), carried away by the mega-kitsch decor of this rather odd place.

Le Bar Sans Nom (map B3, **82**): 49 rue de Lappe 75011. ☎ 01-48-05-59-36. Metro: Bastille. Open 7am to 2am. Closed Sunday, two weeks in August and at Christmas. Beers from 30F to 40F, cocktails 50F. A strikingly authentic bar run by a Parisian South American, his partner and a cosmopolitan team (between them they speak seven languages!). Two rooms – a restaurant, a bar – with refined, baroque decor. Marvellous cocktails and music from all over the world, including previews. Amazing *mojitos*!

Le Kitch (map A2, **83**): 10 rue Oberkampf 75011. ☎ 01-40-21-94-14. Metro: Filles-du-Calvaire. Open daily 11am to 2am, except Satuday and Sunday morning. Set menu 58F at lunchtime. Beers cost around 15F. A little restaurant bar away from the noise of the upper part of the rue d'Oberkampf, decorated with eclectic objects. The tables are multicoloured, there are frescoes of shells on the walls, little gilded cherubs and pink life belts. To recover from the shock, there's only one answer: order a *cucarracha* (28F). 'In the beginning, we used to scare the locals, but things are getting better now.' As you can see.

GOING OUT

Le Cannibale Café (map B–C1, **84**): 93 rue Jean-Pierre-Timbaud 75011. ☎ 01-49-29-95-59. Metro: Couronnes. Open daily 8pm to 2am. Closed lunchtime in August. Set menus 75F at lunchtime, 40F for children. Budget for around 120F without drinks. Lost in the Arab quarter of Belleville, this place has been packed over the last few years. At the time of writing, it had been turned into a meeting place for young women seeking peace and quiet. The tone had been set, although after a few articles had appeared in the press ('*Le Cannibale Café*, a café for women'), the place was invaded by men: 'Is this the man-eaters' café?' Since then, the balance has been re-established between the sexes, and the many charms of this 1930s bistro attract all sorts of people who come for a drink (12F for half a pint of beer), read the papers, see the latest exhibition of photographs or discover world cuisine. There is a fine wine list. Booking is essential.

Le Café Charbon (map B1, **86**): 109 rue Oberkampf 75011. ☎ 01-43-57-55-13. Metro: Parmentier. Open daily 9am to 2am. Budget for around 80F. Beer is 15F for half a pint. An enormous place frequented by former Bastoche trendies and the new Parisian night owls. In the space of a few months this local bar has become one of the most essential places to be seen in the capital. The 1900 frescoes and the clever subdued lighting recreate a turn-of-the-century bistro atmosphere. Ordering a drink at the bar after 7pm is something of a feat. If you want to relax here's a hint: stand in front of a table and don't move until it becomes free. Jump on it and wait for the waitress; the service is quick. At the time of writing the Charbon was planning to triple its capacity with the opening of a concert hall and a mezzanine. Watch this space.

🍸 **Le Cithéa** (map B1, **87**): 114 rue Oberkampf 75011. ☎ 01-40-21-70-95. Metro: Parmentier. Open 10.30pm to 6am. This used to be an old theatre with unpredictable takings, adjoined by a struggling café. The whole thing has been taken over and the two rooms connected, and it has become one of the rare places where you can both see and listen to musicians without having to pay 100F or more. On evenings when there is live music (Wednesday to Saturday) entry is free, even if there is a security guard, and the drinks are reasonably priced (30F for half a pint of beer). There's an Afro-jazz-world-music atmosphere. Come early if you want to see the concert (10.30pm), because young music fans pack the place out. There's an annex just opposite, **L'Estaminet** (cold meats, such as salami, bacon, pâté and ham, and *cassoulet*, for around 80F). A glass wine of costs 12F; no charge for a glass of water. Last orders half past midnight. ☎ 01-43-57-34-29.

🍸 **Satellit Café** (map B2, **81**): 44 rue de la Folie-Méricourt 75011. ☎ 01-47-00-48-87. Metro: Parmentier or Oberkampf. Open Tuesday to Saturday 8pm to dawn (happy hour until 9pm). Closed Sunday and Monday. DJs mix up the rhythms, including funky salsa and jazz. About once a week there are world music concerts (Tuesday, Wednesday or Thursday 9.30pm; entry fee 50F) – maybe a Cajun group, a Slovak band, Armenian musicians, African percussion, or an Italian group singing *a cappella*, anything can happen.

🍸 **La Fabrique** (map B3, **96**): 53 rue du Faubourg-St-Antoine 75011. ☎ 01-43-07-67-07. Metro: Bastille or Ledru-Rollin. Open 11am to 2am. Jazz brunch Sunday from 1pm to 6pm. Happy hour Monday to Friday 5.30 to 8pm (except public holidays). Beers from 14F. Menu 48F at lunchtime. With a refined atmosphere, they brew their own beer here. Whether lager (brewed on the premises), bitter or light ale, they cater for all tastes. The cuisine is simple but high quality. Flambéed tarts, mini-roast beef, sausage by the metre – all accompanied by tasty organic bread.

🍸 **Le Blue Billard** (map B1, **88**): 111–113 rue St-Maur 75011. ☎ 01-43-55-87-21. Metro: Parmentier. Open daily 9am (11am Sunday) to 2am (4am last weekend of the month). Beers from 21F, cocktails 49F. Set meal 50F with a salad, a drink, coffee and an hour on the tables (billiards, pool or snooker). This former camera factory has become a meeting place for lovers of billiards from 7 to 77 years old. Two halls and a mezzanine occupy the space, with no less than five French billiards tables, seven pool tables and six snooker tables (65F to 70F per hour). Free games from noon to 2pm if you're eating at the restaurant which, quite frankly, is not the main attraction. Various games, including chess and backgammon.

🍸 **Le Robinet Mélangeur** (map C1, **85**): 123 boulevard de Ménilmontant 75011. ☎ 01-47-00-

63-68. Metro: Ménilmontant Open 11am (5pm at weekends) to 2am. Closed Saturday lunchtime and Sunday. À la carte only; budget for 60F to 80F without drinks. One of the craziest places in Paris! Yellow, green, red, orange – a cornucopia of sunny colours and friezes on the walls give this tiny restaurant bar a kindergarten-style friendly atmosphere. With the aid of the Blanche d'Abbaye and, especially, the Cévennes wine, you soon get caught up in the atmosphere and swear that you'll be back! Half pint of beer 12F; soups 35F. Afternoon snacks on Saturday and Sunday (25F for a home-made tart).

🍸 **L'Électron Libre** (map B1, **92**): 103 rue St-Maur 75011. ☎ 01-48-06-50-82. Metro: Parmentier. Open nightly 5pm to 2am. Cocktails 26F to 33F, half pint of beer and pastis 10F. There's an increase in price after 10pm. Welcome to the miniature world of brothers Guillaume and Étienne, where experimental music fits in nicely with video art twice a month at cocktail time. DJs from Thursday to Saturday from 10pm. The last real 'local bar' in the Oberkampf area, or so the regulars will tell you.

🍸 **Le Scherkhan** (map C1, **93**): 144 rue Oberkampf 75011. ☎ 01-43-57-29-34. Metro: Ménilmontant Open daily 5pm to 2am. Drinks 14F to 32F. This neighbour of the Café Charbon defines itself as a 'lounge punk' meeting place, where you can have a quiet drink with no hassle, while Sherkhan (Shere Khan), the life-size tiger from The *Jungle Book*, watches over you.

🍸 **L'Armagnac** (map C3, **97**): 104 rue de Charonne 75011. ☎ 01-43-71-49-43. Metro: Charonne. Open daily 7am (10.30am at weekends) to 2am. Closed 1 to 21 August. Drinks around 20F, 16F for half a pint of beer before 10pm. Following in the footsteps of the Café Charbon, here is a new retro place with old mouldings on the ceiling, bistro furniture, ageless decor, with food and drink on the blackboard. Hot and cold *tartines* (around 35F), dish of the day (52F), seven beers on draught, five wines, all sorts of music (Yves Montand, Serge Gainsbourg, and even customers' own CDs). Unpretentious. A warm corner for those shipwrecked at the Bastoche. Brunch at weekends until 3pm (96F).

NIGHTCLUBS

– **Le Balajo** (map B3, **89**): 9 rue de Lappe 75011. ☎ 01-47-00-07-87. Metro: Bastille. Open Wednesday 9pm to 3am (entry fee 80F), Thursday, Friday and Saturday 11pm to dawn, and Sunday 3pm to 7pm. Entry fee 100F with one drink, 60F in the morning. This establishment represents the most sumptuous example of the dance hall *musette*. Originally, *bals-musette* (the name was coined before 1860) were nothing but the small back rooms of bistros, where people from the Massif central used to enjoy their traditional Auvergne dances to the sound of the *cabrette*, a type of bagpipe. Later, as mentioned, the accordion proved more popular and gradually replaced the *cabrette*. Once accepted into the tradition, the accordion was responsible for generating a truly popular form of music known as the *musette*. Dance hall *musettes* first appeared in the 1920s.

Le Balajo was founded in 1936 by Jo France, hence the name 'Bal-à-Jo' (Jo's dance hall). It is a superb place, now one of the headquarters of exotic Paris. Some evenings you have to queue to get in.

– **La Chapelle des Lombards** (map B3, **90**): 19 rue de Lappe 75011. ☎ 01-43-57-24-24. Metro: Bastille. Open Thursday to Saturday and the night before holidays, 10.30pm to dawn. Entry fee and drink 100F on Thursday, 120F on Friday and at the weekend. Entry is free for women on Thursday before half-past midnight. Tropical music: Latin, African and West Indian. There's a highly charged atmosphere, and a strict door policy – the biker look isn't very popular.

– **La Casbah** (map C3, **91**): 18–20 rue de la Forge-Royale 75011. ☎ 01-43-71-04-39. Metro: Ledru-Rollin. Restaurant open Monday to Saturday, club (entry is free) Thursday to Saturday 11pm to dawn. Entry with a drink 100F. Cocktails 70F. Restaurant and bar open 8pm to 2am (4am at weekends). There are a number of set menus from 250F to 450F including drinks (except for the set menu at 250F); main courses at 100F to 150F. A magnificent bar club with Casablanca-style decor, hip clientele and exotic cocktails. But it's also a restaurant offering *pastillas*, *briwattes*, *tajines* and *vin gris* (very pale rosé wine) which you can check out while watching the suggestive swaying of the belly dancers. A guaranteed change of scene!

12TH ARRONDISSEMENT

OPÉRA-BASTILLE ● PLACE DE LA NATION ● THE NEW BERCY QUARTER ● THE BOIS DE VINCENNES

The 12th arrondissement has changed a good deal over the last few years: the former wine storehouses and warehouses now house the Musée des Arts forains (Museum of Fairground Arts), a cinema complex and a few restaurants, and shops are beginning to open in the area. All this is not forgetting the immense 133 square kilometres (50 square miles) of the Parc de Bercy, that hosts anything from football matches to concerts.

WHERE TO STAY

☆ CHEAP

Lux Hôtel Picpus (map C1, **1**): 74 boulevard de Picpus 75012. ☎ 01-43-43-08-46. Fax: 01-43-43-05-22. Metro: Picpus. Double room 260F to 320F and triple room 345F. A stone's throw from place de la Nation, so very practical. Entirely renovated with lots of nickel-chrome and well-equipped rooms. Satellite TV, hairdryer, mini-bar and safe in the larger rooms. It is on the boulevard but double glazed. The fine attic rooms on the 6th floor are available for four to five people (Nos. 637 and 638). There's a generous breakfast.

☆☆ MODERATE

Hôtel des Trois Gares (map A1, **4**): 1 rue Jules-César 75012. ☎ 01-43-43-01-70. Fax: 01-43-41-36-58. Metro: Gare-de-Lyon or Bastille. Double room with washbasin 250F; with shower, toilet, TV and direct telephone from 300F to 360F; with bathroom from 360F to 460F. Behind the smart façade hides a resolutely modern, two-star hotel. The rooms are functional, with refined decor. It is in a quiet street between the Gare de Lyon, Austerlitz and Bastille-Plaisance. A very friendly welcome.

Hôtel Marceau (map A1, **5**): 13 rue Jules-César 75012. ☎ 01-43-43-11-65. Fax: 01-43-41-67-70. Metro: Gare-de-Lyon or Bastille. Double room 370F and 390F with shower or bath and satellite TV. A hand-written page displayed in the reception hall, bought at auction, was written by General Marceau, who fought the Vendéens. The rooms are nicely decorated, some of them are retro, some old looking. There's real charm here, with painted wallpaper and an ancient lift.

Nouvel Hôtel (map C1, **6**): 24 avenue Bel-Air 75012. ☎ 01-43-43-01-81. Fax: 01-43-44-64-13. Metro: Nation. Single room 360F to 380F. Double room with shower 410F, with bath 445F. There are communicating rooms for families at 620F for three people and 690F for four people. Just down the road from the place de la Nation, which provides excellent connections to the main centres of interest in Paris, whether by Metro, bus or RER. The hotel is in a quiet avenue and has an attractive flowery façade and a pretty garden where you can have your breakfast or relax in peace. A charming place and excellent value for money.

☗ **Hôtel Saphir** (map B1, **7**): 35 rue de Cîteaux 75012. ☎ 01-43-07-77-28. Fax: 01-43-46-67-45. Metro: Faidherbe-Chaligny, Reuilly-Diderot or Gare-de-Lyon. Single room 395F. Double room with shower or bath, toilet, TV, mini-bar and direct telephone 470F. Triple room 565F and room for four 615F. Near the Faubourg St-Antoine, this two-star hotel is full of colour. Harmony exists between the pinks, blues, greens or beiges and all rooms are equipped with mod cons. Breakfast is served in a superb arched cellar.

☗ **Agate Hôtel** (map C1, **8**): 8 cours de Vincennes 75012. ☎ 01-43-45-13-53. Fax: 01-43-42-09-39. Metro: Nation or Picpus. Double room 350F or 390F (according to the time of year) with bath or shower, TV, direct telephone, radio and mini-bar. Near the Parc Vincennes, this is a well-run, welcoming little hotel. The decor and paintings are on the theme of . . . well agate, obviously! No problems with noise, most of them overlook the inside garden, and the others are soundproofed.

WHERE TO EAT

☆ BUDGET

✕ **Au Pays de Vannes** (map C2, **20**): 34 *bis* rue de Wattignies 75012. ☎ 01-43-07-87-42. Metro: Michel-Bizot. Open lunchtime only. Closed Sunday and public holidays, as well as in August. Set menus 60F, 75F and 110F. A local bar with a large Breton flag hanging on a wall. The first menu (including drinks) offers several dishes of the day including sauté of pork, roast guinea fowl with leeks, chicken with rice or breast of veal stuffed with braised celery heart. Main courses are surrounded by serious starters (egg mayonnaise, etc.) and desserts ('granny' style *crème caramel*). A good, simple meal, traditionally French and the best value for money in the 12th arrondissement. To start you off, you get a free aperitif. At Saturday lunchtime families come to gorge themselves on oysters straight from Normandy. And for early birds (or night owls) breakfast (23F) is served from 6.30am.

✕ **Le Gave de Pau, Chez Yvette** (map B1, **23**): 147 rue de Charenton 75012. ☎ 01-43-44-74-11. Metro: Reuilly-Diderot or Gare-de-Lyon. Open until 11pm (midnight on Friday and Saturday). Closed Sunday and public holidays, and also for three weeks in August and for eight days between Christmas and New Year. Set menus 70F at lunchtime, 80F in the evening. À la carte, budget for no more than 100F. One of the meeting places for Béarnais people in Paris (the owner is from Pau) and rugby teams from the Île-de-France. The men keep their strength up with the set menu, or *confit de canard* with garlic potatoes, or *magret aux pêches*. The tomato soup (with onions, spaghetti and meat-stock), served in a large bowl, will suit partygoers who need to soak up some of the booze.

✕ **Lolo et les Lauréats** (map B1, **24**): 68 *bis* rue de Reuilly (on the corner with rue Montgallet) 75012. ☎ 01-40-02-07-70. Metro: Montgallet. Non-stop service from 7am to 8pm. Closed Saturday and Sunday and public holidays. Set menu 59F served lunchtime only. À la carte, budget for 120F. A fashionable bistro near the place des Victoires, this place, with its old, long wooden counter, is very popular locally. The wines are sold by the glass (not too expensive) and include several which have won prizes at the *Concours agricole*. The cuisine is pleasant enough and does its best, and the sunny south-facing terrace invites you to relax.

✕ **L'Ogre de Barbarie** (map B1, **26**): 13 rue Claude-Tillier 75012.

☎ 01-43-70-57-92. Metro: Reuilly-Diderot. Closed Saturday lunchtime, Sunday and Monday plus a week at Easter, a week at Christmas, and three weeks in August. At lunchtime there's a set menu at 59F with starter-main course or main course-dessert. In the evening budget for 115F. The former owner of the restaurant Limonaire has set up shop in a discreet little street where the only liveliness comes from the Sonacotra hostel which houses African workers. Their presence explains why the owner organized a month of African storytellers, to the delight of the diners. He used the dinner-and-show formula (dinner 8.15pm, show from 10pm to 11pm, with a minimum charge of 30F). No set menu in the evening, but there are starters from 18F to 22F, main courses 60F and desserts from 18F to 25F. Try lasagne with mint, duck with wild blackberry, or sweet and sour spare-rib, three of the star dishes.

☆☆ MODERATE

✕ **L'Alchimiste** (map B1–2, **22**): 181 rue de Charenton 75012. ☎ 01-43-47-10-38. Metro: Montgallet. Last orders 10.30pm. Closed Sunday, Saturday lunchtime and Monday evening. Set menu 75F at lunchtime, à la carte budget for around 150F, excluding drinks. In a wine bar-style setting, enjoy salmon tartare, *œuf meurette*, sautéed beef with onions, *aiguillette* (rump steak). On the set menu (starter and main course or main course and dessert, served at lunchtime only), *andouillette* at 68F and veal kidneys sautéed with mustard à la carte in the evening prove that the chef knows his bistro cooking. There's a good selection of wines, a few well-chosen apéritifs and a handful of beers.

✕ **Ay! Chihuahua** (map A1, **30**): 36 place de la Bastille 75012. ☎ 01-43-43-79-79. Metro: Bastille. Open daily until 11.30pm. Closed Saturday and Sunday mornings. Set menu 145F served lunchtime and evening. À la carte, budget for around 130F. A wonderfully exuberant Mexican restaurant. In a huge dining room you can sample the traditional Mexican menu (not Tex-Mex) on which *guacamole*, *tacos*, *fajitas* and other *enchiladas* are accompanied by tequila (a choice of 16 from 25F to 50F) and the famous Corona beer. Children's menu at 59F.

✕ **À la Biche au Bois** (map A1, **31**): 45 avenue Ledru-Rollin (corner with the rue de Lyon) 75012. ☎ 01-43-43-34-38. Metro: Gare-de-Lyon. Open until 10pm. Closed Saturday and Sunday, plus mid-July to mid-

Where to stay
- **1** Lux Hôtel Picpus
- **4** Hôtel des Trois Gares
- **5** Hôtel Marceau
- **6** Nouvel Hôtel
- **7** Hôtel Saphir
- **8** Agate Hôtel

✕ **Where to eat**
- **20** Au Pays de Vannes
- **22** L'Alchimiste
- **23** Le Gave de Pau, Chez Yvette
- **24** Lolo et les Lauréats
- **25** Si Seםor
- **26** L'Ogre de Barbarie
- **27** Swann et Vincent
- **28** L'Auberge Aveyronnaise
- **29** Le Santa Luzia
- **30** Ay! Chihuahua
- **31** À la Biche au Bois
- **32** L'Ébauchoir
- **33** Cappadoce
- **35** Les Broches à l'Ancienne
- **36** Les Bombis
- **37** Les Zygomates
- **38** La Sologne
- **39** Square Trousseau
- **40** L'Oulette
- **41** Le Janissaine

Where to go for a drink
- **52** La Liberté
- **53** China Club
- **54** Viaduc Café

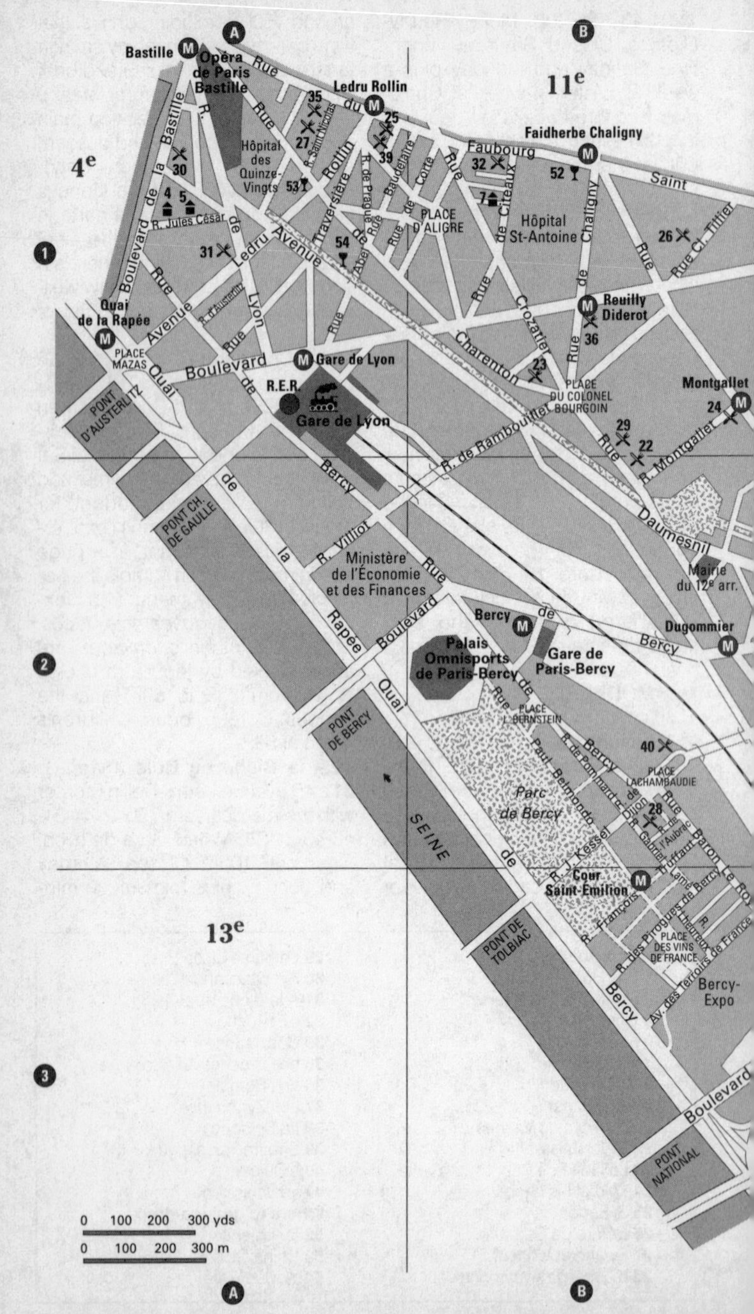

A
B
1
2
3
11e
4e
13e
Bastille
Opéra de Paris Bastille
Ledru Rollin
Faidherbe Chaligny
Hôpital des Quinze-Vingts
Hôpital St-Antoine
PLACE D'ALIGRE
R. Jules César
Quai de la Rapée
PLACE MAZAS
PONT D'AUSTERLITZ
PONT CH. DE GAULLE
Boulevard de la Bastille
Rue de Lyon
Avenue Ledru Rollin
Rue du Faubourg Saint
Rue Traversière
Rue de Charenton
Rue Crozatier
Rue de Cîteaux
Rue de Chaligny
Rue de Prague
Rue Cl. Tillier
Reuilly Diderot
Gare de Lyon
R.E.R.
Boulevard Diderot
PLACE DU COLONEL BOURGOIN
Montgallet
R. Montgallet
R. de Rambouillet
Rue Daumesnil
Mairie du 12e arr.
Dugommier
Rue de Bercy
R. Villiot
Ministère de l'Économie et des Finances
Quai de la Rapée
Boulevard de Bercy
Bercy
Gare de Paris-Bercy
Palais Omnisports de Paris-Bercy
PONT DE BERCY
Quai de Bercy
SEINE
PLACE L. BERNSTEIN
Rue Paul Belmondo
Parc de Bercy
PLACE LACHAMBAUDIE
R. de Pommard
R. de Dijon
Rue Baron Le Roy
R. J. Kessel
Cour Saint-Emilion
R. François Truffaut
R. des Pirogues de Bercy
PLACE DES VINS DE FRANCE
Av. des Terroirs de France
Bercy-Expo
PONT DE TOLBIAC
PONT NATIONAL
Boulevard
4 5 7 22 23 24 25 26 27 28 29 30 31 32 35 36 39 40 52 53 54
0 100 200 300 yds
0 100 200 300 m

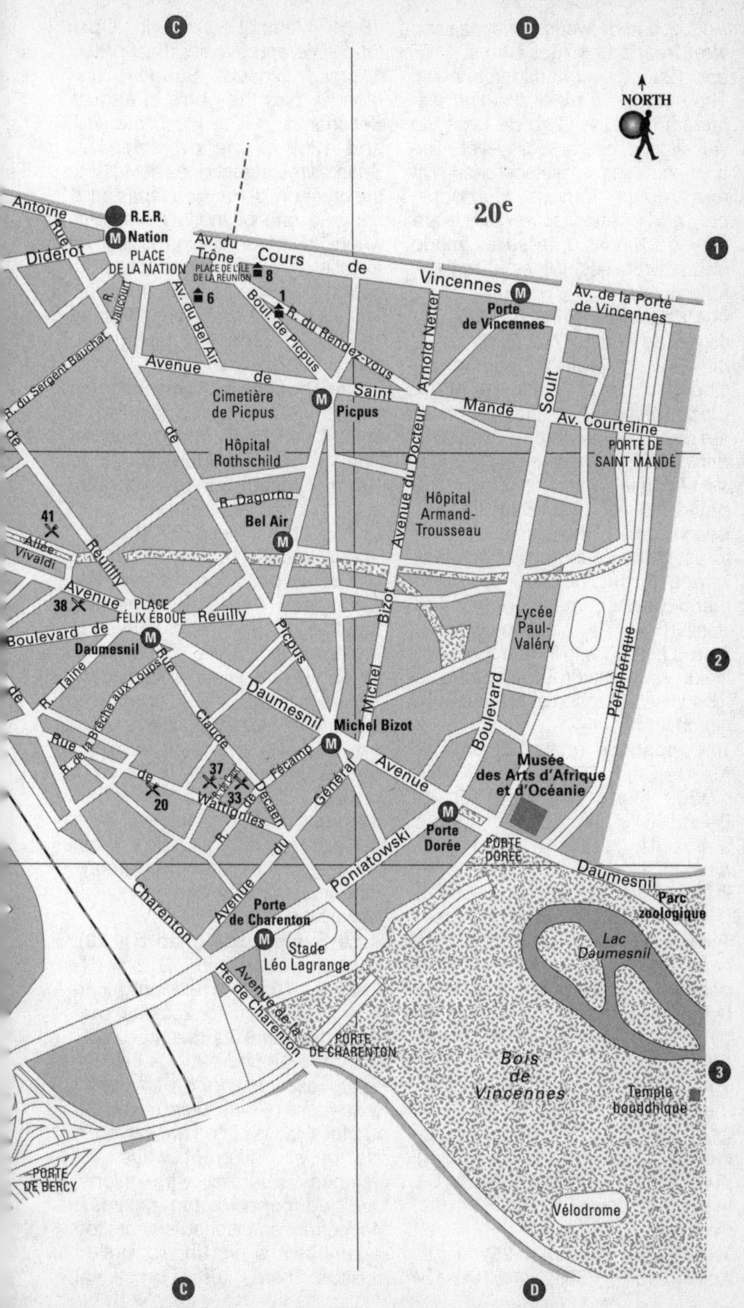

C
D
NORTH
20e
1
2
3
R.E.R.
Nation
PLACE DE LA NATION
PLACE DE L'ILE DE LA RÉUNION
Antoine
Rue
Diderot
Av. du Trône
Cours de Vincennes
Porte de Vincennes
Av. de la Porte de Vincennes
Boul. de Picpus
R. du Rendez-Vous
Arnold Netter
Av. du Bel Air
R. Jaucourt
R. du Sergent Bauchat
Avenue de Saint Mandé
Cimetière de Picpus
Picpus
Soult
Av. Courteline
PORTE DE SAINT MANDÉ
Hôpital Rothschild
R. Dagorno
Bel Air
Hôpital Armand-Trousseau
Avenue du Docteur
Allée Vivaldi
Reuilly
Avenue
PLACE FÉLIX ÉBOUÉ
Reuilly
Boulevard de
Daumesnil
Lycée Paul-Valéry
Périphérique
R. Taine
Rue de la Brèche aux Loups
Rue Claude Decaen
Picpus
Daumesnil
Michel Bizot
Michel Bizot
Boulevard
R. de la Brèche
Rue de Wattignies
Fécamp
Général
Avenue
Musée des Arts d'Afrique et d'Océanie
Porte Dorée
PORTE DORÉE
Poniatowski
Daumesnil
Parc zoologique
Charenton
Avenue du
Porte de Charenton
Stade Léo Lagrange
Lac Daumesnil
Avenue de la Pte de Charenton
PORTE DE CHARENTON
Bois de Vincennes
Temple bouddhique
PORTE DE BERCY
Vélodrome
41
38
37
33
20
1
6
8

August and between Christmas and New Year's Day. Set menus 115F and 128F. It's a good idea to book. The set menus make this fine restaurant near the Gare de Lyon the salvation of many a traveller. The main courses – fillet of beef with mushrooms, Landes *tournedos*, *coq au vin en cocotte noire* – are very traditional. *Pâtisseries* made on the premises. Wines at reasonable prices.

✂ **L'Ébauchoir** (map B1, **32**): 43–45 rue de Cîteaux 75012. ☎ 01-43-42-49-31. Metro: Faidherbe-Chaligny. Open until 10.30pm. Closed Sunday. At lunchtime there are set menus at 68F, including drinks, 85F in the evening. Budget for 170F à la carte. This bistro in the backyard of the Bastille has become one of the essential places to eat in the Faubourg. Its success is due to the excellent set lunch menu (starter, main course and dessert). On the blackboard menu there's herring with fried potatoes or leeks with vinaigrette, *bœuf à la lyonnaise*, fricassée of chicken with lemon, etc.

✂ **Cappadoce** (map C2, **33**): 12 rue de Capri 75012. ☎ 01-43-46-17-20. Metro: Michel-Bizot or Daumesnil. Open noon to 2.30pm and 7pm to 11.30pm. Closed Saturday lunchtime and Sunday and for the last three weeks of August. Set menus 70F to 125F. Polite, discreet Turkish hospitality, and good food here. The *roulé au fromage* (puff pastry filled with cheese) and the aubergine caviar have a very Oriental style; the *pides* (Turkish pizza), grilled meat or kebabs are a treat. There are three well thought-out set menus: vegetarian, light and gourmet. The home-made desserts, including an amazing pumpkin with syrup, are not to be missed. Essential to book in the evenings.

✂ **Si Señor** (map A1, **25**): 9 rue Antoine-Vollon 75012. ☎ 01-43-47-18-01. Metro: Ledru-Rollin. Open lunchtime and evening (last orders 11pm). Closed Sunday and Monday plus the whole of August. Set menus 72F at lunchtime, 90F and 120F in the evening. This Spanish restaurant does not fall into the category of Parisian *tapas* bars, nor is it one of those restaurants where the poor cuisine is just an excuse to drink. Instead, here the cooking is sincere and delicious. There's *tortilla española*, lightly fried squid and Argentine steak seasoned with spicy sauce.

✂ **Les Broches à l'Ancienne** (map A1, **35**): 21 rue St-Nicolas 75012. ☎ 01-43-43-26-16. Metro: Bastille. Open noon to 2.30pm and 8 to 10pm. Closed Sunday, Monday evening and for three weeks around 15 August. Set menu 78F at lunchtime, à la carte budget for around 140F. Half price for children. You can watch free-range chicken, shoulder of pork and sausages turning on their spits . . . licked by the flame of a wide, ultra-modern roasting spit. This spectacle appears to be appreciated by the regulars, who get stuck in to the food, accompanied by a choice of endives, rice or *pommes en lamelles* (sautéed potatoes). As a starter, try dry sausage from Corrèze, green salad or egg mayonnaise. It's a good idea not to wear your best clothes!

✂ **Le Santa Luzia** (map B1, **29**): 179 rue de Charenton 75012. ☎ 01-43-43-47-70. Metro: Montgallet. Open daily 7am to 2am all year round. Set meal 50F, set menu 60F, à la carte around 120F. A French-Portuguese restaurant with mainly Portuguese cuisine, quite rare in the quarter. Dishes of cod are served in five or six different ways; for instance *Lagareiro*, with onions, fried red peppers and potatoes. Mediterranean-inspired starters too – *gambas à la provençale*, stuffed mussels. There is also a simple set menu (egg mayonnaise, steak, dessert and a 25cl bottle of wine or Vittel water included), served daily, which has nothing Portuguese about it but which is popular with the regulars.

✕ **Swann et Vincent** (map A1, **27**): 7 rue St-Nicolas 75012. ☎ 01-43-43-49-40. Metro: Ledru-Rollin. Open daily noon to 2.45pm and 7.30pm to quarter past midnight. Set lunch menu 85F, à la carte around 140F. Excellent *antipasti, charcuterie,* house *gnocchetti, ravioli de ricotta, al pesto* and *all'arrabbiata* sauces (with pepper) poured *à point* onto pasta *al dente.* And the *panna cotta* must be tasted. You may have guessed that this is an Italian restaurant . . . enjoy the retro bistro decor and great big tables, which are almost always full.

✕ **Les Bombis** (map B1, **36**): 22 rue de Chaligny 75012. ☎ 01-43-45-36-32. Metro: Reuilly-Diderot. Closed Sunday and Monday lunchtime. Set menu 75F at lunchtime, drinks included. Budget for at least 150F à la carte in the evening. The Bombis are the inhabitants of Chenove, a little village at the start of the 'wine route', just outside Dijon, which is where the two brothers who started this bistro are from. The one in the kitchen goes for freshness and flavours from France and elsewhere, offering, for instance, skate terrine with melting peppers, and succulent spare ribs. The other, behind the bar, will choose a wine for you from his selection, such as the red Burgundy '96 or Vinsobres '97, both at reasonable prices.

✕ **Le Janissaire** (map C2, **41**): 22–24 allée Vivaldi 75012. ☎ 01-43-40-37-37. Metro: Daumesnil-Montgallet. Closed Monday. Hot and cold *mezze* 24F to 40F, main courses 48F to 74F. Every day, at lunchtime and evening, there's a good value *menu dégustation* at 130F. Authentic Turkish cooking. The decor is resolutely modern with works by contemporary Turkish painters and old tapestries on the walls. The ceiling is decorated with stained glass windows reproducing traditional *kilim* motifs. In the time it takes to drink a *raki* you can discover the richness and variety of the menu. For a starter, there are around 15 cold *mezze* dishes including aubergine caviar, stuffed vine leaves, *œufs de cabillaud*, spiced tomato purée. Go for the assortment (46F), which provides a taste of most of them. Among the hot *mezze* are the inevitable classics – *bôreks* (puff-pastry filled with cheese) and *imam bayildi* (stuffed aubergine). For main courses there are grills, and 30 different dishes, such as *tandir* (baked shoulder of lamb) and *islim* (knuckle of lamb with aubergines and tomatoes). There's a fine list of Turkish wines (70F to 98F). Pleasant modern decor. Booking is recommended in the evening.

☆☆☆ CHIC

✕ **L'Oulette** (map B2, **40**): 15 place de Lachambaudie 75012. ☎ 01-40-02-02-12. Metro: Dugommier or Bercy. Bus Nos. 24 or 62. Service noon to 2.15pm and 8pm to 10.15pm. Closed Saturday lunchtime and Sunday. Set menu 165F. À la carte, the bill will come to around 300F. The decor, which is very New York, filled with green plants, serves as a backdrop for high-class cuisine. The gourmet Paris smart set come here for their fun and to enjoy modern versions of the delicate flavours of the southwest. Try *velouté de potimarron* with cardamom, *onglet* (prime cut) of veal with gentian and grilled chestnuts and, for dessert, *moelleux* with chocolate meringue on the 'seasonal menu' at 250F, including wine. To keep the bill under control, there is a 'market' menu served lunchtime and evening, which very good value. There is a fine selection of wines from the southwest.

✂ **Square Trousseau** (map A1, **39**): 1 rue Antoine-Vollon 75012. ☎ 01-43-43-06-00. Metro: Ledru-Rollin. Open daily until 11.30pm. Set menu 100F at lunchtime and 135F in the evening. À la carte around 160F, excluding drinks. Red velvet and lace curtains hide you away at this 1900 bistro. There is a superb old zinc bar, mosaic tiling, red imitation leather wall seats and moulded ceilings. The set menu and main courses are displayed on large blackboards to an elegant, relaxed clientele. The menu changes every month, according to the market and the seasons. The wine list, which is well designed, has some unusual bottles. A very Parisian place, where it is not rare to see a famous face. There's a terrace in summer.

✂ **La Sologne** (map C2, **38**): 164 avenue Daumesnil 75012. ☎ 01-43-07-68-97. Metro: Daumesnil. Open until 10.30pm (11.30pm Saturday). Closed Saturday lunchtime and Sunday. Menu 165F. There are two other set menus at 215F and 230F. À la carte, budget for 200F. This restaurant is the realm of a chef trained in the best kitchens in France. His menu, with its wide range, makes for interesting reading. Try rabbit terrine flavoured with rosemary, cheek of braised pork casserole with crunchy vegetables, and, for dessert, pear poached in sweet spices, caramelized with honey, and marinated strawberry soup with orange. Those with big appetites may find the portions a bit small. There's a fine wine list at prices which could be a bit lower and more in keeping with the cost of the menu (only five for less than 130F, a factor which has a major influence on the cost of a meal).

✂ **L'Auberge Aveyronnaise** (map B2, 28): 40 rue Gabriel-Lamé 75012. ☎ 01-43-40-12-24. Metro: Bercy. Near the rue de l'Aubrac. Open daily except Sunday evening, closed in August. Set meal 85F at lunchtime, à la carte budget for 150F, without drinks. A country-like establishment. Treat yourself to *aligot de l'Aubrac* and ham on the bone cooked *au foin des monts d'Aubrac*. There's a good set meal with starter plus main course or main course plus dessert. On the menu there's cured ham, sautéed cod with *rouergate* or lamb with parsley and garlic garnish, *charcuterie* and *Fourme* (mild blue cheese) from Laguiole or custard tart *à la louche*. À la carte, Roquefort and Cabecou from the Aveyron.

✂ **Les Zygomates** (map C2, 37): 7 rue de Capri 75012. ☎ 01-40-19-93-04. Metro: Michel-Bizot or Daumesnil. Service noon to 2pm and 7.45pm to 10.15pm. Closed Saturday lunchtime and Sunday, as well as in August. Set menus 80F served at lunchtime only, and 130F. Nothing has changed much in this early 20th-century *charcuterie. The trompe-l'œil* decor, the varnished wood, the marble and the hunt scenes are all very convincing. But the best thing, without doubt, is the very inexpensive cuisine. Goat *cannelloni* and lamb's lettuce salad, pig's tail stuffed with morels, Brie de Meaux and milk chocolate rum baba and verbena ice-cream makes this place a real favourite. It's best to book.

AROUND THE OPÉRA-BASTILLE

★ The **Opéra-Bastille:** 120 rue de Lyon 75012. Metro: Bastille. ☎ 01-40-01-17-89. Reservations: ☎ 08-36-69-78-68 (2.23 F/min.) Seats 50F to 420F for ballet and 60F to 670F for opera. (*For further information see* 'Opéra Garnier' *in the* '9th arrondissement'.)

This great big wedding cake of a building is worth a short historical note. Although the idea of an opera house for the people was not a new one (an official report in 1976 stated: 'The lyric art finds, in the Palais-Garnier, everything it needs to reach as few people as possible while spending as much money as possible'), it was really President Mitterrand's idea and he had the willpower to see it through. He liked the location of the Bastille, on the edge of a working-class quarter, providing a fusion of art and industry. But despite the best intentions, it's not really a democratic place at all.

Six plans were selected. Everyone was expecting that the winner would be the American, Richard Meier, an internationally famous architect, but instead it was the almost unknown Canadian, Carlos Ott, whose name came out of the hat. Many people thought his plan was too modest and not very imaginative, but it was popular with those who feared something too daring. The saga of the construction had both suspense and farce and the entire project was almost stopped because of changes in the political balance of power in 1986.

The story of its creation became rather like a drawn-out soap opera. From 1985 there were resignations and sackings, including the director of the Multi-Purpose Hall, the director of the Bastille project, the chairman and director of the Opera House planning association, the director of the Opera Houses of Paris and the technical director of the Opéra-Bastille. The nomination of Pierre Bergé, chairman and managing director of Yves St-Laurent, as the head of the Opera House after the left wing victory in 1988, in turn generated tensions when, inevitably, all the decisions taken by the previous government were brought into question. In particular, the employment conditions and the 'breadline' salary to be paid to the conductor, Daniel Barenboïm, were renegotiated. A crisis broke out which saw the resignation of the latter and others, including the two directors of the opening show. On the eve of the official inauguration on 14 July 1989 the Opera House finally acquired a head in the person of Korean, Myung Whun Chung. One of the first great works to be put on was Berlioz's *Les Troyens*.

DID YOU KNOW?

The main hall has 2,700 seats and complex machinery (the stage has a number of turntables to allow different shows to be on at the same time), a rehearsal stage, a library, disco, and a video library.

The 17th-century inn Les Grandes Marches, next door, had to be demolished to allow the work to take place and was rebuilt as a restaurant in the same style.

★ In the **rue de Charenton**, near the opera house, stands the famous **hôpital des Quinze-Vingts**, created by St Louis in 1260 to accommodate crusaders who had had their eyes put out in the Holy Land. It could house no more than 300 of them (at the time the term used was '*quinze-vingts*' which, literally, means fifteen-twenties, i.e. 300) and they were organized in the style of a religious congregation. The ophthalmological clinic dates from the end of the 19th century.

★ The **marché d'Aligre**: place d'Aligre 75012. Metro: Ledru-Rollin. 'A market which is not easy to find, but, once you have found it, you'll be back' – that's what all the bargain hunters say about the marché d'Aligre. It was originally the priory of the nearby monastery, who authorized the clothes merchants and the riverside residents to sell to the needy, on the condition that they should sell things very cheaply. Other nobles made similar gestures, so that even the leftovers from feasts at the Louvre ended up in the square each morning. The spirit of the place is still the same, but it's now the second-hand clothes trade which heads the field.

The market takes place every morning except Monday, but Saturday and Sunday are the most interesting days. It's one of the most lively markets in Paris. It's also one of the cheapest. At lunchtime, between place Crozatier and rue Crozatier, it's sheer madness. Some people cross Paris to do their shopping here. In spring, the square looks like a market in Provence or Africa. At the end of the morning, prices fall, given the go-ahead by a great bell. The cafés around the square are usually packed out, but none of them is as good as Le Baron Rouge.

If you're looking for a flea market, stalls can be found at Montreuil or Vanves at the weekend. Good for a rummage, you can sometimes find a real bargain.

If you have time, go and take a look at one of the last wash-houses in Paris, at 9 rue de Cotte. If it weren't for its brick chimney, you could take it for a village hall.

★ The **Coulée Verte** (or *Promenade plantée,* also nicknamed '*viaduc des Arts*' or Viaduct of Arts): open from 8am Monday to Friday; 9am Saturday, Sunday and public holidays. Closes at sundown. There are lots of entrances (about one every 250m/800ft) to this pedestrian walkway. It was developed on the line of a 1.5km (1 mile) stretch of the former Bastille-St-Maur railway line. It stretches right across the 12th arrondissement from the Gare de Lyon (avenue Daumesnil-boulevard Diderot crossroads) as far as the boulevard Périphérique (the ring road which surrounds the Paris Metropolitan area) and between the Porte de Vincennes and the Porte Dorée. The architect Patrick Berger restored the entire stretch. It was bought by the Paris local authority from SNCF (the French national railway company) in 1986. There are two distinct parts: the axis following the avenue Daumesnil, perched on the former viaduct, now transformed into a garden, and the Vivaldi axis (which is for both cyclists and pedestrians), at street level and through a cutting. Along the walk, which is pleasantly lined by bushes, cherry trees and flowerbeds, there are three or four spacious gardens, in particular the Pelouse de Reuilly, where you can stretch out and sunbathe when the weather is fine. Below your feet, housed in the arches along the viaduct, are shops and art galleries, with elegant window displays, and vast bays. You'll find sculptors, stringed instrument makers, cabinetmakers and costumiers . . . . Down in the cutting, 7m (23ft) below everything else, it's all greenery and birds. To finish your walk take the quiet rue du Sahel – which heads towards the noisy *Périphérique*. If you continued, you would reach the Bois de Vincennes.

★ The **Gare de Lyon and Le Train Bleu**: boulevard Diderot 75012. ☎ 01-43-43-09-06 and 01-44-75-76-76. Fax: 01-43-43-97-96. Metro: Gare-de-Lyon. In the 19th-century critics were impressed by the high baroque belfry of the Gare de Lyon. It looks pretty small nowadays, surrounded as it is by high-rise buildings.

With its sumptuous restaurant, Le Train Bleu, the station is worthy of a visit. It was the French President Émile Loubet who inaugurated this restaurant at the end of the 19th century. It's a masterpiece of kitsch and has been listed as an Historic Monument. Coco Chanel, Jean Cocteau, Sarah Bernhardt, Colette, Salvador Dalí, Jean Gabin and many others loved this place. Luc Besson used it as a setting for his film *Nikita*. The restaurant is expensive, but you can always go for the set menu at 250F (lunchtime and evening, wine included), or à la carte for 350F. Open daily. Last orders 11pm. You could also just make do with a cup of tea or a hot chocolate on the Chesterfields in the bar. A perfect place to read the papers or a novel, while you're waiting for a train . . . .

AROUND PLACE DE LA NATION

★ The **place de la Nation**: formerly known as the place du Trône from 1660 to 1880, this is where Louis XIV made his triumphal entrance into Paris. It was rechristened place du Trône-Renversé (meaning the overturned throne) during the Revolution. The guillotine was set up here following complaints from inhabitants of the rue St-Honoré who said that the open carts which carried the condemned were always passing beneath their windows. The guillotine (nicknamed the 'Widow') took just over 1,000 victims in 13 months at place de la Concorde, but at place du Trône-Renversé there were 1,300 executions in 43 days!

★ The **cimetière de Picpus**: 35 rue de Picpus 75012. Metro: Picpus. In winter, open 2 to 4pm daily except Sunday and Monday; guided tour 2.30pm. In summer, open 2pm to 6pm daily except Monday and in August; guided tours 2.30 and 4pm. A cemetery which few Parisians know about, this is where the 1,306 people guillotined in the place de la Nation, including the poet André Chénier, were laid to rest in mass graves. At one end, closed off by a grill, is an enclosure containing the two main mass graves. On the left is a walled-up gate through which the victims passed (you can still see its wooden lintel). The gate is not original (it was changed in 1994) but the lintel is. On 17 June 1794 the executioner, Sanson, had a particularly busy day: he executed 54 people in 24 minutes. La Fayette is also buried here, beneath a very simple tombstone decorated with an American flag. It flew even during the four years of the German occupation.

Since the beginning of the 19th century Picpus has been the cemetery used by descendants of those who were guillotined. From time to time you meet the white figures of the nuns from the Adoration Perpétuelle du Sacré-Cœur. You may even see bees coming out of one of the many beehives all around (there are 16 in all!).

THE NEW BERCY QUARTER

This section covers the whole of the area between Gare de Lyon and the porte de Bercy, the main centres of which are the Ministry of Finance and the parc de Bercy.

★ The **palais Omnisports de Paris-Bercy**: (POPB) 8 boulevard de Bercy 75012. ☎ 01-40-02-60-60. Fax: 01-43-42-09-50. Website: www.bercy.com and www.ticketnet.fr. Metro: Bercy; RER: Gare-de-Lyon (line A). This is the bizarre centre covered with turf and crowned with a blue metallic structure which you can see from a distance. It represents the first section of the conversion work for the transformation of the former wine warehouses into the Parc de Bercy. The POPB was designed to be able to play host to all sorts of events, from showbusiness to sports, and indeed there's something for everyone here, from track cycling to grand opera, via motorcycling, horse-riding, ice-hockey, concerts, go-karting, windsurfing and tennis. No fewer than 45 sporting disciplines, eight operas and over 120 shows have taken place here since 1984. When you have finished being amazed by the turf growing at 45° (not easy to mow!), you can stroll among the warehouses of Bercy.

★ **Le ministère des Finances**: opposite the Omnisports sports centre 75012. Metro: Bercy. In spite of the deliberately monumental choice of building, this construction probably won't cause the same level of controversy as the Pompidou Centre or the Louvre Pyramid. This is because the site is less important from a historical point of view, and the architecture is not as outlandish, even showing an attempt at integration into the environment. It's a product of the 14 years François Mitterrand was in power. In 1981 he said: 'We have to give the Louvre back to the history of France', and announced the transfer of the Finance Ministry which had occupied one of its wings for 110 years.

At Bercy there were two projects drawn up by different architects. During its construction, the most important of them, Paul Chemetov and Borja Huidabro's *'immeuble-pont'* (literally 'bridge building') was the largest office building-site in Europe. Here are a few figures: 225,000m (740,000ft) of flooring, 1,300 foundation piles, 45,000m (148,000ft) of glazed surfaces, 5,000 tons of metal framework. Each of these 'bridges' or porticoes weigh as much as the Eiffel Tower! There is an avenue lined with trees and works of art running alongside it.

The Ministry's other important architectural complex is in rue de Bercy, beside the Gare de Lyon. The work of architects Louis Arretche and Roman Karasinsky, it is a glass complex whose façade made up of numerous projections and recesses breaks up any impression of uniformity.

The flood of people and traffic inevitably caused by the daily arrival of 6–7,000 finance employees meant that the Pont de Bercy would have had to double its capacity, so the new Pont Charles-de-Gaulle between the Pont de Bercy and the Pont d'Austerlitz was opened in 1996.

★ **The former warehouses of Bercy**: for centuries this area (to the east of the Omnisports sports centre and stretching either side of the rue de Dijon) was dominated by the wine trade. Burgundy wine came downriver by barge via the Seine. But this one time bustling stretch of land has now been turned into a 13ha (32 acre) park christened the Jardin de la Mémoire (Garden of Memory) (*see below*). 'The vineyards of Bercy'). Dotted alongside the garden are houses and offices. Note the amazing façade of the American Center, by Frank Gehry. A few warehouses and wine storehouses, in particular the Cour St-Émilion and the Pavillons Lheureux, have been preserved and renovated, as examples of urban industrial architecture. They now house the Musée des Arts forains (*see below*), a wine bar and restaurants, and hold international exhibitions connected with food and wine.

The future Ministry of Agriculture and a business and conference centre is scheduled to be built alongside.

★ **The vineyards of Bercy**: it takes a little over an hour, excluding stops, to walk the 3.5km (2 miles) from the Porte-de-Bercy metro station to the Porte-Dorée Metro station. The area is still known locally as *les vignobles* (the vineyards) *de Bercy* due to its historic involvement with the wine trade.

The **parc de Bercy**, which opened in 1994 was developed in the former Bercy wine warehouses, and intended to be a Garden of Memory. The trees are hundreds of years old. Developed in several stages and finally completed in 1997, the park, measuring more than 13ha (32 acres), became one of the largest parks developed in the city since Haussmann's day. Nine themed gardens dotted with arbours and vines keep to the theme of French-style gardens. An 8m (26ft) high terrace, lined with lime trees, separates the park from the voie Georges-Pompidou. Beautiful trees surround the ornamental lake. Follow the paved path marked by polished granite. Beyond the oak trees you reach large lawns which still bear the scars of construction work.

A house devoted to gardening has been set up in a late 18th-century building which used to house the department of taxes on wines and spirits. This space, surrounded by flowerbeds, is a treasure trove of gardening secrets. Entry is free. There are small exhibition halls on the theme of gardening, plus a library. Information: ☎ 01-53-46-19-19, 41 rue Paul-Belmondo 75012; or ☎ 01-43-28-47-63.

When you leave the park, at the corner of rue Paul-Belmondo, go back up the rue de Dijon towards place Lachambaudie and the church of Notre-Dame-de-Bercy. Before you go under the railway tracks, look for a mark 1m (3ft) up on the span of the bridge commemorating the flooding of the Seine in 1910. Beyond the railway, the rue de Wattignies, the rue de la Brèche-aux-Loups and the rue des Meuniers follow old country lanes. Note the old boundary marks and the mud-scrapers (67 rue des Meuniers). A foot-bridge goes across the disused Petite Ceinture and ends at the Porte de Charenton. An extra 20-minute walk will allow you to take a look at the Bois de Vincennes, leaving from the nearby Porte de Reuilly. The ancient Foire du Trône (funfair) is held in April on the field beside the former fortifications of Paris. The Route de la Croix-Rouge takes you to Lac Daumesnil from where red markers lead you to the Porte-Dorée Metro station on the left.

★ The **musée des Arts forains (Museum of Fairground Arts)**: 53 avenue des Terroirs-de-France 75012. ☎ 01-43-40-16-22. Fax: 01-43-40-16-89. Metro: Cour-St-Émilion. Sometimes open on a one-off basis for individuals (check in advance), otherwise there are organized tours, by appointment only, for groups of at least 15 people. Prices: 75F per adult and 25F per child.

This museum, in the former wine warehouses, has the perfect setting for its rather bizarre subject matter. Steep yourself in the magic of merry-go-rounds, shops and attractions, sometimes on a grand scale, always very elaborate, and brightly lit. These colossal travelling festivals sometimes included up to 1,000 different professions, and you can get a taste of the marvellous atmosphere here. Japanese billiards, trick cycling, German swing-boats named *Fritz* and *Elke*, coconut shies, shooting galleries – it's all here. The exhibits showing various terrifying anatomical phenomena are not for those with a weak disposition: syphilis in close-up, a decapitated head and a scene showing a Caesarean birth, which is strikingly realistic!

Since 1999, two new sections have been created, maintaining the same festive atmosphere and superb decoration that has been used throughout. The *Salons de Musique* encompass a range of old mechanical instruments and waxwork figures of well-known artistic characters from the 1900s, whilst the *Salons Vénitiens* pay homage to the capital of carnival and street artists.

★ The **foire du Trône**: one of the oldest fairs in Paris is held in April-May in the fields at Reuilly. Metro: Porte-de-Charenton. All the old favourites are there – the ghost train, candy floss and scary rides. Aspirant Mike Tysons bash away at one of those machines which test your strength, girls scream as they hang suspended in mid-air, serenaded by old songs played at full blast, kids are dwarfed by monstrous cuddly toys. It's a great big party in a typically Parisian style, which will soon empty your wallet if you're not careful!

THE BOIS DE VINCENNES

The Bois de Vincennes offers the longest walks in Paris. Metro: Château-de-Vincennes, Porte-Dorée or Porte-de-Charenton. In 1926 the politicians decided to annexe the 1,000ha (250 acres) and the four lakes of the Bois de Vincennes to the 12th arrondissement, making it a part of Paris. And yet to get there you have to go to Vincennes, which is not strictly speaking in Paris. The air is clean and apparently encourages you to make wise decisions – or that's what St Louis thought, as he used to dispense justice here. There are also some fine walks, boating lakes and lawns where you can have a picnic. Until the violent storms which hit France in December 1999 there were more than 180,000 trees providing shade from the sun. As in the Bois de Boulogne, oak is the dominant species. Some 70,000 trees fell during the storms or were damaged to such an extent that they had to be cut down. The landscape, of course, has changed and it will take roughly three years to clear up the whole area. In the meantime the majority of the Bois de Vincennes is now open to visitors. At the Lac Daumesnil you can hire bikes at weekends, public holidays and during the school holidays. It gets crowded on Sundays in summer

It's best to take a map with you. Unless you've simply gone for a boating trip on one of the two lakes (Daumesnil or St-Mandé), you can easily get lost – there are over 100km (62 miles) of marked paths. Get a nature trails map from a town hall or the Maison Paris-Nature in the Floral Park (☎ 01-43-28-

47-63). A short walk (7km/4 miles, 2 hours if you don't stop) takes you round the Floral Park and the Lac des Minimes from the Château-de-Vincennes Metro station. You could combine this with a visit to the Floral Park.

Leave from the Château-de-Vincennes Metro station, Fort-Neuf exit, and head towards the Parc floral (Floral Park) de Vincennes. Opposite the Esplanade St-Louis at Vincennes Castle, on the eastern side, there's a blue-and-yellow signposting system which you follow south to reach the Grande Allée Royale, which joins the two parts of the Bois de Vincennes. Towards the east the Petit Circuit meets the panorama of the Route de la Faluère. This part of the Bois de Vincennes has finally brought to fruition some of the old forestry projects of the 18th century. The rosebushes on the southern roundabout of the allée Royale smell gorgeous. Follow the signposts of the Petit Circuit which cuts across the Route de la Belle-Étoile. Thick undergrowth allows you to cross the Route Dauphine and the Route de Bourbon as far as the Plaine St-Hubert. In these large, open, grassy spaces, it's almost like being in the countryside – ideal for a relaxing picnic. On the main road, the avenue du Tremblay, bus 112 takes tired walkers to the château de Vincennes, but note that there aren't many buses on this route. Just like the yellow-and-red circuit of the Grand Circuit du Bois de Vincennes, the Petit Circuit continues along the Route Circulaire. It follows the red-and-white markers of the GR14 (Grand Randonnée 'official' footpath) and a small stream leading to an artificial rockery and the waterfall at the Lac des Minimes. Go a bit further along the banks of the lake to reach the Sentier des Moines (Monks' Path). These monks came from Limousin and were the founders of this 12th-century monastic domain. Return by crossing the Route Circulaire and the avenue du Tremblay towards the Château-de-Vincennes Metro station.

A nature trail, like the one in the Bois de Boulogne, can be followed from the Caserne-des-Gardes No. 325 bus stop. One hour and 12 signposts later you'll be quite familiar with this surprisingly varied environmental area.

You can find all sorts of things at the Bois de Vincennes: a temple of love and romantic grotto at the Lac Daumesnil, horse-riding clubs, cycle-touring tracks, bird-watching trails, *boules* areas and parks for children (at square de la Croix-Rouge and square de St-Mandé). Boat hire: Lac Daumesnil (☎ 01-46-35-21-58); Lac des Minimes (☎ 01-46-36-02-99).

In 1985 a new building, the **Kagyu Dzong** Buddhist temple was erected in the Bois de Vincennes for teaching purposes. This is the home of the International Buddhist Institute, 40 route de la ceinture du Lac-Daumesnil 75012. ☎ 01-43-41-54-48. Metro: Porte-Dorée. Open from April to October for Buddhist ceremonies and teaching seminars and open to the public on condition that they respect the rules of the institute (bare feet and silence). The temple contains the three former Cameroon and Togo pavilions from the Colonial Exhibition of 1931, which originally housed the musée du Bois (Forest Museum). The largest of these is the only one that remains in good condition and is used for celebrating large traditional festivals. The largest Buddha in Europe also sits here. Information: ☎ 01-40-04-98-06.

Don't miss the **Ferme de Paris** (Paris Farm): Route du Pesage 75012. ☎ 01-43-28-47-63. A real farm containing livestock, just a few minutes from the heart of Paris. Witness the birth of calves and lambs early in the year, chicks and other fowl in March, and piglets in September. There are rangers on hand to answer questions, and there's a mini-exhibition.

★ The **Arboretum de l'école du Breuil**: route de la Pyramide, Bois de Vincennes (near the hippodrome) 75012. ☎ 01-43-28-28-94. RER: Joinville-le-Pont. Free during the week, 5F at the weekend. There are a few rare species at this Arboretum, including five conifers which usually shed their needles. Two streams cross the Arboretum, whose groves straddle a charming central path. Armed with the Nature Trails map issued at the entrance (weekends only) you can track some amazing sights from over 300 different species and varieties. In all there are over 2,000 trees. Come in April for the flowers, and October for the leaves.

★ The **Parc floral de Paris**: on the Esplanade of the Château-de-Vincennes. ☎ 01-43-43-92-95. Website: www.parcfloraldeparis.com. Metro: Château-de-Vincennes; RER: Vincennes (line A). Bus No. 112 from Château-de-Vincennes and No. 46 from the Porte-Dorée. Open 9.30am to 7pm mid-September to mid-October, until 6pm for the last fortnight in October and in March, until 5pm late October to late February, 9.30am to 8pm from April to September. Entry fee 10F, concessions for young people aged between six and 18, and lots of other reductions; free for children under six and the unemployed. Come to enjoy 35ha (86 acres) of greenery and flowers. Things to see include the Vallée des Fleurs (Valley of Flowers), the pine forest, the Jardin des Quatre-Saisons (where you can see flowers all year round) and the bonsai trees. There's a playground with over 50 activities, free of charge. Every day from mid-March to the end of August, and on Wednesday, Saturday and Sunday from September to October, there are various attractions which you have to pay for, such as stock-car racing, electric cars, *boules*, the *bateaux-mouches* (6F per ticket), *Parisiennes* (quadricycles) for hire and mini-golf. Free concerts from June to September at 4.30pm in the DELTA (a new concert area with 1,500 seats): on Saturday there's the Paris Jazz Festival, on Sunday an open-air Classical Festival. Free concerts at 2.30pm on Patio 10 in May and at the DELTA area from June to September. Two shops sell gardening accessories and gifts.

★ The **Parc zoologique**: Metro: Porte-Dorée or St-Mandé-Tourelle. ☎ 01-44-75-20-10. Open daily 9am to 5 or 5.30pm in winter, 6 or 6.30pm from 1 April. The ticket offices close half an hour earlier. Entry fee 40F; reduced rate 4 to 16 years and other concessions; free for children under 4. Ask for the free map when you go in.

Fortunately this place is better than many zoos because the setting in which the animals live is at least inspired by their natural environment. When it was built it was a great innovation: the designers had managed to re-create the feeling of distance by using ditches and low walls to separate visitors from animals, making it as 'natural' as possible. But a zoo is still a zoo . . . . The main rock has three observation platforms and a viewpoint giving a panoramic view over Paris. Entry fee 20F. Below there are otters with their own waterfall.

There are a few rare species here such as the giant panda, the okapi and the lemur. You can also see Kaveri, an elephant from Asia, presented to François Mitterrand by Rajiv Ghandi in 1985, and Yen-Yen, a 26-year-old panda, presented to Georges Pompidou by Mao Tse-Tung. Yen-Yen arrived here with Lili, his companion, but unfortunately the great hopes which were founded upon this couple were soon disappointed: Lili was also a male! Expect crowds on Sundays.

★ The **Cartoucherie de Vincennes**: this former cartridge (*cartouche*) factory now houses some of the finest French theatre groups. The vast spaces, which are rare elsewhere in the city, have been put to good use. Buses run, on evenings when there is a show, from the Château-de-Vincennes Metro station.

★ The **château de Vincennes**: ☎ 01-48-08-31-20. Metro: Château-de-Vincennes; RER: Vincennes. Open daily 10am to noon and 1.15pm to 6pm (5pm October to March). There is a tour of the Sainte-Chapelle. The Pavillion du Roi and the Pavillion de la Reine were financed by Mazarin as a 'place where treasures can be kept in case of rioting'! Abandoned as a royal residence in the 18th century, the castle was used as a prison and had a number of famous guests: Fouquet, Diderot, Sade, Mirabeau, to name a few. In the 19th century it was used as a military fortress and suffered serious damage. Since the end of the Second World War a restoration campaign has been attempting to give it back some of its original look. A video traces its history.

★ The **musée des Arts d'Afrique et d'Océanie**: 293 avenue Daumesnil 75012. ☎ 01-43-46-51-61 (answer-machine). For individual visits ring the following number for information: ☎ 01-44-74-85-00. Metro: Porte-Dorée. Bus: PC, 46. Open daily 10am to 5.30pm. Closed Tuesday. This is one of the least-known museums in Paris, and yet it is remarkable. It was initially known as the 'musée des Colonies' (Museum of the Colonies) then, from 1945 to 1960, as the 'Musée de la France d'outre-mer' (Museum of France Abroad), with a large historical section on the 'virtues' of French colonization (this section is unfortunately no longer on show). The progress of the museum, carried out under the aegis of André Malraux, was, after the former colonies became independent, resolutely artistic and aesthetic. The building, constructed in 1931 to mark the Colonial Exhibition, was finally revealed (along with the Palais de Chaillot) as one of the rare examples of concrete architecture from between the wars. The fascinating 100m (328ft) sculpted façade is unique. The artist was asked to express the poetry of the Orient and the intellectual exchange with the West.

The museum is divided into two broad sections: Oceanic (South Pacific) arts and African arts (including North Africa). The Oceanic arts are grouped around an immense hall decorated with frescoes celebrating the apparently civilizing benefits of French colonization. Picasso sometimes came here looking for inspiration.

– **Oceanic arts**: masks from New-Guinea, engraved bamboo, arrows, Kanak hut roof tiles, funeral dummies, Papuan tiles, crocodile carvings.

In the other hall, devoted to Australia, there are engraved stones, paintings on wood and bark telling myths and legends, and acrylic paintings.

– **African arts**: on the 1st floor. Amazing statuettes (see the insignia of Shango, the Yoruba God of Thunder), Yoruba *Chef assis* with his enigmatic face tinted with irony, Ibo *Maternité* (Nigeria), bronzes, a giant ceremonial pipe from Cameroon, masks for initiation rites and musical instruments.

In the other hall there are gold pendants, Ashanti funeral objects, Mossi dancers' hats, fabrics and loincloths.

– **North African arts**: on the 2nd floor. Superb collections showing the finesse of the arts of Morocco, Algeria, Tunisia and the Sahara. In particular, painted wooden doors and chests, chiselled jewels, enamels and precious stones. Also painted ceramics, Tuareg arms and ornaments, richly embroidered fabrics and garments (wedding boleros) and ancient *Koran* manuscripts.

– The **tropical aquarium**: in the basement and an essential part of the visit. A huge renovation project has made it one of the best aquariums in the world, with 300 species, 3,000 individual creatures, 300,000 litres (66,000 gallons) of water (in 100 tanks) and a rare collection of primitive fish, unchanged for 300 million years with rudimentary versions of lungs and fins. Some of them really are amazing, such as the *Melanochromis auratus* which keeps its eggs in its mouth to incubate them and swallows them if they are in danger before spitting them out again. In addition there are enormous catfish, groupers and magnificent tropical fish (clown fish, balloon fish, damsel fish and small sharks). There's also a crocodile pit.

– There are always some interesting temporary exhibitions. Don't forget to take a look, as you come out on the left, at the Salon de Lyautey, known as the 'Salon de l'Asie', and, just opposite, the Paul Reynaud, known as the 'Salon de l'Afrique', with fine art deco work, Guyana palm tree furniture and interesting murals.

– Finally, don't forget to take a look at the Monument à la mission Marchand, another testimony to the 'blessed age of the colonies' (opposite the museum).

WHERE TO GO FOR A DRINK

🍸 **La Liberté** (map B1, 52): 196 rue du Faubourg-St-Antoine 75012. ☎ 01-43-72-11-18. Metro: Faidherbe-Chaligny. Open daily 9am to 2am. Dish of the day 45F at lunchtime. A place with two faces, where the atmosphere changes from lunchtime to evening. At lunchtime, the ambiance is politely 'Faubourg' with relevant dishes (*boeuf bourguignon*, etc.). In the evening the atmosphere is more Bohemian. Wines are sold by the glass and there's no vulgar plonk, just those chosen from the best sources. There are concerts every Thursday evening.

🍸 **China Club** (map A1, 53): 50 rue de Charenton 75012. ☎ 01-43-43-82-02. Metro: Bastille or Ledru-Rollin. Open every evening to 7pm, last orders at 1.30am (3am at weekends). Closed at Christmas. A drink costs from 50F. A classic among classics, this cosy club with its smell of ylang-ylang has survived all the slings and arrows of outrageous fashion without losing an inch of its personality. You'll meet students, Agnès B. lookalike models and groups of flirts with slicked-back hair. Have a game of chess or glance at the international press by the fireside. There is also a restaurant, but it's expensive and nothing special.

🍸 **Viaduc Café** (map A1, 54): 43 avenue Daumesnil 75012. ☎ 01-44-74-70-70. Metro: Bastille or Gare-de-Lyon. Open daily until 4am. Dish of the day 59F; brunch 125F on Sunday. Treat yourself to a rest on the terrace of this neo-bistro. In the evening it's an ideal place for a drink. The terrace has 140 seats in summer. In winter people tend to take refuge inside, either in the bar, or in the large dining room over a meal (last orders 4am). Jazz brunch every Sunday noon to 4pm.

13TH ARRONDISSEMENT

THE BUTTE-AUX-CAILLES ● LES GOBELINS ● THE 'OTHER' 13th

Like many of the arrondissements of Paris, the 13th was once in the countryside. Development began when the Gobelins factory was set up on the banks of the Bièvre, a little river which rose near Trappes, west of Versailles. In 1783 Pilâtre de Rozier landed his hot-air balloon on the hill of the Butte-aux-Cailles, after a journey over Paris of 9 kilometres (5.5 miles) taking 25 minutes.

The working-class character of the area soon became deeply entrenched, with the locals among the first to take up arms during the French Revolution, again in 1848 and then during the Paris Commune.

In the second half of the 19th century and up until the Second World War, several small factories and workshops were established here. Accommodation for the workers was built so that they only had to cross the road to get to work. The inhabitants became very proud of their district and seldom left it. With businesses, cafés and cinemas all to be found locally, they had all they needed on their doorstep. Upon setting off for another arrondissement they would often say: 'I'm going to Paris'.

The 13th was also characterized by its close-knit community. Everyone knew one another and the poor housing and lack of basic comfort pushed people out into the streets and cafés. Over the last 30 years or so the area has undergone a huge transformation, many factories having outgrown it and left.

The 13th arrondissement is made up of three distinct quarters. The Butte-aux-Cailles – clinging to its village character – and the Gobelins area – centred around the Bièvre and what little manufacturing is left – which have retained a certain physical and historical unity in spite of the considerable changes. But there is also the 'other 13th arrondissement', characterised by new building. There is enough here for both nostalgics and modernists to feed their imaginations.

WHERE TO STAY

☆ BUDGET TO CHEAP

La Maison des clubs UNESCO (map A2, **1**): 43 rue de la Glacière 75013. ☎ 01-43-36-00-63. Fax: 01-45-35-05-96. Double room 147F per person, breakfast included. Also single rooms and rooms with three or four beds. Showers and toilet on each floor or, if you're lucky, in your room. It *is* possible to stay in Paris in a quiet area only 10 minutes from the Latin Quarter (bus 21) and for a very reasonable sum. Irreproachably clean. Good welcome. Book 10 days in advance. There's a 2am curfew.

Hôtel Tolbiac (map B2, **2**): 122 rue de Tolbiac 75013. ☎ 01-44-24-25-54. Fax: 01-45-85-43-47. E-mail: htolbiac@club-internet.fr Metro:

Tolbiac or Place-d'Italie. Double room from 170F with washbasin, 210F with shower and toilet. Located five minutes from the Place d'Italie, this vast building (47 rooms) is great if you're on a budget. Go for rooms 19, 29, 39 and 49, which are larger and sunnier. The welcome is pleasant and the rooms are clean. The rue de Tolbiac is fairly noisy but some rooms have double-glazing.

Hôtel Sthrau (map C2, **3**): 1 rue Sthrau 75013. ☎ 01-45-83-20-35. Fax: 01-44-24-91-21. Metro: Nationale, Tolbiac or Porte-d'Ivry. Bus Nos. 62, 83 or 27. Double room 180F with washbasin, 206F with shower, 256F with bath. A modest but clean little hotel for those on a budget, five minutes from the Bibliothèque Nationale de France François-Mitterrand (new National Library). Most of the rooms are very quiet.

Hôtel Coypel (map B2, **4**): 2 rue Coypel 75013. ☎ 01-43-31-18-08. Fax: 01-47-07-27-45. Metro: Place-d'Italie. Double room 185F with washbasin, 220F with shower, 240F with shower and toilet. For three people (one double bed and one single bed) 270F. A standard hotel but it's well run and very close to the Place d'Italie. Satellite TV, lift, double-glazing. Simple but clean and welcoming.

☆☆ MODERATE

Résidence Les Gobelins (map A1, **5**): 9 rue des Gobelins 75013. ☎ 01-47-07-26-90. Fax: 01-43-31-44-05. Metro: Gobelins. Bus Nos. 27, 47, 83 and 91. Double room from 425F with shower and toilet; 445F with bath and toilet. In a remarkably well-preserved medieval street, this hotel gives excellent value for money. Guaranteed peace and quiet, especially with room Nos. 32, 42, 52 and 62, which overlook the rear of the building. TV (Canal +) in all rooms. There's also a little garden for those spring and summer evenings.

Résidence hôtelière Le Vert Galant (map A2, **6**): 41–43 rue de Croulebarbe 75013. ☎ 01-44-08-83-50. Fax: 01-44-08-83-69. Metro: Gobelins or Corvisart. It's 450F for a double room with shower, 500F with bath. A Basque country corner lost in the middle of the 13th arrondissement opposite the jardin des Gobelins; 10 spacious rooms, overlooking the street, with a garden and a lawn. There are vines growing next to the adjoining Basque restaurant, the Etchegorry, which is owned by the same people. There are five smaller rooms. Quiet and with a certain charm. The more expensive rooms are studios with a kitchenette, refrigerator and telephone with direct line. A fine buffet breakfast is served in a loggia, in the middle of the greenery.

☆☆☆ CHIC

Hôtel St-Charles (inset, **7**): 6 rue de l'Espérance 75013. ☎ 01-45-89-56-54. Fax: 01-45-88-56-17. Metro: Corvisart. Budget for 600F for a double room with shower and toilet, and 650F for a room with a bath. In the heart of the Butte-aux-Cailles. The rooms are absolutely impeccable, with TV and Canal +. Go for the higher floors for the view over the church of Ste-Anne and the south of Paris. There's a little indoor garden. The prices are high-ish but justified, especially for the rooms on the courtyard side. There's a car park but you have to pay.

Hôtel La Manufacture (map B2, **8**): 8 rue Philippe-de-Champaigne 75013. ☎ 01-45-35-45-25. Fax: 01-45-35-45-40. Metro: Place-d'Italie. Single room from 420F to 550F, double room from 460F to 600F. Breakfast is included. An elegant 2-star hotel, hidden away in the shade of the town hall, near the famous Gobelins factory. It is run by three meticulous young women who will not allow a single speck of dust in here! There is a very fine entrance with boat decking on the floor and a lounge-bar, which is lovely for an evening drink sitting by the wood fire in winter. A hotel for businessmen and women but also aimed at anyone who wants a different experience of the 13th arrondissement. Air-conditioning, satellite TV. The rooms aren't very large but they are pleasant for a short stay. There is an appetizing buffet in the morning.

WHERE TO EAT

☆ BUDGET

✕ **Virgule** (map B2, **26**): 9 rue Véronèse 75013. ☎ 01-43-37-01-14. Metro: Place-d'Italie. Open to 10pm during the week, 11pm at the weekend. Closed Sunday and Monday lunchtime. There are a number of menus at 64F, 100F and 140F in the evening. Budget for 150F à la carte. A former pizzeria, with a rather banal decor, but it's always full. The set menu at 58F at lunchtime is very good value. The cuisine brings together East and West. Try roast glazed pork or sauerkraut with knuckle of pork and tarte of the day or crème caramel. The set menu at 140F also offers some amazing mixtures (slices of smoked salmon with grapefruit, or cassoulet of the sort made by French grandmothers).

✕ **Menabé L'Île Rouge** (map B3, **22**): 33 rue Damesme 75013. ☎ 01-45-65-04-11. Metro: Maison-Blanche or Tolbiac. Open daily except Sunday and public holidays (or only by booking 48 hours in advance for groups). At lunchtime there's a *Kintana* set meal at 45F. In the evening there are three set meals: *Fy* at 65F, *Manontolo* at 90F and *Tokana* at 130F. Very definitely away from Chinatown and the Butte-aux-Cailles, and set in a quiet street, here is a scale model

Where to stay
- **1** La Maison des clubs UNESCO
- **2** Hôtel Tolbiac
- **3** Hôtel Sthrau
- **4** Hôtel Coypel
- **5** Résidence Les Gobelins
- **6** Résidence hôtelière Le Vert Galant
- **7** Hôtel St-Charles
- **8** Hôtel La Manufacture

✕ **Where to eat**
- **20** L'Espérance
- **22** Menabé L'Île Rouge
- **23** À la Douceur Angevine
- **25** Le Petit Méditerranéen
- **26** Virgule
- **27** Le Timri
- **28** Le Bistrot du Viaduc
- **29** Chez Grand-Mère
- **30** La Touraine
- **31** Chez Françoise
- **32** L'Oncle Benz
- **33** Chez Trassoudaine
- **34** Chez Paul
- **35** L'Avant-Goût
- **36** Au P'tit Cahoua
- **37** L'Anacréon
- **38** Au Cul de l'Oie
- **39** À la Bouillabaisse, Chez Keryado
- **40** Etchegorry
- **41** La Récréative
- **54** Kamukera
- **55** Le Jardin des Pâtes
- **56** Le Terroir

✕ **Asian Restaurants**
- **43** La Lune
- **45** Sinorama
- **46** Paris-Vietnam
- **47** Phuong Hoang
- **48** Bida Saigon
- **49** Lê Lai
- **50** Chanh Seng
- **51** Mer de Chine
- **52** Nouveau Village Tao Tao

Going out
- **63** Chez Gladines
- **61** La Folie en Tête
- **64** Le Merle Moqueur
- **66** OYA Café
- **67** Le Couvent

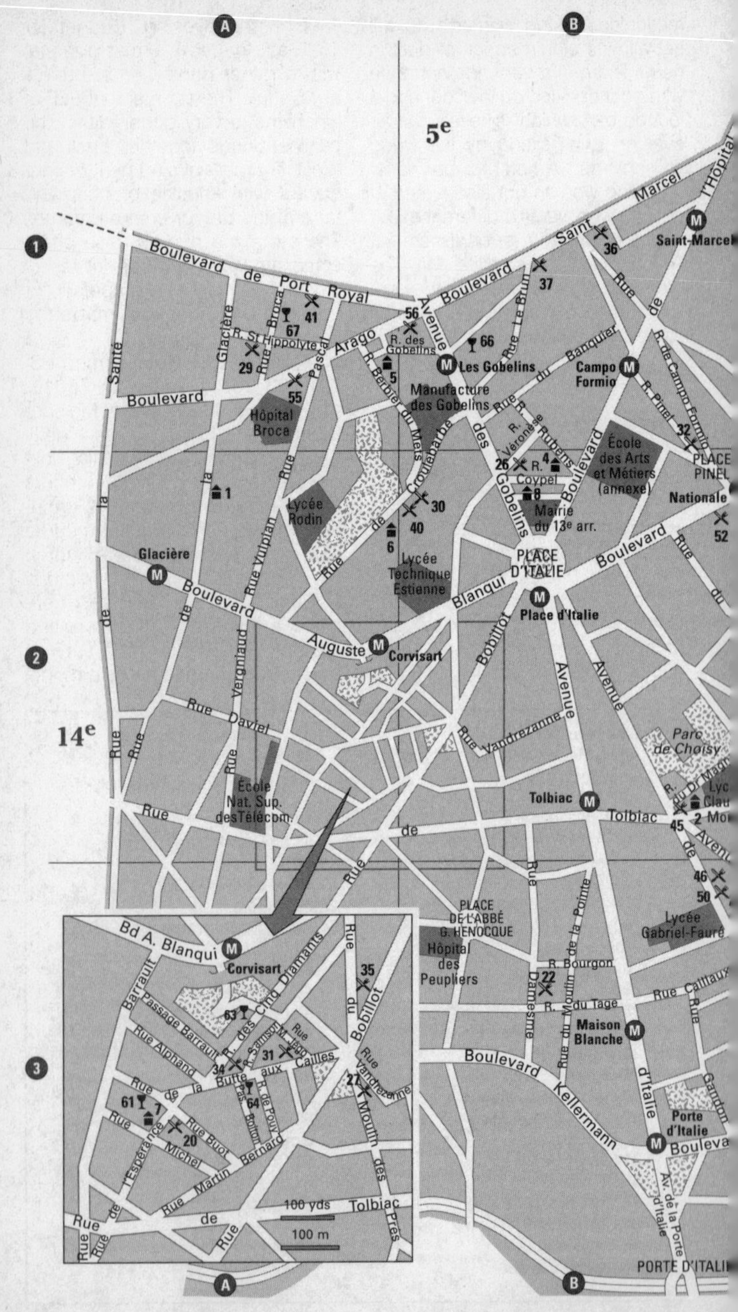
5e
14e
Boulevard de Port Royal
Boulevard Saint Marcel
Boulevard Arago
Boulevard Auguste Blanqui
Boulevard de l'Hôpital
Boulevard Kellermann
Avenue des Gobelins
Avenue d'Italie
Avenue de Choisy
Rue de la Santé
Rue de la Glacière
Rue Broca
Rue Pascal
Rue Vulpian
Rue Le Brun
Rue du Banquier
Rue de Croulebarbe
Rue Bobillot
Rue de Tolbiac
Rue Daviel
Rue Vergniaud
Rue Vandrezanne
Les Gobelins
Campo Formio
Saint-Marcel
Glacière
Corvisart
Place d'Italie
Nationale
Tolbiac
Maison Blanche
Porte d'Italie
Manufacture des Gobelins
Hôpital Broca
Lycée Rodin
Lycée Technique Estienne
Mairie du 13e arr.
École des Arts et Métiers (annexe)
École Nat. Sup. des Télécom.
PLACE D'ITALIE
PLACE PINEL
PLACE DE L'ABBÉ G. HENOCQUE
Hôpital des Peupliers
Parc de Choisy
Lycée Gabriel-Fauré
PORTE D'ITALIE
Bd A. Blanqui
Rue des Cinq Diamants
Rue de la Butte aux Cailles
Passage Barrault
Rue Barrault
Rue Alphand
Rue de l'Espérance
Rue Buot
Rue Michel Martin Bernard
Rue du Moulin des Prés
100 yds
100 m

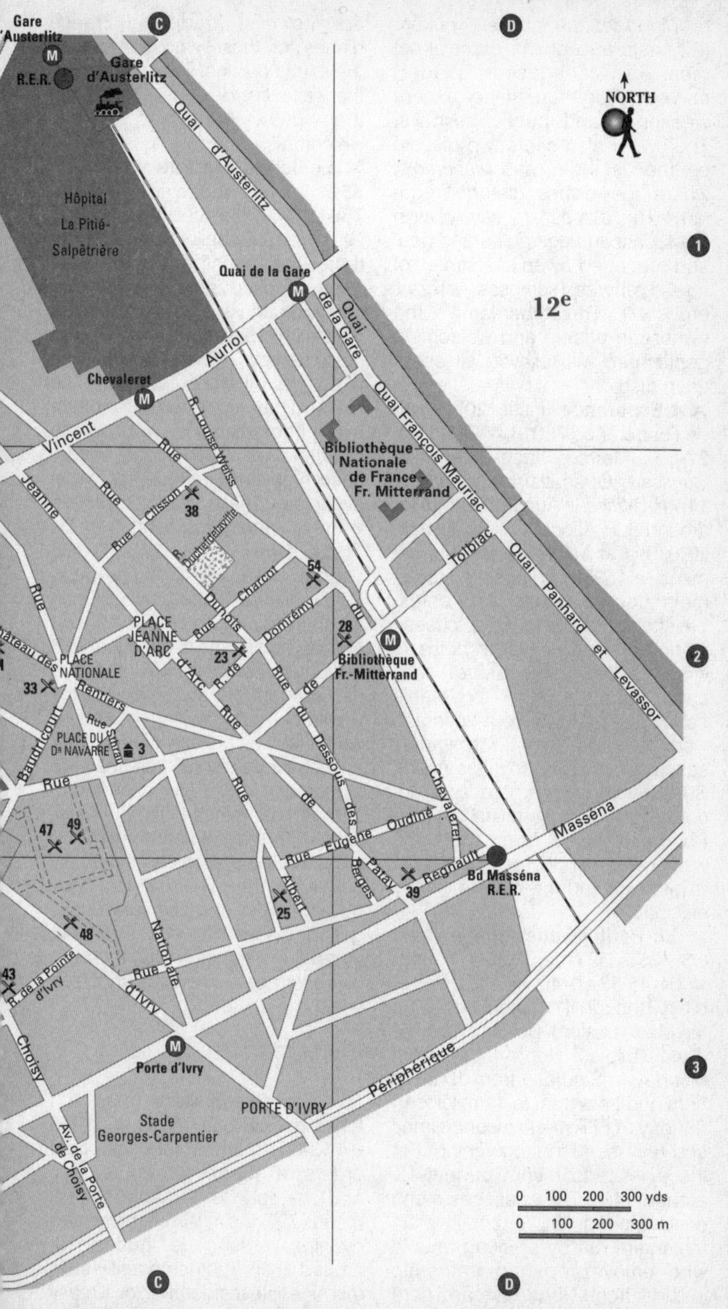
Gare Austerlitz
R.E.R.
Gare d'Austerlitz
Quai d'Austerlitz
Hôpital La Pitié-Salpêtrière
Quai de la Gare
Quai de la Gare
12e
NORTH
Auriol
Chevaleret
Vincent
R. Louise Weiss
Bibliothèque Nationale de France - Fr. Mitterrand
Quai François Mauriac
Tolbiac
Quai Panhard et Levassor
Rue Clisson
38
Jeanne
R. Duchefdelaville
54
Charcot
Dunois
Domrémy
28
PLACE JEANNE D'ARC
PLACE NATIONALE
23
Bibliothèque Fr.-Mitterrand
33
Rentiers
d'Arc
Rue du Dessous des Berges
PLACE DU Dr NAVARRE
3
Baudricourt
Chevaleret
47
49
Rue Eugène Oudiné
Masséna
Patay
Regnault
39
Bd Masséna R.E.R.
Albert
25
48
Nationale
43
R. de la Pointe d'Ivry
Rue d'Ivry
Choisy
Porte d'Ivry
Périphérique
PORTE D'IVRY
Stade Georges-Carpentier
Av. de la Porte de Choisy
0 100 200 300 yds
0 100 200 300 m

of Madagascan culinary culture (22 seats at a push). Express set meal (a Madagascan platter) served every lunchtime except weekends and public holidays. The owner also offers two discovery menus, the *Fy* and *Manontolo*, where the dishes change regularly. The dishes are served with Madagascan vegetables and rice, and preceded by an assortment of hors-d'œuvres (samosas, *accras*, etc.) Mr Razafintsalama, the owner, an affable and welcoming gentleman, will tell you all about each dish.

✕ **L'Espérance** (inset, **20**): 9 rue de l'Espérance 75013. ☎ 01-45-80-22-55. Metro: Place-d'Italie or Corvisart. Open daily. Last orders 11pm. Closed in August. Budget for around 80F. A local cafeteria which is full up at lunchtime with its set menu at 59F, comprising starter, main course (steak and chips, bavette *à l'échalotte*, etc.), cheese or dessert and a quarter bottle of wine. Unbelievable value! À la carte, there's a rather forgettable couscous (though your stomach won't forget it) from 42F (*merguez* sausage) to 75F (royal version). Basically you come here to fill up, not to give a dissertation on gastronomy! Apart from that, the welcome is friendly, the dining room is pleasant and the service is very efficient.

✕ **Le Petit Méditerranéen** (map C3, **25**): 39 rue Albert 75013. ☎ 01-45-83-61-46. Metro: Porte-d'Ivry (though it's quite a way from the Metro station). Bus No. 62 or 27 (Patay-Tolbiac stop). Open from Monday to Saturday from 10am to 3pm and from 6pm to 1am. Closed Sunday. A 58F menu at lunchtimes and 85F menu in the evening. For the à la carte menu, budget for around 140F. The couscous menu costs around 75F. A small, plain restaurant run by a young couple who enjoy preparing authentic cuisine from North Africa. There are, however, traditional French dishes for those who don't fancy the exotic cuisine. The mosaics on the wall were designed by Kamel, the owner. Warm and friendly welcome.

✕ **Le Jardin des Pâtes** (map A1, **55**): 33 boulevard Arago 75013. ☎ 01-45-35-93-67. Metro: Glacière or Gobelins. Open lunchtime and evening (last orders 11pm). Closed Sunday. Budget for 100F with drinks. This is a charming place (in spite of the somewhat hasty service), which will allow you to eat your fill without breaking the bank. They specialize in pasta made from rice flour, rye or wheat, with lots of good things inside. There's a small terrace for warm evenings. (There is another Jardin in the 5th arrondissement).

✕ **Le Timri** (inset, **27**): 41 rue Vandrezanne 75013. ☎ 01-45-65-23-87. Metro: Place-d'Italie. Open lunchtime and evening. Closed Sunday and for the second fortnight in August. Set menu 45F. The chef has brought his know-how all the way from Timri, the village in Kabylia where he was born. A dozen different couscous dishes, from the vegetarian version to the royal (110F) and several *tajines* of lamb (olives-lemons, prunes-almonds, etc.). It's good and the portions are extremely generous. There is also a dish of the day at 48F, plus a few salads and grilled dishes. Try the mint tea. When the weather is fine, there's a lovely terrace on the pedestrianized street.

☆☆ MODERATE

✕ **Chez Grand-Mère** (map A1, **29**): 92 rue Broca 75013. ☎ 01-47-07-13-65. Metro: Gobelins. Last orders 10.15pm. Closed Sunday and 14 July to 15 August. Set menus 79F and 119F lunchtime and evening. À la carte, budget for around 160F. The name really suits this nice little restaurant! You'll really be made welcome. Behind the wine-coloured façade, the dining room opens out onto the essential bistro counter, with a few attractive tables laid out here and there against a background of old-fashioned furniture. Take your pick from one of the set menus – rabbit with mustard or *pot-au-feu à l'ancienne*, served in a pot, with coarse salt and gherkins, in the traditional way. For dessert, there's *tarte Tatin*, and the very simple but delicious crème caramel. There's also a good wine list.

✕ **Le Bistro du Viaduc** (map D2, **28**): 12 rue de Tolbiac 75013. ☎ 01-45-83-74-66. Metro: Bibliothèque or Chevaleret. Bus No. 62. Open lunchtime only, from noon to 3pm. Closed Sunday and public holidays, and for three weeks in August. Set menus 98F and 158F. The decor here is 1930s. Two set menus, with one at 158F offering the very best: roast lobster prepared in various ways according to the season, sole meunière, turbot in red wine with sorrel, or a delicious veal liver. Classic and nicely done.

✕ **La Touraine** (map B2, **30**): 39 rue de Croulebarbe 75013. ☎ 01-47-07-69-35. Metro: Corvisart or Gobelins. Open lunchtime and evening to 10.30pm. Closed Sunday. First set menu 70F lunchtime only, children's menu 50F, à la carte around 180F, excluding drinks. It is advisable to book, especially if you want one of the tables on the terrace. In the evening it's really quiet. There are two large dining rooms with rustic decor. The welcome is charming. Restorative but succulent cuisine like you find in the provinces (pike with *beurre blanc* – a sauce made of butter, vinegar and shallots, lamb's sweetbreads with morels flambéed in Calvados, *pavé* of monkfish wrapped in cabbage, *panaché* of lamb with pickled garlic). Lots of generous menus: at 140F (including drinks, cheese and dessert) and 190F – Gourmet menu. To help your digestion, there's a lovely garden on the other side of the street where you can take a stroll.

✕ **À la Douceur Angevine** (map C2, **23**): 1 rue Xaintrailles (corner with Domrémy) 75013. ☎ 01-45-83-32-30. Metro: Chevaleret. Bus No. 62 (Patay-Jeanne-d'Arc stop). Open Monday lunchtime to Friday and on Thursday evening. Budget for 140F without drinks. The decor here is sober but warm. Note the frieze of green and yellow grapes inherited from a wine fair in Rochefort in 1937 (on the occasion of the visit of President Lebrun). All the produce comes from the 13th arrondissement. There are two to three main courses, such as lamb chops, house *flageolets*, large entrecôte-sautéed potatoes or *potée aux choux* (cabbage and meat stew) for 70F. There is always a different dish of the day, washed down with a very reasonably priced wine by the jug (a quarter bottle costs less than 30F). For aficionados, Anjou from Richou, Muscadet de Couillaud or Cabernet Franc from Lebreton. Traditional French cheeses from small producers and lovely desserts at 30F. When the weather is fine, there is a pleasant terrace straight out of a traditional postcard image of the 13th arrondissement.

✕ **Chez Françoise** (inset, **31**): 12 rue de la Butte-aux-Cailles 75013. ☎ 01-45-80-12-02. Metro: Corvisart or Place-d'Italie. Open lunchtime and evening to 10.30pm (11.15pm on Friday and Saturday). Closed Sunday and in August. Set menus 72F at lunchtime and until 8.30pm, 99F and 146F in the evening. À la carte around 190F. A traditional provincial restaurant in the middle of the most traditional part of the 13th arrondissement. There's a terrace in summer. At lunchtime the regular clientele is made up of local employees, who come to share the lunchtime menu elbow to elbow. There are other more elaborate menus in the evening. Classic French cuisine (monkfish, *confit de canard*, etc.) Paella in the evening from Monday to Thursday.

✕ **L'Oncle Benz** (map B1–2, **32**): 1 rue Campo-Formio 75013. ☎ 01-45-84-39-90. Metro: Nationale or Campo-Formio. Open until 10pm or so during the week and a lot later on evenings when there's a show. Closed Sunday, for a week at Christmas and a week during the wine harvesting season because the owner goes off in search of supplies! Set menus at 63F lunchtime, 89F and 129F in the evening. An à la carte meal comes to around 160F. The cuisine here is French, based on the fruits of the earth (Corsican *charcuterie*, dishes from the south-west of France, etc.). The portions are generous and the range is often renewed, especially as far as the wines by the glass are concerned (more than 60 vintages!). At weekends there are shows from 10pm. When the weather is fine, there are a few tables right on the pavement which you can use as a kind of terrace.

✕ **Chez Trassoudaine** (map C2, **33**): 3 place Nationale 75013. ☎ 01-45-83-06-45. Metro: Nationale. Open lunchtime and evening to 11pm. Closed Sunday and for a fortnight in August. No set menu; budget for around 150F for a full meal without drinks. Arakel and Haigo, two brothers of Armenian origin, got married, one to a Mexican girl and the other to a Dutch girl, and they run this restaurant, oddly put together with the good humour of people who've seen the world . . . . The large, impersonal dining room plays host to a lot of students and also to parties celebrating the end of film shoots. In the smaller and warmer dining room you'll discover both a 'meat' menu and a 'fish' one. *Pavé* du Limousin au poivre gris (90F), veal chops with sorrel (75F), *bavette aux échalotes* (65F), chateaubriand with Roquefort (90F), and, from the sea, grilled seabass (95F), Provençal or Norman *coquilles St-Jacques* and, from time to time (depending on the strength of the current!), an amazing *bouquet du Sénégal* (pink shrimps sautéed with garlic and Cayenne pepper) at 60F.

✕ **L'Appennino**: (map A3, behind inset map) 61 rue de l'Amiral-Mouchez 75013. ☎ 01-45-89-08-15. RER: Cité-Universitaire. Service noon to 2pm and 7.30pm to 10pm. Closed Saturday lunchtime and Sunday, as well for a week in winter. No set menus. Budget for around 200F per person. An establishment which is well known but very discreet. One of the best Italian restaurants in the quarter, specializing in authentic recipes from the north of the country. Here you can be sure of real *antipasti*, such as ricotta salad with basil and red peppers (48F) and, of course, some marvellous Italian-style pasta: *tortelli* with spinach (50F) or pasta with lemon and *rucola*. There are also some fine *escalopines al prosciutto* (82F) or, for real gourmets, a veal liver *à la vénitienne*. Then let yourself be tempted by the mouth-watering plate of Italian cheeses (40F), washed down with a Chianti (54F per half bottle), before giving in and going for one of the delicious house desserts, most of them really original. Efficient service.

☆☆☆ CHIC

✕ **L'Avant-Goût** (inset, **35**): 26 rue Bobillot 75013. ☎ 01-53-80-24-00. Metro: Place-d'Italie. Last orders 11pm. Closed Sunday and Monday, the first week in January and for three weeks in August. Set meal 59F at lunchtime, set menus at 145F and 190F. À la carte, budget for 145F. The Avant-Goût's speciality, pork *pot-au-feu* (98F; served in two instalments), combines rusticity and finesse. The menu offers a choice of five starters, five main courses and five desserts. Pheasant terrine, pork with apple chutney, followed by venison casserole with wild mushrooms and pasta or a salmon with marrow and, to end with, gratin of mangoes and pineapples and spice bread ice-cream demonstrate the talents of the chef. At lunchtime, on the set menu (starter and main course with salad, a glass of wine and coffee included): roast farmhouse chicken with macaroni gratin, roast leg of lamb with French beans. Good wines, with a wine of the month.

✕ **L'Anacréon** (map B1, **37**): 53 boulevard St-Marcel 75013. ☎ 01-43-31-71-18. Metro: Gobelins. Open noon to 2.30pm and 7.30pm to 11pm. Closed Sunday and Monday, and also in August. Set menu 120F at lunchtime and à la carte menu at 180F. Set meals with starter and main course 160F or main course and dessert 150F, taken from the à la carte menu. On this sad-looking boulevard, L'Anacréon is the light at the end of the tunnel for local gourmets. The exceptional set menu at 180F combines the fat of the land with finely-honed produce. One after the other you get rabbit terrine with *foie gras* and vegetables, veal kidneys with mustard, *clafoutis* (fruit baked in batter) with prunes, ice-cream and Armagnac, all made with great talent. The wine complements the cuisine.

✕ **Chez Paul** (inset, **34**): 22 rue de la Butte-aux-Cailles 75013. ☎ 01-45-89-22-11. Metro: Place-d'Italie or Corvisart. Open to midnight, Sunday from noon to 3pm. Closed Christmas and New Year. Budget for 150F to 200F per person. A neo-bistro grafted onto the Butte. The setting is sober but pleasant, with excellent bistro cuisine. The menu is well stocked: ox-tail terrine, *pot-au-feu*, *estouffade de bœuf à la bordelaise*, sucking pig roasted with sage, as well as daily specials on the blackboard. Wines at reasonable prices (Coteaux du Lyonnais 60F and Château de la Bonnelière at 95F are a couple of the best deals). Delicious desserts.

✕ **Le Terroir** (map B1, **56**): 11 boulevard Arago 75013. ☎ 01-47-07-36-99. Metro: Gobelins. Open lunchtime and evening, last orders 10.15pm. Closed Saturday lunchtime and Sunday, a week at Easter, three weeks in August and over Christmas and New Year. Budget for 200F to 250F à la carte. Here is food bursting with flavour, straight from the provinces of France in this discreet bistro. Friends and regulars know what they are doing, they go for the tried and tested house speciality: veal kidneys cooked in a casserole, grilled or with mustard. The menu also offers a fine range of game: amongst the poultry, *andouillettes*, meat and fish from the market are wild boar, hare or partridge, and several mushroom-based dishes. There's a good wine list, and the owner's pride and joy is a Chénas at 98F.

✕ **Au P'tit Cahoua** (map B1, **36**): 39 boulevard St-Marcel 75013. ☎ 01-47-07-24-42. Metro: Gobelins or St-Marcel. Bus No. 67 or 91. Open daily to 11pm. Closed Saturday lunchtime and for three weeks around 15 August. Set menus 65F at lunchtime, 155F in the evening. À la carte, budget for 200F. The decor wavers between a Berber tent and an old-style Moroccan house. Drapes on the ceiling, saffron walls, Oriental-style furniture, a map of colonial Algeria, photos of nubile concubines from Turkish baths, a lounge with wide armchairs and a table where you can have an apéritif or tea before sitting down to eat, as well as Arabian chants and rhythms . . . and, of course, a menu on which couscous and *tajines* reign supreme. A good idea is the generous 'kemia' set meal (with nine courses), which is good if you come with a crowd. During the week there's a set lunch (starter and main course). There is another branch in rue des Taillandiers in the 11th arrondissement.

✕ **Au Cul de l'Oie** (map C2, **38**): 5 rue Clisson 75013. ☎ 01-45-83-04-23. Metro: Chevaleret. Open lunchtime Monday to Friday noon to 2.30pm, in the evening by reservation only and for a minimum of 10 people. There's a gourmet menu at 105F and a '*gourmand*' menu at 163F served lunchtime and evening. À la carte, budget for around 160F, including wine. A rustic interior (there's no lack of bric-à-brac, flowers and plants). À la carte, there are specialities from the south west of France: apple surprise *au crottin de Chavignol*, Landes salad, smoked *magret de canard* with onion preserve, cassoulet of duck, *pavé* with morel sauce and *pommes sarladaises*, omelette with *ceps* served on a salad bed, and dishes of the day which change regularly: fresh fish on Wednesday or Friday, *andouillette* with Meaux mustard. On the wine side, there are excellent Cahors and Madiran. The clientele is generally made up of locals.

✕ **À la Bouillabaisse, Chez Keryado** (map D3, **39**): 32 rue Régnault 75013. ☎ 01-45-83-87-58. Metro: Bibliothèque or Porte-d'Ivry; R.E.R. (line C): Masséna. Open to 10.15pm. Closed Sunday, Monday evening and for the second fortnight in August. Set menu 59F at lunchtime only during the week; in the evening there are menus at 110F and 150F. In this lower part of the 13th arrondissement, not far from the pleasant rue du Dessous-des-Berges, this is a modern, stylized version of a Marcel Pagnol (famous for *Jean de Florette* and *Manon des Sources*)-type bistro. The bouillabaisse does cost 140F, but it is excellent (and it's difficult to find a good one in Paris).

✕ **Etchegorry** (map B2, **40**): 41 rue de Croulebarbe 75013. ☎ 01-44-08-83-50. Metro: Corvisart or Gobelins. Open to 10.30pm. Closed Sunday. It is advisable to book. Set lunch 100F, set menus from 145F to 220F. Victor Hugo, Béranger, Chateaubriand and many other poets used to eat here. The old-fashioned charm is almost intact, the decor is rustic and warm, the windows overlook the Le Gall square, and it's as though you're in the provinces! The cuisine is reputable Basque-Béarnais: *piperade* like in Soule, *manchons de canard* and knuckle of pork with apple and garlic, sheep's cheese, and delicious *îles flottantes* with pink pralines which rivals the fondant Basque gâteau. Everything is freshly made on the premises, even the bread. The first set lunch (starter, main course, cheese or dessert and optional jug of wine) gives good value for money. For a wider choice, go for the menus at 145F or 170F with wine by the jug, or for the gourmet menu at 180F or 220F including wine. On the set menus at 180F and 220F you get a free apéritif or spirit.

✕ **La Récréative** (map A1, **41**): 23 boulevard de Port-Royal 75013. ☎ 01-45-35-03-15. Metro: Gobelins. Bus No. 83 or 91. Open noon to 2.30pm and 7.30pm to 10.30pm. Closed Sunday, for a week at Easter and for a fortnight in August. Set menu 128F served lunchtime and evening. Set lunch at 90F. À la carte, budget for 180F without drinks. In spite of the slightly dated decor, the excellent set menu offers well-cooked dishes such as the pork with ginger and grapefruit. The set menu at 168F refuses to be outdone, with its excellent pear and Roquefort terrine and *émincé* of ham, followed by rabbit with lavender. There are some very entertaining dishes such as the *croustillant* with liquorice mousse or, in season, chocolate gateau with orange and chestnut mousse. The *Menu dégustation* at 220F is a treat for the palate.

✕ **Kamukera** (map C2, **54**): 113 rue du Chevaleret 75013. ☎ 01-53-61-25-05. Metro: Bibliothèque or Chevaleret. Open Monday to Saturday 11am to 2am. Last orders midnight. Closed Saturday lunchtime and Sunday. At lunchtime there's a set menu at 65F; in the evening, à la carte from 130F. Children's menu 45F. In this area, which is in the process of radical transformation (the new Bibliothèque Nationale de France, the new Météor Metro line . . .), here's a great place to eat. The African-West Indian cuisine is varied and very good, although a bit expensive: try stuffed crab, kid goat *colombo* or Aloko braised chicken, and for dessert coconut blancmange, all washed down with Planter's Punch. But what they're really selling is that party atmosphere which only West Indians can truly accomplish! Very friendly service and musical events almost every evening. You'll need to book at weekends.

ASIAN RESTAURANTS

✕ **La Lune** (map C3, **43**): 36 avenue de Choisy 75013. ☎ 01-44-24-38-70. Metro: Porte-de-Choisy. Open daily 8.30am to 10.30pm except Wednesday. Closed 24 December. Soups around 50F. A former Arab restaurant given a quick face-lift. The soups are great but the real pull is the Thai and Cambodian dishes, rather than the Chinese ones. Generous dishes in a basic setting.

✕ **Sinorama** (map B2, **45**): 135 avenue de Choisy, 75013. ☎ 01-44-24-27-81. Metro: Tolbiac. Open daily to 11pm. Set menus 52F and 55F. À la carte, budget for no more than 100F. Yet another Chinese restaurant? To some extent, yes, but this one stands out from a lot of its competitors by offering, à la carte, some less sanitized dishes. The steamed dishes, salt and pepper squid, rice sautéed with pineapple and shellfish are all good. Full at weekends (on Sunday, it's best to arrive before 12.30pm).

✕ **Chanh Seng** (map B3, **50**): 86 avenue de Choisy 75013. ☎ 01-45-70-80-44. Metro: Tolbiac. Open to 11pm. Closed Wednesday. Set menus from 49F to 79F; à la carte, budget for no more than 100F. Run by Vietnamese who were born and lived in Laos, Chanh Seng offers the opportunity to taste specialities from both countries, plus two or three Thai specialities. The Laotian minced beef, Thai chicken with coconut milk, assortment of dried beef and Laotian sausage, papaya salad, the *nems* and steamed ravioli are all delicious and good value. Or try the house speciality: crunchy noodles with vegetables (beef or shrimps).

✕ **Paris-Vietnam** (map B3, **46**): 98 avenue de Choisy 75013. ☎ 01-44-23-73-97. Metro: Tolbiac. Open daily to midnight. Set menus 55F and 75F served lunchtime and evening. Dishes at around 45F. From outside this place looks tiny and unimpressive. Well, you're in for a surprise! The speciality is the Vietnamese fondue for two. Once you've ordered it, it's action stations! Hotplate on the table, a plate with wafer-thin slices of beef, cuttlefish and poultry, covered in coriander and accompanied by fat shrimps, a plate of pasta and *tofu*, and spatulas (to dip the food into the stock) – all these land on your table. All you have to do is tuck in and fill yourself up.

✕ **Phuong Hoang** (map C2, **47**): 52 rue du Javelot 75013. ☎ 01-45-84-75-07. Metro: Tolbiac. Open

11.30am to 2.30pm and 6.30pm to 11.30pm. Set menus from 45F to 160F. À la carte, budget for somewhere between 100F and 150F. Air-conditioned dining rooms; the mezzanine one is really pleasant. There are a few tables outside when the weather is fine. A restaurant specializing in Vietnamese, Thai, Laotian and Chinese dishes. Try the Thai cuttlefish salad, with chicken cooked in a banana leaf, with Singapore-style beef kebab, with pork and caramel. Don't miss the Thai fondue with fresh vegetables, fish, shrimps and meat. The service is fairly quick and courteous.

✕ **Bida Saigon** (map C3, **48**): 44 avenue d'Ivry 75013. ☎ 01-45-84-04-85. Metro: Porte-d'Ivry. Open daily 11am to 10pm. Budget for around 60F for soup and a dessert. A large Vietnamese cafeteria at the end of a corridor at the Galerie Oslo (access by means of the Olympiades escalators, in front of *Paris Store* or the *Tang Brothers'* shop). The menu is classic: 20 or so tasty dishes. The soups (*phó* and Saigonese or Hué) are generously served in large or small bowls (from 38F to 45F); the imperial pasta is crunchy and the steamed rice-cake good and traditional. Spare ribs, chicken grilled with lemon grass and rice and pork dishes with crab stuffed or roasted with caramel for between 42F and 45F. Try the desserts, which are puzzling but rather pleasant: haricot beans with sticky rice, lotus seeds with seaweed. As for the drinks, there is wine, beer, tea (obviously), and excellent fresh fruit juices.

✕ **Lê Lai** (map C2, **49**): 24 rue du Javelot 75013. Terrasse des Olympiades. Entrance through No. 101, rue de Tolbiac (escalators). ☎ 01-45-83-83-33. Metro: Tolbiac. Open noon to 3pm and 7pm to 11pm. Closed Tuesday. Set menus 45F at lunchtime, from 60F at 140F in the evening. Budget for 130F à la carte. More elegant and expensive than the average Asian restaurant in the area. The cuisine is also more *recherché*: here we're talking about the gastronomy of South Vietnam. Very fragrant delicacies, with complex flavours: tamarind, curry, lemongrass, caramel, ginger . . . . There are lots of fish and seafood-based dishes. Try the tamarind with fish or chicken soup, pineapple salad with shrimps served in a pineapple shell, beef kebabs prepared in a thousand and one ways, curried shrimps or pork with caramel (not exactly low in calories, but hey!). If you like taking risks, take a chance on the jellyfish salad . . . . Unusually for a Vietnamese restaurant, they actually have some good wines.

✕ **Mer de Chine** (map C2, **51**): 159 rue du Château-des-Rentiers 75013. ☎ 01-45-84-22-49. Metro: Nationale. Closed Tuesday and mid-July to mid-August. Steamed or traditional set menus 78F at lunchtime only, luxury set menu 118F. À la carte, budget for 180F. Not just another flashy Chinatown eaterie but quality Chinese cuisine. The tables are nicely laid out and the decor has been carefully done. The menu is rich and varied, unlike so many of the predictable menus you'll find if you go into most of its neighbours. As well as the classics, there are some amazing specialities: crêpes with oysters, Taochu-style chicken, jellyfish salad, and seafood-based fondue recipes. Don't be put off by the prices, the tasty fish with tamarind soup can, for instance, be shared between three people, as can the steamed skate sold according to its size (a quarter is enough for two or even three).

✕ **Nouveau Village Tao Tao** (map B–C2, **52**): 159 boulevard Vincent-Auriol 75013. ☎ 01-45-86-40-08. Metro: Nationale. Open daily to 11.30pm. At lunchtime, there are set menus at 65F and 75F, 156F for two people. Budget for 130F à la carte. This Asian restaurant offers a fairly refined setting with green plants all over the place. With its immense ground floor and its first floor, it's almost a whole village on its own! The menu fits in with the decor, with Chinese and Thai or steamed specialities and a few flambéed delicacies which the waiters bring you as fast as they can, prudently protecting themselves with serviettes around their necks! The photos of the dishes in the middle of the wide-ranging menu are a good idea. Try duck with bamboo shoots and spiced coconut milk (a soup) or Thai stuffed crab, spicy chicken with honey and sautéed shrimps, or Peking Duck for two at 240F. There's a proper dessert menu, including grilled Thai custard tart.

THE BUTTE-AUX-CAILLES

Known as 'La Butte' to locals and surrounded by the tower blocks of the Italie district and the Glacière, it is one of the least well-known quarters of the French capital. Today, instead of social decline, it seems to be undergoing an interesting process of renewal.

On a cultural level, things are happening. The Butte-aux-Cailles is no longer the meeting place for criminals its reputation implied, and hasn't been for some time now. Instead it's younger people who are leading the way and bringing the area to life. With them have come bistros: cheap and open late. The difficulties presented by the quarter's distinctive narrow passages and lanes help to keep the Butte off the tourist routes.

A BRIEF HISTORY

The rue du Moulin-des-Prés (Millfields) indicates that, from Gentilly to the Gobelins, there were water mills dotted all along the Bièvre. Jean-Jacques Rousseau loved to collect plants along its banks and to admire the little river of the *butte* (or mound) alongside it. Benjamin Franklin himself came to see the landing of Pilâtre de Rozier's hot-air balloon. The Bièvre didn't have a very good reputation due to the foul smells from the tanneries that washed their leather here, and it was gradually built over. At one time nearly all the inhabitants of the Butte-aux-Cailles were employed in the tanneries.

It was due to the poverty of the area that people began to eat horsemeat. The first horsemeat butcher's opened in Paris, in the place d'Italie, in 1866.

Unlike other areas in the 13th arrondissement, the Butte did not subsequently suffer any great architectural indignities. If you need convincing of this, just take a walk along the rue de la Butte-aux-Cailles and the adjacent streets, or go to the place de l'Abbé-Georges-Hénocque (formerly the place des Peupliers).

WHAT TO SEE

There are a few unusual sites to interest the tourist. There are no grandiose monuments or prestigious shops, but there is something indefinable, even a slightly magical atmosphere. Sadly, the time is approaching when many of the old buildings will be demolished – some even by the time you come to visit – so catch it while you can!

★ In the little garden of the health centre, near the Corvisart Metro station, on the corner with rue Barrault, there is a moving **statue** reminding us that hundreds of children used to live on the streets. The writer Hector Malot describes Rémi crossing the Butte-aux-Cailles in his novel *Sans famille* (Without any Family). The passage Barrault, on the left, is to be avoided if you wear high heels.

★ The rue des Cinq-Diamants (which takes its name from an ancient tavern) leads to the **rue de la Butte-aux-Cailles** (the historic centre of the Butte). The pavement has been widened and apple trees have been planted. There's a village crossroads. All around there are quiet streets, lined with two- or three-storey houses: rue Buot, rue Michal, rue Alphand, passage Boiton . . . .

On the corner of rue des Cinq-Diamants and rue de la Butte-aux-Cailles you'll find a building which has been christened 'la tour de Pise' (The Leaning Tower of Pisa). And it does seem to be struggling to stand upright, the reason for its slightly precarious stance being that the land beneath is riddled with old quarry workings.

★ On the corner of **rue Vergniaud** there is an odd little country-style church used by the Antoinistes, a small spiritualist sect founded in 1913 by a Belgian, Louis Antoine.

★ The **piscine de la Butte-aux-Cailles (swimming pool)**: 5 place Paul-Verlaine 75013. ☎ 01-45-89-60-05. Metro: Place-d'Italie. This is one of the oldest swimming pools in Paris, its neo-Gothic architecture earning it a listing as an historic monument. The inscription on the pediment reminds us that, once upon a time, swimming pools in Paris were health resorts! There is an open-air pool when the weather is fine.

★ **La Cité florale**: a gem which is often overlooked behind place de Rungis. Built in the shape of a triangle in 1928 on fields formerly flooded by the Bièvre this haven of peace is bursting with greenery. A last enclave of resistance to progress in the heart of a quarter covered in concrete. The quarter used to be called 'la Glacière' (the coolbox), because it was here, in the fields flooded by the Bièvre river, that Parisians used to collect the ice in winter to store in their coolboxes for the summer. There was skating, too, on the frozen fields.

The street names almost sing out loud: *rue des Orchidées* and its fine art-deco buildings, peaceful *rue des Glycines* (with a little square with a cherry tree), *rue des Liserons*, which is covered in ivy, *rue des Volubilis, rue des Iris, square des Mimosas*. The houses are mostly made of differently coloured bricks, and the roofs of interlocking orange tiles, giving these lanes a rather original colour scheme.

Looking at a map of Paris you can see from the meandering route that the rue des Peupliers takes, not to mention rue de la Colonie, rue de la Fontaine-à-Mulard, rue Wurtz and rue Croulebarbe too, that they are all following the underground course of the Bièvre river.

★ The **rue de la Fontaine-à-Mulard**: towards the end of the street there's a block of flats by Brillat-Savarin (built in 1951). It's a fine example of social architecture and the use of ordinary brick as an element of decoration. The upper floors form enormous recesses with half-moon shaped balconies, and motifs painted on the walls.

★ **The place de l'Abbé-Georges-Hénocque** (formerly the place des Peupliers) is surrounded by quiet streets such as the rue Dieulafoy, lined with charming houses with rather odd, pointed roofs (built in 1912 by the Association of Employees and Workers of the French Railways).

★ The **Moulin-de-la-Pointe** is an old Parisian village. It's not really supposed to exist any more. When President Pompidou was in power he wanted to raze the area to the ground so as to relieve the pressure on the Porte d'Italie. His death and the coming to power of Giscard d'Estaing put a stop to that. There then followed a decade of indecision over the future of the area: brutal renovation, restoration, limited destruction? However, it would seem that a not-too-brutal renovation was settled upon and the new buildings integrate pretty well with the rest.

There's an interesting attempt to have a little less concrete on the corner of rue du Tage and avenue d'Italie (hardly surprising as it seems that the architect is an Italian!). There are small buildings with a maximum of five floors, with an elegant mixture of exposed stonework and contemporary graphic elements, in broken lines and contrasting colours.

★ The **rue du Moulin-des-Prés**: don't miss the charming square des Peupliers, still so near to the hellish traffic of the rue de Tolbiac. As you go back up rue du Moulin-des-Prés you can see the Butte-aux-Cailles swimming pool (*see above*).

A SHORT WALK AROUND THE AREA

★ **The 13th arrondissement and the Bièvre**: 2km (1.2 miles), 45 minutes non-stop, from the Corvisart metro station to the Cité-Universitaire metro station.

There are few arrondissements so rich in discoveries as the 13th. The former farmyards of the Butte-aux-Cailles, the sunken paving stones of its narrow passages, the fortifications of the city wall and the Parc Montsouris, are all mainly located along the old route of the Bièvre river, which used to provide medieval Paris with its water. Its course, which is partly buried, runs right under many of the buildings in the 13th arrondissement.

Starting from the Corvisart Metro station, go along rue Eugène-Atget and climb up the Butte-aux-Cailles. The rue Jonas and rue Gérard conjure up the image of fortunate landowners from a time when property here was cheap. Walk down rue Simonet until you reach place Paul-Verlaine, whose artesian well is close to the municipal swimming pool with its interesting brick architecture. Not far away the mills of the Prés and the Merveilles were turning on the banks of the Bièvre river 200 years ago. Take the rue de la Butte-aux-Cailles, which still has the atmosphere of an old country path, and then rue Alphand. The passage Sigaud descends towards rue Barrault. Don't miss rue Daviel and the half-timbered architecture of No. 10, built in Anglo-Norman style. Also known as 'Little Alsace', this housing estate opened in 1913 and comprises 40 houses laid out as a garden city.

Opposite, a series of attractive painted villas covered in flowers will give you a total change of scene: is this Ireland, England or is it really Paris?

The rue Michal and rue de l'Espérance lead to the rue de Tolbiac, on the other side of the Butte-aux-Cailles, but still following the course of the river

Bièvre. You reach rue de Rungis and the Cité Florale via rue de l'Espérance and rue Lançon. Heading further west you will enter the 14th arrondissement and reach the Parc Montsouris.

LES GOBELINS

A pleasant area bordering the Mouffetard and the Latin Quarter, whose life revolved around the river Bièvre until the beginning of the 20th century. For many years there were tanneries along its banks (there is still a rue des Tanneries). A dyer, Jean Gobelin, set up a workshop in the 15th century and made his fortune with the discovery of scarlet dye. His many descendants ended up owning so much land and so many houses that people used to talk about 'going to the Gobelins'.

As early as the 16th century ecologists were complaining about the pollution of the Bièvre, and between 1671 and 1906 there were no fewer than 35 rulings and decrees aiming to reduce it. The quarter was very poor, and it is no coincidence that Victor Hugo set a number of episodes of *Les Misérables* here. In 1896 the *école d'imprimerie et d'arts graphiques Estienne* (Estienne School of Printing and Graphic Arts) set up on the corner of rue Abel-Hovelacque and boulevard Auguste-Blanqui. In 1910 all the tanners, dyers and paper manufacturers were compulsorily bought out and the Bièvre was permanently covered over. Subsequently, many renovation projects have altered the face of the quarter.

Today there are many luxury buildings (some of them even showing good taste) and few historic vestiges left. With a little imagination and the aid of a few streets (the rue des Gobelins, for example), you can take a quiet and very pleasant walk.

WHAT TO SEE

★ **La manufacture des Gobelins**: 42 avenue des Gobelins 75013. ☎ 01-44-08-52-00; information: ☎ 01-44-61-21-69. Metro: Gobelins. Bus Nos. 27, 47, 83 and 91. Tours at 2pm and 2.45pm on Tuesday, Wednesday and Thursday; same days for groups but by reservation. All tours are accompanied by a guide. Entry fee 45F; concessions 35F. The old royal factory, founded by Colbert more than 200 years ago, is still producing magnificent tapestries. You can visit the *atelier* (workshop) *des Gobelins,* the *atelier de Beauvais* and *atelier de Savonnerie.* In the Gobelins factory, the tapestries are woven vertically. The motifs and themes are still contemporary. It takes from four to eight years for one to be made by a number of craftsmen.

Then you cross rue Berbier-du-Mets where the *Mobilier national* (National Furniture Store) is located, although it is closed to the public. Furniture for ministries and embassies is kept here. The Bièvre passes right underneath. Note the fine 18th-century façade covered in ivy, seen from the rear of the Gobelins.

The *atelier de Beauvais* and the *atelier de la Savonnerie* are in a modern building. Beauvais tapestries have been made in Paris since 1940 though the workshops at Beauvais were destroyed during the Second World War, but part of the production was relocated in Beauvais in 1989. The *atelier de la Savonnerie* mainly produces carpets, though its name comes from the former soap factory in which it was initially installed by Louis XIII. The carpet for the reconstruction of the King's Room at Versailles was made here.

★ As you come out of the factory try taking a short walk around the area. One of the first things to see is the 16th-century **château de la Reine-Blanche**, which you would never guess is there. To find it you have to go back up the tiny rue Gustave-Geffroy and into no. 4 in the courtyard. You will recognize it by its octagonal tower. It has a fine stone spiral staircase. Note the amazing vertical bannister, which was clearly sculpted from a single tree. As you come back out through 17 rue des Gobelins, note at no. 19 a fine late 14th-century house. In the courtyard there are mullioned windows made of stone.

Below rue Berbier-du-Mets, lines of poplar trees mark what used to be the 'Île aux Singes' (Monkey Island) between the two arms of the river. Jugglers could let their trained monkeys gambol around without having to worry about them escaping.

★ **La Cité fleurie**: 65 boulevard Arago 75013. Metro: Glacière. There have been years of fierce battling to save one of the last places in the quarter where you can get a breath of fresh air, and it has now become an historic monument. The Cité is made up of 30 or so workshops built in the 1880s. It's an extraordinary garden, a jungle of shrubs, bushes and 100-year-old lime trees, sloping gently down to rue Léon-Maurice-Nordmann. At the bottom there are coppices, lawns and an old house – its roof covered with ancient tiles. Some prestigious regular visitors included Gauguin, Modigliani, Rodin and Maillol. The restoration work has not undermined its character. It is still accessible to the public, but the installation of a keypad lock at the entrance suggests that this may not last.

★ **La Cité verte**: 147 rue Léon-Maurice-Nordmann 75013. Metro: Glacière. This Cité comprises an old paved lane lined with artists' workshops made of bric-à-brac and drowning in greenery. One of them even has an outside spiral staircase. The famous sculptor Henry Moore worked here for a while and the craftsman who restored the organs of Notre-Dame still lives here. The whole area is a little wild but has a great deal of charm. Of course, here too the developers have been licking their lips, but after a bitter struggle the artists managed to save the site by getting it listed. Unfortunately, another keypad lock has got the better of the curious visitor, and the public can no longer enter. Opposite, at No. 152, is the little Cité des Vignes (City of the Vines). The rue Léon-Maurice-Nordmann then ends at the sinister Santé Prison.

THE 'OTHER' 13TH

Within the boundary formed by avenue d'Italie, boulevard St-Marcel, the Seine and boulevard Masséna, is the area of the 13th arrondissement which has seen the greatest upheavals. Léo Malet wrote in 1978: 'Pustules of glass and concrete have been erected, and one of them was insolently named *Galaxie* (Galaxy) so that we would be in no doubt that we were entering a new world . . . . I don't want people to think that, under the guise of a love for the picturesque, I am an unconditional advocate for hovels, squalor and sordid conditions. The area did need cleaning up, but it didn't need the kind of decimation last seen in the trench warfare of the First World War! If only we could still find traces of the people who once gave life to the quarter: workers and artisans, modest dropouts and little whores with flowers in their hair, scores of people who may not have been very clever, but who were at least human . . . . I shan't be going back to the 13th arrondissement!'. You may not agree!

The area doesn't really have any monuments of particular note, but it does have a certain charm.

WHAT TO SEE

★ The **chapelle St-Louis and the hôpital de La Pitié-Salpêtrière**: 47 boulevard de l'Hôpital 75013. Metro: Place-d'Italie. There isn't a single Parisian who isn't familiar with this massive silhouette, which is such a well-known landmark. The octagonal dome topped with a lantern is a sort of architectural symbol of a hospital. The entrance is through a courtyard blooming with flowers.

The church has a highly original layout: there are four naves each with four immense chapels. The whole thing surrounds the chancel in perfect symmetry. The unusual construction shows that there was a desire to clearly separate the categories of patients (by class as well as degree of contagiousness). The interior is almost bare; the only pieces on show are a sculpted baptistry and a 17th-century wrought-iron lectern.

The hospital itself occupies an important place in Paris from a historical point of view. A former powder magazine under Louis XIII (hence the name derived from the saltpetre used in the manufacture of explosives), under Louis XIV it became the first hospital set up for the poor, and later a women's prison was added. It was from here that Manon Lescaut (the heroine of the novel by Abbé Prévost) and the famous '*filles du Roy*' – prostitutes, orphans and destitute women – left to populate the French colonies.

In the 19th century the Salpêtrière became an asylum. Incurable patients were locked up and kept in chains, others were crammed into gruesome, squalid rooms. In return for a small donation, families could come and watch the patients' misery from behind glass windows.

Professor Charcot worked at the Salpêtrière in what was, in 1882, the largest neurology clinic in Europe. For six months he had a young student by the name of Sigmund Freud. This is where Freud came up with the theory of the psychoanalysis of the unconscious by observing the results obtained by Charcot's use of hypnosis in the treatment of hysteria.

The Salpêtrière is a veritable city within the city, combining vestiges of the past with totally modern constructions. Starting from the left, you'll see, in the first courtyard, the Bâtiment St-Vincent-de-Paul, the former women's prison. The rue des Archers, with its large paving stones, lined with low, heavily-built 17th-century buildings, plunges you into another world. In front of the Charcot lecture theatre there is an interesting modern white building, elegantly integrating elements of the older architecture.

★ **The Bibliothèque nationale de France François-Mitterrand** (French National Library): Tolbiac site, quai François-Mauriac 75013. ☎ 01-53-79-59-59. Metro: Quai-de-la-Gare or Bibliothèque. Bus No. 62 and 89. Website:

www.bnf.fr. Open Tuesday to Saturday 9am to 8pm, Sunday noon to 7pm. Closed Monday, 1 January, Easter Sunday, 1 and 8 May, Ascension Day, Whit Sunday, 14 July, 15 August, first to the third Monday in September, 1 and 11 November and 25 December.

– **Access** is by the large steps in rue Raymond-Aron (through the Quai-de-la-Gare Metro station), in rue Émile-Durkheim (through the Bibliothèque Metro station and bus 62), or quai François-Mauriac (bus 89). There are two ramps with a moving walkway leading to the reception and a car park which is accessible to visitors with disabilities, and in particular people using wheelchairs. There are also sloping levels and lifts and equipment specially for people with visual impairments.

– **The reading rooms** of the Haut-de-Jardin are accessible to anyone who is 18 or over and prepared to pay the 20F entrance fee. Tickets valid for the whole day. Annual card: 200F, half-price for students. They are closed Monday and public holidays and the first two weeks in September. There are 1,600 places accessible to the general public to view more than 180,000 volumes, including 2,500 periodicals, to which you have free access. The size of the collection is growing rapidly and there is internet access to the catalogue on the first floor.

Taking things in order, you'll find the bibliographical research room, a press room where you can go through 150 daily and 150 weekly French and overseas publications, plus dictionaries and reference works. The audio-visual room presents sound documents, films and CD-ROMs. The science and technology room has reference collections which cover all the basic disciplines. Room D contains over 30,000 volumes devoted to law, the economy and politics. Lliterature and the arts occupy rooms E, F, G and H, which will eventually offer over 120,000 items. The last room on the floor is devoted to philosophy, history and the sciences in general.

The 2,000-seat research library has 13 million volumes which make up the whole of the printed and audio-visual collection acquired by the *dépôt légal* (the formal depositing of one copy of every single book, film, record, etc. produced with the library).

– **Tour**: There are a number of leaflets available to visitors covering technical explanations and details of services offered to the public. There is also an introductory workshop on how to get the most out of the library – including use of the catalogue. There is a tour of the library for individuals. Ring for days and times ☎ 01-53-79-49-49.

– **A brief history** At first a number of people were involved in the BNF project. The historian Emmanuel Leroy-Ladurie, administrator of the Bibliothèque Nationale (the National Library in rue de Richelieu), made a report on how his establishment was suffocating through lack of space. François Léotard, then Minister of Culture, made representations to the Council of Ministers in favour of a second National Library. Also Jacques Attali, who dreamed of a future library where everything would be digital! President Mitterrand entered the fray and ordered the new National Library as the last of his *grands travaux* (great projects). He announced its launch in his speech on Bastille Day 1988.

In August 1989, at the age of 36, Dominique Perrault won the architectural tender for the project. However, there were soon problems and a feeling of bitterness began to develop. With the rue de Richelieu site out of the frame there were divergences of opinion about access for the public (some academics did not want a sort of second Pompidou Centre, with Joe Public disturbing their research), and personal and political rivalries began to rear their heads. In the same way, the question of the transfer of the collections from the Richelieu site to Tolbiac opened up a historical controversy: from what date should books be moved? (1960, the introduction of computerization? 1945, the historic date of the beginning of the post-war period? 1900, the new century? etc.). The question was soon settled: you can't split culture. Apart from the manuscripts, plans and medals, everything was to be transferred to Tolbiac. The President, who had promised that the Library would be open to the general public, decided that part of it would be for the public and the other part for researchers, and never the twain would meet.

Dominique Perrault's architectural concept then received a flood of criticism. Would the four towers in the form of an open book not lead to problems with storage, air-conditioning, circulation of books? Perrault's idea had been to erect translucent 'book silos', where people would be able to watch the books mount up. In order to avoid controversy about books being grilled by the sun, the architect dreamed up an elaborate system. There would be a layer of glass, then 7cm of air, then another layer of glass, then double-sided mahogany wooden flaps. On the inside, an enormous piece of machinery keeps the temperature constant at 18°C (65°F) and 55 per cent humidity. The thermal insulation was to be 10 times more effective than at the rue de Richelieu site.

The towers were to store a third of the works, the rest was to be in the basement. The floors were to be independent so as to avoid the growth of mould – the researcher's greatest fear. In the same vein, the fire safety measures are second to none.

The library has been divided into four departments: literature and arts; science and technology; political, economical and legal sciences; philosophy, history and humanities.

– **Decor and interior layout** The reception hall at garden level is 15 metres (50 feet) high, a harmonious alliance of aluminium, exotic woods and a red carpet (President Mitterrand chose the colour himself).

There are a lot of raw materials: immense 'mesh sides' hang along the walls, slightly superimposed to give the impression of curtains (they are good light reflectors). There are also lots of clever architectural tricks. For instance, the large metal flour sieves, used in the farming and food industry, converted to aesthetically hide the air-conditioning system.

The decor of the audio-visual booths is futuristic and the reading conditions are especially comfortable, with the shape and aesthetics of the chairs given particular thought.

A FEW STATISTICS

– The site measures 7.5ha (18 acres).
– 700,000 square metres (2.2 million square feet) of earth removed.
– Overall cost: 8 billion francs (and note that they did not go over budget, the construction deadlines were met. This is the third of the cost of a nuclear submarine!).

– Height: 80m (260ft) over 22 levels.
– Books transferred from the rue de Richelieu National Library: 12 million.
– Storage capacity: 400km (248 miles) of shelves. The stores will be filled in 2050.
– Number of reading places: 3,500, including 1,900 on the garden level for researchers (660 in the former National Library).
– 8km (5 miles) of rails and 300 hoppers for transporting documents. A book should take a maximum of 14 minutes to reach the reader.
– Running cost: 1 thousand million francs (400 million in the old National Library), but there are 2,000 employees (as against 500 at the Richelieu site). Eventually, 2,700 people should be working here (by comparison, there are 5,000 employees at the National Library in Washington).
– Attendance: 3.6 million users per year.

– **The indoor garden** One of the things which Dominique Perrault is (justifiably) most proud of is the *jardin intérieur* (indoor garden). To avoid having to wait for young trees to take 20 or 30 years to grow he initially picked out 1ha (3 acres) of forest at Fontainebleau and requested it to be transferred, in its entirety, to Tolbiac. Specialists and nurserymen pointed out that this was impossible – the trees would inevitably have died. So Perrault chose pine trees from the Forest of Bord in Normandy, and replanted them elsewhere so that they could spend two years acclimatizing. Over 200 of them survived and were transferred to the library. A few hornbeams and birches add a touch of diversity.

Unfortunately for visitors this garden is only accessible to the gardener, as it is enclosed behind glass.

DID YOU KNOW?

Perrault, not merely a talented architect but evidently an imaginative one, had also dreamed up walkways suspended over the forest to enable a kind of rustic perambulation. But for safety reasons the idea was abandoned . . . .

– **In conclusion** On 30 March 1995 François Mitterrand inaugurated the new building, the last of the *grands travaux* of his second and final seven-year term. In December 1996 the 1,600 reading places in the Haut-de-Jardin rooms (as well as the 180,000 volumes) were opened to the general public. In 1998 the definitive transfer of the collections took place and in autumn of 1998 the BNF was opened to researchers and accredited readers. On the Richelieu site there are still maps and plans, engravings, photographs, manuscripts, medals, coins, musical scores and so on.

THE STRANGE, RUSTIC, UNUSUAL AND SECRET 13TH ARRONDISSEMENT . . .

★ **Le quartier du Chevaleret (Chevaleret area)**: a large part of this area is scheduled to be demolished in the near future. A sizeable portion from the Metro station to the rue Clisson has already been changed and there's little here for the tourist.

In the passage du Chef-de-la-Ville, passage Chanvin and passage Pierre-Gourdault, the workshops are now quiet. But if you go back down rue Charcot towards rue du Chevaleret, on your right you will see a charming little steeple and glimpse a peaceful inner garden. This is the chapel of a

Polish religious institution at 119 rue du Chevaleret (you can't visit it, unfortunately).

Rue du Chevaleret disappears under the rue de Tolbiac and ends at the railway. In rue Cantagrel is the imposing white mass of the Salvation Army building with its splashes of colour, the work of Le Corbusier. This was the first modern building in the 13th arrondissement. There's a good-value self-service restaurant and an auction room.

On the corner of rue Watt and rue du Chevaleret, the Lierre Theatre Company has set up in a former SNCF (French National Railway) warehouse and puts on good shows (☎ 01-45-86-55-83).

★ **Rue Watt**: This is a sinister street, straight out of a detective novel. Nobody actually lives here. It's at its spookiest between midnight and 2am, especially on a windy autumn night, or in winter when it's icy. The pavement is raised, with an iron barrier alongside it on the wall. Although it is deserted, some of its menace was lost when modern streetlights replaced the old ones. The new National Library is nearby and there's even talk of rue Watt disappearing, which would be a shame.

★ **In the rue Nationale area**: go past rue de Patay, where the tarmac has not quite covered the tracks of the tram lines. There's a little bar called La Pente Douce (Gentle Slope). The rue Regnault runs alongside the metro. It is intersected by the rue du Château des Rentiers from which the passage Nationale, lined with small houses, runs into the rue Nationale.

From rue Nationale head into the narrow **passage Bourgoin** and enjoy the delightful smell of honeysuckle and climbing roses. All around is a long succession of spruce little houses with lovely gardens, though there are some more run-down places too. This is where the long-established locals rub shoulders with trendy writers.

★ Beyond rue de Tolbiac, towards boulevard de la Gare, you enter a well-policed, clean and concrete world. Before you do that, however, take a look at the passage des Hautes-Formes (now re-christened **rue des Hautes-Formes**).The name means 'Top Hat Street' so perhaps this is where the bosses used to live in the days when this was a bona fide working-class district.

– You may also appreciate the odd construction on the corner of avenue d'Ivry and rue Baudricourt where a series of buildings harks back to the architecture of the good old days – there are staggered façades, and varied shapes with no feeling of uniformity whatsoever.

★ **Chinatown**: the Asian quarter is dominated by the pagoda-shaped shops on the Terrasse des Olympiades (although apparently they were designed before Chinatown settled here – what a convenient premonition!). Far from being the exclusive domain of the Chinese, there are Vietnamese, Laotians and Cambodians here too, and most of the signs are in three languages: Chinese, Vietnamese and Thai. People of Asian origin now make up more than 13 per cent of the population of the 13th arrondissement. They have managed to erase the cliché of the desperate refugee and the unfortunate boat people, and have created the image of a dynamic and organized community instead.

The Asian community spreads over three main sectors: Masséna, Bandicourt and Dunois and is now well-established here, as they manage many shops and companies: restaurants, supermarkets, jewellers, insurance and doctor's surgeries. Sixty per cent of businesses in Les Olympiades are run by people of Asian origin and there are more than 100 Asian restaurants in the 13th arrondissement alone. Many of their customs are still strongly intact. You may be surprised to see open windows, even when it seems to be cold. This is in accordance with the Chinese belief that the spirits of ancestors should be able to come and go as they please.

The local Asian community's answer to the concrete nightmare in the 13th arrondissement is to decorate it with bright colours and give it life. You've only got to look at the traffic jams around the two large supermarkets in avenue d'Ivry (*Tang*, at No. 48, and *Paris-Store*, at No. 44) to realise this. You can buy exotic fruits, soya, rice and glazed pigs' ears here. Many of these products and vegetables are now grown in France and, suprisingly, tons of soya are grown in the many cellars of the 13th arrondissement! If you're broke you can live on a large bowl of *phò* for quite a while.

– At the beginning of February don't miss the Chinese New Year parade, which is always very lively and colourful. Fierce-looking dragons with wild eyes jump and dance to the accompaniment of bells and drums and the lucky colour of red is everywhere. It's always a really entertaining spectacle.

– You can visit two **Buddhist temples**. The first is in rue du Disque, one of the subterranean streets of the Terrasse des Olympiades (entrance in avenue de Choisy, next to *Tang*). There's a large inscription reading *Autel du culte de Bouddha* (Altar of the Cult of Buddha). There is music on Monday and Wednesday afternoons. It is customary to leave a small donation in the altar's collection box (and make a wish). The other temple is on the Terrasse itself, just along from the Grand Mandarin restaurant. It's the Tchaochu Association in France, a community from the Canton region. Take your shoes off when you go in.

– For fans of Asian music, **Musica** (Centre des Olympiades, at the end of the right wing; ☎ 01-45-86-63-64) brings together more than 1,000 titles from classical music to Asian cover versions of songs by British or American groups.

GOING OUT

🍸 **OYA Café** (map B1, **66**): 25 rue de la Reine-Blanche 75013. ☎ 01-47-07-59-59. Metro: Gobelins. Open 2pm to midnight. Closed Monday. Entrance fee 30F. Play at being a diplomat, get lost in Manhattan, go to private viewings, bluff your way out of things – you can do all this at this unusual café. There are board games and card games imported from Japan, Germany and all over the world at this Japanese-style café where you can sip Japanese tea and nibble a *sen bei*. Appeals to everyone from 7 to 77 years of age. To play costs 35F per person for an unlimited period, with a drink. If you haven't got a partner to go with, you can always strike up a game with someone there.

🍸 **La Folie en Tête** (inset, **61**): 33 rue de la Butte-aux-Cailles 75013. ☎ 01-45-80-65-99. Metro: Corvisart. Open 5pm to 2am. Closed Sunday. Half a pint of beer costs 14F after 10pm. The last caf'-conc' (café with live music) on the Butte. The musical programme on Thursday evening is rich and open, with a bit of everything 'as long as it's good' (accordion music, *ragga*, rock, jazz, etc.) Budget for 40F, including a drink. There is a vast gallery of instruments from all over the world adorning the walls. Don't miss the 'monthly Family Ball', organized in collaboration with *Paname Tropical*. Entrance fee: 70F. The ball has no fixed venue, so ring ☎ 01-45-80-65-99 for information.

🍸 **Le Merle Moqueur** (inset, **64**): 11 rue de la Butte-aux-Cailles 75013. ☎ 01-45-65-12-43. Metro: Corvisart. Open every evening 4pm to 2am. It's 16F for a pint of beer. A lively place, open for over 10 years. The music tends to be rather mad ('everything except classical and techno'), there are musical apéritifs, thirsty crowds and it's always packed out. An institution. Happy hours from 5pm to 8pm.

🍸 **Chez Gladines** (inset, **63**): 30 rue des Cinq-Diamants 75013. ☎ 01-45-80-70-10. Metro: Corvisart. Open lunchtime and evening to 1.30am. Set menu 60F at lunchtime, draught beer 11F before 8pm, 13F afterwards. A local bistro with a friendly, neo-hippy clientele, full of students. There is a good ambiance around the bar, sometimes calm, sometimes electric. A good place for a glass of something good in a warm atmosphere. There's good food from the south west and the Basque country – and it's served until midnight.

🍸 **Le Couvent** 2 (map A1, **67**): 69 rue Broca 75013. ☎ 01-43-31-28-28. Metro: Gobelins. Open to 2am. Closed Saturday lunchtime and Sunday, between Christmas and New Year's Day and for the second fortnight in August. Set menus 59F and 65F at lunchtime, in the evening à la carte only, budget for 85F excluding drinks. In spite of a preference for rock music, blues and Cajun are also included in this bar-restaurant which doubles as a gallery. There's a mixture of students, local craftspeople and journalists from *Le Monde*, which has its headquarters nearby. Le Couvent is also a wonderful testing ground for all forms of artistic expression. Every Friday and Saturday there are acoustic concerts by young talents in the cellar. Every fortnight there is a different exhibition. There are a few generous salads, some hot dishes and usually a good dish of the day and European specialities (goulash, Flemish *carbonnade*).

14TH ARRONDISSEMENT

MONTPARNASSE ● PLAISANCE ● PERNETY ● DENFERT-ROCHEREAU ● MONTSOURIS ● ALÉSIA

This is a fascinating district of Paris, often identified as just Montparnasse. But it also includes the catacombs at Denfert, old-fashioned Plaisance-Pernety and rural Montsouris. They all offer very different attractions, which are perhaps less obvious than the main tourist sights, but which can be just as much fun to explore.

WHERE TO STAY

☆ CHEAP

Maison des Étudiantes (map C1, **1**): 214 boulevard Raspail 75014. ☎ 01-42-18-14-02. Fax: 01-43-20-70-11. Metro: Denfert-Rochereau or Vavin. Bus No. 68, Vavin stop. In summer a double room costs 215F to 290F half board or full board per person, and a single room 265F to 340F. Only available in summer (1 June to 30 September), for students and teachers. Four nights minimum. A survivor – and a successful one – of the spirit of the Left Bank. In the heart of Montparnasse, adjoining the Lycée Paul-Bert, these two 1920s tower blocks, separated by a little garden, are home, for the rest of the year, to around 160 female students who live in spacious rooms with 1 or 2 beds, all with a bathroom and direct telephone. Each floor offers two impeccable showers, a kitchenette and little study rooms. Residents can use the library, a study room and a few classrooms. The self-service restaurant caters for up to 100.

Celtic Hôtel (map C1, **2**): 15 rue d'Odessa 75014. ☎ 01-43-20-93-53 or 83-91. Fax: 01-43-20-66-07. Metro: Montparnasse-Bienvenüe or Edgar-Quinet. Double room with washbasin 250F, with shower or bathroom and toilet 310F to 330F. The only Celtic thing about this little hotel is its name! The rooms are quite large, with marble fireplaces and period furniture. The wallpaper isn't as young as it used to be, but overall it's not bad. It's best to go for a room overlooking the courtyard as they are quieter, because none of the rooms has double-glazing. Book a week in advance if possible.

Hôtel Les Jardins d'Alésia (map **C2, 3**): 34 rue d'Alésia 75014. ☎ 01-43-27-60-80. Fax: 01-43-20-29-09. Metro: Alésia. Bus Nos. 28, 38 and 62. Double room (with bathroom or shower) 320F to 350F. A functional, renovated two-star hotel, with all mod-cons in the rooms. Charming little garden.

Hôtel Le Lionceau (map C2, **4**): 22 rue Daguerre 75014. ☎ 01-43-22-53-53. Fax: 01-43-21-08-21. Metro: Denfert-Rochereau. Double room 230F. A small hotel on a pedestrian street (or at least it's supposed to be) bearing witness in its own way to the evolution of the street and the quarter. Each of the spacious rooms has a different mural decor. Room 18 has a nice mezzanine floor if there are four of you. The bathrooms are cheerful, in blue and white. You have to pay for one night in advance when you book.

☆☆ MODERATE

Foyer Internationale Accueil de Paris (FIAP) Jean Monnet (map D2, **5**): 30 rue Cabanis 75014. ☎ 01-43-13-17-00 (information) and 01-43-13-17-17 (reservations). Fax: 01-45-81-63-91. Metro: Glacière. Budget for 376F for a double room, including breakfast. There are set menus at the restaurant as well as self-service. Originally designated for European students as a place for cultural exchanges, this place offers rooms for individuals – but priority is given to groups (half board only). All the rooms (200 in all, with 500 beds) have a shower and toilet (towels provided). No age limit. It's best to book. Left luggage service.

Hôtel du Parc Montsouris (map C3, **6**): 4 rue du Parc-Montsouris 75014. ☎ 01-45-89-09-72. Fax: 01-45-80-92-72. Metro: Porte-d'Orléans; RER: Cité-Universitaire. Double room with shower, satellite TV and telephone 340F, 400F with bath. Triple rooms 450F. A quiet little hotel. Parc Montsouris is nearby. Renovated and resolutely modern and functional. You may need to book well in advance.

Hôtel Paris-Didot (map B2, **7**): 20 rue Ledion 75014. ☎ 01-45-42-33-29. Fax: 01-45-42-02-58. Metro: Alésia or Plaisance. Bus No. 58 or PC. Rooms 320F to 340F. A nice hotel, with a dark green wooden façade. Each room has brightly coloured Japanese wallpaper. The decor is reminiscent of the warmth of old chalets. There's a generous buffet breakfast (cheese, brioches, cakes) and room service. Nice interior courtyard, double-glazing and a warm welcome.

14TH

Hôtel Saphir (map C1, **8**): 70 rue Daguerre 75014. ☎ 01-43-22-07-02. Fax: 01-40-47-67-78. Metro: Denfert-Rochereau or Gaîté. Double room with shower and toilet 350F, with bathroom and toilet 400F. To say that this two-star hotel is a little gem would be over the top, but it's clean and the welcome is friendly. All rooms have TV and telephone. Go for the rooms on the garden side as the rue Daguerre is pretty noisy, in spite of the double-glazing. Or better still, bribe the staff to exchange your room for one of theirs, in the little house in the middle of the garden! North African cuisine in La Baraka restaurant on the ground floor.

Hôtel Mistral (map B1, **9**): 24 rue Cels 75014. ☎ 01-43-20-25-43. Fax: 01-43-21-32-59. Metro: Gaîté. Double room 240F with washbasin (shower and toilet on each floor), and 340F with shower and toilet. In a fairly quiet street, a stylish hotel behind Montparnasse cemetery. Jean-Paul Sartre and Simone de Beauvoir lived here in the 1930s and during the Second World War. Generous lunch-buffet. All the rooms have been renovated. Telephone and TV in some rooms. For peace and quiet, as usual, ask for the courtyard side. Note that the hotel closes at 11pm.

Cecil Hôtel (map C3, **10**): 47 rue Beaunier 75014. ☎ 01-45-40-93-53. Fax: 01-45-40-43-26. Metro: Porte-d'Orléans. Rooms 390F with shower and toilet, 415F with bathroom and toilet. A well-run family hotel. The rooms are pleasant and comfortable (with cable TV, hairdryer, direct telephone) and there's a terrace bursting with greenery when the weather's fine, overlooking the old inner circle line (but there are no more trains, unfortunately).

Hôtel des Bains (map C1, **11**): 33 rue Delambre 75014. ☎ 01-43-20-85-27. Fax: 01-42-79-82-78. Metro: Vavin or Edgar-Quinet. Rooms from 399F to 410F for two, and 675F for four. A one-star hotel with a discreet façade and undeniable charm. The rooms are tastefully decorated. Double rooms have shower, toilet and TV (11 channels including Canal +). There are quiet, comfortable suites which are much sought after by families, in an annex at the end of the courtyard. Very reasonable, especially as the welcome is excellent. Credit cards are not accepted.

Hôtel du Parc (map B–C1, **12**): 6 rue Jolivet 75014. ☎ 01-43-20-95-54. Fax: 01-42-79-82-62. Website: www.hotelduparc-paris.com. Metro: Edgar-Quinet. Double room from 390F to 420F. 10 per cent reduction if you stay here for at least three nights between 15 July and 30 August. The rooms overlook a charming, quiet, sunny square. They seem to like their peace and quiet here.

Odessa Hôtel (map B–C1, **13**): 28 rue d'Odessa 75014. ☎ 01-43-20-64-78. Fax: 01-42-79-90-71. Metro: Edgar-Quinet or Montparnasse-Bienvenüe. Double room 405F with shower and toilet and at 460F with bathroom. An elegant and well-run place superbly located right in the heart of Montparnasse, at the foot of the Tour Montparnasse. Ask for a room on the 3rd floor or higher – it's less noisy. Cable TV. Double-glazing.

Hôtel Ariane Montparnasse (map B2, **14**): 35 rue de la Sablière 75014. ☎ 01-45-45-67-13. Fax: 01-45-45-39-49. Metro: Pernety or Alésia. A double room costs 450F with bathroom, TV and mini-bar, 435F with shower. An immaculate two-star hotel. The rooms are clean, modern and well equipped. Avoid the rooms on the ground floor.

Hôtel du Moulin Vert (map B2, **15**): 74 rue du Moulin-Vert 75014. ☎ 01-45-43-65-38. Fax: 01-45-43-08-86. Website: www.hotel.moulinvert.com. Metro: Pernety. Double room with bath 400F. A well-equipped hotel, perfect if you're staying in this area. Cable TV, double-glazing and a mini-safe. All credit cards are accepted.

☆☆☆ CHIC

Hôtel Delambre (map C1, **16**): 35 rue Delambre 75014. ☎ 01-43-20-66-31. Fax: 01-45-38-91-76. Website: www.hoteldelambre.com. Metro: Edgar-Quinet or Vavin. Double room 460F with shower and toilet, and 550F with bathroom and toilet. Charm, peace and quiet efficiency – these are the mottos of the Hôtel Delambre, which has changed a lot since the days when it was home to the surrealist André Breton. There's a nice breakfast-buffet in the mornings, satellite TV in the evening. The prices are reasonable for a three-star hotel. In summer you can even sleep with the window open!

Hôtel Daguerre (map C1, **17**): 94 rue Daguerre 75014. ☎ 01-43-22-43-54. Fax: 01-43-20-66-84. E-mail: hotel.daguerre.paris.14@gofornet.com. Metro: Gaîté. For a double room with shower or bath budget for 470F, 650F for a suite for a maximum of four people. This two-star establishment has treated itself to a face-lift. Marble, statues, *trompe l'œil* painting and a romantic patio all hark back to a better era. It continues in the rooms: sparkling cleanliness, a safe, mini-bar, cable TV, and even one or two rooms fitted out for visitors with disabilities, which overlook the little patio. And, what's more, you get a smiling welcome.

Hôtel Le Nouvel Orléans (map C2, **18**): 25 avenue du Général-Leclerc 75011. ☎ 01-43-27-80-20. Fax: 01-43-35-36-57. Metro: Mouton-Duvernet. Double room 450F with shower and toilet, or 500F with bath and toilet. Breakfast-buffet included. Easy to get to by bus and tube, a solid Haussmann-style building which has been renovated and offers rooms with all mod-cons.

If you venture into some of the little streets around you might be forgiven for thinking you were in the countryside . . . .

Hôtel Istria (map C1, **19**): 29 rue Campagne-Première 75014. ☎ 01-43-20-91-82. Fax: 01-43-22-48-45. Metro: Raspail. Rooms 600F, breakfast included. A charming hotel full of literary connections. It was home to the love affair between Elsa Triolet and the poet Louis Aragon, and Raymond Radiguet used to come to meet a woman here, cheating on his gay lover, Jean Cocteau. The British shipping heiress Nancy Cunard escaped from the Plaza to hide her lovers here. The rooms have TV, mini-safe, hairdryer and have recently been renovated.

WHERE TO EAT

☆ BUDGET

✕ **Aux Produits du Sud-Ouest** (map C1, **30**): 21–23 rue d'Odessa 75014. ☎ 01-43-20-34-07. Metro: Edgar-Quinet. Open noon to 2pm and 7pm to 11pm. Closed Sunday, Monday and public holidays, and August. Dish of the day and coffee 32F at lunchtime only. À la carte, budget for 120F. This restaurant-shop offers traditional preserves and tinned food from southwest France at prices which defy all competition. Don't expect Landes gastronomy, but honest dishes using the fruits of the earth such as the platter of *charcuterie* (42F) or the terrines of rabbit or wild boar (17F). Those with smaller appetites can make do with a single course: *cassoulet au confit d'oie*, wood pigeon stew and *confit de canard-pommes sarladaises*. For dessert, an apple tart with Armagnac. Good value for the area.

14TH

✕ **Rehana Store** (map C1, **31**): 30 rue Delambre 75014. ☎ 01-43-22-40-71. Metro: Vavin or Edgar-Quinet. Open 11am to 8.30pm. Closed Sunday. Budget for around 60F or 49F for the set menu. A sort of Punjabi-style general store right in the heart of Montparnasse, this shop is full of spices and bags of rice and has opened a tasting corner where you can try things out for a very reasonable price. *Raïta* with fresh vegetables, vegetable biryani, chicken curry, etc. Perfect if you're feeling a bit peckish before going to the cinema.

✕ **Chez Charles-Victor** (map C2, **32**): 8 rue Brézin 75014. ☎ 01-40-44-55-51. Metro: Mouton-Duvernet. Open to 10.30pm. Closed Saturday lunchtime and Sunday, and public holidays. Set menu 79F served lunchtime and evening. À la carte, budget for around 100F without drinks. Yellow walls, foliage plants, a huge blackboard with dishes of the day, and a cheerful ambiance characterize this place. Veal liver with raspberry vinegar, fillet of seabass with cream, steak tartare and lots of delicious fresh desserts: rhubarb and blueberry crumble, fondant with three sorts of chocolate, etc. The service is efficient. There is a selection of wines straight from the vineyard at 79F.

✕ **La Chopotte** (map B2, **33**): 168 rue d'Alésia 75014. ☎ 01-45-43-16-16. Metro: Plaisance. Bus No. 62. Open lunchtime Monday to Saturday, and Thursday 8pm to 10.30pm. Closed Sunday, public holidays and August. Dish of the day 62F, set menus from 62F to 135F. This place has been transformed into a wine bar. Mâcon, Beaujolais, Chinon – they all slip down smoothly and go nicely with the main courses: *andouillette* with violet mustard (75F), house confit of chicken and *pommes sarladaises* (65F), *piccata* of *onglet* (prime cut) of veal (75F) are displayed on the blackboard as well as other specials, according to the whim of the day.

✕ **Au Rendez-vous des Camionneurs** (map B2, **34**): 34 rue des Plantes 75014. ☎ 01-45-40-43-36. Metro: Alésia. Open to 9.30pm. Closed Saturday and Sunday and August. Set menu 77F served lunchtime and evening. À la carte around 100F. Credit cards not accepted. At lunchtime it's mainly populated with people working nearby, as well as a few artists and models (there is a famous modelling agency not far away) in the evening. Children's portions are available at half price. À la carte there's *magret* of duck with green pepper (for two), and a good rib of beef. As far as value for money is concerned you could hardly do better. Booking is almost essential as there are not many tables.

✕ **La Baraka** (map C1, **8**): 70 rue Daguerre 75014. ☎ 01-43-27-28-20. Metro: Denfert-Rochereau or Gaîté. Open daily to 11.30pm. Set menu 59F at lunchtime only and 79F in the evening. Located on the ground floor of the Hôtel Saphir, this place is lucky enough to have a rare inner courtyard, very pleasant on a long summer evening. The food is plain; go for a kebab and couscous washed down with a little Sidi Brahim, and enjoy the starry night.

✕ **Au Berbère** (map B2, **36**): 50 rue de Gergovie 75014. ☎ 01-45-42-10-29. Metro: Plaisance or Pernety. Open daily noon to 2.30pm and 7pm to 11pm. Set menus 54F to 77F. Popular with locals and well known for its generous couscous – as much as you can eat. Main courses for around 50F. For the *méchoui* (87F) you need to book at least half an hour beforehand.

Where to stay
- **1** Maison des Étudiantes
- **2** Celtic Hôtel
- **3** Hôtel Les Jardins d'Alésia
- **4** Hôtel Le Lionceau
- **5** FIAP Jean Monnet
- **6** Hôtel du Parc Montsouris
- **7** Hôtel Paris-Didot
- **8** Hôtel Saphir
- **9** Hôtel Mistral
- **10** Cecil Hôtel
- **11** Hôtel des Bains
- **12** Hôtel du Parc
- **13** Odessa Hôtel
- **14** Hôtel Ariane Montparnasse
- **15** Hôtel du Moulin Vert
- **16** Hôtel Delambre
- **17** Hôtel Daguerre
- **18** Hôtel Le Nouvel Orléans
- **19** Hôtel Istria

✕ **Where to eat**
- **8** La Baraka
- **30** Aux Produits du Sud-Ouest
- **31** Rehana Store
- **32** Chez Charles-Victor
- **33** La Chopotte
- **34** Au Rendez-vous des Camionneurs
- **35** Cana'Bar
- **36** Au Berbère
- **37** L'Aquarius
- **38** Le Télémaque
- **39** Bistrot Montsouris
- **40** Les Comestibles
- **41** Bistrot du Dôme
- **42** Chez Clément
- **43** Krua Thaï
- **44** Le Château Poivre
- **45** Katmandou Café
- **46** Le Plomb du Cantal
- **47** La Régalade
- **48** L'Amuse-Bouche
- **49** L'Auberge de Venise
- **50** Le Restaurant Bleu
- **51** Vin & Marée
- **52** La Nouvelle Créole
- **53** L'O à la Bouche
- **54** Le Flamboyant
- **55** Il Barone
- **56** Le Pavillon Montsouris
- **57** La Coupole
- **58** Le Vin des Rues
- **59** Severo Bar
- **60** La Mère Agitée

Where to go for a drink/Going out/Where to go for jazz
- **57** Dancing de la Coupole
- **65** Le Dôme
- **66** Le Rosebud
- **68** Magique
- **69** L'Utopia
- **70** Les Mousquetaires
- **71** Le Petit Journal Montparnasse

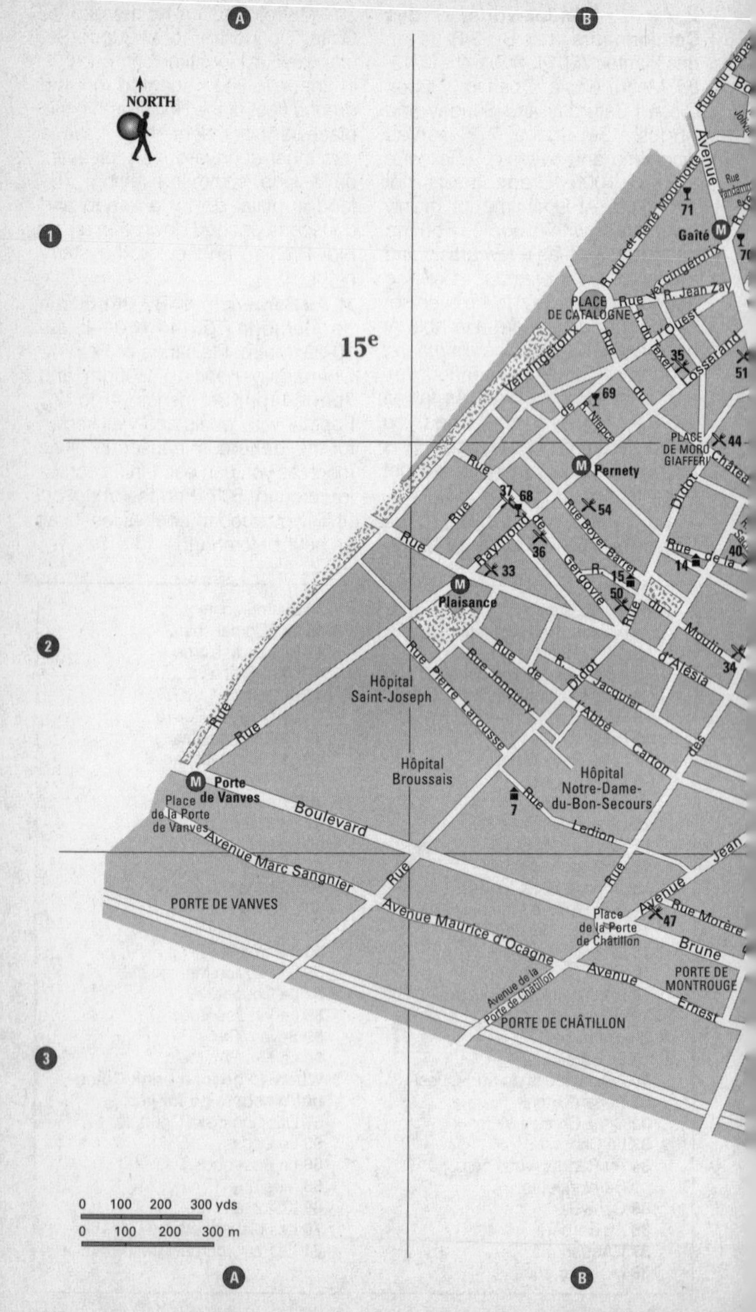
A
B
NORTH
1
2
3
15e
PLACE DE CATALOGNE
Gaîté
Pernety
Plaisance
Porte de Vanves
Place de la Porte de Vanves
PLACE DE MORO GIAFFERI
Hôpital Saint-Joseph
Hôpital Broussais
Hôpital Notre-Dame-du-Bon-Secours
PORTE DE VANVES
PORTE DE CHÂTILLON
PORTE DE MONTROUGE
Place de la Porte de Châtillon
Rue du Départ
Avenue du Maine
R. du Cdt René Mouchotte
Rue Vercingétorix
R. Jean Zay
Rue de l'Ouest
R. du Texel
Rue Losserand
R. Niepce
Rue Raymond Losserand
Rue Boyer Barret
Rue de Gergovie
R. Didot
Rue du Château
Rue de la Sablière
Rue du Moulin
Rue d'Alésia
Rue Pierre Larousse
Rue Jonquoy
Rue de l'Abbé Carton
R. Jacquier
Rue Ledion
Rue des Plantes
Boulevard Brune
Avenue Marc Sangnier
Avenue Maurice d'Ocagne
Avenue de la Porte de Châtillon
Avenue Jean Moulin
Rue Morère
Avenue Ernest Reyer
71
70
35
51
69
44
37
68
54
36
33
15
14
40
50
34
7
47
0 100 200 300 yds
0 100 200 300 m
A
B

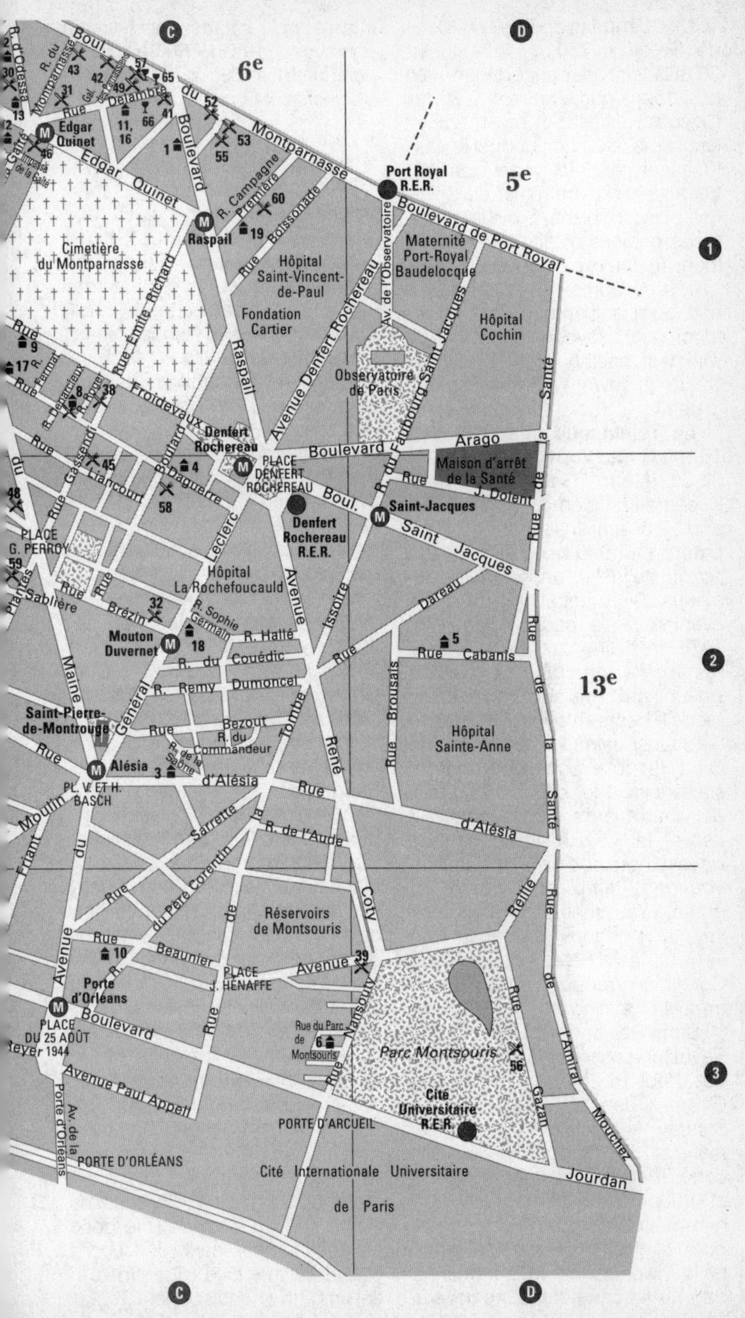

6e
5e
13e
Boulevard du Montparnasse
Boulevard de Port Royal
Port Royal R.E.R.
Edgar Quinet
Raspail
Cimetière du Montparnasse
Hôpital Saint-Vincent-de-Paul
Fondation Cartier
Maternité Port-Royal Baudelocque
Hôpital Cochin
Observatoire de Paris
Av. de l'Observatoire
Avenue Denfert Rochereau
R. du Faubourg Saint Jacques
Boulevard Arago
Maison d'arrêt de la Santé
Rue J. Dolent
Rue de la Santé
Denfert Rochereau
PLACE DENFERT ROCHEREAU
Denfert Rochereau R.E.R.
Saint-Jacques
Boul. Saint Jacques
Rue Froidevaux
Rue Daguerre
Rue Liancourt
Rue Gassendi
PLACE G. PERROY
Hôpital La Rochefoucauld
Mouton Duvernet
R. Hallé
R. du Couëdic
R. Remy Dumoncel
Rue Bezout
R. du Commandeur
Saint-Pierre-de-Montrouge
Alésia
PL. V. ET H. BASCH
Rue d'Alésia
Avenue du Général Leclerc
Avenue René Coty
Rue Dareau
Rue Cabanis
Hôpital Sainte-Anne
Rue Broussais
Rue de la Tombe Issoire
R. de l'Aude
Rue Sarrette
Rue du Père Corentin
Réservoirs de Montsouris
Rue Beaunier
PLACE J. HÉNAFFE
Avenue Reille
Porte d'Orléans
PLACE DU 25 AOÛT 1944
Boulevard Jourdan
Avenue Paul Appell
Rue du Parc de Montsouris
Rue Nansouty
Parc Montsouris
Rue Gazan
Rue de l'Amiral Mouchez
Cité Universitaire R.E.R.
PORTE D'ARCUEIL
PORTE D'ORLÉANS
Cité Internationale Universitaire de Paris

✕ **L'Aquarius** (map B2, **37**): 40 rue de Gergovie 75014. ☎ 01-45-41-36-88. Metro: Plaisance. Open noon to 2.15pm and 7pm to 10.30pm. Closed Sunday. Set menu 65F at lunchtime. À la carte budget for 90F. Whoever said that vegetarian restaurants had to be rather dull? This is a pleasant place, providing generous portions of good vegetarian food. Try the excellent salads, soya *quenelles* (dumplings made of flour and egg), tofu croquettes, mushroom tarts, savoury pasty (made with puff pastry), or nut roast, all washed down with an organic claret!

✕ **Le Télémaque** (map C1, **38**): 15 rue Roger 75014. ☎ 01-43-20-66-38. Metro: Gaîté or Denfert-Rochereau. Open noon to 2.30pm and 7.30pm to midnight (last orders 11pm). Closed Sunday and public holidays, and August. Set menus 60F at lunchtime, 75F in the evening. À la carte, budget for 127F. In a tiny street, this Greek restaurant provides a cuisine which has remained close to its roots. It bears little resemblance to the tourist cafés in the Mouffetard or La Huchette. Some good classic starters include: *pikilia, taramasalata*, then there's *fricassée* (shoulder of lamb with lemon sauce), *bakaliaros* (a cod dish), moussaka, *youvetsi* (lamb and pasta au gratin). You should also try their speciality: chops prepared with vegetables, Feta cheese and Corinthian grapes. The welcome is always charming.

14TH

✕ **Cana'Bar** (map B1, **35**): 22 rue Raymond-Losserand 75014. ☎ 01-43-22-92-15. Metro: Pernety or Gaîté. Open to 11pm. Closed Sunday. At lunchtime there's a set menu at 58F. Budget for 80F à la carte. The set menu (lunchtime only at 1.30pm) is a classic with egg mayonnaise, *terrine de campagne*, *confit* of chicken or spaghetti meatballs (two dishes which change daily). À la carte, there are several interesting salads and main courses such as the 'RMI' (ragout of Irish lamb) at 39F or *boeuf bourguignon* at 44F.

☆☆ MODERATE

✕ **Les Comestibles** (map B2, **40**): 10 rue de la Sablière 75014. ☎ 01-45-45-47-12. Metro: Pernety or Mouton-Duvernet. Closed Saturday lunchtime, Sunday and public holidays, as well as in August. No set menu, budget for around 100F per person. Home-cooked delights abound here. The service is swift and attentive. During the week, the dish of the day is around 60F and the à la carte main courses are between 55F and 80F, and if that's all you have, nobody will mind. The desserts, of which there are lots, are excellent. As a bonus, the restaurant has exhibitions of paintings.

✕ **Bistrot Montsouris** (map D3, **39**): 27 avenue Reille 75014. ☎ 01-45-89-17-05. RER: Cité-Universitaire. Closed Sunday and Monday. Set menu 108F with starter and main course or main course and dessert. À la carte, budget for 200F. Located close to the wonderful Parc Montsouris, the quality of the food and the service are excellent in this charming place, which is more like a country inn than a bistro. The traditional cuisine is in keeping with the decor, carefully thought out. The dishes change according to what's available, with, for instance, delicious seafood *cassoulet* or authentic *blanquette de veau*.

✕ **Chez Clément** (map A1, **42**): 106 boulevard du Montparnasse 75014. ☎ 01-44-10-54-00. Metro: Vavin. Open daily 11.30am to 1am. Squeezed in between two enormous buildings, the Brasserie du Dôme and La Coupole, the good old Clément has certainly found a clientele of their own. (*See* 'Where to eat' *in* '17th arrondissement'.)

✕ **Krua Thaï** (map C1, **43**): 41 rue du Montparnasse 75014. ☎ 01-43-35-38-67. Metro: Edgar-Quinet, Vavin or Montparnasse-Bienvenüe. Open noon to 2.30pm and 7pm to 11.30pm. Closed on Sunday. Set menus 55F to 150F. À la carte, budget for 140F on average. In this 'street of crêpes', this Thai restaurant has already won the heart of the locals, who rush in to enjoy shrimp soup with lemon grass, beef grilled with tamarind, Thai green papaya salad, or mussels sautéed with basil.

✕ **Le Château Poivre** (map B1–2, **44**): 145 rue du Château 75014. ☎ 01-43-22-03-68. Metro: Pernety Last orders 11pm. Closed Sunday, the week of 15 August and at Christmas. Set menu 89F; à la carte, budget for between 160F and 180F. A restaurant which is very popular with the locals. *Andouillette*, *confit*, Hungarian goulash, steak *tartare*... concocted by a friendly owner.

✕ **Le Plomb du Cantal** (map C1, **46**): 3 rue de la Gaîté 75014. ☎ 01-43-35-16-92. Metro: Edgar-Quinet. Open 9am to 1am Tuesday to Saturday. Closed Sunday, Monday and public holidays, and in August. Set menu 80F lunchtime and evening. Main courses around 94F. The rue de la Gaîté (Gaiety Street, obviously!) is no longer as its name might suggest, as it's now been invaded by sex shops and flashy signs giving it the look of a rather out of place 'Pigalle'. There's nothing like a good meal to cheer you up when you see just how low Paris has sunk and here they've got everything you need. Come just for a bowl of soup, followed by a vast omelette, or go straight to the *truffade* (fresh grilled sausage, sautéed potatoes, fresh Tomme cheese, garlic), the Aveyron-style stuffed cabbage, or just a simple plate of Auvergne ham, followed by cheese from the Massif Central for dessert: blue, Cantal, Mont-Salvy. We advise you to take a walk afterwards!

✕ **Katmandou Café** (map C2, **45**): 27 rue Gassendi 75014. ☎ 01-43-20-89-84. Metro: Gaîté or Denfert-Rochereau. Open daily noon to 2.30 and 7pm to 11.30pm. An Indian-Nepalese establishment with elegant decor and perfect service. The cuisine is unpretentious but delicately flavoured (excellent lamb masala) and at prices defying all competition. Set menu 59F at lunchtime only and, for gourmets, there is a generous 'Nepal platter' at 99F, with five starters, a main course, dessert and nan bread.

✕ **La Mère Agitée** (map C1, **60**): 21 rue Campagne-Première 75014. ☎ 01-43-35-56-64. Metro: Raspail. Open Tuesday to Saturday. Sunday and Monday by reservation only (at least 10 people). Dishes of the day 65F and desserts 30F. On the corner of the passage d'Enfer (Passage of Hell!), a few yards from where Jean-Paul Belmondo died in Jean-Luc Godard's film *À bout de souffle* (remade as *Breathless*, with Richard Gere), this is an atypical restaurant serving traditional cuisine. You can eat in the ground floor dining room, which is packed full of cases of wine, or in the smaller arched cellar. There isn't a great deal of choice: two or three starters (crêpe with salmon, terrine of duck, *foie gras*), one or two main courses of the day (roast veal with morels, etc.). It's very fresh, the portions are more than generous and the menu is always changing. There are a few nice wines at very reasonable prices (Gris Meunier de l'Orléanais, Faugères, Muscat de Frontignan for dessert).

☆ ☆ ☆ CHIC

✕ **La Régalade** (map B3, **47**): 49 avenue Jean-Moulin 75014. ☎ 01-45-45-68-58. Metro: Alésia or Porte-d'Orléans. Open till midnight. Closed Saturday lunchtime, Sunday and Monday, for August, and at Christmas and New Year. À la carte 175F. On the edge of the 14th arrondissement, this magical place provides fresh food based on excellent produce served in a retro dining room. As a starter, there's a basket of superb *charcutailles* (cooked pork meat) from Pau. Try the *risotto à l'encre*, squid *façon piballe*, *coquilles* St-Jacques in their shells, root celery tagliatelle, *estouffade* of young wild boar with fresh pasta, seabass, etc. Amazing wine list – they're almost giving it away! You need to book at least five days in advance.

✕ **Bistrot du Dôme** (map C1, **41**): 1 rue Delambre 75014. ☎ 01-43-35-32-00. Metro: Vavin. Open daily. Closed 24 to 31 December. A three-course meal costs around 200–250F. This is the bistro annex to the famous Montparnasse brewery. The fresh fish is excellent, as is the wine list. Fast service. Squid *à la plancha*, grilled turbot *à la béarnaise*, salmon tartare and *solettes meunière* are all as tasty as anything you'd find in a little place beside the sea.

✕ **La Coupole** (map C1, **57**): 102 boulevard du Montparnasse 75014. ☎ 01-43-20-14-20. Metro: Vavin. Open daily 7.30am to 10.30am for breakfast, noon to (last orders) 2am for the brasserie. Set menus 99F at lunchtime, 138F and 188F in the evening. À la carte, budget for around 190F without drinks. This is one of the last of a breed of huge restaurants, once common in Montparnasse. In terms of area, it's the largest restaurant in France.

La Coupole was founded in 1927 in an old wood and coal depot. The founders were former managers of the nearby Dôme who had been sacked. To get their revenge, they decided to set up a rival establishment. From its birth, it was frequented by the arty set: Chagall, Man Ray, Soutine, Joséphine Baker and her lion cub. The decor has barely changed: original art-deco style, columns topped with frescoes, 'cubist' tiling. The clientele is trendy: film makers, advertising and marketing people, architects, etc. It would be impossible to draw up an exhaustive list of all the people who've frequented La Coupole but just a few include Hemingway, Lawrence Durrell, Henry Miller, Luis Buñuel, Salvador Dalí, Pablo Picasso, Colette and Simone de Beauvoir. One 24-year-old writer used to come in, even then with a pipe in his mouth. He became better known as Georges Simenon and his hero, Inspector Maigret, sometimes eats at La Coupole.

La Coupole is also one of the largest 'cafeterias' in Paris. Under its original ownership the food didn't match up to the reputation of the establishment, but that wasn't why people came here – they came to see and be seen. In early 1988 La Coupole was sold. The creator, René Lafon, handed over to Jean-Paul Bücher, the owner of the Flo group, for 60 million francs – or so people say! The latter undertook to respect the establishment's past and its artistic heritage. The restoration work lasted eight months. The famous 33 pillars were reinforced and returned to their original green, with the drapes over the pillars reinstated in their smart colours to mark the 70th birthday of this mythical place, in December 1997. The dining room has 450 seats and the dance hall has also been preserved. It's open at weekends for matinées (tea dances) and in the evening. There are Cuban fiestas on Tuesday evening (*see* 'Going Out'). The cuisine blends continuity and innovation with know-how and the Flo group's recipes. You can still try the famous curry and the no less famous hot fudge ice-cream with hot chocolate and almonds, as well as the old menu favourites steak tartare and cassoulet. Yet these changes have taken the edge off the atmosphere and authors and publishers are now leaving what used to be their 'own' cafeteria.

✕ **L'O à la Bouche** (map C1, **53**): 124 boulevard du Montparnasse 75006. ☎ 01-56-54-01-55. Metro: Vavin; RER: Port-Royal. Open to 11pm. Closed Sunday and Monday evening. Set menus 105F at lunchtime, 140F and 190F in the evening. À la carte, budget for 250F. Franck Paquier, the former chef at La Butte Chaillot, has concocted a watertight menu (which you can break down into starter and main course, or main course and dessert), plus a few daily suggestions on the blackboard. Everything is fresh and consistently well cooked. Try tart with sardines *à la tapenade*, tomatoes preserved with rosemary, fillet of bream with wood mushrooms, vanilla, artichokes and spinach shoots, *grillons* of lamb's sweetbreads with tarragon and mangetout. Desserts include French toast with orange marmalade and vanilla ice-cream, rhubarb *coulis* of red fruit crumble and fromage frais sorbet. The wine cellar is reasonably priced.

✕ **L'Amuse-Bouche** (map C2, **48**): 186 rue du Château 75014. ☎ 01-43-35-31-61. Metro: Mouton-Duvernet. Open noon to 2pm and 7.30pm to 10.30pm. Closed Monday lunchtime and Sunday, as well as for three weeks in August. Set menu 145F served lunchtime and evening, à la carte menu 178F. Gilles Lambert, formerly at Cagna and the Miraville, works with consummate art. If you need proof, try his menu, with starters like artichokes *barigoule*, vegetables with coriander, scampi ravioli with basil, fresh cod risotto, or veal liver with spiced bread. For dessert, the *croustillant* with green lemon mousse is to die for!

✕ **L'Auberge de Venise** (map C1, **49**): 10 rue Delambre 75014. Metro: Vavin. ☎ 01-43-35-43-09. Open to 10.30pm. Closed in August. Set menu 105F served lunchtime and evening. Budget for 150–170F à la carte. Although Montparnasse no longer has the attractions it used to have – except of course a few essential historic monuments such as La Coupole or Le Rosebud – it has not been completely ruined. Its cinemas and good restaurants mean that you can still have fun here in the evening. For instance, there's this Italian inn, where publishers and people from the world of showbiz come. It doesn't matter whether you're rich and powerful or a temporary visiting backpacker here, everyone is welcomed with a smile and gets the same service.

✕ **Le Restaurant Bleu** (map B2, **50**): 46 rue Didot 75014. ☎ 01-45-43-70-56. Metro: Plaisance or Pernety. Open noon to 3pm and 7.30pm to 10.15pm. Closed Sunday, Monday and public holidays, as well as August. Set menu 98F at lunchtime, 120F and 165F in the evening. Taken over by an excellent chef, this old bistro with its peaceful atmosphere, right in the middle of working-class Paris, is worth checking out. The menu goes for the fruits of the earth and combines the seasons of the year – game, terrines, mushrooms, red fruits. The basket of *cochonnailles* (selection of cold meat) from Rouergue is an excellent starter, as is the *pressée de jarrets de veau au persil plat* and goose *foie gras*. To follow, there's fish *cassoulet* with fresh coconut or grilled beef, with fricassée of mushrooms. And for dessert, go for *chaudfroid* of crêpes with preserved orange. On Friday, fish is top of the bill both for starters and main courses.

✗ **Vin & Marée** (map B1, **51**): 108 avenue du Maine 75014. Metro: Gaîté. ☎ 01-43-20-29-50. Open daily to 11.30pm (midnight Friday and Saturday). Budget for around 230F per person à la carte. Here, you'll get fish, fish and more fish, served either on the covered terrace or indoors in a plush setting. No set menu, no à la carte, but there is a big blackboard on which you'll see the fish of the day and the chef's suggestions. For a starter there's salmon tartare, oysters or *accras*. Fish perfectly cooked, prepared and served with professional thoroughness. There are some very popular dishes, such as swordfish steak, *solettes de sable* and *filets de St-Pierre*. There is an interesting selection of wines, with a few on offer sold by the glass. Desserts include Zanzibar babas – the undisputed star. The place has a good reputation, so book ahead.

✗ **La Nouvelle Créole** (map C1, **52**): 122 boulevard du Montparnasse 75014. ☎ 01-43-20-62-12. Metro: Vavin or Port-Royal. Open noon to 2pm and to 10.30pm (11pm at weekends). Set menu 130F. À la carte, budget for 230F to 250F. The decor is pleasant, a sort of totally exotic kitsch effect. Stained-glass windows, coloured wallpaper and naïve frescoes. Garden tables and chairs, with an abundance of real flowers, palm trees and plastic greenery. On the wall, as you go in, you'll see a fine map of Martinique. This place is becoming more and more of a tourist joint and the prices have leapt up. Excellent stuffed crab, *colombo* of tender pork and generous *court-bouillon* fish with delicately spiced and flavoured red beans, and other West Indian specialities. Don't miss the *ti'punch* or the Planter's Punch cocktails, which add plenty of local colour.

✗ **Le Flamboyant** (map B2, **54**): 11 rue Boyer-Barret 75014. ☎ 01-45-41-00-22. Metro: Pernety. Bus Nos. 58 and 62. Last orders 2pm for lunch and 10.45pm in the evening. Closed Sunday evening, Tuesday lunchtime and Monday, as well as August. At lunchtime there is a set menu at 79F; in the evening, there is a set menu at 180F. Children's menu 60F. À la carte, budget for 180F. In the evening booking is essential. One of the best West Indian restaurants in Paris. At lunchtime only (Wednesday, Thursday and Friday), there is a set menu with quarter of a bottle of wine included. À la carte, there is a large choice. Good *accras*. For main courses, there is a choice between the stuffed crab and the shark *touffé*. A nice, family welcome.

✗ **Il Barone** (map C1, **55**): 5 rue Léopold-Robert 75014. ☎ 01-43-20-87-14. Metro: Vavin. Open daily except Sunday lunchtime. Closed Christmas and New Year's Day. Budget for between 200F and 230F without drinks. A little restaurant with unpretentious Italian specialities. Don't be put off as you go in: the first dining room is tiny, so it's best to ask to be seated in the room at the end. People don't come here for the decor (which is very simple), but to satisfy their tastebuds. There's a very good choice of *antipasti* and pasta dishes.

☆☆☆☆ TRÈS CHIC

✗ **Le Pavillon Montsouris** (map D3, **56**): 20 rue Gazan 75014. ☎ 01-45-88-38-52. RER: Cité-Universitaire. Open daily to 10.30pm. Set menus 198F and 298F served lunchtime and evening. Fine 1880s architecture. A mixture of glass and steel and a large glass roof in retro style. Some famous customers include Mata-Hari, who plotted on the 1st floor, and Lenin, who used to eat here after writing his speeches under the pavilion in the park. Jean-Paul Sartre used to eat here every

Saturday lunchtime. The main thing is being able to eat on the terrace in summer, in the park. Try duck with *foie gras*, Challans duckling roasted with honey and Chinese spices (for two), just a couple of the house specialities.

WINE BARS

✕ 𝐈 **Le Vin des Rues** (map C2, **58**): 21 rue Boulard 75014. ☎ 01-43-22-19-78. Metro: Denfert-Rochereau or Mouton-Duvernet. Open lunchtime 12.30pm and at night on Wednesday and Friday if you book, 9pm onwards. Closed Sunday and Monday, as well as from the end of February to the beginning of March and from the beginning of August to the beginning of September. There is no set menu, budget for between 160F and 180F, excluding drinks. In the re-emerging movement of local bistros and wine bars, this place is already well placed. Excellent Lyons-style cuisine, with at least a couple of dishes of the day, which are always substantial. The dishes change daily. For starters, house Beaujolais terrine or Lyons mixed salad. For main courses try sausage with potatoes in walnut oil, braised Beaujolais *andouillette*, casserole of beef with prunes, or *coq au vin*. There is a choice of regional cheeses and house desserts. An amusing blackboard displays the cheaper wines and the menu of the day. There seems to be a certain amount of controversy over the quality of the welcome. Some people say that the owner is difficult (or even impossible), others say that he deliberately cultivates his lack of politeness to recreate the character of the moaning bistro owner of popular films (some people like it!). One thing is certain: this is a 'slow-food' joint. Another thing: the bar is open 10am to 8pm.

✕ 𝐈 **Severo Bar** (map C2, **59**): 8 rue des Plantes 75014. ☎ 01-45-40-40-91. Metro: Mouton-Duvernet. Open 11.45am to 2.45pm and 7pm to 11pm (to 4pm on Saturday). Closed Saturday afternoon and Sunday and for three weeks in July and one week at Christmas. À la carte only, budget for around 130F per person. A modest but authentic wine bar. There are around 60 wines to tempt you and you can try them by the glass. To stop yourself from fainting from hunger, sharpen your appetite with black sausage, steak tartare and chips or Aubrac sirloin with shallots.

MONTPARNASSE

Where does the name 'Montparnasse' come from? During the 18th century students would recite poetry in front of the mound formed by the rubble during the construction of the catacombs. This mound – which has now gone – was at the corner of today's boulevard du Montparnasse and boulevard Raspail, and was named Mont Parnasse (Mount Parnassus) in homage to the Greek poets.

The golden age of the bohemian lifestyle began in 1900: poets, writers, artists, refugees and politicians moved in *en masse* – Modigliani and Utrillo 'emigrated' from Montmartre, Max Jacob, Guillaume Apollinaire, as well as Lenin and Trotsky, who were preparing to emulate the activities of the French a century earlier by launching their own Revolution. Montparnasse is a little like a village, with artists' workshops nestling in flowery cul-de-sacs. After the First World War the quarter began to attract more and more people, many of them coming from abroad. Hemingway, Braque, Chagall, Picasso, Rouault and Klee all frequented the great working-class cafés. This was the golden age of the Paris school, a period when the city was the intellectual capital of the world.

For some years Montparnasse rested on its laurels and continued to attract the crowds, its intellectual aura occasionally being diluted in the alcohol of its bistros and cafés. But the developers had other plans. Exit the old Gare Montparnasse mainline station and enter a brand new one complete with a flashy shopping centre of the sort you can find anywhere in the world, the architectural design of which has no originality. However, there are still some fine remains from the old days. What's more, boulevard du Montparnasse, from the place Bienvenüe to boulevard Raspail, is still lively late into the night and has cinemas, restaurants and cafés to suit all tastes.

THE MONTPARNASSE BRETONS

The Bretons (people from Brittany) settled in the area around the station; poor migrants forced to leave in a rural exodus. A bit like the Asian communities in the 13th arrondissement, the Bretons formed clans at the beginning of the 20th century and opened cafés bearing the name of the town they came from (À la Ville de Guingamp, de Morlaix, de Pont-l'Abbé, de Brest, de St-Malo), started creperies, founded clubs and folk associations (now cultural associations) and generally kept up their own traditions.

The Tour Montparnasse resembles a sort of glass and concrete lighthouse above the sea of rooftops. Being able to see it from their apartment window was a reassuring reminder of their coastal homeland for the Bretons who now populated the 14th and 15th arrondissements.

In rue d'Odessa and rue du Montparnasse, there are lots of creperies giving off the lovely smell of *galettes*. Further on, in rue Delambre, the bar Ty-Jos looks more like an Irish pub than a typical Parisian brasserie. This is one of the main meeting points for wandering Celts. Welshmen and Scots pack in when there's a big game on.

After the bars, the Breton Mission, *Ti-ar-Vretonned,* is still one of the great institutions of Paris. Located at 22 rue Delambre it's run by old M. Quéméner, who is, of course, a Breton. He's made it into a sort of miniature Pompidou Centre for Breton émigrés.

Another unusual place of many is the Breton Social Service. Born out of the 100-year-old foundation *Œuvres des gares*, this service was intended to welcome, guide and help the unemployed and the homeless. Today, it still carries on its work, although the Bretons who arrive in Montparnasse no longer come with empty pockets.

AMERICANS IN MONTPARNASSE

In the 1920s Paris became the adopted home of many Americans. There were a number of reasons for this. Apart from the city's natural attractions, many of them were fleeing from a puritanical America which had introduced Prohibition, while others were making the most of the strength of the dollar.

As for artists, they revelled in the creative and literary melting pot of the time. Hemingway lived at 113 rue Notre-Dame-des-Champs and left a considerable sum to the nearby bar La Closerie des Lilas. The Americans really left their mark in the years between 1920 and 1930, but the Great Depression of 1929, the Spanish Civil War and the Second World War put an end to the love affair.

WHAT TO SEE

★ The **tour Montparnasse:** (*see* '15th arrondissement').

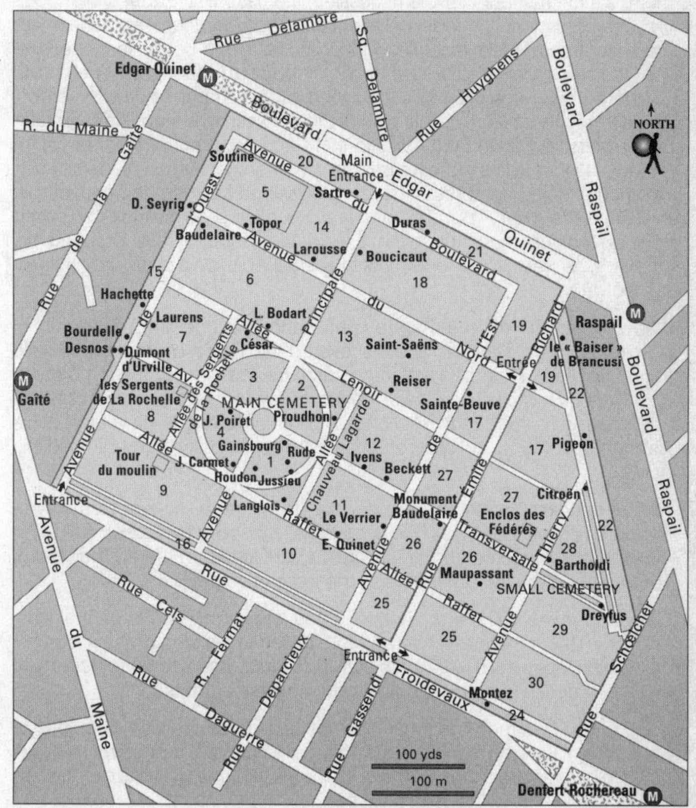

MONTPARNASSE CEMETERY

★ The **cimetière du Montparnasse:** Open 8am (8.30am Saturday, 9am Sunday and public holidays) to 5.30pm (6pm in the summer). A free map is available to visitors from the entrance on boulevard Edgar-Quinet. Created in 1824, this is the third largest cemetery in Paris in terms of area, but one of the most interesting from the point of view of its occupants. It's quite amazing how many famous people have chosen to spend the last few centuries in the shadow of the tower.

The notable graves include those of Baudelaire, Serge Gainsbourg, Rude, Houdon and Bourdelle, Admiral Dumont d'Urville, Robert Desnos, the composer Camille St-Saëns, Proudhon (the anarchist who coined the phrase 'Property is theft'), the critic Sainte-Beuve, Jean-Paul Sartre, Guy de Maupassant, and Dreyfus (of Dreyfus Affair fame).

There are also people whose names are only known because they've got a metro station named after them! Jussieu, the naturalist; Edgar Quinet, philosopher; Boucicaut (founder of the shop *Au Bon Marché*). Also buried here are several publishers including Plon, Larousse, and Louis Hachette. And then there's Stirbois, the guru of the *Front National* (a far-right French political party), who ironically is surrounded by a number of Jewish tombs. There's the great black marble slab of Pierre Laval, who was Prime Minister under Marshal Pétain from 1942 to 1944 and was shot at Fresnes on 15 October 1945. He lies in the tomb of the Chambruns, his son-in-law's family. He should have been buried in the plot reserved for executed criminals in the Cimetière d'Ivry, but it's said that he committed suicide by taking cyanide on the morning of the execution. Although they pumped his stomach, he was already dead, but they still sat him on a chair and shot him symbolically!

A few metres from Laval's tomb stands the little obelisk of the tomb of Admiral Dumont d'Urville, who discovered the *Venus de Milo* and Adélie Land. He died in France's first train crash. Behind him lies the tomb of the poet Robert Desnos, who died of typhus in May 1945 at the Terezin concentration camp (in the Czech Republic). A bit further along is the vault of Louis Hachette, the founder of the French publishing company that originated this guide.

Almost opposite, in the 7th division, stands a superb modern statue symbolizing pain, on the tomb of Henri Laurens (a friend of Braque's). Following the wall which goes along boulevard Edgar-Quinet (in the 20th division), 10m (32ft) before the great gate, is the tomb of Jean-Paul Sartre.

Gainsbourg lies in the first division. If you walk up the great central aisle away from the roundabout, look straight ahead to the 26th division, against the wall on the rue Émile-Richard stands the monument to Baudelaire, with the poet's bust contemplating his body lying in the ground.

If you have any strength left, pay your respects to Bartholdi (the sculptor of the Statue of Liberty) along avenue Thierry. His grave is topped by an angel rising to heaven. Passing his grave, on the left, anyone who has ever owned a 2CV will want to salute André Citroën.

★ The **Observatoire:** 61 avenue de l'Observatoire 75014. ☎ 01-40-51-21-74. RER: Port-Royal. The oldest working observatory in the world, created by Colbert in 1667. It is said that this was the only 17th-century building not to include either wood or iron in its construction: no wood for fear of fire, no iron as it might have affected the magnetic needles. Among other things,

Cassini's division of the ring of Saturn and Neptune was discovered here, and the first modern map of the moon was drawn up. The dome dates from the time of Louis-Philippe and the telescope from Napoleon III. If you want to visit, write to the Service des Visites, 61 avenue de l'Observatoire, 75014 Paris, to go on one of the guided tours which take place on the first Saturday of each month. You really need to apply six months in advance. You'll be shown collections of ancient instruments, a meridian telescope and the cupola housing two equatorial telescopes. In 1959 the observatory, rather absurdly, gave its name to a so-called 'ambush'. The intended victim, François Mitterrand, accused the right wing at that time of trying to assassinate him. This alleged 'Observatoire attack', actually took place in a nearby garden and caused the future President to jump over a hedge. He made himself look quite ridiculous and the incident is mercilessly remembered in French history.

★ **La Gaîté:** from boulevard Edgar-Quinet to avenue du Maine, this street is a reminder that Montparnasse was a very popular venue in the 19th century, with its cabarets, *guinguettes*, theatres and cafés. A lovely mural fresco at the brasserie La Liberté (on the corner of Gaîté – Edgar-Quinet) still bears witness to this. Jean-Paul Sartre, who lived nearby, often used to come to dunk his croissants here. Fast-food outlets and sex shops have now rather spoiled the area. On the site of the Bobino, the most famous theatre on the Left Bank, stands the Hôtel Mercure, close to the fashionable café-theatres. Since the Bobino closed, the street has lost a lot of its liveliness, but there are still plenty of little restaurants, creperies, budget hotels and shops in the lanes all around.

There are also some vestiges of the Belle Époque era: the Théâtre du Montparnasse, with its finely sculpted façade and caryatids. On the ground floor is a popular bistro. Opposite stands the old Théâtre de la Gaîté-Montparnasse, squeezed into a building with a façade which is also beautifully sculpted and is listed as an Historic Monument.

– At 10 rue du Maine is *Breizh*, one of the nicest shops in the area: ☎ 01-43-20-84-60. Metro: Edgar-Quinet or Vavin. Open daily except Sunday, 10am to 1pm and 2pm to 6.45pm, Monday afternoon only, and Saturday to 6.30pm. Books, newspapers, records, gifts, etc., on the theme of Brittany and the Celtic countries. There's a wide choice and the welcome is very polite.

★ The **marché parisien de la Création:** open Sunday 10am to 7pm, at the foot of the Tour Montparnasse, between rue du Départ and rue de la Gaîté. Metro: Edgar-Quinet, Montparnasse-Bienvenüe or Raspail. Website: www.altern.com/ajcplus/Marche.html.

Formerly located near the town hall of the 15th arrondissement and known as the Marché Mouton-Duvernet, it's been here since 1995. Established artists and novices alike come to exchange ideas and sell their work. It has greatly improved since it moved. Photographers, sculptors, painters, jewellers and other creative people have a weekly window where they can exhibit their work. Visitors include tourists and locals.

AN ARCHITECTURAL TOUR

Although Montparnasse is no longer the artistic quarter it used to be, there are still many superb traces of its artistic past. You will find unexpected, amazing things hidden away in the little streets.

★ At 26 **rue Vavin** (actually in the 6th arrondissement but still Montparnasse) there is a fascinating building, built in 1912 by the architect Henri Sauvage. Constructed in tiers, it's covered in white ceramics with luxuriant vegetation at all levels. At the beginning of the 20th century Sauvage created the *Société anonyme des logements hygiéniques à bon marché* (Cheap and Clean Accommodation Ltd), aiming to give the working classes decent accommodation.

★ Not far away, at 216 boulevard Raspail, stands **studio Raspail**, with flats and workshops above it, built in 1932 to a very Cubist design. For its inauguration as an art-house cinema, it showed *Vampyr* by Carl Dreyer. It admitted defeat in 1982, finally beaten by the corporates, after 50 years of loyal and independent service to the cinema.

★ There is another magnificent ceramic façade at 31 **rue Campagne-Première**, a masterpiece of art nouveau (1911) with masks and garlands of roses.

★ At No. 261 boulevard Raspail, the period changes. This is now the headquarters of the **Fondation Cartier pour l'art contemporain**. Metro: Denfert-Rochereau or Raspail. Bus Nos. 38, 68, 91. Information: ☎ 01-42-18-56-50. Website: www.fondation.cartier.fr. Open daily except Monday, noon to 8pm. Created in 1994 by Jean Nouvel, the architect of the Institut du Monde arabe, this glass and steel building is surrounded by a garden, which still houses the mythical Lebanese cedar tree which Chateaubriand planted in 1823. Originally set up in 1984 by Alain Dominique Perrin at Jouy-en-Josas, in lovely surroundings, the aim of the Fondation Cartier is to promote contemporary artists from all over the world, in all their diversity and to support them by commissioning and buying works for its collection. Today, it covers 1,200 square metres (nearly 4,000 square feet) which can be split into modules over two levels for temporary exhibitions. With Les Soirées Nomades, every Thursday at 8.30pm, the Fondation brings together, as part of its programme, dance, music, theatre and cinema (information and bookings: ☎ 01-42-18-56-72).

★ Take boulevard Raspail again and turn right into **rue Schœlcher**. At No. 5 admire the very fine façade: all the balconies and windows are of a different shape. There's a bull's eye forming a balcony framed by a frieze of cascading fruit. At 11 *bis* note the geometrical structure of the flats and workshops with the windows projecting or indented.

★ At 21–23 **rue Froidevaux** there are workshops with immense bow-windows surrounded by little mosaic tiles (1929).

★ A short walk towards the Observatoire will allow you to appreciate the original architecture of the workshops at 3, 3 *bis*, 5 and 7 **rue Cassini**. Opposite, at No. 12, there are a few flats and workshops with a sculpted frieze which epitomises the school of socialist realism.

★ At 126 **boulevard du Montparnasse** pass under a monumental porch; at the end of the second courtyard there is a splendid house with artists' workshops. At 120 *bis*, there is a flower mosaic decor on the façade.

CULTURE

– **Café and Théâtre d'Edgar** (map C1): 58 boulevard Edgar-Quinet 75014. ☎ 01-42-79-97-97 from 2.30 to 7.30pm. Metro: Edgar-Quinet. Closed Sunday. Five shows every evening from 8.15pm to 10.30pm, in both halls. There are seats at 80F and 90F (65F and 70F for students, except Saturday and holidays); cheaper on Monday. One of the oldest and most popular café-theatres in Paris. The decor looks a bit thrown together and the shows don't tend to be anything revolutionary, but they maintain a high standard; eccentric and humorous one-man shows, plays and shows for children.

– **Mission bretonne** (Ti ar Vretoned): (map C1): 22 rue Delambre 75014. ☎ 01-43-35-26-41; answering machine for programmes: ☎ 01-43-21-99-86. Website: www.tav.trad.org. Metro: Vavin or Edgar-Quinet. Open daily Monday to Friday 5pm to 10pm. Closed mid-July to the beginning of September, between Christmas and New Year and some weekends. Lots of Celtic cultural activities, including *Festou-deiz,* concerts of Breton and Irish music. Every Thursday the Irish Association meets (lessons in Gaelic, folk dancing and so on). They ask for a small contribution for the musical events. It's becoming a meeting place for traditional folk music in the Paris region.

PLAISANCE, PERNETY

This is an old working-class area, one which has only been part of Paris for about a century. It falls betwen rue Vercingétorix and avenue du Maine and for a long time was a village. The names of the streets are a reminder of this: rue du Moulin-Vert (Green Mill Street), rue du Moulin-de-Beurre (Butter Mill Street – now gone). The working-class population was displaced by the Haussmann projects which were squeezed in here. Apart from a few residential streets, the Plaisance quarter did not really live up to its name, which refers to pleasure boating. It was one of the most densely populated areas in Paris, and the living and hygiene conditions were very poor. The people working at the large factories all around Paris came and lived here, as did artists, who transformed stables and sheds into workshops. From 1900 to 1950 the area had a life of its own and, despite the slum conditions, there was a very rich local culture, effectively making the inhabitants self-sufficient. The vibrant social life was largely due to the minuscule size of the living quarters – forcing the population into the streets and cafés.

Then, as in the 13th, 19th and 20th arrondissements, the property boom of the 1960s began to take off. The first phase was the development of the Gare Montparnasse. The poor quality of the housing was used as a pretext to replace it with an extension of the business quarter and the introduction of higher-earning properties. The social facilities which were promised along with the Maine-Montparnasse development in the Vandamme sector were substituted with a luxury hotel boasting 1,000 rooms and a shopping centre.

The Vercingétorix radial road project, which was fortunately abandoned, was a typical example of the absurd designs drawn up by the leading town planners of the day. To siphon off the traffic which the new business area was bound to cause, they decided to build a motorway connecting Montparnasse to the Périphérique (Paris Ring Road).

THE AREA TODAY

In times of economic depression there is no longer any question of wiping the area off the map for huge megalomaniac projects. It is claimed that things have stabilized, but with the fall of the Vandamme and Vercingétorix fortresses, in rue de l'Ouest, the life and soul of the place has moved to the area around rue Raymond-Losserand and the Pernety metro station, and things will never be the same. Thanks to a 1948 law on rents, there are still quite a lot of elderly people left to provide the link to the new inhabitants. The newcomers set up cafés, small businesses and cheap restaurants, and thus guarantee a certain amount of activity. One encouraging thing is that in the new, fairly well-off social strata (the 25–35 age group), there is an awareness of green issues and the perils of the concrete jungle which has resulted in the regeneration of some of the local spirit. These are the people who bought and renovated old flats or houses or who can now afford the rents. The changing political face of the community was confirmed by the municipal elections in 1989, when the Greens got their best result in the 14th arrondissement.

There are still a few working-class bistros and characterful restaurants left, and a number of cultural venues have opened up, putting on good shows or concerts. It's best to get around the area on foot and you can still find lots of unusual streets and houses, and plenty of warm smiles (unusual for Parisians!). To the south of rue d'Alésia there are the 'villas', the amazing oases of the 14th arrondissement and the last vestiges of the *village Plaisance* – a privileged, timeless area once outside the city.

A STROLL AROUND THE AREA

From avenue du Maine and rue de l'Ouest, the area has been redeveloped.

★ After his work in Montpelier, the Catalan architect Ricardo Bofill erected a Greek-style temple, pompously named **Les Colonnes** (The Columns) at the corner of rue de l'Ouest and rue du Château. On the plus side there is some local authority housing. The architecture is amazing – the interiors don't look very functional but the shapes are superb.

★ At the centre of the imposing **place de Catalogne**, also the work of Ricardo Bofill, there is a strange *fontaine* (although it seldom seems to work), designed by Shamaï Haber. When it does work, it produces an odd sloping artificial lake (which can look quite pretty at night when it's lit up). The geometry of the square was inspired by Borromini: a semi-circular façade with a vista onto place de l'Amphithéâtre.

★ Just behind the Colonnes stands the **église de Notre-Dame-du-Travail.** It's a curious church with a metallic structure. It's a shame that they've painted over the frescoes representing St Éloi, the patron saint of metallurgists, and St Joseph, the patron saint of woodworkers. There's little left except the frescoes on the apse, painted in the Puvis de Chavannes style. Concerts are held here and the art nouveau-style organ is spectacular.

★ The **rue Vercingétorix** has lost almost all its houses, but it has gained a fine square lined with artists' workshops. At No. 105 is a splendid old-style bakery with enamel decoration on the front and a fine interior ceiling. Now a listed building, it proved the saving grace of the house in which it stands. This is a brilliant place to buy the delicious *fougasse aux anchois et olives* (a flat loaf with anchovies and olives).

At 16 rue de Gergovie stands the workshop of Shamaï Haber, where you can admire some remarkable wrought-iron pieces.

Almost on the outer boulevard stands the little and almost anachronistic provincial Gare d'Ouest-Ceinture railway station, now closed.

Otherwise, around the Pernety metro station, there are a few streets which are reminiscent of the village lanes of old: in the Cité Bauer, rue Plaisance, rue Pernety, rue des Thermopyles, with old bistros and just a few craftsmen and women.

★ In rue d'Alésia, opposite an enormous office complex and trapped behind a service station, a curious, narrow lane runs off in a sideways direction, the **impasse Florimont**. The famous French singer Brassens lived here from 1944 to 1966, enjoying the warmth and friendship of the inhabitants of the cul-de-sac. He died in 1981, leaving around 100 immortal songs. The house he stayed in is still here, at No. 9. If you approach the gate and look up you'll be able to see the window of the room where he composed all his early songs. Unfortunately, the area at the entrance to the cul-de-sac is under threat of demolition, along with the plaque commemorating Brassens. His fans are planning to oppose the town hall's bulldozers and hope to preserve the memory of their hero.

★ **Les puces de Vanves (Vanves flea market)**: avenue George-Lafenestre and avenue Marc-Sangnier. Metro: Porte-de-Vanves. Open Saturday and Sunday dawn to 7pm; in avenue Marc-Sangnier 7am to 1.30pm. After complaints from the riverside residents and regular bric-à-brac traders, the police now regularly patrol this area so the unauthorized traders move their suitcases every five minutes. There are 140 legal traders along avenue Lafenestre. You can get some really good bargains, as long as you're patient and get up early. The casual traders are in avenue Marc-Sangnier.

DENFERT-ROCHEREAU

Situated to the south of Montparnasse, this is another old area with a certain charm, barely touched by renovation. It's a good place to stay and you'll get a feel for its provincial calm. Its fairly central position in the arrondissement, halfway between Montparnasse and Montsouris, means it's also within walking distance of all the main landmarks.

WHAT TO SEE

★ **The villas:** Few Parisians know this part of the 14th arrondissement and its charming little islands of greenery. From Denfert-Rochereau, go down avenue du Général-Leclerc on the left-hand side. Just after the hospice, at No. 19, there's a huge wrought-iron gate announcing the **villa Adrienne**. In 1880 this was just a large garden built on an old quarry, before construction work started 15 years later. The houses formed a sort of garden city in miniature, built by a philanthropic industrialist. Vaguely reminiscent of London's Chelsea, it has a large open garden in the middle and two- or three-storey brick houses, most of them covered in ivy, with little gardens. Instead of a number, each bears the name of a painter, a scientist or a writer: Watteau, Poussin, Lavoisier, Lulli, Molière, Racine. The concierge's house is called Corneille, but don't try to have a picnic here – it's private property.

In rue Hallé the houses suddenly blend into a harmonious rounded shape, sheltering a nice little square. There are a few other rural-like corners in the area: villa Hallé and villa Boulard (in rue Boulard).

In avenue René-Coty, between Denfert and rue Hallé, there's an odd little edifice on a grassy mound. This is the entrance leading to a 17th-century underground aqueduct passing underneath the houses of the quarter (the old Aqueduc d'Arcueil).

★ **The Catacombs:** 1 place Denfert-Rochereau. ☎ 01-43-22-47-63. Metro and RER: Denfert-Rochereau. Bus Nos. 38, 68 and 88. Open Tuesday to Friday 2pm to 4pm, Saturday and Sunday 9am to 11am and 2pm to 4pm. Closed Monday and public holidays. There's an unguided tour, lasting around 45 minutes. You'll need to take a little pocket torch, wear comfortable shoes and wrap up well. Entry fee.

The catacombs date from the end of the 13th century. Cartloads of remains from the great Parisian cemeteries, full after 10 centuries of faithful service, were dumped here. The sub-soil of Paris, holed like Gruyère cheese by the operation of many stone and gypsum quarries (there was even a coal mine on the site of the Hôpital Ste-Anne), turned out to be the perfect site. It is estimated that the remains of 5 or 6 million people were deposited. Among them are those of Mme de Pompadour and probably those of La Fontaine, author of the famous Fables. On 21 August 1944 the catacombs were used as an HQ by the head of the French Resistance, Colonel Rol-Tanguy. Believing them to be an unfinished air-raid shelter, the Germans entrusted the French police with a surveillance operation. However, as the Resistance lost no time in infiltrating the ranks of the police, they were able to use the catacombs to organize a vast clandestine telecommunications network. The place was perfect: 100km (62 miles) of underground passages allowed for speedy getaways and wide-ranging communications, which could not be monitored by the Germans. On 22 August the insurrection began which led to the liberation of the city.

The Catacombs are reached by a spiral staircase leading 20m (65ft) or so underground. On the lintel of the charnel-house, there is an inscription: *Arrête, c'est ici l'empire de la mort* ('Halt, this is the empire of death'). In the galleries the workers entrusted with re-housing the former occupants of the Cimetière des Innocents amused themselves by making shapes 'intended to fire the imagination': bones, piles of skulls, friezes made of femurs and other macabre motifs greet you as you come in.

★ **Place Denfert-Rochereau:** le Lion de Belfort, the work of Bartholdi (of Statue of Liberty fame), contemplates with a cynical eye the daily traffic jams on one of the largest junctions in Paris. The two sculpted friezes are survivors of the 'barrière d'Enfer' (Hell's Gate) built into the wall of the tax collectors' building at the end of the 17th century. Also in the square stood the terminus of the Sceaux railway line, begun in 1846. The third-class fare at the time cost 20 centimes to go as far as Arcueil and 30 centimes as far as Bourg-la-Reine in the southern suburbs.

★ **Rue Daguerre:** the most famous street market in the 14th arrondissement. Agnès Varda, the film director, who has lived here for nearly 50 years, filmed it affectionately in *Daguerréotypes*. However, the street has since undergone a face-lift. There are no more pavement borders or fruit and veg traders, but there is still a certain liveliness, and prices which are among the best in the area. Trotsky, who lived in this street for a while, used to walk around with his shopping bag.

★ The **prison de la Santé:** 42 rue de la Santé 75014. Metro: Glacière; or RER: Port-Royal. There are only tours on exceptional occasions. Built in 1861 by Émile Vaudremer on the site of a former coal market, the prison comprises almost 1,350 cells distributed over five wings in a four-storey building built along rue Messier. When it opened it was unusual in having running water in the cells – the houses in the area didn't even have this facility! It is not a *centrale* (a prison holding offenders serving two years or more); it holds prisoners on remand or serving short sentences. In May 1986 Michel Vaujour escaped from the prison by helicopter. Another notorious inmate was Bernard Tapie, the businessman and disgraced former chairman of the Olympique Marseille football club, who spent some time here in early 1997.

MONTSOURIS, ALÉSIA

To the south of rue d'Alésia, bordered by avenue du Général-Leclerc and rue de l'Amiral-Mouchez, lies a superb area for walking – architecturally fascinating and reminiscent of the countryside.

WHAT TO SEE

★ **An architectural tour:** at 83 rue de la Tombe-Issoire is a peaceful artists' complex. Taking the provincial rue de l'Aude you reach rue des Artistes (also accessible by steps in avenue René-Coty). At 1 rue de l'Aude, an architect's practice occupies the former workshop of a painter. The land had been for sale for 40 years but potential buyers were put off by the unconventional four-storey building erected by the painter. At 3, 5 and 7 Impasse Gauguet there are artists' workshops from the 1930s. The painter Nicolas de Staël occupied one of them.

At 13 rue St-Yves is the *cité du Souvenir,* a group of working-class houses built in 1934 to honour the dead of the First World War 'by a work of life'.

★ The **villa Seurat:** at 101 rue de la Tombe-Issoire, a cul-de-sac lined with pretty houses from around 1925, which once had some well-known occupants. Henry Miller lived at No. 18 from 1934 to 1938 and wrote *Tropic of Cancer* here. Banned as obscene literature in all the English-speaking countries, he was reduced to publishing his books in Paris and almost selling them wrapped in brown paper. Anaïs Nin and Lawrence Durrell lived with him.

★ The **réservoir de Montsouris:** on the corner of rue de la Tombe-Issoire and avenue Reille. Not open to the public. 'Montsouris' (literally 'Mount Mouse'), used to be called 'Moquesouris', referring to a windmill which must have been so poor that even the mice couldn't live off its output. When it was built it was the largest in the world (235m/770ft long and 135m/440ft wide, with outer walls more than 2m/6.5ft thick).

As with a great wine, 'vintages' of water are dated: eg. 'clos' Loing-Lunain 1900 and 'Château' Vanne-Voulzie 1874–1925! There are trout living permanently in this reservoir, as indicators of the purity of the water. Eighty metres (260ft) above sea level, the reservoir looms over the six- or seven-storey buildings on the Left Bank. Because of the difference in height, the water pressure on the top floor of the buildings is always high.

★ **A walk around the 'privileged' areas:** 53 avenue Reille opens onto probably one of the prettiest squares in Paris: square Montsouris. Originally the workshop of the painter Ozenfant, it was the first building by Le Corbusier in Paris in 1922. Since then it has lost its 'sawtooth' roof and a little of its architectural interest. It's still enchanting to tread the great paving stones of the street, between the workshops and houses hiding under their masses of vegetation.

Right at the end, at 14 rue Nansouty, admire the pure lines and elegance of the Villa Guggenbühl.

6 rue Georges-Braque is an artist's residence and workshop. At No. 7 stands the brick-built Reist villa-workshop, with a great glass roof dating from the 1920s. The rue du Parc-Montsouris and the villa of the same name also bring together some large middle-class houses that are crumbling away under the wisteria and honeysuckle. At Nos. 6–10 there is a rococo private residence flanked by earthenware with colourful motifs, which used to belong to the popular French novelist Michel Morphy.

★ The **parc Montsouris:** the second largest park in Paris after the one at Buttes-Chaumont, this park was the only gift made by Baron Haussmann to the people of Paris. In 1867 a copy of the palace of the Bey of Tunis, erected for the Universal Exhibition on the Champ-de-Mars, was built here. Unfortunately it burned down in 1991. The park is wonderfully undulating, with large lawns, thick groves, and rare trees. (The RER railway cuts through the centre – but it is fairly discreet.) There is a large artificial lake and, for children, there is one of the last real roundabouts in Paris.

★ The **cité universitaire (student halls of residence):** Metro: Porte-d'Orléans; RER: Cité-Universitaire. Paradoxically, few Parisians know about this. Like a little country town, it only gets a mention when rival political factions from a particular country square up to one another. The halls of residence extend over 40ha (100 acres) of greenery and house around 6,000 students of which three-quarters come from 122 different countries. It has had some famous occupants: Michel Jobert (who famously said: *Je suis nulle part – je suis ailleurs!,* 'I'm nowhere – I'm somewhere else!'), Raymond Barre, the couturier Pierre Balmain, Habib Bourguiba, and M. M'Bow (former director of UNESCO). There are around 40 countries with their own halls, generally built in the style of the country, which makes a picturesque kaleidoscope of all types of architecture. The Italian hall has a Mediterranean charm, Le Corbusier built the Swiss hall, John D Rockefeller financed the International Hall. Its own post office, sports centre, bookshop, and library means that the complex is virtually self-sufficient. The park stretches over almost 20ha (50 acres) which are open to the public and very pleasant in summer.

Passing visitors can eat in the various university restaurants by paying a slightly higher entrance fee. The one in the international hall is the liveliest and there is also a fast-food outlet.

★ **In Lenin's footsteps:**. Vladimir Ilyich Ulyanov (Lenin) loved the 14th arrondissement. When he arrived in Paris he spent a year living at 24 **rue Beaunier**, a street which runs from opposite the Montsouris reservoir and whose peace and quiet he greatly appreciated (there's a plaque on the wall). He had to put up with the constant complaints of his concierge, who couldn't stand all the comings and goings of his political friends – ugly, hairy, bearded men who looked like conspirators! He moved further away, to 4 **rue Marie-Rose**, and lived there for four years. The concierge there was a little more understanding. There is a plaque on the wall and a little museum (numerous souvenirs and documents on Lenin's time in Paris). For a tour, ring for an appointment with the *Association de la maison de Lénine:* ☎ 01-42-79-99-58.

In the 14th arrondissement, Vladimir Ilyich's life was split between political activity and leisure. In the rue Marie-Rose he would receive visits from the future leaders of the Soviet State: Zinoviev, Kamenev, etc. The Parisian Bolshevik faction met in a café at 11 avenue du Général-Leclerc (then avenue d'Orléans). Lenin had a bank account at the branch of the Crédit Lyonnais in avenue d'Orléans. After a successful hold-up by his friends in Russia, the branch received an enormous sum in gold roubles which Lenin deposited without raising an eyebrow.

Lenin often worked at the Bibliothèque Nationale and made a point of listening to the speeches made by Jean Jaurès at socialist meetings. As for leisure, he divided his time between walking in the Parc Montsouris (which he used to call 'my private garden'!), bicycle rides and chess at the café Le Denfert. He also used to go to the caf'conc' (cafés with live music) in the rue de la Gaîté. Lenin left Paris in 1912 but those who remember him from this time have also passed away. It is said that when he was poverty-stricken he used to sell shoelaces illegally from under an umbrella.

WHERE TO GO FOR A DRINK

🍸 **Le Dôme** (map C1, **65**): 108 boulevard du Montparnasse 75014. ☎ 01-43-35-34-82. Metro: Vavin. Open daily 8pm to 2am. Closed Sunday and Monday in August. Budget for 300F per person. Next to La Coupole. A pleasant terrace, Tiffany lamps, wicker chairs, green plants. On the walls there is an interesting collection of photos to remind us of the great age of the area and the people who used to come here. It's the quietest and most popular (with tourists) of the great Montparnasse cafés. Jean-Paul Sartre used to like to come here in the afternoons.

🍸 **Le Rosebud** (map C1, **66**): 11 *bis*, rue Delambre 75014. ☎ 01-43-35-38-54. Metro: Vavin or Edgar-Quinet. Open daily 7pm to 2am. Closed in August. À la carte only: around 150F. In the 1950s Jean-Paul Sartre and the Montparnasse set often used to come here for a drink. This bar, with its nicely laid out 1930s setting, now plays host to artists, painters, writers and journalists, mostly in their 40s. The L-shaped bar lends itself to customers talking face-to-face. The waiters, with their greying hair, are unmatched when it comes to mixing excellent cocktails; order a Bloody Mary and you'll see what we mean!

🍸 **Magique** (map B2, **68**): 42 rue de Gergovie 75014. ☎ 01-45-42-26-10. Metro: Pernety or Plaisance. Bus No. 62 (Raymond-Losserand stop). Open 8pm to 2am. Closed Monday and Tuesday, and in August. Entrance plus a drink 46F. Live music on Friday and Saturday in this café-concert (café with live music). There's a warm ambiance, with bottles and glasses on the piano around which the audience chatter away. Shows at 11pm (9.30pm during the week). Chanson on Wednesdays and Thursday.

Ɪ **Les Mousquetaires** (map B1, **70**): 7 avenue du Maine 75014. ☎ 01-43-22-50-46. Metro: Gaîté. Open daily 7.30am to 3am (5am at weekends), Sunday 3pm to 2am. Half a pint of beer costs 11F before 9pm, 17F afterwards. Pool or French billiards, no fewer than 11 tables at any time of day or night. The prices vary according to the time of day. The later it gets, the more expensive it gets! 6pm to 5am: 65F per hour for pool, 55F for French billiards. Very popular.

GOING OUT

– **Dancing de La Coupole** (map C1, **57**): 100–102 boulevard du Montparnasse 75014. ☎ 01-43-20-14-20. Open Tuesday, Friday and Saturday evening, Saturday and Sunday afternoon. Entry fee plus drink: 100F in the evening. Cocktails around 70F. Every Tuesday from 9.30pm to 3am all the *aficionados* meet at La Coupole for two nights of 100 per cent Havana fiesta. The turntables pump out the salsa, while on the dance floor there are Cuban dancers brought to Paris especially to give the show that something special. With the aid of a *mojito* or two everyone ends up out there, even those with two left feet. Live concerts at the beginning of the evening.

Ɪ **L'Utopia** (map B1, **69**): 79 rue de l'Ouest 75014. ☎ 01-43-22-79-66. Metro: Pernety Open daily 9.15pm to 4.30am. Closed for around 10 days towards mid-August. No entry fee, drinks cost 50F to 70F according to what's on. Little has changed since it was first set up. The bar has been converted in such a way as to leave more space for the drinkers and rockabilly fans who pack the place out. The programme varies daily and, in the midst of a very varied audience, you might meet 'Hutch' (David Soul, the blond one from *Starsky* and *Hutch*), Laurent Voulzy or Michel Jonasz (two French rock singers).

WHERE TO GO FOR JAZZ

Ɪ **Le Petit Journal Montparnasse** (map B1, **71**): 13 rue du Commandant-Mouchotte 75014. ☎ 01-43-21-97-62. Metro: Montparnasse-Bienvenüe or Gaîté. Open 8pm to 1am. Closed Sunday and 15 July to 15 August. It's 100F for the first drink, 45F after that. A jazz giant with a twin on boulevard St-Michel. Because of the layout of the tables around the stage you always find yourself at a good one. They take great care over the acoustics.

15TH ARRONDISSEMENT

THE TOUR AND THE GARE MONTPARNASSE ● PARC GEORGES-BRASSENS ● PARC ANDRÉ-CITROËN

This is the largest and most highly populated arrondissement in Paris, with more than 200,000 inhabitants trying to resist the incursion of offices and the inexorable rise in prices. Stretching from the Seine to the Gare Montparnasse, it has little to interest the tourist, although its two large parks make for a pleasant stroll.

WHERE TO STAY

☆ BUDGET

Aloha Hostel (map C2, **1**): 1 rue Borromée 75015. Opposite 243 rue de Vaugirard. ☎ 01-42-73-03-03. Fax: 01-42-73-14-14. E-mail: friends@aloha.fr. Metro: Volontaires. Double room: 107F per day off-season; 117F per day in season. Free breakfast. The outside of this 'youth hostel' is nothing special, but regulars don't mind. As soon as you enter reception the tone is set: an American flag and three clocks giving the time in Paris, New York and Sydney, with resolutely rock background music. At least two beds per room and two showers per floor. Common room and tiny kitchen. You have to leave your room between 11am and 5pm (but there's always someone on duty) and they close from 2am.

☆ CHEAP

Le Nainville Hôtel (map B2, **3**): 53–55 rue de l'Église 75015. ☎ 01-45-57-35-80. Fax: 01-45-54-83-00 Metro: Félix-Faure or Charles-Michel. Closed 1pm to 7pm weekends. Closed mid-July to end August. 215F for a double room with washbasin, 300F with shower and 370F with shower and toilet. Satellite TV in all rooms. Right next to the church of St-Jean-Baptiste de Grenelle, a discreet little hotel, with a retro-style café on the ground floor, a friendly owner, and old-style rooms. Ask for a room with a view over the garden of the square Violet (Nos. 30 or 40). Quiet.

Dupleix Hôtel (map B1, **4**): 4 rue de Lourmel 75015. ☎ 01-45-79-30-12. Fax: 01-40-59-84-90. Metro: Dupleix. Around 300F for a double room with shower and toilet. The entrance is hidden between a butcher's and a cheese shop. Coming from the Eiffel Tower and the 7th arrondissement, you're immediately plunged into Parisian conviviality. Ask for a room on the top floor. Clean, family atmosphere and double-glazing. Mini-bar and satellite TV.

Hôtel de la Paix (map B2, **5**): 43 rue Duranton 75015. ☎ 01-45-57-14-70. Fax: 01-45-57-09-50. Metro: Boucicaut or Convention. Bus Nos. 39 and 49. Double room with shower and toilet 300F and 330F. With bath 400F. Free breakfast for children. There's a reduction of 10 per cent except during trade fairs (at the Porte de Versailles). Comfortable and located in a very quiet street, the rooms are nicely decorated in warm, bright colours. The bathrooms are especially well presented: marble, hairdryer and all mod cons.

☆☆ MODERATE

☗ **Pacific Hôtel** (map B1, **6**): 11 rue Fondary 75015. ☎ 01-45-75-20-49. Fax: 01-45-77-70-73. Metro: Émile-Zola or Dupleix. Double room with washbasin 260F, with shower and TV 318F, with bath or shower, toilet and TV 370F. A quiet, charming little hotel; you're welcomed with a smile, and the rooms are simple but practical. It's clean, well run and they have double-glazing.

☗ **Hôtel Amiral** (map C2, **7**): 90 rue de l'Amiral-Roussin 75015. ☎ 01-48-28-53-89. Fax: 01-45-33-26-94. Metro: Vaugirard. 250F for a double room with bathroom, 380F with shower, 400F with bath. A small two-star hotel, discreetly hidden behind the town hall and yet with many qualities: an attentive welcome, pleasant rooms, low prices and access for visitors with disabilities. Room Nos. 7, 25, 26 and 31 all have a balcony and a very Parisian view, with the Eiffel Tower in the distance.

☗ **Hôtel Alsacia-Clarine** (map B2, **8**): 15 rue Mademoiselle 75015. ☎ 01-42-50-20-46. Fax: 01-48-56-01-83. E-mail: hotel.alsacia.paris@wanadoo.fr. Metro: Commerce or Félix-Faure. Double room with bath or shower and toilet between 400F and 460F. Full of charm, this quiet, well-located hotel is mainly used by regulars and people who know about good hotels. A haven of peace and charm. Several better appointed rooms have a view over a little garden and some of them have open beams. TV with Canal +, radio, mini-bar and hairdryer.

☗ **Hôtel Le Fondary** (map B1, **10**): 30 rue Fondary 75015. ☎ 01-45-75-14-75. Fax: 01-45-75-84-42. Metro: Avenue-Émile-Zola. It's 390F for a double room with shower, toilet, direct telephone, TV with Canal + and mini-bar, and from 410F to 425F with bath. You can have your breakfast in a little courtyard in the summer. 10 per cent reduction in August. Well located, in a quiet street near the rue du Commerce, one of the nicest spots in the 15th arrondissement. Modern decor. There's a pretty little patio with a well covered in plants. The prices are quite high, but still reasonable for a two-star.

☗ **Hôtel Lilas Blanc Grenelle** (map C1, **11**): 5 rue de l'Avre 75015. ☎ 01-45-75-30-07. Fax: 01-45-78-66-65. Metro: La Motte-Picquet-Grenelle. A modern, clean and comfortable hotel. Satellite TV, telephone, hairdryer, safe with a code and even a shower gel dispenser. You can admire the fresco painted on the wall of the lounge by Paul Lomré, which is in the *Guinness Book of Records* as the fastest sponge on canvas in the world.

☗ **Carladez Cambronne** (map C2, **12**): 3 place du Général-Beuret 75015. ☎ 01-47-34-07-12. Fax: 01-40-65-95-68. E-mail: carladez@club-internet.fr. Metro: Vaugirard. Double room with shower 430F, with bath 460F. Price in July and August and at weekends is 395F for two, including breakfast. The hotel is named after the Carladez region of Auvergne, where the original owners came from. In a very busy corner of the carrefour Lecourbe-Cambronne, this is a charming hotel. All the rooms are soundproofed, have a mini-bar, satellite TV (with Canal +), hairdryer and direct telephone.

☗ **Hôtel de l'Avre** (map C1, **13**): 21 rue de l'Avre 75015. ☎ 01-45-75-31-03. Fax: 01-45-75-63-26. Website: www.hoteldelavre.com. Metro: La Motte-Picquet-Grenelle. 390F to 410F for a double room with shower or bath, toilet and telephone; 420F to 460F with bath.

Single room 330F. A charming hotel with prices which are relatively low for Paris. In a quiet, narrow street near the noisy carrefour de La Motte-Picquet-Grenelle and five minutes from the Champ-de-Mars. Very friendly welcome, and there is a pleasant garden with chaises longues where you can have your breakfast in the summer. Some rooms overlook the garden. For families there is a room which overlooks the patio with a double and a single bed and scope for adding a folding bed. There are two car parks less than five minutes from the hotel.

WHERE TO EAT

☆ BUDGET

✕ **Le Bistrot d'André** (map A2, **20**): 232 rue St-Charles 75015 (corner of rue Leblanc). ☎ 01-45-57-89-14. Metro: Balard. Closed Sunday, 1 May, Christmas and New Year's Day. Set menu 65F, weekday lunchtime only. Children's menu 43F. À la carte, budget for around 120F without drinks. One of the only bistros which is still going in this area. Pre-war prices for traditional family cuisine – rack of lamb, *gratin dauphinois*, *boeuf bourguignon*, *andouillette* with mustard sauce.

✕ **Ty Breiz** (map D2, **21**): 52 boulevard de Vaugirard 75015. ☎ 01-43-20-83-72. Metro: Montparnasse-Bienvenüe or Pasteur. Open noon to 3pm and 7pm to 10.45pm. Closed Sunday and for three weeks in August. Set menu 63F at lunchtime. For a *galette*, a crêpe and a drink budget for around 100F. This crêperie is always packed so you may have to wait a bit and sometimes the service is a bit brusque, but from 7 to 77 years (children get

Where to stay
- **1** Aloha Hostel
- **3** Le Nainville Hôtel
- **4** Dupleix Hôtel
- **5** Hôtel de la Paix
- **6** Pacific Hôtel
- **7** Hôtel Amiral
- **8** Hôtel Alsacia
- **10** Hôtel Le Fondary
- **11** Hôtel Lilas Blanc Grenelle
- **12** Carladez Cambronne
- **13** Hôtel de l'Avre

✕ **Where to eat**
- **20** Le Bistrot d'André
- **21** Ty Breiz
- **22** Aux Artistes
- **23** La Petite Bretagne, Chez César
- **24** Chez François
- **25** Le Bélisaire
- **26** Les Coteaux
- **27** Le Garibaldi
- **28** Chez Foong
- **29** Au Pois Chiche
- **30** Le Vieil Alger
- **31** Le Triporteur
- **32** La Gitane
- **33** L'Agape
- **34** Da Maurizio
- **35** La Petite Auberge
- **36** Chez Clément
- **37** Woury
- **38** Kushiken
- **39** L'Amanguier
- **40** Swann et Vincent
- **41** Banani
- **42** L'Os à Moelle
- **43** Le Clos Morillons
- **44** El Bacha
- **45** La Papillote
- **46** Les P'tits Bouchons de François Clerc
- **47** Fontanarosa
- **48** Le Bombay Café
- **49** Le Troquet
- **50** Le Bistrot d'Hubert
- **51** Casa Alcade
- **52** Casa Eusebio
- **53** Arti
- **54** Le Mazagan
- **55** L'Heure Gourmande
- **56** Durand-Dupont

Where to go for a drink
- **70** Café Pacifico
- **71** Le Cristal
- **72** Le Bréguet
- **73** L'Inattendu
- **74** Au Bon Coin

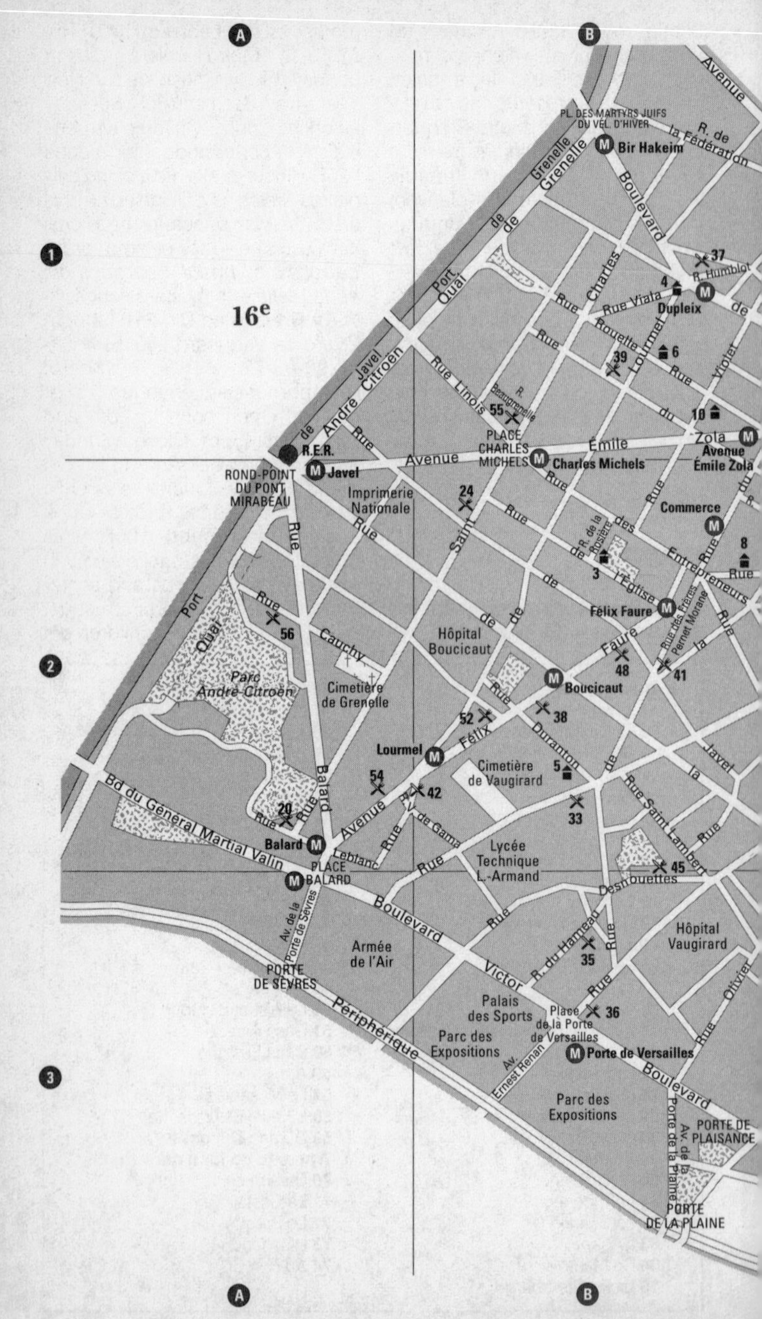
A
B
1
2
3
16e
PL. DES MARTYRS JUIFS DU VÉL. D'HIVER
Bir Hakeim
Dupleix
Javel
R.E.R.
ROND-POINT DU PONT MIRABEAU
Imprimerie Nationale
PLACE CHARLES MICHELS
Charles Michels
Avenue Émile Zola
Commerce
Félix Faure
Hôpital Boucicaut
Boucicaut
Parc André-Citroën
Cimetière de Grenelle
Lourmel
Cimetière de Vaugirard
Balard
PLACE BALARD
Bd du Général Martial Valin
Lycée Technique L.-Armand
Hôpital Vaugirard
Armée de l'Air
PORTE DE SÈVRES
Av. de la Porte de Sèvres
Palais des Sports
Place de la Porte de Versailles
Porte de Versailles
Parc des Expositions
Av. Ernest Renan
PORTE DE PLAISANCE
Av. de la Porte de la Plaine
PORTE DE LA PLAINE
Boulevard Périphérique
Boulevard Victor
Quai de Grenelle
Port de Grenelle
Quai André Citroën
Port de Javel
Rue Linois
R. Beaugrenelle
Rue Saint Charles
Rue de la Fédération
R. Humblot
Rue Viala
Rue Rouelle
Rue Lourmel
Rue du Théâtre
Rue Violet
Rue des Entrepreneurs
R. de la Rosière
Rue de l'Église
Rue des Frères Pernet Morane
Rue Félix Faure
Rue Duranton
Rue de Javel
Rue Balard
Rue Cauchy
Avenue Lebland
Rue de Gama
Rue Saint Lambert
Rue Desnouettes
R. du Hameau
Rue Olivier
Boulevard Lefebvre
37
4
39
6
10
55
24
3
8
56
48
41
38
52
5
54
42
33
20
45
35
36

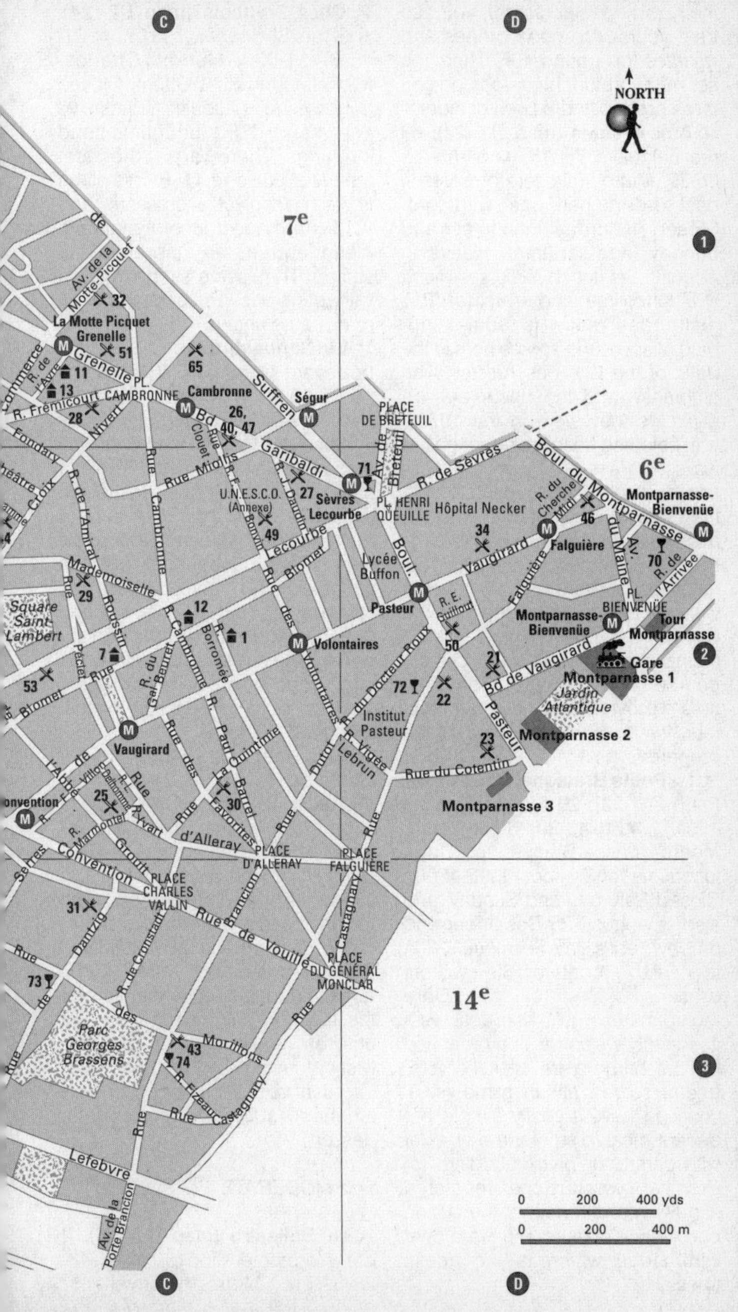
C
D
NORTH
7e
6e
14e
1
2
3
Av. de la Motte-Picquet
32
La Motte Picquet Grenelle
51
65
Grenelle
11
13
PL. CAMBRONNE
Cambronne
Ségur
Suffren
R. Frémicourt
28
Nivert
26, 40, 47
Bd Garibaldi
PLACE DE BRETEUIL
Av. de Breteuil
71
Rue Miollis
R. J. Dardin
27
Sèvres Lecourbe
PL. HENRI QUEUILLE
R. de Sèvres
Boul. du Montparnasse
Montparnasse-Bienvenüe
U.N.E.S.C.O. (Annexe)
49
Bonvin
Hôpital Necker
R. du Cherche Midi
46
34
Falguière
70
R. de l'Arrivée
Lecourbe
Blomet
Lycée Buffon
Boul. Pasteur
Vaugirard
Av. du Maine
Mademoiselle
29
Square Saint-Lambert
12
1
Rue des Volontaires
Volontaires
Pasteur
R. E. Guillout
Montparnasse-Bienvenüe
PL. BIENVENÜE
Tour Montparnasse
Gare Montparnasse 1
50
21
Bd de Vaugirard
Jardin Atlantique
72
22
Institut Pasteur
R. du Docteur Roux
Montparnasse 2
23
Rue du Cotentin
Montparnasse 3
Rousselin
Péclet
7
53
Blomet
R. Cambronne
Borromée
R. du Gal Beuret
R. Paul Barruel
Vaugirard
Rue des Favorites
30
Quintinie
Dutot
R. Vigée Lebrun
25
Convention
d'Alleray
PLACE D'ALLERAY
PLACE FALGUIÈRE
Convention
Groult
PLACE CHARLES VALLIN
31
Rue de Vouillé
Brancion
Castagnary
PLACE DU GÉNÉRAL MONCLAR
Dantzig
R. de Cronstadt
73
74
43
Morillons
Parc Georges Brassens
R. Fizeau
Rue Castagnary
Lefebvre
Av. de la Porte Brancion
0 200 400 yds
0 200 400 m

their own special chairs), you can treat yourself to good crêpes and *galettes* for around 40F. There's a set menu at lunchtime comprising three crêpes and a bowl of cider.

✕ **Aux Artistes** (map D2, **22**): 63 rue Falguière 75015. ☎ 01-43-22-05-39. Metro: Falguière or Pasteur. Last orders half past midnight. Closed Saturday lunchtime and Sunday, and for three weeks in August. Set lunch 58F, set menu 80F lunchtime and evening. This restaurant really is something. Modigliani used to come here in the days of the Cité des Artistes. The ambiance and the decor are the same as they were in the 1970s, with coloured frescoes adorning the walls. There is a very mixed clientele: students, locals, young people from the suburbs out on the razzle, maybe a few artists, eating in a noisy, lively atmosphere. In the evenings at weekends you'll have to wait, but they serve a good kir at the bar. There is a set lunch with starter, main course, chips or salad, or main course and dessert. Generous hors-d'œuvres and no fewer than four ways of having your steak prepared.

✕ **La Petite Bretagne, Chez César** (map D2, **23**): 20 rue du Cotentin 75015. ☎ 01-43-20-96-66. Metro: Montparnasse-Bienvenüe. Open lunchtime only, noon to 2.45pm. Closed Saturday and Sunday, and also in August, 25 December and on New Year's Day. Set menu 63F. À la carte, budget for 80F without drinks. Close to the Gare Montparnasse, this little café, with its friendly welcome, is a great find for the hard-up traveller. For 63F (menu served at lunchtime only), you can have a really simple but decent meal (dish of the day: beef with carrots or black pudding, for example), which is cheaper than a sandwich and a beer at the station bar. A more original dish is the beef with stout, which is the chef's speciality

✕ **Chez François** (map B2, **24**): 106 rue St-Charles 75015. ☎ 01-45-77-51-03. Metro: Charles-Michel. Open to 10.30pm. Closed Sunday and in August. All inclusive set menu 70F lunchtime and evening. There are other set menus at 98F and 118F. This place is reminiscent of a brasserie and yet it's a modest local restaurant, clean and in an unpretentious setting. They serve simple cuisine with generous portions and very reasonably priced.

✕ **Le Garibaldi** (map C2, **27**): 58 boulevard Garibaldi 75015. ☎ 01-45-67-15-61. Metro: Sèvres-Lecourbe. Open lunchtime only 11.30am to 3pm. Closed Saturday and in August. Set menu 72F, à la carte around 100F. At the foot of the elevated railway, this used to be a restaurant for workers. Now office workers and locals try out the simple dining room, which has retained an old counter at the entrance and a turn-of-the-century ceiling. The cuisine is unpretentious and good value. Try crudités, sautéed lamb with green beans, *blanquette de veau*.

✕ **Arti** (map C2, **53**): 173 rue Lecourbe 75015. ☎ 01-48-28-66-68. Metro: Vaugirard. Open daily to 11pm. At lunchtime there is a set menu at 59F, in the evening at 129F. Children's menu 55F. You won't go over 150F à la carte. An excellent Indian restaurant. All the classics of real Indian cuisine at reasonable prices: *samosas*, *raïta*, curry, *biryani*, and a special mention for the tandoori chicken and the Arti chicken. A cheerful setting with wicker furniture and craft artefacts. Excellent value for money on the set lunches (starter, main course, dessert).

☆☆ MODERATE

✕ **Le Bélisaire** (map C2, **25**): 2 rue Marmontel 75015. ☎ 01-48-28-62-24. Metro: Convention.

Open lunchtime and evening, Monday to Friday. Closed at weekends, Christmas and in August. Set menu 94F lunchtime; à la carte budget for around 150F. In a quiet, provincial street, near to the UGC and Gaumont cinemas at the carrefour Convention-Vaugirard. It's named after a 5th-century Byzantine general who defeated the Vandals and the Ostrogoths, and inspired Marmontel, who himself gave his name to this street. This venerable gentleman must be looking down and smiling on this excellent restaurant, run by a cheerful team. There is an old zinc bar at the entrance, a fine provincial dresser in a corner, and a few art-deco touches. French cuisine reviewed and reinterpreted according to the fashion of the day, with generous and well-prepared dishes, and light, creamy sauces: snails with garlic, veal, fish.

✕ **Le Triporteur** (map C3, **31**): 4 rue de Dantzig 75015. ☎ 01-45-32-82-40. Metro: Convention. Open daily lunchtime and evening. Closed Saturday and Sunday and for two weeks in August. Set menus 69F and 79F at lunchtime. In the evening, à la carte only, budget for 150F. In a part of the 15th arrondissement which is deserted when night falls, an old delivery bicycle is exhibited like a museum piece on a platform outside. The vast dining room is divided into two and always full in the evening. The young waiters are quick and very friendly. No à la carte or set menus as in classic restaurants but dishes and wines written up on blackboards which are brought to your table. Try snail ravioli, wild mushrooms, potée with braised cabbage, *pastilla* of guinea fowl or bream roasted *en tapenade*. It's best to book ahead.

✕ **Casa Eusebio** (map B2, **52**): 68 avenue Félix-Faure 75015. ☎ 01-45-54-11-88. Metro: Lourmel. Open till 10.30pm. Closed Sunday and in August. Set meal 58F lunchtime and evening. Budget for 120F à la carte. Eusebio, a former taxi driver from Galicia, has opened this Spanish inn in an old bistro dating from 1913. The decor, made up of pretty mosaics, is in keeping with the Spanish style. *Serrano* ham is laid out on the bar alongside the *manchego* cheese, and other delights include *tortilla* and squid. The Galician-style octopus and the paella (75F) need to be ordered in advance.

✕ **Les Coteaux** (map C1, **26**): 26 boulevard Garibaldi 75015. ☎ 01-47-34-83-48. Metro: Cambronne or Ségur. Open to 10.30pm. Closed Saturday, Sunday, Monday evening and in August. There is a single menu at 140F. Almost underneath the metallic arches of the elevated railway, you soon forget the banal exterior when you see the appetizing menu. A tiny place serving Lyonnaise cuisine, run by a charming couple who know all about the tradition of Lyons. There are 10 tables covered with plastic gingham tablecloths and two great wooden barrels surrounded by high-backed chairs. Depending on what day it is, you can treat yourself to Lyons sausage, cod *à la rhodanienne*, stuffed cabbage, veal *au gratin à la lyonnaise*, oxtail casserole, etc. and 'house' specialities always on the blackboard, such as veal with *sauce gribiche* or *andouillette* with Mâcon wine and Charroux mustard. For smaller appetites, the best solution is to eat sitting around one of the barrels; dishes from 32F to 52F, or dish of the day at 70F. Varied and very well chosen, the wines, straight from the vineyard, are served by the tumbler, glass, in a jug or by the bottle.

✕ **Banani** (map B2, **41**): 148 rue de la Croix-Nivert 75015. ☎ 01-48-28-73-92 and 01-48-28-68-73. Metro: Félix-Faure. Open to 11pm. Closed Sunday lunchtime. Set menus 59F at lunchtime, 99F and

159F in the evening. À la carte at around 150F without drinks. In this large dining room, divided into two sections, you feel you are really in India. At the entrance, a golden *ganesh* highlights the decor; at the back, which is ideal if there is a crowd of you, there's a wooden fresco of a Hindu temple, imported from India. Warm panelling and lights in muted colours make a major contribution to the charm of the place. On the menu are all the flavours of India with no fuss or pretence: real spices carefully measured out, tandoori dishes which are extra fresh and tender, authentic biryanis and massalas to die for! Excellent lamb korma, prawn biryani, vegetable biryani and butter chicken. The nan bread is very fresh and the *lassi* (yoghurt-type drink) excellent. Even the Indian lager is quite good. To end your meal, there are some good desserts (although the choice is a bit limited) and three sorts of tea (iced, honey-cinnamon and with milk). The set lunch gives unbeatable value for money.

✕ **La Gitane** (map C1, **32**): 53 *bis*, avenue de La Motte-Picquet 75015. ☎ 01-47-34-62-92. Metro: La Motte-Piquet-Grenelle. Closed Sunday and public holidays. Budget for around 150F per person. Between the École-Militaire and the Kinopanorama, this lively corner of the 15th arrondissement has more brasseries and sandwich outlets than restaurants, so this place is unusual here. At lunchtime there is an invasion and the dining room stays full until late into the night. The chef changes the menu according to the seasons. Written in chalk on a big blackboard, the main courses, which are as varied as they are tasty, cost between 60F and 80F: *pavé de bœuf Salers*, mullet with mushrooms or lamb kidneys with thyme.

✕ **Chez Foong** (map C1, **28**): 33 rue de Frémicourt 75015. ☎ 01-45-67-36-99. Metro: La Motte-Picquet-Grenelle. Open to 11pm. Closed Sunday and the second fortnight in August. Set menus 56F at lunchtime only, 78F and 85F in the evening. À la carte, budget for 130F. Malaysian cuisine presented through a series of sweet, spicy dishes, artfully prepared by Mr Foong, from Kuala Lumpur. Please note: when they are short-staffed, the service can be very slow indeed and you may have to wait for up to 25 minutes between courses.

✕ **Au Pois Chiche** (map C2, **29**): 3 rue Péclet 75015. ☎ 01-48-28-52-03. Metro: Commerce or Vaugirard. Open lunchtime and evening. Closed Monday and for the whole of August. Booking essential at weekends. Budget for around 130F. A friendly Oriental restaurant with a refined setting. Taste the couscous or lamb *tajine* and wash it down with an Algerian or Moroccan wine.

✕ **Le Vieil Alger** (map C2, **30**): 29 *bis*, rue des Favorites 75015. ☎ 01-48-28-53-37. Metro: Vaugirard. Last orders 10.30pm. It's a good idea to book at weekends and it's absolutely essential at Sunday lunchtimes. No set menu. Budget for around 130F for a full meal, excluding drinks. There's an eastern feel to the decor, good couscous generously served and reasonable prices, making sure that it keeps its good reputation. They are happy to take on group bookings (the back room is perfect for up to 30 people) while still providing a pretty fast service. The couscous with kebabs (70F) and shoulder of lamb (78F) are very popular, as is the 'Vieil Alger' (90F; *méchoui*, which is a North African style barbecue, comprising kebabs and *merguez* sausages).

✕ **El Bacha** (map C2, **44**): 74 rue de la Croix-Nivert 75015. ☎ 01-45-32-15-42. Metro: Cambronne, Commerce or Avenue-Émile-Zola. Open daily 11.30am to 11.30pm. Closed Sunday lunchtime. Set menus at 66F and 96F lunchtime and evening. Budget for 90F à la carte, without drinks. A simple Lebanese restaurant, the specialities include houmous, moutabal (aubergine caviar), *falafels,* and *chawarma.* The grills are all accompanied by bulghur wheat. The cakes here are good, even for people watching their weight, as they're fat-free! Complete dishes at 49F or 56F with a glass of wine or coffee.

✕ **L'Agape** (map B2, **33**): 281 rue Lecourbe 75015. ☎ 01-45-58-19-29. Metro: Convention. Open to around 10.30pm. Closed Saturday lunchtime and Sunday, and also in August. Set meal 95F served daily except Friday evening and at weekends, and another at 120F. The outside looks more cheerful than the inside, which is rather ordinary. But you can eat well, sitting on old-fashioned imitation leather wall seats. The menu is written up in chalk on a blackboard outside: *osso bucco* with ginger, *navarin* of lamb, pork spare ribs with honey and purée of split peas with ginger, *cassoulet* of broad beans and *confit de canard*, fillet of duckling roasted on the bone, seasonal fruit (for two).

✕ **La Petite Auberge** (map B3, **35**): 13 rue du Hameau 75015. ☎ 01-45-32-75-71. Metro: Porte-de-Versailles. Last orders 9.30pm. Closed Sundays, public holidays, August and the last week in December. Booking essential in the evening. Budget for 100–130F à la carte. If post-rugby match sporting ambiance is not your cup of tea, avoid this place when there's a big match on. The dishes of the day, from 46F to 70F, include: streaky salted pork boiled with cabbage, sautéed lamb with haricot beans, *blanquette* of veal, pork spare ribs with lentils, chicken roasted with herbs ... and a quarter bottle of Muscadet or Vin de Pays won't break the bank either.

✕ **Chez Clément** (map B3, **36**): 407 rue de Vaugirard 75015. ☎ 01-53-68-94-00. Metro: Porte-de-Versailles. Open daily to 1am. Near the exhibition park. (*See* Chez Clément *in* '17th arrondissement'.)

✕ **Durand-Dupont** (map A2, **56**): 14 rue Cauchy 75015. ☎ 01-45-54-43-43. Fax: 01-40-60-16-07. Metro: Javel. RER line C; Javel. Open daily noon to 3pm and 8pm to 11.30pm. There are two set meals (85F and 110F). Located near the headquarters of the French pay-per-view channel Canal +, Durand-Dupont is almost their cafeteria, with its clientele of people from the media, TV and showbiz. Customers come here to talk business more than to be seen. The ambiance is warm, both in the choice of bright colours for the decor and the coconut matting on the floor. Artists regularly exhibit their work and some evenings are themed. On the menu are escalope of steamed salmon, leg of lamb roasted with onion marmalade, plates of *charcuterie*, sushi and *gambas*. Brunch on Sunday.

✕ **Woury** (map B1, **37**): 5 rue Humblot 75015. ☎ 01-45-77-37-11. Metro: Dupleix. Last orders 10.30pm. Closed Sunday, in August and at Christmas. Set menu 79F at lunchtime only. Hors-d'oeuvres cost between 32F and 60F, main courses at around 90F. À la carte, budget for 150F. Apart from the essential barbecue, this Korean restaurant (which is a little gloomy) offers some amazing things, such as raw skate with spicy sauce, jellyfish salad, duck with cabbage rolls, or grilled eel. Almost 100 per cent of its clientele are Koreans, but it also welcomes other nationalities!

✕ **Kushiken** (map B2, **38**): 59 avenue Félix-Faure 75015. ☎ 01-45-54-56-32. Metro: Boucicaut. Last orders 10.30pm. Closed Sunday and public holidays. This Japanese restaurant is still not showing its age. The menu is still the same, as is the service – only the prices have changed slightly over the years (but not much!). There is a very simple choice between three set menus: the *yakitori* menu (chicken kebabs) from 80F to 125F; the *robata* menu (seafood and fish kebabs) at 80F; and the lunch menu from 58F to 90F. To drink, real men will go for the *shochu* (sweet potato spirit, or *umeshu* (prune spirit).

✕ **Le Bombay Café** (map B2, **48**): 19 avenue Félix-Faure 75015. ☎ 01-40-60-91-11. Metro: Félix-Faure. Open daily 11am to 11.30pm (last orders). Set menu 49F at lunchtime and in the evening for children; à la carte, budget for 100F excluding drinks. Not really a restaurant, but a coffee shop – and Anglo-Indian to boot! People come here for a snack, a cup of tea, dinner or brunch (89F on Sunday) in a colonial setting, with mahogany furniture and polo equipment as decor. On the house menu-newspaper, the *Bombay Café News,* you'll find tandoori chicken, spicy chicken wings, assorted samosas, chutney and three types of Indian beer.

✕ **Le Mazagan** (map A2, **54**): 136 avenue Félix-Faure 75015. ☎ 01-40-60-13-45. Metro: Lourmel. Closed Sunday. Set menu 125F, including wine and mint tea, at lunchtime. Budget for between 150F and 200F à la carte. A Moroccan restaurant, recommended to all lovers of sweet-savoury-spicy food. The prices are reasonable and it's beautifully simple. Before choosing your lamb *tajine* with a confit of olives and lemons or with onions and raisins, Fes style (a fat-free cuisine), try the fresh stuffed sardines or a *zaalouk* of aubergines with cumin. Or try the *pastilla* with quail (order the day before). Good traditional wines.

✕ **L'Heure Gourmande** (map B1, **55**): 12 rue Beaugrenelle 75015. ☎ 01-45-77-89-24. Metro: Charles-Michel. Last orders 10.30pm. Closed Sunday and the week of 15 August. Set menus 93F to 175F. For several years this family-run place has distinguished itself as one of the best restaurants in the Beaugrenelle quarter. Everything is freshly prepared on the premises. As well as the menu which is changed every three months, the dishes of the day include around a dozen different dishes. Among the starters there could be a plate of three types of salmon, hot goat's cheese salad in breadcrumbs or calves' sweetbreads. For the main courses there might be thigh of *confit de canard* or braised sole with crayfish coulis. The chocolate profiteroles are an absolute treat! The decor is restful, all in grey and pink with a no-smoking dining room.

☆☆☆ CHIC

✕ **Le Troquet** (map C2, **49**): 21 rue François-Bonvin 75015. ☎ 01-45-66-89-00. Metro: Sèvres-Lecourbe. Open lunchtime and evening (last orders 11pm). Closed Sunday and Monday, the first week in January and the first three weeks in August. Set menus 130F at lunchtime 160F in the evening. This delightful place is in a hidden street in the 15th arrondissement, a vast dining room offering delicious food. At lunchtime there's a menu with starter, main course and dessert. In the evening there's no choice, but you're guaranteed to have something tasty, such as creamy carrot soup with cumin, foie gras fried with gingerbread, plaice poached *à la nage* with lemon butter and garnished with wholemeal spaghetti, cheese from the Pyrenees or scrummy *clafoutis* (fruit baked in batter). It's all quite exquisite and the menus change daily. Wines at around 100F. Booking is advisable.

✕ **L'Os à Moelle** (map A–B2, **42**): 3 rue Vasco-de-Gama 75015. ☎ 01-45-57-27-27. Metro: Lourmel. Open to 11pm. Closed Sunday and Monday, and also in August. Set menus 155F at lunchtime, 190F in the evening. The menu-*dégustation* here has four sittings. Depending on what is available at the Rungis market, things may kick off with a *croustillant* of salmon marinated in dill with cucumber juice, followed by a *brouillade* of egg (where the yolk and the egg white is mixed but not beaten) with parmesan and cream of basil, bream roasted in shellfish juice and sweet peppers, and, to end, iced truffle with fresh thyme (the chef's sorbets are exquisite). The wine list is well chosen, at prices which keep the bill within reason.

✕ **La Papillote** (map B2–3, **45**): 22 rue Desnouettes 75015. ☎ 01-48-56-66-26. Metro: Convention. Open to 9.45pm. Closed Saturday lunchtime and Sunday, and also for three weeks in August. Set menu 110F lunchtime and evening (except Friday and Saturday evening). There are other set menus at 145F, 165F and 195F. Children's menu 70F. The only point of interest in an otherwise rather dull area is this minimalist but cosy restaurant (35 tables). The dishes are as well presented as they are tasty. The chef, never lost for ideas, shows great inventiveness. Munster ravioli with *gewürztraminer* and *compotée* of green cabbage; *craquelin à la poire confite* (a crunchy biscuit with pear jelly and a light praline cream). It would be impossible to mention all the original dishes because the menu changes daily. It's best to book.

✕ **Les P'tits Bouchons de François Clerc** (map D2, **46**): 32 boulevard du Montparnasse 75015. ☎ 01-45-48-52-03. Metro: Duroc. Open to 10.30pm. Closed Saturday lunchtime and Sunday. Set menus 115F and 174F lunchtime and evening respectively. This restaurant offers wines at cost price, and you can find some real bargains. The cuisine is not quite up to the wines, and there may be the odd disappointment in a starter or main course. However, it's best to book your table because the cheap wines have been a great success. When the weather is fine there's a terrace, which is best after 9pm, once the traffic on the boulevard dies down.

✕ **Le Bistrot d'Hubert** (map D2, **50**): 41 boulevard Pasteur 75015. ☎ 01-47-34-15-50. Metro: Pasteur. Open daily (including Sunday) to 11pm. Closed Saturday lunchtimes between mid-June and mid-September. At lunchtime there's a set menu at 145F. In the evening there is a menu at 195F, and with wine budget for 230F. There is a large kitchen opening onto the dining room which looks more table d'hôte than true bistro. A veteran in the kitchen, the chef knows all the tricks of his trade. He takes his inspiration from the land and sea – try crab ravioli with thyme or glazed tuna with balsamic caramel on green vegetables. There's a smiling welcome and the service is diligent.

✕ **Casa Alcade** (map C1, **51**): 117 boulevard de Grenelle 75015. ☎ 01-47-83-39-71. Metro: La Motte-Picquet-Grenelle. Open daily to 10.30pm. Closed 24 and 25 December. Set menu 158F; à la carte, budget for around 220F. Here there's a long bar on which there's a large Pyrenees ham, small dishes of olives, and it's decorated with bullfighting posters. A good-natured welcome and warm atmosphere does not distract from the excellent Basque-Spanish cuisine. You'll find fish soup, *pipérade basquaise* (with tomatoes and sweet peppers), cockles, *zarzuela*, red peppers with garlic and roast suckling pig with olive oil purée. The queen of the *casa*, the paella, comes in two versions: for two (260F) and as a main course.

✕ **Da Maurizio** (map D2, **34**): 148 rue de Vaugirard 75015. ☎ 01-47-34-63-45. Metro: Pasteur or Falguière. Open to 11pm. Closed Sunday and in August. Set menu 90F at lunchtime. À la carte, budget for around 160F. Typically Italian, with Maurizio taking charge front of house. A lot of work has gone into setting the scene, the decor has been carefully thought out, and the *commedia dell'arte* is well rehearsed. Every table groans under bunches of flowers, bottles and *antipasti*.

✕ **Swann et Vincent** (map C1, **40**): 32 boulevard Garibaldi 75015. ☎ 01-42-73-30-44. Open daily lunchtime and evening. Closed for three weeks in August. Last orders around 11pm. Booking is essential. Set menu 85F at lunchtime, à la carte around 140F, plus drinks. Allow yourself to be whisked away to Italy. *Penne, tagliatelle al mero, polenta al gorgonzola* – it's all good, fresh and generous. (*See also* Swann et Vincent *in* '12th arrondissement').

✕ **L'Amanguier** (map B1, **39**): 51 rue du Théâtre 75015. ☎ 01-45-77-04-01. Metro: Avenue-Émile-Zola or Charles-Michel. Open daily to midnight. There's a seductive set menu at 98F (starter plus main course or main course plus dessert) and other set menus from 100F to 220F. Not far from Beaugrenelle and its cinema, here is a little haven which has won the heart of the inhabitants of the Charles-Michel quarter. Smooth service and affordable prices all combine to keep everyone happy.

✕ **Fontanarosa** (map C1, **47**): 28 boulevard de Garibaldi 75015. ☎ 01-45-66-97-84. Metro: Cambronne. Open daily to midnight. At lunchtime there is a set meal with starter and main course at 89F, and a set menu at 120F. Budget for 200F à la carte. There's a fine courtyard-terrace which is irresistible in spring (it's covered in winter). The cuisine displays the influence of southern Italy, and especially Sardinia, which is where the owner of the restaurant comes from.

☆☆☆☆ TRÈS CHIC

✕ **Le Clos Morillons** (map C3, **43**): 50 rue des Morillons 75015. ☎ 01-48-28-04-37. Metro: Porte-de-Vanves. Open to 10pm. Closed Saturday lunchtime, Sunday and Monday lunchtime. Set menus at 175F and 285F, à la carte budget for 260F. East meets West on large plates. Try cream of shellfish *au colombo* and with sweet potatoes, glazed tuna and compote of cabbage, Sichuan pineapple marinated in spicy caramel. There is an amazing menu, 'Exploring Spices', with unusual flavours. Good wine list at reasonable prices.

WHAT TO SEE

It's a well-known fact that there are no monuments of note in the 15th arrondissement; however, the Tour Montparnasse and boulevard Montparnasse are both worth a visit.

The rue Lecourbe used to be the main road to Brittany. This is where the built-up areas ended before the Vaugirard district was built.

In the northern part of the arrondissement, in rue Nélaton (Metro: Bir-Hakeim-Grenelle), a monument commemorates the deportation of 13,152 Jews in July 1942. They were initially rounded up and held in the winter Velodrome, which today houses the Ministry of the Interior.

AROUND THE TOUR MONTPARNASSE AND GARE MONTPARNASSE

★ The **tour Montparnasse:** built on the site of the former Gare Montparnasse where, on 25 August 1944, the Germans signed their surrender. A plaque on one of the pillars of the shopping centre commemorates this event. This towering office block was finished in 1973 and is about 200m (656ft) high, dominating the skyline of the surrounding area.

Some fascinating facts: it has dozens of lifts, 40 firemen, 8,000 employees and stands on 56 concrete pillars sunk 80m (262ft) deep to bear the enormous mass of steel and glass. You can go up to the top, for which there's a charge, but it is worthwhile for the excellent views of the city. There's a good bar where you can sip cocktails and look out over the whole of Paris.

★ The **jardin Atlantique:** access by the lifts on either side of the Gare Montparnasse, on boulevard de Vaugirard and rue du Commandant-Mouchotte; also by place des 5-Martyrs-du-Lycée-Buffon, behind the station. Metro: Montparnasse-Bienvenüe, Gaîté or Pasteur. This garden has a very original position – on a platform of more than 3 hectares (7.5 acres), above the railway tracks. An avenue lined with curious tall trees leads to a fountain. There are tennis courts and rest areas crossed by a little pontoon bridge, which is covered in greenery in the spring. Nearby stand the Mémorial du Maréchal Leclerc and the Musée Jean-Moulin.

★ The **musée de la Poste (Post Office Museum)**: 34 boulevard de Vaugirard 75015. ☎ 01-42-79-23-45 (information by telephone). Metro: Montparnasse-Bienvenüe, Pasteur or Falguière. Open every day from 10am to 6pm except Sunday and public holidays. Entry fee 30F, concessions 20F. Free for the under 12s. The 15 rooms with permanent collections have only recently been renovated. The tour starts with a short film giving an introduction to the journey on which visitors are about to embark and the most significant objects in the collection. The first eight rooms are dedicated to the history of the Post Office, from its origins until the present day: its initial transportation by horse and carriage, the appearance of telegraphs, rural postmen in 1830 and the arrival of the public service with price unification in 1848; the transport revolution with the introduction of the train and its sorting carriages and then the evolution of the post office business, with its linked commercial and banking activities, and finally, the arrival of air-mail with the birth of the Aeropostale service and pioneers such as Mermoz. Throughout these rooms there is a variety of unusual and beautiful items on display; a pair of wood-reinforced postilion boots, the first post office map, a collection of letter boxes in various colours and the amazing 'Moulins balls' which were floated down the Seine to ensure the arrival of the post at Parisian destinations during the 1870-71 siege, etc. There are four rooms dedicated to stamps and philately, certain to delight collectors, who can drool over rare national and international stamps as well as contemporary artists' variations on stamp design. The tour is rounded off with an exhibition relating to the place of the post in popular art and society. The temporary exhibitions are suitable for all ages – 'animals on stamps', 'music and paintings on stamps', 'memories of postage stamps' and the like. It's best to ring before coming, especially if you're in a group (information ☎ 01-43-79-23-30). There is a shop plus a stamp collectors' counter open 10am to 6pm Monday to Saturday.

★ The **Chemin du Montparnasse et la cité d'artistes 'du 21':** 21 avenue du Maine 75015. Metro: Montparnasse-Bienvenüe (exit place Bienvenüe). There are around 20 workshops here, one of the last vestiges of what artistic Montparnasse used to be like. It is positively charged with history: Marie Vassilieff's cafeteria was set up here to feed poor artists. In January 1917 Max Jacob organized a meal to celebrate Braque's demobilization. Around the table sat Matisse, Picasso, Juan Gris and Fernand Léger. People like Zadkine, Apollinaire and Chagall also used to visit. Jean-Marie Serreau, one of the forebears of popular theatre, had his workshop here. Roger Blin, who introduced Samuel Beckett to the people of France by putting on *Waiting For Godot,* worked here from 1945 to 1953. Today, occupied by artists, craftsmen and galleries, several associations have happily brought it back to life.

– **Immanence:** ☎ 01-47-34-11-78. The space consists of a workshop aimed at raising awareness of contemporary art in both adults and children. Also an exhibition room.

– Saved at the last hour from the diggers and steam-rollers, the **Chemin du Montparnasse**, ☎ 01-42-22-91-96. Open Wednesday to Sunday, 1pm to 7pm. Entry fee 25F, concessions 20F. A kind of museum to Montparnasse's glory years. Run by an association, it stages temporary exhibitions and also music and poetry evenings (for the latter you need to be a member of the association). The central themes of the exhibitions focus on the artists, painters and poets who have lived and worked in the Montparnasse area 'where the talk has always been more of art than money': the Japanese (Foujita), the Russians (Chagall, Zadkine, Soutine), Prévert and many others.

★ The **musée Bourdelle:** 18 rue Antoine-Bourdelle 75015. ☎ 01-49-54-73-73. Metro: Falguière or Montparnasse-Bienvenüe (exit place Bienvenüe). Bus Nos. 48, 91, 92, 94, 95 and 96. Open 10am to 5.40pm. Closed Monday and public holidays. Entry fee 22F, concessions (including 6-25 year olds) 15F. Temporary exhibitions: entry fee 30F, concessions 20F. There is a series of workshop tours for visitors with impaired vision, who can touch some of the sculptures. There are also children's workshops by appointment (information and bookings: ☎ 01-49-54-73-73). The museum has been housed in these premises since 1949 – where Bourdelle lived and worked until 1929, in the wake of Rodin and other great artists. An extension by the architect Portzamparc made it possible to show all the collections and classify them according to themes. There are almost 500 sculptures as well as studies, sketches, small replicas and plastercasts which allow you to follow the different phases in the creation of a statue. Bourdelle's flat has been kept exactly as he left it, as has his workshop, which is topped by a high glass roof. The documentation room, which houses Bourdelle's archives, is open to researchers only.

– **Large hall:** built for the centenary of the artist's birth. There is an immense Vierge *à l'offrande* with a Baby Jesus. There is also a bas-relief of the theatre on the Champs-Élysées, *La Danse,* with Isadora Duncan and Nijinsky.

– **Small hall:** studies in bronze for monuments (Montceau-les-Mines and Alvéar).

– **Garden:** a bust of Rodin and *La Force.* In the gardens at the rear there is a bronze equestrian statue of General Alvéar and the *Centaure mourant.*

– **Studios:** Bourdelle's studio has hardly changed since his death in 1929 – even the old cast-iron stove is still there. There are some interesting portraits, and don't miss Eugène Carrière's workshop, with an amazing *Madame Félicien Champsaur et sa fille.*

– **Adjoining halls:** paintings, busts, Bourdelle's personal collection and *l'Homme qui marche* by Rodin.

– **New Portzamparc halls:** inaugurated in 1992. A spacious location for the monument to Mickiewicz, former Polish national poet, and the monument to the dead of Montauban (*Têtes hurlantes* or *La Guerre*).

★ The **musée Pasteur:** 25 rue du Docteur-Roux 75015. ☎ 01-45-68-82-83. Metro: Pasteur. Website: www.pasteur.fr. Open daily 2pm to 5.30pm. Closed public holidays and in August. Entry fee 15F, reduction for students. Guided tour lasting 40–45 minutes, by appointment for groups: ☎ 01-45-68-82–73. If a tour has already started you may need to wait a while for the next one. One of the most unusual little museums in Paris, this was Louis Pasteur's house, where he lived for the last seven years of his life. The setting has barely changed at all since his death in 1895. Pasteur was born in Dole (Jura) in 1822. He was a brilliant student, attending the École Normale Supérieure and became a doctor in science, faculty professor, and researcher. He worked on crystallography, so-called 'spontaneous generation', the fermentation of wine and beer, diseases of the silkworm, anthracosis, septicaemia, gangrene and puerperal fever. He also discovered a vaccine for anthracosis, cholera in poultry, swine erysiperlas and, finally, rabies. A busy man indeed.

You can visit the apartment, which is just as he left it. See his room, with portraits of his parents painted by Pasteur himself at the age of 13, his bathroom, with his Member of the Academy's uniform and university gown, and the desk where he wrote up his lab notes in the rue d'Ulm. In the small lounge there is a portrait of Mme Pasteur by Edelfelt. The staircase was specially constructed as he had been the victim of an attack of hemiplegia, which caused him to have problems moving one side of his body. He received the celebrities of the day in the office and large lounge. You can also visit the crypt where he is buried along with his wife. Finally, you can visit the scientific room with an audio presentation of all his work and his laboratory instruments. There is also a very well-prepared information service, which has a photo library, dossiers on the most important subjects of current research, and, of course, about Pasteur and his scientific work.

AROUND PARC GEORGES-BRASSENS

★ **La Ruche (The Beehive):** 52 rue de Dantzig (take the passage de Dantzig). This is a superb rotunda building built by Gustave Eiffel for the Exhibition in 1900. Along with Le Bateau-Lavoir, it was one of the centres of artistic creation in the 20th century. The Wine Pavilion was bought by a wealthy patron of the arts and made available, for a reasonable rent, to struggling artists. Chagall, Soutine and Léger all lived there. La Ruche has, on a number of occasions, had to repel the advances of the bulldozers. Now restored and listed, it still houses artists, painters or sculptors. There are few things more pleasant than to walk in this lovely rambling garden and surround yourself with a wide variety of sculptures.

★ The **villa Santos-Dumont:** squeezed between rue des Morillons and rue de Vouillé, close to the rue de Brancion. A small avenue lined with attractive brick bungalows interlaced with vines leads up to the villa. The family of its founder lived around here until 1991. A further twenty-five houses were erected in the 1920s. Zadkine, the Russian sculptor lived at No. 3 for ten years, Fernand Léger lived at No. 4, and at No. 10 was one of his contemporaries, the designer Franck Margerin. At No. 15, there are some fine mosaics by Gatti, who also lived here.

This quiet place, with its artistic past, also seduced Georges Brassens (who died in 1981), spending the last few years of his life at 42, rue Santos-Dumont (he had previously lived at 9 impasse Florimont).

★ The **parc Georges-Brassens:** corner of rue des Morillons and rue Brancion. This park is built on the site of the old abattoirs of Vaugirard. The two enormous bronze bulls which watch over the main entrance are a monument to this butchers' legacy.

The design of the park is a real success, with all sorts of things for children: little wooden houses, rocks for climbing, artificial hills, etc. An ornamental lake surrounds the great clock, dating from the time of the abattoirs (on one of the façades you can still see the inscription 'Sale by auction'). The Jardin des Senteurs (garden for the senses), running along rue des Morillons is designed for those with a visual impairment. The sounds of the fountains are a guide and plants with particularly pleasant aromas have been carefully selected with labels in Braille. May is the best time of year to go. On Saturday and Sunday mornings a Book Fair is held in rue Brancion. You can find some amazing bargains (get there early – all the pros know that!). The 700 vines (Pinot Noir to be precise) planted in 1985 were harvested for the first time in 1988. According to the specialists, this 'Clos des Morillons' should be very full-bodied, with a good bouquet.

AROUND PARC ANDRÉ-CITROËN

★ The **avenue Félix-Faure:** at No. 24 place Etienne-Pernet there is a superb building (just as you come out of the metro Félix-Faure) entirely in the art-nouveau style. Note the balconies and the door with its wild profusion of plant life. A bit further on, at 40 avenue Félix-Faure, there is a reproduction of the *Renard et le Corbeau* (the Fox and the Crow, from the fable by La Fontaine) above the entrance. At No. 68, in the restaurant, there are some fine tiled panels representing characters dressed in the style of Louis XVI.

★ The **parc André-Citroën:** entrances in rue Balard, quai André-Citroën, rue de la Montagne-de-l'Espérou, rue Cauchy, etc. Metro: Place-Balard; RER: Boulevard-Victor. Open daily 7.30am to 7pm; mid-May to end of August 7.30am to 10pm (opens 9am weekends and public holidays). Inaugurated at the end of 1992, the park is on land formerly occupied by the Citroën factories and covers 14 hectares (34 acres). The work of the architects Patrick Berger, Jean-Paul Viguier, Jean-François Jodry, and the landscape artists Gilles Clément and Alain Provost, this is the largest park to be created since the days of Haussmann.

Its most fervent admirers say it's a sort of modern Versailles with a wide perspective over the Seine, vast lawns, two greenhouses and a lot of water (fountains, pools and canals).

OTHER SIGHTS IN THE 15TH ARRONDISSEMENT

★ At 27 rue de la Convention stands the prestigious **Imprimerie nationale** (National Printworks). It is possible to do a tour, although you have to write to the director in advance, who will organise this. The National Printworks succeeded the Royal Printworks, created in 1640 and initially based at the Louvre. It published the laws decreed during the Revolution, and all the State administrative publications. Today it houses a remarkable museum displaying all sorts of printing techniques. The Imprimerie nationale also publishes its own books, many of them on art and history and always with the highest production values.

★ The **Maison de la culture du Japon (Japanese Cultural Institute)**: 101 *bis*, quai Branly 75015. Information: ☎ 01-44-37-95-01/01-44-37-95-95. Website: www.mcjp.asso.fr. Metro: Bir-Hakeim-Grenelle; RER: Champ-de-Mars-Tour-Eiffel. Open Tuesday to Saturday noon to 7pm (Thursday 8pm). Closed Sundays, Mondays, between Christmas and Epiphany, during August and on public holidays. The decision to create a special space for information about Japan, aimed at the general public, was taken in 1982, but it was not until 1997 that the establishment opened its doors. Designed by Kenneth Armstrong, the innovative and flowing architecture is a replica in glass and steel of the nearby Australian Embassy. It is a superb construction with 11 floors (7,500 square metres/24,600 square feet), only six of which are visible from the exterior and integrates perfectly into its environment. In the evening it looks like a Japanese lantern. There's an exhibition hall (level 2), a multi-purpose theatre (level 3) and a cinema (level 0). They show films, especially on Thursday at 3pm and 5.45pm and you can also take courses in calligraphy, Judo, etc. (information: ☎ 01-44-37-95-95).

– **The library:** on level 3. Open Tuesday to Saturday 1pm to 6pm (8pm on Thursday). Closed Sundays, Mondays and public holidays. Free access. Contains around 15,000 documents, including CDs, video-cassettes and audio-cassettes. As you would expect, you can find books and magazines in Japanese, French and English.

– Every Wednesday, in the superb **tea-room** (level 5), the traditional and sacred tea ceremony takes place at 12.30pm and 6.30pm. It is alternately organized by the Omotesenke and Urasenke schools, two of the most famous academies for training the great masters of the tea ceremony. For bookings relating to the tea ceremony: ☎ 01-44-37-95-95.

★ The amazing **église St-Séraphin** at 91 rue Lecourbe (Metro: Sèvres-Lecourbe or Volontaires) is dedicated to the Russian Orthodox church, but it can't be seen from the outside. You have to venture into the porch to discover this picturesque wooden church, which reproduces all the characteristics of traditional Orthodox churches. The tree passing through it is a reminder that Saint-Séraphin spent a lot of time in the forest. It's almost like being in Moscow! You can visit before or after services. Information: ☎ 01-42-73-05-03.

WHAT TO DO

– The **Kinopanorama** (map **C1**): 60 avenue de la Motte-Picquet 75015. ☎ 01-43-06-50-50. Metro: La Motte-Picquet-Grenelle. An extraordinary cinema with a 180° panoramic screen. The projection and sound quality are exceptional. The best seats are downstairs at the back. You can book in advance at the cinema or through Allociné: ☎ 01-40-30-20-10 (collect your tickets from 2.45pm to 5pm and 6pm to 8.15pm). Entry fee 52F; reduced rate for students, holders of the *Carte Vermeil* and under 12s.

– **Aquaboulevard** (map A3): 4 rue Louis-Armand 75015. ☎ 01-40-60-10-00. Metro: Balard. Bus: PC, 39 or 42; Place-Balard or Louis-Armand stop. Open Monday to Thursday and Sunday 9am to 11pm, Friday and Saturday 8am to midnight. By car, take the Périphérique ring road and come off at the Porte de Sèvres. Entry to the aquatic park 69F during the week, 77F at weekends and public holidays; 50F for under 12s during the week, 56F at weekends and public holidays; free for under 3s (fixed price for four hours, 10F per extra hour). For anyone who doesn't like crowds, the Aquaboulevard is quiet in the mornings from 9am to 10am, except at the weekends.

The Aquaboulevard is a large white liner anchored in the middle of Paris. With its decks, hold and portholes, this 380m (1,250ft) high building is the largest leisure centre in the city. There's an enormous aquatic park with a tropical atmosphere: water at 29°C (84°F), curved banks planted with palm, fig and banana trees, giant American-style waterslides, artificial waves, rivers with currents, jacuzzis and Turkish baths. There are also around 40 sporting activities: tennis (six covered courts and three outdoor, a shop and specialist supervision), squash (six courts), golf (a semi-covered practice course on the terrace) and, of course, restaurants, brasseries and bars.

– **Gymboree** (map A3): 4 rue Louis-Armand 75015. Metro: Balard. ☎ 01-40-71-61-60. Activities and games aimed at young children up to six years of age, accompanied by their parents. Music, imagination and creativity are the keywords here.

WHERE TO GO FOR A DRINK

🍸 **Café Pacifico** (map D2, **70**): 50 boulevard du Montparnasse 75015. ☎ 01-45-48-63-87. Metro: Montparnasse-Bienvenüe. Open daily noon to 3pm and 6pm to 2am. Non-stop at the weekends. Closed 25 December. Set menus 58F at lunchtime, 62F to 75F in the evening. Children's menu 32F. À la carte, budget for no more than 100F. One of the leading Mexican bars in Paris and the most popular meeting place for Paris' small Mexican community. The decor has a plumed serpent, and a *mariachi* feel. The nicest times of the day are the happy hours (drinks at half price) from 6pm to 8pm. There is a superb terrace on the interior courtyard where you can drink until 8pm and then dine until 10pm.

🍸 **Au Bon Coin** (map C3, **74**): 85 rue Brancion 75015. ☎ 01-45-32-92-37. Metro: Porte-de-Vanves. Open 7.30am to 9pm during the week and 6am to 11pm or midnight at weekends. Set menu 70F at lunchtime only. A traditional bistro like many others, except that here, every weekend, it goes mad, with local booksellers, second-hand dealers and locals crowding the bar for a glass of wine (Marcillac, Gamay de Marionet, etc.) and dishes at under 60F. The view over the Parc Georges-Brassens is a crowd puller.

🍸 **Le Cristal** (map D2, **71**): 163 avenue de Suffren 75015. ☎ 01-47-34-47-92. Metro: Sèvres-Lecourbe. Open 8am (6.30pm Saturday) to 1am (2am at the weekends). Closed Sunday. Half a pint of beer 10F, happy hours from 6pm to 2am. Darts and a terrace, which opens as soon as the sun comes out. Always packed out and rocking! A real find in this residential quarter where everything else seems to close early.

🍷 **Le Bréguet** (map D2, **72**): 72 rue Falguière 75015. ☎ 01-42-79-97-00. Metro: Pasteur. Open daily 8am (5pm at weekends) to 1.45am. Closed Sunday and for 10 days in August. Set menu 60F lunchtime and evening. A bar with a difference. Here they broadcast programmes from *Télé Bocal*, 'the first local interactive TV station', on the first Thursday of every month, hold permanent exhibitions and serve 'Molotov' cocktails such as the Sarajevo, and dishes from 20F to 50F. From Mayenne, Vendée, Normandy and Brittany, the four partners, each of whom is madder than the other, have made this seemingly lost cause one of the wildest places in Paris.

🍷 **L'Inattendu** (map C3, **73**): 36 rue de Dantzig 75015. ☎ 01-45-30-11-70. Metro: Convention. Open 11am (3pm Saturday) to 2am. Closed Sunday and public holidays as well as two weeks in August. Dishes from 25F to 45F. Half pint of beer from 15F. What could be more romantic than a moonlit walk around the Parc Georges-Brassens? Not a soul around, no noise, no bistros left open . . . except one: L'Inattendu. Simple and modest, it is very popular with the regulars. The decor is wild – posters from comic strips, an old bike, 'la Perle' (the Pearl), hanging from the ceiling, bistro blackboards and a *Happy Days*-style jukebox. There is a superb selection of earthy wines served by the glass (from 17F) or in a Lyons jug, and delicious *tartines Poilâne* to go with them.

16TH ARRONDISSEMENT

AUTEUIL • PASSY • THE TROCADÉRO • THE BOIS DE BOULOGNE

In 1859, when many outlying communes were annexed to Paris, the villages of Auteuil and Passy became the 13th arrondissement. There was an uproar of protest from the inhabitants. Until then Paris had only been divided into 12 arrondissements, and if a couple were living in sin people used to say: 'They got married in the 13th arrondissement.' The 16th arrondissement, on the other hand, is very definitely the smart part of town.

The larger properties were split up into 'villas' in the 19th century. Although they look quite normal, seen from the street, a 'villa' can actually be concealing a great deal – winding alleys, oases of greenery and magnificent houses. At night the area takes on a look all of its own in the halo of the street lamps. Look up: you'll be surprised by the number of glass roofs and hanging gardens. As you wander around you'll notice that the entrances to the villas are often patrolled by security guards watching you, watching how the other half live.

WHERE TO STAY

☆☆ – ☆☆☆ MODERATE TO CHIC

Hôtel Keppler (northern map D1, **1**): 12 rue Keppler 75116. ☎ 01-47-20-65-05. Fax: 01-47-23-02-29. E-mail: hotel.keppler@wanadoo.fr. Metro: George-V or Charles-de-Gaulle-Étoile. Double room with bath or shower 480F. Free coffee. Near the Étoile, excellent value for money. It's nice to relax in the pastel colours of the lobby or the bar. The rooms are spotless, all of them with a bathroom and TV (satellite and Canal +), but they are not very spacious. There is a view over a fairly gloomy courtyard.

Villa d'Auteuil (southern map B1, **2**): 28 rue Poussin 75016. ☎ 01-42-88-30-37/01-42-88-97-69. Fax: 01-45-20-74-70. E-mail: villaaut@aol.com. Metro: Porte-d'Auteuil. Bus Nos. 52 and 62; Michel-Ange-Auteuil or Porte-d'Auteuil stops. Double room with bath or shower 350F with satellite TV. Located in the nicest part of 16th arrondissement. Around here, the hotels collect stars; this one only has two but it has impeccable rooms, all with bathroom or shower, and is excellent value for money. Very attentive service. The rooms on the street side are quieter thanks to the double-glazing; or ask for a view over the green courtyard.

Queen's Hôtel (southern map B1, **3**): 4 rue Bastien-Lepage 75016. ☎ 01-42-88-89-85. Fax: 01-40-50-67-52. E-mail: contact@queens.hotel.fr. Metro: Michel-Ange-Auteuil. The 22 air-conditioned rooms are distributed over six floors: double room with bathroom and jacuzzi 630F, double room with shower 520F, single room with shower 390F. The fine façade of this hotel has been repainted and all the windows are covered in flowers. An establishment which its owner, a former journalist, has dedicated to the art of his time, as can be seen from the paintings which decorate the lobby and the staircases. The rooms are tastefully decorated, some of them bearing the name of a contemporary painter whose work is on show inside. Satellite TV. The 5th floor gives a fine view over the Villa Michel-Ange.

☗ **Hôtel Ambassade** (northern map C2, **4**): 79 rue Lauriston 75116. ☎ 01-45-53-41-15. Fax: 01-45-53-30-80. Metro: Boissière. Closed from mid-July to the end of August. Double room, depending on the time of year, from 504F to 513F with shower and toilet and 550F to 572F with bath and toilet. Not really for backpackers, you may say to yourself as you arrive in rue Lauriston, and yet this hotel is good value for money, with a relaxed elegance from the reception to the service and the rooms. The latter are not terribly spacious, but well equipped: room service, satellite TV, Canal + and hairdryer.

☗ **Hôtel Boileau** (southern map B2–3, **5**): 81 rue Boileau 75016. ☎ 01-42-88-83-74. Fax: 01-45-27-62-98. Metro: Exelmans. Website: www.cofrase.com/boileau. Double room 480F, with bath, cable TV and hairdryer. Sports fans who are regulars at the Parc des Princes and want to escape from the crowds at big matches will love this charming hotel, overlooking a very quiet little street, near the market in the avenue de Versailles. There is a little patio overlooked by the breakfast room, a bar on the ground floor and a parrot hidden in a corner of the reception!

☗ **Au Palais de Chaillot** (northern map C2, **6**): 35 avenue Raymond-Poincaré 75116. ☎ 01-53-70-09-09. Fax: 01-53-70-09-08. E-mail: hapc@club-internet.fr. Metro: Trocadéro or Victor-Hugo. Double room with shower and toilet 560F and with bath 630F. Right near the Eiffel Tower, this is a really charming two-star hotel, sympathetically restored. The setting is cool and impeccable and all rooms have satellite TV, telephone and a hairdryer. On the ground floor there is a breakfast buffet room. Room service is very efficient. Reserve well in advance.

☗ **Hôtel Le Hameau de Passy** (northern map B3, **7**): 48 rue de Passy 75016. ☎ 01-42-88-47-55. Fax: 01-42-30-83-72. Website: www.hameaudepassy.com. Metro: Passy and Muette; RER: Muette-Boulainvilliers. Double room 610F. Breakfast included. You enter this hotel through a little passage between a leather shop and a hair salon, which leads to a flowery courtyard where the only noise is the singing of the birds. You'll hardly believe that you're only a few yards from the numerous shops in the rue de Passy. Perfect for a weekend break, just down the road from the Trocadéro.

☗ **Hôtel Gavarni** (northern map C3, **8**): 5 rue Gavarni 75016. ☎ 01-45-24-52-82. Fax: 01-40-50-16-95. Website: www.paris-hotel.com/gavarni. Metro: Passy. Individual rooms from 400F to 475F. Double room 510F. The street, hotel and people are all quiet. Two minutes from the rue de Passy, at a gentle stroll, you could easily miss this straightforward hotel. If you're lucky enough to have booked a room, you'll be more likely to meet provincial or foreign politicians than showbiz personalities or tourists in shorts. Quiet, discreet with fitted carpets. You won't be able to resist!

CAMP SITES

☗ **Camping du Bois de Boulogne:** 2 allée du Bord-de-l'Eau 75016. ☎ 01-45-24-30-00. Fax: 01-42-24-42-95. Metro: Porte-Maillot.

Bus No. 244; 'Camping, Le Moulin' stop. There are fixed prices which vary according to the time of year, from 65F to 84F per night for two people with a space where you can put up your tent; 96F to 133F if you've got a vehicle with you (a car or a mobile home). An inclusive price allowing for electricity, water and drainage: 127F to 149F for two. There are also 30 mobile homes available to hire (276F to 486F per night, all with shower, toilet and kitchen). This camp site is 3km (1.5 miles) on foot from the Pont de Neuilly. A private shuttle service operates from Easter to September, 8.30am to 1am. Departures, which are more frequent in season, go from the exit to the metro station and from the Porte Maillot bus station. For drivers, it's well signposted from the Porte Maillot.

This three-star campsite, located between the Seine and Longchamp, has been completely renovated and is open all year round. It has 510 places, in the generous shade of 2,000 privet hedges. It is well equipped with left-luggage lockers, telephone booths, etc. From April there is a supermarket and snack bar. You can stay for up to a month. No bookings, except for the mobile homes on the site. With a car, get here early in the morning in July and August.

WHERE TO EAT

☆ BUDGET

✕ **Les Chauffeurs** (northern map B3, **21**): 8 chaussée de la Muette 75016. ☎ 01-42-88-50-05. Metro: La Muette. Open daily lunchtime and evening to 11pm. Closed 1 May, the second fortnight in August, Christmas and New Year's Day. Set menu lunchtime and evening 68F, à la carte around 120F. On the old-style menu (photocopied in purple ink), there is an anthology of good plain cooking: *sole meunière*, *entrecôte* with shallots, etc., but there is also a menu with vegetable broth, fillet of marinated herring, *pâté de tête* or leek vinaigrette. To follow, try *andouillette*, *blanquette* or chicken-purée, cheese or the house crème caramel. The owners are from Alsace, and very proud of their region's cuisine, so they sometimes slip something onto the menu, like sauerkraut or saveloy.

✕ **La Matta** (northern map B3, **42**): 23 rue de l'Annonciation 75016. ☎ 01-40-50-04-66. Metro: La Muette. Open daily to 11pm. Budget for 100F excluding drinks. A snapshot of Italy hidden at the end of one of those busy streets in this elegant arrondissement, worth checking out for its generous and well-made pizzas (47–74F). The welcome is charming and the service efficient. If you love ice cream and sorbets, it's worth knowing that Pascal le Glacier's shop is in the next street. There's nothing like a good sorbet after a pizza!

✕ **Restaurant GR 5** (northern map B2, **22**): 19 rue Gustave-Courbet 75116. ☎ 01-47-27-09-84. Metro: Rue-de-la-Pompe or Victor-Hugo. Open to 11pm. Closed Sunday. Set menu 80F and 90F at lunchtime only; 120F in the evening. Budget for around 150F à la carte. A former rambler who fell in love with the GR 5 long distance footpath which passed close to his home in Briançon has opened this little place. It is discreet and yet packed out both lunchtime and evening. In the little mountain-cabin-style dining room, the lunchtime menus comprise hors-d'œuvres, a main course such as entrecôte with green pepper or Dijon rabbit, and a dessert. In the evening there's a change of menu, including *tartiflette au reblochon* (a very smelly, but tasty cheese) at

100F and Savoyard *raclette* (fondue-style meal) at 110F, with salami, garlic sausage, dried beef (served in thin slices), green salad and tomatoes, shelled nuts, onions gherkins, and steamed potatoes. There is another set meal: *Raclette à volonté*' (as much as you can eat) for 155F. There's a wine of the month by the bottle, by the 25cl or 50cl jug, with a very good Coteaux du Lyonnais at under 50F.

✕ **La Ferme des Gourmets** (southern map B2, **24**): 82 rue Boileau 75016. ☎ 01-46-47-87-19. Metro: Exelmans. Open lunchtime and evening Monday to Saturday; last orders 10pm. Set menu 80F lunchtime and evening, children's menu 55F. À la carte around 120F without drinks. On one side of the street is the shop and its Provençal designer products, on the other is the restaurant with good *cassoulet au confit*, chicken with rice, etc. There is a terrace in summer, located between two very quiet streets. A nice place with its crowds of local regulars.

✕ **Le Verre et Rouge** (northern map C1, **20**): 30 rue Duret 75016. ☎ 01-45-00-09-29. Metro: Argentine. Open daily to 11pm. Closed Sunday, Monday and public holidays. At lunchtime there is a set meal at 85F; in the evening budget for 200F. In a very 1960s dining room the owners have managed to recreate a local bistro-style atmosphere. Very varied clientele come to enjoy *blanquette de veau à l'ancienne*, streaky salted pork, crème caramel and especially the assortment of the famous *rillettes* and wild boar sausages.

☆ ☆ MODERATE

✕ **Casa Tina** (northern map C–D1, **25**): 18 rue Lauriston 75116. ☎ 01-40-67-19-24. Metro: Charles-de-Gaulle-Étoile. Open daily to 11.30pm. Set menu 89F at lunchtime and 110F in the evening. Budget for around 180–200F à la carte. A Spanish *tapas* bar that doesn't give a stereotypical picture, but one which gives you a more

Where to stay

- **1** Hôtel Keppler *(northern map)*
- **2** Villa d'Auteuil *(southern map)*
- **3** Queen's Hotel *(southern map)*
- **4** Hôtel Ambassade *(northern map)*
- **5** Hôtel Boileau *(southern map)*
- **6** Au Palais de Chaillot *(northern map)*
- **7** Hôtel Le Hameau de Passy *(northern map)*
- **8** Hôtel Gavarni *(northern map)*

✕ **Where to eat**

- **20** Le Verre et le Rouge *(northern map)*
- **21** Les Chauffeurs *(northern map)*
- **22** Restaurant GR 5 *(northern map)*
- **24** La Ferme des Gourmets *(southern map)*
- **25** Casa Tina *(northern map)*
- **26** Le Scheffer *(northern map)*
- **27** Le Lory *(southern map)*
- **28** Le Petit Boileau *(southern map)*
- **29** Le Beaujolais d'Auteuil *(southern map)*
- **30** Restaurant du musée du Vin, Le Caveau des Échansons *(northern map)*
- **31** Le Cuisinier François *(southern map)*
- **32** Driver's *(northern map)*
- **33** Le Bistrot de l'Étoile *(northern map)*
- **34** Le Paris 16 *(northern map)*
- **35** La Gare *(northern map)*
- **37** La Grande Armée *(northern map)*
- **38** Noura *(northern map)*
- **42** La Matta *(northern map)*
- **43** L'Épicerie Russe *(northern map)*

Where to go for an ice-cream/ Where to go for a drink

- **40** Pascal le Glacier *(northern map)*
- **50** Le Totem *(northern map)*

A
B
1
2
3
BOIS
DE
BOULOGNE
Allée
de
Longchamp
Boulevard
de
l'Amiral
PLACE
DU MARECHAL
DE LATTRE
DE TASSIGNY
Porte Dauphine
Avenue
Avenue
Avenue
Foch
R.E.R.
Flandrin
Faisanderie
Rue
des
Belles
Lannes
Rue
la
Spontini
Périphérique
Boulevard
de
Rue
Victor
22
Boulevard
Rue
Avenue
Lycée
Janson-
de-Sailly
Avenue
Henri Martin
R.E.R.
Rue de
la Pompe
Henri Martin
Avenue
Mairie
du 16e arr.
PORTE
DE LA MUETTE
PLACE
DE COLOMBIE
Avenue
Rue
Boulevard
de
O.C.D.E.
Rue
O. Feuillet
Émile
Augier
Suchet
Jardin
du
Ranelagh
Av.
du Ranelagh
21
La Muette
Chaussée de la Muette
Rue
Avenue
Rue
Vital
Rue
7
35
Beauséjour
Rue
Bois le Vent
Boulainvilliers
R.E.R.
Rue
40
R. Duban
Rue de l'Annonciation
R.
Singer
42
PORTE
DE PASSY
Boulevard
de
Boulevard
R.
du
Ranelagh
R. de l'Assomption
Mozart
Avenue
R.
Boulainvilliers
des
Vignes
Rue
Lycée
Molière

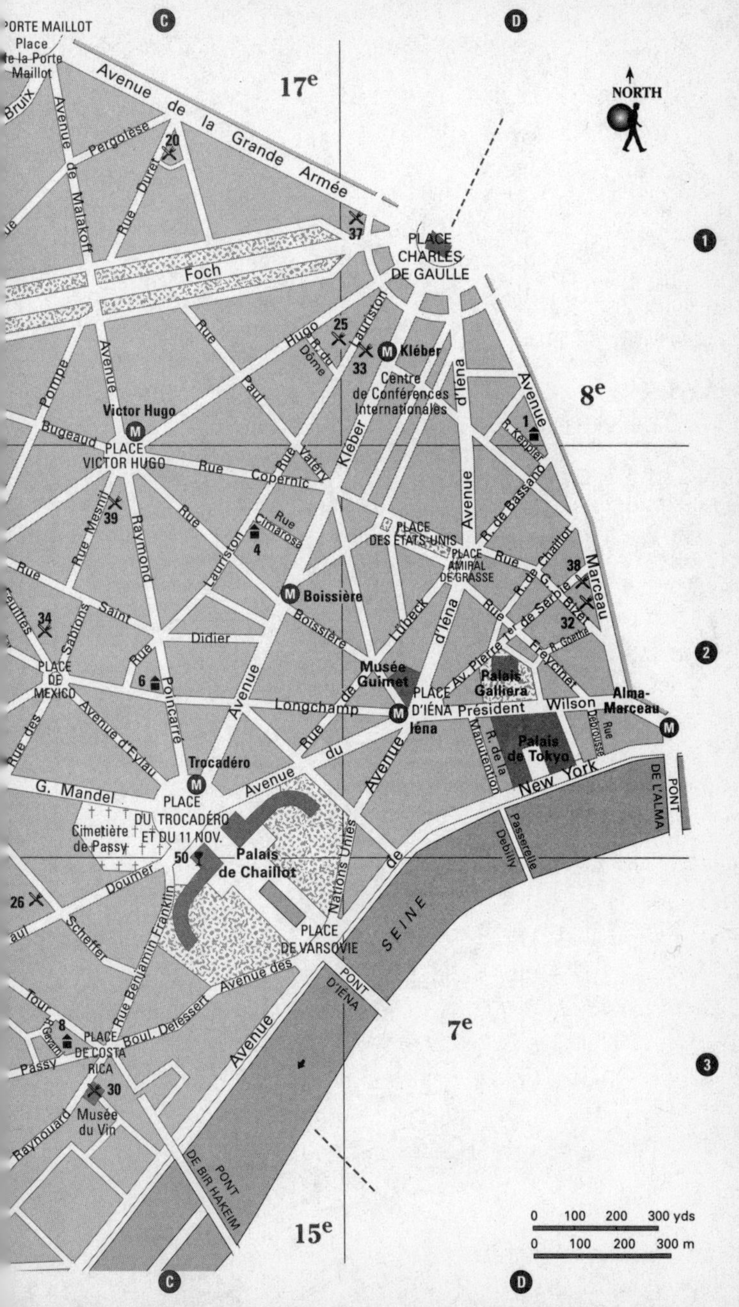
PORTE MAILLOT
Place de la Porte Maillot
17e
8e
7e
15e
NORTH
Avenue de la Grande Armée
Foch
PLACE CHARLES DE GAULLE
Kléber
Centre de Conférences Internationales
Victor Hugo
PLACE VICTOR HUGO
Rue Copernic
PLACE DES ÉTATS-UNIS
PLACE AMIRAL DE GRASSE
Boissière
Musée Guimet
PLACE D'IÉNA
Iéna
Palais Galliera
Palais de Tokyo
Alma-Marceau
Avenue Président Wilson
Avenue de New York
PONT DE L'ALMA
Trocadéro
PLACE DU TROCADÉRO ET DU 11 NOV.
Cimetière de Passy
Palais de Chaillot
PLACE DE VARSOVIE
SEINE
PONT D'IÉNA
PLACE DE MEXICO
PLACE DE COSTA RICA
Musée du Vin
PONT DE BIR HAKEIM
0 100 200 300 yds
0 100 200 300 m

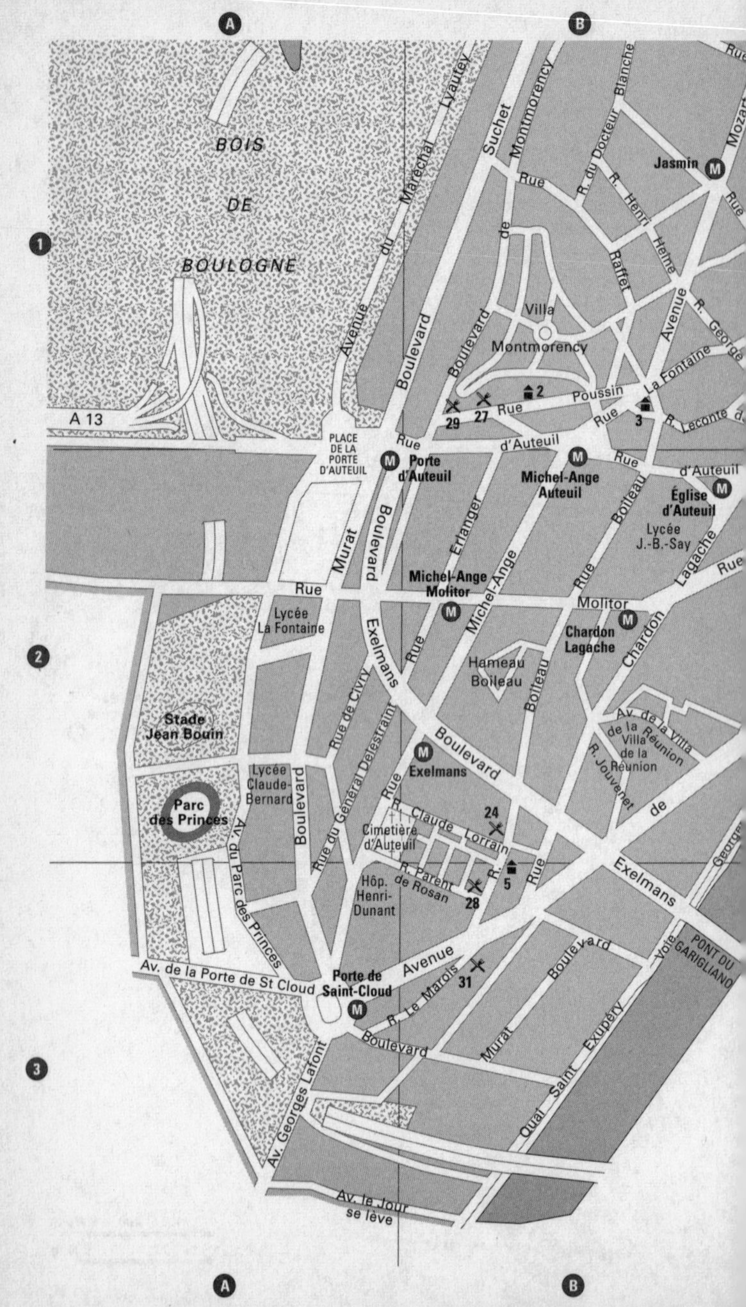
A
B
1
2
3
BOIS
DE
BOULOGNE
A 13
Avenue du Maréchal Lyautey
Boulevard Suchet
Rue de Montmorency
R. du Docteur Blanche
Jasmin
R. Henri Heine
Raffet
Avenue Mozart
R. George
La Fontaine
Villa Montmorency
Boulevard
Poussin
Rue
29
27
2
3
R. Leconte
PLACE DE LA PORTE D'AUTEUIL
Rue d'Auteuil
Porte d'Auteuil
Michel-Ange Auteuil
Église d'Auteuil
Lycée J.-B.-Say
Boileau
Lagache
Murat
Boulevard
Erlanger
Michel-Ange Molitor
Michel-Ange
Molitor
Chardon Lagache
Chardon
Lycée La Fontaine
Exelmans
Hameau Boileau
Av. de la Villa de la Réunion
Villa de la Réunion
R. Jouvenet
Stade Jean Bouin
Rue de Civry
Rue du Général Delestraint
Exelmans
Boulevard Exelmans
Lycée Claude-Bernard
Parc des Princes
R. Claude Lorrain
24
Cimetière d'Auteuil
R. Parent de Rosan
28
5
Hôp. Henri-Dunant
Av. du Parc des Princes
Av. de la Porte de St Cloud
Porte de Saint-Cloud
Avenue
R. Le Marois
31
Boulevard Murat
Voie Georges
PONT DU GARIGLIANO
Quai Saint Exupéry
Av. Georges Lafont
Av. le Jour se lève

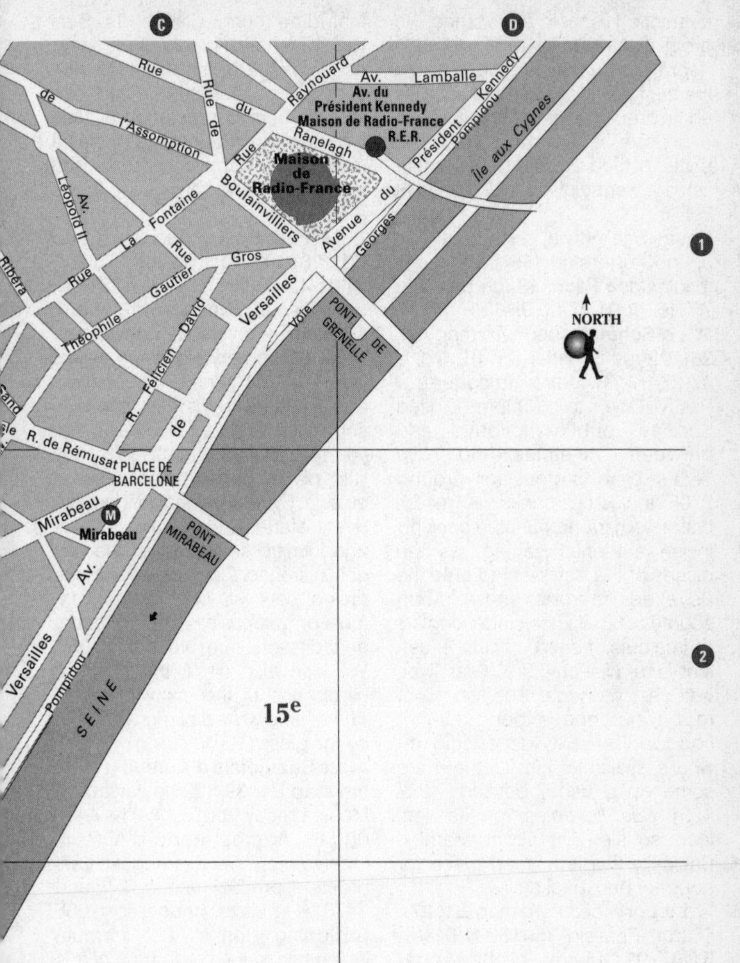
C
D
Rue de l'Assomption
Rue de Boulainvilliers
Rue du Ranelagh
Rue Raynouard
Av. Lamballe
Av. du Président Kennedy
Maison de Radio-France R.E.R.
Maison de Radio-France
Av. du Président Kennedy
Voie Pompidou
Île aux Cygnes
Av. Léopold II
Rue La Fontaine
Rue Gros
Avenue du Georges
Rue Ribéra
Rue Théophile Gautier
R. Félicien David
Av. de Versailles
Voie
PONT DE GRENELLE
R. de Rémusat
PLACE DE BARCELONE
Mirabeau
Mirabeau
PONT MIRABEAU
Av. Versailles
Pompidou
SEINE
15e
NORTH
1
2
3
0 100 200 300 yds
0 100 200 300 m

authentic Hispanic experience. As proof there are *serrano* and *pata negra* hams, chorizo chosen from the best sources, excellent sherries and a fine wine list (though it is a bit expensive, it has to be said). The platter of fried fish and grilled cuttlefish are worthy of an '*Olé*'. Paella at 89F.

Casa Tina's twin restaurant has opened up in the 16th arrondissement: **Casa Paco**, 13 rue Bassano 75016. ☎ 01-47-20-98-15.

✕ **Le Scheffer** (northern map C3, **26**): 22 rue Scheffer 75116. ☎ 01-47-27-81-11. Metro: Trocadéro or Passy. Open to 10.30pm. Closed Sunday, public holidays and between Christmas and New Year's Day. Budget for around 200F including drinks. A model bistro, with irreproachable cooking in an authentic setting, as the dishes of the day painted onto the bevelled mirrors show. Main courses (68–95F) include *onglets* (prime cuts of beef), *confits*, excellent and well-cut pink veal liver, with sherry vinegar. The fish is not to be outdone either: salmon, haddock or sole, depending on what's available. Finally, there are some good family desserts (28–42F): *îles flottantes*, profiteroles, iced soufflé with Grand-Marnier. Basically this is a good place for gourmet backpackers.

✕ **Le Lory** (southern map B1, **27**): 56 rue Poussin 75016. ☎ 01-46-51-47-99. Metro: Michel-Ange-Auteuil. Open daily. Last orders 10.30pm. Closed August. Set menus 120F to 180F. À la carte, budget for 280F. In the warm setting of a small restaurant with embroidered tablecloths and a cosy bar, enjoy honest 'plain cooking', as prepared by Annie, who has been running this kitchen for over 25 years. The first set menu, served lunchtime and evening, is enough on its own to explain the success of the establishment. Excellent value for money, including such dishes as Burgundy snails or the excellent house *terrine* or mussels; then pike *quenelles* (dumpling), or the famous beef bourguignon or veal with *sauce gribiche* (mayonnaise made of chopped hard-boiled egg, capers and herbs); and finally a dessert.

✕ **Le Petit Boileau** (southern map B3, **28**): 98 rue Boileau 75016. ☎ 01-42-88-59-05. Metro: Porte-de-St-Cloud. Open to 10.30pm. Closed Saturdays, Sundays, one week in February and three weeks in August. Set menu 150F lunchtime and evening. In an area which is somewhat deserted in the evening, you may stumble across this cosy little place, with simple, classical cuisine. Every day there are four different starters, four main courses and four desserts. Dish of the day costs around 70F; something like rack of pork with two sorts of potatoes or *andouillette*, etc. Starters and desserts are around 30–35F. You can also sit at the bar and nibble one of the many plates of *charcuterie* while sipping wine sold by the glass (20F).

✕ **Le Beaujolais d'Auteuil** (southern map B1, **29**): 99 boulevard de Montmorency 75016. ☎ 01-47-43-03-56. Metro: Porte-d'Auteuil. Open daily. Closed in August. Last orders 11pm. Set menus 127F and 147F. À la carte, budget for 200F excluding drinks. The formula which has made the fortune of this very old local restaurant is the set menu at 127F, including wine and service. Go for the dishes of the day, such as fresh spinach salad or ham sauerkraut. The roast Provençal rack of lamb isn't bad either. There's a classic dessert menu: chocolate mousse, crème caramel, etc. It's a good idea to book, and if possible get a table on the terrace in summer.

✕ **Restaurant du musée du Vin, Le Caveau des Échansons** (northern map C3, **30**): rue des

Eaux and 5–7, square Charles-Dickens, 75016. ☎ 01-45-25-63-26. Metro: Passy. Open lunchtime only noon to 3pm. Closed Monday and for a week between Christmas and New Year's Day. Set menus 99F lunchtime only, 139F and 160F in the evening. Children's menu 59F. One of the most original restaurants in the arrondissement. At the heart of the 16th arrondissement is the musée du Vin (Wine Museum), in the rue des Eaux (Water Street). It features 14th-century arched cellars, dug into the Chaillot clay by monks who were already tending the vines here in those days. At this superb place, the waiter approaches you at your great wooden table with a glass of wine in his hand, and asks you to try and recognize the wine and if possible the year! You soon discover that the restaurant's main aim is for you to sit down and talk wine with your neighbours while you taste what's on offer. There are lots of wine-based dishes: *coq au vin*, etc. For curiosity value, check out the wine list (200 to 250 items); it is unique and grandiose, and totally outdoes the menu! It covers 12 pages of delights from the Château Yquem 1918 at 7,500F per bottle to the *grands crus* of Bordeaux, Burgundy, Alsace, the Jura, Savoy, the Rhône, the Béarn, the Loire, Beaujolais, Provence, Languedoc, Roussillon, Corsica, Coteaux Champenois – you name it . . . . There are 15 wines available each day by the glass.

✕ **Le Paris 16** (northern map C2, **34**): 18 rue des Belles-Feuilles 75116. ☎ 01-47-04-56-33. Metro: Trocadéro, Rue-de-la-Pompe or Victor-Hugo. Open to 10.30pm. Closed Sunday. Budget for around 150F without drinks. Close to place de Mexico, this Franco-Italian restaurant provides its many regulars with refined, flavourful cuisine. There's antipasti (80F), *bresaola* and artichokes (65F), *rigatoni* with foie gras (69F). Don't forget to book, especially in the evening.

✕ **L'Épicerie Russe (northern map B2, 43)**: 3 rue Gustave-Courbet 75016. ☎ 01-45-53-46-46. Metro: Victor-Hugo or Trocadéro. Open Tuesday to Saturday 10am to midnight, Monday 6pm to midnight. Closed Sunday and one week around the 15th of August. Starters 50–75F, meat or fish dishes 60–140F. Vodka, of course, is the name of the game here – *Gold Wasser* with gold flakes, *Pieprzowka* with pepper, *Impuls* with melon, but also nut, apricot, honey and gin vodkas. In all there are around 60 varieties, not just from Russia and Poland, but also from Romania, Hungary, Bulgaria, Finland, Sweden and Denmark, and even from Ireland, decorating the shelves of this magical place, which serves as a bar, a restaurant and a grocer's shop. As its name suggests (*épicerie* means grocer's), you can come and do your shopping or order your evening meal here. Whichever you go for, you're sure of a good time in the company of Jean-Michel, the owner with a smile as devastating as his house vodka! The real must is definitely the 'Russian Platter' for two (195F): aubergine caviar, taramasalata, salmon, red caviar, stuffed vine leaves, Danish herring, tuna *terrine* on cucumber, shrimp salad, Russian gherkins, all with four *blinis*, a pot of fresh cream, the zest of a lemon and a basket of rye bread. Other dishes on the menu are equally irresistible.

✕ **La Grande Armée** (northern map D1, **37**): 3 avenue de la Grande-Armée 75016. ☎ 01-45-00-24-77. Metro: Charles-de-Gaulle-Étoile. Open daily to 2am. À la carte only, budget for 200F per person. The name refers to Napoleon's army, which conquered much of Europe. There are whole divisions of customers prepared to camp out under the campaign tent amongst the purple and blue uniforms. The cuisine (hamburgers, steak tartare, salmon, coriander omelette, etc.) is delicious and the prices are very reasonable.

☆☆☆ CHIC

✕ **Le Cuisinier François** (southern map B3, **31**): 19 rue Le Marois 75016. ☎ 01-45-27-83-74. Metro: Porte-de-St-Cloud. Open to 10.15pm. Closed Sunday and Monday, for a week in February and all of August. Set menu 160F lunchtime and evening. À la carte, budget for 280–300F. The chef is a real artist in the kitchen, very popular with gourmets, even in this part of the 16th arrondissement, where there are so many other good restaurants. He offers a stunning seasonal à la carte menu at 160F, including coffee. Try cream of celery soup with smoked bacon and a *croute* of autumn mushrooms, braised salmon with tarragon polenta *galette* and corn, rump steak and *crème quercynoise pommes charlotte au jus à l'ail*, pear poached in port and liquorice ice-cream and crème caramel with Oriental orange as a gourmet finale. The produce is excellent and perfectly cooked. Accompany it with a quarter or half bottle of reasonably priced wine of the week.

✕ **Driver's** (northern map D2, **32**): 6 rue Georges-Bizet 75116. ☎ 01-47-23-61-15. Metro: Alma-Marceau or George-V. Open daily, except Saturday lunchtime and Sunday, noon to 2.30pm and 8pm to 11.30pm. Set menu 96F lunchtime only, in the evening budget for 150F à la carte excluding drinks. Not far from the Étoile and a few hundred yards from the *bâteaux-mouches* at the Pont de l'Alma, opposite the largest Orthodox church in France, this is the headquarters for fans of motor sports of all types. The cuisine is the traditional type of the real Parisian bistro. As the menu evolves with the seasons, you can try whelks, side of beef, or leg of lamb, all accompanied by wines from small vineyards such as the Bourgueuil Domaine des Galluches at 85F or the Amourier, Cru Minervois at 90F.

✕ **Le Bistrot de l'Étoile** (northern map D1, **33**): 19 rue Lauriston 75116. ☎ 01-40-67-11-16. Metro: Charles-de-Gaulle-Étoile or Kléber. Open all the year round until midnight Monday to Friday; on Saturday, in the evening only. Closed Sunday, 15 days in August and at Christmas. Set menu 165F at lunchtime or a quick set meal at 135F. À la carte, budget for at least 250F. An independent restaurant with quality, originality and a friendly welcome. The clientele is more suit and tie than jeans and trainers, but that doesn't seem to matter. The cuisine offers new flavours and subtle mixtures, while resolutely sticking to the bistro spirit.

✕ **La Gare** (northern map B3, **35**): 19 chaussée de la Muette 75016. ☎ 01-42-15-15-31. Metro: La Muette. Open daily. Last orders midnight. Set meal 100F at lunchtime, à la carte budget for 190F excluding drinks. This former railway station is extremely popular with the Passy-La Muette clientele. The waiting room has been transformed into a bar (with a charming little terrace), where you sip a *mojito* to a salsa background, and the trackway has been turned into the basement restaurant. It is remarkably comfortable, and the food goes down nicely: Bresse chicken-purée straight from the roasting spit, rack of lamb or *train d'entrecôte* from Nebraska. Two main courses 65F: e.g. glazed spareribs and dish of the day. Steak tartare 75F. There are also very reasonable oysters.

✕ **Noura** (northern map D2, **38**): 27–29 avenue Marceau 75116.

☎ 01-47-23-02-20. Fax: 01-49-52-01-26. Metro: Alma-Marceau. Open daily to midnight. Budget for 100–200F depending on how hungry you are! It's impossible to book; get there early, if possible before 12.30pm. Among the things on the menu are a hors-d'œuvres (six varieties): *houmous, tabouleh,* vine leaves, *falafel, fatayel.* Or give yourself a treat with the excellent *chawarma-poulet-tabouleh* (marinated chicken, thinly sliced, spit-roasted, accompanied by tomato, ground corn, parsley, mint, lemon and olive oil). Lebanese cakes with, in particular, a marvellous *mafrouké* (ground angel-hair pasta with pistachios). There are a few wines by the glass, from the Sancerre white at 24F to the Ksara red at 26F.

WHERE TO GO FOR AN ICE-CREAM

– **Pascal le Glacier** (northern map B3, **40**): 17 rue Bois-le-Vent 75016. ☎ 01-45-27-61-84. Metro: La Muette. Open 10.30am to 7pm. Closed Sunday and Monday and during August. Double cornet 20F, 50F for a half-litre tub. Pascal Combette is an ice-cream maker of genius and his creations are at least as good as those from Berthillon's. He only works with high-quality fruit, and even halts the production of some flavours if he doesn't think the fruit is up to his exacting standards. His blood orange, mirabelle plum and mango sorbets will send shivers of pleasure up your spine. As for the ice-creams, the Tahiti vanilla and dark chocolate-cinnamon will tantalise the taste buds.

AUTEUIL

Before Haussmann set to work on the area people would go out to the village of Auteuil for a day in the country. Chateaubriand, Victor Hugo and the Goncourt Brothers (founders of a famous French literary prize) all used to come here. Two centuries earlier Molière would doubtless have tasted the wine from Altarium, a hamlet with 22 hectares (55 acres) of very well-known vineyard. Today all that remains of this ancient village are a few inns, quiet villas, a garden, and the country atmosphere on market days.

★ The **rue La Fontaine:** there was once a spring here that provided water for the whole of Auteuil. The medicinal waters were discovered by Habert in 1628. They were sulphurous, with the characteristic smell of rotten eggs. They killed off the fish, but were recommended for people suffering from urine retention, kidney stones, jaundice, fever and other ailments. However, these springs (of which there were many) never enjoyed the same reputation as their neighbours at Passy. In 1842 they were rediscovered and a hydrotherapy establishment was founded at 2 rue de la Cure.

The buildings are by Hector Guimard (1868–1942), in his modern style. At No. 14 is the famous Castel Béranger, finished in 1898, also known as *'le Dérangé'* (the Deranged). The building won a prize for its façade – a mixture of steel, wrought-iron and stained glass. At the time it was designed as an 'economic building' (with no bathroom). Molière lived nearby in the 17th century, in what would become avenue Théophile-Gautier, where he received, among others, La Fontaine, Boileau and Racine.

At No. 17 is the tiny façade in red panelling of the Café Antoine, which has remained in good condition since 1911. It has an authentic charm rarely seen in the early days of the 20th century.

On the corner of the **rue Agar**, an unusual, T-shaped street, is a whole block of houses designed by Guimard (1910). Even the guttering is beautifully decorated.

Return to rue La Fontaine; at No. 96 is the site of the house in which Marcel Proust was born and at No. 65, at the junction with rue du Général-Largeau, is a quite spectacular studio-building in multicoloured ceramics by Sauvage (a friend of Guimard's), dating from 1926.

★ The **lycée Jean-Baptiste-Say:** 11 *bis*, rue d'Auteuil. The central part dates from the 17th century. The head teacher's office is listed as an historic monument. You can look around at weekends, but check in first at reception.

★ The **église d'Auteuil:** rebuilt in 1880 in a pastiche of the Roman-Byzantine style, the steeple is reminiscent of the Papal crown. This is where the notorious funeral of French pop star Claude François took place. He was extremely popular in the 1960s and died tragically young.

★ The **parc Ste-Périne:** entrance in rue Mirabeau. This large and pleasant park is a welcome surprise, and particularly good for children.

– Leaving the park at 114 *bis* avenue de Versailles you'll find, just a few steps along the same side of the street, the **Villa de la Réunion** at No. 122. Two quiet streets lead to some fine private residences with a lot of greenery. There are signs saying 'Interdit au public' ('Private Property – No Right of Way') everywhere. At No. 142 stands another of Guimard's projects, dating from 1905. This is the pinnacle of art nouveau, with an inventive richness in the balconies and guttering and a remarkable inner staircase.

★ The **Trois Villas:** 25 rue Claude-Lorrain. These villas have an almost village-like atmosphere, creating a peaceful haven away from the boulevard Exelmans and boulevard de Versailles. Entrances in rue Parent-de-Rosan, at 25 rue Claude-Lorrain, and in rue Boileau for Villa Dietz-Monnin, Villa Émile-Meyer and Villa Cheysson. Rose bushes fill the Villa Dietz-Monnin, lining the paved paths which are too narrow for cars. There are 67 little houses here consisting of just two stories, with little gardens covered in ivy. The atmosphere is a lot more working-class than in the villas of the 'upper' 16th arrondissement.

★ The **cimetière d'Auteuil:** 57 rue Claude-Lorrain. Very quiet and a bit neglected by the public, probably because it doesn't have many big 'stars' in its grounds. Surrounded by rusty railings is the tomb of Doctor Cabanis, who supplied Napoleon with a poisoned loaf of bread at the Fontainebleau abdication. The poison was well past its sell-by date and had absolutely no effect.

The composer Gounod, the painters Gavarni and Hubert Robert, the founder of the newspaper *Figaro*, Villemessant, all lie here in the company of filmmaker Abel Gance and the prolific novelist Pierre Benoit, who was also Mayor of Auteuil. He was in the habit of giving all his heroines a name starting with the letter A.

★ The **rue Boileau:** one of the most typical in the area. It's hard to believe you're still in Paris. It was formerly named the rue des Garennes. At No. 67 Gustave Eiffel set up his aerodynamic laboratory. At No. 62 is the Vietnamese Embassy, a slightly banal, pagoda-style building covered in white tiles. At No. 38 is the Hameau Boileau, which opens onto part of the Boileau estate. Banana trees dominate this haven of peace. Opposite, at No. 41, was 'La Bonne Mort' (the Good Death): a hospice where poor people used to come to die. At No. 34 stands the first private residence built by Guimard, in 1891.

At the crossroads with rue Molitor turn right for another beautiful villa:

★ The **villa Molitor:** intact since it was opened in 1837, this is perhaps the most attractive building in the 16th arrondissement. A wrought-iron gate gives access to the villa and its tree-lined drive. See the guardhouse at the entrance bearing the name of the villa. Johnny Halliday, the French national rock icon, lived in one of the villas for a while, but apparently the roaring of his Harley Davidson and the noise of his guitars were not to everyone's taste in such a quiet area, so he left.

★ The **rue Michel-Ange:** at No. 12 stands the famous Couvent des Oiseaux (literally Convent of Birds), an 'aviary' for young society ladies.

★ The **greenhouses of Auteuil:** 1 *bis,* avenue de la Porte-d'Auteuil. ☎ 01-40-71-74-00. Open daily 10am to 5pm (6pm in summer). You have to pay to get into the garden: 5F, half-price for students. The greenhouses were built at the end of the 19th century on Louis XV's former nurseries. Nostalgia and a tropical ambiance are guaranteed: birdsong, pools with blooming lotuses, and a winter garden. In May and June they host excellent concerts. Also admire the collections of exotic plants all year round (orchids, azaleas, cacti, etc.)

★ The **jardin des Poètes:** avenue du Général-Sarrail. Next to the greenhouses. Open 9am to 5pm. Among other things it houses a bust of Victor Hugo by Rodin.

★ The **villa Montmorency:** main entrance at 12 rue Poussin. Here is a fascinating little complex of 80 villas, created by Émile Pereire in the gardens of the Château de Boufflers, which he had bought in order to complete the railway running around Paris. The idea was to create a form of holiday home. The regulations were quite draconian, so in order to safeguard the original design, there was no interfering with the internal layout: all the houses had to have a garden, trading within the complex wasn't allowed, and, more importantly, it was forbidden for 'ladies of ill-repute to own a villa and to exercise their profession there'. Sarah Bernhardt, Victor Hugo and André Gide all honoured the area with their presence.

★ At 67 boulevard de Montmorency stands the **maison des Goncourt**, which the Goncourt family occupied in 1868 because Jules, who was unwell, needed peace and quiet. It became a literary salon until the death of Edmond in 1896 and contains the famous 'attic', which is also a lounge, museum and library. Émile Zola, Guy de Maupassant and Alphonse Daudet, among others, all used to visit. Unfortunately it's empty at the moment, but there was talk of making it into a museum.

★ At 73 boulevard de Montmorency is the **atelier de Quivilic**. Quivilic was a Breton sculptor. The high wooden door is just big enough to allow blocks of granite to be brought in. The door handles are in the form of women's heads with hats on.

★ The **rue Pierre-Guérin:** a delightful cul-de-sac with scattered paving stones, leading from the rue de la Source, which instantly takes you back in time to the 19th century when life was lived at a slower pace.

The 'village street' look takes you right out of Paris. There are virtually no cars and the private residences, on the left, are also part of the Villa Montmorency. The green gate, with a notice reading *Chien méchant* ('Beware of the Dog'), is all that is left of the little Hôtel Youssoupov, belonging to the Russian prince who killed Rasputin.

★ The **abbaye bénédictine Ste-Marie:** 3 rue de la Source. ☎ 01-45-25-30-07. On Sunday, at 11am mass, you can hear Gregorian chants. A very odd fact, the abbey also has the largest collection of postcards in France. It also has a library, with more than 125,000 volumes, including many classics, which is no longer open to the public.

★ The **fondation Le Corbusier:** 8–10 square du Docteur-Blanche. ☎ 01-42-88-41-53. Metro: Jasmin or Michel-Ange-Auteuil. Open Monday to Friday 10am to 12.30pm and 1.30pm to 6pm (5pm Friday). Closed August and between Christmas and New Year's Day. Entry fee 15F, reduction for groups. Two linked residences built in 1923 by Charles-Édouard Jeanneret. Now listed, one is open for visits, the other houses a documentation centre which is open to the public 1.30pm to 6pm (5pm Friday). Le Corbusier played with 'purist' space and colour and used a sloping walkway instead of a staircase.

★ The **musée Bouchard:** 25 rue de l'Yvette 75016. Metro: Jasmin. Bus No. 22 and PC. ☎ 01-46-47-63-46. Open Wednesday and Saturday 2pm to 7pm. Closed March, June, September and 16 to 31 December. Entry fee: 25F; concessions 15F. One of the most little known museums in Paris. This was the workshop of the sculptor Henri Bouchard (1875–1960), a traditional artist and a disciple of the return to classic values. He won the first Prix de Rome in 1901 and lived here from 1924 until he died. Kept exactly as he left it, the workshop exhibits the sculptor's work, surrounded by his tools. An exponent of 'constructed realism', the lines of his sculptures are highly architectural, even stylized, typified by his *Apollon* on the Terrace de Chaillot. His favourite subject was the labour of workers and peasants and there are many original bronzes and plastercasts and an interesting group of farm animals. Take the tour explaining the different sculpture techniques. There is also a garden.

★ The **rue Mallet-Stevens:** walk back up rue du Docteur-Blanche and turn right. All the houses in this street were built by the cubist architect Mallet-Stevens. There is a great deal of greenery in the street, topped by two huge cedars. The most interesting results of his work can be seen at Nos. 4, 6, 7, 10 and 12.

★ The **rue du Ranelagh:** at the top of this street is a section which has been kept practically intact since the beginning of the 12th century. Halfway along there are some really beautiful private houses.

★ The **lycée Molière:** 71 rue du Ranelagh. The architecture of this building, built in 1886, is quite amazing. Take a look at the two inner courtyards, which are as majestic as a monastery. Closed on Saturday afternoons and Sunday.

– On the other side of the street look down into the cabinetmaker's shop in the basement. It was originally a garage for horse-drawn carriages, before changing its function in 1924. There's a jumble of wood, chairs, planks, tools and shavings. Time has stood still – only the calendar, which is kept up to date, proves that life goes on.

★ The **villa Beauséjour:** 7 boulevard Beauséjour. On the left there is a house in neo-classical style, dating from 1927, with three french windows. Hidden at the end of the aisle on the right are four 'chalets', with logs and friezes. The last one at the end, No. 6, is entirely made of wood. These are Russian *isbas,* built for the Universal Exhibition in 1867 to present Russian products, then reassembled here. They were listed as Historic Monuments in 1992. You can often hear people playing the piano in the evening, at the back of the wooden villas. Chateaubriand had his country house here, in the days when this quarter was just one huge park.

PASSY

★ **La maison de Balzac:** 47 rue Raynouard 75016. ☎ 01-55-74-41-80. Metro: Passy or La Muette; RER: Boulainvilliers or Radio-France-Kennedy (line C). Bus Nos. 52, 32, 70 and 72. Open daily except Monday and public holidays, 10am to 5.40pm. Entry fee 22F; concessions 15F, free for under 18s. For temporary exhibitions: entry fee 30F; concessions 20F; youth ticket (7–26 years) 15F. Balzac lived in this house for seven years under the pseudonym of Widow Breugnol, in an attempt to escape from his creditors. He used to flee from the more perceptive of them through the little door at the end of the garden. 'I like to have a quiet house, between the courtyard and garden, because this is my nest, my shell, the envelope in which I live my life.' It was a busy life. In his writing room Balzac corrected the *Comédie Humaine*, which contains 2,500 characters! You can see some of his personal possessions, including his walking stick and the coffee pot with his initials on it where he kept his 'modern stimulant' – hot coffee. There is a room devoted to the famous Madame Hanska who Balzac married after 18 years of correspondence. Paintings, prints, etc. conjure up other great writers of the time, as well as Balzac's family. Don't miss the 14.5m (50ft) long table on which just a thousand of the characters from the *Comédie Humaine* are listed and categorized. A story reading (in French) of *La canne magique ou l'oeil de Balzac* (The magic walking stick or Balzac's eye) takes place for children from the age of 6 upwards (entry fee); for dates, contact the museum.

★ The **rue Berton:** one of the most charming streets in Paris. Its angled gas lamps and ivy-covered walls recall the days when carriages drove along its narrow roadway. Between rue Berton and la musée du Vin is the pretty little passage des Eaux. The well-guarded private residence in rue d'Ankara was once occupied by the Princesse de Lamballe and later by Doctor Blanche, who treated writers Gérard de Nerval and Guy de Maupassant for mental illness. It is now the Turkish Embassy.

★ The **musée du Vin:** rue des Eaux (which – somewhat ironically – means Water Street!), 75016. ☎ 01-45-25-63-26. Metro: Passy. Go down the steps and turn right. Situated in square Dickens. Open daily 10am to 6pm. Closed Monday and between Christmas and New Year's Day. Entry fee 35F with a tour and a tasting (29–30F for concessions). The rue des Eaux is named after a spring discovered here when the street was being built in 1657. Crowds of people would come for hydrotherapy. The spring disappeared in 1868, once water began to be distributed free of charge. The presence of a museum dedicated to wine is no coincidence since grapes were grown and harvested here. The museum takes the form of winding medieval arched cellars. Here you'll learn all about wine and the reasons why you should drink it (as well as finding out how to get rid of wine stains!), with the aid of displays with strategically placed wax figures. There is a restaurant, Le Caveau des Échansons, open at lunchtime (entry to the museum is free if you eat there); *see* 'Where to eat'.

★ The **théâtre du Ranelagh:** 5 rue des Vignes 75016. ☎ 01-42-88-64-44. Metro: La Muette. A theatre and art-house cinema on the site of the stables of the Château de Boulainvilliers. A patron of the arts decorated the hall of the former 1750 theatre where the composer Rameau gave concerts, surrounded by the incomparably beautiful Flemish Renaissance-style panelling. It was here in 1900 that the first-ever performance in France of Wagner's *Rheingold* was staged. This extraordinary (listed) theatre is also the setting for exhibitions and occasional film shoots. Since 1986 many plays have been staged here and it has become a favourite venue with French theatre-goers.

★ **La maison de Radio France:** 116 avenue du Président-Kennedy 75016. ☎ 01-42-30-22-22. Metro: Passy or Ranelagh; RER: Kennedy-Radio-France (line C). Website: www.radio-france.fr. This 'round house' has a circumference of 500m (1,650ft), with 5km (3 miles) of corridors, 3,500 employees, an archive tower 68m (223ft) high, known as the *Mémoire du siècle* ('Memory of the Century'), 64 studios, and some lovely green spaces all around. Built between 1952 and 1963 in glass and aluminium, it was designed by the architect Henri Bernard and opened on 14 December 1963 by General de Gaulle.

– **Guided tour of the museum and a studio:** daily except Sunday and public holidays, at 10.30am, 11.30am, 2.30pm, 3.30pm and 4.30pm. Entry fee 20F. Groups (by appointment only) must apply in writing. ☎ 01-42-30-21-80 during the week. There are often free concerts and live recordings of radio broadcasts. Ring for information: ☎ 01-42-30-15-16. The house includes the *Salle Olivier Messiaen* (936 seats), where there are concerts by the Philharmonic Orchestra and the National Orchestra, the *Studio Charles Trenet* (257 seats) and the *Studio Sacha Guitry* (250 seats).

★ Opposite, in the middle of the Seine, is a narrow band of land known as the **île aux Cygnes** (Swan Island). Louis XIV had the swans moved here so that people could enjoy looking at them. On a gloomier note, the Protestants who died in the St-Bartholomew's Night Massacre are buried here. Visiting Americans may do a double-take as the island is also home to a scale model of the French-designed Statue of Liberty in New York.

THE TROCADÉRO

★ The **cimetière de Passy:** jutting out over the place du Trocadéro, with the entrance in the rue du Commandant-Schlœsing. Although this cemetery is not very large, there are a great many famous French people buried here: Debussy, Édouard Manet, Louis Renault, Marcel Dassault, Tristan Bernard, Jean Patou, Giraudoux, Gabriel Fauré, Berthe Morisot and the Guerlain and Marnier families. The Cognacq-Jays, founders of the *La Samaritaine* shops and creators of generous charity allowances for large families, lie in a luxurious chapel.

This is the only cemetery in Paris with a heated waiting room. Built in the same style of architecture as the Palais de Chaillot, in the office to the left of the entrance you can see the registers which have been filled in using a quill pen for almost 200 years.

★ The **musée de la Marine:** place du Trocadéro 75116. ☎ 01-53-65-69-69. Metro: Trocadéro. Bus No. 22, 30, 32, 63, 72 or 82. Open 10am to 6pm. Closed Tuesday and 1 January, 1 May and 25 December. Entry fee 38F, reduction for those aged 8–25, free for children aged under 8. Groups by appointment and a guided tour can also be arranged. ☎ 01-53-65-69-53.

This is certainly one of the finest naval museums in the world, rich in rare pieces. It covers the five branches of French Maritime activity: war, trade, fishing, yachting and scientific vessels. Don't miss the figureheads, the gilded wooden poop decorations of the *Réale*, a 17th-century flagship under Louis XIV, as well as the amazing lighthouse glass optics and Napoleon's imperial boat embellished with a gigantic crown. There are also scale models made for each new ship which was to be built that are real works of art. Various collections have since enriched this unique piece of French heritage, and it now includes all types of vessels, from Egyptian boats to supertankers: craft from Tonga, 17th-century galleys, clippers designed for racing, and the king of the liners, the sumptuous *Normandie*.

There is a children's event (8–12 years) on Wednesday at 2.30pm and, for adults, themed visits on Sundays at 3pm.

★ The **musée de l'Homme:** 17 place du Trocadéro 75116. ☎ 01-44-05-72-72. Metro: Trocadéro. Bus Nos. 22, 30, 63, 72 and 82. Website: www.mnhn.fr. Open 9.45am to 5.15pm. Closed Tuesday and public holidays. Entry fee 30F; concessions 20F. This museum covers three areas: prehistory, biological anthropology, and ethnology. Unfortunately, probably due to lack of resources, this museum is somewhat dated compared with others in the city (for example the *Cité des Sciences*). The Africa galleries have rather obsolete exhibitions, although the European galleries have been renovated. Others, such as the Americas, are richer and better laid out. Take a look at the *Tous parents, tous différents* (All parents and all different) and *Six milliards d'hommes* (Six thousand million people), educational exhibitions with interactive terminals and short explanatory talks.

First floor:

There are three permanent exhibitions and also the Afrique noire, Afrique du Nord and Europe (Black Africa, North Africa and Europe) galleries.

– **Tous parents, tous différents (All parents, all different):** this exhibition questions the notion of race through illustrations, interactive terminals and tests that make you realize just how arbitrary the usual classifications are. For children, there is a computer with a choice of 118 pairs of eyes, 66 noses, 81 mouths, 185 hairstyles, etc., so that you can reconstruct the faces of familiar people.

– **Six milliards d'Hommes (Six billion people):** this exhibition invites you to simulate the future of mankind. Armed with a barcode, you wander from terminal to terminal making a personalized trip (terminals in English too).

– **La nuit des temps:** a reconstruction of excavations, skeletons and skulls, and a display of tools, weapons and works of art allow you to follow Man's morphological and cultural evolution. From the first tools, which appeared 2.5 million years ago, and through all the main stages: the acquisition of the notion of symmetry, the birth of a musical sense around 1.2 million years ago, the mastery of fire around 400,000 years ago, tombs and the appearance of art 30,000 years ago, agriculture in the 7th century AD, through to the first metallurgy and writing. It's quite an exhausting trip!

– **Les galeries d'Afrique et d'Europe:** there are some unusual objects here, such as the peak of a hat made from the head of a defeated enemy, the throne of a Cameroon king and tomb ornaments. From North Africa there are some fine Tuareg costumes, an amazing woman's palanquin (a type of sedan chair) and remarkable examples of leatherwork and weaving.

Second floor:

– **La galerie de l'Arctique:** Models in Inuit costumes, a kayak, the inside of an igloo and a stuffed polar bear.

– **La galerie d'Asie** with the Turkish house, a reconstruction of a bazaar with ceramics, brocades, kilims and Oriental slippers. There are also some attractive Indonesian masks and Japanese curios: calligraphy, samurai swords and impressive armour.

– **La galerie d'Amérique:** the most interesting of all the galleries, this was completely renovated for the 500th anniversary of the discovery of the New World, and it offers some real marvels following the archaeology and history of the indigenous American Indian people up to the present day. You'll even find the statuette which inspired Hergé to create the Tin-Tin adventure *L'Oreille cassée.* (the broken ear). The craftsmanship is incredibly rich, with soapstone pipes and containers, elaborate masks, totem poles and a splendid cedar wood statue of a shaman (British Columbia).

There is also a good representation of objects from Central America (Mexico, Belize, Guatemala, San Salvador, Honduras), with the fascinating culture of the 'well tombs' and Mexican stone sculptures. Among the things to see is the *quetzalcoatl* (plumed serpent) in red porphyry (14th century). The list of cultures explored includes the Totonac, Aztec, Olmec, Zapotec and Mayan, the rich Caribbean culture, Taino, (with polished stone axes and yokes) and Andean cultures (with fine weaving and terrifying mummies).

– Don't miss the **salon de Musique**, with its full Javanese gamelan orchestra and the multitude of picturesque musical instruments from five continents. There are some interesting ones, made from very simple materials, and some very old ones, such as the lithophone – a sort of prehistoric xylophone.

– Next door, the **salon des Techniques** is devoted to traditional skills (hunting, fishing, growing crops, agriculture, tools, etc.).

– Note: there are temporary exhibitions and documentary film shows every Sunday at 3pm. On the last Wednesday of each month you can also see an ethnographic film at 6.30pm, leading up, every year, to the ethnographic film review week in March. There are also two concerts a month on Sunday at 3pm with traditional music from all over the world. If you would like more information, check out the details on www.mnhn.fr.

★ The **musée des Monuments français:** Palais de Chaillot, 1 place du Trocadéro 75116. ☎ 01-44-05-39-10 or 39-05 (for bookings). Metro:

Trocadéro. Closed at the time of writing due to renovation and an extension to its collections. The newly renovated museum will be part of a much larger one: the *Cité de l'architecture and du patrimoine* (the Architecture and Heritage Complex) which is due to open its doors in 2003.

★ The **musée Clemenceau:** 8 rue Franklin 75116. ☎ 01-45-20-53-41. Metro: Trocadéro or Passy. Open Tuesday, Thursday, Saturday, Sunday and some holidays 2pm to 5pm. The apartment belonging to the 'le Tigre' (the Tiger), as the French President, Clemenceau, was affectionately known, is now a museum and has remained unchanged since his death in 1929. It has been rather neglected, but nevertheless still gives a rich account of the period, with original panelling, heavy brocades, an impressive library and a lovely U-shaped walnut desk. The garden is particularly attractive.

★ The **musée Guimet:** 6 place d'Iéna 75016. ☎ 01-45-05-00-98. Metro: Iéna or Boissière. Website: www.museeguimet.fr. A large museum dedicated to Asiatic art which has been closed for four years for extensive renovation works. It has now been entirely revamped from top to bottom in a slightly zen spirit (which complements its theme well). Its completely reworked lighting and layout give the Asiatic art the space to breathe that it, perhaps more than any other art form, requires.

★ The **musée du Panthéon bouddhique:** 19 avenue d'Iéna 75016. ☎ 01-40-73-88-11. Metro: Iéna. Open daily except Tuesday 9.45am to 6pm. Entry fee 16F; concessions 12F; free for under 18s. The galleries of this museum trace the religious history of China and Japan from the 4th to the 19th centuries. A magical place set in the middle of a Japanese garden.

★ The **musée d'Art moderne de la Ville de Paris:** 11 avenue du Président-Wilson 75116. ☎ 01-53-67-40-00; recorded information: ☎ 01-40-70-11-10. Metro: Iéna or Alma-Marceau; RER: Pont-de-l'Alma (line C). Bus Nos. 32, 42, 63, 72, 80, 82 and 92. Open Tuesday to Friday 10am to 5.30pm, Saturday and Sunday 10am to 6.45pm. Closed Monday and public holidays. Entry fee 30F; concessions 20F; free for under 18s and reduced rate for access to exhibitions for those aged 7 to 25. There is access for the disabled. Located in one of the wings of the Palais de Tokyo, built for the Exposition Internationale des Arts et Techniques in 1937. The building, originally occupied by carpetmakers from the Savonnerie, was transformed in 1936 into a military warehouse. Today it is home to two museums of modern art, one intended for national consumption, the other for the City of Paris. From the 120 or so plans submitted, the one from architects Dondel, Aubert, Viard and Dastugue was chosen and the museum was created in 1961. The collections come from legacies, donations and purchases, and cover paintings, drawings, engravings and sculptures from the early 20th century to today. There are lots of tours, themed around a work, a painter or an artistic movement. There is a free guided tour to the temporary exhibitions on Thursday at 3pm.

There is the extraordinary 600m (1,960ft) *Fée Électricité* by Raoul Dufy, one of the largest paintings in the world, and permanent exhibits of works by plenty of famous names: the Fauvists, Vlaminck and Derain, Cubists Braque and Juan Gris as well as the famous *Tête d'homme* and *Pigeon aux petits pois* by Picasso, *Fleurs* by Max Ernst and *Rythmes sans fin* by Delaunay. There are also sculptures by Laurens, Lipchitz and Zadkine. In the last hall you'll find Bonnard, Vuillard and Pascin and a very fine *30 Ans ou la Vie en rose* by Dufy. On the ground floor there is a hall devoted to the two versions of *La Danse* by Matisse.

The museum also offers workshops for children and there are some amazing thematic exhibitions which are staged regularly. There is also a good cafeteria and a bookshop.

★ The **musée Marmottan:** 2 rue Louis-Boilly 75016. ☎ 01-42-24-07-02 or recorded message: 01-44-96-50-33. Metro: La Muette. Bus: PC, 63 and 32. Open 10am to 5.30pm. Closed Monday, 1 May and 25 December. Entry fee 40F; concessions 25F. The delightful private residence of the art historian Paul Marmottan contains some very diverse collections from medieval times, the 19th century and the early 20th century. But its main exhibits are an exceptional group of Impressionist works, in particular Monet's famous *Impression, soleil levant*, which was stolen in November 1985 (probably for a private collector). The thieves stole around 10 masterpieces from this museum, although they have all since been found. *Impression, soleil levant* is the most fascinating of a series of 70 canvases painted by Monet in his garden in Giverny, with an amazing array of colours. And to think that by then he was almost blind!

It's impossible to cover all the delights in this museum, but on the ground floor you'll discover halls furnished in Empire style and decorated with paintings and prints, some superb tapestries, wooden statues from the 16th-century Rhine school, stained-glass windows and religious primitive art. There are a few pieces such as the *Vierge à l'Enfant* by Jan Gossaert, known as Mabuse, and a *Crucifixion* by Dierick Bouts. There is also an exceptional collection of illuminations and a stunning geographical Sèvres clock.

The Impressionists are in the basement and include: Monet's famous *Pont de l'Europe, gare St-Lazare, Impression soleil levant, Bras de Seine* and *près Giverny*; Gauguin; Caillebotte; Pissarro; *Claude Monet lisant* by Renoir; Sisley and Berthe Morisot.

On the 1st floor is the Fondation Denis et Annie Rouart (the grandchildren of Berthe Morisot and her husband, who lived in the shadow of the artist). This collection comprises 140 works by the whole of the Impressionist group, to which Berthe Morisot belonged.

★ The **musée Galliera, musée de la Mode de la Ville de Paris:** 10 avenue Pierre-1er-de-Serbie 75016. ☎ 01-47-20-85-23. Metro: George-V, Iéna or Alma-Marceau. Bus Nos. 32, 42, 63, 72, 80, 82, 92. Open 10am to 6pm. Closed Monday and public holidays. Entry at reduced rate for under 25s. Workshops for children on Wednesday and Saturday afternoons. Audio-guides for exhibitions.

For a museum dedicated to fashion you could hardly dream up anything better than this little Italian Renaissance-style palace built at the end of the 19th century and transformed into a permanent exhibition space in 1977. There are over 100,000 exhibits, which makes it one of the leading displays of its kind in Europe. There's no permanent collection, but the themed temporary exhibitions ensure that all the most important treasures are on view. When you come out, you'll know everything, or almost everything, about the history of fashion since 1735. Works on display include those by the great couturiers and creators of fashion since the 17th century. From waistcoats to dresses to crinolines and lace, it is a positive embarrassment of riches.

There is a specialized library accessible by appointment. Ask at the cultural department for information on tours for adults and workshops for children.

★ The **rue Le Sueur** sends shivers down your spine as you walk along its length, between avenue de la Grande-Armée and avenue Foch. It is where, during the Occupation, the abominable Doctor Petiot lured his victims (27 bodies were identified) in order to kill them and burn them (*see below*, 'Bois de Boulogne').

★ The **musée de la Contrefaçon (Museum of Forgery):** 16 rue de la Faisanderie 75016. ☎ 01-56-26-14-00. Metro: Porte-Dauphine; RER: Avenue-Foch (line C). Bus: 82 and PC. Open Tuesday to Sunday 2pm to 5.30pm (except in August and on public holidays). For groups and guided tours booking required. Entry fee 15F. A small museum (three halls) housed in the private residence of the *Union des fabricants pour la protection internationale de la propriété industrielle et artistique* (Union of manufacturers for the international protection of industrial and artistic property) – or protection against counterfeiting. There are notices explaining the financial risks, legal penalties and even the physical dangers of counterfeiting! Among 400 exhibits are fake Negrita rum and Bourjois perfumes, standing next to the authentic products.

★ The **musée Dapper:** 50 avenue Victor-Hugo 75116. ☎ 01-45-00-01-50. Metro: Victor-Hugo. This museum, covering the native arts of pre-Colonial Africa, is closed until the beginnning of December 2000. Phone for more information.

THE BOIS DE BOULOGNE

Throughout the 863 hectares (2,000 acres), there are 140,000 trees, mostly oaks, some of which are over 200 years old, such as the famous oak in the Pré-Catelan area, with a circumference of 6.6m (21ft). The name *Boulogne* comes from a sanctuary dedicated to Notre-Dame de Boulogne by Philippe le Bel. After the Hundred Years' War the forest became a hideout for brigands. Louis XI had the area replanted and it became the site for many fairs and festivals. Henri IV had 15,000 mulberry trees planted and built a silkworm farm. It was Louis XIV who had the first star-shaped avenues designed, to provide wood for the construction of the Naval vessels and for hunting. The Bois became a place for trysts and a very fashionable place for society people to take their constitutionals. At the beginning of the 18th century a number of follies were built (the French word *folie* from which the English word is taken comes from *feuillage*, meaning foliage), elegant residences set in plenty of greenery (*see* 'Parc de Bagatelle'), and the first hot-air balloons were constructed here. The Revolution did not spare many buildings, and the Prussians, who camped here in 1815, did nothing to help. In 1852 Napoleon III gave the Bois de Boulogne to the city of Paris and Haussmann redesigned the Bois to the tastes of the day with grottoes, waterfalls, winding paths, pagodas, lakes and even a reconstructed Swiss chalet! This was all in keeping with Napoleon's tastes for horticulture, which developed while he was in exile in England. More recently the city council has added jogging tracks to the bridlepaths and cycle lanes, but they are not used much.

From place de l'Étoile one way to reach the Bois de Boulogne is to go down avenue Foch, where the most expensive apartments in Paris are located. As you walk down, on the right, is rue Le Sueur where, at No. 21, Doctor Petiot bought a house to use as his 'clinic'. He robbed and killed a large number of people who were threatened with arrest during the Second World War. He would lure them to his house by promising them that they would be able to leave and go to South America, then he tied them up, killed them and, using a pulley, lowered them into the cellar where he immersed them in quicklime. He then burned the remains – and this is what led to his downfall. On the evening of 11 March 1944 people living near the river finally decided to call in the police as there had been a foul smell hanging over rue Le Sueur for two days. The fire brigade forced the door, and, to their horror, they found the cellar full of human remains, and the boiler overflowing with pieces of flesh, skulls, limbs etc. They managed to identify almost 30 bodies, but Petiot escaped and reappeared six months later, at the Liberation of Paris, under a false name, bearded and decorated, and 140 million francs richer. He was soon recaptured and put on trial in 1946, after a rapid investigation during which he confessed to the crimes. There were still mysteries and loose ends about the case, however, and for many months he managed to fool the police by saying that the bodies in the boiler were those of collaborators and Germans. He was guillotined in May 1946, displaying a contempt for his own existence, suggestive, perhaps, of how little he felt for his victims.

You can hire boats on the lac Inférieur (Lower Lake) or Grand lac (Great Lake), covering 11 hectares (27 acres). There are two islands, connected by a bridge, and the largest of them has the café-restaurant Chalet des Îles (expensive). You can hire Pedalos from The Carrefour des Cascades 1.5km/1 mile from the Carrefour du Bout-des-Lacs, between the Lower Lake and the Upper Lake.

Like the Bois de Vincennes, the Bois de Boulogne suffered greatly in the storms of December 1999. Of course, everything possible is being done to clear up the debris, but the landscape has changed quite dramatically and it will be a long time before it is restored to its former glory.

SHORT WALKS IN THE WOODS

★ It is possible to see a lot of the Bois de Boulogne on foot. You can do a complete walking tour (12km/7.5 miles, 4 hours non-stop in a circuit leaving from the metro station at Porte Maillot), or you can cross it, taking the 6km (4-mile), 2-hour route from Porte-Maillot to Porte-d'Auteuil, via the race-course and the mill at Longchamp, the Grande Cascade and the greenhouses of Auteuil. There are also family walks you can take following the yellow and red marked paths.

★ A walk which is easy to do with children, or for those who just want a leisurely stroll, is the Bois de Boulogne **sentier-nature** (nature trail), in the shade of the giant sequoias (4km/2.5 miles, 1.25 hours). You can totally switch off along this route. You start from the corner of avenue de l'Hippodrome and avenue de St-Cloud, near the two lakes (there is a car-park). Following the 12 signs of the nature trail, walk past the Passy boules pitch and cross the Route du Point-du-Jour at Bagatelle, avenue de l'Hippodrome, then the Route de la Vierge-aux-Berceaux, until you reach the carrefour du Lac Inférieur, which brings you back to the beginning.

The signs on the nature trail tell you, among other things, that the sequoias along the route are from California. Their name comes from the Indian chief See-Quayat. Nicknamed 'boxer trees', their red trunks with elastic bark were once used by North American sportsmen as natural punch balls. They were planted here in the 1950s. Pines, chestnut trees and water courses created under the Second Empire add to the charming layout, and if you're quiet you should hear the song of the Bois de Boulogne sparrows, musical thrushes, goldcrests and blackcaps, all competing with the background urban noise. You need to keep your eyes peeled for hedgehogs or squirrels, but there are plenty about.

There are free guided outings to learn about birds, every Sunday morning, (except July and August) in the southern part of the Bois de Boulogne. Meet at 9am, at Porte d'Auteuil, in front of the former RER station: ☎ 01-45-44-20-92). Jacques, the Bird-King, knows how to whistle up any passing sparrows – you won't regret spending your Sunday morning here.

WHAT TO SEE

★ The **Musée national des Arts et Traditions populaires, centre d'Ethnologie française:** 6 avenue du Mahatma-Gandhi 75016. ☎ 01-44-17-60-00. In the Bois de Boulogne. 10 minutes on foot from the metro station and Les Sablons bus stop (bus No. 73). Open 9.30am to 5.15pm. losed Tuesday. Entry fee 22F for the permanent collection, 25F for the temporary exhibitions; free for under 18s, reductions for students and large families.

This museum is devoted to the daily life of the French people over the last 1,000 years. All the objects, tools, costumes and works of religious art which have marked the lives of the French population are on show here. The focus is on rural life, but there are also more abstract exhibits such as songs, stories and legends, recorded on tape. In total there are over 1 million objects and documents. The exhibits trace the roots of French popular culture and explain the diversity of regional dialects and costumes. You'll find idiosyncratic beliefs (a sailor's thanksgiving plaque, religious objects) and customs in abundance. There is a reconstructed room from a Breton house, a fishing boat ready to set sail and an old-fashioned forge of the sort which has long since vanished. Deep, rural France, which is fast disappearing, is brought to life.

There are also temporary exhibitions, conferences and a large information centre. It's a shame that this museum is not better known as it has some exceptional pieces. There are some very interesting explanatory notes, even if some of them are difficult to read because of the rather dim lighting.

★ The **jardin d'Acclimatation:** Bois de Boulogne. ☎ 01-40-67-90-82. Fax: 01-40-67-98-73. Metro: Sablons. Website: www.jardindacclimatation.fr. On Wednesday, Saturday, Sunday, public holidays, and during the school holidays, a train leaves from the Porte Maillot every 15 minutes and trundles through the Bois de Boulogne, then leaves you at the 18-hectare (44-acre) Jardin d'Acclimatation (12F return). This paradise for children is open all year round 10am to 6pm (7pm June to September). Entry fee 13F; concessions 6.5F; free for under 3s. Ask for the free map when you go in. Please note that you have to pay for most of the rides and attractions (on average

13F per ticket); you can buy a book of 16 tickets for 150F or 24 tickets for 200F. You can have a picnic, or take lunch or an afternoon snack in one of the restaurants in the garden.

In 1860, Napoleon III made a gift of this garden to the people of Paris. It is one of the great important sites that has been enjoyed by generations of French families. The latest renovations have made considerable improvements.

Taken over a few years ago by a very dynamic team, the garden has a number of aims: first of all it is a place where you can go for relaxing walks surrounded by peaceful lawns, flowery aisles, animals and a kitchen garden where aromatic herbs, vegetables and fruit trees grow. Compared to the rest of the Bois de Boulogne, the *jardin d'Acclimatation* had a relatively lucky escape during the storms of December 1999, only losing around 100 of its 2,500 trees. It is also an educational space, with some really original workshops, the fascinating Musée en herbe (Museum in the Grass) and the new Explor@dome (*see below*). Finally it is, of course, a place of fun, ideal for kids who find attractions which are made to measure for them – and that's actually pretty rare in Paris.

– **The animals:** they are part of the garden's heritage. The garden was originally intended to accustom animals to the Parisian climate, hence the name *acclimatation*. Apart from the bears, the deer, the monkeys and the aviary, there is a farm with rabbits, hens, cockerels, geese, ducks, pigs, donkeys, sheep and goats, not forgetting the cow.

– **The key attractions:** the *Rivière enchantée* (Enchanted River), which has recently been renovated. On board a little boat, you sail off on a mini-cruise on a vessel worked by a real paddlewheel. There are *tacots* (old cars) in which you can do some 'pretend' driving and the *circuit automobile* (car circuit), where you can learn how to drive a mini-car with real controls all on your own. Along the same lines there is the *Prévention routière* (Traffic Safety), where children can learn about the French equivalent of the Highway Code. Could be useful for any parents who have to negotiate their way along the Périphérique!

– **The games and rides:** there are two sections with loads of games to keep children happy: toboggans, swings, sandpits, paddling pool, tunnels, etc., as well as deckchairs for parents. There is also a sort of fairground, with rides (there is a charge). The *Maison enchantée* (Enchanted House) is a covered games area for under 12s, and there's a foam rubber area for babies from 9 months, a ball pool, mini-toboggans, video-game consoles, CD-ROMs, etc. . . .

– **Sports:** there is a range of different sports on offer. A pony club with beginners and improvers classes, information ☎ 01-45-01-97-97. Cycling (various circuits): ☎ 01-45-01-97-99/06-07-35-40-17/06-13-61-03-37. A golfing green is available for individual practice, lessons in groups or personal tuition as well as a range of activities for youngsters and adults alike, ☎ 01-45-00-16-64.

– **Shows:** the traditional *guignol* (Punch and Judy) is free. Shows on Wednesdays, at weekends, public holidays and holidays, at 3pm and 4pm. The circus is on Wednesday and Sunday at 3pm, Saturday 2.30pm and 5pm (daily during the holidays). And there are various performances at the garden's theatre (☎ 01-40-67-97-86).

– **The Explor@dome:** information and reservations ☎ 01-53-64-90-40. Website: www.exploradome.com. Open daily 10am to 6pm. Access though the garden's Neuilly entrance. Tour 30F; workshop 40F (on top of the fee for the park). Reductions for groups and large families (20F). An interactive space devoted to multimedia and science. Workshops at 10.30am, 2pm and 4pm. There are various themes: meteorology, optical illusions and multimedia. Children never leave empty-handed.

– The **Musée en herbe (Museum in the Grass):** ☎ 01-40-67-97-66. Fax: 01-40-67-92-13. Open daily 10am to 6pm. Entry (on top of the fee for the garden) 17F; concessions 14F. There are special prices for groups from the age of three years upwards. This is a museum specially designed for children. Light years away from the serious nature of traditional museums, here children can play, touch, smell and handle the exhibits. There are temporary exhibitions allowing children to discover art practically and educationally. They specialise in birthday teas, so you may well encounter excited groups of French children milling around as the birthday boys and girls celebrate their *anniversaires*.

★ The **parc de Bagatelle:** Bois de Boulogne. ☎ 01-40-67-97-00. Take the Metro to Porte-Maillot, then bus No. 244 to reach the main gate in the allée de Longchamp. There is another entrance through the Sèvres gate: take the Metro to Pont-de-Neuilly, then bus No. 43. Entry fee 10F; reduction for children aged 6 to 18. Open daily 8.30am to 7.30pm in summer, 9am to 4.30pm in winter. A 24-hectare (60-acre) pleasure park which was a place for lover's meetings in the 18th century. The château was built in 1777, in just two months, for the Comte d'Artois, Louis XVI's brother, following a bet with the Queen. His motto *Parva sed apta* can be translated as 'Small but comfortable'. Obviously the construction work cost a fortune, which is where the expression 'It's a mere bagatelle' comes from.

There are around 10,000 rose bushes of 1,000 different varieties, which give a magnificent display from mid-May to the end of June. It is also worth taking a walk in the garden at the beginning of spring so that you can admire the 1.2 million bulbs which carpet the great lawns, and at the end of the summer you can visit the decorative kitchen garden. Even in winter this romantic park is still enchanting, thanks to the variety of its landscape and the beauty of its lakes, complete with timid moorhens, placid ducks and majestic swans. There are landscaped and formal gardens, a belvedere and hidden gazebos. Near the Sèvres Gate is the restaurant, where you can stop off for tea under the shady foliage.

There are also temporary exhibitions, a gift shop and a bookshop on the subject of the art of gardening. Information: *Association des amis de Bagatelle* ☎ 01-45-01-20-10.

★ The **Pré-Catelan:** Bois de Boulogne. A legend attributes the origin of the name to the story of Arnault Catelan, a young troubadour entrusted with bringing Provençal essences and liqueurs to Philippe le Bel, who lived in Passy. The young musician was murdered by the escort sent by the King. The bandits were hoping to find gold in the casket; but they were tracked down by the smell of the perfumes which they had spilt all over themselves! A pyramid topped with a cross was raised on the site of the crime.

★ The **jardin Shakespeare:** Bois de Boulogne, in the former open-air theatre in the Pré-Catelan. A magical small garden, best visited in summer. Obviously, at weekends you won't be alone. In the evening, between the end of May and the beginning of October, there are theatre performances; it's like finding yourself in the middle of *A Midsummer Night's Dream*. Information: ☎ 01-42-27-39-54 (plays in English in June).

WHERE TO GO FOR A DRINK

🍸 **Le Totem** (northern map C2–3, **50**): 17 place du Trocadéro 75116. ☎ 01-47-27-28-29. Metro: Trocadéro. Open daily noon to 2am. Closed Christmas and New Year's Day. Set menu 129F during weekday lunchtimes, in the evening à la carte only, budget for 180F. Children's menu 70F. Whatever tribe you belong to, come and smoke the pipe of peace at the foot of the largest totem pole in Paris: The Eiffel Tower. Located within the grounds of the Musée de l'Homme, this place has one of the finest terraces in Paris, with a marvellous view over the Iron Lady. The owner has brought an impressive collection of Indian objects over from her native Canada. The resulting decor is elegant and original. Although the place is also a restaurant (service 7.30pm to midnight), sunset over the Invalides at apéritif time is still the best time to come and drink a cocktail.

17TH ARRONDISSEMENT

THE PARC MONCEAU AREA ● LES BATIGNOLLES

Many people think that the 17th arrondissement is really just a little bit added on to the 16th, a sort of suburb of the more elegant arrondissement. Well, they're wrong! Of course, if you restrict your visit to boulevard Malesherbes and Parc Monceau (which holds the record for the number of Louis Vuitton bags per square metre on a Sunday!), it is understandable. On the other hand, if you don't mind going into the slightly more working-class areas, around avenue de Clichy, you will find some things which are easier on the eye . . . and the wallet.

Having said that, well-heeled areas do have some things going for them. In the Parc Monceau (actually in the 8th arrondissement, but most of the people there are from the 17th arrondissement), the children are always beautifully dressed and, on Saturdays, you can watch the brides and grooms coming out of a nearby church to pose for posterity on the lawns in front of the mini-waterfall.

WHERE TO STAY

There are lots of hotels of all categories and at all prices in avenue de Clichy, as far up as the rue des Moines. You can even find some hotels at 55F per night, but there's no guarantee that they'll be either clean or quiet.

☆ CHEAP

Auberge internationale de jeunesse Léo-Lagrange (off map C1, **1**): 107 rue Martre 92110 Clichy. ☎ 01-41-27-26-90. Fax: 01-42-70-52-63. E-mail: paris-clichy@fuag.org. Metro: Mairie-de-Clichy. Single room 171F; double room 128F; multiple rooms (from three to six beds) 115F. Open 24 hours a day. The latest Parisian acquisition by the French youth hostel organization. Some of the rooms have had a well-deserved face-lift. You must have a card but this can be issued on the spot (70F for under 26s, 100F over that). There are 338 beds and toilet facilities on each floor. Linen and breakfast are included in the price. No meals, but they do have a microwave, hotplates, a refrigerator, a dishwasher and a bar. Fast-food restaurants are just on the other side of the street. They also hire out bikes and there's a launderette available.

☆☆–☆☆☆ MODERATE TO CHIC

Hôtel Eldorado (map D2, **2**): 18 rue des Dames 75017. ☎ 01-45-22-35-21. Fax: 01-43-87-25-97. Metro: Place-Clichy. Double rooms with all mod cons (except telephone, but there are phones in the corridors), from 250F to 400F, depending on the size or whether they overlook the garden or the street. Five minutes by car from Montmartre or the Gare St-Lazare, the Eldorado has African-style decor and charming eclectic furniture. The indoor garden houses six exotic rooms, giving both a change of scene and peace and quiet. Artists, models and 'personalities' are regulars. Essential to book.

Hôtel Champerret-Héliopolis (map B2, **3**): 13 rue d'Héliopolis 75017. ☎ 01-47-64-92-56. Fax: 01-47-64-50-44. E-mail: heliopolis@netclic.fr. Metro: Porte-de-Champerret. Double rooms 450F to 495F depending on whether you have a bathroom or a shower, with TV, telephone and hairdryer. Fixed price for three nights, on Friday, Saturday and Sunday only: 1,000F. A very quiet hotel just a few minutes from the Porte Maillot and the Arc de Triomphe, with wooden balconies and a charming patio where you can have your breakfast when the weather is fine and which is overlooked by most of the rooms.

Hôtel Palma (map A3, **4**): 46 rue Brunel 75017. ☎ 01-45-74-74-51. Fax: 01-45-74-40-90. Metro: Porte-Maillot or Argentine. Double room 410F to 430F with shower or bath, and all mod cons. Just down the road from the Palais des Congrès and the Air France terminal, this 37-room hotel with flowery walls and carpets offers a certain amount of luxury at a reasonable price. The service is efficient and courteous. Breakfast is served in the dining room or in your bedroom. Book in advance.

Hôtel Ibéris (map D2, **5**): 167 avenue de Clichy 75017. ☎ 01-46-27-86-45. Fax: 01-46-27-45-19. Metro: Brochant. Double room 430F to 450F with shower or bath, TV, minibar, telephone and hairdryer. Very close to the Porte Clichy, a well-run, cosy two-star hotel with 30 rooms. Double-glazing is vital here as a lot of the rooms are on avenue de Clichy, which is very busy. It's best to ask for the ones overlooking the inside. There's a car-park nearby.

Hôtel Jardin de Villiers (map C2, **6**): 18 rue Claude-Pouillet 75017. ☎ 01-42-67-15-60. Fax: 01-42-67-32-11. Metro: Villiers. Double room from 570F with bathroom. Near Gare St-Lazare and the Air France terminal. Just moments away from the the mainly pedestrian rue de Lévis, where there is a lovely market every day. An impeccable three-star hotel tending towards greenery and flowers, as its name – which means Villiers Garden – suggests. All the rooms have been recently modernized and now have a direct phone line, TV (with Canal +), Satellite TV, minibar, hairdryer and double-glazing. The rooms on the fourth floor with balconies are the most pleasant.

Hôtel Prony (map B2, **8**): 103 *bis* avenue de Villiers 75017. ☎ 01-42-27-55-55. Fax: 01-43-80-06-97. Metro: Pereire. Special prices for backpackers: double room with shower or bath 445F; 395F for a single room, 100F per extra bed, free for children under 12. Satellite TV, double-glazing. Room 32, which is enormous, is particularly good for families of three or four. An excellent hotel close to place Pereire and five minutes from the Porte Maillot, it is part of a chain, but nevertheless has a certain charm. Unusually, breakfast can be served in your room until noon.

WHERE TO EAT

☆ BUDGET

Le 178, Chez Ben Attia (map D1, **20**): 178 avenue de Clichy 75017. ☎ 01-40-25-08-27. Fax: Brochant or Porte-de-Clichy. Open daily except Sunday evening until 10pm. Closed in August. Budget for no more than 70F à la carte. A good Tunisian snack bar with low prices, where the *couscous* is served in generous portions (kebab, 38F, lamb, 40F) and the dishes of the day are traditionally prepared, such as *mermez* at 40F (lamb, chickpeas, tomato, grilled pepper) on

Thursday, or fish couscous on Friday. Every day there's egg *brick* at 20F, *kafteji* at 30F and generous Tunisian or Greek sandwiches at 20F, as well as traditional *chorba* in winter. The clientele is Franco-Tunisian, sometimes with a few Japanese or Latin-Americans who have slipped out of the Hôtel Frantour opposite.

✕ **La Forêt** (map B3, **21**): 10 rue Poncelet 75017. ☎ 01-42-27-84-04. Metro: Ternes. Open lunchtime only. Closed Monday and also in August. Single menu 90F. A tiny, bland bar (the size of a shoebox) packed out every lunchtime with a crowd attracted by the home cooking. *Blanquette de veau*, *cassoulet*, *bœuf bourguignon*, but also couscous and *tandoori* chicken all take their turn on the blackboard at a very reasonable price: 43F. Starters and desserts (house) at 17F. Children are particularly welcome, and dishes are adapted to their tastes and appetites.

✕ **L'Épicerie Verte** (map B3, **24**): 5 rue Saussier-Leroy 75017. ☎ 01-47-64-19-68. Metro: Ternes. Open noon to 8pm. Closed Sunday and in August. Set menus 53F to 83F. À la carte, budget for 60F without drinks. A counter installed at the rear of the shop serves fast-food savoury tarts or a dish of the day based on natural and organic products. There is a courgette, marrow and carrot savoury tart at 28F or a *gratin*-style dish, pies, timbale of fresh pasta *à la provençale* at 43F (with tomatoes, peppers, courgettes and aubergines). After the lunchtime rush you quite often see people from the worlds of fashion and French TV who are fans of the salads here. They also sell organic products to take away.

✕ **Menelik** (map D2, **25**): 4 rue Sauffroy 75017. ☎ 01-46-27-00-82. Metro: Brochant. Open daily until half past midnight (last orders 11.45pm). Booking is recommended at weekends. Set menus 65F served lunchtime and evening, 35F for children. Budget for less than 100F à la carte. If you come by car, you get two hours free parking at the Batignolles car-park at 24 *bis*

Where to stay

1 Auberge Internationale de jeunesse Léo-Lagrange
2 Hôtel Eldorado
3 Hôtel Champerret-Héliopolis
4 Hôtel Palma
5 Hôtel Ibéris
6 Hôtel Jardin de Villiers
8 Hôtel Prony

✕ **Where to eat**

20 Le 178, Chez Ben Attia
21 La Forêt
24 L'Épicerie Verte
25 Menelik
26 Aux Îles des Princes
27 La Gioconda
28 Pizza Lotauro
29 Arcimboldo
30 Shah Jahan
31 Chez Rose
32 L'Impatient
33 La P'tite Lili
34 Restaurant Leclou
35 L'Étoile Verte
36 Le Verre Bouteille
37 Le Café d'Angel
38 Le Vieux Logis
39 Chez Clément
40 Stübli
41 Le Patio Provençal
42 Sud-Ouest Monceau, Claude Laborda
43 Coco et sa Maison
44 Graindorge
45 L'Huîtrier
46 Le Sud
48 Les Bouchons de François Clerc
50 Pau Brazil
51 La Gaieté Cosaque

Where to go for a drink/Where to go for jazz

61 James Joyce's Pub
62 Le Cambridge
65 Nouveau Jazz-Club Lionel Hampton

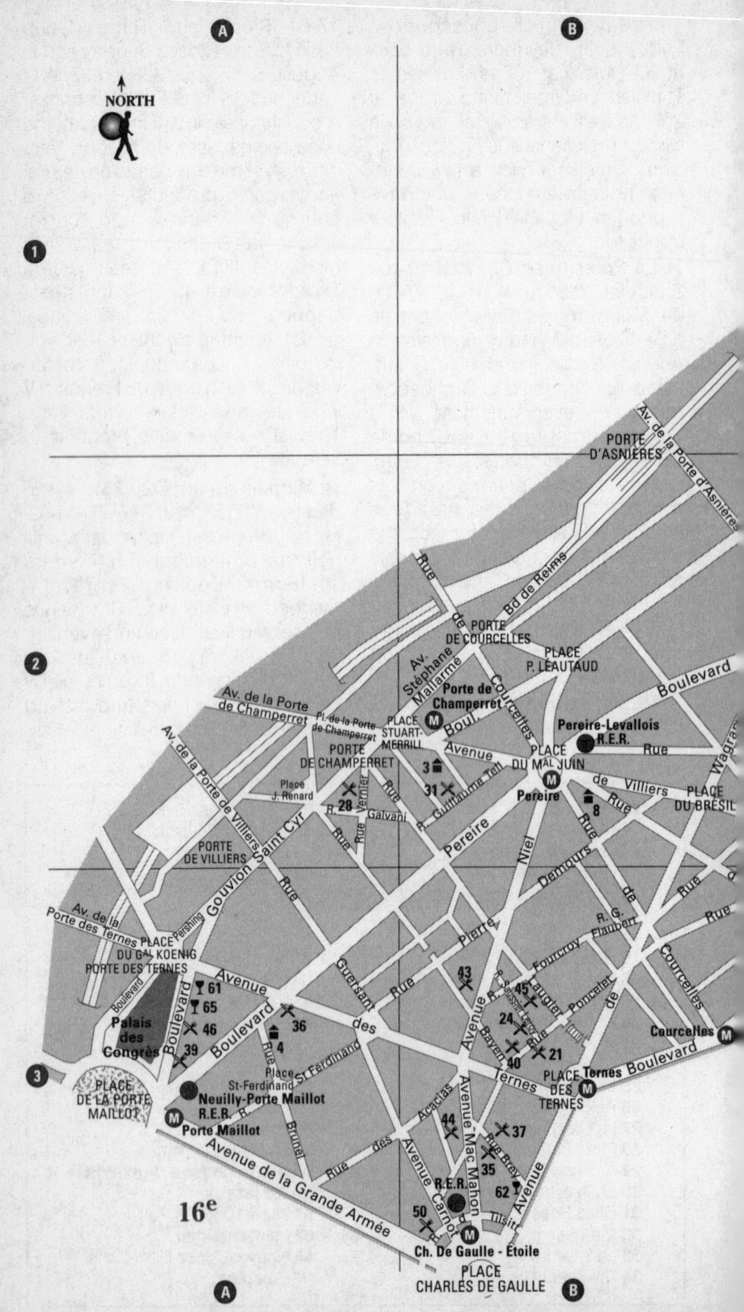
A
B
NORTH
1
2
3
PORTE D'ASNIÈRES
Av. de la Porte d'Asnières
Bd de Reims
Rue de Courcelles
PORTE DE COURCELLES
PLACE P. LÉAUTAUD
Boulevard
Av. Stéphane Mallarmé
Porte de Champerret
Av. de la Porte de Champerret
Pl. de la Porte de Champerret
PLACE STUART-MERRILL
PORTE DE CHAMPERRET
Boul.
Avenue
Pereire-Levallois R.E.R.
PLACE DU MAL JUIN
Pereire
Rue de Villiers
PLACE DU BRÉSIL
Wagram
Av. de la Porte de Villiers
Place J. Renard
R. Galvani
Rue Vernier
R. Guillaume Tell
Pereire
PORTE DE VILLIERS
Gouvion Saint Cyr
Rue Niel
Rue Demours
Rue de Courcelles
Av. de la Porte des Ternes
PLACE DU GAL KOENIG
Pershing
PORTE DES TERNES
Rue Pierre
R. G. Flaubert
Fourcroy
Avenue
Boulevard
Palais des Congrès
Boulevard
Rue Guersant
Rue Laugier
Poncelet
Courcelles
Rue St Ferdinand
Place St-Ferdinand
Avenue des Ternes
Rue Bayen
R. Saussier Leroy
PLACE DES TERNES
Ternes
Boulevard
PLACE DE LA PORTE MAILLOT
Neuilly-Porte Maillot R.E.R.
Porte Maillot
Rue Brunel
Rue des Acacias
Avenue Mac Mahon
Rue Bréy
Avenue Carnot
Avenue de la Grande Armée
R.E.R.
Tilsitt
Avenue
16e
Ch. De Gaulle - Étoile
PLACE CHARLES DE GAULLE
3
4
8
21
24
28
31
35
36
37
39
40
43
44
45
46
50
61
62
65

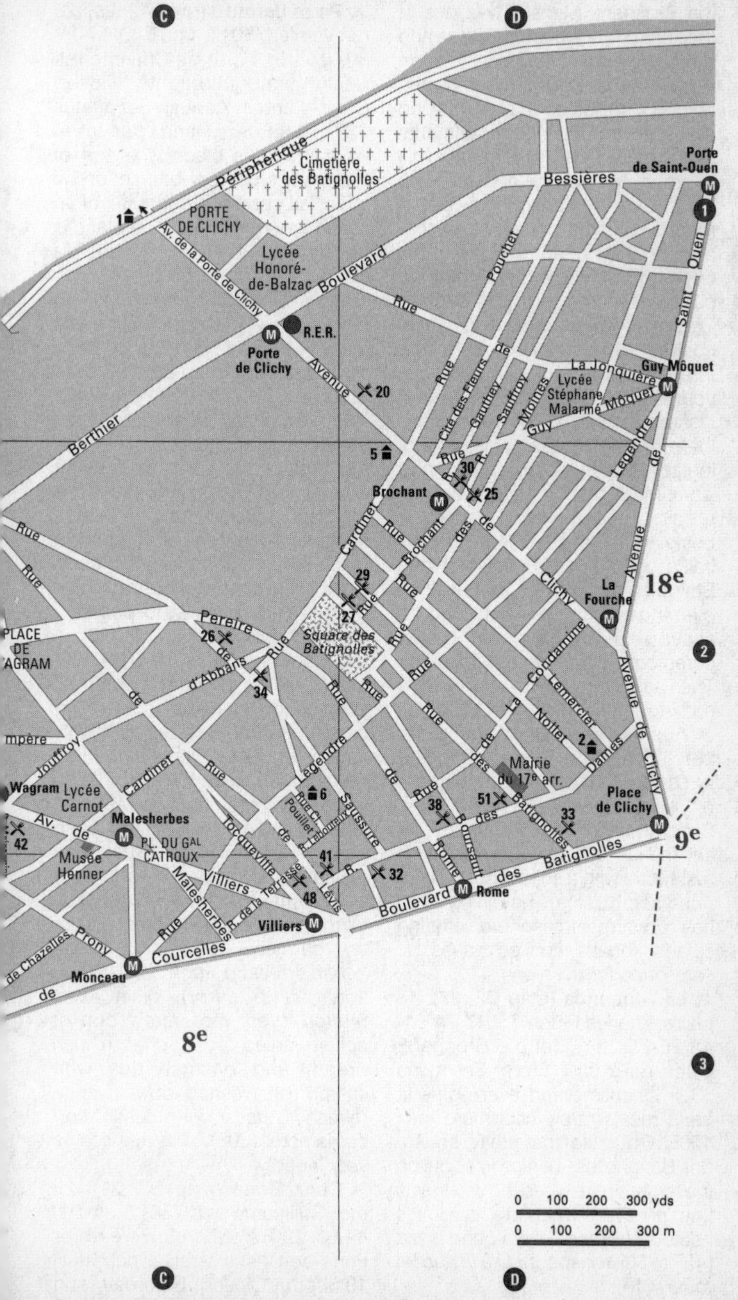
C
D
Périphérique
Cimetière des Batignolles
PORTE DE CLICHY
Av. de la Porte de Clichy
Lycée Honoré-de-Balzac
Boulevard
Berthier
R.E.R.
Porte de Clichy
Avenue
Rue
de
Bessières
Porte de Saint-Ouen
Pouchet
Saint Ouen
La Jonquière
Guy Môquet
Lycée Stéphane Malarmé
Guy Môquet
Cité des Fleurs
Gauthey
Sauffroy
Moines
Legendre
Brochant
Cardinet
Clichy
La Fourche
18e
Avenue de Clichy
Pereire
PLACE DE WAGRAM
de d'Abbans
Square des Batignolles
La Condamine
Lemercier
Nollet
Dames
Mairie du 17e arr.
Place de Clichy
9e
Jouffroy
Wagram
Lycée Carnot
Malesherbes
Av. de Villiers
PL. DU GAL CATROUX
Musée Henner
Tocqueville
Rue Cl. Pouillet
R. Lebouteux
Saussure
R. de la Terrasse
R. Lévis
Rome
Boursault
des Batignolles
Boulevard des Batignolles
Villiers
Rome
Prony
de Chazelles
Courcelles
Monceau
8e
0 100 200 300 yds
0 100 200 300 m

rue Brochant. Menelik was one of the sons of the Queen of Sheba and King Solomon. Originally from Addis Ababa, Solomon (the owner, not the king!) is on to a good thing here and this Ethiopian restaurant fills up thanks to word of mouth. This is probably because he welcomes his guests personally, the dining room is colourful, prices are reasonable, and it's open until late in the evening. Surprisingly, Ethiopian cuisine is rich and highly original. Try *beyayennatou*, an assortment of cooked dishes accompanied by *inreja* pancake, which you eat with your fingers (like all the other dishes, actually!). For vegetarians there are split peas, Swiss chard, lentils, tomato salad, onion and *azifa*. Meat-eaters can try the *ketfo*, a spicy Ethiopian steak tartare. A bottle of Côtes-du-Rhône is 60F, half a jug of wine 25F, beer 18F and Ethiopian tea 15F. On Saturday evening Solomon puts on a show and an Ethiopian coffee ceremony, which is very popular. The atmosphere is young and relaxed.

✕ **Aux Îles des Princes** (map C2, **26**): 96 rue de Saussure 75017. ☎ 01-40-54-01-03. Metro: Wagram or Villiers. Open until 11pm. Closed Sunday lunchtime. Set lunch 70F, set menus 90F to 120F. A Turkish restaurant with a solid reputation for price and cuisine. The dining room has a warm atmosphere, offering salads, kebabs, cooked dishes . . . something for everyone.

✕ **La Gioconda** (map D2, **27**): 18 place Charles-Fillion 75017. ☎ 01-42-26-75-29. Metro: Brochant. Open daily until 11pm. Set menu 130F lunchtime and evening. À la carte meals rarely cost more than 100F. Opposite the pretty square des Batignolles, it's nice to sit out on the terrace here when the weather is fine or even when it's cold (it's heated in winter), with a good pizza (42F to 56F) or spaghetti *à la napolitaine* (41F).

✕ **Pizza Lotauro** (map A2, **28**): 28 rue Vernier 75017. ☎ 01-40-54-05-39. Metro: Porte-de-Champerret. Open until midnight. Closed Sunday and in August. Set menus 65F to 115F. Small and often full at lunchtime, this place is a sort of Italian-style grocery-bar, set up by a Sicilian couple, straight out of an Italian neo-realist film. The place is as simple as they are, but it's perfect if you're a bit broke . . . . The pizzas will fill you up (41F to 62F) as will the generous pasta dishes (42F to 72F).

✕ **Arcimboldo** (map D2, **29**): 7 rue Brochant 75017. ☎ 01-42-29-37-62. Metro: Brochant. Open until 11pm. Closed Sunday and for two weeks at the end of the year. Budget for around 100F including drinks. A pleasant, relaxed *trattoria* with a terrace open in summer. The perfect place for an unpretentious meal, good Italian *charcuterie* and cheese. There is a good tiramisu for dessert.

✕ **Shah Jahan** (map D2, **30**): 4 rue Gauthey 75017. ☎ 01-42-63-44-06. Metro: Brochant. Open all year round, lunchtime and evening until 11.30pm. Booking is highly recommended. At lunchtime there are set menus at 49F and 79F, in the evening set menus at 115F and 130F including drinks. À la carte around 150F. This is a Pakistani restaurant with a decor worthy of a sentimental novel: heavy curtains, mirrors . . . . To soft, insistent music, you can choose either a *sheek kebab*, a lamb *rogh josh* (traditional lamb curry), or a *karai mutton* (very hot lamb curry), accompanied by a cheese *nan* bread, and basmati rice with saffron, all washed down with a refreshing *lassi* with cumin and cardamom (20F). The service is very friendly.

✕ **Chez Rose** (map B2, **31**): 23 rue Guillaume-Tell 75017. ☎ 01-42-67-12-67. Metro: Pereire or Porte-de-Champerret. Open until 10.30pm. Closed Saturday and

Sunday, 30 July to 20 August and 23 December to 2 January. Set meal 75F at lunchtime, 120F in the evening. Budget for around 150F à la carte. This restaurant, in a tiny old butcher's shop near the Porte de Champerret, is very popular with those who like bistros. So much so, a second dining room has been opened to give space for everyone. Dishes of the day at lunchtime may include fresh fish from the market, skate wing with leeks or fricassée of rabbit with basil. In the evening you'll find poached egg with sorrel, *confit* of duckling in a salad with truffle oil, *tarte Tatin* with pears, and *gratin* of red fruit for dessert. Wine of the month at around 70F.

☆☆ MODERATE

✕ **L'Impatient** (map D3, **32**): 14 passage Geffroy-Didelot 75017. ☎ 01-43-87-28-10. Metro: Villiers. Open until 10.30pm. Closed Saturday, Sunday and Monday evening, and also for two weeks in August. At lunchtime there's a menu at 102F, in the evening there are menus from 120F. A good place to eat, tucked away in a passage located between 92 boulevard de Batignolles and 117 rue des Dames, this restaurant lives up to its name. In fact, some evenings you may have to resign yourself to a long wait before sitting down to eat. The reason for this is the impeccable set menus with unbeatable value for money – starter, main course and dessert both at lunchtime and in the evening. You may get sardine fillets grilled with lemon preserve and ice-cream truffle with thyme. The chef even spares a thought for vegetarians, for example the foil parcel of lightly peppered fresh corn (at 70F). There is another set menu at 162F which is more inventive, and a *menu dégustation* at 285F for those bubbling over with the impatience of the true gourmet.

✕ **La P'tite Lili** (map D2, **33**): 8 rue des Batignolles 75017. ☎ 01-45-22-54-22. Metro: Place-Clichy or Rome. Last orders 9.30pm. Closed Saturday lunchtime, Sunday and public holidays, plus the first week of the February holidays. À la carte only, budget for between 130F and 150F. Lili is the mother of Mimi, an ex-theatre props manager who has become a bistro owner. You can see some traces of her former profession in the decoration of her old bistro – she did the whole delightful conversion herself. Comfortable and pleasant, it's worthy of her cooking, which she takes very seriously. On the blackboard are five starters, two main courses and five desserts. All you have to do is take your pick. The Lyons sausage (46F) and the *cochonnailles* (salami, bacon, pâté and ham) or cheese board (56F) are never disappointing. Desserts are equally generous – apple tart or chocolate mousse flavoured with orange. Clever wine selections include Cheverny from Quenioux, Madiran from Laplace. They also sell wine by the glass.

✕ **L'Étoile Verte** (map B3, **35**): 13 rue Brey 75017. ☎ 01-43-80-69-34. Metro: Charles-de-Gaulle-Étoile or Ternes. Open daily lunchtime and evening until 11pm. Set menus 110F and 155F, around 200F à la carte. This institution has been here since 1951. Its name doesn't come from the square of the same name, located five minutes away, but from the offices which used to be on the first floor, where people used to meet to speak Esperanto, the emblem of which was the green star (*étoile verte*). An apéritif and a coffee are included in the set menu at 155F, as is a bottle of Bordeaux for two. Among the star dishes are *noix de St-Jacques à la provençale*, *confit de canard* and calves' sweetbreads.

✕ **Le Vieux Logis** (map D3, **38**): 68 rue des Dames 75017. ☎ 01-

43-87-72-27. Metro: Rome. Open until 11pm. Closed Saturday lunchtime and Sunday. Set menus 65F at lunchtime, 100F in the evening. À la carte around 140F. Created at the end of the Second World War, this is a guaranteed period piece. The door opens onto a tiny bar, from where you glimpse one dining room, followed by another. One of the dining rooms has a courtyard with a glass roof, for when the weather is fine. The menu is entitled *Pourquoi pas?* ('Why not?'). À la carte, *andouillette*, steak tartare and fillet of duck with sautéed potatoes share the limelight. The wines are good value for money and there is always a wine of the month. There are events once a month depending on the owners' moods (magic, French singing, Beaujolais Nouveau and so on).

✕ **Chez Clément** (map A3, **39**): 99 boulevard Gouvion-St-Cyr 75017. ☎ 01-45-72-93-00. Metro: Porte-Maillot. Open daily until 1am. Set menus 85F and 123F at lunchtime and evening. À la carte around 130F without drinks. With cosy decor and a warm atmosphere, this little brother of the other *Cléments* (*see* '2nd, 4th, 8th, 14th and 15th arrondissements') is just as good as the others. This one has the added bonus of a real fireplace with logs burning in winter. Oysters and spit-roasts set the tone on a menu halfway between a bistro and a brasserie. On the menu there is a mixed salad with fresh herbs and beef or spare ribs with honey and spices, and a second menu *Entre Mer and Terre* (Between Sea and Land). Then there is the 'Fishermen's platter' (98F), the '*Grand Bleu*' (118F) or the 'Ocean Globetrotter' (196F). Lots of appetizing desserts too. There is another branch in the 17th arrondissement: 47 avenue de Wagram. ☎ 01-53-81-97-00. Metro: Wagram.

✕ **Stübli** (map B3, **40**): 11 rue Poncelet 75017. ☎ 01-42-27-81-86. Metro: Ternes. Open for tea Tuesday to Saturday 9am to 6.30pm; for the *pâtisserie*, Tuesday to Saturday 8.30am to 7.30pm. Open Sunday morning. Closed in August. Budget for 100F per person for a meal (at lunchtime only). Wonderful cakes, as creamy as a Viennese waltz, tempt passers-by, who have trouble resisting them. *Sachertorte*, *Linzertorte*, Black Forest gateau ... the 1001 sweet delights of the German-speaking world are on parade at this specialist shop (opposite there is a shop devoted to savouries – sausages, etc. as well as beers and spirits). On summer weekends there are a few tables in the street, so you can have brunch (9am to 11.30am Saturday, 9am to 12.30pm Sunday) while watching the cream of 17th arrondissement society go by. Depending on how hungry you are, there is the *Stübli Frühstück* (68F) or the *Wiener brunch*, which is very generous (140F), or just a hot dish. During the week the menu has Austrian and German dishes of the day.

✕ **Le Verre Bouteille** (map A3, **36**): 85 avenue des Ternes 75017. ☎ 01-45-74-01-02. Website: www.leverrebouteille.com. Metro: Porte-Maillot. Open daily noon to 3pm and 7pm to 5am. Closed at Christmas. Three set meals at 90F (at lunchtime only), 110F and 170F. Children's menu at 45F. À la carte, budget for 150F. Le Verre Bouteille receives all the night owls of Paris who come to fill up on solid dishes and generous salads such as the *Nain jaune* (poultry, raisins, curry sauce). Around 30 wines served by the glass. Very lively at the weekend when the time-bell doesn't ring until 4am. A second Verre Bouteille has opened at 5 boulevard Gouvion-St-Cyr 75017. ☎ 01-47-63-39-99. It is only open until midnight.

✕ **Le Patio Provençal** (map C3, **41**): 116 rue des Dames 75017. ☎ 01-42-93-73-73. Metro: Villiers. Open lunchtime and evening until 11pm. Closed at weekends. Budget for around 150F without drinks. All the smells of Provence are on the menu at this restaurant. Little gazebos covered with ivy surround the tables on which there are large bouquets of lavender, thyme and rosemary, all reminiscent of Provence. Start with a dish of two *tapenades* and olives from Provence or with a delicious plate of *mozzarella di bufala* with fresh basil, tomatoes, green salad, mangetout peas and French beans; to follow, the Royans ravioli with basil and cream or sweet peppers with cod flavoured with parsley. But there are also dishes of the day and many house desserts, all washed down with some of the best vintages from the Luberon and elsewhere. Glass of the week at 25F.

✕ **La Gaieté Cosaque** (map D2, **51**): 46 rue des Dames 75017. ☎ 01-44-70-06-07. Metro: Rome or Place-Clichy. Open until 11.30pm. Closed Monday lunchtime, Sunday and for the whole of August. Set menus 59F at lunchtime, 95F and 125F in the evening. Budget for 140F à la carte. This little Russian bistro, run by a couple of former teachers from Moscow, offers wonderful *borscht* and *pelmenis*. In the evening the first set menu has aubergine caviar, *blinis* with *taramasalata* or Russian salad, beef Strogonoff or *pojarski*. All the dishes are accompanied by potatoes *à la campagnarde* and *kacha* (buckwheat). Vodka is 25F per 30ml glass and 170F for 70cl of Zubrovka.

☆ ☆ ☆ CHIC

✕ **Restaurant Leclou** (map C2, **34**): 132 rue Cardinet 75017. ☎ 01-42-27-36-78. Metro: Malesherbes. Open until 10.30pm. Closed Saturday lunchtime, Sunday, some public holidays and in August. At lunchtime there's a set menu at 98F, otherwise budget for 180F à la carte, excluding drinks. An authentic bistro in the middle of nowhere. Great value set menu. Try the black pudding terrine with chestnuts, veal *pot-au-feu* and *crème brûlée* to finish. In the evening there's a 7-hour *confit* of lamb, and delicious warm *moelleux au chocolat*. There is a terrace open in the summer and the wine list is very reasonable

✕ **Le Café d'Angel** (map B3, **37**): 16 rue Brey 75017. ☎ 01-47-54-03-33. Metro: Charles-de-Gaulle-Étoile. Last orders 10.30pm. Closed Saturday and Sunday, for three weeks in August and for Christmas and New Year. Set menus 80F and 95F at lunchtime, 140F and 170F in the evening. In the shadow of the Arc de Triomphe, this bistro is always full. It has a number of advantages: a warm dining room, an open-plan kitchen which everyone can see into, and wonderful inventive food such as crispy pig's trotters, veal kidneys, fish of the day and, to end with, the house chocolate gateau. There are also set menus offering remarkable value for money.

✕ **Sud-Ouest Monceau, Claude Laborda** (map C2, **42**): 8 rue Meissonier 75017. ☎ 01-47-63-15-07. Metro: Malesherbes or Monceau. Last orders 10pm. Closed Sunday and Monday, in August and for a week in April. Booking is recommended in the evening. Budget for 200F to 250F à la carte, including wine. Having gone through the caterer's shop and worked up an appetite, you reach a worthy dining room where well-groomed young executives, businessmen and elderly gentlemen tuck into south-west specialities. The blackboard provides the daily specials: starters like antipasti, *œuf en cocotte* (baked egg cooked in a ramekin) and *foie gras*, among other things; main courses including *cassoulet*, *confit* and *magret* of duck, but also *petit-salé* (streaky salted pork) or *garbure* (soup made with cabbage) and *confit* of goose. The wine list is in keeping with the place and very reasonably priced. The service is very pleasant and decidedly provincial. In the evening it's popular with local families.

✕ **Coco et sa Maison** (map B3, **43**): 18 rue Bayen 75017. ☎ 01-45-74-73-73. Metro: Ternes. Open lunchtime and evening until 11pm. Closed Saturday lunchtimes, Sunday and Monday lunchtimes during the summer as well as two weeks in August. Set lunch menu 150F; budget for 250F à la carte. Coco and Virginie, both from Bordeaux, are the owners here. Over two floors they have recreated a family home, complete with souvenir photos and letters addressed to Gustave Eiffel, their ancestor. The walls, with their warm colourings, match with the panelling, rococo glass chandeliers, old books and large mirrors. Fresh, light starters include *piperade basquaise*, cream of pumpkin soup or peppers marinated in millefeuille with fresh goat's cheese. You won't be able to resist *noix de St-Jacques*, poached John Dory with risotto and Chablis and crispy cabbage, fillet of wild boar or the suggestions of the day and the casserole dishes. No worries about the wines; there are around 40 from 96F to 450F, and a list of more 'prestigious' vintage wines for connoisseurs. Valet-parking (which you have to pay for).

✕ **Graindorge** (map B3, **44**): 15 rue de l'Arc-de-Triomphe 75017. ☎ 01-47-54-00-28. Metro: Charles-de-Gaulle-Étoile. Open lunchtime and evening until 11pm. Closed Saturday lunchtime and Sunday. Book at weekends. Set menus 138F and 168F at lunchtime, 188F and 250F in the evening. À la carte around 200F without drinks. Neo-1930 décor and an inspired chef makes this a popular spot. Red cabbage *à la flamande* or roast Scottish salmon with Ardennes ham, farmhouse Maroilles (cheese) or *fondant* with dark chocolate. À la carte, the *waterzoï de St-Jacques* (a type of broth), shellfish with shrimps from Ostend or the fried *noix de St-Jacques* (scallops) speak of Flanders. Everything is exceptionally fresh and prepared to order. Rather than the wine list, go for the list of Flanders beers, which complement the food well.

✕ **L'Huîtrier** (map B3, **45**): 16 rue Saussier-Leroy 75017. ☎ 01-40-54-83-44. Metro: Ternes. Closed Monday and from mid-July to 31 August. Budget for around 250F per person without wine. This marine bistro, which takes its name from the shellfish-loving oyster-catcher, is a meeting place for captains of industry, young guns from production companies and shellfish fans. The oysters here are straight from Marennes-Oléron.

– Alain Bunel, the owner, has opened a marine snack bar at the nearby Lebon market (**La Cabane de l'Huîtrier** at 1 rue Lebon) where you can swallow a few oysters or nibble an octopus salad, or have crêpes and galettes at any time of the day.

✕ **Le Sud** (map A3, **46**): 91 boulevard Gouvion-St-Cyr 75017. ☎ 01-45-74-02-77. Metro: Porte-Maillot. Open until 11.30pm. Closed Sunday, as well as for Christmas and New Year and two weeks in August. Budget for 300F à la carte, including wine. A corner of Provence in Paris. Stuffed tomatoes with goat's cheese and herbes de Provence, *tapenade* and *anchoïade*, roast fresh tuna, cod *brandade* . . . and the house speciality, *bourride*, a *bouillabaisse* with garlic mayonnaise (168F). When the weather is fine Le Sud is over-run, and it is advisable to book at least 48 hours in advance. There's a bar on the 1st floor with glass roof, lounges and a real fire in winter.

✕ **Les Bouchons de François Clerc** (map C3, **48**): 22 rue de la Terrace 75017. ☎ 01-42-27-31-51. Metro: Villiers. Open until 10.30pm (11pm on Friday and Saturday evenings). Closed Saturday lunchtime and Sunday. Set meal 137F at lunchtime. In the evening there is a single menu at 227F. As in the other Bouchons in the 5th, 8th and 15th arrondissements, the wines are sold at cost price. At lunch local entrepreneurs come to talk business over the set starter plus main course or main course plus dessert and a glass of wine. In the evening the local families take over. There is a menu made up of a starter, a main course, as much cheese as you like and a dessert. Terrace in summer.

✕ **Pau Brazil** (map B3, **50**): 32 rue de Tilsitt 75017. ☎ 01-42-27-31-39. Metro: Charles-de-Gaulle-Étoile. Open 8pm to 2am (last orders midnight). Set menus 198F and 390F to 650F. This very flashy Brazilian restaurant, close to the Arc de Triomphe, with its stunning tropical art-deco interior, is actually the former Étoile swimming pool restaurant, decorated with mosaics dating from 1936. Set meal (except Friday and Saturday), service included, with as much as you can eat from 11 types of meat roasted over the wood fire of the *rodizio*, accompanied by various vegetables and sauces. A furious orchestra leads the dancing as though you were in Rio in the middle of the carnival. Good cocktails (80F) such as *garota d'Ipanema,* based on rum, green lemon and sugar, or the Brazilian national cocktail, the *caïpirinha*. The wines start at 155F.

17TH

LES BATIGNOLLES

Deep in the heart of the 17th arrondissement you will find the Batignolles quarter. At 25 rue de Chazelles an immense statue was erected which rose high above the rooftops. It was Bartholdi's famous *Statue of Liberty*, initially set up in its entirety, before being taken apart and put into crates to be shipped over to New York.

The village of Les Batignolles, as it is still known, has kept a good deal of its provincial character. It actually only became part of Paris by means of a decree issued by Napoleon III in 1860. But this particular New Year's present wasn't terribly popular with the people of Les Batignolles, who decided to keep their village's own traditions. A few small-scale farmers and modest artisans had their second homes here, because the air had a reputation as being very healthy. As Paul Verlaine's family lived at 45 rue Lemercier, the would-be poet spent his childhood in this quarter and studied at the Lycée Chaptal, on boulevard des Batignolles. Stéphane Mallarmé, nicknamed the 'prince of poets', brought together all the Parisian intelligentsia of the day at his home, at 89 boulevard des Baatignolles, for his 'literary Tuesdays'.

WHAT TO SEE

★ Go down the rue des Moines and take a look at the **marché des Moines**, open 8am to 12.30pm and 4pm to 7.30pm; closed Monday and Sunday afternoons. Pretty cheap, ranking third among markets in Paris for value for money.

There's a real mixture here: good fruit and vegetables and craft traders, but there are other forms of culture in the area too: Brazilian in rue des Batignolles, Portuguese in rue Cardinet (with *fado* every day), Corsican and Arabic along avenue de Clichy. Lovers of *couscous* will not be disappointed! Choose from the restaurants L'Étoile du Sud or the Grand Soleil du Maroc.

★ The **avenue de Clichy**, formerly the Grande-Rue-des-Batignolles, hasn't retained any of its provincial character and today seems rather cosmopolitan. And yet during the 19th century it was a very peaceful place, a sort of St-Germain-des-Prés or Montparnasse, frequented by artists. Manet, Degas, Cézanne, Renoir, Pissarro and other illustrious unknowns – at the time – used to meet at The Café Guerbois, which has unfortunately now gone. Here they peacefully plotted to create their own Les Batignolles school, immortalized by Fantin-Latour in a painting which you can see in the Musée d'Orsay.

★ Cross the avenue de Clichy at No. 154 for a stroll around the Les Épinettes quarter. The **cité des Fleurs** was designed in 1847, between avenue de Clichy and 59 rue de la Jonquière (Metro: Brochant), with every owner obliged to plant at least three flowering trees in his or her garden – hence the name. The result is quite fabulous. It's like being in the countryside, with a suprisingly varied spread of styles. A real dream for Parisians starved of pure fresh air. At No. 19 the façade is covered with ivy and further on, at No. 29, you find neo-Renaissance motifs, cherubs under the cornice, exotic bas-reliefs and even white marble inlays. There are some other Renaissance bays and columns at No. 33. Notice the lion's heads above those at No. 40 and some more eccentric constructions at Nos. 31 and 45, which look like a great big cream cake. At the end of the alley, at No. 60, there is a sort of rococo palace, the decoration designed to echo the neighbouring vegetation.

Of course, when you return to avenue de Clichy reality hits a little hard, but you get used to it. The smell of couscous and kebabs has replaced that of chips. The last traditional traders in the area are folding, kicked out by the flood of second-hand clothes dealers. With a little luck you can make some good discoveries.

★ Before entering rue Legendre, stroll down **rue de Lévis** (Metro: Villiers). At No. 8 there used to be a political meeting hall frequented by Victor Hugo, Auguste Blanqui, Gambetta, Ledru-Rollin and Louise Michel, who all lived locally. Nowadays, the voices of the great orators have been silenced to give way to those of the market traders who have invaded the pedestrian streets in a permanent market, worthy of Provence for its fruit, vegetable and flower stalls. There are plenty of great clothes shops here – both expensive and cheap, and also clothes' exchange shops which will take your out-of-date items if they have the right designer labels! Snobbery rules here as well.

You should also take a walk along **rue des Dames**. It's lively, with a real Parisian working-class setting. Verlaine lived at 10 rue Nollet from 1851 to 1865. The Belgian singer/songwriter Jacques Brel lived at 28 rue Lemercier.

★ The long **rue Legendre**, a former Roman road, has many commercial outlets and will lead you to the delightful **place du Docteur-Félix-**

Lobligeois, a provincial little square with a church (Ste-Marie-des-Batignolles) and masses of trees. Some lucky people have balconies overlooking all this greenery.

The inside of the church is nothing special, but the entrance, a copy of the Madeleine, has a touch of charm with its huge white columns. Behind the church is the **square des Batignolles**, the largest of the squares ordered by Napoleon III. All the typical elements of landscaping at the time are here: an ornamental lake, an artificial river, winding alleys. Children under four will love the old roundabout (with a retro Mickey Mouse on his motorbike). There's a roller-skating rink and on Sundays in summer it tends to be very crowded.

★ The **cimetière des Batignolles:** avenue de la Porte-de-Clichy; entrance in the rue St-Just 75017. Metro: Porte-de-Clichy. In this cemetery lie a veritable catalogue of celebrities from Verlaine and André Breton to Gaston Calmette (the editor of the national newspaper *Le Figaro*, murdered by Mme Caillaux in 1914).

★ The **place du Général-Catroux:** better known under its former name of place Malesherbes (Metro: Malesherbes), it is lined with fine private houses whose period architecture often evokes the neo-gothic style. At No. 1, at the junction with avenue de Villiers and boulevard Malesherbes, there is a copy of the Louis XII wing of the Château de Blois, commissioned by Émile Gaillard, a rich banker, and finished in 1878. It is a superb private residence in brick and stone, topped with a slate roof and decorated with wrought-ironwork. The Banque de France has owned it since the beginning of the 20th century. There are plans to demolish it and, as it's not listed, this may well happen. At the centre of the square, Sarah Bernhardt recited Racine's *Phaedra* under the gaze of a statue by Gustave Doré of Alexandre Dumas, author of *The Three Musketeers*. He is kept company by a statue of his son, also named Alexandre, who wrote *La Dame aux camélias*.

★ The **villa des Ternes:** starting at 96 avenue des Ternes, and ending at 39 rue Guersant 75017. Metro: Ternes. Luxury houses and buildings built on the land of the former Château des Ternes from 1822 onwards. There are replicas of country villas, which are quite rare in a city like Paris.

★ The **Ceramic Hôtel:** 34 avenue de Wagram 75017. Metro: Ternes. A fine art-nouveau building, built by Lavirotte in 1904.

WHERE TO GO FOR A DRINK

🍸 **James Joyce's Pub** (map A3, **61**): 71 boulevard Gouvion-St-Cyr 75017. ☎ 01-44-09-70-32. Metro: Porte-Maillot. Open daily 7am (10am Sunday) to 2am. Draught beer 22F for half a pint and 38F for a pint (24F and 40F after 10pm). An alliance of whisky and literature – James Joyce is Ireland's most famous writer – this place welcomes both lovers of good quality booze and future Booker Prize winners. But don't worry if you don't fall into either category – you won't be the only one. The menu is well stocked and prices are reasonable. Among the whiskies, there is a good Black Bushmill (45F).

🍸 **Le Cambridge** (map B3, **62**): 17 avenue Wagram 75017. ☎ 01-43-80-34-12. Metro: Charles-de-Gaulle-Étoile. Open daily 7am to 4am (happy hour 4pm to 7pm). Set menus at 60F and 96F, beer 22F and whiskies 40F to 65F. A real pub, popular with working locals during the day, beer drinkers in early evening, and whisky drinkers later on. Brasserie-style cuisine. On Wednesday, Thursday and at weekends there are some excellent groups playing rhythm 'n' blues or jazz. A haunt for the under 25s.

WHERE TO GO FOR JAZZ

– **Nouveau Jazz-Club Lionel Hampton** (map A3, **65**): Le Méridien Étoile, 81 boulevard Gouvion-St-Cyr 75017. ☎ 01-40-68-30-42. Metro: Porte-Maillot. Open every night. Piano bar on Sunday, concerts from 10.30pm other nights. Entrance fee and drink: 130F, à la carte from 65F. Founded by Moustache, one of the leading figures in French jazz and a great connoisseur, this club opened in 1976 and its stage was canonized one day in November 1984 when Lionel Hampton agreed to lend his name to the place. The result was amazing. Hampton's fame, along with Moustache's eloquence, made it the place to be. All the international stars of jazz and blues – Fats Domino, Cab Calloway, Screamin' Jay Hawkins, Dee Dee Bridgewater, Dizzy Gillespie and BB King, among others – helped to create the unique atmosphere here.

18TH ARRONDISSEMENT

MONTMARTRE ● THE GOUTTE-D'OR

Montmartre is one of the most picturesque areas of Paris and certainly the most popular with tourists. However, it can still spring the odd surprise on the curious, the inquisitive, or on anyone who likes to get off the beaten track.

WHERE TO STAY

☆ BUDGET TO CHEAP

Hôtel du Commerce (inset, **1**): 34 rue des Trois-Frères 75018. ☎ 01-42-64-81-69. Metro: Abbesses or Anvers. This hotel has rooms with 1, 2 or 3 beds, which go from 100F to 180F. 15F for a shower. The prices haven't gone up for ages – ideal if you're broke. The rooms are pretty clean (and actually have double-glazing), even if the bedspreads sometimes have holes in them. No breakfast. Ring the day before to book. The atmosphere of rue des Trois-Frères and the hotel itself have attracted more than one film maker. Credit cards are not accepted.

Hôtel Bonséjour (inset, **2**): 11 rue Burq 75018. ☎ 01-42-54-22-53. Fax: 01-42-54-25-92. Metro: Abbesses. Double room with washbasin 172F and with shower 210F. Right in the middle of Montmartre, in a very quiet area, an interesting little hotel with a few very simple rooms with pretty wrought-iron balconies, giving it a certain touch of class; room No. 51 even has a view of Sacré-Coeur. There is a great atmosphere here, particularly in peak season when all the artists are in the place du Tertre. The hotel has a fine view over a typical Montmartre street. Excellent value for money and an attentive and thoughtful welcome.

Le Village Hostel (map B3, **3**): 20 rue d'Orsel 75018. ☎ 01-42-64-22-02. Fax: 01-42-64-22-04. Website: www.levillage-hostel.fr. Metro: Anvers, Abbesses or Pigalle. Double room with shower, toilet and telephone 147F per person in summer and 137F in winter. A superbly located bed-and-breakfast, very close to Sacré-Cœur. There is a superb half-timbered stairwell. Run by a young American, so it's full of English-speakers. There are 24 spacious rooms for two to six people, in pastel colours and Provençal hues, with exposed beams. Lovely bathrooms. Even less expensive if there are three or four of you. Ask for one of the eight rooms on the fourth, fifth and especially on the sixth floor, which have an incomparable view over Montmartre. It's best to book, especially in summer. There's a bar and breakfast area.

Hôtel Sofia (map B3, **4**): 21 rue de Sofia 75018. ☎ 01-42-64-55-37. Fax: 01-46-06-33-30. Metro: Anvers or Barbès-Rochechouart. Double room with shower and toilet 265F. A few minutes from the hill of Montmartre and away from the noise of boulevard Barbès, this place is in an amazingly quiet shopping area. A clean hotel with a flowery little patio where you can have breakfast when the sun shines. The rooms overlooking the courtyard are even quieter. There is no lift and the staircase is a bit steep. You can hire a TV.

Hôtel Garden Inn-Titania (map B1, **5**): 70 *bis*, boulevard Ornano 75018. ☎ 01-46-06-52-54. Metro: Porte-de-Clignancourt. Double room without shower 170F and with shower 270F. There is a sliding scale of prices for long-term bookings. A hotel where the level of comfort is as simple as any you'll find in Paris (although you do get a TV), and which has passed its day of glory, judging from the façade and the art-deco lobby, both now listed as historic monuments. The rooms are being renovated in turn, and they needed it. It's going to take some time as there are 110 of them! Just down the road from Montmartre and the St-Ouen flea market, the location is ideal for bargain-hunters! Antoine de St-Exupéry, the author of *The Little Prince*, lived here for a long time and director François Truffaut was once the nightwatchman. The film maker even shot his very first footage in the basement of this hotel. One of the least expensive and most interesting places to stay in this arrondissement.

18TH

Style Hôtel (map A2, **6**): 8 rue Ganneron 75018. ☎ 01-45-22-37-59. Fax: 01-45-22-81-03. Metro: Place-Clichy. Double room with bath or shower 295F. There are a few smaller but still impeccable rooms (washbasin and shower on each floor) in the second building, at 190F. A hotel which lives up to its name. The owners have renovated the spacious rooms in the purest art-deco style. There are varnished floors, mirrored wardrobes and bedside Tiffany lamps. A flowery courtyard adds the last touches to the provincial feel. Friendly welcome. Excellent value for money.

Hôtel Caulaincourt (map A2, **7**): 2 square Caulaincourt 75018. ☎ 01-46-06-46-06. Fax: 01-46-06-46-16. E-mail: bonjour@caulaincourt.com. Metro: Lamarck-Caulaincourt. Bus No. 80. Double room with shower and toilet 280F or with bath and toilet 310F. There are a few rooms at 180F, with no shower or toilet. Also a double room at 195F and a triple at 310F which can be booked for 270F if there are only two of you. On the façade, you'll see: '*Ateliers d'artistes*' (Artists' Workshops). This is a perfect spot for cash-strapped romantics. Clean and well-kept. TV in all rooms, except the singles. Those on the fourth floor have a view over Paris and used to be rented out to artists. Near unbeatable value for money.

☆☆ MODERATE

Hôtel Bouquet de Montmartre (inset, **8**): 1 rue Durantin 75018. ☎ 01-46-06-87-54. Fax: 01-46-06-09-09. Website: www.bouquet-de-montmartre.com. Metro: Abbesses. Double room with shower or bath 380F. No TV. Breakfast 30F. The rooms have toilets, are small but decent and all different. Note the alcoves and the original little cupboards and enamel bathrooms. Double-glazing. Pleasant, very well located and a friendly welcome. There is a fine view over Paris from Room 43. You'll need to book in advance.

Hôtel Prima Lepic (inset, **9**): 29 rue Lepic 75018. ☎ 01-46-06-44-64. Fax: 01-46-06-66-11. Metro: Blanche or Abbesses. Double room between 400F and 440F over the courtyard or the street, with shower or bath. At the foot of Montmartre, this is the perfect starting point for walks around the area. The entrance has a *trompe-l'œil* English garden which gives it a fresh feel, reinforced by the garden furniture. Breakfast 30F.

Hôtel Eden-Montmartre (map B2, **10**): 90 rue Ordener 75018. ☎ 01-42-64-61-63. Fax: 01-42-64-11-43. Metro: Jules-Joffrin. Double room with bath or shower and toilet 435F. Satellite TV. A cosy hotel. The clientele is made up of antique dealers from all over the world. Excellent welcome.

Hôtel des Arts (inset, **11**): 5, rue Tholozé 75018. ☎ 01-46-06-30-52. Fax: 01-46-06-10-83. E-mail: Hotel.arts@wanadoo.fr. Metro: Blanche. Double room 440F with shower or bath. In a quiet but very steeply sloping street; right at the end, 100m (330ft) further, is the Moulin de la Galette (*see* 'What to see' *below*). The rooms are modern and fairly spacious. Breakfast is served in a lovely stone-walled cellar. Friendly welcome.

Regyn's Montmartre (inset, **12**): 18 place des Abbesses 75008. ☎ 01-42-54-45-21. Fax: 01-42-23-76-69. Metro: Abbesses. Double room 445F with shower or bath and toilet, and 455F for some of the rooms on the fourth and fifth floors, which have a lovely view over Paris and Montmartre. Fortunately they have double-glazing on all floors. Right in the heart of Montmartre, with a superb view over place des Abbesses. The owner also runs the association *Un village à Paris: Montmartre* (Montmartre: a village in Paris) and may be able to help

18TH

Where to stay
- **1** Hôtel du Commerce
- **2** Hôtel Bonséjour
- **3** Le Village Hostel
- **4** Hôtel Sofia
- **5** Hôtel Garden Inn-Titania
- **6** Style Hôtel
- **7** Hôtel Caulaincourt
- **8** Hôtel Bouquet de Montmartre
- **9** Hôtel Prima Lepic
- **10** Hôtel Eden-Montmartre
- **11** Hôtel des Arts
- **12** Regyn's Montmartre
- **13** Tim Hôtel

Where to eat
- **20** Le Rendez-Vous des Chauffeurs
- **21** Au Port de Pidjiguiti
- **22** Nezbullon
- **24** Wassana
- **25** La Rughetta
- **26** La Farayade
- **27** Pinar
- **28** Le Soleil Gourmand
- **29** Le Moulin à Vin
- **30** La Galerie
- **31** Le Maquis
- **32** Les Feuillades
- **34** Le Restaurant
- **35** Taka
- **36** Le Petit Robert
- **37** La Mazurka
- **38** Sonia
- **39** Pathya
- **40** Chez Paula
- **41** Le Palais du Kashmir
- **42** La Chope de la Mairie
- **43** L'Assiette
- **44** Le Blue's Bar
- **45** Fouta Toro
- **46** Marie-Louise
- **48** Le Cottage Marcadet
- **49** Navel
- **50** À la Goutte d'Or
- **51** Chez Aïda
- **52** Le Nioumré
- **53** Restaurant 'grillades' Le Licite
- **54** Restaurant 'grillades' L'Étoile
- **55** Hôtel-restaurant du Square
- **56** Aux Négociants
- **57** Phuket's Anana
- **58** La Prune d'Ente, Restaurant Dellac
- **59** Piccola Strada
- **60** Le Bistrot d'Asti
- **61** Chez Pradel
- **62** Le Jungle Montmartre

Where to go for a drink/ Going out/Nightclubs
- **70** La Divette de Montmartre
- **73** L'Élysée-Montmartre
- **74** Lux Bar
- **75** Le Divan du Monde
- **76** Le Lapin Agile
- **77** Le Tire-Bouchon
- **78** MCM Café
- **79** La Locomotive
- **82** Le Sancerre
- **83** Les Coulisses
- **84** La Fourmi

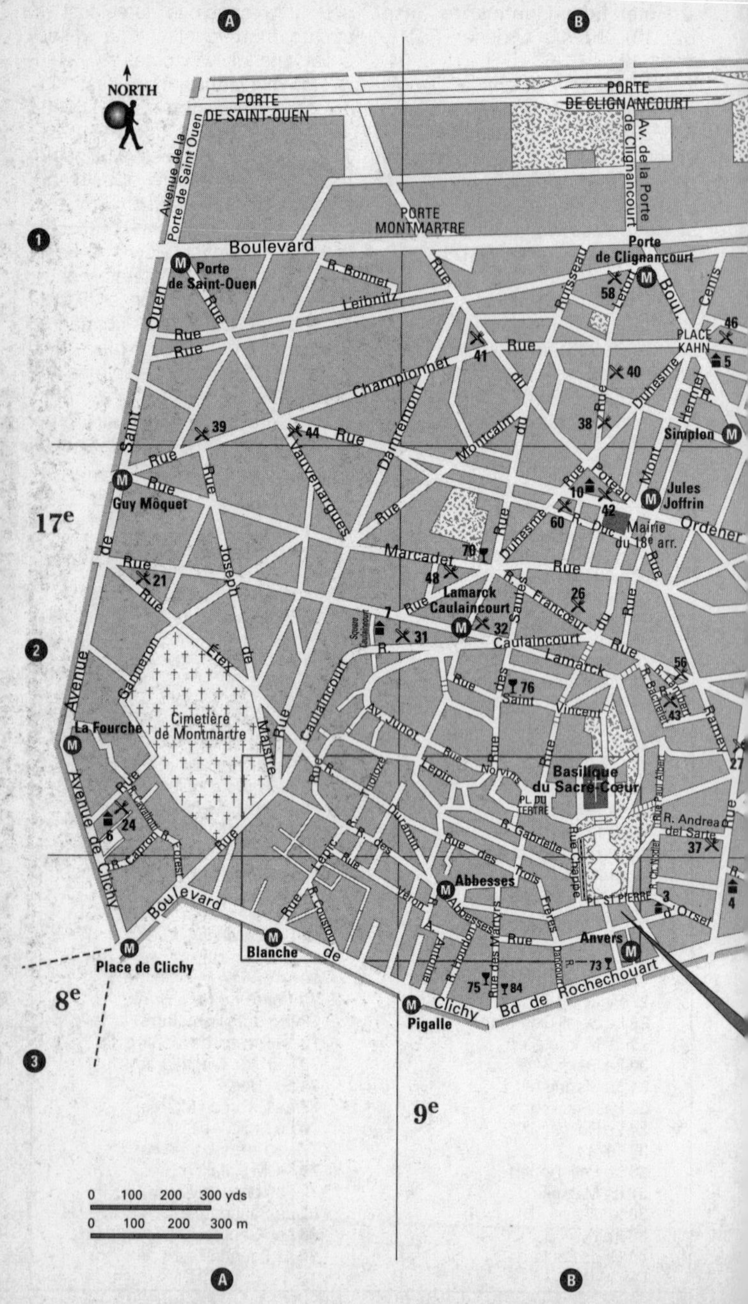

NORTH
PORTE DE SAINT-OUEN
PORTE DE CLIGNANCOURT
PORTE MONTMARTRE
Boulevard
Porte de Saint-Ouen
Porte de Clignancourt
Simplon
Jules Joffrin
Guy Môquet
Lamarck Caulaincourt
La Fourche
Cimetière de Montmartre
Basilique du Sacré-Coeur
Mairie du 18e arr.
Abbesses
Blanche
Anvers
Place de Clichy
Pigalle
Rue Championnet
Rue Marcadet
Rue Ordener
Rue Caulaincourt
Rue Lamarck
Rue Saint Vincent
Av. Junot
Rue Lepic
Bd de Rochechouart
Boulevard de Clichy
Avenue de Clichy
Avenue de Saint Ouen
17e
8e
9e
0 100 200 300 yds
0 100 200 300 m

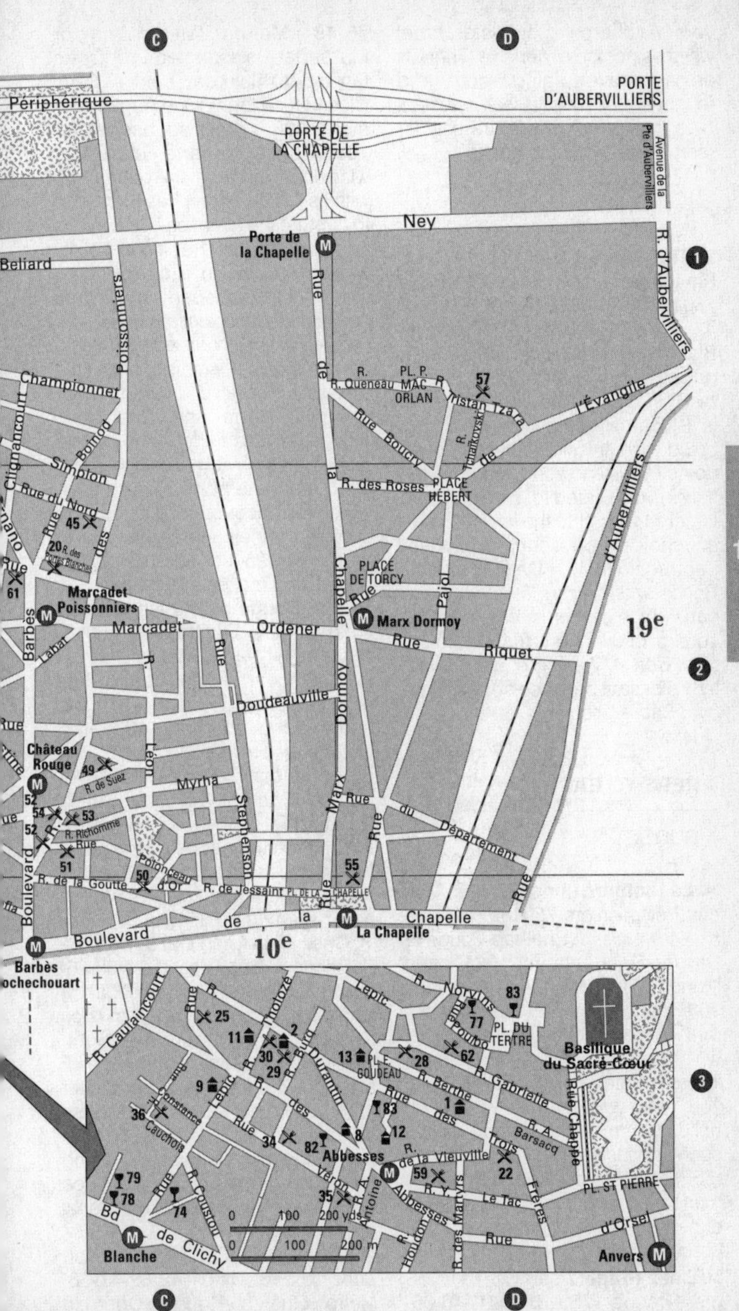

Périphérique
PORTE DE LA CHAPELLE
PORTE D'AUBERVILLIERS
Avenue de la Pte d'Aubervilliers
Ney
Porte de la Chapelle
Beliard
Poissonniers
Rue de la Chapelle
R. d'Aubervilliers
Championnet
R. Queneau
PL. P. MAC ORLAN
R. Tristan Tzara
57
Rue Boucry
R. Tchaikovski
Rue de l'Évangile
Clignancourt
Boinod
Simplon
Rue du Nord
R. des Roses
PLACE HÉBERT
45
20 R. des Portes Blanches
61
PLACE DE TORCY
Rue Pajol
d'Aubervilliers
Marcadet Poissonniers
Marx Dormoy
Marcadet
Ordener
Rue Riquet
19e
Barbès
Labat
R. Léon
Rue Stephenson
Doudeauville
Rue Marx Dormoy
Château Rouge
49
R. de Suez
Myrha
52
54
53
R. Richomme
51
Rue du Département
55
Polonceau
50
R. de la Goutte d'Or
R. de Jessaint
PL. DE LA CHAPELLE
Boulevard
Boulevard de la Chapelle
La Chapelle
10e
Barbès Rochechouart
R. Caulaincourt
Rue Lepic
R. Tholozé
25
11
2
30
29
R. Burq
Durantin
13
PL. E. GOUDEAU
28
R. Norvins
83
77
Rue Poulbot
PL. DU TERTRE
62
Basilique du Sacré-Cœur
R. Gabrielle
R. Berthe
1
Rue des Trois Frères
R. A. Barsacq
Rue Chappe
9
Constance
36
Cauchois
Rue des Abbesses
34
82
8
12
Abbesses
R. de la Vieuville
22
59
R. Y. Le Tac
PL. ST PIERRE
79
78
74
R. Coustou
35
Véron
R. A. Antoine
Abbesses
R. des Martyrs
Houdon
Rue d'Orsel
Bd de Clichy
Blanche
Anvers
0 100 200 yds
0 100 200 m
18TH

you. A charming two-star hotel which is not too expensive. There is an attractive dining room and reception lobby with wall frescoes by a local artist. There are only 22 rooms, so it's best to book.

☆☆☆ CHIC

Tim Hôtel (inset, **13**): 11 rue Ravignan, place Émile-Goudeau 75018. ☎ 01-42-55-74-79. Fax: 01-42-55-71-01. Metro: Abbesses or Blanche. Double room with shower or bath, from 580F to 680F. Breakfast 50F. Situated on a square which is as charming and romantic as you could wish, this fine hotel has been completely renovated. Each of the floors is dedicated to a painter: from the ground floor to the fifth you have a choice between Toulouse-Lautrec, Utrillo, Dalí, Picasso, Renoir and Matisse. Telephone and cable TV in all rooms. View over the square, or over Paris from the fourth floor. Nos. 417 and 517 are particularly pleasant because of their views over Sacré-Cœur.

18TH

WHERE TO EAT

☆ BUDGET

Le Nioumré (map C2, **52**): 7 rue des Poissonniers 75018. ☎ 01-42-51-24-94. Metro: Château-Rouge or Barbès-Rochechouart. Closed Monday. The bill is rarely more than 100F per person. An African restaurant with an excellent atmosphere, which is often full at weekends. There is often a *kora* player on hand. You really will feel like you're on holiday here. Try traditional dishes such as *maffé* (50F), *thieboudienne* (55F) or *yassa* chicken, with onions marinated in lemon. Delicious, not expensive, large portions and a real change of scene.

Chez Pradel (map C2, **61**): 168 rue Ordener 75018. ☎ 01-46-06-75-48. Metro: Jules-Joffrin or Marcadet-Poissonniers. Open Monday to Saturday from 7.30am. Closed for a fortnight in August. Set menu 68F, otherwise budget for 100–110F à la carte, excluding wine. In a lively area, this restaurant, with its 1920s decor, has managed to capture the attention of the locals living by the river. Traditional south-western cuisine in a family atmosphere. The house *foie gras* constitutes an excellent appetiser before *cassoulet* or *magret* of duck. For those with smaller appetites there's Périgord salad with poached eggs and *foie gras*. Alongside these tried and tested dishes there is a menu with some good brasserie dishes, which often varies; all accompanied by a wide choice of wines sold by the glass, by the jug (25cl or 50cl) or bottled and at very reasonable prices.

À la Goutte d'Or (map C3, **50**): 41 rue de la Goutte-d'Or 75018. ☎ 01-42-64-99-16. Metro: Barbès-Rochechouart. Open daily, last orders 10pm, 45F menu lunchtime and evening, à la carte 100–110F excluding drinks. Plenty of light due to its position on the corner of rue de Chartres and rue de la Goutte-d'Or. Couscous and traditional French cuisine, *tajine* and paella if you order it in advance. Very reasonable prices which never seem to go up.

Chez Aïda (map C2, **51**): 48 rue Polonceau 75018. ☎ 01-42-58-26-20. Metro: Barbès-Rochechouart or Château-Rouge. Service from noon to 4pm and 7pm to midnight. Closed Wednesday. Set menu 70F at lunchtime, à la carte budget for 150F including wine. Senegalese specialities from 70F to 90F. A warm, friendly atmosphere. Good *maffés* and *thieboudiennes* (rice with fish – the Senegalese national dish).

Navel (map C2, **49**): 4 rue de Suez 75018. ☎ 01-42-62-47-78. Metro: Château-Rouge. Open to midnight. Closed Monday lunchtime. Set menus 59F and 85F, à la carte budget for no more than 120F. A nicely coloured setting for honest, inexpensive Indian cuisine. Do as the Indians do and accompany your meal with *lassi* (spiced, among others). A few favourite dishes are *kashmir* chicken (with exotic fruit), *madras* shrimps, *murg massala*, lamb with spinach, *rogan josh* and classic tandoori chicken.

✕ **Phuket's Anana** (map D1, **57**): 18 rue Tchaïkovski 75018. ☎ 01-42-05-67-60. Metro: Porte-de-la-Chapelle. Last orders 10.30pm. Closed Saturday lunchtime, Sunday and for a fortnight in August. Set menus 45F to 75F at lunchtime, 55F to 75F in the evening. In a rather unattractive modern complex. A family-run restaurant combining Chinese-Thai cuisine with Madagascan cuisine. A bit unusual, this double identity usually delights customers, who love to vary the menus. There are some Asian dishes, such as shrimp soup with lemon grass, mussels sautéed Thai style and Thai chicken curry. The whole of the Madagascan community meets here on Friday and Saturday evening for lively meals the way they would back home. Watercress and tomato meatballs, tuna *nems*, *sambos* (a sort of *samosa*), vegetable fritters, pork *ravintoto* (ragout of pork cooked with a sort of Madagascan spinach known as *brèdes*) and *romazava*.

✕ Over the last few years a number of **little 'grill' restaurants** run by Algerians cooking the food over bare embers have opened. For instance, at 11 rue des Poissonniers there's **Le Licite** (map C2, **53**), or at 51 rue Myrha there's **L'Étoile** (map C2, **54**), where you can find kebabs with salads and *chorba* (traditional soup). For those who will try anything once in an attempt to eat for next to nothing.

✕ **Hôtel-restaurant du Square** (map D2–3, **55**): 6 place de la Chapelle 75018 (at the end of the square which you see as you come out of the La Chapelle metro station). ☎ 01-46-07-69-74. Metro: La Chapelle. Closed Sunday evening. Last orders 10pm. Set menu 58F served lunchtime and evening. À la carte around 120F. Like a transport cafe in the heart of the city, but rather out of the way. A traditional working-class restaurant with a generous set menu, and good couscous from 46F to 75F. Only really if you're going that way . . . .

☆ CHEAP

✕ **Le Rendez-Vous des Chauffeurs** (map C2, **20**): 11 rue des Portes-Blanches 75018. ☎ 01-42-64-04-17. Metro: Marcadet-Poissonniers. Open noon to 2.30pm (3pm on Sunday) and in the evening until 11pm. Closed Wednesdays and on Thursdays in August. Set menu 65F served until 8.30pm. Otherwise à la carte meal for around 100F excluding drinks. This old café, with its long past, has had a face-lift. Jeannot took over the business on his return from the United States, where he lived for 20 years or so. As a memento of his past, he displays his diploma from *Wine Spectator* magazine from his days as a restaurateur in Seattle. But nothing has really changed: the fine wooden counter, the great mirrors, the tables crowded together and covered with checked oilcloths, the imitation leather wall seats ... it's all here, even the brownish colour of old-style cafés! The set menu, including drinks, brings in clients of all sorts. Come either early or late because it's a fairly small place. Just like in the old days, there's a starter such as celery *rémoulade* or egg mayonnaise, before one of the generous main courses from the daily-changing menu and crème caramel or pear tart to finish off. À la carte, there are main courses like *confit* of duck or *pot-au-feu* (around 65F), all washed down with good, inexpensive wines. The service is a little brusque (it's a bistro, basically!).

✕ **Au Port de Pidjiguiti** (map A2, **21**): 28 rue Étex 75018. ☎ 01-42-26-71-77. Metro: Guy-Môquet. Open to 11.30pm. Closed Monday. Set menus 45F and 50F at lunchtime, 100F lunchtime and evening. This restaurant actually belongs to an African village in Guinea-Bissau. The inhabitants make sure it runs properly and some of the profits go to the village co-operative. Service with a smile. You eat under colourful posters and photos showing social projects in the country. *Thieboudienne* on Wednesday and Saturday, *cachoupa* on Friday and Sunday, as well as the traditional *maffé and kande nasien*. A touch of nostalgia for anyone who knows Africa.

✕ **Nezbullon** (inset, **22**): 20 rue de la Vieuville 75018. ☎ 01-53-41-00-21. Metro: Abbesses. Open to 11pm. Closed Sundays and from 20 December to 10 January. Set main course and dessert 55F lunchtime and evening. Otherwise all main courses are 41F. Nestling in a bend in the street, alongside some hip punk shops, this place displays an insolent youth which is popular with its similarly inclined clientele. Try *tartiflette* (gratin potatoes, onions, bacon, fresh cream and Reblochon cheese – pretty pungent!) served with a mixed salad, as you sip a draught beer. Or go for the *Nez Givré* (literally 'Frozen Nose'!) cocktail (rum and vanilla ice-cream), before attacking a grilled steak with chips and salad.

✕ **Wassana** (map A2, **24**): 10 rue Ganneron 75018. ☎ 01-44-70-08-54. Metro: Place-de-Clichy. Open Monday to Saturday to 11pm, closed Saturday lunchtime. Set menus 65F, 85F and 130F served lunchtime only. In the evening, à la carte is 120F excluding drinks. Well hidden in a discreet street, a real Thai restaurant, with waiters in traditional dress. This place has built itself a good reputation over the years. Succulent Thai soups and admirably flavoured main courses. At lunchtime the first set menu gives amazing value for money.

✕ **La Farayade** (map B2, **26**): 10 rue Francœur 75018. ☎ 01-42-51-53-41. Metro: Lamarck-Caulaincourt or Jules-Joffrin. Open daily to 11pm. Closed Sunday and in August. Set menus 68F and 88F at lunchtime. In the evening budget for at least 150F. A little Lebanese restaurant run by a welcoming Lebanese gentleman. Don't come if you're stressed out and in a hurry. It may not be the best Lebanese cuisine in Paris, but the term 'local restaurant' takes on its full meaning here. At lunchtime have one of the fine platters of Eastern starters or a set menu (starter and main course, plus coffee or tea). There's a large choice à la carte, including specialities based on minced lamb and the traditional plates of *mezze*.

✕ **La Rughetta** (inset, **25**): 41 rue Lepic 75018. ☎ 01-42-23-41-70. Metro: Blanche or Abbesses. Open everyday until 11.30pm but you really must book in the evening because it's often packed out. Closed for three weeks in August and two weeks between Christmas and New Year. Set menu 109F lunchtime and evening, à la carte budget for around 150F. One of the best Italian restaurants in Montmartre in terms of value for money. They don't take advantage of the strategic location and the charming terrace which is heated (in winter) to send the prices through the roof! All sorts of pizzas, of course, but, above all, people come for the large choice of pasta, such as the famous *rigatoni al mascarpone* and *penne à la sicilienne*.

✕ **Pinar** (map B2, **27**): 50 rue de Clignancourt 75018. ☎ 01-42-54-06-20. Metro: Château-Rouge. Open daily except Sunday lunchtime. Set menu 55F, à la carte the bill should be no more than 100F. A little restaurant doing Kurdish and Turkish specialities in a simple setting, which is slightly kitsch but warm, and they've been welcoming regulars from the area for a number of years. Perfect for a quiet, almost provincial evening, away from all the hustle and bustle of Montmartre. Try some Kurdish dishes such as *tava* or *yogurtlu patlican kebab* or the *assiette Pinar*, an assortment of starters such as *taramasalata*, vine leaves, *houmous*, etc. There are a few Turkish wines such as Karmen or Buzbag.

✕ **Sonia** (map B1, **38**): 8 rue Letort 75018. ☎ 01-42-57-23-17. Metro: Jules-Joffrin. Open noon to 2.30pm and 7.30pm to 11.30pm. Closed Sunday lunchtime (open in summer). Set menus 49F and 79F at lunchtime, 99F in the evening. This little dining room (25 seats) is often full, but the welcome is warm and the dishes are tasty. Everything is subtly spiced and perfectly cooked. Nan, madras or vindaloo chicken, *shaki khorma* lamb or *baigan burtha* (Indian-style aubergine caviar).

✕ **Pathya** (map A1–2, **39**): 222 rue Championnet 75018. ☎ 01-42-28-98-68. Metro: Guy-Môquet. Open noon to 3pm and 7pm to midnight. Closed Tuesday. Budget for 50F per person, including drinks. This Chinese restaurant, on the ground floor of a modern building, is extremely popular locally. It's clean, you get a wonderful welcome and a series of interesting dishes (generous ravioli soup with shrimps and perfect dried beef with five spices) and the fast, polite service justify the good reputation.

✕ **Chez Paula (map B1, 40)**: 26 rue Letort 75018. ☎ 01-42-23-86-41. Metro: Porte-de-Clignancourt. Open to 10pm. Closed Saturday and Sunday and in July. There is a set menu 55F at lunchtime and 72F in the evening. À la carte, budget for 130F. A good little local restaurant, which has managed to seduce the local artistic-Bohemian clientele, who like to meet in groups here. Paella on Friday, *fondue bourguignonne* for two if you order it (150F) and grilled *gambas*, pepper steak and good value set menus (starter, main course and dessert).

✕ **Le Palais du Kashmir (map B1, 41)**: 77 rue du Poteau 75018. ☎ 01-42-59-40-86. Metro: Jules-Joffrin. Open daily and all year round to 11.30pm. Set menus 59F and 85F at lunchtime, 90F and 110F in the evening. Unexpectedly in this area, this is perhaps one of the best Indian restaurants in Paris. Also Pakistani cuisine. Don't be put off by the decor, oozing stucco with unlikely looking Doric columns, but allow yourself to be seduced by a delicious, varied cuisine. As a starter, try *pakoras* or *samosas* from the Punjab. Then try *mutton kashmir*, which is excellent, or *mutton shahi korma*. Avoid the wines and go for a house spiced tea (16F). You won't be disappointed.

✕ **La Chope de la Mairie** (map B2, **42**): 88 rue Ordener 75018. ☎ 01-46-06-46-14. Metro: Jules-Joffrin. Open to 10.30pm. Closed Sunday evening. Set meals 75F at lunchtime, 90F in the evening and set menus 90F at lunchtime and 100F in the evening. Dish of the day 50F. A nice little bar, full at lunchtime with butchers and other tradesmen from rue du Poteau, attracted by the set meal (starter and main course or main course and dessert). It offers a choice of around ten starters, six or seven main courses, and a few desserts. Basically it's imaginative family cuisine based on what's available at the market. Musical events at weekends.

✕ **Le Bistrot d'Asti** (map B2, **60**): 14 rue Duc 75018. ☎ 01-46-06-49-68. Metro: Jules-Joffrin. Last orders 10.30pm. Closed Sunday and Monday. Menu at 67F at lunchtime, 95F lunchtime and evening. You can book the restaurant for group meals. This little bistro doesn't look anything special, but behind the dilapidated shop window is a real local cafeteria and a piece of Italy. Delicious food (*crudités*, pasta salad, Italian *charcuterie*, fresh mackerel fillets). The locals dive into the traditional Franco-Italian dishes of the day.

✕ **La Prune d'Este, Restaurant Dellac** (map B1, **58**): 65 rue Letort 75018. ☎ 01-42-64-64-39. Metro: Porte-de-Clignancourt. Open lunchtimes and on Monday, Thursday and Friday evening, with last orders at 9.30pm. Closed Sunday and Bank Holidays. Set menu 65F. À la carte, budget for somewhere between 120F and 180F. Near the Porte de Clignancourt. There are a few specialities on the menu, such as *confit* of duck, beef casserole, or rabbit stewed in wine, but the thing which pulls in the crowds is the set menu served lunchtime and evening. You get a sort of anthology of working-class restaurant cuisine: 12 starters such as egg mayonnaise, *crudités* and rabbit terrine. and main courses which change daily but among which you'll find *cassoulet* and a fish dish on Friday. To end with, there are a dozen desserts including crème caramel, chocolate fondant and apple tart. Good value for money.

✕ **Le Blue's Bar** (map A1, **44**): 30 rue Vauvenargues 75018. ☎ 01-44-85-32-34. Metro: Guy-Môquet. Open to 2am. Closed Saturday lunchtime and Sunday and for three weeks in August. Set menus 62F (lunchtime only) and 89F. À la carte, budget for no more than 130F. Better in the evening. In a fairly quiet area, this is a quiet restaurant. Just 30 or so seats in an attractive arched cellar, where the owner has found a laid-back bar-restaurant formula. As for the restaurant, lunchtime and evening it serves a good set menu which changes regularly (starter, main course and dessert, with a choice of eight main courses, including wine). Occasionally there are a few African dishes. You can dine in a group around a large table. The bar has some specialist beers and whiskies with thirty-five bottled beers and four draught beers from 11F to 37F, and around 40 whiskies from 30F to 45F, as well as some good cocktails. Happy hour from 5pm to 8pm.

✕ **Fouta Toro** (map C2, **45**): 3 rue du Nord 75018. ☎ 01-42-55-42-73. Metro: Marcadet-Poissonniers. Open evenings only. Closed Tuesday. For a full meal, budget for up to 100F. A word of advice: the dining room is small and often full to bursting point. A specialized restaurant which will remind anyone who's ever been there of Africa. Others may find it a bit of a culture shock. They serve some of the best African cuisine in Paris, although the quality can sometimes be a little uneven. *Maffé, thieboudienne* and *yassa* at under 50F. There's a warm atmosphere.

☆☆ MODERATE

✕ **Le Soleil Gourmand** (inset, **28**): 10 rue Ravignan 75018. ☎ 01-42-51-00-50. Metro: Abesses. Open daily to 11pm (we advise you to book in the evening). Budget for around 120F without drinks. At the foot of Montmartre, the Soleil will seduce you with its goodies! Run by two gourmets, one front of house, the other in the kitchen. You can warm yourself in the sun while nibbling at the wonderful savoury tarts at 58F accompanied by fresh rocket or spinach shoots, or a plate of cheeses selected from a great

Parisian cheesemaker, or a southern-style dish made up of *antipasti*. The products have been perfectly chosen and you can see this in the tiniest details such as the bread and the coffee. Don't miss the ice-creams and sorbets (rose petal, almond milk or saffron-honey) from the Pic à Glace, which supplies many large restaurants. Wine by the glass at between 20F and 25F. The decor has a southern feel, with wrought-iron furniture. Elegant Montmartre clientele. Another original feature is that all the furniture is for sale!

✕ **Les Feuillades** (map B2, **32**): 6 rue de la Fontaine-du-But 75018. ☎ 01-46-06-13-40. Metro: Lamarck-Caulaincourt. Open evenings only to midnight. Closed 15 August. Set menu 120F. A quiet, tasteful restaurant with an immaculate white façade slightly away from the hustle and bustle of Montmartre and retaining a discreet charm. There is a little terrace for when the weather is fine. Traditional, simple, but inventive cuisine, as part of a single set menu (starter, main course, cheese or dessert). Dishes such as *confit* of duck, poached skate – nothing but classics. There is a reasonably priced wine list.

✕ **Piccola Strada** (inset, **59**): 6 rue Yvonne-Le-Tac 75018. ☎ 01-42-54-83-39. Metro: Abbesses. Open daily to midnight (we advise you to book in the evening). Set menu 75F at lunchtime, in the evening, à la carte, budget for around 120F. A little restaurant run by an Italian couple. People come here for the delicious pasta and *antipasti*. Among other things, try Trévise salad and *pancetta* or steamed vegetables and other pasta dishes. At lunchtime, the set menu is worth a go, with a starter, main course, dessert and bottle of wine included. À la carte, budget for 75F on average for a main course. The wines are good, but a bit expensive. A few French celebrities come here.

✕ **Le Jungle Montmartre** (inset, **62**): 32 rue Gabrielle 75018. ☎ 01-46-06-75-69. Metro: Abbesses. Open daily from 5pm to 2am. À la carte only, budget for 150F per person on average. Without a doubt the 'earthiest' restaurant-bar in Paris. Here there is no pretence, nothing superfluous, just the bare bones. Authentic African cuisine (fish *pastels*, *aloko*, poulet *yassa*, beef *maffé*, *thieboudienne*), real cocktails (*ti punch*, ginger punch, *bissap* juice, etc.), African music. Starters at around 30F, main courses from 65F. Check out the famous African beer, Flag (25F for a small glass).

✕ **Le Moulin à Vin** (inset, **29**): 6 rue Burq 75018. ☎ 01-42-52-81-27. Metro: Abbesses. Open to 2am. Closed Tuesday, Friday and Saturday lunchtime as well as Sunday and Monday and also for three weeks in August. No set menu, à la carte, budget for around 120F. This authentic wine bistro, located at the foot of Montmartre, gives its customers excellent bistro cuisine (*andouillette* from Duval's, Lyons pistachio sausage and plates of cold meats or cheeses). The main passion of the owner is wine. She lovingly selects the best from the wine producers of the Rhône, Corsica and elsewhere. Wines by the glass from 18F to 25F and bottles from 90F to 600F (for connoisseurs!) Dany, who has a number of strings to her bow, sometimes sings Édith Piaf songs.

✕ **La Galerie** (inset, **30**): 16 rue Tholozé 75018. ☎ 01-42-59-25-76. Metro: Abbesses. Open to 11.30pm. Closed Sunday, Monday lunchtime, Bank Holidays, at Christmas and for a fortnight in August. Set menus 75F and 89F at lunchtime, 145F and 195F in the evening. The charm and elegance of this place, combined with a delightfully light cuisine, have made this former art gallery into a fashionable restaurant among the Montmartre smart set. In a very Parisian atmosphere, there is something for everyone on the menu: *craquant* of shrimps, *mignon de porc* with honey and spices, blancmange with almond milk and orange zest. There is a good choice of wines.

✕ **Le Maquis** (map A–B2, **31**): 69 rue Caulaincourt 75018. ☎ 01-42-59-76-07. Metro: Lamarck-Caulaincourt. Open lunchtime and evening (except Sunday) to 10pm. Set menus 68F at lunchtime, 155F and 200F in the evening (apéritif and coffee included). À la carte (based on what's available at the market), budget for around 180F. Children's menu 45F. A tasteful spot with a few old photos on the wall and an old oak counter which add to the charm. There is a terrace in summer. A good set menu lunchtime – starter, generous dish of the day and a quarter bottle of wine (no dessert). Delicious *brandade* of cod, then poultry *jambonnette* or *magret* of duck with sweet and sour sauce, *tarte princesse aux poires*.

✕ **Le Restaurant** (inset, **34**): 32 rue Véron (corner of rue Audran) 75018. ☎ 01-42-23-06-22. Metro: Abbesses. Open to midnight. Closed Saturday lunchtime, Sunday and Monday lunchtime. Set menu 70F at lunchtime. In the evening there's a set menu at 120F. An inventive restaurant, run by a young owner originally from Cameroon. The simplicity of the scene contrasts with the warm decor (stone, a few dry bouquets, an old Parisian clock) and with the menu, which is full of rash names but is inspired by what's at the market, with a definite southwest tendency. Wine by the glass or at the bar (you only pay for what you drink).

✕ **L'Assiette** (map B2, **43**): 78 rue Labat 75018. ☎ 01-42-59-06-63. Metro: Château-Rouge or Marcadet-Poissonniers. Open noon to 2.30pm and 7.30pm to 10pm. Closed Sunday, Wednesday evening and Bank Holidays. Set menus 59F at lunchtime and 98F in the evening. Children's menu 50F. Budget for 130F à la carte. A real backpacker's heaven, with a brightly coloured façade. There's something good on the blackboard every day – mushroom omelette (58F), *foie gras* (86F) or *confit* of duck (82F). To end with try the chocolate charlotte (the house dessert at 30F). An authentic Périgord set menu for four people is available if ordered in advance and, once a month, also if you order in advance, there is a Ukrainian menu.

✕ **Marie-Louise** (map B1, **46**): 52 rue Championnet 75018. ☎ 01-46-06-86-55. Metro: Simplon. Open lunchtime and evening (last orders 10.30pm). Closed Sunday, Monday evening, public holidays, and for two weeks in February and three weeks in August. Set menu 130F lunchtime and evening. It's a good idea to book. There are maybe 10 restaurants like this left in the whole of Paris. When you come in you could be forgiven for thinking that you'd walked into a middle-class dining room, very 'Old France', where the brass gleams like new. Their clientele is faithful and fairly elderly at Saturday lunchtime. The chef sometimes comes out to say hello to customers he knows. Old-style traditional cuisine: wild rabbit stewed in wine (in season), *coq au vin* (95F), rib of veal (95F), beef *ficelle* for two (190F). Basically, there's a large choice on an attractive menu. Wine by the glass (30F) or bottles from 90F.

☆☆☆ CHIC

✕ **Taka** (inset, **35**): 1 rue Véron 75018. ☎ 01-42-23-74-16. Metro: Pigalle or Abbesses. Open evenings only 7.30pm to 10.15pm. Closed Sunday and Bank Holidays and for the last two weeks in July and August. Set menus 120F and 150F, à la carte budget for 160F with a Japanese beer. A tiny Japanese restaurant at the foot of Montmartre. Often packed out, but if you book you'll be OK. Authentic cuisine perfectly done and always of high quality. You'll find all the great classics loved by connoisseurs: *sushi*, *sashimi* and kebabs. It looks like a Japanese tea house and has an attractive façade.

✕ **Le Petit Robert** (inset, **36**): 10 rue Cauchois 75018. ☎ 01-46-06-04-46. Metro: Blanche. Open evenings only to midnight. Closed Sundays, Mondays and from 20 July to 25 August, as well as in August. Single menu 150F. The whole of gay Paris knows this place. But you don't have to be gay to come here, it's a good Parisian restaurant very close to Montmartre. The set menu is often changed, in tune with the seasons, the market and the owner's mood, with a predilection for southwestern specialities.

✕ **La Mazurka** (map B2, **37**): 3 rue André-del-Sarte 75018. ☎ 01-42-23-36-45. Metro: Château-Rouge or Anvers. Open in the evening to 11.45pm and at lunchtime if you book. Closed Wednesday. Set menus 115, 150 and 180F served lunchtime and evening. À la carte between 150F and 200F. Marek, a Polish citizen, laid his hat and his guitar at the foot of Montmartre a good 10 years ago in this slightly inexpensive-looking but warm setting. He also brought lots of good recipes, such as flambéed sausages, *pierogis* (a type of ravioli), gypsy-style pork ribs, *bigos* (local sauerkraut), beef Strogonoff, *borscht* (beetroot, cabbage and cream soup) and all sorts of *blinis, taramasalata,* eel or smoked salmon. A 25cl jug of vodka costs 130F or 140F. When Marek is in form, he gets out his guitar and sings. You could almost believe that you were in Warsaw or Gdansk, and when the peppered vodka starts to flow, the atmosphere swings – or not. Take a chance.

✕ **Le Cottage Marcadet** (map B2, **48**): 151 *bis*, rue Marcadet 75018. ☎ 01-42-57-71-22. Metro: Lamarck-Caulaincourt. Closed Sunday and in August. Gastronomic menu 210F, including wine. Set meals 120F and 155F. Right in the heart of the 18th arrondissement, here is a little 18th-century salon displaying all the trappings of the culture of the 16th arrondissement. It's in a little old shop, with soberly renovated decor, a few fine paintings on the walls and comfortable old chairs. You'll need to book, of course. The welcome is a little stiff but don't be put off. Sit down, make yourself at home and order from the menu: a starter (such as terrine of pike), a main course (fried perch or *magret* of duck), then salad or a plate of cheeses, and finally dessert (such as *crème brûlée* or gratin of figs). Excellent cuisine at reasonable prices, since the wine is included in the price of the set menu.

WINE BAR

✕ 🍷 **Aux Négociants** (map B2, **56**): 27 rue Lambert 75018. ☎ 01-46-06-15-11. Metro: Château-Rouge or Lamarck-Caulaincourt. Open lunchtime Monday to Friday, and in the evening to 10.30pm Tuesday, Wednesday and Thursday. Closed Saturday, Sunday and public holidays, as well as in August. Budget for around 120F without drinks. Robert Doisneau (the famous photographer who captured *The Kiss*), who you can see in a few photos hung on the walls, used to really like this wine bar, which is still right on form both in the choice of light wines and the honesty of its cooking. Even though he's been here for 20 years, the boss, a former butcher, hasn't forgotten his peasant past – which can make him look a little rugged sometimes! He makes his generous terrines and black sausage himself, chooses his meat with care, has fat ducks brought from the Tarn and checks out vineyards whenever he gets a chance – for example Côte Roannaise, Coteaux du Vendômois, Pinot d'Aunis, Vouvray or Montlouis. Wines by the glass, by the bottle or, according to a dying tradition, at the bar.

MONTMARTRE

A BRIEF HISTORY

St Denis, the Bishop of Paris, had his head cut off on 'la Butte' (the hillock or mound – the affectionate name Parisians use for the hill of Montmartre), and thus it took the Latin name of *Mons Martyrum*, which later became Montmartre. It's interesting to note that St Denis didn't actually like la Butte, and left with his head under his arm to be buried somewhere else (in a cold, grey suburb, later to be called St Denis).

The future Henri IV did like Montmartre however. When he laid siege to Paris, he set up his headquarters at the abbey. The *Vert Galant* (Green Beau), as Henri is known in France, lived up to his reputation as he was on the best of terms with the Mother Superior. The abbey disappeared in the Revolution and its last Mother Superior, who was very elderly, deaf and blind, was nonetheless condemned to the scaffold after Fouquier-Tinville had accused her of 'having plotted against the Republic'!

At the beginning of the 19th century the hill of Montmartre was covered with orchards, vines, little thatched cottages and around 40 windmills (*moulins*). The commune of Montmartre, created during the Revolution, had 638 inhabitants, mostly millers and quarry workers working the gypsum deposits. Gypsum mining (to make plaster) was one of la Butte's main industries; the name place Blanche (which means White Square) reflects the orignal activity of this area. The rural charm of Montmartre was such that people soon began to flock there. One of the consequences of Haussmann's great projects was that crowds of workers and their families, evicted from the city centre, began moving to Montmartre. The rents were less expensive and the wine was not subject to the duty on goods entering the city. On the whole it was a pleasant place to live.

Like the communes of Passy, Montrouge, Vaugirard and Charonne, Montmartre was annexed by Paris in 1860.

Montmartre and the Paris Commune

Parisians were angered when the armistice between France and Prussia, with all its attendant humiliations, was signed on 28 January 1871. The National Assembly, which had taken refuge in Bordeaux and which had a conservative majority, wanted to punish the rebellious capital and so withheld the National Guards' wages. At the same time the Prussians entered Paris and the exasperation of the Parisians was pushed to the limit. This was the context in which Thiers launched a coup by trying to capture the 170 cannons placed on the hill of Montmartre. The local people refused to give them up and the soldiers entrusted with the mission ended up taking the locals' side and arrested their officers. Thiers and the middle-classes fled to Versailles. The central committee of the National Guard organized municipal elections and, on 28 March, an elected council took office at the Hôtel de Ville and adopted the name of the 'Paris Commune'.

The Montmartre of poets, artists, criminals and tourists

For a long time Montmartre remained a real village. Painters, sculptors and poets made it their home towards the end of the 19th century and up until the Great War. Renoir lived in Montmartre and painted it a great deal. Utrillo also managed to render the poetic and melancholic character of its streets and squares in his canvases.

This was also the age of the Bateau-Lavoir, an artists' colony in a great, rickety baroque building, clinging to la Butte, which witnessed the work of so many famous people: Max Jacob, Charles Dullin, Mac Orlan, Harry Baur, Matisse, Braque, Apollinaire and dozens of others. In 1907 Picasso painted what was to become one of his most famous works, marking the birth of Cubism: *Les Demoiselles d'Avignon*.

In the lower part of Montmartre it was one big party. This was the peak of the career of the Moulin Rouge, which opened its doors in 1889, where Parisians rushed to applaud Yvette Guilbert, Jane Avril, Valentin le Désossé, Nini Patte en l'Air or la Goulue. They were immortalized by Toulouse-Lautrec, another adopted *Montmartrois*.

After the First World War, the artists emigrated to Montparnasse. Montmartre then began to fall into the hands of the developers, allowing itself to be concreted over and the *nouveau-riches* moved in. Pigalle and Blanche became an unlikely melting-pot of criminals, prostitutes and scores of pimps and shady characters, mixing with middle-class Parisians and tourists out for a good time.

Utrillo, a boy from la Butte

Of all the painters who have worked in Montmartre, Maurice Utrillo is the only one who was born there (in 1883). His mother, Marie-Clémentine Valadon, was a dressmaker, but also an artist's model. She posed for Berthe Morisot, for Renoir (in *Danse à la ville*), Puvis de Chavannes, and was transformed into a horsewoman for Toulouse-Lautrec. She was also a painter herself, under the name of Suzanne Valadon, and Degas liked her work. Little Maurice was brought up by his grandmother, who often added red wine to his soup to get him to sleep more quickly. This was probably the origin of his alcoholism. At school he moved on to absinthe and soon began to have attacks. The doctors advised his mother to get him interested in painting to keep him away from alcohol. He moved into 12 rue Cortot, and from the age of 15 he painted Montmartre in all its glory. He didn't miss a thing: flights of steps, secret gardens, white façades, all expressed in thousands of brushstrokes. With his mother and her lover, André Utter, he moved into 5 impasse de Guelma (where Braque used to work), then back to 12 rue Cortot (the musician Eric Satie lived at No. 6 in the same street from 1890 to 1898). The relationship between the three of them was somewhat stormy. A neighbour who was also an artist recounted how one day Utrillo threw an iron which crashed through his glass roof, just missing his head.

Utrillo was often held at Montmartre police station, where he was freed in return for a few canvases or drawings. He also left works of art to pay for his slates in the bars. At La Belle Gabrielle in rue St-Vincent (which has now disappeared), the owner, with whom Utrillo was in love, made him clean off all the landscapes he had painted on the walls of the toilet. She was later to regret her decision! After the First World War, Utrillo felt very isolated – all the artists had left for Montparnasse and his friend Modigliani was dead. He divided his time between his new house in the artists' village (11 avenue Junot) and the psychiatric asylum. His mother never stopped trying to protect him. Aged 50, he found a child's catechism on the ground and had himself baptized, then got married. His wife tried to cure his alcoholism and took him to the suburbs, far away from Montmartre. He returned shortly before his death (in 1955) to play himself in *Si Paris m'était conté* by Sacha Guitry. He is at rest in the Cimetière St-Vincent. Nowadays his paintings fetch astronomical sums at auction.

MONTMARTRE TODAY

There are still some of the original inhabitants and craftsmen here, but the small businesses are dying out and being replaced by the more fashionable professions. The advertising agencies, stylists, architects and photographers are taking over, though they are people whose way of life is basically in the vaguely bohemian and libertarian tradition of Montmartre.

There is still a free commune of Montmartre which organizes many parties and events and even has a 'mayor'. As the people of Montmartre have a sense of solidarity (and humour), they have also set up a philanthropic society called the 'Republic of Montmartre'. Poulbot, the father of the famous Montmartre *gamins*, was one of the presidents of this republic. All these traditions keep a real local life going, and it hasn't yet been swamped by the tourist invasion.

Pigalle may be dying slowly from its decades of swindling and changes in the Parisian attitudes to 'forbidden pleasures', place du Tertre may have almost completely sold out to mass tourism, but Montmartre still attracts people from all over the world. Once you get off the beaten track, Montmartre still has some charming corners for walkers and the curious, but its steep staircases may discourage the lazy! Houses showing their age, crumbling walls covered in ivy, paths and wild gardens, sometimes lined with cherry trees – any of these can surprise you at any moment.

Rue d'Orchampt is under threat from concrete!

This little paved street, almost a cul-de-sac, with its courtyards and its flowering interior gardens, has managed to hang onto its provincial charm. Listing this delightful street still haunted by the souls of the artists would save it from concrete forever.

USEFUL ADDRESS

🅸 Syndicat d'initiative du Vieux-Montmartre: 21 place du Tertre 75018. ☎ 01-42-62-21-21. Metro: Abbesses. Open daily 10am to 10pm. The only arrondissement union in Paris, in a building which has just been renovated. Offers a historical and cultural guided tour of Montmartre (minimum 15 people). Duration: 2 hours.

LEISURE AND CULTURE

– **'Un village dans Paris: Montmartre' (Montmartre: a village in Paris):** 18 place des Abbesses or 4 rue Burq 75018. ☎ 01-42-54-45-21. Fax: 01-42-23-76-69. An association of lovers of Montmartre. Every year they publish a practical guide to Montmartre with a brief history, a map, and useful addresses. Available from Metro stations in summer, from the Paris Tourist Office and some shops on la Butte.
Every year (from mid-June to the beginning of July) the association also organizes the **Jazz in Montmartre** festival. Plenty of jam sessions, concerts in various venues around Montmartre, jazz and cinema evenings.

WHAT TO SEE

Don't try and drive to Montmartre. Some people still try to take their cars up as far as place du Tertre; they may as well try getting there by helicopter. You'll only spend hours trying to find somewhere to park and you'll end up on a pavement somewhere, which will annoy the pedestrians.

There is a brand new funicular from place Suzanne-Valadon (Metro: Anvers) for those of you who don't fancy the flights of steps leading up la Butte, or take the Montmartrobus, which is very practical. It goes all over Montmartre from Pigalle to Jules-Joffrin, travelling through all the interesting streets (from 8am to 8pm). This may also seem obvious, but high heels are really not a good idea here as the majority of the streets are cobbled.

★ **Sacré-Cœur:** you can hardly miss the enormous building which has pride of place on la Butte. This basilica is the result of a 'national vow' made by the Catholic Church to expiate the crimes of the Paris Commune. To savour their revenge, the Catholic hierarchy proposed that this 'national temple' be built high up in Montmartre. There was a symbolic value too, as it was to be built on the exact site of the beginning of the Commune. Obviously there was considerable resistance to the plans, passed by the National Assembly in 1873, from the radical MPs to the greens of the day, who denounced the destruction of the Montmartre site and the building's lack of aesthetic appeal. The winner of the tender for the design, Paul Abadie, who was the most conservative and pompous of the architects of the time, chose a Byzantine style. The construction work lasted from 1875 to 1914. When it opened, at the end of the 19th century, Willette, a famous local painter, went along with his friends to yell: 'Long live the Devil!' Émile Zola considered Sacré-Cœur a 'chalky mass, overwhelming, dominating the Paris which gave us the Revolution'.

The basilica was built with stone from Château-Landon (to the southeast of Paris) which, when it rains, secretes a white limy substance which looks like paint. The more it rains, the whiter Sacré-Cœur becomes.

It is worth going up into the *cupola* (you have to pay and there are 237 steep, narrow steps). Entry is through the left-hand side of the church, on the outside. Open 9am to 6pm and until 7pm in summer. There is a wonderful panorama which allows you to look out over the lovely gardens which are usually hidden by high walls, the old cemetery and the fine chevet (apse) of St-Pierre.

It's hard to believe that for the last 110 years, men and women have been praying around the clock in shifts to expiate the sins of humanity. There are even beds so that they can rest between shifts!

★ The **église St-Pierre de Montmartre:** at the intersection of rue St-Éleuthère and rue du Mont-Cenis. Along with St-Germain-des-Prés, this is the oldest (1134), and one of the most attractive churches in Paris and the only remnant of the abbey of Montmartre. Some parts are 12th century, others 15th (the nave) and 17th century. It was built on the site of a Gallo-Roman temple, two of whose columns still decorate the entrance on the inside. For many years the church supported a semaphore signalling station, which made it possible to transmit news of Napoleon's victories from Strasbourg in 6 minutes and from Lille in 2 minutes.

The church deteriorated so much over the 19th century that the ecclesiastical authorities were contemplating demolishing it, especially as it was already looking so shabby alongside the marvel being built on la Butte! Every artist and anti-clerical person in Montmartre was mobilized. They plied the local socialist councillor with such a fine meal and put up such a good argument that they convinced him to defend the cause of the restoration of the church at the municipal council. He must have been effective because he managed to get them to vote in favour of its reconstruction. It was no small paradox, at the time, to see all the atheists become the fiercest defenders of a church, even if it was only to oppose the Catholic hierarchy!

★ The **cimetière du Calvaire:** next to the church is the old cemetery, which dates from the Merovingian period, and can be glimpsed through the heavy bronze gate. It is as romantic and as moving as you could wish for, but you have to wait until 1 November to visit it (it only opens for one day a year, from 8am to 6pm). It is no longer the smallest cemetery in Paris, but it must surely be the most secret. The tomb of the navigator Bougainville is here but that of the sculptor, Pigalle, disappeared during the Revolution. The famous place du Tertre is located in front of the church.

★ The **place du Tertre:** dates back to the 14th century. At Nos. 1, 3 and 9 there are some fine 18th-century houses. The first Montmartre town hall (1790) stood at No. 5. In the morning, at sunrise, it's like crossing a village square. In the evening, there's the rush to the Metro at 6pm. To say that it is popular with tourists is an understatement. You're swamped by people selling poor quality paintings, artists drawing portraits in pencil (two artists per square metre, according to the regulations!), expensive bistros etc., so much so that nowadays the tourists themselves have become a tourist attraction. However, some people like the lively atmosphere, the colours, the lights . . . though some regret that it's all a bit unnatural. It's worth noting that the area has not really changed much in 60 years. Paul Yaki described it: 'there was always a jolly atmosphere on summer evenings, crazy little girls and rich men on the make . . . They'd all noisily admire the faces drawn by the lightning sketchers who had been attracted to this area, like moths to a flame . . . They were followed by people selling faded flowers, tone deaf singers, fiddlers always playing the same tune . . . It was the triumph of bistrocracy!' So, no change there then!

★ The **musée du Vieux-Montmartre:** 12 rue Cortot 75018. ☎ 01-46-06-61-11. Metro: Lamarck-Caulaincourt. Open 11am to 5.30pm. Closed Monday. One of the liveliest museums in Paris. The museum is situated in the fine house owned by Claude de La Rose (known as Rosimond), the actor who replaced Molière as the head of Molière's company and who mimicked him even to the extent of dying on stage just like his predecessor. Rosimond, as an actor, was not entitled to a religious funeral, but thanks to an understanding priest, they managed to bury him at night in a grave for babies who had died before they were baptized.

There is also a very attractive courtyard garden. In 1875 Auguste Renoir rented a part of this rather decrepit country house and painted many of his masterpieces here, the most famous of which is *Le Bal du Moulin de la Galette*, which can be seen at the Musée d'Orsay. Suzanne Valadon and her son Utrillo lived in the studio on the 2nd floor.

There is a permanent, old local bistro bar, fully equipped, a reconstruction of the study of the composer Gustave Charpentier at 66 boulevard Rochechouart, and a great model of Montmartre. The remarkable *Parce Domine* by Willette, a particularly metaphorical work which was once used in Rodolphe Salès' cabaret *Le Chat Noir*, is also here. Historic souvenirs of Montmartre are presented in temporary exhibitions, as well as its cultural life over the ages. There are many testimonies to the rich life of the old cabarets, and earthy, original posters.

★ The **espace Montmartre-Dalí:** 11 rue Poulbot 75018 (just off place du Tertre). ☎ 01-42-64-40-10. Metro: Anvers or Abbesses. Open daily 10am to 6pm. Dalí fans will want to check out this place, which is particularly unusual as it is dug right into la Butte. Dalí was part of the Montmartre intellectual and political set with, among others, Tzara, Picabia and Breton. People associate Montmartre with Dalí's first exhibition in Paris, presented by André Breton in 1929. In 1956, under the amazed eyes of the tourists in place du Tertre, he painted his famous *Don Quixote* using a rhinoceros horn as a paintbrush. Thanks to some very clever special effects, his works are beautifully displayed, especially the sculptures, lithographs and silk-screen prints. They include the famous *Cabinet anthropomorphique, Les Montres molles* and *L'Éléphant spatial*. There's also an interesting series illustrating works such as Boccaccio's *Decameron*, and Ovid's *The Art of Love*.

★ The **halle St-Pierre:** 2 rue Ronsard 75018. ☎ 01-42-58-72-89. Website: www.hallesaintpierre.org. Metro: Anvers or Abbesses. Open daily 10am to 6pm. At the foot of Sacré-Cœur and opposite the St-Pierre market, the former Halles St-Pierre have superb 19th-century wrought iron architecture. They house temporary exhibitions designed around popular, primitive, naïve and unusual art, as well as the **musée d'Art naïf Max-Fourny**, a contemporary art gallery and auditorium. In the Halle St-Pierre you will also find a bookshop specializing in primitive art, naïve art and childhood, and a tearoom/restaurant. There are games and workshops for children.

A ROMANTIC TOUR

As we've already mentioned, to get around Montmartre the best way is on foot. This tour is designed to avoid cars and tourists as much as possible, without returning to place du Tertre.

★ Take rue **Ste-Rustique**, an oasis of peace and quiet only 20m (65ft) from place du Tertre. It is the oldest street in Montmartre, with no pavements, large cobblestones, a stream down the centre and lined with pretty provincial houses.

★ **Rue des Saules**, meaning 'Willow Street', is next. Go on towards the little pink bridge which, as it gets wider, becomes a lovely little country inn. Next up is the 'Château des Brouillards' (Castle of the Mists). Let yourself be sidetracked by **rue de l'Abreuvoir**, between a row of flower-covered village houses and a wild park. In the great curve and depression formed by the end of the street you can glimpse the former watering place for horses. A few paces further on, at No. 22, is the house of the poet Aristide Bruant, and its garden, nicknamed *le vélodrome* (cycle track), which he used to cycle around.

★ The **allée des Brouillards** is very narrow, with steps, a stone balustrade and houses groaning under the weight of ivy. Behind the high walls there are many secret gardens, and the area is still quite charming. Renoir occupied a house at No. 8 in the allée for a while. In March 1997 the little square located on the corner of rue Girardon and the allée des Brouillards was renamed place Dalida and a bust was installed to commemorate the popular French singer. She lived close-by in rue d'Orchamps.

★ In a couple of strides you'll reach **square Suzanne-Buisson**. Art-deco style, terraced and very romantic in the evening, by the light of the street lamps, it is lined with a few houses and a fountain in the middle. Exit in avenue Junot.

★ **Avenue Junot:** the Champs Élysées of Montmartre. The most expensive houses in the area are here and you're never likely to meet too many people. Built across the *maquis* (dense scrubland) in 1910, the avenue is unusually wide, scattered with trees and covered with wooden shacks and huts. Poulbot and many painters lived here. It was like living in the countryside without leaving Paris, with market gardens, poultry and goats (the musée de Montmartre devotes a few showcases to it). Today, there are some fine examples of modern architecture and 1920s art-deco.

★ On la Butte, the last survivor of the great windmills of Montmartre, the **Moulin de la Galette** (corner of rue Girardon and rue Lepic) was built in 1640. Its owners, four brothers, defended it to the bitter end against the Russians in 1814 (one of them was crucified on the sails of the windmill). At the end of the 19th century it became the setting for a famous popular dance hall, immortalized by Renoir. Toulouse-Lautrec used to come here to drink a bowl of hot wine flavoured with cinnamon and chat with the local ne'er do wells.

★ At 11 avenue Junot, in the **hameau des Artistes**, there are large houses and workshops hiding behind the dreamy gardens (no picnicking, it's private property!). A last flight of steps leads to rue Lepic, where Poulbot lived at No. 13.

At No. 23 there is another passageway to 65 rue Lepic. More lanes, more gardens, more nocturnal mystery. The 20 or so trees are the last vestige of the Bois de Montmartre. Even they almost disappeared, victims of a thoughtless plan to build a car park. But the resolute resistance of the local residents and the support of the local people stopped the developers and the local authorities. As Jacques Fabbri, one of the defenders of green spaces, said: 'You feel a bit silly fighting to save a few trees, but we're fighting to save life itself!'

Retrace your steps to the **villa Léandre** which you can get to through 23 *bis* avenue Junot. Plush, green and incredibly peaceful, this villa appears to defy time itself. Max Ernst lived there for a while and there have always been lots of celebrities living in avenue Junot: from the singer Claude Nougaro to actors Jean Marais and Anouk Aimée.

★ Opposite the villa Léandre, take rue Simon-Dereure and enjoy the pleasure of heading back through the allée des Brouillards, then rue Girardon on the left until you reach **rue St-Vincent**, one of the most picturesque in Montmartre, about which poets such as Aristide Bruant have written. It's bordered on one side by the modest **cimetière St-Vincent** (where Utrillo and the writer Marcel Aymé are buried) and on the other by a raised walkway with an iron handrail. Aristide Bruant lived at No. 30. There is a little wood which was planted in 1985. A sign at the entrance reads: 'Don't be surprised by the way this garden looks. Since 1985, we have allowed the plant-life to evolve naturally.' Open Monday and Saturday afternoons only.

The crossroads of rue St-Vincent and rue des Saules is one of the most charming places in Montmartre. The last **vines** on la Butte run down the hill from here. For many years they covered it entirely and produced a wine known as 'Picolo' (which gave the French language the verb *picoler* – to booze). Gamay is the grape variety grown. During the first fortnight in October (generally the first Sunday), they have a party to celebrate the grape harvest. Anatole, the *garde champêtre* (a local policeman) of the free commune of Montmartre, is there, naturally, to make sure everything goes off all right. It's always a really friendly party. At least 300 litres are harvested, and a few hundred bottles of Clos-Montmartre are sold at auction, with the profits going to the elderly of Montmartre. The party ends with a highly colourful parade put on by the various local clubs and societies. The commune, which ages the wine in the town hall cellars, also sells it.

★ The **cabaret Au Lapin Agile:** 22 rue des Saules 75018. ☎ 01-46-06-85-87. Metro: Lamarck-Caulaincourt. A Montmartre institution. It became a cabaret in 1860 under the name *Cabaret des Assassins*. In 1880 the painter André Gill decorated the façade with the famous rabbit jumping out of his cooking pot. At the end of the 19th century it became a restaurant which hosted concerts, initiating the *à la bonne franquette* (informal meal) style. Alphonse Allais, Verlaine, Clemenceau, Renoir and Courteline all came here. Aristide Bruant bought the house in 1903 to prevent it from being demolished and entrusted it to an old gentleman called Frédé, a comic and artist fond of the good things in life, who made the cabaret into the most famous meeting place for the bohemians of Montmartre.

In the meantime, there had been a play on words with the name. The restaurant had become the *lapin à Gill* (André Gill's rabbit) and then *lapin agile* (the agile rabbit). This was where the most famous hoax of the period took place: the perpetrators, Roland Dorgelès, Mac Orlan and Co., got a donkey to paint a canvas using its tail, then exhibited the result at the Salon des Indépendants as an example of the 'excessiviste' trend. Apparently the reviews were mixed! The work of art, entitled *Et le Soleil se coucha sur l'Adriatique*, was even bought for 500F by a collector. The intellectuals of the day were utterly scandalized and there was much amusement in Montmartre. *Le Lapin Agile* had some other famous customers: Picasso, who one day paid for his meals with one of his *Harlequins* (now worth millions!), Francis Carco, Apollinaire, Blaise Cendrars, Max Jacob, Willette, Poulbot – to name but a few. Nowadays it houses the academy of the French *Chanson* (song).

★ After rue St-Vincent, turn right into **rue du Mont-Cenis**, which for a long time was the only way to get to the north of Montmartre. It connected the abbey of Montmartre to the abbey of St-Denis. Berlioz lived at No.22, then a country house, from 1834 to 1836.

★ After passing the huge water tower, rejoin **rue du Chevalier-de-La-Barre**. As you go past salute the brave Jean-François Lefèvre, Chevalier de La Barre, a freethinker and victim of intolerance, whose tongue was cut out before he was beheaded for having refused to salute a religious procession. The street named after him takes a fairly anarchic route. It begins as a street, becomes a flight of steps, and then, where it crosses rue Paul-Albert, it becomes a pedestrian precinct. At night this crossroads, in the pale halo of the street lamps, is one of the most romantic corners of Montmartre. To go back down choose between the rather short passage Cottin or rue du Chevalier, wide and quiet, which reaches rue Ramey. You can also take a short cut by way of rue Paul-Albert.

★ Next cross the gardens of Sacré-Cœur to reach rue Gabrielle; then, further along on the right, is the Escalier du Calvaire. The little **place du Calvaire** is quite charming. A tip: the best place to watch fireworks on Bastille Day or some other event is to the right of the square.

★ **Rue Poulbot:** formerly known as the 'Impasse Traînée', this was a lane as early as the 14th century, wandering and rural. It bears the name of the famous creator of the 'Montmartre urchin' who adorns the walls of so many houses around the world.

★ Go down **rue Norvins** for a short way. At No. 22 you can still see *La Folie Sandrin*, the former lunatic asylum where the writer Gérard de Nerval was treated. On the corner of rue Ravignan, slightly hidden, there is a fountain built in 1835 with an attractive Renaissance façade.

★ **Place Jean-Baptiste-Clément:** named after the former Mayor of Montmartre during the Paris Commune and the composer of one of the loveliest of French songs, *Le Temps des cerises*. Predictably he was paid only 14F for writing this classic French favourite. More than 10 years after the massacres perpetrated by the people of Versailles, this was the tune which made the French people take heart again. For all those years the Commune had been completely surpressed by the authorities, but nobody was fooled. Behind this apparently innocent song everyone could recognize, in the image of the *cerises* (cherries), the allusion to the Red flag and to a rebirth of hope. A cherry tree was planted in the middle of the square to commemorate the song.

★ The small, narrow **rue de la Mire** is a reminder that the Paris meridian passes just near here. Take this street to rejoin rue Ravignan. Below the latter is **place Émile-Goudeau**, one of the most charming squares in Montmartre. At No. 13 is the famous **Bateau-Lavoir** where so many artists stayed. Unfortunately, it had barely been listed when it burned down a few years ago. Now it has been replaced by modern workshops with no great charm, although they have respected the original architecture: one floor overlooking the square and three overlooking a pretty outdoor garden, in rue Garreau. A little shop, next door, tells the story of the Bateau-Lavoir.

One of the first tenants was one Pablo Ruiz Blasco, later known as Picasso. His studio was a real mess and he never changed. Rich and happy at the end of his life, he continued to refer to 'my sort of rubbish bin' when talking about his sumptuous villa. It was at the Bateau-Lavoir that Picasso painted the famous *Demoiselles d'Avignon* who were neither *demoiselles* (single young ladies), nor from Avignon, as actually the artist really wanted to portray the prostitutes of the Barrio Chino in Barcelona. Picasso destroyed traditional forms and shook up the normal techniques to such a point that even his friends thought it was a joke. Among other famous tenants have been Van Dongen, André Salmon, Pierre Mac Orlan, Max Jacob and Juan Gris.

★ The little **rue d'Orchampt**, which is quiet, peaceful and very provincial, was Dalida's private residence. After place Émile-Goudeau, turn right into rue Garreau to rejoin rue Durantin.

★ In **rue Durantin** many artists work in the shops on the street, which means you can watch them at work.

★ The **Villa des Fusains** ends this tour with a flourish. In the extension to rue Durantin, at 22 rue Tourlaque, you'll find the bucolic Villa des Fusains. The façade has false half-timbering and a fine earthenware inscription. Inside, the buildings, drowning in greenery, are former pavilions from the Universal Exhibition of 1889. There are statues strewn around the aisles. Renoir worked here for a while. It is a rather strange, timeless place. Ten years or so later Toulouse-Lautrec lived at No. 7, in a building occupied by artists whose workshops you can still glimpse on the upper floors.

★ **Rue Lepic:** leaves place Blanche and climbs the contour of the hill. Van Gogh lived at No. 56 and Jean-Baptiste Clément (mentioned earlier) at No. 112. At the bottom of the street, between place Blanche and rue des Abbesses, there is a lively market. After your shopping go for a drink at the Lux Bar, at No. 12, which has a superb tiled wall decoration dating from 1910 representing the Moulin-Rouge. Almost opposite, at No. 9, is the tradesmen's entrance of the Moulin-Rouge Palace. At No. 16 passage Lepic starts, lined with lovely houses with hidden gardens. A little further up, **place des Abbesses** has one of the last Guimard-style metro stations, with a glass roof.

★ **Place Blanche** owes its name to the carts which used to transport plaster from the quarries of Montmartre to the construction sites of Paris and which, day in and day out, sprinkled the houses with white.

★ At 65 boulevard de Clichy there is a building housing the little **chapelle Ste-Rita** which is very popular with prostitutes (St Rita is their patron saint) and was also popular with Henry Miller. There is a curious banister in the shape of a snake and the stairwell is decorated in Belle-Époque style.

★ There are a few discreet developments over towards la Butte. Opposite Ste-Rita, at 94 boulevard de Clichy, stands the **cité Véron** with its wrought-iron sign, lined with houses, little gardens and workshops. The poet Jacques Prévert and the writer Boris Vian lived here.

★ At Nos. 58–60 stands the **villa des Platanes**, an unusual courtyard (with a keypad lock), preceded by a monumental porch in surreal baroque, with sculpted wood columns and ceiling. Right at the end there are two luxury houses with entrances framed by columns and sculpted pediments, preceded by horseshoe-shaped flights of steps.

★ **Rue André-Antoine** (formerly rue Élysée-des-Beaux-Arts) turns after passing in front of the wrought-iron gate of a fine house, and ends in steps. Fairly rough at night, you'll find an odd little social mix made up of old drag queens, alcoholics, pickpockets from the metro and petty thieves. **Rue Véron** houses, for the moment, at least, a local population, made up of retired people, a few workers and immigrants.

★ **Pigalle:** this area has a bad reputation; however, it bears the name of a great 18th-century sculptor and has many fine buildings: namely the Napoleon I private residences in avenue Frochot, in avenue Trudaine and its square. Be aware that there are still quite a few petty criminals around, such as pickpockets, but since a series of shootings in 1980 to 1982, the real criminals have become rare. The boulevard de Clichy and boulevard de Rochechouart are lined with a never-ending corridor of sex shops, 'topless cabarets', 'sexodromes', '*lingerie folies*', 'bedsits with all mod cons at the end of the passage' and porn clubs.

If the pleasure here is fake, the poverty is authentic: people take drugs and get drunk so as not to think about tomorrow; women become prostitutes and beg to pay the rent. This motley crew meets in the various cafés along boulevard de Clichy: La Nuit, Le Chat Noir and especially Aux Noctambules (Metro: Pigalle).

In December, and often in June, a fair is set up on boulevard Rochechouart. It's quite a show in itself. Full of lights and colours, with some attractions which are as old as the hills: the snake woman, the fat lady, the sordid little stripteases in unheated shacks . . . all rather sad.

In Pigalle today business is bad. Tourists have become suspicious, and the fear of AIDS has cooled many an ardour. The sex shops and the porn cinemas are suffering serious competition from home videos and pressure from the police has cleared the streets. And although some still come to drool in front of the shop windows and the sex-shop catalogues, it isn't sex that people want to buy nowadays, only a souvenir of it. So the touting for shows is becoming tougher and more aggressive.

On the 9th arrondissement side music has filled the vacuum left by the withdrawal of the sex industry. There are 67 shops within the area marked out by rue Victor-Massé, rue Fontaine and rue de Douai offering a choice of musical instruments, at good prices. Taking advantage of this theme, trendy clubs and bars have replaced some of the cabarets and are contributing to a change in the area's image. L'Élysée-Montmartre, La Cigale and La Locomotive are the new meeting places for Parisian nightlife.

★ The **musée de l'Érotisme:** 72 boulevard de Clichy 75018. ☎ 01-42-58-28-73. Website: www.erotic-museum.com. Metro: Blanche or Pigalle. Open daily 10am to 2am. This is not just another new sex shop in Pigalle. It's a real museum, born from the passion for eroticism and erotic art of three collectors. Their finds are exhibited over seven floors. The basement is highly amusing. Bawdy illustrations, naughty photos and other perversions which are rather heavy on symbolism – basically every sort of lewdness you can imagine. The first three floors take you on a trip around the world of traditional erotic art. The top floors are devoted to contemporary art and temporary exhibitions, renewed every three months.

★ **Avenue Frochot:** (really in the 9th arrondissement, but it's worth the detour!). It begins on the corner of rue Frochot and rue Victor-Massé. A very typical street for an area which does not pull any punches. Come in the evening, towards midnight, and you'll get an overdose of neon lights, sordid touting and bland, lukewarm hot dogs. The street is lined with large, plush villas with pretty gardens, a charming square surrounded by trees and artists' workshops. This is where the great film director Jean Renoir lived.

★ Rue de Steinkerque, rue d'Orsel and above all the famous **marché St-Pierre** are specialists in fabric seconds. You can get some good deals. The shops Reine and Moline also offer some interesting fabrics.

★ The **cimetière de Montmartre:** entrance in avenue Rachel. Open 8am (8.30am Saturday, 9am Sunday) to 5.30pm (6pm in summer). The cemetery is situated in a former gypsum quarry. It has its fair share of celebrities and is also interesting because of the beauty of its sculptures and the architecture of some of the tombs. When you come in, from avenue Rachel, immediately on your right is Sacha Guitry. His tomb always has flowers on it, though no one knows who puts them there. In the first two aisles on the left, is the very

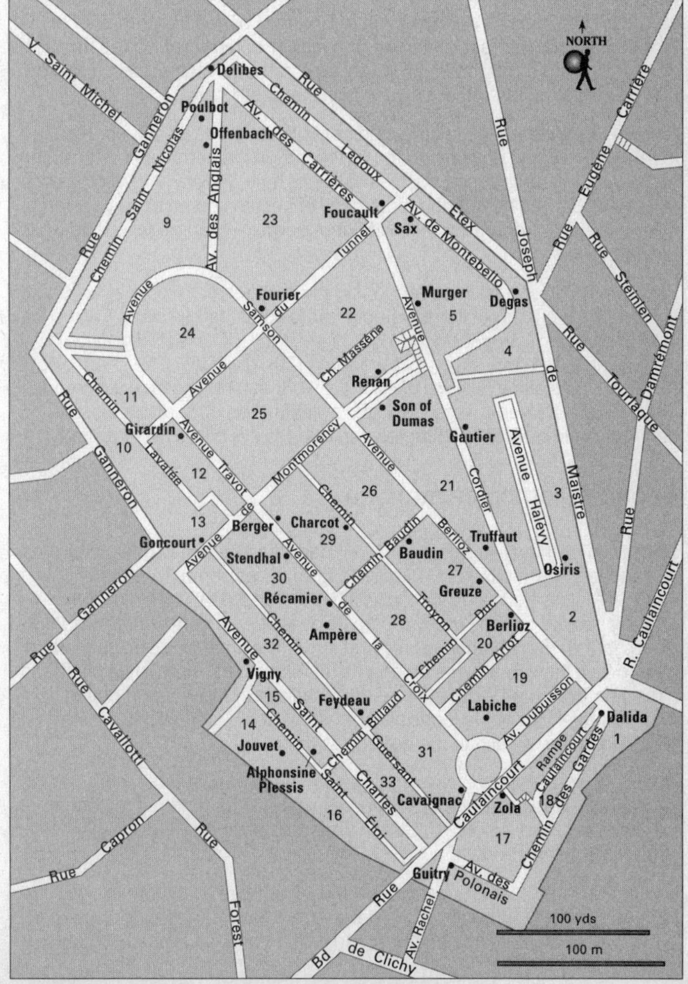

MONTMARTRE CEMETERY

simple tomb of the actor Louis Jouvet and that of Alphonsine Plessis, the model for Marguerite Gautier in *La Dame aux camélias*. It is recognizable because of the kitsch decoration and by the little purple china cushion in front (underneath is the Chemin St-Éloy). At the end of avenue St-Charles lies the poet Alfred de Vigny, and the Goncourt Brothers. In avenue de la Croix lies Henri Beyle, better known as Stendhal. In the same aisles are Mme Récamier, Ampère and Georges Feydeau. In the 5th division are Adolphe Sax (inventor of the saxophone) and the poet Henri Murger. Next door is the painter Edgar Degas. The tomb of Théophile Gautier is in avenue Cordier.

In avenue de Montmorency lies the painter Fragonard and in avenue Berlioz lies the composer Berlioz (between his two wives). During his burial the horses drawing the hearse took fright and bolted so the romantic composer almost escaped from the homage which he would almost certainly have found too ceremonial. Visit the tomb of Charles Fourier, the precursor of the hippie communities and inventor of socialist communes. Zola's remains were moved to the Pantheon though his tomb and bust remain. His wife, however, who he left rather frequently in life, is still here!

In 1984 François Truffaut was buried here. It was his dearest wish. He used to recount how one day he had to film secretly in the cemetery because the authorities refused him permission to shoot here. In May 1987 the French singer Dalida was buried here and many of her fans come to visit her tomb. One of the most recent inmates is Michel Berger – a singer who died while playing tennis.

For anyone interested in surreal or simply picturesque works of art, try to find the bizarre tomb of the architect Laurecisque (1st division), the replica of Michelangelo's *Moses* on the tomb of the banker Osiris (3rd division) and the hexagonal tomb of one Devange (17th division). The mausoleum devoted to Delphine Fix (3rd division) is worth a look: the face is splendid. Finally, those moved by the story of his death (*see* '11th arrondissement'), can visit Baudin and his extremely realistic resting place (27th division).

A LONG TRADITION OF PARTYING

Tourists often have an image of Montmarte as a place of pleasures and debauchery, symbolized by Pigalle ('Pig Alley' as some Americans call it) and the Moulin-Rouge. Historically, it is here and on the slopes of the 9th arrondissement that the many taverns where people came to slum it, flourished. In the 18th century the main street of Montmartre, rue des Martyrs, had no less than 25 taverns among its 58 houses. As for prostitution, it was already a flourishing industry, if we are to believe a police report dating from 1767 complaining of the 'considerable damage caused by the prostitutes, soliciting in the streets, to the corn and rye . . . .'

After a period when the taverns tried to sound respectable, with names such as L'Image Ste-Anne or À St-Louis, in the 18th century they became, for example L'Île d'Amour, Au Caprice des Dames or Au Berger Galant, and were more open about it.

By the early 19th century people were coming here to dance. In 1807 the famous Élysée-Montmartre (72–76 boulevard de Rochechouart) opened. When the weather was fine it attracted a middle-class clientele who, for a while, left Le Bal Mabille or La Grande Chaumière in Montparnasse. But the dance hall burned down in 1900. Rebuilt in 1908 and used as a sports' venue (wrestling and boxing, which were very fashionable), then as a concert hall, L'Élysée-Montmartre was taken under the protection of Monuments Historiques in 1988. Russian troops, camping on Montmartre in 1814, appreciated the pulsating Montmartre nightlife. As they were forbidden to drink, they always ordered their illicit drinks by yelling *bistro, bistro* (quick, quick), which is where the word 'bistro' comes from.

The heyday of la Butte was from 1880 to 1900 – when Montmartre was frenetically alive. New dances – the *chahut*, the can-can, and above all the *quadrille naturaliste* – drove the crowds wild. The dancers' legs emerged from a sea of lace and white skirts, and whenever the audience saw even the slightest bit of ankle they went apoplectic! Some of the girls gained notoriety through being immortalized by Toulouse-Lautrec.

One of the Élysée-Montmartre's competitors, the Moulin-Rouge, ended up overtaking it, with the aid of Toulouse-Lautrec's magnificent posters.

The scandal which really launched the Moulin-Rouge took place on the occasion of the Bal des Quat'z'Arts given by students from the École des Beaux-Arts in 1896. This dance, which had a reputation for being extremely 'loose', did not fail to live up to its billing; after a striptease competition among the prettiest models from the workshops, everyone applauded the first 'complete nude' to appear on a Paris stage. Senator Béranger, president of the *Ligue contre la licence des rues* ('League against vice in the streets') took the affair to court. One model was sentenced to three months in prison, while in the Latin Quarter students erected barricades. For three days rioting had the government in a panic. Windows in St-Germain-des-Prés were shattered, two students were killed by police charges, and the newspapers talked about *La guerre du nu artistique* ('The war of the artistic nude'). The Bastille Day holiday, and the closing of the schools, brought calm, but Paris must still be the only city where anyone has ever died for an artistic nude!

THE LITERARY AND ARTISTIC TAVERNS

Alongside the dance halls there were also literary and artistic taverns where there was singing and satire.

Two such places were the Âne Rouge, and the famous Chat Noir at 84 boulevard Rochechouart. It was a massive hit. In this tiny tavern, just 4m (13ft) wide, crowds came pouring in to listen to everything from barrack-room singing to intense theoretical debates on art. Alphonse Allais was one of the mainstays. Aristide Bruant was the ancestor of the popular cabaret artist. He would rudely harangue tourists, the middle-classes and the fashionable set. His silhouette, with a great black hat and red scarf, and his perceptive songs, will always have a place in popular French memory.

The cabaret was so successful that a newspaper, *Le Chat Noir* (Black Cat), was published to spread the ideas, the controversies and the acerbic and amusing wit aimed at the 'old fogeys of the French Academy' and at the 'mindless boulevard theatre owners'. Alphonse Allais, who was the editor, found his true vocation as a humourist. Students from the Latin Quarter loved the paper in particular, and literary clubs and poets also joined in the satire. Today, *Le Chat Noir* has become a legend . . . and a café, on boulevard de Clichy, which has kept its name.

AND WHAT ABOUT TODAY?

Here and there baroque façades are still true to the memory of the Montmartre of old. Generally speaking, over the last few years the area has become a little more virtuous, and slightly less saucy. The **Élysée-Montmartre** is still standing at 72 boulevard Rochechouart. Boxers were trained here at one time and it has seen all sorts of shows from wrestling and boxing matches, prestigious plays with the Renaud-Barrault company and the Troupe du Soleil and erotic revues, to today's rock concerts and gigs. Over the last few years, it has become very popular with a younger audience. Avant-garde groups or famous artists regularly appear there. **La Locomotive** (*see* 'Where to go dancing') and **La Cigale**, a former theatre which has been done up, have also been huge hits. La Cigale, a caf'-conc' (café with live music) founded in 1887, where Mistinguett and Maurice Chevalier once appeared, had been reduced to a kung-fu centre. A century after it opened however, it has been given a new lease of life as a rock and pop venue.

Nearby, **Le Trianon**, thanks to its architecture, is also a testament to this heyday.

For tourists the **Moulin-Rouge** and the can-can continue to symbolize the grand tradition of Montmartre. However, there are some places which show a more poetic side to the area, such as the artistic and literary pubs and clubs, many of which offer more upmarket shows.

THE GOUTTE-D'OR

The name of this district goes back to the 15th century when the vines growing on the hills produced a white wine called 'Goutte d'Or' (Drop of gold). Marked out by boulevard Barbès, rue Ordener to the north, boulevard de la Chapelle to the south and rue Stephenson, this is an area which has undergone considerable change. Even if those nostalgic for the old Paris don't know where they are anymore, the architecture and urbanisation seem to have prevented the place turning into the ghetto which some people were expecting, and changes have even gone some way to aiding integration. Today 50 per cent of the population is of foreign origin and there are 56 nationalities mixing accents, colours, gestures and the flavours of Africa, Asia and Europe.

A BRIEF HISTORY

Like Belleville, this area has always been a home to immigrants. The first wave came from within France: peasants arrived in the first half of the 19th century, to lend their strength to the triumphant industrialization process. Émile Zola found his characters for *L'Assommoir* here, and this is where Gervaise (the protagonist) had her washhouse. At the beginning of the 20th century there was the first wave of Arab immigration. The Goutte-d'Or was the bastion of the FLN (Front de Libération nationale) during the Algerian war. More recently, West Indians and Africans have moved into the north of the area. But there is still an old French population, reinforced over the years by young people and craftsmen moving in for financial reasons (the rents are lower) or because they appreciate the charm and the village atmosphere.

For a long time the Goutte-d'Or was famous for its 'slaughterhouses', sordid hotels where prostitutes often entertained 60 to 80 clients a day. Tolerated by the public authorities for many years, the hotels were finally closed at the end of the 1970s.

The Goutte-d'Or has always been an enormous national and international business centre. In an area which is actually quite small, there are several hundred businesses with considerable turnover, including Halal butchers' shops, wholesale grocers, fabric shops and jewellers. Bags of couscous, bouquets of aromatic herbs, olives and tinned foods are all sold by the ton. If people are having a party or a wedding they come here to buy fine lamé and embroidered fabrics, or textiles woven or printed in Korea, Taïwan or Holland to patterns designed in Paris. There is a flourishing trade in travel goods as well. You can find all sizes, right up to enormous trunks, at very low prices.

Clothes are also a main feature. Following in the footsteps of the *Tati* phenomenon (a discount clothes chain) many shops are doing good business and offer excellent products. Where else in Paris can you find good second-hand shirts at 5F? And not the least of the pleasures to be gleaned is watching the aspiring middle classes from other areas rapidly swapping their *Tati* plastic bags for one from a more prestigious shop to avoid gossip from their neighbours and concierges!

TODAY

Today the Goutte-d'Or is reaching the end of an in-depth redevelopment process. Half the buildings have been destroyed and replaced by local authority housing. Although the area was in need of restoration, a lot of the inhabitants feared that they would be 'cleaned up' and sent out to some faraway suburb. However, thanks to their resistance and stubbornness, this hasn't happened. As a result, although many houses have been demolished, the area is still laid out like a village, with little streets, courtyards and pretty alleyways. Almost 1,000 families have been rehoused in Paris developments like this, mainly in the 18th arrondissement and a good number of them in the Goutte-d'Or. The area has remained working-class and multicultural. While still large, the North African commercial nucleus has been somewhat restricted here, although one has been created further to the north, around Château-Rouge and the Marché Dejean. Visit the Goutte-d'Or area on Saturday to find authentic local life.

During the rejuvenation of this area the local community came together to tackle the 'standardization' of their culture and to secure housing for the local inhabitants. Today they continue to provide an essential service for the community, dealing with such issues as rehousing, social integration, education for women, schooling and children's activities.

Every year since 1985 a community party has taken place in the first week of July. Completely free of charge and in the open air, there are concerts, dancing, sports activities, exhibitions (photos, paintings, etc.), cinema and so on.

WHAT TO SEE

★ **Rue de la Goutte-d'Or** currently has an amazing number of construction sites. As you enter the street from boulevard Barbès, No. 48 is a modern building, but as you go through the small passageway you discover, in the little courtyard, a garden jealously guarded by two-storey buildings. The **villa Poissonnière** (a well-protected haven of greenery, made up of little Louis-Philippe-style buildings and gardens), starts at 42 rue de la Goutte-d'Or and ends at 41 rue Polonceau. At No. 47 there is a fine building with attractive balconies and a pretty staircase. The columns along the end of rue de la Goutte-d'Or house an oriental *pâtisserie*, good but quite expensive.

★ **Rue des Gardes**, which goes up towards the Square Léon, has been entirely renovated. It's wide, with a row of trees on one side.

★ On **square Léon** there are frescoes along the walls, with one by Geneviève Bachellier showing a sort of idyllic Paris with the sea and a flock of gulls. But the wall is deteriorating and there are no plans to refurbish it. The other frescoes are in good condition.

At 36 **rue Cavé** (bordering the north of the square) there used to be a pawnbroker's.

★ Next is the little **église St-Bernard-de-la-Chapelle**. It's well proportioned, with a tasteful neo-Gothic and neo-Renaissance chevet (apse). There is a lovely porch with a forest of pinnacles. The church was occupied from 28 June to 23 August 1996 by illegal immigrants threatened with deportation.

– There is a **market** under the metro station, on Wednesday and Saturday (one of the least expensive in Paris, along with Aligre and Pantin).

– There are a number of Turkish baths along boulevard de la Chapelle: at No. 54, for women only (open daily 9am to 6pm; 80F; ☎ 01-42-55-07-92) and at No. 120, mixed, open 10am to 7pm; same price: ☎ 01-46-06-77-67.

★ **Rue Caplat** connects boulevard de la Chapelle to rue de la Goutte-d'Or. The art historian François Loyer said that this was a 'coherent urban space of exceptional interest'.

★ Go down rue de Chartres, largely renovated, as far as the crossroads (in the shape of a St Andrew's cross) it forms with **rue de la Charbonnière**, from there you get a fine view over Sacré-Cœur.

★ Further north, starting from boulevard Barbès just after rue de la Goutte-d'Or, there is **rue des Poissonniers** and the **'Château-Rouge'** area. Go up this historic road, where the capital's fish supplies were once brought in. Immediately on the right, where it crosses rue Polonceau, note the temporary mosque (which is to be permanently re-built on boulevard de la Chapelle). Go a bit further down rue Polonceau and, at the exit from the Villa Poissonnière, you'll find a little Japanese Buddhist temple in a former private house (No. 36). Retrace your steps and take rue des Poissonniers again. At No. 9 the shop *Kata Soldes* has set up in an old cinema; go in to look at the decor. Then you reach the 'African market'. In the space of a few years local trade has completely changed, and people come from far and wide to do their shopping here, at the marché Dejean and in **rue Poulet**. Near the Château-Rouge metro station don't miss the chance to buy your fish at the **marché Dejean.** There's a large choice, with all sorts of exotic varieties at amazing prices.

★ As you descend rue Boinod you meet **rue des Amiraux**. The street is named after the admirals who commanded the troops at the Battle of Bourget, on 23 December 1870, during the siege of Paris. Turn left down it, and suddenly, on your left you'll see a huge terraced building, decorated with white tiles. It's by Henri Sauvage, the same artchitect who built No. 26 rue Vavin in Montparnasse. At the time tuberculosis was still raging among the working-class population and he tried to get across a sense of hygiene through his designs, which are reminiscent of the clean look of a hospital. In rue des Amiraux, taking advantage of having more space than in rue Vavin, Sauvage took his ideas about terraced houses to their logical conclusion and here it's a veritable pyramid.

The last street before the outer boulevard is **rue Belliard**. There's nothing much to say about this long street, except that in October 1979 public enemy No. 1, Jacques Mesrine, lived with his girlfriend at No. 35. There was a huge police operation to arrest the man who, for several months since his spectacular and dramatic escape from the Santé prison, had eluded the authorities. On 2 November the police spotted him and trapped him at Porte de Clignancourt. A real ambush, with lots of shooting, brought this urban Robin Hood's time on the run in the 18th arrondissement to an end.

WHERE TO GO FOR A DRINK

🍸 **Le Sancerre** (inset, **82**): 35 rue des Abbesses 75018. ☎ 01-42-58-08-20 or 01-42-58-47-05. Metro: Abbesses. Open daily 7am to 2am. Dish of the day 55F, half a pint of beer 18F after 10pm. Le Sancerre is now the meeting place *de rigueur* for all kinds of locals. Tourists from all over the world and French wine lovers grab the seats as soon as they become free in the dining room or on the terrace.

🍸 **La Divette de Montmartre** (map B2, **70**): 136 rue Marcadet 75018. ☎ 01-46-06-19-64. Metro: Lamarck-Caulaincourt. Open noon (3pm on Monday and Saturday) to 1am. Closed Sunday and for two to three weeks in August. Half a pint of beer 13F, whisky 30F. An old bistro which lives up to its name: 'The *divette* is to operetta what the diva is to opera!'. For the couple who run this local bar – music is their first love – it's a veritable museum of vinyl! On the ceiling, on the walls, behind the wall seats, between the bottles of wine, records, records and nothing but records, except for the picture discs. From the beginning of the 20th century (an old Pathé 1902) to the '50s and '60s (Elvis and the Beatles), they are all there. In total there are almost 2,000 records on show. It's free to look round, but given the price of a half pint of beer it's worth checking out the bar as well. It is also a tobacconist, a caf'-conc' (café with live music) on Friday evening, and a musical gallery (old phonographs and Marconi wireless sets).

🍸 **La Fourmi** (map B3, **84**): 74 rue des Martyrs 75018. ☎ 01-42-64-70-35. Metro: Pigalle. Open daily 8.30am (10.30am on Sunday) to 2am. Half a pint of beer 14F to 20F. A former bistro decorated in the tastes of the day – walls shiny with age, tin bar, 'recycled' chairs, chandeliers – for the sort of very Parisian clientele which everyone wants to attract nowadays. Full of people reading the latest magazines.

🍸 **Lux Bar** (inset, **74**): 12 rue Lepic 75018. ☎ 01-46-06-05-15. Metro: Blanche. Open daily 7am to 11pm. Wine by the glass from 18F, whisky 35F. Salads 48F and *croques poilâne* 39F. A real Montmartre café, whose decor can't have changed since the beginning of the last century. Look at the superb art-nouveau ceramic panels or the amazing bar sculpted from medallions, around which young trendies and old regulars rub shoulders with good humour.

GOING OUT

– **Le Divan du Monde** (map B3, **75**): 75 rue des Martyrs 75018. ☎ 01-44-92-77-66. Metro: Pigalle. Bus 30, 54, 67. A drink costs from 25F. There are children's tea dances the first Sunday in every month, and adult tea dances on the other Sundays from 4pm onwards. During the Second Empire this was a *musette*, then a brasserie, before becoming Le Divan Japonais in 1886, a meeting place which is both Bohemian and artistic, with its newspapers, its singers and its Scala. In March 1894 it was goodbye to Le Divan, and long live the Concert Lisbonne! For the first time ever in Paris young actresses appeared on stage. The first stripteases, the first upheavals and the first scandals were here. Today, at this caf'-conc' immortalized by Toulouse-Lautrec, you get comedy one day, cabaret the next and porn cinema the next! In 1994, after many years of closure, this Parisian institution rose from the ashes, and Le Divan du Monde arrived. The cream of Paris comes here for some eclectic soirées: dance, soul, jazz and Latino concerts, cabaret, celebrations of African culture through dance, fashion and other techno, groove and rock parties, with the best DJs and the top bands of the moment.

– **L'Élysée-Montmartre** (map B3, **73**): 72 bd de Rochechouart, 75018. ☎ 01-55-07-06-00. Metro: Anvers or Pigalle. Entrance fee: 100–120F. Once a month on a Friday this place holds a *Favela Chic* evening from 11pm until dawn. This includes artists from Brazil, bands from Colombia and DJs from all over the South American continent (Orlando de Cali, El Negro Sabroso, amongst others).

– **MCM Café** (inset, **78**): 92 boulevard de Clichy 75018. ☎ 01-42-64-39-22. Metro: Blanche. Open daily 6pm to 5am. Set menus 78F and 98F at lunchtime. Drinks from 18F to 45F during the day; from 22F in the evening. Right against La Loco, within the walls of the former restaurant of the Moulin Rouge, MCM, the music channel, has opened the first 'Live TV Café'. A multiplex space made up of a concert hall, a TV studio (with live shows several times a week), a video game area, two bars and a restaurant. Lots of stars of the small screen here.

– **Le Lapin Agile** (map B2, **76**): 22 rue des Saules 75018. ☎ 01-46-06-85-87. Fax: 01-42-54-63-04. Website: www.au-lapin-agile.com. Metro: Lamarck-Caulaincourt. Events every night except Monday, 9pm to 2am. Entrance and one drink, 130F, then 30F per drink. The doyen of the cabaret clubs of Montmartre. Nothing here has changed – not even a brushstroke has covered the old patina on the walls darkened by smoke from pipes and the old stove. The welcome is as warm as ever. The walls are covered in souvenirs and moving testimonies: the old picture of Christ in front of which Max Jacob used to 'pray', watercolours and paintings by Fernand Léger and André Gill and poems in Bruant's own handwriting. If you come at 9pm you'll have time to explore this little museum of art and poetry in the half-light. The show starts at 9.30pm. This is where the 'greats' began their careers: Pierre Brasseur and Annie Girardot recited poems and Georges Brassens sang here for the first time, but wasn't much of a hit and left after a week. Nowadays, Le Lapin Agile is in some ways to cabaret what *Opportunity Knocks* used to be to British TV, featuring young singers – the stars of tomorrow. There is an excellent four-hour show in which tourists, whether French or not, soon abandon their passive roles and get involved (90F for students during the week).

✗ **Le Tire-Bouchon** (inset, **77**): 9 rue Norvins 75018. ☎ 01-42-55-12-35. Metro: Abbesses. Open daily. Crêpes from 19F to 39F, drinks from 25F to 35F. Very close to place du Tertre. The singer Jacques Brel made his debut here and this was also one of the many places where George Brassens appeared. From 3pm to 9pm it is a crêperie with very reasonable prices. Up to 2am it is a piano-bar with a friendly atmosphere. After 9pm drinks cost from 50F to 70F. Credit cards not accepted.

NIGHTCLUBS

– **La Locomotive** (inset, **79**): 90 boulevard de Clichy 75018. ☎ 01-53-41-88-88. Metro: Blanche. Open 11pm till dawn. Entrance fee: Sunday to Thursday 55F without a drink; Friday 60F before midnight and 100F after; Saturday, entrance and drink 100F. Stuck onto the Moulin-Rouge, this famous 1960s rock club was reopened at the end of 1986 by a group of bouncers. After difficult beginnings (the bouncers were a bit too touchy), some 2,000 young people from the suburbs, plus many English and Italian speakers, now pour into this three-level metropolis. On the ground floor is the concert hall with the latest sound systems and a vast dance floor. In the basement there's a smoking boiler decor and music from the 1950s and '60s. There are bars all over the place with '90s rock music. A mega nightclub. They also do themed nights, such as rock 'n' roll.

– **Les Coulisses** (inset, **83**): 5 rue du Mont-Cenis 75018. ☎ 01-42-62-89-99. Metro: Abbesses. Club open daily 11pm to late. Entry free during the week; 100F with one drink Friday and Saturday. A drink costs 50F. Set menu 160F; otherwise budget for 200F à la carte. A former Montmartre vault rebuilt after the war, then a dance hall, and now one of the most fantastic clubs in Paris, with its baroque world inspired by the *Commedia dell'Arte*. A veritable Venetian *delirium* where you sleep-eat on the first floor before being seduced by the rhythms coming up the stairs, dragging you down and keeping you up until all hours.

19TH ARRONDISSEMENT

BUTTES-CHAUMONT ● BASSIN DE LA VILLETTE ● PARC DE LA VILLETTE

The 19th is one of the lesser-known areas of Paris as far as the visitor is concerned. La Villette, the new complex dedicated to scientific discovery is probably its most well-known feature, but the area has a surprising amount of greenery too. The parc des Buttes-Chaumont and the Bassin de la Villette provide ample space for quiet strolls away from the crowds.

The area is being redeveloped, especially around the Cité des Sciences et de l'Industrie and Stalingrad. The rue de Flandre, one of the most characteristically 19th-century landscapes, has recently undergone a Haussmann-style blitz.

A BRIEF HISTORY

The rue de Flandre follows the old Roman road which linked Paris to the north and to Flanders. The Villette area was a village for many years: 650 inhabitants in 1750, barely 1,800 at the beginning of the 19th century, 12,000 in 1847 and 30,000 in 1860, when it was annexed to Paris. Development began around the Eastern railway line, the Canal de l'Ourcq and the Bassin de la Villette, themselves lined with many warehouses. The nearby livestock market and the abattoirs, and the growth of small scale industries, all made the 19th arrondissement (and more particularly the Villette area) the most industrialized and, therefore, the least residential area of Paris.

WHERE TO STAY

☗ **Hôtel de Crimée** (map B1–2, **1**): 188 rue de Crimée 75019. ☎ 01-40-36-75-29. Fax: 01-40-36-29-57. E-mail: hotel.crimée@free.fr. Metro: Crimée. From 310F for a double room with a shower to 350F with a bath. Rooms for three or four with shower 350F and 400F. Not far from the Cité des Sciences, with simple but comfortable rooms with toilet, cable TV, hairdryer, air conditioning and double-glazing (very useful!). Pay and display parking near the hotel. Warm welcome.

☗ **Hôtel Rhin et Danube** (map C2–3, **2**): 3 place Rhin-et-Danube 75019. ☎ 01-42-45-10-13. Fax: 01-42-06-88-82. Metro: Danube. Bus No. 75. Budget for 350F for a double, 430F for three people and 500F for four people. Rooms/flats with bathroom and well-equipped kitchenettes. A practical hotel in a quiet area resembling a small village, opposite the metro station and near the Buttes-Chaumont and La Villette. At these prices it is worth being a bit out of the centre of Paris (it only takes 10 minutes to get to the Hôtel de Ville). Don't expect a luxury suite or any great charm.

WHERE TO EAT

☆ BUDGET

✕ **Bar Fleuri** (map B3, **9**): 1 rue du Plateau (on the corner with the rue des Alouettes) 75019. ☎ 01-42-08-13-38. Metro: Buttes-Chaumont or Jourdain. Closed Sunday and for the second fortnight in August (in winter they close at around 7pm). Set menus 56F at lunchtime, 69F in the evening. À la carte, budget for 100F without drinks. This little local bistro dates from 1920 and its decor hasn't changed – nor has its name (Flowery Bar), which must relate to the old tiling on the walls, livened up with lots of roses. No menu, but there is an immense blackboard of specials with generous traditional dishes. Five to six choices per section (starter, main course, dessert), half of which change every day.

✕ **Aux Arts et Sciences Réunis** (map C2, **11**): 161 avenue Jean-Jaurès 75019. ☎ 01-42-40-53-18. Metro: Ourcq. Open 11.30am to 2pm and 7 to 9pm. Closed Sunday, Saturday evening and also Christmas and New Year's Day. Set menu 59F lunchtime and evening. This is the restaurant of the headquarters of the Compagnons Charpentiers du Devoir du Tour de France, heroic defenders of the arts of stone, wood and . . . the dining table. Both the atmosphere and the food are rather provincial: escalope, trout and grills. The menu has large portions, with wine included. Dish of the day 41F.

✕ **Le Fleuve Rouge** (map B3, **12**): 1 rue Pradier 75019. ☎ 01-42-06-25-04 Metro: Belleville or Pyrénées. Bus No. 26. Open lunchtime and evening until 10.30pm. Closed Saturday lunchtime, Sunday and public holidays, as well as in August. Set menus at 59F, 70F and 110F lunchtime and evening. The owners here are charming and always find the time to exchange a few words with their customers. There is a cheap menu at 59F, served lunchtime and evening, with generous portions, or try veal kidneys and Vietnamese fondue (order in advance). Gluttons will love it, and the word seems to have been passed to all starving artists, retired people and office employees.

✕ **Café de l'Aubrac** (map C2, **13**): 52 rue d'Hautpoul 75019. ☎ 01-42-39-81-13. Metro: Ourcq. Open lunchtime only Monday to Saturday. Bar open 7am to 8pm. Closed on public holidays. Single menu at 59F. An old provincial local restaurant with good food in a fascinating part of Paris. The classic bistro dishes are all made on the premises: herring with fried potatoes, celery *rémoulade*, ox tongue, *onglet*

Where to stay
- **1** Hôtel de Crimée
- **2** Hôtel Rhin et Danube

✕ **Where to eat**
- **9** Bar Fleuri
- **11** Aux Arts et Sciences Réunis
- **12** Le Fleuve Rouge
- **13** Café de l'Aubrac
- **14** L'Oriental
- **15** La Chouette & Co
- **16** Au Rendez-Vous de la Marine
- **17** L'Heure Bleue
- **18** Soushiya
- **19** L'Hermès
- **20** Le Rendez-Vous des Quais
- **21** Lao Siam
- **22** Chez Valentin
- **24** Le Pavillon Puebla
- **25** Le Relais des Buttes
- **26** Chez Vincent
- **27** La Lanterne
- **28** Au Cochon de Lait
- **29** La Mandragore

Where to go for a drink/ Going out
- **40** Le Café Parisien
- **41** Le Café de la Musique
- **42** Glaz'art

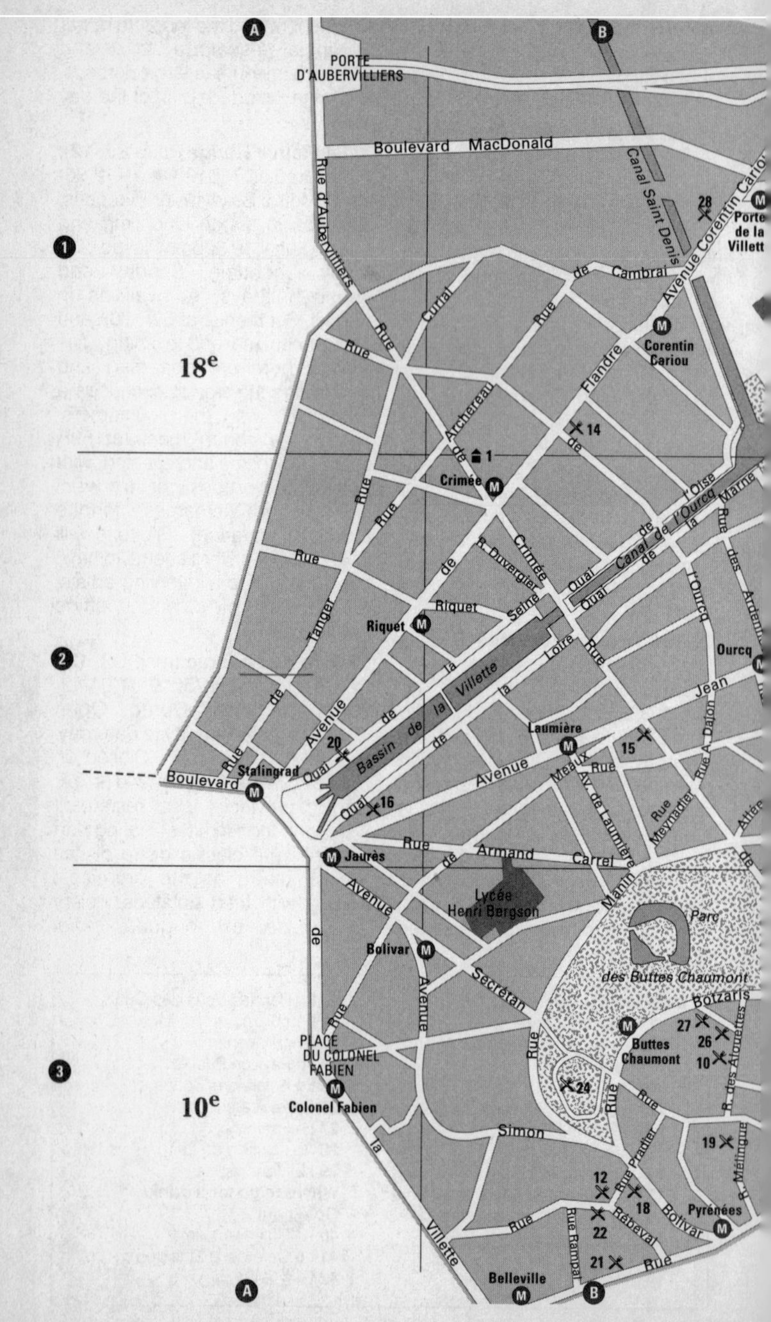

A
B
1
2
3
PORTE D'AUBERVILLIERS
Boulevard MacDonald
Canal Saint Denis
Avenue Corentin Cariou
Porte de la Villett
Rue d'Aubervilliers
Rue de Cambrai
18e
Rue Curial
Rue
Rue
Corentin Cariou
Rue de Flandre
Archereau
14
1
Crimée
Rue
Rue
Rue de Crimée
Quai de l'Oise
Canal de l'Ourcq
Quai de la Marne
Rue des Ardennes
R. Duvergier
Rue Riquet
Riquet
Quai de la Seine
Quai de la Loire
Rue de l'Ourcq
Ourcq
Rue de Tanger
Rue
Avenue Jean Jaurès
Bassin de la Villette
Laumière
15
Rue A. Dalou
20
Stalingrad
Boulevard
Avenue de Meaux
Rue
Av. de Laumière
Rue Meynadier
16
Rue Armand Carrel
Jaurès
Avenue
Lycée Henri Bergson
Rue Manin
Parc des Buttes Chaumont
Bolivar
Avenue Secrétan
Rue Botzaris
Buttes Chaumont
27
26
10
PLACE DU COLONEL FABIEN
Colonel Fabien
10e
Rue
24
Rue
R. des Alouettes
Rue Simon
19
Rue Pradier
12
18
R. Mélingue
Pyrénées
Rue de la Villette
Rue Rébeval
22
Rue Rampal
Avenue Bolivar
21
Rue
Belleville

NORTH
Boulevard MacDonald
Cité des Sciences et de l'Industrie
Géode
Grande Halle
Cité de la Musique
Boulevard
PORTE DE PANTIN
Place de la Porte de Pantin
41
Jaurès
Porte de Pantin
Serrurier
Boulevard
PLACE DU Gal COCHET
Petit
R. Goubet
Milhaud
Manin
Darius
13
Boulevard d'Indochine
Boulevard
Rue David
Brunet
2
PLACE DE RHIN ET DANUBE
40
Danube
PORTE DU PRÉ SAINT-GERVAIS
d'Angers
Serrurier
Périphérique
Hôpital Robert Debré
Pré-Saint-Gervais
d'Algérie
Mouzaïa
Rue du Général
R. de la Liberté
Botzaris
25
17
29
Rue
Rue de
Rozier
Robida
Compans
Crimée
Rue Arthur
Rue des Bois
R. Romainville
Haxo
PORTE DES LILAS
Pte des Lilas
Av. de la
Belleville
Porte des Lilas
R. des Solitaires
PLACE DES FÊTES
Place des Fêtes
R. de Palestine
Fessart
de
Rue de
Télégraphe
Jourdain
Villette
20e
0 100 200 300 yds
0 100 200 300 m
19TH

(prime cut of beef) with shallots. On Friday, Saturday and Sunday there are shows in the evening.

✕ **L'Oriental** (map B1, **14**): 58 rue de l'Ourcq 75019. ☎ 01-40-34-26-23. Metro: Crimée. Open until 11pm. Closed Sunday. Budget for around 90F per person excluding drinks. This Lebanese restaurant, near the rue de Flandre, is quite a find in an area where there aren't many restaurants. The dining room is simple, with music and photos recalling the Lebanon of old. The cuisine is fresh and good. Lots of hot and cold starters, which you can order one by one or as a *mezze* (an assortment of eastern mediterranean hors-d'œuvres; 180F for two): or try the *labné* (mint fromage frais), *tabouleh, falafel* and *houmous*. There are some generous meat dishes for between 48F and 58F and a *kefraya* or a *nakad* (less expensive) to help it go down. Good desserts and they also do takeaways. Pretty full at lunchtime.

✕ **La Chouette & Co** (map B2, **15**): 113 rue de Crimée 75019. ☎ 01-42-45-60-15. Metro: Laumière. Open until 11.30pm. Closed Saturday lunchtime, Sunday and two weeks around 15 August. Set menus 49F and 55F, children's menu 25F. À la carte around 100F. This place used to house the archives of the newspaper *Libération* and has now become a bit of an institution. Children are welcome on the first floor and there's a real fire in winter. Traditional food mixed with good vegetarian cuisine: *houmous, tofu* with wild mushrooms, cod with shrimps flavoured with saffron, and for meat-eaters there is the house speciality, *magret de canard*. The prices are *very* reasonable and there are some very affordable wines; a bottle of Gamay costs 49F. Musical events at weekends.

✕ **L'Heure Bleue** (map C3, **17**): 57 rue Arthur-Rozier 75019. ☎ 01-42-39-18-07. Metro: Place-des-Fêtes. Open until 10.30pm. Closed Saturday lunchtime, Sunday and public holidays, and also for three weeks in August and during the Christmas holidays. Set menu 65F at lunchtime only, children's menu 48F. In the evening budget for 120–150F for the à la carte menu. Located in a little street – you'll need a map to find it – this is a warm, well-lit place, with an attractive wooden bar and a few newspapers for those on their own. Vegetarians are catered for with *tofu*, while for others there's venison paté, savoury tarts or *confit* of duck. For dessert there's a choice between the (excellent) pear tart with ginger, chocolate fondant or house crumble, and lots of other delicious looking dishes.

✕ **Soushiya** (map B3, **18**): 12 rue Pradier 75019. ☎ 01-42-02-85-82. Metro: Buttes-Chaumont or Pyrénées. Open 12.30pm to 2.30pm and 6.30pm to 10pm. Closed Monday. A single set menu served lunchtime and evening at 80F, otherwise budget for around 100F à la carte, excluding drinks. A tiny, tastefully decorated Japanese restaurant. People come here for the mixed *sushi* (depending on what's available) and it's very reasonably priced (a plate costs 90F) as well as very fresh *sashimi* (100F). The tea is free; unfortunately there is no wine (but you can bring your own). Considering how small the place is (10 seats), we recommend that you book and don't smoke. To keep their hands occupied, smokers can learn some origami – something the owner knows all about.

☆☆ MODERATE

✕ **Le Rendez-Vous des Quais** (map A2, **20**): 10 quai de la Seine 75019. ☎ 01-40-37-02-81. Metro: Stalingrad. Open daily until midnight. Set meal of the day 110F served lunchtime and evening, cinema set menu 149F. Children's menu 49F. À la carte, budget for at least 150F. This bistro on the embankment is a port of call for local intellectuals, who seems to have a weakness for the wide, south-facing terrace opposite the Bassin de la Villette. When the sun is shining it gets pretty crowded. Tuck into a salad or main course and a glass of wine while you're waiting for your film at the local cinema. There's a main course plus dessert set meal at lunchtime and during the week. The 'Autour d'un vin' – ('Over a glass of wine') set meal (with dish of the day, a glass of Côtes-du-Rhône, and coffee), is good value. The 'cinema menu' set meal includes the dish of the day, dessert, drink, coffee and cinema ticket.

✕ **Au Rendez-Vous de la Marine** (map A2, **16**): 14 quai de la Loire 75019. ☎ 01-42-49-33-40. Metro: Jaurès. Open until 10pm. Closed Sunday and Monday. Budget for between 140F and 170F. People pack into this charming bistro opposite the Bassin de la Villette, (a former café which is 100 years old). The atmosphere is noisy, especially at lunchtime and on those evenings when there's a singer, two Saturdays per month (in winter only). In summer there are tables on the terrace, with a view over the canal. You get large portions of the reasonably priced main courses. It's a good idea to book.

✕ **Lao Siam** (map B3, **21**): 49 rue de Belleville 75019. ☎ 01-40-40-09-68. Metro: Belleville. Open noon to 3pm and from 6.30pm to 9.30pm. No set menu, budget for around 150F per person. A Sino-Thai restaurant with a refined cuisine (the Thai influence). Try *tourteau à la diable*, quails with grilled garlic, *folies de la mer*, or *pattaya* rice. The dining room is always full of Asian diners, which is a good sign.

✕ **Chez Valentin** (map B3, **22**): 64 rue Rébeval 75019. ☎ 01-42-08-12-34. Metro: Pyrénées. Open until 10.30pm. Sundays and Mondays. At lunchtime there is a set menu at 59F, in the evening budget for 120F à la carte. An Argentine-inspired restaurant, which looks just like a Parisian one. At lunchtime they serve a set menu based on French cuisine, but you can see the South American influence on the evening menu and on the wine list (*tacos, empanadas, quesadillas, chilli con carne,* Chilean and Argentinean wines). Friendly welcome, soft music, a pleasant dining room and good cooking.

✕ **L'Hermès** (map B3, **19**): 23 rue Mélingue 75019. ☎ 01-42-39-94-70. Metro: Pyrénées. Open until 10.30pm. Closed Sunday, Monday, public holidays and in August. Set menus 70F and 130F. À la carte, budget for between 110F and 140F excluding drinks. A sunny dining room, a bistro ambiance and a menu carte flitting between classic and modern dishes. There is a generous set menu at lunchtime (two starters, two main courses and two desserts or cheese), which means it is usually full. The set menu in the evening is more elaborate: lobster *aumônière* with *foie gras*, hare stew *à la royale*, venison and even wild boar.

✕ **La Mandragore** (map C3, **29**): 74 rue Botzaris (on the corner of rue de la Villette) 75019. ☎ 01-42-39-86-18. Metro: Place-des-Fêtes or Botzaris. Last orders 10.30pm. Closed Sunday evening and Monday as well as one week in February and the first three weeks of August. Set menu lunchtime at 70F; 120F and 145F in the evening. Children's menu 100F. Just opposite the entrance to the Parc des Buttes-Chaumont, a charming little restaurant with a rococo façade, huge mirrors, piano and attractive tablecloths. Good French cuisine: you'll find *foie gras, confit de* *canard* and *tarte fine aux pommes*. Wines from 95F. Warm welcome. It's a good idea to book at weekends because it's very popular. In case you were wondering, '*mandragore*' (mandrake) is a plant of the Nightshade family. The subject of many superstitions, it was believed to grow at the foot of the gallows used for hanging criminals.

✕ **Au Cochon de Lait** (map B1, **28**): 23 avenue Corentin-Cariou 75019. ☎ 01-40-36-85-84. Metro: Corentin-Cariou. Open lunchtime only. Closed Sunday and in August. Budget for 120F per person, excluding drinks. This little Porte de la Villette bistro claims to be the 'last bistro of the former abattoirs'. Actually, the owner has been running the place for nearly 40 years and she still uses the same butcher. Try Villette *onglet* (prime cut of beef) at 68F, or the simple set menu with home-made dishes. Good desserts.

✕ The **restaurants of the Porte de la Villette and the Porte de Pantin** are nearly all for meat fans as they're located around the former abattoirs of Paris (now the Parc de la Villette). On the Porte de la Villette and Cité des Sciences side you can still find lots of warehouses and supplies of butchers' equipment.

19TH

☆☆☆ CHIC

✕ **Le Pavillon Puebla** (map B3, **24**): Parc des Buttes-Chaumont 75019; entrance on the corner of rue Botzaris and avenue Simon-Bolivar (in the evening they'll open the park gate for you). ☎ 01-42-08-92-62. Metro: Buttes-Chaumont. Open until 10pm. Closed Sunday, Monday and public holidays. Set menus 190F and 260F lunchtime and evening. À la carte, budget for 400F. This large restaurant, tucked away in the middle of the loveliest park in Paris, is in an ideal location. The setting is truly bourgeois, with its fresh flowers and pretty terrace, delightful when the weather is fine. The cuisine is of a very high standard: *gamba* fritters, iced *bouillabaisse* with saffron, fricassée of suckling pig, and excellent desserts. Obviously it's expensive (very pricey à la carte and with wine), but there is a Catalan menu at 190F with, for example, red mullet with basil and a *galette* with a *fondue* of vegetables, knuckle of lamb with olives, and, to end with, *turrón*-flavoured ice-cream. Cocktail snacks and home-made bread add to the pleasures. Also serves as a tea-room during the day.

✕ **Le Relais des Buttes** (map C3, **25**): 86 rue Compans 75019. ☎ 01-42-08-24-70. Metro: Place-des-Fêtes. Last orders 10.30pm. Closed Saturday lunchtime, Sunday and for three weeks in August. Set menu 178F lunchtime and evening, à la carte budget for around 260F excluding wine. A classic restaurant, whose strong point is the freshness of the produce from Rungis market. There is a courtyard-terrace which is very popular in summer when the heat becomes unbearable. The à la carte menu is a bit pricey; try the set menu, which gives better value for money.

✕ **Chez Vincent** (map B3, **26**): 5 rue du Tunnel 75019. ☎ 01-42-02-22-45. Metro: Buttes-Chaumont or Botzaris. Open until 11pm; on Saturday and public holidays open in the evening only. Closed Sunday. Booking is essential. Set meal 180F at lunchtime, in the evening budget for 200F without drinks. This amazing Italian restaurant is hidden in a little street between former television studios and the Buttes-Chaumont. The dining room is classic but warm, with a bar in the middle where the chef prepares the *antipasti* in front of you. Tasty snacks will ease the wait for the main courses, which are positively enormous: fresh house pasta, *carpaccios* (in particular the one with *coquilles St-Jacques*) at around 90F. The meat or fish dishes vary between 130F and 150F. Good value *dégustation* set meal, with generous portions.

✕ **La Lanterne** (map B3, **27**): 9 rue du Tunnel 75019. ☎ 01-42-39-15-98. Metro: Buttes-Chaumont or Botzaris. Open until 11pm. Closed Saturday lunchtime and on Sunday. Set menus 79F, 119F and 149F. Predictably you'll find a lantern lit in the window of this restaurant. Decent French cuisine. Starters 35F, main courses 79F – such as the *magret de canard* with cider and spice bread, leg of lamb or *steak tartare* – and desserts at 35F. Book a table under a parasol on the pleasant little terrace on the first floor.

BUTTES-CHAUMONT

★ The **Buttes-Chaumont** is another green area of Paris. Metro: Buttes-Chaumont, Botzaris and Laumière. In 1867 this area was transformed into a park under the ubiquitous Baron Haussmann, and the work was carried out by Alphand, an engineer who had a hand in the creation of almost all the parks in Paris. Napoleon III actually saw himself as a '*hygiéniste*', and ordered that every part of Paris should have a green space. He wanted to give the working classes places where they could go for family walks on a Sunday, to keep them away from the taverns.

In the centre of Paris, the Buttes-Chaumont park is a complete surprise. A mountainous mixture of rock and concrete stands in the middle, connected by a suspension bridge and another bridge made of brick. At its summit there is a little temple which provides a splendid panoramic view of the area. The surrounding lake is fed by water from the nearby Canal St-Martin. With waterfalls, criss-crossing rivulets and uneven terrain, the Buttes-Chaumont is an ideal place to take kids. In winter the lake is often frozen over but the rest of the year it is an excellent place for boat trips. There are also concerts in the pavilion.

The famous cave-waterfall, closed in 1945 because it was in danger of collapsing, is now open to the public again. Waffle-sellers and donkey-cart rides complete a perfect day out. Note the old roller-skating rink surrounded by an iron railing.

Everyone loves the *Guignol-Anatole* (☎ 01-43-98-10-95) which is over 150 years old. These marionette puppet shows are a summer tradition in Paris, similar to the English Punch and Judy shows. They show the adventures of Guignol, from age three upwards, in a period setting. Open-air theatre (when the weather is fine) from 1 April to 31 October, Wednesday, Saturday, Sunday, public holidays and in the school holidays. Shows at 3pm and 4.30pm (in July and August there is one show, at 4.30pm). Entry fee 15F.

★ The **église St-Serge:** 93 rue de Crimée 75019. A delightful Russian church, not very well known. The inside, as is often the case with these churches, is splendid; a subdued atmosphere, charming and peaceful.

★ Beside St-Jean-Baptiste-de-Belleville at 6 **rue de Palestine**, is an Orthodox Ukrainian church. Mass is sung every Sunday at 10am.

At the top of rue de Belleville there really is a metro station called 'Place-des-Fêtes' (Party Square), but nowadays there isn't a square and there aren't any parties. Still, go up and take a look anyway at the picturesque **regard de la Lanterne**, on the corner of rue Compans and rue Augustin-Thierry. Built in 1583, it was the head of the aqueduct for the water supply for Belleville.

★ at 11 **rue des Fêtes** there is a superb 17th-century folly, a country house belonging to aristocrats of the time, with *mascarons* (sculpted faces), a balcony and fine roofing. At No. 13 a narrow corridor leads to one of the last estate gardens in the area – around 15 houses with exuberant lilac gardens, trees, a gigantic chestnut tree, a wooden pavilion and total peace and quiet. Note the pretty oval skylights on the roofs.

A SHORT WALK AROUND THE AREA

There are no grandiose monuments or special architecture here, but it is full of secret gardens hiding ivy-clad pavilions with lots of opportunities to take in some local colour.

★ The **villas de la Mouzaïa:** 2km (1 mile), 45 minutes, from either the Porte-de-Pantin or the Pré-St-Gervais Metro station to the Botzaris Metro station. The names of the lanes around here all start with '*villa*' or '*allée*' with connotations of the countryside. From the Porte-de-Pantin Metro station, go around the Lycée d'Alembert and walk back up the pedestrian allée Arthur-Honegger and allée Darius-Milhaud, where birds hide in the hedgerows. In rue Goubet and rue d'Hautpoul the views plunge down over the green space of the Cimetière de la Villette. The rue Manin runs along by the Parc des Buttes-Chaumont and then reaches the heights of Belleville (128.5m/420ft) which loom over the east of Paris. The names 'Bellevue' and 'Belleville' come from these views.

To the south of place Rhin-et-Danube take a walk around the villas which overlook rue de l'Égalité and rue de la Liberté, as well as the lovely rue de Mouzaïa. Villa Amalia is one of the finest: lined with old street-lights and trees, it is a succession of little flowering gardens. In Villa de Fontenay rose bushes spill over onto the street, but in Villa du Progrès you come up against progress: concrete and cranes. Villa Émile-Loubet, on a slope, has a provincial charm, but Villa Bellevue has more colour: the roofs are laid out across one another, in steps. The same goes for Villa des Lilas. The Villa de la Renaissance has some delightful doors covered in ivy (No. 9 for instance). Villa Danube is also bordered by some lovely houses while Villa Marceau is very elegant. In Villa Laforgue, at the end of the path, there's greenery as far as the eye can see. The Villa Boërs overlooks the church steeple. To get back to Paris take rue de Bellevue and rue Arthur-Rozier which lead to the Villa Albert-Rohida, descending a surrealistic flight of stairs to rue de Crimée. You'll soon come to the east of the Parc des Buttes-Chaumont and the Botzaris Metro station.

BASSIN DE LA VILLETTE

★ The **Bassin de la Villette** was dug at the beginning of the 19th century and inaugurated with great pomp and ceremony in 1808, on Napoleon

Bonaparte's birthday. In the 19th century it was often used as an ice-rink during severe winters. Today, the embankments have been converted into a pleasant walk, and the industrial landscape has softened to give way to new, classic architecture. In the evenings you may even be able to spot some crayfish fans, as the fish hide during the day and come out at twilight.

There are two enormous warehouses standing guard at the end of the basin. One of them, a fine building which appeared in the cult French film *Diva,* was badly damaged by fire. Barges used to unload sugar, coal and sand here on the quayside. The sugar was also once stored here, but that stopped in 1990. Today, the remaining warehouse has been transformed into lofts, artists' workshops or photo studios, and houses some elegant, fashionable restaurants.

★ The **pont de Crimée** is the last drawbridge in Paris. It operates by means of rack and pinion gearing set in Greek columns. The company which built it (in 1885) also created the hydraulic lifts for the Eiffel Tower. There are construction dates all over the columns and a fine china plaque on the little house at the entrance to the bridge. The modern building on the corner has made a visible effort to fit in with the local style.

The church, on the quai de la Seine side, couldn't seem to care less about the aesthetic debate surrounding the bridge. There's a sunny market nearby every Sunday and Thursday morning, in place Joinville.

The quai de la Seine seems to be echoing the quai de la Loire with names which still bear witness to the quarter's tradition of a friendly welcome – Le Restaurant des Amis au Bon Accueil and Les Mariniers au Rendez-vous de la Marine.

★ The **rue de Flandre** has, at No. 44, the tiny little Portuguese Jewish Cemetery, with some fine tombs in sculpted marble. It was opened in 1780, which makes it one of the oldest cemeteries in Paris, along with those at St-Germain-de-Charonne and St-Pierre-de-Montmartre. If you would like to visit, ask at the Paris Israeli Consistory. ☎ 01-40-82-26-90.

The shop names around here are pretty down-to-earth. Even though Paris is losing its working class communities, one shop, at the entrance to rue de Flandre, still proudly announces: '*À l'Ouvrier*' (For Workers).

★ The **avenue Jean-Jaurès** and the metro station of the same name are close at hand. Both got their names just after the end of the First World War, replacing 'avenue d'Allemagne' (Germany). This street has seen some historic events: first of all, Louis XVI's flight to Varennes and his return (on 20 and 28 June 1791 respectively), and then, in 1807, the triumphant arrival of the Imperial Guard after the Prussian Campaign. In 1814, on the other hand, it also witnessed the entry of Russian troops with Tsar Alexander, and Austrian and Prussian troops with the King of Prussia. The night before, the armistice had been negotiated with Marshal Marmont in a little inn then located opposite the Villette rotunda.

Rue de Meaux indicates the former country lane leading to Meaux (where the mustard comes from). The old urban landscape around rue de l'Ourcq and rue de Crimée is reminiscent of times gone by but will still, one hopes, be around for a while yet.

PARC DE LA VILLETTE

Metro: Porte-de-Pantin; also accessible through Metro: Porte-de-la-Villette or Corentin-Cariou. Open daily 24 hours, guarded and lit at all times. Guided tours for individuals on Wednesday at 3pm; groups, by reservation. Information: ☎ 01-40-03-75-64 or 01-40-03-74-80. Group bookings: ☎ 01-40-03-74-82. There's a reception pavilion at the Porte-de-Pantin entrance to help visitors find their way around this enormous labyrinth.

Now completed, after many embellishments, the park stretches over 55ha (135 acres), which actually makes it the largest park in Paris. It covers the whole of the old national meat market, between the Porte de Pantin and the Porte de la Villette, at the confluence of the Canal de l'Ourcq and the Canal St-Denis. It comprises the **Cité des Sciences,** the **Cité de la Musique** and the **Grande Halle,** the **Théâtre Paris Villette**, the **Théâtre international de Langue française**, as well as the **Zénith,** the **Géode,** the **Cinaxe**, the **Argonaute**, exhibition halls and venues for circus and cabaret performances.

This vast ensemble was built between 1984 and 1997 and has proved to be quite a success, due to both the content of the 'Cités' and the architecture of the buildings and the park itself. There are more than 3km (1.5 miles) of walks for pedestrians and cycle tracks, and 10 or so themed gardens. It is a cross between the past and the future, arts and science, nature and the city.

The park is the work of Bernard Tschumi, who opted to be modern and design a park with a revolutionary concept. He criss-crossed 35ha (86 acres) with imaginary lines, creating a vast chessboard with squares measuring 120m (390ft) across, and at every intersection put one of what he calls his '*folies*': 25 cube-shaped buildings, each 10.8m (35ft) in dimension and bright red, some highly decorated, with a turret or an external flight of stairs, and some hollowed out. There is an information point, refreshment area and there are usually various activities going on.

Completing the geometry there are two east–west and north–south pedestrian routes running across the park, linking la porte de Pantin with that of la Villette, and linking Paris to the suburbs along the canal d'Ourcq. There is also a meeting place for joggers (*cercle*) and large areas of green (*triangle*).

From mid-July to the end of August there is an open-air cinema, showing classics and art-house films; and dances, also in the open and free, devoted to world music. In the open air as well as in the Grande Halle and the Cité de la Musique, the Villette Jazz Festival takes place at the end of June and beginning of July. Check with the tourist office on the programme.

A BRIEF HISTORY

For a century this whole area was devoted to abattoirs and the livestock market. It was created by Haussmann (yes, him again!) in 1867. The need for slaughterhouses so close to Paris was justified at the time by the lack of refrigeration techniques. The abattoirs of La Villette were part of Paris folklore, as were the slaughtermen and others involved in the bloody business.

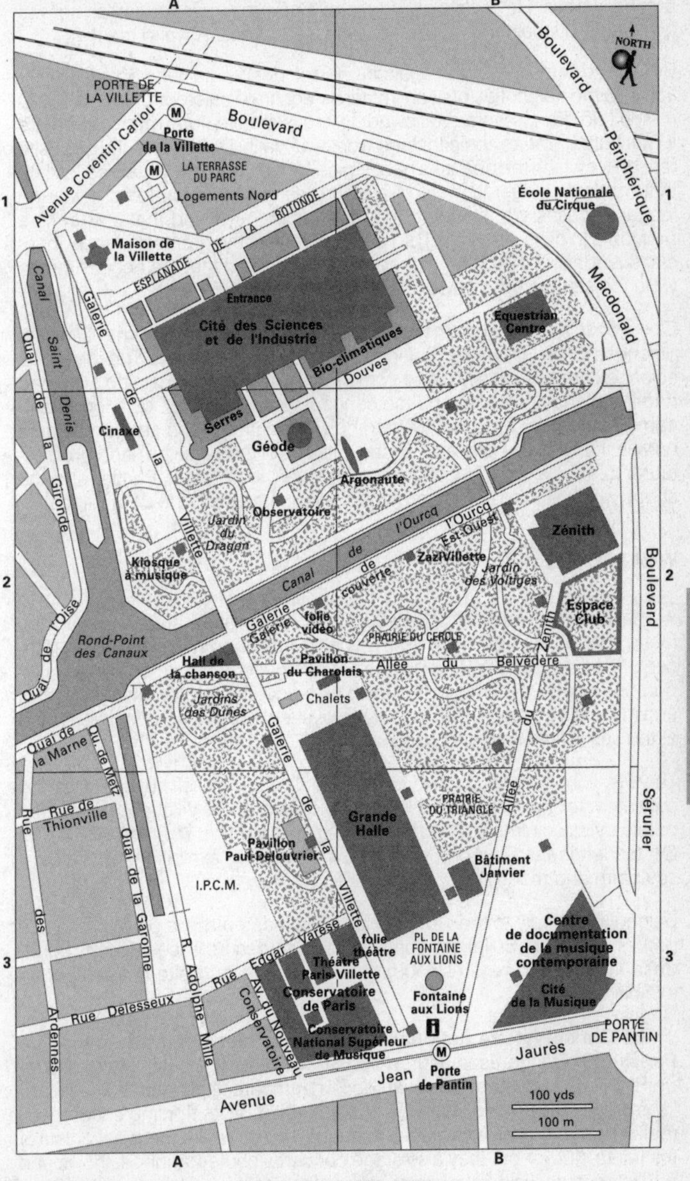

PARC DE LA VILLETTE

The livestock market could hold up to 1,300 cattle at a time. Proust used to come here from time to time to try and pick up the strong, handsome butcher's boys. He always asked them: 'Show me your hands!' as he was fascinated by their enormous, blood-soaked hands. A weird man!

By the end of the 1960s the abattoirs were in desperate need of modernization and the authorities built an immense concrete saleroom. Over 300,000 million (old) francs were swallowed up in this architectural madness before it was halted. It was ironic that the work was halted for exactly the opposite reason for which the abattoirs had originally been built: they realised too late that modern refrigeration and transport techniques meant that it was no longer necessary to slaughter the animals in Paris, and that it was more profitable to do it at source. The result was one of the greatest French financial scandals of the century; they even discovered that the access ramps were too steep for the cows to get up!

One consolation is that the absurd structure now houses the Cité des Sciences et de l'Industrie (Science and Industry Complex). The idea for a science complex initially came from President Giscard d'Estaing, who had had the plans drawn up, and the concept was taken over, developed and carried out under President Mitterrand. The legacy of the abattoirs lingers on with the Grande Halle and, on the outskirts of the park, the handful of restaurants specializing in good meat (around the Porte de Pantin) and the shops which still sell butchers' equipment (around the Porte de la Villette).

WHAT TO SEE

★ The **Grande Halle:** ☎ 01-40-03-75-75 (information and reservations). Metro: Porte-de-Pantin. The former cattle hall is a fine example of 19th-century architecture. Well renovated, it has been transformed into a multi-purpose space for exhibitions, trade fairs and shows. With its glass walls and interesting interior, thanks to walkways and partitions, its architecture is at the same time light and transparent.

The Pavillon Janvier, on the right of the Grande Halle, houses a centre dealing with the history and current activities of La Villette (open to the public by appointment Monday to Friday 1pm to 6pm; ☎ 01-40-03-74-03). On the left is the Pavillon Paul-Delouvrier, hosting exhibitions of statuary, sculpture and modelling.

Belonging entirely to the Grande Halle, but located at the other end of the park, in the white buildings opposite the Cité des Sciences (Metro: Porte-de-la-Villette or Corentin-Cariou), the Maison de la Villette is a temporary exhibition space.

★ The **Conservatoire national supérieur de musique et de danse de Paris:** 209 avenue Jean-Jaurès 75019. ☎ 01-40-40-45-45. Metro: Porte-de-Pantin. Designed by Christian de Portzamparc, this educational establishment for music and dance is characterized by its rippling sheet-metal roof. Its educational aims are very serious – this is where the great artists of the future study – but they also stage concerts, choreographed shows and public courses which are free of charge (subject to availability of places or if you book). A brochure giving the programme is available on request. ☎ 01-40-40-46-46 or 47.

★ The **Cité de la Musique:** 221 avenue Jean-Jaurès 75019. ☎ 01-44-84-44-84. Website: www.cite-musique.fr. Metro: Porte-de-Pantin. Bus Nos. 75, 151 and PC. Open Tuesday to Saturday noon to 6pm, and Sunday 10am to 6pm. Closed Monday.

Also built by Portzamparc (*see above*), and just as original, the concert hall here has 1,200 seats. They put on classical and contemporary music but also jazz, French *chanson* and world music. The complex also has a more intimate amphitheatre, with 230 seats, where they put on concerts in collaboration with the museum – often using old or unusual instruments – and concerts and shows for young people (Wednesday at 3pm). The halls have excellent acoustics, the concerts are of very high quality and the prices are reasonable.

Opened in 1997, the **musée de la Musique** (Music Museum) completes this group with the collection formerly held by the Conservatoire of Paris. Started in 1793, it now possesses 4,500 instruments from the 16th to the 20th century, with 900 permanently on show. The museum is divided into nine areas devoted to European classical music and, to a lesser degree, contemporary and Western music. It is worth noting, however, that the section on the 20th century is closed until January 2002 for major reorganisation. In the meantime this area will be used to house temporary exhibitions. The superb Flemish and Italian harpsichords, lutes, clavichords, mandolins and obscure French horns will amaze you, as will the improbable looking octobass, a huge double-bass 3–4m (10–13ft) high. You can explore the evolution of acoustic instruments before electric Gibson or Fender guitars and the first appearance of electronics (see the amazing Ondes Martenot, 1928). You can listen to the music via the infra-red headphones. Progress does have some advantages! The extracts from operas, concertos or jazz, with serious commentary, charm the ear and broaden the mind. There are also interactive terminals teaching you the history of music, its social role, etc. World and folk music only seem to have temporary exhibitions but there is plenty to keep you occupied with 'themed' tours and workshops for both adults and children.

★ The **Cité des sciences et de l'industrie:** ☎ 01-40-05-80-00 or 01-40-05-12-12 (bookings). Website: www.cite-sciences.fr. Metro: Porte-de-la-Villette (direct access to the Cité). Bus Nos. 75, 139, 150, 152 and PC. There is an underground car park. Open 10am to 6pm (7pm Sunday); different opening times for the Géode and the Cinaxe (*see below*). Closed Monday.

N.B.: for exhibitions with fixed opening times (Cité des Enfants, Techno-Cité) it's best to book, especially during the school holidays.

In the sale room of the former abattoir (which was never actually finished, never mind used!), the Science and Industry Complex deals with issues relating to scientific research, industrial investment and the progress of technology. The architect, Adrien Fainsilber, has spared no expense on the quality of the materials or on the size of the space. From a somewhat forlorn shell he has made a futurist temple, and at the same time adapted it to the early 21st century. In order to push back the enormous façade wall, Fainsilber called on the French company who had worked on the Abu Simbel construction site in Egypt.

The dimensions are impressive: 3ha (7.5 acres) of ground space, 270m (885ft) long, 110m (360ft) wide, 47m (154ft) high – a total of 165,000 square metres (540,000 square feet)! The single entrance hall measures 100m

(328ft) long and 20m (65ft) wide. Above, there are two enormous cupolas suspended over the roof, allowing daylight to flood the reception hall.

This complex is not a museum. All the exhibits, from their presentation to the elements of which they are made up, are prototypes. Since it opened there have been themes as varied as 'The plastic years', 'The blood of men', 'The vine and wine', 'Measurements and excesses', among others.

Another unusual aspect of this futuristic complex is that it is interactive: tap away at a computer keyboard, talk and the machine answers you, push buttons and joysticks, play at setting the world to rights, at drawing portraits, at recognizing the voices of famous people. There's no need to go to the Moon any more, the Moon can come to you!

– **Tour**

There are many aids for visitors taking the tour:

– *Science assistants:* help the public to explore the Cité, its exhibitions and its shows. Ask for a programme when you arrive.

– *Audio headphones:* a headphone set which is tuned in to 40 listening points, enabling each visitor to receive messages individually in five languages (French, English, German, Spanish or Italian) on the scientific exhibits and the architecture of the building.

– For people with impaired vision or any other difficulties in finding their way around, there are messages in French as well as guide strips on the floor. Some of the areas have Braille panels and embossed diagrams. In the multimedia library the Salle Louis-Braille offers access to printed documents, transcribed by voice or in Braille. Assistants are also available, though the sign language specialists only sign French.

– Visitors with disabilities have access to all the exhibitions and services, except the Argonaute submarine.

– There are tours for groups (15 people and upwards).

Here's a taste of just a few of the exhibits:

– **Explora:** 50F, free for children under seven. Over 20 thematic exhibitions occupy the first and second levels, including, for instance:

• *Extreme environments:* here you'll find the *Nautilus* and the head of the *Ariane* rocket, an orbital space station and the decompression centre which replicates space conditions underwater. Further on, the Earth's past is cleverly recreated and brought to life with some excellent displays, as in the Théâtre de l'Ardèche, where you can watch the evolution of a peaceful French valley over 300 million years. There is a geological history of the Earth (rocks and volcanoes), the stars and galaxies (the Big Bang, the fate of a star) and the Théâtre des Galaxies. Don't miss the *planetarium,* an amazing introduction to our own place in the galaxy (there is an astronomic simulator capable of reproducing 10,000 stars and the whole of the solar system). There are events all the year round.

• *The world of Mathematics and Sound:* games for raising awareness of maths and the physics of sound (test how accurate your hearing is, watch a spectrum display of your own voice, etc.)

• *The environment:* this is all about exploring and understanding the climate, ecology and the great environmental issues facing the earth at the beginning of the 21st century. A weather forecasting workshop is accessible to all and there are 52 computer-controlled television screens with films to help you understand ecosystems, with models (including sounds) of a tropical rainforest, the Tunisian desert, cyclones and ocean currents. There are also answers to questions about air and water pollution, toxic waste, acid rain, etc. A piece of computer software tells you what the weather in Paris has been like since 1873 and in 5,000 other cities across the world … probably raining!

- *Man and Health:* a discussion of human health through a series of films and a journey to discover medicines throughout the world. Also the whole history of thinking Man and the secrets of life (conception and birth, measuring biological data, etc.)

- *Communications:* everything you always wanted to know about artificial intelligence, IT and its techniques and the many possibilities of language. You can test your perception of behaviour and look at the 'Reality Screens': images showing scientific observations with the aid of new techniques – thermography, infra-red cameras, medical technology. In the computer department there's a flight simulator using real time images, a strategy game (artificial intelligence at work) and a 'clear' explanation of the basic principles of how a computer works.

On level zero (ground floor) are the *Cité des Enfants* and *Techno-Cité*. The first, as its name (Children's Complex) suggests, is for children, the second is aimed more at teenagers, and, though it doesn't say it anywhere, adults will have just as much fun.

– The **Cité des Enfants:** sessions last an hour and a half from Tuesday to Sunday 10am to 6pm. Price for child and accompanying adult 25F, with a maximum of two accompanying adults per child. Reserved especially for children aged 3 to 5 and 5 to 12 , the 3,800 square metres (41,000 square feet) contains a life-size anthill, carnivorous plants, a televized news bulletin in production, and lots of other attractions. For 3 to 5 year-olds there are computer games, 'today's weather' and an amazing audio-visual 'swimming pool'. There are also lots of very interesting temporary events. It's been such a hit that the exhibition space has almost quadrupled since it opened. Best to book in advance, reservations ☎ 01-40-05-12-12.

– **Techno-Cité:** on level zero (ground floor), for 11 years and upwards. Open to the public Wednesday and Saturday afternoons and during school holidays, reserved for school groups during the week. Sessions last an hour and a half. Price: 25F per person. Take the controls of a helicopter to understand how its rotor works, programme a video game, discover the combination of a safe. Basically the idea is to get your hands dirty and learn about technology. The exhibits encourage you to observe, understand and work using real objects and situations. *Techno-Cité* is organized around five permanent themes: 'Mechanisms in movement', 'Design a piece of software', 'Manufacturing techniques', 'Preparing a prototype', 'Sensors and automation'.

On Level 1 is the *Cinéma Louis Lumière*, the multimedia library, the *Salle Science-actualités* and *Cité des Métiers* (Career Complex):

– **Cinéma Louis Lumière:** offers documentaries, drama and cartoons. Its projection room, fitted for 3D cinema, projects a film in relief (you need special 3D glasses to see it). Ideal for kids.

– The **multimedia library:** open Tuesday to Sunday noon to 6pm. Multimedia library for children open daily noon to 8pm. Contains over 300,000 scientific works, 5,000 periodicals, 3,000 audio-visual documents recorded on video disks (300 hours of programmes). The Salle Louis-Braille offers visitors with impaired vision the opportunity to study written documents thanks to computer equipment.

– The **Salle Science-actualités:** designed to be like a multimedia newspaper hosted by scientific journalists, it specialises in exhibitions and scientific, technical and industrial current affairs. It also puts on a large number of debates and press conferences.

– The **Cité des Métiers:** open Tuesday to Friday 10am to 6pm and Saturday noon to 6pm. Free. Everything you ever wanted to know about careers' advice, employment and training. Advisers answer your questions (by appointment) and there is a whole mass of documents and interactive software available to you. This service is in French only.

– On Level 2, near the cafeteria, you are plunged into the depths of the Mediterranean. Over 250 square metres (2,675 square feet), the **aquarium** houses more than 200 species of fish, shellfish, molluscs and plants from the Mediterranean coastal region. From one showcase to the next you can examine the richness of life at 50m (160ft) under the surface of the water. Free entry.

Adjoining the *Cité des Sciences* (of which they are part: same opening days and same telephone numbers but different timetables, so you should book ahead), the *Géode* and the *Cinaxe* offer excitement and technology and the *Argonaute* will take you into the suffocating world of submarines (access included in the 'Explora' ticket).

★ **The Géode:** shows every hour Tuesday to Sunday 10am to 9pm and also on Mondays, but timetable varies; special opening on bank holiday Monday and school holidays. Entry fee 57F; concessions 44F at weekends and public holidays, except 2pm to 5pm. Bookings: ☎ 01-40-05-12-12.

N.B.: we recommend that you book during the school holidays as there are only 400 seats. However, outside these times and on weekend afternoons you'll generally find room between 10am and noon or 6pm and 9pm. You can buy combined tickets and facilities for group bookings (10 people or more).

This ball of polished steel (the first perfect sphere to be built in the world) will transport you into the future. Since 1986 it has housed a cinema where spectators (nearly 12 million since it opened) are transported by the 1,000m (3,280ft) spherical screen – take a trip on a space shuttle or explore the depths of the Pacific Ocean. The field of vision covers 180° and the effect can take you by surprise! The sensation is increased by excellent acoustics. The strong, sometimes breathtaking images (nose-dives in aeroplanes and all kinds of exciting plunges) can make you feel dizzy. One of the latest films, *Everest*, shows for the first time on the big screen the fascinating story of an expedition to the roof of the world.

★ The **Cinaxe:** next to the *Géode*, open Tuesday to Sunday, 11am to 5pm. Closed Monday. There is a session every 15 minutes. Entry 34F; concessions or group rates: enquire at the ticket desk. Like a flight simulator, this entire cinema moves according to the movements of the images being projected. The spectator feels sensations which, while not as long lasting, are possibly even more impressive than at the *Géode*. You might suddenly plunge into an abyss, then go quickly up again. It's not too good for a weak stomach!

NB.: Not recommended for children under four, pregnant women, people with heart conditions or epilepsy.

★ The **Argonaute:** an authentic submarine, this is the main exhibit in a museum devoted to the technological and human adventure of travelling underwater. Access is included in the 'Explora' ticket. Designed in the 1950s, this submarine used to be one of the jewels in the crown of the French Navy. There's an impressive tour showing the incredible network of tubes and cables, levers, old radar and sonar screens and periscopes; it's almost unthinkably cramped. At the end there are four enormous torpedoes. Unfortunately it is not accessible to those with disabilities.

★ The **Zénith:** 211 avenue Jean-Jaurès 75019. Metro: Porte-de-Pantin. ☎ 01-42-08-60-00. A well-known venue for rock concerts. Initially 'temporary' (set up in six months in 1984) it eventually took root and has now got a good reputation.

ALONG THE BASSIN DE LA VILLETTE AND THE CANAL ST-MARTIN

– **La Guêpe Buissonnière and Le Canotier:** these are authentic barges, not *bateau-mouches* (River Seine tourist boats). For over 20 years they have been plying the canals of Paris, the Seine, and the Marne. Take the time to experience and savour a few moments' peace and quiet, to relax for a few hours to the rhythm of the locks filling and emptying. (*For a more detailed description of the route, see* '10th arrondissement'.)

Barges leave from the Parc de la Villette, then go under the famous pont de Crimée.

19TH

- From end March to mid-November:

– *from the Parc de la Villette:* 2.30pm daily. Leaves from the 'tours folly', in the heart of the park (Metro: Porte-de-Pantin).

– *From the musée d'Orsay:* 9.30am daily. Leaves from the quai Anatole-France, through the car-park of the Musée d'Orsay (Metro: Solférino).

- The rest of the year: on Sunday only.

Price 100F; children aged 4 to 11 55F; *Vermeil* cards and young people aged 12 to 25 (except in the afternoon on Sunday and public holidays) 75F. You have to book by telephone. Information: Paris-Canal, 19–21 quai de la Loire 75019. ☎ 01-42-40-96-97. Also offers themed cruises and fixed prices for tours.

WHERE TO GO FOR A DRINK

Le Café Parisien (map C3, **40**): 2 place Rhin-et-Danube 75019. ☎ 01-42-06-02-75. Metro: Danube. Open 7am until midnight (at least!). Closed Sunday. Half a pint of beer costs 10F. A real local café, not one of the 'yes-it-looks-old-but-it's-actually-brand-new' ones. The neighbouring area was called '*l'Amérique*' (America) because the stones used to build the White House were quarried here. All the attractive houses around, for which today the stars will pay a fortune, were originally accommodation for the quarry workers. Friendly and genuine, at the first ray of sunshine, out come the tables. Lots of cinema posters on the walls and there's a pool table (10F per game) in the back room. There are also concerts some nights.

🍸 **Le Café de la Musique** (map C2, **41**): 213 avenue Jean-Jaurès 75019. ☎ 01-48-03-15-91. Metro: Porte-de-Pantin. Open daily until 1 or 2am (1am on Sundays and Mondays). Budget for around 150F per person, half-price for children. A drink costs 22F. Inside the *Cité de la Musique*, this place has been the subject of some controversy. Although some people like the designer setting of this modern bistro, others say it looks rather '80s ... your decision. The customers tend towards the trendy and so does the cuisine. There is jazz or world music every Wednesday, Friday and Saturday evening from 10.30pm and a wonderful brunch (100F) on Sunday from 11am to 5pm.

GOING OUT

– **Glaz'art** (map C1, **42**): 7–15 avenue de la Porte-de-la-Villette 75019. ☎ 01-40-36-55-65. Metro: Porte-de-la-Villette. Open Wednesday to Saturday 8.30pm to 2am (10pm to 5am on Saturday). Entry from 40F depending what's on. Membership is optional and costs 200F. A drink costs 20F. The *Glaz'art*, a pro-art movement, has taken refuge in a former coach station now rejuvenated as a wonderful multicultural '*caf'-conc*' (café with live music). Overflowing with exhibitions (paintings, sculptures, photos, etc.) in live workshops (stories, theatre ...), concerts, DJs and experimental parties (video, webcam), in understandably arty surroundings.

20TH ARRONDISSEMENT

PÈRE-LACHAISE CEMETERY ● CHARONNE ● MÉNILMONTANT ● BELLEVILLE

A BRIEF HISTORY

The 19th and 20th arrondissements of Paris are relatively recent creations. For many years Belleville and Charonne were just farming towns but, in 1728 Parisians were given permission to start building in Belleville and there was a real rush. These areas had everything – fresh air, property prices which were not as fierce as in Paris and all the advantages of the countryside without Parisian taxes. The Bas de la Courtille (in the current 10th and 11th arrondissements) was covered in *guinguettes* (small restaurants with music and dancing). The word *guinguette* actually represented a mixture of things: from an inn with a reputation for good food and wine to a dance with a rural feel, from the coaching inns (now transport cafés) to a brothel. The upheavals of the Revolution, the Imperial episode, and the Restoration did not have such a profound effect on the way of life in these villages as did the Industrial Revolution, which provided the backdrop to these events.

At the time of the Revolution the village of Belleville had around 1,000 inhabitants. They were mostly market gardeners or wine growers, coopers, a few people of independent means, plus the inevitable *limonadiers* (the word, which means 'café owners', is somewhat ambiguous, because as far as anyone knows lemonade wasn't the main product they were offering for sale). People came from the provinces along with increasing numbers of workers. This growing population was essential for the splendours of the court of the Tuileries though when they erupted onto the political scene, they brought with them the terrors of the Commune.

At the beginning of the 20th century Belleville welcomed a new wave of immigrants. At first people came from the Auvergne; nicknamed the 'Immigrants from the Centre' they became *bougnats* (owners of cafés which originally sold coal, from the Auvergnat term *charbougnat*, meaning collier). The next immigrants to arrive in Paris were Russian and Polish Jews fleeing the pogroms, who became tailors, furriers and fine leather craftsmen. The Armenians, who were escaping from genocide, specialized in the manufacture of shoes. They were followed in 1922 by Greeks leaving Turkey, then by more Jews fleeing from Nazi Germany and Spanish Republicans leaving after Franco's victory. In the 1950s Sephardic Jews came from North Africa as well as North Africans, mainly from Morocco, Algeria and Tunisia. Yugoslavs, Portuguese and Africans soon followed. Belleville continues, as always, to offer asylum to those in need.

The area of Belleville covered in this guide includes the parts of the 10th and 11th arrondissements which used to belong to it before the administrative division in 1860.

THE ORIGIN OF THE STREET NAMES

Something of the history of Belleville, and Ménilmontant and Charonne's agricultural roots can be traced through the street names. Here are a few examples: rue des Gâtines (meaning marshy, sterile land), rue des Bruyères (Briar Road), rue des Fougères (Fern Road), rue des Grands-Champs (Big Field Road), rue de la Plaine (Plain Road), rue des Prairies (Prairie Road – and separating them is rue des Haies – Hedge Road), rue des Amandiers (Almond Tree Road), rue des Pruniers (Plum Tree Road), rue des Mûriers (Mulberry Tree Road), rue des Guigniers (Cherry Tree Road), and even rue des Réglisses (Liquorice Street) – before it was something you bought at the sweet shop, it was a plant growing wild in the hedgerow.

The rue des Montibœufs recalls the cattle (*bœuf* means beef) which sometimes used to struggle up the slopes of Charonne, and *mesnil* means an old farm, hence Ménilmontant. There is also a Porte des Lilas (Lilac Gate), rue des Lys (Lily Street) and rue des Maraîchers (Market Gardeners' Street), and, of course, there is rue des Vignoles (Vineyard Street) with its rue du Pressoir (Wine Press Street); and even a rather strange rue des Panoyaux (Seedless Grape Street!). Last but not least is the Sente des Dorées, which is the hunting term given to stag droppings, an indication that these animals at one time wandered freely around the area.

Surprisingly, out of 72 uniformed marshals, generals and admirals who have given their names to the streets of Paris as a whole, the 20th arrondissement has just one: General Niessel, an obscure officer decorated during the First World War.

WHERE TO STAY

☆ BUDGET TO CHEAP

Auberge de jeunesse d'Artagnan (map C2, **1**): 80 rue de Vitruve 75020. ☎ 01-40-32-34-56. Fax: 01-40-32-34-55. E-mail: paris.le-dartagnan@fuaj.org. Metro: Porte-de-Bagnolet. One night is 115F per person (sheets and breakfast included). A lively youth hostel, open 24 hours a day (but the rooms are closed between noon and 3pm). Self-service, snack bar and even a bar open from 5pm. Grill open in the evening only. Set menus from 35F to 70F. Tex-Mex specialities. The largest youth hostel in France (440 beds), offering double, triple, quadruple and eight-bed rooms. Please note, they're not always as thorough as they might be in cleaning, so check the sheets. For groups, make sure you get them to explain the conditions for your stay properly. There's a pool table and a hall where, every evening, they show a different film in its original language. There is a launderette and a left luggage office. You must have the FUAJ card (which you can buy on the spot). You can book any youth hostel in the world thanks to a sophisticated computer system: the RIBN (Reservations International Booking Network).

Tamaris Hôtel (map C3, **2**): 14 rue des Maraîchers 75020. ☎ 01-43-72-85-48. Fax: 01-43-56-81-75. Metro: Porte-de-Vincennes or Maraîchers; RER: Nation. Small rooms with washbasin 170F for two people. With shower 214F; with shower and toilet 249F; for three or four people, between 215F and 320F. Don't miss breakfast, at only 25F per person. A remarkably well-run little hotel, with rural prices. TV in the lounge. A friendly welcome, and you may be able to negotiate reductions at certain times of the year. We recommend that you book as soon as you know when you're coming!

Eden Hôtel (map B1, **4**): 7 rue Jean-Baptiste-Dumay 75020. ☎ 01-46-36-64-22. Fax: 01-46-36-01-11. Metro: Pyrénées or Jourdain. Bus No. 26. Double rooms with shower from 270F to 295F. A quiet hotel with no great personality but a friendly welcome. Located near the Buttes-Chaumont and Père-Lachaise Cemetery. TV, telephone, lift.

☆☆ MODERATE

Hôtel Pyrénées Gambetta (map B2, **3**): 12 avenue du Père-Lachaise 75020. ☎ 01-47-97-76-57. Fax: 01-47-97-17-61. Metro: Gambetta. Double rooms with shower and toilet 250F to 350F; with bath, 337F to 402F. In a quiet street leading to Père-Lachaise Cemetery, this is a pleasant two-star hotel. The rooms are more than decent, with double beds built into alcoves. They are all equipped with satellite TV with Canal +, as well as a mini-bar. Quiet and cosy in an area that isn't too touristy.

WHERE TO EAT

☆ BUDGET

Au Bon Coin (map B1, **10**): 10–12 rue Pixérécourt 75020. ☎ 01-46-36-67-71. Metro: Télégraphe. Open lunchtime and evening (to 9pm). Closed Saturday, Sunday and August. Single menu 68F. Set menu lunchtime and evening, with a buffet of hors-d'œuvres, a generous main course, platter of cheeses and dessert, wine and coffee (main course on its own 42F). Simple home-cooking to fill you up without breaking the bank. Done out as an old bar which hasn't changed since the 1960s.

Pascaline (map B1, **11**): 49 rue Pixérécourt 75020. ☎ 01-44-62-22-80. Metro: Place-des-Fêtes or Télégraphe. Last orders 10pm to 10.30pm. Closed Saturday lunchtime, Sunday, Monday evening and during August. Set menus 69F at lunchtime, 110F in the evening. À la carte around 110F. A great little restaurant, which fits perfectly into the feel of the area. Treat yourself to home-cooking, generously served. A pleasant dining room

Where to stay
- **1** Auberge de jeunesse d'Artagnan
- **2** Tamaris Hôtel
- **3** Hôtel Pyrénées Gambetta
- **4** Eden Hôtel

Where to eat
- **10** Au Bon Coin
- **11** Pascaline
- **12** Le Torreense
- **13** Restaurant Jardin d'Or
- **14** Chez Carlos
- **15** Aristote
- **16** Chez Jean
- **17** Les Salons de Musique
- **18** Aux Chutes du Carbet
- **20** Café Noir
- **21** La Fontaine aux Roses
- **22** Giacomo Piccola Brescia
- **23** À Roda d'Afiar
- **24** Les Allobroges
- **25** Le Vieux Belleville
- **26** Restaurante Ribatejo
- **27** Paris-Carthage
- **28** Takichi
- **29** Le Bistrot des Soupirs, chez Raymonde
- **30** Le Zéphyr
- **31** Chez Lasseron
- **32** Le Zap Spirit
- **33** Le Krung Thep
- **34** Le Baratin

Where to go for a drink
- **40** Flèche d'Or Café
- **42** Bistrot Le Piston Pélican
- **43** Lou Pascalou
- **44** Le Mercure
- **45** Le Pataquès
- **46** Les Trois Arts
- **47** La Mère Lachaise
- **48** La Maroquinerie

A
B
19e
10e
11e
1
2
3
Télégraphe
Jourdain
Pyrénées
Belleville
Couronnes
Ménilmontant
Gambetta
Père Lachaise
Philippe Auguste
Alexandre Dumas
Avron
Parc de Belleville
Cimetière du Père Lachaise
Boulevard de Belleville
Boulevard de Ménilmontant
Rue de Belleville
Rue des Pyrénées
Rue de Ménilmontant
Rue des Couronnes
Rue Julien Lacroix
Rue des Panoyaux
Rue des Amandiers
R. des Mûriers
Avenue Gambetta
Rue Sorbier
R. de la Bidassoa
Rue Boyer
R. d'Eupatoria
R. des Envierges
Rue Piat
R. Ramponeau
R. Lesage
R. Dénoyez
R. Jouye Rouve
R. J.-B. Dumay
R. Jourdain
Rue Olivier Métra
Ermitage
Rigoles
R. de la Duée
Rue de la Chine
R. du Père Lachaise
Rue des Rondeaux
Cité Aubry
PLA GAMBET
3
10
11
14
16
21
23
25
27
29
30
31
32
33
34
42
43
44
45
46
47
48
0 200 400 yds
0 200 400 m

20TH

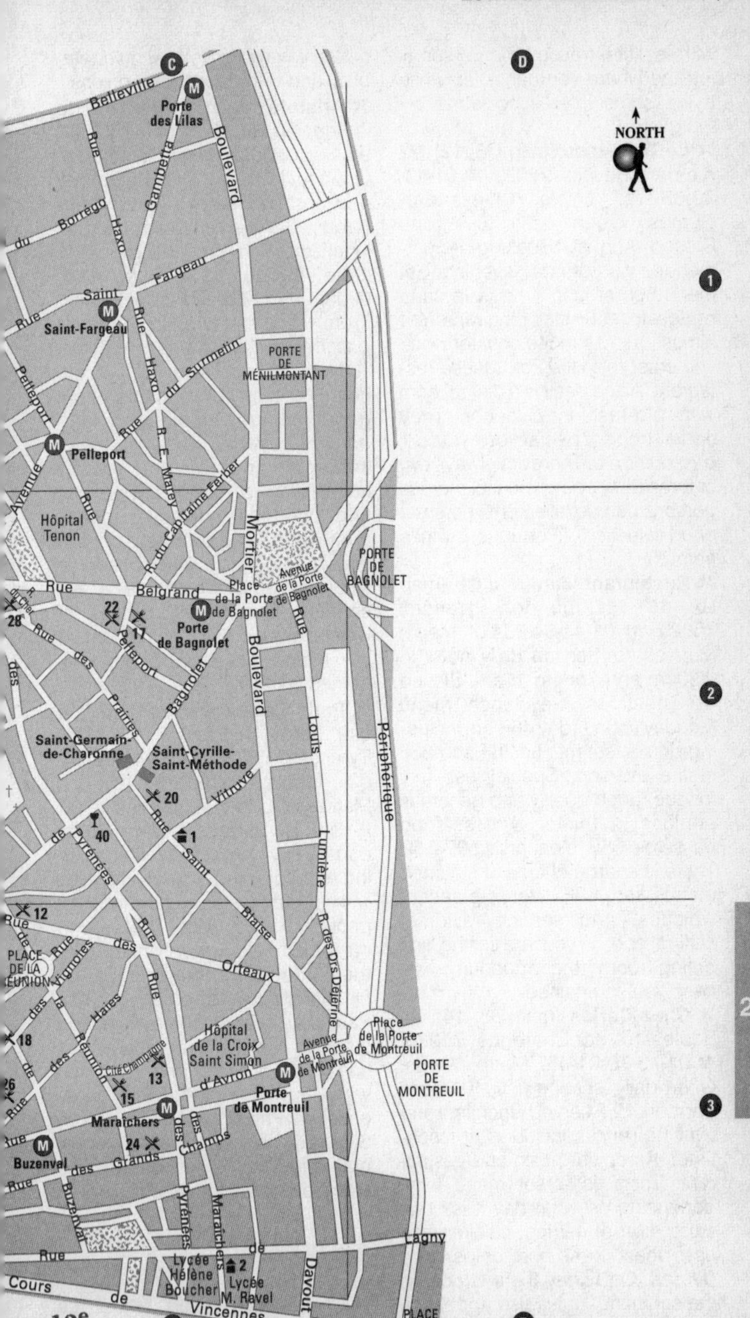

NORTH
Porte des Lilas
Saint-Fargeau
PORTE DE MÉNILMONTANT
Pelleport
Hôpital Tenon
PORTE DE BAGNOLET
Place de la Porte de Bagnolet
Porte de Bagnolet
Saint-Germain-de-Charonne
Saint-Cyrille-Saint-Méthode
Périphérique
PLACE DE LA RÉUNION
Hôpital de la Croix Saint Simon
Place de la Porte de Montreuil
PORTE DE MONTREUIL
Porte de Montreuil
Maraîchers
Buzenval
Lycée Hélène Boucher
Lycée M. Ravel
PLACE DE VINCENNES
12e
20TH

with a little fresco and a sunny terrace where you can relax while trying some interesting wines by the glass.

✕ **Le Torreense** (map C3, **12**): 92 rue de la Réunion 75020. ☎ 01-43-70-33-23. Metro: Alexandre-Dumas. Open daily to 11pm. Closed August. Booking recommended on Saturday evening. Set menu 50F at lunchtime, à la carte budget for 100F including wine. You almost bump into the counter when you enter this little Portuguese restaurant. At the back is a dining room with old-fashioned decor. They serve good specialities: *cozido*, *cassoulet*, etc. There are always two or three tasty cod dishes. Generous portions can be relied on. There is a good selection of Portuguese wines from 75F.

✕ **Restaurant Jardin d'Or** (map C3, **13**): 81 rue des Pyrénées 75020. ☎ 01-44-64-93-20. Metro: Maraîchers. Service daily noon to 2.30pm and 7pm to 11pm. Closed at Christmas. Set lunch menu Monday to Saturday 46F, not including drinks, set menus 75F and 88F in the evening. Specialities: Thai fondue (good quality and generous portions) 210F for two; seafood casserole 55F; meat grills 50F–55F. There is a large choice of steamed dishes at 68F. Very pleasant welcome and service, a quiet setting and, if you are in the first dining room, the aquariums will keep you entertained.

✕ **Chez Carlos** (map B3, **14**): 84 boulevard de Charonne 75020. ☎ 01-43-70-01-45. Metro: Avron. Open daily, service until 10.30pm. Set menu 58F served lunchtime and evening (drinks included at lunchtime). A popular rustic café-restaurant. There is a set menu with, depending on what day it is, tuna salad, fillet of herring, chicken and rice, roast beef and chips, and dessert. On Friday there is cod on the set menu, but it also appears à la carte, cooked in a number of different ways: grilled, with vegetables, and with pepper and onions

✕ **Aristote** (map C3, **15**): 4 rue de la Réunion 75020. ☎ 01-43-70-42-91. Metro: Buzenval or Maraîchers. Open to 11.30pm. Closed Sunday and for two weeks around 15 August. Set menu 52F on weekday lunchtimes. In the evening, à la carte, budget for 80F to 100F. Greek and Turkish specialities. From the starters, try *firinda pastirma* or *firinda sucuk* (meat or Turkish sausage in a foil parcel). From the main courses, apart from generous grilled kebabs and *hunkar beyendi* (rack of lamb, aubergine purée) and *pacha kebab* (leg of lamb, aubergines and potatoes), discover *guvec* (veal and vegetables) or the *yogurtlu* (yoghurt) dishes based on steak or lamb. There are a few seafood specialities. Bottles of wine at around 65F. The customers are mainly locals. You are welcomed warmly.

✕ **Paris-Carthage** (map B1, **27**): 4 cité Leroy (level 317, rue des Pyrénées) 75020. ☎ 01-44-62-24-02. Metro: Pyrénées. Closed Monday. Budget for around 100F. A tiny restaurant nestling in an equally tiny typically Parisian building and adjoining a quiet little alley with a few villas. Hundreds of photos on the walls. The young customers, some of whom take their creature comforts at La Flèche d'Or and others at Lou Pascalou, feel at home here and seem to like the house couscous (large portions) the price of which varies from 40F to 90F. Fish couscous on Friday and *méchoui* on Saturday. In summer the owner puts a few tables outside, and the place becomes almost village like.

☆☆ MODERATE

✕ **Chez Jean** (map B1, **16**): 38 rue Boyer 75020. ☎ 01-47-97-44-58.

Metro: Gambetta or Ménilmontant. Open to 11pm. Closed Saturday lunchtime and Sunday and also the week of 15 August. At lunchtime there are set menus at 49F and 66F, in the evening at 99F and 123F. À la carte around 130F. Jean describes his restaurant as 'the best in rue Boyer' – and the fact that it is also the *only* one doesn't detract from that at all! Good plain cooking with a few exotic dishes. There's a typically 20th-arrondissement trendy working-class hip atmosphere. Accordion and *chanson* on Friday and Saturday evening.

✕ **Le Vieux Belleville** (map B1, **25**): 12 rue des Envierges 75020. ☎ 01-44-62-92-66. Metro: Pyrénées. Open daily except Sunday, Saturday lunchtime and Monday evening. Set menus 59F and 65F served at lunchtime. À la carte, budget for 150F. There isn't much left of the old Belleville around this bistro, perched on the heights of the Parc de Belleville, so here they keep the memories alive. There are sleeves from albums by old *chanson* singers on the walls, and a friendly *guingette* atmosphere around the bar. On Friday evening it's like a *bal musette* dance, with the accordion reigning supreme. The set menus are well put together, including a quarter bottle of wine.

✕ **Aux Chutes du Carbet** (map B–C3, **18**): 31 rue des Vignoles 75020. ☎ 01-43-48-29-87. Metro: Buzenval. Open daily to 2am except Sunday evening and Monday. Set menu 55F at lunchtime; in the evening, budget for at least 120F. In a typically Parisian street with a shady terrace, this is a sort of Creole shed with wallpaper, from where you can hear the sound of the music of the islands. West Indian specialities. At lunchtime it's quieter; on a good night the whole street lights up. Just take the passage des Souhaits (Wish Passage), next to the restaurant, and make a wish that this area and restaurant stay as they are!

✕ **Takichi** (map C2, **28**): 7 rue du Cher 75020. ☎ 01-47-97-03-96. Metro: Gambetta. Open daily except Sunday. Closed for three weeks in August. Set menus 69F and 80F, kebab menus 42F and 49F. Children's menu 42F. This pleasant Japanese restaurant is packed out all day. The secret of its success is a clean appearance and also some very attractive prices. There are two kebab menus at lunchtime (Monday to Friday) which are the house specialities: soup, salad and rice, four chicken kebabs, dessert or coffee, or the same but with beef kebabs. The service is discreet and polite. Takichi 1 set menu has six kebabs; Takichi 2 has seven kebabs; and *sushi* and kebabs set menu, or *sashimi* and kebabs are 128F. For truly gargantuan appetites, there is the *sumo* menu at 140F.

✕ **Les Salons de Musique** (map C2, **17**): 32 rue Pelleport 75020. ☎ 01-43-64-76-60. Metro: Porte-de-Bagnolet. Budget for around 140F. Open evenings only to 11pm. Fans of the marvellous film by Satyajit Ray of the same name will be particularly impressed by this homage to the great film-maker. Although the atmosphere is not exactly that of the film, the resolutely kitsch pop-art Hindu-style *Cage aux Folles* decor (released as *The Birdcage* in America, starring Robin Williams), tapestry with Bengal tigers on the walls, animal rugs hanging from the ceiling, low armchairs made of fake panther, tiger skins, etc. is all pretty surreal! Aubergine curry and lamb massala are part of the show, as are the nans at 20F (plain, cheese or vegetable). The customers are mainly trendies mixed with a sprinkling of locals.

✕ **Le Bistrot des Soupirs, Chez Raymonde** (map B1, **29**): 49 rue de la Chine 75020. ☎ 01-44-62-

93-31. Metro: Gambetta or Pelleport. Open daily except Sunday and Monday. Very remarkable set menus at 79F and 89F lunchtime and evening. À la carte, budget for 150F. You'd hardly suspect that behind this plain façade hides a little gem with a cosy middle-class interior: curtains and flowery tablecloths, panelled walls in the dining room at the back, dotted with framed paintings. Raymonde is attentive to everyone, busy and cheerful. The great flavours of the land are offered at reasonable prices: baked egg with morel cream or Burgundy snails, *andouillette*, rack of lamb in garlic sauce. There is a good choice of wines.

✕ **Chez Lasseron** (map B1, **31**): 1 rue d'Eupatoria (corner of rue Julien-Lacroix) 75020. ☎ 01-43-49-33-14. Metro: Ménilmontant. Closed Sunday. Set menus 50F to 90F, children's menu 50F. The bill rarely comes to more than 100F. After a lifetime spent feeding cinema technicians and stars on set, Lasseron has laid his hat at the foot of the church of Ménilmontant. His colourful little restaurant, with flowery oilcloths and open beams, gives off a happy, modern ambiance. Simple and honest cuisine covering both north and south, from *pot-au-feu* to coriander seasoning. Here they experiment freely with flavours and spices. The menu changes daily, and there are three set menus with some excellent initiatives (oysters in season, affordable wines, unusual apéritifs – try kir with violet) and some good desserts. In the basement a table in an alcove gives small groups some privacy. Booking is advisable.

✕ **Le Zap Spirit** (map B2, **32**): 60 boulevard de Ménilmontant 75020. ☎ 01-43-49-10-64. Metro: Père-Lachaise. Service noon to 2am. Closed Tuesday, Christmas and New Year's Day. Set menu 125F in the evening. Dish of the day 65F to 90F. A cup of tea and a cake costs 27F. Brunch on Sunday (75F). This was the first *souk* restaurant in Paris, and in summer, beneath the huge acacias on boulevard de Ménilmontant, they sometimes throw cushions onto mats so that their customers can eat in authentic style. Actually this is the best time of year to come and eat at its child-size tables. Try the southern *tajine*, cooked for three hours, or crêpes with honey while sipping a mint tea. Relaxed service.

✕ **Café Noir** (map C2, **20**): 15 rue St-Blaise 75020. ☎ 01-40-09-75-80. Metro: Porte-de-Bagnolet or Alexandre-Dumas. Open 7pm to midnight. Closed Sunday, between Christmas and New Year's Day, for the last week in August and the first fortnight in September. Budget for around 130F. At the beginning of the 20th century this was a dispensary. There is not much left of its medical past, and the owners who took over the restaurant in 1991 have collected an amazing amount of bric-à-brac: coffee pots, hats, enamel plates, posters and even two wheelchairs, including a splendid Indian one from 1947. The cuisine is generous: *magret* of duck with lavender honey and with thyme, *filet mignon* with peppered vanilla, parcel of bream with cinnamon ... and what's more, you can smoke Havana cigars, sold individually at the bar.

✕ **Le Krung Thep** (map A1, **33**): 93 rue Julien-Lacroix 75020. ☎ 01-43-66-83-74. Metro: Pyrénées. Open evenings only to 11pm. Sit down comfortably on the threadbare oriental cushions, take a look at the menu, and order your choice – a mango salad, a pot full of sautéed mussels in hot sauce or shrimps with sweet and sour sauce, perhaps. A feast for all the senses in this Thai mirage where the Spanish actress Victoria Abril is said to have set up home.

✂ **Giacomo Piccola Brescia** (map C2, **22**): 31 rue Pelleport 75020. ☎ 01-43-61-07-91. Metro: Porte-de-Bagnolet. Open to 10.30pm. Closed Sunday and Saturday lunchtime, August, Christmas and New Year's Day. Set menu 80F at lunchtime with a drink (Monday to Friday); in the evening, budget for around 200F including drinks. This large, pleasant dining room, with its walls covered in paintings, including a few which actually are quite good, is the realm of Giacomo, a slightly crazy, but very friendly, booming Italian with a gift for business. The place is cosy, with its old butcher's shop furniture, and often full in spite of its unfortunate location and size. The cook is Calabrian and Giacomo is from the north of Italy, whereas the cuisine (especially the dishes of the day) swings between north and south, depending on their mood. You can eat some good house pasta, such as *tagliatelle paglia* and *fieno boscaiola*, preceded by good *antipasti, picatta, osso bucco*, etc. For dessert, tiramisu is the obvious choice.

✂ **À Roda d'Afiar** (map A1, **23**): 14 rue Dénoyez,75020. ☎ 01-46-36-84-95. Metro: Belleville Open to 10pm or 10.30pm. Closed Monday. Set lunch menu 59F; in the evening budget for 130F to 180F per person. 'Spanish specialities', says the business card. True. It's just like being in Spain. At the bar, in front of a collection of fans, the owners speak Castilian Spanish as they play cards or watch a football match. In the adjoining little panelled dining room you can eat a very decent paella or a *fideuà* (the same thing but with noodles instead of rice) with langoustines and the whole works, prepared on request. There are other fish-based main courses and starters which are just as good, and there is also a good *Sangre de Toro*. If you give them notice (a week), they will do some typical delicacies for you, such as *zarzuela* (a pot full of fish), *cocido* (chick pea *pot-au-feu*) or *fabada* (a kind of bean stew).

☆ ☆ ☆ CHIC

✂ **Le Zéphyr** (map B1, **30**): 1 rue du Jourdain 75020. ☎ 01-46-36-65-81. Metro: Jourdain. Last orders 11pm. Closed Saturday lunchtime and Sunday, during the Christmas holidays and for a fortnight in August. Book in the evening. Set menus 72F at lunchtime and 160F lunchtime and evening. À la carte budget for at least 250F per person. The word 'Zephyr' means a soft, pleasant wind, a light breeze. This definition perfectly matches the cuisine which they produce here, but does not give an accurate idea of the establishment. More than just a restaurant, Le Zéphyr manages the *tour de force* of being a lot more than a place with interesting decor and history. There is a superbly conserved 1928 art-deco setting. The set lunch menu comprises a starter, main course and dessert. Gourmets needn't worry, both lunchtime and evening they also offer a set menu, which is flexible and more elaborate, as well as a fine à la carte menu. Depending on the time of year, what would you say to a *terrine* of leeks in nutmeg and langoustine jelly? Or maybe wild boar's ribs with red cabbage and chestnuts, with balsamic sauce? Also, all year round, they do a *confit* of duck, as well as *foie gras* and house brioche bread, which is a meal in itself. You absolutely must finish things off with the warm chocolate fondant with vanilla sauce, or else put your faith in the chef and his fine selection of desserts. As for the wines, there are more than 70 of them at around 110–150F on average. Glasses of wine cost from 75F to 90F. Please note that credit cards are not accepted.

✕ Les Allobroges (map C3, **24**): 71 rue des Grands-Champs 75020. ☎ 01-43-73-40-00. Metro: Maraîchers. Open to 9.30pm. Closed Sunday, Monday, public holidays and during August. Set menus 97F and 180F; à la carte, the bill comes to around 250F. Delicate floral decor, little refinements (from snacks in serviettes held together by raffia to the various little breads) and high-class cuisine; no doubt about it, this is one of the best restaurants in the east of Paris. The two little dining rooms are separated by a corridor where you can glimpse the chef working in the kitchen. The dishes are not lacking in spirit and the pleasure is in the whole meal. Booking is essential, the day before if possible.

✕ La Fontaine aux Roses (map B2, **21**): 27 avenue Gambetta 75020. ☎ 01-46-36-74-75. Metro: Père-Lachaise or Gambetta. Open lunchtime and evening. Closed Sunday evening and Monday, as well as in August. Set menus 120F at lunchtime and 170F in the evening. Children's menu 60F. There is indeed a fountain with roses in it (the name means the Rose Fountain). Actually, the first thing you notice about this elegant little restaurant are the impressive displays of fresh flowers. The menu only offers one set menu, which is a bit more sophisticated in the evening and on Sunday. Everything is included, from the apéritif to the coffee. Very traditional home-cooking: baked smoked salmon, *crêpe de St-Jacques* with chives, cod in a sesame seed crust, *tarte Tatin* flambéed with Calvados.

✕ Restaurante Ribatejo (map B–C3, **26**): 6 rue Planchat 75020. ☎ 01-43-70-41-03. Metro: Avron or Buzenval. Service noon to 2.30pm and in the evening until 5am (during the week, it's best to ring before coming). Closed Monday evening and during August. Set menus 70F and 85F at lunchtime, in the evening budget for 150–180F per person. No, your eyes are not deceiving you, this restaurant is open to 5am in this remote corner of the 20th arrondissement. And what a restaurant! A great big building on the corner of rue des Haies which, at lunchtime, does what everyone else does: cheap set menus. When the evening comes, the house is lit up with blue neon lights and starts to look like a private club. Everyone leaves the room upstairs and goes into the basement, a nightclub-style cellar. A small band sets the tone, and everyone dances under the disco ball in the ceiling. An amazing atmosphere, for lovers of curiosities. Rather good classical Portuguese cuisine, various dishes based on cod, swordfish, etc. A great place to finish the evening, especially at the weekend.

WINE BAR

✕ 🍷 Le Baratin (map A1, **34**): 3 rue Jouye-Rouve 75020. ☎ 01-43-49-39-70. Metro: Belleville or Pyrénées. A little street leading into rue de Belleville and rue Ramponneau. Open from 11am (6pm on Saturday) to 1am; restaurant until midnight. Closed Saturday lunchtime, Monday, and during the first week of January. Set menu 69F lunchtime only; à la carte budget for around 130F. The setting is simple: bare walls decorated with a few paintings and a map of the wine-growing regions of France, a wooden bar and assorted tables. The clientele, often made up of wine experts, gets pretty lively in both of the small dining rooms. Excellent wines (note they don't serve anything as bland as Coca-Cola here) from the Loire in particular. You can also eat simply but well. There's a different risotto every evening, from swordfish to saffron, or maybe ragout of black beans with pork. Main courses between 65F and 68F and if you're hungry you can first have some meticulously prepared starters (30F to 35F). The bill manages to stay reasonable, even if you go a bit over the top, which can happen in this kind of place!

PÈRE-LACHAISE CEMETERY

16 rue du Repos 75020. Entrance on boulevard de Ménilmontant, at the end of rue de la Roquette. ☎ 01-55-25-82-10. Metro: Père-Lachaise. In summer open 8am to 6pm, 8.30am Saturday and 9am Sunday and public holidays; the rest of the year, open 8am to 5.30pm Monday to Friday, 8.30am Saturday and 9am Sunday. Guided tour every Saturday, at around 2.30pm (lasting approximately two hours), and occasionally on Tuesday and Sunday. They also organize lots of themed tours. Their programme is available in any town hall (*mairie*) and there are also free maps and a number of suggested routes for those wishing to seek out writers, musicians, artists and so on.

The Père-Lachaise Cemetery is a unique place to go for a walk. It is by turns tragic, joyous, sinister and playful, with an occasional dose of eroticism and sensuality thrown in for good measure. When Père-Lachaise was created the people of Paris, who were used to being buried in and around churches, showed a certain reluctance to move so 'far' out of Paris. To counteract the problem, the authorities, using a certain amount of skilful publicity, organized the transfer of the remains of Abélard and Héloïse, Molière and La Fontaine. Obviously, the prospect of being buried alongside such illustrious figures exploited people's snobbery and resulted in a freshly discovered enthusiasm for the new cemetery. The town planners of the day, not without a touch of humour, baptized one of the streets bordering the cemetery the 'rue du Repos' (the Street of Rest).

THE PÈRE-LACHAISE VIPS

We can't give you an exhaustive inventory of the cemetery as that would need a whole encyclopaedia. However, you may meet one of the extraordinary Père-Lachaise specialists on your travels, who are always ready to give you information or to tell you an interesting anecdote.

– The tomb of the writer Colette, who died in 1954 (author of, amongst others, *Gigi*) is one of the first on the left of avenue du Puits. Opposite, there is a touching tomb commemorating a blind person, the bust of whom is shown with a pair of white eyes. Returning to the main avenue on the left you will see that Alfred de Musset has an epitaph in the form of a poem: 'Dear friends, when I die, plant a willow tree in the cemetery ....' Unfortunately for him all of the willows planted here seem to die. Next door is the tomb of Baron Haussmann (the town planner) and the engineer Le Bas, who erected the obelisk in the place de la Concorde.

– In the middle of the avenue stands the *monument aux Morts* (Monument to the Dead). On the day of its inauguration, the authorities demanded that the sheet covering the monument should not be removed completely, so that the crowd would not be shocked by the naked buttocks of the statues!

NORTH
Rue Houdart
Rue des Amandiers
Rue Fernand Léger
R. des Mûriers
Rue Désirée
Avenue Gambetta
Square Samuel de Champlain
PL. AUGUSTE MÉRIVIER
Père Lachaise
Avenue Circulaire
72 Avenue
64
Avenue Cail
Av. Frédéric Soulié
47
80
81
71
48 Félix de Beaujour
69
Balzac
49
Delacroix
46
Avenue
65
63
Chemin Errazu
Av. de l'Ouest
Entrance
Duc de Morny
70
Michelet
Nerval
Maquet
Av. des Peupliers
Avenue
Seurat
62
66
68
Bizet
Avenue
Av. des Ailantes
54
Barbedienne
49
53
52
Ch. d'Ornano
67
Louis Blanc
61
Chemin Hautoy
Av. Neigre
Av. de la Chapelle
56
Del Duca
Av. Feuillant
50
Pozzo di Borgo
Boulevard de Ménilmontant
60
57
51
Chapelle
55
58
Thiers
Av. Saint Morys
Passage de la Folie Regnault
Latérale Nord
Monument aux Morts
21
22
59
Av. Circulaire
Haussmann
4
Falguière
Géricault
12
Musset
4
Faure
Talma
Av. Thirion
Colette
Ledru-Rollin
Av. Chapelle
20
Arago
4
Av. Latérale Sud
Bellini
Avenue Principale
3
Bernardin de Saint-Pierre
11
Mlle George
18
10
9
Chopin
13
Main entrance
2
Desproges
Périer
Rue de la Roquette
Comte
8
Rachel
Avenue Casimir Perier
14
Rothschild
7
Héloïse and Abélard
Jim Morrison
Pissarro
5
Chemin
6
Rue de la Folie
Philippe Auguste
73
Serré
Rue de Mont Louis
Av. Philippe Auguste
Boulevard de Charonne

20TH

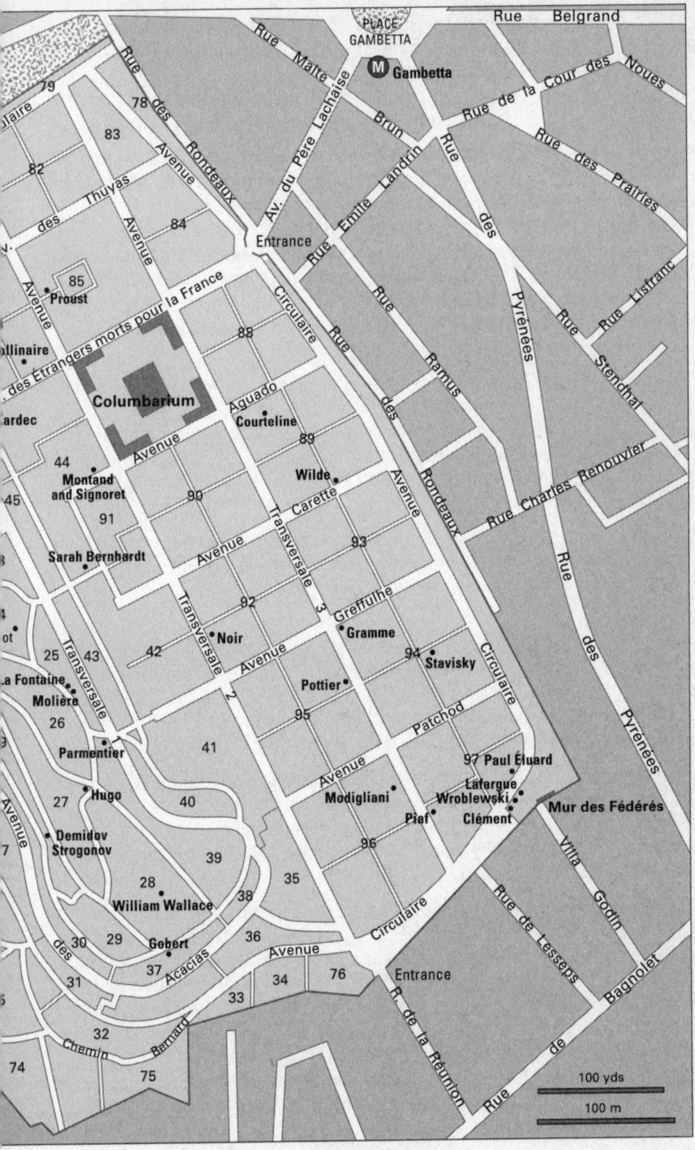

Place Gambetta
Gambetta
Rue Belgrand
Rue Malte Brun
Av. du Père Lachaise
Rue de la Cour des Noues
Rue des Prairies
Rue des Rondeaux
Rue Emile Landrin
Rue des Pyrénées
Rue Lisfranc
Rue Stendhal
Rue Ramus
Rue Charles Renouvier
Entrance
Avenue des Thuyas
Avenue Circulaire
Avenue des Étrangers morts pour la France
Columbarium
Avenue Aguado
Avenue Carette
Avenue Transversale 3
Avenue Transversale 2
Avenue Transversale 1
Avenue Greffulhe
Avenue Patchod
Avenue des Acacias
Chemin Bernard
Mur des Fédérés
Villa Godin
Rue de Lesseps
Rue de Bagnolet
R. de la Réunion
Proust
Courteline
Wilde
Montand and Signoret
Sarah Bernhardt
Noir
Gramme
Stavisky
Pottier
La Fontaine
Molière
Parmentier
Hugo
Demidov Strogonov
William Wallace
Gobert
Modigliani
Piaf
Paul Éluard
Lafargue
Wroblewski
Clément
100 yds
100 m

PÈRE LACHAISE CEMETERY

– In the aisle running along rue du Repos is the great lover and comedienne, Rachel. Nobody knows how many lovers she had (Alfred de Musset and Napoleon III, among others; Victor Hugo, on the other hand, didn't get anywhere with her!). A prince once sent her the following message: 'When? Where? How much?', and she replied: 'Tomorrow. My place. For nothing.'

– A little further along stands the tomb of the Rothschilds with a double 'R' like the double 'L' of Louis XIV. Nearby, on the same side, lies the painter Pissarro. Above lie Abélard and Héloïse, together for all eternity. Curiously, the star-crossed lovers both died at the age of 63, though 20 years apart. Héloïse obtained authorization, even though she was an abbess, to join Abélard in the tomb. The legend says that he opened his arms to receive her! Not far from there is the tomb of Casimir Perier where, every spring, bees return to the nests they have built into the hollow head of his statue.

– Jim Morrison, the lead singer of the Doors, is a bit further out in the 6th division. From avenue Casimir-Perier take the chemin Serré then the chemin Maison, until you reach where it meets the chemin de Lesseps. His fans have marked out the route in chalk. It's a sad fact that this famous singer, who was inspired by Artaud's poetry, ended up dying in a sordid Paris hotel room from an overdose of alcohol and drugs. The tomb is very simple, covered in graffiti and marks of affection.

– Bernardin de St-Pierre, who lies at rest along with another inseparable couple, Paul and Virginie, is one of the most visited tombs. The great actor Talma is buried in the chemin Talma, in a modest sarcophagus.

– After the chemin de la Vierge are the chemin Molière and the chemin La Fontaine, obviously leading to the two great French writers . . . although it is almost certain that they are not actually buried there. Given the fact that the cemeteries in Paris were sold off at the end of the 18th century, it is highly doubtful that their remains were ever found. On the tomb of La Fontaine, of course, there is a representation of one of his fables.

– Take the chemin Camille-Jordan to pay a visit to the marshals. Most of them have tombs which are quite surreal, but the one which takes the prize is without a doubt that of Gobert. This illustrious general, unknown to most people, is shown heroically charging the enemy, killed on his horse at the battle of Baylen in Andalusia.

– Continue along the chemin du Dragons. It is impossible to escape the ghastly tomb of Princesse Demidoff-Strogonoff – it's a marble temple supported by six columns. Around the edifice are decorations of wolves' heads and miners' hammers that remind us that her family became immensely rich thanks to the exploitation of mines in central Asia. There has always been some doubt about her famous will, which is said to have left a considerable amount of roubles for someone to come and live in the vault and keep the princess company. Having said that, some people have tried to actually move in and the authorities occasionally receive applications for the post. The last was as recently as 1983.

– In the chemin Denon (11th division) lies Chopin, although his heart is in Warsaw, immured in the pillar of a church. A charming musical Muse keeps him company at the top of his tomb. Opposite is the late lamented Pierre Desproges, one of the most popular comedians in France, and not far away lies the musician Bellini.

– At this stage of the walk it is more sensible to visit the new part of the cemetery with the Mur des Fédérés and the 'politicians'. Go back to the circular avenue which runs along the eastern wall; once you have gone past side road No. 13 you reach divisions 76 and 97, where all the politicians are buried. In Division 76 there is just a simple plaque commemorating the fact that the last group of Communards were savagely massacred against this wall. In front lie the tombs of Paul Lafargue and Marx's daughter, Jean-Baptiste Clément, the author of *Temps des cerises* and Valery Wroblewski, the Polish General of the Paris Commune, a clear indication of the internationalist character of the movement. This is followed by memorials to those who died in concentration camps.

– In side road No. 3, in the area on the edge of the circular avenue (97th division), lies the tomb of Édith Piaf, which is always covered in flowers. It's not easy to find, because it's on an internal line, on a level with the Léger family. Modigliani is opposite, slightly to the west, on the same level as Kanjovneff (96th division). Next door, buried in the 94th division, lies Gramme, the inventor of the dynamo.

– The tomb of Victor Noir, one of the most famous, is in side road No. 2 (92nd division). It's impossible to miss the tomb as there is always an admiring crowd around it. The murder of Victor Noir, a young journalist aged 22, by Prince Pierre Bonaparte, shocked the whole of France, and even Victor Hugo attended the funeral. An unconventional effigy of Victor Noir captures him at the very moment of his death, his hat discarded at his side. The sculptor has depicted the young man displaying a certain degree of virility *post mortem*. Over the years the place has been polished by thousands of hands, presumably in order to get some of the sexual potency to rub off!

– Admirers of Oscar Wilde will find him in the form of a sphinx in division 89. Its testicles, which were smashed by two shocked lady visitors, were for a long time used as paper weights by the director of the cemetery! Go past the columbarium holding the ashes of the dancer Isadora Duncan, Jules Guesde, the film director Max Ophuls and Pierre Dac. Proust fans will find their idol in division 85 at the edge of side road No. 3.

– Engraved on the tombstone of Apollinaire, who is buried not far from Proust (still on side road No. 2, after the avenue of foreign soldiers who died fighting for France), are a poem and an epitaph in the shape of a heart: 'My heart is like an inverted flame.'

– Next is the tomb with the most flowers in the whole cemetery: that of Allan Kardec, the cult founder of Kardecismo (spiritualism). His tomb, in the shape of a dolmen, is on the corner of the avenue, still on side road No. 2, and the chemin du Quinconce. It is easy to find as you can smell the flowers a mile off. Although not very well known in France, Kardec is read by millions of Brazilians. Umbanda, the Afro-Brazilian religion, is strongly influenced by his spirit philosophy. His loyal followers, usually Brazilians and West Indians, occasionally perform little ceremonies around the tomb.

– Situated in the same division as Kardec is the tomb of Sarah Bernhardt. For someone who lived such an eccentric life this grey, banal last resting place is rather disappointing. Not far away, in division 44, are the tombs of Simone Signoret and Yves Montand.

– At the crossroads of avenue des Thuyas, on the left, you can hardly miss the most megalomaniacal of all the tombs in Père-Lachaise: that of Félix de Beaujour, a little-known diplomat. He saw a chance of securing a place in history with this phallic monument – 16m (52ft) high, it is used as a landmark for locating Père-Lachaise from the higher parts of Paris!

– In the same area lies the tomb of the Alexandre Dumas's 'ghostwriter', Auguste Maquet, on which all the names of Dumas' books are engraved, and the grave of the early 20th century racing driver, Théry, immortalized at his wheel.

– Walk down the chemin du Mont-Louis until you reach the intersection with avenue de la Chapelle and you can admire one of the most interesting sculptures in the cemetery: the Pietà on the tomb of the editor Cino del Duca, who made his name with the newspaper *Nous Deux*. Extremely realistic, the Pietà is shown standing for the first time. Nearby is the obelisk of De Sèze, Louis XVI's defence lawyer.

– In the 67th division, opposite the tomb of the Pozzo di Borgos, who were enemies of Napoleon Bonaparte, is the mausoleum-chapel of the Menier family, famous for their chocolate business. You can almost smell the chocolate in the air. Nearby, there is a woman with a peaceful face, perhaps unable to wake after overdosing on sweet things!

THE OLD VILLAGE OF CHARONNE

This village, annexed just like Montmartre, Auteuil and Vaugirard in 1860, is one of the least well known in Paris, which is why it has managed to retain its original appearance for so long. It developed with the exploitation of the gypsum quarries. In spite of the construction of avenue Gambetta, avenue Belgrand and boulevard de Charonne, the village did not suffer too much from Haussmann's projects, but its population was cruelly decimated by the Versailles repression in 1871. For many years the developers' pickaxes were still unearthing mass graves; in 1897, during the building of a reservoir, almost 800 of these graves were found. The remains were buried in the little cemetery belonging to the church of Charonne and the privet hedge which covers them, along the wall of the presbytery, is designated as another *Mur des Fédérés* for the people.

Charonne is famous for another reason. In February 1962, during a demonstration calling for peace in Algeria, the Charonne metro station was the scene of violent police action which ended with the deaths of nine people – the names of those who died are discreetly commemorated on a simple bronze plaque in the corridors of the station.

A RURAL WALK THROUGH A SECRET VILLAGE

★ Leave the Metro at Gambetta and take the **rue des Prairies**. It has retained a few old houses from its village days, but is now undergoing rapid urbanization. At No. 11 there are some little buildings with interesting architecture: coloured tiles, an exterior spiral staircase and a bow window. The rue des Prairies ends in a spectacular bend above **rue de Bagnolet**, which was smoothed out so that the carts carrying materials for building the surrounding wall could get up the slope. This has resulted in the building of large walls along the whole route, with the houses looming over the road. Opposite, on the other side, there are two typical houses with small horseshoe staircases.

★ **L'église St-Germain-de-Charonne:** 4 place St-Blaise 75020. Bus 76, which goes from St-Germain-l'Auxerrois, passes in front of St-Germain-de-Charonne and also allows you to go through lots of interesting areas on the way (the Marais, the old 11th arrondissement, the whole of the village of Charonne). This is a really delightful church, with a little country-style cemetery. Apart from St-Pierre-de-Montmartre, it is the only church which still has a cemetery of its own. Originally built in the 12th century, it was rebuilt in the 15th century, and then in the 17th century the apse was removed. There were a few additions made in the 19th century and these make it a little masterpiece of asymmetry. Today all that remains of the original building is the steeple. The cemetery is modest but provides a pleasant walk. There are a few tombs: Robert Brasillach, novelist and poet (shot during the Liberation for being a collaborator), the sons of André Malraux (killed in a car accident), and M. Bègue, known as *Père Magloire*, who died in 1837, and claimed to have been Robespierre's secretary. Nobody believed him in the village because he was a drunk and was even buried with a bottle of wine! His friends held a party around his grave and erected a statue bought from a local scrap dealer. The presbytery is surrounded by a beautiful garden.

On the other side of the street there is another, rather less attractive, church. The undertakers were fed up with climbing the steps of St-Germain-de-Charonne and complained to their union about their working conditions, demanding a single-storey church. This was the result.

★ **rue St-Blaise:** this has always been the main axis of the old village. The view over the church from place des Grès, right at the bottom, is one of the most charming in Paris. There are some very pretty bungalows, running all the way along, which have been magnificently restored. At No. 25 there is a fine external staircase with a canopy. There are a few *pâtisseries* and tea-rooms dotted along the road selling delicious pies and tarts at very reasonable prices. At the end of rue Galleron there is a village grocer's with a little terrace and a wrought-iron balcony.

On the corner of rue St-Blaise and rue Vitruve is the pretty place des Grès. On the left, in a recess, one of the first porches leads to a lovely interior garden. If you continue down the passage you'll come to an attractive square.

★ The **rue Vitruve** marks the edge of the village. On the other side the buildings are much the same in design and layout.

★ Return to **rue de Bagnolet**. At No. 120 is the tobacconist-PMU (a kind of betting shop). There is a fine sculpted wood counter, a real zinc bar and engraved windows with little frescoes depicting Charonne. Further on is the Petite-Ceinture bridge built over the railway. For those returning to the Alexandre-Dumas metro station, at 85 rue de Bagnolet, don't miss the lovely Villa Godin, with its attractive houses, trees and flowers, and, at No. 87, the Villa Lesseps. The part of rue de la Réunion running along Père-Lachaise is still paved with large cobblestones. This entrance to the cemetery is quite picturesque and from Nos. 121 to 129 there are some lovely modern houses.

★ Return to the church and take the **escalier Stendhal**, lined with wild gardens. When the weather is fine the little gilded cockerel on the church glistens against the blue sky. Cross **rue Lucien-Leuwen**, one of the few streets in Paris, along with Monte-Cristo, to bear the name of a character from a novel – in this case *Lucien Leuwen* by Stendhal.

Behind the high walls on the right lies what is probably the only real field in Paris with apple trees. All that is missing is a few sheep! This space is protected from development as it covers the city's sewage water supply.

The **Villa Stendhal**, which comes next, was the first road in Charonne to be built with middle-class dwellings. Families from Belleville used to come out here on Sunday to see how the other half lived.

★ **rue Charles-Renouvier** leads into a charming little corner, over rue des Pyrénées via a bridge with stone balustrades, covered in ivy, followed by narrow flights of steps with old street lamps. Finally you will arrive at the rue des Rondeaux, against the eastern wall of Père-Lachaise. A rusty plaque still displays the name: rue Achille. Quiet, lined with bungalows.

★ If you have the energy, finish the walk by paying a visit to the **Campagne à Paris** (The Countryside in Paris), at the Porte-de-Bagnolet metro station. In the first half of the 19th century there used to be a large gypsum quarry in the rue des Montibœufs, but in 1908 they built 100 or so cheap workers houses on top of it. Access is from place Octave-Chanute via the steps.

The charming rue Irénée-Blanc and rue Jules-Siegfried are lined with some pretty houses made of burrstone or brick. In the spring the lilacs smell wonderful, and you could be forgiven for wondering if you were really still in Paris.

MÉNILMONTANT

A WALK AROUND MÉNILMUCHE

★ Start at Père-Lachaise metro station along the **rue des Amandiers** (Almond Tree Street), which has been almost completely rebuilt with newly-designed four-storey, red-brick housing, whilst the rest embody the area's former architecture.

★ The **rue Gasnier-Guy** is a typical street of the old Ménilmuche, paved with large cobblestones. The recesses between the houses have been transformed into gardens.

The rue de la Cloche, which extends along rue de la Voulze, leads up onto a little hill overlooking the crossroads and ends in a flight of steps. Walk up the narrow, roughly cobbled passage with its central gutter to get to rue Villiers-de-L'Isle-Adam. Crossing rue de la Chine, the area commemorates France's Far Eastern expeditions, including rue d'Annam (Annam Street) and rue du Cambodge (Cambodia Street).

★ The **rue Villiers-de-L'Isle-Adam** has a cul-de-sac of the same name leading off to the left (between rue de la Chine and rue Pelleport). At the end there is an enormous red building, which, with its towers, narrow slits and formidable portcullises looks just like a watchtower. This peculiar construction looms over the streets below, which wind through the great arches – you will experience a curious optical effect if you look through them. Built in 1925, this is the famous model housing complex for workers. Today there is nothing very model about it – in fact it's all rather intimidating – so beware if you're easily frightened.

Nearby is the Ganachaud bakery, one of the best in Paris. They make around 30 types of bread in their wood ovens, in all shapes and flavours, as well as a selection of delicious cakes.

★ You might for a moment be tempted to take rue Pixérécourt. Don't, as it only leads to the Impasse de l'Avenir (which means Cul-de-sac of the Future). Head for **rue de l'Ermitage** instead. At No. 49 you can admire the last Belleville-Ménilmuche landscape, providing an idea of what the area used to be like. From the lovely terrace of a modern building you can see the winding lanes, gardens, lawns and, just underneath, the famous **Regard St-Martin** in the rue des Savies. The whole thing exudes a village-like serenity. Adjoining the terrace a narrow flight of stairs leads to the **rue des Cascades**, still lined by a few typical Belleville houses. The name comes from the standpipe situated in an aqueduct which brought water to Paris at the beginning of the 17th century. The water was available to any local inhabitants who passed by. There is another standpipe at 17 rue des Cascades, in the courtyard of a modern building. The **rue des Savies** is charming, with its large milestones. This is where they filmed *Casque d'or* with Simone Signoret and Serge Reggiani. In rue des Cascades the house which was used as a set was saved from a property developer. At the bottom of **rue de la Mare** there is a classic urban landscape: a crooked bridge with steps which crosses the Petite-Ceinture railway.

★ The **Villa Castel:** the rue Henri-Chevreau leads to the last villa in Belleville. Once you reach rue des Couronnes, at No. 83 follow the steps of the picturesque passage Plantin. These are the remaining few steps which used to traverse the whole hill. Go as far as rue du Transvaal to admire the elegant wrought-iron gate marked *Villa Castel*. Along this route there's one pretty little house after another, with flights of steps, elaborate windows and occasional balustrades. All is peaceful. At the end is a little garden and trees. François Truffaut filmed a scene for *Jules et Jim* here. All that is left of the other villas is their signs (the *Faucheurs* – harvesters – at 11 rue des Envierges, the fine gate of the Villa Ottoz, at 43 rue Piat).

★ From **rue Piat** there's a fine panoramic view over Paris.

The **Parc de Belleville** is now finished. When you enter rue Bisson you are immediately faced with a monumental flight of steps (harking back to the architecture of the 1930s). There is a succession of platforms boasting half-moon shaped pools, small waterfalls over steps and jets of water and, right at the top, there's a rocky, cavern-like concrete mass. On the other side, towards the wooden walkway, there are three toboggans for children.

BELLEVILLE

THE NEW AND THE OLD

Belleville is a large area which brings all cultures and all types of people together in a huge melting pot: painters and sculptors looking for inspiration, stars looking for privacy, artisans and old Bellevillois hankering for the past. Alongside them West Indians, Greeks, Spaniards, Asians, Jews and Arabs all rub shoulders and contribute to the dynamism of the area.

★ **Old Belleville** is still symbolized by **rue Dénoyez** and **rue Ramponeau** (lined with dilapidated alleyways). The latter bears the name of a famous 18th century *guinguette* owner. At 8 **rue de Belleville** there is a typical bar which still looks good: Le Vieux Saumur. Even though a whole side of rue Ramponeau is now faced with demolition you can still find quite a few Jewish restaurants, lively bars and grocery shops offering all the lovely smells of the Mediterranean, just 4m (13ft) apart. The whole area is part of a huge renovation project. Initially, almost everything was due to be demolished. The inhabitants have formed the 'Bellevilleuse' association to protect their rights, and especially to fight to keep as many houses as possible for restoration and to maintain the spirit of the area.

Their campaign has prevented the destruction of a Parisian district which is full of historical importance. One symbol of the cultural renewal of the area is the Forge, a former factory in which many artists have squatted. It won a place in the heart of the area through its activities and exhibitions which were opened up to the local population. The Paris authorities and the developers were forced to agree to a respite in the demolition work.

Along **boulevard de Belleville** there are shoe sellers, snack bars and Chinese *pâtisseries*. Towards Ménilmontant metro station you'll find West Indian supermarkets.

★ The **musée Édith-Piaf:** 5 rue de Crespin-du-Gast 75011. ☎ 01-43-55-52-72. Metro: Ménilmontant. Open Monday to Thursday 1pm to 6pm by appointment only. This museum devoted to the famous French singer has photos, sculptures, letters, clothes, etc. and, of course, records, collected by her fans.

★ An interesting **architectural walk**: the whole of the Ramponeau-Bisson, Palikao, Couronnes and Julien-Lacroix sector has been entirely rebuilt. The architecture makes a clean break from the horrors of the 1960s and 1970s. These buildings are much more harmonious and in rue des Couronnes the balconies even ripple. There is a pretty 'unfinished' fresco in rue Bisson (opposite the Cité de Gênes). Admire the superb building at 100 boulevard de Belleville, which has a curious roof in the form of a Mohican haircut.

★ The **rue Jouye-Rouve** leads to former terraced gardens. Right at the top is the Hôtel de la Belle Vue, a boarding house whose days are numbered since the last starving poet was kicked out. It's just like being in Montmartre. At No. 13 there is a new building with a monumental entrance and a staircase leading to the garden. There are two attractive sculptures over the porch in coloured medallions.

★ Go back to **rue de Belleville**. No. 38 has four little courtyards, one after another. No. 40 is decorated in the Belleville nouveau-riche style, with lots of street lights. At Nos. 39 and 41 the painted signs on the ageing façades have now faded. Before we reach the rue des Pyrénées, there is a plaque at No. 72 commemorating Édith Piaf's birthplace.

WHERE TO GO FOR A DRINK

🍸 **Flèche d'Or Café** (map C2, **40**): 102 *bis*, rue de Bagnolet 75020. ☎ 01-43-72-06-87. Metro: Porte-de-Bagnolet. Open daily 10am (6pm on Monday) to 2am. Closed Mondays. Set menus 69F at lunchtime, 95F and 145F in the evening. On Sunday, brunch at 79F. Beers from 22F and cocktails from between 20F and 45F – less expensive during the day. A healthy initiative in a grandiose setting. In May

1995 ten Beaux-Arts students moved into a disused station from the old Petite Ceinture railway on the slopes of a hill overlooking Paris. They brought it back to life with a bar topped with an astonishing locomotive looking as if it was about to crash down onto drinkers. The regulars dress all in black and listen to bands and DJs play a wide range of music. The terrace has a glass roof where you can drink with the trendsetters. Or try some of the original recipes, such as *boeuf réunionnais*. Very relaxed – you don't even have to keep your dog on a lead!

🍸 **Bistrot Le Piston Pélican** (map B3, **42**): 15 rue de Bagnolet 75020. ☎ 01-43-70-35-00. Metro: Alexandre-Dumas. Open 8am to 2am. Set meal 63F at lunchtime, 78F in the evening. Dishes of the day 59F. Half pint of beer at 15F, cocktails from 30F to 45F. All cocktails are 30F during 'happy hour' between 6pm and 9pm. In turn a brothel, a café-grocer's (even today you can see the tanks which allowed customers to fill their *litrons* – containers holding a litre of wine), then a bar, the Pélican got itself in shape again a few years ago, when the orchestra from the 'Piston Circus' (hence the name) entered with a fanfare. In 1996 the musicians from the company, out of breath, handed over to Franck who, at barely 25, has brought a breath of fresh air to a bistro with something of a bad reputation. A lick of paint, some good cooking, and a few metro seats later, and it has made its mark, not without a certain panache; concerts, DJs and theatre, varying every night.

🍸 **Lou Pascalou** (map A2, **43**): 14 rue des Panoyaux 75020. ☎ 01-46-36-78-10. Metro: Ménilmontant Open daily 9.30am to 2am. Half pint of beer: 14F. Since Le Soleil (136 boulevard de Ménilmontant) was banned from holding concerts and no longer has its pleasant terrace, people now come to Lou Pascalou to hear music. No concerts here, either, unfortunately, but there is an atmosphere and as many people as if there were. A former café which has become a real must in the area. In summer the terrace is packed to overflowing.

🍸 **Le Mercure** (map B1, **44**): 84 rue de Pixéricourt 75020. ☎ 01-46-36-64-13. Metro: Place-des-Fêtes. Open 9am to 2am. Closed Sunday and for 10 days in August. Drinks cost around 15F, main courses from 45F. The customers here are mainly aged from 25 to 45, but they do let younger people in! On the walls there are old postcards and photos of people like Elvis Presley, Maria Callas and Léon Davidovich Bronstein. Sometimes there are musical events and puppet shows in the evening. They do food too.

🍸 **La Maroquinerie** (map B1, **48**): 23 rue Boyer 75020. ☎ 01-40-33-30-60. Metro: Gambetta. Open daily 11am to 1am. Closed Sunday except some Sundays in summer (ring to check). 12F for half a pint of beer. On the heights of Ménilmontant, this is a former leather shop converted into a literary café which puts on shows, readings by writers, world concerts and some food. Whether sitting out in the courtyard in the sun, standing at the bar inside, or around the guests' table, this is a good place to come, either at midday or midnight. You have to pay to get in when there's a concert on.

🍸 **Le Pataquès** (map A1, **45**): 8 rue Jouye-Rouve 75020. ☎ 01-40-33-27-47. Metro: Pyrénées. Open Tuesday to Friday 5pm to midnight, Saturday and Sunday 10.30am to 1am. Closed Monday. There's a story attached to this bistro. In the beginning there was Chez Fanfan Lajoy, in rue de la Tourtille, the last old café-grocer's in Belleville. Fanfan's grandmother had opened it in 1932; Fanfan herself grew up there before taking over. A very convivial place, it was the victim of a compulsory purchase order in December 1996. In order to bring it back to life elsewhere and to allow Fanfan to continue to cater for her customers, around 100 regulars set up a 1901 association. They found another den, near the Tourtille, where they could all go once more, with Fanfan in their midst. Unfortunately, she never got used to this new location and ended up packing her suitcases and leaving. So the bar changed its name and became Le Pataquès. Here is the authentic spirit of Belleville, a whole fabric of relationships irrespective of social class, generation and ethnic origin. Nowadays it is also a meeting place for associations and cultural groups, somewhere local artists can exhibit and a concert venue (Saturday and Sunday at 7pm). What better place to have an apéritif before going off to enjoy the delicious cuisine at the Baratin, just opposite.

🍸 **La Mère Lachaise** (map B2, **47**): 78 boulevard de Ménilmontant 75020. ☎ 01-47-97-18-67. Metro: Père-Lachaise. Open daily 8am (10am on Sunday) to 2am. Set menus 55F and 65F, à la carte budget for around 80F. Brunch (75F) on Sunday. Near the Père-Lachaise Cemetery, this new restaurant-bar shines like a new pin. There is a splendid terrace where you can enjoy the sun sitting between groves of green plants and bouquets of flowers, and a back room which is just as remarkable, combining painted wood and earthy colours. Small main courses for around 50F. Good music.

🍸 **Les Trois Arts** (map B1, **46**): 21 rue des Rigoles 75020. ☎ 01-43-49-36-27. Metro: Jourdain. Open daily 7am to 2am. Set menus 47F at lunchtime and 65F in the evening. Budget for 90F à la carte. Half a pint of beer 10F (12F when there are concerts on). In an area which has been flattened by the bulldozers, this is a charming old café. There are concerts (jazz, rock and roll, blues, *musette*, etc.) alternating with little plays in the bar from Thursday to Saturday; and on Sunday, from 6 to 10pm, *l'orchestre national des Trois Arts* (the National Orchestra of the *Trois Arts*) performs. Very good couscous from 65F at weekends, but only if you book.

KNOW YOUR RIGHTS AS A CUSTOMER IN PARIS

Forewarned is forearmed...

It's a good idea to know what pitfalls to look out for and how to avoid being ripped off during your visit to the French capital. So here is a useful reference list which should prepare you for all eventualities!

The welcome: there is no law stating that a hotelier or restaurateur should welcome his customers with a smile. On the other hand, it is hard to imagine a fine being imposed for an unfriendly welcome! In actual fact, each individual manager will receive you in his (or her) own way. Depending on how professionally aware he is, how capable of meeting your needs, and how attractive his personality, the welcome you get can vary from the very best to the absolute pits... There is one simple rule, which all hoteliers and restaurateurs are obliged to follow: they must give their customers the correct information, even on the telephone, with regard to rooms and menus, the level of comfort and the type of cuisine on offer.

Displaying prices: hotels and restaurants are obliged to inform customers of their prices with the use of notices, a board outside or by any other means. This is stated in article 28 of a law imposed on the profession in December 1986. You can therefore only contest exorbitant prices if they are not clearly displayed.

A deposit or payment in advance? When you reserve your room (by phone, fax, letter or e-mail, if applicable) it is not unusual for the hotelier to ask you to pay a deposit, which guarantees your booking. It is always better to pay a deposit, rather than the full amount. Legally there is no set amount for this, but it should be a reasonable proportion of the total amount, say 25–30 per cent, which will ensure that the room is yours. This amount will obviously not be reimbursed if you have to cancel, except in unforeseen circumstances (such as illness or an accident) or if you have agreed a reasonable cancellation period in advance with the hotelier. If, on the other hand, the cancellation is the fault of the hotelier, then he must pay you double the amount of the deposit. This is clearly stated (since 1804!) in article 1590 of the civil code.

Have you ordered enough? It can happen that certain restaurants will refuse to take an order which they consider too small or 'insufficient'. In order to let you make you aware of their feelings, the waiter or the 'patron' (boss) will pull a disapproving face. He may even say that it's losing him money. However, the restaurateur cannot force you to order more – it is illegal.

Water: a simple carafe of tap water is free, as long as it accompanies a meal. Ask for 'de l'eau du robinet' otherwise the waiter will ask you if you want water 'avec gaz' or 'sans gaz' (with or without bubbles) and will charge you accordingly.

Hotels: as with restaurants, hotels are not allowed to exercise unfair sales pressure. In other words, they can't make you reserve extra nights at a hotel of you only want to stay for one. In the same way, they cannot force you to take your breakfast or your meals at the hotel where you are staying; this is illegal and is punishable with a fine. However, the hotelier is free to suggest full or half board. It's a good idea to get the facts before booking a room in a hotel-restaurant. Note that you may also have to pay a supplement if your child shares your room with you.

Menus: often, the first fixed-price menus listed (the least expensive) are only served during the week and by certain times (usually 12.30pm for lunch and 8.30pm for dinner). This should be clearly indicated on the board outside, and it's up to you to check.

The latest trick: not only do you have to pay through the nose in some establishments, but there is a scam to watch out for when paying your bill with cash in a restaurant. When giving you back your change in the customary little dish, the waiter will put the coins in first, then the bill and finally any notes. The idea behind this being that if you're in a hurry you only pick up the notes, leaving the coins hidden under the bill… You have been warned!

Wine: wine menus are not always very clearly laid out. For example, you might think you are ordering a Burgundy at 50F a bottle, but when the bill comes it says 100F. Upon checking the menu you then discover that the price listed was for a **half** bottle, but the print was so small you didn't notice. Watch out for things like this.

Your bottle of wine **must** be uncorked in front of you; in this way you can sure that the bottle does in fact contain what you actually ordered, unless of course you order wine in a carafe ('un pichet').

UNDERSTANDING THE MENU

During your stay you are sure to have a few meals out in a restaurant – after all, what would a trip to France be without sampling the cuisine? This list has been compiled to help you understand the menu and enjoy your meal. Bon appétit!

À point medium rare
Abats offal
Abricot apricot
Acarne sea-bream
Affiné(e) improve, ripen, mature (common term with cheese)
Africaine (à l') african style: with aubergines, tomatoes, ceps
Agneau lamb
Agrumes citrus fruits
Aigre-doux sweet-sour
Aiguillette thin slice
Ail garlic
Aile (Aileron) wing (winglet)
Aïoli mayonnaise, garlic, olive oil
Algues seaweed
Aligot purée of potatoes, cream, garlic, butter and fresh Tomme de Cantal (or Laguiole) cheese
Allemande (à l') German style: with sauerkraut and sausages
Alsacienne (à l') Alsace style: with sauerkraut, sausages and sometimes foie gras
Amande almond
Amandine almond-flavoured
Amer bitter
Américaine (à l') Armoricaine (à l') sauce with dry white wine, cognac, tomatoes, shallots
Amuse-gueule appetizer
Ananas pineapple
Anchoiade anchovy crust
Anchois anchovy
Ancienne (à l') in the old style
Andouille smoked tripe sausage
Andouillette small chitterling (tripe) sausage
Aneth dill
Anglaise (à l') plain boiled
Anguille eel
Anis aniseed
Arachide peanut
Arc-en-ciel rainbow trout
Artichaud artichoke
Asperge asparagus
Assaisonné flavoured or seasoned with; to dress a salad
Assiette (de) plate (of)
Aubergine aubergine, eggplant
Aumônière pancake drawn up into shape of beggar's purse
Auvergnate (à l') Auvergne style: with cabbage, sausage and bacon
Avocat avocado pear
Baba au rhum sponge dessert with rum syrup
Baguette long bread loaf
Baie berry
Baigné bathed or lying in
Banane banana
Bar sea-bass
Barbeau de mer red mullet
Barbue brill
Basilic basil
Basquaise (à la) Basque style: Bayonne ham, rice and peppers
Baudroie monkfish, anglerfish
Bavette skirt of beef
Béarnaise thick sauce with egg yolks, shallots, butter, white wine and tarragon vinegar
Béchamel creamy white sauce
Beignet fritter
Belle Hélène poached pear with ice cream and chocolate sauce
Berrichonne bordelaise sauce
Betterave beetroot
Beurre (Échiré) butter (finest butter from Poitou-Charentes)
Beurre blanc sauce with butter, shallots, wine vinegar and sometimes dry white wine
Beurre noir sauce with brown butter, vinegar, parsley
Bière à la pression beer on tap
Bière en bouteille bottled beer
Bifteck steak
Bigarade (à la) orange sauce
Bisque shellfish soup
Blanc (de volaille) white breast (of chicken); can also describe white fish fillet or white vegetables

Blanchaille whitebait
Blanquette white stew
Blé corn or wheat
Blettes swiss chard
Blinis small, thick pancakes
Boeuf à la mode beef braised in red wine
Boeuf Stroganoff beef, sour cream, onions, mushrooms
Bombe ice-cream
Bonne femme (à la) white wine sauce, shallots, mushrooms
Bordelaise (à la) Bordeaux style: brown sauce with shallots, red wine, beef bone marrow
Boudin sausage-shaped mixture
Boudin blanc white coloured mixture; pork and sometimes chicken
Boudin noir black pudding
Bouillabaisse Mediterranean fish stew and soup
Bouillon broth, light consommé
Bouquet garni bunch of herbs used for flavouring
Bourguignonne (à la) Burgundy style: red wine, onions, bacon and mushrooms
Bourride creamy fish soup with aioli
Brandade de morue salt cod
Bretonne sauce with celery, leeks, beans and mushrooms
Brioche sweet yeast bread
Brochet pike
Brochette (de) meat or fish on a skewer
Brouillé scrambled
Brûlé(e) toasted
Bruxelloise sauce with asparagus, butter and eggs
Cabillaud cod
Cacahouète roasted peanut
Cacao cocoa
Café coffee
Caille quail
Cajou cashew nut
Calmar (Calamar) inkfish, squid
Campagne country style
Canard duck
Caneton (Canette) duckling
Cannelle cinnamon
Carbonnade braised beef in beer, onions and bacon
Carré chop
Casse-croûte snack
Cassis blackcurrant
Cassolette small pan
Cassoulet casserole of beans, sausage and/or pork, goose, duck
Cèpe fine, delicate mushroom
Cerise (noire) cherry (black)
Cerneau walnut
Cervelas pork garlic sausage
Cervelle brains
Champignons (des bois) mushrooms (from the woods)
Chanterelle apricot coloured mushroom
Chantilly whipped cream sugar
Charcuterie cold meat cuts
Charcutière sauce with onions, white wine, gherkins
Chasseur sauce with white wine, mushrooms, shallots
Chateaubriand thick fillet steak
Chaussons pastry turnover
Chemise (en) pastry covering
Chicon chicory
Chicorée curly endive
Chipiron *see* Calmar
Choix (au) a choice of
Chou (vert) cabbage
Choucroute souring of vegetables, usually with cabbage (sauerkraut), peppercorns, boiled ham, potatoes and Strasbourg sausages
Chou-fleur cauliflower
Chou rouge red cabbage
Choux (pâte à) pastry
Ciboule spring onions
Cidre cider
Ciboulette chive
Citron (vert) lemon (lime)
Citronelle lemon grass
Civet stew
Clafoutis cherries in pancake batter
Clou de girofle clove (spice)
Cochon pig
Cochonailles pork products
Cocotte (en) cooking pot
Coeur (de) heart (of)
Coing quince
Colin hake
Compote stewed fruit
Concassé(e) coarsely chopped
Concombre cucumber
Confit(e) preserved or candied
Confiture jam
Confiture d'orange marmalade
Consommé clear soup
Coq (au vin) chicken in red wine sauce (or name of wine)

Coque (à la) soft-boiled or served in shell
Coquillage shellfish
Coquille St-Jacques scallop
Coriandre coriander
Cornichon gherkin
Côte d'agneau lamb chop
Côte de boeuf side of beef
Côte de veau veal chop
Côtelette chop
Coulis de thick sauce (of)
Courge pumpkin
Couscous crushed semolina
Crabe crab
Crécy with carrots and rice
Crème cream
Crème anglaise light custard sauce
Crème brûlée same, less sugar and cream, with praline (*see* Brûlée)
Crème pâtissière custard filling
Crêpe thin pancake
Crêpe Suzette sweet pancake with orange liqueur sauce
Cresson watercress
Crevette grise shrimp
Crevette rose prawn
Croque Monsieur toasted cheese or ham sandwich
Croustade small pastry mould with various fillings
Croûte (en) pastry crust (in)
Cru raw
Crudité raw vegetable
Crustacés shell fish
Cuisse (de) leg (of)
Cuissot (de) haunch (of)
Cuit cooked
Datte date
Daube stew (various types)
Daurade sea-bream
Décaféiné decaffeinated coffee
Dégustation tasting
Diane (á la) pepper cream sauce
Dieppoise (à la) Dieppe style: white wine, cream, mussels, shrimps
Dijonaise (à la) with mustard sauce
Dinde young hen turkey
Dindon turkey
Dorade sea-bream
Doux (douce) sweet
Échalotte shallot
Écrevisse freshwater crayfish
Émincé thinly sliced
Encre squid ink, used in sauces
Endive chicory
Entrecôte entrecôte, rib steak
Entremets sweets
Épaule shoulder
Épice spice
Épinard spinach
Escabèche fish (or poultry) marinated in court-bouillon; cold
Escalope thinly cut (meat or fish)
Escargot snail
Espadon swordfish
Estouffade stew with onions, herbs, mushrooms, red or white wine (perhaps garlic)
Estragon tarragon flavoured
Farci(e) stuffed
Farine flour
Faux-filet sirloin steak
Fenouil fennel
Fermière mixture of onions, carrots, turnips, celery, etc.
Feuille de vigne vine leaf
Feuilleté light flaky pastry
Fève broad bean
Ficelle (à la) tied in a string
Ficelles thin loaves of bread
Figue fig
Filet fillet
Financière (à la) Madeira sauce with truffles
Fine de claire oyster (*see* Huîtres)
Fines herbes mixture of parsley, chives, tarragon, etc.
Flageolet kidney bean
Flamande (à la) Flemish style: bacon, carrots, cabbage, potatoes and turnips
Flambée flamed
Flamiche puff pastry tart
Foie liver
Foie de veau calves liver
Foie gras goose liver
Fond d'artichaut artichoke heart
Fondu(e) (de fromage) melted cheese with wine
Forestière bacon and mushrooms
Four (au) baked in oven
Fourré stuffed
Frais fresh or cool
Fraise strawberry
Fraise des bois wild strawberry
Framboise raspberry
Frappé frozen or ice cold
Friandise sweets (petits fours)
Fricassée braised in sauce or butter, egg yolks and cream
Frisé(e) curly
Frit fried
Frites chips/french fries
Friture small fried fish

Fromage cheese
Fromage de tête brawn
Fruit de la passion passion fruit
Fruits confits crystallised fruit
Fruits de mer seafood
Fumé smoked
Galette pastry, pancake or cake
Gamba large prawn
Ganache chocolate and crème fraîche mixture used to fill cakes
Garbure (Garbue) vegetable soup
Gâteau cake
Gauffre waffle
Gelée aspic gelly
Genièvre juniper
Gésier gizzard
Gibelotte *see* Fricassée
Gibier game
Gigot (de) leg of lamb; can describe other meat or fish
Gingembre ginger
Girofle clove
Glacé(e) iced, crystallized, glazed
Glace ice-cream
Gougère round-shaped, egg and cheese choux pastry
Goujon gudgeon
Goujonnettes (de) small fried pieces (of)
Gourmandises sweetmeats; can describe fruits de mer
Graisse fat
Gratin browned
Gratin Dauphinois potato dish with cheese, cream and garlic
Gratin Savoyard potato dish with cheese and butter
Gratiné(e) sauced dish browned with butter, cheese, breadcrumbs, etc.
Gravette oyster (*see* Huîtres)
Grenouille (cuisses de grenouilles) frog (frogs' legs)
Gribiche mayonnaise sauce with gherkins, capers, hardboiled egg yolks and herbs
Grillade grilled meat
Grillé(e) grilled
Griotte (Griottine) bitter red cherry
Gros sel coarse rock or sea salt
Groseille à maquereau gooseberry
Groseille noire blackcurrant
Groseille rouge redcurrant
Gruyère hard, mild cheese
Hachis minced or chopped-up
Hareng herring
  à l'huile cured in oil
  fumé kippered
  salé bloater
  saur smoked
Haricot bean
Haricot blanc dried white bean
Haricot vert green/French bean
Hollandaise sauce with butter, egg yolk and lemon juice
Homard lobster
Hongroise (à la) Hungarian style: sauce with tomato and paprika
Huile oil
Huîtres oysters
Les claires: the oyster-fattening beds in Marennes terrain (part of the Charente Estuary, between Royan and Rochefort, in Poitou-Charentes).
Flat-shelled oysters: *Belons* (from the River Belon in Brittany);
Gravettes: from Arcachon in the South West);
both the above are cultivated in their home oyster beds.
Marennes are those transferred from Brittany and Arcachon to *les claires*, where they finish their growth.
Dished oysters (sometimes called *portuguaises*):
these breed mainly in the Gironde and Charentes estuaries; they mature at Marennes.
Fines de claires and *spéciales* are the largest; *huîtres de parc* are standard sized.
All this lavish care covers a time span of two to four years.
Hure (de) head (of); brawn, jellied
Île flottante unmoulded soufflé of beaten egg with white sugar
Imam bayeldi aubergine with rice, onions, and sautéed tomatoes
Infusion herb tea
Italienne (à l') Italian style: artichokes, mushrooms, pasta
Jalousie latticed fruit or jam tart
Jambon ham
Jambonneau knuckle of pork
Jambonnette boned and stuffed (knuckle of ham or poultry)
Jarret de veau stew of shin of veal
Jarreton cooked pork knuckle
Jerez sherry
Joue (de) cheek (of)
Julienne thinly-cut vegetables: also ling (cod family)

Jus juice
Lait milk
Laitue lettuce
Lamproie eel-like fish
Langouste spiny lobster or crawfish
Langoustine Dublin Bay prawn
Langue tongue
Lapereau young rabbit
Lapin rabbit
Lard bacon
Lardons strips of bacon
Laurier bay-laurel, sweet bay leaf
Léger (Légère) light
Légume vegetable
Lièvre hare
Limaçon snail
Limande lemon sole
Limon lime
Lit bed
Lotte de mer monkfish, anglerfish
Loup de mer sea-bass
Louvine (Loubine) grey mullet, like a sea-bass (Basque name)
Lyonnaise (à la) Lyonnais style: sauce with wine, onions, vinegar
Mâche lamb's lettuce; small dark green leaf
Madeleine tiny sponge cake
Madère sauce *demi-glace* and Madeira wine
Magret (de canard) breast (of duck); now used for other poultry
Maïs maize flour
Maison (de) of the restaurant
Maître d'hôtel sauce with butter, parsley and lemon
Manchons *see* Goujonnettes
Mangetout edible peas and pods
Mangue mango
Manière (de) style (of)
Maquereau mackerel
Maraîchère (à la) market-gardener style; velouté sauce with vegetables
Marais marsh or market garden
Marbré marbled
Marc pure spirit
Marcassin young wild boar
Marché market
Marchand de vin sauce with red wine, chopped shallots
Marengo tomatoes, mushrooms, olive oil, white wine, garlic, herbs
Marennes (blanches) flat-shelled oysters (*see* Huîtres)
Marennes (vertes) green shell oysters
Marinières *see* Moules
Marmite stewpot
Marrons chestnuts
Médaillon (de) round piece (of)
Mélange mixture or blend
Ménagère (à la) housewife style: onions, potatoes, peas, turnips and carrots
Mendiant (fruits de) mixture of figs, almonds and raisins
Menthe mint
Merguez spicy grilled sausage
Merlan whiting (in Provence the word is used for hake)
Merlu hake
Merluche dried cod
Mesclum mixture of salad leaves
Meunière sauce with butter, parsley, lemon (sometimes oil)
Meurette red wine sauce
Miel honey
Mignon (de) small round piece
Mignonette coarsely ground white pepper
Mijoté(e) cooked slowly in water
Milanaise (à la) Milan style: dipped in breadcrumbs, egg, cheese
Mille-feuille puff pastry with numerous thin layers
Mirabeau anchovies, olives
Mirabelle golden plums
Mitonée (de) soup (of)
Mode (à la) in the manner of
Moelle beef marrow
Moelleux au chocolat chocolate dessert (cake)
Montmorency with cherries
Morilles edible, dark brown, honeycombed fungi
Mornay cheese sauce
Morue cod
Moules mussels
Moules marinières mussels cooked in white wine and shallots
Mousseline hollandaise sauce with whipped cream
Moutarde mustard
Mouton mutton
Mûre mulberry
Mûre sauvage (de ronce) blackberry
Muscade nutmeg
Museau de porc (de boeuf) sliced muzzle of pork (beef) with shallots and parsley with vinaigrette
Myrtille bilberry (blueberry)
Mystère a meringue desert with ice

cream and chocolate; also cone-shaped ice cream
Nature plain
Navarin stew (usually lamb)
Navets turnips
Nid nest
Noilly sauce based on vermouth
Noisette hazelnut
Noisette sauce of lightly browned butter
Noisette (de) round piece (of)
Noix nuts
Noix de veau topside of leg (veal)
Normande (à la) Normandy style: fish sauce with mussels, shrimps, mushrooms, eggs and cream
Nouille noodle
Nouveau (Nouvelle) new or young
Noyau sweet liqueur from crushed stones (usually cherries)
Oeufs à la coque soft-boiled eggs
Oeufs à la neige *see* Île flottante
Oeufs à la poêle fried eggs
Oeufs brouillés scrambled eggs
Oeufs en cocotte eggs cooked in individual dishes in a bain-marie
Oeufs durs hard-boiled eggs
Oeufs moulés poached eggs
Oie goose
Oignon onion
Ombrine fish, like sea-bass
Onglet flank of beef
Oreille (de porc) ear (pig's)
Oreillette sweet fritter, flavoured with orange flower water
Origan oregano (herb)
Orléannaise Orléans style: chicory and potatoes
Ortie nettle
Os bone
Osso bucco à la niçoise veal braised with orange zest, tomatoes, onions and garlic
Pain bread
Pain de campagne round white loaf
Pain d'épice spiced honey cake
Pain de mie square white loaf
Pain de seigle rye bread
Pain complet/entier wholemeal
Pain grillé toast
Pain doré/Pain perdu bread soaked in milk and eggs and fried
Paleron shoulder
Palmier palm-shaped sweet puff pastry
Palmier (coeur de) palm (heart)
Palombe wood pigeon
Palomête fish, like sea-bass
Palourde clam
Pamplemousse grapefruit
Panaché mixed
Pané(e) breadcrumbed
Papillote (en) cooked in oiled paper or foil
Paquets (en) parcels
Parfait (de) mousse (of)
Paris-Brest cake of *choux* pastry, filled with butter cream and almonds
Parisienne (à la) leeks, potatoes
Parmentier potatoes
Pastèque watermelon
Pastis (sauce au) aniseed based
Pâte pastry, dough or batter
Pâte à choux cream puff pastry
Pâte brisée short crust pastry
Pâté en croûte baked in pastry crust
Pâtes fraîches fresh pasta
Pâtisserie pastry
Paupiettes thin slices of meat or fish, used to wrap fillings
Pavé (de) thick slice (of)
Pavot (graines de) poppy seeds
Paysan(ne) (à la) country style
Peau (de) skin (of)
Pêche peach
Pêcheur fisherman
Pèlerine scallop
Perche perch
Perdreau young partridge
Perdrix partridge
Périgourdine (à la) goose liver and sauce *Périgueux*
Périgueux sauce with truffles and Madeira
Persil parsley
Persillade mixture of chopped parsley and garlic
Petit gris small snail
Pétoncle small scallop
Picholine large green table olives
Pied de cheval large oyster
Pied de mouton blanc cream coloured mushroom
Pied de porc pig's trotter
Pigeonneau young pigeon
Pignon pine nut
Piment (doux) pepper (sweet)
Pintade (pintadeau) guinea fowl (young guinea fowl)
Piperade omelette or scrambled eggs with tomatoes, peppers, onions and sometimes ham

Piquante (sauce) sharp tasting sauce with shallots, capers and wine
Pissenlit dandelion leaf
Pistache green pistachio nut
Pistou vegetable soup bound with *pommade* (thick smooth paste)
Plateau (de) plate (of)
Pleurote mushroom
Poché(e), pochade poached
Poêlé fried
Poire pear
Poireau leek
Pois pea
Poisson fish
Poitrine breast
Poitrine fumée smoked bacon
Poitrine salée unsmoked bacon
Poivre noir black pepper
Poivron (doux) pepper (sweet)
Polonaise Polish style: with buttered breadcrumps, parsley, hard-boiled eggs
Pomme apple
Pommes de terre potatoes
dauphine croquettes
château roast
frites chips
gratinées browned with cheese
Lyonnaise sautéed with onions
vapeur boiled
Porc (carré de) loin of pork
Porc (côte de) loin of pork
Porcelet suckling pig
Porto (au) port
Portugaise (à la) Portuguese style: fried onions and tomatoes
Portugaises oysters with long, deep shells (*see* Huîtres)
Potage thick soup
Pot-au-feu clear meat broth served with the meat
Potimarron pumpkin
Poularde large hen
Poulet chicken
Poulet à la broche spit-roasted chicken
Poulpe octopus
Poussin small baby chicken
Pré-salé (agneau de) lamb raised on salt marshes
Primeur young vegetable
Profiterole puffs of *choux* pastry, filled with custard
Provençale (à la) Provençal style: tomatoes, garlic, olive oil, etc.
Prune plum
Pruneau prune
Quenelle light dumpling of fish or poultry
Queue tail
Queue de boeuf oxtail
Quiche lorraine open flan of cheese, ham or bacon
Raclette scrapings from specially-made and heated cheese
Radis radish
Ragoût stew, usually meat but can describe other ingredients
Raie (bouclée) skate (type of)
Raifort horseradish
Raisin grape
Ramier wood pigeon
Rapé(e) grated or shredded
Rascasse scorpion fish
Ratatouille aubergines, onions, courgettes, garlic, red peppers and tomatoes in olive oil
Réglisse liquorice
Reine-Claude greengage
Rémoulade sauce of mayonnaise, mustard, capers, herbs, anchovy
Rillettes (d'oie) potted pork (goose)
Ris d'agneau lamb sweetbreads
Ris de veau veal sweetbreads
Riz rice
Robe de chambre jacket potato
Rognon kidney
Romarin rosemary
Rôti roast
Rouget red mullet
Rouget barbet red mullet
Rouille orange-coloured sauce with peppers, garlic and saffron
Roulade (de) roll (of)
Roulé(e) rolled (usually crêpe)
Sabayon sauce of egg yolks, wine
Sablé shortbread
Safran saffron
Saignant(e) underdone, rare
St-Jaques (coquille) scallop
St-Pierre John Dory
Salade niçoise tomatoes, beans, potatoes, black olives, anchovy, lettuce, olive oil, perhaps tuna
Salade panachée mixed salad
Salade verte green salad
Salé salted
Salmis red wine sauce
Salsifis salsify (vegetable)
Sandre freshwater fish, like perch
Sang blood
Sanglier wild boar
Saucisse freshly-made sausage

Saucisson large, dry sausage
Saucisson cervelas saveloy
Sauge sage
Saumon salmon
Saumon fumé smoked salmon
Sauvage wild
Scipion cuttlefish
Sel salt
Soja (pousse de) soy bean (soy bean sprout)
Soja (sauce de) soy sauce
Soubise onion sauce
Sucre sugar
Tapenade olive spread
Tartare raw minced beef
Tartare (sauce) sauce with mayonnaise, onions, capers, herbs
Tarte open flan
Tarte Tatin upside down tart of caramelized apples and pastry
Terrine container in which mixed meats/fish are baked; served cold
Tête de veau vinaigrette calf's head vinaigrette
Thé tea
Thermidor grilled lobster with browned béchamel sauce
Thon tuna fish
Thym thyme
Tiède mild or lukewarm
Tilleul lime tree
Tomate tomato
Topinambour Jerusalem artichoke
Torte sweet-filled flan
Tortue turtle
Tournedos fillet steak (small end)
Touron a cake, pastry or loaf made from almond paste and filled with candied fruits and nuts
Tourte (Tourtière) covered savoury tart
Tourteau large crab
Tranche slice
Tranche de boeuf steak
Traver de porc spare rib of pork
Tripoux stuffed mutton tripe
Truffade a huge sautéed pancake or galette with bacon, garlic and Cantal cheese
Truffe truffle; black, exotic, tuber
Truite trout
Truite saumonée salmon trout
Turbot (Turbotin) turbot
Vacherin ice-cream, meringue, cream
Vapeur (à la) steamed
Veau veal
Veau pané (escalope de) thin slice of veal in flour, eggs and breadcrumbs
Venaison venison
Verveine verbena
Viande meat
Vichyssoise creamy potato and leek soup, served cold
Viennoise coated with egg and breadcrumbs, fried (usually veal)
Vierge literally virgin (best olive oil, the first pressing)
Vierge (sauce) olive oil sauce
Vinaigre (de) wine vinegar or vinegar of named fruit
Vinaigrette (à la) French dressing with wine vinegar, oil, etc.
Volaille poultry
Yaourt yogurt

INDEX OF STREETS, GARDENS, MUSEUMS AND MONUMENTS

C

D

INDEX OF STREETS

INDEX OF STREETS

INDEX OF HOTELS AND OTHER ACCOMMODATION

INDEX OF RESTAURANTS, NIGHTCLUBS AND BISTROS

C

D

LIST OF MAPS